dBASE IV 2.0 Programming

dBASE IV 2.0 Programming

Cary N. Prague

Windcrest°/McGraw-Hill

New York San Francisco Washington, D.C. Auckland Bogotá
Caracas Lisbon London Madrid Mexico City Milan
Montreal New Delhi San Juan Singapore
Sydney Tokyo Toronto

FOURTH EDITION
FIRST PRINTING
The title of the third edition of this book is *dBASE IV 1.5 Programming—3rd Edition.*

© 1994 by **Windcrest**, an imprint of McGraw-Hill, Inc.
The name "Windcrest" is a registered trademark of McGraw-Hill, Inc.

Library of Congress Cataloging-in-Publication Data

Prague, Cary N.
     dBASE IV 2.0 programming / by Cary N. Prague.
          p.   cm.
     Includes index.
     ISBN 0-8306-4578-0 (paper)
     1. Data base management. 2. dBASE IV (Computer file) I. Title.
QA76.9.D3P7265   1993
005.75′65—dc20   93-21661
                                                                   CIP

Acquisitions editor: Jennifer Holt DiGiovanna
Editorial team: Robert Ostrander, Executive Editor
                John C. Baker, Book Editor
                Jodi L. Tyler, Indexer
Production team: Katherine G. Brown, Director
Design team: Jaclyn J. Boone, Designer
                Brian Allison, Associate Designer
Cover design: Holberg Design, York, Pa.   WP1
Cover photograph: (c) R. Fukuhara/Westlight   4511

This book, my 30th, is dedicated to Lori, a long-lost girlfriend who, by showing me what it's like to have nothing, enabled me to aggressively pursue the countless opportunities in life and business.

Contents

_____ **PART THREE** _____

PROGRAMMING WITH DBASE IV

APPENDICES

Acknowledgments

I want to thank the following people who helped make this book a success:

First to Peter and Nancy Schickler of Button Systems for all their help in updating this book. Also, to Mark Lovely for his assistance on the updated appendices. A special thanks to Thomas J. Brooks, Jr. for renumbering every figure.

To all the folks at TAB and Windcrest books for all their help and encouragement.

A special thanks to my editor John Baker. Thanks for all the care in editing this book and for trying to move up the ship date.

To my partner, Mike Irwin, for always knowing more than me about dBASE!!

A final thanks goes to my family who never sees me but loves me nevertheless. To Karen and my three sons: David, Jeffrey, and Alexander.

About this book

dBASE IV is a very powerful database language. It features the choice of a completely menu-driven interface to create database structures and to add, change, and delete data items or a set of easy to learn commands. dBASE IV also allows the searching, selecting, and displaying of records in the database. Screens can easily be created with the screen painter. Reports can easily be designed and printed. A new advanced query system and view files let the user link as many as ten database files together to produce the most sophisticated reports imaginable. For many users, these commands are sufficient to provide them with simple database queries and reports. Other users, however, would like to unlock the power of dBASE IV as a programming language.

In the ever expanding world of microcomputers today, dBASE IV has gained popularity as a programming language. For many people, it has replaced BASIC or PASCAL. In big business, it is even used as a replacement for COBOL, FORTRAN, and PL/1. dBASE IV has a "full" programming language that is capable of solving almost any data processing problem.

Because of its use of database techniques, dBASE IV makes programming easier than with traditional languages. All normal programming techniques can be used with dBASE IV—decision making, looping, sorting, searching, selecting, displaying, data manipulation, and custom reporting. Full screen selection and data entry menus are simple to design and implement. Many database programming commands can also be integrated into dBASE IV programs. These include setting the programming environment or housekeeping with very simple commands. If a record description needs to be changed after the program is substantially complete, it is a simple task to change the program. It would not be as complicated a task as it is with non-database languages.

Database query commands used to sort, search, and select records are also used as programming commands to replace many programming statements found in traditional languages.

dBASE IV also features a complete Application Generator that can create complete programs or be used as a stepping stone to create your own programs. Reports are simplified by a very powerful report generator, and creating data entry screens is just as simple with the dBASE forms generator. Add this to dBASE's own word processor for creating your program code, and you can program faster than you ever thought possible.

dBASE IV is truly the fourth generation programming generator for the 1990s. This book is written for the computer novice as well as the experienced programmer wishing to add a new language to their toolbox. The book will help both the weekend hacker and the businessman.

It is expected that the reader is a novice and has not even created a database or produced simple reports. The novice will find this book a good introduction to programming concepts and database techniques. The use of dBASE IV is explained in depth with each of these topics. The experienced programmer will find the book a complete guide to making the transition from whatever languages they already know to dBASE IV.

The book is organized into four main parts: "Programming fundamentals," "Database without programming," "Programming with dBASE IV," and "The case study." In each part, you will learn dBASE IV through concepts and practical exercises. You will see how the Ajax Appliance Company creates an order entry system that includes both inventory and customer systems. These examples will help you learn to program. "Programming fundamentals" covers a complete introduction to programming along with comparisons of how dBASE IV differs from traditional programming languages. "Database without programming" explains what a database is and how to efficiently and effectively design and use the databases. You will see how to create an entire application without any programming.

All the database commands are fully explained from both the point of view of the dot prompt and the Control Center. The third part, "Programming with dBASE IV" is subdivided into several chapters. Each shows how to use the appropriate dBASE IV commands taught in each chapter. Each chapter presents the topic as a stand-alone subject and also integrates it with the previously discussed topics. This allows the reader to break down the programming topics into individual subjects and understand how they come together to form the complete program. The Custom System Study links the programs together to form a working, integrated system.

After reading this book, both novice and expert will be prepared to design, code, and implement any problem with the dBASE IV solution.

Part One

Programming fundamentals

1
The business solution

Everyone today is confronted by problems of labor, automation, and rising costs. People in all vocations are realizing that information, instantly available and accurate, holds great importance in meeting these problems head-on. Small businesses, organizations, managers at all levels, are turning to the personal computer to help them solve their portion of these problems.

The computer will not solve your problems for you. It is merely a tool that can implement solutions to problems—provided it has the proper data and instructions. The primary function of your computer system is to accomplish the process of compiling series of trivial items of data into meaningful information, presented in a useful format. Designing this format, determining your system's needs, and defining the data items to be collected are all parts of the implementation plan that you need to establish prior to beginning your computer processing. The task before you is to plan the required solutions, then use the computer to translate those plans into action.

Creating this plan for your business is the most important step in using your computer and dBASE IV to help solve your business problems. Your initial attempt at creating this plan might result in a single application, or even a single program. Eventually, a plan to guide the use of automation throughout your business or organization will emerge. The remainder of this section provides a step by step approach to creating a successful plan for automating your applications and providing you with the information you require to properly manage your business.

The planning process

You should start as soon as possible to form an overall plan for your business. Do not worry about knowing all of the details when you create this high-level plan. Successful planning proceeds from the highest and least-detailed levels down to the detailed actions that implement the plan. Start with what you want to get out of your automated system, and steer the plan toward that goal. If you find that portions of your plan must be changed often as time goes on, then perhaps your overall plan is too detailed. Some change is to be expected, however, because the plan should grow and evolve as your business or organization grows, and as the supporting technology changes.

Planning is problem solving—before trying to implement a solution (see Fig. 1-1). You can try several approaches to the problem, and choose the one that fits your particular situation. If you can visualize the results and side-effects of each approach, you will be less likely to make costly deviations from your overall plan. The solution to your business problem requires an investment of time and money, and you must see to it that both are used to the best effect.

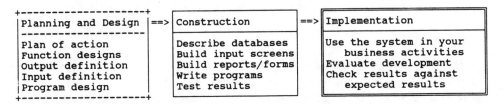

```
+--------------------+      +-------------------+      +-------------------------+
| Planning and Design | ==> | Construction      | ==> | Implementation          |
|--------------------|      |                   |      |                         |
| Plan of action     |      | Describe databases|      | Use the system in your  |
| Function designs   |      | Build input screens|     |   business activities   |
| Output definition  |      | Build reports/forms|     | Evaluate development    |
| Input definition   |      | Write programs    |      | Check results against   |
| Program design     |      | Test results      |      |   expected results      |
+--------------------+      +-------------------+      +-------------------------+
```

1-1   Three phases of a computer system.

If you take the time to plan thoroughly, you will reduce the total time necessary to produce the solution to your business problem. When you are planning a trip in an automobile, you use a good road map and plan your route carefully, resulting in reduced travel time. Without this planning, your trip could take longer and have several detours and wrong turns. Your business plan is a road map to solving your business problem—and few businesses can afford to make wrong turns!

To get the best return for your investment of planning time, you must use the right problem-solving method. The method should start with a definition of the problem, and place planning ahead of action. The need for written documentation of your plan cannot be over-emphasized. This documentation becomes your road map to the goal of solving your business problem.

Proper planning also reduces the time needed for troubleshooting and enhancement of the system after it has been implemented. The documentation produced to define and describe the plan is later used as a manual to describe the inner workings of the system. This aids any effort to fix problems with the system or to add new functions to the system later.

A good plan and good documentation means a successful and flexible system that will fill your business needs well into the future. The first step is to look at the proper way to solve a problem.

Seven-step problem solving

The result of all the actions taken in a computer is the output, which is the reason the program was written in the first place. To assure that a computer program is written properly, every item of information that is required from that program must be defined before the program can be written.

Companies and organizations that already program computers have found that a logical, step-by-step approach to the problem is the easiest to use. When these companies try to come up with a problem solving/documenting method on their own, it is surprising that they all seem to come up with the same answer. Figure 1-2 shows the basic format the various methods give.

```
1. Define the Business Problem

2. Define the Overall System Output

3. Define the Required Data to be Used

4. Determine the Process

5. Create a Function

6. Test the Function

7. Evaluate
```

1-2 The seven-step method.

As with all problem-solving methods (the most well-known of which is the scientific method), the first step in finding the solution is to have an accurate definition of the problem. The solution of this problem will be the application you have for the computer. This is why the type of program you will be writing is known as an application program.

The second step is to determine the output that you need from the system. This keeps your design on course, by setting out the result first. Now that you have your goal written down, you can avoid unnecessary deviations that are not productive.

The third step is to figure out what data items will be used to create the output you have documented. This list will include all of the data you need, and how it is to be placed in computer-readable format. You might have to create new functions within your application for necessary data entry. Defining the input will point this out early in the design process, before any programs are coded that may need to be changed.

The fourth step is to design the process or processes that will turn the input into the output. You might find more data items that are missing from your input or output definitions. You can also check the accuracy of your logic by "playing computer"—making up test cases and following your process design. This will point out any logic problems ahead of time, before they are woven into the fabric of your system.

The first four steps of the seven-step method are called the *design phase* of the system. The next phase is to actually put that design into action by writing the program, testing the processing, and evaluating the test results. These three steps make up the *coding phase* of the system.

The three steps of the coding phase are performed over and over until the system or program is yielding the results that you expect. You code the program, test the logic, then evaluate the results of those steps in terms of readability, speed, and ease-of-use. This evaluation process can also help you in writing future applications, by allowing you to examine which methods work best for you.

The seven-step method can be applied at each level of the system in the same manner. You can use it to design the overall system, a single application, a program, or even a subroutine within a program. You apply the steps in that order, from the highest, most general level down to the most detailed levels. This top-down approach is the most widely accepted method of producing systems that are easy to write and maintain.

As you move down into more detailed levels, the design also becomes more detailed. At a high level, for example, you might have a reference to producing a payroll report. The high-level design might simply say:

Produce payroll report

while the design for the payroll application lists all of the fields, headers, and detail information that the payroll report program must produce. At this point, "produce payroll report" becomes part of the problem description for the next level of detail. The output is defined by specifying the information items that will appear on the report. The required input is then defined, the process mapped, and so forth. The seven-step method is your key to problem-solving at any level.

The solution for your business

A business problem occurs when the current way of performing some business-oriented activity can no longer produce acceptable results. This can happen for a variety of reasons, including a reduction in personnel, an increase in the workload, a need for instantaneous retrieval of information, or the need for a change in the way of doing things. In a company where the entire payroll is four people, including the president, there is probably no need for a computer application to handle payroll. If, however, that company expands to four hundred people, whatever method is used to process the payroll for the smaller group would probably be a seven-days-a-week job when performed for the larger group.

Another example of a problem that would make a small company a candidate for a computer: what if that company with four people on the payroll handles sales to two hundred companies with an inventory that runs into hundreds of thousands of dollars? Unless all four people are doing nothing but inventory control seven days a week, nothing could be shipped!

This example might be a little exaggerated, but it illustrates the point where an automated method of handling the business could be necessary. Then, once the computer was installed, as an afterthought, the payroll could be computerized if time and resources permit.

Once there is a complete, clearly written definition of the problem, coupled with a complete, clearly written specification for the output, these two documents are used as the basis for the rest of the problem solution. Any such important documents should be finished prior to coding any computer programs, the textbook writers tell you. So why do most companies spend less time at these activities than at program coding?

The answer is obvious. As shown in Fig. 1-3, the time spent up-front in design of a programming system is inversely proportional to the time that will be spent coding. In simpler terms, when the design of a program is complete and well-documented, the programs almost code themselves! When the proper amount of design is skipped over in the name of "productivity," coding takes many times longer, because mistakes that should have been eliminated in the design phase did not surface until the program-coding phase.

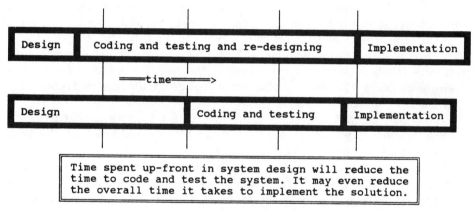

1-3 The system time-line.

Defining the problem

Whatever the business need, the correct first step in finding a solution to it is defining just what has to be done, and when, how much, etc. This overall statement of objective is necessary to keep the process of finding the solution on course, without troublesome wrong turns and side issues.

A problem definition should state why action is necessary, and just what is expected from any solution. A problem definition should also avoid precluding a solution by placing restrictions on its achievement. In other words, do not include any mention of what tools are to be used to construct the final solution, whether computer-based or not.

It is also important to include a description of the expected results in the problem definition. The description should not be vague, but as complete as possible. This will help determine just what information is needed to produce the result. If a computer solution is to be implemented, extensive data entry work is necessary to make the required information available to the computer system. Data entry time must also be taken into account when creating cost estimates of the new system.

For example, the "produce payroll report" application mentioned earlier requires that a database exists containing employee information, such as their Social Security Number, name, and hourly rate. This information must be entered and available before the "produce payroll report" application can actually be used. The length of time necessary to enter this information depends on the number of employees.

A well-written problem definition reduces the time spent on speculation; this makes the solution available faster.

Defining the output

The next step after completing the problem definition is to define the exact content of what the solution is to produce—in short, *define the output. Output* is any product that is essential to solving the business problem. The output in a payroll system is the checks, reports to management about the hours worked, vacation or sick time reports, reports to the IRS, and the pay stubs. These vary in form, and some, at least from an employee's point of view, seem irrelevant. However, each output form helps to solve a part of the total business problem. There might also be files to be kept for year-end reporting; these are also output.

A complete output definition should include a description of each data item to appear in the output. A proper description should include the data type (character or numeric), a name for each variable to be used, the length of the item, and its source, whether from an already existing file or through calculation. The necessity of this step should be apparent: without knowing the exact output specifications, it would be impossible to determine what input is needed.

It is unlikely that all the input that a new computer system must use will be available in usable form. Problems of data entry must, therefore, also be considered. If existing files are to be used, determine whether they are available for use, when are they available for use, and what format they are in. Consideration of these key points at this time can save time and sweat later.

Use a large sheet of paper, and lay out your reports in the format you want (see Fig. 1-4). As when you are writing a program, you will not know the exact values that will be printed. You can use example data if you already have some collected, or you can guess at the sizes you will need. For example, most names are less than 20 characters long, so you can use twenty X's to mark the space that a name will take. There are exceptions to every rule, of course; when you make this type of rule for your system, you must be able to accommodate all of the cases that you might encounter.

Always use the largest field size that a data item can be to make your

```
Report Date: MM/DD/YY

Quantity          Description           Price Each        Amount

   QTN       X---------DESC----------X     999.99        $99,999.99
   QTN       X---------DESC----------X     999.99        $99,999.99
   QTN       X---------DESC----------X     999.99        $99,999.99
   QTN       X---------DESC----------X     999.99        $99,999.99
   QTN       X---------DESC----------X     999.99        $99,999.99
   QTN       X---------DESC----------X     999.99        $99,999.99
   QTN       X---------DESC----------X     999.99        $99,999.99
   QTN       X---------DESC----------X     999.99        $99,999.99
                                                        ----------
                              Total Amount:            $999,999.99

                              Discount: (xx%)       ($ 99,999.99)
                                                      ------------
                              Amount Due:             $999,999.99
                                                      ============
```

1-4 A columnar report.

report layouts. You must allow some room for growth here, as well. You might never have to expand the length of name fields, for example, but numeric fields, like dollar amounts, will grow as your business does.

Not all output is in the form of reports. Sometimes, you might only need a screen display to see the information you need (Fig. 1-5). This is especially true in interactive systems, where each step leads to another until the final result is achieved. Another reason to use screen displays as output is to save paper, which is consumed quickly and irretrievably. You can keep costs down by using paper output sparingly; screen output is much cheaper.

```
                    CUSTOMER INFORMATION

            Name:     :▓▓▓▓▓▓▓▓▓▓▓▓▓▓:

            Address:  :▓▓▓▓▓▓▓▓▓▓▓▓▓▓:

1-5  Screen display output.  City:     :▓▓▓▓▓▓▓▓▓▓▓▓▓▓:

            State:   :▓:    Zip:  :▓▓▓▓▓:

            Date of Birth: :▓▓/▓▓/▓▓:

            Credit Limit: :▓▓▓▓▓▓▓:
```

The output from a program may be in the form of a file that is stored for other programs to use. This might be some intermediate step in the processing chain, or might be information that would be stored in paper files without a computer. Computer storage saves you space, because paper files are bulky. Computer storage also saves you time, because retrieving individual records is much faster than pawing through filing cabinets full of forms.

Be sure to document your output description thoroughly, including notes on the source of the information, and format changes or calculations needed to arrive at the result.

Defining the input

The next step in the design phase is defining the input necessary to produce the output that was just defined.

If you carefully noted the source of all of the data items when creating the output definition, the input definition should just be a case of describing these data items and their format. They may need to be entered by hand, in which case this is probably a good time to find out who will do the work.

In new systems, probably all the input data items needed will be entered by hand. Fortunately, with dBASE IV, this is a task that is performed more easily than with most other languages. When you define what your data files/databases will look like, dBASE IV will allow you to immediately start entering data. dBASE IV generates input screens which allow easy entry of the items to be stored.

This means that you can start data entry as soon as you have defined your input. As you are creating the system that will use that data, someone else could be entering the data you need. This can save you some time, and also means that data will be available to test your programs when they are completed.

You should also choose the formats that you will want the data entered in (see Fig. 1-6). For example, dates can be entered several different ways, including those shown here:

```
MM/DD/YY
MM/DD/YYYY
YY/MM/DD
DD/MM/YYYY
```

You must choose a method of entering and displaying the data when creating your input definition. Remember, the computer can change formats faster than you can; the data can be entered one way, stored another way, and reported in still another format.

Another consideration is how easily the data can be typed by someone at the keyboard. It is slower to enter numeric fields, such as dollar amounts, with commas and decimal places. Numeric fields should be entered as just numbers, and the formatting taken care of by the software or your own program.

You can logically arrange the data items on the data entry screen in such a way that data entry is faster and more accurate. To make the entry faster, you can group all of the character and numeric data items in separate groups. This means that the person doing the data entry does not have to keep switching between the numeric keypad and the letters on the keyboard.

Accuracy of the input data is important, because the computer system is only as good as its data. You can arrange the data items on the screen so that

```
Date can be entered as:

   MM/DD/YY      (American)
   YY.MM.DD      (ANSI)
   DD/MM/YY      (British)
   DD-MM-YY      (Italian)
   DD.MM.YY      (French/German)
   MM/DD/YYYY    (American - Four-digit year)
```

```
... stored in file as:

         YYYYMMDD
```

```
... and finally reported:

   MM/DD/YY      (American)
   YY.MM.DD      (ANSI)
   DD/MM/YY      (British)
   DD-MM-YY      (Italian)
   DD.MM.YY      (French/German)
   MM/DD/YYYY    (American - Four-digit year)
   (or in a format that you create)
```

1-6 Examples of date and number reformatting.

the data entry person can spot mistakes with a single glance. Your process should also contain edits to tell the operator what items are in error, and allow them to be corrected. When you are creating your input definition, you can specify what edits are to be performed on each data item, specifying ranges and allowable values.

Defining the process

Now the problem has been defined, the output specifications have been written, and the input determined. With these documents firmly in hand, you are ready to define the actual process of turning the input "data items" into the output "information."

The overall functions of the system, as set out in the problem definition, must each be divided into their component functions. This is when the actual process of programming takes place. The problem, output, and input definitions were the beginning of this process, but only now is the actual process defined. This can be done using many different methods.

The process design can take many forms, and is usually a matter of personal taste. The most tried-and-true methods are charting methods, such as flowcharts, PERT charts, and so forth. These methods have been used to describe processes, even non- computer processes, for a long time. There are specialized symbols that describe processes, decisions, and terminal inter-action. If you can visualize the system in this manner, charting might be the best method for you to use.

The problem with charting methods is that each revision means redraw-ing the chart. This makes use of flowcharting awkward for documentation, especially at the detailed level. Each time the detail changes, the chart must be redrawn. Computer applications are evolving, dynamic systems, and the details change frequently while the results remain constant.

More recently, a form of process design called *pseudocode* has become more popular among computer programmers as a superior way of describing computer application processes. Pseudocode makes use of logical constructs that are common to most computer languages to create a generic process description that can be applied in any language. This form of design is flexible and exact—and also takes the form that the final system will take. The logic used in pseudocode should look the same as the program logic it represents (for example, as shown below in Fig. 1-7).

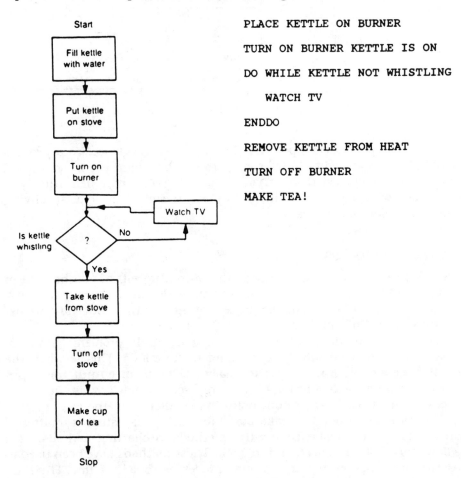

PLACE KETTLE ON BURNER

TURN ON BURNER KETTLE IS ON

DO WHILE KETTLE NOT WHISTLING

    WATCH TV

ENDDO

REMOVE KETTLE FROM HEAT

TURN OFF BURNER

MAKE TEA!

1-7 An example of a flowchart and pseudocode.

Interactive processes can be described by yet another method. You interact with the computer system via the keyboard and monitor screen, which allows you to design the system around this interaction. This "give-and-take" approach is called *storyboarding*.

Storyboarding is a method used by directors and writers to design the action in a movie or television show. Each scene is drawn by hand, showing relationships of objects to each other in the picture, noting the look of special effects, and so forth. The storyboard is like an extremely detailed comic book of the final result. You can use this same method to describe an interactive computer process.

The storyboard shown in Fig. 1-8 is based on the screen display that the users see when they are interacting with your system. Each data item is shown in the position it will hold on the screen, and the source and/or destination of each item is described. Any editing information, formatting, or other processing is also noted. The storyboards will, when complete, contain the complete documentation and data dictionary for the system.

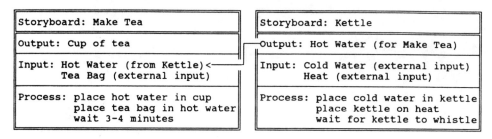

1-8 An example of a storyboard.

Charting, pseudocoding, and storyboarding might not be the only answers to creating a process definition. For example, storyboarding is an excellent way of describing the overall system, but is difficult to apply to the detail levels. You could use all three methods at one point or another during the design.

The highest levels of the system rarely change, so a charting method could be used to document their actions. Storyboards could then be used to describe the interactions between operator and machine, and detailed programming logic could be described with pseudocode. All of the tools at your disposal should be used to make the final system a success.

Planning concepts

As various methods of implementing computer strategies have evolved over the years, the most successful systems are those that are structured from the top down. The design starts with the overall plan, then continues down, level by level, to the detailed actions. The seven-step method of design can be applied at each of the levels and functions of the business system.

Top-down planning

Whether you are writing a single program, creating an entire application system, or compiling a computer plan of action, the process is goal-oriented.

If you start with a clear definition of the problem and the required result, the process is just a matter of filling in the details. The benefit of top-down design is that it is easy to spot processes that are extraneous and do not lead to the goal. This keeps your system development from deviating into unproductive areas.

At the top levels of the system, the general structure and expected results of the system are defined. This overall design becomes the framework for the detailed designs you will develop later (see Fig. 1-9). The results of each function identified within the system should lead to that final result.

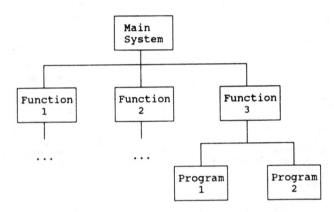

1-9 The format of a hierarchy chart.

The middle levels of the design describe the functions necessary for the system to produce that result. These may be general functions, like "file maintenance and update," "data entry," "monthly reports," and so forth. This level of design shows the relationships between the functions within a system, and how the intermediate results are used to create the final result.

The lowest levels of the design describe individual actions of a single function and intermediate results that the function will produce. This should be the most detailed of the designs, describing the source and disposition of each data item that is to be processed. Calculations and formatting procedures should be noted as a guide to later program coding. Pseudocode should be used to describe any logical algorithms that the system is to follow. You should make the pseudocode parallel the processing of your final program as much as possible.

The details get filled in as you go (see Fig. 1-10). If your design framework is sound and logical, the details will be quickly dispensed with. Top-down design and construction create a system that new functions simply "plug into," without change to your existing structure. The next step is to create a model of your system so that you may check the form of the results and determine their desirability.

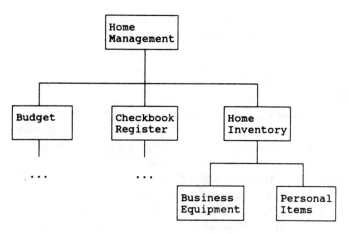

1-10 An example of a system hierarchy.

The system prototype

Before the actual coding of the system begins, you can create the screen and report formats that you will use. dBASE IV makes this easier by providing report formats and screen formats that can be used outside of the programming language.

If you use the storyboard technique of design for your interactive processes, then you can create a system prototype directly from the storyboards. The prototype shows how well the storyboards relate to each other, and how a user of your system will move from screen to screen.

The other advantage to using a system prototype is that most of the display and data entry screens for the application system are created and tested before the rest of the system. This saves time during the actual program coding. You can use the screens for training a data entry person, or even start data entry while application development is still continuing.

You have to test your prototype with the people who will be doing the actual work. In many cases, this will be you yourself—which means you must rely on your own judgment. If something is awkward or difficult to do, it will show up during the prototype and not later, when the damage may be irreversible. The navigation from screen to screen should be logical and easy to understand.

Report formats can be adjusted to fit preprinted forms, before the system is started. You can find data items and information that might be missing from your design. Make sure that the formats you have chosen fit your own needs, because every business problem, every situation, is a little different.

You can create your prototype in dBASE IV outside of the programming that might be necessary later. You can interactively use the screens to add, change, and delete records before the program exists. Test data can be entered for use in debugging the programs later.

Your system prototype becomes the framework where your new applications will reside. The relationships of the screens to each other and to the final results help you to further divide your system into more manageable pieces.

Divide and conquer

The methods most often used by professional programmers to define processes are flowcharting and pseudocoding. They are representative of the two categories of process mapping. Charting a process involves drawing a pictorial representation of the flow of control, with symbols that depict the functions. Pseudocoding defines the process in terms of the functions, using a structured style that mirrors the workings of computer programs.

Dividing a function into its component functions makes the program coding phase go faster. This is because each piece of the solution is easier to master than the entire solution all at once. By dividing the functions in up-front design time, coding becomes faster and more controlled. The overall process might be too big, cumbersome, or complicated to try to understand all at once. You will probably be able to see the individual pieces easier than the entire system. You can divide the system to conquer its processing, as shown in Fig. 1-11.

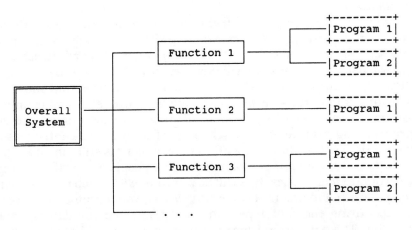

1-11 Dividing to conquer.

Using the top-down approach, you first design your overall computer plan of action. Don't worry about the individual details of how to arrive at the results—just specify the results that you want to obtain. The next step is to decide what input data is necessary to produce the output that you have specified. If you are detailed and exact in defining what you want to see, the design process is much easier.

Next, you divide the overall design into the individual functions that lead to the specified results. If your ambition is to produce mailing labels for customer mailings, then you need a file of customer information from which to print the labels. The existence of such a file means that you have to have some way of entering data into that file, or a data entry function. You will also need a way to change and remove records from this file once it has been created—a file maintenance function. Finally, you need a function that actually formats and prints the labels.

Divide each function into separate applications for the computer. The data entry function noted, for example, might consist of an "add customers to file" application and a "list newly added customers" function, so that the data entry operators can check their work. The file maintenance function might be divided into "change customer" and "delete customer."

The applications can also be approached as individual design processes. Each application is divided into individual working units, which become the programs, reports, and screens necessary to do the work. Dividing your business problem into these smaller units makes it easier for you to understand the problem, and solve it.

The form of the plan

Now for the second phase of our project: the coding phase. In the design phase you defined the problem, the output, the input, and the process. Now it is time to code and test the new system.

Documenting the plan

The reference materials you need during your coding phase are the manuals for whatever software you are using, the problem definition, output definition, input definition, and the process definition. These materials, aside from the reference manual, are the documentation for your system.

The design definition and the program code form a package that is necessary for future changes that might occur to the system. When a system is to be changed or enhanced, the programmer refers to the documentation package for a clearer understanding of the system. This enables the programmer to find the easiest, least-change method for the enhancement.

A poorly assembled documentation package can make changes difficult, if not impossible, to implement. Some companies keep outdated computer equipment, some dating back to the early 1960s. Why? Because the programs were written then, and the documentation has become scattered, scrambled, and lost during the interim. In some cases, the source language for the program itself has been lost, rendering all change impossible. Their attitude toward this is "The programs still work fine, and we don't have the time to rewrite and re-document the system." Usually, the cost of keeping the old equipment is much greater than the cost of developing a new, rewritten, and documented system. The point of this is that the documentation package is important to you and to your business. Write them well, and keep two copies of everything!

Because the source code of the program is part of the documentation package, it is important to write it in a readable manner. Even the pseudocode or flowchart should be painstakingly written, so that when you come back to it later, you can understand how the process works.

Many professional programmers find themselves working on systems they designed and wrote years in the past, scratching their heads in wonder at how they could have forgotten what they did. With readable, understandable documentation, this is a much easier task.

One way of making programs (and pseudocode) more readable is to indent subordinate code. Any code that is inside a loop, for example, should be indented to differentiate it from the main code. This one act alone makes the program much easier to read.

Another method of making a program easier to read is to start each function at the top of a new page. In some languages, it is necessary to put comments in the code, showing the break between the end of one subfunction, and the start of the next.

Finally, comment statements are available in virtually all computer languages. Use them to your advantage. By commenting effectively, and changing those comments when necessary, you can put some documentation directly into the code. This is especially helpful when a complicated process is present; you can explain the process in plain language to programmers who might change the program in the future. Remember, it could be you!

How large an audience?

When a mime performs, he or she adjusts the size of the movements they use to fit the size of the audience. The mime must be sure that people in the farthest seats can see the movement, because a mime's movement is the only vehicle with which to tell the story. A routine performed for ten people, therefore, will look different if performed for fifty, or a thousand. The mime expands the gestures and makes the actions broader. Likewise, you must judge the amount and quality of application documentation that you create by the size of your audience.

The size of your audience might also dictate what documentation you have to produce. In large companies, there are strict guidelines for the types of final documentation that must be made available before the system can be implemented. Software companies must provide manuals to their customers on the technical, business, and operational aspects of their systems. The individual private user might not need to have all of these pieces of documentation, but just a well-documented design.

If you are doing everything yourself, you would be making a grave mistake if you did not accurately and completely document your system. Your documentation, however, might be in the form of handwritten notes, program listings, and sample reports. A larger audience might require a manual to the system, training guides, business specifications, and so forth. The method of reproduction also changes, from handwritten notes and copies, to printed originals and copies, to typeset and bound manuals.

You should spend time at each step of the design process documenting your plans and ideas. Make guesses when you are not sure; you can change the plans if they appear to be unworkable. If your documentation is good enough, you should be able to spot the flaw before a single program that relies on that flaw is written.

If you produce documentation at each design step, the documentation should be 99% complete before the coding is actually started. Provide this documentation to other interested parties for their views and suggestions. This helps you improve your system and its functions, before any actual programs have to be changed. Your system will be easier to implement and also more complete if you follow these guidelines.

Always make copies of everything

Security is a major issue that should be built into your computer plan of action. Computer security is your plan for the protection of your computer automation investment. This means protecting not only the equipment that you bought, but the software packages, like dBASE IV, that you have purchased, the programs that you have spent your time creating, and the data that you have entered. Your machine, programs, and data are assets to your business or organization. You should be protected against their sudden loss.

You should be able to recover all of your data and programs, even if the originals or working copies are totally destroyed. If you rely on your computer for daily activity, activity should continue with little delay in such a circumstance. This is the only way to protect the investment of your time in the automated system. Your business cannot afford to be put on hold while technical difficulties are resolved.

There are three main issues in computer security: first, the security of the data from error or destruction; second, the security of the data, programs, and hardware from human tampering and theft; third, protection against fire, flood, and other natural disasters. Your computer plan of action should address each of these three areas (Fig. 1-12).

Protecting your data against error and destruction is the easiest form of protection to implement. Data editing routines in programs guarantee that the data entered into the databases is as error-free as possible. Cross-checking results also point out errors in the data. Protection against accidental destruction is simply a matter of making copies.

You should *Always Make Copies Of Everything*. Follow the dBASE IV procedures for creating a backup copy of the dBASE IV software. Back up your own data files as often as you feel is necessary. Have a backup computer system quickly available for times when there might be hardware problems.

How often is "necessary"? Each situation is different, but there are some simple guidelines. You should make new backup copies of your files immedi-

Type:	Method:	Guards against:
Physical security	Hardware backup	Fire, theft, natural disaster
	Software backup	Accidental erasure
	Data backup	Accidental erasure, vandalism
Data security	Audit trails	Embezzlement, fraud
	Limited access	Sabotage, vandalism
	Supervision	Espionage

1-12 Security considerations.

ately after updating or changing them in any way. This guarantees that there are copies of the most up-to-date files available in case of emergency. If you update your files daily, this calls for daily copies.

You should keep these copies in archive for at least two generations. For example, if you are making copies of your data files every day, three days' worth of copies should be available. This means that if the most recent copy is bad for any reason, you will lose at most two days of updates. The chances of three sets of backup copies being bad are very small.

For maximum data file protection, you should make two copies after each day's work is completed. One copy is stored *on-site*, or at the location where the computer system is. If something goes wrong with the main working files, there is a copy immediately available for recovery. The second copy should be stored *off-site* in some other location—in a separate building, in a vault, or at your home. If something is wrong with both the working files and with the on-site copy, the off-site copy can be used for recovery.

Many people, to their chagrin, ignore the importance of adequate backup copies of their data. "Backups are a hassle" and "I don't have the time" are the usual excuses. This stage lasts until the first time they lose an important file or have to reenter 10,000 records by hand—after which they make backup copies with a vengeance! Creating adequate backup copies will save you time and stress when something does go wrong.

You might not need to address the idea of human tampering and sabotage, depending on the sensitivity of your application. Most companies do not really have the need to protect their data that closely. Sometimes, putting protection on a system is a lure for those who simply like to break protection schemes. All that is really necessary, in most circumstances, is a lock on the computer room door.

If you do have worries about human-caused damage, an adequate number of backup copies should cover this type of loss. If your data is sensitive, and must be kept from prying eyes, there are several types of encryption available. Encryption packages allow you to "scramble" your data according to a password that you provide. Only a person with the same password could unscramble the file to look at it.

You should be able to recover your entire system in the event of a disaster. This, again, is a matter of scale—a home computer, for example, might not be as important as the computer for a small business. Off-site copies of programs and data are the mainstay of a disaster-recovery plan. If a large business loses their computer system due to fire or other disaster, there is usually a backup system held in reserve in another location. This off-site system can pick up the workload in a minimum amount of time, allowing the company to continue with business as usual.

You can make a deal with a friend, a neighbor, or even a competitor for mutual aid in the event of a disaster. Your remote site should be a safe distance from the original site, so that they do not both become involved in the same disaster.

The center of all of these security methods is adequate backup copies of the software, programs, and data files. *Always make copies of everything*, and you will reduce the time necessary to recover your system should the need arise.

2
The programming process

There are two major styles of programming: interactive and passive. *Passive* programs are processes that can run from start to finish with no interruption by the operator. Sometimes called *batch* programs by professional programmers, passive programs make up most of the work cycle at large installations. Huge numbers of transactions are accumulated during normal business hours, and then processed on the second and third shifts. The series of passive programs process these transactions, update files, create reports, print special forms, and so forth. All this happens with little or no direct input from the computer operators; the operations staff has enough to do! They place the transactions (either cards, tape, or disks) into the proper units, put paper in the printers, align the forms, and determine the order that the programs are to be run in.

The idea of batch processing meant that once the program had started the user had to wait while the program ran all its coded instructions without interruption. *Interactive* programming is having a conversation with the program. The program prints certain questions on the screen, and the user must answer them to allow the program to continue running.

The problem with doing this in the past was that terminals were not widely used to perform program execution—they were used to enter and modify programs. The computer operations staff, the trained professionals who really run the computer in large installations, were too busy doing their job to answer questions from the program.

Interactive processing

The increasing use of terminals and the advent of microcomputers has made interactive programming possible, because interactive programming requires extensive communication with the operator. This type of program would not be welcome in a batch environment, because in big shops there are large numbers of programs running at any given time; the operations staff cannot (and will not!) devote much attention to an individual program. Microcomputers, however, are ideal for interactive programming. They are usually run as *dedicated systems*, which means that only one program can be running at a time.

Interactive programs handle just one transaction between the operator and the system at a time. The operator requests a function, enters the data, and a file is updated. The operator enters another function, and a report is produced. *Interactive* means that the operator can control what functions are performed, and in what order. Interactive programming also helps alleviate operator boredom by showing that the system is working, and by giving the operator control over the outcome.

Terminal operators, who may or may not be programmers, are now running their own jobs and controlling their execution from the terminal. Because they are the primary operators for their little piece of the system, and would probably just sit and watch the program run anyway, they have time to respond to questions from the program. The interaction shows the operator the progress of the program and lets him or her know that the work is still being performed.

Microcomputers have brought interactive programming to its peak. Game programs are the most obvious and notorious type of interactive program. They translate the input of the game controller (joystick) into motions of graphic characters on the display screen, and dole out rewards and punishments for improper use of the controller. Interactive business programs do much the same thing—if the data is entered incorrectly, the program will pass error messages back to the user who will immediately reenter the field.

Another way of interacting with programs, other than using question/answer format, is with full-screen menus. Menus are lists of functions that you might want to perform with the system, and that you have programmed previously. The operator can choose the function to be performed by choosing the desired option from a list of possible functions.

The systems that you create for your business can be either interactive or noninteractive in nature. The most often-used programs you will write are interactive programs, such as when you are entering, changing, or deleting records. There are times when you would also use noninteractive processing, such as for printing statements for customers, or producing an inventory report.

The interaction of operator, program, and database is your application for the computer. The result of this interaction is the information that you need to increase your effectiveness in serving the customer and to make your business more efficient. This chapter shows you the methods of writing both interactive and noninteractive programs.

Logical constructs

Programs are series of instructions that tell the computer what operations are to be performed in the order they are to be performed. The operations that can be performed are determined by the software you are using. dBASE IV is a fully functioning database management system and programming language. This means that the available operations in dBASE IV are at such a level that by combining and arranging the operations, you can achieve any desired result.

The most important part of learning how to program is to learn how the operations can be arranged to achieve the maximum effect. The result is like learning a human language, such as Spanish or French, by learning the proper grammar first, then learning the meaning of the words. This is not possible with a human language, of course, but a computer language is constructed according to some logical rules. If you learn the construction of a program first, you will be able to build a program in almost any computer language. The only thing left to do after that is to learn the proper commands and their functions, because you already know how to put them together.

Figure 2-1 shows the logical constructs that can be found and used in most computer languages, including dBASE IV. By arranging, nesting, and combining these constructs, you can create a program to achieve any possible result that you may need. There are also added bonuses—the program will be *easy to write*, because you will have already constructed the logical framework; it will be *easy to change*, because you can add new constructs as needed, like building blocks; and it will be *easy to read*, because everything will fall into the logical framework. These three "EZ2s" are the marks of a good program.

```
┌─────────────────────────┐
│      SEQUENCE           │
├─────────────────────────┤
│  statement ...          │
│  statement ...          │
│  statement ...          │
└─────────────────────────┘
```

```
┌─────────────────────────────────────┐
│  CASE-WHEN-OTHERWISE                 │
├─────────────────────────────────────┤
│  CASE variable name OF               │
│     WHEN value1                      │
│        process for value1            │
│     WHEN value2                      │
│        process for value2            │
│     . . .                            │
│     WHEN valueN                      │
│        process for valueN            │
│     OTHERWISE                        │
│        process for other values      │
│  ENDCASE                             │
└─────────────────────────────────────┘
```

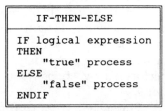

```
┌─────────────────────────────────┐
│         IF-THEN-ELSE            │
├─────────────────────────────────┤
│  IF logical expression          │
│  THEN                           │
│       "true" process            │
│  ELSE                           │
│       "false" process           │
│  ENDIF                          │
└─────────────────────────────────┘
```

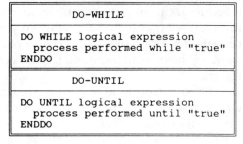

```
┌─────────────────────────────────────┐
│              DO-WHILE                │
├─────────────────────────────────────┤
│  DO WHILE logical expression         │
│     process performed while "true"   │
│  ENDDO                               │
└─────────────────────────────────────┘
```

```
┌─────────────────────────────────────┐
│              DO-UNTIL                │
├─────────────────────────────────────┤
│  DO UNTIL logical expression         │
│     process performed until "true"   │
│  ENDDO                               │
└─────────────────────────────────────┘
```

2-1 The logical constructs.

Sequence

The logical construct sequence is just that: one statement following another. This is the simplest form of construct, and simply depicts one action following another. The others (IF-THEN-ELSE, DO WHILE, DO UNTIL, and CASE) are decision statements, and most languages have them in one form or another. These constructs are used to create a program in pseudocode, so that you can see and trace the logic of your program. If the logic does not work in pseudocode, it will not work in a real computer language, either.

The logical constructs can also be represented by flowchart symbols. Thus, you can use either a pseudocoding or a charting method to build the system. If you use the logical constructs, your program will be logically sound no matter which design method you use.

It might be necessary, in some languages, to use the statements available to create the logical constructs. In dBASE IV, the constructs exist in the forms shown in Fig. 2-1 (except for DO UNTIL). Notice that there are no input/output type statements used in pseudocode. That is because the design process should not be tied down in the exact form to be used. This type of design allows flexibility, so that a change of computers or software does not affect the design. The only necessary references to input and output might be statements such as the following:

```
GET A RECORD
GET NEXT RECORD
WRITE A LINE
```

Sequence shows one operation following another. Each operation is performed, then the next, and so forth (Fig. 2-2). The reason that sequence is important is that each operation in the sequence could also be a logical construct. There could be a series of IF statements, for example, or a DO loop with a sequence of instructions taking place inside the loop.

IF-THEN-ELSE

The IF-THEN-ELSE logical construct is the simplest form of decision statement (see Fig. 2-3). It asks a question by making a comparison, for example, IF PAYROLL CODE IS 2. There are two possible results from a comparison of this type: true or false. If the comparison in the IF is true, then whatever processing is invoked in the THEN part of the statement is performed, and when completed, the next statement following the IF construct is performed. If the result is false, the ELSE section is performed.

Some IF statements have only a THEN following them: if the comparison is false, the THEN unit is not performed, and control falls to the next statement.

By the way, IF-THEN-ELSE statements, and for that matter ALL the logical constructs, are, or can be considered, individual statements. There-

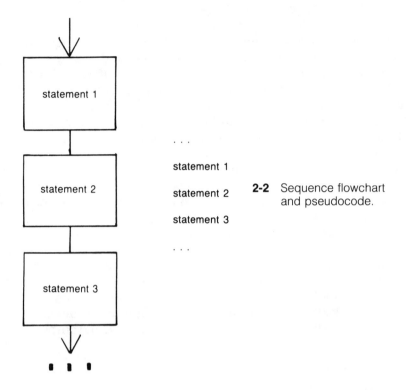

statement 1

statement 1

statement 2

statement 2   **2-2** Sequence flowchart
                        and pseudocode.

statement 3

statement 3

fore, the THEN unit of an IF-THEN-ELSE construct can also have an IF statement in it. This is called nesting by programmers, and is valid. Take care, however, that IFs and THENs match up with the proper ELSEs. This can be done by using indentation to contrast statements on different nesting levels. Also, don't nest too deeply, because this can become unwieldy and unreadable. If necessary, create another function!

In dBASE IV, the IF statement looks like this:

```
IF conditional expression
     statements to be performed if true
ELSE
     statements to be performed if false
ENDIF
```

Notice that there is no word THEN in the statement. dBASE "understands" that the statements between the IF and the ELSE or ENDIF are the THEN part of the construct. If the expression is false, dBASE looks for an ELSE in the code, otherwise if an ELSE is present, performs the statements following it. If there is no ELSE, the ENDIF is reached, and the next statement is executed.

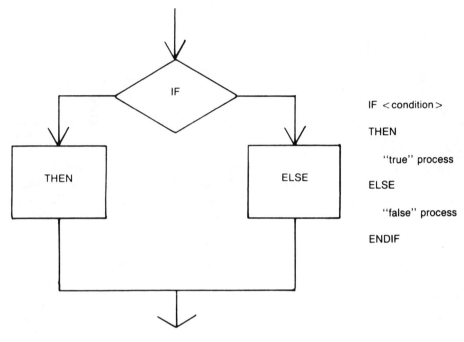

IF < condition >

THEN

    "true" process

ELSE

    "false" process

ENDIF

2-3 IF-THEN-ELSE flowchart and pseudocode.

Indentation is important in IF-THEN-ELSE constructs to make the code easier to read and understand. Each level of indentation represents a nesting level.

As an example of how IF-THEN-ELSE constructs are executed, suppose that a program does some special processing when a date is in November. The pseudocode would look like this:

```
IF MONTH =11
THEN
    perform "November processing"
ELSE
    perform "normal processing"
ENDIF
```

In this example, the conditional expression is MONTH = 11 on the line starting with IF. The expression asks a question to which there can be only two possible answers: "Is month equal to 11? Yes or no."

When the system sees an expression like this, it examines the value of the variable MONTH and compares it to the literal value 11. If they are equal, the system signals a "true" or "yes" answer for the question, and the process contained in the THEN unit of the construct is performed. If the value of MONTH is not equal to 11, the ELSE unit gets control, and that processing is performed. Here are other examples:

```
IF STATE = "CT"
THEN ...
IF ZIP = 06040
THEN ...
IF DATE = EXPIRE:DATE
THEN ...
```

In the third example above, the contents of the variable DATE are compared against the contents of the variable EXPIRE:DATE. Again there are only two possibilities: the contents are either equal or not equal, so the expression is either true or false. There is no other answer to a conditional expression.

Using the logical operators AND, OR, and NOT, you can create complex conditional expressions. The rules for evaluating complex conditional expressions are expressed by the logical truth tables, as shown in Fig. 2-4.

AND – both sides must be true for expression to be true				OR – only one side must be true for expression to be true		
A	B	A AND B		A	B	A OR B
T	T	T		T	T	T
T	F	F		T	F	T
F	T	F		F	T	T
F	F	F		F	F	F

NOT – reverses the logical value of the expression	
A	NOT A
T	F
F	T

2-4   The logical "truth tables."

In complex expressions, each conditional expression is evaluated separately, and then the results of the ANDs and ORs are evaluated according to the AND and OR rules, for example:

```
IF STATE = "CT" AND ZIP = 06040
THEN ...
```

In this example, the value of the variable STATE is compared against the literal CT. Likewise, the value of the variable ZIP is compared to 06040. Only if *both* of these conditions are true is the entire expression true. If either is false, the entire condition is false. You can replace the conditions in the statement with the values you want to test, like this:

```
IF "true" AND "true" ...
```

If you look at the AND truth table in Fig. 2-4, you will see that the result of "True" and "True" is "True," meaning that the entire expression is true if each part of the expression is true.

In the following example, the two simple conditions are made into a complex expression by joining them with an OR:

```
IF STATE = "CT" OR STATE = "MA"
THEN ...
```

It is obvious that at least one of these conditions must be false; STATE cannot have two different values! However, the OR rule states that only one of the joined expressions need be true for the entire condition to be true. Here, if the value of STATE is CT, the condition is true. The condition is also true if the value is MA. If anything other than these two values is in STATE, the condition is false.

In more complicated conditional expressions, two expressions connected with an AND can be connected to still other expressions:

```
IF (STATE="CT" OR STATE="MA")
AND NAME ="SMITH"
THEN ...
```

In this example, the condition inside the parentheses is evaluated first, and then ANDed against the evaluation of the third expression. If the variable STATE contains either CT or MA, the condition in the parentheses is evaluated as true (by the OR rule). Then the value of the variable NAME is compared with the literal value SMITH. Therefore, this complex condition is true if NAME is equal to SMITH, and if the STATE is either CT or MA.

When evaluating complex conditional expressions, it is important to (1) evaluate the expressions inside parentheses *first*, and (2) remember the AND and OR rules. Also, don't make conditions too complex, for readability's sake; the KISS ("Keep It Simple, Stupid") method is the best compromise.

DO-WHILE/DO-UNTIL

DO-WHILE is another type of conditional statement (see Fig. 2-5). A DO-WHILE is a series of statements that is performed over and over, while the condition remains true. Each time the loop of statements is performed, the condition is reevaluated, and, if true, the process in the loop is performed again.

Programmers use DO-WHILE loops to perform a series of statements as long as some condition is true. This condition can be internal to the program, for example:

```
SET COUNTER TO 1
DO-WHILE COUNTER < = 15
    ...
    statements
    ...
    add 1 to counter
ENDDO
```

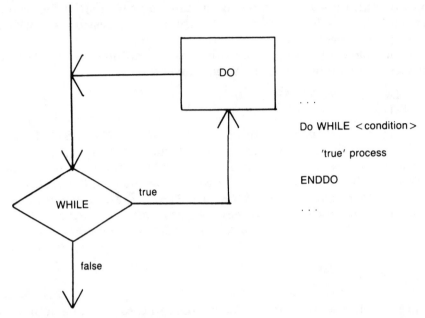

DO
. . .

Do WHILE <condition>

'true' process

ENDDO

. . .

true

WHILE

false

2-5 DO-WHILE flowchart and pseudocode.

The DO-WHILE loop will be performed fifteen times; each time through the loop the counter is incremented by one. The condition in the DO-WHILE statement (COUNTER< =15) is tested immediately after each time the counter is incremented. When the value of COUNTER exceeds fifteen, the loop is ended, and control passes to the statement following the ENDDO.

Another way that DO-WHILE is used is to test for a condition external to the program. One such condition is *end-of-file*, which answers the question "Are there any more records to read?" Using a DO-WHILE loop with an end-of-file type of condition means that the loop will be performed once for each record in the file, regardless of the number of records. Most "major function" routines are based on this type of loop:

> *read a record*
> DO-WHILE *more records*
>
> ...
> *statements*
> ...
> *read next record*
> ENDDO

The condition is external to the program; the loop will be performed once for each record in the file. If records are added to the file in the future, the program will still work because the condition tests when the end of file is reached regardless of the number of records in the file.

Notice also that the condition is tested after both "read" statements. The condition is tested at the start of the loop, as well as after each subsequent read as it reaches the ENDDO. While the condition remains true, the loop is executed. When the condition becomes false, the statement after the ENDDO is executed, and the program continues from there.

The DO-WHILE logical construct takes the following form in dBASE IV:

DO-WHILE *conditional expression*
    statements to be performed as long as the condition is TRUE
ENDDO

The loop continues to be executed as long as the conditional expression tests true; it is tested each time the ENDDO is encountered. The end of the DO-WHILE is marked by an ENDDO in dBASE IV. If the condition is already true when the DO statement is reached, the loop is skipped, and processing continues with the first statement following the ENDDO.

DO-UNTIL is a logical construct that has no corresponding dBASE IV command (Fig. 2-6). The difference between DO-UNTIL and DO-WHILE is that where a DO-WHILE loop is performed *while* a condition tests true, a DO-UNTIL loop is performed *until* a condition becomes true.

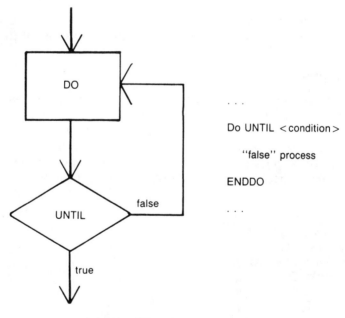

Do UNTIL <condition>

"false" process

ENDDO

2-6   The DO-UNTIL logical construct.

Another difference between DO-WHILE and DO-UNTIL is that the statements in a DO-UNTIL loop are always performed once, even if the condition is true when the loop is executed the first time. The effect is as if the condition is tested at the bottom of the loop instead of the top as in a DO-WHILE loop.

In dBASE IV, because there is no DO-UNTIL loop command, you must create this construct by using existing dBASE IV commands. The usual way is to reverse the DO-WHILE condition by using the logical .NOT. operator:

```
USE CUSTFILE
DO WHILE .NOT. EOF ( )
      DO CUSTPROC
ENDDO
```

The problem with the code shown is that the commands inside the loop are not executed if the condition tests true the first time. There are two ways of working around this problem. One way is to repeat all the instructions before the loop, so that they are executed before the condition is tested. The second is to base a DO-WHILE loop on a logical memory variable, or switch, that is set by an IF statement at the bottom of the loop. The next example shows this method:

```
USE CUSTFILE
DO CUSTPROC
DO WHILE .NOT. EOF ( )
      DO CUSTPROC
ENDDO
```

Fortunately, the need for a DO-UNTIL loop is rare—most of the processing you will need to perform will be adequately handled using DO-WHILE.

CASE structures

The final logical construct is the CASE structure. A CASE is a decision where there can be more than two processes performed for various values of a variable. For instance, the variable SEX appears to have only two possible values. However, there are three: male, female, and invalid. Here the CASE condition has three possible processes to perform: one for male, one for female, and one for invalid data. The CASE figure would look like this:

```
CASE SEX
      WHEN MALE
            male processing
      WHEN FEMALE
            female processing
      OTHERWISE
            invalid sex code processing
ENDCASE
```

There can be any number of WHEN conditions in a CASE figure, and each of those can head a process that can contain nested logical constructs, except other CASE figures in dBASE IV. Some other languages do permit nested CASE statements.

The CASE construct in dBASE IV is a form of the DO command (see Fig. 2-7). The format looks like this:

```
DO CASE
    CASE expression 1
        commands to be performed if condition 1 is true
    CASE expression 2
        commands to be performed if condition 2 is true
    CASE expression 3
        commands to be performed if condition 3 is true...
    OTHERWISE
        commands to be performed if all previous are FALSE
ENDCASE
```

Each condition is evaluated and, if true, the commands are performed until the next CASE, the OTHERWISE, or the ENDCASE is reached. Then the next statement following the ENDCASE is performed, and the program continues from there. If no condition in a CASE is true, the OTHERWISE unit is executed, if present, until the ENDCASE is reached.

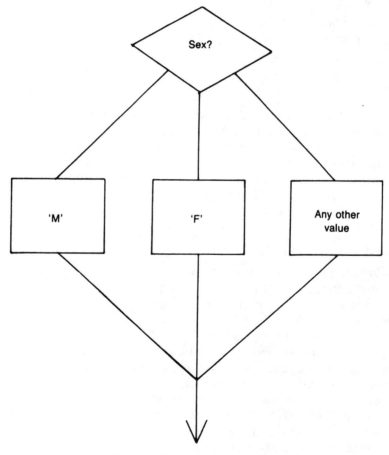

2-7 Case flowchart and pseudocode.

Remember that all the logical constructs are themselves statements, and can be used inside other constructs. This is called *nesting* the constructs, and is one way of combining the constructs to build the final process.

The SCAN construct

To make programming slightly more convenient, dBASE IV includes a construct called SCAN, which is really a different way of coding a DO-WHILE logical construct. Consider this example of processing database records with a DO-WHILE:

```
read a record
DO WHILE more records
    IF condition specifying record selection criteria
        statements
    ENDIF
        read next record
ENDDO
```

This can be replaced with a SCAN construct in dBASE IV. The format of the SCAN construct is:

```
SCAN [scope] [WHILE/FOR condition]
    commands
ENDSCAN
```

The advantage to using the SCAN construct is that you can specify which records are to be processed in the WHILE condition. You can also process all the records in the database, because the processing does not stop when the condition is true. The database is scanned for records matching the WHILE condition, and the statements in the loop are executed for that record. When the statements are completed, the next record matching the criteria is found and processed, and so forth.

Subroutines

Just as logical constructs can be nested to create complex processes, programs can also be nested. One program can be executed from inside another program, and so forth. The second most-common statement in programs is the *subroutine call*

The subroutine is a subprogram. The subroutine call causes a subroutine or subfunction to be performed. When the function is complete, control returns to the next statement after the call. This is the way that the hierarchy of function is described in computer language terms. Each major function module calls the functions listed in the second level in the function chart, and they in turn, call the next level. Figure 2-8 is an illustration of how the flow of control moves when using subroutines.

One advantage to using subroutines is that you can build the program top-down, the same way that the design is created. The high-level programs

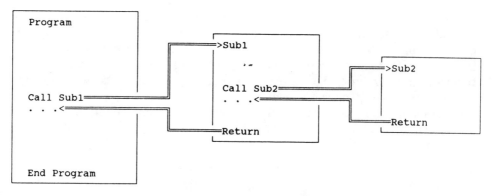

2-8 The flow of control when calling subroutines.

are coded first, calling subroutines to do detailed functions. The subroutine can be left empty until the high-level program has been tested, creating a program "stub."

The "program stubs" are empty lower-level modules that have not yet been coded. By looking at the function chart, you will know what subfunctions there will be, so it is possible to set up stubs for them. As each subfunction is coded, it can then be placed in the stub, and lower-level stubs added. You can actually write your programs this way, and test each level as it is created. The high-level modules are the ones that will be executed most often, because the lower levels are often executed as the result of IF or DO-WHILE conditional statements. The most often used programs should also be the most-tested programs, and "stub" subroutines allow you to do this.

Programming in modules

Subroutines and logical constructs illustrate that programs are constructed from smaller parts, like children's building blocks. The difference is that each program piece holds the level below it, as opposed to supporting the piece above it. Another advantage to this is that your design can emphasize the result of each piece of the system. You can reduce a large, complex system into a series of smaller, easy-to-understand modules—in effect, dividing to conquer.

After the first three design steps:

- Define the problem
- Define the output
- Define the input

is the part where you actually construct your system:

- Define the process

In top-down design, you create the highest level first, moving down from level to level, until the entire system is defined. The seven design steps also apply to each section of the system down to the lower levels. There is no difference between designing an inventory system and designing the function to add a record to the inventory database. In each case, you follow the seven design steps to create the proper process.

For example, if you are creating an inventory system, the highest level of the system might appear as in Fig. 2-9.

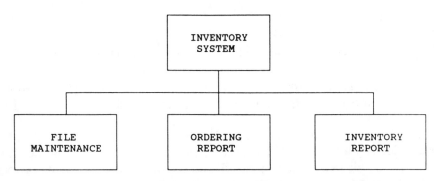

2-9 The highest level of the Inventory System.

The overall system has subsections, each of which performs a major function of the system. Each of these sections can also be divided into functions, as the File Maintenance function is divided in Fig. 2-10.

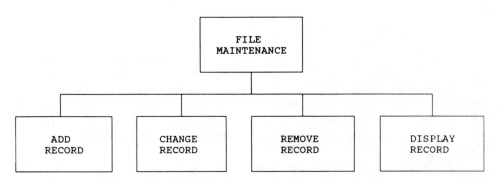

2-10 The inventory File Maintenance function.

The programs at the highest level, such as the box labeled "Inventory System" in Fig. 2-9, become simple processes that guide the user to the lower level functions. This usually means that the higher-level modules are really menus for the operator to choose a function from. Figure 2-11 shows a pseudocode example of a menu processing program.

```
SET EXIT TO "N"

DOWHILE EXIT = "N"

  DISPLAY MENU SCREEN
  READ OPTION

  CASE

    WHEN OPTION = 1 PERFORM "ADD RECORD"
    WHEN OPTION = 2 PERFORM "CHANGE RECORD"
    WHEN OPTION = 3 PERFORM "REMOVE RECORD"
    WHEN OPTION = 4 PERFORM "DISPLAY RECORD"
    WHEN OPTION = X SET EXIT TO "Y"

    OTHERWISE WRITE "INVALID OPTION" ON SCREEN AND BEEP

  ENDCASE

ENDDO
```

2-11 The File Maintenance menu pseudocode.

You can see, in Fig. 2-11, that the pseudocode reflects the hierarchy charts shown in Fig. 2-10. The line "perform add record" represents the program that will actually perform that function. This level can be designed using the same design steps used to reach the higher levels (see Fig. 2-12).

```
Problem definition: Add a new record to the inventory file.

Output: A completed, ready-to-use inventory record.

Input: All fields defined on inventory record.
       Key field must be unique.

Process:
              ACCESS inventory file
              SET ORDER NUMBER TO NOT BLANK

              DO WHILE ORDER NUMBER NOT BLANK

                 DISPLAY SCREEN
                 GET ITEM NUMBER FROM OPERATOR
                 VERIFY ITEM NUMBER

                 IF NEW NUMBER
                 THEN
                   DISPLAY SCREEN
                   GET REMAINING DATA ITEMS
                   ADD RECORD TO FILE
                 ELSE
                   WRITE "ITEM NUMBER ALREADY ON FILE" ON SCREEN AND BEEP
                 ENDIF

              ENDDO
```

2-12 The "add record" design.

Generic subroutines

Another advantage of using the "building block" approach to programming is that one module may be used in several places, or even in several different application systems. This can be done by making the subroutines generic.

A generic subroutine is one that works at any point in the system, as long as the same input is supplied to the subroutine. Also, a generic subroutine should work with any data passed to it—that is, the incoming data should be edited to be certain that the subroutine will work.

The processing performed by subroutines vary, but you can be consistent in the way in which you create them. The data items passed to the subroutine and data produced as a result of the subroutine should be defined, as you define the output and input for a system or program. The order in which you pass the data items can also be the same from subroutine to subroutine, as well as the way in which a subroutine indicates that an error has occurred during processing. If your subroutines are consistent in their interaction with the system, the programs you create will be easier to write and understand.

Another advantage to creating generic subroutines is that the routines can be used in other application systems in the future. For example, the add, change, delete, and display functions for one database can be cloned for use with another database for a different application. This can save you time when creating new applications for your business.

A generic subroutine usually does not use database fields; in fact, it might only perform a minor process in the conversion, editing, or tabulating of database data. A generic function can either be one that is performed so often that it is inefficient to repeat the code, or a function that, because of size or coding structure, would be impractical to include in the main program.

One example of a generic module would be a routine to convert a dBASE date-format memory variable into a character string containing the Julian date, as shown in Fig. 2-13. This subroutine could be called using the DO ... WITH command, because the subroutine will use unique memory variable names; the subroutine may also use PUBLIC memory variables for its receiving and sending areas. Whenever the Date-to-Julian conversion is to occur, this subroutine will be called to perform the task.

Utility modules

You can also use subroutines in different functions without modifying the routines at all. Subroutines that can be used in this way are called *utility modules*.

Utility modules are usually used to perform one basic function in a system. For example, an "add record" function for a database file might call a subroutine to determine if the value of key fields entered by the operator already exist on the database. If you are adding records to an employee database, you would want to be sure that you were not entering duplicate

```
STORE ' 1  2  3  4  5  6  7  8  9 10 11 12 ' TO monsrch
STORE '000031059090120151181212243273304334 ' TO daysb4

STORE CTOD('10/15/1975') TO gdate

STORE VAL(SUBSTR(daysb4,AT(' '+STR(MONTH(gdate),2),monsrch),3)) TO jdays

STORE jdays + DAY(gdate) to jdays

IF MONTH(gdate) > 2
   IF INT(YEAR(gdate)/100) # (YEAR(gdate)/100)
      IF INT(YEAR(gdate)/4) = (YEAR(gdate)/4)
         STORE jdays + 1 TO jdays
      ENDIF
   ELSE
      IF INT(YEAR(gdate)/400) = (YEAR(gdate)/400)
         STORE jdays + 1 TO jdays
      ENDIF
   ENDIF
ENDIF

STORE INT(YEAR(gdate) * 1000) + jdays) TO jdate
```

2-13   The Juilian-Date conversion subroutine.

records accidentally. Figure 2-14 shows a partial flowchart for "add record" with a utility that finds a record with the given key.

If the key exists, a "true" value is returned by the subroutine, along with the record number. If a "false" value is returned, then the record does not exist. This utility module can be used in the change and delete functions as well, to retrieve the record for an existing key.

Utility modules can be created for accessing single database records, or for other application needs such as calculating sales tax. Another example is a utility module that would reformat a name into various forms for use in reports, letters, or bills.

Flowcharting, pseudocoding, and storyboards

The documentation for your system should be the result of your design process. You have already determined the output that you need, and the input necessary to create that result. After you have decided what data items you need to work with and store, you then design the process that builds the output. The plan layout is a description of the method by which the input becomes the output.

The plan layout

There are several different methods that you can use to map the process. The methods involve either charting or coding the process plan. Most people tend to choose either one method or another when deciding how to build their own system. The real power, however, comes from the ability to use either method equally well, or even to combine the methods into a flexible tool for process design.

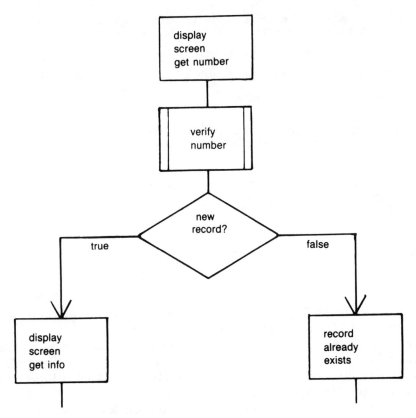

2-14 The partial "add record" flowchart.

Charting methods entail building a graphic representation of the process, using symbols or pictures. There are several types of process charting, each designed to show different aspects of the plan. A PERT chart, for example, shows the tasks involved in a process and the order in which they should be completed. Computer programming is more linear than task oriented—most often, tasks are performed one after the other, even if the second task does not require the result of the first task. This is because computers are "single-threaded;" only one process may be performed at a time.

The most common process-charting method relating to computers is flowcharting. Flowcharts are used by engineers and programmers to map the flow of a process. The flowcharting symbols represent the tasks, decision points, and input/output operations required in the final process.

Coding methods, most notably pseudocode, became more prevalent in the early and mid 1970s. Using plain language logically structured by using the logical constructs, a pseudocoded program accurately reflects the workings of a computer program written in a real computer language.

A newer hybrid of these two methods is storyboarding. The storyboard is a representation of an input screen, an output report, or a stored database file. The idea is to show the data items and variables needed at each step of the process, and the processing required to reformat the data items or to calculate information using the data items.

Whichever method you finally choose, the map of the process becomes the main reference document to use when writing the actual programs for the application system. This document will also become the manual of how to use the system, and will also aid you when you are going to make changes to the system later.

Using flowcharts

Flowcharting has been in use since the inception of computers in the business environment. There are some advantages and disadvantages that you should be aware of before choosing flowcharts as the standard for your business. First, the pictorial representation of the logic of a program is readable, that is, it can be understood easily and by anyone. Unfortunately, the opposite is true for drawing them: they are difficult to envision, cumbersome to change, and because of this are usually not finished before coding starts. Coding is simpler to most people than flowcharting. A system design should be living and evolving as new, more efficient paths are discovered. The flowcharts have to be redrawn each time a change is made.

By using the flowchart symbols shown in Fig. 2-15, a programmer or process designer can show the flow of paperwork through a department. Think of the rectangles as "desks." The paperwork moves from desk to desk along the lines of control. If there is a decision, a choice between desks, the decision point is denoted by a diamond, as shown in Fig. 2-16.

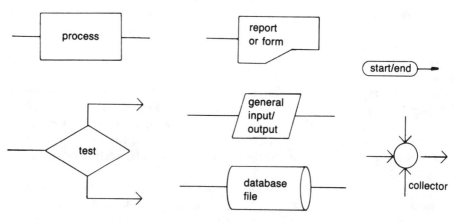

2-15 The flowcharting symbols.

Any process, whether a computer process or not, can be depicted with a flowchart. For example, Fig. 2-17 shows a flowchart of boiling water for tea. In many programming classes, this type of flowchart is used to drill future

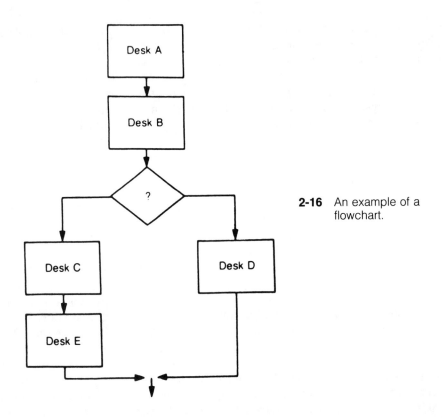

2-16 An example of a flowchart.

programmers in breaking a process down into its simplest components. If you want to practice flowcharting, try "answering the telephone," or "choosing a television show." As you find simpler and simpler steps to break the process into, you will find yourself drawing and redrawing your flowchart.

Note that the following examples use the logical constructs discussed earlier in this chapter. All processes can be defined in terms of these constructs.

Another type of process is a search to find certain records in the database. For example, suppose a company is looking through its employee records, choosing records that meet certain criteria. The employees that meet the qualifications are going to be asked if they would like to transfer to a foreign branch office. The process could be defined (flowcharted) as shown in Fig. 2-18.

The flowchart in Fig. 2-18 really works; that is to say, it will perform the requested process. However, it is not consistent or readable. Notice that all the diamond blocks have "NO" legs on the left, except the last one, which has a "YES". This flowchart falls short on readability and consistency.

A better way of depicting the process can be accomplished by using the logical construct flowchart. Notice that in Fig. 2-19, every diamond block has the YES leg out to the right side. The entire process is contained in a read loop, where the records are read. After each READ operation, a question is

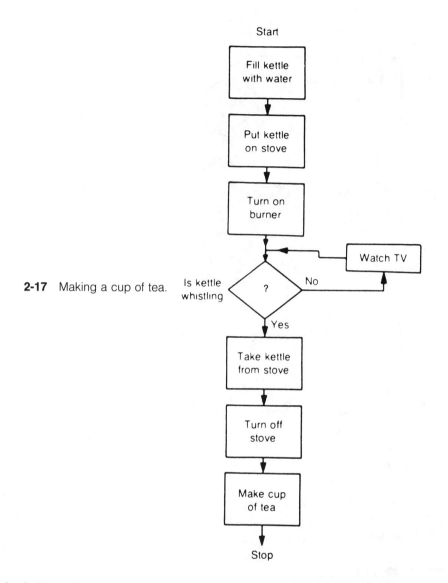

2-17 Making a cup of tea.

asked: "Are there any more records to read?" This determines if the last record has been processed.

Another thing you might notice is that the flowchart could define the logical structure of a program, or could show the flow of paperwork in the office. If the "records" were sheets of paper in a file cabinet, and all the questions were answered by human examination of the document, this flowchart would still be valid. A process definition does not have to be computer-based.

On first sight, the second flowchart seems to be larger and more complicated than the first. However, each logical construct is apparent, and the resulting chart is much more readable.

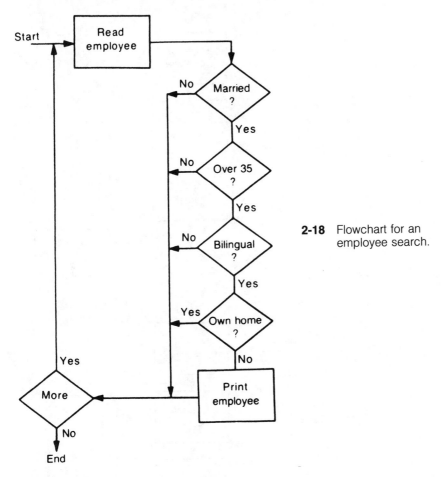

2-18 Flowchart for an employee search.

You can see the problems with trying to modify flowcharts. Usually the whole chart must be redrawn. In a growing, evolving system design, this can be a drawback.

Pseudocoding

In recent years, pseudocoding has become an important addition of the programmer's toolbox. It reduces programming into the simplest relationships of data. This is done by using the logical constructs that appear in some form in most computer languages.

With logical constructs, processes may be mapped out in general terms, and slowly become more detailed, until the final solution has evolved. Each subfunction may be worked with until it is solved, eventually becoming a part of the system.

This "divide and conquer" method of problem-solving is the answer to the problem of complexity. Functions are reduced to subfunctions of less complexity, and are divided again into units of even less complexity, until a detailed,

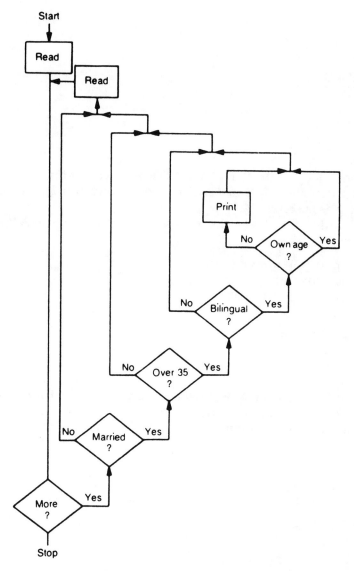

2-19 Logical construct flowchart.

accurate map of the process has been obtained. Coding is now just a matter of translating the pseudocode into a real computer language. Coding takes less time, and testing can be started at the same time as coding commences.

Pseudocode is a representation of a logic flow, but unlike the pictorial flowchart, pseudocode is written in plain language. This fact makes it easier to change and/or rewrite than a flowchart. The first example in Fig. 2-16 showed the flow of paperwork from desk to desk in an office. That same process, shown as pseudocode, would look like this:

```
DESK A
DESK B
IF X
THEN
     DESK C
     DESK E
ELSE
     DESK D
ENDIF
...
```

The diamond block, with its YES and NO legs, becomes an IF-THEN-ELSE logical construct. The THEN part is done if condition X is true, the ELSE part if condition X is false.

The "waiting for the tea kettle" process in Fig. 2-17 would look like this in pseudocode:

```
PLACE KETTLE ON BURNER
TURN ON BURNER THAT KETTLE IS ON
DO WHILE KETTLE NOT WHISTLING
     WATCH TV
ENDDO
REMOVE KETTLE FROM HEAT
TURN OFF BURNER
MAKE TEA!
```

The DO WHILE construct is a loop that is performed over and over again while the condition ("kettle not whistling") is true.

For a final example of pseudocode, let's look at the process flowcharted in Fig. 2-18:

```
READ EMPLOYEE
     DO WHILE MORE EMPLOYEES
     IF MARRIED
     THEN
          IF OVER 35
          THEN
               IF BILINGUAL
               THEN
                    IF OWNS HOME
                    THEN
                         NOTHING
                    ELSE
                         PRINT EMPLOYEE
                    ENDIF
               ENDIF
               ENDIF
          ENDIF
     READ EMPLOYEE
ENDDO
```

First, notice the IF OWNS HOME construct. The THEN leg of the flow has no process associated with it. That construct could be changed to a negative comparison by the addition of NOT:

```
...
IF DOES NOT OWN HOME
THEN
     PRINT EMPLOYEE
ENDIF
...
```

Also notice that there is a series of IF-THEN-IF-THEN.... These constructs could be replaced by a single IF if you make the condition complex. This is accomplished by connecting the conditions with AND. The final version of the pseudocode would look like this:

```
READ EMPLOYEE
DO WHILE MORE EMPLOYEES
     IF MARRIED AND OVER 35 AND BILINGUAL
     THEN
          IF DOES NOT OWN HOME
          THEN
               PRINT EMPLOYEE
          ENDIF
     ENDIF
     READ NEXT RECORD
ENDDO
```

The pseudocode has become simpler than the flowchart by use of a complex condition. It is much easier to combine expressions in pseudocode than to type all those conditions in that little diamond block! Because pseudocode is so easily changed, it is much more desirable than a flowchart for a design tool. Flowcharts are excellent documentation tools, however; they should be drawn after the design is complete.

Storyboarding the system

The storyboarding approach allows you to envision each step of the process being designed. Each board contains data items to be entered from a screen, printed on paper, calculated, displayed on the screen, and stored for future use. After all the data items are laid out this way, your task is to connect the boards using calculation, storage, and other dBASE operations.

Storyboards are connected to each other by way of the logical constructs used in programming. dBASE programs use this type of logic to manipulate the data items, in effect connecting the storyboards to one another. For example, if a data item is a percentage, the user could enter the number as 40, indicating 40%. A section of code could change this number to .40 for calculation and storage purposes. This conversion is the connection between the storyboard of the input screen and the storyboard for the database file.

These connections between the storyboards can be pseudocoded using simple terms, and directly translated into a dBASE process.

There can be processes that are performed on data items before they reach the storyboard, and that are performed after the storyboard is completed. For example, if the storyboard represents a screen display, the data items can be manipulated before they are displayed, or after they are entered on the screen. The calculations or reformatting that takes place before the storyboard is reached is called *pre-processing*, while the processing that follows the storyboard is called *post-processing*.

The first step of the process is always to define your problem, then to choose an alternative to solve it. There are usually many ways to solve any one problem, and also many different methods of implementing each solution. You must make the choice for your own individual situation. The problem-solving techniques used in this book work for the design of almost any process.

You have decided that you need more information, or more accurate information, or more available information. You want to be able to see some representation of that information—a display screen, a report, or a graph. When you have decided what information you need to see, write down those items you wish to see. Group the items into the format you want, and make any notes that you might think are applicable.

Planning a computer system is actually like writing a story backwards, because you start with the output (what you need), then work backwards to determine the required input (what you enter). Applying this idea to the storyboard approach, the first boards that you create will have the final results that you expect from the system. The next set of boards should contain the necessary items required to produce those results. Finally, you will reach a point where all the information must come from an outside source. This is the information that you must enter into the system in order to reach the final results.

The first storyboards are used to collect the items that the system is required to produce. For example, you might want the system to produce a list of all your customers' names and addresses. Perhaps you want to address envelopes, or to create mailing labels. Your first storyboard might look like Fig. 2-20.

Your next task is to determine what is necessary to produce this label. You could, for example, enter the name and address each time you want to produce labels. This would change your $1000 computer into a typewriter! Another alternative is to save a file of customer names and addresses that you could expand and modify as your customer list changes.

You now create a storyboard that describes this file, such as shown in Fig. 2-21. You can now create the "bridges" between the customer file storyboard and the mailing labels storyboard, changing the stored data into the format for printing on the labels. The bridge takes the form of processing to be performed on the data items before printing can occur. For example, the customer file items last name, first name, middle name, title, and suffix must

```
Storyboard name: MAILING LABELS

Data items:

        customer name (title first middle last)
        street address
        mailing address (if different than street address)
        city
        state
        zipcode

Planned output: adhesive labels (1-up)

Output format:

(name)                XXXXXXXXXXXXXXXXXXXXXXXXXXXXXX
(street addr)         XXXXXXXXXXXXXXXXXXXXXXXXXXXXXX
(mailing addr)        XXXXXXXXXXXXXXXXXXXXXXXXXXXXXX
(city, state zip)     XXXXXXXXXXXXXXXXXXXXXXXXXXXXXX
```

2-20   Storyboard: Mailing labels.

```
Storyboard name: CUSTOMER FILE

Data items:

        last name      - (primary order on this field) 30 characters
        first name     - (secondary order on this field) 30 characters
        middle name    - 15 characters
        title          - 10 characters
        suffix         - 10 characters
        street address - 35 characters
        mailing address- 35 chars. (if different than street address)
        city           - 20 characters
        state          - 2 characters
        zipcode        - 9 characters
```

2-21   Storyboard: Customer file.

be arranged and grouped to print the label as indicated. City, state, and zipcode must also be rearranged for the label.

To indicate this on the storyboard, add notations to the preprocessing part of the mailing labels storyboard. Your notations might look like those in Fig. 2-22.

Now you can move on to the next step: showing where the data items on the customer file storyboard came from. This means that you need some data entry screen format to get these values into the customer file. A new storyboard is created for the input data items. If a customer name is needed in an output board, there will have to be an input board with the corresponding data item to be entered. The only information that is available to the computer is that which you enter. You can sort, calculate, and infer new information from the stored data, but that data must be entered item by item at some point.

As you build the input storyboard, document relationships between the data items and the output information that they will yield. You could indicate

```
Storyboard name: MAILING LABELS

Data items: (All data items come from CUSTOMER FILE)

          customer name (title first middle last suffix)
          street address
          mailing address (if different than street address)
          last addr line (city state zipcode)

Pre-processing:

     customer name
          join "title" "first name" "middle name" "last name" "suffix"
          (all of these items from Customer File)

     zipcode2 (from Customer File)
          format "zipcode" from 999999999 to 99999-9999

     last addr line
          join "city" "state" "zipcode2"

Planned output: adhesive labels (1-up)

Output format:

(name)             XXXXXXXXXXXXXXXXXXXXXXXXXXXXXX
(street addr)      XXXXXXXXXXXXXXXXXXXXXXXXXXXXXX
(mailing addr)     XXXXXXXXXXXXXXXXXXXXXXXXXXXXXX
(last addr line)   XXXXXXXXXXXXXXXXXXXXXXXXXXXXXX
```

2-22 Storyboard: Mailing labels with preprocessing.

that a year-to-date-purchases output item is really "sales subtotal accumulated through a time period." You could also specify detailed calculations, and differing values based on other data items. Validation information should also be listed, such as whether the information is to be numeric and/or entered in a special format.

The same storyboard can be used to show all maintenance functions. When you are maintaining a database or file, you always need a way to add, change, delete, and view records. All data items on the file can be entered or changed by this process. For example, Fig. 2-23 shows a customer file data entry/maintenance storyboard.

As the system grows more complex, you will find that some storyboards are used as output from one process and as input to the next. The collection of storyboards leading from the input to the final result are the computer system. Once you have created all the storyboards, you can arrange and rearrange them for different functions. For example, Fig. 2-24 shows three different ways to arrange the storyboards customer file, customer file data entry, and mailing labels.

The three arrangements show that first, data moves from the data entry storyboard to the mailing label storyboard. Second, the customer file storyboard can send and receive data from/to the two other storyboards. Third, the customer file storyboard and the mailing labels storyboard can be used to produce labels from an existing and up-to-date file; that is, if there are no changes to make to the customer file, the data entry storyboard is not used.

```
Storyboard: CUSTOMER FILE DATA ENTRY/MAINTENANCE

Data items: (All data items come from user entry or Customer File)

        last name       - (primary order on this field) 30 characters
        first name      - (secondary order on this field) 30 characters
        middle name     - 15 characters
        title           - 10 characters
        suffix          - 10 characters
        street address  - 35 characters
        mailing address - 35 chars. (if different than street address)
        city            - 20 characters
        state           - 2 characters
        zipcode         - 9 characters
                          formatted 99999-9999, stored as 999999999

Post-processing and editing:

    "title" "first name" "middle name" "last name" alphabetic

    zipcode -- numeric
```

2-23 Storyboard: Customer file data entry/maintenance.

The important thing to remember is timing—a storyboard must exist from input before it can be used for storage or output. The boards should be grouped by business function. As more detail is added, you can expand your data lists and relationships to include new edits, cross-edits, and formats.

You use logical statements on the storyboard to describe the actions to be taken. Each statement must use a data item that is referenced on either the current storyboard or another storyboard. To be sure to create a workable system, statements must use these data items according to certain rules. You can create new data items on a storyboard, but it must be composed of the result of an operation with already existing data items.

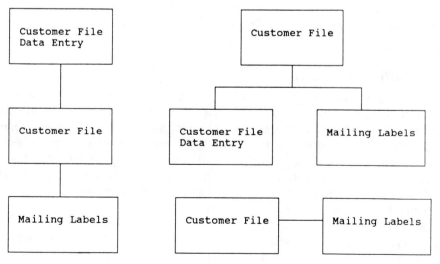

2-24 Three arrangements of storyboards.

Storyboarding is in itself a hybrid process. Not only are the storyboards themselves used to represent the "stopping points" of the data items, but pseudocode is used to map pre- and post-processing that occurs around the storyboard. The best "process designers" are those who can use a variety of methods to get the job done. You might find that you can connect the storyboards using the flowcharting symbols, thereby creating a three-way hybrid for your process design.

Creating a prototype

It is possible to start working on your system right away, and also increase the effectiveness of your system. You can create a prototype of your system, developing the menus and screens needed in the system, before the programs are written.

The advantage to this arrangement is that the screens and menus that make up the user interface of your system can be tested and changed (if necessary) early in the process. The arrangement and number of data items on a data entry screen will probably mean that any program using that screen would have to be modified to accommodate the change.

Creating a system prototype also enables data entry to begin, while the rest of the functions are still being designed and coded. The process design you have created can be used to find problems with screen navigation or general system handling that should be changed before the system is really used.

A system prototype also allows the eventual end-users to see the setup of the application system, so that they can learn the system. The ultimate end-user of the system, whether that user is a manager, secretary, or even yourself, can offer suggestions to make the system easier to use. The important thing is to get this kind of feedback before the system is so far completed that a change would be difficult or impossible.

Debugging the plan

When you have finished your pseudocode for a function, it is necessary to "test it out," that is, to examine it for logical correctness. Or, to put it another way, make sure it does what you want it to do! To check out your pseudocode, read each statement one at a time. This is the way the computer will execute your statements when you translate your pseudocode into dBASE IV code. Point a pencil to each line as you read it, to mark the statement where the control is. When you execute conditional statements, examine the flow of control for both true and false conditions.

In CASE figures, test the flow for every WHEN condition. In an IF-THEN-ELSE logical construct, when the IF condition is true, the statements in the THEN unit are executed, and then control passes to the statement following the ENDIF. For example, consider the following:

1. IF month = 2
2. THEN month name is "February"
3. ENDIF
4. ...

If month does equal 2, the flow of control (using the line numbers) would be 1-2-3-4. On the other hand, if month was anything other than 2, the flow would be 1-3-4. With no ELSE unit for a false condition, control passes out of the IF-THEN construct to the next statement (line 4).

If the IF construct includes an ELSE unit, slightly different processing occurs:

1. IF state = "CT"
2. THEN perform "in state"
3. ELSE perform "out of state"
4. ENDIF
5. ...

A true condition in the example above (state equal to "CT") would execute statements 1-2-2-5. The ELSE unit is skipped over by control when the condition is true. A false condition in the above example would execute statements 1-3-2-5; the THEN unit would be skipped over.

In a CASE construct, control is passed to the statements in the WHEN unit where the condition tests true, and then jumps to the statement following the ENDCASE. If no WHEN condition tests true, control jumps to the OTHERWISE, if any. For example, consider the following:

1. CASE
2. WHEN state = "CT"
3. perform "in Connecticut"
4. WHEN state = "MA"
5. perform "in Massachusetts"
6. WHEN state = "NY"
7. perform "in New York"
8. OTHERWISE
9. perform "other state"
10. ENDCASE
11. ...

When this construct is executed, and the value of state is "CT", the statements will be performed 1-2-3-10-11. If state is "MA", the flow of processing would be 1-2-5-10-11; for state of "NY", the flow would be 1-6-7-10-11. If the state was anything other than "CT", "MA", or "NY", the processing would be statements 1-8-9-10-11.

In a DO-WHILE construct, a loop of statements is performed as long as a condition is true. In the following example, a counter is incremented and then tested by the DO-WHILE:

1. set counter to 1
2. DO WHILE counter < = 3
3. add counter to total
4. add 1 to counter
5. ENDDO
6. ...

First, the variable counter is set to one. The DO-WHILE then tests variable counter against a literal (3). While counter remains at three or below, this loop is executed. The flow of processing would be 1-2-3-4 (counter now 2)-5-2-3-4 (counter now 3)-5-2-3-4 (counter now 4)-5-2 (condition now "false")-5-6. The variable TOTAL would now contain six (1 + 2 + 3), while counter would be set to four.

Notice the loop was performed three times, while counter was one, two, and finally three. The incrementation to four made the condition false and the statements inside the loop were not performed after counter became four.

Another aid in testing your pseudocode is to write any variable names down on a separate sheet of paper, and write in the values you wish to test. As the values change, cross out the old values and write in the new ones. This will show the exact values of the variables at each statement in the code.

The name for this type of careful examination of the process design is walk-through, and it is invaluable as a testing tool. By getting the design right before the actual computer program is written, you can save yourself much aggravation at having missed problems in your design. Your program might even work the first time, if you take the time to design it properly and test the design.

This testing and walk-through is performed not only on your program layouts, but on your plan at every level. By carefully thinking and bench-checking your plan, you create a uniform and complete system. You might not find all the problems, and you might even miss some "whoppers," but you will eliminate most of the time-consuming rewriting and reworking that occur when the design is not properly tested.

3
Bringing it together

dBASE IV allows you to process, store, maintain, query, and report data without writing programs at all. The real power of dBASE, however, can only be realized by creating your own customized systems using the dBASE programming language.

The dBASE programming language

There are two basic methods of using dBASE IV. First, you can use the dBASE IV Control Center, accessing the dBASE functions from the menus. The second way is to enter the commands directly from the dBASE prompt, also called the *dot prompt*. Many new dBASE users find that the Control Center, called *The Assistant* in earlier versions of dBASE, helps them to access the power of the software without remembering a lot of commands. As a dBASE user becomes more experienced, however, they find that they are hampered by the necessity of using the menu system and want to enter commands directly. dBASE IV can accommodate both of these methods.

The Control Center can be entered by issuing the command ASSIST at the dot prompt. You can also specify that the Control Center is to be entered directly upon entry to dBASE IV by using the file CONFIG.DB. This file is used to store your own default environment for dBASE—part of which is the first command to be executed upon entry to dBASE IV. If you want to enter the Control Center directly upon entry to dBASE, include the line:

    COMMAND = ASSIST

in the CONFIG.DB file. This file can be created and updated using a standard text editor, dBASE's own built-in editor, or by using the special CONFIG.DB editor included in DBSETUP. You will be greeted with the Control Center main menu, as shown in Fig. 3-1.

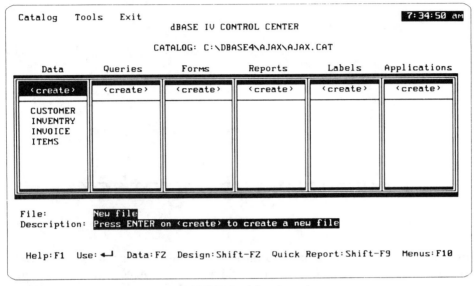

3-1 The dBASE Control Center main menu.

The experienced dBASE user can access the power of dBASE directly from the dot prompt by entering dBASE commands. You can also configure dBASE so that it is easier for you to use, for example, by changing the dot prompt to something more readable or explanatory. In the CONFIG.DB file, enter the line:

PROMPT = dBASE>

and the dot prompt becomes the dBASE > prompt. No matter how you set your prompt, dBASE commands can be entered directly. You can open database files, request reports, display your data, use the EDIT, BROWSE, and APPEND features to manipulate your data. The first command you should know is how to leave dBASE IV once you are through using it. That command is QUIT.

The first section of this book is an explanation of how applications are built. You should plan and build your applications according to these guidelines before you even try to start up the dBASE software. Later, you may change these guidelines to conform more with the way your organization operates or to conform to your personal style.

If you are trying dBASE (or any other database software) to see if it fits your needs, you should try writing a small application using the software. You could build a telephone/address book or a customer directory. These applications are simple and can be quickly designed. You can then try to implement this small application using dBASE to see how the software behaves during use.

The design for this trial application should be small enough that it can be implemented quickly—say in a few minutes. You can create the database file, then use the dBASE commands to perform data entry, update, and reporting. The next step is to make the application more sophisticated by creating a menu, data entry screen formats, and customized reports. Then you can create your own programs to perform these functions. Each level of sophistication that you add to the trial application should teach you more about the software and how to use the many facilities of dBASE IV.

For example, a telephone book application is one of the easiest to create and modify. You can use this simple application to test how the database software, in this case dBASE IV, works for you. You create a database design, and the application functions to add, change, delete, and report the entries. You can then expand on this "mini-design" by adding a screen format, a report format, and a menu to tie the functions together. These can be used to add levels of complexity to the simple telephone book application.

Another reason to try out an easy application is so that you can test your understanding of the software. You know how your trial application, like the telephone book database, should work—so it is just a case of finding the right commands to accomplish the task. You might learn more about the software from your efforts to get the trial application working.

With your completed design firmly in hand, the first step is to build your database file. The database design that you have completed can be entered into the dBASE catalog as a single database file or as a series of files. The data item definitions in your design each become a separate field in the database file.

From the dBASE Control Center main menu, you can choose the ⟨create⟩ icon under the database heading. You can also create a database file using the CREATE command from the dot prompt. Using either method, you arrive at a database definition screen, as shown in Fig. 3-2.

Enter all of the data items that you have decided belong in a group as fields on the database. The field name, data type, length, and number of decimal places are entered into the database definition screen. This creates the structure of a single database file. If your data design calls for more than one group of data items, each group is entered as a separate database file. You can enter all of your database files in this manner.

When you have completed entering the field definitions for a database, dBASE prompts you for input with the question:

Input records now? (Y/N)

You can reply Y to this question, and immediately begin entering data into the file. dBASE IV provides you with a default screen format to use for every database. This default format consists of all of the database fields, identified by the field name, starting in the upper left corner of the computer monitor.

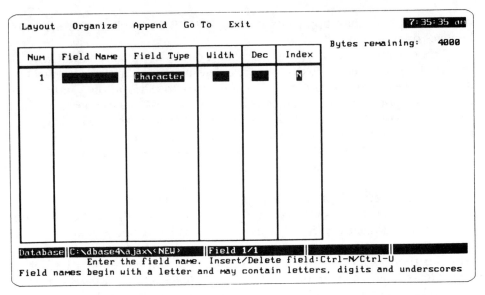

3-2 The database definition screen.

You can start entering data into a database as soon as it is created, even if no other part of the application is done.

The default screen format is only an expedient—real data entry efforts require a well-formatted and well-designed screen layout. dBASE IV lets you generate a screen layout via the CREATE SCREEN process. Enter this process either by using the CREATE SCREEN command at the dot prompt or by choosing the ⟨create⟩ icon under the Screen column on the Control Center main menu. The screen format editor allows you to move fields around the screen, specify formats and values for input fields, and to place text on the screen wherever needed. You can design your own screens to meet your specific needs.

A default report format in dBASE IV, called a quick report format, creates a report format much like the default screen format—headings are database field names, values are not formatted. You can also define more sophisticated reports using a customized report format. Report formats are a description of how fields in a database file should be printed on a report. Report formats are defined in much the same way as a screen format, using the CREATE REPORT process. CREATE REPORT allows you to generate reports in any format you need.

The dBASE programming language consists of all of the dBASE commands; the IF-THEN-ELSE, DO-WHILE, CASE, and subroutine logical structures, and the environment setting commands. These types of commands, along with the use of dBASE built-in functions, memory variables, and database fields, allow you to create application programs in dBASE IV.

The dBASE commands are those operations that actually cause some external or internal change as a result of their execution. For example, an assignment statement changes the contents of a memory variable or database field. An APPEND BLANK command causes an empty record to be added to a database file.

dBASE commands differ from the logical constructs IF-THEN-ELSE, DO-WHILE, and the CASE structure. While the commands cause an action to occur, the logical constructs cause the flow of execution within the program to change. The IF-THEN-ELSE construct, for example, causes one set of commands to be executed if a comparison is true, and causes a different set of commands to be executed if the comparison is false. Nothing changes except the flow of execution within the program—but the commands that are executed because of the IF-THEN-ELSE can cause other changes.

The environment settings of dBASE IV allow you to change the overall configuration of dBASE during the execution of a program. For example, you can change whether or not the alarm sounds for errors with SET BELL OFF. SET commands affect the environment that the program is executing in. These commands can be entered as program commands or can be set in the CONFIG.DB file. You can alter the environment for a particular purpose, such as changing the format of date variables, changing the delimiters for screen displays, or allowing the deletion of database files.

The command language, the logical structures, functions, and environment settings are used together to form your application programs in dBASE IV.

The logical constructs in dBASE IV code

The logical constructs of structured programming can be used to build dBASE programs. Each of the constructs exists in the programming language of dBASE IV. (See Fig. 4-1.)

The iterative DO-WHILE construct allows repetitive execution of a series of commands. This construct is a common framework to use when building a program. For example, the pseudocode and program code in Fig. 3-3 shows one use of the DO-WHILE loop.

The DO-WHILE loop in Fig. 3-3 executes a process that is driven by the records in the database. In other words, the statements between the DO-WHILE and END-DO statements will be executed once for each record in the database file, until there are no more records. This is a common way of writing a process where all of the records in a file must be accessed.

Subroutine calls can be used in a program as a single statement. The purpose of a subroutine is to perform some specific task and return some information to the calling routine. Each subroutine is coded as a separate program. If you follow the structured design procedures, the outermost or *top-most* programs will be designed first, and coded first. You can then test these outermost "shell" programs. When they are correct, you can code and test the next level of subroutines, and so forth. This process ensures that your most-often-used programs are tested most often.

IF-THEN-ELSE and CASE structures, as shown in Fig. 3-4, are used to

```
USE PPHONE INDEX LNAMEX

GO TOP

TESTCHAR = SPACE(1)                          && set up break test variable

DO WHILE .NOT. EOF()                         && stop at End Of File

      BRKCHAR = SUBSTR(LASTNAME, 1, 1)  && test first character

      IF BRKCHAR # TESTCHAR                   && if new section ...

           DO HEADING                         && print section heading
           TESTCHAR = BRKCHAR                 && save first character

      ENDIF

      DO PRTLINE                              && print record from PPHONE

      SKIP                                    && get next record

ENDDO

* end of program
```

3-3 The DO-WHILE loop used in a program.

change processing in particular circumstances. The circumstances are contained in the condition specified in either the IF or WHEN statements. The condition of an IF or WHEN statement can be a comparison of two values, a compound comparison, or a logical field. Built-in functions can also be used as part of the comparison or as a logical value. dBASE logical fields and logical built-in functions contain either a .T. ("true") or .F. ("false") value.

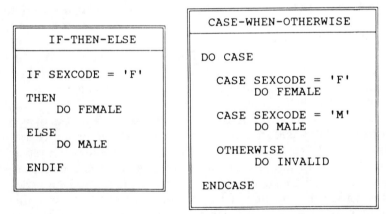

3-4 The IF-THEN-ELSE and CASE structures.

These are the logical values that dBASE uses to represent the result of a comparison, so that a logical field can be used directly in place of a comparison, as shown in Fig. 3-5.

The difference between the IF-THEN-ELSE and CASE structures is that the IF-THEN-ELSE is only effective on "true/false" questions—ones where

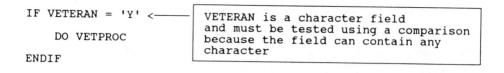

```
IF VETERAN = 'Y'  <───── VETERAN is a character field
                          and must be tested using a comparison
        DO VETPROC        because the field can contain any
                          character
ENDIF
```

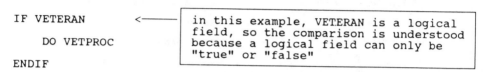

```
IF VETERAN        <───── in this example, VETERAN is a logical
                          field, so the comparison is understood
        DO VETPROC        because a logical field can only be
                          "true" or "false"
ENDIF
```

3-5 Using a logical field instead of a comparison.

there are only two values possible as an answer. The CASE structure can be used to interrogate data where more than two values are expected. For example, a data field called VETIND might indicate whether or not an employee has served in the Armed Forces. This criteria has only two possible values, YES and NO. If you are processing a database record that had the field VETIND, and some processing is based on the contents of VETIND, you would use an IF-THEN-ELSE construct. In the dBASE language, you would normally use a logical field for this type of data item.

However, if you were editing an input field called SEXCODE that has allowable values M and F, you would use a CASE structure. This is because there are actually three possible values in this input field—M, F, and invalid. If different processing is to be performed for each of these values, an IF-THEN-ELSE construct might become overly complicated, where a CASE structure would not.

Using all the logical constructs together, you can build any process you need. The logical constructs can be nested or used in sequence. A completed construct can be considered a single logical statement. Figure 3-6 shows a program using the logical constructs.

The programming language that is built-in to dBASE IV almost requires that you properly structure your programs. There are no labels in the language, and therefore no unconditional branch-to-label statements. The logical structures formed in pseudocode are exactly mirrored in the syntax of the language.

Structured coding means more than just eliminating GO TO statements from a language. Structured coding also means that each discrete group of code, or module, must be self-contained. Each procedure or program should have one and only one entry point and one and only one exit point.

dBASE allows you to return control to a calling routine just by using the RETURN statement. In a structured environment, there should only be one of these in a routine.

```
USE PPHONE INDEX LNAMEX          && open database and index

GO TOP                           && input/output statement

TESTCHAR = SPACE(1)              && assignment statement

DO WHILE .NOT. EOF()             && DO-WHILE

    BRKCHAR = SUBSTR(LASTNAME, 1, 1) && assignment statement

    IF BRKCHAR # TESTCHAR        && IF-THEN-ELSE

        DO HEADING               && subroutine call
        TESTCHAR = BRKCHAR       && assignment  statement

    ENDIF                        && end of IF-THEN construct

    DO PRTLINE                   && subroutine call

    SKIP                         && input/output statement

ENDDO                            && end of DO-WHILE construct

* end of program
```

3-6 A program with logical constructs.

As with most "rules," the structured programming guidelines are made to be bent. In an interactive program, especially systems with several levels of menus, the operator might require a way to avoid the intervening menus when going back to the top. This means at least one extra RETURN statement, the RETURN TO MASTER, must be included in the lower-level menus. RETURN TO MASTER tells dBASE to return control to the first routine in the hierarchy, the top-most level.

This is an excellent example of coding trade-offs during application development. The coding necessary to reproduce the workings of the RETURN TO MASTER statement would take a prohibitive amount of time. The possible bending of structured programming guidelines can be weighed against the ease of coding, and the understandability of the final code. The RETURN TO MASTER statement is obvious in its intent, and requires no further coding.

Two other unstructured commands in dBASE IV are the LOOP and EXIT statements. These commands are used to bypass normal DO-WHILE loop processing.

The EXIT statement causes control to pass from inside a DO-WHILE loop to the first statement following the ENDDO; the condition is not tested again. The EXIT statement constitutes a second exit point from the loop, making this loop unstructured (Fig. 3-7). There should never be more than one entrance into or exit from a logical construct. Use of this statement is a flagrant violation of structured principles and should be avoided at all costs.

The LOOP statement bends the rules, but does not break them. LOOP tells dBASE to go immediately to the top of the DO WHILE loop, to once again test the condition. This can be necessary, because it bypasses unwanted processing without actually exiting the loop.

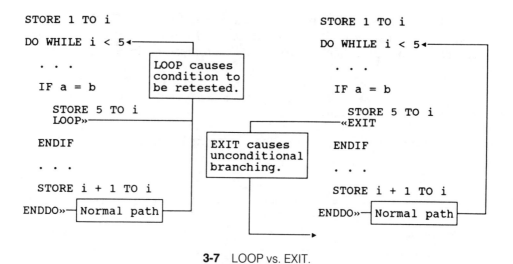

```
STORE 1 TO i                              STORE 1 TO i

DO WHILE i < 5                            DO WHILE i < 5
                  ┌──────────────┐
   . . .          │ LOOP causes  │           . . .
                  │ condition to │
   IF a = b       │ be retested. │           IF a = b
                  └──────────────┘
      STORE 5 TO i                              STORE 5 TO i
      LOOP»                                     «EXIT
                  ┌──────────────┐
   ENDIF          │ EXIT causes  │           ENDIF
                  │ unconditional│
   . . .          │ branching.   │           . . .
                  └──────────────┘
   STORE i + 1 TO i                          STORE i + 1 TO i
         ┌──────────────┐                          ┌──────────────┐
ENDDO»──┤ Normal path  │                   ENDDO»──┤ Normal path  │
         └──────────────┘                          └──────────────┘
```

3-7 LOOP vs. EXIT.

The efficiency of any program can be improved by skipping over statements that are truly unnecessary, based on certain conditions. The key here is the term *conditions*, because they are what slow down a program.

Any statement that requires a decision on the part of the interpreter takes longer than those that don't. This is another common-sense rule: The more a single statement has to do, the longer it will take. The statements that take the least amount of time are STOREs (assignment statements). The value to store is in memory, and the area it is being stored in is in memory; the move is all but instantaneous.

DO-WHILE loops, IF-THEN-ELSE conditions, and CASE structures take more time. In these cases, dBASE is retrieving two or more values from memory, and comparing them character by character, and then storing a value ("true" or "false") to yet another area of memory.

The statements that take the most time are input/output statements such as LOCATE and REPLACE. The interpreter must call the operating system to actually get the record and place it at a certain point in memory called the *buffer*.

Keeping this in mind, you should begin to see little ways in which your programs can be made more efficient. Contrary to the beliefs of some programmers, when the code is complete and the program works, the project is *not* finished.

The source code postmortem is another of the tools used by professional programmers to increase the efficiency of the systems that they write. This means going line-by-line through the final version and looking for places to tighten it. This can be aided by having another programmer or other disinterested party sit down with you to "walk through" the code.

For example, a program might need to check for a certain character to be in a specific position in a character string. If the character is A, the remainder of the field contains one format; if it is B, there is a slightly different format, and so forth. Rather than checking each possibility with SUBSTR( ), it is much better to use SUBSTR( ) once at the beginning, move the value to a memory variable, and then test that variable instead of the sub string (Fig. 3-8).

```
Poor code should be tightened ...

IF (SUBSTR( TEST, 1, 1) = 'A') .OR. (SUBSTR( TEST, 1, 1) = 'B')



                ... so that unnecessary functions are eliminated.

  STORE SUBSTR( TEST, 1, 1) TO TEST2      && call function just once
  IF (TEST2 = 'A') .OR. (TEST2 = 'B')      && and test memvar
```

3-8 Tightening the code.

Another "speed-eater" occurs when statements are performed within a loop. If the same value is being moved to the same variable each time through the loop, the statement can be moved outside the loop, probably to a position just before or after it. Even though a STORE statement does not take much time, when it is repeated over and over again in a loop, the time can add up.

Sample programs

The best way to learn any piece of software is to use it—and dBASE IV is no exception. Even with the Control Center menus, using dBASE is still a learning process. As you use the software, you discover better ways to perform the processes that you create. Each application program will be easier than the last, because you will start understanding the sequence of events that needs to occur for dBASE to do its job.

You might start this learning curve with a sample application that you can create easily. You might predesign this application so that you can use it as a test application when evaluating any database software package. The application should also be easy and small enough that you can remember a good portion of it—you might have to create the application without your notes. If you are evaluating a software package in a computer store, for example, you may try the first level of your system, such as creating the database or writing a simple screen format.

You should also be able to make your test application more sophisticated by using more of the features of dBASE. This will enable you to learn the features of the software by actually using them. The results of your test application should be easily verified, so that you can identify and correct errors quickly.

One example of this type of application is the personal telephone directory. You might create a database of telephone numbers, names, and addresses, then store records in the file, and try to print a list of the records. After you have done this much, you might make the application more sophisticated by using a screen format for input and display of the records. Also, try to retrieve records by name, and create a report format for the list. You can then even move on to create a menu for your application. At each level of sophistication, you are learning something new about dBASE IV.

The database design is fairly easy—only a limited number of data items are associated with a personal phone directory. For example, the following list of data items are all that are required:

- Telephone number
- Name (last, first, middle initial)

You can break name down into its components, or use a single field for the name. Telephone number could also be divided into the separate field's area code and telephone number. You can change your definitions of these fields, so that you can try to handle them in several different formats. You can optionally add:

- Street address
- City
- State
- Zipcode

to create an address book as well. This means that you might also create mailing labels by using the label format of dBASE IV, adding another function to your test application.

The database file for this test application, as shown in Fig. 3-9, is created by starting the dBASE software, going to the dot prompt, and entering:

CREATE PPHONE

or by choosing the ⟨create⟩ icon under the Database column in the Control Center.

After you enter the database definition, the software will prompt you with the message:

Input records now?

Answering Y to this question will allow you to start entering records immediately, using a default screen format, as shown in Fig. 3-10.

You might enter a small number of records into the database for testing purposes. After you finish entering the records, press the enter key on an empty screen, and you will return to the dot prompt (or the Control Center menu). Now, try to reaccess the database and change one of the records. This will show you how to retrieve the correct record and make the change. You might then attempt to add a new record to the file, or delete a record from the

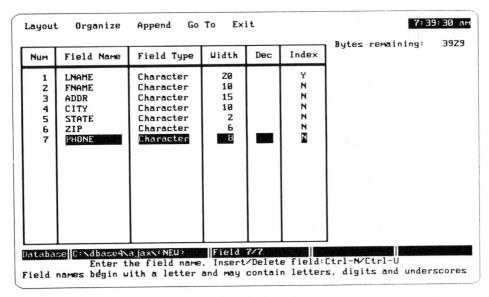

3-9 The PPHONE database.

file. This will show you how all of the basic file operations work interactively with dBASE IV. The commands that you use from the dot prompt are the same commands that you would use in a program to perform the operation.

Once you feel comfortable with the actions of the various file commands such as EDIT and APPEND, you might try to display a list of the records you

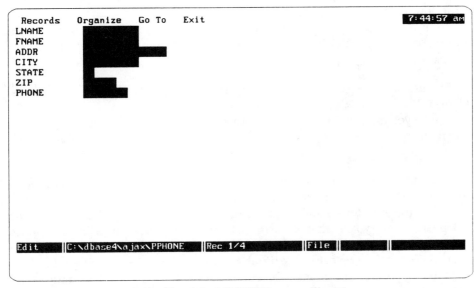

3-10 The default PPHONE screen format.

have in the database. The DISPLAY or LIST commands list the records on the screen, as shown in Fig. 3-11.

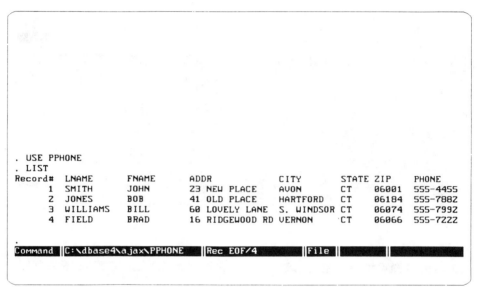

```
. USE PPHONE
. LIST
Record#  LNAME      FNAME      ADDR            CITY         STATE ZIP     PHONE
      1  SMITH      JOHN       23 NEW PLACE    AVON         CT    06001   555-4455
      2  JONES      BOB        41 OLD PLACE    HARTFORD     CT    06184   555-7882
      3  WILLIAMS   BILL       60 LOVELY LANE  S. WINDSOR   CT    06074   555-7992
      4  FIELD      BRAD       16 RIDGEWOOD RD VERNON       ·CT   06066   555-7222
.
 Command  C:\dbase4\ajax\PPHONE    Rec EOF/4        File
```

3-11 A display of the PPHONE database.

The USE command in Fig. 3-11 opens the database file, in this case PPHONE, so that you can access those records. The DISPLAY command causes all of the records on the database to be displayed. This same command can be used to print the list by adding TO PRINTER.

If you had been following these steps, you can see that you would have used all of the basic input and output functions that any application system would need. You would have created a database, added records to it, changed records in it, deleted records from it, listed the records to both the screen and printer. These functions are the most basic of any system, and you should be familiar with the way that dBASE IV performs them.

Customizing your processing

Now that you have completed the basic requirements necessary for a personal phone directory system, you can start using the features of dBASE IV to make the application more sophisticated. You can customize the phone directory to your own style and needs—and as you do that, you will learn more of the use of dBASE IV features.

An easy first step is to create a simple report format for your PPHONE database. You must first access the database with the USE command, then enter CREATE REPORT to create the report format. As with all dBASE IV functions, you may also create a report format using the Control Center menu. Using either method, the report format menu is presented, as shown in Fig. 3-12.

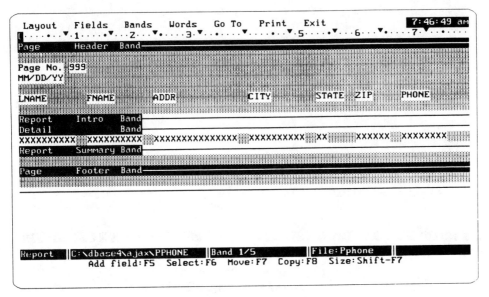

3-12 The report format menu for PPHONE.

You might choose to create a *quick format*, which is a simple list of all fields in the database with their field name as a column heading. You can specify your own headings, change the formats of your fields, and add your own headings and footings to create a customized report. Then, you might print the report to see how the various formats actually look on paper. In the process of doing all this, you will see how to create and use a dBASE IV report format.

Another step you can take to customize your test application is to create a screen format for editing your database records. The screen format is created by using the CREATE SCREEN command or by using the Control Center menu. The screen format work area, with the PPHONE default format, is shown in Fig. 3-13.

You can change the screen format by moving the fields, adding meaningful titles, placing your own personal heading on the screen, and so on. The final screen format can be used by EDIT and APPEND for customization of data entry. For example, the commands that you would use at the dot prompt to add new record to the file, would be:

```
USE PPHONE
SET FORMAT TO PPHONE
APPEND
```

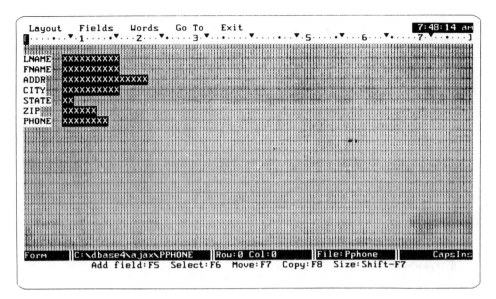

3-13 The custom PPHONE screen format.

You can add a further level of sophistication to your test application by using a generated menu to link all of the functions. This is done by entering CREATE APPLICATION from the dot prompt or by using the Control Center menu. This process allows you to create a horizontal bar menu or a pop-up menu from which you can access all of your application functions. Figure 3-14 shows a sample menu for the personal phone directory application.

By creating your own small application, you have learned about the way dBASE IV works. You can use some of the features, and can create a simple application using dBASE. As you move along into creating more complex applications, you already have an understanding of the basic features and operations of dBASE IV. You can concentrate your efforts on using the more sophisticated features and functions, when you have the basic knowledge in hand. dBASE IV is not an adversary to be conquered, but a tool to be used.

Types of processing

There are two major categories of processing. Processing where there is a human operator, who enters information and sees results, is called *interactive processing*. Processing without human intervention is called *deferred processing* or *batch processing*.

Interactive processing in real time

Interactive processing means that interaction between the human operator and the program is required to achieve the results. For example, if the function is

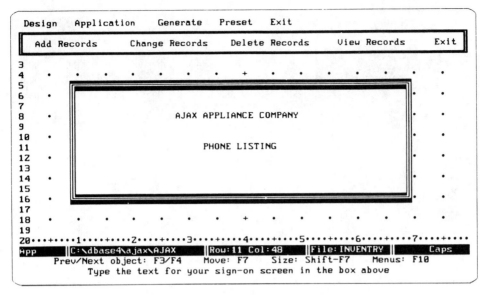

3-14 A sample menu for the PPHONE application.

to add records to a database file, the operator enters data values, while the software edits the values and either updates the database file or returns an error to the operator. The interaction takes place almost like a human conversation—in fact, interactive processing is sometimes called *conversational processing* for this very reason. Also, because the changes to the database file happen as the operator finishes each operation, this type of processing is also called *real time processing*.

Each interaction between the operator and the application program is called a transaction. The transaction causes your application system to take some action with the database—retrieve a record, position to a record, add a record, change a record, and so on.

The easiest way to represent transactions between the operator and the database is using the storyboard approach. Each point of interaction—menu, function, database, report—becomes a storyboard in the application design. Each storyboard is connected to the others by the data items that are passed between them.

The personal phone system would, for example, have one storyboard each for the database, for the report format, for the screen format, for the add a record function, for the change/delete function, and for the report function. Figure 3-15 shows the interaction of these storyboards.

The menu storyboard shows each of the options available in this application and relates the options to the storyboards that perform those functions (see Fig. 3-16).

The storyboards for add a record and change a record both refer to the storyboard for the screen format (see Fig. 3-17). The screen format may be

```
┌─────────────────────────┐
│ PERSONAL PHONE DIRECTORY │
└─────────────────────────┘
```

These functions should be performed by the system:

    1. Maintain a personal phone directory database file by being able to:

        A. Add records to file

        B. Remove records from file

        C. Change existing records

    2. Produce a printed or displayed copy of the phone directory records

        A. Display records on screen

        B. Print records on paper

3-15 Phone directory: The application functions.

Application: PERSONAL PHONE DIRECTORY
Storyboard: MAIN MENU

Menu functions:

1. Add records
   Purpose: addition of entries to personal phone directory
   Title on menu: "ADD RECORDS"
   Menu prompt: "Add names/numbers to phone directory"
   Processing storyboard: "ADD RECORDS"

2. Remove records
   Purpose: deletion of entries from the personal phone directory
            for correction or file size reduction
   Title on menu: "REMOVE RECORDS"
   Menu prompt: "Delete names/numbers from phone directory"
   Processing storyboard: "REMOVE RECORDS"

3. Change existing records
   Purpose: modification of existing entries in personal phone directory
            for correction purposes
   Title on menu: "CHANGE RECORDS"
   Menu prompt: "Change phone directory information"
   Processing storyboard: "CHANGE RECORDS"

4. List records
   Purpose: to report or look up names in the phone directory
   Title on menu: "LIST RECORDS"
   Menu prompt: "Display or print phone directory entries"
   Processing storyboard: "LIST RECORDS MENU"

5. Exit application
   Purpose: to return to prevailing computer environment
   Title on menu: "EXIT"
   Menu prompt: "Leave the Personal Phone Directory"

3-16 Phone directory: Menu storyboard.

used in both functions with the same field edits. The report format is also a storyboard used by the report function. The storyboards in this application are small and simple, because the personal phone directory is a small, simple application.

```
Application: PERSONAL PHONE DIRECTORY
Storyboard: ADD RECORD

    Purpose: addition of entries to personal phone directory

    Title on menu: "ADD RECORDS"

    Menu prompt: "Add names/numbers to phone directory"

    Functional information:

        Key field:      Last name, non-unique
        Other edits:    Validity edits only, no cross-editting
        Screen format:  PPHONE2
        Database:       PPHONE2, all fields
        Error handling: Return error to operator

    Processing:

            Add empty record to end of database.
            Edit the record.
            Save changes.
            Add next record or return to menu.

- - - - - - - - - - - - - - - - - - - - - - - - - - - - - - - - - - - - - - - -

Application: PERSONAL PHONE DIRECTORY
Storyboard: CHANGE RECORD

    Purpose: modification of existing entries in personal phone directory
             for correction purposes

    Title on menu: "CHANGE RECORDS"

    Menu prompt: "Change phone directory information"

    Functional information:

        Key field:      Last name, non-unique
        Other edits:    Validity edits only, no cross-editting
        Screen format:  PPHONE2
        Database:       PPHONE2, all fields
        Error handling: Return error to operator

    Processing:

            Ask operator for Last name (optionally First name too).
            Find the record and display it.
            Edit the record.
            Save changes.
            Get next Last name or return to menu.
```

3-17 Phone directory: The "add" and "change" storyboards.

The database storyboard depicts the place where all of the entered records are stored for later use. The database storyboard is also the central focus of a database application system. The purpose of a database system is to store data for use in generating the information you need. The database file is the physical file, present on some storage medium such as a floppy disk or fixed (hard) disk. The storyboard for the database contains information about each data item to be stored on the file, including the item's name, what other storyboard or source the item came from, how the item is to be stored, the purpose of the data item, and its next destination(s).

The storyboards depict your interactive application system in a way that is easily understood (see Fig. 3-18). Each point of interaction between the application program and the operator is explicitly defined. You might test the effectiveness of your interaction by following the descriptions on the storyboards. If you use storyboards as a design tool, you might also use them as a documentation tool and also as a training tool if necessary.

```
Application: PERSONAL PHONE DIRECTORY
Storyboard: DIRECTORY DATABASE


    Purpose: storage of personal phone directory entries and information.

    Field:              Database name:        Type:         Length:

*  Last name            LNAME                 C                10
   First name           FNAME                 C                15
   Address line         ADDR1                 C                25
   City                 CITY                  C                15
   State                STATE                 C                2
   Zipcode              ZIPCODE               C                9
   Telephone number     PHONE                 C                10

   * indicates key field.

   Special display formats:

      ZIPCODE:     99999-9999 (last 5 positions optional)
      PHONE:       (999)999-9999
```

3-18 Phone directory: The database storyboard.

Once the storyboards are complete, you can create the application system using dBASE IV. The first step is to use the CREATE command to create the database file. If your database is to be named PPHONE, you would enter:

.CREATE PPHONE

at the dot prompt. Then use the item definitions on the database storyboard to fill in the requested information for dBASE, as shown in Fig. 3-19.

dBASE IV creates a physical file called PPHONE.DBF. The first part of the file name is the name of the database specified in the CREATE command. The second part of the name, after the period, is called the *file extension*. The DBF is the standard dBASE file extension for a *database file*. You may enter your own file extension. If you want to use your own file extensions instead of the extensions that are automatically recognized by dBASE, you must specify the extension on every command that requires the file name. For example, to create the PPHONE database with the extension of OWN, you would enter:

.CREATE PPHONE.OWN

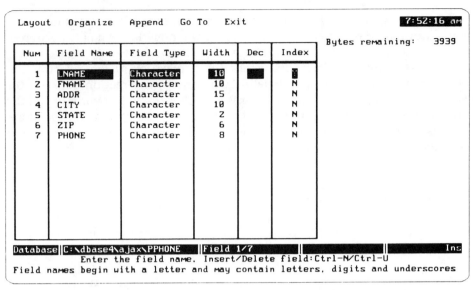

3-19 Phone directory: The database definition.

at the dot prompt. Any other command that requires the file name must now also use the file extension.

After you create the database, you can immediately start using it. You can start entering records into the file either by answering Y to the Input records now? prompt at the end of the CREATE process, or by entering:

```
.USE PPHONE
.APPEND
```

at the dot prompt. The USE command tells dBASE to open the database file PPHONE.DBF. APPEND is the command used to add records to the end of a database file. In this example, dBASE would use the default screen format, which is just a list of field names and input areas. This is the first of your application functions—the add record function—in its most rudimentary form. You can also perform the other functions with single commands. The change/delete function is the command EDIT, while the report function can be performed with the command DISPLAY TO PRINT.

Now you can continue to build the application from the storyboards, creating a screen format, a report format, and a menu to link the application functions.

Deferred processing

Deferred processing is processing that occurs without operator interaction. Instead of directly changing the database with each interaction, the transaction might be formatted and saved on a database file. This transaction file can then be used by another program to actually perform the operations.

Deferred processing can save operator time on more complex, longer-running applications. If several files need to be updated or complex processing is performed between each operator interaction, there may be processing lags for the operator, periods of time where they are waiting for the computer to finish an operation. If this processing is deferred until lunch time or after business hours, for example, the operator can enter changes more effectively. Editing the values on the input screen is done immediately, but the real processing is deferred until later.

For example, if you have a customer invoice system, you may add and change records interactively, but you might defer printing of monthly bills until nonbusiness hours. Producing a bill from invoice records would be a process that would require large numbers of input/output operations with the database, that would not require the operator's direct control.

Another example of deferred processing is to defer printing long reports, allowing you to keep the printer free during business hours. You can use an application program to create a report database instead of directly printing the report.

Reporting is not the only function of a system that can benefit from the technique of extracting data from several files and producing a new file of combined data. Extract files can also be used for other types of processes.

The new file can contain data in exactly the same format as the parent databases, or calculations and conversions can be performed on the extracted data. Calculations can also be split between programs, because extracting data assumes there are two parts to the process—the extract program and the main function program (see Fig. 3-20).

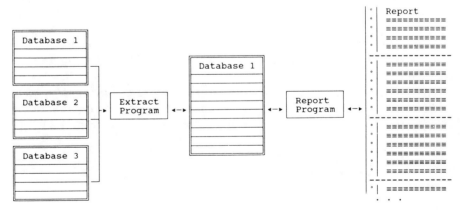

3-20 The extract process.

Installations with more than one computer can also benefit from data extracts. The extracted files can be copied onto a floppy diskette and transported between computers for inquiry or report purposes. The most difficult part of learning the extract process is believing that two programs performing a single function can sometimes run faster than one that performs the same function. In the first place, the extract program does most of the necessary input/output operations, while the main program does the major part of the calculations. If the extract file is properly designed, the main process will execute faster because of the rearrangement.

This technique should be used anytime the existing database structure is compromised. This usually occurs when a program, while using the normal structure, breaks the limitations of dBASE; the system can also reach *breakpoint*, meaning that the processing for a time period takes more time than the period contains. The process might require more than fifteen open files or that the data is accessed is too slow for real-time processing.

The extraction technique requires that the main process, the one for which the data will be extracted, be examined for clues to the data structure that will accommodate the needs of the program and the user. Once this structure is determined, it is turned into a dBASE database and used to store the extracted data.

The extract program is written in such a way that the limitations broken by the main process are not also broken by the extract program. This can be done in several ways, such as storing record numbers and closing databases when not needed to avoid having too many files open at once. The extract program, because it has been removed from the main process, can include techniques that could not have been used in that program. This "divide to conquer" strategy is often used in data processing.

Processing before displaying screen data

Processing is performed on an interactive basis, in two places. First, processing may be performed prior to the user receiving information from the program; second, processing may be performed after the user has finished with the information. These are generically called pre-processing and post-processing.

Interactive programs may perform some kind of pre-processing before displaying a screen. Usually, preprocessing involves setting up memory variables and system options for the operation that follows (Fig. 3-21).

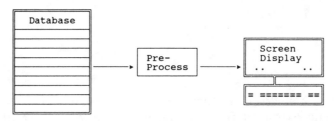

3-21 Pre-processing.

Data can be retrieved from the database file and reformatted for display to the user during pre-processing. The data item may be stored in one way, then displayed in another. This means that you might decrease the potential size of your database file by storing data items in the most efficient format, then using a pre-process to reformat the item into a more readable format for the user.

An interactive process can also have an interactive pre-process. For example, the "add record" function might be used to add a record to a database whose records each have a unique key. The pre-process to the add record program might have the user enter the new record's key field value, then check the database file for any duplicate key values. This way, all of the key values on the database will be unique, because you have performed an edit of the key value during the pre-process.

Processing entered data

Post-processing occurs after the user finishes with a particular entry and presses the enter key. Using the add record function as an example, the post-process edits the entered data item values, creates the new database record, and places the values onto the record. There is usually more post-processing to an interactive program than pre-processing because the largest part of data editing has to occur after the data is entered (Fig. 3-22).

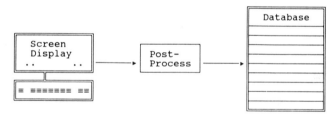

3-22 Post-processing.

In dBASE IV, some editing is performed as a function of the screen format itself. Screen input fields designated as numeric cannot accept any characters other than numerics. Date fields must have valid date values when they are entered, and logical fields must also have only those values allowed for logical fields.

The screen format can also specify a range of acceptable values for a numeric or date field. Editing the data type of an input value and range-editing are performed outside of your application program by using the dBASE IV screen format.

One type of edit that cannot be performed by the screen format is editing for reasonability. *Reasonability editing* means that the entered data is compared against other fields on the database or on the same record to assure that the entered data is correct. In a payroll system, for example, the program might not allow an entry in an "overtime hours worked" field if the "regular hours worked" field is less than 40. Here, the program determines that the entry of overtime hours is "unreasonable" given the number of regular hours worked. This type of editing changes from one application program to another.

After all of the data editing has been performed, the record can finally be added to the database file. The dBASE commands to cause this to happen are:

APPEND BLANK
REPLACE *field name* WITH *memory variable* ...

Now that you have been introduced to the basic concepts of database program design and construction, the next chapters will show you examples of how application systems are built.

4
Case study in design
Ajax Appliance Company

Up to this point, you have seen a lot of material on the generic term *programming*. The first three chapters could be used for almost any computer language. In the remainder of this book we will talk specifically about dBASE IV and relate each concept used in the first section to some real-life problems and real-life solutions.

This chapter discusses system design. You will see an entire system designed from the ground up—or actually from the report down. This design will afford you many opportunities to see how a system is really designed and then implemented. If you think that some of the design assumptions or ideas seem a little strange, they probably are. Remember, in order to show most of the power and features of dBASE IV in one small book it was necessary to take some "author liberties" in creating the examples in this book.

The examples of Ajax Appliance Company, a fictitious entity, will be used throughout this book to serve as a case study. Whether you are a programmer in a large corporation or a small businessman you will find the lessons taught in the case studies will serve as a basis for almost any program that you write.

This chapter designs three separate subsystems—customer, inventory, and invoice. Each system design uses completely different techniques. In reality, a system would be designed using one technique. However, to teach you three different ways to accomplish the same basic thing, it is important to show you more than one user interface.

The customer system uses five separate programs to display a customer operation selection menu and then to add, change, delete, and simply display your data. Reports are created both with the label and report forms and by completely programming them from scratch. A very traditional design is shown here to handle all the data entry and reporting tasks.

The inventory system uses only two programs to handle all menu control and data entry tasks. Two format files are used for input and display. A very nontraditional prototyping design method is taught in this section of the chapter. Using pre- and post-processors, you will see how to quickly and easily create an entire module while maintaining flexibility for error checking and successfully completing data entry tasks.

Finally, the invoice system ties everything together. Using several relations including simple parent-child, multiple children, and a one-to-many relationship, you will see how complex systems are designed and built. Using a combination of traditional and nontraditional approaches, you will see how to perform multi-file input and output. We will also show you how to integrate dot prompt commands into your programs in order to save many programming statements for things dBASE can do already.

You will learn about menus, windows, user-defined functions, and many other new dBASE IV commands as you build your system. However, before you can start programming, you must create your design. That is the focus of this chapter.

The sixteen-step method for design and programming

To program a system, you must first complete a series of tasks known as design. The better your design is, the better your program will be. Also, the more you have thought through your design, the faster you can complete any system. Design is not a necessary evil nor is its intent to produce voluminous amounts of documentation. The sole intent of design is to enable the designer to produce a clear-cut path to follow for the programmer. Often, people are one and the same. It is especially wise to make your design as complete as possible for you may have to follow it!

In the previous chapter, you learned our seven-step method for developing procedures:

1. Define the problem
2. Define the output
3. Define the input
4. Determine the process
5. Code
6. Test
7. Evaluate

Figure 4-1 shows a modified version of this method designed especially for dBASE IV. Two distinct phases are design and programming. Each one is separate yet integrated with the other. By completing a good design, you can create a good system.

Throughout this chapter is a very detailed design of the system that will be created in the last two sections of this book. Both the design and the

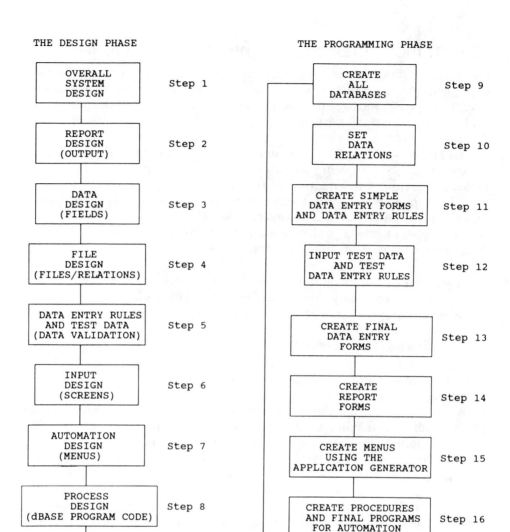

4-1 The 16-step design and programming flowchart.

system will show you almost all there is to know about dBASE IV, both to create and use databases and to create complete turnkey systems. As you read through the design, remember that this is created before the programming takes place. The designers however, knew what they wanted.

As we go through each step, we will examine the design in terms of the outputs and the inputs. Though you will see the actual components of the system (customer, inventory, invoice) a lot, remember the focus of this chapter is how to design each step. As you see the Ajax Appliance System designed, pay attention to the design not the actual system.

Step 1: the overall design from concept to reality

All software developers and programmers face similar problems. The first set of problems you encounter is gathering the end users requirements. The end user is typically your client, your coworker, or you! It is important to understand the overall needs of the system before you can zero in on the details.

Our eight-step design method and eight-step programming methodology shown in Fig. 4-1 can help you create the system you need and at a price, measured in time or dollars, that you can afford.

Ajax Appliance is a medium-sized wholesale business that primarily sells major appliances to retail dealers and occasionally to the general public. They sell refrigerators, washers, dryers, stoves, and microwave ovens. Basically, Ajax Appliance needs to automate several tasks:

- Tracking customers—names, addresses, and status information
- Tracking inventory—items, and quantities in stock
- Recording sales which includes producing invoices and warranty agreements
- Producing sales reports

In order to create a system to handle all of Ajax's needs, the designers must follow good design procedures to avoid redesigning the system as they move from step to step. All of the bugs should be worked out in design, not in programming. Developing applications with dBASE IV can be a very quick process as long as the design has been done well and completely.

The design process is an iterative procedure. That is, as each new step is finished, all the previous steps must be checked to make sure nothing in the basic design has changed. If you decide, when creating a data entry rule (design step 5) that you need another field not already on the database to validate a field you have already defined, then you have to go back and follow each previous step to add the field. You need to make sure to add the field to each report where you want to see the field. You also need to make sure it was on an input screen along with a data file. Only then could you use this new field in your system.

Now that Ajax has defined their overall systems in terms of what they want to do, they can begin the next step of report design.

Step 2: report design—placing your fields

Design work should be broken up into the smallest level of detail that you know at the time. You should start each new step by reviewing the overall design objectives. In the case of Ajax Appliances, their objectives are to:

- Track customers—names, addresses, and status information
- Track inventory—items, quantities in stock, on order

- Recording sales (which includes producing invoices and warranty agreements
- Produce valid reports

Generally, you start at the beginning or wherever you feel most comfortable. If the design of one part of the system is critical to understanding another part of the system, you should work in an order that is logical and makes sense.

What is report design?

Report design begins by "laying out" the report form either by hand or by using the computer to design what data you want on the report and what each basic layout looks like. You can get fancy and use a computer-based drawing package or simply use an ASCII text editor and create something very simple. Of course the easiest way is still pencil and paper.

Laying out fields in the report

When you look at the forms created in this section with a simple ASCII editor (The IBM Personal Editor) you may wonder. What came first, the chicken or the egg? In other words, did the report layout come from first or the data items and text that make up the form? Well, actually they are conceived together.

Begin by getting a rough idea of what fields you need in the report and then lay them out on the paper. After looking at the report form, you may wish to add or remove some of the items.

It is not important how you lay out the fields in this conception of a report. However, the more time you take now, the easier it is when you actually create the report. Some people go as far as to place grid lines on the report so they know the exact location each field is to occupy on the report. In this case, we just do it visually.

The customer directory

Ajax Appliance begins with designing the tasks of tracking customers. The first report they need to develop is a report sorted by customer number or company name that lets them see all the data for that customer. This is also known as a *data dump*. The report lets you see every field and the values for a file while displaying it in an easy-to-read fashion. A data dump can simply be a list of all the information in the file arranged into rows and columns or it can be a full-page form showing only one or a few records on the page.

They have already decided on some of the fields for the customer file. First, of course is the customer's name and address. In their case, they will refer to the customer's name as company name as they usually deal with companies and not individuals. They can also use this field to put in an individual's name instead of the company name.

Address consists of the customer's street, city, state, and zip code. They also record the company's phone number.

Another field that they will maintain on their file and use on their report is the last transaction date. This field will be used to let Ajax know when to remove a customer from the file. They have decided that they will remove a customer from the file if they have not purchased anything in the last two years. Because they plan to purge the invoice file each year they would not be able to find this information out any other way.

If you have not thought out your system in detail, you might not discover items like this until you create later forms such as an invoice form. It then becomes readily apparent that you need these fields. Later you will learn about some fields that must be in the customer file that have not been discovered yet.

There is one final and very important field that Ajax knows must be in the database and in their report. Ajax Appliance Company already has several customers in their file with the same or very similar names, or companies that have multiple locations. The company name would not be a good key field as it may not be unique. Ajax has decided to assign a customer number to each customer. This way they can enter only a few characters and retrieve the record for a company with a long name.

With that information in mind Ajax creates the report form shown in Fig. 4-2.

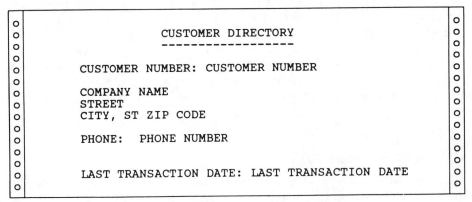

4-2 The Customer directory report design.

Customer number cross reference

Now that Ajax has created the customer directory that shows each customer and all of their fields, they also have to create a report that lets them find each customer number quickly. Because Ajax Appliances already has several customers in their file with the same or very similar names they decided to assign a customer number to each customer. Therefore, the next report Ajax wants is a report showing the company name and their corresponding customer number. They would keep this next to the computer. When a customer invoice is to be entered, they would be able to cross-reference the company name based on the correct customer number. Because there is the possibility of customers with multiple locations, the report has to have enough of the location to allow the people at Ajax to know to which customer they are sending their merchandise.

Ajax Appliance creates the report shown in Fig. 4-3. The X's represent any character to be placed in the field while the 9's represent only numbers to be placed in the field. The A's mean that only alphabetic characters may be placed in the field. These are called templates and will be explained later in the book. The numbers in the middle of the field serve to estimate the size of the display of the field. In the normal print size you can fit about 85 characters across an 8½"×11" sheet of paper that would be used in a standard dot matrix or laser printer.

```
          CUSTOMER NUMBER CROSS REFERENCE
          ------------------------------

     COMPANY          CUSTOMER
      NAME            NUMBER      STREET           CITY     STATE

  x-----20-----x     AA-999   x----20----x    x---20---x    AA
  x-----20-----x     AA-999   x----20----x    x---20---x    AA
  x-----20-----x     AA-999   x----20----x    x---20---x    AA
  x-----20-----x     AA-999   x----20----x    x---20---x    AA
  x-----20-----x     AA-999   x----20----x    x---20---x    AA

  x-----20-----x     AA-999   x----20----x    x---20---x    AA
  x-----20-----x     AA-999   x----20----x    x---20---x    AA
  x-----20-----x     AA-999   x----20----x    x---20---x    AA
  x-----20-----x     AA-999   x----20----x    x---20---x    AA
  x-----20-----x     AA-999   x----20----x    x---20---x    AA

  x-----20-----x     AA-999   x----20----x    x---20---x    AA
  x-----20-----x     AA-999   x----20----x    x---20---x    AA
  x-----20-----x     AA-999   x----20----x    x---20---x    AA
  x-----20-----x     AA-999   x----20----x    x---20---x    AA
  x-----20-----x     AA-999   x----20----x    x---20---x    AA

  x-----20-----x     AA-999   x----20----x    x---20---x    AA
  x-----20-----x     AA-999   x----20----x    x---20---x    AA
  x-----20-----x     AA-999   x----20----x    x---20---x    AA
  x-----20-----x     AA-999   x----20----x    x---20---x    AA
  x-----20-----x     AA-999   x----20----x    x---20---x    AA
```

4-3 The Customer cross-reference report design.

The numbers on the report form are there for two reasons. The first reason is to determine how much of the paper each field will use when it prints. The second reason is to let Ajax know the size of the field in the database. When you create fields with dBASE IV, you need to know the length. Though dBASE IV can handle almost any size fields in its databases, you still must tell dBASE IV how big a field will be. On input forms you can allow as much space as you want and scroll in the input field box to see it all if it is bigger than the box. But, on output reports and forms you are potentially limited to the physical size of the paper. You will learn more about this when we actually create the report forms.

When you are creating tables of information as this report shows, it is important to create the report with field lengths to help you position the data. In the first report, it was not necessary as the field lengths would never exceed the size of the paper where only one field occupied a line (see Fig. 4-3).

Field types and lengths

You can see from the report design that several field lengths and field types have been determined. dBASE has several different field types. These include:

- Character
- Numeric (Fixed Point)
- Float (Floating Point)
- Date
- Logical (True or False)
- Memo (Unlimited text)

This report shows us one of those data types—the character data type. Character fields can be any type of alphanumeric value including the twenty-six letters from A to Z, the numbers 0 through 9, and every special character known to ASCII. Character fields have a fixed length from 1 character to 254 characters. Each of the fields on the report are composed of alpha or alphanumeric values. The customer number is made up of two alpha characters followed by a dash and then three numeric characters. The entire field,.however, is said to be alphanumeric because it includes both letters and numbers.

Numeric and Float fields can contain only numbers, a negative sign, and a decimal point. Numeric fields may be 20 digits while Float fields may be 19.

Date fields are always eight positions and are typically MM/DD/YY. Using several dBASE functions you can change the separator from a slash to a period or dash and can also change the position of month, day, and year.

Logical fields are always one character and are either T or F. The logical field is used when the value is one thing or another. An example of this might be taxability. A customer pays state sales tax or they don't.

Memo fields are the most interesting type of field. They can hold over half a million bytes per database but only take up 10 characters per field. Until you enter data into a memo field, the field takes up only 10 characters. They are used to hold large amounts of textual data such as a description of all the features of a refrigerator.

Customer mailing labels

The last report that Ajax Appliances needs is the mailing labels. Many times they need to send mailings to all their customers. Having labels generated makes it very easy. As this is the third report using the customer file, it is becoming easier to create the report forms. Labels are nothing more than part of the customer directory arranged into two columns (if you are using two column labels). Ajax creates the design shown in Fig. 4-4.

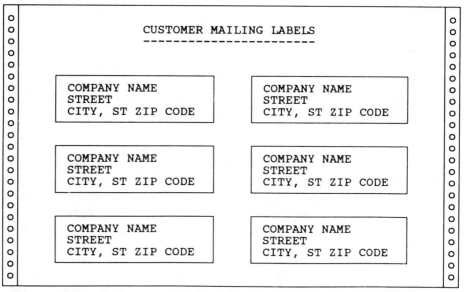

4-4 The Customer mailing label design.

This design completes the customer reports that Ajax has envisioned. It is now time to begin the inventory reports.

Inventory valuation report

Inventory reports are very similar to the customer reports. Ajax Appliance Company has had a manual inventory system for a long time.

The first report they create is an inventory valuation report that tells them the net worth of their inventory at the retail price. With that information in mind Ajax creates the report form shown in Fig. 4-5.

This is an example of a fancier design. The vertical lines are added to define the columns. It is still not to scale. Looking at the page, you can see that about 85 characters have been defined including the vertical lines. When

```
 INVENTORY VALUATION REPORT

 ITEM                                QTY      QTY              INVENTORY
NUMBER   BRAND     TYPE  DESCRIPTION IN STOCK ON ORDER  PRICE  VALUATION
AAAA-999 x--10--x x--12--x x----25---x  9999    9999  9999.99 price*qty
                                                                ---------
                                                                 total
```

4-5 The Inventory valuation report design.

the report is actually created, Ajax may find that some lines need to be expanded while others need shortened. In design, it is only important to make sure there are enough columns on the report. If there are not enough, you might have to switch to a form type of report instead of a tabular or column-oriented report.

The first field Ajax needs on the report is the item number. Because this is the key to the item and must be on the report. The next two fields BRAND and TYPE allow them to tell one item from another. However, sometimes this is not enough. Perhaps the customer needs a little more information. Maybe the item comes in several colors with a different item number differentiating one color from another. The items also need a short description field to allow Ajax to describe the item to the customer.

Like the customer file, Ajax Appliance uses a unique number to identify the item and to make data entry easier. They have chosen an eight-character field where the first two characters will be the first two letters of the BRAND name. The next two characters will be the first two letters of the TYPE. This will all be followed by a dash and three sequential numbers.

Because this is an inventory valuation report, Ajax needs to know the quantity in stock and the price. They also need to know the quantity on order because that measures their additional short-term inventory carrying cost. Because the prices change constantly it is important to keep the retail price on file. The discount the customer gets determines the final price the customer pays. Their discount will be based on their level of purchases. By using the retail price as a benchmark, Ajax can make sure that each customer is treated fairly and, at the same time, keep a tight handle on margins.

The reason for an inventory system is to keep track of the quantity of each item you sell and to always know how many you have available for sale. In an appliance company, this is even more essential. When a company needs to sell an item today, they will only wait a short time for you to get it. If the item isn't already on order, the company will never satisfy most customers needs.

Ajax tracks two inventory quantities. The first quantity is quantity in stock. This quantity is the most important of the numbers as it tells exactly how many of an item sit in the warehouse ready for sale. The other quantity is the quantity on order. Ajax can better manage their inventory if they know how many appliances they may have in stock soon. Without this figure, it is easy to double and triple order your restocking orders.

The inventory valuation report that Ajax will develop is a report sorted by item number or item name that lets them see all their valuation data for that item. The most important part of the report is the inventory valuation. This is the dollar value (at retail) of their inventory. This can be used to help the management know what items need to be moved more than other items. A total at the end is also useful for calculating their monthly inventory valuation for insurance or profit reasons.

The final field on the report is a *calculated field*. It is the calculation of quantity in stock times price. Calculated fields do not reside in a dBASE database. In fact, they don't reside anywhere. The result of the calculation is available anytime so why store the result? When the report is run the calculation is made and the result is printed in the report. When you program this report, you will also see how to create a total for all the individual item valuations.

Item number cross reference

Now that Ajax has created the inventory valuation report that shows a valuation of each item and a grand total, they also have to create a report that lets them find each item number quickly. Because Ajax Appliances already has some fairly long descriptors and many with similar item descriptions, they decided to assign an item number to each item. Therefore, the next report Ajax wants is a report showing the item name and their corresponding item number. They would keep this next to the computer and when an invoice had to be entered they would be able to cross-reference the item based on the correct item number.

Remember, the X's represent any character that can be placed in the field while the 9's represent only numbers that may be placed in the field. Remember, these are called templates and will be explained later. The numbers in the middle of the field serve to estimate the size of the display of the field (Fig. 4-6).

This report is to be sorted by the BRAND name and TYPE so the number can be quickly found for an item. The short item description is also on the report so if there are any records that are the same BRAND and TYPE with maybe a different color, you could tell this from the short description. It is quite possible that another report just like this might be desired, except that the data would be sorted by item number. This way when someone asks, "What is an FRRE-001?," you can quickly look up the number FRRE-001 and tell them it is, for example a FROSTY Refrigerator.

```
ITEM NUMBER CROSS REFERENCE
---------------------------

                           ITEM            ITEM
   BRAND        TYPE     DESCRIPTION       NUMBER

 x--10--x     x--12--x   x-----25-----x   AAAA-999
 x--10--x     x--12--x   x-----25-----x   AAAA-999
 x--10--x     x--12--x   x-----25-----x   AAAA-999
 x--10--x     x--12--x   x-----25-----x   AAAA-999
 x--10--x     x--12--x   x-----25-----x   AAAA-999

 x--10--x     x--12--x   x-----25-----x   AAAA-999
 x--10--x     x--12--x   x-----25-----x   AAAA-999
 x--10--x     x--12--x   x-----25-----x   AAAA-999
 x--10--x     x--12--x   x-----25-----x   AAAA-999
 x--10--x     x--12--x   x-----25-----x   AAAA-999

 x--10--x     x--12--x   x-----25-----x   AAAA-999
 x--10--x     x--12--x   x-----25-----x   AAAA-999
 x--10--x     x--12--x   x-----25-----x   AAAA-999
 x--10--x     x--12--x   x-----25-----x   AAAA-999
 x--10--x     x--12--x   x-----25-----x   AAAA-999
```

4-6   The Inventory cross-reference report design.

The salesperson inventory report

The last inventory report that Ajax will develop is a report sorted by item number that lets Ajax's salespeople see all the data for each item. This data dump will become their catalog for their salespeople. This form report will let them see every item, its complete BRAND, TYPE, and DESCRIPTION, the current price, and availability of each item.

The last item on the report is a complete description of all of the features of the product. The size, colors available, energy rating, whether or not it has an icemaker and if it is in the door, etc. This type of data lends itself to the *memo field*. This field type lets you have an unlimited amount of text in the field. It only uses ten characters of storage space until you begin to enter data into it, and then it only uses as much space as the number of characters you enter. As you will see in Part two, the memo field has some other unique features that make it an excellent data type for large amounts of information.

The report form shown in Fig. 4-7 shows this field occupying a rectangular area at the bottom of the screen. Memo fields can occupy a space any size you desire and, depending on their contents, can be adjusted as you see fit.

This report form also shows a line separating the identifying area of the screen from the data area. When this report is created you will see how to do that, too.

```
SALESMAN INVENTORY REPORT
-------------------------

ITEM NUMBER:   ITEM NUMBER

     BRAND:   BRAND         TYPE:   TYPE

DESCRIPTION:   DESCRIPTION
----------------------------------------------------------

     PRICE:   PRICE

                              IN STOCK      ON ORDER
INVENTORY QUANTITIES:           999           999


  FEATURES:

      MMMMMMMMMMMMMMMMMMMMMMMMMMMMMMMMMMMMMMM
      MMMMMMMMMMMMMMMMMMMMMMMMMMMMMMMMMMMMMMM
      MMMMMMMMMMMMMMMMMMMMMMMMMMMMMMMMMMMMMMM
      MMMMMMMMMMMMMMMMMMMMMMMMMMMMMMMMMMMMMMM
      MMMMMMMMMMMMMMMMMMMMMMMMMMMMMMMMMMMMMMM
```

4-7 The Inventory salesperson report design.

Invoices

The next section of the overall design states that producing invoices and warranty agreements are a necessary output of the system. Ajax will produce a warranty agreement for each item based on the warranty for that item—that should make you think. Where do we get the warranty period from? It's not on the inventory database. Well, it should be. This is the iterative process we described earlier. You are going to have to go back and consider a field called warranty for inclusion in the inventory database as well as some of the inventory reports. For now, let's deal with just the invoice. You'll see another method to "find" these hidden fields.

Figure 4-8 shows the design for the invoice report. As you can see, the invoice consists of many fields. First is the invoice identification information. A unique invoice number will suffice to uniquely identify each invoice. Ajax Appliance Company has decided to use a simple eight-character identifier—four numbers, a dash, and three numbers. The first four numbers are the year and the month. For example, March 1988 would be 8803. The last three numbers are just a sequential numbering from 001 to 999 for the month. Ajax Appliance Company does not presently exceed 999 invoices or warranties per month nor do they anticipate this in the near future.

The invoice date is next. This date should be initially retrieved from the system date. The operator should still be allowed to change it in case they are putting in yesterday's invoices and do not want them dated today.

```
              AJAX APPLIANCE COMPANY - INVOICE
              --------------------------------

    INVOICE NUMBER: nnnn-nnn          CUSTOMER NUMBER: aa-99
                                      COMPANY NAME
    INVOICE DATE: mm/dd/yy            STREET
                                      CITY, ST ZIP CODE

    ------------------------------------------------------------

    QTY   ITEM #   BRAND   TYPE   DESCRIPTION    PRICE    EXTENSION
    ---   ------   -----   ----   -----------    -----    ---------

    999   AAAA-999  x-10-x x-12-x x---25---x  99,999.99  999,999.99
    999   AAAA-999  x-10-x x-12-x x---25---x  99,999.99  999,999.99
    999   AAAA-999  x-10-x x-12-x x---25---x  99,999.99  999,999.99
    999   AAAA-999  x-10-x x-12-x x---25---x  99,999.99  999,999.99
    999   AAAA-999  x-10-x x-12-x x---25---x  99,999.99  999,999.99
    999   AAAA-999  x-10-x x-12-x x---25---x  99,999.99  999,999.99
    999   AAAA-999  x-10-x x-12-x x---25---x  99,999.99  999,999.99
    999   AAAA-999  x-10-x x-12-x x---25---x  99,999.99  999,999.99
    999   AAAA-999  x-10-x x-12-x x---25---x  99,999.99  999,999.99
    999   AAAA-999  x-10-x x-12-x x---25---x  99,999.99  999,999.99
    999   AAAA-999  x-10-x x-12-x x---25---x  99,999.99  999,999.99
    999   AAAA-999  x-10-x x-12-x x---25---x  99,999.99  999,999.99
    999   AAAA-999  x-10-x x-12-x x---25---x  99,999.99  999,999.99
    999   AAAA-999  x-10-x x-12-x x---25---x  99,999.99  999,999.99
    999   AAAA-999  x-10-x x-12-x x---25---x  99,999.99  999,999.99
    999   AAAA-999  x-10-x x-12-x x---25---x  99,999.99  999,999.99
                                                         ----------
                                    Sub Total            999,999.99

                                    Discount 99%          99,999.99
                                                         ----------
                                    Taxable Amount        99,999.99

                                    Tax 99.9%             99,999.99
                                                         ----------
                                    Total Amount         999,999.99
                                                         ==========
```

4-8 The Invoice design.

Next is the customer's name and address. This appears at the top of the invoice. The customer number should also be on the invoice to cross-reference the name and address that appears. In fact, only the customer number has to be entered. The system should automatically retrieve the customer information as a display-only set of fields.

Each invoice can have many items on the invoice. Each item has several fields. These include the quantity purchased, which item they purchased, the item brand, type, description, and price. Each line on the invoice will have these fields. There should also be a field called EXTENSION which multiplies the quantity sold times the price. This is done for each item on the invoice. Again, because this is a calculation, it occurs at print time and is not stored on the database.

After the fields for each item are the summary fields. The first is the Sub Total calculated by summing all of the extensions. Next each customer receives a discount which is a percentage of the subtotal. This percentage is maintained in the customer file and is a subjective number based on the amount of sales and the longevity as a customer.

After subtracting the discount from the subtotal, the report shows a taxable amount. If the customer is subject to tax, the tax is calculated based on the current tax rate. Adding the tax to the taxable amount gives the total. This is the amount the customer pays on the invoice.

Later you see where the tax rate comes from and another way to handle a rate that only appears once. As you see, it doesn't belong in any database but rather should be stored in a memory variable file. You will learn about these later.

If you look at the invoice report design you will see that at the bottom of the invoice, the actual discount and tax percentages are to be shown. These are also done at print time.

Warranty agreement

Each invoice item requires a warranty agreement. This tells the customer how long the item will be warranted for and how much an extended year of warranty might cost.

The warranty agreement document is signed by the customer. It is a mail merge type document consisting of large amounts of text with fields in the middle of the text. This is a different type of report than the column or reports you have seen so far. It will be described fully in chapter 13.

Specifically, the warranty agreement states the terms and conditions of the warranty along with the quantity and item being warranted. It also includes most of the information from the invoice including the date, customer, and other descriptive information. When the invoice is printed there will be a separate warranty agreement for each item on the invoice. The warranty agreement design is shown in Fig. 4-9.

All the fields that appear on the warranty agreement come either from one of the databases or are calculated based on Ajax Appliance Company's policies. The warranty agreement number is the invoice number with a two-digit suffix. The suffix is the sequential item numbers from a single invoice. The warranty agreement date is the same as the invoice date.

The company name and address information comes from the invoice by way of the customer file. The quantity and description information comes from the item on the invoice. The original free warranty period is also on the warranty agreement. This must come from the inventory file and this field will have to be added to our design. Don't run back yet and add it to the reports. Let's wait and see if there are any more surprises. The warranty expiration date is calculated as the current date plus the number of months the warranty is good for. After that, the client can purchase a one-year extension. The price for a one-year warranty extension is 10% of the retail price.

Monthly sales report

The final report desired by Ajax Appliances is a monthly report of the total sales and net profit. This is a report showing the month and the total billings

```
┌─────────────────────────────────────────────────────┐
│ o                                                 o │
│ o            AJAX APPLIANCE COMPANY               o │
│ o              WARRANTY AGREEMENT                  o │
│ o            --------------------                 o │
│ o                                                 o │
│ o  WARRANTY AGREEMENT NUMBER: 9999-999-99         o │
│ o                                                 o │
│ o  WARRANTY AGREEMENT DATE:   mm/dd/yy            o │
│ o ----------------------------------------------- o │
│ o                                                 o │
│ o  This warranty agreement is between the Ajax Appliance o │
│ o  Company and:                                   o │
│ o                                                 o │
│ o        COMPANY NAME                             o │
│ o        STREET                                   o │
│ o        CITY, ST ZIP CODE                        o │
│ o                                                 o │
│ o  This agreement maintains that Ajax Appliance Company o │
│ o  will warranty QTY TYPE(s) in accordance with the o │
│ o  manufacturers warranty terms. BRAND warranties this o │
│ o  product for a period of WARRANTY months.       o │
│ o                                                 o │
│ o  The TYPE being warrantied is a DESCRIPTION.    o │
│ o                                                 o │
│ o  This warranty will expire on DATE+WARRANTY. At the o │
│ o  end of that period you may purchase our standard o │
│ o  warranty for an additional year for each item for o │
│ o  only PRICE/10.                                 o │
│ o                                                 o │
│ o  This agreement is legal and binding in the state o │
│ o  of confusion and cannot be broken.            o │
│ o                                                 o │
│ o   Signed,                                       o │
│ o                                                 o │
│ o  -------------------------    ------------------------- o │
│ o  Ajax Appliance Company        COMPANY NAME    o │
│ o                                                 o │
└─────────────────────────────────────────────────────┘
```

4-9   The Warranty agreement design.

for the month sorted by company and invoice number and grouped by company. All of the items are "rolled up" or totalled for each invoice. The discount is also shown along with the net profit.

This report gives us an opportunity to learn about rolling up totals and aggregating data that has the same key and multiple occurrences such as invoice and customers numbers. The individual item extensions from each invoice are summed to show only the total for each invoice. We want subtotals by customer as well as grand totals for all invoices (Fig. 4-10).

Step 3: data design—what fields do I have?

Now that you have decided what you want for output, it is time to begin to understand how you will get the data into a system to make it available for the reports you have already defined, as well as ad hoc queries.

What is data design?

The next step in the design phase is to take an inventory of all the data fields that is needed to accomplish the output. One of the best ways to do this is to take each report and list the data items that are found in the report. As you do

```
o    |                  MONTHLY SALES REPORT - MONTH ENDING month year              |  o
o    |                                                                              |  o
o    |                                                                              |  o
o    |  COMPANY    INVOICE    INVOICE     INVOICE                       NET         |  o
o    |   NAME      NUMBER      DATE       AMOUNTS      DISCOUNT        PROFIT        |  o
o    |                                                                              |  o
o    | x----20----x  9999-99  mm/dd/yy  $999,999.99  ($99,999.99)  AMOUNT-DISC      |  o
o    | x----20----x  9999-99  mm/dd/yy  $999,999.99  ($99,999.99)  AMOUNT-DISC      |  o
o    | x----20----x  9999-99  mm/dd/yy  $999,999.99  ($99,999.99)  AMOUNT-DISC      |  o
o    |                                  -----------  ------------  -----------      |  o
o    |  comp total                      $999,999.99  ($99,999.99)  AMOUNT-DISC      |  o
o    |                                                                              |  o
o    | x----20----x  9999-99  mm/dd/yy  $999,999.99  ($99,999.99)  AMOUNT-DISC      |  o
o    | x----20----x  9999-99  mm/dd/yy  $999,999.99  ($99,999.99)  AMOUNT-DISC      |  o
o    | x----20----x  9999-99  mm/dd/yy  $999,999.99  ($99,999.99)  AMOUNT-DISC      |  o
o    |                                  -----------  ------------  -----------      |  o
o    |  comp total                      $999,999.99  ($99,999.99)  AMOUNT-DISC      |  o
o    |                                  -----------  ------------  -----------      |  o
o    |  grand total                     $999,999.99  ($99,999.99)  AMOUNT-DISC      |  o
o    |                                  ===========  ============  ===========      |  o
o    |                                                                              |  o
```

4-10 The monthly sales report design.

this, you should note the items that are found in more than one report. Make sure that an item with the same name in one report is really the same data item in another report.

Another step to take is to see if you can begin to separate logically the data items. Later you will have to group these data items into logical file structures and then map them onto understandable data entry screens. Customer data should be entered as part of a customer file process, not part of an invoice entry.

Ajax Appliances has created many reports. They also fit into three basic categories: customer information, inventory information, and sales information. As each report is searched for data items, keep this in mind in order to best segregate the data items.

Customer data

First each report must be examined. Ajax starts with the three customer reports and lists the data items as shown in Fig. 4-11.

```
CUSTOMER DIRECTORY        CUSTOMER NUMBER CROSS REFERENCE       MAILING LABELS
------------------        -------------------------------       --------------

CUSTOMER NUMBER               CUSTOMER NUMBER
COMPANY NAME                  COMPANY NAME                       COMPANY NAME
STREET                        STREET                             STREET
CITY                          CITY                               CITY
ST                            ST                                 ST
ZIP CODE                                                         ZIP CODE
PHONE NUMBER
LAST TRANSACTION DATE
```

4-11 The data items found in the customer reports.

As you can see, all of the data fields pertaining to customer were actually found in the first report. This type of data searching is the easiest because the customer reports all deal with one file.

Notice some of the techniques we employed for positioning the data. The customer directory used all of the customer fields and is complete. The customer number cross-reference report used only the first five fields and is placed on the same lines as the customer directory. The mailing labels, however, do not use the first field (customer number) or the last two fields. As such, only the fields that are used are placed on the paper. These fields are placed on the same lines as their counterparts in the other customer reports. This allows us to see which items are in which reports more easily. We can look across a row instead of looking for the same names. Because the relative row and the field names are the same, it is easy to make sure we have all the data items. Though not critical for this small database, this will become very important in the invoice file.

You may also note that we still have not added the discount field. This is because it's not "officially" on any of the Customer reports—yet. It will be, but let's wait until we complete the invoice data items analysis first.

Inventory data

The inventory file, like the customer file, deals with one file and is shown in Fig. 4-12.

INVENTORY VALUATION	ITEM NUMBER CROSS REFERENCE	SALESMAN INVENTORY REPORT
ITEM NUMBER	ITEM NUMBER	ITEM NUMBER
BRAND	BRAND	BRAND
TYPE	TYPE	TYPE
DESCRIPTION	DESCRIPTION	DESCRIPTION
PRICE		PRICE
QTY IN STOCK		QTY IN STOCK
QTY ON ORDER		QTY ON ORDER
INVENTORY VALUATION		
		FEATURES

4-12   The data items found in the inventory reports.

Again it is obvious that these are stand-alone files that have been well designed. Potentially, only the invoice file might have been designed, and the realization of the need for a customer file and an inventory file might have come later. Then these steps would have all been redone to design the customer and inventory file. In this case study, we assume that Ajax Appliance Company has already had some experience designing some systems, and that they automatically assumed that customer and inventory files are part of any sales system.

These reports lay out a little differently than the customer file. There is no single report containing all the fields. The first report, inventory valuation, does not contain the FEATURES field that the salesman inventory report does. At the same time, the salesman report does not contain the inventory valuation field. The cross-reference report only contains a few fields that are contained in the other two reports.

Later when we begin to work on file design, we will use all of the fields in the first and third reports to prepare one database that has all the necessary fields. The warranty field and the customer discount field will be considered later.

Invoice data

Now for the difficult part—determining the fields that compose the invoice, warranty agreements, and monthly sales reports. Upon examining the multitude of fields and calculations in the many documents you will see, you may start to see which fields actually belong to or will come from other files and which files might make up an invoice subsystem.

For now, every field on the reports should be included. Many fields will not be in the final file structure. Calculations will be excluded because they are made up of other fields. Some calculated fields are stored on the database. Your ability to accept larger files and your need for data that could be calculated should dictate the practicality of placing calculated fields in the database. The invoice function's data items are shown in Fig. 4-13.

INVOICE	WARRANTY AGREEMENTS	MONTHLY SALES REPORT
INVOICE NUMBER		INVOICE NUMBER
	WARRANTY AGREEMENT NUMBER	
INVOICE DATE		INVOICE DATE
	WARRANTY AGREEMENT DATE	
CUSTOMER NUMBER		
COMPANY NAME	COMPANY NAME	COMPANY NAME
STREET	STREET	
CITY	CITY	
ST	ST	
ZIP CODE	ZIP CODE	
QTY	QTY	
ITEM #		
BRAND	BRAND	
TYPE	TYPE	
DESCRIPTION	DESCRIPTION	
PRICE		
EXTENSION		
SUB TOTAL		
DISCOUNT %		TAX AMOUNT
DISCOUNT AMT		TOTAL AMOUNT
TAXABLE AMOUNT	PRICE/10	
TAX %	WARRANTY	
TAX AMOUNT	DATE+WARANTY	
TOTAL AMOUNT		NET PROFIT (TOTAL-DISC)

4-13 The data items found in the invoice and sales reports.

As you can see in Fig. 4-13, the invoice contains the most fields. However, both the warranty agreement and the monthly sales report contain some unique fields. In fact, the monthly sales report has very few fields at all. Only the last field net profit is unique to the report. As you can see in the warranty agreement column, some of the fields aren't given names. They just appear as calculations such as PRICE/10, and DATE+WARRANTY. This will make it easier to spot calculated fields later.

Combining the data

Once all the data is best displayed using each report, consolidate the data by function and then compare the data across functions. In this case, first look at the customer reports and create one set of data items by combining the different fields. Do the same for the inventory file. These two are very easy because the first report's data fields in each function are almost all-inclusive.

The Invoice data items might present some different problems due to many different items including some calculated fields. Placing a different field on each line helps. Fields only on one report are in a row on the page that contains that one item. For a field like company name that is in each invoice report, the field is on each column in its row. This makes it very easy to make sure you have all of the data items. The three functions can be put next to each other as shown in Fig. 4-14.

```
CUSTOMER DATA ITEMS        INVENTORY REPORT        INVOICE DATA ITEMS
-------------------        ----------------        ------------------

CUSTOMER NUMBER            ITEM NUMBER               INVOICE NUMBER
COMPANY NAME               BRAND                  *  WARRANTY AGREEMENT NUMBER
STREET                     TYPE                      INVOICE DATE
CITY                       DESCRIPTION            *  WARRANTY AGREEMENT DATE
ST                         PRICE                     CUSTOMER NUMBER
ZIP CODE                   QTY IN STOCK           +  COMPANY NAME
PHONE NUMBER               QTY ON ORDER           +  STREET
LAST TRANSACTION DATE   *  INVENTORY VALUATION    +  CITY
                           FEATURES               +  ST
                                                  +  ZIP CODE
                                                     QTY
                                                     ITEM #
                                                  +  BRAND
                                                  +  TYPE
                                                  +  DESCRIPTION
                                                  @+ PRICE
                                                  *  EXTENSION
                                                  *  SUB TOTAL
                                                  @? DISCOUNT %
                                                  *  DISCOUNT AMT
                                                  *  TAXABLE AMOUNT
                                                  &? TAXABLE
                                                  ?  TAX %

                                                  *  TAX AMOUNT
  * Calculated                                    *  TOTAL AMOUNT
  + Found in Another Database                     *  PRICE/10
  ? Should be Moved to Another Database           ?  WARRANTY
  @ Should be in Two Databases                    *  DATE+WARRANTY
  & Needs to be Added                             *  NET PROFIT (TOTAL-DISCOUNT)
```

4-14 Comparing the data items from the three functions.

Each field must be examined to determine if it can be calculated or if it can be accessed from another file. The customer file and inventory file are almost at their "normalized" values. The invoice file is the file that must be most closely examined. Some of the fields can be placed in one of the other files or even eliminated.

A good method to use is to develop some sort of "key" or "legend" for fields that should be moved or eliminated. Figure 4-14 shows the keys that we used here. Data is examined for five possibilities as each item is checked. Calculated fields are marked with an asterisk. These fields will probably be eliminated from the database because they can be calculated.

If data in one database is already found in another database it is marked with a plus sign. For example, customer data is the invoice and can and should be retrieved at print time. This way, if the customer address changes it will be reflected in the hardcopy.

If data is found in a database but it really belongs somewhere else for storage purposes, it is marked with a question mark. For example, the warranty period field only appears in the invoice file right now. It should only be in the inventory file.

Data marked with a at-sign should be in two places. Common examples of this are price and discount. Although the price of an item is stored in an inventory file and retrieved by the invoice at print time, it is important to store another copy of the price on the invoice file. If the price changes next week on the inventory file and you reprint the invoice, you don't want the customer to get the new price. Price is fixed at the moment of purchase. The same is true for discount. If the customer has a 10% discount today, but because they buy a large order next week you give them 15%, you do not want to apply that retroactively. If you reprint the invoice from last week and the discount is not stored in the invoice database, then you see the new discount.

Finally, as you examine the data you might hear some "oops, I forgot one" as you remember a field that is necessary. In this example, the indicator of taxability is needed. It has been written into the invoice file but needs to be moved to the customer file. An item may be marked with more than one indicator. Items with no indicators should be left alone.

Most of your work will come from systems that use more than one file. Because the customer and inventory systems only need data from their own files, it is relatively easy to define their items. However, the invoice file takes a long time. Let's look at the invoice file in detail.

Invoice number is the key to the invoice data and must be kept. However, the warranty agreement number is simply the invoice number with a two-digit sequence number. The sequence number is simply the sequence of the number of items on the invoice. This sequence can easily be calculated from the invoice. Because an invoice automatically creates the warranty agreements, there is no reason to keep separate numbers on the file. This field can be eliminated from the file.

The invoice date is important to tell when the invoice was created. The warranty agreement date is always the same as the invoice date. Therefore, the warranty agreement date should be eliminated.

Customer number is a field that links the invoice to the customer file. Through this field, any information in the customer file can be retrieved and displayed or used by the invoice program. This field must be part of the invoice file. It is not marked with an at sign because it is used as a link to another database. However, data that is retrieved through the link would be marked.

The customer data that appears as part of the invoice can be retrieved through the customer number and is not needed. The company name and address information will not be part of the invoice file.

The quantity field is needed in the invoice file to tell how many of each item the customer purchased. There will be multiple occurrences of this field, and several others that make up each line item on the invoice.

The item number field tells the invoice which item the customer is purchasing. The ITEM # also links the invoice file to the inventory file to retrieve data about the item in the invoice. This field certainly needs to remain in this file.

The brand, type, and description fields can all be brought in from the inventory file and need not be part of the actual invoice file.

PRICE is one of the most interesting fields in the file. At first glance, you might think that this field is not needed in the invoice database because the price can be looked up in the inventory file. However, prices change. If PRICE is not captured in the invoice file itself, there would be no way to know what the price was on the date of the invoice. PRICE must be captured in the invoice file from the inventory file at the time of purchase. The PRICE field needs to be on both the invoice and inventory databases. This is not redundant because the price on the invoice file is the price at time of purchase while the price on the inventory file is the current retail price.

The field extension contains the formula QTY*PRICE. This can be calculated at any time; it does not need to be on the database.

SubTotal is an intermediate total calculated by adding all of the extensions. This too can be calculated at any time.

The discount percentage is a subjective measure assigned by the general manager based on a number of factors including how long the customer has been buying from Ajax, their yearly dollar volume, and how much support the customer requires. This field should really be on the customer database as well as the invoice file. This is an example of where planning still cannot help.

Until you actually think about where this field will be when doing the data design, you would not know that it really needs to be in the customer file, too. The iterative process of design was needed to flush out this field. The discount amount is calculated by multiplying the discount percentage by the subtotal of the extensions.

The taxable amount is calculated by subtracting the discount from the subtotal. This amount can be calculated and need not be stored on the database. However, tax is dependent on the customer's tax status. Out-of-state customers are never taxed. Because Ajax Appliance Company is a California company, any state codes other than CA are not taxable. Also if the customer is a reseller or remarketer, there is no tax.

Even though they have created those rules, Ajax needs a field to determine the company's tax status. Again, they decide to use the customer file to maintain this field. Because it doesn't exist already, it will be added.

Tax amount will not be stored on the database. The amount of tax is calculated by multiplying the taxable amount by the tax rate. The present tax rate for California where this fictitious business resides is 7.5%. Because there will only be one rate it makes no sense to put it in a database. The one tax rate can be stored in a "memory variable file" discussed later.

The final calculation of the invoice is the total after discounts and taxes. This Total Amount is a very important field to Ajax, but it can always be calculated.

Why are some of the calculated fields not stored in the database? Very simply it comes down to a matter of what is important to you. In dBASE IV, you can always recalculate your data and see it very quickly. For some people, a few seconds of calculation time may not be worth the wait. They may want to store a certain total on the database itself. Recalculation has ramifications if data changes or in storage space, but it is a widely acceptable practice. Although we do not advocate storing calculated fields on any database, it can be done. You will have to recalculate if data changes, however. dBASE IV has no calculated field type.

If Ajax frequently does ad hoc reports concerning their gross sales before discount, taxes paid, their total invoice amount after discount, and taxes, they could choose to leave these calculated fields on the database. Otherwise each ad hoc report would have to duplicate all of the extension, discount, tax, and final calculations to show these fields. Remember, it takes up room and slows down the system.

The last few fields in the Invoice Data Items column are from the warranty agreement and the monthly sales report. With the exception of the warranty field, they all can be calculated. The warranty field is a perfect example of a "hidden" field. Until you see this field in the invoice file, you forget that it never existed only in the warranty report. In actuality, it needs to be part of each inventory record so the salesman can know how many months the item is under warranty. The warranty field needs to be moved to the inventory database.

If you have not thought out your system in detail, you might not discover items like these until you create later forms such as an invoice form. Then it becomes readily apparent that you need these fields.

Step 4: file design—organizing the fields

Once data design is completed, the next step is to make the final organization of the data into files. This is of key importance because once you enter data into a database and decide to add fields, you must go to all the existing records and enter the new field values. This is especially important to files that have related fields.

Transforming fields into files

Creating the final set of files is easy if you have been paying attention. By looking at the marks in Fig. 4-14, you can see which fields need to be eliminated, which need to be added or moved, and finally which fields will simply remain in their original database.

After using the marks as a guide, the final set of data is created as shown in Fig. 4-15. As you can see the files have shrunk noticeably. Fewer fields are in each file, and the task should now be more manageable.

```
CUSTOMER DATA ITEMS        INVENTORY REPORT        INVOICE DATA ITEMS
-------------------        ----------------        ------------------

    CUSTOMER NUMBER            ITEM NUMBER             INVOICE NUMBER
    COMPANY NAME               BRAND                   INVOICE DATE
    STREET                     TYPE                    CUSTOMER NUMBER
    CITY                       DESCRIPTION             DISCOUNT
    ST                         PRICE                   QTY
    ZIP CODE                   QTY IN STOCK            ITEM #
    PHONE NUMBER               QTY ON ORDER            PRICE
    LAST TRANSACTION DATE      WARRANTY
    DISCOUNT                   FEATURES
    TAXABLE


MEMORY FILE
-----------
    TAX RATE
```

4-15 Separating the data by function and eliminating duplicates.

Redesigning your reports

Once the files are created, you can recreate any reports that are in need of fields. Each field should be used at least once in some report. Because several fields were added to the customer file, you must return to the previous design steps and see if anything needs to be changed. The customer file had both the discount field and the taxable indicator field added to it. The customer report must be redesigned to accommodate the new fields. The final customer directory is shown in Fig. 4-16.

```
                    CUSTOMER DIRECTORY
                    ------------------


        CUSTOMER NUMBER: CUSTOMER NUMBER

        COMPANY NAME
        STREET
        CITY, ST ZIP CODE

        PHONE:   PHONE NUMBERS

        DISCOUNT: DISCOUNT

        TAXABLE: TAXABLE

        LAST TRANSACTION DATE: LAST TRANSACTION DATE
```

4-16 Another look at the customer directory report design.

The inventory database also had one new field added to it—the warranty length. The salesman inventory report must be modified to display the length of the warranty in months. To make sure the salesman knows it is months and not years, an indicator is added after the number of months indicating that the time period is months. The final salesman inventory report is shown in Fig. 4-17.

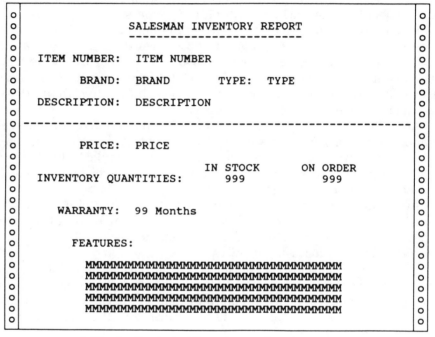

4-17 Another look at the salesman inventory report.

Setting relations

Later in this book, you will learn all about using multiple files and how relations are set in dBASE IV. For now, we briefly cover this topic and design the relations between the various files we have identified. We will also see why one of the files needs to be split into two files to work more effectively.

Files can be related to each other so that information in one file is accessible to another. In dBASE IV systems, you will usually have several files related to each other. Relations are established by having fields in both files sharing a common value. The field names in both files need not be the same, only the values have to match. For example, in the invoice file you will have the customer number. By relating the customer number in the invoice file to the customer number in the customer file you can retrieve all there is to know about the customer. This will save you from having to store the data in two places.

Not duplicating data is the first reason to have a relation-table lookup. A field in one file is used to look up other data in another file. Another table lookup relation from the invoice file to the inventory file uses the item number field. As each item is entered, data about the item such as price and availability is passed from the inventory file to the invoice file.

A second reason is that as you decide how to relate the files that you have already designed, you must also decide how to handle multiple occurrences of data. For each line item in the invoice, in this system design the quantity and item number information have multiple occurrences.

When you have multiple occurrences of data, you should split the files into two files. In this design, place the line item data of the invoice in a separate file from the single occurrence invoice items such as invoice date or customer number. This new Itemsfile is related by invoice number from the invoice file. The inventory file used to verify each line item would then be related to the item file instead of the invoice file.

An individual file might have several relations to different files. In this example, the invoice file is related both to the customer file and to the items file. You can have more than one relation to the same file but this is rare. Because each file usually has one unique key this would be highly unlikely if your data was properly designed.

After you have decided on your final data items in each file, you must decide on your relations. The invoice file is the central focus of the system. The invoice file needs to be related to the customer file to retrieve customer information when processing invoices.

The invoice reports need information from the customer file. The customer number entered as part of an order automatically retrieves the customer's name and address. Though name and address information is not stored as part of the order record, it is used to confirm that the correct customer number has been entered.

The invoice file and the items file relate to each other by invoice number. The items file for each invoice has multiple records, but each record in the items file will share the same characteristics as the main record in the invoice file. That is, for each item in the items file, you could trace the relationship back to the invoice file and then to the customer file to see the same customer information for each item of an invoice.

The Items file will be related to the inventory file. The items file retrieves the price and item information from the inventory file. It also updates the inventory file as items are purchased.

The final files and their relations are shown in Fig. 4-18. As you see, the arrows point to the relation. Only the invoice file has multiple relations—one to the item file and one to the customer file. Because the invoice file is related to the item file, and the item file is related to the inventory file, this is a *chained relation*. By tracing relations backwards, you see which customers have which invoices and purchased which items.

Besides the four database files which have been designed, a memory file contains the single tax rate for California. If more than one tax rate were

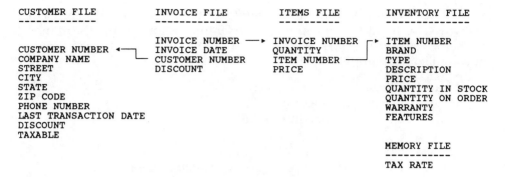

```
CUSTOMER FILE          INVOICE FILE          ITEMS FILE          INVENTORY FILE
-------------          ------------          ----------          --------------
                       INVOICE NUMBER ──►  INVOICE NUMBER  ┌─►  ITEM NUMBER
CUSTOMER NUMBER ◄─┐     INVOICE DATE         QUANTITY             BRAND
COMPANY NAME      └──   CUSTOMER NUMBER      ITEM NUMBER ────┘    TYPE
STREET                 DISCOUNT              PRICE                DESCRIPTION
CITY                                                             PRICE
STATE                                                            QUANTITY IN STOCK
ZIP CODE                                                         QUANTITY ON ORDER
PHONE NUMBER                                                     WARRANTY
LAST TRANSACTION DATE                                            FEATURES
DISCOUNT
TAXABLE
                                                                MEMORY FILE
                                                                -----------
                                                                TAX RATE
```

4-18 A design for the files and their relationships.

needed to be maintained, then you would have to create another file of states and tax rates and perhaps relate the customer file to it. Because Ajax only plans to charge sales tax in California, only one rate is necessary.

Step 5: data entry rules and test data

The next step is to define your fields and files in much further detail.

Designing field names, types, and sizes

First, you must name each field. The name should be easy to remember yet descriptive, so that you recognize the function of the field by its name. The name should be long enough to describe the field, but not so short that it becomes cryptic. Rules you must follow when creating field names require that field names:

- Are 1–10 characters in length
- Contain no blank spaces
- Must start with a letter

The only non-alphanumeric character allowed in a field is the underscore.

You must also decide what data type each of your fields will be. In dBASE IV you have the option of several data types:

- Character
- Numeric (Fixed Point)
- Float (Floating Point)
- Date
- Logical
- Memo

These will be explained in more detail in the next section of the book. One of these data types must be assigned to your field. You also have to specify the storage length and, for numeric or float fields, the number of decimals. This allows you to specify the maximum length for input, storage, and the number of characters that you can see at a time. In dBASE IV, the limits as to the size of your data fields are:

Character fields	1–254 characters
Numeric fields	20 maximum digits
Float fields	19 maximum digits
Date fields	Always 8 characters (MM/DD/YY)
Logical fields	1 character (T or F)
Memo fields	10 characters used for memo marker

Numeric and float fields may have decimals but the entire number must be at least two greater in size than the decimal value to allow for the sign and decimal point. For example:

5.1	5	total positions, 1 decimal	999.9
8.2	8	total positions, 2 decimal	99999.99
12.5	12	total positions, 5 decimal	999999.99999
4.2	4	total positions, 2 decimal	9.99

One last item to design when you are thinking about your data is whether or not you want any of the fields ordered in your database. Usually the key fields such as customer number, item number, or invoice number are needed to help you find desired values quickly. You may also want your data sorted by some other field such as a customer's name or state. dBASE IV gives you the ability to specify an automatic sort directive known as an index when you create your database. Because of this, it is also a good idea to design the indices you want.

Designing data entry rules

The last major decision to make is data validation. Data validation is used when data is input to make sure that only "good" data gets into a system. Good data can be defined as data that passes certain tests that you define. There are several types of data validation.

- Template validation
- Range validation
- List validation
- Existence validation

Template validation makes sure that the data entered meets some criteria for its form. For example you can verify that a name contains only letters. You could verify that phone numbers either contain seven numbers or three numbers, a dash, and four numbers. You could verify a phone number for a left parenthesis, followed by three numbers, followed by a right parenthesis, a space, three numbers, a dash, and finally four numbers. dBASE IV has an excellent facility for template checking (see Part Two).

Range validation is used for numeric or date fields and simply ensures that the number or date entered falls within a certain range. As you will see later in this book, dBASE IV allows you to specify range checking when you create a screen form that uses the data.

List validation means that you verify that the data entered matches a value on some list. You might enter the list as part of a screen form verification, you could verify that some other data file contains the value, or you could match it to a global variable.

The final type of validation is *existence checking*. This simply verifies that the value either does or does not already exist in some other place, usually in the same or another data file.

The customer file

The customer file database table design is shown in Fig. 4-19. As you design the final set of specifications for the database, restate your design and create a summary of each field, why it exists, and how it will be used.

CUSTOMER FILE FIELD NAME	DATA TYPE	DISPLAY SIZE	INDEX	TEMPLATE RANGE CHOICES
CUSTNO	CHAR	6	Y	AA-999
COMPANY	CHAR	20	Y	
STREET	CHAR	20		
CITY	CHAR	20		
STATE	CHAR	2		AA
ZIP	CHAR	10	Y	99999-9999
PHONE	CHAR	13		(999)999-9999
LST_TXND	DATE	8		01/01/87-12/31/99
DISCOUNT	NUMERIC	2		0-50%
TAXABLE	LOGIC	1		YES, NO

4-19 The data entry rules and templates for the customer file.

An inventory of your customers is as important as an inventory of your parts. The customer file will be used in order to serve customers for various reasons. Every business needs to maintain basic information about their customers. A customer directory showing a printout of all or selected customer groups is important to check profitability or growth in the business' target markets. A mailing label or mailmerge program is also essential to communicate monthly specials to the customers or just tell the customers when you will be closed.

The invoice reports use the customer number entered to retrieve automatically the customer's name and address. This information is used only to confirm that the correct customer number has been entered.

Other customer information is needed to complete the order. The customer's tax status determines if tax is necessary on the order. The discount is used to give the customer a discount on the subtotal of the order. The last transaction date simply tells when was the last time a customer bought something. Every few years the inactive customers will be purged from the file.

CUSTNO is two characters followed by a dash and three numbers. The two characters must be the first two characters of the company name. The three numbers will be sequential. This is the key field used to identify the customer. When new customers are added, an existence verification is made to make sure that the customer number doesn't already exist. An index named CUSTNO will be created to access the customer numbers in order.

COMPANY is the name of the company. It is 20 characters long. It also has an index to report the data in company order.

STREET, CITY, STATE, and ZIP make up the address information. The STATE is a two-character state abbreviation. List verification can be used to verify one of the fifty states. ZIP is five or nine characters. If it is nine characters, a dash separates the first five from the last four characters. An index for ZIP allows mailings to be sorted and labels printed in zip code order to save postage.

PHONE uses a template to make sure that all numbers are entered and that area codes have proper parentheses and dashes.

LST_TXND is posted from the invoice program each time a new invoice is created for the customer. It must be in the range of 1/1/87 through 12/31/99. (This will have to be modified in the year 2000.)

DISCOUNT is subjectively based on how much the customer buys and how long they have been a customer. DISCOUNT will be in the range of 0–50%.

TAXABLE is either Yes or No (T or F), taxable or nontaxable depending if the customer is a reseller.

The inventory file

The next file is the inventory file as shown in Fig. 4-20. The inventory file exists for several reasons. First, it keeps track of Ajax's second most important asset, its inventory. Such items as the inventory number, brand, type, and description help identify the item. The price and warranty length fields are used during the order process to fill in important information about the order. The inventory quantities help the managers control the reorder process.

ITEMNO is four characters followed by three numbers. The four characters are the first two characters of the item brand followed by the first two characters of the item type. The three numbers are sequential. An index on ITEMNO will allow searches on this key field.

BRAND is the brand of the item. It is 10 characters wide. Because there is an infinite number of brands, there are no special data entry rules. An index

INVENTORY FILE FIELD NAME	DATA TYPE	DISPLAY SIZE	INDEX	TEMPLATE RANGE CHOICES
ITEMNO	CHAR	8	Y	AAAA-999
BRAND	CHAR	10	+TYPE	
TYPE	CHAR	12		REFRIGERATOR DISHWASHER WASHER DRYER RANGE MICROWAVE
DESC	CHAR	25		
PRICE	NUMERIC	7.2		9999.99
QTY_STK	NUMERIC	3		999
QTY_ORD	NUMERIC	3		999
WARRANTY	NUMERIC	2		0-24
FEATURES	MEMO	10		

4-20 The data entry rules and templates for the inventory file.

is built by BRAND and TYPE together. Though this may not make the index unique, it will give the database a good way to be sorted for the salesman's book of products.

TYPE is the various types of items that Ajax Appliance Company sells. These include refrigerators, dishwashers, washers, dryers, stoves, and microwaves.

There are many ways to implement known (or changing) lists of items in dBASE IV. As you learn about screens and programming, you will see many of these different ways.

DESC is a short 25-character description of the item. This way, when there are several items with the same type and brand, you will be able to distinguish them. Though they have different item numbers, you still will not be able to identify the specific item without a short description.

PRICE is a numeric field. PRICE is passed to the items file for each item on the invoice. The maximum price of an individual item is $9,999.99.

Two quantities are maintained on the database, QTY_STK and QTY_ORD. These are the in-stock and on-order quantities. Both have a maximum of 999 units.

The WARRANTY amount is a two-digit numeric field. This is the number of months the item can be under warranty. The maximum is 24 months, while some items will have no warranty at all.

Finally, on the file is the FEATURES field. This is a memo field and allows the salespeople to view long descriptions of the item. Because there is no limit (well, almost no limit) to the size of a memo field, they can store all sorts of information about the item—Its energy efficiency, the dimensions of the item, companion products such as ice makers for refrigerators, *Consumer Reports* reviews, or even the next model higher in quality. Regardless of for what it is used, memo fields have many excellent uses.

The invoice files

The invoice and items files are shown in Fig. 4-21. INVNO is four numbers followed by three numbers. The first four numbers give the year and month. The three numbers will be sequential. A procedure verifies the invoice number during an add or change to conform with the rule. It also initializes automatically the next invoice number.

INVOICE FILE FIELD NAME	DATA TYPE	DISPLAY SIZE	INDEX	PATTERN/ RANGE/ CHOICES
INVNO	CHAR	8	Y	9999-999
INVDATE	DATE	8	Y	01/01/87-12/31/99
CUSTNO	CHAR	6		AA-999
DISCOUNT	NUMERIC	2		from customer file

ITEMS FILE FIELD NAME	DATA TYPE	DISPLAY SIZE	INDEX	PATTERN/ RANGE/ CHOICES
INVNO	CHAR	8	Y	9999-999
QTY	NUMERIC	3		999
ITEMNO	CHAR	8		AAAA-999
PRICE	NUMERIC	7.2		from inventory file

4-21 The data entry rules and templates for the invoice and items file.

INVDATE is the system date and cannot be changed without changing the system date first. This will be allowed when the program starts and the user is asked to input the desired date. This can override the system date which will be the initial value.

CUSTNO is a validated customer number from the customer file. If the customer number does not exist, an error box is displayed. The user then has to return to the customer file to add the new customer.

DISCOUNT is also stored in this file. Although the discount can be retrieved from the customer file at any time, it may not receive the correct discount. The discount the customer receives might change depending on how much they buy and how fast they pay. When an order is taken, the total cost should reflect the discount in effect at that time. If the discount on the customer file changes at a later date, then the customer should only receive the new discount for subsequent purchases.

Those items make up the invoice file. Each item appears once in an invoice. The invoice items however appear as multiple records in the items file, one record for each invoice item.

Four fields make the items database. The first field is INVNO. The invoice number automatically copies from the invoice file and should never have to be entered. It is of utmost importance to keep the invoice number in both the invoice and items file the same. If they are not the same, then the items will be lost from the invoice.

QTY is the number of items the customer wants. This number is entered for each item on the invoice.

ITEMNO is entered as the item number the customer desires. After the item number is selected, it will be checked. First, the item number must be validated against the item file. If the item does not exist, an error box is displayed and the item number must be reentered. You cannot enter an item number that is not on the file. When adding new items to the invoice, the quantity of the item must not exceed the quantity in stock. An error box will be provided indicating the quantity available if a quantity greater than the in-stock amount is entered. The system will then return to the quantity field to allow the user to change the quantity or item number. Inventory quantities will be reduced for new sales.

PRICE is automatically retrieved from the inventory file. Like the customer discount, this field could be retrieved from the inventory file at any time. Also like the discount field, the price field constantly changes. The customer is entitled to the price of the item at the time they purchased it.

This takes care of defining the data entry rules and database items. Later, when you build your database you will be able to follow this design and save a lot of time. Remember, the more time you spend planning up front the quicker the programming steps will go. For each hour you spend planning, you should save at least two in programming and testing.

Creating test data

Once you have defined your data entry rules and what your database looks like, it is time to create test data. Test data should be prepared very scientifically in order to let you test many possible conditions. Test data should have many purposes. It should let you test data entry. Do all the conditions you programmed generate the proper acceptance or error messages? You may find some conditions you should have tested for that you did not think about. What happens when someone enters a blank into a field? How about numbers in a character field? dBASE automatically traps such things as bad dates or characters in date or numeric fields, but you must take care of the rest.

You will create two types of test data. The first is simply data to allow you to "populate" or fill the databases with meaningful data. This will be the initial "good" data that should end up in the database and be used to test output. Output would mainly consist of your reports. The second type of test data is used to test data entry. This includes designing data with "errors" that will display every one of your error conditions along with "good" data that should test some of your acceptable conditions.

Test data should allow you to test routine items such as you would normally find in your data. You should also test for limits. Put in data that is only one character long for some fields or every field. Create several records that use every position in the database (and therefore every position in the data entry screen and reports, too). When you create invoices, create some with no items and some with the maximum number of items. Use the same item number twice, can the system handle it? Do you want the system to handle it?

Create customer names that are very similar. Can the system handle that? Create some bad test data. Enter data that tests every condition. Try to enter a customer number that already exists. Try to change a customer number that is not on the file. Enter prices and quantities that test the system limits. If someone orders 999 units of 10 items, can the system still total correctly?

These are just some of the things to consider when testing your system. Of course, testing your system begins with the test data. Figure 4-22 shows the test data for the customer database.

```
                        CUSTOMER FILE TEST DATA
                        -----------------------
```

CUSTNO	COMPANY	STREET	CITY	STATE	ZIP	PHONE	LST_TXND	DISCOUNT	TAXABLE
C6	C20	C20	C20	C2	C10	C13	D8	N2	L
AP-001	APPLIANCE CITY	210 SKY LANE	OXNARD	CA	95677-	(415)555-4772	07/25/88	15	Y
AP-002	APPLIANCE CITY	360 ACE AVE	HOLLYWOOD	CA	95245-	(213)555-4766	08/10/88	15	N
AP-003	APPLIANCE WORLD	20695 BLUE BIRD AVE	SAN FRANCISCO	CA	95564-	(415)555-3353	08/19/88	0	Y
AV-001	AVON APPLIANCE	1687 NEW PLACE ROAD	LOS ANGELES	CA	98887-	(415)555-7963	05/16/88	15	Y
BO-001	BOB'S BRANDS	BOB'S DRIVE	SANTA FE	NM	84545-4545	(434)555-3444	05/31/86	0	N
CA-001	CARY'S COOLERS	60 STRAWBERRY HILLS	WINDSOR	CT	06773-	(203)555-7799	08/21/88	50	N
CR-001	CRAZY FREDDIES	1820 171ST ST	NEW YORK	NY	15545-	(212)555-9974	10/11/88	5	N
ER-001	ERNIES TV	456 SNOW PLOW AVE	BLEAUVILLE	CA	94454-8946	(213)555-4975	11/29/88	10	Y
FR-001	FRIENDLY APPLIANCE	26 CHOCOLATE AVE	HERSHEY	PA	15554-	(717)555-6274	07/01/88	15	N
JA-001	JACKEL & HYDES	357 BAT COURT	LAWRENCEVILLE	PA	14434-	(717)555-3656	05/24/88	25	N
JI-001	JIMS HOT AND COLD	55 SKINNER RD	VERNON	CA	95565-8784	(213)555-6473	07/13/88	5	N
RA-001	RANGES ON THE HOME	23 OLD OKIE DR	OKLAHOMA CITY	OK	73344-	(564)555-3248	12/31/88	35	N
RO-001	RON'S REFRIGERATORS	141 HOLLOW OAK PLACE	SAN JUAN CAPISTRANO	CA	95564-6877	(213)555-5764	07/05/87	10	Y
TH-001	THE HOME SHOPPE	25 APPLIANCE LANE	SARATOGA	CA	93434-	(415)555-8355	01/29/88	35	N
WA-001	WASHER WAREHOUSE	15525 MARINER DR	LOS ALTOS	CA	97688-	(213)555-9843	06/30/87	15	N
WE-001	WEST'S WHITE GOODS	26 DENNIS LANE	CUPERTINO	CA	92324-3342	(213)555-0478	11/14/88	10	N

4-22 Test data for the customer file.

Testing for the customer file is easy. Because this is a stand-alone file, much of the testing can be done at data entry time. In this figure, all you see is the final database. Later, when you see the invoice test file, you will see conditions defined as well.

Sixteen customer records have been defined. Try to enter a customer number twice. Also, try to enter a discount over 50%. Because both of these errors can be easily trapped by dBASE, you will see some error messages.

In Fig. 4-22, you can see that the data was typed onto a piece of paper. This is not yet in a dBASE database. It is strictly used for design. Each field name has been entered at the top of each column. Below each field name is a size indicator along with the data type. The exact number of characters has been allowed for, the maximum of each field. CUSTNO is a 6-character field, COMPANY is a 20-character field, etc. Below these column headers are the actual data.

Notice some of the data that has been created. Ron's Refrigerators is our maximum size test case. Each field in Ron's Refrigerators is at its maximum size. This will allow us to see where we have not allowed enough space in screens or reports. The first two records are both for Appliance City which has two locations. This will also be a test to make sure that our program (that you will design and program) can meet that condition. Other than those conditions, the data will simply be entered. This is a simple file.

Figure 4-23 shows the test data for the inventory database. Again, the first field ITEMNO is the unique key. No one record is used here to fill all the field lengths. The FROSTY Refrigerator FRRE-001 contains the largest description. COLDPOINTS is the only BRAND name that fills the field. Various other records fill the price and quantity fields. Because of the large amount of numeric data and the fact that many quantity totals times price will be summarized, you will have to wait to run the reports to see if the summary field sizes are large enough. If the maximum price is $9,999 and the maximum number of items is 999, then you would need a field capable of handling 10 million dollars. In reality though, the retail price probably won't exceed $1,500, and the quantity in stock may not exceed 100. That's only $150 thousand. Hundred thousands to ten millions is a difference of two display characters.

```
                          INVENTORY FILE TEST DATA
                          ------------------------
```

ITEMNO	BRAND	TYPE	DESC	PRICE	QTY_STK	QTY_ORD	WARRANTY	FEATURES
C8	C10	C12	C25	N7.2	N3	N3	N2	M10
CODR-001	COLDPOINTS	DRYER	SUPERSPIN I	489.99	82		12	TBA
CODR-002	COLDPOINTS	DRYER	SUPERSPIN II	689.99	58		12	TBA
WHDR-001	WHOLEPOOL	DRYER		899.99	36		18	TBA
HIMI-001	HITECH	MICROWAVE	1500 WATT	229.99	127		6	TBA
HIRA-001	HITECH	RANGE		689.99	89		12	TBA
RURA-001	RUSTIC	RANGE	WOOD TRIM	659.99	0	100	12	TBA
WHRA-001	WHOLEPOOL	RANGE		929.99	28		18	TBA
FRRE-001	FROSTY	REFRIGERATOR	1 DOOR TOP FREEZER W/ICE	699.99	112		6	TBA
FRRE-002	FROSTY	REFRIGERATOR	2 DOOR SIDE BY SIDE	899.99	78		12	TBA
FRRE-003	FROSTY	REFRIGERATOR	2 DOOR UPRIGHT	1199.99	6	5	60	TBA
CORE-001	COLDPOINTS	REFRIGERATOR	MINI-MAX	229.99	17		6	TBA
WHRE-001	WHOLEPOOL	REFRIGERATOR		469.99	23	40	6	TBA
COWA-001	COLDPOINTS	WASHER		369.99	89		6	TBA
WHWA-001	WHOLEPOOL	WASHER		739.99	36		6	TBA
WHWA-002	WHOLEPOOL	WASHER	DELUXE MODEL	969.99	2	30	12	TBA

4-23 Test data for the inventory file.

There are really no special requirements for this test data. However, this test data will be used by the invoice test data. You should make sure that this data allows you to test the many error conditions necessary for proper design of the invoice file. The prices must be high enough to test the maximum field size in the invoice report. There must be enough of some items so the quantity won't drop to zero, and a small enough quantity of others so that zero and out of stock conditions can be tested.

Some of the other data that was entered allows us to check quantity on order data. Some quantity on orders have inventory left, while others are already at zero.

You may also notice that the memo field data in the inventory file has just been coded TBA. This means "To Be Addressed." It is not important to enter anything specific here. When you get to data entry, you can enter anything you like.

The final test data to enter is for the invoice file. This data is used to test a myriad of data entry and output conditions. Because it should be designed to perform a very comprehensive test, another column called "Testing Objectives" is added to the design, as shown in Fig. 4-24.

Even though the data is entered in two separate databases, the design is shown here as one database that actually looks like an invoice. Remember, much of the data in the invoice is either retrieved from another file or is calculated. There are very few fields that need to be entered.

Seven invoices are shown in this design. Of course, you can add more if you really want. Five of the invoices are for 8/88 and two are for 9/88. The five invoices of August are where most of the effort will be spent in design and testing. Invoice data entry and testing cannot commence until both the customer and invoice data have been entered. Besides just entering the invoices, you will have to check the output reports to make sure that the right data is being retrieved from the customer and inventory files.

The first invoice entered should be 8804-001. This corresponds to the first invoice entered in August 1988. Later, this number will be automatically generated by a program that you will create. The customer to be entered is JA-001. This number exists on the customer file. Once you enter the main invoice information, you enter data for the items. Four items are shown. All of these items should enter with no problems. Your first goal is to try data that should work, to try the normal data entry procedures.

Once you enter that invoice, you should start to try some error conditions. Try to enter 8804-001 again. Did you get an error message? Enter a customer number that doesn't exist. Again, you should get an error message, and you should be able to continue. The customer for this second invoice will be Ron's Refrigerators. We'll enter many invoices for this customer to test the various reports and roll-up programs later.

This invoice tests many different conditions. Enter ten items, and then try to enter an eleventh which should be rejected. Attempt to enter an item that doesn't exist. Enter a quantity for an item number that exceeds the quantity in stock. Enter an item that uses the same item twice—this should be permissible.

In the third invoice, enter successive records that are out of stock. We should be able to eventually enter a good record. The fourth invoice and fifth invoice will again use Ron's Refrigerators. Enter a large quantity and a zero

INVNO	INVDATE	CUSTNO	QTY	ITEMNO	
C8	**D8**	**C6**	**N3**	**C8**	**TESTING OBJECTIVES**
⌐	⌐	⌐	⌐	⌐	------------------
8808-001	08/01/88	JA-001	2	WHRE-001	JUST ADD A FEW RECORDS
			7	HIRA-001	TO TEST ADD ROUTINES
			3	FRRE-003	NO ERROR MESSAGES
			10	FRRE-001	
8808-002	08/01/88	RO-001	25	FRRE-001	TEST RON'S REFRIGERATORS
			15	FRRE-002	TEST 10 ITEMS TEST OVERSTOCK
			2	FRRE-003	* WILL ONLY LEAVE 1 IN STOCK
			11	CODR-001	
			9	WHWA-002	* ONLY 2 IN STOCK
			7	WHWA-001	
			15	HOWA-001	* ITEM DOESN'T EXIST - MAKE COWA
			9	CODR-001	2ND CODR - OK ALSO LAST ITEM
8808-003	08/02/88	WA-001	5	COWA-001	
			6	WHWA-001	
			3	WHWA-002	* SHOULD BE 0 IN STOCK - FORGET
			5	RURA-001	* SHOULD BE 0 IN STOCK - REPLACE
			5	WHRA-001	
8808-004	08/02/88	RO-001	7	FRRE-001	2nd RON'S REFRIGERATORS
			120	HIMI-001	LARGE QUANTITY
			0	WHWA-002	TEST FOR 0 QUANTITY
8808-005	08/05/88	RO-001	5	FRRE-001	3rd RON'S REFRIGERATORS
					ONLY 1 LINE ITEM
8809-001	09/01/88	RO-001	10	FRRE-001	TEST ANOTHER MONTH ON FILE
			9	FRRE-002	ALSO RON'S REFRIGERATORS
			5	WHRE-001	
			10	COWA-001	
			6	CODR-001	
8809-002	09/15/88	WE-001	5	HIRA-001	
			12	CODR-001	
			8	CODR-002	

4-24 Test data for the invoice file.

quantity. The fifth invoice will test for only one line item. Somewhere you may want to try to enter an invoice that has no items.

Besides adding records, you are going to have to test changing and deleting invoices and invoice items. This will be up to you to design a list of possible conditions. As you complete the pseudocode section of this design, you will see all of the error conditions thought out.

The last two invoices will test another month. Can you enter a September invoice if the month is August? That's for you to decide in your design and then create test data for. The two September invoices will simply be entered and used to test for output reports, and to make sure that the program can correctly separate different months of data.

Remember, test data serves two purposes. It gives you a chance to test validation and error conditions, along with giving you a database that can be used to check all of your reports. You may have to tweak the test data as you go, but having a good starting point is important.

Step 6: screen design

Once the data and file relationships are established, it is time to design your screens. Screens are made up of the fields that can be input or viewed in the edit mode. If at all possible, your screens should look very much like the forms that you might use in a manual system. This makes for the most user-friendly system.

Designing data entry screens

When performing screen design, it is important to place all three types of objects on the screen. This includes:

- Data Fields
- Text
- Lines and Boxes

Your data fields should be placed where you want them. When entering data, the cursor will move from top to bottom, left to right. You can make the entry size any size you want. You should make sure that as you place the fields, you leave as much space around them as you will use. Calculated fields that are display only can also be a part of a data entry screen.

Fixed text includes your field labels and other text that makes the screen more readable to you, the computer user. Fixed text can also include your company name or data entry instructions.

The final type of object you can place on your screen is lines and boxes. Lines and boxes allow you to cleanly segregate your data items into areas to make it easier to see the different fields in your data entry. For example, in the invoice screen, you would segregate the many quantities and items in the item file itself, from the data items that only occur once in the invoice.

When performing screen design, you have already determined your data items and what the reports should look like. Screen design should simply consist of creating the screen in dBASE IV by placing the fields you desire on the work surface (see Part Two). For now, a more simplified set of screen storyboards is shown in Fig. 4-25 through 4-27.

The customer screen

The customer data entry screen shown in Fig. 4-25 is the first screen we will design. It is very simple and simply consists of text and fields, along with some lines and boxes for emphasis. The unique key field, which is customer

```
        AJAX APPLIANCE COMPANY
        CUSTOMER DATA ENTRY SCREEN

    CUSTOMER NUMBER:    AA-999


     Company    XXXXXXXXXXXXXXXXXXXX
     Street     XXXXXXXXXXXXXXXXXXXX
     City       XXXXXXXXXXXXXXXXXXXX
     State/Zip AA  99999-9999


     Telephone Number   (999)999-9999
     Last Transaction   MM/DD/YY
     Discount Percent   99
     Taxable Flag       X
```

4-25 The Customer file data entry screen design.

number, is centered at the top of the screen and is separated from the other fields. This is very normal. We also have separated the address information from the other information about the customer by using some horizontal lines.

In the Inventory data entry screen, you will see that we also will separate the identifying fields from the actual data fields. At the top of the Customer screen is a header to indicate what screen this is. It is very important in a data entry screen that the type of screen be identified at the top. When an operator uses many screens and many systems, this greatly eliminates confusion.

```
               AJAX APPLIANCE COMPANY
               INVENTORY DATA ENTRY SCREEN

            ITEM NUMBER: AAAA-999

          BRAND                    TYPE
       XXXXXXXXXX              XXXXXXXXXXX

       ITEM DESCRIPTION: XXXXXXXXXXXXXXXXXXXXXXXXX


     QUANTITY IN STOCK          QUANTITY ON ORDER
          999                         999

               PRICE: 99999.99

          WARRANTY PERIOD: 99 MONTHS

      ┌ FEATURES: ─────────────────────────────
      │
      │
```

4-26 The Inventory file data entry screen design.

```
         AJAX APPLIANCE COMPANY - INVOICE FORM

                                   ┌─────CUSTOMER NUMBER: AA-9999─────┐
  INVOICE NUMBER: 9999-99          │ COMPANY NAME                     │
                                   │ STREET                           │
  INVOICE DATE:    mm/dd/yy        │ CITY, ST ZIP CODE                │
                                   └──────────────────────────────────┘

LINE QTY   ITEM #    BRAND      TYPE      DESCRIPTION       PRICE    EXTENSION
  9. 999 AAAA-999 X-BRAND-X X--TYPE--X X------DESC------X  9PRICE9  9QTY*PRI9
  9. 999 AAAA-999 X-BRAND-X X--TYPE--X X------DESC------X  9PRICE9  9QTY*PRI9
  9. 999 AAAA-999 X-BRAND-X X--TYPE--X X------DESC------X  9PRICE9  9QTY*PRI9
  9. 999 AAAA-999 X-BRAND-X X--TYPE--X X------DESC------X  9PRICE9  9QTY*PRI9
  9. 999 AAAA-999 X-BRAND-X X--TYPE--X X------DESC------X  9PRICE9  9QTY*PRI9
  9. 999 AAAA-999 X-BRAND-X X--TYPE--X X------DESC------X  9PRICE9  9QTY*PRI9
  9. 999 AAAA-999 X-BRAND-X X--TYPE--X X------DESC------X  9PRICE9  9QTY*PRI9
  9. 999 AAAA-999 X-BRAND-X X--TYPE--X X------DESC------X  9PRICE9  9QTY*PRI9
                                                                  ----------
                                              Sub Total         999,999.99
                                              Discount 99%       99,999.99
                                                                  ----------
                                              Taxable Amount    999,999.99
                                              Tax 99.9%          99,999.99
                                                                  ----------
                                              Total Amount      999,999.99
```

4-27 The Invoice data entry screen design.

The inventory screen

As shown in Fig. 4-26, the screen is divided in two areas by a line across the screen. Above the line is the identifying information. The item number is the unique key field and is at the top of the screen below the main header. To identify what the item number refers to, however, takes the three fields: brand, type, and description. The brand and type are shown on the same line, because they might make the description unique. However, as some manufacturers have more than one item of the same type, it is necessary to see a short description.

Below the line is the data items. The two quantities are shown first, followed by the price and warranty period. You may notice that some of the data fields are below the descriptions rather than to the right. You may also notice that some lines contain more than one description and field. This is all permissible. You can place text and data fields anywhere you want. Later, you can specify the order that the cursor will move from field to field.

Finally, at the bottom of the screen is the FEATURES field which will be a memo field. The data is shown enclosed in a window. Memo fields give you the option of being automatically displayed in a window. You will choose this option when creating the data entry screen later in Part Two.

The invoice screen

The last data entry form is the invoice form. This screen is actually made of several screens. The first screen displays the data from the invoice file, while the second screen displays data from the items file. A potential third screen will display the subtotal and total calculations. This will be implemented using the new windows features of dBASE IV. Because a data screen can only allow data from one file at a time, we have to use some innovative coding. Through programming, we can overcome this restriction, but you still must program this multi-file data entry, and cannot use the screen form generator as you will soon see.

The screen, as shown in Fig. 4-27, has only a few fields on the screen. At the top of the screen is the main header. This main header needs to be at the top of each screen. Only three fields are actually entered. The invoice number will be automatically calculated. It can also be entered or simply confirmed. The invoice date uses the system date as its default, and you can change the date or simply confirm it. Another condition that may have to be "trapped" is if the date or invoice number is changed, should they be compared to each other to make sure that they are still in sync? Remember that the invoice number is comprised of the month and year of the date, followed by a sequential number.

The customer number, upon being entered, automatically retrieves and displays the customer's address. The city, state, and zip code will be displayed as one string using some functions you will see later.

Once the main invoice information is entered, you can enter the item data. You have to enter only the quantity and item number. The brand, type, description, and price are retrieved from the inventory file. The extension is calculated after each quantity and item number is verified. Later, you will see the design for the menu that allows you to choose and enter each of the items that make up the invoice.

The bottom of the invoice is simply a mass of calculations. Each time an item is added, changed, or deleted, the screen is redisplayed and the totals recalculated.

Once screen design is done, you essentially have completed all the steps that you can do without any programming. The first six steps of this process might be called screen and data design. The last two steps—menu and process design—are where you will program with dBASE IV. In the rest of this chapter, you will see how to do menu and process design. In Part Two of this book, you will see how to make your data and screen design come to life. In Part Four, you will see how to take the programming steps necessary to complete the design as shown earlier in the chapter.

Step 7: automation design (menus)

Menus are the key to a good system. The operator must be able to follow the system in order to go from place to place. Usually each program is a menu choice. So, in your design, you must decide how to group the menus. From examining the overall design and looking at all the systems you have, you can start to see a distinct set of combinations. The data entry and report screens, and reports that have been designed so far are shown in Fig. 4-28. Reindexing files is a maintenance item that you will see later.

In dBASE IV, menus can be created two different ways. First, you can create menus with standard screen commands to display a lot of text

```
MENU SELECTIONS
----------------
      CUSTOMER DATA ENTRY
      PRINT CUSTOMER DIRECTORY
      PRINT CUSTOMER CROSS REFERENCE
      PRINT CUSTOMER MAILING LABELS
      INVENTORY DATA ENTRY
      PRINT INVENTORY VALUATION REPORT
      PRINT ITEM NUMBER CROSS REFERENCE
      PRINT SALESMAN INVENTORY REPORT
      INVOICE DATA ENTRY
      PRINT INVOICE
      PRINT WARRANTY AGREEMENT
      PRINT MONTHLY SALES REPORT
      REINDEX FILES
```

4-28 The programs that will be necessary in the system.

describing each menu choice along with a single entry area for user input at the top or bottom of the screen. Generally, the choices are in the form of a number, and each item on the menu has a number associated with it. Look at the menu and choose the number next to the choice that you want. This is similar to data entry screens.

The other alternative is to use the new menu commands in dBASE IV to create bar menus or pull-down menus. You can also create pop-up menus that pop-up anywhere on the screen. In fact, using the new dBASE IV menu commands, you can create menus that look just like the dBASE IV menus used to create screens, reports and databases in dBASE IV. Before designing the type of menu you want, it is more important to know what each option is and the suboptions that will follow.

There are customer programs, inventory programs, and invoice programs. Looking at the list of programs, you can create the traditional menu design shown in Fig. 4-29. The disadvantage of this type of menu is that it is not easily expandable. It takes up much of the screen and leaves no room for anything else on the screen. It also forces you to choose the selection by number, rather than visually. Although it has been a stable design for many years in computer systems, it no longer is the recommended method.

Some of these processes will be dependent upon other processes. A menu item can allow the separation of the dependencies. For instance, when a new invoice is entered, it should bring up a menu choice to ask the operator if they want to print the Warranty Agreements. They may choose to print nothing, the invoice or both "reports." Suppose, the paper jams and the output is destroyed. The operator must have a way to reprint the invoice or warranty agreement.

A more contemporary design looks like Fig. 4-30. The Invoice and other pulldowns are shown below their actual placement. As you can see in this design the different systems have their own pull-down menus. All the user would actually see is the "bar" menu at the top, showing the three different systems, the Other option, and the Exit option. As the cursor is moved to each bar menu option, a menu appears below the bar text. It is called a pull-down menu because it appears to pull down from the single text on top of the screen. As you move the cursor from the bar, the pull-down menu disappears and the next bar menu choice appears.

```
        AJAX APPLIANCE COMPANY
        MAIN SELECTION MENU

        ENTER SELECTION: __

CUSTOMER SYSTEM          INVOICE SYSTEM           INVENTORY SYSTEM
---------------         --------------          ----------------

1. DATA ENTRY           5. DATA ENTRY            9. DATA ENTRY

2. DIRECTORY            6. PRINT INVOICE         10. VALUATION REPORT

3. CROSS REFERENCE      7. WARRANTY AGREEMENT    11. CROSS REFERENCE

4. MAILING LABELS       8. SALES REPORTS         12. SALESMAN REPORT


        OTHER PROCESSING              EXIT PROCESSING
        ----------------              ---------------

        13. REINDEX FILES             15. EXIT TO DOT PROMPT

        14. PACK FILES                16. EXIT TO DOS
```

4-29 Menu design using traditional menus.

Once you are inside a pull-down menu, use the up and down arrow keys to select one of the choices inside the menu. As you move from menu to menu, a different choice is highlighted. When you press Enter, the choice that was highlighted is run.

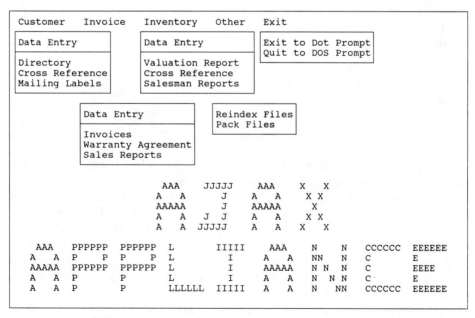

4-30 Menu design using bar and pull-down style menus.

One last feature of the pull-down menu screen is the advantage of having a lot of leftover screen. As you can see in the design in Fig. 4-30, Ajax Appliance has plenty of room to display their logo. As you see the process design created, you will learn more about menus and what they can do for you.

Step 8: process design

Now that the reports, screens, menus, and data items are designed, and the overall processes have been considered, it is time to begin to design the detailed processes that will complete your system.

Tools of process design

There are many ways to design the details including flowcharting, pseudo-coding, and storyboarding. *Flowcharting* is used to define the overall process and to tell which action comes after each preceding action. *Pseudocoding* lets you put into generic words the specific actions that need to be automated. Finally, *storyboarding* includes the design of your screens, reports, error messages, and finally menus and windows.

Just as you have designed your report formats, and screen formats you will also be designing programs and windows. Windows are rectangular areas that can be placed anywhere on the screen and be any size. They allow communication to and from the operator and sit on top of whatever is already on the screen. There are several uses for windows:

- Error messages
- Help screens
- Menu choices
- Confirmation messages
- User fill-ins

Error messages and help screens usually are one way communication. They simply give the operator a message, and any key is pressed to continue. They would most likely be used when an edit check failed, when some other item is incorrect, or when the user pushes a predetermined help key.

Windows can be any size, anywhere on the screen. Anything can be placed inside a window including text, screens, fields, and menus. These allow two-way communication to the user. Windows can be used for custom menus, or to allow the input of a password or any parameter to a system. Because they sit on top of what is already on the screen, they don't disturb the normal program flow. Because all of the dBASE IV tools are available to you, it is easy to create customized systems.

In dBASE IV, the *procedures* or *programs* are created with your favorite editor, word processor, or the internal dBASE Editor. Procedures can occur anytime. You decide when a procedure is called or run, and whether one procedure calls another.

You will see many different types of procedures in this system, including traditional programming design where many modules are used for each function. In the customer system, a separate program is used for adds, changes, deletes, and programs, and a separate program it used for each report. You will see this technique demonstrated in the customer system.

You will also learn a technique used with data entry screens known as pre- and post-processing. Procedures that occur before data entry are called *pre-processors*. If the procedure occurs after leaving the data entry screen, it is called a *post-processor*. Only a couple of modules are used for all of the functions. By using the dBASE screen and report generators, very little code is needed.

When you get to the invoice system, a combination of traditional and contemporary programming is demonstrated to show you how to write the most productive systems quickly.

A good way to start developing the design for the procedures you need is to list all the screens and reports you have already designed. Because each one may require a program, you can assume that most of your programs will be defined by that list.

All of the screens and reports you have designed will become an integral part of your program. They will either be called by the program, or the code they produce will be integrated into your program.

Two extra programs in this figure were not in the figure during menu design. The first is an opening program. Traditionally, systems will have some sort of beginning program that contains their logo and perhaps where password validation and date checking take place. The other program is the program that contains the main menu and all the appropriate actions. The new program list is shown in Fig. 4-31.

```
PROGRAMS
--------
OPENING SCREEN
MAIN MENU
CUSTOMER DATA ENTRY SCREEN
PRINT CUSTOMER DIRECTORY
PRINT CUSTOMER CROSS REFERENCE
PRINT CUSTOMER MAILING LABELS
INVENTORY DATA ENTRY SCREEN
PRINT INVENTORY VALUATION REPORT
PRINT ITEM NUMBER CROSS REFERENCE
PRINT SALESMAN INVENTORY REPORT
INVOICE DATA ENTRY SCREEN
PRINT INVOICE
PRINT WARRANTY AGREEMENT
PRINT MONTHLY SALES REPORT
```

4-31 Programs that might contain procedures.

The opening screen

When you create complicated systems, you may also have programs that do very little, but perform important functions such as the opening screen program used to get the system password and to confirm the system date.

This screen would be the first screen the operators see when they run the main program in a dBASE IV system that you design.

A flowchart to show the sequence of events in this program is shown in Fig. 4-32. This flowchart tells us that first the opening screen is displayed. Next, the user enters the Password and System Date. The password and date is verified. If the password is invalid, an error condition occurs, and an error window is displayed. The user then must enter the correct password in three attempts. If the user fails to enter a valid password, then the user is taken out of the program. If the user enters a valid password, then the menu system is run.

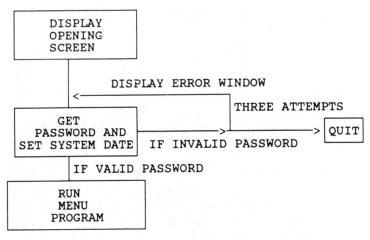

4-32 The flowchart for the process of the opening screen.

Flowcharts used to be the prime medium that an analyst used to communicate process flow to a programmer. Many times the analyst and the programmer are the same person. Nothing is more embarrassing to analysts then not remembering why they created a design that does not make any sense to program. Today, pseudocode is more widely accepted as a standard to show process flow. Flowcharts become nearly impossible to follow as they become large. When a new function is added, flowcharts typically have to be redrawn.

Pseudocode should be used to show the desired procedure in more detail. For this small program it might look something like Fig. 4-33. As you can see from the figure, understanding the process flow from viewing the pseudocode is easier than from examining the flowchart. If you don't agree, read some of the page-long pseudocode later in this book. Some of the fifty-line pseudocodes used to be ten-page flowcharts. You may also notice that the pseudocode is more detailed than the flowchart. You can see that before allowing the reader to enter the password and system date, they must first be retrieved from their storage locations. You can see that a screen must be displayed in order to get the password. Though any programmer knows this, it wasn't readily apparent in the flowchart.

```
OPENING SCREEN

GET THE SYSTEM DATE FROM THE SYSTEM
RETRIEVE THE CURRENT SECRET PASSWORD FOR COMPARISON TO OPERATOR INPUT
LOOP FOR THREE TIMES OR UNTIL PASSWORD IS CORRECT AND DATE IS VALID
DISPLAY A SCREEN TO GET THE PASSWORD AND VERIFY THE DATE
IF PASSWORD IS NOT VALID DISPLAY WINDOW WITH PASSWORD ERROR MESSAGE
AFTER THREE INVALID PASSWORD TRIES QUIT
```

4-33   The pseudocode for the process of the opening screen.

Finally, a storyboard is created showing the screen you would use. This screen is very important, because it leaves no doubt as to what the screen should look like. This screen is shown in Fig. 4-34. The screen contains several text and field areas to show the user where to enter the password and verify the date. After both had been done, the system would verify the password and date. If the date is invalid, dBASE's automatic date checker would not let you leave the date entry area. If the password is invalid, an error window could be displayed as demonstrated below.

4-34   The screen for opening the program.

The main menu

The menus that you will use were designed in the seventh step. Eventually, a choice has to be made whether to use the dBASE IV bar and pull-down menus in a program, or use the more traditional full-screen text menus. Because both menus are already designed in a storyboard, you might want to draw a flowchart of the menu selections. Though flowcharts are not used much in process design, they are still used frequently in menu flow analysis. Later, you can expand this to encompass all of the logic of other programs. For example, a menu item is designed to print an invoice or warranty agreement. This same program is also called from the invoice data entry. You will see that logic later.

The flowcharts for the menus are shown in Fig. 4-35. The main menu gives us the choice of calling any of four other system menus or programs. The choices are the customer system, the invoice system, the inventory system, or the other processing program.

In this set of flowcharts, each system is represented by a separate flowchart. In Fig. 4-35, flowchart A is the customer system. The customer system has four modules that can be called. These include a data entry module and a module for each report. The invoice process in flowchart B is very much the same. Flowchart C is the inventory system. The inventory system is a straightforward process much like the customer system. Flowchart D, the other processing category, has only two processes. Reindexing files is explained later. Exiting the system is an important function, because it lets you exit from the system in a controlled manner.

Because Ajax had decided to use a bar and pull-down menu system to call other programs, it can be added to the original opening screen pseudocode. Based on the items in the menu, the revised pseudocode would look like Fig. 4-36 on page 204.

The original pseudocode has already been explained. A loop is set up for the menus to keep appearing after each choice is finished. For example, the first time into the menu, the operator chooses to do some customer data entry. After that is complete, the operator is returned to the menu and allowed to make additional choices, until choosing Other Processing and selecting EXIT to end the program. As each bar menu choice is selected, a pull-down menu automatically appears. Later, you will see that the program code is very similar to the pseudocode.

The customer data entry system processes

You are about to begin to design three different modules of the Ajax Appliance Company system. Normally, when you design a system, you would use one consistent interface. If you have attempted to use the sample programs that come with dBASE IV, you have seen the Ashton-Tate Furniture Company system. Every program looks and acts and is written exactly the same. While that makes for a nice consistent system, it does little to teach you contemporary techniques.

In this customer system, you will see traditional programming techniques. Using the "fillin" technique, you will see how traditional menus work. We will also show you a way to make it a little more contemporary in just a few statements. You will also see traditional module design. The data entry functions of add, change, delete, and display (view) are each a separate module, and you will see how to create memory variables. Each report is also a separate module although each report itself uses reports you created in the report writer.

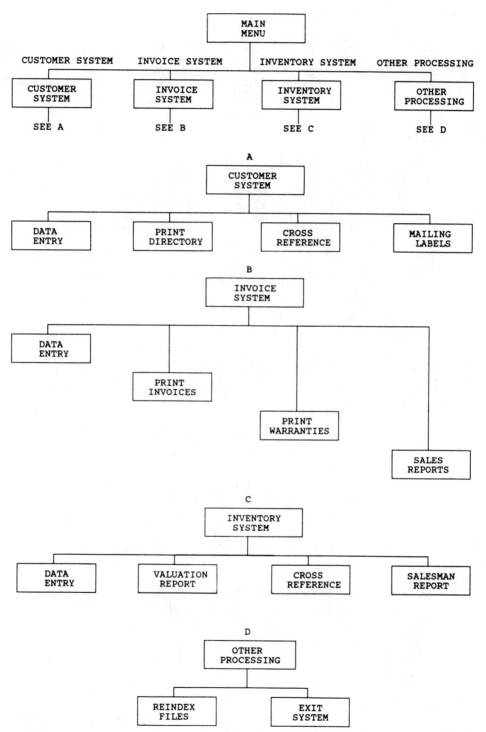

4-35 The flowchart for the main, customer, invoice, inventory, and other menu flows.

```
OPENING SCREEN AND MAIN MENU

GET THE SYSTEM DATE FROM THE SYSTEM
RETRIEVE THE CURRENT SECRET PASSWORD FOR COMPARISON TO OPERATOR INPUT
LOOP FOR THREE TIMES OR UNTIL PASSWORD IS CORRECT AND DATE IS VALID
   DISPLAY A SCREEN TO GET THE PASSWORD AND VERIFY THE DATE
   IF PASSWORD IS NOT VALID DISPLAY WINDOW WITH PASSWORD ERROR MESSAGE
   AFTER THREE INVALID PASSWORD TRIES QUIT
END LOOP

IF PASSWORD IS VALID
    DISPLAY BAR MENU
      CASE CHOICE
        WHEN CUSTOMER SYSTEM
          DISPLAY PULL DOWN MENU
          CASE CHOICE
            WHEN DATA ENTRY DO CUSTOMER DATA ENTRY
            WHEN DIRECTORY DO CUSTOMER DIRECTORY
            WHEN CROSS REFERENCE DO PRINT CUSTOMER CROSS REFERENCE
            WHEN MAILING LABELS DO CUSTOMER MAILING LABELS
        WHEN INVOICE SYSTEM
          DISPLAY PULL DOWN MENU
          CASE CHOICE
            WHEN DATA ENTRY DO INVOICE DATA ENTRY
            WHEN PRINT INVOICES DO PRINT INVOICES
            WHEN WARRANTY AGREEMENTS DO PRINT WARRANTY AGREEMENTS
            WHEN SALES REPORTS DO SALES REPORTS
        WHEN INVENTORY SYSTEM
          DISPLAY PULL DOWN MENU
          CASE CHOICE
            WHEN DATA ENTRY DO INVENTORY DATA ENTRY
            WHEN VALUATION REPORT DO PRINT VALUATION REPORT
            WHEN CROSS REFERENCE DO INVENTORY CROSS REFERENCE
            WHEN SALESMAN REPORT DO PRINT SALESMAN REPORTS
        WHEN OTHER PROCESSING
          DISPLAY PULL DOWN MENU
          CASE CHOICE
            WHEN REINDEX FILES THEN REINDEX FILES
            WHEN PACK FILE THEN PACK FILES
        WHEN EXIT SYSTEM
          DISPLAY PULL DOWN MENU
          CASE CHOICE
            WHEN EXIT TO DOT PROMPT THEN CANCEL
            WHEN EXIT TO DOS PROMPT THEN QUIT
      ENDCASE
    ENDLOOP
```

4-36 The pseudocode for the process of the opening screen.

When you see the design for the inventory and invoice files, you see a much more contemporary design that takes advantage of dBASE IV's power. Here, you will see many types of menus, windows and even user-defined functions.

For now, let's begin by designing a customer menu. Figure 4-37 shows what a typical customer menu screen might look like. The company name is at the top of the page, and the selection entry area is also there. The various choices are listed below with a number in front of each choice.

This menu would be "called" from the main menu when the user chooses Data Entry from the Customer System menu choice. Once the user enters the

```
             AJAX APPLIANCE COMPANY
               CUSTOMER DATA ENTRY


         ENTER SELECTION ==>  __

         1. ADD CUSTOMER INFORMATION

         2. CHANGE CUSTOMER INFORMATION

         3. DELETE A CUSTOMER

         4. VIEW CUSTOMER INFORMATION

         X. EXIT CUSTOMER DATA ENTRY
```

4-37   The screen for the customer data entry menu.

choice—a number from 1 through 4 or an X to exit—the program would "call" another program to actually perform the function.

A more sophisticated screen is shown in Fig. 4-38. Notice the entry area is gone, and there are simply five choices. These would be created with a pop-up menu. As the user pressed the up or down arrow keys, a different selection would be highlighted. When the user presses Enter, the selection is made. Also, a user could simply press the first letter of the choice to select the desired function. dBASE IV automatically takes care of this in the pop-up menu creation process.

```
             AJAX APPLIANCE COMPANY
               CUSTOMER DATA ENTRY

          ADD CUSTOMER INFORMATION

         CHANGE CUSTOMER INFORMATION

            DELETE A CUSTOMER

          VIEW CUSTOMER INFORMATION

          EXIT CUSTOMER DATA ENTRY
```

4-38   The alternative screen for the customer data entry menu.

The program to create this is very simple. The menu is displayed either by traditional programming commands or by the new menu commands of dBASE IV. The program then must loop while checking the user response. Once a correct response is found, the program branches to the next program or returns to the main menu from where the customer menu was called. In effect, it either moves up or down the flowchart that you saw in Fig. 4-35. This pseudocode is shown in Fig. 4-39.

Regardless of the menu chosen, this process pseudocode will be the same. Until the EXIT choice is chosen, the program lets one choice after another be made.

```
DISPLAY MENU
  DO WHILE .NOT. EXIT
   CASE CHOICE
      WHEN ADD CUSTOMER INFORMATION DO ADD CUSTOMER
      WHEN CHANGE CUSTOMER INFORMATION DO CHANGE CUSTOMER
      WHEN DELETE A CUSTOMER DO DELETE CUSTOMER
      WHEN VIEW CUSTOMER INFORMATION DO VIEW CUSTOMER
      WHEN EXIT RETURN
  ENDDO
```

4-39 The pseudocode for the customer data entry menu.

Four functions are on the menu, and each of the functions needs some pseudocode to determine in overall terms how it will operate. Remember that pseudocode is meant to be generic. When you say "Display Menu" or "Access Customer File," you are telling the programmer (who may be you) to write the necessary code to accomplish that function. We will do this in Part Three.

The pseudocode and error message design for adding a customer is shown in Fig. 4-40. When adding a customer, you must check to see if the customer already exists because you don't want to add them again. You begin by accessing the customer file. Once you have read the file into memory, you begin a loop. The commands inside the loop will be run over and over again until some condition is satisfied. In this pseudocode, you have decided that the condition to exit the loop will be blanks or nothing entered into the customer number field. Therefore, to begin the loop, you initialize the customer number field to non-blanks by filling it with any character. Once this is done the loop can begin.

A data entry screen is displayed. Data may be entered into every field. When the screen is displayed, the customer number field is filled with blanks. You can then enter a customer number. If you enter nothing, then the loop will end and you will return to the main customer menu. That is how this design states that the system knows that data entry is complete—nothing will be entered into the key field.

Now if you examine the pseudocode carefully, you might notice that the code really doesn't say how the customer number field gets blanked out. The next command after adding a customer is to CLEAR DATA FIELDS. This would seem to imply that the customer number field should be cleared, too. Then, because it is blank it would cause the loop to fail, and only one record could be entered at a time. In actuality, the field is cleared prior to the screen being displayed and not before. When the data entry occurs, the customer number field is immediately checked to see if it is empty. If it is, the program does not execute any more commands, and control is returned to the customer system menu.

Once the data is entered, the customer number is verified. In the case of an add, it is verified to see that it does not exist. If it is not found on the file,

```
ADD A CUSTOMER

ACCESS CUSTOMER FILE
SET CUSTOMER NUMBER TO NOT BLANK
DO WHILE CUSTOMER NUMBER NOT BLANK
  DISPLAY SCREEN
  ENTER DATA
    VERIFY CUSTOMER NUMBER
    IF NEW NUMBER
      THEN
        ADD CUSTOMER DATA
        CLEAR DATA FIELDS
      ELSE
        DISPLAY ERROR WINDOW - CUSTOMER NUMBER ALREADY ON FILE
    ENDIF
ENDDO
```

```
                    *** ERROR ***

          CUSTOMER NUMBER ALREADY ON FILE
            ENTER A NEW CUSTOMER NUMBER

              PRESS ANY KEY TO CONTINUE
```

4-40   The pseudocode and error window for the customer add routine.

then it is a new customer number. This new number is added to the files, and the fields cleared to make room for new data. If it is found, however, an error message is displayed. This message is also shown in Fig. 4-40.

The loop continues letting us enter new data until a blank field is entered. Once a blank field is entered, the program will end. We will be returned to the main customer menu.

Besides the add customer function, there is a change customer function. This is different from the add customer because you must first decide which customer you will change. The change customer pseudocode is found in Fig. 4-41.

This routine is similar in that one loop continues until a blank customer number is entered. However, after that, it is somewhat different. The data entry screen is displayed, and the customer number only is entered. Next, customer number is verified. This time, the verification looks to make sure that the number exists. When it finds the customer record, it retrieves the rest of the data and displays it on the data entry screen. You can then make changes to the data. After making the changes, the record is updated, and the fields are cleared for the next request. If the customer is not found, an error message is displayed.

Deleting a customer is similar to changing one except that after successfully finding the customer number, you look at the data without being able to make changes. This lets you confirm that the number you entered is the customer that you want to delete. The Delete Customer pseudocode is shown in Fig. 4-42.

After finding the record you want to delete and displaying the customer data, a message window should appear asking if you really want to delete the

```
CHANGE A CUSTOMER

ACCESS CUSTOMER FILE
SET CUSTOMER NUMBER TO NOT BLANK
DO WHILE CUSTOMER NUMBER NOT BLANK
   DISPLAY SCREEN
   ENTER CUSTOMER NUMBER
      VERIFY CUSTOMER NUMBER
      IF FOUND()
         THEN
            RETRIEVE CUSTOMER DATA
            CHANGE DESIRED FIELDS
            UPDATE RECORD
            CLEAR DATA FIELDS
         ELSE
            DISPLAY ERROR WINDOW-CUSTOMER NUMBER NOT ON FILE
      ENDIF
ENDDO
```

```
          *** ERROR ***

     CUSTOMER NUMBER NOT ON FILE
     ENTER ANOTHER CUSTOMER NUMBER

        PRESS ANY KEY TO CONTINUE
```

4-41 The pseudocode and error window for the customer change routine.

record. If the user chooses to delete the record, then the record is deleted and a message to that effect is displayed. Notice that the message window contains a menu. Windows can contain anything! If the user decides not to delete the record, then a message to that effect is displayed.

The final set of pseudocode for viewing a customer is shown in Fig. 4-43. This pseudocode is exactly the same as the delete pseudocode except that there is no delete confirmation. The data is simply displayed, and a continuation message is displayed on the screen. You must make sure that the placement of the message does not obscure any of the data.

A typical error window is shown in Fig. 4-44. The advantage of a window over a simple one-line error message is that it draws more attention to itself and is harder to miss. Sometimes a simple one-line error message can be overlooked. On the negative side, however, sometimes a window obscures the very information to which it refers. Error messages sometimes have this problem. You might want to tell the user that a customer does not exist, but the window might be sitting on top of the customer number, blocking it. Figure 4-44 shows a correctly positioned customer add error window. Here, customer number can clearly be seen.

If a window must obscure the information, then you can always include the information in the window. In the case of delete and display routines, you often are not displaying error boxes but confirmation or continuation boxes. These boxes should be designed so that the user can see enough data to make proper decisions. As we work with the inventory system, you will see this more clearly. For these data entry screens we work with simple error messages as designed and get fancier later.

```
DELETE A CUSTOMER

ACCESS CUSTOMER FILE
SET CUSTOMER NUMBER TO NOT BLANK
DO WHILE CUSTOMER NUMBER NOT BLANK
   DISPLAY SCREEN
   ENTER CUSTOMER NUMBER
      VERIFY CUSTOMER NUMBER
      IF FOUND()
         THEN
            RETRIEVE CUSTOMER DATA
            DISPLAY DELETE CONFIRMATION WINDOW
            IF CONFIRM
               DELETE RECORD
               MESSAGE = 'RECORD DELETED'
             ELSE
               MESSAGE = 'RECORD NOT DELETED'
            ENDIF
            CLEAR DATA FIELDS
        ELSE
            DISPLAY ERROR WINDOW-CUSTOMER NUMBER NOT ON FILE
      ENDIF
ENDDO
```

```
+-------------------------------------------+
|                                           |
|           *** CONFIRM DELETE ***          |
|                                           |
|            DO YOU REALLY WANT TO          |
|            DELETE THIS RECORD             |
|                                           |
|                                           |
|   [NO]                           [YES]    |
|                                           |
+-------------------------------------------+
```

```
+-------------------------------------------+
|                                           |
|              *** ERROR ***                |
|                                           |
|        CUSTOMER NUMBER NOT ON FILE        |
|       ENTER ANOTHER CUSTOMER NUMBER       |
|                                           |
|        PRESS ANY KEY TO CONTINUE          |
|                                           |
+-------------------------------------------+
```

4-42   The pseudocode and message windows for the customer delete routine.

Designing customer report processes

Reports are produced from the main menu rather than the customer menu. When a function is complete, the operator returns to the main menu rather than the Customer menu as with the data entry functions.

The first report process that is designed is the customer directory. Here we create the screen design first and then the pseudocode. Unlike the data entry screens already designed, this is a process screen and is designed separately and before the pseudocode. Figure 4-45 shows the design of the customer directory print screen.

This design lets the user have the option of choosing only one customer to print or to print all the customers. After something or nothing is entered into the customer number field, the user is placed in the pop-up menu at the bottom of the screen. The user then has the option of printing the directory or canceling the print and leaving the Print menu.

```
VIEW A CUSTOMER

ACCESS CUSTOMER FILE
SET CUSTOMER NUMBER TO NOT BLANK
DO WHILE CUSTOMER NUMBER NOT BLANK
   DISPLAY SCREEN
   ENTER CUSTOMER NUMBER
      VERIFY CUSTOMER NUMBER
      IF FOUND()
         THEN
            RETRIEVE CUSTOMER DATA
            DISPLAY INFORMATION
         ELSE
            DISPLAY ERROR WINDOW-CUSTOMER NUMBER NOT ON FILE
      ENDIF
ENDDO
```

```
+----------------------------------------+
|             *** ERROR ***              |
|                                        |
|      CUSTOMER NUMBER NOT ON FILE        |
|      ENTER ANOTHER CUSTOMER NUMBER      |
|                                        |
|         PRESS ANY KEY TO CONTINUE      |
+----------------------------------------+
```

```
+----------------------------------------+
|                                        |
|         PRESS ANY KEY TO CONTINUE      |
|                                        |
+----------------------------------------+
```

4-43 The pseudocode and message windows for the customer view routine.

An error message and accompanying logic should also be designed in case a nonexistent customer number is entered. You could also simply not print anything. A good design should trap normal error messages, but

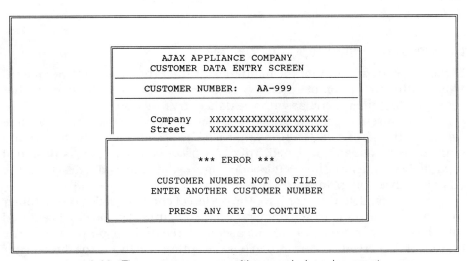

4-44 The customer screen with error window placement.

```
               AJAX APPLIANCE COMPANY
               CUSTOMER DIRECTORY PRINT


             ENTER THE CUSTOMER NUMBER TO PRINT
           OR LEAVE BLANK TO PRINT ALL CUSTOMERS

                                    ┌─────────────────────┐
           CUSTOMER NUMBER:         │                     │
                                    └─────────────────────┘


             ALIGN PAPER AND CHOOSE A MENU OPTION

                    ┌────────────────────────┐
                    │    PRINT DIRECTORY     │
                    │                        │
                    │    CANCEL PRINTING     │
                    └────────────────────────┘
```

```
                    *** ERROR ***

            CUSTOMER NUMBER NOT ON FILE
            ENTER ANOTHER CUSTOMER NUMBER

               PRESS ANY KEY TO CONTINUE
```

4-45   The customer directory print screen and error window.

sometimes the cost of trying to account for every permutation is cost—and time—prohibitive.

The pseudocode for this screen is shown in Fig. 4-46. First, the screen is displayed without the menu. Next, data entry is allowed in the customer number field. If something is entered, then validate the customer number. Once a valid customer number or a blank is entered, the menu is displayed. If the Print Directory choice is made, then the one customer or all customers will print. If the Cancel Printing choice is made, then the user returns to the main menu.

```
CUSTOMER DIRECTORY PRINT

   DO WHILE NOT CANCEL PRINTING
      DISPLAY SCREEN TO CONFIRM THE PRINTING OF THE DIRECTORY
      ALLOW ENTRY INTO THE CUSTOMER FIELD
      IF AN ENTRY IS MADE
         VERIFY CUSTOMER EXISTS
         SELECT ONLY THAT CUSTOMER
      DISPLAY POP-UP MENU
      IF PRINT DIRECTORY
         PRINT DIRECTORY
       ELSE
         LEAVE PRINT ROUTINE
      ENDIF
   ENDDO
```

4-46   The customer directory print pseudocode.

Later, you will see that for this print module and others we simply use the report forms you will create in chapter 13. In some cases, we will also show you how to write your own program code to produce reports. Because the dBASE IV report writer is so powerful, you would have little reason to want to write reports from scratch.

Once the customer directory is finished it is time to design some logic for the cross-reference report. This report is all or nothing. The screen as shown in Fig. 4-47 is displayed with the menu active. The user then chooses either to print the entire cross-reference report or to print nothing. The pseudocode for this report is the same as the customer directory, only this report has no loop and no customer number data entry. The screen is simply displayed, and a menu choice allowed.

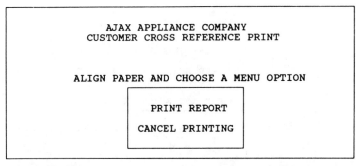

4-47 The customer cross-reference report print screen.

The final report to be produced in the customer system is not actually a report but a series of mailing labels. As you can see in Fig. 4-48, the menu has three choices. The first choice produces an alignment test. This is a standard practice of label programs and allows you to make sure that your labels are lined up with your printer. It "wastes" a few labels by printing X's or the character of your choice across all label positions. If the labels are misaligned, you realign the printer and test them again. Once they are right, you choose Print Labels to print the actual labels. Later, you will use the labels you create in the label generator in Part Two.

Figure 4-49 shows the pseudocode for this printing program. A simple loop continues until the Cancel Printing option is chosen. Until then, the system runs the label form program, either printing actual labels or alignment labels. You can print as many sets of alignment labels as necessary before printing the actual labels.

This completes the design for the programming of the customer system. Because of dBASE IV's ability to handle many tasks without programming, you have seen very little program design in the customer system. Remember, between the customer system and other systems is little interaction. As you see the rest of the system design unfold, you will see some fairly complicated

```
          AJAX APPLIANCE COMPANY
          CUSTOMER LABELS PRINT

      ALIGN LABELS AND CHOOSE A MENU OPTION

          ┌────────────────────────┐
          │    ALIGNMENT TEST      │
          │                        │
          │     PRINT LABELS       │
          │                        │
          │    CANCEL PRINTING     │
          └────────────────────────┘
```

4-48   The customer labels print screen.

programming. Each programming step is described along with the code in Parts Two and Three.

The inventory data entry system processes

The Inventory system uses a new type of program design known as pre-and post-processing. Before the data entry function is performed, certain things happen. This is pre-processing. In this example, the user decides whether to add, change, delete, or view data. The user also enters the key field-item number. Then the pre-processor continues and decides whether the item number exists in the case of a change, delete, or display or does not exist in the case of an add. If either condition is not satisfied, the appropriate error message is displayed. If the condition is satisfied, then the pre-processor continues and in the case of an existing record, positions the record pointer and displays a data entry screen to allow changes to the record or a display of the record depending on the function. If the function is an add, then a new record is created and data entry allowed into it. All this is handled in a single program.

Once the data entry or review is complete, the post-processor is invoked. In the case of an add or change, it performs some more complicated error checking that the screen itself does not. In the case of a delete, it sets up a delete confirmation message.

```
CUSTOMER LABELS PRINT

    DISPLAY SCREEN TO CONFIRM THE PRINTING OF THE DIRECTORY
    DO WHILE .NOT. CANCEL PRINTING
      DISPLAY POP-UP MENU
      IF ALIGNMENT TEST
        PRINT TEST LABELS
      IF PRINT LABELS
        PRINT LABELS
      IF CANCEL PRINTING
        CANCEL PRINTING
    ENDDO
```

4-49   The customer labels print pseudocode.

In the customer system, you saw a very simple design. The inventory system has a more complex design that begins to take advantage of the power of dBASE IV.

A standard format screen is used to capture the data entry and perform limited error checking. Instead of having separate modules with code that produces the screen, we use the format file that you create in Part Two. One program handles all data entry for the inventory system.

The inventory menu and pre-processor screen is shown in Fig. 4-50. First, the user chooses a menu item as in the customer file. Then, an entry area is displayed for the item number. Once the function is chosen and the enter key is pressed, the preprocessor validates the existence or non-existence of the item number and displays the data entry screen for all of the inventory data items. The pseudocode for this menu and the data entry process is shown in Fig. 4-51.

```
            AJAX APPLIANCE COMPANY
            INVENTORY DATA ENTRY


                ADD NEW ITEM

          CHANGE ITEM INFORMATION

              DELETE AN ITEM

          VIEW ITEM INFORMATION

          EXIT INVENTORY DATA ENTRY
```

```
            AJAX APPLIANCE COMPANY
            INVENTORY DATA ENTRY
        DATABASE ADD/CHANGE/DELETE/VIEW


          ENTER ITEM NUMBER: _____
```

4-50 The inventory system data entry menu.

Although this pseudocode is longer and more complicated than the Customer system, it is simply one module and therefore potentially easier to maintain. Look at the pseudocode to see how it works. The menu pseudocode simply allows the user to choose a menu item and then calls the data entry screen.

```
INVENTORY DATA ENTRY MENU

    DISPLAY MENU
    DO WHILE .NOT. EXIT
     CASE CHOICE
        WHEN ADD NEW ITEM DO INVENTORY DATA ENTRY WITH ADD
        WHEN CHANGE ITEM INFORMATION DO INVENTORY DATA ENTRY WITH CHANGE
        WHEN DELETE AN ITEM DO INVENTORY DATA ENTRY WITH DELETE
        WHEN VIEW ITEM INFORMATION DO INVENTORY DATA ENTRY WITH VIEW
        WHEN EXIT RETURN
    ENDDO


INVENTORY DATA ENTRY

DO WHILE NOT EXIT INVENTORY SYSTEM
  DISPLAY SCREEN TO ALLOW ENTRY OF ITEM NUMBER BEING USED
  ALLOW ENTRY INTO THE ITEM FIELD
  IF AN ENTRY IS MADE
     STORE INTO MEMORY VARIABLE
    ELSE
     EXIT OUT OF DO WHILES
  ENDIF
  ACCESS INVENTORY FILE
  IF ADD
     CHECK FOR ITEM NUMBER EXISTENCE
     IF FOUND()
        DISPLAY DATA ENTRY SCREEN WITH ERROR WINDOW
        LOOP BACK TO NEW DATA ENTRY
       ELSE
        ACCESS INVENTORY FILE
        APPEND BLANK RECORD
        REPLACE KEY FIELD WITH ITEM NUMBER
        USE FORMAT FILE ALLOWING GET'S IN NON-KEY FIELDS
        ALLOW DATA ENTRY DIRECTLY INTO FILE
     ENDIF

    ELSE   && CHANGE OR DELETE OR VIEW
     CHECK FOR ITEM NUMBER EXISTENCE
     IF .NOT. FOUND()
        DISPLAY DATA ENTRY SCREEN WITH ERROR WINDOW
        LOOP BACK TO NEW DATA ENTRY
       ELSE
        ACCESS INVENTORY FILE
        POSITION RECORD POINTER ON ITEM NUMBER RECORD
        USE FORMAT FILE ALLOWING GET'S IN NON-KEY FIELDS
        ALLOW DATA ENTRY DIRECTLY INTO FILE
        IF DELETE
           DISPLAY DELETE CONFIRMATION WINDOW
           GET CONFIRMATION
           IF Y
             DELETE RECORD
           ENDIF
        ENDIF
     ENDIF
  ENDIF
ENDDO
```

4-51 The inventory system data entry pseudocode.

The main loop controls the program until the exit choice is made. The preprocessor screen is displayed, and a blank item number is placed in the area. If a blank item number is entered, then the program assumes you are through and the user is exited from the program and returned to the main menu.

Once the item number is entered, the inventory file is accessed and the item number verified. If it is an ADD, the check is for the item number existence. If the number is found, an error window is displayed on the pre-processor screen. These error message windows are displayed in Fig. 4-52. If there is no problem with the item number validation then a new record is added to the file with just the key field and the validation loop closed.

```
┌─────────────────────────────────────┐   ┌─────────────────────────────────────┐
│          *** ERROR ***              │   │          *** ERROR ***              │
│                                     │   │                                     │
│   ITEM NUMBER ALREADY ON FILE       │   │    ITEM NUMBER NOT ON FILE          │
│   ENTER ANOTHER ITEM NUMBER         │   │    ENTER ANOTHER ITEM NUMBER        │
│                                     │   │                                     │
│   PRESS ANY KEY TO CONTINUE         │   │    PRESS ANY KEY TO CONTINUE        │
└─────────────────────────────────────┘   └─────────────────────────────────────┘
            ┌──────────────────────────────────────────┐
            │          *** CONFIRM DELETE ***           │
            │                                           │
            │         DO YOU REALLY WANT TO             │
            │         DELETE THIS RECORD                │
            │                                           │
            │    [NO]                        [YES]      │
            └──────────────────────────────────────────┘
```

4-52   The inventory system windows.

If the function is CHANGE, DELETE, or VIEW, then the check is made to make sure that item number does exist. If it is not found, then an error message is displayed stating that the item number is not found and the user must reenter item number. If the item number is found, then the inventory file is accessed and the pointer established to the record. Again the validation loop is closed and the system proceeds.

After the first loop is the post-processor. The data entry screen is displayed. The function type determines whether you can add or change the data or just view the record. If it is an ADD or CHANGE, data entry is allowed. If it is a VIEW or DELETE, then the user can only view the data. In the case of a DELETE, the post-processor places a confirmation on the screen after viewing the record. The user is then asked if he or she really wants to delete the record. If the user does want to delete the record, then it is deleted. As you can see in Fig. 4-52, the confirmation window has a menu in it. This is another technique you will learn in this book.

Once the data entry or viewing process is complete for each record, the user returns to the pre-processor screen for entry of a new item number or to complete the process and return to the main menu. Figure 4-52 shows the last part of this design—the three windows necessary to the system. The first two windows sit on top of the pre-processor screen. They could sit on top of existing text and can be thought of as floating slightly above what is underneath. When they are through being displayed, whatever is underneath again becomes visible. You see as you complete this system that sometimes windows and menus fit nicely into blank or unused space on a screen. Sometimes, however, they obscure something underneath. Good design minimizes this problem.

The first window is the error message when attempting to add an existing item number. Conversely, the second error window appears if you try to change, delete, or view a nonexistent item number. These windows stay on-screen until a key is pressed. Then the user can again try to enter a valid item number into the item number entry area.

The last window in Fig. 4-52 is the Delete Confirmation window. This is displayed on the data entry screen after the user has viewed a record that he or she wants to delete. The cursor will be on the left menu item—[NO]. The user then has the option of pressing Enter and not deleting the record or pressing the right arrow to move the cursor to [YES] and pressing Enter to delete the record.

The inventory reports

Inventory reports are so similar to the customer reports that there is very little reason to design them. The inventory valuation report and cross-reference report will always be printed out in their entirety and the design in Fig. 4-47 can be used.

The salesman report should be able to print one item at a time or all of them. The design for the customer directory in Figs. 4-45 and 4-46 should be used substituting the item for the customer number. When you create the program, that should also act as a starting point for the code.

With this in mind it is time to move to the invoice system. This system is actually a system within a system and will help you learn all about the intricacies of dBASE IV.

The main invoice screen process design

The creating of an invoice is a two-part process. Data is being entered into two different databases. First, the invoice database contains the information that occurs once for each invoice. Also, the items database contains a separate record for each item on the invoice. This invoice example will be very "clean." All of the data in the first screen belongs to one database, and all of the data in the second screen belongs to another database. Because of this, you could use a format file to input the data. However, it is more complicated than that. In the first screen shown in Fig. 4-53, you can see that there are three data fields for input along with a display of the customer information from another database. This could be done by a format file with pre- and post-processors but you will find it is easier to use the same concepts learned in the customer file and create the screen yourself with program commands.

Figure 4-53 displays the invoice form. You can assume that this first design is the add function. This form combines everything you have seen so far. Instead of using a pre-processor screen, everything will happen on this screen. Data entry is restricted to the invoice number, invoice date, and customer information.

The best place to start is in the beginning. In this screen and file, the beginning is the invoice number. The invoice number is automatically created during an add.

```
┌─────────────────────────────────────────────────────────────────────────┐
│              AJAX APPLIANCE COMPANY - INVOICE FORM                        │
│                                   ┌──CUSTOMER NUMBER: AA-9999──┐          │
│   INVOICE NUMBER: 9999-99         │ COMPANY NAME               │          │
│                                   │ STREET                     │          │
│   INVOICE DATE:   mm/dd/yy        │ CITY, ST ZIP CODE          │          │
│                                   └────────────────────────────┘          │
├─────────────────────────────────────────────────────────────────────────┤
│ LINE QTY  ITEM #   BRAND     TYPE     DESCRIPTION      PRICE    EXTENSION  │
│                                                                           │
│                                                                           │
│                                                                           │
│                                                                           │
│                                                                           │
│                                                                           │
│                                                                           │
│                                                                           │
│                                                                           │
│                                                                           │
│                                                                           │
│                                                                           │
│                                                                           │
└─────────────────────────────────────────────────────────────────────────┘
```

4-53 The main invoice menu.

The invoice date is determined from the system date. It is automatically filled in from the system date during the invoice pre-processor procedure and needs no special attention.

Any customer entered into the Sale/Rental system must be verified. Many of the data items in the Sale/Rental file are dependent upon information in the customer file. There are many approaches to verifying a customer number. The simplest is to force the user to enter a customer number that is found on the file. However, this is unrealistic. Many times a customer number might be entered incorrectly or a new customer has not been added to the customer file yet. It is also possible that a new customer walks in and has never purchased anything before.

If the customer number entered by the operator is not on the file, you might display an error window and force them to go back through the menus and enter the customer number in the customer file. However, a better way is to automatically pass the customer number to the customer file data entry screen and let the operator enter the customer information. This can be done automatically. After the customer information is entered, the program should return the operator to the Sale/Rental data entry screen to continue entering the sale or rental information.

The customer address information could be set to Display only and changes not allowed during data entry. But this prohibits the changes when a customer says during the sale, "Oh, by the way, I moved." Instead, the post-processor on customer number should move the entry point out of the customer section, and if the user wants to change the customer address, he or she would have to do so knowingly by moving the insertion point into the customer address fields. Figure 4-46 shows pseudocode for this post-processor.

Invoices: multi-file data entry

So far you have seen two distinct methods for performing data entry. When you create the program code, you will see how this is different as well. The invoice program starts out like the customer and inventory programs in that you have a menu controlling the functions of add, change, delete, and view. This menu is shown in Fig. 4-54.

```
              AJAX APPLIANCE COMPANY
                INVOICE DATA ENTRY

                 ADD NEW INVOICE

            CHANGE INVOICE INFORMATION

               DELETE AN INVOICE

             VIEW INVOICE INFORMATION

             EXIT INVOICE DATA ENTRY
```

4-54   The invoice menu.

Beginning the process   You may think it is redundant to show, draw or design this menu because it is very similar to the other menus you have seen, but remember—you may only be doing the design, not the programming. It is important to spell out as much of the system as possible. You will find programming is much easier for you or for others, because design gives you time to think, to make sure that you have maintained consistency throughout your system, and to account for everything. When you actually program the system, you might start with the customer or inventory data entry menu programs and modify them to create the invoice data entry menu program. But, in design, you should spell out exactly what you are going to do.

In some respects, it is more important to get your storyboards for screen and report figures right than your pseudocode. In testing, your program may eventually work correctly but the screens and menus may not be what you want. The storyboard figures ensure that the system has the "look and feel" you designed.

Adding the invoice data   The creating of an invoice is a two-part process. Data is entered into the invoice database with the information that occurs once for each invoice, and also in the items database with separate record for each item on the invoice. This invoice example is straightforward because the data in the first screen belongs to one database and the data in the second screen belongs to another database. Because of this, you could use a format file to input the data. However, in the first screen shown in Fig. 4-53, you can see that there are three data fields for input along with a display of the customer information from another database. This could be done by a format file with pre- and post-processors, but you will find it is easier to use the concepts learned in the customer file and create the screen yourself with program commands.

The first invoice screen asks for information specific to that invoice, such as, the invoice number, customer number, and invoice date. When this information is entered, a second screen is displayed for adding items. The second screen has room to enter eight items. For this case study, that will be the maximum. Through more complex programming you could redisplay the screen with enough space for eight more items each time you had filled every successive group of eight items.

Verify any customer entered into the invoice system because many of the data items in the invoice file are dependent upon information in the customer file. Remember that a CUSTOMER NUMBER might be entered incorrectly, the new customer might not have been added, or this customer has never made a purchase before.

If the customer number entered by the operator is not on the file, you might display an error window and force them to go back through the menus and enter the customer number in the customer file. Although there are more complex ways to handle this problem, keep this design simple and require the customer to exist before creating an invoice.

Begin by looking at the add new invoice function. Figure 4-53 displays the top of the invoice form. Instead of using a pre-processor screen, everything happens on this screen. Data entry is restricted to the invoice number, invoice date, and customer.

Start with the invoice number. The invoice number is automatically created during an add and calculated by using the system date and a sequential number. The left side of the invoice number is the year and month (YYMM). To the right of the dash is a sequential number. A simple algorithm can be used to create the invoice number and search for the next unused number. In Fig. 4-55, the pseudocode for this screen, you can see this algorithm.

The current date is retrieved and the year and month "plucked" from the date. This "builds" the left side of the invoice number. A dash is added. Once this is done the sequence number 001 is added to create the rest of the invoice number. Because the invoice file will be indexed by this number, a FIND can be used to see if the number already exists. If it is found, one is added to the right side of the number and again the invoice file is checked to see if the item exists. This sequential search continues until an unused invoice number is found. Because Ajax Appliance company only has a few hundred invoices a month, this process should take no more than ten seconds even if there are close to a thousand invoices for that month in the file. The way the algorithm works is to index directly into the first record for that month and then sequentially search after that. The index itself never takes more than one second and the sequential search can look at a hundred records per second.

Invoice date is determined from the system date. It is automatically filled in from the system date during the invoice pre-processor procedure and needs no special attention.

```
INVOICE DATA ENTRY ADDITIONS (SCREEN 1)

SELECT DATABASE FILES
DO CALCULATE NEXT INVOICE NUMBER
CREATE BLANK MEMORY VARIABLES
DO WHILE MORE INVOICE NUMBERS
   DISPLAY EMPTY TOP OF THE INVOICE FORM
   ALLOW ENTRY INTO THE INVOICE, DATE, AND CUSTOMER NUMBER FIELDS
   IF INVOICE NUMBER IS BLANK
      EXIT BACK TO DATA ENTRY MENU
   ELSE
      VERIFY INVOICE NUMBER
      CHECK FOR INVOICE NUMBER EXISTENCE
      IF NOT FOUND()
         IF CUSTOMER NUMBER IS BLANK
            DISPLAY ERROR WINDOW
            LOOP BACK TO NEW DATA ENTRY
         ENDIF
         CHECK FOR CUSTOMER NUMBER EXISTENCE
         IF FOUND()
            GET CUSTOMER INFORMATION
            DISPLAY CUSTOMER INFORMATION
            APPEND BLANK RECORD
            REPLACE DATABASE FIELDS WITH MEMORY VARIABLE VALUES
            UPDATE LST_TXND IN CUSTOMER FILE
            DO ADD ITEMS ROUTINE
            DO CALCULATE NEXT INVOICE NUMBER
            EXIT BACK TO NEW DATA ENTRY
         ELSE
            DISPLAY CUSTOMER NUMBER NOT FOUND ERROR WINDOW
            LOOP BACK TO NEW DATA ENTRY
         ENDIF
      ELSE
         DISPLAY INVOICE NUMBER ON FILE ERROR WINDOW
         LOOP BACK TO NEW DATA ENTRY
      ENDIF
   ENDIF
ENDDO
CALCULATE NEXT INVOICE NUMBER

GET CURRENT DATE
STRIP THE MONTH AND YEAR AND BUILD THE LEFT SIDE
MAKE THE RIGHT SIDE '001' AND CONCATENATE WITH A DASH
IF THE RECORD IS FOUND IN THE FILE
   THEN
      DO WHILE THE RECORDS ARE FOUND IN THE FILE
         ADD ONE TO RIGHT SIDE
         REBUILD THE WHOLE FIELD
      END
      NEWRECORD IS FOUND WHEN THE LOOP IS EXITED
   ELSE
      NEWRECORD = LEFT SIDE CONCATENATED WITH "-001"
ENDIF
```

4-55 The pseudocode for the main invoice screen.

In Fig. 4-55, you can see the customer information that was drawn from the customer file. This information is displayed on the add invoice screen so that the operator may then judge if the correct customer number was chosen. If the customer did not exist in the customer file, an error message is displayed, but in the program Ajax cannot guard against an incorrect customer number entry. The computer can't read minds! The customer information is displayed immediately, so the operator can doublecheck to see that the correct customer's name matches the entered customer number.

The pseudocode for the top part of the data entry process is shown in Fig. 4-55. First, the database files are selected and the next invoice number is calculated. A loop allows for more than one invoice during the session. The invoice number is "blanked out" to signal a completion of data entry.

Verification begins with the invoice number. Even though invoice number is calculated, it may be changed by the operator. If it is not found, then the customer number is verified first, to make sure that something was entered and then to make sure that the customer number is on the file. If either condition fails, an error window is displayed and data entry into those fields is again allowed.

Once all the information is verified, the customer name and address is displayed. A new record is added to the invoice file with the invoice number, date, and customer number. The "last transaction date" field is also updated in the customer file to indicate that there is some activity for that customer and not to eventually purge them from the file at the end of the year.

Figure 4-56 shows the three possible error windows that might be generated. By designing these windows now, you will save a lot of time later. Notice each window is exactly the same size and looks almost the same. This consistency makes it easy to program many windows quickly. You can even create a library of windows and call them from the library when needed.

```
*** ERROR ***                         *** ERROR ***

CUSTOMER NUMBER CANNOT BE BLANK    CUSTOMER NUMBER NOT ON FILE
    ENTER A CUSTOMER NUMBER        ENTER ANOTHER CUSTOMER NUMBER

  PRESS ANY KEY TO CONTINUE         PRESS ANY KEY TO CONTINUE
```

```
               *** ERROR ***

        INVOICE NUMBER ALREADY ON FILE
        ENTER ANOTHER INVOICE NUMBER

          PRESS ANY KEY TO CONTINUE
```

4-56   The error windows for add invoice data.

Adding items to the invoice   Once this is all done it is time to add items to the invoice. Figure 4-57 shows a completed data entry screen design. All three parts of the screen are shown. The middle part is where the items are entered. The bottom of the screen is where the totals are displayed are calculated and displayed automatically.

Notice that the company and address information is displayed on this screen, also. This is another double check; if the operator gets confused about which invoice is being entered, the name information might help them figure it out.

The quantity and item number for eight items can be entered on this screen. If there are less than eight items, the operator enters the invoices, enters blanks on a line (actually just presses the enter key again), and the

```
                      AJAX APPLIANCE COMPANY - INVOICE FORM
                                         ┌──CUSTOMER NUMBER: AA-9999──┐
       INVOICE NUMBER: 9999-99           │ COMPANY NAME               │
                                         │ STREET                     │
       INVOICE DATE:    mm/dd/yy         │ CITY, ST ZIP CODE          │
                                         └────────────────────────────┘

   LINE QTY   ITEM #    BRAND     TYPE       DESCRIPTION      PRICE    EXTENSION
     9.  999 AAAA-999 X-BRAND-X X--TYPE--X X------DESC------X 9PRICE9  9QTY*PRI9
     9.  999 AAAA-999 X-BRAND-X X--TYPE--X X------DESC------X 9PRICE9  9QTY*PRI9
     9.  999 AAAA-999 X-BRAND-X X--TYPE--X X------DESC------X 9PRICE9  9QTY*PRI9
     9.  999 AAAA-999 X-BRAND-X X--TYPE--X X------DESC------X 9PRICE9  9QTY*PRI9
     9.  999 AAAA-999 X-BRAND-X X--TYPE--X X------DESC------X 9PRICE9  9QTY*PRI9
     9.  999 AAAA-999 X-BRAND-X X--TYPE--X X------DESC------X 9PRICE9  9QTY*PRI9
     9.  999 AAAA-999 X-BRAND-X X--TYPE--X X------DESC------X 9PRICE9  9QTY*PRI9
     9.  999 AAAA-999 X-BRAND-X X--TYPE--X X------DESC------X 9PRICE9  9QTY*PRI9
                                                                     ----------
                                              Sub Total             999,999.99
                                              Discount 99%           99,999.99
                                                                     ----------
                                              Taxable Amount        999,999.99
                                              Tax 99.9%              99,999.99
                                                                     ----------
                                              Total Amount          999,999.99
```

4-57 The complete data entry screen.

invoice is filed. When the eighth item is entered, the operator gets a message that the invoice is full, and a new invoice must be created.

When a blank line is entered on the screen, the program knows that the operator is finished adding items. The pseudocode for adding invoice items is found in Fig. 4-58.

First a loop is set up to get each new item. Line counters keep track of which line to display the cursor on. The subtotal field is created and initialized to zero so totals can be displayed at the bottom of the screen.

Each time a line is entered, the program verifies that the item number exists on the item file and that the quantity in stock is sufficient to fill the order. If either of these conditions are not met, an error window appears. Once these items are verified, the inventory quantity is reduced in the inventory file.

The description information is retrieved along with the price and displayed on the line. Extension is calculated to be quantity times price and places the new invoiced item into the invoice items file. If the item number is not on the file, an appropriate error message is displayed. As long as the item number entered is not blank, the system continues to add records to the file. When the operator has entered eight records the data entry will also stop.

After each new record is entered, the subtotal is displayed at the bottom of the screen as shown in Fig. 4-57. Using the taxable indicator and the discount amounts in the customer file, TAX and DISCOUNT and all intermediate totals are also calculated and displayed. These totals are updated each time a new invoice item is added.

Figure 4-59 shows four possible error windows for the add items function. These include the item number verification for both it being blank and not found, the quantity exceeded, and finally the full invoice. Notice the

```
INVOICE ITEMS ADD DATA ENTRY - SCREEN 2

DO WHILE MORE INVOICE ITEMS
   SET UP LINE COUNTERS
   ZERO OUT THE SUBTOTAL FIELD
   GET THE QUANTITY AND ITEM NUMBER FOR THE LINE ITEM
   SET ITEM COUNT BASED ON NUMBER OF ITEMS
   IF QUANTITY = 0
      EXIT ITEM DATA ENTRY
    ELSE
      VERIFY THE ITEM NUMBER
      IF ITEM NUMBER IS BLANK
         DISPLAY BLANK ITEM ERROR WINDOW
         LOOP BACK TO ITEM DATA ENTRY
      ENDIF
      IF ITEM NUMBER IS FOUND IN INVENTORY FILE
         RETRIEVE PRICE
         IF QUANITY DESIRED IS > QUANTITY IN STOCK
            DISPLAY INSUFFICIENT QUANTITY ERROR WINDOW
            LOOP BACK TO ITEM DATA ENTRY
         ENDIF
         REDUCE THE INVENTORY QUANTITY
         RETRIEVE THE DESCRIPTION INFORMATION
         DISPLAY THE COMPLETE LINE ITEM INCLUDING EXTENSION
         UPDATE THE SUBTOTAL
         DISPLAY TOTALS INCLUDING DISCOUNT AND TAX
         ADD THE RECORD TO THE ITEMS FILE
         UPDATE THE ITEM COUNTERS
         IF THAT IS THE EIGHTH ITEM
            DISPLAY INVOICE IS FULL ERROR WINDOW
            EXIT ITEM DATA ENTRY
         ENDIF
       ELSE
         DISPLAY ITEM NOT ON FILE ERROR WINDOW
      ENDIF
   ENDIF
ENDDO
```

4-58   The Invoice item additions pseudocode.

quantity box. A value is placed inside the box when it is displayed telling the
operator how many items were left in the file. Remember, anything can go
inside an error or message window—text, fields, menus, and as you will soon
see, data entry.

```
+------------------------------+      +------------------------------+
|        *** ERROR ***         |      |        *** ERROR ***         |
|                              |      |                              |
|  ITEM NUMBER CANNOT BE BLANK |      |    INVOICE FORM IS FULL      |
|     ENTER AN ITEM NUMBER     |      |    CREATE A NEW INVOICE      |
|                              |      |                              |
|   PRESS ANY KEY TO CONTINUE  |      |   PRESS ANY KEY TO CONTINUE  |
+------------------------------+      +------------------------------+

+------------------------------+      +------------------------------+
|        *** ERROR ***         |      |        *** ERROR ***         |
|                              |      |                              |
|  NOT ENOUGH QUANTITY IN STOCK|      |   ITEM NUMBER NOT ON FILE    |
|  REDUCE THE QUANTITY TO QTY_STK|    |  ENTER ANOTHER ITEM NUMBER   |
|                              |      |                              |
|   PRESS ANY KEY TO CONTINUE  |      |   PRESS ANY KEY TO CONTINUE  |
+------------------------------+      +------------------------------+
```

4-59   The Invoice item additions error and message windows.

Changing the invoice data Ajax Appliance is now ready for the next box on the hierarchy—the change invoice function. This function is very similar to the add items function in that the invoice number is entered and the date or customer number can be changed. Perhaps the invoice was entered with yesterday's date but it was really today's invoice. Perhaps the customer was entered wrong or the wrong location was used. These all can be corrected by a change function.

The screen for this would be exactly the same as the add invoice screen. The only difference is how it is used. The invoice number would not be automatically calculated because it is a change function and the computer has no way of knowing which invoice you want. Also data entry initially is allowed only in the invoice number to retrieve the invoice date and customer number from the invoice file. The pseudocode for this as shown in Fig. 4-60 is very similar to the add function. Again, the only difference is that only the invoice number is initially entered.

```
INVOICE DATA ENTRY CHANGES (SCREEN 1)

SELECT DATABASE FILES
CREATE BLANK MEMORY VARIABLES
DO WHILE MORE INVOICE NUMBERS
   DISPLAY EMPTY TOP OF THE INVOICE FORM
   ALLOW ENTRY INTO THE INVOICE FIELD
   IF INVOICE NUMBER IS BLANK
        EXIT FROM DO WHILE
     ELSE
        VERIFY INVOICE NUMBER
        CHECK FOR INVOICE NUMBER EXISTENCE
        IF FOUND()
            RETRIEVE DATA FROM INVOICE FILE
            FIND CUSTOMER RECORD
            RETRIEVE DATA FROM CUSTOMER FILE
            DISPLAY TOP OF INVOICE
            ALLOW CHANGES TO INVOICE DATE OR CUSTOMER NUMBER FIELDS
            IF CUSTOMER NUMBER HAS BEEN CHANGED SET AN ERROR CONDITION
            DO WHILE CUSTOMER NUMBER IS NOT VALIDATED
                IF CUSTOMER NUMBER IS BLANK
                    DISPLAY BLANK CUSTOMER ERROR WINDOW
                  ELSE
                    VERIFY CUSTOMER NUMBER
                    IF FOUND
                        STORE CUSTOMER INFORMATION TO MEMORY VARIABLES
                        REDISPLAY NEW CUSTOMER INFORMATION
                      ELSE
                        DISPLAY CUSTOMER NOT FOUND ERROR WINDOW
                    ENDIF
                ENDIF
            ENDDO
            DISPLAY WINDOW AND MENU TO DECIDE IF ITEM CHANGES ARE TO BE MADE
            IF YES
                DO ITEM CHANGES
            ENDIF
          ELSE
            DISPLAY INVOICE NUMBER NOT FOUND ERROR WINDOW
        ENDIF
   ENDIF
ENDDO
IF ITEMS WERE DELETED
   PACK THE ITEMS FILE
ENDIF
RETURN TO DATA ENTRY MENU
```

4-60 The Invoice item changes pseudocode—screen 1

Once the main invoice is updated, a message window with a menu is displayed asking the operator if any items need to be changed. This way the operator does not have to wait to see all the items displayed if they only wanted to change the customer number on the invoice. If changes are made, then the change items program is called. One item to look at in this pseudocode is at the bottom. A statement checks to see if any items are deleted. If any are, the file is packed. You will see more about this later. The reason this statement is shown in this pseudocode and not in the change items pseudocode is that packing can take a few minutes. If you are deleting items from several invoices, you only need to pack the file once. If this statement was in the items pseudocode, you might tell your program to pack the file after each invoice's items are deleted instead of after all of the invoices are changed.

The invoice changes error windows are shown in Fig. 4-61. The only new one is the "change items?" window and that is actually a modification of the inventory or customer delete confirmation window. Reuse as much of other programs as you can to make coding simpler and faster.

```
        *** ERROR ***

 CUSTOMER NUMBER CANNOT BE BLANK
     ENTER A CUSTOMER NUMBER

     PRESS ANY KEY TO CONTINUE
```

```
       *** CHANGE ITEMS? ***


 [YES]                        [NO]
```

```
        *** ERROR ***

   CUSTOMER NUMBER NOT ON FILE
 ENTER ANOTHER CUSTOMER NUMBER

     PRESS ANY KEY TO CONTINUE
```

```
        *** ERROR ***

   INVOICE NUMBER NOT FOUND
 ENTER ANOTHER INVOICE NUMBER

    PRESS ANY KEY TO CONTINUE
```

4-61   The Invoice item changes error windows—screen 1.

Changing the invoice items   The next function is the change invoice items function. This is the most sophisticated function in this program and will be presented more than explained. You need a lot of experience to create programs like this from scratch, but by studying the pseudocode and programs, you should be able to understand how to copy and modify these programs for use in a multi-file environment. Functions that come under the "change invoice" heading are add items, change the quantity of an item, change an item number, and remove an item.

When the screen is first displayed, all of the items that are found on the invoice are displayed. Then, a menu appears as shown in Fig. 4-62 that allows the user to control the changes to the individual items. They can add an item if the invoice does not have eight items already, they can change an item's quantity or item number, and finally they can delete an item.

```
                AJAX APPLIANCE COMPANY - INVOICE FORM

                                             ┌─CUSTOMER NUMBER: AA-9999─┐
  INVOICE NUMBER: 9999-99                     COMPANY NAME
                                              STREET
  INVOICE DATE:   mm/dd/yy                    CITY, ST ZIP CODE
                                             └──────────────────────────┘

LINE QTY  ITEM #    BRAND      TYPE      DESCRIPTION       PRICE    EXTENSION
  9. 999 AAAA-999 X-BRAND-X X--TYPE--X X------DESC------X 9PRICE9  9QTY*PRI9
  9. 999 AAAA-999 X-BRAND-X X--TYPE--X X------DESC------X 9PRICE9  9QTY*PRI9
  9. 999 AAAA-999 X-BRAND-X X--TYPE--X X------DESC------X 9PRICE9  9QTY*PRI9
  9. 999 AAAA-999 X-BRAND-X X--TYPE--X X------DESC------X 9PRICE9  9QTY*PRI9
  9. 999 AAAA-999 X-BRAND-X X--TYPE--X X------DESC------X 9PRICE9  9QTY*PRI9
  9. 999 AAAA-999 X-BRAND-X X--TYPE--X X------DESC------X 9PRICE9  9QTY*PRI9
  9. 999 AAAA-999 X-BRAND-X X--TYPE--X X------DESC------X 9PRICE9  9QTY*PRI9
  9. 999 AAAA-999 X-BRAND-X X--TYPE--X X------DESC------X 9PRICE9  9QTY*PRI9
                                                         ----------
        ┌─────────────────────────────┐  Sub Total        999,999.99
        │      ADD A NEW ITEM          │  Discount 99%      99,999.99
        │   CHANGE ITEM INFORMATION    │                  ----------
        │      DELETE AN ITEM          │  Taxable Amount   999,999.99
        │      EXIT ITEM CHANGES       │  Tax 99.9%         99,999.99
        └─────────────────────────────┘                  ----------
                                          Total Amount     999,999.99
```

4-62 The Invoice item changes screen and menu.

The pseudocode for this logic is shown in Fig. 4-63. Let's begin at the top. First, a loop is set up at the top of the program. This handles different items and eventually lets you out of the process. The first group of pseudocode displays all the items and the totals on the screen. Then, the data entry menu is displayed. If the operator chooses to exit, this program ends, and the operator is returned back to the main invoice program to change another invoice or to exit back to the original invoice menu.

Once the menu is displayed, the user makes a choice to add, change, or delete. The next section of the pseudocode handles positioning of the cursor for the actual data entry. If an item is to be added, a check is first made to see if the invoice has eight items already. If it does an error window is displayed. If not, then the count of items is updated, and the cursor is positioned at the line following the last item entered.

If an item is to be changed or deleted, then there is an extra step. A message window appears and asks for the line number that is to be changed or deleted. If a line number of zero is entered, the process is aborted, and the data entry menu is redisplayed. This might happen when the user chooses the delete function when the user meant to change or add an item. Next, the line number is checked to make sure that it contains data. If there are only three items on the invoice you cannot ask to change item number seven. Once a valid line number is entered, the changes can begin.

If the function is an add, there is no line number data entry. The cursor is automatically positioned at the next available line by the original routine that counted the lines. The next block of pseudocode handles actually adding items. In fact this block of pseudocode and later the program code was copied right from the add items function you just saw. Why not? It's the same! A loop is set up to check for invalid quantities and item numbers. The quantity and

```
INVOICE ITEMS DATA ENTRY - SCREEN 2

DO WHILE NOT RETURN TO INVOICE DATA ENTRY
  DISPLAY ALL THE ITEMS FOR THE INVOICE
  DISPLAY THE TOTALS FOR THE INVOICE ITEMS
  SET ITEM COUNT BASED ON NUMBER OF ITEMS
  DISPLAY DATA ENTRY MENU
  IF EXIT ITEM CHANGES
    LOOP BACK TO INVOICE ITEMS PROGRAM
  ENDIF
  IF ADD ITEM                              && LINE NUMBER TO POSITION CURSOR
    IF CNT < 8 (MAXIMUM NUMBER OF ITEMS)
        ADD 1 TO COUNT
      ELSE
        DISPLAY INVOICE IS FULL ERROR WINDOW
    ENDIF
  ENDIF
  IF CHANGE OR DELETE ITEM
    DO WHILE INVALID LINE NUMBER
      DISPLAY WINDOW ALLOWING DATA ENTRY FOR LINE NUMBER
      IF LINE NUMBER = 0
        LOOP BACK TO DATA ENTRY MENU
      ENDIF
      IF LINE NUMBER > LAST LINE NUMBER
        DISPLAY LINE NUMBER IS GREATER THAN THE LAST LINE ERROR WINDOW
      ENDIF
    ENDDO
  ENDIF
  IF ADD ITEM                                        && ADD A NEW ITEM
    DO WHILE INVALID ENTRY
      GET QUANTITY AND ITEM NUMBER
      IF QUANTITY = 0
          EXIT ITEM DATA ENTRY
        ELSE
          VERIFY THE ITEM NUMBER
          IF ITEM NUMBER IS BLANK
              DISPLAY BLANK ITEM ERROR WINDOW
              LOOP BACK TO ITEM DATA ENTRY
          ENDIF
          IF ITEM NUMBER IS FOUND IN INVENTORY FILE
              RETRIEVE PRICE
              IF QUANITY DESIRED IS > QUANTITY IN STOCK
                  DISPLAY INSUFFICIENT QUANTITY ERROR WINDOW
                  LOOP BACK TO ITEM DATA ENTRY
              ENDIF
              REDUCE THE INVENTORY QUANTITY
              RETRIEVE THE DESCRIPTION INFORMATION
              ADD THE RECORD TO THE ITEMS FILE
            ELSE
              DISPLAY ITEM NOT ON FILE ERROR WINDOW
          ENDIF
      ENDIF
    ENDDO
  ENDIF
  IF CHANGE ITEM
    FIND THE LINE NUMBER AND POSITION CURSOR
    DO WHILE INVALID CHANGES
      ALLOW CHANGES TO THE QUANTITY AND ITEM NUMBER
      IF QUANTITY = 0
        DISPLAY QUANTITY CANNOT BE 0 ERROR WINDOW
        LOOP BACK TO DATA ENTRY
      ENDIF
      VERIFY THE ITEM NUMBER
      IF ITEM NUMBER IS BLANK
        DISPLAY BLANK ITEM ERROR WINDOW
      LOOP BACK TO ITEM DATA ENTRY
    ENDIF
    IF ITEM NUMBER IS FOUND IN INVENTORY FILE
```

4-63 The Invoice item changes pseudocode—screen 2.

```
            RETRIEVE PRICE
        IF QUANITY DESIRED IS > QUANTITY IN STOCK
            DISPLAY INSUFFICIENT QUANTITY ERROR WINDOW
                LOOP BACK TO ITEM DATA ENTRY
            ENDIF
            ELSE
                DISPLAY ITEM NOT ON FILE ERROR WINDOW
                LOOP BACK TO ITEM DATA ENTRY
            ENDIF
            EXIT FROM ERROR CONDITIONS
        ENDDO
    ENDIF
    IF DELETE ITEM
        FIND THE LINE NUMBER AND HIGHLIGHT LINE
        DISPLAY WINDOW AND MENU TO CONFIRM DELETE
        IF YES
            DELETE ITEM
        ENDIF
        UNHIGHLIGHT LINE
    ENDIF
```

4-63 Continued.

item number must be entered, and the item number must exist on the file
with enough quantity in stock to cover the order. If that is all verified, the
item is added to the file, the lines are redisplayed along with the descriptions
and extensions, and the totals are redisplayed at the bottom of the screen.

The change item function is very similar. First, the line number that was
entered is used to position the cursor. The original values found on that line
are preserved for data entry. After that it's the same as the add function. The
changes or lack of changes are verified to make sure that the quantity and
item number are not blank, that the item number exists, and the quantity in
stock is sufficient to cover the quantity desired. If that's all verified, the item
is added to the file, the lines are redisplayed along with the descriptions, and
extensions and the totals are redisplayed at the bottom of the screen.

The delete function is a little simpler because no data entry takes place.
The entire line selected for deletion is highlighted and then the now-standard
delete confirmation box is displayed. If the user answers affirmatively, the
item is deleted. When the lines are redisplayed, the item no longer appears.

That is all there is to the pseudocode of changing items. It is very modular
and straightforward with the process being divided into small groups of
code. Finally, all of the error windows, message lines, delete confirmations,
and the line number data entry boxes are displayed. These are shown in
Fig. 4-64.

Deleting and viewing invoices Deleting invoices is very easy. Using almost the
same code as the first part of the change pseudocode, an entry screen is
displayed that only allows the invoice number to be entered. Once a valid
invoice number is entered, the invoice is retrieved and the entire invoice
displayed including the line items and totals. Then a delete confirmation box
is displayed. If the operator wants to delete the invoice, the invoice and all
associated items are deleted. This pseudocode is shown Fig. 4-65. In this
process, the packing is done to both files after all invoices are deleted.

```
        *** ERROR ***                         *** ERROR ***

    INVOICE FORM IS FULL              NOT ENOUGH QUANTITY IN STOCK
    CREATE A NEW INVOICE              REDUCE THE QUANTITY TO QTY_STK

  PRESS ANY KEY TO CONTINUE            PRESS ANY KEY TO CONTINUE


     ENTER LINE NUMBER                       *** ERROR ***
     OR ENTER 0 TO EXIT
                                      ITEM NUMBER NOT ON FILE
       LINE NUMBER: _                 ENTER ANOTHER ITEM NUMBER

                                       PRESS ANY KEY TO CONTINUE


        *** ERROR ***                         *** ERROR ***

  LINE NUMBER IS GREATER THAN          QUANTITY CANNOT BE 0
     LAST LINE NUMBER                  CHANGE THE QUANTITY

  PRESS ANY KEY TO CONTINUE           PRESS ANY KEY TO CONTINUE


        *** ERROR ***                    *** CONFIRM DELETE ***

  ITEM NUMBER CANNOT BE BLANK          DO YOU REALLY WANT TO
    ENTER AN ITEM NUMBER               DELETE THIS RECORD

  PRESS ANY KEY TO CONTINUE          [NO]                    [YES]
```

4-64 The Invoice item changes error windows—screen 2.

```
INVOICE DELETES

SELECT DATABASE FILES
DO WHILE MORE INVOICE NUMBERS
   DISPLAY EMPTY TOP OF THE INVOICE FORM
   ALLOW ENTRY INTO THE INVOICE FIELD
   IF INVOICE NUMBER IS BLANK
        EXIT FROM DO WHILE
     ELSE
        VERIFY INVOICE NUMBER
        CHECK FOR INVOICE NUMBER EXISTENCE
        IF FOUND()
              RETRIEVE DATA FROM INVOICE FILE
              FIND CUSTOMER RECORD
              RETRIEVE DATA FROM CUSTOMER FILE
              DISPLAY TOP OF INVOICE
              DISPLAY ALL ITEMS ON BOTTOM OF INVOICE
              DISPLAY THE TOTALS ON THE INVOICE
              DISPLAY WINDOW AND MENU TO DECIDE IF YOU REALLY WANT TO DELETE
              IF YES
                 DELETE THE INVOICE AND ALL ASSOCIATED ITEMS
              ENDIF
           ELSE
              DISPLAY INVOICE NUMBER NOT FOUND ERROR WINDOW
        ENDIF
   ENDIF
ENDDO
IF ITEMS WERE DELETED
   PACK THE INVOICE FILE
   PACK THE ITEMS FILE
ENDIF
RETURN TO DATA ENTRY MENU
```

4-65 The Invoice delete pseudocode.

Figure 4-66 shows the invoice view pseudocode. This program is the same as the delete program except there is no delete confirmation window and no records are deleted.

```
INVOICE VIEW

SELECT DATABASE FILES
DO WHILE MORE INVOICE NUMBERS
  DISPLAY EMPTY TOP OF THE INVOICE FORM
  ALLOW ENTRY INTO THE INVOICE FIELD
  IF INVOICE NUMBER IS BLANK
      EXIT FROM DO WHILE
    ELSE
      VERIFY INVOICE NUMBER
      CHECK FOR INVOICE NUMBER EXISTENCE
      IF FOUND()
          RETRIEVE DATA FROM INVOICE FILE
          FIND CUSTOMER RECORD
          RETRIEVE DATA FROM CUSTOMER FILE
          DISPLAY TOP OF INVOICE
          DISPLAY ALL ITEMS ON BOTTOM OF INVOICE
          DISPLAY THE TOTALS ON THE INVOICE
        ELSE
          DISPLAY INVOICE NUMBER NOT FOUND ERROR WINDOW
      ENDIF
  ENDIF
ENDDO
RETURN TO DATA ENTRY MENU
```

4-66   The Invoice view pseudocode.

Invoice system reports   Three reports are associated with invoices:

- The invoice form
- The warranty agreement
- The monthly sales report

The programs for the invoices and warranty agreements are basically the same. Figure 4-67 shows the screen to print either the invoices or warranty agreements. Instead of asking for a single invoice number, a range of invoices is allowed. There must be error checking to make sure both "ends" exist, and then the printing can be limited to a certain range of invoices or warranty agreements. Like other printing programs, the user has the option of printing the forms or canceling the prints.

Figure 4-68 shows the last report, the monthly sales report screen. This lets you enter a year and month to print. The only unique item here is the data entry of a partial date field. The pseudocode for this design is shown in Fig. 4-69. First, the print window is displayed. The month and year are entered. Next, the items that are found for the month and year must be retrieved, and totals are calculated for each invoice. This report is at the invoice level, not at the item level. Next the totals are resorted by company and invoice date. Finally, the report is produced.

```
              AJAX APPLIANCE COMPANY
                  INVOICE PRINT

       ENTER THE INVOICE NUMBER RANGE TO PRINT


     BEGINNING INVOICE              ENDING INVOICE
     ┌─────────────────┐         ┌─────────────────┐
     │                 │         │                 │
     └─────────────────┘         └─────────────────┘

          ALIGN PAPER AND CHOOSE A MENU OPTION
              ┌───────────────────────────┐
              │      PRINT INVOICE        │
              │                           │
              │      CANCEL PRINTING      │
              └───────────────────────────┘
```

4-67   The Invoice/warranty print storyboard.

```
              AJAX APPLIANCE COMPANY
              MONTHLY SALES REPORT PRINT


          ENTER MONTH/YEAR:  ┌────────┐
                             │  mm/yy │
                             └────────┘


          ALIGN PAPER AND CHOOSE A MENU OPTION
              ┌───────────────────────────┐
              │      PRINT REPORT          │
              │                           │
              │      CANCEL PRINTING       │
              └───────────────────────────┘
```

4-68   The monthly sales report print storyboard.

```
MONTHLY SALES REPORT

DISPLAY PRINT WINDOW
GET THE MONTH AND YEAR DESIRED
SELECT THE ITEMS FILE
TOTAL ON INVOICE NUMBER FOR INVDATE YEAR AND MONTH = YEARMONTH
USE FIELDS QTY*PRICE,QTY*PRICE*DISCOUNT TO NEW DATABASE
RESORT BY COMPANY NUMBER AND INVOICE DATE
PRODUCE MONTHLY REPORT
```

4-69   The monthly sales report print pseudocode.

A final comment

This concludes the design for Ajax Appliances. It is a good idea before you try any system to create a complete design, albeit not as extensive as this design. However, with a design as complete as this one, the programming time might be cut by over 90% because as you will see in Part Three the programming becomes very easy when design is completed up front. Without knowing any of the actual programming commands of dBASE IV, this design enables you to have thought out some of the more complicated tasks for which you will create procedures. As you read the next sections of this book, remember that going from pseudocode to dBASE IV code is very simple once you understand the basics.

Part Two

Database without programming

So far, you have seen the concepts of programming and systems design. You have seen a case study of The Ajax Appliance Company in design. Now, you will see how to actually create the system shown in that design. This part will show you how to use the dBASE IV user interface. This includes everything other than the actual program commands used to create turnkey systems. You will see that in Part Three.

In this part, you will first see how to install and run dBASE IV. You will examine the two distinct ways to run dBASE IV—the Control Center and the dot prompt. After a complete tour of the Control Center, you will create your first database and then create all of the databases designed in the Ajax Appliance Company case study.

With your databases created, you will see adding, changing, and deleting your data. You will see how to sort and index your data, and how to begin to turn your raw data into meaningful information. Before learning the various WYSIWYG work surfaces, you will learn how to use more than one database at a time.

Once all of the data functions have been mastered, turn your attention to the information functions. The QBE or Query By Example function lets you ask queries or questions about your data. You will learn about data entry screens and reports and printing. Finally, the dBASE IV application generator creates the basics of the Ajax Appliance Company system without any programming. However, you will also see the limitations of the Applications Generator and why you need to learn how to program to really create custom systems in dBASE IV. For now, you will concentrate on all the non-programming tasks that make it easy for you to program later.

Overview of changes in dBASE IV 2.0

The following sections contain an overview of the enhancements to the dBASE language in version 2.0. Borland has added new development tools, made significant improvements to the performance of the dBASE environment, and created many new features to the language itself.

dBASE IV 2.0 new features: a quick look

dBASE IV version 2.0 performance has been drastically increased with speed improvements at nearly every level of the product. In addition, version 2.0 incorporates many new and enhanced commands to make application development easier and quicker. These new enhancements to dBASE can be categorized into several broad groups:

- Performance improvements—Every aspect of dBASE IV has been fine-tuned to create dramatic performance improvements. Average task usage is 8 to 10 times faster than dBASE IV version 1.5 and twice as fast as Microsoft FoxPro 2.0.

- Virtual memory manager—dBASE IV dynamically allocates memory so that, the more memory there is available, the more it will use. It provides a solution for users who need to run large dBASE applications and previously had insufficient memory available. dBASE IV version 2.0 works on systems with as little as 1Mb of extended memory.
- Language enhancements—Thirty-one new and enhanced commands and functions have been added to make programming in dBASE IV easier and quicker than ever before. Expanded mouse functionality and event handling let programmers enhance dBASE IV programs with graphic-like elements such as radio buttons, check boxes, and check lists.
- Expanded debugger—Several new functions make it easier for dBASE IV developers to debug their programs.
- Faster and easier installation—dBASE IV installation has been completely revamped to make it virtually automatic. It is easy for novice users to install dBASE IV. After installation, however, advanced users still can customize dBASE IV for the way they work. Simplified installation is especially useful to IS Managers who must regularly install multiple copies of the software.

Virtual memory management

dBASE IV version 2.0 includes a new Virtual Memory Manager that allows dBASE IV to access up to 16Mb of extended memory. By default, dBASE IV now uses as much extended memory as is available on the system or 5Mb, whichever is greater. If the system has less than 5Mb of extended memory, dBASE IV version 2.0 creates a swap file on the hard disk to store software code and data segments. The intelligent Virtual Memory Manager dynamically allocates memory to use all of the system's available memory.

With virtual memory management, you can run dBASE IV version 2.0 with as little as 1Mb of extended memory, provided you have sufficient hard disk space for dBASE IV to create the swap file. As a result, dBASE IV version 2.0 can run on a wide range of boundary for applications and data is removed.

With the Virtual Memory Manager, it is possible to execute extremely large DOS applications from within dBASE IV. For example, WP = BRIEF.EXE would allow kilobytes of conventional memory.

Language enhancements

Several enhancements to the dBASE language provide developers with additional flexibility in menu construction and event handling. In dBASE IV version 2.0, there are more ways to create and control menus in mouse operations. The programmer can create easy-to-use applications that generate less code.

Menu pop-up and bar commands   A number of new commands and functions improved the use of pop-ups and bars. A *pop-up menu* is a screen window containing special prompts, messages, and a border. A *bar* is a single prompt or option that appears in a defined pop-up.

The new BARCOUNT( ) function returns the number of bars in the active or specified pop-up. This is useful for processing items in a dynamic pop-up.

The new BARPROMPT( ) function returns the text that appears in a given bar of the active or specified pop-up. Now, a developer can process a list of files, other than .DBF files, to build a pick list.

The new ON BAR command executes a specified command when any bar in a pop-up is highlighted.

The new ON POPUP command carries out a specific command when a bar of the specified pop-up is highlighted.

The new ON SELECTION BAR command carries out a specific command when users select a specified bar in a pop-up.

The enhanced ON SELECTION POPUP command carries out a specific command when any one of the bars in a pop-up is selected.

The new ON EXIT BAR command executes a specified command when the highlight leaves the bar in a pop-up.

The new ON EXIT POPUP command executes a specified command when any bar in a specified pop-up is exited.

Menu and pad commands Several new commands let developers capture additional menu and pad events and attach code to their dBASE IV programs.

The new PADPROMPT( ) function returns the text that appears in a given pad of the active or specified menu.

The new ON MENU command executes a specified command when any pad in a menu is highlighted.

The enhanced ON PAD command now allows you to carry out a specific command when users highlight a specific pad in a menu.

The new ON SELECTION MENU command carries out a specific command when one of the menu pads is selected. This command reduces the amount of code required by attaching one command to replace several ON PAD commands.

The new ON SELECTION PAD command carries out a specific command when one of the menu pads is selected.

The new ON EXIT MENU command executes a specified command when any pad in a specified menu is exited.

The new ON EXIT PAD command executes a specified command when a pad in a specified menu is exited.

Mouse functionality New mouse functions provide developers with new functionality for managing object-based menu resources. With these new functions, developers will need to generate less code to get more visually-appealing results.

SET MOUSE ON/OFF now is supported.

The MROW( ) and MCOL( ) functions return the current mouse position. MCOL( ) returns the column position of the mouse cursor on the screen. MROW( ) returns the row position of the mouse cursor on the screen.

The ISMOUSE( ) function returns a logical true (.T.) or false (.F.) that indicates whether a mouse driver has been installed or not.

The ON MOUSE command will execute a command when the user clicks the left mouse button.

Additional new commands and functions

The AT( ) function now takes an optional third argument, which is the Nth occurrence of the matching string to look for. The AT( ) function returns a number that shows the starting position of a character string (substring) within a larger string or memo field. AT( ) starts the search from the first character of the string or memo field being searched.

The RAT( ) function, like the AT( ) function, returns a number that shows the starting position of a character string (substring) within a larger string or memo field. RAT( ) starts the search from the last character of the string or a memo field.

The KEYMATCH( ) function indicates whether or not a specified expression is found in the index keys of a specified index.

The MEMORY( ) function has been enhanced to accept new values. It enables developers to find out more about how dBASE IV is managing memory so that they know if there's enough memory available to run particular functions. MEMORY( ) reports on:

- The amount of memory available
- The amount of memory in the heap
- Low DOS memory
- The amount of extended memory that is unallocated
- The amount of physical memory being managed by the Virtual Memory Manager
- The amount of memory that is being used by the buffer manager

The TIME( ) function now takes an optional argument. This will cause the hundredths of seconds to be returned in the time string.

Additional features in dBASE IV include:

- Support for VGA mode displaying 50, 43, and 25 lines so that users can view more data on each screen
- DOS Protected Mode Interface (DPMI) compliance, which eliminates performance degradation when dBASE IV is run from within Windows or OS/2

The dBASE IV Compiler for DOS brings new capabilities to the dBASE IV version 2.0 application development environment. Based on dBASE IV version 2.0, the dBASE IV Compiler provides dBASE developers with a package of tools to easily develop and distribute their applications. The dBASE IV Compiler converts a dBASE application to a fully-functional executable (.EXE). Developers can distribute .EXEs royalty-free, without shipping a runtime module. Fast code is generated for all versions of dBASE IV and dBASE III PLUS. The dBASE IV Compiler is fully compatible with all previous versions of dBASE III PLUS and dBASE IV. Chapter 24 explains this new development tool in great detail.

An overview of the changes in dBASE IV 1.5

dBASE IV 1.5, which was shipped in March 1992, is the latest version of the most used personal computer database management system. dBASE IV 1.5 is the successor to the last major release, dBASE IV 1.1, which was shipped in July 1990. dBASE IV 1.0 originally was shipped in September 1989.

dBASE IV 1.5 new features: a quick summary

dBASE IV 1.5 is a backward compatible extension of previous versions of dBASE IV. Its major enhancements can be summarized in several broad categories:

- Easier-to-use and more efficient installation routine
- Increased number of work areas from 10 to 40
- Enhanced single-user and network performance and reduced memory requirements
- Mouse support for menu selection and navigation within the various design screens, browse and edit
- Many new features in Query-By-Example including:
  - ~ Editable views using multiple files
  - ~ Automatic selection of query method for improved performance
  - ~ Calculated fields now support aggregate and summary operators
  - ~ Calculated fields now support linking fields
  - ~ Improved support for existing index usage within a query
- Open architecture control center
- Low-level I/O functions
- New or enhanced programming commands including:
  - ~ Smart key filter for improved record selection
  - ~ Enhanced blank support
  - ~ New index functions
  - ~ Enhanced keyboard command
  - ~ New SCROLL clause for @ SAY/GET commands to scroll an area of the screen

A detailed summary of the new features in dBASE IV 1.5

Many new features have been added to dBASE IV 1.5. They fall into several major categories.

- Enhanced installation routine
- Usability and productivity enhancements
- Indexing and data selection enhancements
- New control center and QBE design screen features
- Enhancements for developers

Enhanced installation routine

The dBASE IV 1.5 installation routine has been improved to make it easier for the end user to get dBASE IV 1.5 up and running. The install also is faster. This is very important for corporations that have to install many copies of dBASE IV 1.5. The improvements are described in the following sections.

Automatic sensing of CGA systems   The installation routine automatically senses the video card and monitor to determine whether monochrome or color should be used. It then decides which colors are displayed most appropriately.

Disk caching installation has been automated   The system automatically examines the computer's memory to determine the type of memory available. If LIM (expanded) memory is found, it is used for caching. If no LIM memory is found, dBASE searches for extended memory and uses it. If no extra memory is found, the cache is not enabled.

Windows 3.x preparation   The necessary dBASE files and icons are included in a dBASE group, so dBASE IV 1.5 can be run easily from within Microsoft Windows 3.x. The Windows PROGMAN.INI file is updated to include the group and five customized files are copied to the destination file. A dBASE IV 1.5 PIF file is set up to work with either 386 enhanced mode or standard mode. Required memory is set to 450K, while the 386 enhanced advanced option is set to all available memory. This setup also creates a dBASE IV 1.5 icon.

Improved network installation and automatic network detection   This makes it easier to set up and use dBASE IV 1.5 on a network. A single network access control file, which can be placed in any directory, has replaced the network subdirectory that used to be necessary. A new configuration option called CONTROLPATH has been added to point to the network control files. Most importantly, dBASE IV 1.5 automatically starts in multi-user mode if a network is detected.

Developers edition has been eliminated   The template language compiler now is included in the standard edition. This allows the developer to change the templates that come with dBASE IV 1.5, so code generation from the Control Center design screens can be customized.

The royalty free RunTime facility now is offered separately for those who want to distribute their applications.

International editions and translations installation enhanced These now are easier to install and provide more flexibility because the installation routine can accept a variable number of disks without changing the installation program itself. Additionally, configuration for international options has been automated through the users current code page. Install automatically will set international options for decimal points, numeric separators, currency symbols and alignment, date formats, and time formats in the CONFIG.DB configuration file. Finally, dBASE IV 1.5 will use collation tables to store language-specific information about sorting high-order characters. An extra bit has been added to allow up to 63 collation groups for languages such as Czech and Polish.

New dBINFO utility This utility makes information about your system available to you and to Borland product support. dBINFO provides such information as the DOS version, memory configuration, hardware information (including machine type), BIOS type and date, processor, coprocessor, monitor, video card type, and keyboard and mouse information. It also provides a listing of TSRs and a listing of CONFIG.SYS, AUTOEXEC.BAT, and CONFIG.DB files. dBINFO also provides a quick facility for commenting out lines of an AUTOEXEC.BAT file.

More efficient and extensive data compression added Efficiencies have been added to the installation routine by using PKUNZIP rather than self-extracting files. This saves 13K in overhead per disk. Additionally, the tutorial files now are compressed to save disk space.

Usability and productivity enhancements

The overall performance and usability of dBASE IV has been enhanced greatly in this release. From simply running faster in all areas to improved usability on networks, these enhancements make dBASE IV more usable for both Control Center users and developers. Increased ease of use from the installation program, the new help system, and the expansion of work areas and mouse support make dBASE IV more powerful as well.

Mouse support One of the most significant improvements in dBASE IV 1.5 is the addition of mouse support to the most important areas of the product. Mouse support is available in all Control Center operations including menu navigation, file name selection, prompt boxes and expression builders, work surface field selection and movement, and list boxes and even assists with navigation through hot keys in the navigation line.

 The mouse pointer appears as a solid block in normal operations but changes to an up or down arrow when positioned on the top or bottom borders of a scrollable list. Mouse support also works in the dot prompt to move the cursor to the location of the mouse pointer and in the help screen to navigate through the hot keys.

 In the Browse screen, the mouse can be used to move the cursor to any value in the table. Memo fields can be selected for editing and zoomed by using the mouse clicks and double clicks. In most design screens, the mouse can be used to select, move, and size fields and text. Lines and boxes can be selected and sized with the mouse.

The most exciting use of mouse support besides menu selection is found in the ability to selectively move to @ GET areas in a data entry form. This allows the user to select and enter data in fields in a non-sequential mode. Additionally, complete protection has been built in for the developer to allow fields to maintain required data entry in a sequential order. In dBASE programs, the mouse is usable in menus, data entry screens, and list pop-ups.

Increased number of work areas from 10 to 40   The number of work areas in dBASE IV 1.5 has been increased to 40 from the 10 available in dBASE IV 1.1. This popular request allows developers to create more powerful applications and removes the need to juggle their database files in and out of only 10 work areas. Work areas now are dynamically allocated. Using fewer than five work areas will leave more memory available than in dBASE IV 1.1, which automatically allocated space for all 10 work areas. The SET CATALOG command no longer uses work area 10 but now uses an invisible work area. All commands and functions that are affected by work areas have been enhanced to recognize the 40 work areas, including database usage and cleanup, status commands, and work area functions such as SELECT( ) and CATALOG( ).

Improved caching performance   The DBCACHE utility (Hyperdisk) has been improved, making it more robust, especially for use with Windows 3.*x* and DOS 5.0. It also has been improved to give additional compatibility with TSRs and other caches.

Printer driver enhancements   Printer drivers have been improved to remove old and outdated drivers and have been replaced with newer printer drivers. Family entries have been added to make it easier to pick industry standard printers from manufacturers such as Epson, Hewlett Packard, and Okidata. Most importantly, Postscript and Postscript-compatible printers now are supported in dBASE IV 1.5.

Selectable CONFIG.DB files   A switch has been added to the dBASE IV 1.5 command line to allow the user to specify a different CONFIG.DB file for different applications. This allows the user to control all of the selectable parameters such as color, database search methods, and editors without having to hardcode them into programs.

Help system improvements   The dBASE IV 1.5 help system has been improved to provide even more helpful context-sensitive information. For the first time, every menu operation and every command now has online help. The online tutorial also has been improved to make learning dBASE even easier.

Indexing and data selection enhancements

The dBASE IV .MDX (Multiple Index File) format was a major enhancement from previous versions of dBASE. By allowing up to 47 index tags per .MDX file and automatically opening and maintaining all of the index tags in the production index file the responsibility of the user to maintain the indexes was eliminated. In dBASE IV 1.5, efficiencies have been added to speed up changes to the database. Additionally, new functions and commands allow for much faster and more efficient searching methods.

Improved indexing algorithm In dBASE IV 1.1 every index was updated as a record was added, changed, or deleted. In dBASE IV 1.5, each index tag is assigned an internal marker to describe how it should be handled. Some indexes will be updated after each record is added, changed, or deleted. Some will be rebuilt after all the records have been changed. Others will be ignored completely if the index is not touched during a data operation. The end result is that performance is greatly enhanced when updating a large amount of records.

Additionally, the developer can determine how indexes are updated by the commands REPLACE, APPEND FROM, BLANK, and UPDATE through the use of the new REINDEX keyword. If the data to be changed is part of a non-controlling index key expression and the change includes a WHILE or ⟨scope⟩ clause, the index is not rebuilt until all the changes have been made.

New and improved index functions In dBASE IV 1.1, there were a number of index functions that allowed the developer to extract needed information about the indices used with a database. There are five new index functions that enhance a developer's ability to control and obtain information about existing indices.

- DESCENDING( ) indicates whether an index tag was created with the DESCENDING keyword.
- FOR( ) indicates whether an index tag was created with the FOR option.
- TAGCOUNT( ) gives the number of active indexes in the specified .MDX file or work area.
- TAGNO( ) gives the position of the specified index in the list of active indexes.
- UNIQUE( ) indicates whether an index tag was created with the UNIQUE keyword.

In addition, TAG( ) and KEY( ) have been improved to give the user more information about the controlling index when no arguments are supplied. Error handling also has been improved when an incorrect argument is supplied.

Data selection enhanced with smart key filter A smart key filter has been added to dBASE IV 1.5 with the command SET KEY TO. This allows a specific selection of records based on an existing index to be selected. Because only the index information is used and not the data, performance is improved significantly. By taking advantage of existing indexes, dBASE IV 1.5 can go directly to the beginning of a set of records and work with only the records that belong to the set. The order in which the records are handled is set by the index, not by the way the arguments were entered. This is a better method than INDEX FOR because no partial index is created. Disk space is saved as well as the time it takes to create the partial index.

SET KEY also can work with SET FILTER to create and use complex data selection quickly. While SET KEY first defines a valid selection range, SET FILTER can be used to select specific records. For example, in a sales file, SET KEY could be used on an index file of states to find the set of all records in California, while SET FILTER then could limit the selection to customers with balances over 60 days. This would be much faster than any other previous record selection method in dBASE IV.

New Control Center and QBE design screen features

New enhancements have been made to the Control Center and its design surfaces. The Control Center's architecture itself has been opened up, so its design surfaces are more flexible. This allows the developer to run programs before a surface is accessed and, when a file is saved, to allow for customized use of the Control Center screens. This is fully described in the next section entitled "Enhancements for developers."

The most important changes in the Control Center screens have been made to Query-By-Example (QBE), which will result in QBE users being able to use the queries design screen for many more types of complex queries without any programming. Overall, QBE now will provide greater flexibility, better performance, and improved ease of use.

Editable multi-file views   In dBASE IV 1.1, a major limitation of QBE was that a query created from more than one file was read-only. This actually was not a limitation of dBASE's architecture but a conscious decision to maintain data integrity.

In dBASE IV 1.5, this restriction has been lifted. Views created with multiple files now are editable. The only restriction is that calculated fields (which don't exist on the database files) remain read-only. The user can selectively add read- only restrictions on any fields when the query is created. This gives much more flexibility to the user while maintaining data integrity. When using the multi-file view in Browse or Edit fields can be changed but records cannot be added or deleted.

Automatic and user-selectable query optimization   In previous versions of dBASE IV, record selection was performed with a SET FILTER or an INDEX FOR command. With the addition of the smart key filter command SET KEY, QBE now can choose between three different methods to select records. QBE now can automatically select the most efficient method of record selection, which optimizes query speed to produce results faster and let data be displayed faster. The user also can override the automatic optimization of a query and select one of the three methods to be used for record selection.

File linking allowed on calculated fields   File linking allows data from more than one file to be used. In dBASE IV 1.1, only database fields or index tags could be used as links. In dBASE IV 1.5, calculated fields can be used as file links. This allows users to create complex relationships without adding fields to database files to perform a link or create additional index tags.

Calculated fields now deletable   In dBASE IV 1.1, once a calculated field was created, it could not be deleted from the calculated field skeleton. dBASE IV 1.5 adds a menu option to delete any or all calculated fields from the query. This makes it easier to ask what-if type questions without creating new queries.

Improved summary operations with calculated fields   Calculated fields have been enhanced to allow summary operators such as SUM, AVERAGE, MIN, MAX, CNT, and STD to be used. In addition, the aggregate operator GROUP BY also can be used within calculated fields. This will allow such queries as "What is the total sales (QTY*PRICE) of my sales file by customer?" Previously, a report had to be created to see this type of information.

Improved handling of complex index tags   In dBASE IV 1.1, index tags created with FOR or UNIQUE parameters were not treated as index tags. In dBASE IV 1.5, index tags created with the FOR or UNIQUE parameters now are handled as complex tags when Include Indexes is used. This allows you to display all the attributes for an index tag when using an index tag in a query. Complex index fields also can contain aggregate operators such as SUM and CNT and the GROUP BY operator.

Ascending or descending index indicator   When Include Indexes is used in QBE a pound symbol is displayed next to database fields to let the user know that the field also is an index. The pound symbol also is displayed next to complex index tags. In dBASE IV 1.5, the pound symbol has been replaced with an up or down triangle indicating that an index is ascending (up) or descending (down). If a database field is used in two tags, one ascending and one descending, the pound symbol is used.

Option to keep speedup indexes   When necessary, dBASE IV creates temporary index tags during a query. You now can instruct QBE to keep the index tags so they can be used again. This speeds up subsequent executions of the same query or any query using the index.

Re-creation of lost index tag   If an index tag is used in a query that has been deleted, all relevant information about a tag is saved so it can be correctly recreated if it is needed when a query is run.

Eliminating duplicate records in a join   When two files are linked together with fields from both databases in the view, the user generally does not want a join, because any duplicate records displayed when records in one database match a particular value in the other database are indistinguishable in the view. In dBASE IV 1.5, when fields from only one of the linked files are in the view, QBE treats the second file as a filter instead of a join. This allows the user to see only records that have a match; however, because they are used as a filter, only the first record for each match is shown. This is equivalent to putting the FIRST keyword in front of the linking variable.

Improved Shift–F1 Pick list expression builder   A new column has been added to the queries design screen expression builder list which is displayed by pressing Shift–F1. The column called QBE Operators displays operators unique to QBE such as GROUP BY, LIKE, SOUNDS LIKE, FIRST, EVERY, etc.

View skeleton wrap around   In dBASE IV 1.5, navigating in the view skeleton automatically will wrap around just as the file skeleton allows. This saves several keystrokes when working in QBE.

Enhancements for developers

Many new enhancements targeted at the serious developer have been added. These include opening up the architecture of the Control Center, low-level I/O functions, improved support for blank values, and many new programming commands while retaining backward compatibility with previous versions of dBASE IV.

In dBASE IV, there always has been a close relationship between the various design surfaces and the dBASE programming language, especially because each of the design surfaces generates executable dBASE program commands. dBASE programming commands have been added to take advantage of new design surface changes.

Open architecture Control Center   The architecture of the Control Center has been opened up so that its design tools are more flexible. Programs can be run before, after, and during the use of all of the design screens, including databases, forms, queries, reports, labels, applications, browse and edit screens, and entry and exit from the Control Center itself. This allows the advanced developer use of the Control Center in programs to enhance, customize, or scale it to meet the needs of the final user. Third-party add-ins now can be incorporated into the Control Center for easy access if desired. All of this is controlled by new keywords in the CONFIG.DB file to make it easy to control usage. Because you now can specify custom CONFIG files within dBASE IV 1.5, the programmer has complete flexibility over multiple configurations.

Conditional compilation   dBASE IV 1.5 now includes the ability to add compiler directives inside program files. These directives tell the compiler which pieces of dBASE IV code to leave out of the .DBO file. This is particularly useful to developers who create applications for multiple environments such as DOS, UNIX, VMS, and MAC and also for developers who create programs for different versions of dBASE IV or different types of dBASE IV such as the server edition or RunTime. Compiler directives can be nested up to 32 levels. The new directives include: #define, #undef, #ifdef, #else, and #endif.

Low-level file I/O   Low-level file I/O functions have been incorporated into dBASE IV 1.5 to provide the advanced developer with greater flexibility when manipulating files. This can be particularly useful when the need arises to import or export data file formats not currently supported through dBASE IV. These options include:

FCREATE( )	Creates a file
FOPEN( )	Opens an existing file
FCLOSE( )	Closes a file
FGETS( )	Reads a line terminated string
FPUTS( )	Writes an ASCII string to a file
FREAD( )	Reads a specific number of characters from a file
FWRITE( )	Writes a specific number of characters to a file
FSEEK( )	Seeks a specified position in a file
FFLUSH( )	Flushes the current system buffer to disk
FERROR( )	Returns file I/O error status
FEOF( )	Returns end of file status

Variable parameter passing   dBASE IV 1.5 allows developers to pass a variable number of parameters to a procedure, rather than a set number of parameters as determined by the PARAMETERS statement. dBASE IV 1.5 also keeps track of the number of parameters passed by the WITH clause. Developers also can use the new PCOUNT( ) function to find out how many parameters were passed.

Enhanced blank support   The first step toward true null support has been taken with the inclusion of enhanced blank support. This has been done without requiring the additional development changes that would be required by tri-state logic and the addition of a null character. Blank support has been enhanced to provide the ability to fill individual fields or records with blanks—CHR(32). Logical, numeric, and date fields all now can be blanked. The new ISBLANK( ) function tests whether a field, memory variable, array element, or other expression is blank. For statistical work, averages and other statistics now can be handled correctly when no data has been entered into a field.

Improvements to RUN( ) function   The RUN( ) function has been improved in two ways. Parameters can be included that instruct RUN( ) to attempt to free more memory when rolling out to DOS. This leaves only a 10K shell of dBASE in RAM. This allows many more programs to run from within dBASE IV 1.5. RUN( ) also now sends a command string directly to DOS without preceding it with COMMAND.COM /C. This makes it possible to return the called commands error code rather than an error code from COMMAND.COM.

Enhanced KEYBOARD( ) command   KEYBOARD( ) has been enhanced with the ability to pass extended ASCII keys like function keys or cursor keys (such as Ins, Del, PgUp, PgDn, etc.) as part of an expression. This enhanced keyboard control provides significant benefits when automating tasks.

SCROLL clause in @ command   A SCROLL clause has been added to the @ command to provide users with the ability to scroll the contents of a specified region of the screen. This makes it possible to display a lot of information in a specified area. A WRAP keyword also has been added to indicate whether text moving out of a boundary of the region should be brought back to fill in the row being vacated at the opposite boundary. This will prove invaluable for displaying textual information on the screen and for creating simulated windows when necessary.

Enhanced SET DESIGN   The SET DESIGN command allows an advanced developer to prevent the end-user of a program from entering design modes of queries, forms, reports, and labels. In dBASE IV 1.1 the value of SET DESIGN was a global setting, meaning that, if a sub-procedure or a UDF turned the setting off, it would stay off. In dBASE IV 1.5, the value of SET DESIGN will be local. This allows SET DESIGN to be turned off in a sub-procedure but remain on when the procedure returns control to the main program.

File information enhancements   In dBASE IV 1.5, developers have the ability to obtain specific information about files from the operating system. The following functions have been added:

TIME( )	The value of the time the file was last updated
FDATE( )	The value of the date the file was last updated
FSIZE( )	The value of the size of the file in bytes

Toggle to turn off the Organize menu   In the Browse and Edit screens, the Organize menu allows the user to physically sort a database, create or modify index tags, or reset the controlling index. Through the addition of the new NOORGANIZE keyword to the BROWSE, EDIT, CHANGE, INSERT, and APPEND commands, the developer is assured that their programs' index integrity is preserved.

New field count function   A new function FLDCOUNT( ) has been added to provide developers with the ability to determine how many fields are in each record of an open database file.

Additional procedure libraries   Users and developers frequently want to store commonly used procedures and UDFs in a procedure library. dBASE IV 1.1 supported only one active procedure library at a time. In dBASE IV 1.5, a new command, SET LIBRARY TO, establishes a global procedure library. This is designed for users who want a default collection of procedures available all the time. Developers then can use the SET PROCEDURE TO command for more program specific needs.

Additionally, a new CONFIG.DB setting, SYSPROC =, has been added to let users specify a high-level library of procedures. This library will be searched as soon as a given procedure or function is not found in the built-in dBASE IV procedure and functions. This feature gives developers a set of procedures and functions that are found quickly. These procedures take precedence over other procedure libraries established with the lower priority SET PROCEDURE and SET LIBRARY commands.

More arguments for the SET( ) function   The SET( ) function now returns values for more arguments than in dBASE IV 1.1. This includes some of the new SET commands. These arguments include BORDER, DATE, DEVICE, INDEX, LIBRARY, MARK, ORDER, POINT, SEPARATOR, SKIP, and WINDOW. This will allow more flexibility in programs that need to know the current settings of these arguments.

Enhanced QUIT command   The QUIT command now has a WITH *<errorcode>* parameter to return a value to indicate whether dBASE was exited correctly. This is invaluable when dBASE is called by external applications.

Network user ID function   dBASE IV 1.5 now provides the ability for users who are signed on to the network or other multi-user systems to check the identification of a user. The new ID( ) function returns the name of the current user as a character string.

dBASE home directory function   A new function, HOME( ), has been added to tell the user which directory dBASE IV 1.5 was loaded from. This function is useful in network environments and also helps developers make their applications more robust.

DEXPORT command   In dBASE IV 1.1, users could set an environment variable named DTL_TRANSLATE to tell dBASE IV to create a BNL file with an .NPI extension whenever the design for a form, report, or label was saved. In dBASE IV 1.5, developers have more control over the creation of .BNL files. dBASE IV 1.5 uses the default extensions of .SNL for screens, .FNL for reports, and .LNL for labels. The DEXPORT command lets developers create a .BNL file at any time. This is especially useful with the open architecture of the Control Center.

New template language functions   Several new functions have been added to the dBASE IV Template language.
   DGEN( ) executes the internal template interpreter. This performs the program instructions in the template file. If a layout object is specified, DGEN( ) generates a dBASE program as specified in the layout object. This allows programs to dynamically recreate Control Center generated program code without entering the actual design screens.
   ARGUMENT( ) returns the character string (if any) passed to the template compiler DGEN as the second argument.

TOKEN( ) is used to indicate how to tell the difference between one argument and the next.

IMPORT( ) converts a .DBF, .QBE, .UPD, or .CAT file into a template layout object.

An overview of the changes in dBASE IV 1.1

dBASE IV 1.1 continues the enhancements that dBASE IV 1.0 started. The following discussions describe the changes to each section.

Changes to the Control Center work surfaces

Changes to the Control Center work surfaces are the inclusion of the Organize menu in Browse and Edit screens and the changes to QBE.

Most notable is the inclusion of the Organize menu from the Data work surface in the Browse and Edit screens. This gives you the ability to create new indices and change the active index and see your data in different orders without leaving the Browse or Edit screens. In dBASE IV 1.0, you had to specify indices in the Data work surface and then move to the Browse screen. Now you can view your data in the Browse or Edit screens and change the sorted order of the data easily. After you specify a new index in the Browse or Edit screen using the Organize menu, you will see the data instantly rearranged on the screen. This allows you to see the data in any order you specify without having to leave the Browse work surface.

The Queries work surface was also changed to allow you to see more fields in the file skeleton. In dBASE IV 1.0, each field box in the file skeleton was 15 characters wide. In dBASE IV 1.1, the size of the field box is initially the size of the field name. As you enter criteria or sort directives in the field boxes, the size of the box expands. By shrinking the field box size, you can see more fields in the file skeleton on the screen at the same time.

Changes to programming commands

SET DIRECTORY TO This new command lets you specify a drive and directory to serve as the default path for dBASE to look for and store data to. Presently the SET DEFAULT TO command only lets you choose the disk drive. This command lets you choose the drive and directory and is equivalent to the DOS Change Directory (CD) command.

To change to a subdirectory of the current directory you would enter:

SET DIRECTORY TO MYDATA

To change to a new subdirectory off the current root directory you would enter:

SET DIRECTORY TO\MYDATA

To change to a new subdirectory on a different disk drive you would enter:

SET DIRECTORY TO:\DBASE\EXAMPLES

Finally, to change to the parent directory of the current subdirectory on the C drive (assuming you were in the C drive), you would enter:

SET DIRECTORY TO C:

This command will give you a lot more flexibility because dBASE remembers where all of the base dBASE files are and lets you change the subdirectory for data purposes while still retaining the path information that currently exists.

INDEX ON...FOR   One of the more serious limitations of dBASE IV 1.0 is the ability to create *partial* indices. These are indices that only contain keys for a subset of the database. For example, suppose you wanted to work with the customers in California and wanted to see the data in order from the largest sales to the smallest sales. However, you wanted to make changes to the data and only wanted to see these customers. You could use QBE, but that would create a read-only file. You could write the view as a new database that only contained a subset of the data, but then you would have to manage putting the changed data subset into the original database.

The other problem with this example is the speed of using the Browse screen with a filter. Though a filter will only let you see the data you want, searching the database is very slow because searches are performed in a record by record sequence.

The solution is to use a partial index. The new FOR parameter of the INDEX command solves this problem. To only work with the California records and still retain the speed you desire you would create a partial index. For example:

INDEX ON SALES TAG CASALES FOR STATE = 'CA' DESCENDING

This creates an index and accomplishes the same task as a filter only allowing you to see the records whose value of state is CA and placing in order of sales from largest to smallest. You can then work with the database and have instant access to all records in the Browse screen.

KEYBOARD   The KEYBOARD command allows you to place values in the type-ahead buffer that can be executed as if the user had typed them in. This gives you many new possibilities in controlling the systems that you create. For example, suppose you want to control data entry screens by reading the keys that are pressed. You can easily trap for certain keys with the ON KEY LABEL command but there is no way to easily exit the screen if that is what you want to do. By using the KEYBOARD command, you could place an ESC into the type-ahead buffer to leave the screen without saving the changes or you could place a Ctrl–End into the type-ahead buffer to leave the screen and save any changes. To do this, you would enter:

KEYBOARD CHR(27)   && Enters an Esc into the buffer

or

KEYBOARD CHR(14)   && Enters a Ctrl—End into the buffer

The KEYBOARD command clears the type-ahead buffer before it executes the characters in the KEYBOARD command.

@ **GET VALID REQUIRED...RANGE REQUIRED**   The way data validation is handled has changed in dBASE IV 1.1. In dBASE III Plus, each field was validated with the RANGE or VALID clauses of the @ GET only if the data had changed. For example, suppose you were validating the range of a date field to be yesterday, today, or tomorrow for the purposes of validating a sales entry. Your statement read:

@ 10,15 GET HIRE_DATE RANGE DATE ( )—1, DATE ( )+1

What happened if you went to that record six months later to change the sales amount? As long as you didn't change the data in the HIRE_DATE field no revalidation of the HIRE_DATE data would occur. You could change the sales amount field and move on.

In dBASE IV 1.0, you could not do this! Data validation occurred whether the data was changed or not. This required you to not use RANGE clauses and instead use the VALID clause. You had to set up complicated expressions or UDF's which would check for a change and return a .T. to the VALID clause if there was no change and skip the revalidation.

In dBASE IV 1.1, this has been fixed. Data validation with the RANGE or VALID clauses now only works when the field is changed. This did, however, add another problem. What happens if you must have the field revalidated whether the data changed or not? dBASE IV 1.1 also adds a new parameter, REQUIRED. The REQUIRED parameter goes after a VALID or RANGE clause to force the revalidation of the field regardless of the change. For example:

@ 10,15 GET HIRE_DATE RANGE REQUIRED DATE( )—1, DATE( )+1

would cause a revalidation of the field when the cursor leaves the field or the data is saved. It also causes a revalidation when the form is a multipage form, and the user moves from one page to the next. Before the pages are changed, all REQUIRED fields are validated on the current page.

REPLACE FROM ARRAY   dBASE IV allows you to declare and use arrays. Version 1.1 of dBASE IV includes commands to COPY TO ARRAY and to APPEND FROM ARRAY. For some reason the REPLACE FROM ARRAY was not included in dBASE 1.0. It is however in v1.1. This allows you to selectively or globally replace values in an array. For example, suppose you want to use an array to store memory variables for data entry. You might first declare the array and then use COPY TO ARRAY to store the database values to the array. Next, you would perform the edits using the array memory variables and then replace the values in the database with the values in the array. For example:

```
USE data1 ORDER item
DECLARE getdata [5]

......
*Some code to position the record pointer could go here

......
COPY TO ARRAY getdata NEXT 1
CLEAR
@ 5,10 SAY 'PART NUMBER:      '+getdata[1]
@ 7,10 SAY 'PART NAME:      '+getdata[2]
@ 9,10 SAY 'DESCRIPTION:      '+getdata[3]
@ 11,10 SAY 'PRICE:      '+getdata[4]
@ 13,10 SAY 'QTY_INSTK:   '+getdata[5]
READ
REPLACE FROM ARRAY getdata
```

SAVE SCREEN and RESTORE SCREEN   SAVE and RESTORE SCREEN commands are not new. They simply have never been documented. These commands allow you to save the entire screen and then after you do anything to the screen you can recall the original screen and its contents. This is called saving and restoring the screen.

Saving and restoring screens is another method of preserving the screen. You would save your screen to a file, perform some other functions on the original screen or on a completely different screen, and when you are done simply restore the screen to its original state. A common sequence of code might be:

```
SAVE SCREEN TO myscreen
DO DISPALL
RESTORE SCREEN FROM myscreen
```

SET CURSOR   Sometimes you do not want the user to see the cursor. When you SET CURSOR OFF, the cursor is hidden. You would then use SET CURSOR ON to redisplay the cursor.

SET MESSAGE TO...[AT row, col]...   The SET MESSAGE TO command has existed for several versions of dBASE. It became very important in dBASE IV because many commands now included messages such as menus, data entry fields, and validation commands. The one deficiency in the message output is that it was solely confined to the last line of the screen. Line 24 in a 25-line screen and line 42 in a 43-line EGA screen.

The new AT parameter of the SET MESSAGE command lets you specify the row and column that messages will be displayed on. A common example would be:

```
SET MESSAGE TO 'Enter your data as displayed' at 5, 10
```

5
Starting dBASE IV

Installing dBASE IV on your machine is very simple thanks to the dBASE IV installation program. If you haven't already installed dBASE on your machine, you should do so now. It is very easy.

Installing dBASE IV on your computer

Start by placing the install disk in any floppy drive you choose. Type INSTALL and the installation program will begin. You will be asked to switch disks many times as you go through the installation. When you first begin the installation procedure, your hard disk will be checked for enough space to install dBASE IV. You will need a minimum of 5Mb of hard disk storage. If you don't have that much, dBASE will advise you of this and let you delete some files before trying again.

Once you type INSTALL, you will have to switch disks to enter your identification information. This screen is shown in Fig. 5-1. This screen requires that you enter your company name, your name, and the dBASE IV serial number. If you can't remember any of these, you can enter anything for the company and individual names, including asterisks. For the serial number you must enter a valid Borland serial number.

Once you have entered this successfully you change disks several times to complete the installation.

Next, you can modify your settings by entering DBSETUP at the DOS prompt. Choose Modify Existing CONFIG.DB, and you will see the settings screen. Press Enter to select Drivers to set up your printer.

In Fig. 5-2, the printer choice menu is shown open on the desktop. You can choose from a list of available printers by pressing Shift–F1. Many times

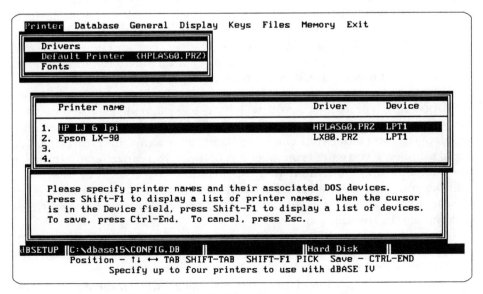

```
Install
  Software Registration

  User Name    ....................    Cary Prague

  Company Name    ..................    Windcrest Books

  Serial Number    ................    KD711B10000005


        Before using this product for the first time,
        you must fill in this registration form.  Once
        you save the form, you must reinstall to change it.

        Use Ctrl-End to save this form once you have
        provided the requested information.


INSTALL  A:\                                    720K Floppy
        Enter registration information.  Save - CTRL-END  Cancel - ESC
```

5-1 The dBASE IV installation identification screen.

when things appear desperate and you are totally confused when using dBASE IV, you might find that Shift–F1 will bring up a menu of choices. You can install several different printers that dBASE IV can recognize and that can be accessed from within the dBASE IV print menu when you want to print something.

```
Printer  Database  General  Display  Keys  Files  Memory  Exit

  Drivers
  Default Printer   (HPLAS60.PRZ)
  Fonts


      Printer name                          Driver      Device

  1.  HP LJ 6 lpi                           HPLAS60.PRZ  LPT1
  2.  Epson LX-90                           LX80.PRZ     LPT1
  3.
  4.

    Please specify printer names and their associated DOS devices.
    Press Shift-F1 to display a list of printer names.  When the cursor
    is in the Device field, press Shift-F1 to display a list of devices.
    To save, press Ctrl-End.  To cancel, press Esc.

dBSETUP  C:\dbase15\CONFIG.DB            Hard Disk
        Position - ↑↓ ↔ TAB SHIFT-TAB  SHIFT-F1 PICK  Save - CTRL-END
              Specify up to four printers to use with dBASE IV
```

5-2 The dBASE IV main installation screen.

Once you select your printer, you can select from many other options.

That is all there is to installing dBASE IV. If you have any further questions, you should consult the Getting Started manual in your dBASE package.

Starting dBASE IV

dBASE is started from your hard disk by simply entering DBASE at the DOS prompt as shown in Fig. 5-3. If you want to start it from a data subdirectory, just use the DOS PATH command to point to the subdirectory that includes dBASE IV. As shown in Fig. 5-3, dBASE resides in the subdirectory \DBASE4. Our data will reside in the Ajax subdirectory of the DBASE4 subdirectory. Therefore, the PATH command was used to tell DOS where to find dBASE.

```
C:\>CD \DBASE4\AJAX

C:\DBASE4\AJAX>PATH C:\DBASE4

C:\DBASE4\AJAX>DBASE
```

5-3   Starting dBASE IV from DOS.

Once you have entered the PATH command if necessary, you can start dBASE. As you can see in Fig. 5-3, the command DBASE starts dBASE IV. First, a DBASE introductory screen is displayed followed by the license agreement screen.

You can press Enter to pass the license agreement screen that appears after this introductory screen, or if you wait about 15 seconds, it will go away automatically.

One of two screens appears after the license agreement screen. One of the screens is almost blank except for a message telling you to type a dBASE command and press the Enter key. This screen has a dot in the lower left corner of the screen called the dot prompt. The other screen will be filled with a lot of text, lines, and boxes. It should be titled "dBASE IV Control Center."

Running dBASE IV—the Control Center and the dot prompt

There are several ways to run dBASE IV. The simplest for some people is to use the Control Center, a menu-driven interface to most of the functions of dBASE IV. The former Assistant found in dBASE III Plus required you to know the commands of dBASE. However, the Control Center is simply a way to access all the various work surfaces that make up dBASE IV without having to remember the various commands. A work surface is a screen where certain functions are performed. This will be covered later.

The dBASE Control Center is used to help you access the work surfaces to create, update, sort, and query your data. The Control Center lets you create queries, forms, reports, labels, and complete applications without requiring you to have any knowledge of dBASE IV. If you want the Control Center to appear automatically when you start dBASE IV you must put the command:

COMMAND=ASSIST

in your CONFIG.DB file. The CONFIG.DB file is a file on your dBASE directory that determines how dBASE is configured upon startup. You can control such things as the size of memory variables (more about them later), storage, defaults of environment commands, default colors, date handling, and much more. Most of the SET commands described in Part Three can be set in the CONFIG.DB file. Using the CONFIG.DB file, you can have dBASE start with any defaults you choose.

The other method of operating dBASE IV is to use the dot prompt shown in Fig. 5-4. When you see the dot prompt, then dBASE is waiting for you to enter a dBASE command. You can change the dot prompt to anything you want by using the PROMPT parameter in the CONFIG.DB file. To change the prompt to:

DBASE>

You would enter

PROMPT = DBASE>

in the CONFIG.DB file.

To leave the Control Center and use the dot prompt commands of dBASE, just press the Esc key from the Control Center. To get into the Control Center from the dot prompt, press F2 or type ASSIST at the dot prompt. Although the Control Center is no longer called the Assistant, you still use the command ASSIST to access it.

No matter how you run dBASE, your results will be the same. Even experienced dBASE users will find that the Control Center is invaluable for saving time. Almost everything you can do in the dot prompt can be done with the Control Center. There are however, many things that dBASE program commands can do that the Control Center cannot.

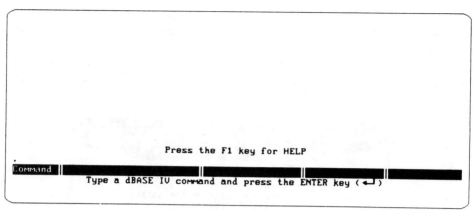

Press the F1 key for HELP

Command

Type a dBASE IV command and press the ENTER key (↵)

5-4 The dBASE IV dot prompt.

The six work surfaces

Six official work surfaces in dBASE IV correspond to the six panels in the Control Center:

Data	Creates and displays database files
Queries	Manipulates and extracts data
Forms	Creates and accesses custom input screens
Reports	Creates and prints reports
Labels	Creates and prints labels
Applications	Creates and runs programs

A work surface is where you do your work. Database structures are created in the Data work surface, screen forms in the Forms work surface, etc. These work surfaces perform similar functions to the old screens of dBASE III Plus although they are radically different. The chapters of this section, detail each work surface which has its own menus and operating instructions, although you will find that many keystrokes are universally the same throughout dBASE IV. Some of the various work surfaces are shown in the introduction to this section entitled "An Overview of the Changes in dBASE IV."

There also are two other "unofficial" work surfaces, EDIT and BROWSE. These are not "official" work surfaces because they are not shown as panels in the Control Center. However, as you will soon learn, they have all the features of a work surface and can be accessed from the Control Center with a single keystroke. You will see the Control Center and all its work surfaces in depth in the next chapter.

The help system

If you ever need general help, you can press F1. Depending on whether you are in the Control Center or the dot prompt, you then will get the main help menu shown in Fig. 5-5. The menu has five choices. The choices give you a short "course" on dBASE IV. You can choose to see the syntax on any command or function.

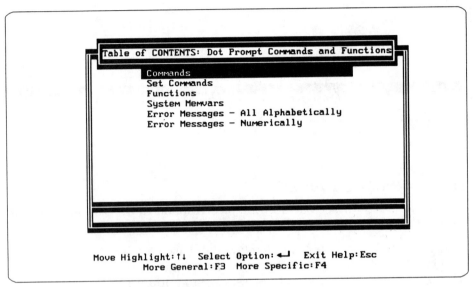

5-5 The dBASE dot prompt main help menu.

If you make an error entering a command in the dot prompt, dBASE tells you something is wrong. It then asks you if you want to Edit or Cancel the incorrect command or get help. If you tell dBASE that you want help, it retrieves the appropriate help screen.

You really can't make a mistake in the Control Center. You can, however, get help whenever you want by pressing F1.

Quitting dBASE

It is just as important to know how to leave a program as it is to start a program. If you are in the dot prompt, you simply can enter QUIT at the dot prompt:

    . QUIT

If you are in the Control Center, you can return to the dot prompt several ways. First, you simply can press Esc in the Control Center. You will receive a message box asking you if you really want to quit. If you move the menu choice to Yes and press Enter (or just press Y), you will be returned to the dot prompt.

The other way to leave the Control Center is to use the Exit menu. You can choose the Exit menu by pressing Alt–E. The menu will open and present you with two choices:

Exit to dot prompt
Quit to DOS

If you want to exit to the dot prompt simply press Enter to select Exit to dot prompt where the menu bar should be.

If you want to quit completely out of dBASE IV to DOS, then either move the menu bar to the Quit to DOS choice and press Enter or press Q. Either way, you leave dBASE and return to the DOS prompt.

The following message should appear on your screen:

*** END RUN   dBASE

You then are in the DOS prompt and can continue on with your normal work.

6

The Control Center and the dot prompt

This chapter discusses the dBASE Control Center work surfaces and catalogs. You will see how to navigate around the Control Center using special function keys. Finally, you will see how to choose items from menus and get help when you need it.

The Control Center

It is very important to read the entire chapter. There are many places where you will not fully understand the material until you have completed the lesson. Then everything should be "tied" together and you will be an instant Control Center expert.

What is the Control Center

The Control Center is an interface between you and the powerful dBASE command language. It gives you a way of communicating with dBASE through a system of menus and visual interaction with your files. The Control Center translates your menu choices and keystrokes (Fig. 6-1) into dBASE code or commands. At this point, you do not need to interact directly with dBASE commands at the dot prompt, because the Control Center makes it easier for you to learn and to use dBASE.

The Control Center can help you move from work surface to work surface with very little effort. It will actually improve your productivity if you are working with databases, queries, forms, reports, labels, and applications.

The different areas of the Control Center

The Control Center is divided into three distinct areas. The top of the screen contains pull-down menus used to run various functions. The center of the

Normal	Help	Data	Previous	Next	Field
Shift +	Pick	Design	Find Previous	Find Next	Find
	F1	F2	F3	F4	F5

Normal	Extend Select	Move	Copy	Zoom	Menus
Shift +	Replace	Size	Ditto	Quick Report	Macros
	F6	F7	F8	F9	F10

6-1 The dBASE function keys for enhanced keyboards.

screen lists all of your work surface files that are part of your system. As you will see, this display is controlled by your catalog. The active file and its description are also shown in the work surface panels. The bottom of the screen contains the navigation and message lines.

The navigation line at the bottom of the screen provides currently available information on keystrokes. The message line is used to explain a particular function of the menu selection currently highlighted. It is located below the navigation line at the bottom of the screen.

You can move your cursor only within the panels in the center of the screen or, once F10 is pressed, you can use the menus. Within a menu, the arrow keys are used to move the highlight. You may also use the Home and End keys to go to the top and bottom, or beginning or end, of most menus.

Work surfaces and the Control Center panels

The main area of the Control Center is divided into six columns also known as panels. These include:

Data	Creates and displays database files
Queries	Manipulates and extracts data
Forms	Creates and accesses input screens
Reports	Creates and prints reports
Labels	Creates and prints labels
Applications	Creates and runs programs

Each panel lists all of your files in each work surface. The right and left arrow keys will move the cursor from one panel to the next. Notice the word ⟨create⟩ appears at the top of each panel. So far we have yet to create something.

Each of these panels keeps track of the files that you have created. The six panels correspond to six of the work surfaces where you can design your data. These include Database File Design, Query Design, Forms Design, Report Design, Label Design, and Application Design.

When you create any of the previous types of files and give them names, the names appear in the panel below the operation name. For example, screen form filenames are displayed in the Forms panel and report filenames are displayed in the Reports panel.

Everything you create in the Control Center is linked to its original database file. Some files are above the line in a panel while others are below. When you use or activate a database file by highlighting it and pressing Enter, you will see all the files that are associated with that database file also move above the line. This helps you to know what belongs to what. A form developed to be used with data from the CUSTOMER database file might be useless with INVOICE database file.

Notice that BROWSE and EDIT are not considered "work surfaces" and are not Control Center panels. This is because they are the result of your other operations. Your data is simply displayed in either BROWSE or EDIT modes.

Navigating in the Control Center panels

There are a few important keys to learn before using the Control Center. The most important thing to remember is that the Esc key always takes you back to the Control Center. You may have to press it a few times and confirm that you want to get out of whatever you are doing, but it will always take you back.

The standard arrow keys move you from panel to panel in the center of the screen. Home and End take you to the beginning or end of the panels. If you wish to open the pull-down menus, you can press F10.

The Control Center displays all of your files segregated by type in the different panels. Use your cursor to select the file you want to use and then by pressing one of three keys you decide what to do with the file.

Generally, there are three keys to understand when using the Control Center:

Enter	The Selection Key
F2	The Data Key
Shift–F2	The Design Key

Enter, the Selection key, is used in each panel when selecting ⟨create⟩ to create a new design for a database, query, screen, report, label, or application. Selecting a file in the Data panel makes the database active. Selecting a file in the Reports or Labels panel opens a Print menu and lets you print the report or labels. If the option Instruct is on, it displays selection menus for each panel as an alternative to using the Data and Design keys.

F2, the Data key, displays your data. Once files are displayed in your Control Center, you use this key to actually see your data.

Shift–F2, the Design key, puts you into the correct work surface to design or modify a database, query, form, report, or application. This differs from the Data key which displays your data.

Pressing these keys will produce the following results depending on the type of file you have chosen in the various Control Center panels.

Panel	Enter	Data(F2)	Design (Shift—F2)
	Display	*Data In...*	*Modify the...*
Data	Open a Database	BROWSE/EDIT	Data Structure
Queries	Open a View	BROWSE/EDIT	Query
Forms	EDIT using the Form	Screen Form	Form
Reports	Print a Report	BROWSE/EDIT	Report
Labels	Print a Label	BROWSE/EDIT	Label
Applications	Run the Application	No effect	Application

Remember, that you can always get to BROWSE or EDIT by pressing the Data key F2. You can also get into any work surface by pressing the Design key Shift—F2.

Remember the four keys:

- Enter
- F2 (Data)
- Shift—F2 (Design)
- Esc

Using them moves you around the Control Center and all the work surfaces without ever choosing a menu. Do not forget the Esc key quits whatever you are doing and potentially may not save your work if you desire.

Using a mouse in the Control Center

dBASE IV allows use of a mouse in several areas, including:

- Control Center navigation
- Browse and Edit navigation
- Design surface navigation
- Data entry screens
- Menus

When you first start dBASE, if you have a mouse attached to your computer and the mouse driver is enabled, dBASE will take advantage of the mouse.

In the Control Center, the mouse can be used for all operations including menu selection and navigation, filename selection, and prompt boxes. Moving the mouse to a menu or Control Center panel and clicking on the desired object will position the highlight on the object or open a menu. A second click (known as double clicking) actually will select the object. This is the same as pressing Enter. In the example of menus, opening the menu with the first mouse click is the same as pressing F10, while the second click is equivalent to pressing Enter. Remember that the first click positions the highlight much the same as the arrow or Tab keys work and that the second click is the same as pressing Enter. If you keep that in mind, you'll always understand how to use the mouse in any situation.

At the bottom of the Control Center screen is the navigation line. Each of the key definitions are selectable, because, when a mouse is active, they act as hot keys. These are an alternative to keystrokes such as Shift–F2 or Shift–F9.

In the Browse screen, the mouse can be used to move the cursor to any value in the table. You can even move to any character in any value. When the value you want to select is not in view, you can use the mouse to navigate to the desired value. The mouse pointer appears as a solid block in normal operations but changes to an up or down arrow when positioned on the top or bottom borders of a scrollable list. It appears as a left or right arrow on the left or right borders. When the pointer changes to an arrow, you can hold the left mouse button down and the data will scroll in the direction of the arrow.

Memo fields can be selected for editing and zoomed by using a mouse click and double click.

In most design screens, the mouse can be used to select, move, and size fields and text. Lines and boxes can be selected and sized with the mouse. The mouse also works in the expression builders, work surface field selection list boxes, and the menus.

The most exciting use of mouse support besides menu selection is found in the ability to selectively move to @ GET areas in a data entry form. This allows you to select and enter data in fields in a nonsequential mode. Additionally, complete protection has been built in, so fields that must be entered in order or validated for required data entry are not violated.

In dBASE custom programs, the mouse is usable in menus, data entry screens, and list pop-ups.

Mouse support also works in the dot prompt to move the cursor to the location of the mouse pointer and in the help screen to navigate through the hot keys.

The dBASE function keys

In dBASE, the ten function keys initiate various commands. Figure 6-1 illustrates the location of the function keys and their associated commands on an enhanced keyboard for use within the dBASE Control Center.

Figure 6-2 illustrates the function keys for a standard keyboard using the Control Center in dBASE.

To access any of the function key commands, simply press the associated function key. For example, to ask dBASE for help, press F1. To view the database data, press F2. The location of the function key does not affect its function. To use any of the commands that require Shift, hold Shift down and press the function key. For example, to print a quick report, hold Shift and tap F9.

Getting help

You can get help at any time by pressing the Help (F1) key. The dBASE help program is context sensitive. That means when you press the Help key, the

Normal	Help	F1	F2	Data
Shift +	Pick			Design
Normal	Previous	F3	F4	Next
Shift +	Find Previous			Find Next
Normal	Field	F5	F6	Extend Select
Shift +	Find			Replace
Normal	Move	F7	F8	Copy
Shift +	Size			Ditto
Normal	Zoom	F9	F10	Menus
Shift +	Quick Report			Macros

6-2 The dBASE function keys for standard keyboards.

help information that is displayed is determined by what you are working on when you ask for help.

Getting help by pressing F1 makes it easy to get quick information on a topic without picking up a manual or book. The help menu is positioned over your work. You need only to press Esc to return to your work. The help menu allows you to move a screen forward or back, print the screen to your printer, and search for additional information by using a table of contents or index.

Sooner or later, most of us need some extra help from the computer software. If you don't know quite how to do something or if you make a mistake, your program should help you out. dBASE provides several kinds of help depending on your circumstances.

Help boxes Help boxes appear only when you request help. The help boxes look like the one shown in Fig. 6-3. Help boxes are context sensitive. This means that the contents of the box that pops-up depends on where in dBASE you are working at the time. If you are in the Control Center and press F1, you will receive help about the Control Center. Likewise, if you are in the EDIT screen, you will receive help about the EDIT screen.

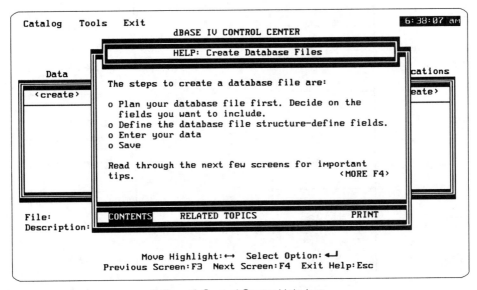

6-3 A Control Center Help box.

Many of the screens have multiple pages. You can move forward within help by pressing F3. You can also press F4 to move back a page.

Help box options At the bottom of each help box are several options. Select the options by pressing the arrow keys. At least three choices are at the bottom of each help box. The first choice is Contents. Choosing this option places you in one of the table of contents screens so you can choose a new help topic. This aspect of help is also context-sensitive; the screen you are shown depends on where you call help from.

The next option is Related Topics. When you choose this option, it displays a list of help topics similar to the one you were just reading about, and lets you choose which topic you want to view next.

The third option in this figure is Print. Choosing this causes dBASE to automatically print out the help screen information in a neat format. When the manual is nowhere in sight, and you find yourself constantly flipping back and forth between the help box and actually performing the task, the print option is invaluable.

Once you begin to move around inside the help boxes, a new option appears between Related Topics and Print options—the Backup option. This lets you retrace your steps backwards throughout the help system. This option is an alternative to pressing F3 to back up.

Exiting help When you have had all the help that you need, you can leave the help system and return to the place where you had been previously working by pressing the Esc key.

A tour of the menus

The Control Center contains two separate areas where you do your work. You have already seen about the six panels. The second area is the menus area, near the top of the screen. There are three menus:

- Catalogs
- Tools
- Exit

The middle menu in the Control Center is the Tools menu as shown in Fig. 6-4. The first option is for the creation of macros which let you record and play back your keystrokes. The next two items let you import and export "foreign" files. Foreign files are non-dBASE files that store their data differently than dBASE IV. The fourth item, DOS utilities, gives you access to DOS directly from a menu system and lets you perform all of the DOS commands without leaving dBASE. The next selection, Protect data, lets you assign a password to both dBASE and your data. Assigning a password protects your files from others' access to them.

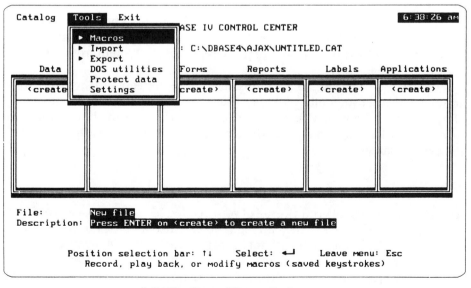

6-4 The Control Center Tools menu.

The last item in the Tools menu is Settings. This is where you would go to view or change the various settings that affect the way dBASE runs. Menus are opened by pressing F10 and visually selecting the choice you want. You can also open menus by pressing the Alt key with the first letter of the menu. The tools menu is opened by pressing Alt–T from the Control Center. You can then enter S for Settings. The screen should look like Fig. 6-5.

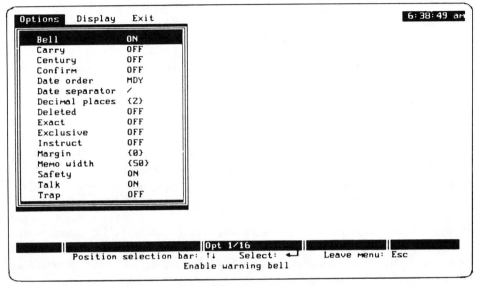

6-5 The Control Center settings submenu.

The Options submenu opens automatically and shows 16 settings. There are also two other menus entitled Display and Exit. Display lets you select colors for the various parts of the screen. The Exit menu returns you to the Control Center.

Figure 6-6 displays a brief summary of the sixteen settings and their actions with their defaults. Some of these are very important because they affect some very obvious ways that dBASE runs. Most of the settings are toggles, that is, when you select the setting, you can press Enter to change the default values.

Catalogs

A catalog is a means of grouping all of your related files for easy access. As you create a file, it is added to the catalog. You can also add files to your catalog that are already on your disk but not known to the catalog. A file can belong to one or more catalogs. A catalog may consist of many files of different types.

As you begin with the Control Center, notice that the catalog name appears above the six panels and is labeled UNTITLED.CAT.

SETTING	DEFAULT	DESCRIPTION
Bell	ON	dBASE beeps when you enter data past the field width.
Carry	OFF	Does not carry the data of the previous record to the next record when adding records.
Century	OFF	Displays dates without the century.
Confirm	OFF	Automatically skips to the next field when data entry fills the field width.
Date order	MDY	Displays dates as month/day/year. Toggle allows other date display options as day/month/year or year/month/day.
Date separator	/	Separates date parts with slashes (dashes or periods).
Decimal Places	{2}	Displays data with 2 decimal places and dBASE uses 2 decimal places in internal calculations. Change number in brackets with UP or DOWN arrow keys, or with numeric keypad. Maximum number of decimal places is 18.
Deleted	OFF	When ON allows you to skip over records marked for deletion.
Exact	OFF	When ON, requires exact character string comparison matches.
Exclusive	OFF	Prevents shared use of a file in a network
Instruct	ON	Sets the help level to display help boxes when <Enter> is pressed in the Control Center
Margin	{0}	Starts printed output {x} columns from the left. You can change the bracketed number with the UP or DOWN arrow keys or with the numeric keypad.
Memo width	{50}	Default width for displaying memo fields.
Safety	ON	Asks for confirming message before overwriting files.
Talk	ON	When ON, Displays results of commands on the screen.
Trap	OFF	Turns the debugger on and off

6-6 The settings defaults.

Catalogs are very important to dBASE IV. If you used dBASE III Plus, then you already may be familiar with catalogs. You can use the dBASE catalogs to help you remember what each database file is for and to keep track of all the files that are related to each database file. Each database file can have several supporting files: queries, custom screen forms, report forms, label forms, and applications.

Once a catalog is activated, each time you create a new dBASE database file or a supporting file such as a query, screen form or a report form, the name of the file is added to the catalog. To help you remember what each file is for, the catalog also lets you enter a description of each file. Catalogs are always active in dBASE IV. The last catalog you use reappears the next time you enter dBASE IV. The first time you begin dBASE IV, a catalog entitled UNTITLED.CAT is created for you. The .CAT extension tells dBASE that it is a list of your files. There is also a master catalog CATALOG.CAT that keeps track of all your catalogs. Its purpose is to maintain consistency among catalogs.

The real value of the catalog lies in its ability to keep an inventory of all the supporting files that you have for each of your database files. You can create index files, report form files, format (custom screen) files, query files, and label form files from each database file you have. If you have several of these supporting files for each of your database files, the disk directory becomes cluttered, and you might have difficulty remembering what each file is for and which database file it belongs to. The catalog does this remembering for you.

Using catalogs   You can open the catalog menu by pressing F10 or by typing Alt–C. The screen should look like Fig. 6-7. The catalog menu has two sections. The top section interacts with the catalogs. The bottom section works with the various files that are in the catalogs.

When you select the first option, Use a Different Catalog, a list pops up on the right side of the screen. When you choose a catalog from the list, dBASE displays the names of files associated with that catalog.

The next choice is Modify catalog name. This choice lets you rename the selected catalog. It doesn't affect any of the files in the catalog, it just lets you rename the catalog.

Each catalog or file that you use in dBASE IV has a description associated with it. The last choice in the top section, Edit description of catalog, lets you enter or modify a catalog description. You can enter any one-line description in the highlighted box that is displayed when you choose this option.

The bottom half of the Catalog menu lets you work with the files that are in the catalog. The first choice, Add file to catalog, lets you add an existing file into the catalog. The file can be part of another catalog that was created outside of the active catalog.

The next option, Remove highlighted file from catalog, removes a selected file from the catalog and stops tracking the file. It doesn't delete the file from your disk drive—unless you ask it to when it prompts you—it merely removes it from the catalog.

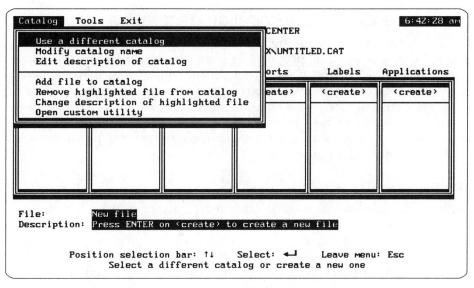

```
 Catalog   Tools   Exit                                    6:42:28 am
        Use a different catalog                  CENTER
        Modify catalog name                      X\UNTITLED.CAT
        Edit description of catalog
                                          orts      Labels      Applications
        Add file to catalog
        Remove highlighted file from catalog      eate>    <create>      <create>
        Change description of highlighted file
        Open custom utility




     File:           New file
     Description:    Press ENTER on <create> to create a new file

              Position selection bar: ↑↓    Select: ↵    Leave menu: Esc
                  Select a different catalog or create a new one
```

6-7   The Control Center with Catalog menu.

The last option in the menu, Change description of highlighted file, allows you to change the description of a file. Just as the catalog has a description, each file also has a description. You normally maintain these descriptions in the individual work surface where the file was created, but by choosing this option you can change them from the Catalog menu as well.

Deleting files   dBASE provides a couple of ways to remove files permanently from your disk. Don't delete anything, right now, while you are reading this section. But do read on to learn how it's done for later use.

You have already learned that you can remove a file from a catalog by selecting a file, and choosing Remove highlighted file from catalog from the Catalog menu, and answering Yes to the first prompt. This option also deletes the file from the disk, if you answer Yes to the second prompt,

Do you also want to delete this file from the disk?

Another way you can remove a file from the catalog, and potentially delete it from the disk, is by highlighting the file and pressing the Del key. dBASE IV displays a menu asking you if you want to remove the file from the catalog. If you wanted to delete the file from the disk you would also want to remove it from the catalog, so you would press Y for Yes. After removing the file from the catalog, dBASE asks if you really want to delete the file from the disk. Answering Yes deletes the file permanently from the disk.

The final option, Open Custom Utility, lets you run an external program through the open architecture feature of the dBASE IV Control Center. This is for advanced users.

Screen, report, and application generators

In the early years of programming, everything that went on inside a computer had to be programmed by people. The computer hardware could perform certain functions, but only if the functions were initiated in some fashion—usually by receiving a specific electronic impulse at a specific point. The impulses were initiated by software commands, each of which had to be entered by a human being. The operating system, the application programs, and the utility functions were all programs aimed at getting the hardware to perform the proper functions.

The purpose of generators

Some of the low-level programs, such as a routine putting letters on a computer screen, were repetitive and could be used in many situations. The only difference is the actual words written on the screen, not the routine writing them. This same philosophy applies not only to screen writing, but also to report printing, disk storage, and other computer functions.

These lower-level functions became utilities—programs useful in many different circumstances to perform a specific function. The difference between each time these tools are used is the input provided.

This same philosophy is being applied to higher functions within application systems. For example, the only difference between an add function for two different databases is the fields used in the function. The basic function of adding a record to the file is the same.

dBASE IV includes generators to produce menus, data-entry screens, reports, and basic application systems. The functions that can be generated automatically are very sophisticated and can fulfill the requirements for most application systems.

The screen generator allows you to place database fields in any chosen position on the screen, arrange text around the fields, and place headings and borders on the screen to give your applications a professional look. Using a generator means that you do not need to know how to write the program yourself—you can place the fields, text, and borders where you want and let dBASE do the rest.

The dBASE software will generate the code that allows the computer to display your screen exactly as you have designed it. The software also takes care of receiving input data from the screen and performing basic editing functions, such as validating the data type of the input. dBASE IV checks that numeric fields contain only numeric data and that date fields are correct. You also can specify that data in particular fields must be within a certain range of values.

Producing reports from stored database fields is another easily automated process. Customized report formats are handled the same as a screen format, where text and fields can be placed in any position. Columnar reports display field values along a line or several lines with headings, footers, totals, and subtotals placed as specified by the entered design. The generated report format also can be used to format fields for printing, such as placing hyphens in a Social Security number or telephone number.

A menu is a text screen that you display from within an application program. The menu gives the application user a set of choices or options for the tasks that the application can perform. The user then chooses which function to do, either by entering a number or letter that corresponds to that function or by moving a highlight with the cursor keys and pressing the enter key to choose the highlighted option.

Creating a menu is easier than producing a screen format. A menu is mostly text information. Once the text is entered and placed on the screen, you need only to identify an operation to perform when an option is chosen. dBASE IV allows you to create different types of menus, including bar and pop-up menus. Using these types of menus, you can produce either menus that "pop up" anywhere on the screen, or you can combine a horizontal bar and pop-up menus to simulate a "pull-down" menu.

Easy-to-use menus will enhance any interactive applications that you will create. The first part of your system that a user will see is the main menu. Users will spend most of their time moving from menu to menu in your application system. The menus also represent the hierarchy of your application system, showing how the functions of the system relate to each other.

dBASE IV can help you generate screens, menus, and reports using your database design. dBASE also includes an Application Generator that will help you to develop application programs to use for your system. Application generators are programs that help you create your own application programs. General procedures—such as the add, change, delete, and display functions—can be created by a program because only the database and fields change. Remember also that you can generate screen formats to use with the database. The creation of a generic function simply involves providing the format file names and the name of the database file.

While you can generate many parts of an application system using dBASE, the generated code probably will not meet all of your requirements, dBASE IV allows you to customize the generated code created by the Application Generator by adding routines to the generated programs. Complete customization might require that you create your own application programs, but you still can reduce development time and problems by using the dBASE IV Application Generator.

Generator concepts

The idea behind a program generator is that certain standard routines can be created and used in almost every circumstance. The procedure for creating a screen format is almost the same from database to database. This is why dBASE can present a "standard" screen layout when you create a database before you have coded a program. This same reasoning applies to reports, especially columnar reports. Also, some application functions can be generated.

For example, each database file should have an add, change, delete, and display function. These functions are necessary for maintenance, even if you have programs that are responsible for updating the database. If the program makes a mistake or somehow an error is entered, these basic functions can be used to make spot corrections and adjustments.

Screen generators and report generators are dependent upon entered text and the fields in a particular database or set of databases. Once you put the text (such as headings and titles) and database fields where you want them, it is easy to generate program code to create the display screen or report page. dBASE IV takes this a step farther by creating this format code in a condensed, quickly executed form, instead of using the dBASE language that some earlier screen generators used.

Application generators use the same general philosophy to create dBASE code for an application function.

Some editing and range checking can be programmed as a part of the screen format. Other application functions can be generated in the same manner. Most functions can be created generically to work in a wide variety of situations.

Screen layouts and what you can do with them

One of the obstacles facing the programmer who wants to write readable modules in dBASE is programming the input, output, and text areas of the screen. The preponderance of commands necessary to draw a screen for a menu or full-screen input function can clutter a program. Screen formats, once decided, change rarely over the life of the system. During development of the system, they might change more frequently, but not as much as the surrounding code. Given the complexity and number of commands, changing a program each time a screen changes is clumsy and unworkable.

Nothing could be done about the complexity of changing screens until the screen format file was added to dBASE. Screen format files allow the programmer to separate the code to display screen formats from the program code, making both sets of code easier to understand and adapt.

All you have to do is create the screen. The screen format generator of dBASE IV allows you to place text and database fields on the screen wherever necessary. You can specify the acceptable data type to be accepted into the field and a range of acceptable values. This way, the basic editing of the input data can be accomplished outside of the program. You accomplish this in a style known in the industry as a WYSIWYG environment ("What You See Is What You Get"—pronounced "wizeewig"). Type text where you want it to appear on the screen. You also can move place-holders for the fields and specify the field names of the fields to place there.

The screen format file contains the compiled version of "@...SAY...GET" commands necessary to build the screen, to define the input fields, and to edit any entered values. The file can be viewed as a type of program file, because it contains executable statements.

Using screen format files also is advantageous if the textual information is changed or new fields are added to the screen. The existing programs do not have to be changed. For example, the company name usually appears at the top of every screen in a system. If the company name changes, or you are developing the system for sale, changing the name involves changing only the screen format files, and not the programs.

One screen format can be used in several programs. Any change made to the screen immediately is reflected in all of the programs. If a new field is added that requires special processing, that portion of the program would have to be added or changed. The basic input and output of the screen format is only changed in one place—the screen format file itself.

The dBASE IV Application Generator also can generate very sophisticated menus for your applications. The entire menu system can be designed very quickly in a WYSIWYG environment, just like the screen formats. You can create pop-up menus, menu bars both vertically and horizontally, and standard "pick a choice" menus.

Reporting concepts

Data processing reports have had the same columnar format for many years. The original data processors were accountants, who liked to see numbers in tables and columns. They could visualize the trends of the business simply by looking at these columns of numbers. Such an ability is either an inborn talent or earned through many years of experience.

Today, the world of computer reporting has changed so that almost any report, graph, picture, or model can be represented in any format. Graphs can be plotted with great precision and clarity; reports can be displayed on a terminal screen—and rearranged at will. A model of the business can be shown on a computer screen with animated graphics showing the flow of goods in and out of the company.

Reports are messages from your application about the actions happening internally to the system. Reports also are the vehicle for moving the business-oriented information from the computer system, where it was gleaned from data, to the manager or executive who can change that information into action.

Computer reports also include customer bills and statements, mailing labels, payroll records and checks, and so forth. Any document that your customers see represents your company to them. If the form appears cold and impersonal, that is the impression they will receive. The final recipients or users of the form also should have a part in its design, but they usually do not. The system designers decide if the form is one that they could use themselves.

Designing a computer report or form is a process just like other forms of design. First, the purpose of the report is defined. Then, all of the people who are involved in producing and using the report have to agree what data items need to be shown on the report in order to produce enough accurate information. Given this fact, it is relatively easy to produce an automated process to create reports. The dBASE IV report generator is a sophisticated tool for creating reports in almost any format you choose. Before discussing the report generator, however, it is necessary to outline some basic reporting concepts.

The tabular, or columnar, report format still is by far the most popular. The problem is that data processors used to looking at this type of report, can "see" the real world represented by the numbers and other information; however, people who do not have this background often need more pictorial methods of describing the data, such as charts or graphs.

Reports produced for higher levels in a company necessarily become less and less detailed. They need to see summaries of the data, not the individual elements. This is necessary to keep business on track. More detailed reports are needed at levels closer to the actual business of the company, where the detail can be dealt with.

Columnar reports have given way in past years to full-page forms. This probably is because of the general proliferation of forms that has filtered to industry from the government. Forms for taxes, grants, contracts, health care benefits, insurance, car registration, driver's license—all of these forms are used by almost everybody at one time or another.

Computer reports can be printed on forms, or in a "forms" arrangement. The reason is to speed the human acquisition and transfer of the data. What this really means is that the completed form is used as a data entry document for a screen format that looks the same as the form, then the most detailed reports also take the same form. This way, quickly needed information can be spotted at the same location on any of the forms at any step in the process.

Another reason that forms are used is the speed at which data can be entered in this manner. Pattern recognition and use is a basic human function; to data entry supervisors and programmers, this means that data entry personnel can enter data items from paper forms and onto screen forms much faster than they could if the incoming data is in a columnar format.

When forms are used in this manner, the detailed output document can be used as a *turnaround* document. This means that the completed report form also can be used for data entry input. The form is changed, either with corrections or updates, and goes back into the front-end of the process.

The dBASE IV report generator can be used alone or within the Application Generator. You can generate columnar reports or custom forms with very little difficulty. Like the screen format, you create the report format by typing text and specifying the fields in a WYSIWYG format.

If you are creating a simple columnar report for a database, the fields in the database definition are listed on the screen. You specify the fields that you want, and the generator will arrange the detail lines of the report accordingly. You can indicate that a field is to be totalled, and the generator will place a total line at the bottom with the totals lined up under the proper column. You also can enter titles, column headings, and titles for the report.

You can mix fields from two related databases in the same generated report. Also, you can use the editing and data formatting functions of the dBASE language to change the format of printed fields so that they are more acceptable to the recipient of the report.

The advantage to using generated report formats, as with screen formats, is that changes to the report can be made without affecting the other application programs in a system. If you wrote a program to print a report, instead of using the report generator, a change to any field or heading would mean a change to all of the programs that print that report.

Working in the dot prompt

Up to this point you have been learning about the dBASE IV Control Center. This is a "front-end" that actually sits on top of dBASE IV and has been translating every action you have made into some dBASE IV program code or command. There is no need in most cases for you to understand these commands because the Control Center makes it easier to use dBASE IV, especially if you are just getting started.

The dot prompt mode is primarily used for programmers or for when you are looking for something so simple that the Control Center actually would take longer. Because this is a book on programming, we use many dot prompt commands as we go. As we introduce new work surfaces from the Control Center, you will see the dot prompt command to enter that same work surface. In the next five chapters, we work primarily with the dot prompt as we learn how to create and manage databases, display and find information, how to sort and index many databases, and work from the work surfaces. When you examine queries, forms, reports and applications, you primarily use the Control Center.

Begin by going to the dot prompt and look at some commands that can help you work.

Removing the status bar

First we need to go to the dot prompt. If your computer is already in the dot prompt, then you are ready. If you are in the Control Center, to exit press Alt–E and then choose Exit to dot prompt. Your screen should look like Fig. 6-8 only without the error box. If you want to remove the status bar, enter

. SET STATUS OFF

at the dot prompt. Don't type the period before the command. This is only to show you that the dot prompt is active. If you want to see it again, enter:

. SET STATUS ON

As we move into later chapters, you will see many of the dot prompt commands necessary to do your work. For now, let's just look at some other uses of the dot prompt.

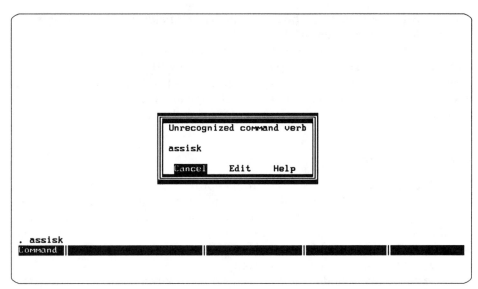

6-8 An error box with dot prompt assist.

Error boxes

Generally you cannot make an error in the Control Center. dBASE IV controls your movements through the menus and doesn't require you to enter any commands. When you are entering commands in the dot prompt however, you may find yourself making mistakes now and then.

As you enter either commands or data you may upon occasion make a typographical error. For example, suppose that you are working within the dot prompt mode and you decide to enter the Control Center. Instead of pressing F2 (ASSIST), enter the command ASSIST at the dot prompt with a typographical error. Figure 6-8 shows the error box for this situation.

dBASE does not recognize this command as entered. You have three choices: to cancel the command and try again, to edit or fix the command, or to ask for help. How much dBASE understands of the command determines where in the help library it places you. If it has no idea, it will place you in the help table of contents.

An electronic blackboard

The dot prompt gives you access to one more power that the Control Center does not—the dBASE blackboard. A simple command called the "question mark" allows you to ask direct questions from dBASE and receive direct answers.

A simple expression might be to add two numbers together:

```
.? 5 + 8
    13
```

dBASE returns the value 13 which is the sum of 5 plus 8. You can also use the electronic blackboard for any calculations with your database. Suppose you had an inventory database and you want to know the current value of BRAND. First let's go to the top of the database. Then display the current value of BRAND:

```
. GO TOP
. ? BRAND
FROSTY
```

dBASE tells you the value of BRAND is FROSTY for the current record. If you wanted to see the value of the current item's QUANTITY*PRICE:

```
. ? QUANTITY*PRICE
          5849.85
```

You might notice that character answers are left justified and numeric answers are right justified. This is normal.

There are also some other operators besides the question mark known as aggregate operators because they automatically work with all of your data. One of these is SUM. SUM gives you a total of an individual field, group of fields, or even calculated fields. This example produces the sum of both the quantities and the quantity times price:

```
. SUM QUANTITY, QUANTITY*PRICE
15 records summed
      quantity        quantity*price
      8354            647309.67
```

The concepts of commands, the dot prompt, and the electronic blackboard are put to good use in the next few chapters as you learn about operators, functions, and the query work surface. As you learn these new concepts, remember that you have both the Control Center and dot prompt available to you at all times.

7
Creating a database

Database is the term given to both the physical and logical means of storing your data in a computer system. A database is a physical file residing on a hard disk or floppy disk medium; a database is also the data that the physical file contains. In the most simple terms, the database is all data available to a company, organization, or individual.

Database files and the database design

An endless number of databases are available. In one sense, the telephone directory is a database. In a business environment, one of the most common databases is a file of customers. A customer file can be used for sales, billing, and marketing purposes, and is found in almost every business where the customer base is more-or-less stable. For example, a supermarket would probably not have a customer file, while a copier sales-and-maintenance company would most likely have this type of database.

Some businesses have a base of regular customers who are billed once a month, along with in-house retail sales to the public. An auto parts store, for example, might keep a list of automobile dealerships and shops that they regularly supply with parts. The auto parts store would also have retail sales that would be tracked using a different method than that used for the large buyers.

A customer database, in its simplest form, contains customers' names (a company name or an individual's name), addresses, and phone numbers (see Fig. 7-1). This basic file can be used in conjunction with other files, such as a customer accounts file for outstanding balances, and a file of items purchased. In a retail business application, other files, such as inventory files, price files, and item description files, might be used to administer inventory, billing, and purchasing applications. Together, all these files make up the database for the business.

Customer database data items	
Data item name	Sample values
CUSTNO	123456, WO8802, AP-001
COMPANY	"Appliance City", "Crazy Freddies"
STREET	"123 First St", "PO Box 10023"
CITY	"Allentown", "South Windsor", "Duff City"
STATE	"PA" or any of the other 50 postal codes
ZIP	12345-6789, 14153
PHONE	(123)456-7890

7-1   The data items for a customer database.

Another example of a database application is a dictionary system. This database would be comprised of two files, the dictionary file and the thesaurus file. The dictionary file contains a single entry for each defined word, with each entry containing three fields: the word, the part of speech (noun, verb, etc.), and its definition. The thesaurus file contains many entries for each word, with each entry comprised of two fields, the search word and another word with the same meaning. Used together, these files could form the basis for a spelling-checker program.

Database constructs

Databases   Although a database is all of the information available to a computer application, a dBASE IV file is also called a database. The database file used by dBASE IV is a standard file created by the operating system and handled like other files. The dBASE IV software is the key that can unlock the data stored in that file. The operating system cannot manipulate the data stored inside the database file; the operating system can only manipulate the file itself.

The database file is stored on a computer medium, most likely on a floppy disk or a hard disk. The file name that is assigned to this file by dBASE IV consists of the database name that you provide, and the file extension of .DBF (for "database file"). For some application programs, a single database file may be all that is needed to perform a function. The personal phone directory application used in the first section of this book, for example, contains only a single database file.

In most cases, several database files might be necessary to form the complete database structure for the application. A key field from one database file is stored on another file as an information field. For example, an invoice file should contain all of the information necessary to create a customer invoice. This information would normally include the customer's name and address so that the invoice could be mailed to the customer in question. If there were several invoices for the same customer on the file, this would lead you to believe that the name and address information would be duplicated for each invoice.

If a second file, called a customer directory, is also available, there would be no need to duplicate the name and address information on each invoice. The invoice database file would contain only the customer number; this customer number would also be the key field of the customer directory database file. Using this method, each time an invoice is to be created and mailed to the customer, the name and address information is retrieved from the customer directory (see Fig. 7-2). This method not only saves space on the invoice database file, but eliminates the problem that would occur when a customer's address changes. Instead of updating many invoices, the information is changed only once—in the customer directory file.

COMPANY	CITY	STATE	ZIP	PHONE
APPLIANCE CITY	OXNARD	CA	95677-	(415) 555-4772
APPLIANCE CITY	HOLLYWOOD	CA	95245-	(213) 555-4766
APPLIANCE WORLD	SAN FRANCISCO	CA	95564-	(415) 555-3353
AVON APPLIANCE	LOS ANGELES	CA	98887-	(415) 555-7963
BOB'S BRANDS	SANTA FE	NM	84545-4545	(434) 555-3444
CARY'S COOLERS	WINDSOR	CT	06773-	(203) 555-7799
CRAZY FREDDIES	NEW YORK	NY	15545-	(212) 555-9974
ERNIES TV	BLEAUVILLE	CA	94454-8946	(213) 555-4975
FRIENDLY APPLIANCE	HERSHEY	PA	15554-	(717) 555-6274
JACKEL & HYDES	LAWRENCEVILLE	PA	14434-	(717) 555-3656
JIM'S HOT AND COLD	VERNON	CA	95565-8784	(213) 555-6473
RANGES ON THE HOME	OKLAHOMA CITY	OK	73344-	(564) 555-3248
RON'S REFRIGERATORS	SAN JUAN CAPISTRANO	CA	95564-6877	(213) 555-5764
THE HOME SHOPPE	SARATOGA	CA	93434-	(415) 555-8355
WASHER WAREHOUSE	LOS ALTOS	CA	97688-	(213) 555-9843
WEST'S WHITE GOODS	CUPERTINO	CA	92324-3342	(213) 555-0478

7-2 An example of a database.

Using these methods, you can build a database structure that can be used by different application programs for varying purposes.

Records Each entry in a database file is called a record. The record is the data for one entity in the database. In a customer directory file, for example, each record represents one customer. In an invoice file, each entry would represent one invoice, while in an invoice-items file, each entry would represent one line item on the invoice, and so on.

A record is the smallest unit of information on the database. Within a database record, fields contain detailed data for that record. Fields are the smallest units of data on the database—but that data does not mean anything without being related to a specific entry.

Database processing, and all data processing in general, is performed in terms of database records. An invoice database would be processed record by record, testing to see if the invoice has been paid, accessing the proper record on the customer directory file for address information, and accessing one or more records on the invoice-items file to create the line items for the invoice. When all of the processing is completed for one invoice record, the next is retrieved and the process starts over again.

Fields   Each database record contains detailed fields that describe the record. If you were to look at a database as a table of information, each line on the table would be a record, while each column would be a database field. The database fields each have their own name or title. The customer directory file has the following fields:

NAME, STREET, CITY, ST, ZIP, and PHONE

You define these fields when you create the database. You can then enter values for these fields into the database. Whenever you wish to use this data, refer to each field by its name. The field names exist to help you use the data that you have stored. You can use field names in various dBASE commands, or you can print reports using the field names for column headings.

Good database design

The first thing you do, after you have decided the functions that your application will perform, is to begin the database design. Your database should have all the fields needed to arrive at the output you want your system to produce. These input or storage fields are all that belong on your database. Any fields that can be calculated should not be included on the database; calculations can be performed faster and more accurately by the computer.

When you are creating a database, keep these limits in mind:

1. Databases can have a maximum of 255 fields.
2. Total length of a record cannot exceed 4,000 characters.
3. Databases can have up to 1 billion records, with a maximum size of 2 billion characters.

As you can see, the only real limitation in dBASE IV is the number of fields. The limitation occurs with the hardware that you are using—a 360K floppy disk, for example, could not hold as many large records as a 20-megabyte hard disk could hold. Later, you will see a method of estimating how large a medium you need to store your own database files.

The first task that you may decide to computerize is your customer file. This is a standard type of database file, and would include the customer's name, address, and phone number. Should the database look like Fig. 7-3?

No, of course not! If you define your database this way, it would be very

Data item	Type	Length
NAME	Character	20
ADDRESS	Character	29
PHONE	Character	10
Total		59

7-3 A database that is difficult to query.

difficult to ask questions and group common types of customers. Rather, divide the database into a format that is easier to get answers from, such as is shown in Fig. 7-4.

Data item	Type	Length
LAST_NAME	Character	10
FIRST_NAME	Character	10
STREET	Character	12
CITY	Character	10
STATE	Character	2
ZIP	Character	5
AREACODE	Character	3
NUMBER	Character	7
Total		59

7-4 A database that is easier to query.

The size of the database has not changed, but it is now easier to use if, for example, you wish to see all customers in Connecticut or Massachusetts. By dividing "conglomerate" fields into their smallest parts, you have gained the ability to manipulate the data with more flexibility.

Note that there is a field called STREET, which is also a conglomerate of several items. You could have divided it into STREET#, STRTNAME, and STRTTYPE, but only in rare circumstances would you actually use these data items. You might never care how many people lived on "lanes" as opposed to "streets" and "roads". You might never ask to see customers who lived at addresses whose number was 32. While you may ask to see all customers who live on Main Street, this can be done regardless of the street number.

What is a database structure?

Each individual database file has a structure that you define when you create the database. The database structure is the "dictionary" to your data—in fact, you will sometimes hear the database structure referred to as the "data dictionary". The database structure is made up of several elements, including the database name, the name of each field, the maximum size of each field, and data type of each field.

Database names The database name should be something meaningful. Actually, all names you use in an application computer system should be meaningful. Remember, some day someone else may have to use this program, or worse: YOU may have to revisit the program after two or three years. Even though you have two lovely children named Sue and Bobby, these names are inappropriate in your computer system. Choose names that indicate what the database contains. In dBASE IV (and using a PC- DOS or MS-DOS operating system) the four rules for creating a database name are shown in Fig. 7-5.

1. The name may be a maximum of eight characters.
2. The first character of the name must be a letter.
3. The other seven characters may be letters, numbers, or underscores.
4. No blanks allowed in the name.

7-5 Database naming rules.

Good database names include: CUSTOMER for a customer file, INVN-TORY for an inventory file, SALE_OCT for an October sales file. Examples of illegal names are 1957SALE (must start with a letter), CUSTOMERS (name too long), and CAR PART (no blanks allowed).

When using dBASE, there is another rule to formatting database names. You may have several database files open at the same time. Each database file occupies a dBASE work area named by a letter A (for the first open area) through J (for the tenth open work area). You can specify a database field by using either the database name or the alias of the work area in a "pointer" construct, for example:

CUSTOMER—>COMPANY

The "dash-greater than" symbol is a pointer—and a way of specifying which database that a field is in. Not only is this good "in program" documentation, but the pointer symbol also allows you to have fields with the same name in different database files.

You could also specify the work area alias (letter A through J) for the database name. For example, if the CUSTOMER database is open in the first work area, the company name could also be referenced as:

A—>COMPANY

In this light, you can see why creating databases with a name A, B, C, and so forth could be very confusing. These names are considered illegal in dBASE IV. Also the letter M, which is used to denote memory variables, should not be used as a database name.

By properly naming your files you will be able to easily recognize and use your databases—and so will everybody else!

Field names   Each field has a field name that you use to search, sort, report, change, or manipulate the data in any way. Each field name in a file must be unique. You can use the same name in different files; when two files share a common key field, the same field name should be used.

As with database names, each field name should be meaningful. Use NAME to represent a person's name, and ZIP_CODE for the zip code. Remember, these names will be used extensively in your programs, so they should be easily recognizable and, if possible, short. This way it will be easier to enter the field name in calculations or expressions. The rules for dBASE IV field names are shown in Fig. 7-6.

1. The name may be a maximum length of ten characters.
2. The first character of the name must be a letter.
3. The other nine characters may be letters, numbers, or underscores.
4. No blanks allowed in the name.

7-6 Field naming rules.

Examples of good names include CUSTOMER, QTY (as long as you note somewhere that QTY means "quantity"), and CITY_ST. Unacceptable names include CUSTOMER_NAME (more than 10 characters), CITY ST (no blanks allowed), or 52_WKS (must start with a letter).

Another method to be avoided is to use the database name in the field name. For example, you might use CUSTNAME for "customer name" where NAME would work just as well. dBASE IV allows you to use the database name when referring to a field, by using a "dash-greater than" (—>) connector: CUSTOMER—>NAME is more readable than CUSTNAME, and is different from SUPPLIER—>NAME or ITEM—>NAME.

Fields Fields in dBASE refer specifically to database fields. You can store intermediate information or data as memory variables (sometimes called *memvars*). Other variables called system variables contain information about the dBASE environment, and thereby make that information available to your programs. Memory variables and system variables also conform to the rules that apply to fields on a database file.

Field names allow us to identify an item of data, such as NAME or ZIP_CODE. The program does not have to be sensitive to the actual contents of these fields in order to move or manipulate them. For example, the computation for Connecticut state sales tax is:

TAX = SUBTOTAL * 0.075

That is to say, the tax is 7.5% (as of this writing) of the taxable subtotal. In this example, the actual value of SUBTOTAL and the resulting value to be placed in TAX are unimportant. The calculation is written the same way no matter what the value that is stored in SUBTOTAL.

To change a field, you can directly input data into the field, you can edit a value already there, or you can use an assignment statement to replace the value in it. No matter what, you always have control over the contents of a field.

Field types dBASE IV supports several different data types, as shown in Fig. 7-7. Each data type conforms to certain rules that govern that type of data.

7-7 The dBASE IV field data types.

Character
Date
Logical
Memo
Numeric
Float

Character fields are fields that will not be used in mathematical expressions. Character fields may contain any value—letters, numbers, special characters, anything! Don't forget that values of all numbers, such as zip codes and social security numbers, can also be character fields, because they will never be used in calculation.

Date fields are special fields used to store dates in a format that can be used in calculations. Date fields are usually used in standard American format of MM/DD/YY (month, day, year). The date field is physically stored in a YYYYMMDD format, so date fields are always eight characters long when stored on the database. Aside from the default MM/DD/YY format, dates can also be displayed in DD/MM/YY format for Canadian and European application, and also with "." or "–" in place of the "/" separator.

Logical fields are data items with only two possible values, true or false. They are always one position in length: either T or F. These are used as a "check-list" type of variable. A field name of VETERAN may be a logical field. If the person is a veteran, the field is set to T, if not it is set to F.

Memo fields contain text that you want to associate with a database record. For example, an EMPLOYEE database may have a memo field containing note on an individual employee's accomplishments for the year for use in a review. A customer file might have a memo field that contains a record of customer interaction or correspondence. This is information that is useful to you for record-keeping, but not information that can be processed easily, unlike invoice amounts and inventory counts. You can think of them as notes that go with a record. When you create screens that contain memo fields, the memo fields are displayed differently than other fields. The word "memo" appears in a four-character entry area. When you press PgDn, you enter the dBASE word processor to enter your memo field data. Memo fields take up ten characters apiece on the database file. The actual text information is stored in a database text file (with the extension .DBT). You can store an almost unlimited amount of text for a single database record.

Numeric fields contain numbers to be used in calculations. When entered on the screen, they also might contain a decimal point and a sign. There are two numeric data types in dBASE IV, the N or fixed-point numeric and the F or floating-point numeric. In business applications, the most common type of numeric field is the fixed-point numeric. Most business applications have calculations that may be dollars and cents (two decimal places) or percentages that may have several decimal places. The results required are almost always between two and five decimal places, which is the range that the fixed-point numeric data type would be used for.

Floating-point numbers are more often used in scientific calculations that require a greater degree of accuracy. The floating-point numeric type is used to store numbers that are very large or very small, such as the width of a bacterium or the distance to another galaxy. This type of notation is also called "scientific notation," where a base number, the characteristic is multiplied by a power of ten, the mantissa. This data type is not used in business applications.

Field and database rules   Just as some rules apply to the formation of field names, some rules apply to the contents and format of the fields themselves (Fig. 7-8).

CHARACTER	- maximum length 254 characters
DATE	- always 8 characters, in a valid date format
LOGICAL	- maximum length of 1 - T (for True) or F (for False)
MEMO	- variable length -- up to 64,000 characters
NUMERIC	- maximum 20 digits
FLOAT	- maximum 19 digits

7-8   The dBASE IV rules for data types.

Like other software, dBASE IV has some limitations although it is capable of creating virtually any application system. dBASE IV can theoretically contain up to one billion records on a database with two billion bytes. However, no storage devices today can store that much data easily and practically. The capabilities of the available hardware are not as great as the theoretical limits of the software.

The largest record possible in a database file is 4000K—that is to say, the sum of the field lengths cannot exceed 4,096,000 characters. Memo field files are "limited" to one billion bytes. These limits are obviously very high, and it is very rare that they are ever tested by a normal application program.

There may be a maximum of 255 fields in a database file. You can have up to 99 files open at one time, including 10 open databases, 10 index files per database, 1 memo field file, 1 format file, and 32 procedure files (or programs). You can open and close files as needed to eliminate any bottleneck that may occur.

Long before you have ever approached these limits, you will have moved on to a different set of software. Remember that these limits are set in laboratory conditions, and real experience is needed to see where the practical limits fall. Your own application could possibly need more than ten open database files at one time—in which case, you might write a program to work around this limitation. Chances are, however, that any application program you write will not even come close. Careful planning and design of your application will point out any potential bottlenecks early enough in the application design that you can choose an alternative solution.

Creating the database structure After you designed an application's data needs and arranged the data items into logical groups, you are ready to define the data to the dBASE IV software. Each group of logically connected data items that are fully dependent on a key field will become a single dBASE IV database file.

In order to create a database definition, use the dBASE CREATE command or use the ⟨create⟩ icon in the "Data" panel of the Control Center to get started. Either way, the same process is executed by dBASE to let you create a new database. The CREATE command would be entered at the dot prompt in the following manner:

```
. CREATE CUSTOMER
```

This starts the process of defining a new database file called CUSTOMER. This database is designed using the specifications found in Fig. 4-19 in chapter 4. The actual database file on the disk will be called CUSTOMER. DBF.

If you start the database creation process from the Control Center, you will see the database definition screen shown in Fig. 7-9. If you had started the process from the dot prompt, the name of the file would already be displayed in the status bar.

dBASE IV is now ready for you to describe the database. You will be asked to enter three, four, or five items for each field. Each column must have a Field Name, Type, Width, and Index. While you have to enter a field width for character fields, and a width/number of decimal places for numeric fields, other data types behave differently. For example, logical fields always have a length of one, date fields always have a length of eight, and memo fields always have a length of ten. These definition items default to the correct size when you enter the data type in the Type column, saving you time and keystrokes.

Numeric field widths are the total width of the field, including any signs, the decimal places, and the decimal point. Make sure that you leave enough room for the entire field. A field defined with a width of 5 and 2 decimals can hold a number only as large as 99.99. The total length is five, including the

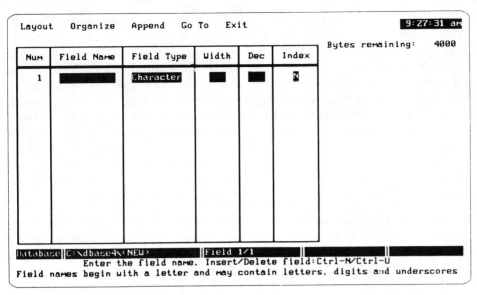

```
  Layout    Organize    Append    Go To    Exit                        9:27:31 am
                                                          Bytes remaining:    4000
 ┌─────┬────────────┬────────────┬───────┬──────┬───────┐
 │ Num │ Field Name │ Field Type │ Width │ Dec  │ Index │
 ├─────┼────────────┼────────────┼───────┼──────┼───────┤
 │  1  │ ▓▓▓▓▓▓▓▓   │ Character  │ ▓▓▓   │ ▓▓▓  │   N   │
 │     │            │            │       │      │       │
 │     │            │            │       │      │       │
 │     │            │            │       │      │       │
 │     │            │            │       │      │       │
 │     │            │            │       │      │       │
 │     │            │            │       │      │       │
 │     │            │            │       │      │       │
 │     │            │            │       │      │       │
 │     │            │            │       │      │       │
 └─────┴────────────┴────────────┴───────┴──────┴───────┘
 Database  C:\dbase4\<NEW>              Field 1/1
            Enter the field name.  Insert/Delete field:Ctrl-N/Ctrl-U
 Field names begin with a letter and may contain letters, digits and underscores
```

7-9   The create database screen.

decimal point. There are two decimal places, leaving only two places to the left of the decimal point.

You must also decide if a field will be used as an index for keeping track of the data in the order of the field values. You'll learn more about this later. For now, you will follow the design in chapter 4, Fig. 4-19, and index the database by the CUSTNO, COMPANY, and ZIP fields as you create them.

You are now ready to enter your definition of the fields in your database. First, enter the name of the field, followed by the other required information. The first field name entered is called CUSTNO. It is a character field six characters long.

The right top corner of the screen shows the number of bytes remaining. A record can have 4000 characters. As you add fields to the definition, each field's length is subtracted from 4000. The first field used 6 bytes, leaving 3994 bytes.

You can move from field to field making changes after you have already defined a field. To insert a field between two existing fields, use the Ctrl–N keystroke. You can delete an existing field with the Ctrl–U keystroke. When you are through entering fields, press Ctrl–End or just press Return on a blank field.

As soon as the field name is entered, the cursor moves to the Type column to enter the proper data type for the field. You can see the various choices by pressing the Spacebar. One of the six choices must be entered: character, numeric, float, date, logical, or memo.

As you finish entering one field, the cursor automatically moves down to the next field to let you begin entering its definition. After you enter each column's name, type, width, and index, you can change fields you defined by using the cursor keys to move between the field names.

Figure 7-10 shows the completed database structure with seven fields defined. The total length of the database record is 103 characters.

```
 Layout    Organize   Append   Go To   Exit              9:29:53 am

                                               Bytes remaining:    3898
 ┌─────┬────────────┬────────────┬───────┬──────┬────────┐
 │ Num │ Field Name │ Field Type │ Width │ Dec  │ Index  │
 ├─────┼────────────┼────────────┼───────┼──────┼────────┤
 │  1  │ CUSTNO     │ Character  │   6   │      │   Y    │
 │  2  │ COMPANY    │ Character  │  20   │      │   Y    │
 │  3  │ STREET     │ Character  │  20   │      │   N    │
 │  4  │ CITY       │ Character  │  20   │      │   N    │
 │  5  │ STATE      │ Character  │   2   │      │   N    │
 │  6  │ ZIP        │ Character  │  10   │      │   Y    │
 │  7  │ PHONE      │ Character  │  13   │      │   N    │
 │  8  │ LST_TXND   │ Date       │   8   │      │   N    │
 │  9  │ DISCOUNT   │ Numeric    │   2   │  0   │   N    │
 │ 10  │ TAXABLE    │ Logical    │   1   │      │   N    │
 │ 11  │            │ Character  │       │      │   N    │
 │     │            │            │       │      │        │
 │     │            │            │       │      │        │
 │     │            │            │       │      │        │
 │     │            │            │       │      │        │
 └─────┴────────────┴────────────┴───────┴──────┴────────┘
 Database C:\dbase4\<NEW>              Field 11/11
             Enter the field name.  Insert/Delete field:Ctrl-N/Ctrl-U
 Field names begin with a letter and may contain letters, digits and underscores
```

7-10 The complete database.

When you have finished entering all of the database fields, you press Ctrl–End to end the definition of the database. At this point, there is a difference in dBASE IV processing that depends on how you arrived at the Create Database work area. If you went to the dot prompt and entered:

. CREATE CUSTOMER

you would continue on to the Input data records now? prompt. If, however, you used the ⟨create⟩ icon on the Control Center menu, you would now be required to enter the name of your database. dBASE opens a small window on the screen where you may enter the database name, as shown in Fig. 7-11.

dBASE then asks if you wish to begin entering records at this point (Fig. 7-12). You may choose to begin entering data into your database immediately, using a default screen format. You could also reply N to this question, and you would be returned to the dot prompt.

You can list the database structure by entering the command:

. DISPLAY STRUCTURE

Figure 7-13 shows the structure for this database.

Notice that the total length is listed as 103 bytes. This is correct. dBASE adds one character to mark a record that has been deleted. Later, you will see

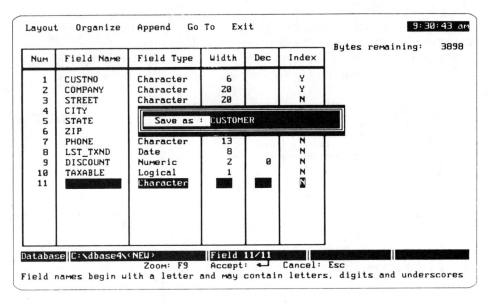

7-11 Entering the database name.

that you can delete records and recall them. You can "hide" the deleted records from processing and, when you are sure that you want to delete them permanently, you can delete them completely off the file.

The DISPLAY STRUCTURE command also displays the number of records in the database (presently zero) and the date of last update. DISPLAY

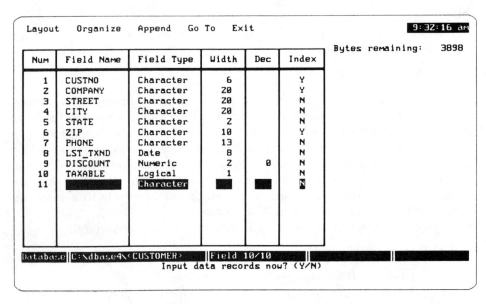

7-12 The Input data records now? prompt.

```
. use customer
. display structure
Structure for database: C:\DBASE4\CUSTOMER.DBF
Number of data records:     16
Date of last update  : 03/15/92
Field  Field Name  Type      Width   Dec   Index
    1  CUSTNO      Character      6            Y
    2  COMPANY     Character     20            Y
    3  STREET      Character     20            N
    4  CITY        Character     20            N
    5  STATE       Character      2            N
    6  ZIP         Character     10            Y
    7  PHONE       Character     13            N
    8  LST_TXND    Date           8            N
    9  DISCOUNT    Numeric        2            N
   10  TAXABLE     Logical        1            N
** Total **                    103
.
Command  C:\dbase4\CUSTOMER          Rec  1/16          File
```

7-13 Reviewing the database.

STRUCTURE can be abbreviated as DISP STRU—all dBASE commands can be abbreviated to four characters for ease of use. Some of the examples in the rest of this chapter contain the 16 records that you designed in chapter 4. If you need to remember these, refer back to Fig. 4-22. You might put them in now if you are following along or read chapter 8 first before you fill the databases with data.

You have now finished defining the CUSTOMER database structure. At the end of the chapter you will also want to define the INVENTRY, INVOICE, and ITEMS files that were designed in chapter 4.

Files, indices, and catalogs

Another part of your database structure, in an overall sense, is the way that a database file interacts with your application and with other files. Related databases and the means to relate them must be part of your data design for your application. All of the files that can be used with your database should be documented for future reference. When you first create your database file, you are already using the database file itself—but you have the option of creating an index file. You have also already created an entry in the catalog file. You should be able to identify all of the files associated with your database.

Almost immediately, you might want to change the order of records in your database. For example, you might enter all of your customers or have two or more data entry clerks enter the information for you. You might then want to combine all of the customer records into a single dBASE database file. If the customer file is to be ordered by customer number you could, at the very beginning of creating your application, sort the file by this data item. The final result is your ready-to-use customer database.

Your application might also require that you place the database into order by last name for certain functions. This seeming contradiction is easily performed by using an index file or index tag, and indexing the database by last name. An index could also be created for customer number, even though your database is already sorted into this order.

Each record on the database file is assigned a record number. If you think of a dBASE IV database like a table of values, then the fields become the columns of the table, and the records become the rows in the table. The tabular view of a database can be seen using the dBASE IV BROWSE command, as shown in Fig. 7-14.

```
 Records    Fields    Organize    Go To    Exit                    9:35:27 am

 CUSTNO COMPANY              STREET              CITY                 STATE ZI

 AP-001 APPLIANCE CITY       210 SKY LANE        OXNARD                CA   95
 AP-002 APPLIANCE CITY       360 ACE AVE         HOLLYWOOD             CA   95
 AP-003 APPLIANCE WORLD      20695 BLUE BIRD AVE SAN FRANCISCO         CA   95
 AV-001 AVON APPLIANCE       1687 NEW PLACE ROAD LOS ANGELES           CA   98
 BO-001 BOB'S BRANDS         BOB'S DRIVE         SANTA FE              NM   84
 CA-001 CARY'S COOLERS       60 STRAWBERRY HILLS WINDSOR               CT   06
 CR-001 CRAZY FREDDIES       1820 171ST ST       NEW YORK              NY   15
 ER-001 ERNIES TV            456 SNOW PLOW AVE   BLEAUVILLE            CA   94
 FR-001 FRIENDLY APPLIANCE   26 CHOCOLATE AVE    HERSHEY               PA   15
 JA-001 JACKEL & HYDES       357 BAT COURT       LAWRENCEVILLE         PA   14
 JI-001 JIM'S HOT AND COLD   55 SKINNER ROAD     VERNON                CA   95
 RA-001 RANGES ON THE HOME   23 OLD OKIE DR      OKLAHOMA CITY         OK   73
 RO-001 RON'S REFRIGERATORS  141 HOLLOW OAK PLACE SAN JUAN CAPISTRANO  CA   95
 TH-001 THE HOME SHOPPE      25 APPLIANCE LANE   SARATOGA              CA   93
 WA-001 WASHER WAREHOUSE     15525 MARINER DR    LOS ALTOS             CA   97
 WE-001 WEST'S WHITE GOODS   26 DENNIS LANE      CUPERTINO             CA   92

 Browse   C:\dbase4\CUSTOMER      Rec 1/16          File

                         View and edit fields
```

7-14 The tabular view of a database using BROWSE.

dBASE numbers the rows with this record number; this number is used in all of the record and database manipulation that dBASE performs. The software "keeps track" of the current record by maintaining a current record pointer, which contains the record number of the current database record. You can change the current record pointer using the GO command. For example, the commands:

. USE CUSTOMER
. GO 15

cause dBASE to open the database file CUSTOMER.DBF, then to change the current record pointer to 15, "positioning" dBASE to the fifteenth physical record on the database file.

When you create a dBASE database, you have the option of marking any field as an index field. An index contains the key field or expression along with the record number of the record associated with that key field. The index is in order by that key field, so that when the dBASE software is using the index to "order" the database, the records appear in a different logical order. You can also create an index from EDIT and BROWSE. This allows you to reorder the records as you are viewing them.

There are two types of index files. In prior versions of dBASE each index resided in a single file, which had an extension of .NDX. Up to seven index files could be used and updated at one time with a database. The .NDX type of index file is still supported by dBASE IV.

When you are using an index file, the order of the records that you see on the database depends on the order of the key field in the index. The physical order of records is not important. For example, the command:

. GO 1

changes the current record pointer to the first physical record on the file. This is not necessarily the same record as would appear on the file first were it in order by some field. The commands GO TOP and GO BOTTOM are used to move to the first and last record, respectively, based on the index order.

dBASE IV has the ability to store multiple indexes in a single file, which has the file extension of .MDX (for multiple-index). Each .MDX file (or *mindex*) contains the information for 47 index expressions, and thereby taking the place of 47 old- style .NDX files. Each individual index is called a tag in the .MDX file.

A multiple-index file that has the same file name as the database that the mindex is used with is called a production .MDX file. For example, the CUSTOMER.DBF file that you have created is associated with CUSTOMER-.MDX, if you have indexed any fields. Because you indexed the database by the CUSTNO, COMPANY, and ZIP fields, an .MDX file was created with three tags. The following sequence of commands:

. USE CUSTOMER
. INDEX ON CUSTNO TAG CUSTNO

would create an index tag labeled CUSTNO in the file CUSTOMER.MDX if it didn't already exist. If CUSTOMER.MDX did not exist, it too would be created. To create another tag for the field STATE, enter the command:

. INDEX ON STATE TAG STATE

and the tag STATE is added to the mindex file. Indexing your databases makes the process of relating two or more databases easier and more efficient for the dBASE software. Indexing also allows you to rearrange data and to directly access records in a database.

All of the files directly involved in your database, including the database (.DBF) file, the mindex (.MDX) file, and the database text (.DBT) file (if present), and other related files are stored in a dBASE catalog (.CAT) file. The catalog file holds lists and descriptions of other types of dBASE IV files. Using a catalog file helps you keep files grouped for easier access and use. If you have many applications, you may have one or more catalog files for each application.

You might start your actual definition of the application to the dBASE IV software by creating the application's catalog. For example, you probably don't have any catalog entered yet. Or, perhaps you already created the Ajax catalog as shown in chapter 6. Regardless, if you need to create a new catalog (in this case study—Ajax), your first step would be either to enter the command:

. SET CATALOG TO Ajax

or to use the ⟨create⟩ icon on the Control Center Catalog menu, as shown in Fig. 7-15. New catalogs are created by opening the Catalog menu of the Control Center and choosing Use a different catalog. In either case, the catalog file Ajax.CAT is created. As long as Ajax is the catalog file in use, any new files will be added to the catalog.

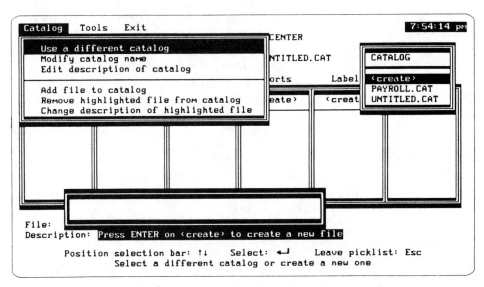

7-15   Creating a new catalog with the Control Center.

Using a catalog file enables you to use the "look up" feature of many dBASE file commands. For example, if you wanted to open a database file, but you were not quite sure of the name of the file, you could enter:

. USE ?

dBASE IV then accesses the currently-open catalog file and displays a list of database files that could be substituted for the ? in the USE command. You can move the highlight with the cursor keys and choose the database file that you want. This is useful not only for switching between files, but also if you have a bad memory for database names.

However, the beauty of the Control Center is that all of the files in your catalog are always displayed in the panels. Figure 7-16 shows the result of the CUSTOMER file being added to the catalog. If the catalog was in use when the CUSTOMER file was created, then it would be added automatically. In this case the menu choice Add file to catalog was made from the Catalog menu of the Control Center.

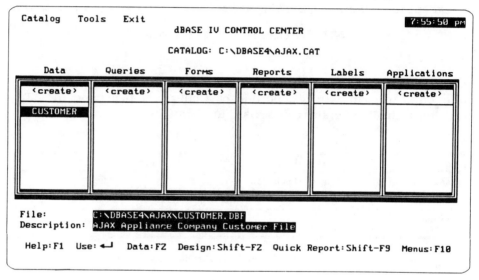

7-16   An example of using a catalog.

Defining fields

Fields have guidelines controlling their size and allowable values.

dBASE IV data types

The six field data types are character, numeric, float, date, logical, and memo.

Character   Character fields are used to store names, addresses, and other small amounts of textual data. A character field, defined on screen without a picture, accepts any character (see Fig. 7-17).

When combined with the PICTURE clause, character fields can contain any type of data in any format. This can be useful in temporary storage of dates in formats other than the common dBASE date formats.

Character fields or character string memory variables can be used in performing character operations. The most common character operation is an assignment—a character value can be copied from one character field to another. Character fields can be concatenated with other character fields

```
Character Fields:
```

Data type:	C
Maximum Length:	254 characters
Minimum Length:	1 character
Allowable Values:	All codes* from X'00' to X'FF' Usually alphanumeric

*Exception: Ctrl-Z (X'1A') which marks end of file.

7-17 The character field specifications.

using the "+" and "−" operators of dBASE IV (Fig. 7-18). The SUBSTR( ) function is used to extract a portion of a character field, and the AT( ) function or the "$" operator can be used to identify the contents.

Operation	Statement	Resulting value in VAR
Assignment (=)	VAR = 'ABCDEF'	'ABCDEF'
Concatenation (+)	VAR = 'DR ' + 'JONES'	'DR JONES'
Trimmed Concatenation (−)	VAR = 'JOHN ' − 'JONES'	'JOHNJONES '

7-18 The character operations.

Character fields are stored as a string and padded with blanks. The LEN( ) function returns a numeric value that is the length of the character string. This only applies to memory variables that are assigned strings of varying lengths. Character fields residing on a database always show a length that is the same as the field length, unless the TRIM( ) function is used as well.

Numeric Numeric fields can be used for any type of arithmetic data. Any purely mathematical function or operation must have numeric variables as its component operands. Numeric fields are stored as character strings in a dBASE database, right-justified and blank filled. dBASE translates these numbers into binary/hexadecimal values for calculations.

The length of a database numeric field is specified on the Create screen, including sign and decimal point. A field of length 7 with 2 decimal places can contain values in the range 9999.99 to −999.99 (see Fig. 7-19).

In dBASE, almost any place a numeric value may be used, a numeric result of a calculation or function may be substituted. The calculation or function is done first, and the resulting value used in the statement (see Fig. 7-20).

```
┌─────────────────────┐
│ Numeric Fields:     │
└─────────────────────┘
```

Data type:	N
Maximum Length:	20 characters, including decimal point and signs Maximum decimal places: 18*
Minimum Length:	2 characters
Allowable Values:	Digits 0 through 9, +, -, .

```
┌──────────────────────────────────────────────┐
│ * Note: the number of decimal places must be  │
│         at least 2 less than the total length.│
└──────────────────────────────────────────────┘
```

7-19 The numeric field specifications.

Float   Floating point fields are also numeric fields that are used in calculations. The difference is that floating point fields yield results that are more accurate than standard fixed-point arithmetic. These numbers are used in scientific calculations where great precision is needed. The real difference between the Numeric data type and the Float data type is in how dBASE IV stores the fields internally (see Fig. 7-21). You could choose to use either data type in your application. You should be consistent within your application.

Date   Date fields are stored as character strings eight characters long in the format YYYYMMDD (Fig. 7-22). This is the most utilitarian format of the Gregorian date that is commonly used. The advantage of storing dates in this format is that numeric comparisons of greater or lesser values work correctly without the need for multiple comparisons and conversions.

dBASE IV also allows a limited range of calculations to be performed on date fields. Days may be added to a date, yielding another date; dates may also be subtracted from one another, yielding the number of days between them.

Operation	Statement	Resulting value in VAR
Assignment (=)	VAR = 123.45	123.45
Addition (+)	VAR = 42 + 64	108
Subtraction (-)	VAR = 42 - 64	-22
Multiplication (*)	VAR = 42 * 64	2688
Division (/)	VAR = 42 / 7	6
Exponent (**)	VAR = 2 ** 8	256

7-20 The numeric operations.

Data type:	F
Maximum Length:	19 characters, including decimal point and signs Maximum decimal places: 15*
Minimum Length:	2 characters
Allowable Values: Digits 0 through 9, +, -, .	

* Note: the number of decimal places must be at least 2 less than the total length.

7-21 The floating point specifications.

Dates in dBASE can be stored with up to five digits of century, allowing a vast range of dates to be stored. This means that historical scholars could create a time line using dBASE IV, using memo fields to store a narrative text. The database might then be used to produce time lines and other educational aids.

A new SET command, SET CENTURY ON, allows you to display and enter dates with a full four digits of year. This can be very helpful; the year 2000 A.D. is fast approaching, and many systems might become obsolete simply because they are geared toward 19*xx* dates. All formats of date are changed to display four-digit years by SET CENTURY ON.

When SET CENTURY OFF is entered, the full year may not be entered with @GET; the format is strictly MM/DD/YY (based on the particular type of date—see the next part). Using this format, the century number 19 is always assumed. Dates greater than 12/31/1999 and less than 01/01/1900 may be calculated with, but not displayed in, a date field—unless SET CENTURY is ON.

Date Fields:

Data type:	D
Length:	8 characters
Stored as:	YYYYMMDD
Default display:	MM/DD/YY
Allowable Values: Valid date values	

7-22 The date field specifications.

The correct century can always be accessed by using the YEAR( ) function. By using PICTURE, the CTOD( ) function, and a memory variable, dates outside of the twentieth century can be converted to dBASE date format without the use of SET CENTURY.

dBASE IV can be used to store other date formats that are not software supported—which means, of course, you must program the conversion yourself. This would mean that you could store the information in a character string, then format the date and edit it using a separate program or user-defined function.

dBASE IV accepts input into date fields in the format MM/DD/YY when SET CENTURY is OFF, MM/DD/YYYY when SET CENTURY is ON. When SET CENTURY is OFF, the year, even though only two digits long, is stored as 19YY on the database.

dBASE IV allows several formats of Gregorian date, notably the American, ANSI (American National Standards Institute), British, French, German, and Italian. Figure 7-23 shows the various date format names and the resulting date formats, assuming SET CENTURY is OFF.

SET DATE command	Date format
SET DATE AMERICAN	mm/dd/yy
SET DATE ANSI	yy.mm.dd
SET DATE BRITISH	dd/mm/yy
SET DATE ITALIAN	dd-mm-yy
SET DATE FRENCH	dd/mm/yy
SET DATE GERMAN	dd.mm.yy
SET DATE JAPAN	yy/mm/dd
SET DATE USA	mm-dd-yy
SET DATE MDY	mm/dd/yy
SET DATE DMY	dd/mm/yy
SET DATE YMD	yy/mm/dd

7-23   The dBASE IV date formats.

The maximum flexibility is offered by dBASE IV, because the character inserted between the parts of a date may also be changed to any character the user may desire. The command SET MARK TO allows you to change the inserted character in any of the previous date formats. For example, if you wanted to insert exclamation points into your date values, you could enter the commands:

```
. SET DATE MDY
. SET MARK TO "!"
```

If you display a date field after this, the format is changed to the MM/DD/YY format, except that exclamation points replace the diagonals. The date 12/31/88, for example, would appear as:

12!31!88

The most useful form of date is the YYYYMMDD format of the standard Gregorian date that dBASE stores its dates in. This format allows dates to be compared, since the format is in ascending order of change. This means that the date 19860704 tests greater than 19851231. This would not be the case using any other arrangement. This format can be achieved by using the ANSI date format with SET CENTURY ON.

Logical   The dBASE Logical data type is for fields that contain simple "yes" or "no" values. Logical fields are also known as binary (or bit) switches because they have only two possible values. Logical fields provide a readable way to test control information in a program. The logical field name can be created in such a way as to make decision statements understandable at a glance (see Fig. 7-24).

Logical Fields:	
Data type:	L
Maximum Length:	1 character
Minimum Length:	1 character
Allowable Values:	T, t, F, f, Y, y, N, n

7-24   The logical field specifications.

For example, an employee database might have a field that indicates whether or not a person is a veteran of one of the Armed Forces. Rather than using this following statement to interrogate the value:

IF EMPLOYEE—>VETIND = 'Y' ...

this much more readable statement can be used

IF EMPLOYEE—>VETERAN ...

Logical fields are stored in a database record as single characters (length one) with values of T, t, Y, and y interpreted as true; the characters F, f, N, and n are considered false. In an IF statement, only the variable name is used; comparisons using logical fields do not work in dBASE IV.

Memo Database systems do not often offer a way of storing large amounts of text. After all, that is not really a function of a database, because text is random rather than being in a readily identifiable format. There is no easy way of breaking the text into discrete data items, because most text is meaningful only in conjunction with the rest of the text in the document.

What is a memo field? dBASE IV, however, allows text lines (i.e., a document) to be stored with the database information. The actual text is stored separately from the "real" data, but can be accessed as if it were physically present on the database record by means of a memo field. The physical memo field on the database record is not a field that the dBASE user can access. It contains information that helps dBASE find the textual information, which is actually stored in another file. Such referencing fields are called pointers. The memo field points to the stored text.

Any number of memo fields may exist in a database, although, most often, only one is necessary (see Fig. 7-25). Each memo field in the database uses 10 characters on the database file, and at least 512 characters in the associated .DBT file. The .DBT (DataBase Text) file is created when a memo field is placed on a database; only one .DBT file is associated with the database file, no matter how many memo fields the database contains.

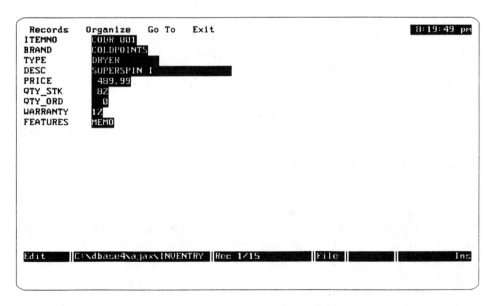

7-25 An example of a memo field.

The maximum length of a memo field is 64K characters, if you are using the dBASE internal word processor. You may select your own favorite word processor or editor to edit the memo fields; the limit to the size of the memo is based on the limits of the editor you are using.

Memo fields can be used for several purposes, depending on the requirements of the dBASE user (you). One way of using a memo field is to place a history of changes made to a particular database record, called a change log. When a record is changed, the operator can enter the memo text and add a line describing the change, the date, and so forth. This type of honor-system audit trail can save confusion later, especially in the order that changes occurred.

Another way that a memo field could be used is to store resumes in a personnel system, or a work history for an employee. They can be used to store descriptions of items, appointment reminders, and exceptional processing conditions for the record.

How do memo fields differ from character fields? A character field contains a single, unique data item that happens to be character in format. One example of a character field is a NAME field—the NAME can be used in many ways throughout the system, for reports, mailing labels, and screen titles. NAME becomes a single field on the database because it is used in so many different ways. Character fields have the advantage of being flexible, in that they can be rearranged and used in any order.

A memo field, on the other hand, is used to store text—which is usually a free-form document, meant to be read as a single unit. The text is not actually used by the application system at all except to display it in its entirety with no modifications.

For example, you might store the mailing label for a customer in a memo field on the database record. Then, instead of reformatting the character fields on the database record, you could simply print the memo field on the label. This is not a good practice—if the character fields already exist, and you add their values to a memo field, there would be duplication of data on the database.

A database cannot be indexed or sorted based on data stored in a memo field. dBASE IV has functions that allow you to access and manipulate memo fields from within a program. You could store character information in a memo field and retrieve this information later for use in program processing. This would require greater access time, causing the program to take longer than if the formatted data was already part of the database.

How do you use memo fields? A memo field is created by choosing Memo as the field type of a field when you are defining your database. Each memo field uses ten characters on the database record. This field contains a pointer to the text information. The text is stored in another file, with the extension .DBT.

You cannot put data into the field directly on the screen. The screen display for the memo field simply says "memo"—until you press Ctrl–PgDn or Ctrl–Home (see Fig. 7-26). Doing this opens up the dBASE word processor, where you may then add or change the text lines in the memo field. You can also define a window to show some of the memo field text on the screen (see Fig. 7-27).

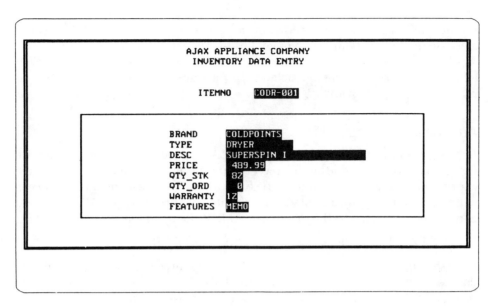

7-26 A memo field marker displayed on screen.

Once the word processor is activated, dBASE retrieves the text from the memo-storage file. The contents of the memo field are then displayed over the current screen. The screen is not erased from memory—dBASE just "overlays" the screen with the full-screen text editor. This process is called windowing; pressing Ctrl–PgDn opens a window to the memo text. This

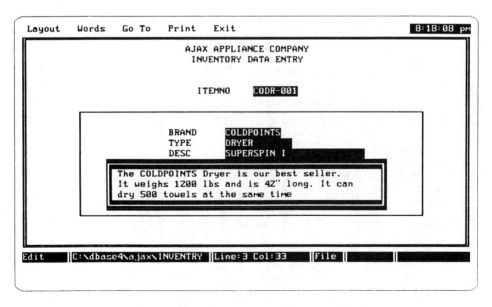

7-27 Memo text displayed in a window.

method allows you to view or edit the contents of the memo field. You could also use the F9 or Zoom key to open a full-screen window for text entry.

The memo field can also be printed. The report generator of dBASE IV allows you to print a memo field, using an area that you can change to whatever width you want.

Automatic indexing

As you are defining fields during the CREATE process, you can specify the fields that are to be the main key of your database. This will be the key expression that would be used for the first index of the database. This process will create an index tag and place the tag into the "production" .MDX file. You can create other tags in the production .MDX file by using the command:

. INDEX ON <key expression> TAG <tagname> [FOR <comparison>]

All of the tags in the production .MDX file are updated continuously while the database is open with the production .MDX file. The SET ORDER TO command determines the current master index—that is to say what index order the database will appear in. SET INDEX can be used to open other .MDX or .NDX files. All open indexes are updated if the database file is updated.

If you are using the dBASE IV Control Center, you can also change the order of your database and create new index tags. The Organize menu, as shown in Fig. 7-28, contains the options necessary. You may also access the Organize menu from the BROWSE and EDIT work surfaces.

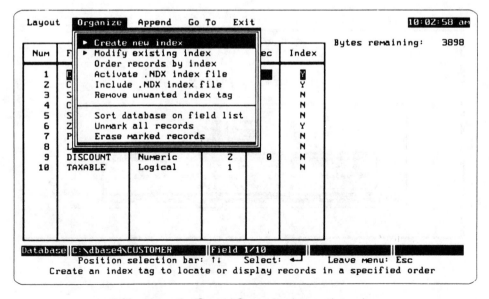

7-28 Using the Control Center to change the order.

A total of 47 indexes can be open at once, including .NDX files and .MDX tags. This means that if you have a completely full .MDX file, containing 47 index tags, no other index files could be open at the same time.

You also do not have to rely on automatic index updating. You could, from within an application program, reindex the file via the program command REINDEX. REINDEX updates all open index files.

The physical database

The dBASE programmer has little reason for knowing the physical internal structure of a database, other than curiosity. dBASE IV performs all of the operations necessary to retrieve and replace records, so that the dBASE user has no real need to know the file structure.

What can be realized from studying the physical structure of a dBASE database is the knowledge that dBASE is not performing a magical function. There are reasons that dBASE behaves in the manner it does, mostly dependent on the database file organization. The techniques used by dBASE IV in file storage and retrieval can be applied to other applications, even those written in dBASE.

A dBASE database is divided into three main areas: the header, the field descriptions, and the data. The information stored in the header and field descriptions is what makes dBASE "tick;" this describes the data stored in the data area and provides other information so that dBASE can perform the operations it does.

The database header area contains general information about the database. This information includes the number of data records contained on the database, the date of the last update to the database, the length of each data record, and an indicator that specifies whether or not a memo field exists on the database (Fig. 7-29). The header also contains a pointer to the first record in the data area.

The field that stores the number of records on the database is a 32-bit number, which is where the dBASE specification of a "1,000,000,000" record limit comes from. This may be the largest number that can fit into a 32-bit binary field, but that many records, depending on their size, would be beyond the storage capacities of most machines.

In computer processing, 32-bit numbers work like other binary numbers. The data is stored with the bytes in reverse order; the leftmost byte of the number contains the rightmost two hexadecimal digits (Fig. 7-30).

The date of last update contained in the header is also stored in binary; one byte each is allocated to year, month, and day. Other numbers on the database header are in the "normal" low byte-high byte 16-bit binary format. The first character of the header indicates if a memo field is contained in this database, so that dBASE can prepare for its access. Finally, a large area of the header is not used; this is reserved for use by dBASE at a later date.

Each field on the database is represented by an entry in the field description area. Each entry is 32 characters long, and contains all informa-

dBASE database

		Position	Length	Description
Header (32 bytes)		0	1	X'03' (constant) (X'83' if database contains memo fields)
Field descriptor (32 bytes each)				
Field descriptor		1	1	Last update date year
Field descriptor		2	1	Last update date month
. . .		3	1	Last update date day
Data		4	4	Number of records
		8	2	Position of first record
		10	2	Record size
		12	2	Reserved
		14	1	Incomplete transaction flag
		15	1	Encryption flag
		16	12	Reserved for network use
		28	1	Production .MDX file flag
. . .		29	3	Reserved

7-29 Database header structure.

tion necessary for dBASE IV to recognize and work with the data in that field. Included are the field name, its length, the number of decimal places, and the data type. Also, a large area is reserved for future expansion, and a field is an internal memory pointer to a dBASE buffer. This last field can only be deciphered and used by dBASE IV (Fig. 7- 31).

The data area of the database contains all of the data records in the order they were placed on the file. No special codes go between records, because the record length is available from the header area. Each record contains one more character than the field descriptions allow for, the "unseen" deletion indicator; this field is accounted for in the header's record length field (see Fig. 7-32).

Each field in the data area is stored as a character string. The number of characters is defined by the field length; there are no varying-length fields,

Number 1653 in hexadecimal:	X'0675'
16-bit number stored as:	75 06

Number 28667010 in hexadecimal:	X'01B56C82'
32-bit number stored as:	82 6C B5 01

7-30 32-bit numbers.

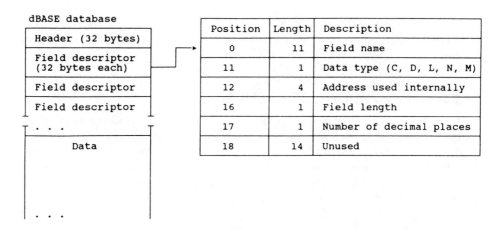

Position	Length	Description
0	11	Field name
11	1	Data type (C, D, L, N, M)
12	4	Address used internally
16	1	Field length
17	1	Number of decimal places
18	14	Unused

dBASE database

Header (32 bytes)

Field descriptor (32 bytes each)

Field descriptor

Field descriptor

. . .

Data

. . .

7-31 The field description structure.

nor is any compression performed to rid the file of unneeded blanks. Character, float, and numeric fields are stored as they are viewed; numeric and float fields contain blanks in place of leading zeros.

Date fields are stored as character strings, in the format YYYYMMDD. The four-digit year is also used in a slightly different manner; the first position can represent one or two digits, depending on the year. If a date with five positions of year is placed in a date field, the first position of the stored field contains a hexadecimal code that represents the first two digits. Dates with four digits of year, or less, will be stored in character-string format.

Logical fields contain the value placed into them by the full-screen operation or REPLace command used to store the value. The values Y, y, T, and t represent "true" or "on" switches; N, n, F, and f are "false" or "off" values. These values are also redisplayed during full-screen operations.

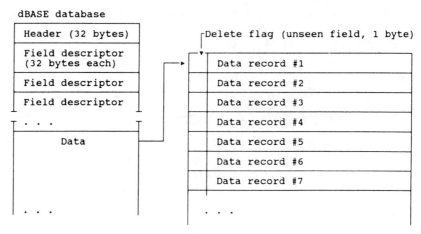

7-32 The data structure.

Memo fields use ten characters of storage on the record. This area stores a pointer into the memo field file (.DBT) associated with the database being accessed.

Calculating your database size

You can plan the amount of disk space you need for a database by using a simple formula. This will aid you in planning the application system for your computer, and for planning for the future of that system.

dBASE IV has a database header that consists of certain fields in certain positions. If you know the format of the header area, you can determine the approximate size of a database file with great accuracy.

The dBASE IV database header area has 32 characters for overall database information, another 32 characters each for each field definition, and 1 character that separates the header from the data area. If you know approximately how many records are placed on a certain database file, the length of the fields on the record, and the number of fields, you can take an accurate guess at how much disk space the database file will use. The formula is:

32	(length of database header)
+ (32 * number of fields)	(length of field definitions)
+ 1	(length of separator)
+ (approximate number of records * record size)	

Each database record also has an indicator that flags deleted records in the file. Add one to the total of the field lengths to arrive at the actual record size.

For example, the total of the field lengths in the CUSTOMER database is 102. Add 1 for the delete flag, making the record size 103. There are 10 fields on the database, so the number of characters or bytes needed to store a database that contains 1000 records would be:

32 + (32 * 10) + 1 + (1000 * 103)

or approximately 103,353 characters (see Fig. 7-33).

Changing a database definition

Once you have created and saved a database, you can change the database definition and still keep any data that may have been entered. This is so that you can correct mistakes or add fields to the database if needed. The command:

. MODIFY STRUCTURE

lets you change the database structure.

```
Structure for database: C:\DBASE4\CUSTOMER.DBF
Number of data records:      16
Date of last update    : 09/05/88
Field   Field Name   Type        Width    Dec    Index
    1   CUSTNO       Character      6               Y
    2   COMPANY      Character     20               Y
    3   STREET       Character     20               N
    4   CITY         Character     20               N
    5   STATE        Character      2               N
    6   ZIP          Character     10               Y
    7   PHONE        Character     13               N
    8   LST_TXND     Date           8               N
    9   DISCOUNT     Numeric        2               N
   10   TAXABLE      Logical        1               N
** Total **                       103
```

Size computation:

Database header size	32 characters	
Field descriptors (10 * 32)	320 characters	(10 * 32 characters)
Separator	1 character	
Data area for 50 records	5150 characters	(50 * 103 characters)
Total	5503	

7-33   The customer file definition and size computation.

The Modify Structure menu, shown in Fig. 7-34 on page 312, is used to change the database structure. The modify structure screen is the same menu used to create the database definition during the CREATE process. Once you choose the database you want to work with, dBASE displays the database structure in exactly the same form.

```
 Layout   Organize   Append   Go To   Exit                    9:49:58 am

                                               Bytes remaining:    3898
 ┌─────┬────────────┬────────────┬───────┬──────┬────────┐
 │ Num │ Field Name │ Field Type │ Width │ Dec  │ Index  │
 ├─────┼────────────┼────────────┼───────┼──────┼────────┤
 │  1  │ CUSTNO     │ Character  │   6   │      │   Y    │
 │  2  │ COMPANY    │ Character  │  20   │      │   Y    │
 │  3  │ STREET     │ Character  │  20   │      │   N    │
 │  4  │ CITY       │ Character  │  20   │      │   N    │
 │  5  │ ▮▮▮▮▮      │ Character  │ ▮▮▮   │ ▮▮▮  │   N    │
 │  6  │ STATE      │ Character  │   2   │      │   N    │
 │  7  │ ZIP        │ Character  │  10   │      │   Y    │
 │  8  │ PHONE      │ Character  │  13   │      │   N    │
 │  9  │ LST_TXND   │ Date       │   8   │      │   N    │
 │ 10  │ DISCOUNT   │ Numeric    │   2   │  0   │   N    │
 │ 11  │ TAXABLE    │ Logical    │   1   │      │   N    │
 └─────┴────────────┴────────────┴───────┴──────┴────────┘

 Database C:\dbase4\CUSTOMER        Field 5/11
            Enter the field name. Insert/Delete field:Ctrl-N/Ctrl-U
 Field names begin with a letter and may contain letters, digits and underscores
```

7-34   Modifying the database.

Once on the Modify Structure menu, use the cursor keys to move between the fields. Rename the field simply by typing the new name, or change the definition of the field by entering the new length or data type.

The Ctrl–N key sequence allows you to insert a new field between two existing fields. By moving the cursor to an existing field and pressing Ctrl–N, the fields below move down one row, allowing a new field to be defined. The Ctrl–U keystrokes delete the field where the cursor currently positioned.

When you change a database structure, the data that is already in the database file is copied to a temporary storage area. After the database structure is changed, the data is copied back into the data structure on a field by field basis, going by the names of the old fields versus the names of the new. This means that if you change a field name, the data is not copied in from the temporary file. If you add a new field, all the existing records will contain no data for that specific field.

Cloning a database structure

dBASE IV also gives you many facilities to maintain and manipulate your database files. You can clone database structures to new files, copying all or part of the data to the new file. You can also import and export dBASE data into standard data format, or into several popular data formats for other database software.

To clone a database structure without change and without copying any records, you can use the command:

. COPY STRUCTURE TO ⟨dbname⟩

If you clone the structure of a database or part of the structure to create a new database file, you can then use the MODIFY STRUCTURE command to change the cloned structure in any way needed. This allows you to build a new database but retain the existing fields. You could copy the data with the same command, by removing the word STRUCTURE:

. COPY STRUCTURE TO CUSTNEW FIELDS COMPANY, PHONE, ZIP

This command would create a new database called CUSTNEW.DBF that contains the fields COMPANY, PHONE, and ZIP. The MODIFY STRUCTURE command then allows you to add new columns to the database as needed.

The COPY STRUCTURE command lets you copy field definitions without any data to create a new database. If you do not specify any fields on the COPY command, all of the database fields are copied to the new database. To create a new database with only the COMPANY, PHONE, and ZIP fields you would enter the command:

. USE CUSTOMER
. COPY STRUCTURE TO CUSTNEW FIELDS COMPANY, PHONE, ZIP

The COPY command is also used to export data. You can create several types of data files, as shown in Fig. 7-35.

DELIMITED WITH BLANK--Fields are separated with blanks instead of with commas and quotes.
DELIMITED--Standard delimited file, each field separated by a comma, character fields enclosed in quotes.
SDF--System Data Format--Data is in normal ASCII format, each field the size specified in the database definition.
DIF--Visicalc file format.
SYLK--Multiplan spreadsheet format.
WKS--Lotus spreadsheet formula.
DBASEII--dBASE II database.
RPD--Rapidfile database.
FW2--Framework II database.

7-35 The data export options.

You can use any of these formats by specifying the keyword TYPE and one of the types listed in Fig. 7-35 with the COPY command. For example, to create a Lotus 1-2-3 file:

```
. USE CUSTOMER
. COPY TO CUSTNEW FIELDS COMPANY, PHONE, ZIP TYPE WKS
```

The dBASE EXPORT command creates PFS file formats, as well as DBASEII, RPD, and FW2 formats. The format of the EXPORT command is:

```
. USE CUSTOMER
. EXPORT TO CUSTNEW TYPE PFS
```

Completing the Ajax Appliance databases

In chapter 4, you learned about a design for a complete system. Before going on, you should create all of the databases that are defined between Figs. 4-9 and 4-21. You have already defined the CUSTOMER database file. You must still define the INVENTRY, INVOICE, and ITEMS file.

Return to the Control Center or the dot prompt and enter the "Data" work surface. Create the three databases as shown in Figs. 7-36, 7-37, and 7-38.

Once you have created the databases you should enter data into them as designed in Figs. 4-22, 4-23, and 4-24. You will be using this data throughout this book. If you aren't ready to enter data yet, then wait until you read chapter 8 and then you should feel comfortable about entering data.

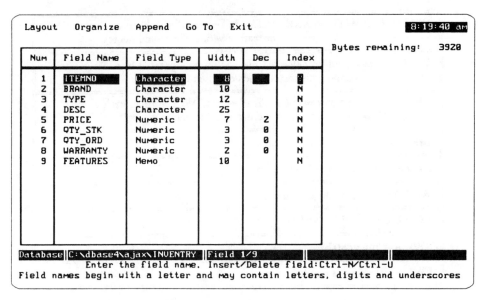

7-36 The INVENTRY database.

Final form of information

The plan of action that you created for your computer application has brought you to this point. You planned your application of computer technology for your business or organization. You determined the data items it is

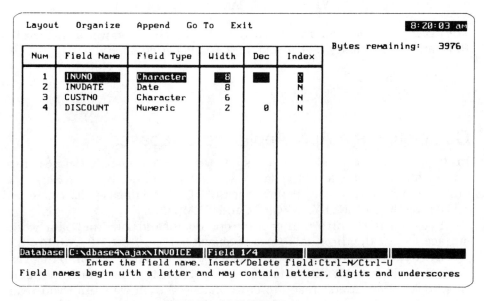

7-37 The INVOICE database.

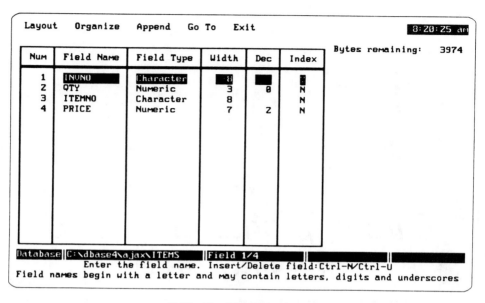

7-38 The ITEMS database.

necessary to store to achieve the information results that you want and need. You created the physical files to hold these data items, and you entered data into the data files.

You may now be able to use the computer and the dBASE IV software for simple tasks, such as keeping a phone list, or a list of customer addresses. Now that the database has been created, you must be able to put information into the file and retrieve information from the file.

Your final goal is to use this information to help your business or organization. You may be able to meet some of these informational goals by simply looking at your data in a different order, or by asking questions like: "Which customer orders how much of which item?" or "How well do blue widgets sell?"

Your actions as you explore your database mirror the actions of programs that process your data later. For now, you must determine how the data is to be presented by the system and entered into the system.

For example, if you are creating a customer invoice system, you have entered the current list of customers, the item descriptions, and prices. You have created an invoice and invoice items files so that new purchases by customers can be added to the files as they happen.

You now need some way of entering the invoice data. Will the data be entered from a form, or will it be entered at the point of sale? Will the system need to print the invoice immediately, or as a monthly billing? What will the bills, invoices, and data entry screens look like?

The next chapter in this part deals with the use of the low-level features of dBASE IV to enter, manipulate, store, change, and delete information in a dBASE IV database.

8

Entering, changing, and deleting data

Data can be entered into your database as soon as you have finished the database definition. If you answer Y to the prompt Input records now? after completing the database definition, you will be allowed to enter records using the simplest of data entry forms.

The simplest of data entry forms

This "quick-and-dirty" data entry facility is a great advantage to people who are developing systems in dBASE IV. You can begin the data entry process while you are designing or writing the remainder of your application system. The quick format that dBASE IV creates can be used to enter new records onto the file, to change records already on the file, and to delete records from the file. These, along with the facility to display and print records on the database, are the basic functions needed to maintain the records of a single database.

The computer screen and keyboard caused a revolution in data processing. No longer were the results of a data entry clerk's work a series of unreadable holes in a card. The data can now be displayed on the screen in any format desired. The simplest type of data entry screen format is just simply listing the fields on the database file, along with an area that matches their respective lengths.

dBASE IV can use the quick screen format in any place where dBASE uses full-screen data entry. For example, Fig. 8-1 shows the quick screen layout for the file CUSTOMER.DBF.

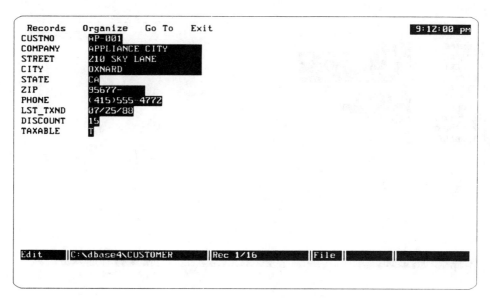

```
   Records    Organize   Go To   Exit                      9:12:00 PM
  CUSTNO     AP-001
  COMPANY    APPLIANCE CITY
  STREET     210 SKY LANE
  CITY       OXNARD
  STATE      CA
  ZIP        95677-
  PHONE      (415)555-4772
  LST_TXND   07/25/88
  DISCOUNT   15
  TAXABLE    T






  Edit        C:\dbase4\CUSTOMER        Rec 1/16        File
```

8-1 Quick screen layout for CUSTOMER.DBF.

Adding records

Adding records to a database file is called "appending" records—so it is not surprising that the dBASE command for this action is APPEND. APPEND causes a new record to be added to the end of the current database file, using data entered by the operator via the quick screen format provided by dBASE IV. For example, the commands:

```
. USE CUSTOMER
. APPEND
```

cause the CUSTOMER.DBF file to be opened and a new record to be added at the end of the file. This new record would receive its values from the data entered on the quick screen format, as shown in Fig. 8-2. Note that the status line shows the current record is 17/17, meaning that the current record pointer is positioned to a new, blank record on the file. The entered values on this screen would be placed into the new database record by dBASE.

Adding records to a database file can be accomplished in several ways. Using the APPEND BLANK command adds a blank record to the end of the database without displaying the data entry screen format. This allows a program to add a record and fill in the values using the REPLACE command. Another method is to use the dBASE EDIT command and paging beyond the end of the current file. dBASE IV allows you to add records.

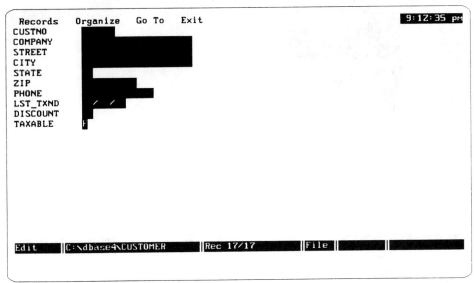

```
    Records    Organize    Go To    Exit                        9:12:35 pm
    CUSTNO
    COMPANY
    STREET
    CITY
    STATE
    ZIP
    PHONE
    LST_TXND      /    /
    DISCOUNT
    TAXABLE    F




   Edit    ||C:\dbase4\CUSTOMER    ||Rec 17/17      ||File ||
```

8-2 Adding a new record to the database.

Changing records

Another function of any database management software is to allow the user to change the data values in records on the database. As with most functions, there are several ways to change database records in dBASE IV.

The EDIT command, like the APPEND command, lets you use the simple data entry form, or a data entry form that you have created, to view and change the values of fields in the database. The dBASE IV command CHANGE is a synonym for EDIT; CHANGE behaves exactly like the EDIT command.

During the data entry phase of your application, there are times when the data entry operator (which could be you!) needs to correct records that have already been entered into the database. The EDIT command can be used, along with the default quick screen format, to edit data values and change any mistakes that are noticed. The commands:

```
. USE CUSTOMER
. EDIT 1
```

open the CUSTOMER database, change the record pointer to point to the first physical record, and display an EDIT screen with the first record's values filled in (see Fig. 8-3). You may then change the values and move from record to record, making changes as needed.

The BROWSE command can also be used to alter data while viewing the database in a tabular format. Using the Tab key, you can move from field to

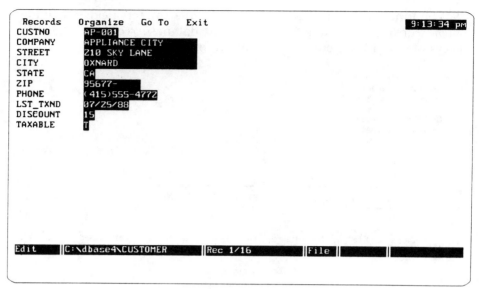

```
   Records    Organize   Go To   Exit                            9:13:34 PM
   CUSTNO     AP-001
   COMPANY    APPLIANCE CITY
   STREET     210 SKY LANE
   CITY       OXNARD
   STATE      CA
   ZIP        95677-
   PHONE      (415)555-4772
   LST_TXND   07/25/88
   DISCOUNT   15
   TAXABLE    T




   Edit      C:\dbase4\CUSTOMER        Rec 1/16          File
```

8-3 EDITing a record.

field and make changes. You can also scroll through the database using the
PgUp and PgDn keys. The database record that appears at the top of a
BROWSE display is the current record. This means that if you use the
command:

   . EDIT 15

then switch to BROWSE, the fifteenth record would appear at the top of the
BROWSE display.

Finally, a program can be used to retrieve information from the database,
change the values via calculation or new input, and put the new values on the
database in place of the old values. An application where the data changes
constantly would, most likely, be updated interactively. A very simple application, like the personal phone directory, would probably not need a program
to update the database. Most applications, however, require some program
updating of the database.

Deleting records

Each database record includes a one-character field as its first field. This is
used to mark a deleted record. This is the extra character noted on the
DISPLAY STRUCTURE report, where the field lengths do not seem to total
correctly.

When the DELETE command is issued for a record on a database, dBASE
places an asterisk in the delete mark character of the record. This indicates to
dBASE, for commands like PACK and COPY, which records are to be ignored.

The function DELETED( ) can access this unseen field, providing a logical true/false indicator for the current database record. DELETED( ) always works with the current database record (see Fig. 8-4).

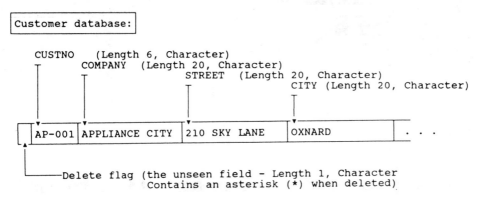

8-4 The unseen field.

The SET DELETED TO command can set the dBASE environment to accept or reject deleted records. If SET DELETED is ON, most dBASE commands will ignore deleted records; with SET DELETED turned OFF, the deleted records are treated as any other record. The DELETED( ) function can then be used for processing dependent on this fact.

Database records can be undeleted simply by moving a space into this unseen field in the record. The programmer, however, cannot directly access this field. The dBASE command RECALL recalls deleted records in this manner. *Note*: a RECALL ALL will not work with SET DELETED ON.

Deleted records are always indexed. Direct-access commands like DISPLAY RECORD 7 or GO 7 will display/access the record even if it is deleted and SET DELETED is ON.

Packing deleted records

You might ask, "How do deleted records get removed from the database?" The answer is through the PACK command. The unwanted records, the records marked for deletion, are physically removed from the database by this process. A related command, ZAP, removes all records from the database file.

The PACK command copies a database to itself, while ignoring any records marked for deletion. This process reduces the size of the database file and also causes the database to be reindexed, if any index files are currently open. Figure 8-5 shows the actions taken while packing the Customer database.

The ZAP command marks all database records for deletion, then PACKs the database file—effectively removing all records from the database, permanently. This command is used mostly to "clean out" temporary database files used in a process.

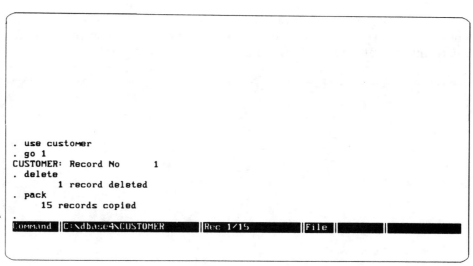

```
. use customer
. go 1
CUSTOMER: Record No     1
. delete
         1 record deleted
. pack
      15 records copied
.
```

`Command ‖C:\dbase4\CUSTOMER       ‖Rec 1/15        ‖File ‖            ‖`

8-5 PACKing the CUSTOMER database.

Before the next process begins, for example, a temporary file is ZAPped, leaving an empty database for use in the process. The database structure remains intact, but all of the records have been removed, as shown in Fig. 8-6.

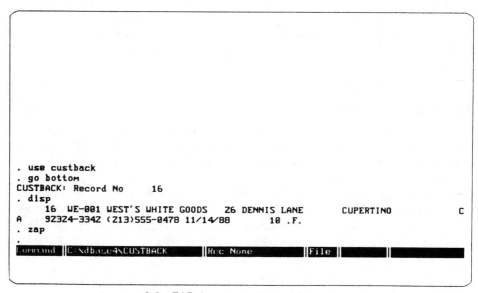

```
. use custback
. go bottom
CUSTBACK: Record No     16
. disp
     16  WE-001 WEST'S WHITE GOODS   26 DENNIS LANE       CUPERTINO          C
A     92324-3342 (213)555-0478 11/14/88        18 .F.
. zap
.
```

`Command ‖C:\dbase4\CUSTBACK       ‖Rec None        ‖File ‖            ‖`

8-6 ZAPping a temporary database.

The SET SAFETY ON/OFF command causes a prompt to be displayed (or not displayed) when a ZAP or PACK command is executed. Figure 8-7 shows the results of a SET SAFETY command.

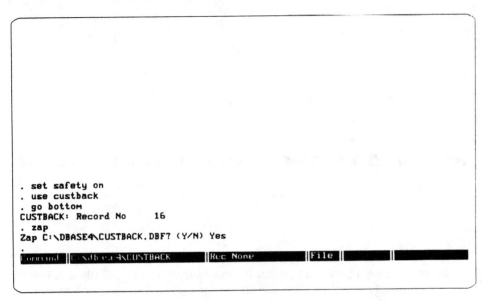

```
. set safety on
. use custback
. go bottom
CUSTBACK: Record No      16
. zap
Zap C:\DBASE4\CUSTBACK.DBF? (Y/N) Yes
.
Command   C:\db as 4\CUSTBACK      Rec None          File
```

8-7 The effects of SET SAFETY on a ZAP command.

Different ways to work with data

Business information has been historically recorded on forms—formatted pieces of paper that are stored in drawers in a filing cabinet. Now that data has become electronically encoded, it is still easier for the human clerks and accountants to see the information in the same format, or one close to the original format.

Using the edit work surface

Most data entry is, therefore, performed on the computer screen in a formatted display that can look like the original paper for that information. The screen format might also look like the data collection forms, surveys, invoices, bills, or checks.

The default data entry screen can be used to update databases "on-the-fly," or for error correction. If you are building several applications, you might want to become familiar with all aspects of dBASE IV. The quick screen formats allow you to be immediately productive when using a dBASE database.

APPEND The APPEND command causes a new record to be added to the database, and the current record pointer is positioned to this record. The quick screen format is displayed, and you can enter data into the database record. During the APPEND process, each time you reach and enter the last field on a particular record, dBASE APPENDs a new blank record. Continue entering records in this manner until you finish. Pressing Ctrl–End finishes the process. The APPEND command format is shown in Fig. 8-8.

```
APPEND      [ BLANK ]

            [ FROM filename /? ┌ [ TYPE ]  SDF                            ┐
                               │           DELIMITED [ WITH BLANK ]       │
                               │           DIF                            │
                               │           FW2                            │
                               │           RPD                            │
                               │           SYLK                           │
                               │           WKS                            │
                               └           WK1                            ┘

                  [ FOR < condition > ]
```

8-8 The APPEND command.

The default screen format, and most other screen formats, allow you to move between fields on the screen using the cursor control keys (the "arrow" keys), changing the values as needed. The PgUp and PgDn keys allow you to move between the records.

EDIT The EDIT command allows you to view and change the values on a particular record. The quick screen format is used again, this time to display the current record. For example, the commands:

```
. USE CUSTOMER
. EDIT
```

display the values contained in the first record in the file CUSTOMER.DBF.

EDIT differs from APPEND in that there are more options available to control the EDIT process. Figure 8-9 shows the syntax for the EDIT command.

```
EDIT  [ NOINIT ]     [ < record number > ] [ FOR/WHILE < condition > ]
      [ NOFOLLOW ]
      [ NOAPPEND                             [ FIELDS < field list > ]
      [ NOMENU
      [ NOEDIT
      [ NODELETE
      [ NOCLEAR ]
```

8-9 The EDIT command.

The EDIT process is the usual method for updating and changing database records interactively. You can use the cursor keys to move to any of the fields, then change the value that is there. EDIT also allows you to delete records by pressing Ctrl–Y.

When you are using the EDIT work surface, you can use several special keystrokes to control the EDIT session. The Ctrl–End and Esc keystrokes, for example, cause you to exit from the EDIT work surface back to the dot prompt or Control Center, depending on where you entered EDIT from. The cursor control keys cause the cursor to be moved within fields and records, while the PgUp and PgDn keys allow you to move between records.

Figure 8-10 shows all the key combinations for the EDIT work surface. The F3 and F4 keys cause you to move to the next and previous fields, respectively. If the field that you advance to happens to be a memo field, the "word wrap" work surface, or dBASE word processor, is automatically opened for you. Ctrl–PgUp causes you to move to the first record on the database, while Ctrl–PgDn moves you to the last record.

Function keys	
F1 Help	Enters dBASE Help system
F2 Data	Toggle between BROWSE/EDIT (Control Center)
F3 Previous	Moves back one field (will open memo field)
F4 Next	Moves to next field (will open memo field)
F9 Zoom	Open text window to full screen size
F10 Menus	Access EDIT menus
Un-aided keys	
PgUp	Moves up one record
PgDn	Moves down one record
Up arrow	Moves cursor up one field
Down arrow	Moves cursor down one field
Esc	Exit the EDIT session, ignoring changes to current record
Del	Delete character
Ctrl- keys	
Ctrl-Home	Enter memo field
Ctrl-End	End EDIT session, saving changes
Ctrl-U	Delete/Un-delete record toggle
Ctrl-PgUp	Move to first record
Ctrl-PgDn	Move to last record

8-10   EDIT special key combinations.

If you advance past the last record on the database while using EDIT, the EDIT process allows you to add records, unless the NOAPPEND option was used. This means that you can use EDIT to append records in the same way as APPEND.

dBASE IV has an added Edit menu that can be displayed during the EDIT process. This menu gives you interactive control over the EDIT procedure. The menu that is displayed is a set of pull-down menus that aid you in file navigation, searching for records with particular values, and generally directing EDIT. The Edit menu can be removed by using the NOMENU option on the EDIT command.

The Record menu, as shown in Fig. 8-11, allows you to add new records, to mark records for deletion, to "initialize" a record by blanking all of the fields, to lock records when you are using dBASE in a multiple-user environment, or to undo changes that you have made to a record.

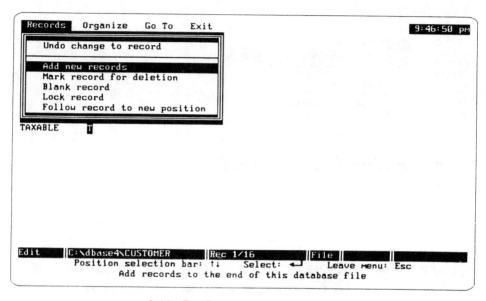

8-11 The Record EDIT menu option.

The Undo change to record returns the values of fields in the record to the values the record had when you first displayed it. If you use the PgDn key and move to another record, the values are permanently changed—that is, you would have to change them again, yourself. If you have not left the record, you can reset the original values by using Undo.

The Add new records option moves you to the end of the database and appends a blank record for you to enter values into. You could also do the same by moving to the end of the database and allowing EDIT to prompt you for adding records. The Mark records for deletion does just that—although you could do the same by using the Ctrl–U keystroke.

The Blank record option changes or erases all of the values in a record. These values then can be replaced, or the record could be left blank. This is used in some multi-user environments to maintain positions in the database. The Lock record option is also used in a multi-user environment to keep other users from editing the values on a record that you are currently editing.

The Follow record to new location option takes effect if you change the value in a field used for an index. If the new value of the field causes the record to change location in the file relative to the other records, and you use the PgUp or PgDn keys, you would see the records displayed as if the record had changed locations. If this option is set to OFF, the records will not appear to change order until the next EDIT session.

The Organize menu (added to the Edit work surface in dBASE IV Release 1.1 and shown in Fig. 8-12) allows you to create new index tags or to sort the database records directly from the EDIT work surface.

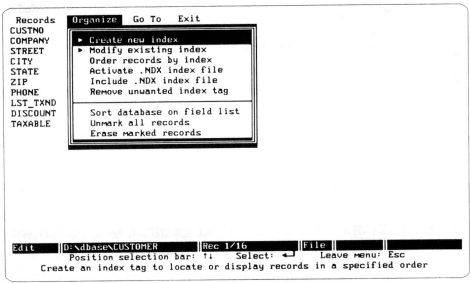

8-12   The Organize menu of the EDIT work surface.

The Create New Index option of the Organize menu allows you to create a new index tag (or file). Modify Existing Index allows you to change an existing index tag by changing or adding to the key fields of the file. Order records by index causes the chosen index tag to become the "master" index for the current database. This means that the records will appear to be in order by the keys specified in the chosen index tag. The Remove unwanted index tag option of the Organize menu allows you to remove index tags from the .MDX file.

The options to Activate and Include .NDX files are included for compatibility with earlier versions of the dBASE software. While .NDX index files can still be used, using .MDX tags is much more efficient. Each .NDX file represents just one index tag in an .MDX file. Sort database on field list gives you the ability to sort physically your database records directly from the EDIT work surface.

The Unmark all records and Erase marked records work with database records that have been marked for deletion. When you DELETE a database record, a delete marker is placed in the records, but the record does still exist on the database. You can, while using the EDIT work surface, choose to delete records from the database. Choosing the Unmark option removes the delete marker from all records, thereby undeleting them. Choosing Erase marked records causes the records to be physically deleted from the file.

The functions that are available from this menu are discussed in chapter 9 "Sorting and indexing."

The Go To menu, in Fig. 8-13, gives you a menu method of navigating in the database. You can quickly move to the top or bottom of the database by choosing that option—or you can move to any record by providing a specific record number. You might also perform record searches, or even use the index to locate a particular record or set of records.

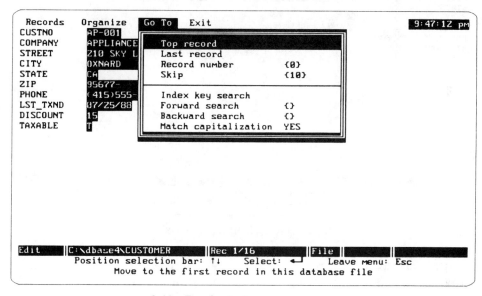

8-13   The Go To EDIT menu option.

The Go To menu contains several methods to allow you to control your position within a database. This is most useful in large databases with many records. The Top record and Last record options allow you to position to the first or last database record. If the database is indexed, the first or last record is in the index order. Otherwise, the database is displayed in natural order, and the first and last records are the records that are physically at the beginning and end of the database. The Record number option allows you to position to a particular physical record in the database. The Skip option allows you to jump forward or backward by a specified number of records.

You can also use an index to control your position, even use a search criteria based on fields not in an index. The Index search option allows you, when an index is being used, to enter a search value for the index key field. The record that most nearly matches the requested value is displayed if SET NEAR is ON. The Forward search and Backward search options allow you to test for specific values in any database field, whether it is an index key or not. The

Match capitalization option allows you to toggle whether or not you have to exactly match the capitalization of the searched-for value.

The Exit menu, shown in Fig. 8-14, allows you to exit from dBASE or from EDIT. If you exit from EDIT, you are returned to the Control Center main menu (if you entered EDIT from there) or to the dot prompt.

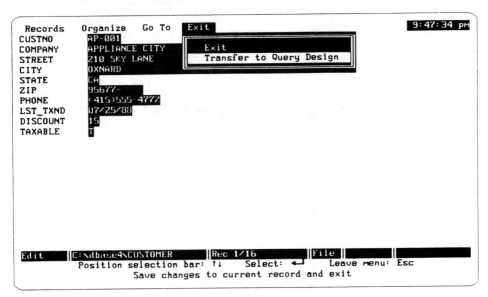

8-14 The Exit EDIT menu option.

EDIT works with either the quick screen format created by dBASE, or can be used with a customized screen format that you create yourself.

Using the BROWSE table

BROWSE is one of the most powerful dBASE commands. BROWSE displays your records on the screen in a tabular format. Scroll to the left or right to see all fields on the records, and scroll up and down to see all the records. You can move from field to field, and you can change the values in the fields.

Figure 8-15 shows the Browse screen after either pressing F2 from the Control Center menu or by entering:

```
. USE CUSTOMER
. BROWSE
```

from the dot prompt. The entire CUSTOMER database is displayed. You can move freely between fields and records, changing any of the values you want. You can even delete individual records by pressing the Ctrl–U keys. When you delete a record, the status line displays the letters Del on the right to let you know that the record is deleted. You can undelete the record by pressing Ctrl–U again.

```
 Records    Fields    Organize    Go To    Exit                    9:48:20 pm
┌────────┬─────────────────────┬────────────────────┬────────────────────┬─────┬──┐
│ CUSTNO │ COMPANY             │ STREET             │ CITY               │STATE│ZI│
├────────┼─────────────────────┼────────────────────┼────────────────────┼─────┼──┤
│ AP-001 │ APPLIANCE CITY      │ 210 SKY LANE       │ OXNARD             │ CA  │95│
│ AP-002 │ APPLIANCE CITY      │ 360 ACE AVE        │ HOLLYWOOD          │ CA  │95│
│ AP-003 │ APPLIANCE WORLD     │ 20695 BLUE BIRD AVE│ SAN FRANCISCO      │ CA  │95│
│ AV-001 │ AVON APPLIANCE      │ 1687 NEW PLACE ROAD│ LOS ANGELES        │ CA  │98│
│ BO-001 │ BOB'S BRANDS        │ BOB'S DRIVE        │ SANTA FE           │ NM  │84│
│ CA-001 │ CARY'S COOLERS      │ 60 STRAWBERRY HILLS│ WINDSOR            │ CT  │06│
│ CR-001 │ CRAZY FREDDIES      │ 1820 171ST ST      │ NEW YORK           │ NY  │15│
│ ER-001 │ ERNIES TV           │ 456 SNOW PLOW AVE  │ BLEAUVILLE         │ CA  │94│
│ FR-001 │ FRIENDLY APPLIANCE  │ 26 CHOCOLATE AVE   │ HERSHEY            │ PA  │15│
│ JA-001 │ JACKEL & HYDES      │ 357 BAT COURT      │ LAWRENCEVILLE      │ PA  │14│
│ JI-001 │ JIM'S HOT AND COLD  │ 55 SKINNER ROAD    │ VERNON             │ CA  │95│
│ RA-001 │ RANGES ON THE HOME  │ 23 OLD OKIE DR     │ OKLAHOMA CITY      │ OK  │73│
│ RO-001 │ RON'S REFRIGERATORS │ 141 HOLLOW OAK PLACE│SAN JUAN CAPISTRANO│ CA  │95│
│ TH-001 │ THE HOME SHOPPE     │ 25 APPLIANCE LANE  │ SARATOGA           │ CA  │93│
│ WA-001 │ WASHER WAREHOUSE    │ 15525 MARINER DR   │ LOS ALTOS          │ CA  │97│
│ WE-001 │ WEST'S WHITE GOODS  │ 26 DENNIS LANE     │ CUPERTINO          │ CA  │92│
│        │                     │                    │                    │     │  │
└────────┴─────────────────────┴────────────────────┴────────────────────┴─────┴──┘
 Browse    C:\dbase4\CUSTOMER        Rec 1/16           File
                         View and edit fields
```

8-15   BROWSE of the CUSTOMER database.

You can add new records by moving the cursor beyond the last record. A displayed message asks you to confirm that you are entering a new record. The keyword NOAPPEND of the BROWSE command prevents the adding of records.

When you are using the BROWSE work surface, several special keystrokes control the BROWSE session. The Ctrl–End and Esc keystrokes, for example, cause you to exit from the BROWSE work surface back to the dot prompt or Control Center, depending on where you entered BROWSE from. The cursor control keys cause the cursor to be moved within fields and records, while the PgUp and PgDn keys allow you to move between records.

Figure 8-16 shows all the key combinations for the BROWSE work surface. The F3 and F4 keys move you to the next and previous fields respectively. If the field that you advance to happens to be a memo field, the "word wrap" work surface, or dBASE word processor, is automatically opened for you. Ctrl–PgUp moves you to the first record on the database, while Ctrl–PgDn moves you to the last record.

When you are through viewing data in the BROWSE table, you can press the Esc key to return to the Control Center main menu. If you make changes to the values of fields in the database, you press Ctrl–End to exit from BROWSE. The Ctrl–End key sequence tells dBASE to save all of your changes.

You can limit the number of fields displayed for each record, and you can also limit the BROWSE to certain records in the database. The FIELDS and FOR/WHILE keywords give special instructions to dBASE IV for handling your data.

Function keys	
F1 Help	Enters dBASE Help system
F2 Data	Toggle between BROWSE/EDIT (Control Center)
F3 Previous	Moves back one field (will open memo field)
F4 Next	Moves to next field (will open memo field)
F9 Zoom	Open text window to full screen size
F10 Menus	Access BROWSE menus

Un-aided keys	
PgUp	Moves up one page
PgDn	Moves down one page
Up arrow	Moves cursor up one row
Down arrow	Moves cursor down one row
Tab	Moves forward one field
Shift-Tab	Moves backward one field
Esc	Exit the BROWSE session, ignoring changes to current record
Del	Delete character

Ctrl- keys	
Ctrl-Home	Enter memo field
Ctrl-End	End BROWSE session, saving changes
Ctrl-U	Delete/Un-delete record toggle
Ctrl-PgUp	Move to first record
Ctrl-PgDn	Move to last record

8-16 BROWSE keystrokes.

You can use the FIELDS clause to limit the number of fields that you want. For example:

. BROWSE FIELDS CITY COMPANY PHONE

displays the BROWSE table, but only with the fields CITY, COMPANY, and PHONE. The rest of the records in the database are hidden from view. They are still there, but you can only edit the fields displayed in the BROWSE table.

The Browse menu is displayed at the top of the BROWSE table. This menu allows you to position the display to any record in the database. The current record is the first line of the displayed data.

The Record menu, as shown in Fig. 8-17, allows you to add new records, to mark records for deletion, to "initialize" a record by blanking all of the fields, to lock records when you are using dBASE in a multiple-user environment, or to "undo" changes that you have made to a record.

The Undo change to record returns the values of fields in the record to the values the record had when you first displayed it. If you move the highlight away from the current record, the values are permanently changed—that is, you would have to change them again yourself. If you have not left the record, you can reset the original values by using Undo.

The Add new records option moves you to the end of the database and appends a blank record for you to enter in values. Moving to the end of the database and allowing EDIT to prompt you for adding records is the same.

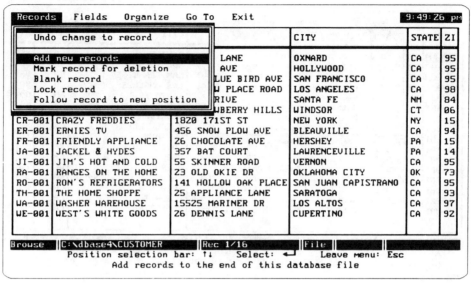

```
 Records   Fields   Organize   Go To   Exit                9:49:26 pm
┌─────────────────────────────────┐          │CITY          │STATE│ZI
│  Undo change to record          │          │              │     │
├─────────────────────────────────┤  LANE    │OXNARD        │ CA  │95
│  Add new records                │  AVE     │HOLLYWOOD     │ CA  │95
│  Mark record for deletion       │ LUE BIRD AVE│SAN FRANCISCO│ CA │95
│  Blank record                   │ U PLACE ROAD│LOS ANGELES  │ CA │98
│  Lock record                    │ RIVE     │SANTA FE      │ NM  │84
│  Follow record to new position  │ BERRY HILLS│WINDSOR      │ CT │06
└─────────────────────────────────┘
 CR-001 CRAZY FREDDIES      1820 171ST ST      NEW YORK          NY   15
 ER-001 ERNIES TV           456 SNOW PLOW AVE  BLEAUVILLE        CA   94
 FR-001 FRIENDLY APPLIANCE  26 CHOCOLATE AVE   HERSHEY           PA   15
 JA-001 JACKEL & HYDES      357 BAT COURT      LAWRENCEVILLE     PA   14
 JI-001 JIM'S HOT AND COLD  55 SKINNER ROAD    VERNON            CA   95
 RA-001 RANGES ON THE HOME  23 OLD OKIE DR     OKLAHOMA CITY     OK   73
 RO-001 RON'S REFRIGERATORS 141 HOLLOW OAK PLACE SAN JUAN CAPISTRANO CA 95
 TH-001 THE HOME SHOPPE     25 APPLIANCE LANE  SARATOGA          CA   93
 WA-001 WASHER WAREHOUSE    15525 MARINER DR   LOS ALTOS         CA   97
 WE-001 WEST'S WHITE GOODS  26 DENNIS LANE     CUPERTINO         CA   92

 Browse   ║C:\dbase4\CUSTOMER ║Rec 1/16     ║File ║
         Position selection bar: ↑↓   Select: ←┘   Leave menu: Esc
            Add records to the end of this database file
```

8-17 The Record BROWSE menu option.

The Mark records for deletion does just that—although you could also use the Ctrl–U keystroke.

The Blank record option erases all of the values in a record. These values might then be replaced, or the record might be left blank. In some multi-user environments, this option maintains positions in the database. The Lock record option is also used in a multi-user environment to prevent other users from editing the values on a record that you are currently editing.

The Follow record to new location option takes effect if you change the value in a field used for an index. If the new field value changes the record's location in the file relative to the other records, the records are displayed as if the record had changed locations. If this option is set to OFF, the records do appear to change order until the next BROWSE session.

The Organize menu (added to the BROWSE work surface in dBASE IV Release 1.1 and shown in Fig. 8-18) allows you to create new index tags or to sort the database records directly from the BROWSE work surface.

The Create New Index option of the Organize menu allows you to create a new index tag (or file). Modify Existing Index allows you to change an existing index tag by changing or adding to the key fields of the file. Order records by index causes the chosen index tag to become the "master" index for the current database. This means that the records will appear to be in order by the keys specified in the chosen index tag. The Remove unwanted index tag option of the Organize menu allows you to remove index tags from the .MDX file.

The options to Activate and Include .NDX files are included for compatibility with earlier versions of the dBASE software. While .NDX files can still be

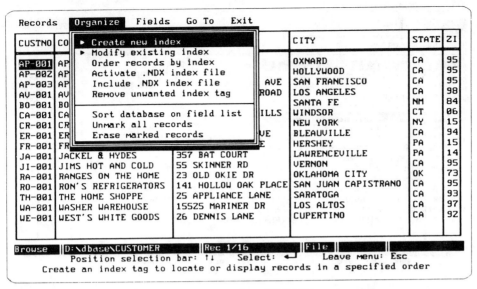

8-18 The Organize menu of the BROWSE work surface.

used, using .MDX tags is much more efficient. Each .NDX file represents just one index tag in an .MDX file.

Sort database on field list gives you the ability to sort physically your database records directly from the BROWSE work surface.

The Unmark all records and Erase marked records work with database records that have been marked for deletion. When you DELETE a database record, a delete marker is placed in the records, but the record does still exist on the database. You can, while using the BROWSE work surface, choose to delete records from the database. Choosing the Unmark option removes the delete marker from all records, thereby undeleting them. Choosing Erase marked records causes the records to be physically deleted from the file.

The functions that are available from this menu are discussed in chapter 9, "Sorting and indexing."

The Fields menu, as shown in Fig. 8-19, gives you several options to control the fields in a BROWSE display. The Lock fields on left option allows you to hold fields on the screen display. For example, you could lock the fields CUSTNO and COMPANY, while letting the rest of the CUSTOMER fields scroll. This lets you see all of the data, but without losing your place.

The Blank field option erases the value of a field on the screen. Freeze field means that you may only change the values of the specified field. The Size field option allows you to shrink or expand the amount of room that a field takes on the BROWSE display.

The Go To menu, in Fig. 8-20, gives you a menu method of navigating in the database. Move to the top or bottom of the database by choosing that option—or move to any record by providing a specific record number. You can

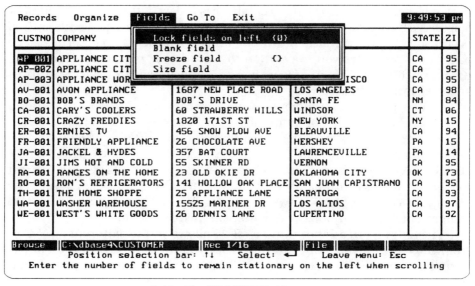

8-19 The BROWSE Fields menu.

also perform record searches, or even use the index to locate a particular record or set of records.

The Go To menu contains several methods to allow you to control your position within a database. This is most useful in large databases with many records. The Top record and Last record options allow you to position to the

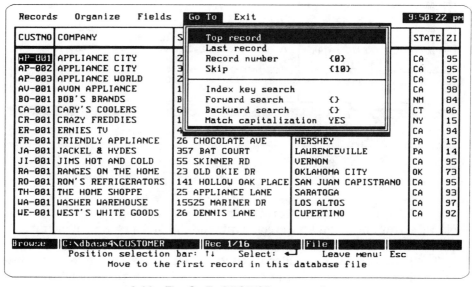

8-20 The Go To BROWSE menu option.

first or last database record. If the database is indexed, this means the first or last record by the index order. Otherwise, the database is displayed in natural order, showing the physical beginning and end of the database. The Record number option allows you to position to a particular physical record in the database. The Skip option allows you to jump forward or backward by a specified number of records.

You also can use an index to control your position, even use a search criteria based on fields not in an index. The Index search option allows you, while using an index, to enter a search value for the index key field. The record that most nearly matches the requested value will be displayed if SET NEAR is ON. The Forward search and Backward search options allow you to test for specific values in any database field, whether it is an index key or not. The Match capitalization option allows you to toggle whether or not you have to exactly match the capitalization of the searched-for value.

The Exit menu, as shown in Fig. 8-21 allows you to exit from dBASE or from BROWSE. If you exit from BROWSE, you are returned to the Control Center main menu (if you entered BROWSE from there) or to the dot prompt.

```
  Records    Organize    Fields    Go To    Exit                 9:50:48 pm

 ┌────────┬─────────────────────┬───────────────────────────────────┬───────┬──┐
 │CUSTNO  │COMPANY              │STREET      ┌─────────────────────┐ │STATE  │ZI│
 │        │                     │            │   Exit              │ │       │  │
 │AP-001  │APPLIANCE CITY       │210 SKY L   │ Transfer to Query Design│CA   │95│
 │AP-002  │APPLIANCE CITY       │360 ACE AVE └─────────────────────┘  │CA   │95│
 │AP-003  │APPLIANCE WORLD      │20695 BLUE BIRD AVE SAN FRANCISCO     │CA   │95│
 │AV-001  │AVON APPLIANCE       │1687 NEW PLACE ROAD LOS ANGELES       │CA   │98│
 │BO-001  │BOB'S BRANDS         │BOB'S DRIVE         SANTA FE          │NM   │84│
 │CA-001  │CARY'S COOLERS       │60 STRAWBERRY HILLS WINDSOR           │CT   │06│
 │CR-001  │CRAZY FREDDIES       │1820 171ST ST       NEW YORK          │NY   │15│
 │ER-001  │ERNIES TV            │456 SNOW PLOW AVE   BLEAUVILLE        │CA   │94│
 │FR-001  │FRIENDLY APPLIANCE   │26 CHOCOLATE AVE    HERSHEY           │PA   │15│
 │JA-001  │JACKEL & HYDES       │357 BAT COURT       LAWRENCEVILLE     │PA   │14│
 │JI-001  │JIMS HOT AND COLD    │55 SKINNER RD       VERNON            │CA   │95│
 │RA-001  │RANGES ON THE HOME   │23 OLD OKIE DR      OKLAHOMA CITY     │OK   │73│
 │RO-001  │RON'S REFRIGERATORS  │141 HOLLOW OAK PLACE SAN JUAN CAPISTRANO│CA │95│
 │TH-001  │THE HOME SHOPPE      │25 APPLIANCE LANE   SARATOGA          │CA   │93│
 │WA-001  │WASHER WAREHOUSE     │15525 MARINER DR    LOS ALTOS         │CA   │97│
 │WE-001  │WEST'S WHITE GOODS   │26 DENNIS LANE      CUPERTINO         │CA   │92│
 └────────┴─────────────────────┴───────────────────────────────────┴───────┴──┘
  Browse    C:\dbase4\CUSTOMER      Rec 1/16        File
        Position selection bar: ↑↓    Select: ↵    Leave menu: Esc
              Save changes to current record and exit
```

8-21 The Exit BROWSE menu option.

BROWSE uses a tabular format that can be modified by freezing fields, holding certain fields on the screen while scrolling others, and allowing only certain fields to be changed.

The BROWSE table can also be used to display a screen of records, but not to allow the user to change that screen. This "display table" function would require a small program that uses the KEYBOARD command.

You would choose a database file, and position the cursor at the first record to appear on the list. Then, by using the commands:

KEYBOARD CHR(27)
BROWSE NOCLEAR

you would cause a BROWSE table to be displayed. However, the KEYBOARD command has placed an Esc character into the keyboard buffer. This has the same effect as the user typing BROWSE NOCLEAR, then pressing the Esc key to leave BROWSE. The KEYBOARD command places characters into the keyboard buffer, just exactly as if the user had typed them in from the keyboard. The NOCLEAR option of the BROWSE command tells dBASE not to clear the screen when the BROWSE function is ended. The records are displayed in an easily readable format, and the user cannot use the features of the BROWSE work surface to change the database field values.

Using memo fields

The final work surface for entering data into your database is the memo field work surface. This is actually the dBASE word processor, an editor included in dBASE for text entry. The memo field takes ten characters in a database file, but the entire text is actually stored in another file.

Memo files   Each database that contains memo fields has another file, a database text file, that contains the text of the memo fields. This file has the same name as the database, only with the extension .DBT. For example, Fig. 8-22 shows the Database Design work surface containing the structure of the CUSTOMER database.

```
 Layout    Organize    Append    Go To    Exit                    9:51:34 PM

                                                        Bytes remaining:    3898
 ┌─────┬──────────────┬──────────────┬───────┬──────┬────────┐
 │ Num │ Field Name   │ Field Type   │ Width │ Dec  │ Index  │
 ├─────┼──────────────┼──────────────┼───────┼──────┼────────┤
 │  1  │ CUSTNO       │ Character    │   6   │      │   Y    │
 │  2  │ COMPANY      │ Character    │  20   │      │   Y    │
 │  3  │ STREET       │ Character    │  20   │      │   N    │
 │  4  │ CITY         │ Character    │  20   │      │   N    │
 │  5  │ STATE        │ Character    │   2   │      │   N    │
 │  6  │ ZIP          │ Character    │  10   │      │   Y    │
 │  7  │ PHONE        │ Character    │  13   │      │   N    │
 │  8  │ LST_TXND     │ Date         │   8   │      │   N    │
 │  9  │ DISCOUNT     │ Numeric      │   2   │  0   │   N    │
 │ 10  │ TAXABLE      │ Logical      │   1   │      │   N    │
 └─────┴──────────────┴──────────────┴───────┴──────┴────────┘

 Database C:\dbase4\CUSTOMER          Field 1/10
           Enter the field name.  Insert/Delete field:Ctrl-N/Ctrl-U
 Field names begin with a letter and may contain letters, digits and underscores
```

8-22   The CUSTOMER database structure.

Ten fields are defined on the CUSTOMER database. To add a memo field as an eleventh field, you need only to move to the end of the field list and enter the new field. Figure 8-23 shows a new memo field, called NOTES, added to the CUSTOMER database.

```
  Layout    Organize    Append    Go To    Exit                      9:52:00 PM
                                                    Bytes remaining:      3888
 ┌──────┬───────────────┬─────────────┬───────┬───────┬─────────┐
 │ Num  │  Field Name   │  Field Type │ Width │  Dec  │  Index  │
 ├──────┼───────────────┼─────────────┼───────┼───────┼─────────┤
 │  1   │ CUSTNO        │ Character   │   6   │       │    Y    │
 │  2   │ COMPANY       │ Character   │  20   │       │    Y    │
 │  3   │ STREET        │ Character   │  20   │       │    N    │
 │  4   │ CITY          │ Character   │  20   │       │    N    │
 │  5   │ STATE         │ Character   │   2   │       │    N    │
 │  6   │ ZIP           │ Character   │  10   │       │    Y    │
 │  7   │ PHONE         │ Character   │  13   │       │    N    │
 │  8   │ LST_TXND      │ Date        │   8   │       │    N    │
 │  9   │ DISCOUNT      │ Numeric     │   2   │   0   │    N    │
 │  10  │ TAXABLE       │ Logical     │   1   │       │    N    │
 │  11  │ NOTES         │ Memo        │  10   │       │    N    │
 │  12  │               │ Character   │       │       │    N    │
 │      │               │             │       │       │         │
 └──────┴───────────────┴─────────────┴───────┴───────┴─────────┘
 Database C:\dbase4\CUSTOMER         Field 12/12
              Enter the field name. Insert/Delete field:Ctrl-N/Ctrl-U
 Field names begin with a letter and may contain letters, digits and underscores
```

8-23 The CUSTOMER database with a memo field.

The field NOTES can now be used to store text data about the customer, personal information, reminders about customer dealings, or any other data. This is data that is for your own use, because the memo text is not for use in calculations or other computer record-keeping.

Figure 8-24 shows a BROWSE table of the new CUSTOMER database. The fields CUSTNO and COMPANY have been locked on the left. The right-most column is the memo field NOTES.

Notice that the NOTES column contains only the word memo. The lowercase memo means that the memo field has not been used, in other words, the memo field is empty. When text has been entered into the memo field, the marker changes to uppercase: MEMO.

To enter data, move the highlight to the memo marker, then press Ctrl–Home. The dBASE word processor will be opened, as shown in Fig. 8-25. Note that a line of text has been entered.

Ctrl–End saves the text and returns you to the BROWSE table, as shown in Fig. 8-26 on the next page. The marker now says MEMO in uppercase, because text has been entered into the memo field.

Getting data into a memo field The dBASE word processor, known in dBASE IV as the "word wrap" work surface, is the main method for entering text into memo fields. When you open this work surface by pressing Ctrl–Home on a

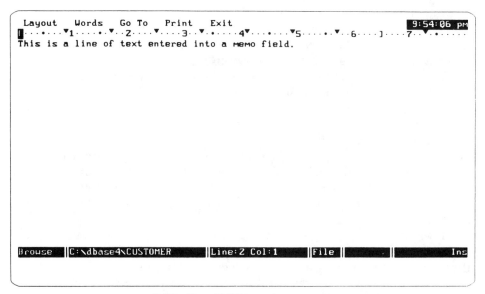

```
  Records   Fields   Organize   Go To   Exit                    9:53:06 pm

 ┌────────┬───────────────────────┬─────────────┬──────────┬─────────┬─────────┬──────┐
 │CUSTNO  │COMPANY                │PHONE        │LST_TXND  │DISCOUNT │TAXABLE  │NOTES │
 ├────────┼───────────────────────┼─────────────┼──────────┼─────────┼─────────┼──────┤
 │AP-001  │APPLIANCE CITY         │(415)555-4772│07/25/88  │      15 │T        │memo  │
 │AP-002  │APPLIANCE CITY         │(213)555-4766│08/10/88  │      15 │F        │memo  │
 │AP-003  │APPLIANCE WORLD        │(415)555-3353│08/19/88  │       0 │T        │memo  │
 │AV-001  │AVON APPLIANCE         │(415)555-7963│05/16/88  │      15 │T        │memo  │
 │BO-001  │BOB'S BRANDS           │(434)555-3444│05/31/86  │       0 │F        │memo  │
 │CA-001  │CARY'S COOLERS         │(203)555-7799│08/21/88  │      50 │F        │memo  │
 │CR-001  │CRAZY FREDDIES         │(212)555-9974│10/11/88  │       5 │F        │memo  │
 │ER-001  │ERNIES TV              │(213)555-4975│11/29/88  │      10 │T        │memo  │
 │FR-001  │FRIENDLY APPLIANCE     │(717)555-6274│07/01/88  │      15 │F        │memo  │
 │JA-001  │JACKEL & HYDES         │(717)555-3656│05/24/88  │      25 │F        │memo  │
 │JI-001  │JIM'S HOT AND COLD     │(213)555-6473│07/13/88  │       5 │F        │memo  │
 │RA-001  │RANGES ON THE HOME     │(564)555-3248│12/31/88  │      35 │F        │memo  │
 │RO-001  │RON'S REFRIGERATORS    │(213)555-5764│07/05/87  │      10 │T        │memo  │
 │TH-001  │THE HOME SHOPPE        │(415)555-8355│01/29/88  │      35 │F        │memo  │
 │WA-001  │WASHER WAREHOUSE       │(213)555-9843│06/30/87  │      15 │F        │memo  │
 │WE-001  │WEST'S WHITE GOODS     │(213)555-0478│11/14/88  │      10 │F        │memo  │
 └────────┴───────────────────────┴─────────────┴──────────┴─────────┴─────────┴──────┘

 Browse     C:\dbase4\CUSTOMER        Rec 1/16         File

                       View and edit fields
```

8-24 A BROWSE of the CUSTOMER database.

memo marker, type the text that you want in the memo field. The "word wrap" feature causes the text to be formatted into lines without breaking words in half. The default setting for the width of a memo field is 50 characters.

The word wrap work surface is displayed whenever you enter a memo field. Other than Ctrl–Home, you might also use the F9 "Zoom" key to enter

```
  Layout   Words   Go To   Print   Exit                    9:54:06 pm
 ▌····•···▼1···•··▼··2···▼···3··▼·•····4▼··•···▼5·····▼··6····]····7·▼·•·····
 This is a line of text entered into a memo field.

















 Browse     C:\dbase4\CUSTOMER        Line:2 Col:1      File                Ins
```

8-25 The dBASE word processor.

| Records | Fields | Organize | Go To | Exit |

CUSTNO	COMPANY	PHONE	LST_TXND	DISCOUNT	TAXABLE	NOTES
AP-001	APPLIANCE CITY	(415)555-4772	07/25/88	15	T	MEMO
AP-002	APPLIANCE CITY	(213)555-4766	08/10/88	15	F	memo
AP-003	APPLIANCE WORLD	(415)555-3353	08/19/88	0	T	memo
AV-001	AVON APPLIANCE	(415)555-7963	05/16/88	15	T	memo
BO-001	BOB'S BRANDS	(434)555-3444	05/31/86	0	F	memo
CA-001	CARY'S COOLERS	(203)555-7799	08/21/88	50	F	memo
CR-001	CRAZY FREDDIES	(212)555-9974	10/11/88	5	F	memo
ER-001	ERNIES TV	(213)555-4975	11/29/88	10	T	memo
FR-001	FRIENDLY APPLIANCE	(717)555-6274	07/01/88	15	F	memo
JA-001	JACKEL & HYDES	(717)555-3656	05/24/88	25	F	memo
JI-001	JIM'S HOT AND COLD	(213)555-6473	07/13/88	5	F	memo
RA-001	RANGES ON THE HOME	(564)555-3248	12/31/88	35	F	memo
RO-001	RON'S REFRIGERATORS	(213)555-5764	07/05/87	10	T	memo
TH-001	THE HOME SHOPPE	(415)555-8355	01/29/88	35	F	memo
WA-001	WASHER WAREHOUSE	(213)555-9843	06/30/87	15	F	memo
WE-001	WEST'S WHITE GOODS	(213)555-0478	11/14/88	10	F	memo

| Browse | C:\dbase4\CUSTOMER | Rec 1/16 | File |

View and edit fields

8-26 The BROWSE table with MEMO marker.

the word wrap work surface. Also, if you are using the F3 Previous or the F4 Next keys, the word wrap work surface is opened for you automatically when you move to a memo field.

In the word wrap work surface, you can enter text as with any word processor. The text in a memo field is entirely free-format. This means that the appearance of the text is completely up to you. The memo field should contain only text that is to be printed or displayed. If some value is entered that is required in a calculation, it would be difficult and time-consuming to extract that needed data item inside a program. It is possible to do this, but it is costly in processing time and programming time.

You can move text around, insert new lines, copy text from one location to another, and delete text from the memo field. The F6 "Extend select" key allows you to select an area of text to move, copy, or delete. You press F6, move the cursor to the end of the area you wish to select, then press Enter. An area of text is now highlighted, as shown in Fig. 8-27.

Once you have selected an area of text, the F7 Move key moves that text to a new location. You move the cursor to the location that you want the text to be moved to and press F7. F8 Copy allows you to copy the text to another position in the memo field. If you press the Del key, the selected text is deleted.

If you press F6 once, you begin the select process at a character level. If you press F6 twice, the current word is selected automatically. If you press F6 three times, the entire paragraph is selected automatically.

Several other editing key combinations that you can use while in the word wrap work surface, are shown in Fig. 8-28. Ctrl—T deletes the current

```
Browse  ║C:\dbase4\CUSTOMER    ║Line:1 Col:33   ║File ║        ║       Ins
```

8-27 Using F6 (Extend select) on text.

word, while Ctrl–Backspace deletes the previous word. Using the cursor-left and -right keys, you can move the cursor quickly to the beginning of the next word. Ctrl–N lets you insert a new line of text. Finally, Ctrl–End lets you leave the memo field, saving any changes that you have made. If you want to leave the memo field without saving your changes, use the Esc key.

The word wrap work surface also has a menu that you can reach by using the F10 Menus option, or by pressing the Alt key in combination with the first letter of the menu choice. Figure 8-29 shows the Layout menu for the word wrap work surface when editing a memo field.

The Menus option is used in other work surfaces for other options, but in a memo field its only purpose is to save the text of the memo field. This is useful when you are entering a lot of text, and want to save it in small sections.

The Words menu of the word wrap work surface shown in Fig. 8-30, gives you several options that allow you to not only manipulate the text inside a memo field, but also to manipulate the work surface itself. You can change the ruler that is displayed at the top of the screen, or get rid of it completely by using the Hide ruler toggle. You can also import text into the memo field by using the Write/read text file option.

The Go To menu, as shown in Fig. 8-31, allows you to position yourself in the memo field. The Go To line number option positions you to a particular line in the memo field text. Forward/backward search lets you search for a text string in the memo field. The Replace option allows you to search for a text string, then replace it with another. Finally, the Match capitalization option allows you to toggle whether or not the case of the text is ignored in the search.

```
┌─────────────────────────────────────────────────────────────────────┐
│ Function keys                                                         │
├─────────────────────────────────────────────────────────────────────┤
│ F1 Help              Enters dBASE Help system                         │
│ F6 Extend Select     Starts selection of text and fields             │
│ F7 Move              Move selection to new location                   │
│ F8 Copy              Copy selection to another location               │
│ F9 Zoom              Open text window to full screen size             │
│ F10 Menus            Access Work Surface menus                        │
├─────────────────────────────────────────────────────────────────────┤
│ Un-aided keys                                                         │
├─────────────────────────────────────────────────────────────────────┤
│ PgUp                 Moves up one page                                │
│ PgDn                 Moves down one page                              │
│ Up arrow             Moves cursor up one line                         │
│ Down arrow           Moves cursor down one line                       │
│ Esc                  Exit the word-wrap session,                      │
│                          ignoring changes                             │
│ Del                  Delete current selection                         │
├─────────────────────────────────────────────────────────────────────┤
│ Ctrl- keys                                                            │
├─────────────────────────────────────────────────────────────────────┤
│ Ctrl-End             End word wrap session, saving changes            │
│ Ctrl-Y               Delete line                                      │
│ Ctrl-T               Delete previous word                             │
│ Ctrl-PgUp            Move to first line                               │
│ Ctrl-PgDn            Move to last line                                │
│ Ctrl-Right arrow     Move to next word                                │
│ Ctrl-Left arrow      Move to previous word                            │
└─────────────────────────────────────────────────────────────────────┘
```

8-28 Word Wrap work surface keystrokes.

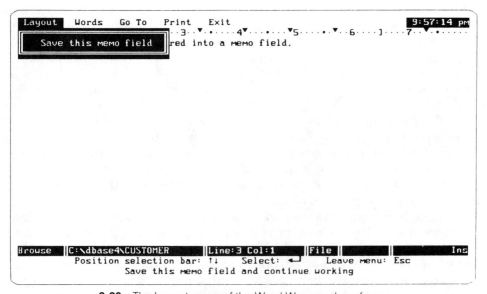

8-29 The Layout menu of the Word Wrap work surface.

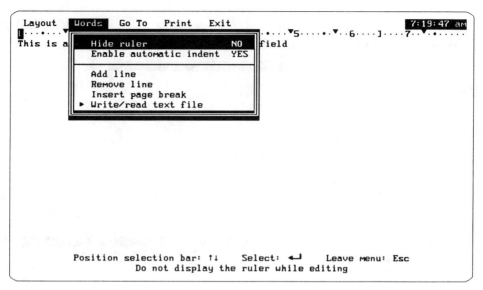

8-30 The Words menu of the Word Wrap work surface.

The Exit menu allows you to exit from the word wrap work surface (see Fig. 8-32). If you exit without saving the changes you have made, the value of the memo field returns to the value it had prior to your entering the word wrap work surface. Otherwise, the new value is saved, and you return to the place where you pressed Ctrl–Home.

8-31 The Go To menu of the Word Wrap work surface.

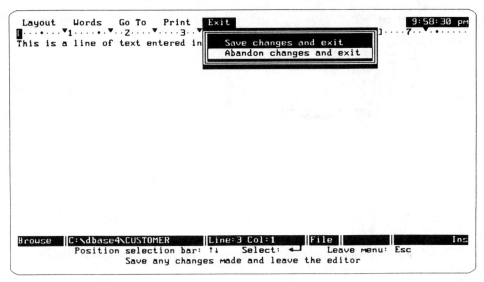

8-32 The Exit Word Wrap work surface menu option.

Getting data out of a memo field There are several methods to reporting, displaying, and printing the text that is stored in a memo field. Use the Print menu of the word wrap work surface, or the dBASE Report Generator, to print the contents of the memo field. You could also write the text of the memo field to another text file. You can even display the memo field on a screen format, using a window to show a scroll-able form of the text contained in the memo field.

The text you enter into a memo field may be of any nature. It could be just a list of changes made to the database record, to show an audit trail of activity. If the database contained data for a personnel department in acompany, a memo field could be used to hold the results of an employee's yearly reviews, or a list of skills the employee possesses. In a customer database, a memo field might be used to keep a record of customer correspondence. A salesman who has a customer database might even keep personal data about a client, such as their children's names and birthdays.

The Print menu of the word wrap work surface, as shown in Fig. 8-33, lets you print the contents of a memo field on the printer. There are several options for printing, and this menu is discussed at greater length in chapter 13 on reports. You can also use a memo field in a report format. When you specify the memo field to be included, dBASE IV gives you a column for the field that is 50 characters wide. An example of a report with a memo field is shown in Fig. 8-34 on the next page.

The Write/read text file option of the Words menu lets you copy text from the memo field into an external text file. Text that has been selected using F6

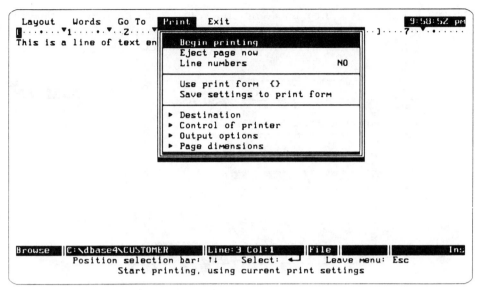

8-33 The Print menu of the Word Wrap work surface.

Extend select is copied to an external text file that you name (see Fig. 8-35). This text file can then be used outside of dBASE, or you can edit it from the dot prompt by issuing the command:

. MODIFY FILE *filename*

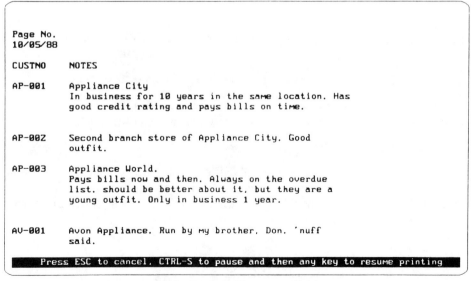

8-34 Report with a memo field.

Markers and windows The most common way of displaying memo fields is by displaying them on the screen. Besides the "word wrap" work surface, you can use a window to display the memo field text directly.

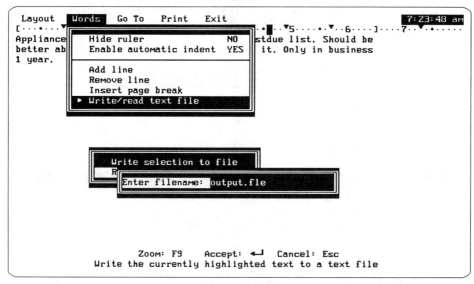

8-35 Exporting text.

The usual way of seeing a memo field is the memo field marker. When you press Ctrl–Home on the memo marker, you "open a window" into the text, because when you exit the word wrap work surface, you return to the display that you came from.

You can create windows to display memo fields on the screen without causing the entire screen to be taken up by the word wrap work surface. The command:

. DEFINE WINDOW *windowname* FROM *row1, col1* TO *row2, col2*

tells dBASE to reserve a window at those screen coordinates. The window can be associated with a memo field display by using the command:

. SET WINDOW OF MEMO TO *windowname*

Now, when you use the EDIT or BROWSE screens, and you access the memo field, the window that opens is defined by the row and column numbers in the DEFINE WINDOW command. For example, if you enter these commands from the dot prompt:

. USE CUSTOMER
. DEFINE WINDOW CNOTES FROM 10,40 TO 20,70
. SET WINDOW OF MEMO TO CNOTES
. EDIT

you are in the EDIT work surface, positioned to the first record of the CUSTOMER database. If you then move to the marker for the memo field NOTES and press Ctrl–Home, the memo field is displayed in the defined window, as shown in Fig. 8-36.

8-36 The memo field window.

The actual programming command that supports memo field windows is the @...GET command, in conjunction with the DEFINE WINDOW and SET WINDOW OF MEMO commands. The command is:

> @ *row,col* GET *memofield* WINDOW *windowname*

This form of the command opens the defined window when the marker is accessed and Ctrl–Home is pressed. The same command with the OPEN operand:

> @ *row,col* GET *memofield* OPEN WINDOW *windowname*

opens the window automatically on the screen. If you want to edit the text in a memo field, you are still required to press Ctrl–Home, but the text is displayed in the defined window.

Bringing outside data into memo fields   Data in a dBASE memo field can be copied from an external text file in the word wrap work surface by using the Words menu. The size of a memo field is limited to 5,000 characters, including carriage returns, so there is a limit to how much data you can import into a memo field.

The Write/read text file option of the Words menu allows you to copy external text files into a dBASE memo field. You choose this option and enter the name of the external file, as shown in Fig. 8-37.

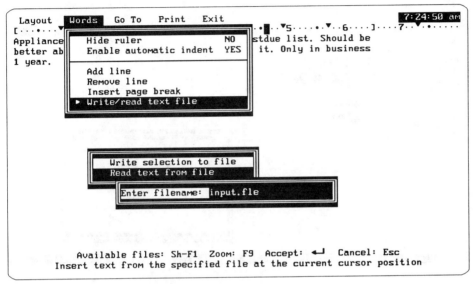

8-37 Copying an external text file.

A common practice before memo fields were included in dBASE was to store textual information in a file as a group of character fields. These pseudo-text records are stored on a separate database, related by the key field of the record they applied to. The only other field on the record would be a 50-character field containing one line of text. This pseudo-text database could be manipulated, edited, and printed like any other. The widespread use of this type of text manipulation leads to the creation of the memo field.

People who use this technique now want to change their character-field text data into a memo field, thus reducing or eliminating the programming necessary for the use of the character databases. In small systems, this can be done very easily. First, the character fields for each main record are copied to a separate SDF (Standard Data Format) file, which become the external text files. Then the main database can be modified to include the new memo field. Finally, the database is edited, the memo fields accessed, and each external text file copied into the memo field by using the Write/read text file option of the Words menu. Small amounts of text can be converted into a memo field in this manner.

9
Sorting and indexing

One of the most important features in dBASE IV is the ability to reorder data. Most of the time you want your database in a certain order. Possibly, you may want to see your customers in alphabetical order by name. You might also want a list by their state. There are even times you might want a list of customers in the order of the customer who owes the most money to the one who owes the least money.

A new order

Ordering data in dBASE IV is done by sorting and indexing.

Reordering data

One way to rearrange data in a file is to sort the data. This means to physically move the records into the order you want. When you sort a database, dBASE moves each and every record to put the database in the order you request. Each time you change the order, dBASE must move the records. Each time you add a record, the data must also be re-sorted. To sort 1000 records using dBASE IV could take as much as several minutes, depending on the length of your record and the complexity of your sort.

Fortunately, dBASE also provides a second, faster method of rearranging records. Indexing is a method where a separate list of "pointers" is kept. This list contains the order of the records in the database based upon the sort order that you specified, also called an index expression or index key. A database can be indexed much faster than it can be sorted. Indexes also allow multiple rearrangement in a short period of time. Indexing a database assigns values to a list of pointers, which is a fairly fast operation, while sorting means physically rearranging the data, a fairly slow operation.

When you view your data with an index, your data appears to have been rearranged, but in reality dBASE IV arranges the display of your data into the order specified by the master index.

To illustrate the concepts of sorting and indexing, look at the database CUSTOMER displayed using a BROWSE table, as shown in Fig. 9-1.

```
┌──────────────────────────────────────────────────────────────────────────┐
│  Records   Fields   Organize   Go To   Exit              [11:30:55 am]     │
│ ┌────────┬────────────────────┬─────────────────────┬───────────────────┬──────┬───┐ │
│ │CUSTNO  │COMPANY             │STREET               │CITY               │STATE │ZI │ │
│ ├────────┼────────────────────┼─────────────────────┼───────────────────┼──────┼───┤ │
│ │AP-001  │APPLIANCE CITY      │210 SKY LANE         │OXNARD             │CA    │95 │ │
│ │AP-002  │APPLIANCE CITY      │360 ACE AVE          │HOLLYWOOD          │CA    │95 │ │
│ │AP-003  │APPLIANCE WORLD     │20695 BLUE BIRD AVE  │SAN FRANCISCO      │CA    │95 │ │
│ │AV-001  │AVON APPLIANCE      │1687 NEW PLACE ROAD  │LOS ANGELES        │CA    │98 │ │
│ │BO-001  │BOB'S BRANDS        │BOB'S DRIVE          │SANTA FE           │NM    │84 │ │
│ │CA-001  │CARY'S COOLERS      │60 STRAWBERRY HILLS  │WINDSOR            │CT    │06 │ │
│ │CR-001  │CRAZY FREDDIES      │1820 171ST ST        │NEW YORK           │NY    │15 │ │
│ │ER-001  │ERNIES TV           │456 SNOW PLOW AVE    │BLEAUVILLE         │CA    │94 │ │
│ │FR-001  │FRIENDLY APPLIANCE  │26 CHOCOLATE AVE     │HERSHEY            │PA    │15 │ │
│ │JA-001  │JACKEL & HYDES      │357 BAT COURT        │LAWRENCEVILLE      │PA    │14 │ │
│ │JI-001  │JIM'S HOT AND COLD  │55 SKINNER ROAD      │VERNON             │CA    │95 │ │
│ │RA-001  │RANGES ON THE HOME  │23 OLD OKIE DR       │OKLAHOMA CITY      │OK    │73 │ │
│ │RO-001  │RON'S REFRIGERATORS │141 HOLLOW OAK PLACE │SAN JUAN CAPISTRANO│CA    │95 │ │
│ │TH-001  │THE HOME SHOPPE     │25 APPLIANCE LANE    │SARATOGA           │CA    │93 │ │
│ │WA-001  │WASHER WAREHOUSE    │15525 MARINER DR     │LOS ALTOS          │CA    │97 │ │
│ │WE-001  │WEST'S WHITE GOODS  │26 DENNIS LANE       │CUPERTINO          │CA    │92 │ │
│ └────────┴────────────────────┴─────────────────────┴───────────────────┴──────┴───┘ │
│ │Browse  ││C:\dbase4\CUSTOMER   ││Rec 1/16      ││File ││          ││          │      │
│                        View and edit fields                                │
└──────────────────────────────────────────────────────────────────────────┘
```

9-1   The CUSTOMER database.

Keys

You can see that the CUSTOMER file is in order by customer number—that is to say, the value in the field CUSTNO. You can arrange the data into order by the contents of a field, in ascending or descending sequence. The field or fields that you specify as containing the values to be sorted are called the keys. The first field in a list of fields to be sorted on is called the primary key, while the rest are called secondary keys.

Normally, a database is sorted by an ascending key. The record with the lowest value in the key field becomes the first record and the record with the highest value of the key field becomes the last record. Character values are sorted from A to Z, with all lowercase characters coming after the uppercase characters. The lowercase letters have higher values than the uppercase Z. Numbers are sorted from the lowest negative value to the highest positive value. These orders are reversed in a descending sort.

Ascending sorts

If the CUSTOMER database was sorted by STATE, the data would be physically rearranged to look like Fig. 9-2. The commands to sort the CUSTOMER database on STATE are:

```
. USE CUSTOMER
. SORT ON STATE TO CUSTST
```

Each record is moved to a new position in the database. If two or more state codes began with the same letter, the sort would take the second letters into consideration. If two fields have exactly the same value, then the order is kept the same as before the sort.

```
Records    Fields    Organize    Go To    Exit                    11:31:59 am

CUSTNO  COMPANY                STREET               CITY                  STATE  ZI

ER-001  ERNIES TV              456 SNOW PLOW AVE    BLEAUVILLE            CA     94
AP-001  APPLIANCE CITY         210 SKY LANE         OXNARD                CA     95
AP-002  APPLIANCE CITY         360 ACE AVE          HOLLYWOOD             CA     95
AP-003  APPLIANCE WORLD        20695 BLUE BIRD AVE  SAN FRANCISCO         CA     95
AV-001  AVON APPLIANCE         1687 NEW PLACE ROAD  LOS ANGELES           CA     98
WE-001  WEST'S WHITE GOODS     26 DENNIS LANE       CUPERTINO             CA     92
WA-001  WASHER WAREHOUSE       15525 MARINER DR     LOS ALTOS             CA     97
JI-001  JIM'S HOT AND COLD     55 SKINNER ROAD      VERNON                CA     95
RO-001  RON'S REFRIGERATORS    141 HOLLOW OAK PLACE SAN JUAN CAPISTRANO   CA     95
TH-001  THE HOME SHOPPE        25 APPLIANCE LANE    SARATOGA              CA     93
CA-001  CARY'S COOLERS         60 STRAWBERRY HILLS  WINDSOR               CT     06
BO-001  BOB'S BRANDS           BOB'S DRIVE          SANTA FE              NM     84
CR-001  CRAZY FREDDIES         1820 171ST ST        NEW YORK              NY     15
RA-001  RANGES ON THE HOME     23 OLD OKIE DR       OKLAHOMA CITY         OK     73
JA-001  JACKEL & HYDES         357 BAT COURT        LAWRENCEVILLE         PA     14
FR-001  FRIENDLY APPLIANCE     26 CHOCOLATE AVE     HERSHEY               PA     15

Browse   C:\dbase4\CUSTST        Rec 1/16          File

                           View and edit fields
```

9-2 The CUSTOMER database sorted by STATE.

Descending sorts

If you sorted the CUSTOMER database by the field DISCOUNT in descending mode, using the command:

```
. SORT ON DISCOUNT DESCENDING TO STDDISC
```

the data would look like the database in Fig. 9-3. The data is again rearranged. The highest discount is displayed first, and the lowest discount is last. Sorting data does not disturb the order of the fields on the database. The entire record is moved regardless of which field is used as the key.

CUSTNO	COMPANY	ZIP	PHONE	LST_TXND	DISCOUNT	TAXAB
CA-001	CARY'S COOLERS	06773-	(203)555-7799	1988.08.21	50	F
RA-001	RANGES ON THE HOME	73344-	(564)555-3248	1988.12.31	35	F
TH-001	THE HOME SHOPPE	93434-	(415)555-8355	1988.01.29	35	F
JA-001	JACKEL & HYDES	14434-	(717)555-3656	1988.05.24	25	F
AP-001	APPLIANCE CITY	95677-	(415)555-4772	1988.07.25	15	F
AP-002	APPLIANCE CITY	95245-	(213)555-4766	1988.08.10	15	F
AV-001	AVON APPLIANCE	98887-	(415)555-7963	1988.05.16	15	T
FR-001	FRIENDLY APPLIANCE	15554-	(717)555-6274	1988.07.01	15	F
WA-001	WASHER WAREHOUSE	97688-	(213)555-9843	1987.06.30	15	F
RO-001	RON'S REFRIGERATORS	95564-6877	(213)555-5764	1987.07.05	10	T
ER-001	ERNIES TV	94454-8946	(213)555-4975	1988.11.29	10	T
WE-001	WEST'S WHITE GOODS	92324-3342	(213)555-0478	1988.11.14	10	F
CR-001	CRAZY FREDDIES	15545-	(212)555-9974	1988.10.11	5	F
JI-001	JIM'S HOT AND COLD	95565-8784	(213)555-6473	1988.07.13	5	F
BO-001	BOB'S BRANDS	84545-4545	(434)555-3444	1986.05.31	0	F
AP-003	APPLIANCE WORLD	95564-	(415)555-3353	1988.08.19	0	T

Browse   C:\dbase4\STDDISC   Rec 1/16   File

View and edit fields

9-3 The database sorted by descending DISCOUNT.

The concept of indexing

In the examples shown in Figs. 9-1 through 9-3, the data records were physically rearranged by the SORT command. Figure 9-4 shows a conceptual model of the STATE sort done with an index. As you can see, the index is a separate list that contains the order of the database.

Customer file   Customer index

#	CUSTNO	COMPANY			
				>CARY'S COOLERS	5
1	010001	CRAZY FREDDIES	. . .	CRAZY FREDDIES	1
2	012000	FRIENDLY APPLIANCE	. . .	ERNIES TV	3
3	013001	ERNIES TV	. . .	FRIENDLY APPLIANCE	2
4	014001	JACKEL & HYDES	. . .	JACKEL & HYDES	4
5	021001	CARY'S COOLERS	. . .		

9-4 The database with index pointers.

Indexing a database is much faster than sorting because you are simply setting up the pointers. In reality, the pointers do not look like those in Fig. 9-4, but rather the index records are put into the key sequence, with a pointer to the database records.

Another analogy of index pointers is the index in the back of a software product catalog. The products are contained in the index by the product type, manufacturer, and by the product name. There are three separate indices all pointing to the same page in the catalog. The index takes much less space than the catalog itself, because it only contains pointers to the products—the pointers, in this case, being page numbers. dBASE's index pointers are actually record numbers for the records in the database.

Multiple field sorting and indexing

The application for a more complex database, such as the payroll database in Fig. 9-5, will probably need to sort the data in more complex ways.

```
 Records    Fields    Organize    Go To    Exit                    12:40:41 pm
┌──────────┬────────┬──────────┬─────────┬──────────┬───────────────────────┐
│ EMPLNO   │ DEPTNO │ SALARY   │ PAYGRADE│ HIREDATE │ BIRTHDATE             │
├──────────┼────────┼──────────┼─────────┼──────────┼───────────────────────┤
│111-22-3333│ 4100  │ 12135.00 │ 02      │1988.12.01│1954.01.04             │
│222-33-4444│ 4100  │ 17655.00 │ 03      │1988.01.01│1957.08.04             │
│333-44-5555│ 4100  │ 10200.00 │ 01      │1988.01.01│1952.09.19             │
│444-55-6666│ 4000  │ 21000.00 │ 04      │1987.06.01│1956.12.22             │
│555-66-7777│ 4700  │ 19200.00 │ 04      │1986.01.01│1960.10.18             │
└──────────┴────────┴──────────┴─────────┴──────────┴───────────────────────┘
 Browse    C:\dbase4\PAYZ              Rec 1/5          File
                          View and edit fields
```

9-5 A payroll database example.

You might want to sort or index on multiple fields. For example, the manager of a payroll department might want to see the payroll database by department and the highest paid to lowest paid individual. This does not mean that the database has to be stored and maintained in two different files and in two different orders. This means that the manager wants to see the database in the order of department, and within the records of a department to see records in the descending order of salary. This is called a multiple field sort.

After sorting the payroll database in ascending order by department and at the same time by descending salary, the database looks like Fig. 9-6. The database is now sorted by department. Within each department, the records are sorted from the highest salary to the lowest salary. This lets the manager choose the highest paid from each department.

You can sort on a maximum of ten fields. As you sort on more fields, however, you begin to break up your database into detail that rarely is needed. If name is your primary key, then a secondary key is only needed where two names are the same. A large corporation might process millions of

```
Records    Fields   Organize    Go To    Exit
┌──────────┬───────┬──────────┬─────────┬──────────┬────────────┐
│ EMPLNO   │DEPTNO │SALARY    │PAYGRADE │HIREDATE  │BIRTHDATE   │
├──────────┼───────┼──────────┼─────────┼──────────┼────────────┤
│444-55-6666│4000  │21000.00  │04       │1987.06.01│1956.12.22  │
│222-33-4444│4100  │17655.00  │03       │1988.01.01│1957.08.04  │
│111-22-3333│4100  │12135.00  │02       │1988.12.01│1954.01.04  │
│333-44-5555│4100  │10200.00  │01       │1988.01.01│1952.09.19  │
│555-66-7777│4700  │19200.00  │04       │1986.01.01│1960.10.18  │
│          │       │          │         │          │            │
└──────────┴───────┴──────────┴─────────┴──────────┴────────────┘
 Browse    C:\dbase4\PAY3          Rec 1/5          File
                      View and edit fields
```

9-6   Multiple field sorting.

records a day for expenses. Fields may include operating company, department, expense code, date, and amount. Hundreds of records might have the same operating company, department, expense code, and date. Each might have different amounts. That is an example where a multiple field sort is necessary.

You can also produce multiple keys for indexes as well. The problem with SORT is that, once the records are in a particular order, the only way to change the order is to rewrite the records. Indexes allow the database to be used in many different orders, by varying key fields, all of which are updated as records are added to the database.

Sorting the database with dBASE

The SORT command structure is shown in Fig. 9-7. When you sort a file in dBASE, you are actually sorting a copy of the original data. dBASE asks you for a name of the new database to be created. The SORT command creates this new database. The database can be sorted by character, numeric, or date fields. Logical fields and memo fields are not to be accepted by either the SORT or the INDEX commands.

Sorting on one field

Why would you ever use a SORT command? After all, indexing is faster than sorting, and you can reindex at any time that you want, without hurting or rearranging the original data.

```
SORT TO <FILENAME>   ON   <FIELD1> [ /A /D /C ]

                     [ , <FIELD2> [ /A /D /C ] ] ...
                     [ , <FIELDn> [ /A /D /C ] ]

                     [ ASCENDING / DESCENDING ]
```

9-7 The dBASE IV SORT command.

There are some very good reasons for using the SORT command. Imagine that your business or organization has several operators involved in data entry, each entering a specific portion of the CUSTOMER database. After all of the data entry is complete, each operator has a dBASE database that resembles the CUSTOMER database used as an example here; one operator has a database called CUST1, the second has CUST2, and so forth. First, all the customer records must be placed into the same database file, using the commands:

. USE CUSTOMER
. APPEND FROM CUST1
. APPEND FROM CUST2

  ...

until all of the customer records have been placed into the CUSTOMER database. The records put into the database in this manner are in the order that they were entered. The database could now be indexed by the customer number or by name—dBASE and your application programs still process in the expected manner using the index.

The application programs that process this database or perform searches in this file, also work slightly more efficiently if the database is in some order. The primary key of the CUSTOMER database is CUSTNO or customer number. After all of the records from the operators' databases are appended to the full CUSTOMER database, the database can be sorted into physical sequence by CUSTNO. Periodically, during the lifetime of an application system, the files need to be reorganized for efficiency.

To use the SORT command, you must first have an active database. Enter the command:

. USE CUSTOMER

You then could issue the command:

. SORT TO SORTCUST ON CUSTNO

to sort the records into physical sequence by CUSTNO. The CUSTOMER database has been copied into a new database, the SORTCUST database. You can recover the original environment by using the commands:

. DELETE FILE CUSTOMER.DBF
. RENAME SORTCUST.DBF TO CUSTOMER.DBF

Note that, in the DELETE FILE and RENAME commands, you must use the .DBF extension when referring to the database files.

The SORT options /A, /C, and /D allow you to specify, on a field-by-field basis, whether the field is to be sorted in Ascending or Descending order. The /C option tells the SORT command to treat all alphabetic characters as if they were uppercase—that is to say, the case of the field is ignored during the SORT. In dBASE IV, this is also called dictionary order. If you wanted to sort the database by CUSTNO in descending order and ignoring case, the command would be:

. SORT TO SORTCUST ON CUSTNO /DC

Other SORT options allow you to choose certain records to be copied, instead of the whole database. You can create smaller files for use on other machines or for back-up purposes.

You can also SORT databases from the dBASE IV Control Center. After you have selected/opened a database on the Control Center main menu, you could enter the Design work surface by pressing Shift–F2. You should access this menu from the BROWSE and EDIT work surface (F2). The Organize menu, as shown in Fig. 9-8, allows you to SORT the database.

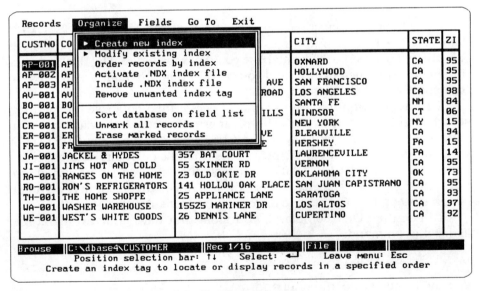

9-8 The Organize menu.

Choosing the Organize menu option Sort database on field list gives you the option of entering the fields to be sorted. You can also choose the sort order (ascending/descending) on a field-by-field basis. What the Control Center is actually doing is building a SORT command just like the one that you enter from the dot prompt. Figure 9-9 shows the Sort Database on Field List menu with the field STATE chosen as the sort key.

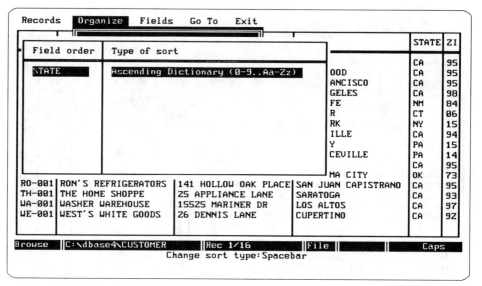

9-9 Choosing the sort key fields.

The only field selected is STATE. After you enter the field name in the Field order column, you can then move to the Type of sort column, which is already prefilled with the option for an ascending ASCII sort. You can change this sort order by pressing the Spacebar. Each possible value for the sort order will be displayed—you can choose the order you want by pressing Enter. Figure 9-10 shows the four sort orders allowed for each field.

9-10 The sort order options of Organize.

```
Ascending ASCII (0..9A..Za..z)

Descending ASCII (z..aZ..A9..0)

Ascending Dictionary (0..9Aa..Zz)

Descending Dictionary (Zz..Aa9..0)
```

As you use the Control Center, the command is being created for you. When you have completed entering the sort key fields, the Control Center asks for the name of the new database to copy the sorted records into (Fig. 9-11). The new database is called CUSTST.DBF. The file extension .DBF is automatically added to the name you enter if you do not specify a file extension. The new file name must also be different from the original file name, because the original database is still open. If you try to sort the database to a database that already exists, you will be prompted to overwrite the file.

The final command is generated by the Control Center when you press the Enter key after entering the new database name. The result is shown in Fig. 9-12. Note that you could have performed the same SORT by issuing the USE CUSTOMER and the SORT command from the dot prompt.

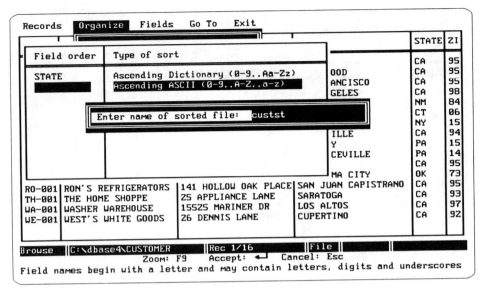

				STATE	ZI
				CA	95
Field order	Type of sort			CA	95
			OOD	CA	95
STATE	Ascending Dictionary (0-9..Aa-Zz)		ANCISCO	CA	98
	Ascending ASCII (0-9..A-Z..a-z)		GELES	NM	84
				CT	06
	Enter name of sorted file: custst			NY	15
			ILLE	CA	94
			Y	PA	15
			CEVILLE	PA	14
				CA	95
			MA CITY	OK	73
RO-001	RON'S REFRIGERATORS	141 HOLLOW OAK PLACE	SAN JUAN CAPISTRANO	CA	95
TH-001	THE HOME SHOPPE	25 APPLIANCE LANE	SARATOGA	CA	93
WA-001	WASHER WAREHOUSE	15525 MARINER DR	LOS ALTOS	CA	97
WE-001	WEST'S WHITE GOODS	26 DENNIS LANE	CUPERTINO	CA	92

Browse   C:\dbase4\CUSTOMER   Rec 1/16   File

Zoom: F9   Accept: ←   Cancel: Esc

Field names begin with a letter and may contain letters, digits and underscores

9-11   Naming the SORTed database.

You will now find a new file called CUSTST.DBF on your disk. It contains the same fields and records as the original file CUSTOMER.DBF, except that the records are rearranged by the value of the STATE field.

Records   Organize   Fields   Go To   Exit

CUSTNO	COMPANY	STREET	CITY	STATE	ZI
AP-001	APPLIANCE CITY	210 SKY LANE	OXNARD	CA	95
AP-002	APPLIANCE CITY	360 ACE AVE	HOLLYWOOD	CA	95
AP-003	APPLIANCE WORLD	20695 BLUE BIRD AVE	SAN FRANCISCO	CA	95
AV-001	AVON APPLIANCE	1687 NEW PLACE ROAD	LOS ANGELES	CA	98
BO-001	BOB'S BRANDS	BOB'S DRIVE	SANTA FE	NM	84
CA-001	CARY'S COOLERS	60 STRAWBERRY HILLS	WINDSOR	CT	06
CR-001	CRAZY FREDDIES	1820 171ST ST	NEW YORK	NY	15
ER-001	ERNIES TV	456 SNOW PLOW AVE	BLEAUVILLE	CA	94

SORT TO C:\DBASE4\custst.

| WA-001 | WASHER WAREHOUSE | 15525 MARINER DR | LOS ALTOS | CA | 97 |
| WE-001 | WEST'S WHITE GOODS | 26 DENNIS LANE | CUPERTINO | CA | 92 |

Browse   C:\dbase4\CUSTOMER   Rec 1/16   File

9-12   Sorting from the Control Center.

The Control Center main menu, as shown in Fig. 9-13, now shows more than one database in the Database column. You must choose the CUSTST database or USE it to make it active. Once you open the new file, select the F2 Data option to BROWSE the database, as you saw in Fig. 9-2.

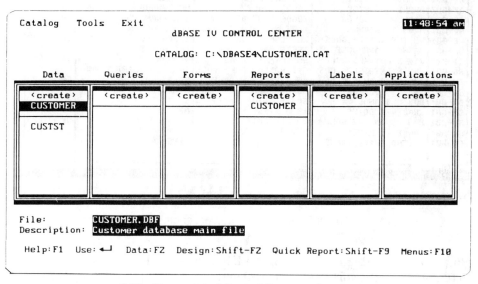

9-13 The updated Control Center main menu.

The data is now in order by the values contained in the STATE field. All the California records are first followed by the Connecticut record, and so on. The order of the records within each state may not necessarily be the same as the order in the original database.

Sorting on descending keys

To sort any field by descending order merely requires the option /D be added after any field that you want sorted into descending order. The statement to sort the file into descending order by STATE would be:

```
. SORT TO CUSTSTD ON STATE /D
```

This would create a file called CUSTSTD.DBF with the same records, except that the records from Pennsylvania would be first, then Oklahoma, and so forth to Connecticut. Figure 9-14 shows the CUSTSTD database after the descending sort on STATE. Character, date, float, and numeric fields can be sorted in descending order.

Sorting on multiple fields

When you sort a database by multiple fields, you are really creating sorts within a sort. You can specify up to ten sort fields in the SORT statement,

CUSTNO	COMPANY	STREET	CITY	STATE	ZI
ER-001	ERNIES TV	456 SNOW PLOW AVE	BLEAUVILLE	CA	94
AP-001	APPLIANCE CITY	210 SKY LANE	OXNARD	CA	95
AP-002	APPLIANCE CITY	360 ACE AVE	HOLLYWOOD	CA	95
AP-003	APPLIANCE WORLD	20695 BLUE BIRD AVE	SAN FRANCISCO	CA	95
AV-001	AVON APPLIANCE	1687 NEW PLACE ROAD	LOS ANGELES	CA	98
WE-001	WEST'S WHITE GOODS	26 DENNIS LANE	CUPERTINO	CA	92
WA-001	WASHER WAREHOUSE	15525 MARINER DR	LOS ALTOS	CA	97
JI-001	JIM'S HOT AND COLD	55 SKINNER ROAD	VERNON	CA	95
RO-001	RON'S REFRIGERATORS	141 HOLLOW OAK PLACE	SAN JUAN CAPISTRANO	CA	95
TH-001	THE HOME SHOPPE	25 APPLIANCE LANE	SARATOGA	CA	93
CA-001	CARY'S COOLERS	60 STRAWBERRY HILLS	WINDSOR	CT	06
BO-001	BOB'S BRANDS	BOB'S DRIVE	SANTA FE	NM	84
CR-001	CRAZY FREDDIES	1820 171ST ST	NEW YORK	NY	15
RA-001	RANGES ON THE HOME	23 OLD OKIE DR	OKLAHOMA CITY	OK	73
JA-001	JACKEL & HYDES	357 BAT COURT	LAWRENCEVILLE	PA	14
FR-001	FRIENDLY APPLIANCE	26 CHOCOLATE AVE	HERSHEY	PA	15

Browse ║C:\dbase4\CUSTST   ║Rec 1/16   ║File ║   Ins

View and edit fields

9-14 CUSTOMER data sorted into descending order by state.

simply by listing them in the command. In the Control Center, you can list up to ten fields on the sort fields list. You can use the /A, /D, and /C options with each field as you wish.

For example, suppose you wanted to sort the CUSTOMER file by STATE, and that within each STATE, you want to see records with the highest DISCOUNT through the lowest DISCOUNT. To create a new database called CUSTDISC.DBF, you would enter the following:

. USE CUSTOMER
. SORT TO CUSTDISC ON STATE, DISCOUNT /D

You could also perform this sort from the Organize menu in the Control Center, as shown in Fig. 9-15.

Figure 9-16 shows the result of this statement applied to the CUSTOMER database. In the figure, some fields are locked so that the results can be clearly seen.

Sorting on multiple field types

dBASE IV allows you to sort on character fields, numeric and floating-point fields, and on date fields. Memo fields cannot be used in a sort because their data physically resides on a different file, the .DBT files associated with the database. Logical fields cannot be used in a sort, because they have only two values, and the values .T. and .F. have no logical "which comes first" relationship.

Fields containing character data are sorted according to their ACSII codes. There are 256 of these codes, but usually, character fields are either

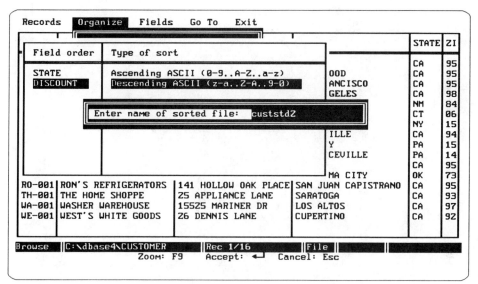

9-15 The multiple-field sort from the Control Center.

```
   Records    Organize    Fields    Go To    Exit

 CUSTNO COMPANY                 STREET                 CITY                  STATE ZI
 TH-001 THE HOME SHOPPE         25 APPLIANCE LANE      SARATOGA              CA    93
 AV-001 AVON APPLIANCE          1687 NEW PLACE ROAD    LOS ANGELES           CA    98
 WA-001 WASHER WAREHOUSE        15525 MARINER DR       LOS ALTOS             CA    97
 AP-002 APPLIANCE CITY          360 ACE AVE            HOLLYWOOD             CA    95
 AP-001 APPLIANCE CITY          210 SKY LANE           OXNARD                CA    95
 ER-001 ERNIES TV               456 SNOW PLOW AVE      BLEAUVILLE            CA    94
 WE-001 WEST'S WHITE GOODS      26 DENNIS LANE         CUPERTINO             CA    92
 RO-001 RON'S REFRIGERATORS     141 HOLLOW OAK PLACE   SAN JUAN CAPISTRANO   CA    95
 JI-001 JIMS HOT AND COLD       55 SKINNER RD          VERNON                CA    95
 AP-003 APPLIANCE WORLD         20695 BLUE BIRD AVE    SAN FRANCISCO         CA    95
 CA-001 CARY'S COOLERS          60 STRAWBERRY HILLS    WINDSOR               CT    06
 BO-001 BOB'S BRANDS            BOB'S DRIVE            SANTA FE              NM    84
 CR-001 CRAZY FREDDIES          1820 171ST ST          NEW YORK              NY    15
 RA-001 RANGES ON THE HOME      23 OLD OKIE DR         OKLAHOMA CITY         OK    73
 JA-001 JACKEL & HYDES          357 BAT COURT          LAWRENCEVILLE         PA    14
 FR-001 FRIENDLY APPLIANCE      26 CHOCOLATE AVE       HERSHEY               PA    15

 Browse   C:\dbase4\CUSTSTD2        Rec 1/16          File
```

9-16 The multiple-sorted CUSTOMER database.

letters, numbers, or spaces. At times, character fields can contain hyphens, slashes, commas, periods, question marks, and exclamation points. The ACSII codes for these characters and their sequence are shown in Fig. 9-17.

Using the /A or ascending options of the SORT command, the order is: numeric digits, uppercase alphabetics, and lowercase alphabetics (space, 0

Character	Decimal ASCII value	Character	Decimal ASCII value	Character	Decimal ASCII value
space	32	K	75	f	102
0	48	L	76	g	103
1	49	M	77	h	104
2	50	N	78	i	105
3	51	O	79	j	106
4	52	P	80	k	107
5	53	Q	81	l	108
6	54	R	82	m	109
7	55	S	83	n	110
8	56	T	84	o	111
9	57	U	85	p	112
A	65	V	86	q	113
B	66	W	87	r	114
C	67	X	88	s	115
D	68	Y	89	t	116
E	69	Z	90	u	117
F	70	a	97	v	118
G	71	b	98	w	119
H	72	c	99	x	120
I	73	d	100	y	121
J	74	e	101	z	122
!	33				
'	44				
-	45				
.	46				
/	47				
?	63				

9-17 The ascending ASCII character order.

through 9, A through Z, a through z). In a descending sort, of course, this order is reversed (z through a, Z through A, 9 through 0, space).

The /C option tells dBASE to ignore the case of the values where alphabetic characters are concerned. This changes the order to numbers first, then letters (space, 0 through 9, and Aa through Zz). This is also called dictionary order when using the Control Center. Characters other than alphabetics continue to be sorted in ASCII code order.

Numeric and float fields sort in ascending or descending order according to their numeric values. Date fields sort in order by their values, from the earliest date to the latest, no matter what date format was used. This means that 12/31/1986 would sort before 01/01/1989 in an ascending sort.

Other restrictions apply to the SORT command. For example, you cannot sort a file onto itself. This is helpful, because the original data is kept, and a new copy created. This way, if anything goes wrong with the SORT—you may have accidentally entered the wrong sort fields or a power failure could occur during the SORT—the original data is still available. SORT also requires that the new database being created is not already open in one of the other dBASE work areas, for the same reason.

Indexing the database with dBASE

Indexing is similar to sorting, except that no data is moved. A file of "pointers" is created, rather than a file of data. While sorting rearranges the data and copies that data to a new database, indexing creates a file of pointers. The pointers define the order of the records in the database file.

If you have arranged your database into a physical sequence, and you wish to maintain this physical sequence, then you must re-SORT the database each time a new record is added. When you use an index, the pointers are automatically updated as you add new records or change the index key fields in existing records.

The CUSTOMER database is shown in Fig. 9-18. A new record, with the customer number of SA-001 has been added to the database. This customer number would fall into order between RO-001 and TH-001, if the database were sorted in physical sequence. If the database was indexed by CUSTNO, the data records would appear to be in order by CUSTNO. If you entered the commands:

. USE CUSTOMER
. INDEX ON CUSTNO TAG CUSTNO
. SET ORDER TO TAG CUSTNO

the CUSTOMER database would appear as shown in Fig. 9-19.

Records	Organize	Fields	Go To	Exit		

CUSTNO	COMPANY	STREET	CITY	STATE	ZI
AP-001	APPLIANCE CITY	210 SKY LANE	OXNARD	CA	95
AP-002	APPLIANCE CITY	360 ACE AVE	HOLLYWOOD	CA	95
AP-003	APPLIANCE WORLD	20695 BLUE BIRD AVE	SAN FRANCISCO	CA	95
AV-001	AVON APPLIANCE	1687 NEW PLACE ROAD	LOS ANGELES	CA	98
BO-001	BOB'S BRANDS	BOB'S DRIVE	SANTA FE	NM	84
CA-001	CARY'S COOLERS	60 STRAWBERRY HILLS	WINDSOR	CT	06
CR-001	CRAZY FREDDIES	1820 171ST ST	NEW YORK	NY	15
ER-001	ERNIES TV	456 SNOW PLOW AVE	BLEAUVILLE	CA	94
FR-001	FRIENDLY APPLIANCE	26 CHOCOLATE AVE	HERSHEY	PA	15
JA-001	JACKEL & HYDES	357 BAT COURT	LAWRENCEVILLE	PA	14
JI-001	JIMS HOT AND COLD	55 SKINNER RD	VERNON	CA	95
RA-001	RANGES ON THE HOME	23 OLD OKIE DR	OKLAHOMA CITY	OK	73
RO-001	RON'S REFRIGERATORS	141 HOLLOW OAK PLACE	SAN JUAN CAPISTRANO	CA	95
TH-001	THE HOME SHOPPE	25 APPLIANCE LANE	SARATOGA	CA	93
WA-001	WASHER WAREHOUSE	15525 MARINER DR	LOS ALTOS	CA	97
WE-001	WEST'S WHITE GOODS	26 DENNIS LANE	CUPERTINO	CA	92
SA-001	SUZIE'S APPLIANCES	123 FOURTH ST	SELDOM SEEN	PA	15

Browse	C:\dbase4\CUSTOMER	Rec 1/17	File	Caps

9-18 The non-indexed CUSTOMER database (natural order).

You can index a database at any time, whether there are data records in it or not. Once you index a database, you never have to index it again as long as the index file is opened at the same time as the database or opened via the SET INDEX TO command.

dBASE IV allows you to create multiple-index files, each containing up to 47 separate indexes. The individual indexes within a multiple-index file are called index tags. You can also create separate index files that each contain a

CUSTNO	COMPANY	STREET	CITY	STATE	ZI
AP-001	APPLIANCE CITY	210 SKY LANE	OXNARD	CA	95
AP-002	APPLIANCE CITY	360 ACE AVE	HOLLYWOOD	CA	95
AP-003	APPLIANCE WORLD	20695 BLUE BIRD AVE	SAN FRANCISCO	CA	95
AV-001	AVON APPLIANCE	1687 NEW PLACE ROAD	LOS ANGELES	CA	98
BO-001	BOB'S BRANDS	BOB'S DRIVE	SANTA FE	NM	84
CA-001	CARY'S COOLERS	60 STRAWBERRY HILLS	WINDSOR	CT	06
CR-001	CRAZY FREDDIES	1820 171ST ST	NEW YORK	NY	15
ER-001	ERNIES TV	456 SNOW PLOW AVE	BLEAUVILLE	CA	94
FR-001	FRIENDLY APPLIANCE	26 CHOCOLATE AVE	HERSHEY	PA	15
JA-001	JACKEL & HYDES	357 BAT COURT	LAWRENCEVILLE	PA	14
JI-001	JIMS HOT AND COLD	55 SKINNER RD	VERNON	CA	95
RA-001	RANGES ON THE HOME	23 OLD OKIE DR	OKLAHOMA CITY	OK	73
RO-001	RON'S REFRIGERATORS	141 HOLLOW OAK PLACE	SAN JUAN CAPISTRANO	CA	95
SA-001	SUZIE'S APPLIANCES	123 FOURTH ST	SELDOM SEEN	PA	15
TH-001	THE HOME SHOPPE	25 APPLIANCE LANE	SARATOGA	CA	93
WA-001	WASHER WAREHOUSE	15525 MARINER DR	LOS ALTOS	CA	97
WE-001	WEST'S WHITE GOODS	26 DENNIS LANE	CUPERTINO	CA	92

Browse   C:\dbase4\CUSTOMER   Rec 1/17   File

9-19   The indexed CUSTOMER database.

single index. Multiple-index files have an extension of .MDX, while index files have an extension of .NDX.

Index files contain information necessary to quickly locate a particular record in a database. The key field of the record, which can be any field in the record, is stored in a tree-type chain; this means that the desired record number can be obtained with a minimal number of disk reads. The record is accessed directly, so that the search-and-wait time is very short.

Indexing on one field

An index is created by the INDEX command shown in Fig. 9-20. The field specified after the ON becomes the key field for that particular index. The key and the record number of each record is stored in the index, and a tree structure is built. The name of the index is specified in the TO clause; this name becomes the name of the index tag, or the name of the .NDX file.

```
INDEX ON <key expression>

        TO <ndx file name> [ FOR <condition> ]    && single-index file

    or ...

        TAG <tag name> [ OF <mdx file name> ]     && multi-index file

            [ FOR <condition> ]
```

9-20   The INDEX command.

Indexing can also be performed from the dBASE IV Control Center, through the Organize menu. This menu is available from the DESIGN, BROWSE, and EDIT work surfaces. You can create a new index tag or file, change the controlling index for the data, and modify an existing index tag or file. For example, Fig. 9-21 shows the CUSTNO index tag being created for the Customer file.

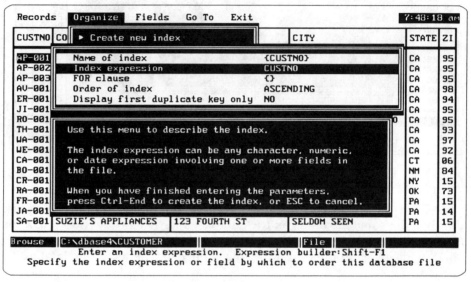

9-21 The CUSTNO index tag created from the Control Center.

You can index the database on a single field using the Create new index option or by entering Y in the index field column on the Design work surface itself.

In the following example, the database CUSTOMER is being indexed by the field STATE. After you have entered the index name and field name, the screen would look like that in Fig. 9-22.

The dot prompt code to index the database by STATE is:

```
. USE CUSTOMER
. INDEX ON STATE TAG CUSTST
```

To view the database in the indexed order, you must tell dBASE the order that you want. This can be done by using separate commands:

```
. USE CUSTOMER
. SET ORDER TO TAG CUSTST
```

or the ORDER can be part of the USE command

```
. USE CUSTOMER ORDER TAG CUSTST
```

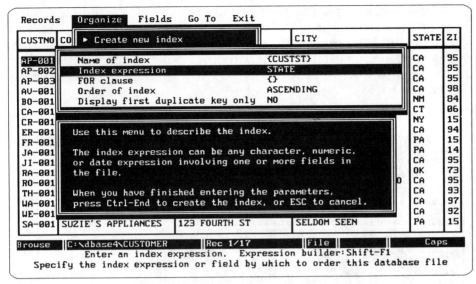

```
  Records    Organize   Fields   Go To   Exit
 CUSTNO CO    ▶ Create new index                        CITY            STATE ZI
 AP-001     Name of index              {CUSTST}                          CA  95
 AP-002     Index expression           STATE                            CA  95
 AP-003     FOR clause                 {}                               CA  95
 AV-001     Order of index             ASCENDING                        CA  98
 BO-001     Display first duplicate key only  NO                        NM  84
 CA-001                                                                 CT  06
 CR-001                                                                 NY  15
 ER-001     Use this menu to describe the index.                       CA  94
 FR-001                                                                 PA  15
 JA-001     The index expression can be any character, numeric,        PA  14
 JI-001     or date expression involving one or more fields in         CA  95
 RA-001     the file.                                                  OK  73
 RO-001                                                              0  CA  95
 TH-001     When you have finished entering the parameters,            CA  93
 WA-001     press Ctrl-End to create the index, or ESC to cancel.      CA  97
 WE-001                                                                 CA  92
 SA-001  SUZIE'S APPLIANCES    123 FOURTH ST      SELDOM SEEN           PA  15

 Browse   C:\dbase4\CUSTOMER      Rec 1/17        File              Caps
        Enter an index expression.  Expression builder:Shift-F1
    Specify the index expression or field by which to order this database file
```

9-22 Indexing by state.

dBASE IV creates a special multiple-index file, called a production .MDX file, that has the same file name as the database file. The production .MDX file is created when you INDEX using a tag name, without specifying an .MDX name. The production .MDX file is opened whenever the database is opened.

If a single-index, or .NDX file, is being used, or if a multiple-index file other than the production .MDX file is being used, you must explicitly open the index in the USE command. You create a separate index by using the commands:

. USE CUSTOMER
. INDEX ON STATE TO CUSTST

This command creates a file called CUSTST.NDX that contains the index. To use this file, and to have it automatically updated, you must explicitly open the index file by:

. USE CUSTOMER INDEX CUSTST

or

. USE CUSTOMER
. SET INDEX TO CUSTST

Indexing on descending fields

dBASE IV allows you to create an index in a descending order. The descending option of the INDEX command causes the index to be built with the highest value first. The descending option refers to the entire index expression; indexing on multiple fields in multiple directions requires careful planning. You can index on a single field in a descending order by using the command:

    . INDEX ON CUSTNO TAG DCUSTNO DESCENDING

This command creates a new tag, DCUSTNO, in the production .MDX file for the CUSTOMER database (CUSTOMER.MDX).

Indexing on multiple fields

Just as the SORT command lets you sort on more than one field, the INDEX command lets you index on more than one field. Indexing requires you to build a single expression, called the index expression, to define the index order. The index expression is changed into a value, then the index tag or file is built. If the index expression is:

    . INDEX ON DISCOUNT + 10 TAG DISC10

then the numeric expression (DISCOUNT + 10) would be evaluated. The index order would be numeric by the value of the expression resulting from using the DISCOUNT value on each database record.

To index a file by multiple fields, you must concatenate the fields together. This means that you must convert the fields in the expression to the same data type. Most of the time, this means character.

The advantage of character fields is that they can be concatenated into a single string of characters. For example, to index the CUSTOMER database by STATE and COMPANY, you enter:

    . INDEX ON STATE + COMPANY TAG STCO

For the first record of the CUSTOMER database, the previous index expression would result in:

    "CA" + "APPLIANCE CITY"

and the final index value would be

    "CAAPPLIANCE CITY"

Concatenation of character strings is accomplished with the "+" operator. STATE + COMPANY concatenates the values of those fields. STATE becomes the primary key, while COMPANY becomes the secondary key. You can concatenate as many fields as you want, as long as the total length of the concatenated key is less than 100 characters.

Indexing on multiple field types

You cannot (directly) index a database by fields of different types. You can convert numeric and date fields to character, then concatenate them into a character string. To index on the STATE field and the numeric field DIS-COUNT with a length of two, enter:

```
. INDEX ON STATE + STR(DISCOUNT, 2) TAG STATEAM
```

Any dBASE built-in function can be used in an index expression. The character field STATE can be used directly, but the DISCOUNT field must be converted to character via the STR( ) function, which converts numeric values to the character data type.

Date fields can be changed to character and used in an index expression by using the DTOC( ) ("date-to-character") function. A standard date, how-ever, is in the wrong format. For example, the date:

```
12/31/87
```

is before:

```
01/01/88
```

If these dates were viewed as character strings, then the 12/31/1987 date is larger than 01/01/1988, and would therefore fall after that date in a character index. The problem is the format: the month is first, followed by the day and year. This does not sort chronologically. A solution to this problem is to use the command:

```
. SET DATE ANSI
```

to convert the date field to "year, month, day" format. Then using the commands:

```
. SET DATE ANSI
. INDEX ON STATE + DTOC(LAST_TXND) TAG STDATE
```

you can create the index tag. You should always store and use dates in your application systems in the ANSI order, to avoid confusion. It is also a good idea to use the SET CENTURY ON command, too, so that dates after the year 2000 will index correctly.

While the entire expression can be changed to descending, it is possible to index on descending numeric and date data fields by using a little calculation. Numeric fields can easily be used as a descending index by themselves. For example, to index in descending order by DISCOUNT, the Customer database could be indexed:

```
. INDEX ON DISCOUNT TAG CUSTDISC
```

By adding a negative sign in front of the numeric key, you are telling dBASE to index by the negative of the value. The file would thus appear to be in descending order. When used as a part of a character index expression, however, you must use a different method.

If you know that the number you are using is 2 digits long, you can subtract the number from 99 to get the inverse value called a nines-complement. To index the CUSTOMER database by ascending STATE and descending DISCOUNT, enter:

```
. INDEX ON STATE + STR((99 – DISCOUNT),2) TAG STATEAM
```

Date fields can also be changed in this manner to get a descending date sort. Date fields can be subtracted to give the number of days between the dates. If you subtract a date value from a date of 9999/12/31, you get a complement form of the date value. This can then be used as a date value. The command to create such an index would be:

```
. SET DATE ANSI
. SET CENTURY ON
. INDEX ON STATE + STR(({9999/12/31} – LAST_TXND),7) TAG STDATE
```

The "{ }" brackets denote a date literal. In prior versions of dBASE, this would be CTOD('9999/12/31'), using the character-to-date built-in function.

Conditional indexing

In dBASE IV version 1.1, you can specify a FOR ⟨condition⟩ parameter in the INDEX ON command. This allows you to create partial indexes based on conditions present on the database records. The index tags built in this manner only have entries for the records that meet the specified criteria.

A database using a conditional index behaves in the same way as a database using a "normal" index tag in conjunction with the SET FILTER TO option. For example, the commands:

```
USE CUSTOMER
INDEX ON COMPANY TAG CO
SET FILTER TO STATE = 'CT'
...
```

cause the CUSTOMER database to be indexed by company name. The filter then restricts the records that are displayed to those with a STATE field value equal to 'CT.' In version 1.1, you can use a conditional index to accomplish the same result:

```
USE CUSTOMER
INDEX ON COMPANY TAG CO FOR STATE = 'CT'
...
```

The conditional index creates an index file which only has entries for the records that have a STATE Field value of 'CT'. This means that the index file will be smaller, because only a part of the database is actually indexed. When you are using large databases, the size of the index file might be a factor in deciding to use conditional indexing.

Using multiple-index files

Multiple-index files, or .MDX files, can contain up to 47 index tags. Each tag behaves like a dBASE III Plus index (.NDX) file. So where the command:

. INDEX ON CUSTNO TO CUSTNO

would create an index file called CUSTNO.NDX, the command:

. INDEX ON CUSTNO TAG CUSTNO OF NEWORDER

creates a new index tag in the NEWORDER.MDX file.

If you specify TAG without specifying a file name, the Tag becomes part of the production .MDX file. This multiple-index file is always associated with the database.

Multiple-index, MDX files

Multiple-index and single-index files are opened either as a function of the USE command or by using the SET INDEX TO command.

If a multiple-index file is open, then all of the index tags contained in the file are automatically updated as records are added to the database. The production .MDX file is opened automatically along with the database, if it exists.

To use a multiple-index file other than the production .MDX file, use the command:

. SET INDEX TO NEWORDER TAG CUSTNO OF NEWORDER

or

. USE CUSTOMER INDEX NEWORDER ORDER TAG CUSTNO OF NEWORDER

You can also specify a number of index files with the SET INDEX TO command. You can specify up to ten filenames, either .NDX files or .MDX files. You do not have to specify the name of the production .MDX file, which is opened automatically.

Production .MDX files

The easiest way to use indexes in dBASE IV is to place all of the index tags that you need for a database in the production .MDX file. This is a file containing index tags that have the same name as the database file. For example, the CUSTOMER database would have a production .MDX file called CUSTOMER. MDX.

If you use the production .MDX file, you never have to open the index with a separate command. You can change the database order by simply issuing the command:

SET ORDER TO TAG *(tagname)*

If you use readable names for your index tags within the production .MDX file, you can change up to 47 orders instantly. These index tags are updated automatically whenever the database is open and records are added or removed (via PACK).

If you create an index tag and do not specify an "OF" option, dBASE assumes that the tag is to be placed in the production .MDX file. If one does not exist, it is created automatically.

Tags

The dBASE index file or tag is a structure called a B+ tree. This hierarchical tree structure contains the keys of each record in the database and the associated record number. Each place where the tree branches is called a node; the highest node in the structure is called the root node. The B in "B+ tree" stands for binary—each node point has two and only two hierarchical paths leading to the next lowest level of the tree.

Each node contains a key value. During a SEEK or FIND operation, the node value is compared to the value of the key being sought. The relationship of this key value to the node key is determined; if the value being searched for is greater than the node key one path is followed, otherwise the second path is followed. The paths eventually lead to the lowest level containing the keys of all database records and their record numbers (Fig. 9-23).

The search continues through the nodes of the tree until the matching

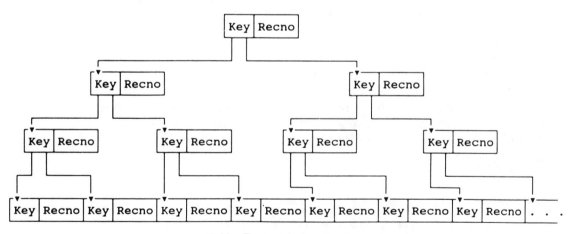

9-23 The tree index structure.

lowest-level node, called a leaf node, is reached. The record number is then used to quickly retrieve the database record. The number of searches necessary to reach the correct leaf is very small; most keys can be found in three index accesses (the system's, not yours).

Converting .NDX files to .MDX tags

dBASE IV has a command that allows you to copy an .NDX or single-index file into a multiple-index file as a tag. The command is:

. COPY INDEXES ⟨ndx file names⟩ TO ⟨mdx file name⟩

If the "TO" option is omitted, the new tag is created in the production .MDX file. Up to 47 index files can be turned into tags in a single COPY INDEXES command.

You might create index files to test new index orders. If one of these new orders is found to be useful, you can copy it into the production .MDX file.

Associating the index with a multiple index file

You can also copy index tags contained in an .MDX file to a single-index .NDX file with the command:

COPY TAG ⟨tag name⟩ OF ⟨mdx file name⟩ TO ⟨ndx file name⟩

Only a single tag name is allowed in the COPY TAG command, because the .NDX file can only hold one index order.

Using a database with indices

dBASE IV lets you maintain more than one index for a database. As long as all the indices are active, each new record is updated in each index.

SET INDEX TO

The SET INDEX command, as shown in Fig. 9-24, is the command used to set up the index environment. The example shows three active index files for the database CUSTOMER. Each time a record is added or deleted, all of the index tags and single index files represented by the list are updated. If you list the database with any command, the database is shown in natural order—the original physical sequence.

```
[SET INDEX TO < list of ndx or mdx file names >

[ ORDER <ndx file name> / TAG <tagname> [ OF <mdx file name> ] ]
```

9-24 The SET INDEX command.

You can choose the order of the database with the ORDER option of the USE command or with the SET ORDER command. You can also specify the order in the SET INDEX command:

. SET INDEX TO NEWORDER ORDER TAG CUSTST OF NEWORDER

You can specify up to 10 .MDX files in a SET INDEX command. The production .MDX file is automatically assigned to the database—in fact, if you do specify the production .MDX file, dBASE ignores the reference. The production .MDX file, if it exists, is always open for index updating. Theoretically, you could have up to 11 .MDX files open—the ten that you specify and the production .MDX file.

You can also specify up to seven single-index (.NDX) files in the SET INDEX command. You can mix .MDX and .NDX files in this list, but the SET ORDER command does not allow you to change the index order to an .NDX file.

The best idea is to create .MDX files as you need them. If you are upgrading from a previous release of dBASE, you should convert all of your single-index files into tags. If a database is used in several different application systems, each application could have a separate .MDX file.

SET ORDER TO

The SET ORDER TO command allows you to access the database by any index's order or by the natural order. You can specify the name of the TAG for the order. Figure 9-25 shows the syntax of the SET ORDER TO command.

```
SET ORDER TO <number> / TAG <tagname> [ OF <mdx file name> ]
```

9-25 The SET ORDER TO command.

Here, the primary index is CUSTST. If you enter BROWSE, the data is in order by STATE. The command:

. SET ORDER TO TAG ⟨tagname⟩ OF ⟨mdx file name⟩

allows you to choose index tags from other .MDX files. You can have a limitless number of index orders for a given database, because you can have any number of .MDX and .NDX files.

.NDX files are not used by their names in the SET ORDER command. In fact, if you are using any .MDX file at all, including the production .MDX file, you cannot SET ORDER TO an .NDX file. If you are using only .NDX files, you can change the order to the third index file in the list (issued in the SET INDEX command) by entering the command:

SET ORDER TO 3

The command:

SET ORDER TO 0

resets the database to its natural order.

REINDEX

If you USE a database without specifying any indexes or orders, any index tag in the production .MDX file is updated automatically if the database is changed. It is possible, however, for other index files to become "out of step" with the database. For example, you may forget to specify a file in the SET INDEX command. You could rebuild all of the indexes using the INDEX ON command; dBASE gives you an easier method in the REINDEX command.

After you have issued the USE, SET INDEX, and SET ORDER commands to set up the index environment you want, the REINDEX command rebuilds all open index tags and files. You simply enter:

. REINDEX

and the rest is handled by dBASE. Figure 9-26 shows the results of a REINDEX command on the Customer database.

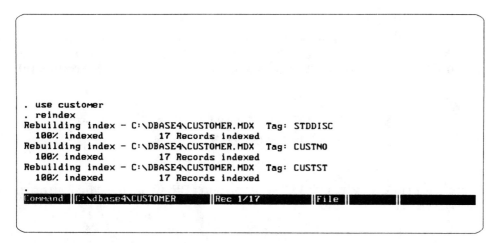

9-26   The REINDEX command in action.

The REINDEX command was used frequently in prior versions of dBASE, because it was possible to open a database without opening an index file. In dBASE IV, you always have the production .MDX file open, so that the index tags contained therein are always updated.

SET NEAR

The SET NEAR command is a new addition to the dBASE language. If you execute an index search using the SEEK or FIND commands, prior versions of dBASE simply gave you an indication that the value that you were searching for was not found. If you now enter:

. SET NEAR ON

either from the dot prompt or by placing it in the CONFIG.DB configuration file, you can change that action. With SET NEAR ON, you are positioned to the record with the next-highest key value in the database, instead of at the beginning or end of the file. This is more like the actions of most database management systems, and unlike the previous versions of dBASE.

SET NEAR OFF causes dBASE to behave as it always did. If you search for a value, and that value is not found, you will be positioned either at the beginning or end of the database file.

Displaying the database and index status

The command:

. DISPLAY STATUS

gives you information about the current dBASE environment. The currently open databases, what work areas are being used, their associated index (.MDX and .NDX) files, memo (.DBT) files, screen and report format files—all of these are displayed so that you can quickly grasp the current setup.

The DISPLAY STATUS command also shows you the current values of the programmable function keys, and the current value of SET options. For example, the CUSTOMER database has the following tags in its production .MDX file:

1. CUSTNO—indexed on customer number
2. CUSTST—indexed on state
3. STDDISC—indexed on state and descending discount

```
Currently Selected Database:
Select area:  1, Database in Use: C:\DBASE4\CUSTOMER.DBF   Alias: CUSTOMER
Production   MDX file:   C:\DBASE4\CUSTOMER.MDX
          Index TAG:       STDDISC  Key: state+str((99-discount),2)
          Index TAG:       CUSTNO  Key: custno
          Index TAG:       CUSTST  Key: state
          Memo file:    C:\DBASE4\CUSTOMER.DBT

File search path:
Default disk drive:  C:
Print destination:   PRN:
Margin =       0
Refresh count =      0
Reprocess count =    0
Number of files open =    6
Current work area =    1

ALTERNATE  - OFF   DELIMITERS - OFF   FULLPATH   - OFF   SAFETY     - ON
AUTOSAVE   - ON    DESIGN     - ON    HEADING    - ON    SCOREBOARD - ON
BELL       - ON    DEVELOP    - ON    HELP       - OFF   SPACE      - ON
Press any key to continue...
Command  C:\dbase4\CUSTOMER          Rec 1/17          File
```

9-27 DISPLAYing the database environment.

Figure 9-27 shows the DISPLAY STATUS for this environment. Note that all of the index tags are listed, as well as the name of the production .MDX file. If you choose one of the tags as the prevailing order, the display would appear as shown in Fig. 9-28. Notice that in Fig. 9-28, the CUSTST tag has the word Master beside it. This means that the CUSTST tag has been chosen, via the SET ORDER command, as the prevailing order for the CUSTOMER database.

```
Currently Selected Database:
Select area:   1, Database in Use: C:\DBASE4\CUSTOMER.DBF    Alias: CUSTOMER
Production    MDX file:   C:\DBASE4\CUSTOMER.MDX
              Index TAG:     STDDISC  Key: state+str((99-discount),2)
              Index TAG:     CUSTNO  Key: custno
   Master Index TAG:        CUSTST  Key: state
         Memo file:   C:\DBASE4\CUSTOMER.DBT

File search path:
Default disk drive: C:
Print destination:  PRN:
Margin =        0
Refresh count =      0
Reprocess count =      0
Number of files open =     6
Current work area =     1

ALTERNATE  - OFF   DELIMITERS - OFF   FULLPATH  - OFF   SAFETY     - ON
AUTOSAVE   - ON    DESIGN     - ON    HEADING   - ON    SCOREBOARD - ON
BELL       - ON    DEVELOP    - ON    HELP      - OFF   SPACE      - ON
Press any key to continue...
Command  ||C:\dbase4\CUSTOMER    ||Rec 1/17     ||File ||
```

9-28   The master index.

Notice also that the key expressions are displayed alongside the index tags that represent them.

Displaying the index keys

You can also display the index key of a particular tag by using the dBASE built-in function KEY( ). KEY( ) returns you the key expression of a particular index tag or file. The syntax of the KEY( ) function is shown in Fig. 9-29.

```
KEY( [ <mdx file name>, ] <number>, [ ,<work area alias> ] )
```
9-29   The KEY( ) built in function.

The number that you give this function is the relative position of the index tag within the .MDX file. If you do not name an .MDX file, the production .MDX file is searched first, followed by all open .MDX and .NDX files. In other words, if you specify KEY(50), dBASE returns the key of the fiftieth tag, starting with the production .MDX file and continuing through all files listed in the SET INDEX or USE command. For example, if you opened the CUSTOMER database, and asked for the key of the third tag, dBASE would respond as shown in Fig. 9-30.

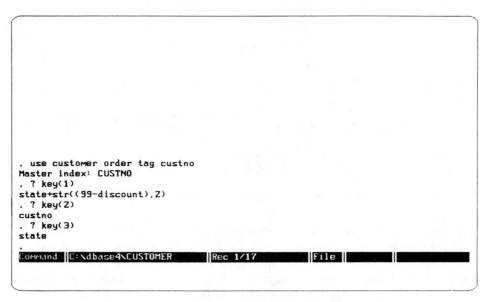

```
. use customer order tag custno
Master index: CUSTNO
. ? key(1)
state+str((99-discount),2)
. ? key(2)
custno
. ? key(3)
state
.
Command  C:\dbase4\CUSTOMER      Rec 1/17      File
```

9-30   Using the KEY( ) built-in function.

10
Working with more than one database

The customer and invoice system example in this book shows how databases can contain information that is related, but physically separate. If you are processing the invoices, for example, the controlling database is the invoice file itself—but that database is supported by and related to both the customer database and the file containing the line items for the invoice.

The concepts of relational databases

The invoice file, the invoice items file, and the customer file are all physically separate files. The invoice file, however, does contain the key of the customer record that it is related to—and it is easy to open the CUSTOMER database, then use LOCATE or SEEK/FIND to retrieve the correct customer. The same is true of the invoice items file—each record contains the invoice number of the related invoice. dBASE IV provides a method to link these databases automatically, using the key fields.

An indexed database may be related by its key field to other databases using the SET RELATION TO command. This command tells dBASE to reposition the related file each time the relation field, in this case customer number, is changed. Thus, when your program is processing an invoice, the customer information is instantly available simply by referencing the required data item by an alias name. The format of the command is:

SET RELATION TO *⟨field name⟩* INTO *⟨alias⟩*

The database identified by the alias must be indexed by the field referenced by *⟨field name⟩*. The field must also be present on the database in the current work area. Each time a new value is received into the current partition, the database *⟨alias⟩* is repositioned automatically.

This feature allows you to process one file sequentially and refer to related data in another without extra processing. For example, the invoice items file contains the invoice number to identify the invoice being processed (Fig. 10-1). The current discount rate (as of the date of the invoice) is contained on the invoice file, along with all other non-repeating information.

```
Structure for database: C:\DBASE4\INVOICE.DBF
Number of data records:        7
Date of last update   : 11/01/88
Field  Field Name   Type         Width    Dec    Index
   1   INVNO        Character      8                 Y
   2   INVDATE      Date          8                 Y
   3   CUSTNO       Character      6                 N
   4   DISCOUNT     Numeric       2                 N
** Total **                      25
```

```
Structure for database: C:\DBASE4\ITEMS.DBF
Number of data records:       26
Date of last update   : 11/01/88
Field  Field Name   Type         Width    Dec    Index
>  1   INVNO        Character      8                 Y
   2   QTY          Numeric       3                 N
   3   ITEMNO       Character      8                 N
   4   PRICE        Numeric       7        2        N
** Total **                      27
```

10-1 The invoice and invoice items databases.

By using SET RELATION TO, the invoice file can automatically be positioned to the correct invoice each time a new invoice items record is retrieved (Fig. 10-2). Related files may be used to produce a report format that includes fields from multiple databases.

SET RELATION can be used to relate one database file to one or more other open files. For example, the invoice items file could be related to both the invoice database and to the item description database with the same command. The following commands show how this environment could be set up:

```
. USE INVOICE ORDER TAG INVNO IN A
. USE ITEMS ORDER TAG INVNO IN N
. USE INVENTRY ORDER TAG ITEMNO IN C
. SELECT INVOICE
. SET RELATION TO INVNO INTO ITEMS
. SELECT ITEMS
. SET RELATION TO ITEMNO INTO INVENTRY
```

each time a new invoice item is retrieved, the invoice database in work area A would be repositioned to the correct invoice record, while the item description database in work area C would be positioned to the description record

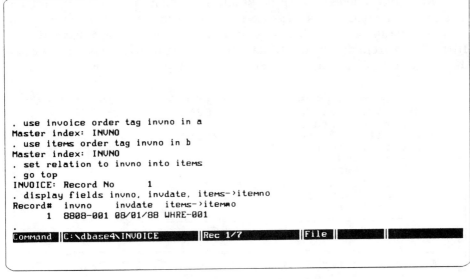

```
. use invoice order tag invno in a
Master index: INVNO
. use items order tag invno in b
Master index: INVNO
. set relation to invno into items
. go top
INVOICE: Record No      1
. display fields invno, invdate, items->itemno
Record#  invno     invdate  items->itemno
     1   8808-001 08/01/88 WHRE-001
.
┌────────┐ ┌──────────────────────┐ ┌────────┐ ┌────┐
Command  C:\dbase4\INVOICE          Rec 1/7    File
```

10-2 Using the SET RELATION.

that corresponds to the item record. All of this positioning takes place automatically after the SET RELATION TO command.

Multiple files can also be related by setting relations from one file to another, and then from that file to still another, and so forth. Using the previous invoice example, you could relate the invoice database to the invoice items database in work area B, while relating the invoice items database to the inventory database which would be open in another work area. This technique is called chaining (Fig. 10-3).

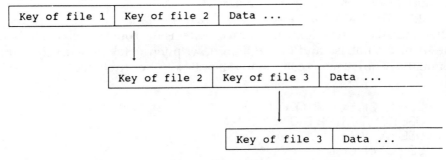

10-3 Chaining relations.

Sometimes, although not frequently, dBASE IV seems to lose its place during an operation on related databases. This usually occurs when the related database is repositioned independently of the active database. dBASE automatically repositions the related database, but only if the record in the active database is reaccessed. This can be done simply by using the GO command to GO to the current record, with the command:

```
. GO RECNO( )
```

while the active work area is SELECTed.

Another way of defining a relationship between dBASE databases is to use the RECNO( ) option of SET RELATION. This creates a synchronous linkage between the files; each time one file is repositioned, the second file is positioned to the same record number. This is used for relating databases that are not indexed. For example, if the customer database were to be used to hold accounting information, while a separate database contained the name and address information, there would be a one-to-one relationship between the files—one account record for each name-and-address record. The files could be related using the commands:

```
. USE CUSTOMER IN A
. USE CUSTADDR IN B
. SELECT A
. SET RELATION TO RECNO( ) INTO B
. GO TOP
...
```

A numeric value or expression can be used to replace the RECNO( ) option in the SET RELATION TO command; the related database is positioned to the record number that corresponds to the result of the expression.

Normalization

If normalization is performed on a set of data fields, then, in all but the very simplest of applications, a multiple number of database files are required by the application. The "extra" databases are needed to hold the values of multi-valued fields, such as ITEMNO in an invoice/inventory system. The key on the main record is usually a number; the database that contains the meanings of the keys contain that item number and a description of that item. This "item description" database could be used across applications, from the invoice to the inventory system.

Another time when multiple databases are used is when the entity contains a set of data that is processed more frequently than other data relating to the entity. For example, in an invoice system, the name and address of a customer is used for reports or printing statements (only another type of report, after all). The inventory system needs the number of items sold, and the item description; these fields would be processed, but the customer name and address information would not be referenced. This indicates that the fields used in calculations and for storage of the amounts would be on a separate database. Reducing the physical size of the database means reducing processing time.

Most applications will deal with a number of databases. This does not say that databases cannot cross application boundaries. The purpose of normalization is to eliminate redundant data, so application programs, which might originally have stored their own data in unique databases, should now be allowed to access databases that are primarily used for other applications.

dBASE IV allows for several methods for using multiple databases. To choose one of these features for your own systems, you must take into account the time needed to process by each method, how easy the method is to understand, and how well each method works for you.

Opening multiple work areas

Once you break up your database into multiple databases there must be some way to address the various databases. The databases shown in Figs. 10-4 through 10-7 show the databases used as examples.

Records	Fields	Organize	Go To	Exit		8:05:02 am

CUSTNO	COMPANY	STREET	CITY	STATE	ZI
AP-001	APPLIANCE CITY	210 SKY LANE	OXNARD	CA	95
AP-002	APPLIANCE CITY	360 ACE AVE	HOLLYWOOD	CA	95
AP-003	APPLIANCE WORLD	20695 BLUE BIRD AVE	SAN FRANCISCO	CA	95
AV-001	AVON APPLIANCE	1687 NEW PLACE ROAD	LOS ANGELES	CA	98
BO-001	BOB'S BRANDS	BOB'S DRIVE	SANTA FE	NM	84
CA-001	CARY'S COOLERS	60 STRAWBERRY HILLS	WINDSOR	CT	06
CR-001	CRAZY FREDDIES	1820 171ST ST	NEW YORK	NY	15
ER-001	ERNIES TV	456 SNOW PLOW AVE	BLEAUVILLE	CA	94
FR-001	FRIENDLY APPLIANCE	26 CHOCOLATE AVE	HERSHEY	PA	15
JA-001	JACKEL & HYDES	357 BAT COURT	LAWRENCEVILLE	PA	14
JI-001	JIMS HOT AND COLD	55 SKINNER RD	VERNON	CA	95
RA-001	RANGES ON THE HOME	23 OLD OKIE DR	OKLAHOMA CITY	OK	73
RO-001	RON'S REFRIGERATORS	141 HOLLOW OAK PLACE	SAN JUAN CAPISTRANO	CA	95
TH-001	THE HOME SHOPPE	25 APPLIANCE LANE	SARATOGA	CA	93
WA-001	WASHER WAREHOUSE	15525 MARINER DR	LOS ALTOS	CA	97
WE-001	WEST'S WHITE GOODS	26 DENNIS LANE	CUPERTINO	CA	92

Browse	C:\dbase4\CUSTOMER	Rec 1/16	File	

View and edit fields

10-4 The sample CUSTOMER database.

There are four databases—INVENTRY, INVOICE, ITEMS, and CUSTOMER. The INVENTRY database and the CUSTOMER database are known as static databases, meaning that the data does not change frequently. These databases are used to perform the function of tables, where the static data can be found.

The active databases are the INVOICE and the ITEMS databases, both constantly growing and changing. Data is entered into the INVOICE and ITEMS databases with each new order and data is retrieved from the

```
 Records    Fields    Organize    Go To    Exit                    8:05:32 am
┌─────────┬──────────┬───────┬──────────────────────────────────────────────┐
│ INVNO   │ INVDATE  │CUSTNO │DISCOUNT                                        │
├─────────┼──────────┼───────┼──────────────────────────────────────────────┤
│ 8808-001│ 08/01/88 │JA-001 │    25                                          │
│ 8808-002│ 08/01/88 │RO-001 │    10                                          │
│ 8808-003│ 08/02/88 │WA-001 │    15                                          │
│ 8808-004│ 08/02/88 │RO-001 │    10                                          │
│ 8808-005│ 08/05/88 │RO-001 │    10                                          │
│ 8809-001│ 09/01/88 │RO-001 │    10                                          │
│ 8809-002│ 09/15/88 │WE-001 │    10                                          │
│         │          │       │                                                │
│         │          │       │                                                │
│         │          │       │                                                │
├─────────┴──────────┴───────┴──────────────────────────────────────────────┤
│ Browse   │C:\dbase4\INVOICE    │        │Rec 1/7     │        │File │       │
└────────────────────────────────────────────────────────────────────────────┘
                          View and edit fields
```

10-5   The sample INVOICE database.

CUSTOMER and INVENTRY files for verification and reporting purposes. A customer cannot order an item that is not in the INVENTRY file. Likewise, an order cannot be created for a customer not on the customer file. This does not mean that the system refuses orders from new customers—it means that a

```
 Records    Fields    Organize    Go To    Exit                    8:06:01 am
┌─────────┬─────┬────────┬──────────────────────────────────────────────────┐
│ INVNO   │ QTY │ ITEMNO │ PRICE                                             │
├─────────┼─────┼────────┼──────────────────────────────────────────────────┤
│ 8808-001│   2 │WHRE-001│   469.99                                          │
│ 8808-001│   7 │HIRA-001│   689.99                                          │
│ 8808-001│   3 │FRRE-003│  1199.99                                          │
│ 8808-001│  10 │FRRE-001│   699.99                                          │
│ 8808-002│  25 │FRRE-001│   699.99                                          │
│ 8808-002│  15 │FRRE-002│   899.99                                          │
│ 8808-002│   2 │FRRE-003│  1199.99                                          │
│ 8808-002│  11 │CODR-001│   489.99                                          │
│ 8808-002│   2 │WHWA-002│   969.99                                          │
│ 8808-002│   7 │WHWA-001│   739.99                                          │
│ 8808-002│  15 │COWA-001│   369.99                                          │
│ 8808-002│   9 │CODR-001│   489.99                                          │
│ 8808-003│   5 │COWA-001│   369.99                                          │
│ 8808-003│   6 │WHWA-001│   739.99                                          │
│ 8808-003│   5 │WHRA-001│   929.99                                          │
│ 8808-004│   7 │FRRE-001│   699.99                                          │
│ 8808-004│ 120 │HIMI-001│   229.99                                          │
├─────────┴─────┴────────┴──────────────────────────────────────────────────┤
│ Browse   │C:\dbase4\ITEMS     │        │Rec 1/26    │        │File │        │
└────────────────────────────────────────────────────────────────────────────┘
                          View and edit fields
```

10-6   The sample ITEMS database.

ITEMNO	BRAND	TYPE	DESC	PRICE	QTY_STK	QTY
CODR-001	COLDPOINTS	DRYER	SUPERSPIN I	489.99	82	0
CODR-002	COLDPOINTS	DRYER	SUPERSPIN II	689.99	58	0
WHDR-001	WHOLEPOOL	DRYER		899.99	36	0
HIMI-001	HITECH	MICROWAVE	1500 WATT	229.99	127	0
HIRA-001	HITECH	RANGE		689.99	89	0
RURA-001	RUSTIC	RANGE	WOOD TRIM	659.99	0	100
WHRA-001	WHOLEPOOL	RANGE		929.99	28	0
FRRE-001	FROSTY	REFRIGERATOR	1 DOOR TOP FREEZER W/ICE	699.99	112	0
FRRE-002	FROSTY	REFRIGERATOR	2 DOOR SIDE BY SIDE	899.99	78	0
FRRE-003	FROSTY	REFRIGERATOR	2 DOOR UPRIGHT	1199.99	6	5
CORE-001	COLDPOINTS	REFRIGERATOR	MINI-MAX	229.99	17	0
WHRE-001	WHOLEPOOL	REFRIGERATOR		469.99	23	40
COWA-001	COLDPOINTS	WASHER		369.99	89	0
WHWA-001	WHOLEPOOL	WASHER		739.99	36	0
WHWA-002	WHOLEPOOL	WASHER	DELUXE MODEL	969.99	2	30

Browse   C:\dbase4\INVENTRY   Rec 1/15   File

View and edit fields

10-7   The sample INVENTRY database.

new customer must first be added to the CUSTOMER database before an order can be entered.

In order for your application to use the four databases, they all have to be opened at the same time. This is accomplished by using the ten work areas of dBASE IV.

Each dBASE work area can contain an open database file and its supporting files—the production .MDX file, other open index files, an associated database text file, screen and report format files, etc. Relationships between the databases are actually opened between the work areas. You designed this relationship pattern when you designed your data and normalized it into distinct groups of items. The keys of these groups become the keys to your databases and help you to relate the files into the integrated whole that you started with.

The dBASE work areas are identified in one of two ways. First, they can be identified by the numbers 1 through 10, or by the letters A through J. The other way is to use a work area alias, usually the name of the open database file. You can choose your own alias by using the ALIAS option of the USE command. The full form of the USE command is shown in Fig. 10-8.

The IN option of the USE command allows you to specify the work area the database is to be opened in. To open the CUSTOMER database in work area A, for example, you could enter the command:

    . USE CUSTOMER IN A

```
USE database name    [ IN work area ]

                     [ INDEX index name ]

                     [ ORDER [ ndx file name ] / [ TAG tag name ] ]

                     [ ALIAS alias name ]
```

10-8 The USE command.

The SELECT command is also used to move from one work area to another. You could have used the commands:

```
. SELECT A
. USE CUSTOMER
```

to accomplish the same thing. The SELECT command is used to change work areas when the databases are already open.

To activate the four database areas in the invoice (or accounts receivable) system, enter:

```
. USE INVOICE ORDER TAG INVNO
. USE ITEMS ORDER TAG INVNO IN B
. USE CUSTOMER ORDER TAG CUSTNO IN C
. USE INVENTRY ORDER TAG ITEMNO IN D
. SELECT INVOICE
```

The first area is automatically area A, if you have not changed the current work area after entering dBASE. Generally, you should set up your databases in the order of importance, with the frequently-updated databases first and the static databases last. The final SELECT command tells dBASE to make the INVOICE file the currently active database.

The SELECT command can reference the work areas either by their number/letter or by the alias name. An alias name can be assigned in the USE command:

```
. USE CUSTOMER ORDER TAG CUSTNO IN A ALIAS FRED
```

After this command has been issued, any of the commands:

```
. SELECT FRED
```

or

```
. SELECT A
```

or

```
. SELECT CUSTOMER
```

could be used to make the CUSTOMER database the currently-active database.

The special notation "—>" is used to reference data items that reside in a database other than the one currently selected. If you set up your environment with the commands:

```
. USE INVOICE ORDER TAG INVNO
. USE CUSTOMER ORDER TAG CUSTNO IN B
. SELECT INVOICE
. SET RELATION TO CUSTNO INTO CUSTOMER
. GO TOP
```

you would be positioned at the first record in the INVOICE database. dBASE IV will have already positioned the CUSTOMER database to the corresponding CUSTOMER record—that is to say, the record that contains the same value for CUSTNO as is contained on the record in the INVOICE file. You could then DISPLAY the current value of the field COMPANY in the CUSTOMER file by using the notation:

```
. DISPLAY CUSTOMER—)COMPANY
```

The "—>" looks like an arrow and represents a pointer to another work area that is not currently selected.

The command DISPLAY STATUS shows all of the work areas, their name, their alias, all supporting files that are open, key field for the indexes, which is the master index, and also shows which is the currently selected database. Figure 10-9 shows the result of this command in the four-database environment described.

```
Currently Selected Database:
Select area:   1. Database in Use: C:\DBASE4\INVOICE.DBF    Alias: INVOICE
Production   MDX file:  C:\DBASE4\INVOICE.MDX
     Master Index TAG:     INVNO  Key: INVNO
             Index TAG:     INVDATE  Key: INVDATE

Select area:   2. Database in Use: C:\DBASE4\ITEMS.DBF    Alias: ITEMS
Production   MDX file:  C:\DBASE4\ITEMS.MDX
     Master Index TAG:     INVNO  Key: INVNO

Select area:   3. Database in Use: C:\DBASE4\CUSTOMER.DBF    Alias: CUSTOMER
Production   MDX file:  C:\DBASE4\CUSTOMER.MDX
     Master Index TAG:     CUSTNO  Key: CUSTNO
             Index TAG:     COMPANY  Key: COMPANY
             Index TAG:     ZIP  Key: ZIP

Select area:   4. Database in Use: C:\DBASE4\INVENTRY.DBF    Alias: INVENTRY
Production   MDX file:  C:\DBASE4\INVENTRY.MDX
     Master Index TAG:     ITEMNO  Key: ITEMNO
             Index TAG:     BRANDTYPE  Key: BRAND+TYPE
Press any key to continue...
Command  C:\dbase4\INVOICE          Rec 1/7          File
```

10-9 The DISPLAY STATUS command.

Relating two databases

Two databases can be related using a common key field. This relation can exist in a language and system like dBASE with SET RELATION TO or its equivalent. Even if dBASE did not have this convention, however, you could perform the task by changing work areas, locating a record with the desired key value, then making the information available to the program. This method requires using a program to accomplish the relationship. dBASE IV supplies the means to perform these tasks automatically.

Figure 10-10 shows the INVOICE and ITEMS databases in a conceptual picture of a relation. As the key changes in the INVOICE file, the record pointer in the ITEMS file is automatically repositioned on the record with the key of the same value. This is known as a parent-child relation—the "controlling" database, the INVOICE database, is the parent, while the subordinate database ITEMS is the child.

```
SELECT INVOICE ...
```

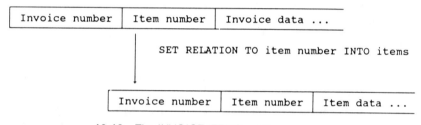

10-10   The INVOICE-ITEMS relation.

INVOICE is selected as the parent file. The command:

```
. SET RELATION TO INVNO INTO ITEMS
```

sets the proper relationship between the databases. As long as SET RELATION is in effect, the record pointer in the child file moves each time the parent file's key value changes.

This ability enables you to perform the normalization of your data. Data items that would normally be associated with an invoice, for example, would include the customer name and address. If this information was repeated on each invoice, then there is always a chance that an address or name is wrong in your invoice file, somewhere. The normalization process separates redundant and unrelated data items into discrete files, with no possibility of duplicated data. The database can be updated more easily, and the information that you receive from it is more reliable.

Multiple relations

In dBASE IV, you have the ability to open relationships from one work area to all of the other work areas. This means that a single database can have multiple children. There are other ways to use multiple related databases.

You can "chain" one work area to another using SET RELATION. Figure 10-11 shows chaining between three work areas. The INVOICE file is the primary file and the start of the chain. It is related to the ITEMS file by the field INVNO. As the current value of the INVNO changes in the INVOICE file, the record pointer in the ITEMS file is repositioned to the first occurrence of the value of the field INVNO in the ITEMS that matches the current value of INVNO in the INVOICE file.

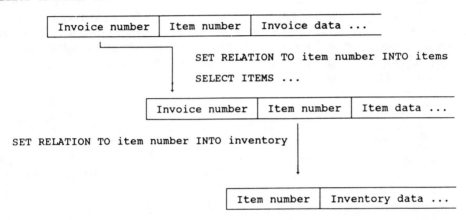

SELECT INVOICE ...

| Invoice number | Item number | Invoice data ... |

SET RELATION TO item number INTO items

SELECT ITEMS ...

| Invoice number | Item number | Item data ... |

SET RELATION TO item number INTO inventory

| Item number | Inventory data ... |

10-11 A relation for INVOICE to ITEMS to INVENTRY.

The ITEMS file also has a relation to the INVENTRY file. The ITEMNO field is used to relate the ITEMS file to the INVENTRY file. As the current value of the ITEMNO field in the ITEMS file changes, the record pointer in the INVENTRY file is also repositioned. This creates a chain known as:

INVOICE.DBF—>ITEMS.DBF—>INVENTRY.DBF

The record pointer in the ITEMS file can be changed by changing the record pointer in the INVOICE file to a different key value, which in turn can also change the record pointer in the INVENTRY file. As a new order number is entered, the first corresponding record in the ITEMS file is available along with the record in the INVENTRY file that corresponds to the item number.

Now use these concepts in a real example. Figure 10-12 shows a simple relation being created and used in a LIST statement. A simple relation is set between the ITEMS file and the INVENTRY file, using the key field ITEMNO. The LIST command displays the INVNO, QTY and ITEMNO fields from the ITEMS file without any special notation because the ITEMS file is the currently selected file.

The BRAND, TYPE, and PRICE fields from the INVENTRY file are also displayed according to the value of the ITEMNO. The special notation INVENTRY—> must be used because the DESC and PRICE fields are not on the currently selected database.

A calculation is also performed from the QTY field on the ITEMS file and the PRICE on the INVENTORY file. The resulting display is shown in Fig. 10-12.

```
. USE INVOICE ORDER TAG INVNO IN A
Master index: INVNO
. USE ITEMS ORDER TAG INVNO IN B
Master index: INVNO
. USE INVENTRY ORDER TAG ITEMNO IN C
Master index: ITEMNO
. SELECT ITEMS
. SET RELATION TO ITEMNO INTO INVENTORY
. LIST INVNO,QTY,ITEMNO,INVENTRY->BRAND,INVENTRY->TYPE,INVENTRY->PRICE,QTY*INVENTRY->PRICE
```

Record#	INVNO	QTY	ITEMNO	INVENTRY->BRAND	INVENTRY->TYPE	INVENTRY->PRICE	QTY*INVENTRY->PRICE
1	8808-001	2	WHRE-001	WHOLEPOOL	REFRIGERATOR	469.99	939.98
2	8808-001	7	HIRA-001	HITECH	RANGE	689.99	4829.93
3	8808-001	3	FRRE-003	FROSTY	REFRIGERATOR	1199.99	3599.97
4	8808-001	10	FRRE-001	FROSTY	REFRIGERATOR	699.99	6999.90
5	8808-002	25	FRRE-001	FROSTY	REFRIGERATOR	699.99	17499.75
6	8808-002	15	FRRE-002	FROSTY	REFRIGERATOR	899.99	13499.85
7	8808-002	2	FRRE-003	FROSTY	REFRIGERATOR	1199.99	2399.98
8	8808-002	11	CODR-001	COLDPOINTS	DRYER	489.99	5389.89
9	8808-002	2	WHWA-002	WHOLEPOOL	WASHER	969.99	1939.98
10	8808-002	7	WHWA-001	WHOLEPOOL	WASHER	739.99	5179.93
11	8808-002	15	COWA-001	COLDPOINTS	WASHER	369.99	5549.85
12	8808-002	9	CODR-001	COLDPOINTS	DRYER	489.99	4409.91
13	8808-003	5	COWA-001	COLDPOINTS	WASHER	369.99	1849.95
14	8808-003	6	WHWA-001	WHOLEPOOL	WASHER	739.99	4439.94
15	8808-003	5	WHRA-001	WHOLEPOOL	RANGE	929.99	4649.95
16	8808-004	7	FRRE-001	FROSTY	REFRIGERATOR	699.99	4899.93
17	8808-004	120	HIMI-001	HITECH	MICROWAVE	229.99	27598.80
18	8808-005	5	FRRE-001	FROSTY	REFRIGERATOR	699.99	3499.95
19	8809-001	10	FRRE-001	FROSTY	REFRIGERATOR	699.99	6999.90
20	8809-001	9	FRRE-002	FROSTY	REFRIGERATOR	899.99	8099.91
21	8809-001	5	WHRE-001	WHOLEPOOL	REFRIGERATOR	469.99	2349.95
22	8809-001	10	COWA-001	COLDPOINTS	WASHER	369.99	3699.90
23	8809-001	6	CODR-001	COLDPOINTS	DRYER	489.99	2939.94
24	8809-002	5	HIRA-001	HITECH	RANGE	689.99	3449.95
25	8809-002	12	CODR-001	COLDPOINTS	DRYER	489.99	5879.88
26	8809-002	8	CODR-002	COLDPOINTS	DRYER	689.99	5519.92

10-12 A data relation with the LIST command.

The DISPLAY STATUS command is used to show the current relations in Fig. 10-13. Notice that area 2 is the currently selected database. The ITEMS database is related into INVENTRY with the ITEMNO field. The previous example showed the second and third links of the chain undisturbed by the first link which was not in use.

The record pointer in the ITEMS file can be changed by changing the record pointer in the INVOICE file to a different key value, which can also change the INVENTRY file's record pointer. As a new order number is entered, the first corresponding record in the ITEMS file is available along with the record in the INVENTRY file that corresponds to the item number.

```
Select area:  1, Database in Use: C:\DBASE4\INVOICE.DBF   Alias: INVOICE
Production   MDX file:  C:\DBASE4\INVOICE.MDX
   Master Index TAG:     INVNO  Key: INVNO
         Index TAG:      INVDATE  Key: INVDATE
   Related into: ITEMS
   Relation: invno

Currently Selected Database:
Select area:  2, Database in Use: C:\DBASE4\ITEMS.DBF   Alias: ITEMS
Production   MDX file:  C:\DBASE4\ITEMS.MDX
   Master Index TAG:     INVNO  Key: INVNO
   Related into: INVENTRY
   Relation: itemno

Select area:  3, Database in Use: C:\DBASE4\INVENTRY.DBF   Alias: INVENTRY
Production   MDX file:  C:\DBASE4\INVENTRY.MDX
   Master Index TAG:     ITEMNO  Key: ITEMNO
         Index TAG:      BRANDTYPE  Key: BRAND+TYPE
         Memo file:      C:\DBASE4\INVENTRY.DBT

Press any key to continue...
Command  C:\dbase4\ITEMS          Rec 1/26          File
```

10-13 DISPLAY STATUS with a data relation.

Multiple children

In dBASE IV, the ability to relate one database to another has been expanded. You can now relate one database to several others, creating multiple child relationships. This is especially useful when processing data from several files through a single controlling file. Prior versions of dBASE allowed you to chain relations from work area to work area, but the multiple child method is much easier to use.

For example, the invoice file in the application described in this chapter could be used as the controlling file, with relations set into both the invoice items database and the customer database. The INVOICE database contains one record for each invoice; each record contains the data items that occur singly for each invoice, as well as a key field (INVNO) and a customer number (CUSTNO) to relate into the CUSTOMER database for name and address information. The ITEMS database contains one record for each item on an invoice. All of the invoice items are stored on one database file, because the INVNO key field is contained on the item record. The end result of relating these databases is to create an invoice form—a statement to send to the customer. You could also use the database environment to create a report of outstanding invoices and delinquent customers. You could set up the database environment by the commands:

```
. USE INVOICE ORDER TAG INVNO IN A
. USE ITEMS ORDER TAG INVNO IN B
. USE CUSTOMER ORDER TAG CUSTNO IN C
. SELECT INVOICE
. SET RELATION TO INVNO INTO ITEMS, CUSTNO INTO CUSTOMER
```

The database environment would look like Fig. 10-14. With this environment, you could process each record in the INVOICE database, while the record pointers in the CUSTOMER and ITEMS databases are repositioned every time the values of the fields CUSTNO and INVNO change in the INVOICE database.

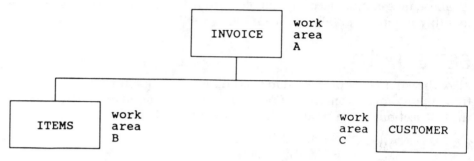

10-14 The INVOICE environment.

You could add another level of relation to this environment, so that the description of each invoice item could be placed on the invoice form. You would do so by opening the INVENTRY database in an unused work area (D), then setting a relationship between the ITEMS database already open in work area B. In addition to the commands used earlier, you would need:

```
...
. USE INVENTRY ORDER TAG ITEMNO IN D
. SELECT ITEMS
. SET RELATION TO ITEMNO INTO INVENTRY
```

Now the database environment would appear as shown in Fig. 10-15.

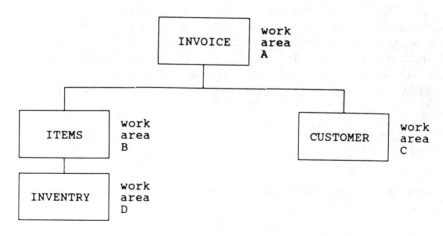

10-15 Multiple levels of relationships.

Each time dBASE repositions the record pointer on the ITEMS database, the correct INVENTRY record is also accessed. The secondary relation from the ITEMS database into the INVENTRY database allows you to produce a statement containing the number of items purchased (field ITEMS—>QTY) and what the item is (fields INVENTRY—>BRAND, INVENTRY—>TYPE, and INVENTRY—>DESC) on each of the detail lines. Data from each of the database files can be used in a single output report, such as a customer's monthly statement or (ahem!) late notice.

SET SKIP TO

All of the commands presented in this chapter are equally useful when used from a program or from the dot prompt. The database environment used in the last section can be created with these commands:

```
. USE INVOICE ORDER TAG INVNO IN A
. USE ITEMS ORDER TAG INVNO IN B
. USE CUSTOMER ORDER TAG CUSTNO IN C
. USE INVENTRY ORDER TAG ITEMNO IN D
. SELECT INVOICE
. SET RELATION TO INVNO INTO ITEMS, CUSTNO INTO CUSTOMER
. SELECT ITEMS
. SET RELATION TO ITEMNO INTO INVENTRY
```

In order to use the environment thus created in most languages you would need to write an application program to make use of all the data items. The program would have to advance the record pointer on the ITEMS database, because more than one record exists on the ITEMS database for each invoice on the INVOICE database. The relationship only positions the record pointer at the first record in a series—in this example, the first of a group of ITEMS records that all have the same value in the INVNO field. Somehow, you need to capture the data on all of the ITEMS records that apply to a single invoice.

The SET SKIP TO command gives you this ability (Fig. 10-16). This command tells dBASE to reposition the record pointer in the specified database until the key value in the related database changes. Only when this occurs does dBASE move the record pointer in the controlling database. SET SKIP TO, in effect, automatically repositions the record pointer in child databases without moving the record pointer in the controlling database.

```
SET SKIP TO [ alias name 1 ]  [, alias name 2 ]  [, alias name 3 ] . . .
```

10-16   The SET SKIP TO command.

If you would add the following command to the environment described earlier:

```
...
. SELECT INVOICE
. SET SKIP TO ITEMS
```

```
. USE INVOICE ORDER TAG INVNO IN A
Master index: INVNO
. USE ITEMS ORDER TAG INVNO IN B
Master index: INVNO
. USE CUSTOMER ORDER TAG CUSTNO IN C
Master index: CUSTNO
. USE INVENTRY ORDER TAG ITEMNO IN D
Master index: ITEMNO
. SELECT ITEMS
. SET RELATION TO ITEMNO INTO INVENTRY
. SELECT INVOICE
. SET RELATION TO INVNO INTO ITEMS, CUSTNO INTO CUSTOMER
. SET SKIP TO INVOICE
. LIST INVOICE->INVNO,CUSTOMER->COMPANY,ITEMS->QTY,INVENTRY->PRICE
```

Record#	INVOICE->INVNO	CUSTOMER->COMPANY	ITEMS->QTY	INVENTRY->PRICE
1	8808-001	JACKEL & HYDES	2	469.99
2	8808-002	RON'S REFRIGERATORS	25	699.99
3	8808-003	WASHER WAREHOUSE	5	369.99
4	8808-004	RON'S REFRIGERATORS	7	699.99
5	8808-005	RON'S REFRIGERATORS	5	699.99
6	8809-001	RON'S REFRIGERATORS	10	699.99
7	8809-002	WEST'S WHITE GOODS	5	689.99

```
. SET SKIP TO ITEMS
. LIST INVOICE->INVNO,CUSTOMER->COMPANY,ITEMS->QTY,INVENTRY->PRICE
```

Record#	INVOICE->INVNO	CUSTOMER->COMPANY	ITEMS->QTY	INVENTRY->PRICE
1	8808-001	JACKEL & HYDES	2	469.99
1	8808-001	JACKEL & HYDES	7	689.99
1	8808-001	JACKEL & HYDES	3	1199.99
1	8808-001	JACKEL & HYDES	10	699.99
2	8808-002	RON'S REFRIGERATORS	25	699.99
2	8808-002	RON'S REFRIGERATORS	15	899.99
2	8808-002	RON'S REFRIGERATORS	2	1199.99
2	8808-002	RON'S REFRIGERATORS	11	489.99
2	8808-002	RON'S REFRIGERATORS	2	969.99
2	8808-002	RON'S REFRIGERATORS	7	739.99
2	8808-002	RON'S REFRIGERATORS	15	369.99
2	8808-002	RON'S REFRIGERATORS	9	489.99
3	8808-003	WASHER WAREHOUSE	5	369.99
3	8808-003	WASHER WAREHOUSE	6	739.99
3	8808-003	WASHER WAREHOUSE	5	929.99
4	8808-004	RON'S REFRIGERATORS	7	699.99
4	8808-004	RON'S REFRIGERATORS	120	229.99
5	8808-005	RON'S REFRIGERATORS	5	699.99
6	8809-001	RON'S REFRIGERATORS	10	699.99
6	8809-001	RON'S REFRIGERATORS	9	899.99
6	8809-001	RON'S REFRIGERATORS	5	469.99
6	8809-001	RON'S REFRIGERATORS	10	369.99
6	8809-001	RON'S REFRIGERATORS	6	489.99
7	8809-002	WEST'S WHITE GOODS	5	689.99
7	8809-002	WEST'S WHITE GOODS	12	489.99
7	8809-002	WEST'S WHITE GOODS	8	689.99

10-17 SET SKIP TO and the DISPLAY command.

the ITEMS database would be repositioned until the relationship is no longer true—that is to say, until the value of INVNO changes on the current ITEMS record. Only after that happens will a new record be accessed in the INVOICE database.

If you set up the environment listed previously:

```
. USE INVOICE ORDER TAG INVNO IN A
. USE ITEMS ORDER TAG INVNO IN B
```

```
. USE CUSTOMER ORDER TAG CUSTNO IN C
. USE INVENTRY ORDER TAG ITEMNO IN D
. SELECT ITEMS
. SET RELATION TO ITEMNO INTO INVENTRY
. SELECT INVOICE
. SET RELATION TO INVNO INTO ITEMS, CUSTNO INTO CUSTOMER
. SET SKIP TO ITEMS
```

then you can use the REPORT FORM command to create all of the invoices at once, without using a program. SET SKIP TO affects the operation of all commands that use the FOR and/or WHILE options. Many dBASE commands use the FOR/WHILE options, including LIST/DISPLAY, REPORT FORM, and LOCATE. Figure 10-17 shows the result of commands with and without SET SKIP TO.

Note that the semicolon character in dBASE denotes the continuation of a program statement. There is no continuation at the dot prompt, you simply keep typing the entire command. You can enter up to 1024 characters in a single command.

Using SET SKIP, SET RELATION, the dBASE work areas, indexing, and the proper design techniques, the database environment that these commands have created can be used to create customer invoices by using a single dBASE command, instead of writing an application program to perform the same task.

```
 Layout   Organize   Append   Go To   Exit                    8:40:04 am
                                                    Bytes remaining:   3975
 ┌─────┬─────────────┬─────────────┬───────┬─────┬────────┐
 │ Num │ Field Name  │ Field Type  │ Width │ Dec │ Index  │
 ├─────┼─────────────┼─────────────┼───────┼─────┼────────┤
 │  1  │ INVNO       │ Character   │   8   │     │   Y    │
 │  2  │ INVDATE     │ Date        │   8   │     │   Y    │
 │  3  │ CUSTNO      │ Character   │   6   │     │   N    │
 │  4  │ DISCOUNT    │ Numeric     │   2   │  0  │   N    │
 │  5  │ PAID        │ Logical     │   1   │     │   N    │
 └─────┴─────────────┴─────────────┴───────┴─────┴────────┘

 Database C:\dbase4\INVOICE        Field 5/5
               Enter the field name. Insert/Delete field:Ctrl-N/Ctrl-U
 Field names begin with a letter and may contain letters, digits and underscores
```

10-18 The INVOICE database with field PAID.

```
. use
. use customer order tag custno in b
Master index: CUSTNO
. use invoice order tag invno in a
Master index: INVNO
. set relation to custno into customer
. display all for .not. (invoice->paid) fields customer->company
Record#   customer->company
      1   JACKEL & HYDES
      3   WASHER WAREHOUSE
      4   RON'S REFRIGERATORS
      6   RON'S REFRIGERATORS
.
Command  C:\dbase4\INVOICE          Rec EOF/7        File
```

10-19 Display of the INVOICE database for non-paid customers.

"Displaying related records

The primary purpose of all the relationships and database definitions is to get information from your data. The act of relating databases ensures that your data stays simple—that time and careless updating does not make your data complex and confusing. The elimination of redundancy represented by the normalization process creates the separated groups of data items that become database files. Use that data to generate information to help your business or organization to grow and prosper.

One simple way to use this information is to group your customers by some criteria. You may want to examine your Invoice file to see how many unpaid invoices there are. You could also find out what customers are consistently late in paying, which customers do not pay at all, which of your customers spend the most money. This information can be used to determine discount rates or late charges.

For example, suppose that the database structure of the INVOICE database is changed to include a field called PAID. PAID would be a logical field and would be set to "true" (.T. in dBASE) if the invoice has been paid. The new database structure would appear as shown in Fig. 10-18.

You might now ask the question: "What customers have unpaid invoices outstanding?" You could answer this question by using the following dBASE commands:

```
. USE CUSTOMER ORDER TAG CUSTNO IN B
. USE INVOICE ORDER TAG INVNO IN A
```

```
. SET RELATION TO CUSTNO INTO CUSTOMER
. DISPLAY ALL FOR .NOT. (INVOICE—>PAID) FIELDS CUSTOMER —>COMPANY
```

This command would display a list of customer names with outstanding invoices, as shown in Fig. 10-19. If a company had five outstanding invoices, the company name would appear five times. Adding the invoice date to the list of fields would also show you how long the invoice had been outstanding.

There! You have received useful information from your stored data—and just the data that you would normally store in a file as a means of managing your business. You would probably store this information whether you had a computer or not! Without a computer, however, you would not be able to quickly change the data, or produce other information that is not specifically given. If this information is retrievable in this easy-to-use format so quickly, then just think of the possibilities when you use customized programs that can access up to ten different databases in this manner.

11
QBE (query by example)

So far in chapters 7 through 10, you have seen how to create and use a database. You have seen the DISPLAY and LIST commands, how to select certain fields for the display, and how to filter only the records that meet the criteria that you set. You also have seen sorting and indexing and using more than one database.

In this chapter, you will see queries are a way to perform the many operations that you have already seen without having to know any dBASE dot prompt code. In fact, for the rest of this section, use just the Control Center as you now use all of the WYSIWYG work surfaces. After you complete this chapter, you should be able to decide whether you want to use the dot prompt or the Control Center. You will find that both have uses throughout your daily work.

You have primarily used the CUSTOMER database although you should have created the other three databases used by Ajax Appliance Company. These include the INVENTRY, INVOICE, and ITEMS databases. In this chapter, you will use all of the databases to demonstrate the power of queries. If you have not already created these databases and want to follow along in the examples, make sure you create them as designed in chapter 4 and shown again in chapter 7. Queries are used for character, numeric, logical, and date data.

Figure 11-1 shows the Control Center as it might look now with only the databases showing in the panels. Make sure you have a catalog active named Ajax if you are going to follow along and place the four database files into the catalog as you learned about in chapter 6.

Query concepts
Remember, queries perform operations from the Control Center.

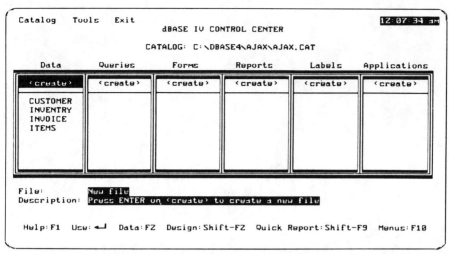

11-1 The Control Center with four database files.

Types of queries

The two basic types of queries are view queries and update queries. View queries are used to look at your data in a different way than the data appears in a single database. With the view query you can perform all of the various operations you have already learned including:

- Selecting files
- Selecting fields
- Selecting Records (Filtering)
- Sorting
- Creating new calculated fields
- Aggregating and Totalling (SUM, MIN, MAX, AVG)
- Grouping

As you will see all of these operations are defined using a single screen known as the Query work surface. The technique employed is known as QBE (Query by Example) because you tell dBASE what you want to do by providing it with examples of the result. As you will see, it is very easy and very visual.

The other type of query is the update query. While the view query only lets you look at your data, the update query allows you to actually change your data. You can work with several different operations. These include:

APPEND	Adds records from other files
MARK	Marks records for deletion
REPLACE	Changes data values in the database
UNMARK	Unmarks records for deletion

The query work surface

Let's begin by looking at a typical query screen. Make sure you have the INVENTRY database active. Check Fig. 8-23 to make sure all 15 records you have are the same as in the figure. If not, update the database so that it matches exactly.

You should be in the Control Center. Whenever you begin a query you should first select a database file. Make the INVENTRY database active by pressing Return on INVENTRY in the Data panel. This will place it "above the line." If it is already active then you are all set to create your query.

Choose the ⟨create⟩ option in the queries panel of the Control Center. Press Return and your screen should look like Fig. 11-2. This is the Query work surface ready for you to work in it.

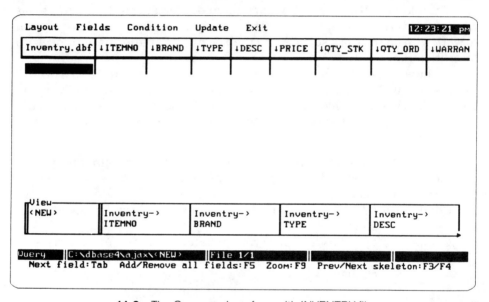

11-2 The Query work surface with INVENTRY file.

The Query work surface has three distinct areas just as every work surface in dBASE IV has. So far, you have learned about the Data, Edit, and Browse work surfaces. As you can see, the Query work surface is similar. At the very top of the screen are the menus. Menus are always activated in dBASE IV by pressing the function key F10. This specific work surface has five menus, and we discuss each as you use them.

The bottom area of the work surface is the status area that you have seen in other work surfaces. The status bar tells you many things. It tells you the name of the work surface, the current drive, directory, and name of the query which in this case is unnamed so it says NEW. It also tells you that there is one file on the work surface. As you add more database files on to the work surface, the status bar immediately reflects that.

Below the status bar is "navigation help." This is where you receive messages or prompts and find help with common navigating keys. In this case there are four different operations listed including how to move from field to field, how to add or remove fields, how to zoom (or see more than the present screen size allows), and finally how to move from one file to another.

The field area of the Query work surface contains a section for each field in the currently open database. As you enter criteria that is wider than the field area, it expands automatically.

The sizes of the field entries can be adjusted by using Shift⌐F7 (Size). This is done by placing the cursor on the field entry, then pressing Shift⌐F7. You use the cursor keys to adjust the size of the entry, and press Enter when you are done. You can make some field entries smaller, so that more entries will fit on the work surface.

The middle of the screen, however, should interest you the most. This is where all of your work takes place. This area lets you place the files you want to work with on the work surface and then decide what information you want to extract from them.

At the very top of the screen are the menus which are activated in dBASE by pressing the Menus key (F10) or using Alt with the first letter of the menu option. This work surface has five menus; each will be discussed as you use them. For now a brief description of the five menus on the Query work surface will suffice:

Layout	Adds and removes files to query and saves the query.
Fields	Adds and removes fields to view and creates calculated fields.
Condition	Adds, removes and shows a condition box for the entire query.
Update	Specifies and performs update operations to databases.
Exit	Returns to work surfaces, saves or abandons query changes.

File skeletons

Right now the two different types of file skeletons are displayed on the work surface. These are data file skeletons and view skeletons. Data file skeletons are simply a list of the fields in your database. Each file skeleton represents a different database. Each field in the file skeleton occupies one position. Data file skeletons are used for entering the sort directions and record selections that make the query screen work. They help you ask questions of your data. View skeletons only display the fields used in your answer. Your answer is a temporary database to be used by you in BROWSE or EDIT screens or in custom reports.

The file skeleton lists all of the fields in the database. You can have more than one file skeleton on the work surface. This is the case if you use two or more databases that are to be combined. You will be working with only one file skeleton on the work surface in this exercise.

The INVENTRY database skeleton is the current file skeleton. The name of the database appears at the top left box on your screen. To the right you see the first three fields only. When there are more fields in the database, a small arrow points to the right under the last field of your screen. The Tab and Shift⊥Tab keys are used to move the cursor horizontally to different fields in the skeleton. Most of your work takes place in this skeleton.

The area under the database name is known as the "pothandle" because it sticks out like the handle of a pot. The space below the pothandle is used for operations that tell dBASE to change data values or update the entire file. The area below the individual fields is used for operations that change the display of the file without changing the data such as sort and filter commands.

You can see only the first three fields because that is all that will fit. Regardless of the size of your fields or the number of fields in the database, you will see only the first three fields. You can tell that there are more fields because there is a right arrow on the far right side of the file skeleton. This lets you know that there are more fields. In order to get to those fields, you must move your cursor beyond the third field by using the Tab key.

You can have as many data file skeletons as you need on the surface, but you will only be able to see a few at a time. You will see how to navigate among skeletons when you have many on the work surface.

View skeletons

The lower part of the screen shows the second skeleton on the work surface known as the view skeleton. The view skeleton always appears as the last skeleton on the work surface regardless of the number of file skeletons. The view skeleton displays the fields that you see in your ANSWER. Only the fields in the view skeleton appear when you browse or edit the data.

Currently, all fields in the file skeleton are in the view skeleton. This is a default when you create a query with an open database. Four fields are shown in the view skeleton. When there are more fields in the view skeleton (as there are now), a small arrow points to the right under the last field of your screen. The Next (F3) and Previous (F4) keys are used to move the cursor from one skeleton to the next.

Think of all the skeletons other than the view skeleton as the question. The view skeleton is where you enter the sort directions and record selections. Think of the view skeleton as the answer because it lets you determine which fields you want to see. Only if a field is in the view skeleton can you work with the data in BROWSE or EDIT or custom reports.

Working with your data

How do you actually work with the data? In the dBASE Query work surface, you translate your questions into dBASE queries. You don't actually ask English questions like "Show me all my WASHERS and sort the data by BRAND." Rather you enter dBASE query commands into the area underneath each field in the file skeletons. For example, if you wanted only to see your refrigerators you might enter REFRIGERATOR underneath the TYPE field in the INVENTRY file skeleton. When you looked at your data in the BROWSE screen, you would only see refrigerators.

Enter your selections into the data file skeleton and tell dBASE what data you want to see and how to sort your data. You also can add, remove, and move fields around in the view skeleton. When you are done, you can tell dBASE to save your selections. This is known as a view because you view a specific portion of your data. The saved selections are saved in a query file that can be modified at any time by choosing the file in the Control Center.

When you run a query, dBASE translates your selections into dBASE commands and then creates a temporary database to display your data. You might use the view of your data several ways. You can BROWSE the data in a BROWSE table. You will see only the records you asked for when you entered selection criteria. Your data is also sorted if you told dBASE to sort it. You can also see your data in the EDIT mode one record at a time.

Another way to use your data in a view is to use it as the database in a custom report. Rather than running a report with all your data, you might use the selected data from a view in a custom report. Also, you might create a view made up of multiple databases and use that in your report instead as you will see in this chapter.

Field selection

Field selection is the process of including or excluding fields from the view skeleton. You may at times be interested in only certain fields from a database. You can choose what fields will appear in your view skeleton and in what order.

Field selection is accomplished by placing the cursor on the corresponding field in the file skeleton and using the Fields key (F5). This would remove or add the field in the view skeleton. An arrow pointing down preceding the field name in the file skeleton indicates that field is in the view skeleton.

To tell if a field is in the view skeleton, look at the field in the database skeleton. If a downward pointing arrow is in the field box to the left of the field name, then the field is included in the view skeleton. Whatever is included in the view skeleton appears in BROWSE or EDIT screens or in your reports. You may have as few as one field in the view skeleton or as many as all the fields in the database skeletons.

Remember that you can always view your data with the F2 key. If you were to press F2 right now, you would simply see the BROWSE or EDIT screen with all of your fields and records. As of yet, we haven't made any requests of our data.

You can decide which fields will appear in the view skeleton and in what order. Right now, all of the fields in the INVENTRY file appear in the view skeleton. dBASE IV automatically places all of the fields in the database into the view skeleton when you create a query. Four fields are shown in the view skeleton. Just as at most three fields show in the database skeleton, at most four fields show in the view skeleton.

If you want to remove a field from the view skeleton, you can move the cursor to the same field in the file skeleton or view skeleton and press F5 to remove the field from the view skeleton. Also press F5 on a field in the file skeleton if you want to add that field to the view skeleton.

Sorting

Asking for information in a certain sequence is called sorting. By selecting fields to be sorted, you can sequence your answers. When a database is sorted in dBASE, a sorted copy of the original database is made and the data is rearranged. In a query, a temporary database is created and data is rearranged using an index. Remember that the temporary database is deleted when you are through with the query. Because queries can be saved, the temporary database can be re-created at any time.

Filters

A filter is the process of selecting certain records from the database. If you want to know how many people were hired in a certain year, this information can be retrieved from the database by using a query.

Whenever you select records, you should think of the query as a question. Though in dBASE IV questions are asked by entering selection criteria in the entry areas of the fields affected, you might think of the question in more human terms. In English, the questions as simple as "Show all the records whose list price is over 300" or as complicated as "Show all the refrigerators and microwaves whose gross margin is more than $125 sorted by brand name."

Queries on your data might be a little different depending on the data type. Numeric queries are probably the easiest because numbers can't be confused with variable names like character values might be. Numeric queries can be one number, a range of numbers, or sometimes a list of numbers. Character queries must have the values enclosed in quotes, while date queries must have the values enclosed in curly braces to differentiate them from variables with the same name. Logic data is enclosed by periods and must be either T or F. Several special operators besides greater than, less than, and equal to are used with character variables.

Filters perform the same operation as the FOR clause of a LIST or DISPLAY. When combined with field selection and sorting, filters form a powerful combination to help you see your data precisely as you want to.

Calculated fields

You might want to include a field in your view that is not in any of your databases but can be calculated using data from your databases. These calculated fields are created by taking fields from your databases, constants, operators, and even the dBASE IV functions to create (in some cases) fields made up of very complex calculations.

The view

When you complete the Query work surface, you have constructed a query which might include a question which identifies what information you are interested in, what information you wish to view, and how the information is to be organized, sequenced and presented. To view the answer to query, simply use the Data key (F2). This changes the screen to the edit or browse view and shows you the answer to your query.

If you wish to switch to the alternate mode, simply use the Data key again. You can switch between browse and edit repeatedly by pressing this key. When you want to return to the query work surface, press the Design key (Shift–F2).

Remember that the data in a view cannot be changed. It is a read-only file that exists as long as you are in the query. It is a virtual database—it only exists in memory. You can save the results of a view as a new database file. You might, of course, save the items entered in a query and re-create the results with the current data at any time.

The query code

As you create each part of a query by filling in the QBE work surface, dBASE IV code is being produced. A file with a .QBE extension is created. You can later access and change this file and use it in programs. This file contains the following dBASE command verbs to tell dBASE what you want to do:

USE	Open a Database
SET RELATION	Relate Multiple Databases
INDEX ON	Re-sort the Data
SET FIELDS	Choose certain fields
SET FILTER	Select certain records

As you complete each section of this chapter you will see the dBASE IV .QBE file displayed as a figure and discussed. You might build several queries in this chapter that can be used with the Application Generator later.

Creating and using views

Creating and using a query can be thought of as a step-by-step process.

The seven-step design method

Although you don't have to perform every step of this process, you should perform them in the order shown. It doesn't really matter if you sort before you select records or vice-versa. But you should enter all your selections before saving the query and viewing your data:

Step 1—Select your database file in the Control Center
Step 2—Create a new query
Step 3—Place your desired fields into the view skeleton
Step 4—Enter sort directions in the file skeletons
Step 5—Enter record selections in the file skeletons
Step 6—Create any new calculated fields
Step 7—Use the query in BROWSE, EDIT, or a custom report

You can create as many queries as you need to. Queries can use the same databases or many different databases. As you see some of the examples in this chapter, you will see the power of queries and how they let you work with your data the way you need to!

Queries can be very simple to construct and can instantly provide you information about your data. You should think of each query as answering a question. Construct your queries a field at a time and first think about sorts, fields to be included in the query and what data to look at.

Using the keyboard in query design

Some navigating keys that you should know when using the Query screen are listed in Fig. 11-3. The most important ones deserve some extra explanation. The first special keys to know are the ones that move you from skeleton to skeleton. These are the F3 and F4 keys. The F3 key takes you to the previous skeleton while F4 takes you to the next skeleton. Practice this by first pressing F4. The cursor should move from the pot handle of the INVENTRY skeleton to the pot handle of the view skeleton. Move the cursor back to the INVENTRY database skeleton by pressing F3.

To move from field to field within a skeleton, use the Tab and Shift–Tab key combination. The Tab key takes you forward in your fields while the Shift–Tab combination takes you to previous fields in your skeleton. The cursor normally starts in the pot handle before the first field (ITEMNO). If you press the Tab key four times, the cursor is in the DESC field. The ITEMNO field moves out of sight and all the other fields will "slide" over so the new field can be displayed. More fields are to the right of the DESC field as shown by the arrow on the right side of the DESC box. The first field showing (BRAND) now has a left arrow being displayed in the left side of its box indicating that more fields to the left are out of sight. Move the cursor back to the pot handle by pressing Shift–Tab four times.

Another important key is the Zoom key (F9). When you are typing in a field area and run out of room, the area automatically scrolls to the left and right. When you want to see more characters at once than the entry area displays, the F9 key zooms the area into a much larger area of approximately 78 characters across by 12 lines. This should give you enough characters to

```
┌─────────────────────────────────────────────────────────────────┐
│ Function keys                                                     │
├─────────────────────────────────────────────────────────────────┤
│ F1  Help              Enters dBASE Help system                    │
│ F2  Data              View Data and perform query                 │
│ F3  Previous          Moves to previous skeleton                  │
│ F4  Next              Moves to next skeleton                      │
│ F5  Fields            Add/Remove a field from the view skeleton   │
│ F6  Extend Select     Select more than one field in view skeleton │
│ F7  Move              Moves a field in the view skeleton          │
│ F9  Zoom              Open text window to full screen size        │
│ F10 Menus             Access EDIT menus                           │
│ Shift-F1 Pick         Display a pick list                         │
├─────────────────────────────────────────────────────────────────┤
│ Un-aided keys                                                     │
├─────────────────────────────────────────────────────────────────┤
│ <Tab>                 Moves to next field entry area              │
│ <Shift Tab>           Moves to previous field entry area          │
│ Up arrow              Moves cursor up one level in an entry area   │
│ Down arrow            Moves cursor down one level                 │
│ PgDn                  Go to next page of file skeletons           │
│ PgUp                  Go to previous page of file skeletons       │
│ Home                  Move cursor to pothandle of skeleton        │
│ Esc                   Exit the Query session ignoring changes     │
│ Del                   Delete character                            │
├─────────────────────────────────────────────────────────────────┤
│ Ctrl- keys                                                        │
├─────────────────────────────────────────────────────────────────┤
│ Ctrl-Home             Enter memo field                            │
│ Ctrl-End              Save query and exit                         │
│ Ctrl-U                Delete/Un-delete record toggle              │
│ Ctrl-PgUp             Move to first row in current column         │
│ Ctrl-PgDn             Move to last row in current column          │
│ Ctrl-Enter            Save and continue                           │
└─────────────────────────────────────────────────────────────────┘
```

11-3 The Query work surface navigation keys.

type anything you want. Press F9 to open up a zoom window. Pressing F9 again shrinks the area back to its original size.

The F10 key gives you access to the five menus at the top of the screen that are standard for all work surfaces.

Mathematical operators

To create a calculated field, you must code or build a formula using mathematical operators, fields, and values. Mathematical operators are the symbols used to indicate addition, subtraction, multiplication, and division. The following mathematical operators will be useful as you create calculated fields:

Symbol	Definition
+	addition
−	subtraction
*	multiplication
/	division
**	exponentiation
( )	parenthesis

Adding files to the query

When you create a query with a database file active, you automatically get a file skeleton and a view skeleton that contains all of the fields from the database. If however, you create a query with no databases active, you get neither a file skeleton nor a view skeleton.

Let's first discuss how to select a database and place it on the work surface as a file skeleton. This is done by using the Layout menu. This menu is used to add files to the work surface. It has two basic uses: to add a file when none were active when the query was created, and to add more than one database to the work surface when creating a query that uses more than one database. This menu is also used to link more than one database when more than one database is on the work surface. You will see more of this menu when you see how to create queries involving more than one database. This menu is shown on the work surface in Fig. 11-4.

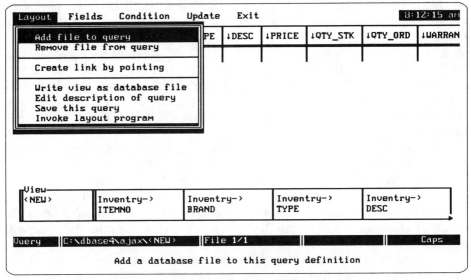

11-4 The Layout menu on the Query work surface.

If you are following along in this example, then you should already have the INVENTRY database on the Query work surface. If you are in the Query work surface but have no files open, use the menu choice Add file to query to add the INVENTRY file to the query. This is functionally equivalent to the dot prompt command:

USE INVENTRY

Later in this chapter, you will see that each action in the query creates one or more lines of standard dBASE code.

Manipulating fields

You might not want all of the fields in your database. You also might want to change the order that they appear when you use the BROWSE or EDIT modes. Using just a few simple cursor keys you can add, delete, or change the order of your view fields.

Adding and deleting fields   Fields are added or removed by pressing the F5 or Fields key. When the cursor is in the pot handle (the area farthest to the left under the file skeleton name), all fields in the database are added or removed from the view skeleton. If all the fields are removed, the view skeleton is removed as well. Once the first field is added back to the view skeleton the view skeleton again appears on the work surface.

Individual fields are added to the view skeleton by pressing F5 when the cursor is in the entry area of a field in the file skeleton. Individual fields are removed by placing the cursor in the field to be removed in either the file skeleton or the view skeleton.

Suppose you want to remove the DESC field from the view skeleton. Because all operations take place in the database skeletons, move the cursor to the DESC field in the INVENTRY file skeleton or the DESC field in the view skeleton. After you move the cursor to the DESC field, press F5 once. The DESC field in the view skeleton will flash several times and then it will disappear into the INVENTRY skeleton. The space from the now-missing field is closed up in the view skeleton and the down arrow in the DESC field of the INVENTRY skeleton disappears to indicate that it is no longer in the view skeleton.

Suppose you remove a field and then add it again. Move the cursor to the BRAND field and press F5. Again, the field would disappear from the view skeleton. You could re-add the field by pressing F5 again with the cursor on the BRAND field in the file skeleton. This time the field would scoot to the right. It has now added it to the end of the view skeleton. You must be in the database skeleton to add a field. If you are in the view skeleton, nothing will happen.

Suppose you did these things to the database. Let's see the results of these changes. Remember, you removed the DESC field from the view and removed and re-added the BRAND field at the end of the view skeleton. Press F2 to view the data. As you can see in the BROWSE screen shown in Fig. 11-5, the DESC field is nowhere in sight and the BRAND field is shown last. The DESC field is not gone; it is simply not shown on the BROWSE screen. In order to transfer back to the query design, you must open the Exit menu and choose Transfer to query design. After pressing Return, you will find yourself in the Query screen again. You can also press the Design (Shift–F2) key to return to the Query screen.

Changing field order   The last thing to demonstrate before concluding is moving fields in the view skeleton. Press F4 so the cursor moves to the view skeleton which is the next skeleton. Notice the last line of the screen contains

ITEMNO	TYPE	PRICE	QTY_STK	QTY_ORD	WARRANTY	FEATURES	BRAND
CODR-001	DRYER	489.99	82	0	12	MEMO	COLDPOINTS
CODR-002	DRYER	689.99	58	0	12	memo	COLDPOINTS
WHDR-001	DRYER	899.99	36	0	18	memo	WHOLEPOOL
HIMI-001	MICROWAVE	229.99	127	0	6	memo	HITECH
HIRA-001	RANGE	689.99	89	0	12	memo	HITECH
RURA-001	RANGE	659.99	0	100	12	memo	RUSTIC
WHRA-001	RANGE	929.99	28	0	18	memo	WHOLEPOOL
FRRE-001	REFRIGERATOR	699.99	112	0	6	MEMO	FROSTY
FRRE-002	REFRIGERATOR	899.99	78	0	12	memo	FROSTY
FRRE-003	REFRIGERATOR	1199.99	6	5	60	memo	FROSTY
CORE-001	REFRIGERATOR	229.99	17	0	6	memo	COLDPOINTS
WHRE-001	REFRIGERATOR	469.99	23	40	6	memo	WHOLEPOOL
COWA-001	WASHER	369.99	89	0	6	memo	COLDPOINTS
WHWA-001	WASHER	739.99	36	0	6	memo	WHOLEPOOL
WHWA-002	WASHER	969.99	2	30	12	memo	WHOLEPOOL

Browse   C:\dbase4\ajax\INVENTRY   Rec 1/15   File

View and edit fields

11-5 Browsing a view with fields moved around.

some navigation keys you haven't seen yet. The F6 key selects fields. The F7 key allows you to move them.

Let's move the BRAND field so it is again in its original position in the view skeleton. Move the cursor until it is on the BRAND field in the view skeleton. In this skeleton, the cursor moves along the top of the skeleton. There is no entry area in the view skeleton because it is simply a list of the fields to appear in the "answer" displayed with the BROWSE or EDIT screen. Press F6 to begin the selection process. The field becomes highlighted. Return is pressed to complete the selection process.

Now it is time to move the fields. First, the F7 key is pressed to tell dBASE you are going to move the selected area. Then, Shift–Tab is pressed until the field is again after the ITEMNO field. That's all there is to it. Press F2 to again verify that your data is now in this order. Figure 11-6 shows this process in progress.

If you are following along with this book, then save the query for later use. In fact, we use this query over and over again to demonstrate different queries using the INVENTRY database. The reason for this is simply so we can show you the results with all the fields displayed. By eliminating the DESC field from the display, everything fits on the screen at once. We saved the query and called it INVNTRY1.

These statements are functionally equivalent to the dot prompt command:

```
_SET FIELDS TO ITEMNO,TYPE,PRICE,QTY_STK,QTY_ORD,
WARRANTY,FEATURES,BRAND
```

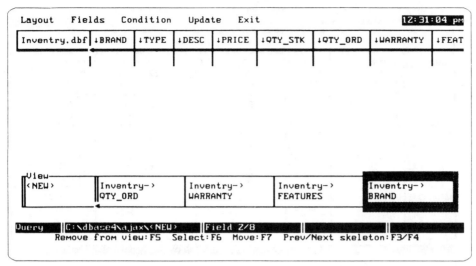

11-6 Moving fields in the view skeleton.

Sorting

So far, we have seen how to select a database file and begin our query. We also briefly talked about placing fields into the view file. The next step is to decide how to display our data records. By choosing fields to be sorted, you can decide the order to display your records. As you learned earlier, this is called sorting. If you already have indices built, you might use those in place of specifying a new sort.

As you have also learned, when an actual database is sorted, a copy of the original database is made and the data is rearranged. In a query, a temporary database is created, and the data is indexed.

So far the data has been used in its "natural" order. The data happened to be entered in order by TYPE, but it has not been sorted. There are two indexes in the .MDX file, but none are active. You are about to ask your first "question." The question is "Show me my data sorted by BRAND in alphabetical order." Remember, all "questions" are answered by placing query commands in the entry areas below the field names in the file skeletons. You don't really ask an English-like question. In this example, we are only working with one skeleton, INVENTRY. Because the question is to sort the data by BRAND in alphabetical order (ascending), we must tell dBASE to sort the data in the BRAND field.

The first step is always to move the cursor to the field you are going to work with in the file skeleton. In this case, it is BRAND. So, move the cursor to BRAND. Remember, press the Tab and Shift–Tab keys to move the cursor forward and backward. If BRAND is out of sight, use these keys to bring it into view and move the cursor into the field's entry area.

Because you don't know what to put in the entry area, let's let dBASE do it automatically. Make sure your cursor is in the INVENTRY skeleton in the

BRAND field. Press Alt–F to open the Fields menu. This menu lets us work with fields and also sort our data. Next, you would choose Sort on this field by typing S.

The Type of Sort box should open up on the work surface. Depending on your data, you will select either ASCII or Dictionary. A general guideline is that if your data is character data and is made up of mixed case (upper and lower), then you should use Dictionary. Otherwise it probably won't matter. Move the cursor to Ascending Dictionary. The screen should look like Fig. 11-7. Pressing Return completes the entry.

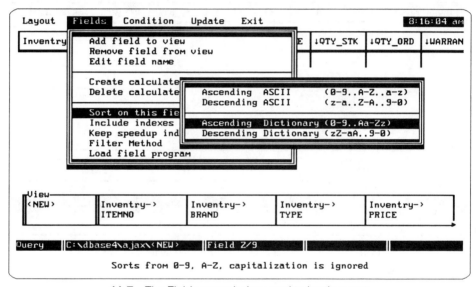

11-7 The Fields menu being used to begin a sort.

When you press Return, the code AscDict1 appears in the BRAND box to tell us that Ascending Dictionary has been selected. You might press F2 to see that your data has been rearranged into BRAND name order.

In order to transfer back to the query design, you must open the Exit menu by pressing Alt–E and choose Transfer to query design. After pressing Return, you will find yourself in the Query screen again. You can also press the Design (Shift–F2) key to return to the Query screen. We are now going to sort our data a second way.

You do not have to use the menus to create a sort. You can type the proper code along with a number in the entry area of the file skeleton.

Although your data is sorted by BRAND, it is unsorted within BRAND. In other words, if you look at all the COLDPOINTS equipment, you will see it is in no special order. In chapter 9 you saw sorts within sorts. Let's sort each group of BRANDs by TYPE in descending order. This means that you want an additional sort by TYPE in reverse alphabetical order.

Move the cursor to the TYPE column. Choose Sort on this field by first pressing Alt–F to open the Fields menu. Next, type S to start the sort type selection. The sort box should open up on the work surface. This time select Descending ASCII. The characters Dsc2 will appear in the TYPE entry area. This tells you that it is the second sort of the query and that it is in descending order. Figure 11-8 shows the BRAND and TYPE entry areas with the sort code that was already entered.

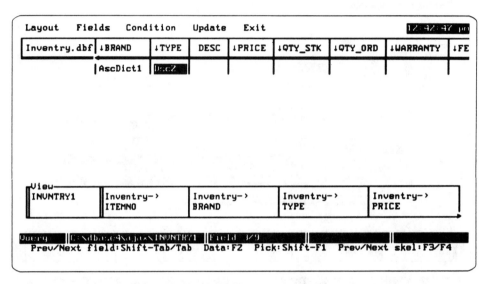

11-8   The BRAND and TYPE entry areas with sort code.

Ignoring the number on the end of the sort type, there are four different sort codes:

Asc   Ascending ASCII
Dsc   Descending ASCII
AscDict   Ascending Dictionary
DscDict   Descending Dictionary

To see how the sorted data looks, press F2. Your data should now be sorted by BRAND. If you look at each group of BRANDs, you will see that they are grouped from Z to A by TYPE. You can return to the query screen by pressing Shift–F2.

When you enter these sort directives, you are actually telling dBASE to index your data or to use previously created indices or, in this case, to sort your data. If it can, dBASE generates an index command or uses an existing index. It checks your .MDX file before creating a new index tag. However, in this case, because you want one ascending tag and one descending tag it must sort the data to a temporary database that is deleted after the query is looked at. These directives are functionally equivalent to the dBASE dot prompt commands:

```
SORT TO QBE_12 ON BRAND/AC,TYPE/D
```

If you had simply been doing a single sort on BRAND, it would have generated an index like this:

```
INDEX ON BRAND TAG BRAND
```

or

```
SET ORDER TO BRAND
```

if the index tag already existed.

Before moving on, let's save the query. Press Alt–L to open the Layout menu. Type S to Save this query. Because you have already saved this as INVNTRY1, change the name to INVNTRY2. When you are asked for the name, type INVNTRY2 for the name of the query. After the query has been saved press Esc and confirm to abandon the query. You will be sent back to the Control Center. Because you first saved the query, it has been saved and now both names appear in the queries panel of the Control Center.

Filtering

The process of filtering allows you to see only records that meet certain criteria that you have set for your data. In the following section, we will create queries on all data types in this chapter. You will see both very simple queries as well as queries involving several fields of different types and different databases.

Queries on your data may differ depending on the type of data you are asking about. Numeric queries can be one number, a range of numbers, or a list of numbers. Character queries can also be one value or a list of values, but must have the values you are looking for enclosed in quotation marks to distinguish them from variable names. Date queries can be a single date or a list or range of dates and must have the date(s) you are looking for enclosed in curly braces to distinguish them from numeric values. Logic fields can only be specified as .T. or .F..

The next step is to begin to select records. Just as the type of sort and sort number are expressed as a "code" in the entry area, record selection is expressed in terms of operators, fields, and values. Valid questions can be asked by placing these in the entry areas of the database field skeleton. Examples of valid questions are:

```
>= 300
"REFRIGERATOR"
< PRICE
$ "HARTFORD"
Sounds Like "Cary"
> {02/23/89}
.F.
```

Query optimization In dBASE IV 1.0, record selection always was performed with a SET FILTER command. Although this works, it requires the entire database to be searched for records meeting the search criteria. It can take a long time for the computer to display the first screen of matching records as it searches the entire database file in sequential order for the first screen of matches.

In dBASE 1.1 a new command INDEX ON...FOR... allowed a partial index to be created that matched those records in the database in order of the search criteria. Because those records were indexed and only the records that were needed were in the index file, it was much faster. In dBASE IV 1.1 the index itself could be used as a sort directive but not as a filter without using the entire set as a filter. In dBASE IV 1.5, you can specify a partial set of the indexed set as the filter. This makes it very fast.

In dBASE 1.5, another new command, known as a smart key filter, was added. The command SET KEY [*range*] lets you create a partial index that goes a step farther for searching speed. When the data to be filtered is found in a narrow range this option is the fastest.

With these three choices, QBE now can choose between the three different methods to select records. QBE also can automatically select the most efficient method of record selection, which optimizes query speed to produce results faster and lets data initially be displayed faster. The user also can override the automatic optimization of a query and select one of the three methods to be used for record selection if they want.

The Query screen often combines SET KEY with SET FILTER to filter a subset of the data for an even smaller subset. Figure 11-9 shows the Filter Method toggle menu in the Fields menu of the Query work surface. The four choices are:

SET FILTER
INDEX FOR
SET KEY
Optimized

Optimized always will choose the fastest method for the type and size of your database. You can cycle through the four choices by using the Enter key. First letter selection also works within the toggle.

Relational operators To select specific information in your database, you generally code or build the query using relational operators, fields, and values. A relational operator is used in making a comparison. The relational operators for numeric comparisons are:

Operator	Definition
<	less than
<=	less than or equal to
=	equal to
>	greater than
>=	greater than or equal to
<> or #	not equal to

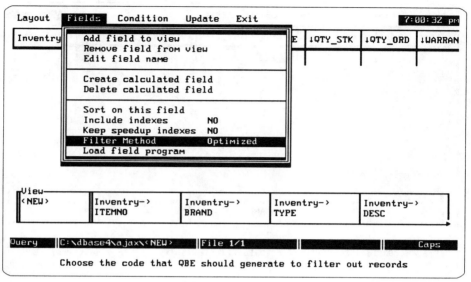

11-9 The IQ! optimizer.

The relational operators for character comparisons are:

Operator	Definition
=	equal to
<> or #	not equal to
$	contained in
Like	pattern match
Sounds Like	Soundex match

AND and OR   There is no real AND or OR in the query work surface. As you will see as you go through the various examples, when more than one query is entered on the same line as another, they are ANDed together. When they are on different lines, they are ORed together. As you go through the various queries you will see this.

Searching on numeric fields   Numeric queries are usually very simple because you are placing only numbers and operators in the entry area. The first question we will answer is "How many items do we sell whose list price is over $750.00?" What we must do is to place the "filter" >750 in the entry area of the PRICE field in the INVENTRY skeleton. One of the easiest ways is to simply type it in.

If you want to follow along, then create a new query with the INVNTRY1 database selected. All your fields except the FEATURES field should be in the view skeleton. Move the cursor to the PRICE field in the INVENTRY skeleton and type >750 (Fig. 11-10).

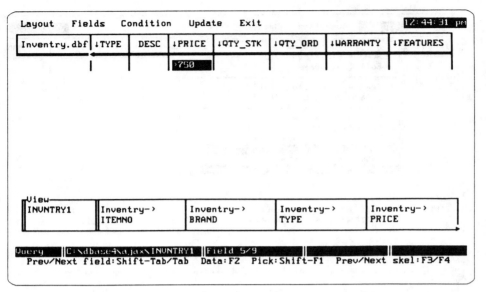

11-10 Selecting records whose value of PRICE > $750.

When you press F2, you will see only the data for those records whose value in the price field is over 750. If the amount you wanted to see was greater than or equal to 750, you would enter:

>=750

in the entry area.

If you wanted to ask the question "Show me all the records whose list price is between 750 and 900," this would require entering a range in the entry area. Ranges are entered for numeric variables by separating the values with a comma. You would enter:

>750,<900

in the PRICE entry area. Queries placed on the same line are joined together with AND. This expression says, "Show me the data whose price is greater than 750 and less than 900." Figure 11-11 shows this entered into the PRICE entry area.

When you press F2, the data is displayed and you should only see two records. As you enter new record selections, make sure you erase old ones or you may get results you didn't want. In this chapter, we are showing you how many queries are built.

In reality, each query will probably start with a new screen unless you were looking at smaller and smaller groups of your data. You can erase old questions by simply moving the cursor to the entry area and pressing the Del key enough times or by pressing Ctrl–Y in the entry area that you want to clear. Let's clear the query in the PRICE entry area.

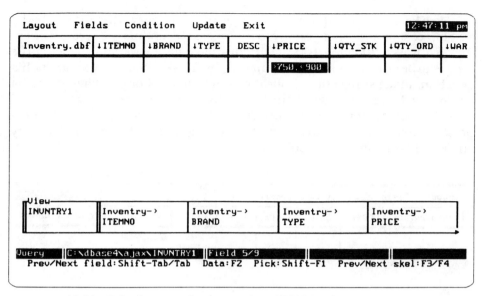

11-11 Selecting records whose value of PRICE > $750 and < $900.

Suppose you want to see which items have a QTY_STK less than 10 and a QTY_ORD greater than 0. You are again asking an AND question. You would enter < 10 in the QTY_STK entry area and < 0 in the QTY_ORD entry area (Fig. 11-12).

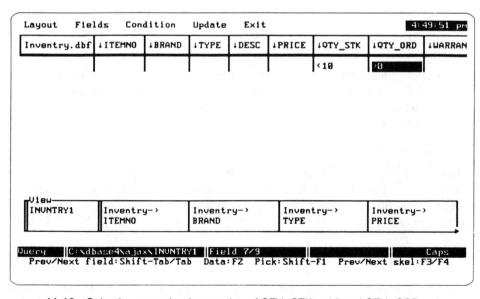

11-12 Selecting records whose value of QTY_STK < 10 and QTY_ORD > 0.

Now look at an OR question. If you wanted to know which items had a very low cost or a very high cost, you might ask, "Show me the records where the PRICE is < 300 or > 1000." OR questions are answered by placing the ranges to be selected on separate lines in the file skeleton entry area. To this question, make sure your old questions are removed or you have started a new query. Move the cursor to the PRICE entry area. First enter < 300. Next, press the Down arrow. A new line opens in the entry area. Enter > 1000. Now press F2 to see your high and low cost items. Figure 11-13 shows an OR query and Fig. 11-14 shows the result.

```
 Layout    Fields    Condition    Update    Exit                    4:52:09 PM

  Inventry.dbf  ↓ITEMNO   ↓BRAND   ↓TYPE   ↓DESC   ↓PRICE   ↓QTY_STK   ↓QTY_ORD   ↓WARRAN

                                                   <  300   ████████
                                                   >  1000



 ┌View──────
 ║ INVNTRY1       Inventry->     Inventry->     Inventry->     Inventry->
 ║               ITEMNO          BRAND          TYPE           PRICE

 Query     C:\dbase4\ajax\INVNTRY1  Field 6/9                              Caps
     Prev/Next field:Shift-Tab/Tab   Data:F2   Pick:Shift-F1   Prev/Next skel:F3/F4
```

11-13 Selecting records whose value of PRICE < $300 or > $1000.

For complicated queries, just remember that everything on the same line is joined together with ANDs while entries on separate lines are joined together with ORs. In the last example, we were asking for the equivalent of the dot prompt command:

DISPLAY FOR PRICE < 300 .OR. PRICE > 1000

A final example might use another variable as its value instead of a number. For example, if you wanted to verify that the values of all the QTY_ORD field were higher than the values of the QTY_STK field to make sure that you were ordering enough items, you could enter the following in the QTY_ORD entry area:

> QTY_STK

This tells the query to display all the records whose value of QTY_ORD was higher than the value of QTY_STK. Of course, this would show you all the

ITEMNO	BRAND	TYPE	PRICE	QTY_STK	QTY_ORD	WARRANTY	FEATURES
HIMI-001	HITECH	MICROWAVE	229.99	127	0	6	memo
FRRE-003	FROSTY	REFRIGERATOR	1199.99	6	5	60	memo
CORE-001	COLDPOINTS	REFRIGERATOR	229.99	17	0	6	memo

Browse   C:\dbase4\ajax\INVNTRY1   Rec 4/15   View   Caps

View and edit fields

11-14   The records whose value of PRICE < $300 or > $1000.

records where it was true. You really want to see all the records where this was not true. You would probably want to just enter:

< QTY_STK

to see all the records that didn't meet the stocking requirements.

Searching on character fields   Character queries usually don't use operators such as greater than or less than but usually use the following operators:

=	equal to
#	not equal to
$	contained in
Like	pattern match
Sounds Like	Soundex match

Character queries are always enclosed in quotes to avoid conflict with variable names. In the last example in numeric queries you saw how the variable QTY_STK was used as part of a query. If you had a variable whose value was the seven-letter word QTY_STK, you could have a conflict. By requiring quotes around character values you avoid this problem.

Begin with a simple query. Press Esc to get out of the current query and get back to the Control Center. Start a new query with the INVNTRY1 view open and type REFRIGERATOR in the TYPE entry area. Make sure you enter the word REFRIGERATOR in quotes as shown in Fig. 11-15. Press F2 and you will see only your refrigerators listed. If the system only beeps and displays the message No records selected, then dBASE hasn't found any records. Maybe you typed it wrong or forgot to put it in capital letters or in quotes. Transfer back to the query screen when you are done by pressing Shift–F2.

```
 Layout   Fields   Condition   Update   Exit              4:58:04 pm
┌──────────────┬─────────┬─────────┬─────────┬──────┬───────┬─────────┬─────────┐
│ Inventry.dbf │ ↓ITEMNO │ ↓BRAND  │ ↓TYPE   │ ↓DESC│ ↓PRICE│ ↓QTY_STK│ ↓QTY_ORD│
├──────────────┼─────────┼─────────┼─────────┼──────┼───────┼─────────┼─────────┤
│              │         │         │"REFRIGERATOR"│  │       │         │         │
│              │         │         │         │      │       │         │         │
└──────────────┴─────────┴─────────┴─────────┴──────┴───────┴─────────┴─────────┘


 ┌View─────────────────────────────────────────────────────────────────────┐
 │ INVNTRY1  │ Inventry-> │ Inventry-> │ Inventry-> │ Inventry->            │
 │           │ ITEMNO     │ BRAND      │ TYPE       │ PRICE                →│
 └───────────────────────────────────────────────────────────────────────────┘
 ┌Query─┬────────────────────┬──────────────┐
 │Query │C:\dbase4\ajax\INVNTRY1│Field 3/9  │
       Prev/Next field:Shift-Tab/Tab   Data:F2   Pick:Shift-F1   Prev/Next skel:F3/F4
```

11-15 The records whose value of TYPE is REFRIGERATOR.

Suppose that you want to see all the records for REFRIGERATOR and RANGE. You wouldn't put the two values on the same line because that says, "Show me all the records whose value of TYPE is 'REFRIGERATOR' and 'RANGE'." Because each record only has one value for the field TYPE you would never get any records, unlike numeric fields which let you request a range of values. In character fields, you are requesting a list of values and those are always ORed together by putting them on different lines. The question is really "Show me all the records whose value of TYPE is 'REFRIG-ERATOR' or 'RANGE'." To do this you must first enter "REFRIGERATOR" and then press the Down arrow to open a new line and type "RANGE". If you look at your data now you will see more records.

Now let's get a little more detailed. Follow along with this example in dBASE if you like or just sit back and follow the pictures. Suppose you want to see all the REFRIGERATORs and RANGEs that were made by WHOLEPOOL. You would first enter "REFRIGERATOR" on the first line of TYPE and "RANGE" on the second line of TYPE. Next you would enter "WHOLEPOOL" on both lines of BRAND. Why both lines of BRAND? You cannot put parentheses around queries in the QBE screen so you must somehow tell dBASE that you want to see the WHOLEPOOL refrigerators and the WHOLEPOOL ranges. This is equivalent to saying either:

```
. DISPLAY ALL FOR BRAND='WHOLEPOOL'; .AND.
TYPE = 'REFRIGERATOR'
OR BRAND='WHOLEPOOL' .AND. TYPE = 'RANGE'
```

or

```
. DISPLAY ALL FOR BRAND= 'WHOLEPOOL' .AND.;
(TYPE = 'REFRIGERATOR' .OR. TYPE = 'RANGE'
```

Figure 11-16 shows this query.

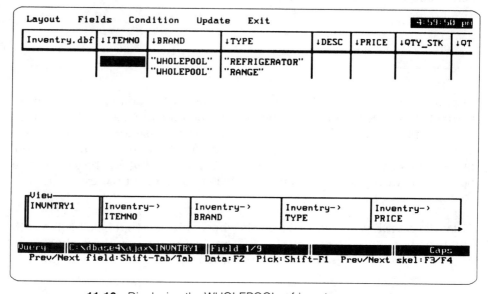

11-16 Displaying the WHOLEPOOL refrigerators or ranges.

The other operators available in character queries help you see different portions of your data. The # (not equal) or <> operator can allow you to see everything but the value you enter. For example, entering #"WHOLEPOOL" in the BRAND entry area shows everything but the WHOLEPOOL equipment.

The $ (contains) operator is useful when you have a lot of data that is similar but not exact matches. Suppose that some of your TYPE data contains the value "REFRIGERATOR" while other items contain the word "REFRIGERATORS". Maybe still others are misspelled and contain REFERIGER-ATOR". Still others might be entered incorrectly with two words such as "UPRIGHT REFRIGERATORS". You could list each of these entries on separate lines, but you would still not be assured of matching all of the values. If you entered $ "REF" in the TYPE entry area, you would ask dBASE IV to find all the records whose TYPE contained the value "REF". This would take care of all the records as long as somewhere in the TYPE field was the value "REF". It doesn't matter whether it is in the beginning, middle, or end of the value as long as somewhere in the value it was found.

Another use of this may be cities. If you had city data and wanted to find all the cities in Connecticut that contained "Hartford", which would include East Hartford, West Hartford, and just plain Hartford you could use the entry $ "Hartford". As long as the characters Hartford were found anywhere in the value the record would be selected.

Another variation of this is the "Like" operator. This lets you enter wildcards in an expression to find a value. Suppose you were looking for an inventory item number identified by a code instead of its TYPE and BRAND. Suppose that the code consisted of four characters followed by three numbers. Some sample codes might be:

    WHRE-001
    GRER-003
    FRRE-003
    CORE-001
    RERA-001

Suppose you wanted to find all the records where the middle two characters of the code were RE. You couldn't use the $ operator because RE is found in different places in all of those variables. You would use the "Like" operator. The "Like" operator uses two wildcard symbols, "*" and "?". The ? symbol takes the place of a single character. If you were looking for the second two positions to be RE, you would enter the following in the entry area:

    Like "??RE-???"

This tells dBASE IV to select all records whose value for that field begins with any two characters, then contains RE-, and contains any three characters after that. You could also have used the wildcard "*" in the following way:

    Like "??RE-*"

The * wildcard says anything else is acceptable for any length. Generally the * is used to represent many characters and is used at the beginning or at the end of a search pattern.

The last character operator to learn is the "Sounds Like" operator. This operator uses a method known as SOUNDEX to see if something sounds like something else when spoken. A good example is names. If you were looking for a person named Cary and weren't sure how it was spelled you could enter:

    Sounds Like "Cary"

This would return such spellings as:

    Cary
    Carrie
    Kerry
    Karrie
    Carry

So, you can see that the "$", "Like", and "Sounds Like" operators can play a valuable role in finding data whose values aren't exactly known.

This completes your use of the INVNTRY1 view for queries. You will be using the INVENTRY database file later when you learn about using multiple database files in a query.

The next types of query you will see are date and logic queries. For these, you will again use the CUSTOMER file. If you want to follow along, create a new view using the CUSTOMER file. Include only the CUSTNO, COMPANY, STATE, PHONE, LST_TXND, DISCOUNT, and TAXABLE fields.

Searching on date fields Dates are a little different from numeric or character queries because they require that proper dBASE dates be used. Because you cannot directly enter data in the internal form of a dBASE date, you must tell dBASE to convert what you enter. There are several ways to do this. When you initially enter data into a date field in EDIT or BROWSE, it is automatically converted to an internal date format. In order to enter date data to compare against internally stored date formats, simply enclose your date in braces { }. Curly braces is the preferred way to enter date data into dBASE IV rather than the CTOD function used in previous versions of dBASE.

The first type of question you might enter with dBASE is to ask for a single date or a range of dates. Suppose, for our example, you wanted to ask "What customers last had a transaction on August 21, 1988?" You would enter:

{08/21/88}

in the entry area for LST_TXND. This tells dBASE to convert to characters '08/21/88' to the dBASE IV internal date format so they can be compared against the date value in the field LST_TXND. If you wanted to check a date range such as "What customers last had a transaction between July 1, 1988 and August 31, 1988." You would enter:

> {07/01/88}, < {08/31/88}

This is shown in Fig. 11-17 in the zoom mode of the query screen.

Another date query you can use involves DATE( ), the function to determine the system date. Suppose you wanted to see all the customers that haven't made a transaction in the last 30 days. You would enter:

< DATE( ) –30

in the LST_TXND entry box. This lets you see the records where the value of LST_TXND is less than 30 days ago. So, as you can see, the Query screen makes it easier for you to enter queries against date fields than in the dot prompt modes, but with the same result.

Searching on logical fields Like the date data type, the logical data type also allows queries against it. If you want to see all of the customers who are taxable, enter:

.T.

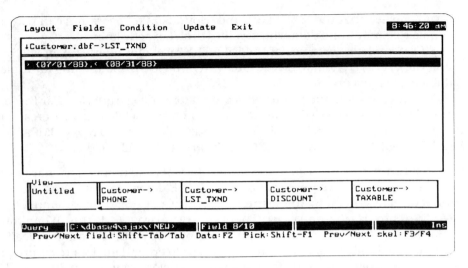

11-17 Searching for dates between 7/1/88 and 8/31/88.

in the TAXABLE data entry area. When you press F2, you would only see the data that was taxable. If you wanted to see the data that was not taxable, then you would enter a .F. in the TAXABLE field entry area.

Compound conditions   Not all queries are made up of one simple question as described in the previous examples. You might want to combine more than one question in a single query. The following examples show how to create combined queries with a modified version of the CUSTOMER database. As you review the following examples, notice the wording of the objective for the words AND/OR and how they relate to the way the query is written. The comma on the same line separating the conditions implies an AND condition. When one value is listed below the other, this implies an OR condition.

Figure 11-18 shows different compound conditions. Logical conditions cannot be both .T. and .F. (true and false) for the same field unless ORed with another condition. Conditions cannot be written where the field value is one value AND another (i.e., STATE cannot be both CA and NM for the same customer).

Although you interact with the dBASE query work surface differently in filtering than with the FOR clause of a DISPLAY or LIST command, the result is almost the same. Remember, the DISPLAY or LIST output is only for a moment. The query can be saved and the result of the query used in a BROWSE or EDIT form, a report, or even a LIST or DISPLAY. The work you do in a query is used to create a view, which to dBASE IV seems to be just another database, albeit read-only.

Calculated fields

When you want to look at data that does not exist in your database, but can be created from data contained in your database, this requires creating new

Layout   Fields   Condition   Update   Exit

Customer.dbf	COMPANY	STATE	LST_TXND	DISCOUNT	TAXABLE

OBJECTIVE:

List customers who have discounts between 10 and 40 percent.				>10,<40	
List customers who are non taxable and are in California.	"CA"				.F.
List customers in Calfornia or New Mexico that have had a transaction in the last 60 days.	"CA" "NM"	>DATE()-60 >DATE()-60			
List customers in Calfornia or New Mexico that are taxable or all customers who are nontaxable.	"CA" "NM"				.T. .T. .F.

11-18 Compound conditions.

fields known as calculated fields. These fields exist only during the query or with operations that use the query.

Once again, if you are following along, reuse the INVNTRY1 view active. This query is used later in this chapter, so make sure that you use the existing query and actually create the calculated field as instructed.

Calculated fields are created by using the Fields menu. Press Alt–F to open the Fields menu and then choose Create Calculated Field as shown in Fig. 11-19. A new file skeleton appears called Calc'd Flds. In this skeleton you can enter into either the top or the bottom entry areas. The bottom entry area is used for sort and selection criteria just like the database skeleton. The top entry area is used to tell dBASE how to derive or calculate its value. The line above the top box is used later when you give the field a name.

In order to create the name of a calculated field when you add it to the view skeleton, wait until you have finished creating the calculation, and dBASE will ask you for the name. For example, create a new field that calculates the retail inventory value of each item. The inventory value is calculated by multiplying the QTY_STK*PRICE. Assume you want to call that variable INVVALUE. You could enter:

QTY_STK*PRICE

in the upper entry box.

When you want to create complicated calculated fields and you need to use certain functions or operators that you can't always remember, dBASE provides a Pick box to help you create your calculations and expressions.

Instead of typing it in directly, enter QTY_STK*PRICE to get the inventory cost, but do it a little differently. You are going to use the dBASE IV "expression builder" to enter the expression.

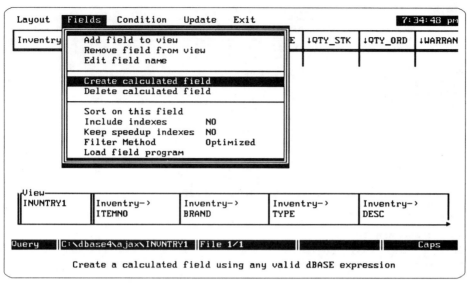

```
   Layout   Fields   Condition   Update   Exit                    7:34:48 pm
  ┌─────────┬────────────────────────────────┬──┬────────┬────────┬────────┐
  │ Inventry│  Add field to view             │E │↓QTY_STK│↓QTY_ORD│↓WARRAN │
  │         │  Remove field from view        │  │        │        │        │
  │         │  Edit field name               │  │        │        │        │
  │         │ ┌────────────────────────────┐ │                              
  │         │ │ Create calculated field    │ │                              
  │         │  Delete calculated field       │                              
  │         │                                │                              
  │         │  Sort on this field            │                              
  │         │  Include indexes         NO    │                              
  │         │  Keep speedup indexes    NO    │                              
  │         │  Filter Method        Optimized│                              
  │         │  Load field program            │                              
  │         └────────────────────────────────┘                              
  │                                                                          
  ┌─View────────────────────────────────────────────────────────────────────
  │INVNTRY1 ││Inventry->  │Inventry->  │Inventry->  │Inventry->              
  │         ││ITEMNO      │BRAND       │TYPE        │DESC                    
  └────────────────────────────────────────────────────────────────────────
   Query    C:\dbase4\ajax\INVNTRY1  File 1/1                         Caps
       Create a calculated field using any valid dBASE expression
```

11-19 Creating a calculated field with the Fields menu.

If you look at the bottom of the screen, you will see a list of function keys that do something. We are going to use the function key combination Shift–F1. This is known as the Pick key because it allows you to build expressions from menus instead of typing them in.

There are several good reasons to use this method. Suppose you have many fields and you can never remember what you called them. If you look at the INVENTRY.DBF file skeleton at the top of the screen, you will notice that only the first three fields are showing. The rest are out of sight, wrapped around the back of your monitor. You can get to them, as you have learned, by using the Tab key, but there is another way to remember what those exact names are.

Did you call the retail price field PRICE or RETAIL? If you can't remember, you can't enter the formula to calculate total price. The Pick menu will tell you the field names.

Make sure your cursor is in the upper entry box for the newly created calculated field. Press Shift–F1". The Pick menu should appear as in Fig. 11-20.

The Pick menu has four columns labeled:

Fieldname   Operator   Function   QBE Operator

Below each column is a list of all the possible choices. Move around in this menu box with the cursor arrow keys. You are going to "build" the expression QTY_STK*PRICE. Move the cursor to QTY_STK in the Fieldname box and press Return. The fieldname QTY_STK is automatically placed in the calculated field box and the Pick menu goes away.

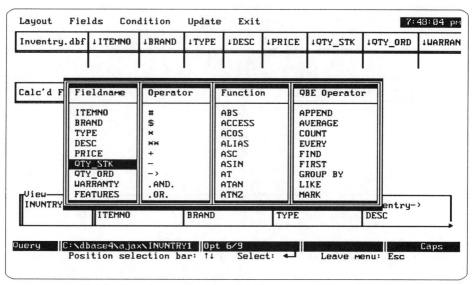

11-20 Creating a calculated field formula with the pick box.

Press Shift–F1 again to redisplay the Pick menu. Now move the cursor to the third choice in the Operator column. This is the multiplication symbol. Press Return, and again the asterisk is placed in the calculated field box next to the field QTY_STK. Finally, press Shift–F1 again, and choose PRICE in the Fieldname box. You have now completed the expression!

Now, you still must add the field to the view skeleton. Whenever you create a calculated field in the query screen, you are only telling dBASE that it now exists and here's how to calculate it. You still haven't told dBASE IV that you want to use it to view your data. Until you tell dBASE to place the field in the view skeleton, you will not be able to see it in an Edit or Browse screen.

Your field is also as yet unnamed. The Fields key (F5) is the easiest way to add the field to the view skeleton, and at the same time, name the field. Press F5 to place a field in the view skeleton. If you only wanted to name the field but not add it to the view skeleton, you could use the menu choice of Edit field name in the Fields menu. If you are following this example, press F5 and type in the name INVVALUE to name the field. The name appears above the calculation as shown in Fig. 11-21 on page 426.

Before you go on, let's do a few things. First remove the FEATURES field from the view skeleton by selecting it on either skeleton and pressing F5. This is needed to make the BROWSE table, you will soon be seeing, fit with the calculated field. Now save the results. Press Alt–L to open the Layout menu, and then type S to Save this query. dBASE will ask you to confirm the name. Remember, you originally started with INVNTRY1. Let's call this query

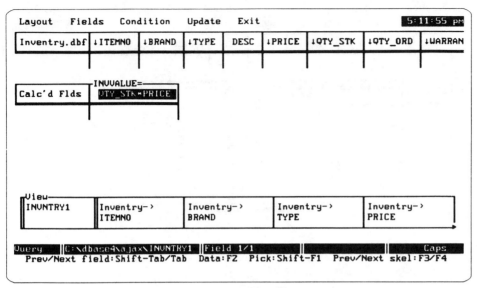

11-21 The calculated field on the Query.

INVVALUE. Change the name of the .QBE file to INVVALUE and press Return. The query is now saved in its present form. You can press F2 to view your new fields as shown in Fig. 11-22 on the next page. When you are through, press Esc to return to the Control Center.

ITEMNO	BRAND	TYPE	PRICE	QTY_STK	QTY_ORD	WARRANTY	INVVALUE
CODR-001	COLDPOINTS	DRYER	489.99	82	0	12	40179.18
CODR-002	COLDPOINTS	DRYER	689.99	58	0	12	40019.42
WHDR-001	WHOLEPOOL	DRYER	899.99	36	0	18	32399.64
HIMI-001	HITECH	MICROWAVE	229.99	127	0	6	29208.73
HIRA-001	HITECH	RANGE	689.99	89	0	12	61409.11
RURA-001	RUSTIC	RANGE	659.99	0	100	12	0.00
WHRA-001	WHOLEPOOL	RANGE	929.99	28	0	18	26039.72
FRRE-001	FROSTY	REFRIGERATOR	699.99	112	0	6	78398.88
FRRE-002	FROSTY	REFRIGERATOR	899.99	78	0	12	70199.22
FRRE-003	FROSTY	REFRIGERATOR	1199.99	6	5	60	7199.94
CORE-001	COLDPOINTS	REFRIGERATOR	229.99	17	0	6	3909.83
WHRE-001	WHOLEPOOL	REFRIGERATOR	469.99	23	40	6	10809.77
COWA-001	COLDPOINTS	WASHER	369.99	89	0	6	32929.11
WHWA-001	WHOLEPOOL	WASHER	739.99	36	0	6	26639.64
WHWA-002	WHOLEPOOL	WASHER	969.99	2	30	12	1939.98

11-22 The calculated field in the BROWSE Table.

Global conditions

Sometimes you might design a query that is extremely complicated. It might not make sense to enter selection criteria in many different fields, especially when multiple ANDs and ORs are needed. Sometimes a condition spans several databases and simply cannot be done through entering conditions in the field entry areas themselves. For this reason, dBASE IV is the only product on the market to feature global condition boxes. This allows you to create a selection criteria that affects all of your databases.

To illustrate a global condition query, continue to use the INVNTRY1 query. Begin by pressing Alt–C to open the Condition menu. This menu has three choices. You can add, delete, or decide if you want to see the condition box on the screen after you have created it. Press Return to "Add condition box". Figure 11-23 shows the condition box on the Query work surface and the Condition menu pulled down.

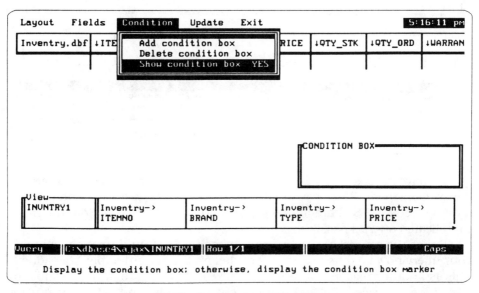

11-23 Creating a condition box.

Inside this box you can write any type of query. For example, answer a question that combines many of the conditions we have already asked for: "Show me all the records for everything but REFRIGERATORs for all brands other than FROSTY that have a PRICE > 750 or any HITECH items." This query uses data from the TYPE, BRAND, and PRICE fields. You might place each query criteria in each separate field entry area. However, it is easier to specify the whole query at once. Either using the pick menus or simply typing it in you could enter the following condition into the condition box:

(TYPE #'REFRIGERATOR'.AND.BRAND#'FROSTY'.AND.PRICE>750).
OR.BRAND='HITECH'

Figure 11-24 shows this condition box filled out in zoom mode.

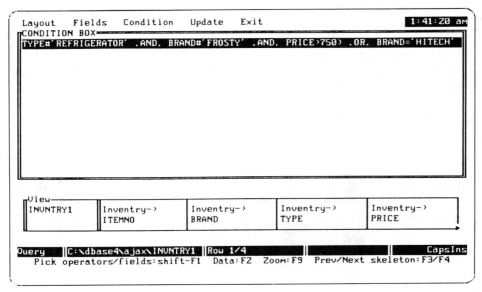

11-24 Query screen with condition box filled in.

We have purposely filled the condition box on separate lines. You can see it is in zoom mode. When you are in the condition box, press F9, and you will have a screen of 78 characters wide and 20 lines deep to handle the most complicated queries possible.

Delete the condition box by again pressing Alt–C and then choosing D. Your query now is in its previous form before the condition box was added. This is another reason for condition boxes. If you go to all the trouble of creating sorts, select fields, create calculated fields, and set up aggregate operators, you might want to try these formats with several record selection criteria. By using the global condition box, you can add complicated queries and then erase the record selection portion much faster than having to go to many data fields and erase selection criteria.

Totalling: SUM, AVG, MIN, MAX, and CNT

Besides sorting and selecting, a group of operators known as *aggregate operators* allow you to ask for certain accumulations of numeric values. These include:

SUM   Totalling
AVG   Averaging
MIN   Minimum Values
MAX   Maximum Values
CNT   The Number of Records
STD   Standard Deviation
VAR   Variance

Unlike normal filtering, these work to produce a single record in the answer set which contains the aggregate value requested.

Let's start a new query. Move your cursor to the QTY_STK field and enter:

SUM

Do the same thing to the QTY_ORD field. Now press F2 and you will see the result of the query as shown in Fig. 11-25. The SUM of the in-stock quantities is 783, and 175 for the on-order quantities.

Records	Fields	Organize	Go To	Exit				4:35:38 am
ITEMNO	BRAND	TYPE		PRICE	QTY_STK	QTY_ORD	WARRANTY	FEATURES
▮					783	175		MEMO

Browse   C:\dbase4\ajax\INUNTRY2   Rec 1/1   View   ReadOnly   Ins

View and edit fields

11-25 Summing the quantities.

If you add a selection criteria to the query, you can see the SUM for that selection. For example, enter WHOLEPOOL in the BRAND entry area. Now press F2. You should see only the sum of the WHOLEPOOL equipment.

You can place aggregate operators in any numeric field. If you have them in more than one entry area, you will see the results of all of them at once, as you saw in Fig. 11-25. You can only have one aggregate operator per entry area at the same time. If you want to see the SUM and AVG of a numeric field, you must run two separate queries. Some of the operators, such as MIN and

MAX, can also be used in date fields to show the oldest or youngest data. Placing MIN in a date field type will show the oldest date.

Grouping

You might want to see your information grouped by another variable. For example, suppose you wanted to see the total of the quantities in stock for each brand regardless of TYPE. You can leave the operator SUM in the quantity fields, and put the GROUP BY operator in the BRAND field. Figures 11-26 and 11-27 show the query and the result.

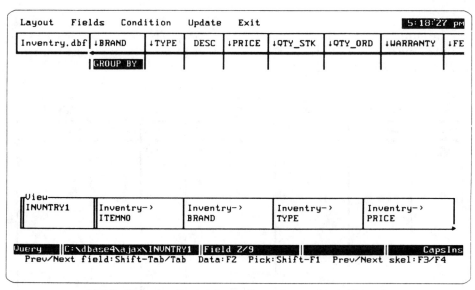

11-26 Summing the total quantity and grouping by brand.

GROUP BY automatically sorts your data into ascending sequence, so you can see your data in the proper groups.

Using calculated fields in grouping and aggregate operations

Sometimes you need to create summaries or groupings for fields that don't exist in the database. An example could be the following:

Display the total inventory valuation

Inventory valuation could be calculated by multiplying QTY_STK by PRICE. By using an aggregate operator in a calculated field, you can perform this example. Figure 11-28 shows an example of a complicated query using

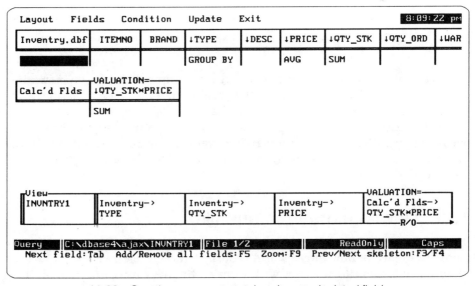

```
 Records   Fields   Organize   Go To   Exit                    1:23:09 am
┌─────────┬───────────┬─────────┬─────────┬────────┬────────┬────────┬─────────┐
│ ITEMNO  │ BRAND     │ TYPE    │ PRICE   │QTY_STK │QTY_ORD │WARRANTY│FEATURES │
├─────────┼───────────┼─────────┼─────────┼────────┼────────┼────────┼─────────┤
│▓▓▓▓▓▓▓▓▓│COLDPOINTS │         │    .    │   246  │    0   │        │ MEMO    │
│         │FROSTY     │         │    .    │   196  │    5   │        │ MEMO    │
│         │HITECH     │         │    .    │   216  │    0   │        │ MEMO    │
│         │RUSTIC     │         │    .    │     0  │  100   │        │ MEMO    │
│         │WHOLEPOOL  │         │    .    │   125  │   70   │        │ MEMO    │
│         │           │         │         │        │        │        │         │
└─────────┴───────────┴─────────┴─────────┴────────┴────────┴────────┴─────────┘
 Browse    C:\dbase4\ajax\INVNTRY1  Rec 1/5           View  ReadOnly        Ins
                          View and edit fields
```

11-27   BROWSE screen with result.

several aggregate operations and a grouping involving a calculated field. In Fig. 11-28, a new field (VALUATION) has been created by using the calculation QTY_STK*PRICE. This new calculated field will be added to the view (not to the database file) and will display the result of the calculation.

```
 Layout   Fields   Condition   Update   Exit                  8:09:22 pm
┌──────────────┬────────┬───────┬───────┬──────┬───────┬─────────┬─────────┬─────┐
│ Inventry.dbf │ ITEMNO │ BRAND │↓TYPE  │↓DESC │↓PRICE │↓QTY_STK │↓QTY_ORD │↓WAR │
├──────────────┴────────┴───────┼───────┼──────┼───────┼─────────┼─────────┼─────┤
│▓▓▓▓▓▓▓▓▓▓▓▓▓▓                  │GROUP BY│     │ AVG   │  SUM    │         │     │
                 ┌─VALUATION=───────
 ┌──────────────┐│↓QTY_STK×PRICE
 │ Calc'd Flds  ││
 └──────────────┘├──────────────────
                 │ SUM
                 └──────────────────

 ┌View──────────────────────────────────────────────────────┌─VALUATION=──────
 │INVNTRY1     ││Inventry->  │Inventry->   │Inventry->  │Calc'd Flds->
 │             ││TYPE        │QTY_STK      │PRICE       │QTY_STK×PRICE
                                                          └─R/O───────────→
 Query     C:\dbase4\ajax\INVNTRY1  File 1/2              ReadOnly     Caps
    Next field:Tab   Add/Remove all fields:F5   Zoom:F9   Prev/Next skeleton:F3/F4
```

11-28   Creating aggregate totals using a calculated field.

The SUM operator tells dBASE to calculate the total of all valuations, rather than one for each record. However, notice the Inventory file skeleton. There is a GROUP BY operator in the TYPE field. This means that the valuation field will display totals by group rather than a single occurrence for all the records. This is equivalent to subtotals by group. There is also an aggregate operator for PRICE and QTY_STK. The query will display the average PRICE and total QTY_STK for each TYPE.

Figure 11-29 shows the results of the query. The data is displayed in order of TYPE and totals for QTY_STK and VALUATION are displayed along with the average PRICE for each group.

```
 Records    Organize   Fields   Go To    Exit
┌──────────────┬────────┬───────┬──────────────┬────────────────────┬───┐
│ TYPE         │QTY_STK │PRICE  │VALUATION     │DESC                │QT │
├──────────────┼────────┼───────┼──────────────┼────────────────────┼───┤
│ DRYER        │   176  │693.32 │   112598.24  │                    │   │
│ MICROWAVE    │   127  │229.99 │    29208.73  │                    │   │
│ RANGE        │   117  │759.99 │    87448.83  │                    │   │
│ REFRIGERATOR │   236  │699.99 │   170517.64  │                    │   │
│ WASHER       │   127  │693.32 │    61508.73  │                    │   │
│              │        │       │              │                    │   │
└──────────────┴────────┴───────┴──────────────┴────────────────────┴───┘
 Browse   │C:\dbase4\ajax\INVNTRY1│ Rec 1/5          │View│ReadOnly│  Caps
```

11-29 Displaying aggregate totals using a calculated field.

A calculated field also can be used with a group statement. If you wanted to group records by the calculated field and then sum or average one of the fields in the file skeleton, you could do that too.

Calculated fields are very powerful. They can be used for file linking as well as aggregation within a query. Whenever you use a calculated field, it will be read-only. Key fields should never allow themselves to be changed without proper program control.

Queries with more than one file

So, it is time to see the true power of queries. Later in the book, you will see some examples of how queries and reports interact together, and how even data entry forms can interact with queries to give you editing capabilities over only a portion of your data.

Linking files

In this section, you will see how to link databases together. You will create several query files needed to produce your reports that were designed in chapter 4. Before going forward, look at Fig. 11-30.

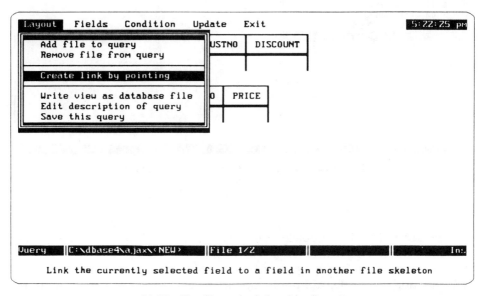

11-30 The file and relationship diagram.

Figure 11-30 shows how the files will be linked together. The INVOICE is the "main" database in the system. The INVOICE file is linked both to the CUSTOMER file and to the ITEMS file. The ITEMS file is linked to the INVENTRY file.

First go to the Control Center. Four databases should be in the Data selection panel: CUSTOMER, INVENTRY, INVOICE, and ITEMS. First, if any of the databases is active, put it away by choosing it and pressing Return. All of your databases should now be below the line. From the Control Center, choose ⟨create⟩ in the query panel to create a new query. You should now be in a blank query screen with no databases displayed, as shown in Fig. 11-31. The Layout menu should be open, allowing you to select a file to add to the work surface. The Layout menu opens automatically if you have no active files.

We need to place both the INVOICE and ITEMS files on the desktop at the same time. Choose Add file to query from the Layout menu. A list of databases will appear.

Select INVOICE and press Return. The file skeleton is placed on the desktop. Next we need to place the ITEMS skeleton on the desktop. Again, press F10 to open the Layout menu, and again choose Add file to query, but this

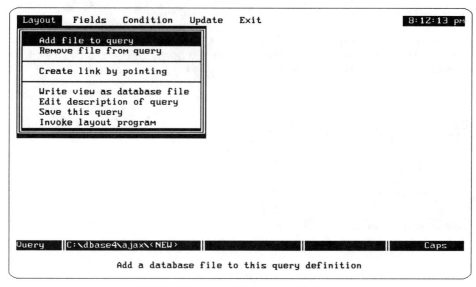

```
 Layout   Fields   Condition   Update   Exit                    8:12:13 pm
┌─────────────────────────────────┐
│ Add file to query               │
│ Remove file from query          │
│                                 │
│ Create link by pointing         │
│                                 │
│ Write view as database file     │
│ Edit description of query       │
│ Save this query                 │
│ Invoke layout program           │
└─────────────────────────────────┘




 Query    ║C:\dbase4\ajax\<NEW>      ║        ║        ║        ║      Caps

               Add a database file to this query definition
```

11-31   The empty Query work surface.

time select the ITEMS database, and press Return. Both databases should now be on the work surface.

Until you tell dBASE how these files are related, you can only work with each file independently. Although you can select fields from each file to be placed on the view skeleton, they will have no meaning until they are linked by their common key, which we know is INVNO.

The next step is to tell dBASE how the files are related. We know that they are related by INVNO. Because in this example the field INVNO appears in both databases, we will link the field INVNO in the INVOICE file to the field INVNO in the ITEMS file.

To create the link, the easiest way is to use the option Create link by pointing in the Layout menu. You can see this menu again in Fig. 11-32. In order to use this choice, you must have at least two files on the desktop.

Before opening the Layout menu, move the cursor to the first field that you want to use in the relation. This is the INVNO field in the INVOICE database. Once the cursor is in the INVNO entry area in the INVOICE database (the top skeleton), open the Layout menu by pressing Alt–L and type C to Create link by pointing.

After you type C, the menu will disappear and the word LINK1 should appear in the INVNO entry area. The cursor is still in this box. You are now half done. You have told dBASE IV where the link begins, but you still need to tell it what to link to. You must tell dBASE which field in the other database contains the same value as records in this database. In this example, the other field is also the INVNO field in the ITEMS database.

If you look at the message line at the bottom of the screen below the status line, you will see that dBASE is waiting for you to complete the link. You first

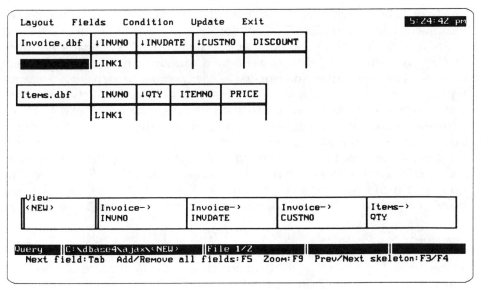

```
 Layout   Fields   Condition   Update   Exit              5:24:42 pm
┌──────────────┬────────┬─────────┬─────────┬──────────┐
│ Invoice.dbf  │↓INVNO  │↓INVDATE │↓CUSTNO  │ DISCOUNT │
├──────────────┼────────┼─────────┼─────────┼──────────┤
│              │LINK1   │         │         │          │
└──────────────┴────────┴─────────┴─────────┴──────────┘

┌──────────────┬────────┬─────────┬─────────┬──────────┐
│ Items.dbf    │ INVNO  │↓QTY     │ ITEMNO  │ PRICE    │
├──────────────┼────────┼─────────┼─────────┼──────────┤
│              │LINK1   │         │         │          │
└──────────────┴────────┴─────────┴─────────┴──────────┘


┌─View─────┬──────────┬──────────┬──────────┬──────────┐
│<NEW>     │Invoice-> │Invoice-> │Invoice-> │Items->   │
│          │INVNO     │INVDATE   │CUSTNO    │QTY       │
└──────────┴──────────┴──────────┴──────────┴──────────┘
 Query     C:\dbase4\ajax\<NEW>      File 1/2
   Next field:Tab   Add/Remove all fields:F5   Zoom:F9   Prev/Next skeleton:F3/F4
```

11-32 Creating a link between two files.

must move the cursor to another file. Press F4 to go to the next skeleton. The
cursor will move to the pot handle of the ITEMS database. Now press Tab to
move it to the INVNO field of that database. Press Return to complete the task.
The word LINK1 also appears in the INVNO box of the ITEMS database. You
are done—you have linked the two databases as shown in Fig. 11-33!

```
 Records   Fields   Organize   Go To   Exit            12:28:36 am
┌────────┬─────────┬────────┬───┬────────┬─────────┐
│ INVNO  │ INVDATE │CUSTNO  │QTY│ ITEMNO │ PRICE   │
├────────┼─────────┼────────┼───┼────────┼─────────┤
│8808-001│08/01/88 │JA-001  │  2│WHRE-001│  469.99 │
│8808-001│08/01/88 │JA-001  │  7│HIRA-001│  689.99 │
│8808-001│08/01/88 │JA-001  │  3│FRRE-003│ 1199.99 │
│8808-001│08/01/88 │JA-001  │ 10│FRRE-001│  699.99 │
│8808-002│08/01/88 │RO-001  │ 25│FRRE-001│  699.99 │
│8808-002│08/01/88 │RO-001  │ 15│FRRE-002│  899.99 │
│8808-002│08/01/88 │RO-001  │  2│FRRE-003│ 1199.99 │
│8808-002│08/01/88 │RO-001  │ 11│CODR-001│  489.99 │
│8808-002│08/01/88 │RO-001  │  2│WHWA-002│  969.99 │
│8808-002│08/01/88 │RO-001  │  7│WHWA-001│  739.99 │
│8808-002│08/01/88 │RO-001  │ 15│COWA-001│  369.99 │
│8808-002│08/01/88 │RO-001  │  9│CODR-001│  489.99 │
│8808-003│08/02/88 │WA-001  │  5│COWA-001│  369.99 │
│8808-003│08/02/88 │WA-001  │  6│WHWA-001│  739.99 │
│8808-003│08/02/88 │WA-001  │  5│WHRA-001│  929.99 │
│8808-004│08/02/88 │RO-001  │  7│FRRE-001│  699.99 │
│8808-004│08/02/88 │RO-001  │120│HIMI-001│  229.99 │
└────────┴─────────┴────────┴───┴────────┴─────────┘
 Browse    C:\dbase4\ajax\INVOICE    Rec 1/7      File  ReadOnly
                        View and edit fields
```

11-33 A link between two files.

Now examine what we have done. The word LINK1 is known as an example. We have told dBASE to look for the same word in both places, and when it finds it, to join the databases. The word LINK1 means nothing. dBASE uses the word LINK followed by a number when it automatically creates a link by pointing. You can just as easily cursor to each entry area and type any word. As long as the word is the same in two skeletons, the databases will be joined. You could have used a word there like DOG, CAT, WINDOW, or even something meaningful like LINK1. By using the word LINK1, dBASE attempts to tell you it means this is used as a link.

Don't be confused with other words you can put in the QBE screens. Your record selections or "filters" that go in quotes such as "RANGES" are placed in quotes to avoid conflict with example variables. There are also a small number of reserved words that cannot be used for LINK words. These include:

GROUP BY, SUM, AVG, MIN, MAX, CNT, STD, VAR, FIRST, EVERY

These are all keywords that mean something in the query screen. You have learned most of them already in this chapter.

Files can be linked by database fields, index tags, and calculated fields.

So far, all you have done is create the link. We haven't looked at the data yet. Let's create our view skeleton by selecting the fields we want in the "answer." Suppose we want the following data table:

INVNO	(from the INVOICE file)
INVDATE	(from the INVOICE file)
CUSTNO	(from the INVOICE file)
QTY	(from the ITEMS file)
ITEMNO	(from the ITEMS file)
PRICE	(from the ITEMS file)

In this chapter, you learned how to select the fields that you want to appear in the view file. The only difference here is that now you can select from either database file.

The first field, INVNO, comes from the INVOICE file. Make sure the cursor is in the INVOICE file. Remember that F3 and F4 move you from file to file. Position your cursor to the INVNO field and press F5. The field flashes for a second, and jumps down to the bottom of the screen to begin the view file.

Move one box to the right and select INVDATE in the INVOICE file. After pressing F5, that field is added to the view file. Next is the CUSTNO field which also comes from the INVOICE file. Tab to the right until the CUSTNO field is selected. Then press F5 to add it to the view file.

The next field comes from the ITEMS file. First, you must press F4 to move to the ITEMS file skeleton. Next, use the Tab key to move to the QTY field. Again, press F5 to add that field to the file skeleton. Do the same with the ITEMNO and PRICE fields, and you are all done.

Notice that the file name in the view file for the QTY field tells us that it came from the ITEMS database, and not from the INVOICE database.

Whenever you create a view skeleton, it always tells you what database the field comes from. You may have not noticed it before because you were only working with one file. Now it is important so you can see from which file your data came. The INVOICE —> INVNO is marked as R/O, which stands for read-only. You cannot change a key field's data.

Although we took three fields from the INVOICE file and three fields from the ITEMS file, you do not have to select fields this way. You can select fields from either database anytime. You can now select a field from the INVOICE file again, and then another from the ITEMS file. It doesn't matter where the fields come from or in what order. The first four fields of the view file are shown in Fig. 11-34 along with the two file skeletons.

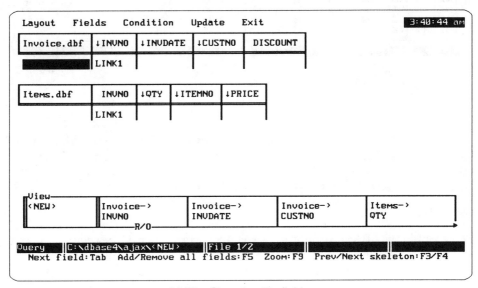

11-34 Choosing the fields.

The complete query screen should look like Fig. 11-34. All that is left now is to see our data. Let's first predict what we should see. We have asked to see the first three fields in the INVOICE database along with their corresponding items from the ITEMS database. This means that for each invoice in the file, you should see all of the items that make up the invoice. From the ITEMS file, you will see the ITEMNO, QTY, and PRICE fields. The data in the INVOICE file will be repeated for each item in the ITEMS file.

Let's examine the results. Get into BROWSE by pressing F2 (or F2 twice). If you are in EDIT, please get into BROWSE. The screen should look like Fig. 11-35.

Using the FIRST keyword

As you can see in Fig. 11-35, all of your data is shown (or at least what will fit on the screen). For each corresponding record in the ITEMS file from the

INVNO	INVDATE	CUSTNO	QTY	ITEMNO	PRICE
8808-001	08/01/88	JA-001	2	WHRE-001	469.99
8808-001	08/01/88	JA-001	7	HIRA-001	689.99
8808-001	08/01/88	JA-001	3	FRRE-003	1199.99
8808-001	08/01/88	JA-001	10	FRRE-001	699.99
8808-002	08/01/88	RO-001	25	FRRE-001	699.99
8808-002	08/01/88	RO-001	15	FRRE-002	899.99
8808-002	08/01/88	RO-001	2	FRRE-003	1199.99
8808-002	08/01/88	RO-001	11	CODR-001	489.99
8808-002	08/01/88	RO-001	2	WHWA-002	969.99
8808-002	08/01/88	RO-001	7	WHWA-001	739.99
8808-002	08/01/88	RO-001	15	COWA-001	369.99
8808-002	08/01/88	RO-001	9	CODR-001	489.99
8808-003	08/02/88	WA-001	5	COWA-001	369.99
8808-003	08/02/88	WA-001	6	WHWA-001	739.99
8808-003	08/02/88	WA-001	5	WHRA-001	929.99
8808-004	08/02/88	RO-001	7	FRRE-001	699.99
8808-004	08/02/88	RO-001	120	HIMI-001	229.99

Browse ║C:\dbase4\a.jax\CARY ║Rec 1/37 ║View ║ ║

11-35 Displaying the linked data.

INVOICE file, there is a record displayed in the view. Suppose you only wanted to see the first occurrence of each invoice's item—just enough to tell you that there were some items. This would require using the FIRST operator. You would change the LINK1 expression in the ITEMS file to:

FIRST LINK1

This would tell dBASE to only show the first occurrence of the related records. This changes the SET SKIP TO statement that dBASE builds when it links multiple databases through QBE.

Using the EVERY keyword In the previous figure, you saw all of your data (that would fit on your screen). This is the normal situation because all of your data is "good" data. That is, each invoice in the file has one or more matching items. Suppose that you had no items in the file. Would you still have seen the first part of the invoice with blanks for the items portion? The answer might surprise you. No!

If you know the definition of a JOIN, you know that the definition states that for each record in a main database (INVOICE) that matches a record in the second database (ITEMS) there should be a record—and there is. If, however, you had an INVOICE record with no items, it will never match a value in the ITEMS database and those records will not show up in your view file.

dBASE IV has correctly joined the files based on the way a JOIN works. The simple linking of files to produce this type of JOIN really only works when both files have corresponding keys. In an invoice system where the main invoice information is input separately from the items, you will hopefully have corresponding records. You might use this type of query if you had limited the record selection to only invoices that had been completely filled out. This type of JOIN helps us locate mistakes or omissions.

If you have any doubt that your data is in good shape, then you might need to use a slightly different form of the LINK statement to make sure that every record in the main (parent) file appears, regardless if it has any matching keys in the child file. This would simply require changing the word LINK1 in the INVOICE file so that it reads:

EVERY LINK1

Nothing else changes. The LINK1 in the ITEMS database remains the same. This tells dBASE to display every record in the INVOICE file whether or not there is a match to a corresponding INVNO key in the ITEMS file.

If we display all of the records regardless of any matching, what would be displayed for INVOICE records with no corresponding records in the ITEMS file? One record would be in the view file for each of these "unmatched" INVOICE records, and the fields in the view file that comes from the ITEMS file (QTY, ITEMNO, PRICE) would be blank.

If we reversed the EVERY operator and placed it in the ITEMS file instead of the INVOICE file, then the result would be very different. First of all, if there were any records in the ITEMS file that had no corresponding records in the INVOICE file, you would see only the ITEMS data in the record. The INVNO, INVDATE, and CUSTNO fields would be blank. Even though there is data for the INVNO field in the ITEMS database, you have asked the View file to take the INVNO data from the INVOICE database. Since there would be no match, the INVNO data would be blank. When using the EVERY operator, you should make sure that the common field (INVNO) is placed in the view file from the database that contains the EVERY operator.

What actually happens is that if you use the EVERY operator, the database that you use it in becomes the primary database, and all relations are set from that database.

You cannot have the EVERY keyword in both databases. This is simply a restriction in the dBASE IV QBE processor. Although this example does not lend itself to this situation, you can probably think of a good one that does. For example, how can you find customers that have no invoices? You could join the customer file to the invoice file by CUSTNO and use the EVERY operator to see which records have no data for the INVOICE fields. That would tell you your answer.

Filtering with multiple databases If you wanted to view only the data for a certain invoice or group of invoices, you could certainly do that by adding a filter expression such as >= "8808-003", <= "8809-001" in the INVNO entry area. Or, you could only see invoices for Ron's Refrigerators by placing the query = "RO-001" in the CUSTNO entry area.

Suppose that you only wanted to see the data for only the items that had a PRICE > 750. You would simply have to add a filter to the database that contains the field. You can mix "filters" and "links" in your database skeletons to further limit the data displayed. To see just the PRICE > 750 items, move the cursor to the price entry area in the ITEMS database and place > 750 in the entry area. This limits the display to those items as shown in Fig. 11-36.

```
Records   Organize   Fields   Go To   Exit
┌────────┬─────────┬────────┬───┬────────┬─────────────────────────────┐
│ INVNO  │ INVDATE │ CUSTNO │QTY│ ITEMNO │ PRICE                       │
├────────┼─────────┼────────┼───┼────────┼─────────────────────────────┤
│8808-001│08/01/88 │JA-001  │  3│FRRE-003│1199.99                      │
│8808-002│08/01/88 │RO-001  │ 15│FRRE-002│ 899.99                      │
│8808-002│08/01/88 │RO-001  │  2│FRRE-003│1199.99                      │
│8808-002│08/01/88 │RO-001  │  2│WHWA-002│ 969.99                      │
│8808-003│08/02/88 │WA-001  │  5│WHRA-001│ 929.99                      │
│8809-001│09/01/88 │RO-001  │  9│FRRE-002│ 899.99                      │
│8812-001│12/31/88 │AV-001  │  3│FRRE-003│1199.99                      │
│8812-001│12/31/88 │AV-001  │  1│WHWA-002│ 969.99                      │
│        │         │        │   │        │                             │
│        │         │        │   │        │                             │
│        │         │        │   │        │                             │
│        │         │        │   │        │                             │
│        │         │        │   │        │                             │
│        │         │        │   │        │                             │
│        │         │        │   │        │                             │
├────────┴─────────┴────────┴───┴────────┴─────────────────────────────┤
│ Browse   C:\dbase4\ajax\CARY      Rec 3/37       View                 │
└──────────────────────────────────────────────────────────────────────┘
```

11-36 Displaying the linked data.

Look at the data. There is no invoice number 8808-004. This is because no items from the invoice have prices greater than $750. The other invoices are only displaying the items that are over $750. Suppose you wanted to see all of your invoices regardless of whether they had any items over $750. Could you use the EVERY operator to see all of the invoices even if one had no items whose PRICE value was over $750? The answer is no. The EVERY operator acts as a filter. If you already have a filter such as > 750, this filter takes precedence.

You can have as many filters as you want. The filters can get very complicated. If you place a filter at the INVOICE (parent) level, then that can affect the whole query. If you place the expression = "RO-001" in the CUSTNO entry area of the INVOICE file skeleton, and > 750 in the PRICE entry area of the ITEMS skeleton, then any invoices that are not for Ron's Refrigerators will not be displayed even it the items pass the PRICE filter. The query simply becomes an AND. It says to display all the records for Ron's Refrigerators (Customer Number = "RO-001") whose value of PRICE in an item is greater than $750. Whether or not you have filters in your data, the important thing to remember about multiple databases is to make sure your links are correct.

Completing the view for the invoice   So far, you have linked the INVOICE and ITEMS files together. Now it's time to create the last two links to make up the Ajax Appliance System as displayed in Fig. 11-30.

You should have already created the first link from the INVOICE to the ITEMS file. If you have any filters, remove them before continuing. First, you should add the CUSTOMER file to the query. Using the Layout menu, choose the Add file to query option and select the CUSTOMER file. Once the file appears on the work surface, you can link the INVOICE file to the CUSTOMER file. Place the cursor in the CUSTNO field entry area in the INVOICE file skeleton.

As you have learned earlier in this section of this chapter, select the Create link by pointing option. The example, LINK2, appears in the entry area. Press F4 twice to move the cursor to the CUSTOMER file skeleton, and then move the cursor to the CUSTNO entry area. Press Enter to complete the link. The example variable LINK2 appears in the CUSTNO field of the CUSTOMER file skeleton. The files are now linked together.

Before viewing the data, we should make a little more room for the BROWSE screen so you can see more on one screen. Remove the INVDATE field from the view skeleton, and then add the COMPANY field from the CUSTOMER file after the CUSTNO field in the view skeleton. The query screen is shown in Fig. 11-37. Notice how the INVOICE file is linked to two different files, and both INVNO and CUSTNO are read-only in the view skeleton.

When you are through, press F2 to see the data as shown in Fig. 11-38.

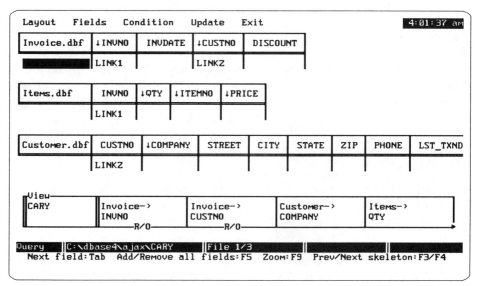

11-37   Linking three files.

```
 Records   Organize   Fields   Go To   Exit

┌────────┬────────┬──────────────────────┬────┬────────┬─────────┐
│ INVNO  │ CUSTNO │ COMPANY              │ QTY│ ITEMNO │ PRICE   │
├────────┼────────┼──────────────────────┼────┼────────┼─────────┤
│8812-001│ AV-001 │ AVON APPLIANCE       │ 111│ FRRE-001│  699.99 │
│8812-001│ AV-001 │ AVON APPLIANCE       │   1│ FRRE-001│  699.99 │
│8812-001│ AV-001 │ AVON APPLIANCE       │   3│ FRRE-003│ 1199.99 │
│8812-001│ AV-001 │ AVON APPLIANCE       │   1│ COWA-001│  369.99 │
│8812-001│ AV-001 │ AVON APPLIANCE       │   2│ FRRE-001│  699.99 │
│8812-001│ AV-001 │ AVON APPLIANCE       │   3│ FRRE-001│  699.99 │
│8812-001│ AV-001 │ AVON APPLIANCE       │   1│ WHWA-002│  969.99 │
│8901-001│ AV-001 │ AVON APPLIANCE       │   5│ FRRE-001│  699.99 │
│8901-001│ AV-001 │ AVON APPLIANCE       │   8│ WHWA-001│  739.99 │
│8901-001│ AV-001 │ AVON APPLIANCE       │   1│ COWA-001│  369.99 │
│8901-001│ AV-001 │ AVON APPLIANCE       │ 100│ HIMI-001│  229.99 │
│8808-001│ JA-001 │ JACKEL & HYDES       │   2│ WHRE-001│  469.99 │
│8808-001│ JA-001 │ JACKEL & HYDES       │   7│ HIRA-001│  689.99 │
│8808-001│ JA-001 │ JACKEL & HYDES       │   3│ FRRE-003│ 1199.99 │
│8808-001│ JA-001 │ JACKEL & HYDES       │  10│ FRRE-001│  699.99 │
│8808-002│ RO-001 │ RON'S REFRIGERATORS  │  25│ FRRE-001│  699.99 │
│8808-002│ RO-001 │ RON'S REFRIGERATORS  │  15│ FRRE-002│  899.99 │
└────────┴────────┴──────────────────────┴────┴────────┴─────────┘

 Browse    C:\dbase4\ajax\CARY      Rec 4/16        View
```

11-38 Displaying the data.

The final step is to add the INVENTRY database file so you can see more information about the items such as the description of the item. The file is added to the work surface by again choosing Add file to query from the Layout menu. After selecting the INVENTRY file, it is added as the fourth file skeleton. Because you can only see three skeletons at a time, it pushes the INVOICE skeleton out of sight above.

In order to link the ITEMS skeleton to the INVENTRY file skeleton, the example variable LINK3 (or anything else) is entered in the ITEMNO field in both the ITEMS and INVENTRY file skeleton. The completed file skeletons are shown in Fig. 11-39.

You can see that three separate links are shown. After adding the item's description to the view file, the data appears in Fig. 11-40. Later, this view is used to create the invoices along with the invoice reports. The only difference is that all of the fields will be selected for the view.

Update queries

The last subject to look at in our comprehensive look at queries is updating large amounts of data through an operation known as updating. There are actually four types of update operations:

APPEND	Adds records from other files
MARK	Marks records for deletion
REPLACE	Changes data values in the database
UNMARK	Unmarks records for deletion

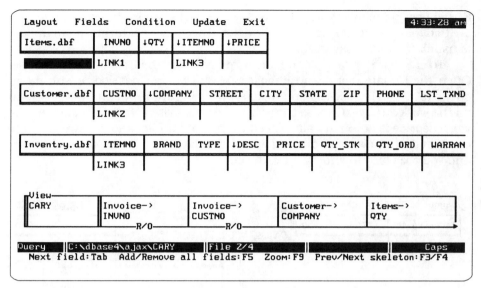

11-39 Completing the file skeletons.

The update operation is placed in the pot handle of the file to be updated. Updating takes two steps. The first step is to define the operation in the pot handle and determine which records will be affected and how. The second step is to perform the operation.

You can enter the update operation in the pot handle, or you can open the Update menu in the Query work surface to choose the update operation.

INVNO	CUSTNO	COMPANY	QTY	ITEMNO	PRICE	DESC
8812-001	AV-001	AVON APPLIANCE	111	FRRE-001	699.99	1 DOOR TOP FREEZER W
8812-001	AV-001	AVON APPLIANCE	1	FRRE-001	699.99	1 DOOR TOP FREEZER W
8812-001	AV-001	AVON APPLIANCE	3	FRRE-003	1199.99	2 DOOR UPRIGHT
8812-001	AV-001	AVON APPLIANCE	1	COWA-001	369.99	
8812-001	AV-001	AVON APPLIANCE	2	FRRE-001	699.99	1 DOOR TOP FREEZER W
8812-001	AV-001	AVON APPLIANCE	3	FRRE-001	699.99	1 DOOR TOP FREEZER W
8812-001	AV-001	AVON APPLIANCE	1	WHWA-002	969.99	DELUXE MODEL
8901-001	AV-001	AVON APPLIANCE	5	FRRE-001	699.99	1 DOOR TOP FREEZER W
8901-001	AV-001	AVON APPLIANCE	8	WHWA-001	739.99	
8901-001	AV-001	AVON APPLIANCE	1	COWA-001	369.99	
8901-001	AV-001	AVON APPLIANCE	100	HIMI-001	229.99	1500 WATT
8808-001	JA-001	JACKEL & HYDES	2	WHRE-001	469.99	
8808-001	JA-001	JACKEL & HYDES	7	HIRA-001	689.99	
8808-001	JA-001	JACKEL & HYDES	3	FRRE-003	1199.99	2 DOOR UPRIGHT
8808-001	JA-001	JACKEL & HYDES	10	FRRE-001	699.99	1 DOOR TOP FREEZER W
8808-002	RO-001	RON'S REFRIGERATORS	25	FRRE-001	699.99	1 DOOR TOP FREEZER W
8808-002	RO-001	RON'S REFRIGERATORS	15	FRRE-002	899.99	2 DOOR SIDE BY SIDE

11-40 Displaying the data.

Either way, as soon as you place the update operation in the pot handle, you are told that the view skeleton will be deleted because the "target" of an update is usually the database itself.

To create an update, create a new query using the INVENTRY database. Open the Update menu and choose Specify Update Operation. A sub-menu opens to let you choose the update operation. Figure 11-41 shows this menu on the work surface. Choose the Replace records in INVENTRY.DBF choice. The word Replace is automatically placed in the pot handle, and you are asked to confirm that you want to proceed with an update operation. Choose Proceed, and you are ready to enter your criteria.

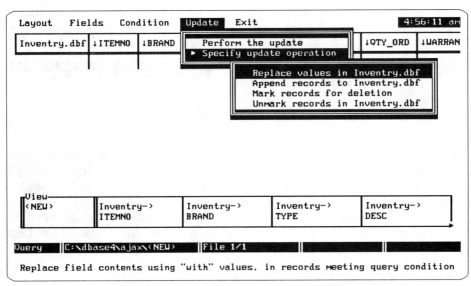

11-41   Query screen with Update menu.

The records you want to affect are decided by entering selection criteria in exactly the same way as with record selection. Let's assume that you want to raise the list price of all REFRIGERATORs by 12%. You would enter REFRIGERATOR in the TYPE entry area and enter

    with PRICE * 1.12

in the PRICE entry box as shown in Fig. 11-42. Go ahead and do this. When you are done, you normally would open the Update menu and choose Perform the update. Don't do this now. If you had, all of your data for refrigerators would have the PRICE field increased by 12%.

Saving the view as a new database

Suppose you want to create a new database, and include only the data from a presently existing query if you were to look at it in the BROWSE screen.

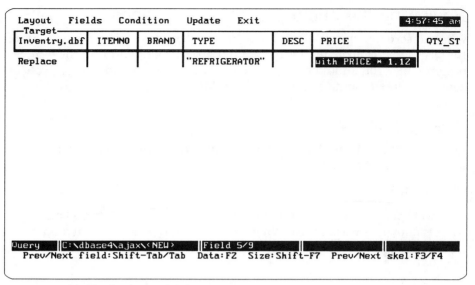

11-42 Replacing PRICE with PRICE * 1.12 for REFRIGERATORs.

dBASE IV provides the capability to take the present query view file, which up to now only exists in memory, and write it out as a database file.

On the Layout menu, this option is called Write view as database file. When you use this option, it allows you to take the current view of your databases including the open files and their relations, fields you have placed in the view file, sorts you have specified, and the records you have selected, and this option creates a new database with only the information from the current view. The new database is a real database with only the filtered information in the sorted order that you specified. The new database is a single database created from all of the instructions. You can use it like any other database. The original databases that make up the view are untouched. All you do is create a new database.

Using QBE in programs

When you create a query, dBASE IV creates a file known as a query file with the file extension .QBE. Thus, the INVOICES query you created has the file name INVOICES.QBE.

The statements which occupy the file INVOICES.QBE is a regular ASCII file. You can use any editor to view, modify, copy, and generally use the commands right in your program. If you are familiar with QBE, but just starting out in programming, the query screen is a good place to set up your view for your program and then copy the statements to make the database section of your program.

Reviewing the query program commands

When you create a query, dBASE IV actually interprets what you have done on the QBE screen and generates dBASE dot prompt commands in the form of a program file. You should be exposed to all of the commands in case you see some code like it, and need to understand it in the future.

Opening databases

Files are made active with the USE command. You could enter the following to make the ITEMS file active:

```
. USE ITEMS
```

This will open the ITEMS database without any indexes open and place it in what is known as work area 1. When you use only one database at a time, it is not important which work area you place the database in. The default work area is 1.

Next, you could open a second work area and open our child database. Work areas are open with the SELECT command or the IN option of the USE command. You could select work area 2 and open a second database:

```
. SELECT 2
. USE INVENTRY
```

or you could enter:

```
. USE INVENTRY IN 2
```

Indexing the related file

Child databases must be indexed in order to establish the relation from the parent files. When generating code from the query screen, dBASE checks to see if an index exists for the field to be used in the child file. If no index exists, it indexes the file. When you write your own code, you also know if the file is indexed. If it isn't, you would enter (in this example):

```
. INDEX ON ITEMNO TAG ITEMNO
```

However, when you created the INVENTRY file, you should have automatically indexed the file by ITEMNO by placing a Y in the index column of the database create screen. Because the database is already indexed by ITEMNO, you would enter:

```
. SET ORDER TO TAG ITEMNO
```

or

```
. USE INVENTRY IN 2 ORDER ITEMNO
```

if you wanted to combine the statements with the USE command.

Now you see how to open both work areas that are needed, and place database files into them. Because we will establish the relation from the ITEMS file to the INVENTRY file, you have to make the ITEMS work area active again, unless you use the "IN" option. If you use the SELECT method, then the INVENTRY database is active in work area 2.

Once you USE a database, you can select its area in several ways. The first way is by the original work number you gave it. Another way is by its alias. An alias for a database is another name by which it is known. Each database is automatically known by an alias, which is its name regardless of the area it was placed in. Once you establish the work area and open the database, you can make that area active by using the database name again, instead of the work area number.

Selecting and relating the files

Let's select the ITEMS file by its alias. Although we know it's in work area 1 and could simply enter SELECT 1, it is easier to enter the alias names when you have many work areas in use:

. SELECT ITEMS

This now returns control to the ITEMS database. The INVENTRY database is still open in the second work area. The last task is to relate the ITEMS database to the INVENTRY database so fields from both databases are available as though they were one database. That's basically the whole concept behind relational databases. You can maintain separate databases for simplicity and to make data entry more simple and efficient, but for reporting you need the databases to appear as one. Once two databases are related, they appear as one, and data from both can be displayed quickly and easily.

The command to relate two databases is fairly easy. The SET RELATION command is used to do this. The parent database must be selected as your database currently should be. A relation is set from the field in the parent database into the indexed child file. The command:

. SET RELATION TO ITEMNO INTO INVENTRY

sets this relation between the ITEMS file and the INVENTRY database. Because the first work area is selected where the ITEMS database was placed, dBASE knows about that database. The SET RELATION command assumes that you are in the parent file. The field specified in the TO clause describes the field in the parent database that will be used as the link to the child file. The field ITEMNO in the parent file is used to link to the child file. The other half of the link in the child file is the index key. Because the INVENTRY file is indexed by ITEMNO, there will be a valid match. The name of the fields used in the link and the index do not have to be the same. Both files contain the field names ITEMNO. However, this is not necessary. The values of both fields must match.

The INTO clause specifies the name of the child file. Once this link is established, you can begin to see your data. Many commands in dBASE IV now treat your relation as a single database, while other commands simply understand that the link makes the fields from both files available.

Remember that the type of relationship is totally dependent on your data, and not on the relation you establish. Regardless of your data, you will always use the same SET RELATION command to establish the relation. Because of your data, you have established a many-to-one relationship. There is more than one record with the same value of ITEMNO in the ITEMS file, but only one matching record is in the INVENTRY file, although the record in the inventory file is used again and again. In the ITEMS file, there are multiple records for each ITEMNO because, different invoices use the same items.

There is one more command to learn in setting relations that, in this example, has little relevance, because you have a something-to-one relationship. (Something is either one or many.) When you have a something-to-many relationship, you may want to control how many levels of duplicates are displayed. The command SET SKIP TO takes care of this. If you don't list a child file in a SET SKIP TO command, you will only see the first occurrence of a duplicate parent record.

Let's assume you had a relation from the INVOICE file to the ITEMS file. Without the command:

. SET SKIP TO ITEMS

only the first ITEM of each invoice would be displayed. In this example, however, where the ITEMS file forms a many-to-one relationship, the SET SKIP TO command can be left out or blank.

Once the relations are set, you could stop and use the DISPLAY, LIST, EDIT, or BROWSE commands to select your records and fields. However, there are a few more commands to understand.

Selecting the fields

First, you must decide which fields are to appear in the view file used to display the data. The command SET FIELDS TO is used to accomplish this task. For the example of a four-file view file the command would be:

. SET FIELDS TO INVOICE—>INVNO, CUSTOMER—>CUSTNO,
    CUSTOMER—>NAME,ITEMS—>QTY,ITEMS—>ITEMNO, ;
    INVENTRY—>BRAND, INVENTRY—>TYPE,INVENTRY—>PRICE

Notice that the same form of selecting a field in a database is used here as in the view file of the query screen. The database name is placed first, followed by an arrow constructed from a dash and a greater than sign, followed by the field name itself. At the end of the top and middle lines is a semicolon indicating that the line is continued. This is optional in the dot prompt, but mandatory if used in a program file.

Setting the filters

Once the fields are decided, you can set any filters to decide which records are displayed. Filters are separately set in each work area. If we were to filter the INVENTRY database for only the refrigerators that cost more than $750, we would enter one of three forms. This is automatic if the filter method is set to optimized:

```
. SET FILTER TO (TYPE = 'REFRIGERATOR' .AND. PRICE > 750)
. INDEX ON ITEMNO TAG REFPR FOR TYPE =
    'REFRIGERATOR' .AND. PRICE > 750
. SET KEY TO 'REFRIGERATOR' SET FILTER TO PRICE > 750
```

Filters have the exact same form as record selection used with the DISPLAY or LIST commands. Instead of setting a filter, you could have typed:

```
. DISPLAY ALL FOR (TYPE = 'REFRIGERATOR' .AND. PRICE > 750)
```

All of these commands entered separately at the dot prompt create various parts of the view. The view isn't just something you create in the QBE screen. The current view determines the open databases, indices, and relations. It also includes the field and record selections. Whether you enter the commands from the dot prompt or use the Query screen, the result will be the same. You have built a "window" into your database that only includes what you want within your view. Just as you can save your queries, you can save all the dot prompt commands that you enter to create a view. To do this you would type:

```
. CREATE VIEW FROM ENVIRONMENT
```

dBASE would ask you for a file name and save all of the commands you had entered to a file, much like the Query screen says your commands.

As you have seen in this chapter, there are several ways to decide how to see your data. The number of ways to look at your data are infinite, and only limited by your imagination and database design. You have learned the importance of designing databases that limit redundancies. Because of the ability to set your relations, you can have your data presented any way you want.

12

Creating and using screens and forms

So far in this section, you have seen how to create and use a database, how to sort and index your data, how to use multiple databases, and finally how to query a database. In this chapter, you will see the process of designing input screens for your databases. A good design not only makes entering data into a database more fun, but, when done correctly, it can affect the productivity and integrity of the data that can be added or changed in your database.

Understanding the design process

With careful planning, a good design for an input screen reduces the potential of collecting incorrect information. This is accomplished by designing a concise, uncluttered screen. The screen might contain simple directions or suggestions for input and might provide feedback when information is input incorrectly.

Design your screens so that the user will be able to enter the information quickly and accurately. People using the information in the database, after it has been input, expect that all the information is correct and accurate. However, those who enter the data in the database sometimes make mistakes. It is important in designing your input screens so that the data is checked and validated at the time it is entered and the screens do not allow bad data in the database.

In this chapter, you will design just one screen form—the inventory data entry screen. However, you will learn everything there is to know about creating and using a screen form and then using the program code produced by the form generator in your program. Both the customer screen and the invoice screen will be created strictly by program commands as shown in chapter 4. However, you will see how to add data validation commands to the code you will create later in this book and will see how BROWSE screens can be used to validate data.

The screen form design created in chapter 4 will be built in this chapter. You will also learn to add messages, data validation commands, lines, and boxes to the form. If you don't remember this design, it is in Fig. 12-1.

```
                    AJAX APPLIANCE COMPANY
                 INVENTORY DATA ENTRY SCREEN

              ITEM NUMBER: AAAA-999

              BRAND                    TYPE
              XXXXXXXXXX              XXXXXXXXXXX

       ITEM DESCRIPTION: XXXXXXXXXXXXXXXXXXXXXXXXXX

          QUANTITY IN STOCK          QUANTITY ON ORDER
                999                         999

                   PRICE: 99999.99

              WARRANTY PERIOD: 99 MONTHS

          ┌ FEATURES: ──────────────────────────────┐
          │                                          │
          │                                          │
          └──────────────────────────────────────────┘
```

12-1   The inventory data entry screen design.

Creating special customized screens such as that shown in Fig. 12-1 was once a source of woe for computer users. Beginners couldn't do it, and programmers hated doing it. The result was nearly always dull screens with terse messages. Today, an increasing number of software packages are making it easy for anyone to create special screens.

Custom screens offer more than just a pleasing appearance. These screens allow you to make better use of the limited screen space. By adding lines and boxes they let you segregate common data items, change the order you can edit the data, and most importantly, they can also provide complete edit checking of the data.

Without a custom screen, you get a standard screen like you have seen in the EDIT mode. All of the field names along the left side and the fields themselves next to each field name. This screen is adequate for a default screen. Because you know what you want the screen to look like, you can, however, always improve on a standard form.

Basic steps in the design process

There are six basic steps to creating a good data entry screen:

Step 1—Define the database of the system
Step 2—Use Quick Layout to place the fields on the work surface

Step 3—Rearrange the fields and text labels
Step 4—Define lines and boxes
Step 5—Define areas of color
Step 6—Define data validation rules

Next, we will examine each of these steps as we build the inventory data entry screen.

Step 1: Define the database of the system

First, you should familiarize yourself with the database and its structure when you begin to design an input screen. It is important to know what fields will be used in the database for your input form. In special situations, you might want to design an input screen which only allows access to certain fields in a database. It is important to know the field types and sizes that you will use in the design to appropriately lay out the information on the screen.

You will be working with the INVENTRY database that you created back in chapter 7. To create a custom form, you must have the database in use that will use the custom screen. If you were not using that database when you entered the work surface you can choose the Use different database file or view choice from the Layout menu. In this example, you will select the INVENTRY database.

You may choose any database or view. However, if you choose a view that uses multiple databases you will not be able to add, change, or delete records. You will only be able to display records. dBASE IV cannot handle multi-file data entry without programming!

Step 2: Use quick layout to place the fields on the work surface

An input screen is typically comprised of 25 rows and 80 columns. You can lay out your design on paper before attempting to create the input screen.

The fields in the design should be placed in a logical order for the person who will be using the input screen. If the input screen user will be entering information from a form, you should lay out the fields in your screen design in the same order as they appear on the form.

The Quick Layout option is used to automatically place your fields on the work surface. They are placed on the work surface with the field name on the left and the field itself on the right. This is the default Edit screen.

Step 3: Rearrange the fields and text labels

Once the quick layout is completed, begin to move the fields and text labels into the position that you desire. You should include any instructions that may be helpful for the person inputting information using your screen. Make sure the instructions are simple, easy to understand, and will be important to the person who inputs the information.

Too much text on the screen makes inputting information difficult and tends to be distracting. The text should form boundaries around the input fields and make it easy for the user to understand where the data is to be entered.

Step 4: Define lines and boxes

Include lines and boxes in your design only if it helps organize the information on the screen. Lines and boxes should be used to highlight and attract attention to areas on the screen. Use lines and boxes to form boundaries around the input fields in your design or to highlight text significant to the data collection process. Too many lines or boxes can be distracting.

If you look at the design in Fig. 12-1, you can see that there is a box designed around the entire screen and a line dividing the key fields from the rest of the data fields. There is also a box around the memo field indicating that the memo field will be displayed inside a window.

Step 5: Define areas of color

In screen design, color may also be used to attract attention. Keep in mind that not all people see colors in the same way. Some people find it difficult to distinguish different colors. Also be aware of the equipment that will be used to collect information. It is quite obvious that use of color in your design will have no value if the screen is displayed on a monochrome or single color monitor.

If you decide to use color, be careful in your selection. Avoid using low contrasting colors which are difficult to see. For example, you might want to use red to attract attention when an error is detected during input.

Step 6: Define data validation rules

You can check the data input at the screen and provide feedback when the data is incorrect. This process is called data validation. Two types of data validation can take place. Data can be edited for format or correctness. Editing data for format is comparing each character of the input to a template or picture. Data is edited for correctness by checking the entire field against other values.

To make data entry easier, messages can be displayed at the bottom of your screen each time the cursor moves to a different field. Error messages can be displayed when the data entered does not meet the data validation rules.

To define data validation rules for each field of the input screen design, you must know what values are valid and what values are not. The more rules you can think of during the screen design, the better the validation process will be. The more validation you perform on your data, the more accurate the data in your database will be.

It is important to check the data input into the INVENTRY database. Let's consider what validation you will use in the INVENTRY form design. Figure 12-2 shows the design of the INVENTRY database created in chapter 4.

INVENTORY FILE FIELD NAME	DATA TYPE	DISPLAY SIZE	INDEX	TEMPLATE RANGE CHOICES
ITEMNO	CHAR	8	Y	AAAA-999
BRAND	CHAR	10	+TYPE	
TYPE	CHAR	12		REFRIGERATOR DISHWASHER WASHER DRYER RANGE MICROWAVE
DESC	CHAR	25		
PRICE	NUMERIC	7.2		9999.99
QTY_STK	NUMERIC	3		999
QTY_ORD	NUMERIC	3		999
WARRANTY	NUMERIC	2		0-24
FEATURES	MEMO	10		

12-2 The inventory database data entry rules and patterns.

First, you might have a rule that says the ITEMNO field must consist of four letters followed by a dash and three numeric digits. This validation is performed by using a template. A template describes what characters are valid for input.

Suppose you do not want to allow lowercase letters in the BRAND or DESC fields. In the INVENTRY form you can convert mixed case input to capital letters using a picture for each field. The picture is used to convert, translate, and/or embed characters in a field. In a phone number field, you might use a template to specify the parentheses around the area code and a dash after the first part of the number, but you might use a picture to tell dBASE to make those special characters part of the stored data.

You are required to validate that the data entered for the BRAND field match one value from a list of acceptable values. This is accomplished by using a multiple choice picture. The multiple choice picture does not allow the value of a field to be typed at the keyboard. Instead, the space bar changes the value in the input field until the desired value appears, preventing typographical errors when the input must be a specific value.

Date-defined fields provide automatic date validation. This prevents invalid input of month, day, and year combinations. The WARRANTY field in the INVENTRY database must fall within a pre-determined range. A number can be validated to fall within a range of two numbers, to be greater than a certain number or to be less than a certain number using Edit options. The data validation rules for the INVENTRY form are summarized in Fig. 12-2.

Using the dBASE IV screen/form designer

Once you understand the basics of creating and using forms, it is time to create the INVENTRY form.

The forms work surface

Let's start by going to the Control Center and making the INVENTRY file active by choosing it and pressing Return to bring it above the line. Once the INVENTRY file is active, you can move the cursor to the ⟨create⟩ line of the Forms panel and press Return. The Forms work surface appears as shown in Fig. 12-3.

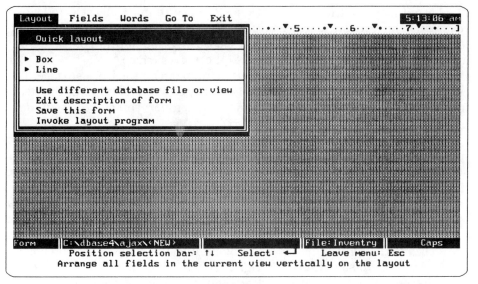

12-3 The Forms work surface.

Of course you can also enter the Forms work surface from the dot prompt by entering the following commands:

```
. USE INVENTRY
. CREATE SCREEN INVENTRY
```

If you entered the screen form from the Control Center, then you will later name the form INVENTRY.

The Forms work surface is used to lay out labels and fields needed to produce the custom screen. When the information is laid out on the work surface, it can be stored in a disk file. When the information on the work surface is saved, a form program is created and stored on disk. The form program is used to display the screen. The form can be modified from the Forms work surface.

Once the screen form appears on the work surface, add the fields. This form gathers the information that dBASE needs to produce this custom screen and stores the information in a disk file. The filename for this screen form must conform to the standard rules for disk filenames. dBASE automatically adds the .SCR file identifier to this filename. When the screen has been completely defined, dBASE uses the screen file to produce a second file called a format file. dBASE automatically assigns the format file the same name as the screen file, but uses an .FMT file identifier. When you use the screen for the first time, dBASE IV compiles the .FMT file into an object module and gives it an .FMO extension.

Using the quick layout feature

The Layout menu of the Forms work surface is automatically selected when you access the work surface. If a database has not been accessed before going to the work surface, the Use different database file or view option of the Layout menu can be used to define the fields to the work surface.

In Fig. 12-3, you can see the Layout menu open on the work surface. The cursor bar is on the Quick Layout choice. This choice places all of the fields from the database onto the work surface. Remember, you can only edit data in one database at a time.

The Quick Layout option of the Layout menu is used to place the field names and fields on the work surface in the same layout found on the EDIT screen. This technique is faster than adding the fields to the work surface one field at a time.

Once you press Return on Quick Layout, your data is placed on the work surface. It looks exactly like the EDIT mode's default form. As you can see in Fig. 12-4, all of the field names are lined up along the left side and the fields are placed to the right. There is also a blank line at the top of the screen.

If you were to save this form right now, it would perform just like the EDIT screen. This gives you a starting point to create your screen.

Navigating the forms work surface

In the next section, you will practice techniques in navigating the work surface. The arrow keys move the cursor around the work surface one character at a time. The cursor moves left and right faster using Tab and Shift–Tab.

Fields are moved by moving the cursor to any part of the field and using the Move key (F7). When you use this technique to move a field, the field is selected and a shaded box the size of the field can be moved around to a new location of the work surface. When the shaded box is in the position you want the selected field moved to, press the Enter key which in turn moves the field from the old location to the new location.

Text labels on the work surface can be moved by using the Select key (F6) and the arrow keys to highlight the area to be moved. When the Select key is

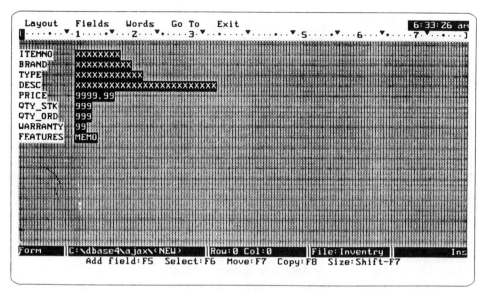

```
 Layout   Fields   Words   Go To   Exit                    6:33:26 am
[ · · · · ▼ · 1 · · · ▼ · · · 2 · · · ▼ · · · · 3 ▼ · · · · · ▼ · · · · ▼ · · · 5 · · · · ▼ · · · · 6 · · · ▼ · · ▼ · · · · 7 · ▼ · · · · · ]

 ITEMNO     XXXXXXX
 BRAND      XXXXXXXXX
 TYPE       XXXXXXXXXX
 DESC       XXXXXXXXXXXXXXXXXXXXXXX
 PRICE      9999.99
 QTY_STK    999
 QTY_ORD    999
 WARRANTY   99
 FEATURES   MEMO
```

```
 Form      C:\dbase4\ajax\<NEW>        Row:0 Col:0      File:Inventory       Ins
           Add field:F5  Select:F6  Move:F7  Copy:F8  Size:Shift-F7
```

12-4 The Quick Layout.

pressed, a shaded square the size of one character marks the first corner of a selected area. The arrow keys are then used to highlight the remaining area to be selected. The Enter key is used to mark the opposite corner of the selected area. An area that has been selected can be moved using the Move key, the arrow keys and the Enter key. You can also select multiple fields and text by using the Select key.

Selected labels and fields can be removed from the work surface using the Delete key. If you decide to select a different area of the work surface, use the Esc key to remove the shaded selected area.

You compose your screen from the work surface. The work surface should initially resemble Fig. 12-4. This is the starting point for creating the custom screen. Note that the field areas are in reverse video. Character fields are filled with Xs, numeric fields with 9s, date fields with MM/DD/YY, logic fields with Y, and the memo field with MEMO.

You can move the cursor to any position on screen with the help of the cursor control keys. The Left and Right arrow keys move the cursor one space in the direction of the arrow. The Up and Down arrow keys move the cursor one line up or down. To move the cursor to the beginning (or the end) of the line, press the Ctrl key and the Left (or Right) arrow at the same time. The status bar keeps track of the cursor position. It will be helpful to refer to the status bar and the message area at the bottom of the screen for the cursor column and row position information and messages which help locate labels and fields on the work surface. The status bar lists your starting position in the left top corner as Row:0 Col:0, as shown in Fig. 12-4.

The form menus

The Forms screen has five menus:

- Layout
- Fields
- Words
- GoTo
- Exit

Menus in the Forms work surface are opened in the same way as any other menu in dBASE IV. You can either press the F10 key and select the menu with the arrow keys or press the Alt key with the first letter of the menu choice.

You have already seen the Layout menu in Fig. 12-3. The Layout menu has three sections. First, you can perform a Quick Layout of all your fields. The middle section is used to create lines and boxes in your form. Finally, the last section of the Layout menu lets you choose a database to work with, edit the description of the form, or to save the form and continue working.

The Fields menu is shown in Fig. 12-5. The menu has two main purposes. First, you can add, remove, or modify a field from your database or field you have calculated from fields in your database. You will see how to add or modify a field later in this chapter. When you select Remove field, a list of all your fields is displayed and you can choose the field to delete. If you already have a field selected on the work surface it is easier to simply press the Delete key.

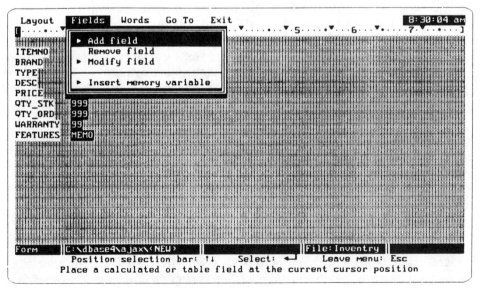

12-5 The Fields menu.

You can also add memory variable fields to the screen which are not part of the database structure. Their primary function is to display calculations involving a field and a value or several fields. For example, if you had quantity and price fields on the database (like the inventory database), a memory variable could multiply the fields to get a total value.

If you had added a field to the screen as a memory variable that was not calculated, you could change it here. When you choose the last option Insert memory variable, you can create a memory variable of any type that can be used for data entry. Unlike a calculated database or memory field that is only used for display, a memory variable can be used for data entry. You will have to modify the format file if you expect to add the memory variable to your database file. This is used a lot with the application generator to allow input of control parameters.

The next menu is the Words menu as shown in Fig. 12-6. This menu contains a variety of choices all dealing with the way the data looks. The first option Style is not used in forms. The next two options Display and Position let you work with colors and centering commands. The next two commands let you work with the ruler at the top of the screen. The last option Enable automatic indent is only used for the word wrap editor found in the program editor or the word wrap band of reports.

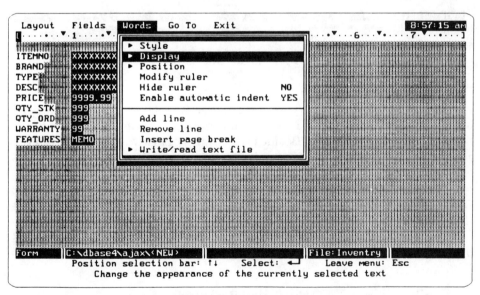

12-6 The Words menu.

The bottom half of the menu lets you add or delete lines on the work surface, insert page breaks into reports (but not forms), and write the form as a text file or read a text file of labels into the work surface. This is one good way to add your labels after you have spent time designing complex screens of text. You can add your fields, lines, and boxes after importing the text.

The Go To menu shown in Fig. 12-7 lets you quickly go to places on the screen. Sometimes you may find yourself creating long screens of many pages. This will allow you to quickly go to any line on the screen.

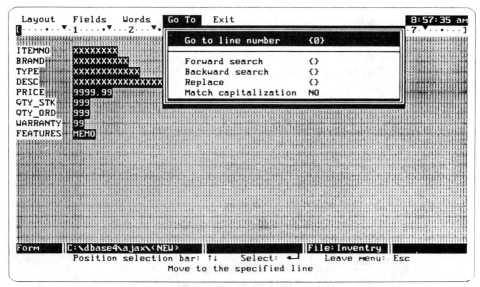

12-7 The Go To menu.

The Go To menu also lets you perform search and replace functions. This way if you decide to change a specific name or title, you can quickly change it throughout the entire form. Besides a forward or backward search from the current cursor position, you can also decide if matching capitalization is important.

The Exit menu allows you to save all your changes and return to the Control Center or dot prompt or abandon all changes you made from the last time you saved the form.

You will see these menus again when you build the inventory form used by the programs in this book.

Placing labels and text where you want them

Now it is time to continue creating the inventory screen. If you don't choose the Quick Layout, you will work with a blank work surface. The F5 or Add Field key allows you to add fields to the work surface from the current database. Of course you can also open the Fields menu and choose Add field. Either way, you can place a new field on the work surface.

You can put the fields anywhere on the screen—and in any order. Figure 12-8 shows the first step in moving screen fields around. In order to move the fields and labels most efficiently, it is best to start by placing all of the fields and labels at the bottom center of the screen. Then, fields can be moved into position from top to bottom without interference by other fields already on the work surface but not yet in position.

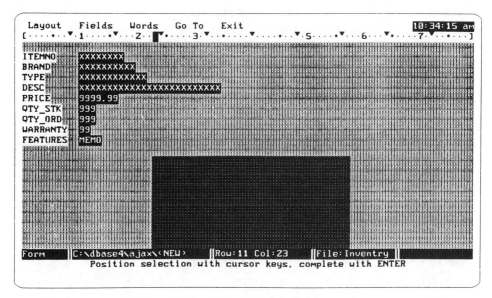

12-8 Moving all of the fields.

Figure 12-8 was created by first selecting all of the fields and labels. This was accomplished by first moving the cursor to the top left corner of the fields. Then press the F6 or Extend Select key. The cursor keys are then used to move to the bottom right corner of the fields. As the cursor is moved, a highlighted rectangle is created that gets larger as more fields and labels are selected. Once all of the fields are selected, the Enter key is pressed. This completes the selection, and the highlighted area remains.

There are two ways to move the rectangle and its contents. First F7 or Move can be pressed to make the highlighted area mobile. The cursor keys can then move it wherever you want. Figure 12-8 shows this area already moved into position. All that is left is to press Enter and the fields and text are moved. You can also move the cursor to the left corner of where you want the area to be moved to and press F7. Either way the area will be moved.

Once the fields and text are out of the way, you can begin to move each individual field and text label into the approximate final position.

To do this, you must first change the highlighted area. You can unhighlight an area by pressing Esc. You can then highlight a new area. For example, after removing the highlight the cursor is moved to the I in the

ITEMNO text label and F6 is pressed to begin the selection. In this example, pressing the Tab key three times highlights the ITEMNO label and field. Pressing Esc completes the highlighting process. Next, the cursor is moved according to the design and F7 is pressed. When the process is complete, the ITEMNO label and field should start at about 3,32 or row 3, column 32. Remember that row 3 is the fourth row from the top because the rows are numbered from 0 to 24. The columns are numbered from 0 to 79. Figure 12-9 shows this first field moved on the work surface.

Once you have mastered moving one field, you have mastered moving them all. Remember, you can move groups of fields, groups of text labels, or both. Whatever moves your fields the fastest is the method you should employ.

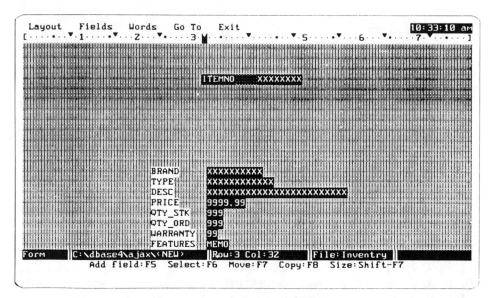

12-9 Moving the ITEMNO field.

Follow the design in Fig. 12-1. Move all the fields into their approximate position. This is shown in Fig. 12-10.

It doesn't look like much yet, but it soon will. Note that some of the field labels are above the fields themselves. This was done by moving the text and field separately.

Also notice that the PRICE field comes after the quantity fields even though this is not the order of the database structure. The order of the database structure doesn't matter. Your cursor moves left to right and top to bottom when it allows your data. At the end of this chapter, you will learn a secret for controlling the cursor movement when you enter data.

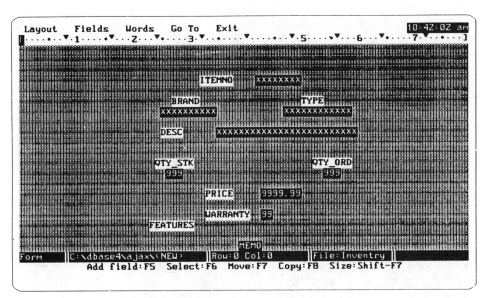

12-10 Completing moving all the fields.

Adding and changing text

Now it is time to change the field names where necessary and to add more text to make the screen more readable. You might need to fine tune the position of some of the fields as you add the text to make the screen more centered. You also might need to add or delete blank lines.

There are several ways to add and delete blank lines. Lines can be added from the current cursor position by pressing Ctrl–N. When you add a blank line everything below the cursor moves down one line and a blank line appears below the cursor. Lines are deleted by pressing Ctrl–U.

You can also add and delete lines through menu selections. The Words menu contains choices for adding and deleting lines. If you have trouble remembering the key combinations, the menus will work just as well.

To enter new text on the screen, move the cursor to where you want the text to be and type it in. Later, if you don't like where you placed it, you can move it by first selecting it with the F6 key and then moving it with the F7 key. In this example, we will add some text at the top of the screen. We will also change some of the field name text identifiers to make them more to our liking.

When you move text or fields on top of existing text or fields, you will see a message that asks:

Delete covered text and fields? (Y/N)

This allows you to place moved text or fields on top of existing text or fields and automatically deletes the covered portion before doing so. It does, however, give you the chance to preserve what is underneath before it is deleted.

Figure 12-11 shows the screen after text has been added and changed. The screen is starting to look better. Labels are now in place. There is even a label after the warranty period as well as before it. This extra text makes it easier for the operator to remember the unit of measure.

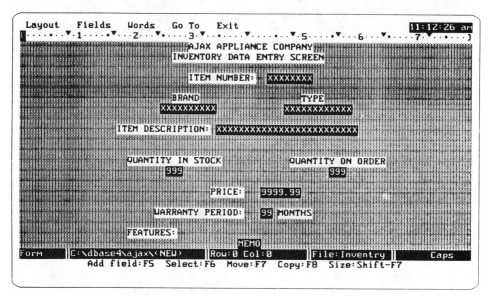

12-11 Completing text entry and changes.

Notice that we have also added some text at the top of the screen and changed the text for many of the field labels. Changing the text in this screen does not change the actual field names on the database. Only by going to the database work surface can you do that. Changing text in this screen applies to this data entry screen only!

Drawing lines and boxes

Adding lines and boxes is another step that you should consider in creating forms. Lines and boxes are selected from the Layout menu. Once you choose one of these selections you are asked whether you want a single line or a double line.

The next step is to place the left corner of the line or left top corner of the box on the screen. After you place the left corner press Return. This "locks" the left corner in place. As you use the cursor keys, the line or box expands to cover the area to the cursor. When your box covers the desired area press Return again. Each box is created this way. Lines are "drawn" by moving the arrow keys. Lines do not have to be horizontal. You can draw vertical lines or make corners or connect two lines. Lines that pass through other lines will correctly create corners or crosses.

Lines and boxes are shown entered on the work surface in Fig. 12-12. This completes most of the entry for the form.

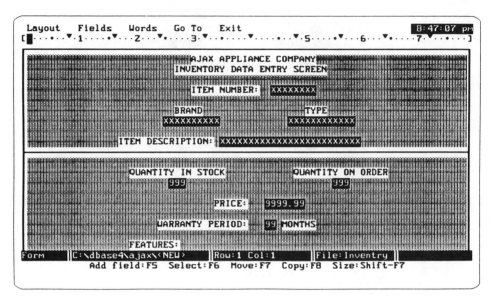

12-12 Completing lines and boxes.

Many other changes had to be made to make the screen look like Fig. 12-12 and to conform to the original design. First, because the box around the entire screen had to go through line 0, the titles had to be moved down one line. In fact, everything had to be moved down one line. The Add line command was used from the Words menu to do this. You will notice that the bottom of the box is out of sight. Remember that although the screen form only shows about 20 lines at a time, 25 lines can be used by the screen when displayed.

The memo field marker is also out of sight after the new line was added. Finally, a line was added across the screen from columns 1 to 78. The line was also continued into the box and the corners connected to make perfect T's where the line meets the box.

You may find it easier if you have an EGA or VGA system to work in 43-line mode. This will let you see all of your screen at once so you are not constantly paging up and down. Of course, you can press F2 (Data) at any time to see how your screen would look and then press Shift–F2 (Design) to get back to the Forms work surface.

Figure 12-13 shows the screen as it presently exists. If you are following along just press F2. Pressing Shift–F2 returns you to the Forms work surface. Once you return to the work surface, you can continue working. If you need to erase a box simply select it and press Delete. You can also move boxes by pressing F7 after the box is selected. Lines must be deleted one character at a time or by selecting the entire line with the F6 key.

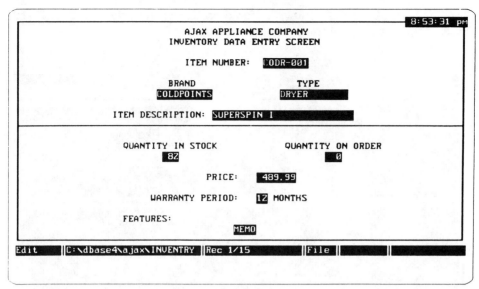

```
                                                              ┌─────────┐
                                                              │8:53:31 PM│
                                                              └─────────┘
              AJAX APPLIANCE COMPANY
              INVENTORY DATA ENTRY SCREEN

                  ITEM NUMBER:   CODR-001

              BRAND                    TYPE
              COLDPOINTS               DRYER

          ITEM DESCRIPTION:  SUPERSPIN I

      QUANTITY IN STOCK              QUANTITY ON ORDER
             82                             0

                      PRICE:    489.99

              WARRANTY PERIOD:   12 MONTHS

          FEATURES:
                             MEMO

 Edit     C:\dbase4\ajax\INVENTRY  Rec 1/15        File
```

12-13 Viewing the screen.

Composing the data entry form is an iterative process. Each time you add some text, a line, a box, or move a field around, something else probably needs to be moved as well. Make sure you always keep in mind what the final screen should look like as you go through this process.

Memo field markers and windows

The last item to change before we go on to data validation is to change the way that the memo field FEATURES will appear. This is changed through an item on the Field Box. Either move your cursor to the MEMO marker or choose Modify field in the Fields menu and choose FEATURES. The field box will open for the FEATURES field.

An option that applies only to the memo field type is at the bottom of the field box. This option affects the display of the memo field itself. The memo field is displayed as a small "marker" on the work surface.

Figure 12-14 shows the Modify field box for the FEATURES memo field. The selection Display as was highlighted showing the current value as MARKER. It was changed to the other option WINDOW by pressing Enter. A memo display window is a rectangular area that is bounded by lines that display a portion (or all) of your memo data. Think of it as a window to your memo file.

When you select WINDOW, you should also select the type of border lines that will surround the window. Choices include Single and Double. Once the WINDOW selection is made, you can select the Border Lines choice (Fig. 12-14).

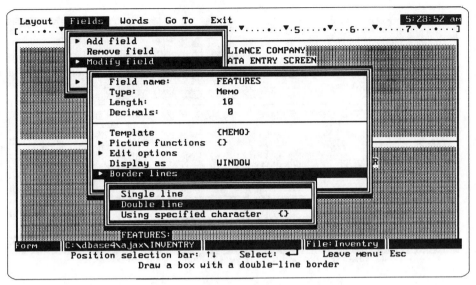

12-14 Creating a memo window.

Once you make this selection, a memo window appears on the work surface as shown in Fig. 12-15. Luckily, this box behaves like any other box. You can select it with the F6 keys (though it is initially selected). You can then

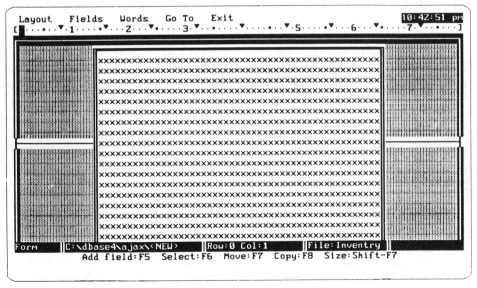

12-15 The initial memo window.

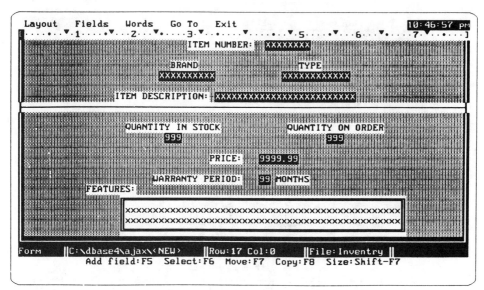

12-16 The final memo window on the work surface.

move it with F7 or resize it with the Shift–F7 keys. Figure 12-16 shows the memo window on the work surface after the FEATURES text has been moved as well. The figure shows the bottom part of the screen.

Testing the screen form

Before going on to add the "bells and whistles" such as editing options and picture displays, you should test the screen. Though you get a pretty good idea of what the screen will look like while creating it, there is nothing like a good test drive to make sure it works the way you would expect. Once you are happy with the layout, you can name the screen and then save it. If you entered the screen through the dot prompt, then you have already named it.

Press Alt–E to open the Exit menu. Next choose the save option. You are asked to name the screen. Call it INVENTRY. When you are done you are returned to the Control Center or dot prompt. From the Control Center, place the cursor on the form name and press F2. You should be placed in an EDIT screen using the form. The first record in the database is displayed. If you are in the dot prompt, you must tell dBASE IV to use the format. Use the following commands:

```
. SET FORMAT TO INVENTRY
. EDIT
```

Figure 12-17 shows the final version of this screen.

Notice that the status bar is forcing the memo field window to shrink and be placed on the last line of the main box. Also notice that the clock seems out of place. Later, you will modify the format file slightly to fix all of these problems.

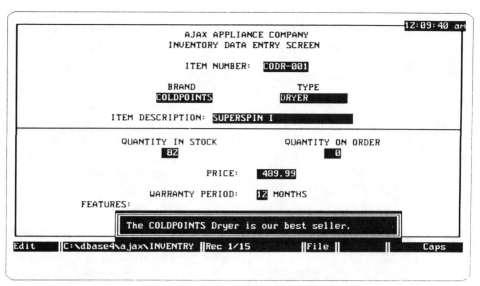

```
                                                                12:09:40 am
          AJAX APPLIANCE COMPANY
          INVENTORY DATA ENTRY SCREEN

                ITEM NUMBER:  CODR-001

            BRAND               TYPE
         COLDPOINTS          DRYER

      ITEM DESCRIPTION: SUPERSPIN I

       QUANTITY IN STOCK         QUANTITY ON ORDER
              82                        0

                    PRICE:  489.99

              WARRANTY PERIOD:  12 MONTHS
        FEATURES:
               The COLDPOINTS Dryer is our best seller.

Edit      C:\dbase4\ajax\INVENTRY   Rec 1/15      File           Caps
```

12-17 The INVENTRY screen.

The EDIT and APPEND commands will now use the special screen format in place of the standard display. To turn off the special format, use the command CLOSE FORMAT or you can "unselect" it in the Control Center by again choosing it and pressing Return to send it "below the line." If you close the database you are using, the FORMAT file will automatically close. When you reopen the database, you must again choose the form or use the SET FORMAT TO command with the format filename to reestablish the custom screen.

If you are using several database files at the same time, you might have a custom screen for each. That means that you can have a separate format file in each dBASE work area.

Data validation

Once you have placed all of the fields on your screen it is time to look at each individual field and decide if you can enhance its capabilities to handle input.

The two primary concerns of data entry is to (1) enter the data quickly, and (2) enter the data accurately. There is a fine balance between these two areas of concern. How you approach the balance of fast data entry against accurate data entry is one of those items determined by your personal style. A system developer expects all information stored in the computer to be completely correct and accurate. People are doing the data entry, however, and they are prone to errors. You will find it is prudent to check for valid data at the time it is entered and not allow bad or incorrect data into the system.

The data entry program checks for accuracy in the incoming data by a process called editing. There are three types of data editing: format editing, correctness editing, and validity editing. The two ways of performing this editing are by using input formats on each character of the input as specified by templates and picture functions and by using edit options to check the entire field.

Modifying a field

Editing data begins by modifying a field on the screen. You can modify any field by selecting the field and pressing F5 or by choosing the Fields menu and selecting Modify field. Either way the field box appears which lets you manipulate different characteristics about the field during data entry. The field box is shown for the BRAND field in Fig. 12-18.

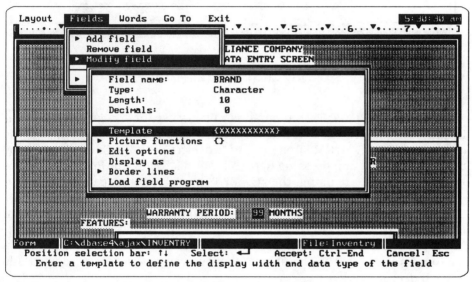

12-18 Modifying the BRAND field's characteristics.

The top half of the box contains the field's name, data type, length, and number of decimals. Because this comes from the field's database structure you cannot change any of these.

dBASE naturally provides a limited measure of control to facilitate data entry. Only numbers can be entered into numeric fields, and only valid dates can be entered into date fields. We can, however, provide a great deal more control for data entry through the custom screen. For example, we can restrict the data entry for character fields to the letters a–z, and we can force the entry to uppercase A–Z. We can also restrict the entry of date or numeric data to a range of values. This can be done with the help of the templates, picture functions, and edit options.

In the BRAND box, five selections are at the bottom of the box. The last two selections are only available for memo fields and have already been explained. The other three selections affect the way the field looks, how data is entered into a field, and whether or not the input is accepted as valid input.

Templates

A template lets you specify what can be placed into a field at the individual character level. A list of the character template symbols is shown in Fig 12-19. The BRAND template is simply ten X's indicating that any character can be entered into each of the ten positions. In Fig. 12-19 you can see some of the more common symbols.

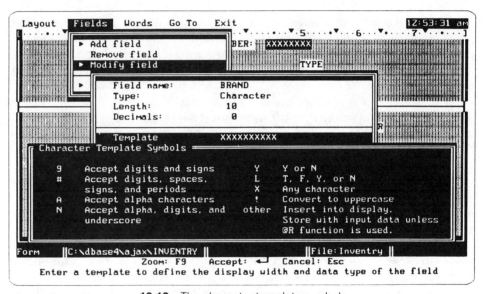

12-19 The character template symbols.

An X indicates that any character can be entered into each of the positions marked by an X.

An A indicates that only a letter, A through Z (upper- or lowercase) can be entered in that position of the field.

An N indicates that letters or numbers may be entered in that position of the field.

A # indicates that numbers, blanks, or signs (plus or minus) may be entered in that position of the field.

A 9 indicates that only a digit 0 through 9 or a plus or minus sign may be input or displayed in that position of the field.

The Y character is used to verify that the input is either the letter Y or N in that position of the field and can be used for character or logical fields.

The L character is used strictly for logical fields and verifies that the input is Y, N, T, or F.

The ! character allows any character, number or special symbol to be entered, and instantly converts lowercase letters to uppercase and stores the input in uppercase in your database.

Your ITEMNO field requires you to enter four alphabetic characters followed by a dash and three numbers. You must set up the template or "mask" in the ITEMNO field:

AAAA-999

A phone number template that allowed the area code and number and required the parentheses and dash would be:

(999) 999-9999

A blank space acts as a mask preventing data entry or display into that position of the field. Some of the other template symbols are used for specific purposes. The Y and L template symbols are used strictly for logic fields. The ! symbol instantly converts lowercase letters to uppercase and stores it that way.

Be aware that any other symbol other than those listed in Fig. 12-19 appears not only as you type in the data, but it also becomes part of the record itself. The parentheses in the phone number template is a good example of this. However, you can make these symbols not be part of the record by using the R picture function, as you will soon see.

When you use any of the template symbols such as the A template that only allows alpha characters and you attempt to enter a number the cursor simply will not move. Nothing gets entered and the cursor just sits on the entry area.

When you use a symbol not on the list like the parentheses, your cursor will skip over that symbol as you enter the other template data. The phone number field would appear like this when you see the blank field.

Figure 12-19 only shows the character templates. Numeric and logic fields have their own sets of templates. You should look at these different sets. The numeric templates are shown in Fig. 12-20.

The "$" and "*" characters in numeric fields can be used to create a "check-protected" format to display or print dollar figures. Any leading zero that is matched with an asterisk or dollar sign is replaced by that character.

The "," template symbol automatically inserts commas in the appropriate place when data is entered.

Any other symbols in a template appear as the data is entered on the screen and become part of the data in your database.

The logic templates are either L or Y. The L template allows T, F, Y, or N while the Y template only allows Y and N.

Pictures

Picture functions are used to control various characteristics of a particular field. Unlike templates, picture functions are not specified on a character by

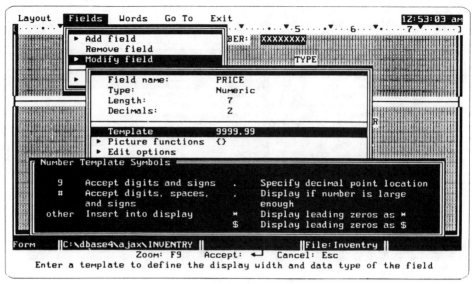

12-20 The numeric template symbols.

character basis. Instead, picture functions control the way an entire field is displayed on the screen.

Some of the characteristics for numeric fields include the use credit/debit identification (i.e., CR, DB), parentheses around negative numbers, use of dollar signs, commas, exponential notation, display leading zero values and blanks for leading zero values. Each characteristic is controlled from the Picture option of the Field description menu and can be turned on or off.

Some of the characteristics for character fields include the use of uppercase conversion, scrolling within a specified width, alphabetic characters only, and multiple choice.

Figure 12-21 shows the character picture functions. Character data may be edited and displayed using picture functions. The alphabetic functions are: A, !, R, S, and M. The A function (alphabetic characters only) tells dBASE to accept only alphabetic characters in the input field. The ! (uppercase conversion) is a direction to change all lowercase letters to uppercase. The R (literals not part of data) function removes the insertion characters before storing the value to a field. If you have used template characters other than the pre-defined characters, these new characters called insertion characters are placed in the field as part of its value. The R function keeps this from happening.

The S (scroll within display data) function creates a scrollable field that is *n* characters wide; *n* must be a positive integer. As you enter the data into an entry area that is smaller than the field width, the data scrolls to let you enter all of your data. For example, you can define an input area 10 characters long for a database field which is actually 20. Only 10 characters are displayed on

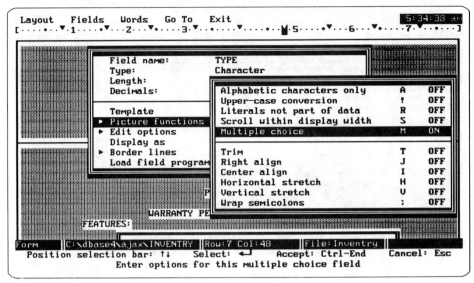

```
  Layout   Fields   Words   Go To   Exit                    5:34:38 am
  [ · · · · • · · ▼·1 · · · · ·▼· · · ·2 · · ·▼• · · · · 3·▼ · · • · · · ·▼· · · · · ·▮·5· · · · ·▼· · ·6· · ·▼• · · · ·7·▼ · · • · · · ]

           ┌──────────────────────────────────────────────────────────┐
           │  Field name:       TYPE                                   │
           │  Type:             Character                              │
           │  Length:          ┌────────────────────────────────────┐ │
           │  Decimals:        │ Alphabetic characters only    A  OFF│ │
           │                   │ Upper-case conversion         !  OFF│ │
           │  Template         │ Literals not part of data     R  OFF│ │
           │ ▶ Picture functions│ Scroll within display width  S  OFF│ │
           │ ▶ Edit options    │ Multiple choice               M  ON │ │
           │   Display as       │                                    │ │
           │ ▶ Border lines    │ Trim                          T  OFF│ │
           │   Load field program│ Right align                 J  OFF│ │
           │                   │ Center align                  I  OFF│ │
           │                 P │ Horizontal stretch            H  OFF│ │
           │                   │ Vertical stretch              V  OFF│ │
           │                   │ Wrap semicolons               :  OFF│ │
           │          WARRANTY PE└────────────────────────────────────┘ │
           │FEATURES:                                                   │
           └──────────────────────────────────────────────────────────┘
  Form     C:\dbase4\ajax\INVENTRY   Row:7 Col:48      File:Inventry
         Position selection bar: ↑↓     Select: ◄┘      Accept: Ctrl-End     Cancel: Esc
                      Enter options for this multiple choice field
```

12-21   The character picture functions.

the screen; after the first 10 characters are entered, the field will scroll out of sight on the left side of the field. The information is still there in this "window" and can be changed by using the cursor movement keys.

The final function at the top of the box is the M (multiple choice) picture function. This is one of the best functions available in dBASE IV. When you choose this function, you are asked to enter the allowable choices. Press Enter and a box appears so you can enter your choices for TYPE into the multiple choice entry area that appears once you turn this picture function on. Enter:

REFRIGERATOR,DISHWASHER,WASHER,DRYER,STOVE,MICROWAVE

When you use the data entry form the first option REFRIGERATOR appears in the TYPE entry area. With the cursor in the entry area, you would press the Spacebar. Each time you press the Spacebar, a different value from the list appears. After the last value is shown, the first one returns and the list continues. You are restricted to choose one of the values in the list. This is an excellent way to limit the data entry to allowable values.

The bottom of the box contains five functions common to both character and numeric picture functions. These are only used for the reports and label work surfaces.

Numeric picture functions affect the display and storage of the entire field as well as character picture functions. Figure 12-22 shows the numeric picture functions.

The numeric picture functions are: C, X, (, L, Z, $, and [CAR]. These allow global editing on numeric data, where the whole number is affected.

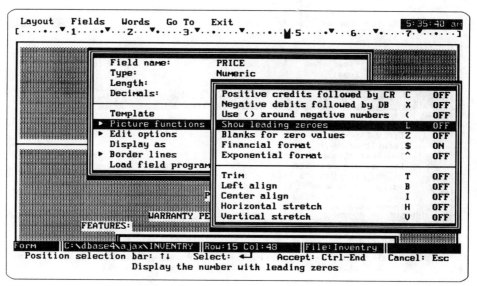

12-22 The numeric picture functions.

Only the last four can be used in data entry screens. The L (show leading zeros) function displays leading zeros in a field. The Z (blanks for zero values) function displays a blank field when the value is zero. Financial format ($) automatically places dollar signs and commas around numbers as you enter them while the exponential format ([CAR]) places numbers in scientific notation.

When used properly and together, these picture functions and templates can enhance the data entry process. Most of your entry will probably be the simple character or numeric variety. But, when some field needs some individual attention, these tools can help your operator do their data entry.

Editing options

Many editing options allow you to display messages, trap errors and display error messages, carry data forward, decide if data entry should be allowed in a field, and what range should the data be within.

Figure 12-23 shows the Edit Options menu for the WARRANTY field already filled in.

Allowing editing (Editing allowed) The first option in the Edit Options menu is the Editing allowed option, used to allow or restrict input to a field. Input might be restricted when information is entered into the database file by some other process like a program. If the Editing allowed value is NO, the cursor will not move into the field when data entry is performed. In this example, it is YES, so the WARRANTY field can be entered or changed.

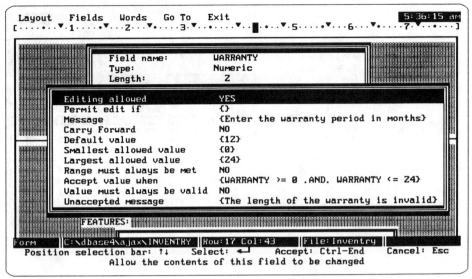

12-23 The editing options.

Conditional editing (Permit edit if) Editing Allowed lets you determine if the field is "editable." This option goes one step further. It lets you determine at the time the record is displayed on the screen if it's editable. A normal example might be a Social Security form example used by the government. One of the fields on the form could be a logical field called DECEASED. If the value of DECEASED is true, then you would not want to allow an entry except to the fields that might have to do with final payments and death benefits. This option would give you selective access to which fields you need to change and which should be display only.

Conditional editing allows you to control when a field value may be input or modified based on a condition. In our inventory example, there are no fields where this would be used. An imaginary situation might be that data entry into the QTY_ORD field would only take place when no stock is left in the QTY_STK field. This would let you enter data into the QTY_ORD field only when the value of QTY_STK was 0. The cursor would skip over the QTY_ORD field, and the field would not even be highlighted if QTY_STK was greater than 0. This restriction would only apply when using the form which uses this feature for a field. This means that the field's value can still be changed when this form is not used.

Displaying messages (Message) It is important to help the person using the form to enter information accurately. Be sure the person knows what field the cursor is on at all times. dBASE IV forms have the ability of displaying messages at the bottom of the screen, allowing you to prompt for input.

These messages are in addition to labels on the screen. You can prompt for input or provide examples of valid information for a specific field using

402   Database without programming

messages on the screen. The messages referred to in this section are not error messages. Instead, the messages are designed to prompt the person to enter data.

The message option lets you display a message centered at the bottom of the screen below the status bar when the cursor first moves into that field on the form. In this case, the message Enter the warranty period in months appears when the cursor moves into the WARRANTY field.

In our case study, we have entered a message for every field. You will see this later when you examine the .FMT or format file.

Carrying data forward (Carry Forward)   The Carry Forward option allows you to select at the field level whether or not the value from a field in the last record entered is copied to the next record. When using this option, a person can simply press the Enter key if the information is the same for the new record as in the previous record. This reduces the time to input information into the database. It is good practice to use this option when several records are entered together which contain the same values for a field.

One of the options in the Settings option of the Tools menu is CARRY. This lets an entire record be copied to the next record when entering data to make it easy to enter data that changes only slightly from record to record. However, this option copies the entire record. If you only want a few fields with the CARRY option at the record level, you are out of luck.

The Carry Forward option in Fig. 12-22 allows you to select at the field level whether or not the value from a field in the last record entered is copied to the next record. This gives you control on a field level basis and lets you copy only parts of records to make data entry easier.

For example, suppose you are entering all the invoices today for the AV-001 company—all 40 of them. You would design your entry form to carry forward the date and company number fields.

Default data (Default value)   This lets you determine what value the entry form should show each time a new record is entered. The default value will not override a carry forward. Common default values include today's date or a system date, the most common choice from a list of choices, or any data that is repetitive among records. The default value for the WARRANTY field is 12.

Range checking (Smallest/Largest allowed value)   To ensure that a numeric field's value entered is not lower than a pre-determined minimum value the option Smallest allowed value can be used. Similarly, the option Largest allowed value can be used to ensure that a numeric field's value is not greater than a pre-determined maximum value.

You do not have to use both options. You might desire to verify that a number be no greater than a certain value and can be any value less than the maximum positive or negative. You might desire to verify that a number be no less than a certain value and could be any higher value.

Primarily, these options are used with numeric and date fields to perform range checking. By using both options, you can check to see that a number is larger than the Smallest allowed value and smaller than the Largest allowed value. You can also make sure that an entered date falls within one or both ranges. In this example the WARRANTY range is between 0 and 24. Only data that falls within that range will be accepted.

Required ranges (Ranges must always be met)   The yes/no option allows you to specify whether the range should be checked when editing data. When the cursor moves to that field and no change is made, the range is checked only if this option is set to YES. If it is set to NO, the data is checked only when data is added or changed.

Accepting valid values (Accept value when)   Accept value when is one of the most powerful of all the dBASE IV editing commands because it lets you enter a field and not leave until this choice is satisfied. Any valid dBASE condition can be placed here including range checking expressions, logical comparisons, checks for characters strings, date verification, lists of choices, etc. Any expression that can be added to a DISPLAY FOR command can be added here.

In this example, the phrase WARRANTY > = 0 .AND. WARRANTY < = 24 has been entered indicating that any value greater than 24 or less than 0 will be rejected. Now, this is actually redundant because it is simply a numeric range check, but it is used here to illustrate how it works.

You could if you wanted, however, have the comparison be with values in other fields, too. For example, you could compare the BRAND field with a list of valid brands. You can have the most complex expressions here including ANDs, ORs, and parentheses around the expression.

Once the cursor enters the field, it will not leave until the data has been accepted. By using this option with many of the fields, you can write a nearly foolproof edit-checking routine without ever writing one programming command.

Required values (Value must always be valid)   This option is used to allow existing values that don't meet the accept value when checking to pass. When set to NO, only new data or changed data is validated. When set to YES, the data in the field is validated even if it doesn't change, as long as the cursor moves onto the field.

Displaying error messages (Unaccepted message)   This last option displays a custom message centered below the status bar telling the user why the data is not being accepted. Entering invalid data triggers the message.

These are the various options that provide the capabilities for complete input data entry and validation. Whether you are entering a few simple fields with no special data concerns or creating a screen that will be part of a complex system where "data integrity" must be perfect, the screen form can help you.

When a person makes a mistake inputting information according to the validation rules you have defined, it is important that you provide appropriate feedback so they can correct the error. Error messages allow you to provide feedback when input errors are detected.

Error messages may not be feasible for most character fields. Typically, character fields, such as the BRAND, TYPE, and DESC fields are not possible because there are no real unacceptable values to check against.

These choices in the Edit options menu will take some time to input if you use them for every field, but they can make for a very powerful system. In the next part of this chapter, you will see how they are translated into program commands in the format file.

Format files and their uses

When you create a custom screen, you are creating a screen and choosing options that are saved in an .SCR (screen) file. This file is used to recreate your screen form in case you want to change it. When you are through working with the .SCR file a format file is created with the file extension .FMT. This format file contains programming commands that are run by dBASE IV. If you want, you can actually take the format file and integrate it into a custom program you might write someday.

Look at the format file that dBASE IV creates from this screen and a few of the options you entered as shown in Fig. 12-24. You can see pictures, templates, and edit options as well as the positioning of the statements, lines, and boxes. There are also many housekeeping commands that set up the way the form works.

The form is divided into three sections, each of which is commented. These sections are the initialization code, the @ SAY GETS Processing, and the exit code.

The middle section interests us the most. In fact, under program control or after you have created the screen format you can eliminate the first and last sections.

The first section is used to set up the environment for the format file. First three environment options are checked:

- SET TALK
- SET DISPLAY TO
- SET STATUS

The status of your environment when you began the screen (format file) creation process determines the action of these options.

The SET TALK code makes sure the TALK setting is off. It also makes sure that after the file is closed, the environment is reset to what it was initially. This is the reason for the variables lc_status, lc_talk, and other system variables you see. They store the state of the environment at a point in time.

The SET STATUS code displays the status bar. If you want the status bar off in your screen, then make sure it is off before you start creating the screen.

Finally, a window is defined for the memory field. The window's size reflects the resizing of the window box during the creation of the screen.

```
*.-----------------------------------------------------------------
* Name.......: INVENTRY.FMT
* Date.......: 3-16-92
* Version....: dBASE IV, Format 1.5
* Notes......: Format files use "" as delimiters!
*.-----------------------------------------------------------------

*-- Format file initialization code ------------------------------------------

*-- Some of these PRIVATE variables are created based on CodeGen and may not
*-- be used by your particular .fmt file
PRIVATE ll_talk, ll_cursor, lc_display, lc_status, ll_carry, lc_proc

IF SET("TALK") = "ON"
  SET TALK OFF
  ll_talk = .T.
ELSE
  ll_talk = .F.
ENDIF
ll_cursor = SET("CURSOR") = "ON"
SET CURSOR ON

lc_status = SET("STATUS")
*-- SET STATUS was OFF when you went into the Forms Designer.
IF lc_status = "ON"
   SET STATUS OFF
ENDIF

*-- Window for memo field Features.
DEFINE WINDOW wndow1 FROM 19,18 TO 21,68 DOUBLE

*-- @ SAY GETS Processing. -------------------------------------------------

*--  Format Page: 1
@ 0,0 TO 21,79
@ 1,30 SAY "AJAX APPLIANCE COMPANY"
@ 2,27 SAY "INVENTORY DATA ENTRY SCREEN"
@ 4,30 SAY "ITEM NUMBER:"
@ 4,44 GET Itemno PICTURE "@! AAAA-999" ;
   MESSAGE "Enter the Item Number"
@ 6,27 SAY "BRAND"
@ 6,50 SAY "TYPE"
@ 7,25 GET Brand PICTURE "XXXXXXXXX" ;
   MESSAGE "Enter a Brand Name"
@ 7,47 GET Type PICTURE "@M REFRIGERATOR,DISHWASHER,WASHER,DRYER,RANGE,MICROWAVE" ;
```

12-24 The dBASE format file.

```
    MESSAGE "Press <spacebar> to Select a Type"
@ 9,17 SAY "ITEM DESCRIPTION:"
@ 9,35 GET Desc PICTURE "XXXXXXXXXXXXXXXXXXXXXXXXXX" ;
    MESSAGE "Enter a Description for the Item"
@ 9,79 SAY "|"
@ 10,0 SAY "|————————————————————————————————————————————————|"
@ 11,0 SAY "|"
@ 12,19 SAY "QUANTITY IN STOCK"
@ 12,48 SAY "QUANTITY ON ORDER"
@ 13,26 GET Qty_stk PICTURE "999" ;
    RANGE -200,999 ;
    MESSAGE "Enter the Quantity in Stock"
@ 13,55 GET Qty_ord PICTURE "999" ;
    RANGE 0,750 ;
    MESSAGE "Enter the Quantity On Order"
@ 15,34 SAY "PRICE:"
@ 15,43 GET Price PICTURE "@$ 99999.99" ;
    RANGE 50,1999 ;
    VALID PRICE >= 50 .AND. PRICE <= 1999 ;
    ERROR "Price must be between $50 and $1999" ;
    MESSAGE "Enter the Price for the Item"
@ 17,24 SAY "WARRANTY PERIOD:"
@ 17,43 GET Warranty PICTURE "99" ;
    RANGE 0,24 ;
    VALID WARRANTY >= 0 .AND. WARRANTY <= 24 ;
    ERROR "The length of the warranty is invalid " ;
    DEFAULT 12 ;
    MESSAGE "Enter the warranty period in months"
@ 17,46 SAY "MONTHS"
@ 18,12 SAY "FEATURES:"
@ 19,18 GET Features OPEN WINDOW wndow1
*-- Format file exit code ----------------------------------------------

*-- SET STATUS was OFF when you went into the Forms Designer.
IF lc_status = "ON"  && Entered form with status off
   SET STATUS ON     && Turn STATUS "ON" on the way out
ENDIF
IF .NOT. ll_cursor
  SET CURSOR OFF
ENDIF

RELEASE WINDOWS wndow1

RELEASE lc_fields,lc_status
*-- EOP: INVENTRY.FMT
```

The next part of the code is the main part of the code. This is where the screen is built and data entry is allowed. Each entry into this section is a dBASE command. The basic command is the @ command. It is most often used in this form:

@ *row,column* SAY *'display text'* GET *field*

The various picture options, templates, and edit options are part of the @ command. The SAY and GET options can be combined on one line. In that case the field is displayed one character space after the last character displayed with the SAY. The SAY must be before the GET. Each command can include all of the editing options. The very first line:

@ 0,0 TO 21,79

draws a single-lined box from positions 0,0 to 21,79. If it were to be a double-lined box the option DOUBLE would follow the 21,79.

Next comes two lines that put the title at the top of the screen. @ 1,30 means row 1 column 30. The title is placed in quotes because it is a character string. Fields can also go into the @ SAY and they don't require quotes.

Look at an example of a GET and a PICTURE and TEMPLATE clause. The ITEMNO field demonstrates that. The command:

@ 4,44 GET itemno PICTURE "@! AAAA-999"

shows both. The @! is the uppercase picture while the AAAA-999 is the template for the field. Pictures and templates are activated with the PICTURE parameter, but the picture is preceded by the @ sign. The template follows any picture. If there are no pictures, then there will be no @ sign.

Now look at the Edit options. The WARRANTY field provides the best example of all the edit options:

```
@ 17,24 SAY '"WARRANTY PERIOD:"
@ 17,43 GET warranty PICTURE "99" ;
      RANGE 0,24 ;
      VALID WARRANTY >= 0 .AND. WARRANTY <= 24 ;
      ERROR "The length of the warranty is invalid " ;
      DEFAULT 12 ;
      MESSAGE "Enter the warranty period in months"
```

The RANGE clause is set for 0,24. Also, a redundant VALID clause checks for errors and triggers an error message. The ERROR message is displayed with the ERROR clause. There is a DEFAULT amount of 12. Finally, a data entry MESSAGE is displayed.

Notice the semicolons at the end of some lines. This means that the command is being continued on another line.

The last part of the format file is the exit code. The same SET commands are reversed (if necessary) and the window and environment variables are released.

If you want, you can remove the STATUS checking code and either turn it ON or OFF. In this example, it will be turned OFF. However, if the screen form is modified, the format file is regenerated.

You will see more about these commands in the last part of this book. For now, just understand the way that a format file works, and how you really don't need to know anything about it.

Before we leave this subject, take one more look at the screen generated by the format file as shown in Fig. 12-24. The memo field is shown with data entered into it, and a message is displayed at the bottom of the screen in Fig. 12-25.

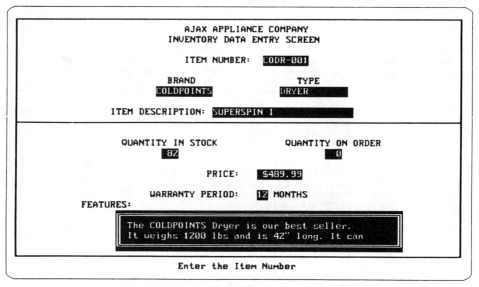

12-25 The dBASE final screen.

By combining data entry with data display and validation, the screen form proves an invaluable tool for any system. This tool makes custom screens possible for the beginner and saves time for the expert. You can create custom screens by using a word processor to construct format files, but it is much more work to actually create the format commands that dBASE IV automatically generates. Without the forms screen, you cannot visually see what your screen will look like until you are actually done.

EDIT and BROWSE

The format file can be used with APPEND or EDIT mode as well as BROWSE mode. The format file is activated by using the SET FORMAT TO command. To use the INVENTRY file, activate the format file. Then, to EDIT the data you could enter the following commands:

```
USE INVENTRY
SET FORMAT TO INVENTRY
EDIT
```

If you are using the Control Center, select the INVENTRY file in the Forms panel and press F2. If the INVENTRY data file is not already active, you will be asked if that is the database you want to use.

You can also use the APPEND command to enter new data into a database under format control. The big surprise is that under certain conditions you can also use the BROWSE commands and have all the pictures, templates, and editing options active during the BROWSE command as you can see in Fig. 12-26.

```
┌─────────────────────────────────────────────────────────────────────────────┐
│  Records    Fields    Organize    Go To    Exit            12:15:49 am        │
├──────────┬───────────┬───────────┬─────────────────────┬────────┬────────┬───┤
│ ITEMNO   │ BRAND     │ TYPE      │ DESC                │QTY_STK │QTY_ORD │PRI│
├──────────┼───────────┼───────────┼─────────────────────┼────────┼────────┼───┤
│ CODR-001 │ COLDPOINTS│ DRYER     │ SUPERSPIN I         │    82  │      0 │$4 │
│ CODR-002 │ COLDPOINTS│ DRYER     │ SUPERSPIN II        │    58  │      0 │$6 │
│ WHDR-001 │ WHOLEPOOL │ DRYER     │                     │    36  │      0 │$8 │
│ HIMI-001 │ HITECH    │ MICROWAVE │ 1500 WATT           │   127  │      0 │$2 │
│ HIRA-001 │ HITECH    │ RANGE     │                     │    89  │      0 │$6 │
│ RURA-001 │ RUSTIC    │ RANGE     │ WOOD TRIM           │     0  │    100 │$6 │
│ WHRA-001 │ WHOLEPOOL │ RANGE     │                     │    28  │      0 │$9 │
│ FRRE-001 │ FROSTY    │ REFRIGERATOR│1 DOOR TOP FREEZER W/ICE│112│   0 │$6 │
│ FRRE-002 │ FROSTY    │ REFRIGERATOR│2 DOOR SIDE BY SIDE │    78  │      0 │$8 │
│ FRRE-003 │ FROSTY    │ REFRIGERATOR│2 DOOR UPRIGHT      │     6  │      5 │$11│
│ CORE-001 │ COLDPOINTS│ REFRIGERATOR│MINI-MAX           │    17  │      0 │$2 │
│ WHRE-001 │ WHOLEPOOL │ REFRIGERATOR│                   │    23  │     40 │$4 │
│ COWA-001 │ COLDPOINTS│ WASHER    │                     │    89  │      0 │$3 │
│ WHWA-001 │ WHOLEPOOL │ WASHER    │                     │    36  │      0 │$7 │
│ WHWA-002 │ WHOLEPOOL │ WASHER    │ DELUXE MODEL        │     2  │     30 │$9 │
│          │           │           │                     │        │        │   │
├──────────┴───────────┴───────────┴─────────────────────┴────────┴────────┴───┤
│ Browse   C:\dbase4\a.jax\INVENTRY  Rec 1/15          File                     │
├───────────────────────────────────────────────────────────────────────────────┤
│                      Enter the Item Number                                     │
└─────────────────────────────────────────────────────────────────────────────┘
```

12-26 The dBASE screen in BROWSE.

First, if you enter the BROWSE mode from the Control Center with a format file active, it will be used. If you enter APPEND or EDIT with a format file active and then press F2, you will be in the BROWSE screen with all the format controls. The @ SAY and GET positions are ignored.

If you want to use the BROWSE command from the dot prompt and activate a format file, you must add the FORMAT parameter to the BROWSE command. The form would then be:

```
USE INVENTRY
SET FORMAT TO INVENTRY
BROWSE FORMAT
```

Using it in a program

Of course, this code would also work under program control. The format files can save you a lot of time in many ways. First, instead of programming @ SAY and @ GET commands, you can simply create a form and use it with BROWSE or EDIT. Second, if you insist on writing programs you can use the screen form to help you get the screen positions right the first time.

The .FMT files can be edited with any ASCII editor or by the dBASE Editor. To edit the INVENTRY format file you might enter:

```
. MODIFY COMMAND INVENTRY.FMT
```

This allows you to edit the format file code to your desires. Finally, you can extract the parts of the code you want and add it to your favorite program.

Whatever you decide, the format file can serve many purposes. You will see this format used in the INVENTRY program you will create in Part Three. You will also see these statements of editing, pictures, and templates in the code in Part Three for the customer and invoice files.

13

Creating and using reports and labels

Reports are the backbone of business today. If you can't write a good report, you might as well not have any information. Using the design found in chapter 4, you will see how to create all three types of reports as well as labels.

Reports and the AJAX Appliance case study

Nine reports were designed in chapter 4. These included:

- CUSTOMER DIRECTORY—Simple form report
- CUSTOMER CROSS REFERENCE—Simple column report
- CUSTOMER MAILING LABEL—Simple mailing labels
- INVENTORY VALUATION REPORT—Column report with calculations and totals
- ITEM NUMBER CROSS REFERENCE—Simple column report
- SALESMAN INVENTORY REPORT—Form report with memo field
- INVOICE—Complex form report with multiple databases, multiple records in a database, and extensive calculations
- WARRANTY AGREEMENT—Mailmerge report
- MONTHLY SALES REPORT—Complex column report with totalling, roll up, groupings, row and column totals, templates, and functions

These reports will each be presented with their original design along with screen figures of the final report or label forms and complete explanations of the steps involved to create each type of report. Before you see how each one of these reports was created, you must first learn the basics of report writing and learn several of these reports in complete detail.

Two of the inventory reports are used to demonstrate simple column and form reports. After you see how to do these two simple reports, you will see the other seven reports.

The four types of reports

Computer-generated reports have had the same columnar format for many years. The original data processors were accountants, and they liked the numbers in tables and columns to visualize the trends of the business.

Today, the world of computer reporting has changed so that almost any report, graph, picture, or model can be represented in any format. Graphs can be plotted with great precision and clarity; reports can be displayed on a terminal screen—and rearranged at will. A model of the business can be shown on a computer screen, with animated graphics showing the flow of goods in and out of the company. The column report is now only one way to look at your data.

Several types of reports are commonly used in business and available through the dBASE IV Report Generator. These are:

- Column reports
- Forms reports
- Mail-merging

Column reports like the one shown in Fig. 13-1 are reports organized into rows and columns much like the BROWSE table. Each record becomes a row in the table. The only real difference from a browse mode is that you can create customized headers for both the page and each column, and you can

INVENTORY VALUATION REPORT

ITEM NUMBER	BRAND	TYPE	DESCRIPTION	QTY IN STOCK	QTY ON ORDER	PRICE	INVENTORY VALUATION
CODR-001	COLDPOINTS	DRYER	SUPERSPIN I	82	0	489.99	40179.18
CODR-002	COLDPOINTS	DRYER	SUPERSPIN II	58	0	689.99	40019.42
WHDR-001	WHOLEPOOL	DRYER		36	0	899.99	32399.64
HIMI-001	HITECH	MICROWAVE	1500 WATT	127	0	229.99	29208.73
HIRA-001	HITECH	RANGE		89	0	689.99	61409.11
RURA-001	RUSTIC	RANGE	WOOD TRIM	0	100	659.99	0.00
WHRA-001	WHOLEPOOL	RANGE		28	0	929.99	26039.72
FRRE-001	FROSTY	REFRIGERATOR	1 DOOR TOP FREEZER W/ICE	112	0	699.99	78398.88
FRRE-002	FROSTY	REFRIGERATOR	2 DOOR SIDE BY SIDE	78	0	899.99	70199.22
FRRE-003	FROSTY	REFRIGERATOR	2 DOOR UPRIGHT	6	5	1199.99	7199.94
CORE-001	COLDPOINTS	REFRIGERATOR	MINI-MAX	17	0	229.99	3909.83
WHRE-001	WHOLEPOOL	REFRIGERATOR		23	40	469.99	10809.77
COWA-001	COLDPOINTS	WASHER		89	0	369.99	32929.11
WHWA-001	WHOLEPOOL	WASHER		36	0	739.99	26639.64
WHWA-002	WHOLEPOOL	WASHER	DELUXE MODEL	2	30	969.99	1939.98

461282.17

13-1 A sample column report.

have subtotals and totals on your numeric fields. Common examples of column reports could include sales and inventory reports, your bank statement, and even a simple balance sheet or income statement.

Forms reports, new to dBASE IV, give you unlimited control over your data as shown in Fig. 13-2. Usually created with one record or several records per page, form reports let you place data anywhere on a page and create all types of new totals and summaries. Common examples of form reports include invoices, checks, and tax forms.

```
                    SALESMAN INVENTORY REPORT

          ITEM NUMBER:   CODR-001

                BRAND:   COLDPOINTS   TYPE:   DRYER

          DESCRIPTION:   SUPERSPIN I
-----------------------------------------------------------------------
                PRICE:   $489.99
                         +---------------------------+
  INVENTORY VALUATION:   | IN STOCK          ON ORDER |
                         |    82                   0  |
                         +---------------------------+
             WARRANTY:   12 MONTHS

          FEATURES:
                 The COLDPOINTS Dryer is our best seller.
                 It weighs 1200 lbs and is 42" long. It can
                 dry 500 towels at the same time
```

13-2 A sample form report.

Mail merging is very similar to a forms report except it is usually very heavily text-based with data placed in between the text. This type of report shown in Fig. 13-3, is also known as a word-wrap report, because the text must be adjusted depending on the size of the data that is placed in between the text lines. A common mail-merge report is a letter to a customer about an overdue bill.

Mailing labels are also a type of report but are created from the Label work surface. A sample set of labels is shown in Fig. 13-4.

dBASE IV handles all of these types of reports with ease and all using the same report form. In fact, whether you are creating a column, form, or mail-merge report, dBASE uses the exact same work surface and menus to accomplish them. The only difference is how you lay out the report and what it looks like.

The quick report

The quick report is a report that can automatically be generated at any time from many of the work surfaces and from the Control Center. These include:

- Data
- Query
- Form
- Browse
- Edit

```
                    AJAX APPLIANCE COMPANY
                       WARRANTY AGREEMENT

WARRANTY AGREEMENT NUMBER: 8808-001-04

WARRANTY AGREEMENT DATE:    08/01/88
------------------------------------------------------------------------

This warranty agreement is between the Ajax Appliance Company and:

        JACKEL & HYDES
        357 BAT COURT
        LAWRENCEVILLE, PA 14434-

This agreement maintains that Ajax Appliance Company will warranty 10
REFRIGERATOR(s) in accordance with the manufacturers warranty terms.
FROSTY warranties this product for a period of 6 months.

The REFRIGERATOR being warrantied is a 1 DOOR TOP FREEZER W/ICE.

This warranty will expire on 05/21/89. At the end of that period you may
purchase our standard warranty for an additional year for each item for only
70.00.

This agreement is legal and binding in the state of confusion and cannot be
broken.

 Signed,
---------------------------------       -----------------------------------
    Ajax Appliance Company                    JACKEL & HYDES
```

13-3 A sample mail-merge report.

Using the active database or view, it will create a column report which includes all of the fields in the query or view. All the numeric fields are totalled, and the field names are used for the column headers.

You can create a quick report to view or print your data in a formal manner. Notice the help line at the bottom of most screens. You will see that the keystroke to access the Quick Report is Shift–F9.

When you press these keys, the computer generates a report program for you before it actually prints the report. You will not be able to go on until the computer finishes generating the program and produces the output either on your screen or your printer.

A print menu appears for you to decide any special print parameters and the destination of the output. A quick report in progress is shown in Fig. 13-5. No matter where you create the report from, all you will see is a print menu. Later, you will learn that the quick report uses the same format as the Quick Layout.

The Quick Layout is a way of automatically placing all of your fields on the Reports work surface as well as your column headers and totals for numeric fields. You will see this quick layout and its output when you create your first column report.

The basic steps of report design

Reports are messages from your application about the actions happening internally to the system. Reports are also the vehicle for moving the business-

```
APPLIANCE CITY              APPLIANCE CITY
210 SKY LANE                360 ACE AVE
OXNARD,CA 95677-            HOLLYWOOD,CA 95245-


APPLIANCE WORLD             AVON APPLIANCE
20695 BLUE BIRD AVE         1687 NEW PLACE ROAD
SAN FRANCISCO,CA 95564-     LOS ANGELES,CA 98887-


BOB'S BRANDS                CARY'S COOLERS
BOB'S DRIVE                 60 STRAWBERRY HILLS
SANTA FE,NM 84545-4545      WINDSOR,CT 06773-


CRAZY FREDDIES              ERNIES TV
1820 171ST ST               456 SNOW PLOW AVE
NEW YORK,NY 15545-          BLEAUVILLE,CA 94454-8946


FRIENDLY APPLIANCE          JACKEL & HYDES
26 CHOCOLATE AVE            357 BAT COURT
HERSHEY,PA 15554-           LAWRENCEVILLE,PA 14434-


JIMS HOT AND COLD           RANGES ON THE HOME
55 SKINNER RD               23 OLD OKIE DR
VERNON,CA 95565-8784        OKLAHOMA CITY,OK 73344-


RON'S REFRIGERATORS         THE HOME SHOPPE
141 HOLLOW OAK PLACE        25 APPLIANCE LANE
SAN JUAN CAPISTRANO,CA 95   SARATOGA,CA 93434-


WASHER WAREHOUSE            WEST'S WHITE GOODS
15525 MARINER DR            26 DENNIS LANE
LOS ALTOS,CA 97688-         CUPERTINO,CA 92324-3342
```

13-4 Sample labels.

oriented information from the computer system, where it was gleaned from data, to the manager or executive who can change that information into action.

Designing a computer report or form is a process just like other forms of design. First, the purpose of the report is defined. Then, all of the people who are involved in producing and using the report have to agree what data items need to be shown on the report in order to produce accurate and plentiful

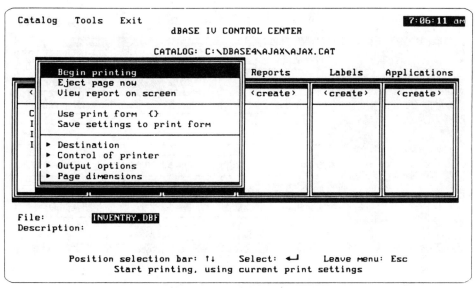

13-5 The Quick Report menu.

information. Finally, the report itself is defined, including placement of all data fields and text identifiers, totals, subtotals, and even such things as the quality of the print on the page.

dBASE IV lets you create your reports by means of a "What You See Is What You Get" (WYSIWYG) interface. Text, including column headers, report headers, lines, and boxes as well as fields, calculations, and summaries are placed anywhere on an area that serves as a representation of the printed page known as the work surface. By creating a template for the report generator to follow, you can see the format of your report before it is printed. Figure 13-6 shows a complete report form. Notice how every data field and text item on the report work surface visually lets you see where the data will actually be placed on the report.

This visual interface lets you place your text and fields anywhere on this work surface. You can be sure that its exact positioning determines where the actual printed output goes. dBASE uses this template in order to map in the data. Each record fills a part of the template like jello into a mold.

Designing your reports is best done by taking a blank piece of paper and sketching out what the report will look like. You would place your titles and column headers on the page and then put all of the fields from your database in the approximate positions. Last, you would add calculations and totals. Creating the report form with dBASE IV is a similar process. In this chapter, we use the following steps to create simple reports:

1. Assemble your data into a database or view.
2. Choose the Quick Layout option or add the fields you want.
3. Delete unwanted fields and text.

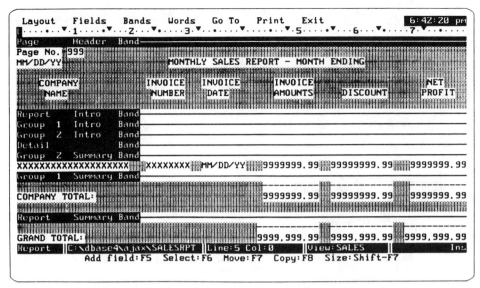

13-6 Visualizing the data with the WYSIWYG interface.

4. Move fields and text into final position.
5. Create calculated and summary fields.
6. Create group bands, headers, and footers.
7. Add final column headers, text, lines, boxes, and styling.

As we create our report, we'll look at each of these steps in detail.

The different bands of the report work surface

Reports generally have standard areas. Figure 13-7 shows these standard areas. These are the same types of areas that dBASE uses to organize its report generator. This is the column report we will create in this chapter. This report is an inventory valuation report.

At the top of page is the *page header*. Items that are placed in this area include page numbers, dates, titles, and—in column reports—the column headings themselves.

Another type of area is known as a *report area*. It only appears at the beginning and end of the entire report. The report intro can be used for such items as a cover letter or just a title that might appear by itself on the report. The report summary usually is more important because it contains grand totals for the entire report. Often a report has a report summary but no report intro. This is perfectly acceptable. Although headers and footers come in matched pairs, you do not have to use both in a report.

Likewise, *page summaries* are not often used. They appear at the end of each page and often contain no text or data. They would be used only when some type of totals or explanation is needed on each page.

THE VARIOUS PARTS OF THE REPORT

Page No. 1
12/23/89

AJAX APPLIANCE COMPANY
SALES REPORT

	INVOICE NUMBER	INVOICE AMOUNT	DISCOUNT	PROFIT
Page Header				
Group Heads	COMPANY: ABC			
Detail	999 999 999	999 999 999	999 999 999	999 999 999
Group Footer	TOTAL ABC	999	999	999
Group Header	COMPANY: DEF			
Detail	999 999 999	999 999 999	999 999 999	999 999 999
Group Footer	TOTAL DEF	999	999	999
Report Footer	GRAND TOTAL	999	999	999

13-7 A report's general areas.

The next type of area is the *group area*. There is no real limit to the number of group areas a report may contain, but it often gets very confusing if there are more than three or four groupings. In Fig. 13-7, only one grouping is shown for each TYPE. Each grouping has both a header and a footer. The header is used to identify the data that the group represents, while the footer shows subtotals.

Lastly (or in the middle), are the *detail lines* themselves. The detail lines contain the actual data from the database that goes into the report. As the report is produced, the data appears one line at a time in the detail line area.

Reports are prepared with the help of a reports work surface. The Reports work surface lets you enter the information onto a screen that becomes a template for the report. It creates a disk file that contains the information to prepare the report. Because it is a disk file, you can use it over and over again and make as many copies of the report as you like—whenever you want. Because the database file is the source of data, any changes in data content are automatically reflected in the final report. Report forms are prepared using the Reports panel from the Control Center or from the CREATE REPORT command in the dot prompt. They are changed with the Reports panel or the MODIFY REPORT command.

The dBASE IV Report Generator lets you place your text and fields into areas known as bands. There are four types of bands in dBASE IV as shown in Fig. 13-8:

- Page bands
- Report bands
- Detail bands
- Group bands

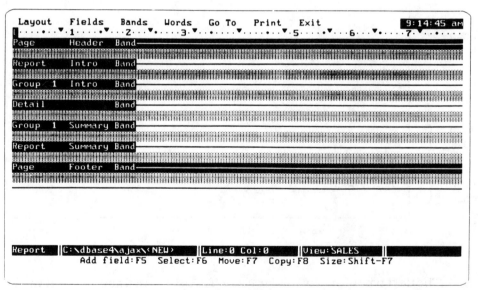

13-8 An empty report screen with a group band.

Page, report, and group bands come in matching sets. The header (also known as the *intro*) comes before the detail lines and the footer (also known as the *summary*) comes after the detail lines. Headers are usually used for identification such as a title, page number, date, or even a common data value. Footers are used for totals, summaries, and other statistical measures.

The page header comes first. Whatever appears in this band appears at the top of every page. The fact that a new page is being produced is what triggers this band to print.

The report intro comes next, but only appears once in the very beginning of the report. It is often used to place a cover memo or a title page for the report.

For each subtotal or grouping you want on the report, you will have a pair of group bands numbered 1 to the number of groupings on your report. In our inventory example, there is just one group band and that is grouped by BRAND. Group bands do not appear automatically as the other bands do. You must tell dBASE that you want a grouping and on what field or expression.

Detail bands are just that; they are where the detail of the report goes. The data that makes up the report is generally found in the detail band, one record used for each page or line, depending on the type of report.

Bands can be opened and closed. If a band is closed, its data will not print. This is very useful for summary reports where the detail is not desired.

Group summary bands come next and are used for subtotals for the group. The report summary band is used for grand totals as anything in this band appears once at the very bottom of the report. The last band is the page footer band. This band appears at the bottom of each page and is used for totals based on individual pages.

The report work surface gathers the information that dBASE needs to produce this custom report and stores the information in a disk file. The filename for this report form must conform to the standard rules for disk filenames. dBASE automatically adds the .FRM file identifier to this file-name. When the report has been completely defined, dBASE uses the .FRM file to produce a second file. dBASE automatically assigns the file the same name as the report file, but uses an .FRG file identifier. When you actually use the report for the first time, dBASE IV compiles the .FRG file into an object module and gives it an .FRO extension.

Navigating the report work surface

In the next section, you will practice techniques in navigating the work surface. You have already learned most of them in the forms work surface. The arrow keys move the cursor around the work surface one character at a time. The cursor moves left and right faster using Tab and Shift–Tab.

Fields are moved by moving the cursor to any part of the field and using the Move (F7) key. When you use this technique to move a field, the field is selected and a shaded box the size of the field can be moved around to a new location of the work surface. When the shaded box is in the position you want the selected field moved to, press the Enter key which in turn moves the field from the old location to the new location.

If you want to move a field from one report band to another, then you have to first select the field you want to move by pressing F6. Then, move the cursor to the position in another report band and press F7. The field will move to the new band. Pressing Enter completes the move.

Text labels on the work surface can be moved by using the Select (F6) key and the arrow keys to highlight the area to be moved. When the Select key is pressed, a shaded square the size of one character marks the first corner of a selected area. The arrow keys are then used to highlight the remaining area to be selected. The Enter key is used to mark the opposite corner of the selected area. An area that has been selected can be moved using the Move (F7) key, the arrow keys, and the Enter key. You can also select multiple fields and text by using the F6 (Select) key.

Selected labels and fields can be removed from the work surface using the Del key. If you decide to select a different area of the work surface, use the Esc key to remove the shaded selected area.

You compose your screen from the work surface. The field areas are shown in reverse video. Character fields are filled with X's, numeric fields are filled with 9's, date fields with MM/DD/YY, logic fields with 'Y', and memo fields with V's.

You can move the cursor to any position on screen with the help of the cursor control keys. The Left and Right arrow keys move the cursor one space in the direction of the arrow. The Up and Down arrow keys move the cursor one line up or down. To move the cursor to the beginning (or the end) of the line, press the Ctrl key and the Left or Right arrow at the same time. The status bar keeps track of the cursor position. Refer to the status bar and the message area at the bottom of the screen for the cursor column and row position for helpful information and messages to locate labels and fields on the work surface. The status bar lists your starting position in the left top corner as Line:0 Col:0. The Line indicator refers to the line of the band you are in. If you move the cursor to the band border, it will tell you that you are band x/y, where x is the band number on the screen and y is the total number of bands on the work surface. In Fig. 13-8, there are seven bands.

The report menus

Before we go on, look at a few of the menu choices available to us in the report screen. Menus in the Reports work surface are opened in the same way as any other menu in dBASE IV. You can either press the F10 key and select the menu with the arrow keys or press the Alt key with the first letter of the menu choice.

The first is the Layout menu as shown in Fig. 13-9. This menu is used to perform quick layouts and to draw lines and boxes on the work surface. In fact, we will add some lines and boxes when we create the form report later in this chapter. You will see the Quick Layout procedure in detail when you create your first report.

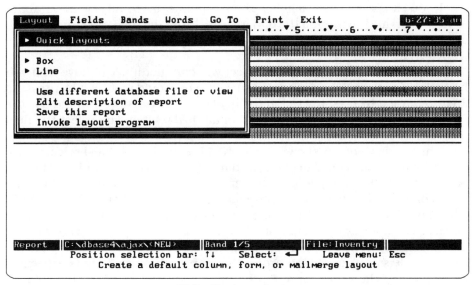

13-9 The Layout menu.

The Layout menu is also used to select the database or view that will be used in the report. You can also edit the description of the report and save the report from this menu without returning to the Control Center.

The next menu is the Fields menu. This menu lets you add, remove, or modify fields in the database, view, or work surface as shown in Fig. 13-10.

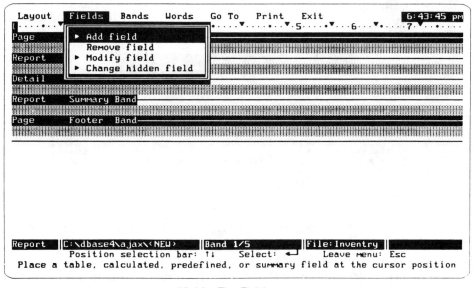

13-10 The Fields menu.

If you choose Add Field, a field box opens showing you all of your database or view fields and giving you the opportunity to create calculated, predefined, or summary fields. You can also add a field at any time by pressing F5 on the work surface.

Once a field is on the work surface, you can modify or remove it. If you have already selected it on the work surface, you would modify it by pressing F5 or remove it by pressing Del. If the field is not selected, you would use the Fields menu and it will give you a list of all fields. When you select the field from the fields list, the operation is performed.

The Bands menu, as shown in Fig. 13-11, contains the most selections of all the menus and is used to create and modify group bands and affect other bands as well. The top part of the menu lets you add, remove, and modify group bands. When you add a group band, you must tell dBASE what fields will be used to determine the grouping. These can include database or view fields, calculated expressions, or even a number of records. You will see different group bands during this chapter. The last option in the top part of the menu lets you repeat the group intro on each page. This is especially important if data will be on more than one page and will need the column headers or group headers repeated.

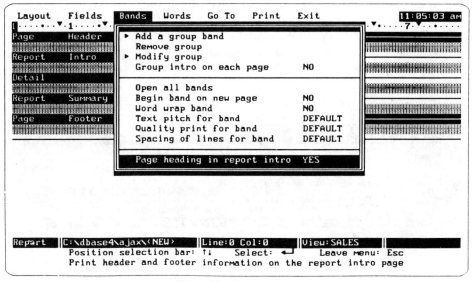

13-11 The Bands menu.

The next part of the menu is used to affect different things in any of the bands. Once you select a band, you can choose these options.

Bands can be opened and closed by pressing Enter on a band border. If a band is closed, it does not print. This is used to create summary reports. The last report in this chapter, the SALES report, uses this method.

Bands can begin on a new page. If you want to have a new page for each group you would turn the option Begin band on new page on.

The next option, Word wrap band, lets you make the band a text band used for mail merge reports. As data within the band expands beyond the right margin, the text and fields will "wrap" to the next line just like in a word processor.

The last three choices affect the printing quality of the band. The text pitch is the size of the print. Choices include Default, Pica, Elite, and Condensed. These choices are dependent on your printer. The Quality print includes Default, Yes, and No, and is also dependent on your printer. Finally, the line spacing is Default, Single, Double, and Triple. Usually if you choose default for any of these then no control code is sent to the printer. If you choose any other options, then the appropriate control code for your printer is sent to the printer before printing.

The final part of this menu allows you to suppress the normal page headers and footers in the report intro band. Because the report intro is usually used for a cover sheet, the page headers and footers are probably unwanted.

Another menu to examine is the Words menu (Fig. 13-12). We will use this extensively in the report form. For now, let's just examine some of the choices.

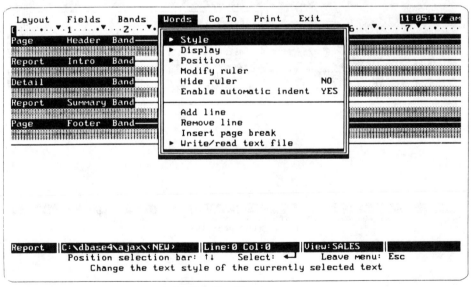

13-12 The Words menu.

The Style menu opens to reveal print styles such as Bold, Underline, Italic, Superscript, and Subscript; it also places the selected text or fields under a different printer font if you have selected them in your setup. The

Display menu lets you choose colors on a color system and is only used for forms. The Position item affects whether fields are left, right, or centered within the entry area. Once you have set your margins with Ruler, you can center headings easily. Enable automatic indent is used in word wrap bands to allow the new lines to be indented one tab character.

The bottom of the menu lets you perform some critical functions that you will need to know—mainly adding and deleting blank lines in the form. New blank lines can also be added by pressing Return at the end of a line if *insert* is on. To remove a line, you can use the Remove line option or press Ctrl–Y. The Insert page break option allows you to determine where page breaks go in specific bands. The last item lets you write the report form as a text file or read a text file of labels into the work surface. This is one good way to add your labels after you have spent time designing complex screens of text. You can add your fields, lines, and boxes after importing the text.

The Go To menu is shown in Fig. 13-13. This lets you quickly go to places on the screen. Sometimes you may find yourself creating long screens of many pages. This menu allows you to quickly go to any line on the screen.

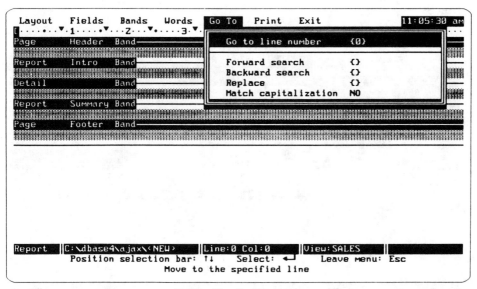

13-13 The Go To menu.

The Go To menu also lets you perform search and replace functions. If you decide a specific name or title needs to be changed, you can quickly change it throughout the entire report. Besides a forward or backward search from the current cursor position, you can also decide if matching capitalization is important.

The Print menu which you saw lets you determine many print options as you can see in Fig. 13-5. The Print menu for the Quick Report is the same menu you can open in the Report work surface. The print menu is described fully in chapter 14.

Finally, the Exit menu gives you the options of saving all your changes and returning to the Control Center or dot prompt or abandoning all changes you had made from the last time you saved the report.

You will see these menus again as you build the various reports that are used in this book's programs.

Simple column reports

To create a report form, you must give dBASE information about the page layout as well as about what is to go into the report. When you create a report, you must be using the database that you will be reporting on, or in the case of using multiple databases, you must make sure that you have related the databases or that a query screen is active. Once all your data is assembled, it is time to begin.

Assembling your data

Before you create a report using the Reports work surface, you must get all of your data into one database or one view. If you are only working with one database, then that database is put in use or made active before the report is begun. If you need access to data from multiple databases, then create a view using the QBE screen or the dot prompt commands that let you set your relations and link your data together.

If you are planning to ask for subtotals or groupings, you should make sure your data is sorted or indexed into that order or else your groupings might turn into a large mess. Creating a group band tells dBASE to produce a header and footer for each change in the group field of the database. If the data is not sorted in the group order, the data will appear to dBASE as having many different groupings when actually the data is not ordered correctly.

To begin to create our first report, let's go to the Control Center and make sure the INVENTRY file is active. If any queries are active, close them before continuing. Move your cursor to ⟨create⟩ on the reports panel and press Return. The Reports work surface opens to let you begin creating your report.

The quick layout

The Layout menu opens automatically because dBASE assumes that you will start with Quick Layout. Press Return to open the Quick Layout option. The three choices are shown in Fig. 13-14. For this first example, let's use the Column layout choice. Press Return on this choice.

We have chosen to use a column report because it is the most common type of report used in business. It has many standard areas and provides

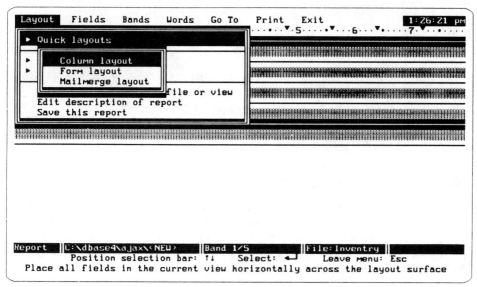

```
 Layout   Fields   Bands   Words   Go To   Print   Exit        1:26:21 PM
                                       ···•···▼·5···•▼···6···▼·····7·▼··•····
 ► Quick layouts
   ┌───────────────────────┐       ▐▊▊▊▊▊▊▊▊▊▊▊▊▊▊▊▊▊▊▊▊▊▊▊▊▊▊▊▊▊▊▊▊▊▊▊▊▊▊▊▊▌
 ► │    Column layout       │       ▐▊▊▊▊▊▊▊▊▊▊▊▊▊▊▊▊▊▊▊▊▊▊▊▊▊▊▊▊▊▊▊▊▊▊▊▊▊▊▊▊▌
 ► │    Form layout         │       ▐▊▊▊▊▊▊▊▊▊▊▊▊▊▊▊▊▊▊▊▊▊▊▊▊▊▊▊▊▊▊▊▊▊▊▊▊▊▊▊▊▌
   │    Mailmerge layout    │
   │                   file or view ▐▊▊▊▊▊▊▊▊▊▊▊▊▊▊▊▊▊▊▊▊▊▊▊▊▊▊▊▊▊▊▊▊▊▊▊▊▊▊▊▊▌
   │ Edit description of report     ▐▊▊▊▊▊▊▊▊▊▊▊▊▊▊▊▊▊▊▊▊▊▊▊▊▊▊▊▊▊▊▊▊▊▊▊▊▊▊▊▊▌
   │ Save this report               ▐▊▊▊▊▊▊▊▊▊▊▊▊▊▊▊▊▊▊▊▊▊▊▊▊▊▊▊▊▊▊▊▊▊▊▊▊▊▊▊▊▌
   └───────────────────────┘

  ▊▊▊▊▊▊▊▊▊▊▊▊▊▊▊▊▊▊▊▊▊▊▊▊▊▊▊▊▊▊▊▊▊▊▊▊▊▊▊▊▊▊▊▊▊▊▊▊▊▊▊▊▊▊▊▊▊▊▊▊▊▊▊▊▊▊▊▊▊▊▊▊▊▊▊▊▊▊




 Report   ║C:\dbase4\ajax\<NEW>║  ║Band 1/5║         ║File:Inventry║
                Position selection bar: ↑↓    Select: ↵     Leave menu: Esc
       Place all fields in the current view horizontally across the layout surface
```

13-14   The Quick Layout menu on the Reports work surface.

great flexibility in creating an almost unlimited number of subtotals and totals. Because the detail data is usually placed in neat rows and columns, it is an easy report to understand regardless of the data or business industry.

Rather than tell dBASE which fields you want to use from your database and where to place them on the form, dBASE has an option known as the Quick Layout. This allows you to have dBASE place all of your fields in the detail band on the form in either a column, form, or mail-merge layout. It places column headings in the page header band and also adds page numbers and the date in the page header band. In column reports, it creates automatic totals for your numeric fields and places them in the report summary band.

This can give you a quick start to creating your report. In fact, this is the exact same layout used by the Quick Report option (Shift–F9) available in most work surfaces. By placing all of your data on the form, you can then begin to place it where you want it and then concentrate on making the report look good.

If, however, you only want a few fields on the form, then you might need to start with a blank form. In that case, you would place your fields on the form one at a time by using the Add field option of the Fields menu or F5.

Instantly, all of the fields in the INVENTRY database are placed on the screen. Examine Fig. 13-15. You can see that the data has been placed in the various bands on the report surface. The page header band contains a blank line and then the text Page No. along with a field to hold the current page number. The date also appears on a third line in the report work surface's page header band. You will see later how certain predefined fields such as Date, Time, Pageno, and Recno can be placed on the work surface.

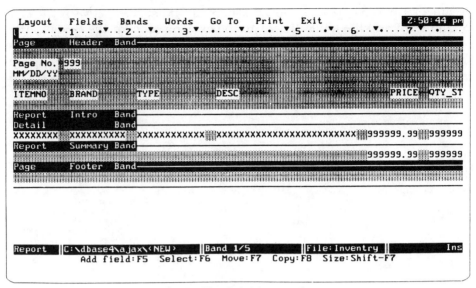

13-15 The Quick Layout data.

After skipping another line, the column headers are also placed on the work surface in the page header band. These headers will be printed at the top of each page. Each band is expandable to allow you to place almost any number of lines in each band. Another line is skipped after the headers. There is nothing in the report intro band. This is not usually used because it only appears once at the beginning of the report, and when it is, it is usually used for a report cover or cover letter that might precede the entire report.

After the intros come the detail line. This is where your actual data is placed. If you look at Fig. 13-15, you will see X's where your character fields are and 9's where your numeric fields are. You would also see MM/DD/YY where your date fields are, L where a logic field is, and V's where memo fields are.

In this figure, you can only see the first six fields because that is all that will fit in the first 80 characters on the screen. You will have to "pan" the screen to the right to see the rest of your fields.

Once you start to work on the work surface and you move your cursor to one of the fields, it will display the field name below the status bar, along with the field type and length. You can also remember which field is which by looking at the headers in the page header band.

Numeric fields are automatically totalled and placed in the report summary band. Because totals occur once per report, it makes sense to place grand totals in the report summary band. If you also wanted totals at the end of each page as well, you could place totals (or anything else) in the page footer band.

Look at Fig. 13-16 to see what this report would generate if it were printed now. Notice a few things on the report. There is no report title because we haven't created one yet. There are no spaces between the last detail record and the totals. There are no explanations for the fields in the report summary; they just appear. The total for the price fields makes no sense whatsoever. Finally, the memo fields that have data are taking up multiple lines. The report is printed in compressed print so it shows up on one page. This is controlled by the Print menu and is covered in the next chapter.

```
Page No.    }
11/22/88

ITEMNO     BRAND        TYPE           DESC                        PRICE  QTY_STK  QTY_ORD  WARRANTY  FEATURES

CODR-001   COLDPOINTS   DRYER          SUPERSPIN I                489.99       82        0        12  The COLDPOINTS Dryer is our
                                                                                                      best seller.
                                                                                                        It weighs 1200 lbs and is 42"
                                                                                                      long. It can
                                                                                                        dry 500 towels at the same
                                                                                                      time

CODR-002   COLDPOINTS   DRYER          SUPERSPIN II               689.99       58        0        12
WHDR-001   WHOLEPOOL    DRYER                                     899.99       36        0        18
HIMI-001   HITECH       MICROWAVE      1500 WATT                  229.99      127        0         6
HIRA-001   HITECH       RANGE                                     689.99       89        0        12
RURA-001   RUSTIC       RANGE          WOOD TRIM                  659.99        0      100        12
WHRA-001   WHOLEPOOL    RANGE                                     929.99       28        0        18
FRRE-001   FROSTY       REFRIGERATOR   1 DOOR TOP FREEZER W/ICE   699.99      112        0         6  The Frosty Refrigerator is a
                                                                                                      cool seller.
                                                                                                        Make sure that we offer any
                                                                                                      buyer
                                                                                                        an extended warranty for 1
                                                                                                      year.

FRRE-002   FROSTY       REFRIGERATOR   2 DOOR SIDE BY SIDE        899.99       78        0        12
FRRE-003   FROSTY       REFRIGERATOR   2 DOOR UPRIGHT            1199.99        6        5        60
CORE-001   COLDPOINTS   REFRIGERATOR   MINI-MAX                   229.99       17        0         6
WHRE-001   WHOLEPOOL    REFRIGERATOR                              469.99       23       40         6
COWA-001   COLDPOINTS   WASHER                                    369.99       89        0         6
WHWA-001   WHOLEPOOL    WASHER                                    739.99       36        0         6
WHWA-002   WHOLEPOOL    WASHER         DELUXE MODEL               969.99        2       30        12
                                                                10169.85      783      175       204
```

13-16 Output from the column quick report.

This is probably not the way our report should look. Let's get started changing around the fields and producing the report the way we want it. We should first look at our design completed in chapter 4 for the Inventory Valuation Report. Figure 13-17 shows this design. Some fields have been removed such as the Warranty and the Features field. The PRICE field has been moved after the quantity fields. A text header has been added in the first band. Finally a calculated field called INVENTORY VALUATION has been created and contains the value of the QTY_STK field multiplied by the PRICE field.

The custom layout

Once all of your data has been placed on the form using the Quick Layout, you may want to delete some of the fields that aren't needed for that report. When you delete fields, you will also need to delete the field column headers.

				INVENTORY VALUATION REPORT				
ITEM NUMBER	BRAND	TYPE	DESCRIPTION	QTY IN STOCK	QTY ON ORDER	PRICE	INVENTORY VALUATION
AAAA-999	x--10--x	x--12--x	x----25---x	9999	9999	9999.99	price*qty
							total

13-17 The inventory valuation report design.

Deleting unwanted objects   Deleting a field is easy. First, you move the cursor to the field. When the cursor touches any part of the field, it is highlighted. When it is highlighted, just press Delete and the field will disappear from the work surface. Of course, you might also use the Remove Field option of the Fields menu.

Before we learn how to print the report, let's make some changes to the report form so it will print the report in Fig. 13-17. The first thing we want to do is delete some of the unwanted fields from the work surface and create our subtotals. The WARRANTY and FEATURES field will be deleted from the work surface.

Figure 13-18 shows the Fields menu open and the Remove Field option selected. All of the fields on the report work surface are listed, including summary fields. All of the fields are in alphabetical order. From this menu, the WARRANTY and the FEATURES fields can be deleted. The summary field SUM(WARRANTY) must also be deleted. Whenever you delete a field from the detail band, it probably makes sense to delete its column header as well.

Because the WARRANTY and FEATURES field headers are next to each other, it is easy to delete them. Using the arrow keys, move the cursor to the W in WARRANTY in the page header band. You will notice that the entire text field does not highlight as it would with a database field. This is because this is not a field but text. Text is something you actually type on the work surface and dBASE really doesn't know where text begins and where it ends. In order to select text you have to use the Select key (F6) to select more than one character. Once you press the F6 key, everything you touch with the cursor is selected until you press Return.

Next, press the F6 (Extend Select) key. This begins the process of highlighting text. Using the arrow or tab keys, move the cursor to the S in FEATURES. The highlight expands from the W in WARRANTY to the S in FEATURES. Pressing Esc completes the selection. You can now do several

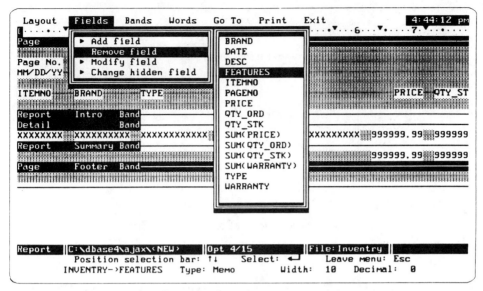

13-18 Removing fields from the work surface.

things with a defined selection. You can move or copy the text or, in this case, you can delete the text. Press Del to delete the text.

After you have completed this, delete three summary fields that are not needed. Totalling prices makes no sense unless you are looking for averages, and in this example, we don't want totals for the quantity fields. Move the cursor to the report summary band. As you move through each band, the band border is highlighted to tell you which band is active. Select the PRICE total. Next press F6 to continue the selection and press the End key. This selects both the quantity fields as well (Fig. 13-19). You can delete all of the fields at once by pressing Delete. All the report summary fields are now gone.

At this time, you might want to move your fields into the desired position. If you had removed fields that were between other fields, you would want to close up the space or add new space to allow room for any new fields you want to place on the work surface. In this way, you can save moving them twice. Creating report forms is a very interactive activity. Each time you do one task (adding, deleting, or moving a field) you might create a few more tasks. One thing that is always the same though is the visual ability to continue to improve the look of the report as you develop it.

Moving fields and text Your screen should look like Fig. 13-19 with the summary fields missing. Move the PRICE field and its header after the quantity fields, and then close up the space by moving all the fields.

Let's move the PRICE column header first. First position the cursor on the P in PRICE in the page header band. Next press the F6 key to begin the selection. Then press the Tab key to highlight the entire text. Press Enter to complete the selection. Finally, press the F7 key to move the item. Once F7 is

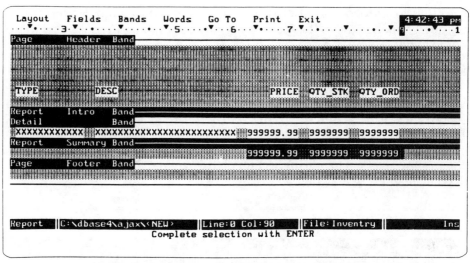

13-19 Removing summary fields from the work surface.

pressed, position the PRICE text a few characters to the right of the QTY_ORD text. Press Enter once the text is in its final position.

Now do the same thing with the PRICE field in the detail band. The only difference between moving text and moving a field is that once you place the cursor on any part of a field, the entire field is automatically selected.

Before we go on, we will close up the space left by the moved field. The text and fields in the bands need to be adjusted. You cannot simply delete blank spaces in the report screen. The only way to close up blank spaces is to move the fields or text that need to be moved to close up the space. All of the quantity and price data need to be moved to the left to close the gap left by the moving of the PRICE field.

Let's move the fields first. First, select the PRICE field, and then press F6 to highlight it and both the quantity fields. Once this is done, press Return to complete the selection. Once the selection is complete, it is time to move the fields. With both fields highlighted, press the F7 key to move the items. Now as you use the cursor keys to move the text to the left, you will see a rectangle representing the text moving across the work surface. When the left side of the rectangle is a few spaces to the right of the DESC field, press Return to finish moving the fields. You may receive the message Delete covered text and fields? (Y/N). dBASE is just warning you that the original fields are being covered. Press Y to accept this selection.

The space in the detail band is now closed up. However, there is still space between the text headers. This time, move all three text headers, QTY_STK, QTY_ORD, and PRICE, at once. Start your selection with the leftmost character in the selection, the Q in QTY_STK, and press F6. Now Tab over until all three text words are selected. Press Return to complete the selection. To move the selection, press F7 and move the rectangle a few spaces to the right of the end of the DESC field, just above the QTY_STK field in the detail band.

Changing text labels You are almost done with the text now. All that is left to do is to change the text labels so they mean more and conform to our design. Change the text labels as shown in Fig. 13-7. You can add a line to the page header band by pressing Enter on the last line of the page header band with insert mode on. You can also use the Add line option of the Words menu.

Text labels can be changed by simply typing over what is there or by using the Ins and Del keys to add and remove letters. Once the text is changed, the screen should resemble Fig. 13-20.

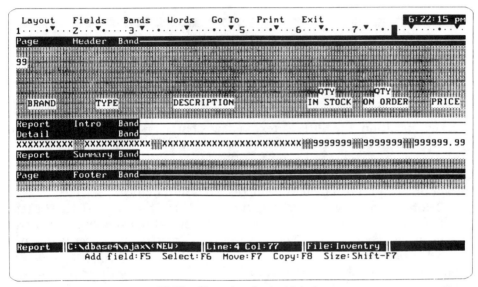

13-20 Changing the text labels.

Remember that the ITEMNO field is also on the work surface but is out of sight to the left. The next step is to add new fields. You must add the field for PRICE*QTY and a summary and header for that calculated field.

Adding new fields Fields can be added by moving the cursor to the area you wish to add them in and pressing F5. Let's begin by creating the inventory valuation field. In order to get this, we need to multiply QTY_STK*PRICE to get the valuation at list price.

Move the cursor just to the right of the PRICE field in the detail band. Press F5 to add a field. A special type of selection box opens on the work surface, as you see in Fig. 13-21.

This box lets you place fields on the work surface. The box has four columns—INVENTRY, CALCULATED, PREDEFINED, and SUMMARY. The first column shows you the name of your database or view. Because we are

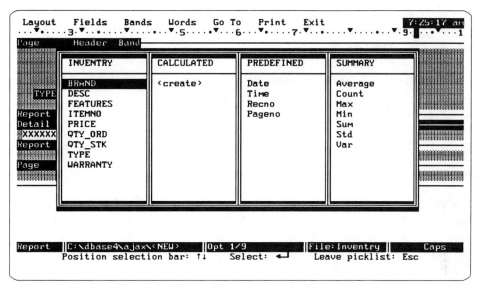

13-21 Creating a new field.

using a single database named INVENTRY, that is the title of the column. All of the fields in the database are shown. We can place any of them on the work surface by merely selecting one and pressing Return. However, now we are going to create a calculated field—QTY_STK*PRICE.

Adding calculated fields You can have several types of calculated fields. The first type is valid dBASE expressions or calculations. Calculations can be as simple as multiplying one number by another, calculating a date, changing a logical field into YES or NO, or concatenating two text fields. They can also be rather complex to include table lookup and multiple occurrences of a field. No matter what type of calculation you want to do, dBASE IV can handle it through a series of menus that appear when you press F5 to Add a field to the report form.

Another type of field that can be added to the form is the Predefined field. These are four fields that are automatically kept track of by dBASE IV and can be used on the report. These include:

- Date—The current system date
- Time—The current system time
- Recno—The record number being printed
- Pageno—The current page number being printed

They are used by simply adding them to the work surface.

The final type of field is a summary field. dBASE IV is capable of creating many types of numeric summaries including:

- Average—The average of a group of numbers
- Count—The number of records
- Max—The largest value
- Min—The smallest value
- Sum—The total of the numbers
- Std—The standard deviation of a group of numbers
- Var—The variance of a group of numbers

Move the cursor to the ⟨create⟩ label in the CALCULATED column. Press Return. Yet another menu opens and is ready for us to name and describe this field.

The Field menu   This Field menu is shown in Fig. 13-22. The first entry lets you name the field. We have called it INVVAL. To enter this in the field, move your cursor to the brackets beside Name and press Return. You can now enter the name INVVAL. When you are through, press Return. The Description field is optional, and simply used for documentation. This has also been filled in already.

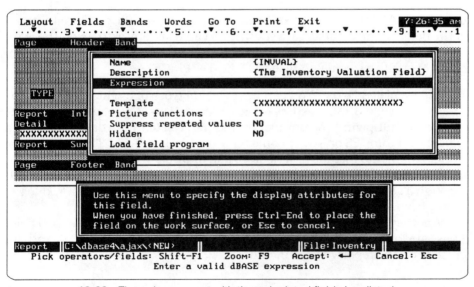

13-22   The column report with the calculated fields box listed.

Now, you could simply type the calculation QTY_SHP*PRICE. This would create a calculated field called INVVAL whose formula is the value of QTY_SHP times the value of PRICE. However, for complicated expressions or when you need to remember the name of a field or a function, you will want to use a method known as the *Pick list*.

The Pick box   Instead of typing the calculation in directly, let's do it a little differently. You are going to use the dBASE IV expression builder, also known as the *Pick list*, to enter the expression.

If you look at the bottom of Fig. 13-22, you will see a list of function keys that do something. We are going to use the function key combination Shift–F1. This is known as the Pick key, because it allows you to build expressions from menus instead of typing them in. There are several good reasons to use this method.

Suppose you have many fields and you can never remember what you called them. Did you call the retail price field PRICE or RETAIL? If you can't remember, you can't enter the formula to calculate total price. The Pick menu will tell you.

Make sure your cursor is in the Expression line for the calculated field in progress. Press Shift–F1. The Pick menu should appear as in Fig. 13-23. The Pick menu has three columns labeled:

Fieldname   Operator   Function

Below each column is a list of all the possible choices. You move around in this menu box with the cursor arrow keys. You are going to "build" the expression QTY_STK*PRICE. Move the cursor to QTY_STK in the Fieldname box and press Return. The fieldname QTY_STK is automatically placed in the calculated field box, and the Pick menu goes away.

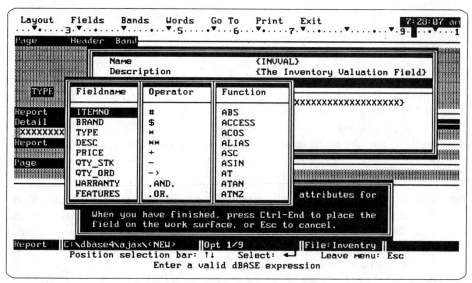

13-23   Creating a calculated field formula with the pick box.

Press Shift–F1 again to redisplay the Pick menu. Now move the cursor to the third choice in the Operator column. This is the multiplication symbol. Press Return and again the asterisk is placed in the calculated field box next to the field QTY_STK. Finally, press Shift–F1 again and choose PRICE in the Fieldname box. Press Ctrl–End and you have now completed the expression!

Don't worry about the lower half of the menu. This is used for changing what the field will look like. We will accept the defaults. When you are all through, press Ctrl–End. This will give you a new field on the work surface. It should appear just to the right of the PRICE field. If not, you can use the steps you saw to move a field and move it next to PRICE.

Adding summary fields   After calculated and predefined fields are added to the form, you might need to add Summary records. dBASE IV is capable of creating many types of numeric summaries including Average, Count, Max, Min, Sum, Std, and Var. dBASE IV takes care of any accumulations and calculation to produce the desired summary. You just tell it what field to monitor and it takes care of the rest. You can create summaries on any numeric field whether it is in the database or calculated.

When you choose one of these summaries, you are asked how to break the summary. Your choice at this point is at the report or page level because you have not yet defined any group breaks. The summary fields are usually placed into the report summary or page footer bands.

In the report summary band, there are presently no fields. Let's create totals for our new calculated field. First, move the cursor to the report summary band underneath the column for the new field. Once again, you can press F5 to add a field. The same box opens as in Fig. 13-21. You may notice that this time our new calculated field is listed in the Calculated column. What we are going to do now is create a Summary field. We are going to SUM the new field INVVAL.

Move the cursor to the SUMMARY column of the Add fields box and place the cursor on Sum. Press Return, and the screen changes to show you the Summary field entry area. As you can see in Fig. 13-24 which has already been filled in, this menu lets you decide which operation to perform (in this case SUM), which field to sum, and how often to recalculate the sum. The Name and Description fields are optional and are only used for documentation. In this case, we want to sum the INVVAL field and reset the total only at the REPORT level. Later, we'll see how to create a group subtotal on BRAND or TYPE.

Adding new text   You should now have a new field on the work surface along with a summary for the field. However, this field needs a name. Although you called the field INVVAL, this name does not just appear in the page header area, you have to enter it. Move the cursor to the page header band. Place the cursor where you want to enter the text. Once you are there, just type away. Use the cursor keys to move freely about that area. In fact, using Fig. 13-25 as a guide, change all the text in this area to be in our final form according to Fig. 13-25.

Add the report title as shown in Fig. 13-25. The title of the report is INVENTORY VALUATION REPORT. A line of dashes has also been added above the summary field. First, a blank line is added to the band, and then the

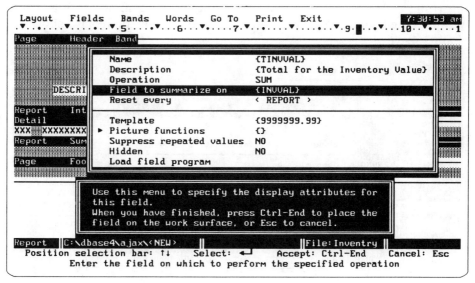

13-24 Creating a summary field.

dashes are typed in. If you use the Spacebar or use the Backspace keys, you might notice holes in the background. This is normal and lets dBASE tell you where blank spaces have been entered on the form. They don't do anything, they are just there to inform you.

Before going on, save the form by using the Save this report option of the Layout menu, and name the report INVVALUE. Let's print the report before

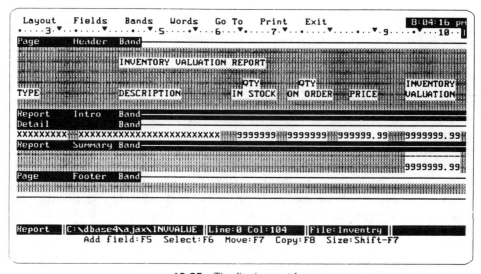

13-25 The final report form.

returning to the Control Center. The printed report shown in Fig. 13-26 was produced from data input during the testing of the design shown in chapter 4.

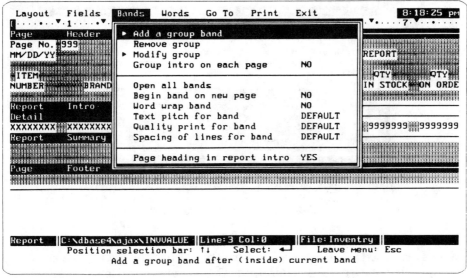

13-26 The column report with the Bands menu open.

You will see how to print the report or any report in chapter 14. The report shown in Fig. 13-1 was printed in compressed print mode so 133 characters can fit on a standard piece of paper.

This completes the report as designed for the inventory valuation report. Before going on, you should see how to create group bands. Even though this is not in your design, it is a good time to learn it.

Creating group bands

Besides page headers and report summaries that create report totals, there may be a need for a more detailed breakdown of your data. Perhaps you want subtotals by several different dimensions. This is most appropriate when you have many occurrences of a key such as TYPE. In our INVENTRY example, several items of each TYPE are among the various brands. In this chapter, you have seen in Fig. 13-1 a subtotal by TYPE. This is known as a grouping, because the data has been grouped by a field (TYPE). Data can be grouped by any field or expression in the database. The only caveat is to make sure that the data is sorted by the group expression.

A menu choice is required to create a group band. When you add a group band, you are asked to decide how the grouping will be. Is it an individual field or a dBASE expression that tells dBASE when one group ends and a new one begins? Group bands like most others come in pairs—an intro and a summary. The group intro band usually contains some identifier to tell what the value of the group field is. The group summary is usually used for subtotals. dBASE automatically takes care of resetting the totals each time a new group value occurs.

Although there is no real limit to the number of group breaks, you will see that it gets very complicated if you have more than a few. Although dBASE keeps track of everything for you, it is still difficult to make good looking reports with a lot of group breaks.

All that is left now is to group the data by TYPE. Your data must be sorted or indexed by TYPE to effectively use a grouping. In this case, the data's natural order is by TYPE and is already in that order. If not, you would have to go back to the Data menu in the Control Center and index the database by TYPE before printing the report.

Group bands let you create intros and summaries based on the value of a field changing. Once you sort the database by TYPE, you will see the data in TYPE order. First will come all three DRYERs followed by the MICROWAVE and the three RANGEs. Finally, the five REFRIGERATORs and three WASHERs are last. In our very small database, only one TYPE has a single occurrence; this will prove to be redundant. Totals are necessary only when there is more than one item in a grouping, but will print for each group regardless of whether there is one detail item or one thousand.

In this example, we want to see a subtotal for each TYPE that we carry in the inventory for the inventory valuation field. We have already done that for our grand report total, and now we simply want subtotals. Let's begin by creating a group band.

Bands are created by using the Bands menu choice. You should still be in the INVVALUE report. Make sure you are in the page header band. Press Alt–B to open the Bands menu. This menu is shown in Fig. 13-26. There are choices to add, remove, and modify group bands. To add a group band your cursor must be in the page header area. When you add a group, you are adding an intro and a summary band. You must tell dBASE on which field you want to group. This database must be sorted or indexed on this field or be in the natural order by this field or the groupings will be a mess because the data won't be in order. dBASE prints a new group intro at the beginning of each new group and a group summary at the end of each group. The data usually should be in order by the group field.

Some of the other options in this menu let you start a band on a new page, create word-wrap bands, and even change the type or quality of the printing along with the line spacing for that band. You can even close a band, which will let you print the report as if the closed band wasn't even there.

Let's create the group band for TYPE. With the Bands menu open, select Add a group band. Press Return and the screen changes to ask you how to group the data. You have three choices—field value, expression value, or record number. In this case, we want to work with a single field, so choose Field Value, and press Return again. The last menu in this sequence allows us to choose a field to GROUP BY. Choose the TYPE field as shown in Fig. 13-27.

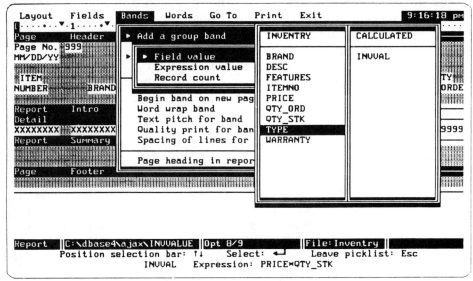

13-27 Choosing a group field.

A new band appears on the screen ready for us to enter an intro and summary.

To start, keep the intro simple. First put the text on the work surface Type: by typing it in the Group 1 Intro band as shown in the finished form in Fig. 13-30. After completing the text, add the TYPE field. Press F5 and add the TYPE field next to the text TYPE:. The field should appear in the Group 1 Intro band (Fig. 13-29).

Now, the TYPE field already appears in the report. Normally, when you add a group band, you remove the field that the grouping is near from the body of the report. For now, you will leave the TYPE field in both places.

To create the subtotals for the INVVALUE field, you need to again add a summary field; except this time the subtotals are added to the Group 1 Summary band. Move the cursor to the Group 1 Summary band, and place it above the INVVALUE summary in the Report Summary band. When you add this new summary field, you must make sure you reset every {TYPE} instead of every {Report} as you did earlier. Otherwise, the process is the same. Review the process of creating the summary fields if you need help. The summary screen is shown in Fig. 13-28.

Don't forget to label the group summary band by adding TYPE TOTAL: followed by the TYPE value. The final report screen is shown in Fig. 13-29.

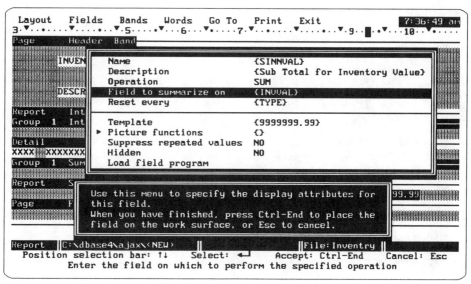

```
 Layout   Fields   Bands   Words   Go To   Print   Exit        7:36:49 am
3.▼....▼..5....▼....▼...6...▼....7.▼...▼.........▼.9.▮..▼...10..▼....
 Page        Header   Band
             INVEN  ┌─────────────────────────────────────────────────────┐
                    │  Name                     {SINNVAL}                   │
             DESCR  │  Description              {Sub Total for Inventory Value} │
                    │  Operation                SUM                         │
 Report    Int      │▶ Field to summarize on    {INVVAL}                    │
 Group  1  Int      │  Reset every              {TYPE}                      │
                    │                                                       │
 Detail             │  Template                 {9999999.99}               │
 XXXX  XXXXXXX      │▶ Picture functions        {}                         │
 Group  1  Sum      │  Suppress repeated values NO                         │
                    │  Hidden                   NO                         │
 Report    S        │  Load field program                                 │
                    └─────────────────────────────────────────────────────┘
 Page      F  ┌───────────────────────────────────────────────────┐ 99.99│
              │ Use this menu to specify the display attributes for │
              │ this field.                                         │
              │ When you have finished, press Ctrl-End to place the │
              │ field on the work surface, or Esc to cancel.        │
              └───────────────────────────────────────────────────┘
 Report  ║C:\dbase4\ajax\<NEW>║                    ║File:Inventry║
      Position selection bar: ↑↓    Select: ◄┘    Accept: Ctrl-End   Cancel: Esc
               Enter the field on which to perform the specified operation
```

13-28 Creating the group summary.

You can print this report, as you will soon see. The printed report is shown in Fig. 13-30. If you decide to save this report, make sure you rename it by using the Save this report option of the Layout menu and calling it something like INVVALU2.

```
 Layout   Fields   Bands   Words   Go To   Print   Exit        9:31:11 pm
[....▼.1....▼..2....▼..3.▼.......▼.........▼.5....▼..6..▼....7.▼....
 Page        Header   Band
 Page No. 999
 MM/DD/YY                                        INVENTORY VALUATION REPORT
  ITEM                                                             QTY      QTY
 NUMBER     BRAND        TYPE            DESCRIPTION          IN STOCK  ON ORDE
 Report    Intro   Band
 Group  1  Intro   Band
 Type: XXXXXXXXXXX
 Detail            Band
 XXXXXXX  XXXXXXXXX  XXXXXXXXXX XXXXXXXXXXXXXXXXXXXXXXX  9999999  9999999
 Group  1  Summary Band
 Type Total: XXXXXXXXXXX
 Report    Summary Band

 Page      Footer  Band

 Report  ║C:\dbase4\ajax\INVVALUE║Line:0 Col:0║    ║File:Inventry║
       Add field:F5  Select:F6  Move:F7  Copy:F8  Size:Shift-F7
```

13-29 Creating the group summary.

```
Type: MICROWAVE
HIMI-001   HITECH       MICROWAVE    1500 WATT                    127      0    229.99      29208.73
                                                                                         ----------
Type Total: MICROWAVE                                                                     29208.73


Type: RANGE
HIRA-001   HITECH       RANGE                                     89       0    689.99      61409.11
RURA-001   RUSTIC       RANGE        WOOD TRIM                     0     100    659.99          0.00
WHRA-001   WHOLEPOOL    RANGE                                     28       0    929.99      26039.72
                                                                                         ----------
Type Total: RANGE                                                                         87448.83


Type: REFRIGERATOR
FRRE-001   FROSTY       REFRIGERATOR 1 DOOR TOP FREEZER W/ICE     112      0    699.99      78398.88
FRRE-002   FROSTY       REFRIGERATOR 2 DOOR SIDE BY SIDE          78       0    899.99      70199.22
FRRE-003   FROSTY       REFRIGERATOR 2 DOOR UPRIGHT                6       5   1199.99       7199.94
CORE-001   COLDPOINTS   REFRIGERATOR MINI-MAX                     17       0    229.99       3909.83
WHRE-001   WHOLEPOOL    REFRIGERATOR                              23      40    469.99      10809.77
                                                                                         ----------
Type Total: REFRIGERATOR                                                                 170517.64


Type: WASHER
COWA-001   COLDPOINTS   WASHER                                    89       0    369.99      32929.11
WHWA-001   WHOLEPOOL    WASHER                                    36       0    739.99      26639.64
WHWA-002   WHOLEPOOL    WASHER       DELUXE MODEL                  2      30    969.99       1939.98
                                                                                         ----------
Type Total: WASHER                                                                        61508.73


                                                                                         ----------
Grand Total:                                                                             461282.17
```

13-30   Printing the final report with a group summary.

Completing the rest of the column reports

Now that you have finished the inventory valuation report, in the next part of this chapter, you will complete the rest of the simple reports. These include the:

- Item number cross-reference
- Customer cross-reference

These reports are very simple and will now be described. They may be simple, but a few things may surprise you.

The item cross-reference report

Let's begin with the design from the item number cross-reference report as shown in Fig. 13-31. This design shows a report with only four fields. You could place the fields on the work surface one at a time. Also, you could use the Quick Layout, then delete all the fields you don't need, and move around the fields into the final position. However, this would take a long time. A third method is to create a view with only those four fields and in the order of the report. You could then use the Quick Layout.

```
┌─────────────────────────────────────────────────────────────┐
│ o                                                         o │
│ o          ITEM NUMBER CROSS REFERENCE                    o │
│ o          ---------------------------                    o │
│ o                                                         o │
│ o                              ITEM            ITEM       o │
│ o     BRAND      TYPE        DESCRIPTION      NUMBER       o │
│ o                                                         o │
│ o   x--10--x    x--12--x    x-----25-----x   AAAA-999     o │
│ o   x--10--x    x--12--x    x-----25-----x   AAAA-999     o │
│ o   x--10--x    x--12--x    x-----25-----x   AAAA-999     o │
│ o   x--10--x    x--12--x    x-----25-----x   AAAA-999     o │
│ o   x--10--x    x--12--x    x-----25-----x   AAAA-999     o │
│ o                                                         o │
│ o   x--10--x    x--12--x    x-----25-----x   AAAA-999     o │
│ o   x--10--x    x--12--x    x-----25-----x   AAAA-999     o │
│ o   x--10--x    x--12--x    x-----25-----x   AAAA-999     o │
│ o   x--10--x    x--12--x    x-----25-----x   AAAA-999     o │
│ o   x--10--x    x--12--x    x-----25-----x   AAAA-999     o │
│ o                                                         o │
│ o   x--10--x    x--12--x    x-----25-----x   AAAA-999     o │
│ o   x--10--x    x--12--x    x-----25-----x   AAAA-999     o │
│ o   x--10--x    x--12--x    x-----25-----x   AAAA-999     o │
│ o   x--10--x    x--12--x    x-----25-----x   AAAA-999     o │
│ o   x--10--x    x--12--x    x-----25-----x   AAAA-999     o │
│ o                                                         o │
└─────────────────────────────────────────────────────────────┘
```

13-31 The item number cross-reference design.

In this example, the fields were added one at a time from the original INVENTRY database. Because the labels had to be reentered anyway, it was just as easy to add the labels as to retype them.

This report contains no subtotals, totals, or calculated fields. The report form is shown in Fig. 13-32. As you can see, there is a group band in the form. Because there are obviously no subtotals, you might ask why is there a group band.

The answer is simple. If you examine the design in Fig. 13-31, you will notice that there is a blank line every 5 lines. This is accomplished by using the Record count option of the group band as shown in Fig. 13-33, and setting it to 5.

Notice that the group intro band is closed and the group summary band is open although it is empty. Actually, there is something in it—a blank line! This is the line that separates every fifth record. If the group intro band was also open, there would be two blank lines between every fifth record. Either band can be open as long as only one band is open and the open band contains a blank line.

The final printed report is shown in Fig. 13-34. The data was ordered by BRAND and TYPE before running the report. This report is named ITEM-CROS.

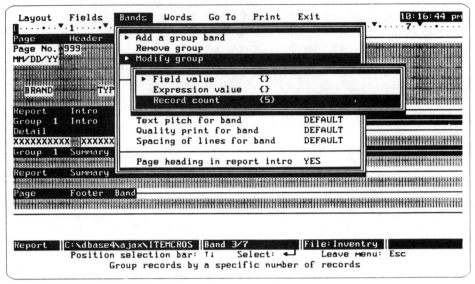

13-32 The item number cross-reference report form.

The customer cross-reference report

The customer cross-reference report is exactly the same as the inventory cross-reference report. As you can see from the final report form shown in Fig. 13-35, it too contains a group band in order to skip a line every fifth record. Five fields from the customer database are used in this report named CUSTCROS.

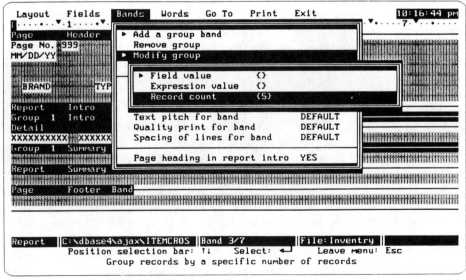

13-33 The record count option of the group band.

		ITEM	ITEM
BRAND	TYPE	DESCRIPTION	NUMBER
COLDPOINTS	DRYER	SUPERSPIN I	CODR-001
COLDPOINTS	DRYER	SUPERSPIN II	CODR-002
WHOLEPOOL	DRYER		WHDR-001
HITECH	MICROWAVE	1500 WATT	HIMI-001
HITECH	RANGE		HIRA-001
RUSTIC	RANGE	WOOD TRIM	RURA-001
WHOLEPOOL	RANGE		WHRA-001
FROSTY	REFRIGERATOR	1 DOOR TOP FREEZER W/ICE	FRRE-001
FROSTY	REFRIGERATOR	2 DOOR SIDE BY SIDE	FRRE-002
FROSTY	REFRIGERATOR	2 DOOR UPRIGHT	FRRE-003
COLDPOINTS	REFRIGERATOR	MINI-MAX	CORE-001
WHOLEPOOL	REFRIGERATOR		WHRE-001
COLDPOINTS	WASHER		COWA-001
WHOLEPOOL	WASHER		WHWA-001
WHOLEPOOL	WASHER	DELUXE MODEL	WHWA-002

13-34 The final item cross-reference report.

Because there are no significant differences, you can create this report the same way you created the inventory report. You will use both of these reports later when you create the menu-based system.

Reports like these can be created in just a few minutes. Although you will later see how to program one of these reports, you will find that the Reports

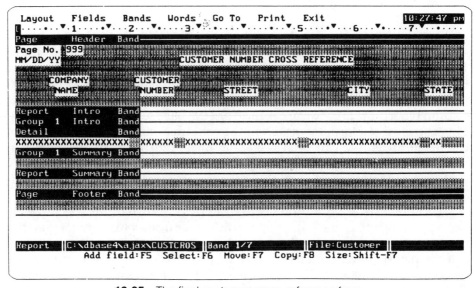

13-35 The final customer cross-reference form.

work surface can save you many hours of programming and can be incorporated right into your menu-based systems. The final printed customer cross-reference report is shown in Fig. 13-36.

```
Page No.    1
11/22/88                        CUSTOMER NUMBER CROSS REFERENCE
          COMPANY         CUSTOMER
           NAME           NUMBER        STREET                CITY            STATE

APPLIANCE CITY            AP-001    210 SKY LANE          OXNARD              CA
APPLIANCE CITY            AP-002    360 ACE AVE           HOLLYWOOD           CA
APPLIANCE WORLD           AP-003    20695 BLUE BIRD AVE   SAN FRANCISCO       CA
AVON APPLIANCE            AV-001    1687 NEW PLACE ROAD   LOS ANGELES         CA
BOB'S BRANDS              BO-001    BOB'S DRIVE           SANTA FE            NM

CARY'S COOLERS            CA-001    60 STRAWBERRY HILLS   WINDSOR             CT
CRAZY FREDDIES            CR-001    1820 171ST ST         NEW YORK            NY
ERNIES TV                 ER-001    456 SNOW PLOW AVE     BLEAUVILLE          CA
FRIENDLY APPLIANCE        FR-001    26 CHOCOLATE AVE      HERSHEY             PA
JACKEL & HYDES            JA-001    357 BAT COURT         LAWRENCEVILLE       PA

JIMS HOT AND COLD         JI-001    55 SKINNER RD         VERNON              CA
RANGES ON THE HOME        RA-001    23 OLD OKIE DR        OKLAHOMA CITY       OK
RON'S REFRIGERATORS       RO-001    141 HOLLOW OAK PLACE  SAN JUAN CAPISTRANO CA
THE HOME SHOPPE           TH-001    25 APPLIANCE LANE     SARATOGA            CA
WASHER WAREHOUSE          WA-001    15525 MARINER DR      LOS ALTOS           CA
WEST'S WHITE GOODS        WE-001    26 DENNIS LANE        CUPERTINO           CA
```

13-36 The final customer cross-reference form.

Simple form reports

In this section of the chapter, we examine creating two simple form reports:

- Salesman inventory report
- Customer directory

We begin with the salesman inventory report as designed in chapter 4, and shown in Fig. 13-37. This design shows that the report occupies many lines. This is known as a *form report*, because the information is *not* placed into neat little rows and columns. The majority of information in a form report appears in the detail section rather than in the headers or footers. In fact, in this column report, the only two areas used are the page header and detail areas. This is typical of a form report. Even the column or data headers are part of the detail areas. We can even see some lines and boxes in the report to separate some data items from others. dBASE IV is capable of creating very sophisticated form reports including tax forms, invoices, checks, or practically anything that doesn't fit into neat rows and columns.

Form reports are traditionally used to place your data in specific locations on the printed page. The primary difference from column reports is that usually a form report record is spread out on the whole page, where the column reports have as many records on a page as will fit. Form reports are usually much fancier than column reports because there is more room to work with.

```
                    SALESMAN INVENTORY REPORT
                    -------------------------

  ITEM NUMBER:   ITEM NUMBER

        BRAND:   BRAND         TYPE:   TYPE

  DESCRIPTION:   DESCRIPTION
 ------------------------------------------------------------

        PRICE:   PRICE

                              IN STOCK       ON ORDER
  INVENTORY QUANTITIES:         999             999


     WARRANTY:   99 Months


     FEATURES:

          MMMMMMMMMMMMMMMMMMMMMMMMMMMMMMMMMMMMMMMM
          MMMMMMMMMMMMMMMMMMMMMMMMMMMMMMMMMMMMMMMM
          MMMMMMMMMMMMMMMMMMMMMMMMMMMMMMMMMMMMMMMM
          MMMMMMMMMMMMMMMMMMMMMMMMMMMMMMMMMMMMMMMM
          MMMMMMMMMMMMMMMMMMMMMMMMMMMMMMMMMMMMMMMM
```

13-37 The salesman inventory report design.

This is a simple example, but you will later see that by using several databases, you can create very complicated reports such as an invoice form or a tax form. Invoices are especially difficult, because they combine all of the features of a form and a column report. They appear as a form report because they take up an entire page, but they also contain a portion of the report that is created as a column report. The many items in an invoice including quantities, part numbers, descriptions, and price are the detail portion of an invoice report. The page headers and footers act as a form and contain many lines including descriptions and summaries. In this chapter, we complete a simple form with all of its fields in the detail band.

Creating the initial form

Creating a form report is much the same as creating a column report. In fact, the step-by-step method learned to create column reports is again used with some omissions. More time is spent in making the form pretty than in worrying about totals. A form can have totals such as would be found on an invoice, and it can also contain other information that doesn't require totals.

Let's start from the Control Center. Make sure that you have made the INVENTRY database active. Next you will create the form report, so move the cursor to ⟨create⟩ in the Reports panel and press Return.

The Layout menu opens automatically, because dBASE assumes that you will start with Quick Layout. Press Return to open the Quick Layout option. The three options of this menu are listed. Rather than individually placing each one of your data items on the work surface, you can automatically place all of them in one of these forms. For this first example, let's use the Forms layout choice. Press Return on this choice.

Instantly, all of the fields in the INVENTRY database are placed on the screen. Examine Fig. 13-38. You can see that the data has been placed in the various bands on the report surface. The page header band contains the text Page No. along with a field to hold the current page number. Also, the date appears on a third line in the report work surface.

13-38 The inventory Quick form layout.

The detail band contains all of the fields from the database. Instead of being arranged in a single line across the report as in the column reports, they are arranged down the band in two columns. The first column contains the field names, while the second column contains the fields themselves. Also, no summaries are created. In a form report, dBASE assumes that you are not looking for any totals and doesn't calculate any.

Moving the text and fields

In this form, all of the data that you want is found on the work surface. There will be no fields to delete. The next step is to simply move the fields into the approximate position on the work surface for the report.

Using the function keys shown in the bottom of the screen in Fig. 13-38, you can begin to place the fields on the work surface. Remember, the goal is for the report to look like Fig. 13-37. You will add details like lines and boxes later.

You can add a page header for the report and move some of the fields around, as shown in Fig. 13-37. There is no one right way to move the fields around. An efficient method is to place all of the database fields on the work surface, then add new fields, rearrange the fields again, add lines and boxes, rearrange fields again, and then finish any little details. The key to this, as you can see, is constant rearranging. Each time you have new information as to the final form of the form, you should take advantage of it and move the fields.

Another good way is to first move all of the fields and text labels to the bottom center of the screen. This gets all of the objects "out of the way." You can begin to arrange the objects starting with the top rows and ending with the bottom. This way, as you move your first few fields into final position, the rest of the fields don't have to be constantly moved around. Your objective is to make the screen look like Fig. 13-39.

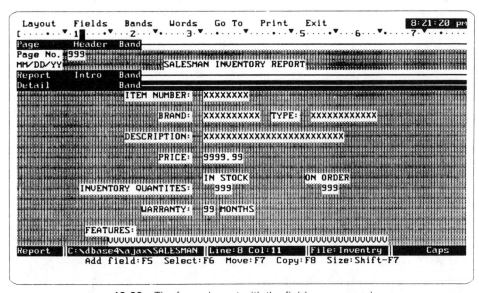

13-39 The forms layout with the fields rearranged.

Remember, you can move selected fields and text by using the F7 key. If you need help in remembering how to select and move fields, you might want to look back in the column reports section earlier in this chapter.

Drawing lines and boxes

So far, you have created a form report and arranged the fields and text on the work surface. The next step is to add lines and boxes. Although our design did not call for any boxes, you should create a line and a box in this next section.

Text can "dress up" the report and make it more readable, but you can also make it fancier and draw attention to specific areas on the report through the use of lines and boxes. Lines and boxes placed on the template will also print out in the report. Lines can help segregate parts of the form from one another, while boxes can specifically draw attention to parts of the report. Drawing these lines and boxes is very easy, as you will see. They are drawn visually by choosing one corner and then making the box grow both horizontally and vertically until it encloses the desired area.

Adding lines and boxes is another step that you should consider in creating reports. Lines and boxes are selected from the Layout menu. Once you choose one of these selections, you are asked whether you want a single or double line, or if you want to pick your own character. The next step is to place the left corner of the line or left top corner of the box on the screen. After you place the left corner, press Return. This "locks" the left corner in place. As you use the cursor keys, the line or box expands to cover the area to the cursor. When your box covers the desired area, press Return again. Each box is created this way. Lines are nothing more than flat boxes with no height.

Boxes are shown entered on the work surface in Fig. 13-40. This completes the entry for the report. When you see the final printout this report form generates, you might be surprised to see that the line and box also prints out. dBASE IV is one of the few programs that actually prints out lines and boxes.

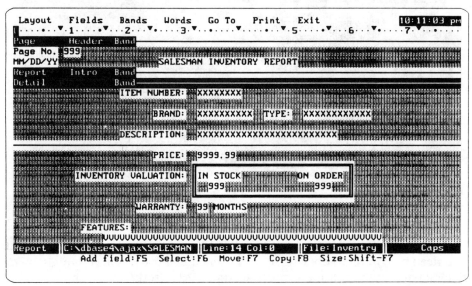

13-40 The forms layout with lines and boxes.

Reports and memo fields

Memo fields are represented by V's on the work surface because they have the *vertical stretch* picture function. This means that if the memo field data exceeds the width of the V's, then the data continues below the original V's. This means that the data stretches vertically for as many lines as needed to fit each set of data on the page.

Because some memo field data might be longer than others, this function allows the data to stretch to fit whatever space is necessary. You can make the width of the template of V's as wide or as narrow as you want. Wherever it finds the memo field, it will put the memo data.

Customizing and styling data with pictures and templates

It is important to not let data fields just display by themselves without any explanation of what the data means. Some field's output may be readily apparent to you, but it may be foreign to the reader, and therefore need some clarification. Make sure that all of your columns have column headers, and all of your non-column oriented fields have labels either to the left or just above them. By labeling your fields, calculations, and summaries, you will make your form a lot more readable. Take a good look at your report template. Print it out. Is it as nice as it should be? How can you improve the look further?

Styling is another important feature in dBASE IV. This lets you change the font type to any one of six font types that you can install when you first install dBASE. You can also choose whether a field is bold, italic, underlined, superscript, or subscript. Styling can bring you another step closer to the perfect report.

As you can see in the Style menu shown in Fig. 13-41, the underline option has been turned on. The title in the page header band has been underlined. If you style something, make sure you turn off the style where you want it to end. Styling is turned on in one place and off in another. It does not work by selecting a block of text or group of fields.

If you have not already moved all of your fields exactly where you want them and added the appropriate column headers and text to make the form more readable, now is the time.

Before we go on and print the form, there is one thing left to do. You can affect the way a field is displayed without creating new fields, too. The Modify field option in the Fields menu lets you change the field. Besides changing the display size of the field, you can use the option Picture functions to change the display of fields. This menu appears in Fig. 13-42.

Character and numeric functions have separate menus. There are many different numeric functions. You can put the debit and credit symbols around numbers. You can also place parentheses around negative numbers. You can also show leading zeros or blanks, in place of a value of zero. Finally, you can specify a financial format with dollar signs and commas. You can also combine several functions such as the $ and (function to affect the number even more. In this figure, we have added the dollar sign to the PRICE field. When you do this, the size of the field is increased by one. However, if you want to add commas, you will have to change the field template. You will see

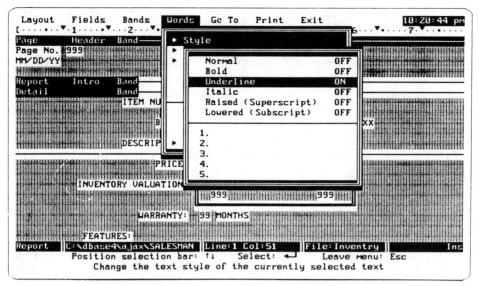

13-41 The Style menu.

this in more detail when you complete the invoice report. This subject is also covered in the forms chapter.

The bottom part of the menu handles numbers that exceed the length you have allowed for them. You can tell dBASE IV to trim a field if it exceeds the allowed length. You can also left- or center-align the field within the display area. As numbers are usually right-aligned, there is no need for that option.

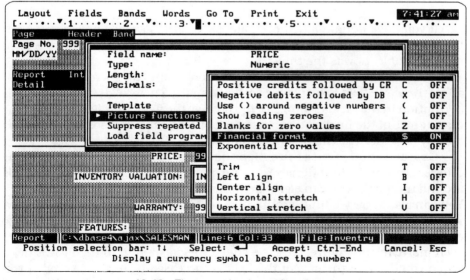

13-42 The numeric picture functions.

The last two choices let you determine how to expand the field when the field exceeds its allotted size. The default is vertical stretch. This means that if it exceeds its width, it uses the area below it to place the characters that exceed the field length. If you turn on *horizontal stretch*, then dBASE IV uses the area to the right of the field. You should be cognizant of any fields that might be in the way if the field stretches, to avoid conflict.

This should complete the report form named SALESMAN. It might seem like a lot of work, but it really isn't. You were able to create a very complex report by visually selecting and placing your fields. In fact, as this author created the final form from scratch, it only took three minutes to produce the report.

When you print the form, it comes out on multiple pages—one form to a page. You will also have to add a page break by using the Bands menu option Begin band on new page in the first band of the form. You can also use the option Insert page break in the Words menu. A sample page from the report is shown in Fig. 13-43.

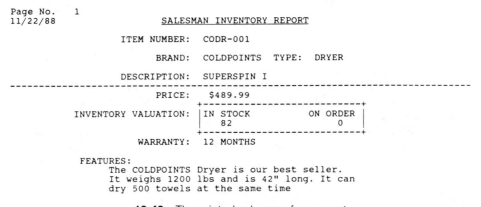

13-43 The printed salesman form report.

The customer directory—another form report

Another simple form report is the customer directory. This completed report form is shown in Fig. 13-44. You might notice that the center of the form has a lot of text without any labels near it. This is where the customer's address information is stored. This is one of the rare instances that labels are not needed.

How fields look on the work surface is one task we haven't tackled yet. When you place a field on the work surface, the field will be displayed at that location in the printed report. You can also change the way fields are displayed. For example, numeric fields can be displayed with dollar signs, commas, parentheses around negative numbers, etc. Although you have seen how to do that, you still have a few more things to learn. You can also

```
[.......▼.1.....▼...2...▼.....3.▼......▼...▼.5.....▼...6...▼..▼.....7.▼...▼......
Page No. 999
MM/DD/YY                            CUSTOMER DIRECTORY


Report    Intro    Band
Detail             Band

                    CUSTOMER NUMBER:  XXXXXX

                    XXXXXXXXXXXXXXXXXXX
                    XXXXXXXXXXXXXXXXXXX
                    XXXXXXXXXXXXXXXXXXX,  XX  XXXXXXXXX

                    PHONE:        XXXXXXXXXXXXX

                    DISCOUNT:   99

                    TAXABLE:    Y

                    LAST TRANSACTION DATE:  MM/DD/YY
Report  C:\dbase4\ajax\CUSTDIR   Line:12 Col:39   File:Customer
         Add field:F5  Select:F6  Move:F7  Copy:F8  Size:Shift-F7
```

13-44 The customer directory form.

transform a field from one type of data to another. Logic fields provide a good example of this.

Logic fields pose a special challenge, and a great opportunity to display their data better. A logic field exists to tell us something is either true or false. However, on a report, the value .T. or .F. is not that attractive. Using the IIF (Immediate IF) function, you can transform data from one form to another.

This example involves the logic field TAXABLE. Let's create a new field that uses the logic field in a calculation. We want to make the value of this new field YES if the value of TAXABLE is true, and NO if it is not. To do this, we first must delete the logic field and then add a new field by pressing F5. After the box opens up, move the cursor to the ⟨create⟩ label in the CALCULATED column. Press Return. A submenu opens, and is ready for us to name and describe this field. The submenu is shown in Fig. 13-45.

The areas have been filled in. The top area names the new field TAX-ABLE2. The calculation is shown as:

    IIF(TAXABLE,'YES','NO')

This is the IIF (Immediate IF) command. It says, if the value of the field TAXABLE is true, then set the value of TAXABLE2 to 'YES'. If it is false, then make the value of TAXABLE2, 'NO'. The value of the logic field TAXABLE is unchanged. The value was simply used in a calculation. When the report is produced, the value YES or NO is shown in place of T or F for each record.

Figure 13-46 also shows the template menu open. Because the calculated field created by the IIF function is a character field, a default template of 10 Xs is created. You would need to change the size of the template to 3 characters.

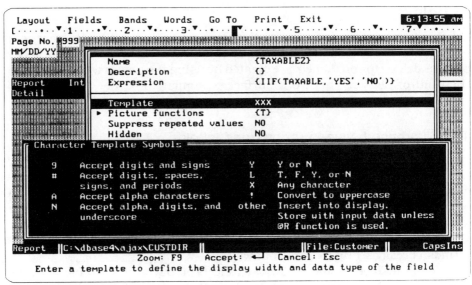

13-45 Changing a logical field.

When you change a template, the menu is automatically opened; this helps you change the templates to something else when you can't remember the different symbols you can choose from.

```
                    CUSTOMER DIRECTORY


        CUSTOMER NUMBER:   AP-001

        APPLIANCE CITY
        210 SKY LANE
        OXNARD,                    CA 95677-

        PHONE:       (415)555-4772

        DISCOUNT:    15

        TAXABLE:     YES

        LAST TRANSACTION DATE:   07/25/88
```

13-46 Printout of the customer directory.

When you're done with this form, you can name it CUSTDIR. The first page of the printed directory is shown in Fig. 13-46.

This completes our work with simple form reports. You still must learn how to create column and form reports from more than one database, and you need to learn how to create complex reports such as an invoice. Before you see how to create these important reports, you should learn how to create simple labels using the customer file. You will see that labels are created using another work surface called the Labels work surface.

Labels

Labels can take many forms, from the standard mailing labels that are sent out to customers, to labels that might be stuck on an item containing the price and description. Labels are created by using the Labels work surface in the Control Center. This work surface is similar to other work surfaces, except that it is a very small work surface. In fact, it looks just like a label.

The difference between reports and labels

Theoretically, anything you can put into a label can be put into a report. Why then, if you have a report work surface, do you need labels too? The answer is easy. Labels can have multiple occurrences across and down the page. A record could fill one label in the top left corner of a sheet of labels, then the second record would fill a label in the top middle of the label sheet, and the third record would fill the label in the top right of the label sheet. The report form isn't really set up to print that way.

Computer labels come in standard sheets of rows and columns. The total number of labels on each sheet varies according to label size and the layout of the labels on the sheet. The number of columns across a sheet of labels is called *the number of labels*. What kind of labels should you choose? First of all, they need to be big enough. After that, it will depend on how you are going to use them. If you will be printing hundreds of labels at a time, you will be happier with three or four across. Most printers can print multi-column labels faster than single-column labels, because it takes time to advance the printer for each new line. On the other hand, if you are going to print only a handful of labels, you might be happier with single-column labels.

To create and print labels, you would first go to the Labels work surface and create the label form. Once this is created, you can print the labels any way you want. Once you have created a label form, you can make changes to it at any time. You can also determine at print time how many labels across the page to print, along with different spacing to accommodate virtually any type of label sheets.

The Label form

Printed labels have long been a favorite of time-conscious business people. Although there are many uses for printed labels, the most common is the old-fashioned mailing label. Let's use the CUSTOMER database which contains the COMPANY, STREET, CITY, STATE, and ZIP fields to create our labels.

We'll use these fields to create a simple set of labels. Start by going to the Control Center and making the CUSTOMER file active by choosing it and pressing Return to bring it "above the line." Once the CUSTOMER file is active, you can move the cursor to the ⟨create⟩ line of the Labels panel, and press Return. The Label work surface appears as shown in Fig. 13-47.

The label form looks very similar to other work surfaces you have already seen. The menu on top contains many of the same options you have already

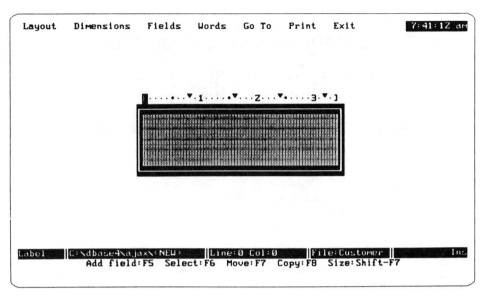

13-47 The Labels work surface.

used. Later, you will see some of the differences. Once the label form appears on the work surface, it is time to choose the size of your labels.

Defining the dimensions

To set the dimensions of a label, you would use the Dimensions menu, as shown in Fig. 13-48. Let's look at the bottom half of the menu first. You can set many of the label's size dimensions yourself, or use one of the many predefined sizes that come set up with dBASE IV. As you can see, in Fig. 13-48, these options include:

- Width of Label—Number of characters across the label
- Height of Label—Number of lines in each label
- Indentation—Size of left margin in characters
- Lines between labels—Lines between labels up and down
- Spaces between label columns—Characters between labels across
- Columns of labels—Number of labels across the sheet

These selections give you the ability to create labels of almost any size or dimension. Sometimes, however, you may not want to take the time to measure your label sheet. You can also use the predefined sizes submenu which opens when you press Enter on the Predefined size option.

Our design, in chapter 4, calls for two labels across the page. Therefore, we have chosen the option $^{15}/_{16} \times 3\frac{1}{2} \times 2$. This is a standard predefined size which makes the label 35 characters across and 5 rows up and down. When

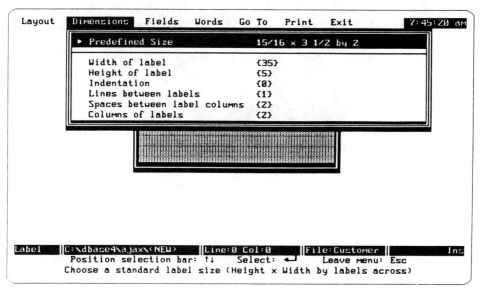

```
Layout   Dimensions  Fields   Words   Go To   Print   Exit        7:45:20 am
      ┌─────────────────────────────────────────────────────┐
      │ ▶ Predefined Size              15/16 × 3 1/2 by 2     │
      │  ┌───────────────────────────────────────────────┐   │
      │  │ Width of label              {35}              │   │
      │  │ Height of label             {5}               │   │
      │  │ Indentation                 {0}               │   │
      │  │ Lines between labels        {1}               │   │
      │  │ Spaces between label columns {2}              │   │
      │  │ Columns of labels           {2}               │   │
      │  └───────────────────────────────────────────────┘   │
      └─────────────────────────────────────────────────────┘

Label   │C:\dbase4\ajax\<NEW>  ││Line:0 Col:0 ││File:Customer ││        Ins
         Position selection bar: ↑↓    Select: ◄┘    Leave menu: Esc
       Choose a standard label size (Height x Width by labels across)
```

13-48 The Dimensions menu.

you choose this, the label in the center of the form will resize itself to your exact specifications. If you change the Width of Label to 50, it will get wider. If you change the Height of Label to 3, it will get smaller.

The default size is the second one in the list above. To select another from this list, press Return to open the submenu. Use the Up or Down arrow key to highlight the choice that is closest to your labels. When you choose a predefined size, the other menu options, such as Width of label, are automatically assigned values to match the particular selection. If you need to, you can change the default height and width even after selecting one of the values in the list. That is just a starting point.

All the options assume that your printer is set to print 10 characters per inch and 6 lines per inch. Computer printers can print at just about any print density. The three most common are 10, 12, and 17 characters per inch (pica, elite, and compressed). If your printer is set to other than 10 characters per inch (cpi) and 6 lines per inch, you will need to make appropriate adjustments in the options settings. The option settings below will need to be changed only if your printer is set to a nonstandard configuration or if you are not using one of the dBASE standard label sizes.

Adding fields

Fields are added to the label form by pressing the F5 (Add) key. You can also select Add Field from the Fields menu. Once you press the F5 key, the Fields menu appears over the label form, as shown in Fig. 13-49.

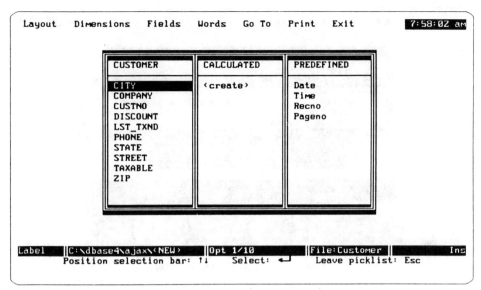

```
┌─────────────────┬──────────────────┬──────────────────┐
│ CUSTOMER        │ CALCULATED       │ PREDEFINED       │
├─────────────────┼──────────────────┼──────────────────┤
│ CITY            │ <create>         │ Date             │
│ COMPANY         │                  │ Time             │
│ CUSTNO          │                  │ Recno            │
│ DISCOUNT        │                  │ Pageno           │
│ LST_TXND        │                  │                  │
│ PHONE           │                  │                  │
│ STATE           │                  │                  │
│ STREET          │                  │                  │
│ TAXABLE         │                  │                  │
│ ZIP             │                  │                  │
└─────────────────┴──────────────────┴──────────────────┘
```

Label   C:\dbase4\ajax\<NEW>   Opt 1/10   File:Customer   Ins
              Position selection bar: ↑↓   Select: ↵   Leave picklist: Esc

13-49   The fields box.

This menu box lets you place fields in the label form. The box has three columns called CUSTOMER, CALCULATED, and PREDEFINED. The first column shows you the name of your database or view. Because we are using a single database named CUSTOMER, that is the title of the column. All of the fields in the database are shown in alphabetical order. We can place any of them on the work surface by merely selecting one and pressing Return. Now let's create a mailing address label that simply has the three lines:

COMPANY
STREET
CITY, STATE, ZIP

Place the COMPANY and STREET fields on the first two lines of the label. Once the fields are placed on the label, they can be moved around freely if they need to be by using the F7 (Move) key. Choose COMPANY first and press Return. A series of Xs will appear in the label form to show the placement of the field when the label is printed. Creating the CITY, STATE, and ZIP line is a little trickier. This will be created as one line, not three separate fields. We use a method known as *concatenation*, because we place one character field next to another. Figure 13-50 shows this new field being created from the other three fields. The field box is shown in zoom mode at the bottom of the screen. Remember, whenever you need more room, just press the F9 key to "zoom" the entry area. You can unzoom the entry area by again pressing F9.

The new field is the concatenation of the fields CITY, a comma, STATE, a space, and the ZIP field. You could also have created these fields on the label

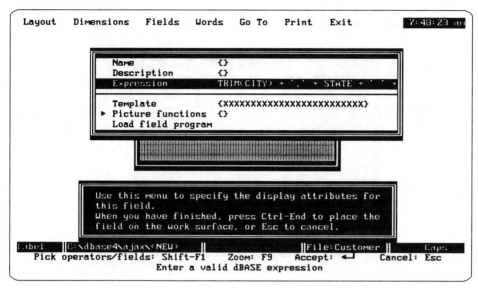

13-50 Entering a field.

separately, but it wouldn't have been as much fun. No, actually it's a good idea to learn about the TRIM function now. Because of the T picture function, the TRIM function in the beginning of the expression wasn't necessary. But, when you program, you will need to understand this function. The field CITY is a 10-character field. What happens normally if the actual city name is only five characters? There will be five blanks before anything else prints. The TRIM function (like the T picture function) removes any extra spaces at the end of a field. Once you enter this, the final screen will look like Fig. 13-51.

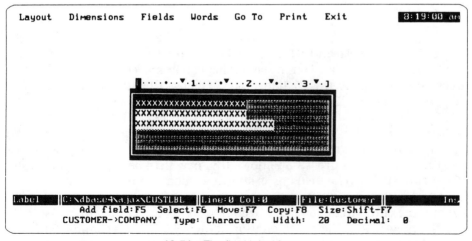

13-51 The final label form.

The three blocks of Xs correspond to the three fields. In the figure, you can see the first group selected. You can also see, at the bottom of the screen, that the field information is showing, telling you the field name, type, width, and number of decimals. As you move the cursor to each field, the display changes, showing you the different field names.

Once the fields are in the label form, you can add text to the label form or move the fields around by using the F6 (Select) and F7 (Move) keys. You can also add and delete lines by using options found in the Words menu. The label can be as large as you set up the dimensions to be. You can save this label form as CUSTLBL.

Printing the labels

Once the label is defined, you might want to print it. The Print menu is shown in Fig. 13-52. The print options are very similar to the options you will see in the next chapter. The main difference is in the third option, Generate sample labels. This option generates several sample labels from your database. This allows you to align your paper before the final print. Once you select this option, you can continue to generate sample labels until you are satisfied, and then print the actual labels.

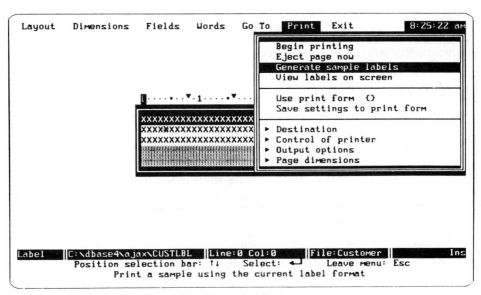

13-52 The Label Print menu.

Whatever data is defined or selected will print on the labels. You can select the data using the QBE screen or using another form of the LABEL command from the dot prompt. The LABEL FORM command can also be used to print selected labels using the FOR command. Suppose that you want to print labels for CUSTOMERs in California. You might enter:

. LABEL FORM CUSTLBL FOR STATE='CA' TO PRINT

The output from this command would be labels for only those customers having CA as the value of STATE.

In this chapter, we have examined the commands that you can use to prepare labels and the work surface itself. You can use these commands to prepare labels for a variety of uses. You are not restricted to preparing mailing labels. Use labels for inventory shelves, file folders, book plates—anywhere that you might otherwise use a gummed label. A final print of the first sheet of all your labels is displayed in Fig. 13-4.

Reports from more than one database

Creating reports with multiple databases is no different than creating reports with a single database. This is because when multiple databases are linked together in the query screen, they appear as one database to the report writer. The only real complexity occurs when there are multiple occurrences of the detail data for the same key. In the next section of this chapter, you will see how to handle multiple databases in the report writer.

Creating the view for the final reports

Before we move on to the next section, let's make sure we have a view that contains the linked databases. In the QBE chapter, you should have created a view called INVOICES. This consisted of placing the INVOICE, ITEMS, CUSTOMER, and INVENTRY databases in the query and placing all of the fields in the view skeleton. It also required linking the INVOICE file to both the ITEMS and CUSTOMER file, while the ITEMS file is linked to the INVENTRY file.

If you need to recreate this view, you can start with INVOICES and place the other databases in the query. You can select all of the fields from all the databases for the view file (except the duplicates of the linking keys for INVNO, CUSTNO, and ITEMNO). Remember, you can select all of the fields from a database by pressing F5 in the pot handle of the database. You can call this new view INVOICES when you save it. This links the databases together and gives you access to all information in the files.

An example of the query screen is shown in Fig. 13-53. Remember, that the INVENTRY file is out of sight. The ITEMNO field is where the other LINK3 is found.

Complex forms: the invoice

The first complex report that you will see is the invoice. This is one of the most complex and common reports that you will face. An invoice combines all of the features of a form report with all of the complexity of a column report.

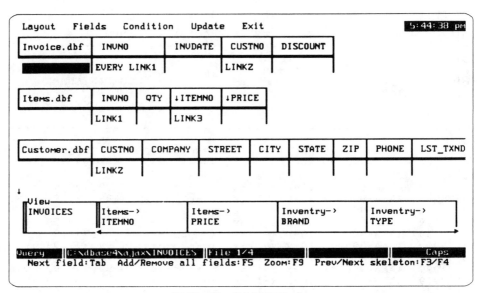

```
  Layout   Fields   Condition   Update   Exit                    5:44:38 pm
 ┌─────────────┬────────┬──────────┬────────┬──────────┐
 │ Invoice.dbf │ INVNO  │ INVDATE  │ CUSTNO │ DISCOUNT │
 ├─────────────┼────────┼──────────┼────────┼──────────┤
 │ ███████████ │ EVERY LINK1 │      │ LINK2  │          │
 └─────────────┴────────────┴───────┴────────┴──────────┘

 ┌───────────┬───────┬─────┬──────────┬─────────┐
 │ Items.dbf │ INVNO │ QTY │ ↓ITEMNO  │ ↓PRICE  │
 ├───────────┼───────┼─────┼──────────┼─────────┤
 │           │ LINK1 │     │ LINK3    │         │
 └───────────┴───────┴─────┴──────────┴─────────┘

 ┌──────────────┬────────┬─────────┬────────┬──────┬───────┬─────┬───────┬──────────┐
 │ Customer.dbf │ CUSTNO │ COMPANY │ STREET │ CITY │ STATE │ ZIP │ PHONE │ LST_TXND │
 ├──────────────┼────────┼─────────┼────────┼──────┼───────┼─────┼───────┼──────────┤
 │              │ LINK2  │         │        │      │       │     │       │          │
 └──────────────┴────────┴─────────┴────────┴──────┴───────┴─────┴───────┴──────────┘
 ↓
 ┌View──────────────────────────────────────────────────────────────────────────────┐
 │ INVOICES    │ Items─›  │ Items─›  │ Inventry─›  │ Inventry─›  │
 │             │ ITEMNO   │ PRICE    │ BRAND       │ TYPE        │
 └───────────────────────────────────────────────────────────────────────────────────┘
 Query    C:\dbase4\ajax\INVOICES  File 1/4                              Caps
   Next field:Tab  Add/Remove all fields:F5  Zoom:F9  Prev/Next skeleton:F3/F4
```

13-53 The INVOICES view.

Examining the invoice design   In chapter 4, you designed what the invoice would look like. This invoice design is again shown here in Fig. 13-54. As you can see, in this design, the invoice has three distinct parts. The first part is the identification area that will be in the page header area. This includes the report title, invoice number and date information, customer information, and column headers for the items. This area uses data from two different databases, INVOICE and CUSTOMER. This is a traditional form report.

The middle of the invoice is the detail section containing a column-type report which displays the quantity, item number, description, and price along with the extension of quantity times price.

The bottom part of the report is the summary band. This band contains the summary of the extensions and then the calculations of discount and tax, along with the intermediate calculation of taxable amount, and finally total amount.

Creating a complex form   Creating a complex form usually starts without a Quick Layout, because there are simply too many fields to rearrange. Because most of the fields don't have the field names alongside them and those that do are reentered anyway, it makes more sense to enter each field individually. Figure 13-55 shows the Add field option of the Fields menu.

As you can see, many fields are in the INVOICES section. In fact, there are more fields than will fit in the box. You have to scroll down to see more of the options. Begin by placing on the screen those items you want, and then moving them into the desired positions. Because you have already learned how to place and move fields, and also to create lines and boxes, we can skip right to the completed first part of the design shown in Fig. 13-56.

```
o                                                                      o
o              AJAX APPLIANCE COMPANY - INVOICE                        o
o              -------------------------------                         o
o                                                                      o
o    INVOICE NUMBER: nnnn-nnn              CUSTOMER NUMBER: aa-99       o
o                                          COMPANY NAME                o
o    INVOICE DATE: mm/dd/yy                STREET                      o
o                                          CITY, ST ZIP CODE           o
o                                                                      o
o  -----------------------------------------------------------------   o
o                                                                      o
o   QTY    ITEM #   BRAND   TYPE   DESCRIPTION     PRICE     EXTENSION  o
o   ---    ------   -----   ----   -----------     -----     --------   o
o                                                                      o
o   999  AAAA-999  x-10-x  x-12-x  x---25---x   99,999.99  999,999.99  o
o   999  AAAA-999  x-10-x  x-12-x  x---25---x   99,999.99  999,999.99  o
o   999  AAAA-999  x-10-x  x-12-x  x---25---x   99,999.99  999,999.99  o
o   999  AAAA-999  x-10-x  x-12-x  x---25---x   99,999.99  999,999.99  o
o   999  AAAA-999  x-10-x  x-12-x  x---25---x   99,999.99  999,999.99  o
o   999  AAAA-999  x-10-x  x-12-x  x---25---x   99,999.99  999,999.99  o
o   999  AAAA-999  x-10-x  x-12-x  x---25---x   99,999.99  999,999.99  o
o   999  AAAA-999  x-10-x  x-12-x  x---25---x   99,999.99  999,999.99  o
o   999  AAAA-999  x-10-x  x-12-x  x---25---x   99,999.99  999,999.99  o
o   999  AAAA-999  x-10-x  x-12-x  x---25---x   99,999.99  999,999.99  o
o   999  AAAA-999  x-10-x  x-12-x  x---25---x   99,999.99  999,999.99  o
o   999  AAAA-999  x-10-x  x-12-x  x---25---x   99,999.99  999,999.99  o
o   999  AAAA-999  x-10-x  x-12-x  x---25---x   99,999.99  999,999.99  o
o   999  AAAA-999  x-10-x  x-12-x  x---25---x   99,999.99  999,999.99  o
o   999  AAAA-999  x-10-x  x-12-x  x---25---x   99,999.99  999,999.99  o
o   999  AAAA-999  x-10-x  x-12-x  x---25---x   99,999.99  999,999.99  o
o   999  AAAA-999  x-10-x  x-12-x  x---25---x   99,999.99  999,999.99  o
o                                                           ----------  o
o                                          Sub Total      999,999.99   o
o                                                                      o
o                                          Discount 99%    99,999.99   o
o                                                          ----------  o
o                                          Taxable Amount  99,999.99   o
o                                                                      o
o                                          Tax 99.9%       99,999.99   o
o                                                          ----------  o
o                                          Total Amount   999,999.99   o
o                                                         ==========   o
o                                                                      o
```

13-54 The INVOICE report design.

The first thing you might notice is that there is no title. Ajax Appliance decided that they will print on an invoice form, and therefore, don't need a title. You might also notice that the page number and date are in the page header band, while the invoice information is in the Group 1 Intro band. Why is this? What group is in the report?

Well, the answer is the group in the INVNO field. This is because the report consists of more than one invoice, and an invoice can span multiple pages. Therefore, the only band left for each invoice's header and footer is the group band. For each new invoice, a new group intro is produced. This intro will print the invoice number and date along with the customer information. After this is printed, a line is drawn across the screen followed by the column

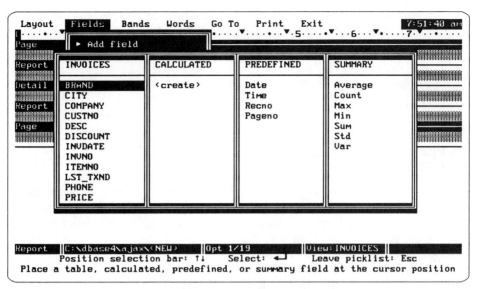

Page   ► Add field

Report   ┌─ INVOICES ──┬─ CALCULATED ─┬─ PREDEFINED ─┬─ SUMMARY ──┐
Detail   │ BRAND   │ <create>   │ Date   │ Average   │
          │ CITY   │   │ Time   │ Count   │
Report   │ COMPANY   │   │ Recno   │ Max   │
          │ CUSTNO   │   │ Pageno   │ Min   │
Page   │ DESC   │   │   │ Sum   │
          │ DISCOUNT   │   │   │ Std   │
          │ INVDATE   │   │   │ Var   │
          │ INVNO   │   │   │   │
          │ ITEMNO   │   │   │   │
          │ LST_TXND   │   │   │   │
          │ PHONE   │   │   │   │
          │ PRICE   │   │   │   │
          └─────────────┴──────────────┴──────────────┴────────────┘

Report ║C:\dbase4\ajax\<NEW>   ║Opt 1/19   ║View: INVOICES ║
         Position selection bar: ↑↓   Select: ↵   Leave picklist: Esc
   Place a table, calculated, predefined, or summary field at the cursor position

13-55 Add Field option of the Fields menu.

headers. Because this will happen once for each new invoice, invoices with many items can print correctly.

No calculations are in the top part of the form, only text and fields from the view. All of the relations needed to retrieve the customer information are handled by the view. The city, state, and zip code is a concatenated field created the same way as the field you saw in the label section.

```
Layout  Fields  Bands  Words  Go To  Print  Exit          3:09:19 pm
[....•...▼.1....•▼...2...▼....3.▼..•....▼.....•....▼.5....•▼...6...▼....7.▼..•....
Page       Header  Band
Page No. #999
MM/DD/YY
Report     Intro   Band
Group 1    Intro   Band

Invoice Number: XXXXXXXX              Customer Number: XXXXXX
Invoice Date: MM/DD/YY                         Company: XXXXXXXXXXXXXXXXXXXX
                                                        XXXXXXXXXXXXXXXXXXXX
                                                        XXXXXXXXXXXXXXXXXXXX
                                                        XX, #XXXXXXXXXX

QTY   ITEM #    BRAND       TYPE          DESCRIPTION        PRICE
---   -----     -----       ----          -----------        -----

Detail         Band
Report  ║C:\dbase4\ajax\INVOICE ║Line:0 Col:0    ║View: INVOICES ║
          Add field:F5  Select:F6  Move:F7  Copy:F8  Size:Shift-F7
```

13-56 The top part of the invoice.

Once the Group 1 Intro is created with the invoice information, it is time to create the detail information as shown in Fig. 13-58. This consists of a single line with the following fields:

QTY
ITEMNO
BRAND
TYPE
DESC
PRICE
EXTENSION

The final field extension is simply a calculation of QTY*PRICE. Remember, calculated fields are created by simply choosing the ⟨create⟩ option from the fields box. Remember to name the field when you complete the expression, so you can use it later for summaries. These fields are placed on the work surface in the detail band, one field at a time.

Finally, the lower half of the invoice is shown in Fig. 13-57. You might notice that in Fig. 13-56, the far right side of the invoice was out of sight. In Fig. 13-57, the left side of the invoice is out of sight. In this report, you will have to do a lot of scrolling to create the invoice.

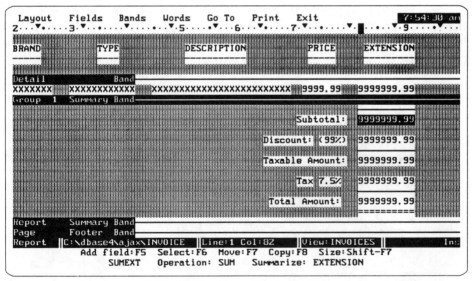

13-57 The bottom part of the invoice.

The bottom of the invoice is created in the Group 1 Summary band. For the same reason the page header could not be used, the page footer could not be used. If an invoice spans multiple pages, then you wouldn't want a set of totals at the bottom of each page.

There are five fields all created in the Group 1 Summary band. These include one summary field and four calculated fields. The first field is the summary field. This is a summary field called SUMEXT that sums the EXTENSION field from the detail band and resets the total every INVNO. The summary field here is created using the SUMMARY panel of the field box in the same way you saw earlier in this chapter when you created the inventory valuation report. The other four fields are calculated fields and include:

Calculated Field Name	Calculation Expression
DISCDOL	SUMEXT*(DISCOUNT/100)
TAXAMT	SUMEXT-DISCDOL
TAX	TAXAMT*.075
TOTAMT	TAXAMT+TAX

The DISCDOL field calculation box is shown in Fig. 13-58. You must complete this box for each calculated field on the report.

You should name each field when you create it and enter the expression. If you don't name the field, you can't use it in a later calculation. Figure 13-58 shows the DISCDOL field calculation in the field box.

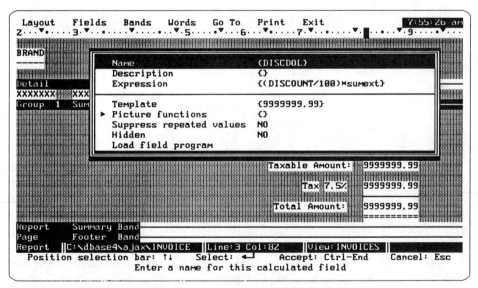

13-58 Calculations of the DISCDOL field.

Notice that the discount is displayed as part of the text label. This is accomplished by simply displaying the DISCOUNT field on the report. The tax rate was created at a fixed 7.5% rate for simplicity. In reality, you would probably have a state tax table as another relation from the customer file.

Finally, some underlines throughout the work surface were created with the line options, while some are simply dashes. The final invoice printout is shown in Fig. 13-59.

```
Page No.   1
11/22/88

   Invoice Number:   8808-001              Customer Number: JA-001
      Invoice Date:   08/01/88                    Company: JACKEL & HYDES
                                                            357 BAT COURT
                                                            LAWRENCEVILLE
                                                            PA, 14434-

 ----------------------------------------------------------------------------

 QTY    ITEM #      BRAND       TYPE        DESCRIPTION        PRICE    EXTENSION
 ---    ------      -----       ----        -----------        -----    ---------

   2   WHRE-001   WHOLEPOOL   REFRIGERATOR                     469.99      939.98
   7   HIRA-001   HITECH      RANGE                            689.99     4829.93
   3   FRRE-003   FROSTY      REFRIGERATOR  2 DOOR UPRIGHT    1199.99     3599.97
  10   FRRE-001   FROSTY      REFRIGERATOR  1 DOOR TOP FREEZER W/ICE 699.99 6999.90
                                                                        ----------
                                                           Subtotal:   16369.78

                                                    Discount: (25%)     4092.45
                                                                        ----------
                                                    Taxable Amount:    12277.34

                                                         Tax 7.5%        920.80
                                                                        ----------
                                                       Total Amount:   13198.14
                                                                        ==========
```

13-59   The invoice printout.

A mail-merge report: the warranty agreement

A mail-merge report contains a lot of text. This could be thought of as a form letter where some information is filled in throughout the letter. There is no difference from a standard form report except that it uses a special type of band called the "word-wrap" band. This band allows the text to be adjusted when fields of different lengths are inserted. It is very similar to the way a word processor works. When you type past the end of a line, the next line begins. If you add some new text in the middle of a line, all of the text shifts accordingly.

Let's produce a mail-merge document to serve as a warranty agreement for our customers, for each item they purchase. Figure 13-60 shows the warranty agreement we want to send out for each of the items on the invoice. We will need information from all of the files. We can use the INVOICES query file again to create our warranty agreement.

```
┌─────────────────────────────────────────────────────────┐
│o                                                        o│
│o              AJAX APPLIANCE COMPANY                     o│
│o               WARRANTY AGREEMENT                        o│
│o               --------------------                      o│
│o                                                         o│
│o  WARRANTY AGREEMENT NUMBER: 9999-999-99                 o│
│o                                                         o│
│o  WARRANTY AGREEMENT DATE:   mm/dd/yy                    o│
│o ------------------------------------------------------- o│
│o                                                         o│
│o  This warranty agreement is between the Ajax Appliance  o│
│o  Company and:                                           o│
│o                                                         o│
│o        COMPANY NAME                                     o│
│o        STREET                                           o│
│o        CITY, ST ZIP CODE                                o│
│o                                                         o│
│o  This agreement maintains that Ajax Appliance Company   o│
│o  will warranty QTY TYPE(s) in accordance with the       o│
│o  manufacturers warranty terms. BRAND warranties this    o│
│o  product for a period of WARRANTY months.               o│
│o                                                         o│
│o  The TYPE being warrantied is a DESCRIPTION.            o│
│o                                                         o│
│o  This warranty will expire on DATE+WARRANTY. At the     o│
│o  end of that period you may purchase our standard       o│
│o  warranty for an additional year for each item for      o│
│o  only PRICE/10.                                         o│
│o                                                         o│
│o  This agreement is legal and binding in the state       o│
│o  of confusion and cannot be broken.                     o│
│o                                                         o│
│o                                                         o│
│o   Signed,                                               o│
│o                                                         o│
│o                                                         o│
│o  --------------------        ------------------------   o│
│o  Ajax Appliance Company          COMPANY NAME           o│
│o                                                         o│
└─────────────────────────────────────────────────────────┘
```

13-60 The warranty agreement design.

The mail-merge report   Let's look at some conceptual views of word wrapping. The text might be entered onto the work surface as follows. Each field name in capital letters represents a field placed within the text:

This agreement maintains that Ajax Appliance Company will warranty QTY TYPE(s) in accordance with the manufacturer's warranty terms. BRAND warranties this product for a period of WARRANTY months.

When the report is produced, however, it might print out like this:

This agreement maintains that Ajax Appliance Company will warranty 100 REFRIGERATORS in accordance with the manufacturer's warranty terms. WHOLEPOOL warranties this product for a period of 24 months.

As you can see in the second example, some text was forced to different lines than the original form template, because of the length of the data. This is what word wrap is supposed to do, and is also the underlying concept behind mail merging.

Each field you enter on the work surface should also have the horizontal stretch picture function turned on, so that any field you place on the work surface will correctly flow around any text. Sometimes the display width you place on the work surface for a field is not sufficient to hold all its characters. This is especially true when calculated fields are used that can vary widely in size or when numeric fields are styled with commas and dollar signs.

Mail merging works because you type in text onto the work surface. Data fields are intermingled with the text. When the report is produced, each record will have a separate page in the data file. The value for each field for a given record is placed where the field was placed in the text.

When you enter a field in the reports work surface, the field size and type is shown by the template—Xs for character fields, 9s for numeric fields, L for logic fields, and MM/DD/YY for date fields. Because the mail-merge layout is really a report, it works the same way.

Creating the warranty agreement You can again start from the Control Center. Choose the INVOICES view in the queries panel, and press Return to make this view active. Next, create a new report. As always, the Layout menu opens automatically, because dBASE assumes that you will start with Quick Layout. Press Return to open the Quick Layout option. Now, choose the Mail-merge layout and press Return.

All you get is a relatively empty work surface, as you can see in Fig. 13-61. There are no fields placed on the work surface and no column headers. Why should there be? You have asked for a mail-merge report. Because dBASE has no information about which fields you might want to use and what your document will say, it cannot place anything on the work surface for you. dBASE has, however, done some very important things for you.

dBASE has closed all of the bands except the detail band. Because all of the work in a mail-merge document occurs in the detail band, this is a good idea. Next, the options Word Wrap and Begin band on new page have been turned on in the Bands menu. Because we are creating a mail-merge document, we will want our text to wrap around the data fields. This is probably the most important part of mail merging.

Let's create our warranty agreement. You can begin by entering the text as you want it placed on the letter. Figures 13-62 and 13-63 show you the two halves of the WARRANTY report.

The top part of the warranty agreement contains some title lines and the warranty agreement number and date. These are in the page header band. There is no real reason to do this, other than it places text in a band that doesn't need to have word wrap. On the other hand, the warranty agreement number or date obviously will never exceed the right margin of the page, and therefore won't wrap, so there is no reason why everything wasn't done in the

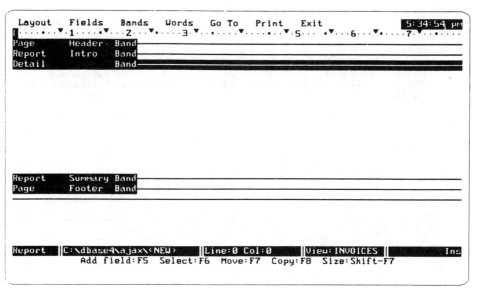

13-61 The mail-merge Quick Layout.

Detail band, other than to show you that you are not limited to this band in the mail-merge report.

Adding your text and fields is the same in the word-wrap band as in the non-word-wrap bands. Just type in your text, and when you come to a field you want to add, press F5. Press F5 to view the list of database, calculated,

13-62 The warranty report—part 1.

```
█ · · · · · ·▼·1· · · ·▼· · · ·2· · ·▼· · · · ·3·▼· · ·· · · · ·▼· · · · ·· ·▼·5· · · · ·▼· · ·6· · ·▼· · · ·· ·▼· ·7·▼· ·· · · · ·

   The XXXXXXXXXXXX being warrantied is a XXXXXXXXXXXXXXXXXXXXXXXXX.

   This warranty will expire on MM/DD/YY. At the end of that period you may
   purchase our standard warranty for an additional year for each item for only
   9999999.99.

   This agreement is legal and binding in the state of confusion and cannot be
   broken.

    Signed,



   ---------------------------------        ---------------------------------
       Ajax Appliance Company                 XXXXXXXXXXXXXXXXXXXX
```

```
Report    Summary Band
Page      Footer  Band
```

```
Report   ║C:\dbase4\ajax\WARRANTY ║Line:26 Col:0    ║View:INVOICES ║
              Add field:F5   Select:F6   Move:F7   Copy:F8   Size:Shift-F7
```

13-63 The warranty report—part 2.

predefined, and summary field names. You can also press Alt–F to open the Fields menu and choose Add Field. Either way, you will choose the new field to be entered and decide if you want to change the field's template or picture display. Placing fields in the mail-merge layout is no different than in the column or report layout.

There are sixteen different fields to add in this layout. The first field is the warranty agreement number. This is actually made up of two fields. The invoice number makes up the first part of the warranty agreement. Because there is a separate page (and warranty agreement) for each line item on the invoice, you can use the Predefined field Pageno, as the item counter. A dash separates the two fields.

The warranty agreement date is also the same as the invoice date, and that field is used for the warranty date. Five fields from the customer file make up the company name and address information.

The first paragraph in the warranty agreement after the customer information contains four fields. The QTY field comes from the ITEMS database; the rest of the fields come from the INVENTRY database. The next sentence also contains two fields from the INVENTRY database.

The next paragraph contains two calculated fields. The date that the warranty expires can be loosely calculated as the invoice date plus the number of warranty months times 30 (days per month). This gives a date that is only a few days from exactly the number of months in the warranty. You could create a more complicated calculation, but we will save that for a later book. The cost of the additional warranty is the price per item divided by 10, or one tenth the cost of the item.

The rest of the document is strictly text. The printed warranty agreement is shown in Fig. 13-64.

```
                         AJAX APPLIANCE COMPANY
                          WARRANTY AGREEMENT

WARRANTY AGREEMENT NUMBER: 8808-001-03

WARRANTY AGREEMENT DATE:   08/01/88
------------------------------------------------------------------------
This warranty agreement is between the Ajax Appliance Company and:

        JACKEL & HYDES
        357 BAT COURT
        LAWRENCEVILLE, PA 14434-

This agreement maintains that Ajax Appliance Company will warranty 3
REFRIGERATOR(s) in accordance with the manufacturers warranty terms.
FROSTY warranties this product for a period of 60 months.

The REFRIGERATOR being warrantied is a 2 DOOR UPRIGHT.

This warranty will expire on 10/27/93. At the end of that period you may
purchase our standard warranty for an additional year for each item for only
120.00.

This agreement is legal and binding in the state of confusion and cannot be
broken.

  Signed,


--------------------------------       ---------------------------------
    Ajax Appliance Company                    JACKEL & HYDES
```

13-64 The printed warranty agreement.

Both labels and mail-merge documents can help you communicate to your customers, suppliers, and co-workers. Combined with reports and the QBE screen, you should now be able to use your data efficiently and productively.

Complex column reports: the monthly sales report

The final report to complete is the sales report. In some respects, this report is the hardest to create, and on the other hand, it is very simple. However, a few "tricks" are involved. First, let's look at the design as shown in Fig. 13-65.

Designing a "roll-up" report The sales report contains two different group totals and a grand total. The two different groups are COMPANY and INVNO. There are subtotals for each customer, and you are "rolling" up the items into each invoice. Rolling up means to summarize without seeing the detail. In fact, the trick to this report, or any roll up, is to not print out the detail records. But, how do you do that when you need the detail records to perform the summary calculations?

The answer is to simply *close the detail band.* By closing the detail band, you stop the data from printing in the detail band. This appears to provide a roll up.

```
o                    MONTHLY SALES REPORT - MONTH ENDING                    o
o                                                                           o
o   _____       o
o                                                                           o
o      COMPANY       INVOICE     INVOICE      INVOICE                NET     o
o       NAME         NUMBER       DATE        AMOUNTS     DISCOUNT   PROFIT  o
o   _____       o
o   x----20----x    9999-99     mm/dd/yy    $999,999.99  ($99,999.99) AMOUNT+DISC o
o   x----20----x    9999-99     mm/dd/yy    $999,999.99  ($99,999.99) AMOUNT+DISC o
o   x----20----x    9999-99     mm/dd/yy    $999,999.99  ($99,999.99) AMOUNT+DISC o
o                                           -----------  ----------- ---------- o
o    comp total                             $999,999.99  ($99,999.99) AMOUNT+DISC o
o                                                                           o
o   x----20----x    9999-99     mm/dd/yy    $999,999.99  ($99,999.99) AMOUNT+DISC o
o   x----20----x    9999-99     mm/dd/yy    $999,999.99  ($99,999.99) AMOUNT+DISC o
o   x----20----x    9999-99     mm/dd/yy    $999,999.99  ($99,999.99) AMOUNT+DISC o
o                                           -----------  ----------- ---------- o
o    comp total                             $999,999.99  ($99,999.99) AMOUNT+DISC o
o                                           -----------  ----------- ---------- o
o    grand total                            $999,999.99  ($99,999.99) AMOUNT+DISC o
o                                           ===========  =========== ========== o
o                                                                           o
```

13-65   The sales report design.

Creating the sales view with multiple key sorting   To create the sales report, you must first create a new view to hold the data. This view is shown in Fig. 13-66. Notice in the view, that the inventory file is not part of the view. The report

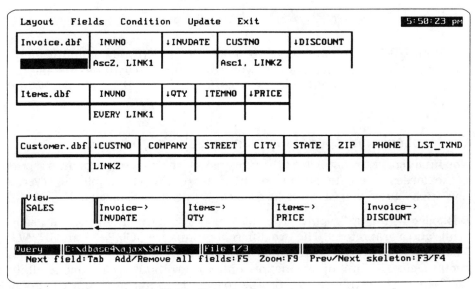

13-66   The sales report query.

only has three database fields and three calculated fields. The three database fields come from the customer file and the invoice file. There are also three calculated fields. They are:

Field	Expression
INVOICE AMOUNT	QTY*PRICE
DISCOUNT	−1*INVOICE AMOUNT*(DISCOUNT/100)
NET PROFIT	INVOICE AMOUNT+DISCOUNT

When you look at this data, you can see that the inventory file is not needed. Let's examine the calculated fields.

In the view, the data contains two sort directives. First, the data must be sorted by COMPANY. Within each company, it must be sorted by INVNO. This arranges the data in proper order to produce the report grouped by COMPANY and invoice. The EVERY keyword appears in the ITEM file to make sure that all items are selected.

The sales report   The final sales report can now be created, as shown in Fig. 13-67. The page header band is used to enter the title of the report and the column headers. The title could have another field that would be passed by a program running the report to limit the month ending date and to fill in the month ending area of the title. In this example, no area is completed.

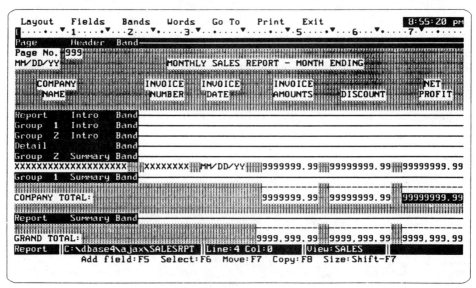

13-67   The sales report form.

Data has been entered in the detail band for the invoice amount, discount, and net profit as shown in the previous table. The detail band is then closed, and these calculations won't print. According to the design, the discount is to be a negative number. This is accomplished by multiplying the calculation by negative one and then adding the invoice amount to the discount to get net profit.

Once the detail band is completed, the two group bands can be created. Create the Group 1 band first, and make the COMPANY the field to group by. The inner group, Group 2, is the INVNO field to be used for the roll-up. As you add each new band, they become inside bands and increase the level of detail. There is no data in either group intro band. All of the data goes into the summary bands.

The Group 2 summary band (INVNO) contains all six fields. The first three fields are the identifying fields of company name, invoice number, and invoice date. The next three fields are simply summaries of the calculations in the detail band that are reset every INVNO.

The Group 1 summary band is the COMPANY band and only contains the totals by company. As you can see, some text is at the far left of the band. The three fields are summaries of the fields in the detail band and are reset every time the COMPANY changes.

Finally, the report summary band holds the same three summaries, only this time, they are reset every report making a grand total.

So, this report is very similar to the first report you saw—the inventory valuation report. By learning the tricks of closing the detail band, you can accomplish anything.

The final work to do is to change all of the summary field's picture functions to add dollar signs and to place parentheses around negative numbers. This is accomplished by selecting the picture function options $ and (for each field. When you use these picture functions, the fields all expand by one character. You might have to move the fields to realign them on the decimal points. The last totals in the report summary band also have their templates modified to add a comma if the total is over one thousand dollars. The final printed report is shown in Fig. 13-68.

```
Page No.    1
11/22/88                     MONTHLY SALES REPORT - MONTH ENDING

       COMPANY          INVOICE   INVOICE     INVOICE                      NET
        NAME            NUMBER      DATE       AMOUNTS      DISCOUNT       PROFIT

JACKEL & HYDES          8808-001  08/01/88     16369.78  (   $4092.45)  $12277.34
                                             ----------   -----------   -----------
COMPANY TOTAL:                               $16369.78  (   $4092.45)  $12277.34

RON'S REFRIGERATORS     8808-002  08/01/88     55869.14  (   $5586.91)  $50282.23
RON'S REFRIGERATORS     8808-004  08/02/88     32498.73  (   $3249.87)  $29248.86
RON'S REFRIGERATORS     8808-005  08/05/88      3499.95  (    $350.00)   $3149.96
RON'S REFRIGERATORS     8809-001  09/01/88     24089.60  (   $2408.96)  $21680.64
                                             ----------   -----------   -----------
COMPANY TOTAL:                              $115957.42  (  $11595.74) $104361.68

WASHER WAREHOUSE        8808-003  08/02/88     10939.84  (   $1640.98)   $9298.86
                                             ----------   -----------   -----------
COMPANY TOTAL:                               $10939.84  (   $1640.98)   $9298.86

WEST'S WHITE GOODS      8809-002  09/15/88     14849.75  (   $1484.98)  $13364.78
                                             ----------   -----------   -----------
COMPANY TOTAL:                               $14849.75  (   $1484.98)  $13364.78

                                             ----------   -----------   -----------
GRAND TOTAL:                                $158,116.79  ( $18,814.14)$139,302.65
```

13-68   The sales report.

Using reports in programs

Just as you can enter the work surface with the CREATE REPORT command, you can also modify the form with the MODIFY REPORT command. Make sure that your databases have been selected before using these commands. If you attempt to modify a report without the proper database active, or with a database whose structure has been altered, you won't be able to work with those fields and might not even be able to get back into the form until those fields have been recreated.

You can also run the report from the dot prompt. The command:

```
. REPORT FORM SALES
```

would send the form to the screen, while the command:

```
. REPORT FORM SALES TO PRINT
```

would send the report to the printer. You can even add filter commands right in the REPORT FORM command itself. Suppose you wanted to see all of the data for the month ending July 1989. You would enter:

```
. REPORT FORM SALES ; FOR YEAR(INVDATE)='89'
   .AND. MONTH(INVDATE)=7
```

This completes the reports section. In the next chapter, you will see how to print anything you want.

14
Printing

In dBASE IV you have a myriad of printing options available to you. Anything can be printed. Your database structure, the data in any database, results of a query, reports, labels, and even the documentation generated by any application. Some of these items have their own print menus while some you have to retrieve using the dBASE editor.

You can also print any of the program code you write or any of the code generated by dBASE IV. Because the code is in regular ASCII files, you can print it using the dBASE Editor or any text editor.

Finally, there are your queries, screen form, report, and label definitions. You can print the program files these screens generate, but you might need to produce output of the screen or report definitions themselves. You can print any screen by using the computer hardware's PrtSc (print screen) key along with the DOS graphics command. However, you can print perfect reproductions of your screens in dBASE by using one of the many screen dump programs that exist today. We used a product called HotShot Graphics to produce all of the screen dumps found in this book. This $199 package produces excellent quality dumps and has many features needed by documentation personnel and writers alike. The company that makes HotShot Graphics is called SymSoft and is in Incline Village, Nevada.

This chapter will show you how to print almost anything. It focuses on printing all of the work you have accomplished in Part Two of this book. The program commands and parameters to handle printing from within programs is covered mostly in Part Three.

Configuring dBASE IV for your printer

The dBASE IV Installation program allows you to enter a printer type, name, and printer port. In that way, you could enter several printers to be used with dBASE IV for different types of printing. When you enter your printers into this program, dBASE stores your entries and creates several lines in the CONFIG.DB file.

The CONFIG.DB file is where all of your parameters are stored that dBASE uses to begin the program. This includes which colors will be active, which printers will be used, any starting commands, set statement defaults, and other things that globally affect dBASE IV.

If you look at your CONFIG.DB file (it's a regular ASCII file that you can edit with the dBASE editor), you will probably see a PDRIVER statement and at least a PRINTER 1 statement.

Suppose that you had two printers attached to your computer, one, a Hewlett Packard Laserjet II and one an Epson FX-185. You would tell dBASE that you had each printer when you initially set up dBASE. For the HP Laserjet II, you might even tell dBASE to use it two different ways. One way would be portrait where the paper is printed normally while the other is landscape where the paper is printed sideways. To do this, you would configure dBASE with three printers. The HP in Portrait mode, HP Landscape mode, and Epson FX. You also need to tell dBASE which printer port each is hooked up to. Your choices are parallel ports LPT1, LPT2 or LPT3 or serial ports COM1, COM2, or COM3.

You also tell dBASE which printer is the default. What dBASE does is copy the files from your installation disk to the hard disk and updates your CONFIG.DB file. The following lines are what you might find in the CONFIG.DB file:

```
PDRIVER = HPLAS100.PR2
PRINTER 1 = HPLAS100.PR2 NAME "HP LJ II" DEVICE lpt1
PRINTER 2 = HPLASL.PR2 NAME "HP LJ II Landscape" DEVICE lpt1
PRINTER 3 = FX85_1.PR2 NAME "Epson FX-185" DEVICE lpt1
```

The PDRIVER command names the default printer. The PRINTER commands define each printer that will appear in the print menus. The print driver file name is first displayed. This is a file on your disk. Besides these three files are the files GENERIC.PR2 and ASCII.PR2. These drivers are used when you do not select any of these printers in the dBASE print menus or when you are printing to a file. The NAME parameter displays what you will see in your menu selections while the DEVICE parameter defines the printer port. Figure 14-1 shows the dBASE Destination Print menu open with the first choice. The names shown in the menu and in the configuration file have been shortened so they will better fit within the menu selection areas. For some reason, when Ashton-Tate supplied these names, they made them too long to fit within the entry area and when they are

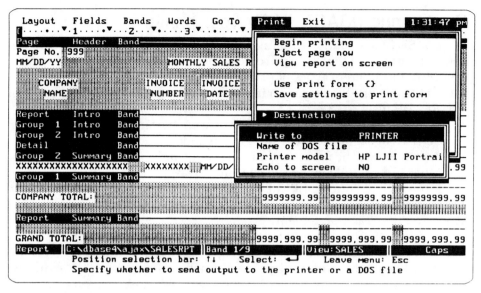

```
 Layout   Fields   Bands   Words   Go To   Print   Exit              1:31:47 pm
[······▼·1····▼···2···▼·····3·▼········▼·         ┌──────────────────────────┐
 Page      Header   Band─────────────             │ Begin printing           │
 Page No. 999                                     │ Eject page now           │
 MM/DD/YY                        MONTHLY SALES R   │ View report on screen    │
                                                  │                          │
    COMPANY               INVOICE   INVOICE        │ Use print form  {}       │
      NAME                NUMBER    DATE           │ Save settings to print form│
                                                  ├──────────────────────────┤
 Report    Intro    Band                          │ ▶ Destination            │
 Group  1  Intro    Band──────────   ┌────────────┴──────────────────────────┐
 Group  2  Intro    Band──────────   │ Write to              PRINTER         │
 Detail             Band──────────   │ Name of DOS file                      │
 Group  2  Summary  Band             │ Printer model         HP LJII Portrai │
 XXXXXXXXXXXXXXXXXXX  XXXXXXXX MM/DD/ │ Echo to screen        NO           .99│
 Group  1  Summary  Band             └───────────────────────────────────────┘
                                     ─────────────────────────────────────────
 COMPANY TOTAL:                       9999999.99  99999999.99  99999999.99
                                     
 Report    Summary  Band──────────────────────────────────────────────────────
                                     ─────────────────────────────────────────
 GRAND TOTAL:                         9999,999.99  9999,999.99  9999,999.99
 Report   C:\dbase4\ajax\SALESRPT   Band 1/9      View:SALES         Caps
          Position selection bar: ↑↓    Select: ◄┘    Leave menu: Esc
          Specify whether to send output to the printer or a DOS file
```

14-1   The dBASE print destination selections.

automatically shortened by dBASE, you can't tell the HP Laser printer modes apart.

You might find it is easier to change the CONFIG.DB file rather than to use the dBASE Install program when you want to change printers. Just remember to copy the print drivers from the installation disk as well as adding the files to your CONFIG.DB file.

Using the print menus

The Print menu is displayed from a variety of places. These include the quick report or form print menus in many of the work surfaces. Several work surfaces have their own print menus. These include:

- dBASE Editor
- Data work surface
- Reports work surface
- Labels work surface

Although the menus are essentially the same in each of these work surfaces, each menu has some slight differences as you will see. For example, the label menu has a choice to produce sample alignment labels while the editor work surface print menu lets you line number the file you are printing.

The Print menu

In order to start the printing process, you should choose the Print menu as shown pulled down in Fig. 14-2. Let's examine a standard report menu along with all of the options of its submenu.

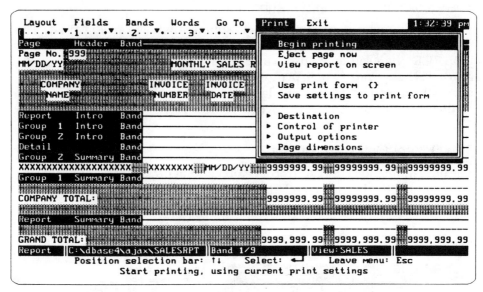

14-2 The dBASE Print menu in the Reports work surface.

This menu is the same menu that pulls down from any of the other work surfaces and also the quick report. This menu has many options and four submenus.

The Print menu in the Reports work surface is divided into three main areas. The first option at the top of the menu is the Begin printing command. This is the go signal to tell dBASE IV to start printing to wherever you told it to print using whatever print settings you told it to use. It is usually the last thing you do before starting to print. Before you print the report, you should make sure all of your other print options are selected.

The next option Eject page now sends a form feed to the printer and can be used to align the printer before starting.

The last option in the first section lets you send the output to the screen instead of the printer. If you would rather see the output on the screen, choose this option.

The next two options in the middle of the menu let you save common print settings. After you have created a set of print choices that you might use often, you can save just those settings using the Save settings to print form option. You can then give the settings a name. Later when you decide you want to activate those settings you can use the Use print form { } option to activate the settings that you previously saved.

The last four options bring up individual submenus and are used to control the printing to an even finer detail.

The Destination of Printout submenu

The first submenu is the Destination submenu shown in Fig. 14-1. This menu lets you choose between the PRINTER and a DOS FILE. If you choose a DOS FILE, then you must also name that file using the second option. You also have the option of which printer to print to. You should have selected this during your system setup. The last option lets you not only print to the printer or a file but also lets you see it on the screen.

The Control Options submenu

The next submenu is the Control of Printer submenu. This assumes that you are printing to the printer. This menu shown in Fig. 14-3 has several sections.

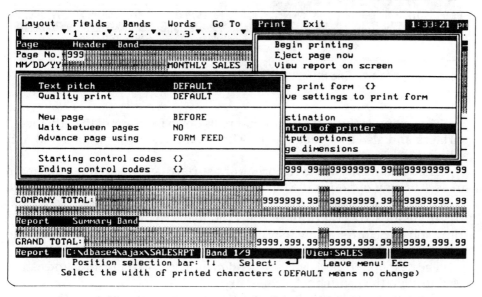

14-3 The dBASE control of printer menu.

The first option lets you choose the text pitch such as PICA, ELITE, or COMPRESSED. The second option determines if letter quality is to be turned on for your printer. The pitch is simply the style or size of the print, and the quality determines whether the text is letter quality or not. On laser printers, this can be set with either option.

In the middle section are three options. The first lets you choose from NONE, BEFORE, AFTER, or BOTH and determines when dBASE sends a page eject to the printer in relation to a page break. Normally, you want the AFTER option although the default in dBASE III PLUS was BOTH. This caused many problems because it added a page eject before it started printing. If you set the option Wait between pages to YES, then you are prompted to put a new piece of paper in the printer or confirm to continue the printing. The last option in the section lets you tell dBASE whether to send a line feed or a form feed to advance the page. Some of the older printers take advantage of this option.

The last section lets you add your own control codes to the output either before the print starts or after it is finished. This allows you to send control characters for complex control of both dot matrix and laser printers.

Control characters differ from printer to printer. For example, the code to use "compressed" print on an Epson printer would be {015}. Double strike would be {027}{071}. You can also translate the "backslash" and ASCII code combinations into their ASCII character equivalents. {027}{061}would become {ESC}G. However, on a Hewlett Packard Laser printer, the compressed font is known as "line printer" and is accessed by entering {ESC}s16.66H.

The Output Options submenu

The next submenu is the Output options submenu shown in Fig. 14-4. This lets you determine how much of the report prints. You can specify the starting and ending pages to print but it assumes you know the

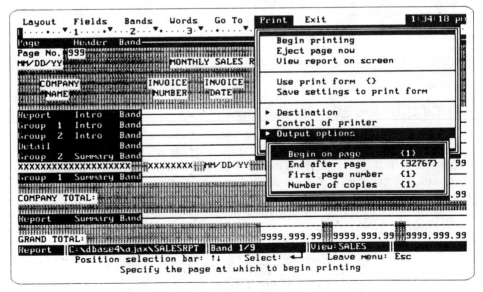

14-4 The dBASE Output Options submenu.

page numbers. You can also start the page numbering on something other than page 1. The last menu option lets you choose the number of copies.

The Page Dimensions submenu

The last submenu is the Page dimensions menu (Fig. 14-5). It has three simple choices. You can select the length of the page before sending a page break. Also you can specify the number of characters from the left to reserve for a blank margin while printing. The last option lets you select single, double, or triple spacing.

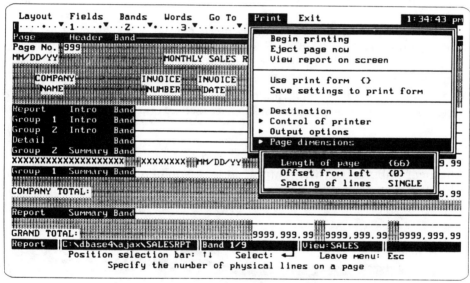

14-5 The dBASE Page Dimensions submenu.

Printing database structures

Database structures can be printed easily from the Data work surface. Figure 14-6 shows the Print menu opened on the Data work surface. It is the same Print menu that you have used in other places in dBASE IV. What it prints is the database structure of your data. You can choose the full range of print options as you have learned already in this chapter.

From the dot prompt, you can also print your database structure with the dot prompt command:

    . LIST STRUCTURE TO PRINT

A printed database structure is shown in Fig. 14-7. Notice that the printed structure also includes the number of records in the file.

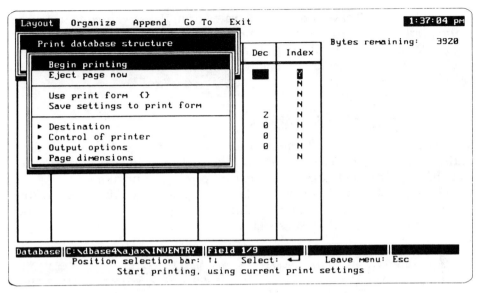

```
  Layout  Organize  Append  Go To  Exit                    1:37:04 pm

    Print database structure               Dec  │ Index     Bytes remaining:    3920
      Begin printing                                  Y
      Eject page now                                  N
                                                      N
      Use print form  {}                              N
      Save settings to print form             Z       N
                                              0       N
    ▶ Destination                             0       N
    ▶ Control of printer                      0       N
    ▶ Output options                                  N
    ▶ Page dimensions                                 N




  Database C:\dbase4\ajax\INVENTRY  Field 1/9
          Position selection bar: ↑↓   Select: ↵     Leave menu: Esc
            Start printing, using current print settings
```

14-6   The Print menu on the Data work surface.

```
Page #      1

Structure for database: C:\DBASE4\AJAX\INVENTRY.DBF
Number of data records:      15
Date of last update   : 01/23/84
Field   Field Name  Type        Width    Dec   Index
    1   ITEMNO      Character        8              Y
    2   BRAND       Character       10              N
    3   TYPE        Character       12              N
    4   DESC        Character       25              N
    5   PRICE       Numeric          7      2       N
    6   QTY_STK     Numeric          3              N
    7   QTY_ORD     Numeric          3              N
    8   WARRANTY    Numeric          2              N
    9   FEATURES    Memo            10              N
**  Total **                       81
```

14-7   The printed database structure.

Printing raw data

Raw data can be printed in several ways. If you use the quick report, you actually are printing a column report and this should not be considered raw data.

Printing raw data means printing your data in a completely unformatted form. The way to do this is again use the TO PRINT option of the LIST command. The LIST command will list your data in a "natural" fashion. The commands to list your INVENTRY file would be:

```
. USE INVENTRY
. LIST ALL TO PRINT
```

This would print all of your data in its "raw" form. If you wanted to use some of the print options, then you would have to create a report, use the quick column layout, and close the page header and report summary bands. This would just leave the detail band active and therefore that is all that would print.

Printing reports and labels

Reports and labels can be printed either from within the Reports or Labels work surfaces or by choosing the Report or Label name in the Control Center and pressing Enter. This will bring up the appropriate print menu.

You have already seen the standard report print menu earlier in this chapter. The Labels menu is a little different. Figure 14-8 shows the Label print menu on the Labels work surface.

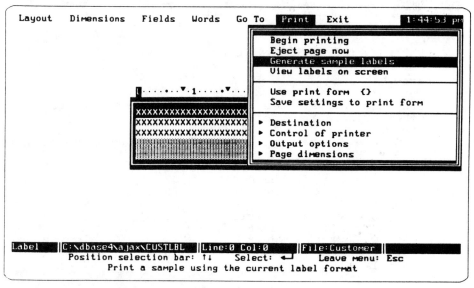

14-8   The Print menu on the Label work surface.

Notice the extra line in the Print menu. It allows you to generate sample labels. This will print a row of labels with X's taking the place of the fields. After the sample labels print, you are asked if you want another row of sample labels or if you are ready to print the real labels. When you are printing labels to an impact printer, it is necessary to be able to generate sample labels in order to properly align the labels with the printing on the page.

Printing program code generated by dBASE IV

The files that are generated by dBASE are regular ASCII text files and can be printed from dBASE or outside dBASE. When you create queries, forms, reports, labels, or applications, dBASE generates a file of program code. By knowing the name of that program code, you can retrieve it inside of dBASE using the editor and then use the print menus to print the code. You can also retrieve it using any text editor or word processor outside dBASE and print it using that program's print facilities. Figure 14-9 shows the Print menu of the dBASE editor.

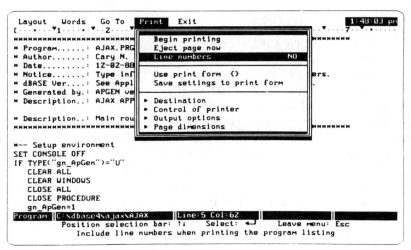

14-9   The Print menu on the Editor work surface.

Below is a table of the various work surface file names and the names of the program files they create. These program files can be printed:

Work surface & filename		Generated program name	How file is printed
Database	*.DBF	None	Print Menu in the Work
Surface			
Query	none	*.QBE	ASCII Program File
Forms	*.SCR	*.FMT	ASCII Program File
Report	*.FRM	*.FRG	ASCII Program File
Label	*.LBL	*.LBG	ASCII Program File
Application	*.APP	*.PRG	ASCII Program File
		*.DOC	ASCII Text
Documentation			

Remember, data in the .DBF files can be printed by using reports or by using the LIST or DISPLAY commands with the TO PRINT parameters.

Of course, you can always print ASCII text files with the DOS COPY command. Assume you wanted to copy a program file called INVOICE.PRG to your printer which was attached to the parallel printer port LPT1. You would enter:

```
COPY INVOICE.PRG LPT1:
```

at the DOS prompt. Remember that this will only copy the file to the printer. It does not send a form feed to the printer so you will have to eject the last page yourself.

Printing memo fields

Memo fields seem to have a mind of their own. The length of the memo field template created in a report determines the number of characters that will print across the page. The memo field template can be moved or resized in a report to determine where and to what length the memo data will print. Memo field templates always have the V picture function. This is the vertical stretch and means that if there is more data to print than the length of the template allows, then the data will continue on the next line. If you have too much data and too short a template, then the data will take up many lines, "stranding" the rest of your data on the first line. This might produce huge gaps from the start of one record to the next, even spanning many pages. You must be careful to plan your memo field data carefully so you get your desired result.

A command that affects the default width of memo field data when it prints is the command:

```
SET MEMOWIDTH TO 50
```

Fifty is the default, but you can change it to anything you want. You can also put the following parameter in your CONFIG.DB file:

```
MEMOWIDTH = 50
```

Printing list command output

Many LIST commands have output that can be directed to the printer by adding the parameter TO PRINT on the end of the command. Some of these include:

- LIST—Lists raw data (You can specify fields, scope, and filters).
- LIST FILES—Lists files like the DOS DIR command.
- LIST HISTORY—Lists all commands in the history buffer.
- LIST MEMORY—Lists all memory variables and other items defined in memory. This includes:
  - ~ Print system memory variables
  - ~ Other system memory variables
  - ~ Defined windows
  - ~ Defined popups, menus, and pads
  - ~ Remaining memory available

- LIST STATUS—Lists a group of statistics about the current environment. This includes:
  - ~ Current work area
  - ~ Database name with drive, path, and alias
  - ~ Open index filenames and tags
  - ~ Open memo filenames
  - ~ Filter formulas
  - ~ Database relations
  - ~ Format files
  - ~ File search path
  - ~ Default disk drive
  - ~ Print destination
  - ~ Loaded modules
  - ~ Currently selected work area
  - ~ Left margin setting
  - ~ Currently open procedure file
  - ~ Reprocess and refresh count
  - ~ The setting for DEVICE (Screen, print, or file)
  - ~ Currency and delimiter symbols
  - ~ Number of files open
  - ~ ON command settings
  - ~ Settings for ON/OFF SET commands
  - ~ Function key assignments

By using these LIST options and directing their output to the printer, you can get a lot of information about your environment and save it for future reference. As you begin to program in the next part, you will find printed output invaluable for solving your problems.

We will examine some of the printing programming commands in the next part. For now, these commands and the ability to use the Print menu should get you through any Control Center challenges you might encounter.

15
Application generator

The dBASE IV Application Generator is a valuable tool that can help you create applications.

Understanding applications

So far you have learned how to use many of the various work surfaces that are necessary to create, input, change, view, and report the data you need to satisfy your information requirements. You have worked with the following work surfaces:

- Data—Create new databases
- Edit and Browse—Input and view data
- Queries—Create views of your data
        Select only certain fields and records
        Create calculated fields
        Sort, summarize, and group data
        Link two or more files
- Forms—Develop complex data input screens
        Create custom edit and validation rules
- Reports—Develop custom output reports and output forms
- Labels—Produce mailing type labels

In fact, your Control Center screen should look like Fig. 15-1 right now with files listed in every panel except the Applications panel.

There is still one panel in the Control Center that we haven't used. This is the Applications panel that lets you either write custom programs or use the Application Generator to create complete applications.

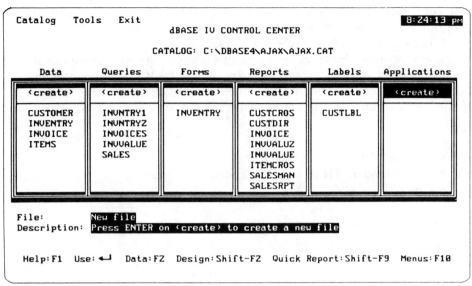

15-1 The Control Center files.

Whether you use the Applications Generator or design custom programs, you will find that the work in your work surfaces will not be lost. The databases, forms, reports, and labels you create in the various work surfaces will prove very valuable when made part of a program.

Why would you need a program

You have seen most of dBASE IV's work surfaces and can now create databases, add records, and produce reports, however, you have only begun to harness the power of a database. The true power of a database is its language to let you write *turnkey* systems better known as applications.

A turnkey system is a system that can be operated by a person totally unfamiliar with the database system but who knows the business side of the system. Let's take a typical payroll system. With what you have seen, you could create employee files, tax files, and company files. You could enter data to each file and perform simple edit checking. You could probably even create a report to print the checks.

You need a program to simplify access to each individual database and to add calculations, complex data transfers, and even more complex editing, forms, and reports that are possible in the Control Center work surfaces.

What a program is

A program is nothing more than a collection of dBASE dot prompt statements that, when correctly put together in some logical fashion, perform a repetitive task. These program statements can also act as a "taxi driver" taking you from one place in the system to another. Menus are a good example of programs. Programs are stored in files with the file extension .PRG.

Programs are made up of most of the same commands that you can enter in the dot prompt. However, some programs also use statements that are meaningless at the dot prompt. Programs are built around sequences of statements. These statements also include the *logical* constructs, a fancy name for program statements allowing control over a program. These include:

- Looping (DO WHILE... ENDDO)
- Conditions (IF THEN ELSE ... ENDIF)
- Cases (DO CASE ... ENDCASE)

You will see more about these constructs in chapter 16.

Menus

Traditionally, systems interact with humans through some sort of interface. Menus are the most common type of interface today. dBASE program commands provide tools for all of the same types of menus that are used in the dBASE IV Control Center. These include:

- Horizontal bar menus (at the top of the screens)
- Pull-down menus (that can be attached to a bar menu)
- Pop-up menus
- Pick lists (fields, files, values)

A menu is nothing more than a screen that you display from within an application program. This particular type of screen is one where you give the application user a set of choices or options for the tasks that the application can perform. The user then chooses which function to do, either by entering a number or letter that corresponds to that function, or by moving a highlight with the cursor keys and pressing the Enter key to choose the highlighted option.

Creating a menu is even easier than producing a screen format. A menu is mostly text information. Once the text is entered and placed on the screen, the only thing left is to identify an operation to be performed when an option is chosen. dBASE IV allows you to create different types of menus, including bar and pop-up menus. Using these types of menus, you can produce either menus that pop up anywhere on the screen, or you can combine a horizontal bar and pop-up menus to simulate a pull-down menu like the type in the dBASE IV Control Center.

Menus that are easy to use will enhance any interactive applications that you create. The first part of your system that users see is the main menu, and users spend most of their time moving from menu to menu in your application system. The menus also represent the hierarchy of your application system, showing how the functions of the system relate to each other.

How generators work

The idea behind a program generator is that certain standard routines can be created and used in almost every circumstance. The procedure for creating a screen format is almost the same from database to database. In fact, this is the reason that dBASE can present a "standard" screen layout when you create a database, before you have even coded a program. This same reasoning applies to reports, especially columnar reports; some application functions can also be generated.

For example, each database file should have an add, change, delete, and display function. These functions are necessary for maintenance, even if you have programs that are responsible for updating the database. If the program makes a mistake, or somehow an error is entered, these basic functions can be used to make spot corrections and adjustments.

Screen generators and report generators are dependent upon entered text and the fields in a particular database or set of databases. Once you put the text (such as headings and titles) and database fields in the places you want to see them, it is an easy matter to generate program code to create the display screen or report page. dBASE IV takes this a step farther by creating this format code in a condensed, quickly executed form.

Application generators use the same general philosophy to create dBASE code for an application function. For example, the basic format of a dBASE "add record to database" function is the same regardless of the data involved.

The generated code could be used for any given database by changing the name of the screen format used. Some editing and range checking can be programmed as a part of the screen format. Other application functions can be generated in the same manner. Most functions can be created generically—and they will work in a wide variety of situations.

The difference between programs and applications

A program in dBASE terms should be thought of as the individual dBASE statements that perform a certain function. It usually takes many programs working together to make an application. An application is what the many programs are called when placed together to form one logical task.

For example, a payroll system could be an application. The various add, change, delete, display, calculate, and print tasks could each be programs. Additionally, an overall menu system might control all of these programs which itself is also a program. Today, with dBASE IV, you no longer have to be concerned with these individual programs. It is the application itself that has become important.

In dBASE II, everything you wanted to do had to be programmed. There were few if any tools to assist you in this process. Screens, reports, menus, even data entry processes had to be programmed from the dot prompt. dBASE III introduced screen forms that let you create the form for input and output. An application generator existed, but it lacked sophistication and did not allow very customized applications.

The built-in application generators

dBASE IV includes generators to produce menus, data entry screens, reports, labels, and basic application systems. Each separate work surface generates dBASE code that can be modified, merged into custom programs, or used with the Application Generator. The functions that can be generated automatically are very sophisticated and fulfill the requirements for most application systems. Where the generator is not enough, it can be modified to varying degrees from simple additions of a few lines of code to complete changes using the original generated code as a starting point. Figure 15-2 lists these generators.

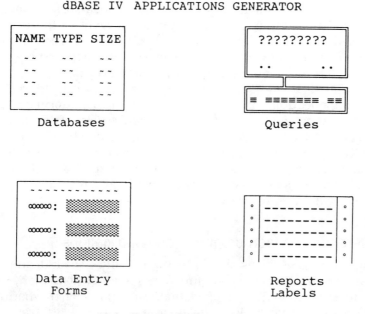

15-2 The dBASE IV generators.

As you have learned, the screen generator allows you to place database fields in any chosen position on the screen, arrange text around the fields, and place headings and borders on the screen to give your applications a professional look. Using a generator means that you do not need to know how to write the program yourself—you can place the fields, text, and borders where you want them and let dBASE do the rest.

The dBASE software will generate the code that allows the computer to display your screen exactly as you have designed it. The software also takes care of receiving input data from the screen and performing basic editing functions, such as validating the data type of the input. dBASE IV checks that numeric fields contain only numeric data and that date fields are correct. You can also specify that data in particular fields must be within a certain range of values.

The screen generator also allows advanced edit validation that you can design yourself to only allow in the system data that meets your most stringent conditions. The screen generator also displays messages when the cursor enters a data entry field and a different message when bad data is entered. You can even determine if the field should be for display only or if the user can make any additions or changes.

Producing reports from stored database fields is another process that can be easily automated. Customized report formats are handled the same as a screen format, where text and fields can be placed in any position. Columnar reports display field values along a line or several lines, with headings, footers, totals and subtotals placed as specified by the entered design. The generated report format can also be used to create new calculated fields, produce subtotals, totals, and even format fields for printing, such as placing hyphens in a Social Security Number or telephone number.

The dBASE IV Application Generator

dBASE IV can help you generate screens, menus, and reports using your database design or view created in the query screen. dBASE also includes an Application Generator that will help you to develop application programs to use for your system.

Application generators are programs that help you to create your own application programs. General procedures can be created by a program because the only change between these procedures are the database and fields that are used. Add to this the fact that you can generate screen formats to use with the database, and the creation of a generic function is simply a matter of providing the format file names and the name of the database file.

While you can generate many parts of an application system using dBASE, most likely the generated code will not meet all of your requirements. dBASE IV allows you to customize the generated code created by the Application Generator by adding routines to the generated programs. Complete customization may require that you create your own application programs, but you might still reduce development time and problems by using the dBASE IV Application Generator as a starting point.

Application generator concepts

You can program your design two ways with dBASE IV. The first is to use the Application Generator to automatically create most if not all of your program.

The second, of course, is to do it yourself by using the actual dBASE programming statements.

The idea behind the Application Generator

Use the Application Generator to reduce your coding time by generating the basic functions of a system, and do the more complex programming yourself as you get better at it. You can mix your code and the Application Generator's to create as powerful a system as you can design quickly and easily.

Several standard functions that most application generators can create include menus, add routines, change routines, delete routines, display routines, and printing routines. These are the routines needed to maintain and enter the data of any database. The basic functions are generally the same for all databases. The dBASE IV Application Generator can do a lot more including running your programs in windows on the screen, creating help screens, and even allowing batch routines to backup your database. However, we concentrate on the simple functions in this chapter.

One of the best uses of the Application Generator is to create the menus that the terminal operator would use to access your application system. You can quickly build a menu system to run the system. The Application Generator can generate the code for standard functions. Later, you can add routines to the generated code to produce a customized application that fits your own needs.

The idea behind the Application Generator is to allow non-programmers to generate application functions quickly. Simply put, an application generator is a program that creates another program based on some form of input. The input can be in the form of both a work surface where you create menus and also based on selections made interactively via a menu, as in the case of the dBASE IV Application Generator.

The Application Generator is a system that combines the other facilities of dBASE IV into an application. The Application Generator actually provides the "glue" to hold the built-in functions of dBASE together. The existing BROWSE, EDIT, and APPEND features are combined with your screen formats, report forms, and database layouts or views into an application.

The "glue" is formed by a series of menu screens that the generator builds for you. You specify a database name, the type of menu you would like to use, the screen and report formats that you would have the application produce, and even a sign-on screen for your application. The dBASE IV Application Generator then generates dBASE program code that displays the menus and causes them to perform the functions you specified. Figure 15-3 shows a conceptual view of the generation process.

Just as the user creates a series of menus, the user also interacts with the Application Generator via a system of menus and screens. Through a step-by-step process, the application developer is led through the definition of the application from the top level down to the detailed functions.

The reason that application generators like the Application Generator

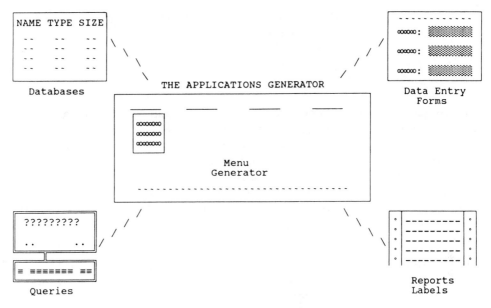

15-3 The application generation process.

work is because the programs that perform common database functions are similar in structure. In fact, the only difference between, for example, the Add functions for two different databases is the name of the program, the name of the database accessed, and the names/definitions of the individual fields. These are supplied to the application generator by the programmer, and the changes are made to the stock ADD function from the generator's library of functions.

The Application Generator creates a basic menu structure for each application. The action to be performed for each choice may be defined as one of the stock functions, or can include *custom* programs (those created outside of the Generator). The creation of such a menu is also a stock function, because there are fewer differences between menu programs than between Add functions: the only changes are the options on the menu.

Using an application generator is relatively easy; the programmer fills in the blanks, and the code is generated automatically by the program. The application can be quickly entered, and the programs be available for testing a very short time, usually minutes, after the creation of the database.

Designing applications: a step-by-step approach

Before you begin using the Application Generator, you should take a few minutes and think about your design. You have already seen how to design and build databases, screen forms, and reports. You learned that during design, you make sure that:

- Databases had to include all of the data that would be necessary for any and all of your information needs.
- Screen forms had to include all of the data from the databases.
- Each report had to include the fields and calculations that were necessary for the report.

Creating an application is no different. You must make sure that each form you have already created (or will create) is accessible through the menu system that you design. Each menu choice you create must have an action assigned to it. Typical actions would include displaying another menu, displaying a data entry form, performing a calculation, or printing a report.

In earlier chapters, you saw that you design databases by knowing what data would be necessary for the various reports. You hopefully started with reports and then worked backwards to databases and screens. The process to create an application is similar except now you work forwards.

Step 1　Take an inventory of your various screen forms, reports, and labels. These are what your menu will bring you to. Do you have all that you will need? If not, create them now!

Step 2　Decide which database file or view will be the main source of information. Make sure you have built all of the views necessary to the retrieval of your information in any form you desire, including indices and relationships between files.

Step 3　Design your main menu. What type of menu will it be? What choices will it have? What action will each choice cause?

Step 4　Design each submenu (if any).

Step 5　Assign an action to each menu choice.

Step 6　Add custom code to parts of the application.

Step 7　Generate the Application.

Actually, most of the steps are done for you before you even begin. You have already designed your databases, screen forms, and reports. All you really need to do is think about your menus that act as your glue to hold the application together. The path to designing an application is shown in Fig. 15-4.

The many types of menus

We have seen several types of menus in this book. If you are working with only one database and you only want a few simple functions such as data entry and report printing, you probably want one simple menu versus a hierarchy where one menu calls another. In fact, dBASE has an automatic "quick generation" feature that creates one simple menu to run your application if you only want to use one database, one screen form, and one report form.

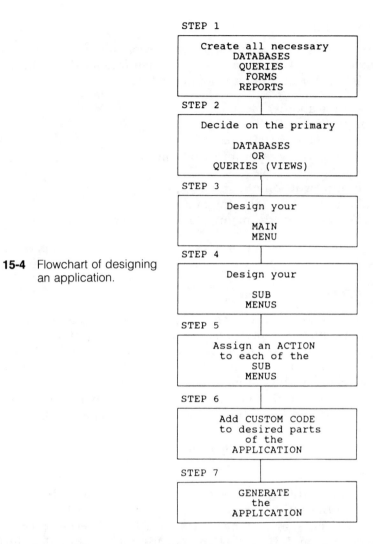

STEP 1

```
Create all necessary
      DATABASES
      QUERIES
      FORMS
      REPORTS
```

STEP 2

```
Decide on the primary

      DATABASES
         OR
      QUERIES (VIEWS)
```

STEP 3

```
Design your

       MAIN
       MENU
```

STEP 4

```
Design your

       SUB
       MENUS
```

STEP 5

```
Assign an ACTION
to each of the
       SUB
       MENUS
```

STEP 6

```
Add CUSTOM CODE
to desired parts
    of the
  APPLICATION
```

STEP 7

```
   GENERATE
      the
  APPLICATION
```

15-4 Flowchart of designing an application.

There are many types of menus. The most common is the horizontal bar menu which runs across the top of the screen horizontally. A light bar (or big fat cursor) moves from choice to choice, highlighting each option until you decide to press Return to select. Most bar menus also let you press the first letter of the choice so you have to make the first letter of your choices unique.

Attached to each bar menu choice can be a pull-down menu. A pull-down menu is displayed either automatically when the cursor is placed on the bar menu option or after the Return key is pressed on the option. The dBASE IV Application Generator allows you to easily create both types of pull-down menus—those that open manually and those that open automatically. A pull-down menu in dBASE IV is actually a pop-up menu that appears to pull down from a bar menu. It actually sits on top of a bar menu and appears to pull down when open.

Action screens

Once you create your menus and give each menu its choices you will determine an action for each menu. Each menu choice should be assigned an action. Actions include but are not limited to:

- Opening another menu
- Displaying a BROWSE table
- Displaying an EDIT screen
- Printing with a report or label form
- Running a DOS file
- Running a dBASE Program
- Running one dBASE command
- Take no action (the menu choice is for display only)

As we go through several examples, you will see the various uses for these menus and actions.

A design for Ajax Appliance

So far you have created databases, screen forms, and reports. In this section, we create a simple example from these input and output tools. In order to do this example, you should make sure you have all of your database fields and views. Also make sure you have all the screen forms, reports, and labels that were completed in the last eight chapters. Review Fig. 15-1 for a list of all the files that are used. You can build these from inside of the application generator by going from the generator to the proper work surface at the appropriate time.

If you don't feel like building these files for the culmination of our Ajax Appliance example, just sit back and relax. Our explanation and figures should be sufficient for you to understand the Application Generator.

Basically, in this system we have two chores—data entry and reporting. We can do both now by using the Control Center or the dot prompt to call up individual records, append new ones, or delete unneeded records. We can print reports from the Control Center or the dot prompt using the forms we created or with the quick report option.

What we need to do is to add a menu around our various forms and to use the generator to add even more functionality to the system. For example, the report form can be used in many different reports. We can determine through a menu which records are selected for the report and even if the report should only include summarized data when it prints. The same form can serve for many tasks as you will see.

Starting the Application Generator

The Application Generator can be started (like most work surfaces) from either the dot prompt or the Control Center. Figure 15-1 shows the main Control Center screen with the ⟨create⟩ choice highlighted in the Applications panel.

Choosing this will begin the Applications process. dBASE will ask you if you want to write a dBASE program using the dBASE Editor or if you want to use the Application Generator. Because you want to have dBASE automatically create your application choose the Application Generator choice. You can also start the Application Generator by entering:

. CREATE APPLICATION AJAXQ

at the dot prompt. In this case, we have named the application AJAXQ because the first application you will create will be a quick application for the AJAX Appliance Company.

Once the generator starts, you will be placed in a new work surface. This surface has many menus (in fact they constantly change depending on what you are doing) and many screens behind the menus. Nearly everything you do in this work surface is guided by menus and screens.

Objects, menus, items, and actions

Examine some of the terminology you should understand in order to use the Application Generator. The work surface is like other work surfaces in that you manipulate *objects* on the work surface. In the forms and reports screens, your objects consisted of the fields, lines, and boxes that you arranged on the work surface.

In the Application Generator, your objects are menus. You will place on the surface all of the menus that make your system perform its tasks. In this example, we create one horizontal bar menu and three pop-up menus that become pull-down menus.

Each menu has a series of choices. These choices are called *items*. Each menu can have as many choices or items as you desire. When you want to work with the entire menu you would use the Menu menu at the top of the screen. When you work with an individual item in a menu you would use the Item menu at the top of the screen. Until you have created your first menu, these two items won't even appear on the menu bar. Instead, you will see the Application choice as you work with the entire application.

Each item in a menu must be assigned an *action*. That way when you choose the item, something happens. As described earlier in this chapter, actions can be anything from calling another menu to using another work surface to running a dBASE program.

To define an action usually means filling out a screen. There are close to a hundred different screens in this tool. In this chapter, you see a small but important group of these screens.

Defining the application

Figure 15-5 shows the Application Definition box open on the work surface. This is the first thing you must fill out upon entering the work surface. If you haven't already given the application a name, this is where you do it. You also can optionally enter a description for the application that shows up in the catalog. Every application needs a main menu, and you must tell dBASE the name and type of menu even if you haven't created it yet. You also must assign the database or view that controls the application. Later, you can change the database for different menu choices.

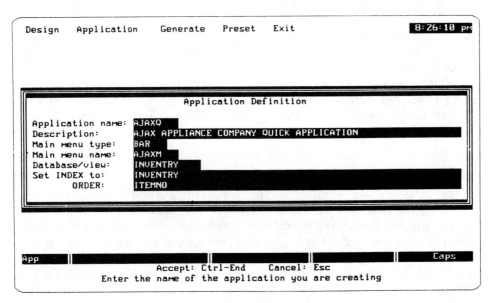

```
 Design    Application    Generate    Preset    Exit          8:26:10 pm



 ┌──────────────────────────────────────────────────────────────────────┐
 │                      Application Definition                            │
 │  Application name:  AJAXQ                                              │
 │  Description:       AJAX APPLIANCE COMPANY QUICK APPLICATION           │
 │  Main menu type:    BAR                                                │
 │  Main menu name:    AJAXM                                             │
 │  Database/view:     INVENTRY                                           │
 │  Set INDEX to:      INVENTRY                                           │
 │         ORDER:      ITEMNO                                             │
 └──────────────────────────────────────────────────────────────────────┘



 App                                                             Caps
              Accept: Ctrl-End      Cancel: Esc
         Enter the name of the application you are creating
```

15-5   Defining the application.

Figure 15-5 has already been filled in, telling us that the INVENTRY file is the main file used and that the main menu is a bar menu named AJAXM. In reality, we are filling out this screen for nothing. We are first going to create a quick application and that does not use this definition screen. You will need to use it when you create the main application.

Once the initial parameters are defined, an object is automatically placed on the desktop. This is the "sign-on" banner that the user might see when the application starts. Because we are not going to use this, we can move right to creating the quick application.

Creating a quick application

If you are only using a single database and want a very quick application, one option automatically generates a "quick" application. You are limited to a single database, screen, and report file. The application is a simple full-screen menu that lets you perform data entry and report or label printing.

Figure 15-6 shows the Applications menu opened on the work surface. Many choices affect the entire application. The first two choices let you reedit your responses when you initially started the generator. The third choice lets

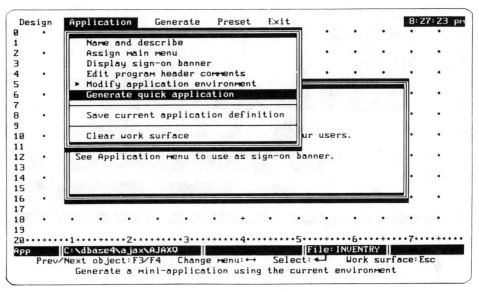

15-6 The Application menu.

you decide whether the sign-on banner will be displayed when the application is started. The next two choices allow you to change the way code is generated, including the addition of a header message such as a copyright into the generated code along with changing colors and environment settings.

The important choice here is the Generate quick application choice. This lets you generate an entire application without creating menus or assigning actions. If you have one database, one screen format, and one report, it can be a big help. When you choose this option the screen in Fig. 15-7 is displayed.

This screen has eight entry areas. The top half of the screen lets you enter your database, screen format file, report format file, and label format file. Each of these must exist before you attempt to use the screen with the quick generator. If you have trouble remembering the names of the files you have created, you can always press Shift–F1 for a list of the appropriate files from which you can pick.

The middle part of the screen lets you enter the name of your index file and, in the case of multiple indices, lets you choose the order that the data should be displayed in.

Finally, the bottom of the screen shows some documentation displayed when the system runs; this will show up on the main menu as a header.

You can see that the INVENTRY database is being used. The INVENTRY screen format file you created earlier in this book is also entered. The INVVALUE report is entered. No labels are entered because the only labels entered were for the CUSTOMER file. The index file and order is also entered. Finally, at the bottom of the screen, the author and menu heading is entered.

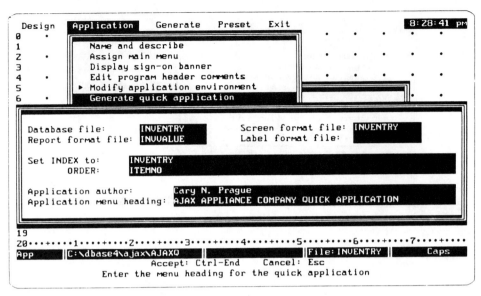

15-7 The quick application screen.

The menu heading is very important because that is what the operator of the system will see on the automatically generated menu.

Once you have completed the screen press Ctrl–End and the application will be generated. You can then run the application from the Control Center by choosing it and pressing Return or by using the dot prompt command DO with the application name. Figure 15-8 shows this application running in dBASE IV.

As you can see, the menu heading is at the top of the page. A menu in the center of the page contains all the choices you need to run this quick application. Choosing Add Information uses the INVENTRY format file with the APPEND command to let you add new records. Change Information does the same with the EDIT command. Browse Information uses the BROWSE function to let you see all (or a lot) of your records at once. The Discard Marked Records selection issues a PACK command. The Print Report choice runs the REPORT FORM command and prints the INVVALUE report. You can also choose to reindex the database or exit back to the Control Center or dot prompt. This is as far as you can go with the quick application. If you want to create a customized application, you must use the full application generator.

A complete application

Creating quick applications is fast and easy, but sometimes you need a lot more control over your application than a quick generation gives. The rest of this chapter is devoted to explaining the basics of generating an entire application.

```
┌──────────────────────────────────────────────────────────────────┐
│▐Fri. 03/13/92      AJAX APPLIANCE COMPANY QUICK APPLICATION    8:31:50 pm▌│
│                                                                          │
│                  ╔═══════════════════════════╗                          │
│                  ║ Add Information            ║                          │
│                  ║ Change Information         ║                          │
│                  ║ Browse Information         ║                          │
│                  ║ Discard Marked Records     ║                          │
│                  ║ Print Report               ║                          │
│                  ║ Reindex Database           ║                          │
│                  ║ Exit From AJAXQ            ║                          │
│                  ╚═══════════════════════════╝                          │
│                                                                          │
│  ██║C:\dbase4\ajax\INVENTRY ║Rec 1/15          ║File ║  ██             │
│              Add records to database INVENTRY                             │
└──────────────────────────────────────────────────────────────────┘
```

15-8 Running the quick application.

Defining the application

Creating a complete application begins like a quick application with creating the system parameters and the sign-on screen. Once this is accomplished, we turn our attention to building menus. First, reexamine the first two steps.

Figure 15-9 shows the Application Definition box open on the work surface. Again, this is the first thing you must fill out upon entering the work surface. If you have not already given the application a name, this is where you do it. You also can optionally enter a description for the application that shows up in the catalog. Every application needs a main menu, and you must tell dBASE the name and type of menu even if you have not created it yet. You also must assign the database or view that controls the application. Later, you can change the database for different menu choices.

Figure 15-9 has already been filled in telling us that the INVOICE file is the main file used and that the main menu is a bar menu named AJAXBAR.

Once the initial parameters are defined, the sign-on or welcome banner is automatically placed on the desktop. You have control over this if you do not want the user to see the sign-on banner. Initially, the banner has predefined text indicating the version of the Application Generator you are running. Figure 15-10 shows a customized message. You can move your cursor around inside the box, delete old text, and add new text. You also delete all the text quickly by pressing Ctrl–Y several times.

The application sign-on screen has several special properties. It can be resized by using the Shift–F7 keys or moved with the F7 key. It cannot be deleted although it can be not displayed at run time. It is used as a "reference"

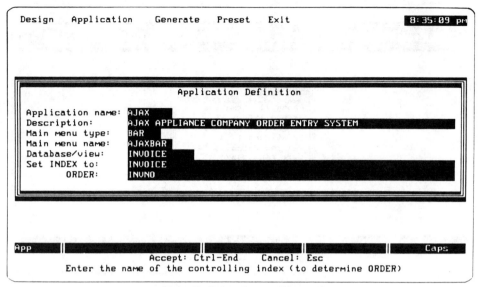

15-9 Defining the application.

point for the desktop. As you add more objects (menus) to the desktop, this one object is the one that must be selected to generate the application. After the application is saved and you modify the application, all you will see is this object. The other objects must be reloaded separately. You will also see that you must save all the other objects separately.

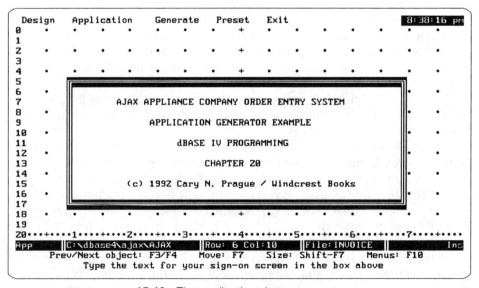

15-10 The application sign-on screen.

Generating a horizontal bar menu

Begin this application by defining a main menu. In this example, we use a horizontal bar menu at the top of the screen. The process is begun by using the Design menu. Figure 15-11 shows the Design menu open on the work surface. This menu has several choices. These choices let you select the type of menu or list. In our example, we select the Horizontal bar menu choice. Once this choice is selected, a pop-up box opens on the right of the screen.

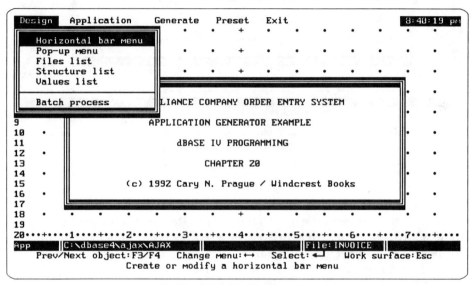

15-11 Selecting the Bar menu.

A list of all the bar menus previously defined appears along with a ⟨create⟩ tag. Choose the ⟨create⟩ tag to create a new menu. Once you choose this, another screen appears as shown in Fig. 15-12 and allows you to enter the name, description, and message line prompt for the horizontal bar menu. As you can see, they have been filled in.

Once filled in, you can press Ctrl–End and an empty box appears at the top of the screen. This rectangle stretches from one side of the screen to the other and is three lines in height. It waits for you to put the menu items inside it. You can move the empty (or filled) menu box anywhere on the screen. You can even place it on the bottom of the screen. You might want to have a title on the final screen, and so you would move it down a few lines. Moving objects around the work surface will be covered soon. For now, leave it alone and concentrate on filling it.

The cursor is inside the box waiting for you to enter your items. You define the options in the menu bar by moving the cursor on the work surface to the place where you want the option to appear, then pressing the F5 function key. You then type the option name, and press F5 again when

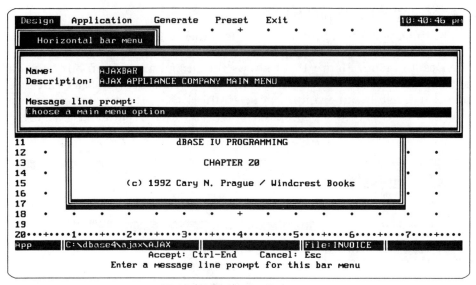

15-12 Defining the Bar menu.

complete. This registers the option name, now known as a menu item, to the Application Generator. After you have entered all of the application items that you need, you can then specify a prompt to be displayed when that item is chosen, and attach an application function to the item.

Figure 15-13 shows this filled-in menu. Four choices have been created. Each one is created by pressing F5 to begin the selection and F5 to end it. This way you can have options with blank spaces between the words.

The four choices will allow the user to perform data entry using the EDIT command, to display data using the BROWSE command, and to print reports and labels that you have already created in other chapters of this book. The final selection EXIT simply returns you to the calling program—either the Control Center or the dot prompt.

You are not limited to using a horizontal bar menu for your main application menu. You could use a pop-up window to display a vertical bar menu, choosing an option by moving the cursor up and down the menu, instead of side-to-side as with a horizontal menu bar.

It is important to note that objects (menus) are stored separately from the application. This way menus can be shared among applications, and you are not limited to the size of an application because you can move these objects on and off the work surface. When you complete entering each menu, you should use the Save this menu choice to save the menu. Saving the application saves the main application, not the individual menus.

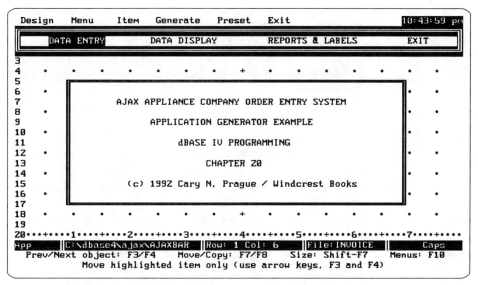

15-13 Defining the Bar menu choices.

Navigating the work surface

Before we create a pop-up menu, it is important we understand how to move around the work surface as well as to move objects around the work surface. First, you move from object to object using the F3 (Previous Object) and F4 (Next Object) keys. In Fig. 15-13, two objects were defined—the sign-on screen and the bar menu.

Objects can be moved around the screen by using the F7 key. This is very important when positioning pop-up menus that will become pull-downs. You can also size the menus to fit the items inside by using the Size key Shift–F7. These important keys are always displayed at the bottom of the screen and are consistent with other work surfaces. A complete list of navigation keys is found in Fig. 15-14.

Adding pop-up menus

Once the main bar menu is created, you can create your pop-up menus if you want them. This example has three submenus—one for the data entry, one for the data display, and one for reports. The exit menu choice will simply quit from the application.

Pop-ups are created in the same way as bar menus initially. The Design menu is used to add a pop-up menu to the work surface. Once on the work surface, you can add items without pressing any special keys as with bar menus. You just enter the text inside the box as you want. Each line becomes a separate menu choice.

Function Key	Explanation
F1 *Help*	Provides Help wherever you are in the Applications Generator.
F3 *Previous*	Moves cursor to the *previous* object on the work surface, making that object current.
F4 *Next*	Moves cursor to the *next* object on the work surface, making that object current.
F5 *Field*	Marks beginning and end of an item when entering it in a horizontal bar menu (Enter may also be used instead of the second F5 to finish).
F7 *Move*	Allows moving an object to a new location on the work surface, or an item and all its attributes to a new location in the object or to a different object of the same type.
F8 *Copy*	Allows copying an item to another location in the same object or to a different object of the same type.
F9 *Zoom*	Displays or removes the Applications Generator menu bar and information lines, giving a full screen on which to lay out objects.
F10 *Menus*	Moves cursor from an object on the work surface to the Applications Generator menu bar. If in a menu, selects the current option.
Shift-F1 *Pick*	Displays a list when the cursor is on a field that allows a selection.
Shift-F7 *Size*	Allows changing of the length and width of the frames that enclose an object.

Navigation key	Action
Left arrow	Moves cursor one position to the left.
Right arrow	Moves cursor one position to the right.
Up arrow	Moves cursor one position up.
Down arrow	Moves cursor one position down.
Del	Deletes current character.
Home	Moves to the first field or option.
Ins	Toggles Insert on and off.
End	Moves to the last field or option.
Spacebar	In a field with choices, cycles through the choices. In an object, editing frame or dialog box, enters a space at the cursor position.
Esc	In an editing frame or dialog box, cancels the changes made and exits. In the Applications Generator menu, exits to the current object on the work surface. In an Applications Generator submenu, exits to the calling menu. In an object, cancels all unsaved changes made to any object during the current session and asks whether to exit the Applications Generator. Also, cancels a move or copy.

15-14 Navigating the work surface.

You can resize the pop-up with the Shift–F7 keys to shrink or stretch it horizontally or vertically. You can center the text by moving the text with the insert key. You can move the lines around with the F7 key.

Once the pop-up is defined, you should move it to exactly where you want to see it pop up. If it is going to be a pull-down menu then it should reside directly underneath the bar menu choice. Figure 15-15 shows the data entry pop-up menu placed on the work surface. When you place these objects on the work surface they won't all be there when the application runs. Only the sign-on banner (if you request it), the main menu, and any text objects are displayed. All other menus only display when they are called from other menus.

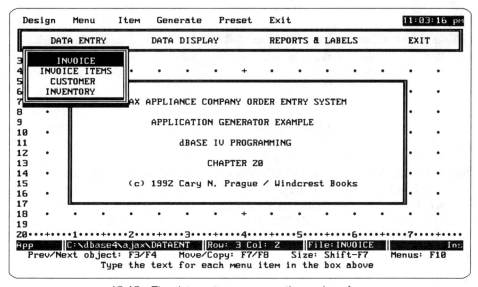

15-15   The data entry pop-up on the work surface.

When you press F7 to move the pop-up menu, you are asked if you want to move the entire frame or an item. If you are moving the entire menu, choose Entire frame. If you really want to move your items around without retyping them, then choose the latter. Once you complete the first menu, you should place the other pop-ups you will need on the work surface.

Figure 15-16 shows all of the pop-up menus on the desktop. Again, only one at a time will really show up. But, when you are designing your menus it is good to see the relative position of one to another.

As you can see in the Data Entry pop-up menu, four choices correspond to each of the databases. Data entry can only take place in one database at a time without programming, so in order to simulate data entry in an invoice, both the invoice and the invoice items must be entered separately in the Application Generator.

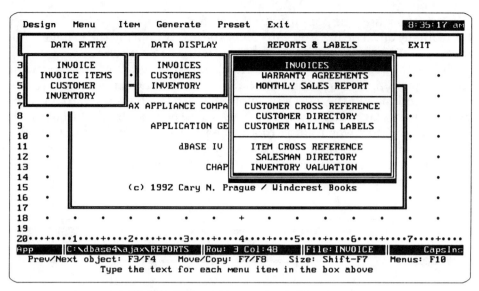

| Design | Menu | Item | Generate | Preset | Exit | 8:35:17 am |

| DATA ENTRY | DATA DISPLAY | REPORTS & LABELS | EXIT |

```
 3      INVOICE            INVOICES          INVOICES
 4   INVOICE ITEMS        CUSTOMERS      WARRANTY AGREEMENTS        •   •
 5     CUSTOMER           INVENTORY     MONTHLY SALES REPORT
 6    INVENTORY
 7                AX APPLIANCE COMPA  CUSTOMER CROSS REFERENCE      •   •
 8    •                               CUSTOMER DIRECTORY           •   •
 9                     APPLICATION GE  CUSTOMER MAILING LABELS
10    •                                                            •   •
11    •                  dBASE IV     ITEM CROSS REFERENCE         •   •
12    •                                SALESMAN DIRECTORY
13                          CHAP      INVENTORY VALUATION          •   •
14    •
15                (c) 1992 Cary N. Prague / Windcrest Books
16    •                                                            •   •
17
18    •     •     •     •     •     •     +     •     •     •     •       •
19
20 ••••+••••1••••+••••2••••+••••3••••+••••4••••+••••5••••+••••6••••+••••7••••+••••
App   ║C:\dbase4\ajax\REPORTS ║Row: 3 Col:48 ║║File:INVOICE ║        CapsIns
  Prev/Next object: F3/F4    Move/Copy: F7/F8    Size: Shift-F7    Menus: F10
              Type the text for each menu item in the box above
```

15-16 All the objects on the work surface.

The second pop-up is the BROWSE command used for data display. If you assume that no data entry takes place, you can use the INVOICES.QBE file that you created in the QBE chapter to look at the invoice data linked together. The INVENTRY and CUSTOMER files can be browsed directly.

The last pop-up lists the names of all the reports created in chapter 13. You will have to specify a different database or view for each report as each is different than the default INVOICE file that you entered in the application definition screen.

The Menu menu

Figure 15-17 shows the Menu menu. This menu name varies depending upon the object you are in. When you are in the bar menu it says Menu. If we were in a list, it would say List and contain options that were appropriate for list menus.

Choosing menu options The first item lets you reopen the initial screen that you saw when you created the bar menu. You can change the name, description, and message line prompt. The next item lets you change the main database controlling the application for an individual menu; this item is discussed in the next part of this chapter.

Write help text actually lets you create a custom help screen for the menu. If the users press F1 when in the menu, they will see the help screen that you create here. To create a help screen, simply make this choice and enter text anywhere you want in the screen. The help screen automatically is attached to the menu. We examine this more in the next part of this chapter.

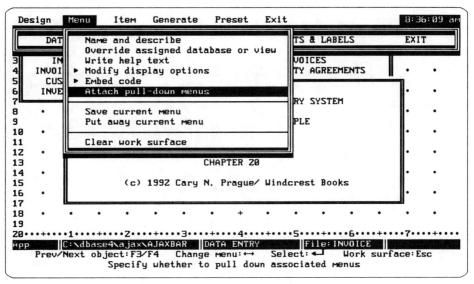

```
        DAT                                          TS & LABELS        EXIT
   3    IN    Name and describe                     UOICES
   4  INUOI   Override assigned database or view    TY AGREEMENTS    •   •
   5   CUS  ▸ Write help text
   6  INUE  ▸ Modify display options                                 •   •
   7         Embed code
   8    •    Attach pull-down menus                 RY SYSTEM         •   •
   9         Save current menu                      PLE
  10    •    Put away current menu                                   •   •
  11
  12    •    Clear work surface                                      •   •
  13                         CHAPTER 20                              •
  14    •                                                            •   •
  15              (c) 1992 Cary N. Prague/ Windcrest Books           •   •
  16    •                                                            •   •
  17
  18    •    •    •    •    •    •    •    +    •    •    •    •    •    •
  19
  20••••+••••1••••+••••2••••+••••3••••+••••4••••+••••5••••+••••6••••+••••7••••+••••
App      C:\dbase4\ajax\AJAXBAR   DATA ENTRY        File: INVOICE
    Prev/Next object:F3/F4    Change menu:↔    Select:↵    Work surface:Esc
               Specify whether to pull down associated menus
```

15-17   The Menu menu.

The next item lets you specify the colors and line types for the various objects and menu boxes. Color is a good thing to avoid changing. Unless you are tracking sales figures for Rainbow Brite, it is a good idea to stick to a couple basic colors.

Embed code lets you actually place a few lines of dBASE Program code either before or after a menu item action. We'll save this choice for an advanced session.

The final selection in the first section of this menu is Attach pull-down menus. This allows you to automatically have pop-ups appear when a bar menu is chosen. This makes the pop-up menu into a pull-down menu.

Remember that each menu is a separate entity and can be saved, put away, or retrieved separately from the application. The middle two choices allow us to save or put away the object. It can be retrieved by using the Design menu and choosing it again. The very last choice lets you clear the work surface of all objects.

Creating help screens   Let's look at a typical help screen. Help screens can be added at the menu level or at the individual menu choice level. When the user is on the menu item and presses F1, the defined help screen is displayed. When you choose Write help text, the screen in Fig. 15-18 is displayed.

As you can see, the screen has already been filled in. When F1 is pressed by the user in the bar menu, this screen appears. That's all there is to it. You can add help screens for each menu choice in the system.

Making pop-up menus into pull-down menus   The last choice in the first part of the Menu menu in Fig. 15-17 is Attach pull-down menus. If you choose this and then confirm the choice, when you move the cursor in the application to the

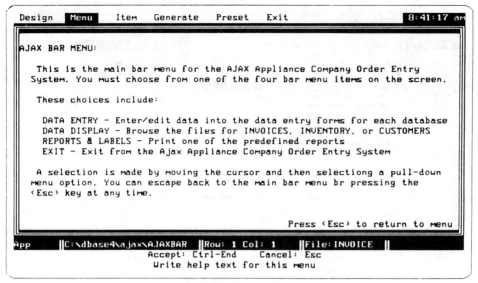

```
 Design   Menu    Item   Generate   Preset   Exit          8:41:17 am
╔═══════════════════════════════════════════════════════════════════╗
║AJAX BAR MENU:                                                       ║
║                                                                     ║
║   This is the main bar menu for the AJAX Appliance Company Order Entry║
║ System. You must choose from one of the four bar menu items on the screen.║
║                                                                     ║
║   These choices include:                                            ║
║                                                                     ║
║   DATA ENTRY - Enter/edit data into the data entry forms for each database║
║   DATA DISPLAY - Browse the files for INVOICES, INVENTORY, or CUSTOMERS║
║   REPORTS & LABELS - Print one of the predefined reports            ║
║   EXIT - Exit from the Ajax Appliance Company Order Entry System    ║
║                                                                     ║
║   A selection is made by moving the cursor and then selectiong a pull-down║
║ menu option. You can escape back to the main bar menu br pressing the║
║ <Esc> key at any time.                                              ║
║                                                                     ║
║                         Press <Esc> to return to menu               ║
╚═══════════════════════════════════════════════════════════════════╝
 App    ║C:\dbase4\ajax\AJAXBAR ║Row: 1 Col: 1   ║File: INVOICE ║
                Accept: Ctrl-End      Cancel: Esc
                Write help text for this menu
```

15-18   Creating a Help screen.

menu that the pull-down is attached to, it automatically opens as soon as the cursor touches the menu option. Otherwise, the pull-down doesn't open until Return is pressed. Of course, if the bar menu item's action is not to open a pull-down menu nothing will happen. Make sure you do not forget to assign an action to each menu item.

Choosing actions

The essence of an application is its ability to do a lot of things. Choosing an action for each menu item is how the generator works. A menu item can have many actions.

The Item menu   Figure 15-19 displays the Item menu. This menu has many choices like the Menu menu. Remember that any choice you make here deals with the menu item only. Some of the choices include the ability to change databases at the item level or to run dBASE code before or after the action is taken. You can skip the item entirely if a certain condition is met just as some options only work at certain times in dBASE IV menus. You can position the record pointer to a specific record or change the index order.

Another feature is the ability to define a window. A window is a portion of the screen where anything can run such as a BROWSE screen or report output, except that it sits on top of the screen itself and all output is confined to the borders of the window. It is just like creating a pop-up menu in that you can only operate within the box.

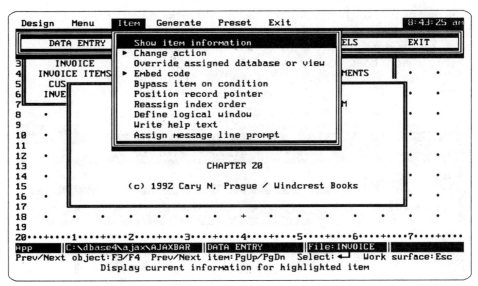

15-19 The Item menu.

Writing help text and changing the message line prompt are the last two choices which can be made at the item level.

Choosing an object or item   This section is about assigning actions to our menus. First, place the cursor on the item you want to assign an action to. If the item is found in the current object, then just move the cursor to the item you want to assign an action to. If the item you want is in a different object, then use the F3 or F4 keys to first move to that object and then select the item.

Due to memory restrictions of large applications, you might not be able to have all of your objects on the work surface at once. If you have created your application from the Control Center you can reclaim some memory by entering the application to create or modify it from the dot prompt.

However, you can freely move an object onto the work surface, assign actions to each item, and then put away the object. When the application is generated, all of your objects will be brought together to form the application regardless if you could actually see them on the work surface. Simply think of the Application Generator work surface as a train station. Trains go in and out, but if you want to they can all be in the same place at once!

Once you select the item, you can use the Item menu. First check the current status of a menu item. Figure 15-20 shows you the results of Show item information on the DATA ENTRY item of the AJAXBAR bar menu. In this case, the cursor is on the DATA ENTRY item of the AJAXBAR bar menu. The current database and view is displayed. As yet, no action has been chosen so this item will:

"Display text (no action)"

This means that the bar menu item is only there for looks. Until we assign an action, it does not do anything. To change an action, we must choose Change action on the Item menu. Figure 15-21 shows the Change action submenu. There are eight basic choices as you can see.

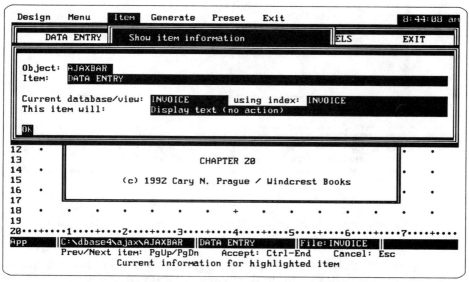

15-20 Displaying the item information.

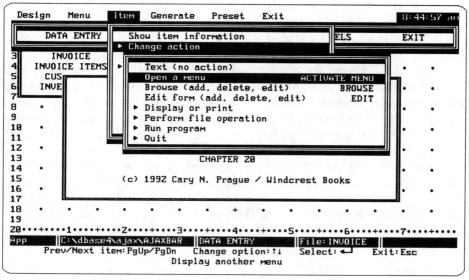

15-21 Changing an action.

- Text (no action)
- Open a menu
- BROWSE
- EDIT
- Display or print
- Perform file operations
- Run program
- Quit

Opening menus The first action we are going to choose is to Open a menu. This displays another box as shown in Fig. 15-22 which asks you for the menu type and menu name. Remember that not only is each menu stored separately, but the different types of menus have different file extensions. You can have a bar menu and a pop-up menu with the same name if you desire, so dBASE IV must ask you both the menu name and menu type.

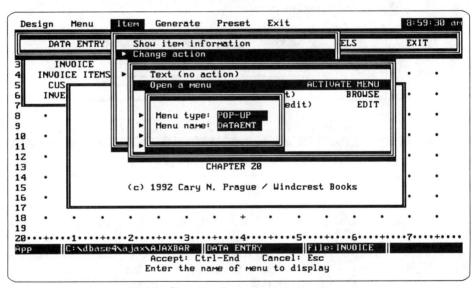

15-22 Choosing the menu name and type.

In Fig. 15-22, you can see that the DATA ENTRY menu calls the pop-up menu DATAENT. That is how one menu calls another. If you have chosen to Attach pull-down menus to the bar menu choice, then the pop-up is displayed as soon as the cursor touches that selection, simulating a pull-down menu. If not, the pop-up won't appear until Return is pressed.

Any type of menu can call other menus or lists. Bar menus can open bar menus, pop-ups can call bar menus, even pop-ups can open other pop-ups. There is no real limit to the number of menus in a chain. However, if you fill the screen with menus, your user will easily get lost and confused.

After you take care of the data entry menu, you must do the same for the data display and report menu choices. Although the Attach pull-down menus choice works for the entire bar menu, you still must choose the Open a menu item for each bar menu choice.

The Quit option   The last bar menu selection that you created is to quit the system. You now have to tell dBASE what this selection will do. This is also one of the actions that is chosen from the Item menu. Figure 15-23 shows this selection process.

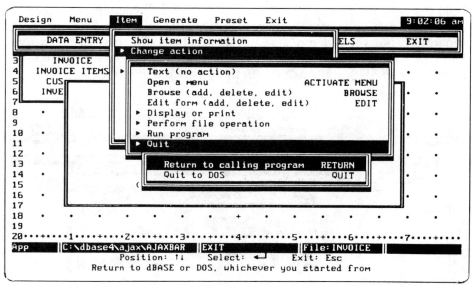

15-23   Choosing a quit option.

Once you place the cursor on the Quit menu item and select the Quit choice from the Item menu, another menu appears. As you can see, there are two choices. You can have the system return to the place that it was started from, such as the Control Center or the dot prompt. You can also have the system leave dBASE and quit to DOS.

Changing databases   Some of the items in the DATA ENTRY, DATA DISPLAY, and REPORTS menu choices will not be using the INVOICE database. This is the database that you created as the default database of the system. Any database or view can be the default database. The items in the various menus will use many of the other databases and views that were created in this book. Depending on the choices you make, you might need to use a different database than the default database. For example, in the DATA ENTRY pop-up menu, use the INVOICE database when entering data into the INVOICE database. However, when entering data into any of the other databases, you will have to change the database to the proper database. In some of the reports and for the INVOICE data display, you will have to override the

INVOICE database with the proper view. You can change databases at the menu or item level. In fact, you will see that the Item menu has many of the same choices as the Menu menu.

To change a database at the item level, we will choose Override assigned database or view as shown in Fig. 15-24. The current selection is shown at the top of the box. We filled in the bottom of the box with the database and order we want to use.

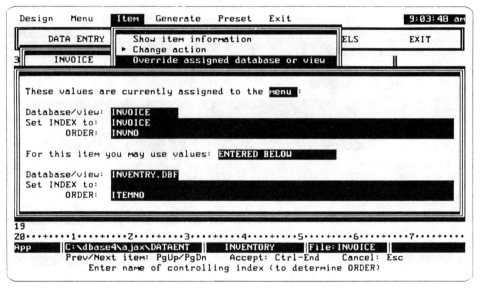

15-24 Changing the database.

Because this change was made at the item level, only items in the INVENTORY choice of the DATA ENTRY menu reflect this change. If you make the change at the Menu level, all of the items would have the override on the database.

The middle of the screen tells the system whether you will be using the currently assigned database or view or the values ENTERED BELOW. This comes in very handy when you have changed the database at the menu level and many of the choices use a different database. The new databases will be filled in automatically in the bottom part of the screen for every item in the menu, but you can selectively override it by changing the option For this item you may use values: to DISPLAYED ABOVE.

Adding/changing/deleting records Data entry is performed by means of the BROWSE or EDIT choices. These use the standard work surfaces you are used to seeing in dBASE IV. The Application Generator provides you with a series of menus to access all of the features of the BROWSE and EDIT screens.

In Fig. 15-23, the choice Edit form (add, delete, edit) lets us perform data entry. The cursor was in the DATA ENTRY pop-up menu object on the INVENTORY item.

Choosing the EDIT action opens the screen in Fig. 15-25. This opens the standard EDIT work surface that you have seen. You can tell what object and item you are in by looking at the status bar. The item is listed in the center of the status bar while the object is named in the second field of the status bar.

15-25 The EDIT screen.

In order to open the EDIT screen in a very controlled environment, you are asked to fill out a "questionnaire" in the form of a screen. This screen first asks for the format file name and whether you will be in APPEND mode adding new records or EDIT mode changing existing records. Because this action is performing data entry, we do not know if the user is adding or changing records. Because, the EDIT mode allows you to add, change, or delete records, we will choose that mode. The INVENTRY format file is entered in the top left part of the screen because there is a format file for the inventory database. The other three databases have no format files and, when those menu items are given the EDIT action, there will be no format file. If we did not know the name of the format file or wanted to create one, we would press Shift–F1 to retrieve a list of format files or to ⟨create⟩ a new screen format.

Any time you are asked to fill in a blank in the Application Generator, you can press Shift–F1 to see a list of files or other choices. In many of the file selection windows is a ⟨create⟩ icon. This icon lets you go to a work surface and create a new file. In the case of a format file, you are placed in the Forms work surface and can create a new form. The same is true of databases, reports, and labels.

The middle half of the screen lets you select only certain fields and records to work with just like the query screen does. This can be especially useful in segregating certain records for editing such as the "FROSTY" brand of refrigerators. You can choose the fields to be displayed and in what order, filter desired records by inputting any valid dBASE expression, choose how many records to work with using the SCOPE (ALL, NEXT 20, etc.), or even determine a condition to be met using FOR and WHILE logic.

The bottom of the screen lets you toggle seven different parameters to determine if certain operations will be allowed. We will allow records to be added, changed, and deleted. You could, however, limit the action to only additions for the Inventory records. Other toggles let you display the menu at the top of the screen for the user to use and affect the way new records are added.

You would fill out one of these screens for each item in the pop-up menu. Remember to change databases for the inventory, customer, and items files. Because the default is the invoice file, you don't have to worry about that one. Our design calls for the EDIT screen to be used for adding, changing, and deleting records, and the BROWSE screen for viewing the records.

Viewing records Once you assign each of the items to the EDIT screens, you should assign the Data Display menu choices. These use the BROWSE choice. The Browse choice as shown in Fig. 15-26 opens the BROWSE screen to allow you to enter the parameters for the viewing of more than one record at a time in the BROWSE screen. Our design calls for additions, changes, and deletions to be made in the EDIT screen, one record at a time, while viewing of the data would happen all at once in the BROWSE screen.

The BROWSE screen is slightly different from the EDIT screen, just as the BROWSE work surface is different than the EDIT screen. The top of the screen lets you decide which fields and records will be displayed. In this example, we allow all the records to be displayed.

The middle of the screen features choices from the Browse menu normally found at the top of the work surface. You can:

- Lock fields.
- Freeze a field for editing.
- Determine the maximum column width.

You can also perform editing from a format file by using the data validation and display commands from a format file.

The bottom of the screen contains most of the same option toggles from the EDIT screen. In this example, we want the BROWSE screen to be used strictly for display so we could not allow additions, changes, or deletions. You can also decide if the BROWSE menu will be displayed at the top of the screen and if the field names will be compressed into the first line of the screen.

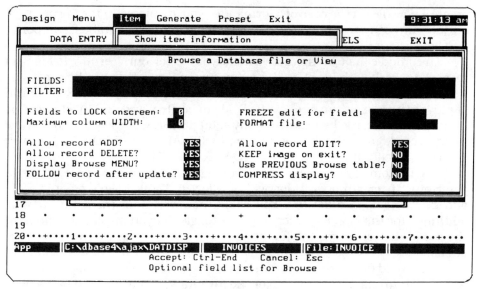

DATA ENTRY ║ Show item information   ║ELS   EXIT

Browse a Database file or View

FIELDS:
FILTER:

Fields to LOCK onscreen: 0   FREEZE edit for field:
Maximum column WIDTH: 0   FORMAT file:

Allow record ADD?   YES   Allow record EDIT?   YES
Allow record DELETE?   YES   KEEP image on exit?   NO
Display Browse MENU?   YES   Use PREVIOUS Browse table? NO
FOLLOW record after update? YES   COMPRESS display?   NO

17
18   .   .   .   .   + ...
19
20 ...+....1....+....2....+....3....+....4....+....5....+....6....+....7....+....
App ║ C:\dbase4\ajax\DATDISP ║ INVOICES ║File:INVOICE ║
              Accept: Ctrl-End   Cancel: Esc
              Optional field list for Browse

15-26 The BROWSE screen.

This example requires that three items be assigned actions. Each of the items in the DATA DISPLAY pull-down menu must have the databases overridden. The INVOICES choice uses the INVOICE.QBE view file, while the CUSTOMER and INVENTORY choices use their respective databases. Before going on to the Reports menu, you should complete assigning actions to all of the other menus and their items.

Changing databases to a view   None of the items in the Reports menu choices will not be using the INVOICE database. The items in this menu use all of the other databases and views that were created in this book.

Changing a default database to a view is very similar to changing to another database, as you have already seen. First, you must choose Override assigned database or view as shown in Fig. 15-27.

The current selection is shown at the top of the box. Shift–F1 has been pressed for a list of databases and views. The box on the far right of the screen was displayed. Look at the top of that box. See the ⟨create⟩ tag. If you choose ⟨create⟩, dBASE IV would allow you to create a new database or view without leaving the Application Generator.

In the Reports and Labels menu, the first choice is Invoices. In the database selection box on the right side of the screen, the cursor is on the INVOICES.QBE choice. When Enter is chosen, the entry area will be filled in with the view name. That view would then be used for the report.

Printing reports or labels   The bar menu choice Reports and Labels that you have designed has many items. This group of options should let you print your data using the various report and label forms that you created in the

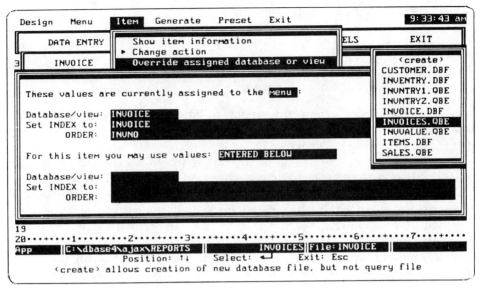

15-27 Changing the database to a view.

reports chapter. For these you would use the reporting actions. The Display or print action in the Change action submenu of the Item menu controls these actions, as shown in Fig. 15-28. Make sure you have placed your cursor in the Invoices item of the Reports and Labels pop-up before choosing the action.

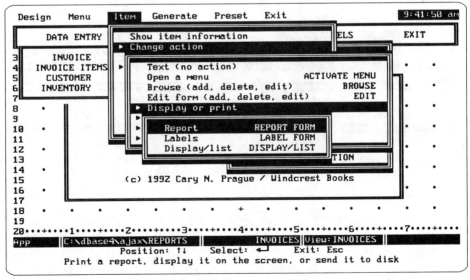

15-28 Selecting a report type.

There are three choices for reporting:

- REPORT FORM
- LABEL FORM
- DISPLAY/LIST

The first two choices let you run a report or label form. The last option runs the LIST or DISPLAY dot prompt commands after first letting you choose the fields and records to be displayed or listed.

In this example, we use all of the report forms we created earlier. By selecting Report, the screen changes as shown in Fig. 15-29. This screen gives you access to all the power of the report form. First, you can enter the name of a report form you have already created. If you can't remember the name, then press Shift–F1 as you can see in Fig. 15-29 and a list of all the report forms on your disk is displayed. If you have not created them yet, you can choose the ⟨create⟩ marker and enter the Reports work surface. After creating the report form, you will be returned to the Application Generator and can finish completing the screen.

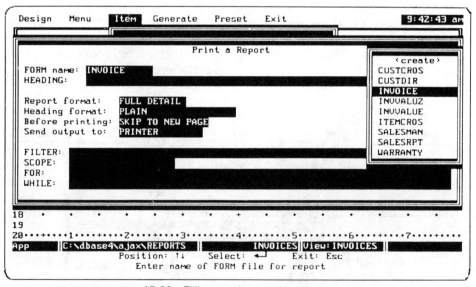

15-29 Filling out the report screen.

You can enter a heading that is displayed at the top of the report when it is printed using the Heading entry area. This does not take the place of anything in your report form, it simply adds to the top of it. You can also decide if you are going to print all of the detail lines in the report or just summaries by using the Report format toggle. Other toggles let you determine the heading format, whether or not lines are skipped or pages are ejected before printing, and where the output should be sent.

The bottom part of the screen lets you determine which records to process as part of the report. In our example, we will not enter anything into these fields. We have chosen a simple report, each record based on a single database or view. The first report choice in our menu system, Invoices, requires simply that we fill out the report screen as you have seen. This would print all of the invoices. However, suppose you only wanted the invoices for Avon Appliance or you only wanted the invoices that were created today?

This last section of the report screen gives you great flexibility in creating many menu items using the same report. For example, instead of just having the one menu item that says Invoices, you could have created the following three choices under the reports menu:

- Complete invoice report
- Avon appliance invoices
- Summary of invoices for the last 24 hrs

All three of these reports would use the same report form. The first, Complete invoice report, would have no special filter parameters. The second might have the filter:

COMPANY =' AVON APPLIANCE'

while the last choice might have the filter:

INVDATE = DATE .OR. DATE( )−1

and place summary in the report detail box.

Although each choice uses the same report form, each choice produces a different looking report, including different data. The last report would even have eliminated the detail data and just produced a summary report.

Each choice in the Reports and Labels pop-up menu must be assigned a report or label form to use to print the report. The labels screen is a little different.

The labels screen used for the customer labels selection is shown in Fig. 15-30. The label form is called CUSLBL. The output can be sent to the screen, a file, or, as in this example, to the printer. The Print sample option generates sample labels for alignment. The filter and scope parameters are the same for the labels as for reports.

Generating the application

After you have defined your menus and assigned your actions to each item, you can generate the program that displays these menus and performs the actions by using the Generate option on the Application Generator's menu as shown in Fig. 15-31. Before you Begin generating, however, you must tell dBASE which "template" to use to generate the code. A template is a road map

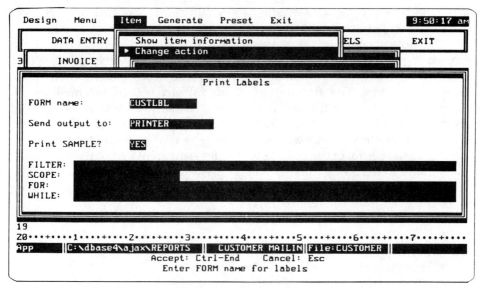

15-30 The labels screen.

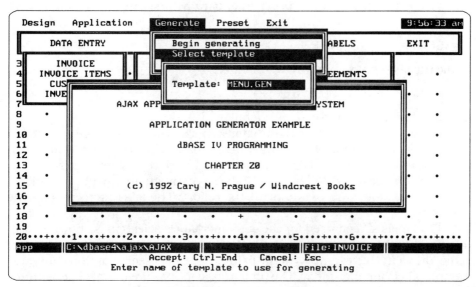

15-31 Generating the code.

for the generator to follow in generating its code based on the work you did on the work surface. A template called MENU.GEN is provided to generate your code. Don't worry about the other templates or custom templates. The MENU.GEN template will do an excellent job generating the code for you. When you choose the Select template option on the Generate menu, you will be asked for the template. Enter MENU.GEN and then press Begin generating.

If Display during generation is ON, then dBASE IV opens a window and shows you the dBASE program code as it is generated. If it is off, you will not see the code generated but it will happen. This program code is placed in a dBASE .PRG file so that you can execute the application from the dot prompt by using the command DO ⟨name⟩, where the ⟨name⟩ is the application name. You can also select the AJAX application from the Control Center Application panel and press Return to run the application. The running application is shown in Fig. 15-32. The first menu is pulled down, ready for you to select an item.

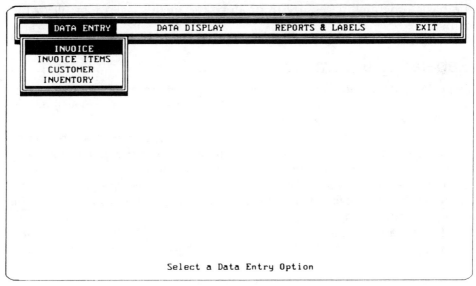

15-32 Running the application.

Benefits of the generator

Saving development time is especially important when starting an application that will require a large data entry effort at the outset. If, for example, a company wanted to computerize their customer list, someone must actually enter all of the information on their existing customer list into the computer. Simple data entry functions (add, change, delete, and browse) might be quickly provided using an application generator, allowing data entry to proceed while the application is still being developed. These functions can then be replaced by customized programs or revised to fit the needs of the system.

The dBASE IV Application Generator is a very advanced application program generator. The program code necessary to create bar and pop-up menus is very complex—but this code is also generic. The program for one horizontal bar menu has to perform the same tasks as any other program that displays a horizontal bar menu. The difference is the items that are displayed on the menu and the actions that each item initiates.

You provide the names of the items, the associated prompts, their placement on the screen, and the actions to be performed when you create the menu using the Application Generator. Even variables such as the color of the boxes, bars, and lines can be changed. All of these options are plugged into the basic code to produce each type of menu, thus creating an application-specific menu for any situation. This approach is like that of a professional programmer, who saves routines for use later when a similar routine is needed. The Application Generator already has the basic programs necessary to produce the menus—you just fill in the blanks!

Generating documentation

The dBASE IV Application Generator will also generate documentation for the programs it generates. The documentation file is a technical overview of each function in the application.

You could use the documentation file that is generated as a reference when modifying your application. You could also use the generated documentation, along with your own design documentation, to create a manual for your application system. Such a manual could be used not only for your own reference, but also to train and guide the people who would actually be using the application.

To generate documentation, return to the Control Center and choose the AJAX application. Press Shift–F2 to return to the application work surface. You will notice that your menus are not on the work surface. Menus are stored separately from the work surface. You must reload all the menus by first choosing the menu type from the Design menu, and then reloading each menu from the menu list. After reloading the four menus, you are ready to create the documentation. Open the Generate menu and select the DOCU-MENT.GEN template. This tells dBASE to create documentation instead of running a program. When you then choose the Begin generating choice, a file called AJAX.DOC is created. You can print the file by going into the dBASE editor and choosing the print menu choice. The documentation produced by this file is shown in Fig. 15-33. This can serve as a guide to how each choice should be made throughout this chapter.

This sophisticated approach to generating applications and documentation makes the dBASE IV Application Generator a valuable tool. You can increase the speed with which you create prototype applications for review, and also decrease the amount of time needed to create a full application system. This process will be a great advantage to you as you create your own dBASE IV application systems, both now and into the future.

Application Documentation for System: AJAX.PRG

Application Author: Cary N. Prague
Copyright Notice..: (c) 1988 Cary N. Prague/TAB Books
dBASE Version.....: 1.0

Display Application Sign-On Banner: No

Main Menu to Open : AJAXBAR.BAR

Sets for Application:

```
    Bell        ON
    Carry       OFF
    Centry      OFF
    Confirm     OFF
    Delimiters  OFF
    Display Size 25 lines
    Drive
    Escape      ON
    Path
    Safety      ON
```

Starting Colors for Application:

```
 Color Settings:
    Text          : W+/B
    Heading       : W/B
    Highlight     : GR+/BG
    Box           : GR+/BG
    Messages      : W+/N
    Information    : B/W
    Fields        : N/BG
```

Database/View: INVOICE
Index File(s): INVOICE
Index Order: INVNO

===

Menu/Picklist definitions follow:

Layout Report for Horizontal Bar Menu: AJAXBAR

Screen Image:
```
     0        10        20        30        40        50        60        70
    >....+....|....+....|....+....|....+....|....+....|....+....|....+....|....+.
00:
01:     DATA ENTRY        DATA DISPLAY        REPORTS & LABELS        EXIT
02:
03:
04:
05:
06:
07:
08:
09:
10:
11:
12:
13:
14:
15:
16:
17:
18:
19:
20:
21:
22:
23:
24:
    >....+....|....+....|....+....|....+....|....+....|....+....|....+....|....+.
```

15-33 Documenting the application.

15-33 Continued.

```
Setup for AJAXBAR follows:
-------------------------

 Description: AJAX APPLIANCE COMPANY MAIN MENU
 Message Line Prompt for Menu: Choose a main menu option

Colors for Menu/Picklist:
-------------------------
 Color Settings:
   Text           : W+/B
   Heading        : W/B
   Highlight      : GR+/BG
   Box            : GR+/BG
   Messages       : W+/N
   Information     : B/W
   Fields         : N/BG


Help Defined for Menu AJAXBAR:
------------------------------

 AJAX BAR MENU:

    This is the main bar menu for the AJAX Appliance Company Order Entry



 Page: 3   Date: 12-02-88 10:42a

    System. You must choose from one of the four bar menu items on the screen.

    These choices include:

      DATA ENTRY - Enter/edit data into the data entry forms for each database
      DATA DISPLAY - Browse the files for INVOICES, INVENTORY, or CUSTOMERS
      REPORTS & LABELS - Print one of the predefined reports
      EXIT - Exit from the Ajax Appliance Company Order Entry System

    A selection is made by moving the cursor and then selectiong a pull-down
    menu option. You can escape back to the main bar menu br pressing the
    <Esc> key at any time.


                              Press <Esc> to return to menu



Bar actions for Menu AJAXBAR follow:
------------------------------------
Bar: 1
 Prompt: DATA ENTRY
 Action: Open a Popup Menu Named: DATAENT
--------------------------------------------------------------------------------

Bar: 2
 Prompt: DATA DISPLAY
 Action: Open a Popup Menu Named: DATDISP
--------------------------------------------------------------------------------

Bar: 3
 Prompt: REPORTS & LABELS
 Action: Open a Popup Menu Named: REPORTS
--------------------------------------------------------------------------------

Bar: 4
 Prompt: EXIT
 Action: Return to calling program
--------------------------------------------------------------------------------


Page: 4   Date: 12-02-88

Layout Report for Popup Menu: DATAENT
-------------------------------------
```

15-33 Continued.

```
Screen Image:
    0        10        20        30        40        50        60        70
   >....+....|....+....|....+....|....+....|....+....|....+....|....+....|....+.
00:
01:
02:
03:    ┌─────────────────┐
04:    │     INVOICE     │
05:    │  INVOICE ITEMS  │
06:    │    CUSTOMER     │
07:    │    INVENTORY    │
       └─────────────────┘
08:
09:
10:
11:
12:
13:
14:
15:
16:
17:
18:
19:
20:
21:
22:
23:
24:
   >....+....|....+....|....+....|....+....|....+....|....+....|....+....|....+.
```

Setup for DATAENT follows:

 Description: DATA ENTRY POP UP
 Message Line Prompt for Menu: Select a Data Entry Option

Colors for Menu/Picklist:

 Color Settings:
    Text   : W+/B
    Heading   : W/B
    Highlight   : GR+/BG
    Box   : GR+/BG
    Messages   : W+/N
    Information   : B/W
    Fields   : N/BG

Bar actions for Menu DATAENT follow:

Bar: 1
 Prompt: INVOICE
 Action: EDIT

Page: 5 Date: 12-02-88 10:43a

Bar: 2
 Prompt: INVOICE ITEMS
 Action: EDIT
 New Database/View: ITEMS
 New Index Order: ITEMNO

Bar: 3
 Prompt: CUSTOMER
 Action: EDIT
 New Database/View: CUSTOMER
 New Index Order: CUSTNO

Bar: 4
 Prompt: INVENTORY
 Action: EDIT
 Format File: inventry.fmt
 New Database/View: INVENTRY
 New Index Order: ITEMNO

15-33 Continued.

Layout Report for Popup Menu: DATDISP

Screen Image:
```
     0        10        20        30        40        50        60        70
    >....+....|....+....|....+....|....+....|....+....|....+....|....+....|....+.
00:
01:
02:
03:                          ┌─────────────────┐
04:                          │    INVOICES     │
05:                          │    CUSTOMERS    │
06:                          │    INVENTORY    │
                             └─────────────────┘
06:
07:
08:
09:
10:
11:
12:
13:
14:
15:
16:
17:
18:
19:
20:
21:
22:
23:
24:
    >....+....|....+....|....+....|....+....|....+....|....+....|....+....|....+.
```

Setup for DATDISP follows:

 Description: AJAX APPLIANCE COMPANY DATA DISPLAY POP-UP MENU
 Message Line Prompt for Menu: Select a data display option

Colors for Menu/Picklist:

 Color Settings:
   Text   : W+/B
   Heading   : W/B
   Highlight   : GR+/BG
   Box   : GR+/BG
   Messages   : W+/N
   Information   : B/W
   Fields   : N/BG

Bar actions for Menu DATDISP follow:

Bar: 1
 Prompt: INVOICES
 Action: Browse File
 New Database/View: INVOICES.QBE

Bar: 2
 Prompt: CUSTOMERS
 Action: Browse File
 New Database/View: CUSTOMER
 New Index Order: CUSTNO

Bar: 3
 Prompt: INVENTORY
 Action: Browse File
 New Database/View: INVENTRY
 New Index Order: ITEMNO

15-33 Continued.

Page: 8 Date: 12-02-88

Layout Report for Popup Menu: REPORTS

Screen Image:
```
   0         10        20        30        40        50        60        70
   >.....+....|....+....|....+....|....+....|....+....|....+....|....+....|....+.
00:
01:
02:
03:                                               ┌──────────────────────────┐
04:                                               │        INVOICES          │
05:                                               │   WARRANTY AGREEMENTS     │
06:                                               │   MONTHLY SALES REPORT    │
07:                                               ├──────────────────────────┤
08:                                               │  CUSTOMER CROSS REFERENCE │
09:                                               │    CUSTOMER DIRECTORY     │
10:                                               │  CUSTOMER MAILING LABELS  │
11:                                               ├──────────────────────────┤
12:                                               │   ITEM CROSS REFERENCE    │
13:                                               │    SALESMAN DIRECTORY     │
14:                                               │   INVENTORY VALUATION     │
15:                                               └──────────────────────────┘
16:
17:
18:
19:
20:
21:
22:
23:
24:
   >.....+....|....+....|....+....|....+....|....+....|....+....|....+....|....+.
```

Setup for REPORTS follows:

Description: AJAX APPLIANCE COMPANY REPORTS POP-UP MENU
Message Line Prompt for Menu: Select a report or label to print

Colors for Menu/Picklist:

 Color Settings:
   Text   : W+/B
   Heading   : W/B
   Highlight   : GR+/BG
   Box   : GR+/BG
   Messages   : W+/N
   Information   : B/W
   Fields   : N/BG

Bar actions for Menu REPORTS follow:

Bar: 1
 Prompt: INVOICES
 Action: Run Report Form INVOICES.frm
 Print Mode: Send to Default Printer

 Page: 9 Date: 12-02-88 10:43a

 New Database/View: INVOICES.QBE

Bar: 2
 Prompt: WARRANTY AGREEMENTS
 Action: Run Report Form WARRANTY.frm
 Print Mode: Send to Default Printer
 New Database/View: INVOICES.QBE

Bar: 3
 Prompt: MONTHLY SALES REPORT
 Action: Run Report Form SALESRPT.frm
 Print Mode: Send to Default Printer
 New Database/View: SALES.QBE

```
Bar: 4
 Prompt: _____
 Action: Text only defined for this option - NO ACTION
-------------------------------------------------------------------------------

Bar: 5
 Prompt: CUSTOMER CROSS REFERENCE
 Action: Run Report Form CUSTCROS.frm
 Print Mode: Send to Default Printer
 New Database/View: CUSTOMER
 New Index Order: CUSTNO
-------------------------------------------------------------------------------

Bar: 6
 Prompt: CUSTOMER DIRECTORY
 Action: Run Report Form CUSTDIR.frm
 Print Mode: Send to Default Printer
 New Database/View: CUSTOMER
 New Index Order: CUSTNO
-------------------------------------------------------------------------------

Bar: 7
 Prompt: CUSTOMER MAILING LABELS
 Action: Run Label Form CUSTLBL.lbl
 Command Options:
  SAMPLE
 Print Mode: Send to Default Printer
 New Database/View: CUSTOMER
 New Index Order: CUSTNO
-------------------------------------------------------------------------------

Bar: 8
 Prompt: _____
 Action: Text only defined for this option - NO ACTION
-------------------------------------------------------------------------------

Bar: 9
 Prompt: ITEM CROSS REFERENCE
 Action: Run Report Form ITEMCROS.frm
 Print Mode: Send to Default Printer




 Page: 10   Date: 12-02-88 10:43a

 New Database/View: INVENTRY
 New Index Order: ITEMNO
-------------------------------------------------------------------------------

Bar: 10
 Prompt: SALESMAN DIRECTORY
 Action: Run Report Form SALESMAN.frm
 Print Mode: Send to Default Printer
 New Database/View: INVENTRY
 New Index Order: ITEMNO
-------------------------------------------------------------------------------

Bar: 11
 Prompt: INVENTORY VALUATION
 Action: Run Report Form INVVALUE.frm
 Print Mode: Send to Default Printer
 New Database/View: INVVALUE.QBE
-------------------------------------------------------------------------------


End of Application Documentation
```

Part Three

Programming with dBASE IV

In the first part of this book, you learned how to program from a conceptual viewpoint and how to design a system. You put that knowledge to work as you worked through the design in chapter 4. In Part Two, you saw the various work surfaces of dBASE IV and how to create each type file. You also saw how to add a menu system to these tasks and make a "turnkey" system. You also saw some of the limitations of the Application Generator and the various work surface files.

In this part, you will see all of the commands that you will need to know to create a custom system—the system you designed in chapter 4. This part will be strictly a dot prompt command part as you learn how to create a complete system from scratch!

You will see the dBASE programming philosophy and then see many of the commands and functions that are commonly used. You will see some special chapters devoted to menus and windows—the new features of dBASE IV. Finally, you will see how to test and debug a program and some technical facts about compiling and linking your programs.

In Part Four, you will see the programs that make up the Ajax Appliance Company system.

16
Programming commands

When you have entered your database structure and set up your database files, you are ready to begin programming. You should review your design so that the tasks to be performed by your application are clear in your mind. This is where your design techniques will be put to the test. The quality of your design and pseudocode will determine how long it will take to code and test your application programs.

Programming the dBASE way

There are two ways to program your design with dBASE IV. You can either use the Application Generator provided with dBASE IV, or you can create the programs yourself using the dBASE Editor or your own favorite editor.

An application generator will write programs for you. There are several standard functions that most application generators can create, including menus, add routines, change routines, delete routines, display routines, and printing routines. dBASE's Application Generator lets you design custom-made forms and reports to enhance your application. You can also add your own dBASE code to the code that the generator produces to form a "hybrid" program. Any application generator, however sophisticated, will still leave areas where your own programs will be needed to "fill in the gaps." When you need totally customized programs, you will have to use the dBASE command language.

dBASE IV even gives you the best of both worlds. You can use the Application Generator to create sophisticated menus and screen layouts—then either choose the "canned" code that Generator creates or write your own routines to be attached to the menus for custom applications.

It is important to understand the dBASE programming environment, no matter which method you choose to create your application programs. This chapter will show you how to set up your dBASE environment, how to create your own executable program files, and how to use memory variables to enhance your processing.

Getting started

dBASE IV identifies the files it works with by using a variety of file extension names. You have already seen the use of .DBF for database files, .MDX for multiple-index and .NDX for single index files, and the .DBT extension of a database text file. dBASE programs, or *command files*, have an extension of .PRG. Program files contain the dBASE commands necessary to perform a task in dBASE IV.

Creating and using command files

Command files can be created by using the dBASE command MODIFY COMMAND, which places you into the dBASE Editor. From the dot prompt, you would enter:

. MODIFY COMMAND *name*

The Editor first searches the disk for a file with the name *name*.PRG, substituting *name* with your entered program name. In most dBASE commands, when you enter a file name, you can also specify your own extension names. It is much easier to use the default file extensions expected by dBASE IV. You can also specify the disk drive where the file should (or does) reside.

Once you have entered the dBASE Editor, you can enter any of the dBASE commands that you would want to execute. This is where your application design comes in—you must specify, in dBASE language, the exact sequence of actions that are to be taken by the program. In a command file, you can use the commands that do not seem very useful from the dot prompt, such as DO WHILE, LOCATE, CONTINUE, and the IF-ELSE construct.

For example, if you issue the command:

. MODIFY COMMAND JIM

dBASE would search for a command file named JIM.PRG. If it existed, it would be loaded into the Editor work surface so that you can change the program. If the file did not exist, you would be presented with an empty work surface for entering a new program.

The command file can be executed from either the dot prompt or from within another command file. The commands that you enter are interpreted by dBASE and executed exactly as they are entered, one at a time, until the end of the file is reached, or a command is executed that tells dBASE to return control to the dot prompt or the Control Center.

The dBASE Editor

The dBASE Editor is a WORDSTAR-like editor that is used for editing program files. The Editor is adequate for most editing work. It allows you to move from the beginning to the end of a file by scrolling you either forward or back one page at a time, using the PgUp and PgDn keys. You can insert or delete lines as needed. There is also a search command to find words or command phrases within the program. Figure 16-1 shows a simple program in the dBASE Editor work surface.

```
Layout   Words   Go To   Print   Exit                        9:03:45 am
█·····▼1·····▼··2····▼····3··▼··········4▼·····▼5·····▼··6····▼··7·▼·······
* sample program in dbase iv

use invoice order tag invno in a
use items order tag invno in b
use customer order tag custno in c
use inventry order tag itemno in d
select items
set relation to itemno into inventry
select invoice
set relation to invno into items, custno into customer
set skip to items, invoice

* end of program




 Program  C:\dbase4\JEHSET            Line:2 Col:2
```

16-1 The dBASE editor.

The dBASE Editor is adequate for most purposes and for minor additions to the programs. If you do not have your own favorite file editor, the dBASE Editor will serve. While other editors on the market are very sophisticated, the dBASE Editor is utilitarian in nature. After all, the Editor is an addition to a package, not the entire package in itself, and therefore is built as small as possible.

The dBASE Editor, in spite of this, is a full-featured editor and can be used for program development. You can enter program statements, move and copy lines from one place to another, delete lines, and perform search/replace operations. The Editor menus provide the same flexibility as shown in the dBASE Editor when accessing database memo fields.

In version 1.5, the dBASE Editor is mouse-driven. All menus are accessible with the mouse, and blocks of code can be highlighted using the mouse, replacing the F6 highlighting selection. You can position the mouse cursor at the beginning of the block to be highlighted, then, holding the mouse button down, drag the mouse cursor to the end of the desired block. When the button is released, the block will be highlighted.

The dBASE Editor is resident in memory, which makes it faster and easier to use than an external editor. It is made to be used in the dBASE environment. You can edit files of unlimited size, with command lines up to 1024 characters long. This is an *impractical limit*, meaning that most application programs will never test the limits of the dBASE Editor.

When you use the MODIFY COMMAND command, and the program already exists, the Editor will create a backup copy (with the extension of .BAK) of the original program. This way, if you accidentally erase half of the program or lose the file due to a power failure or disk error, you will still have an original copy. This .BAK file is erased whenever you edit the program the next time.

The F6 (Extend select) key allows you to select an area of text to move, copy, or delete. You press F6, move the cursor to the end of the area you wish to select, then press Enter. An area of text will now be highlighted, as shown in Fig. 16-2.

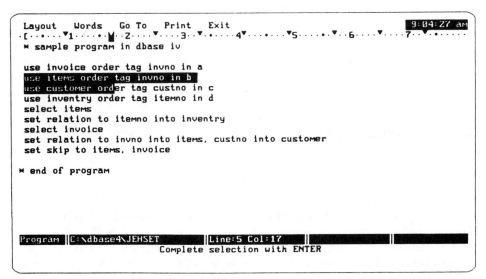

```
Layout   Words   Go To   Print   Exit                      9:04:27 am
 [.....▼1....▼..2....▼...3..▼.....4▼....▼5....▼..6...▼...7.▼......
 M sample program in dbase iv

use invoice order tag invno in a
use items order tag invno in b
use customer order tag custno in c
use inventry order tag itemno in d
select items
set relation to itemno into inventry
select invoice
set relation to invno into items, custno into customer
set skip to items, invoice

M end of program




Program  C:\dbase4\JEHSET          Line:5 Col:17
                  Complete selection with ENTER
```

16-2 Using F6 (extend select) on program code.

Once you have selected an area of text, the F7 (Move) key will move that text to a new location. You move the cursor to the location that you want the text to be moved to and press F7. F8 Copy allows you to copy the text to another position in the memo field. If you press the Del key, the selected text will be deleted.

If you press F6 once, you will begin the select process at a character level. If you press F6 twice, the current word is selected automatically. If you press F6 three times, the entire paragraph is selected automatically.

There are several other editing key combinations that you can use while in the dBASE Editor, as shown in Fig. 16-3 on the next page. Ctrl–T deletes the current word, while Ctrl–Backspace deletes the previous word. Using the cursor-left and -right keys (the arrow keys), you can move the cursor quickly to the beginning of the next word. Ctrl–N lets you insert a new line of text.

Function keys	
F1 Help	Enters dBASE Help system
F6 Extend Select	Starts selection of text and fields
F7 Move	Move selection to new location
F8 Copy	Copy selection to another location
F9 Zoom	Open text window to full screen size
F10 Menus	Access Editor menus
Un-aided keys	
PgUp	Moves up one page
PgDn	Moves down one page
Up arrow	Moves cursor up one line
Down arrow	Moves cursor down one line
Esc	Exit the Editor, ignoring changes
Del	Delete current selection
Ctrl- keys	
Ctrl-End	End Editor session, saving changes
Ctrl-Y	Delete line
Ctrl-T	Delete previous word
Ctrl-PgUp	Move to first line
Ctrl-PgDn	Move to last line
Ctrl-Right arrow	Move to next word
Ctrl-Left arrow	Move to previous word

16-3 dBASE editor keystrokes.

Finally, Ctrl–End lets you leave the program file, saving any changes that you have made. If you want to leave the file without saving your changes, the Esc key will do just that.

The dBASE Editor also has a menu that you can reach by using the F10 Menus option, or by pressing the Alt key in combination with the first letter of the menu choice. Figure 16-4 shows the Layout menu for the dBASE Editor when editing a program. This option is used in other work surfaces for other reasons, but in program editing, its only purpose is to save the program. This is useful when you are entering a lot of statements, and want to save the program in small sections. You can also copy routines into separate files by using F6 Select to choose the statements to copy.

The Words menu of the dBASE Editor, as shown in Fig. 16-5, gives you several options that allow you to not only manipulate the lines inside a program, but also to manipulate the Editor itself. You can get rid of the ruler by using the Hide ruler toggle. You can automatically indent subsequent lines to match the previous line by using the Enable Automatic indent menu item. You can also import text into the memo field by using the Write/read text file option.

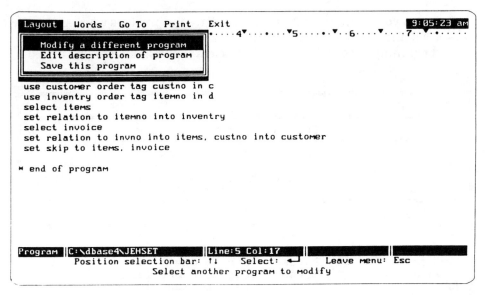

16-4 The Layout menu of the dBASE editor.

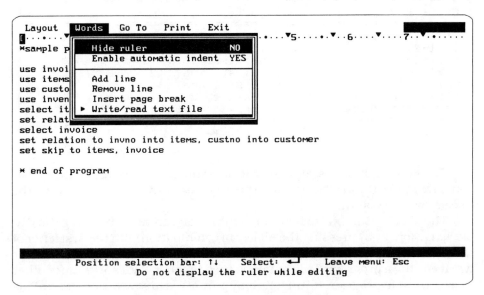

16-5 The Words menu of the dBASE editor.

The Go To menu, as shown in Fig. 16-6, allows you to position yourself in the program. The Go to line number option positions you to a particular line in the file, while Forward/backward search lets you search for a text string. The Replace option allows you to search for a text string, then replace it with another. Finally, the Match capitalization option allows you to toggle whether or not the case of the text will be ignored in the search.

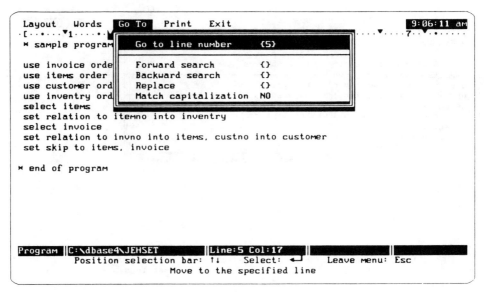

```
 Layout   Words   Go To   Print   Exit                              9:06:11 am
·[·····▼1······
  ⋈ sample program ┌──────────────────────────────────────┐ ····7··▼····
                   │   Go to line number        {5}       │
  use invoice orde │                                      │
  use items order  │   Forward search           {}        │
  use customer ord │   Backward search          {}        │
  use inventry ord │   Replace                  {}        │
  select items     │   Match capitalization     NO        │
  set relation to itemno into inventry└────────────────────┘
  select invoice
  set relation to invno into items, custno into customer
  set skip to items, invoice

  ⋈ end of program




 ┌─────────┐┌──────────────────────┐┌────────────────┐┌─────────────────────
 │Program  ││C:\dbase4\JEHSET      ││Line:5 Col:17   ││
 └─────────┘└──────────────────────┘└────────────────┘└─────────────────────
          Position selection bar: ↑↓    Select: ↵      Leave menu: Esc
                         Move to the specified line
```

16-6   The Go To menu of the dBASE editor.

The Print menu of the dBASE Editor allows you to print a hardcopy listing of your programs. This is very helpful when you are creating documentation for your application programs. The Print menu gives you total control over the printing of the program. You can select portions of the command file to print using the F6 Extend Select option, or you can print the entire program. The Print menu is shown in Fig. 16-7.

The Exit menu, shown in Fig. 16-8, allows you to exit from the dBASE Editor. If you exit without saving the changes you have made, the program will be returned to the way it was prior to your entering the dBASE Editor. Otherwise, the new program with all of your changes will be saved, and you will return to the dot prompt.

Choosing your favorite word processor

You can use any word processing software such as KEDIT, Microsoft WORD, Framework III, WORDSTAR, WordPerfect, IBM's Personal Editor, or Multimate. Whatever editor you choose, it must create a plain ASCII text file. In word processors like DisplayWrite 4, this causes you to take an extra step to translate the document file into an ASCII text file.

You might find that text editors such as Personal Editor or KEDIT actually work better than full-fledged word processors. The command files you create are nothing more than a series of dBASE commands strung together in the right way. There is no real limit to the number of statements you can have in a single command file. You will find that good programming techniques dictate that you should break up your programs into small workable modules of no more than one or two hundred statements. The

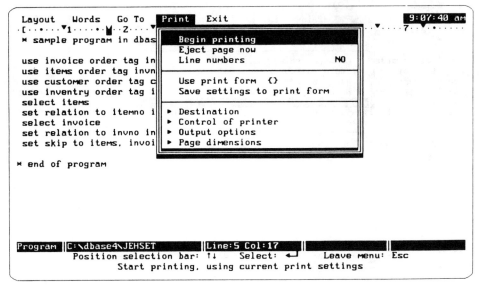

16-7 The Print menu of the dBASE editor.

programs or program modules should be readable and understandable, and should not exceed three or four screen-fulls—or about 60 to 80 statements.

To choose your own favorite word processor, you must change the dBASE configuration. There is a file in your dBASE directory called CONFIG.DB. This file contains values for various SET commands and other

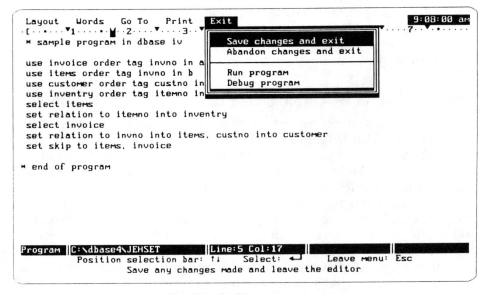

16-8 The Exit dBASE editor menu option.

options that are activated when you start dBASE IV. CONFIG.DB allows you to customize your dBASE environment to your own needs. The CONFIG.DB file is created when you install dBASE IV, or can be modified with the dBSETUP procedure supplied with dBASE.

The TEDIT option of CONFIG.DB lets you choose the word processor that should be used when MODIFY COMMAND is executed. To change the word processor, you would place the statement:

TEDIT=*filename*

into CONFIG.DB. The *filename* is the name of your favorite editor. WORD-STAR is executed as WS, Framework III is known as FW, Personal Editor is PE, KEDIT is either KEDIT or K. For example, to make KEDIT the chosen editor, you would place the following line into your CONFIG.DB file:

TEDIT=KEDIT.EXE

The other word processor you can specify is the one for memo fields. Whenever you press Ctrl–Home in a memo field, the dBASE Word wrap work surface is activated. You can specify the name of a word processor to be used in memo field editing with the statement:

WP=*filename*

placed in the CONFIG.DB file.

Make sure that your word processing files are in the same disk and directory as dBASE, or that you have specified a PC-DOS Path command if the word processor is contained somewhere other than the current directory.

Splitting long command lines

Most computer screens are designed to show 80 characters on each line of the screen. This can sometimes be a drawback to writing readable program statements, because many statements require more than 80 characters. If you continued to type the program statement, regardless of the length of the line, you would need to scroll to the right and left to read the entire line. This may not cause you a problem when you are writing a program—but later, when you are reading that same program to find and fix an error, you will find that oversized statements are tedious, difficult, and nearly impossible to maintain.

The semicolon (;) character is used to specify that a program statement is to be continued on the next line. For example:

ACCEPT "Enter your choice for the menu: ";
TO menuchoice

This ACCEPT command may have been able to fit on one line, but it shows the use of the semicolon as a continuation character. You should take care that you do not split a calculation or other expression unless it is absolutely necessary—and even then, be sure to test the statement thoroughly. If you need to, break long expressions into shorter expressions, and use more statements. It is better to write a readable program in the long run.

You can also use the semicolon to make a program statement more readable. For example, the following REPLACE command:

```
REPLACE ALL    FOR STATE = 'CT' ;
               SALESTAX WITH 0.075, ;
               TAXAMT WITH SALEAMT * SALESTAX
```

might be short, but the continuation is used to separate the parts of the command into easy-to-read groups. This separation can make the statement more readable by allowing you to quickly see the clauses that make up the command.

When you are entering long lines interactively at the dot prompt, you can just keep on typing. dBASE will accept commands up to 1024 characters long at the dot prompt.

Commenting your code

As you write your programs, it is nice to embed your thoughts and reasons for performing routines and using certain statements directly in the program. This is another step to readability—the notes can be used as references later, when finding problems or enhancing the program. If you work in a large company, chances are that someday, someone else might be looking at or changing your program code. The "neat coding trick" that you thought up today will be long forgotten in six months. You may have left the company, leaving that poor hapless individual with no reference to what you were doing. There is a scenario that is much worse—the person looking at your code in six months may be YOU! You may not remember your own train of thought from a Tuesday afternoon, six months ago, when you had the idea of writing a particular program in a particular way.

Therefore, most computer languages have a method of embedding comments directly in the program code, either on a line by themselves, or on the same line with a program statement. dBASE IV supports both types of commenting.

A full-line comment is created by starting the line with a single "*," like this:

```
* This is a comment
```

or by using the word NOTE, as in this example:

```
NOTE This is also a comment
```

Comments can be of any length, up to the 1024 character line limit.

You could use a technique known as *flower-boxing* to create comments that are easily seen to be important. At the beginning of a program you might have several lines of comments enclosed in a "flower box." For example:

```
* * * * * * * * * * * * * * * *
*                           *
*   MAIN MODULE    *
*   SYSTEM ABCD    *
*                           *
* * * * * * * * * * * * * * * *
```

Your comments should stand out from your program statements—and they should not interfere with your ability to read and understand your program statements. Use your own judgment in this matter. As you gain experience in writing dBASE IV programs, you will decide for yourself how much commenting is too much.

Comments can be placed on the same line as a program statement by using "&&" between the code and the comment. For example:

```
STORE 0.075 TO SALESTAX       && CT state sales tax is 7.5%
```

The "&&" commenting method can be used in several ways. You could place comments on every line of program code. You could also only comment those statements that you feel need to be commented on. Using the "same line" comment means that you are losing some of that valuable line-space (80 characters, remember?) to the comment.

There is another alternative—put the comment on the same line, but more than 80 characters from the beginning of the line. This means that your program statement will occupy your full attention—but if you need to look at the comments, you could scroll to the right to look at the comment. This places the comments on a "second page," just out of sight but immediately available.

By commenting your program code as you write it, you will save a lot of time and grief later on. Make your comments precise and readable (more readable than your code!) so that you will have no misunderstandings in the future.

There are several database access commands that you will see in this section of the chapter. These commands will allow you to open and use databases, choose index orders, add, change, and delete data, and finally to close the databases when you are through.

Database access commands

You will see several database access commands in this section of the chapter. These commands will allow you to open and use databases, choose index orders, add, change, and delete data, and finally to close the databases when you are done.

USE

The USE command lets you open an existing database file. If you have any .MDX index files they are also opened automatically. If you have the dBASE III style .NDX index files you have to specify them in order to use them. The USE command also automatically opens a .DBT memo file if the database contains memo fields.

A typical USE command looks like this:

. USE INVENTRY

If you wanted to open an .MDX or .NDX file specifically, add the INDEX clause to the command:

. USE INVENTRY INDEX INVENTRY

The INDEX parameter does not have to open an index file with the same name. Your index files can be any name you want. If both an .MDX file and an .NDX file exists with the name you specify, the .MDX file takes precedence.

If you want to activate a specific index tag in the .MDX file you can use the ORDER parameter:

. USE INVENTRY ORDER TAG ITEM

USE ? displays a menu of the .DBF files that are cataloged when the catalog is open. When the catalog is not open, USE ? displays all of the .DBF files in the current directory.

Later in this chapter you will see how to open more than one database at a time in different work areas.

APPEND BLANK

The APPEND command is used in native dBASE dot prompt to display a data entry form on the screen to add data to a database. Usually when using custom command files to add data to databases, a different form of the APPEND command is used.

The APPEND BLANK command is used to add a blank record to the bottom of the database. Once the blank record is added, the blank values in all the fields can be replaced with actual field values by using the REPLACE command.

While the REPLACE command lets you change existing fields, the "APPEND BLANK" command is needed to add new records. This command adds a totally blank field to the end of the database. APPEND BLANK is usually followed by a REPLACE to fill the fields. An indexed database automatically is indexed by either command. If an APPEND BLANK command is performed and no REPLACE ever follows it, a blank record will be in the file.

The APPEND BLANK command should not be used unless a REPLACE immediately follows it. You should do all your error checking first, and then use the APPEND BLANK and REPLACE commands.

The normal form of the APPEND BLANK command is simply:

. APPEND BLANK

REPLACE

So far you have seen several commands that manipulate variables in memory. Also, several commands manipulate data in a database. The first is the REPLACE command.

You will see the REPLACE command used often in programming, especially when records are added or changed in a database through programming. Changing data using a program is a multi-step process involving the REPLACE command. When using the EDIT command, your data is updated automatically.

Let's first look at adding a new record to a database. To use the REPLACE command a database must be open. When the REPLACE command is issued, the current record fields are REPLACEd by the command for those fields specified in the REPLACE command. If you wish to place a numeric memory variable into a character field or vice versa, the STR or VAL conversion functions must also be used. These are explained in the next chapter on the function library.

Assuming you have data for the fields you want to add to a new record, use the following commands to first place values into some memory variables, then to open the database, add a blank record, and replace the database values with the values from the memory variables:

```
. STORE 'AVON APPLIANCE' TO COMP
. STORE 'CA' TO ST
. STORE 25000 TO ES
. USE CUSTOMER
. APPEND BLANK
. REPLACE COMPANY WITH COMP,STATE WITH ST,EST_SALES WITH ES
```

The simple REPLACE adds data to the three fields of the database. Usually the values come from screen input, not from a direct assignment statement.

Only the fields in a database that you wish to change from being blank to having data need to be referenced by the REPLACE command. Generally, when a screen is READ and the user's data input is evaluated, the data is placed in temporary storage while it is validated. Once validated, the data must be placed in the database. When you are adding new records, it is easy as the APPEND BLANK command is used as shown.

However, when you are changing existing records, there are a few more steps because you aren't simply inputting new data into empty memory variables. First, you must take a copy of the data fields from the database and place them into the memory variables you create. The steps are:

- Create memory variables for all fields in the database.
- STORE each database field to its memory variable.
- Create a screen using the memory variables.
- Let the user change any or all of the fields.
- Validate the changes.

- After validation, REPLACE all the fields in the database with the values of the memory variables.

Adding new records is very much the same except the following steps are used:

- Create memory variables for all fields in the database.
- APPEND BLANK to create a blank record in the database.
- Create a screen using the memory variables.
- Let the user enter data in all of the fields.
- Validate the changes.
- After validation, REPLACE all the blank fields in the database with the values of the memory variables.

When you add or change values in the database with an index, each index is updated by the key field. Later, when you see AJAX create their add or change programs, you will see this process.

The REPLACE command also lets you change the value of a field in a database without a screen. You can change just one record or all the records in a database. The simplest form of the REPLACE command is the following:

REPLACE SALARY WITH SALARY * 1.1

This multiplies the salary at the current record pointer in the open database by 1.1 (10%) to give everyone a raise. You can also extend the scope of the REPLACE command to selected records:

REPLACE SALARY WITH SALARY * 1.1 FOR NAME = 'SMITH'

Now, only the people named SMITH receive a raise. You can also have the REPLACE command change all the records in the database with the ALL scope command:

REPLACE ALL SALARY WITH SALARY * 1.1

You can also have the REPLACE command use other columns in the database or variables you have created. For example:

REPLACE ALL INVNTRY WITH ONHAND + PURCH

This would add the columns ONHAND to PURCH in the open database and change the value of INVNTRY in the open database.

You can also use a memory variable in the REPLACE statement whose name is the same as a name of a field in the database:

REPLACE PCT WITH AMT/M—>AMT

This changes the field PCT in the database to the value of the field AMT divided by the memory variable AMT. The notation "M—>" is only necessary if a field on the database has the same name as a memory variable. Remember, in that case, the field always takes precedence unless the "M—>"

notation is used. The variable AMT could have been created with the SUM command as the sum of the field AMT in the database. This would let you calculate the percentage of each employee's salary to the total payroll. The SUM command would have looked like this:

```
SUM AMT TO M—>AMT
```

REPLACE FROM ARRAY

This variation of the REPLACE command allows for the replacing of fields in a record with values from a predefined array. Data is copied from the first row of the specified array into fields of the active database file. The first array element is copied to the first field, the second element to the second field, and so on. The process stops when there are no more fields or there are no more elements to process. The syntax of the command is:

```
REPLACE FROM ARRAY array name [FIELDS field list] REINDEX
    [FOR condition] [WHILE condition]
```

This command specifies the array to use, what fields to update on the database, whether to reindex the file after updating, and optionally whether to use a criterion specified in the FOR and/or the WHILE conditions to select the records to be updated.

BLANK

BLANK is a command that will fill fields of a database according to the data type of the specified field. The syntax of the command is:

```
BLANK [FIELDS field list/LIKE/EXCEPT skeleton] [REINDEX] [scope]
    [FOR condition] [WHILE condition]
```

where the FIELDS option lets you specify certain fields to clear to blank, including the optional LIKE and EXCEPT options. You can specify a REINDEX after the BLANK processing by including that option in the command. You can select certain records within the database by specifying a FOR and/or WHILE condition.

INSERT

The INSERT command lets you add a new record to the database after the location of the current record pointer. It is usually used with non-indexed files. This command lets you place a record between two existing records. This is the only way to add a record in a physical spot in the database other than at the end. The INSERT command by itself:

```
. INSERT
```

gives you a full screen entry form just like APPEND. With INSERT, the record is added in between two existing records, and not to the bottom of the file.

If the database is indexed, the record is added to the bottom of the file regardless of the file pointer. The index is updated normally. If it is crucial to place a record in a certain physical location in an indexed file, you could remove the index with the SET INDEX TO command, INSERT the record, set the index to the correct index, and then use the REINDEX command to rebuild the index.

If you need to insert a record in the first position, you can move the record pointer to the top of the file with the command:

```
. GO TOP
```

or

```
. 1
```

then use the form of the INSERT command:

```
. INSERT BEFORE
```

When the INSERT command is used in a program, it is generally used like the APPEND BLANK command. The command:

```
. INSERT BLANK
```

inserts a blank record after the record pointer, and then the REPLACE command fills the record with data.

DELETE

The DELETE command is used to delete records no longer wanted. This will not physically remove the record but only mark it for removal.

In order to remove the record, a PACK command must be given. The PACK command copies the entire file without copying the marked records to a new database and then renames it back to the original name. The old database with the marked records is then deleted. If the file is indexed, the new file is reindexed.

One problem you might have is that as you DELETE records, they are still found by search commands. The function "DELETED( )" can be used to see if they are marked for deletion and are just "hanging around" until the PACK command is given:

```
USE CUSTOMER ORDER TAG COMPANY
FIND 'AVON APPLIANCE'
IF .NOT. DELETED( )
    DELETE
ENDIF
```

The ".NOT. DELETED( )" phrase checks to see if the record is marked for deletion even if it is found. This is especially useful when PACKs are done infrequently and searches of a database might yield deleted records. This in effect makes them invisible. You can also use the SET DELETED ON command to make deleted records invisible.

The DELETE command marks the current record in the database for deletion. Later in the program, the database can be PACKed. Because PACKing a database means copying all the records, it can take some time. Only use a PACK command when you have to, not every time you delete one record.

If you want to delete *all* the records in a database and pack it at the same time, you can use the command:

    ZAP

Be very careful as this command instantly deletes all the records in the database, and they can't be RECALLed.

CLOSE ALL/DATABASES

The CLOSE ALL command closes all the files of every type and returns you to work area one. If you want to close all your open files without affecting memory:

    .CLOSE ALL

CLOSE DATABASES has no effect on work area 10 if a catalog is open. Beyond closing all the database files, it also closes any associated index (.NDX or .MDX) files, memo files (.DBT), and any format (.FMT) files. To close only the database you have currently selected, use the USE command with no parameters instead of CLOSE. To close all the database index, and format files you have opened:

    . CLOSE DATABASES

Input commands

These commands concern the ACCEPT and INPUT commands.

ACCEPT

The ACCEPT command is used to allow the entry of a single value from the keyboard. You can display a message and then accept input from the keyboard. The ACCEPT command is used extensively in command files to make interactive decisions:

    ACCEPT "Enter a disk drive specification: " TO CHOICE

When this command is run the screen displays the following:

    Enter a disk drive specification:

You can then enter a disk drive specification. Your answer is set to the variable CHOICE, or whatever variable you use in the ACCEPT command. You do not have to define the variable you use in advance. The data type of whatever you enter is used as the data type of the variable created. You can now use the variable CHOICE in any expression or statement that allows variables. The variable exists until it is cleared or its value changed.

The ACCEPT command can use a memory variable for a prompt:

```
STORE "Enter your choice ==>" TO ENTC
ACCEPT ENTC TO CHOICE
```

This displays the prompt Enter your choice ==>, then lets the user input a value to be placed in the memory variable CHOICE. This form of the ACCEPT command lets you place the ACCEPT command in a loop and lets you change the prompt.

The ACCEPT command is sometimes used in conjunction with a TYPE command as a substitute for a menu. The TYPE command is run first displaying text that gives menu choices. The ACCEPT command is then used to get the choice. This code might look like this:

```
TYPE MENUTXT
ACCEPT "Enter your menu selection: " TO MENC
```

and might produce a screen like this:

```
AJAX APPLIANCE COMPANY

1 - Customer System
2 - Employee System
3 - Order System
4 - Inventory System

Enter your menu selection:
```

The top part of the screen would be found in the MENUTXT file and displayed with the TYPE command. The bottom entry line is displayed with the ACCEPT command. No matter what is entered by the user, it is accepted as a character string.

INPUT

The INPUT command is very similar to the ACCEPT command except that the INPUT command requires delimiters to be entered by the user to input the response as a character field. The same is true for data input—it would have to be converted from character to date when it is input.

The examples below show the input of a character variable, numeric variable and a date variable:

```
INPUT "Enter the company name ==> " TO NAME
       Enter the company name ==> "AVON APPLIANCE"
```

INPUT "Enter the company sales ==>" TO SALES
    Enter the company sales ==> 250000

INPUT "Enter the last sales date ==>" TO LSD
    Enter the last sales date ==> {05/15/88}

Screen display commands

The screen display commands control the way the screen appears.

?/??/???   The "?" command is used to write literals and variables to the screen or printer. Remember, literals are constants such as a title while variables are those fields which receive data: The ? writes whatever follows it after issuing a line feed and carriage return. The "??" command displays whatever follows it starting at the current screen or printer position. The ??? is used solely to send printer control codes to the printer.

    The ? command is used at the beginning of a line and writes the line to the device specified. An example of the ? command is:

```
? 'Order Number: ' + ORDRN
   Order Number: 203
```

The phrase "Order Number: " is enclosed in single quotes to show that it is a literal. The ORDRN field is a variable; it is not enclosed in quotes. The value of ORDRN is substituted into the example.

    The line is printed starting at the beginning of the next line. Subsequent lines are printed following the original line.

    Notice a "+" between the literal and variable. The "+" is a connector between literals or variables which allows them to be concatenated. Concatenation is the term that means putting strings together. In math, $1+1=2$, in concatenation "1" + "1" = "11". There is also another symbol for concatenation. The "−" concatenates fields but eliminates any blanks between the fields. The following example shows the difference:

```
? 'Order Number: ' + ORDRN yields Order Number: 231
'? 'Order Number: ' − ORDRN yields Order Number: 231
```

The number of concatenations on a line is unlimited. You can combine many variables and literals:

```
'Dear ' + NAME
'On' + DATE + ' You bought ' + AMT + 'Widgets'
```

WAIT   The WAIT command stops processing temporarily. It is a way to freeze the command file until a key is pressed. Accompanied by a prompt, it can be a valuable command:

```
WAIT "Enter any letter to continue" TO HOLDIT
```

This example stops processing and displays the message:

Enter any letter to continue

When a key is pressed, its value is stored to the variable HOLDIT.

If no prompt is specified with the WAIT command the prompt Press any key to continue... is displayed.

TYPE   The TYPE command displays a screen full of text from an external file:

TYPE MYSCRN.TXT

The DOS file MYSCRN.TXT is displayed on the screen. If there are more than 24 lines, the top scrolls off the screen.

The TYPE command is very similar to the DOS TYPE command except that it displays the contents of an ASCII file starting with the current screen position. This TYPE command displays menu text, help screens, or even external files that might need to be incorporated into a system.

TEXT-ENDTEXT   The TEXT-ENDTEXT commands also display blocks of text to the screen. You can create a block of text, and when dBASE finds the TEXT command, dBASE begins displaying it without any evaluation until the ENDTEXT command is encountered. An example of the TEXT-ENDTEXT command and the ACCEPT command is shown in Fig. 16-9.

```
TEXT

              Ajax Appliance System

              1 - Customer System

              2 - Employee System

              3 - Order System

              4 - Inventory System

ENDTEXT

ACCEPT "Enter your selection ===>  " TO CHOICE
```

16-9   The TEXT-ENDTEXT command.

@ SAY   This command allows literals or variables to be exactly positioned on the screen. The "@" command signals that the literal or variable following the "SAY" should be displayed on the screen or printed.

Using full-screen commands. The exact location depends on the line and column. The line and column can be numbers or variables. The line can be a number from 0 to 24 for screens. The "column" can be 0 to 79 for 80-column screens.

This command is the most used in programming because of its ability to put any output at any location of the screen. Whether you are programming menus or screens of any kind, the @ SAY command is very necessary. An example of this is the following:

```
@ 5,15 SAY 'Dear'
@ 5,20 SAY NAME
@ 6,15 SAY 'On'
@ 6,18 SAY DATE
@ 6,27 SAY 'You bought'
@ 6,37 SAY AMT
@ 6,42 SAY 'Widgets';
```

You can also use these together if you wish with concatenation and the ? command:

```
@ 5,15 SAY 'Dear ' + NAME
? 'On ' + DATE + ' You bought ' + AMT + ' Widgets'
```

This allows the exact positioning of the first line, and the second line follows right behind it using the ? command.

Picture templates and functions. There is also an advanced form of the @ SAY command called the "@ SAY PICTURE" command. This works exactly the same as the PICTURE templates and functions in the @ GET commands described later in this chapter. Instead of affecting how the data is input, it affects how the data is output. You can determine what a variable looks like when it is output. This is usually used with numeric variables to form an edit mask. Some examples are found in Fig. 16-10.

```
        STORE 12345 TO XYZ
    1.  @ 5,10 SAY XYZ PICTURE   '99999'
    2.  @ 5,10 SAY XYZ PICTURE   '$$$,$$$.99'
    3.  @ 5,10 SAY XYZ * 50 PICTURE   '**$,$$$,$99'
    4.  @ 5,10 SAY XYZ * 50 PICTURE   '999'


    1.          12345
    2.          $12,345.00
    3.          **$617,250
    4.          250
```

16-10   Examples of PICTURE clauses.

As noted in Fig. 16-10, examples 3 and 4, you can also have expressions in the @ SAY command. Any mathematical expression or string expression may appear here.

As can be seen from Fig. 16-10, the same number looks very different because of the edit mask. Be very careful not to specify an edit mask that does not contain enough digit selectors such as #, 9, X, A, $, or *. If there are not enough the number is shortened from left to right as in Fig. 16-10, example number 4.

The complete list of PICTURE templates and functions are shown in Figs. 16-11 and 16-12. The functions (,^, $, B, C, D, E, L, X, and Z are used for output with numeric numbers. The functions !, A, D, E, I, J, R, and T are used with character string output. Many examples of templates and functions are in the section on the @ GET command.

9	Only Digits 0-9 for character fields
	Digits 0-9 and + , − , . for numeric fields
#	Only Digits 0-9 and + , − , . and spaces can be input
A	Allows only letters (A-Z) to be input
L	Allows only logical data (T,F)
Y	Allows only logical data (Y,y,N,n) and converts to uppercase
N	Allows only letters and digits
X	Allows any character to be input
!	Converts letters to uppercase
$	Displays dollar signs in place of leading zeros
*	Displays asterisks in place of leading zeros
.	Specifies decimal position
,	Displays a comma if there are digits to the left of the comma

16-11 PICTURE TEMPLATES.

C	Displays CR (credit) after a positive number
X	Displays DB (debit) after a negative number
(	Encloses negative numbers in parentheses
B	Left justifies numeric data
Z	Displays zero as a blank
D	American date format
E	European date format
A	Alphabetic characters only
!	Converts letters to uppercase
^	Converts numbers to scientific notation
$	Displays data in currency format
L	Displays leading zeros
M	Multiple choice—allows only specified choices
R	Uses literals in template and not in database
S<n>	Limits field width display but allows horizontal scrolling

16-12 PICTURE FUNCTIONS.

Drawing lines and boxes. You can draw lines or boxes on the screen with the new @ TO command in dBASE IV. When you think of your screen, think of it in terms of X,Y coordinates. The screen is 24 lines down by 80 columns across. The lines are numbered 0 to 23 while the columns are numbered 0 to

79. The top left corner of the screen is coordinate (0,0), top right (0,79), bottom left (23,0), and bottom right (23,79). The middle of the screen is about (12,40).

The command to draw a horizontal line from near the top left corner to near the top right corner would be:

@ 2,5 TO 2,75

To draw the same line using a double line you would enter:

@ 2,5 TO 2,75 DOUBLE

A vertical line down the left side of the screen would be drawn with such coordinates as:

@ 4,5 TO 22,5

By choosing two points, neither of which are on the same line, you would draw a box. The following commands would draw a small box near the center of the screen:

@ 9,30 TO 15,50

Figure 16-13 shows the program and screen used to display the screen in Fig. 16-13.

Filling screen areas with color. The @ FILL lets you paint areas of the screen with color. @ FILL works just like @ TO except that instead of drawing a line,

```
Edit: A:BOXES.prg
SET TALK OFF                              <
SET ECHO OFF                              <
@ 2,5 TO 2,75                             <
@ 4,5 TO 22,5                             <
@ 9,30 TO 15,50 DOUBLE                    <
```

16-13 Drawing lines and boxes.

@FILL encloses the area in the foreground and background color you specify. In the following example, the screen would be changed to white letters on a red background in the rectangle formed from positions 1,25 to 10,55:

```
@ 1,25 FILL TO 10,55 COLOR W/R
```

The color parameter of the @ SAY command specifies the colors for the SAY variables. The SAY command uses standard colors. They follow the same rules as these options in the SET COLOR command. Foreground and background colors can be specified for each one:

```
@ 1,25 SAY TEXT COLOR W/B,R/B
```

If you omit the color code, the standard and enhanced colors will be left unchanged. If you leave out the standard code, but want to change the enhanced colors, place a comma in front of the enhanced code so the comma parser can determine that the standard code has not been changed:

```
@ 1,25 SAY TEXT COLOR ,R/B
```

Clearing parts of the screen. You can clear parts of the screen in much the same way as you can draw lines and boxes on parts of the screen. The command:

```
@ 10,25 CLEAR TO 10,35
```

clears the horizontal area on line 10 from columns 25 to 35. You can clear a vertical line the same way by changing the coordinates.

A rectangular area can be cleared by entering the right coordinates. Most of the center of the screen is cleared with the command:

```
@ 3,10 CLEAR TO 20,70
```

Only a small border is not cleared around the outside of the screen. If you enter the command as:

```
@ 10,20 CLEAR
```

everything will be erased from 10,20 to the bottom right corner 23,79.

CLEAR   The CLEAR command clears the entire screen. The command CLEAR can appear anywhere in a command file and clears the screen to make it ready for new output commands. The CLEAR command can be used by itself or it can be coupled with an IF clause in a command file.

Scrolling part of the screen   You can shift a part of the screen up, down, left, or right. This might be useful when writing special programs for scrolling through a file of data. The syntax of the command is:

```
@ row1,column1 TO row2,column2 SCROLL [UP/DOWN/LEFT/RIGHT] [BY expN]
[WRAP]
```

The BY option allows for moving a section of the screen by more than one row or column at a time. The WRAP option redisplays the text that goes off one side of the screen back onto the other, creating a wrapping effect for the display.

@ GET

Entering data   The @ GET command is the cornerstone of building screens with many variables that can be all entered at one time and then manipulated. The general form of the @ GET command is:

@ *line,column* GET *variable*

This command allows input to be read from the screen directly into the named variable. The location for the retrieval of input from the screen may be exactly positioned with the @ *line,column* GET command. The @ GET command signals that an area should be set up and defined by reverse video or the delimiter of choice with a length equal to the variable length. The variable can be predefined as a new variable or it can be a field from a database. If the field name exists as a memory variable, that is, a variable created with a STORE command outside of a database, and also exists as a field in an open database, the length from the database field is used.

Normally, the reverse video area is blank unless the variable presently has data in it. If the memory variable or database field has data in it, the data is displayed in the field. The cursor is positioned to the beginning of the field ready to receive input. If more than one field is to be input, the cursor is positioned to the first.

dBASE IV does not stop to "read" all the GETs until a READ command is issued. This causes dBASE IV to stop and look for all pending GETs. If there is no READ command, there is no input from the screen.

The exact location depends on the line and column. The line and column can be numbers or variables. Line can be a number from 0 to 23, while column can be 0 to 79 for 80-column screens.

Generally, the @ GET command is preceded by a @ SAY command. An example of this is found in Fig. 16-14.

16-14   Using the @ GET command.

```
STORE '            ' TO NAME
@ 5,15 SAY 'Enter Your Name'
@ 5,31 GET NAME
READ

            Enter Your Name
```

The single @ GET followed by the READ lets you input the one field in the example. Multiple fields can be input the same way with multiple GETS and only one READ statement.

In Fig. 16-15, you can see multiple @ SAY and @ GET commands. The first four fields already have data in them and new data can now be entered. The last field is blank as no data is present. Notice the @ SAY and @ GET are on the same line. Also notice the @ GET command has no line and column specification. If they are on the same line, the @ GET is assumed to be one character to the right of where the @ SAY ends.

```
STORE 'CAROL ZARSKY     ' TO NAME
STORE '212 Auburn Rd.   ' TO ADDR
STORE 'Springfield, MA  ' TO LOCATION
STORE '05774' TO ZIP
STORE          TO BIRTH
@  5,15 SAY 'Enter Your Changes:'
@  7,10 SAY 'NAME       'GET NAME
@  8,10 SAY 'ADDRESS    'GET ADDR
@  9,10 SAY 'LOCATION   'GET LOCATION
@ 10,10 SAY 'ZIP CODE   'GET ZIP
@ 11,10 SAY 'BIRTHDATE 'GET BIRTH
READ
```

16-15 Using multiple @ GET commands.

```
        Enter Your Changes

        NAME       CAROL ZARSKY
        ADDRESS    212 Auburn Rd.
        LOCATION   Springfield, MA
        ZIP CODE   05774
        BIRTHDATE    /  /
```

You can enter data in any of the fields on the screen that are included in the @ GET to READ commands. You can move back and forth from one field to another. When you press Return on the last field, the data is actually "READ."

Picture templates and functions The "@ GET" command also has several advanced forms. The first is the "@ GET PICTURE" command. Use this option to restrict the type of data that may be entered into a variable or to format the data displayed. The clause can consist of a function, which is preceded by an @ symbol, and affects all the input or output characters, and/or a template, which affects input or output on a character-by-character basis. A PICTURE clause can be any character expression, although it is usually a string of characters delimited by quotation marks. If the clause is a memory variable, it is enclosed in parentheses.

The PICTURE option can also accept character expressions that are variables containing function and template symbols. Formatting contained in variables works no differently than function and template symbols used in a program or on a command line.

Functions can also be used with the FUNCTION option; these do not need to be preceded with the @ symbol. Please note that the PICTURE and FUNCTION options can each be used only once on any one command line.

Here you can determine what a variable will look like when it is input or output. This is used with numeric variables to form an edit mask. Figure 16-16 shows some of these picture clauses in use.

```
STORE 0 TO QTY
STORE '          ' TO BIRTH
STORE '              ' TO PARTNO
STORE '                ' TO PHONE
@ 5,15 SAY 'Enter Your Changes:'
@ 7,10 SAY 'QUANTITY   'GET QTY PICTURE '999'
@ 8,10 SAY 'BIRTHDATE 'GET BIRTH PICTURE '99/99/99'
@ 9,10 SAY 'PARTNO    ' ;
     GET PARTNO PICTURE 'AAA-XX-999'
@ 10,10 SAY 'PHONE NO. ' ;
     GET PHONE PICTURE '(999)999-9999'
READ

          Enter Your Changes

     QUANTITY
     BIRTHDATE   / /
     PARTNO      -  -
     PHONE NO. (   )   -
```

16-16 Using @ GET picture clauses.

As can be seen from Fig. 16-16, the edit templates specified in the @ GETs allow special characters to be inserted in the fields. Templates also restrict input to certain types of data. The quantity field is straightforward and allows up to three numbers to be inserted. The birthdate field accepts six numbers with each set of two being separated by slashes. The part number uses some of the more interesting digit selectors for GET commands (see Fig. 16-11). Part Number is an eight-digit field with the first three as alphabetic only (A-Z), the next two as any character or number, while the last three must be numbers (0-9). Phone Number is a ten-digit field of all numbers with parentheses and a dash in the field. The two examples in Fig. 16-16 show the @ SAY and @ GET on separate lines. This is allowed as long as the @ SAY line ends with a semicolon (;). The various PICTURE templates were shown in Fig. 16-11.

Also, a variety of special functions can affect how data is input to the entry form. For example, if the PICTURE clauses are used without the special function @R when these fields are saved, they are saved with the special characters. Birthdate will grow to eight characters, Part Number to ten, and Phone Number to thirteen. All these fields must be defined as character fields except quantity, because of the use of special characters. You might enter a "−" sign in front of quantity to show a negative value or a "." to show decimal places. These characters also take up room. If decimals are to be stored, the database field must be defined to eight decimals.

However, a number of special functions are used with the template characters to affect data entry and storage. Figure 16-12 showed the various functions that affect the @ GET and @ SAY commands. Several of these need explanation. While the template symbols tell where individual characters might flow, the functions affect the entire entry area. Some of the functions are strictly used for output with the @ SAY functions, while some are used with both input and output commands.

The functions B, D, E, and Z are used for input with numeric numbers. The functions !, A, D, E, S, and R are used with character string input. Figure 16-17 shows the same example as shown in Fig. 16-16 with PICTURE functions added.

```
STORE 0 TO QTY
STORE '          ' TO BIRTH
STORE '            ' TO PARTNO
STORE '              ' TO PHONE
@ 5,15 SAY 'Enter Your Changes:'
@ 7,10 SAY 'QUANTITY  'GET QTY PICTURE '@B 999'
@ 8,10 SAY 'BIRTHDATE 'GET BIRTH PICTURE '@D 99/99/99'
@ 9,10 SAY 'PARTNO      ' ;
    GET PARTNO PICTURE '@R! AAA-XX-999'
@ 10,10 SAY 'PHONE NO. ' ;
    GET PHONE PICTURE '@R (999)999-9999'
READ

        Enter Your Changes

    QUANTITY  :   :
    BIRTHDATE :  / / _ :
    PARTNO    :   - - :
    PHONE NO. :(   )   -     :
```

16-17 Using the picture functions.

The QTY field has the @B function added. The number is left justified when entered. The BIRTH field accepts data entry in the American date format MM/DD/YY due to the @D format. If the @E function is used, the entry field would expect the date in the European date format DD/MM/YY.

The PARTNO field has two functions. First, the @R function keeps the dashes from being added to the database when the field is placed on the database. The ! function is combined with the R function to convert any letters entered to uppercase. Finally, the PHONE number field also uses the @R function to keep the special characters from being added to the database.

One function that isn't shown is the @S*n* function. This allows a field to be entered that is much larger than the entry area. Suppose you have a company name field. The average company name is 15 characters wide. You do, however, have 5 customers which take 25 characters. Because you need as much room as you can on your form, you decide to create the entry area as only 15 characters, but the field itself is 30 characters. By using the @S function, you can enter more than the 15 characters shown on the screen. After you enter the 15th character, the additional characters will scroll previous characters off the screen to the left. You can "pan" the field with the Ctrl–F and Ctrl–A keystrokes. For example:

@ 10,10 GET COMPANY PICTURE '@S15 AAAAAAAAAAAAAAA'

A final note about changing numbers—when you enter numbers into the system, it sometimes does not look correct. This is because the system stores numbers right-justified, but you are entering them left-justified. Figure 16-18 shows the various ways numbers are handled.

```
                            QUANTITY  :    0:   (Before Entering)
                            QUANTITY  :23  0:   (After Entering 23)
                            QUANTITY  :   23:   (After Hitting Enter)
16-18  Examples of numeric
       justification.       QUANTITY  :  205:   (Before Entering)
                            QUANTITY  :2135:    (After Entering 213)
                            QUANTITY  :  213:   (After Hitting Enter)
```

RANGE specifications   You can perform limited data validation with the RANGE option of the @ GET command. This lets you specify range checking with the RANGE command. You can specify a lower and an upper limit. For example, the command:

@ 10,15 GET SALARY RANGE 0,15000

only accepts numbers between 0 and 15000. If you attempt to enter a number outside the range, dBASE IV prompts you until you enter a number within the range. Date ranges can also be accepted with the function CTOD:

@ 10,15 GET DOB RANGE {'01/01/21'}, {'12/31/68'}

only accepts people whose birthdates were between January 1, 1921, and December 31, 1968. You can combine templates, functions and ranges like this:

@ 10,15 GET SALARY PICTURE '@B 999,999.99' RANGE 0,125000

There is an optional addition to the RANGE command, the REQUIRED statement. If present, it makes the system check the range clause whenever the cursor is positioned at the GET instruction where it is present. It does not allow for skipping through the field if the REQUIRED option is present right next to the RANGE statement.

Multiple choice fields   The multiple choice field is actually a special version of a function. The M function allows for multiple choices. When you create an input field with the multiple choice function, you can change the choices by pressing the Spacebar—just like creating a database field type. A normal form of this would be:

@ 10,25 SAY 'ENTER THE ANIMAL TYPE' ;
    GET ANIMAL PICTURE '@M COW,DUCK,HORSE,GOAT,SHEEP'

When the screen is displayed, the first choice is displayed in the field entry area. When the cursor is placed in the field and the Spacebar is pressed, the field changes from COW to DUCK to HORSE, etc. The user can also press the first letter of the desired selection.

Data validation The @ command has many other data validation options. Some examples are shown in the following paragraphs.

@ row, col. Without any options, the @ command clears the specified row beginning at the specified column position.

DEFAULT. Use the expression to put a preset value into a GET variable; it must match the GET variable's data type. The expression is evaluated only when you add records to a database file. The DEFAULT expression appears in the GET variable, and pressing Enter assigns the value to the GET variable. A DEFAULT value is overridden by any value brought forward by a SET CARRY command.

MESSAGE. expC must be a valid character expression, which then appears when a READ is executed and the cursor is placed in the GET field associated with the message. If SET STATUS is ON, the message is centered on the bottom line of the screen. If SET STATUS is OFF, the message does not appear. This command temporarily overrides a SET MESSAGE expression.

VALID. This option can state a condition that must be met before data is accepted into the GET variable. If the condition is not met, the message Editing condition not satisfied, or the message you defined with the ERROR option appears. No checking takes place if you press Enter without pressing any other key.

As with the RANGE statement, there is an optional addition to the VALID command, the REQUIRED statement. If present, it makes the system check the VALID clause whenever the cursor is positioned at the GET instruction where it is present. It does not allow for skipping through the field if the REQUIRED option is next to the VALID statement.

ERROR. expC is any valid character expression. Use this option to display your own message when the VALID *condition* is not met. Your message overrides dBASE IV's message, Editing condition not satisfied.

WHEN. You can provide a condition that is evaluated when you try to move the cursor into a GET field. If the condition is true, the cursor moves into the field for you to edit. If the condition is false, the cursor skips the field and moves to the next one.

WINDOW window name. When you use the @ command with GET variable, and the variable is a memo field, you can use the WINDOW option to open a separate editing window. Put the cursor on the memo field and press Ctrl–Home to open the window; Ctrl–End closes the window. The word MEMO you see on screen is in uppercase if the field contains text. If the field is empty, memo is in lowercase letters. The *window name* is the name of a window you have already defined. Without the WINDOW option, dBASE IV uses full-screen editing. The editor within the window is the one you specified in the CONFIG.DB file.

OPEN WINDOW window name. The editing window for your memo field can be opened by default. You don't need to open and close it if OPEN is included in the WINDOW option. You do use Ctrl–Home and Ctrl–End to enter and exit the window. A typical input screen's data might look like Fig. 16-19.

```
@ 1,29 SAY "AJAX APPLIANCE COMPANY"
@ 2,30 SAY "CUSTOMER DATA ENTRY"
@ 6,28 SAY "CUSTOMER NUMBER:"
@ 6,45 GET csn PICTURE "@! AA-999" ;
    MESSAGE "Enter a new customer number"
@ 8,26 SAY "COMPANY NAME:"
@ 8,40 GET cmp PICTURE "@! XXXXXXXXXXXXXXXXXXXX" ;
    MESSAGE "Enter the company name"
@ 10,32 SAY "STREET:"
@ 10,40 GET str PICTURE "@! XXXXXXXXXXXXXXXXXXXX" ;
    MESSAGE "Enter the customers street address"
@ 11,34 SAY "CITY:"
@ 11,40 GET cty PICTURE "@! XXXXXXXXXXXXXXXXXXX" ;
    MESSAGE "Enter the customers city"
@ 12,33 SAY "STATE:"
@ 12,40 GET stt PICTURE "@!M CA,CT,NM,NY,OK,PA" ;
    MESSAGE "Enter the customers state"
@ 13,30 SAY "ZIP CODE:"
@ 13,40 GET zp PICTURE "99999-####" ;
    MESSAGE "Enter the customers zip code"
@ 15,33 SAY "PHONE:"
@ 15,40 GET phn PICTURE "(###)999-9999" ;
    MESSAGE "Enter the customers phone number"
@ 17,17 SAY "LAST TRANSACTION DATE:"
@ 17,40 GET ltd ;
    RANGE {01/01/80},DATE()+60 ;
    WHEN LTD # {  /  /  } ;
    MESSAGE "Enter the last transaction date"
@ 19,30 SAY "DISCOUNT:"
@ 19,40 GET dis PICTURE "99" ;
    VALID DIS>= 0 .AND. DIS <= 50 ;
    ERROR "The discount is not valid (0-50) Re-enter the discount"
    MESSAGE "Enter the customers discount"
@ 21,31 SAY "TAXABLE:"
@ 21,40 GET tax PICTURE "L" ;
    DEFAULT .T. ;
    MESSAGE "Enter the customers tax status"
```

16-19 Input screen data validation commands.

Changing colors and highlighting   The @GET command uses enhanced color, and follows the same rules as these options in the SET COLOR command. A foreground or background color may be specified.

The enhanced color codes can stay unchanged by omitting the color code. If you want to change the enhanced color code, but leave the standard code the same, place a comma in front of the enhanced code so the comma parser will know that the standard code has not been changed:

> @1,30 GET TEXT COLOR ,R/B

During the current @ command the colors you specify will override the SET COLOR command.

READ and READ SAVE

While the READ command lets you enter your data into the entry fields, the READ command also clears all the GETs after editing. If you use the field names and enter data directly to a database and are using the APPEND

BLANK command between passes through the @ GETs and the READ, the fields are cleared and appear empty for the next set of data entry. If you are using memory variables you will have to blank them out or the last data entered will remain.

If you are using the field names and the APPEND BLANK to enter data, a special form of the READ command, READ SAVE keeps your old data active.

SAVE/RESTORE/RELEASE SCREEN

These three commands allow for the saving, restoring, and releasing of full-screen images to and from memory. The main purpose of these commands is to allow for overlaying one screen on top of another, doing some special processing, then restoring the old screen to its original display. The format of these commands are as follows:

```
SAVE SCREEN TO screen1
    do some special processing
    on top of the original screen
RESTORE SCREEN FROM screen1
RELEASE SCREEN screen1
```

KEYBOARD

There is a command, KEYBOARD, that allows you to enter a string of characters into the keyboard buffer, just as if the operator entered them. You can specify a character string, a CHR( ) value, or a key label. The syntax is:

```
KEYBOARD expC [CLEAR]
```

The expression will be entered into the keyboard buffer immediately. If the CLEAR option is specified, the keyboard buffer will be cleared before inserting the desired keystrokes into the buffer.

KEYBOARD PgDn CLEAR

KEYBOARD PgDn CLEAR will clear the keyboard buffer and put a PgDn key into it, just as if the operator pressed the PgDn key. dBASE IV will read the character in the buffer when you execute a command that expects keyboard input, such as READ, BROWSE, or EDIT.

SET FORMAT TO

SET FORMAT TO lets you use a form with the READ, EDIT, APPEND, INSERT, CHANGE, or BROWSE commands. The form is stored as a format (.FMO) file, which is compatible with a dBASE IV (.FMT) extension. The SET FORMAT TO command activates the format file named in the command for use with the full-screen editing commands. It also updates a catalog if one is open and SET CATALOG is ON. If you want to see a directory of all the files with an .FMT extension in the active database file, make sure a catalog is open and type: SET FORMAT TO ?. Each work area that has an open database file can have an open format file.

CLEAR/ALL/FIELDS/GETS

When you use the CLEAR command, three things happen. First, the screen is erased. Second, the cursor is repositioned to the lower left-hand corner of your screen; and third, all the GETs that are pending are now released. Several options can be used with CLEAR, but each must be used separately.

CLEAR ALL closes every database file that you have open, releases all memory variables (non-system), array elements, and pop-up and menu definitions. If a catalog file is open, it is also closed by this command.

CLEAR FIELDS releases the fields list created by the SET FIELDS command. Note that this command clears all fields, including those in other work areas.

CLEAR GETS allows you to release all the @...GETs that have been issued since the last CLEAR ALL, CLEAR GETS, or READ command. The default value is 2000 @...GETs permitted by dBASE IV before a CLEAR GETS or READ command must be issued.

Data manipulation commands

Two commands, SUM and TOTAL, are discussed next.

SUM

If you want to total numeric expressions to memory variables or arrays, use SUM. All database records are summed unless it has been otherwise specified by a scope by a FOR or WHILE clause. Also, if there is no expression list, all the numeric fields are summed.

The sum for each numeric expression is placed into the memory variable list or array. The sum of the first numeric expression is put in the first variable or array element, and so on down the list. If you run out of memory variables or elements in the array, only the existing variables or elements are filled. If there are more variables or array elements than are needed, the extras are not filled and contain the original values.

Each named array has to be one-dimensional. SUM produces a type F numeric variable:

```
. USE INVENTRY
. SUM QTY_STK,QTY_STK*PRICE
15 records summed
    QTY_STK QTY*STK*PRICE
1456    756835
```

TOTAL

The TOTAL command sums the numeric fields of the active database file and creates a second database file to hold the results. The TO database file contains the numeric fields that total all the records that have the same key value in the original database.

The TO filename has to include the drive designator if it is not on the default drive. Unless you specify otherwise, a .DBF extension is assumed. Also, unless you specify a scope, or a FOR or WHILE clause, all the records are totaled. All the numeric fields in the record are totaled unless you limit them with the FIELDS list.

The ON option subtotals groups by the expression specified in the ON clause providing the data is sorted or indexed by the data in the ON clause. You must INDEX or SORT the active database file on the key (ON) field. If the TO filename already exists, TOTAL gives a warning prompt before overwriting the file unless SET SAFETY is off.

If an asterisk (**) shows up in the field, the total is too large for the field size. To avoid or correct this, use MODIFY STRUCTURE to increase the size of the fields in the active database to their maximum or your largest total:

```
. USE INVENTRY ORDER BRAND
. TOTAL ON BRAND TO INVBRAND
. USE INVBRAND
. DISP ALL OFF BRAND QTY_STK
```

```
      BRAND QTY_STK

      FROSTY      120
      HIRA        375
      HITECH      198
      RUSTIC      605
      WHOLEPOOL 364
```

If you are following the examples in this part, you might notice that many use fictitious data not found in this book anywhere else. In Part Four, you will see the original data again.

Working with multiple tables

So far, you have seen commands for working with one database. This part looks at working with multiple databases, index and query files, and catalogs.

SELECT

By using the SELECT command, you can choose the work area in which you want to open a database file. You can also specify a work area in which a database file is already open. As you first enter dBASE IV, the active work area is work area number 1. You can use work areas from 1 to 40, and from letters A to J. Beyond work area 10, you must use the number or an alias. Each area that is selected can contain an open database file.

Suppose you want to have two files open in work area 1 and 2 with the following commands, and then you want to return to work area 1:

```
. USE INVENTRY
. SELECT 2
. USE ITEMS
. SELECT 1
```

You can use each of the work areas to open files associated with the database files, like query and index files. SELECT can also change work areas so that the open database file in the selected work area will become the active database file:

```
. SELECT DESIGNS
. USE CURRENT
. SELECT BILLINGS
```

USE

The USE command opens databases as you have already seen. However without the IN= clause, it opens the database in the current work area. If you want to change work areas to open a database, you normally use the SELECT clause and then USE the database in the new work area. You can save one step with the IN= clause. Suppose you want to open the INVENTRY and ITEMS databases and again end up in work area 1:

```
USE INVENTRY IN 1
USE ITEMS IN 2
```

This opens the INVENTRY database in work area 1 and then opens the ITEMS database in work area 2. This also leaves the active work area active. This saves having to return to the original work area and to switch work areas with the SELECT command.

SET RELATION TO and SET SKIP TO

When more than one database is open, you can form relations between them. Let's examine a typical example like the one you have seen already in this book:

```
. USE INVOICE ORDER TAG INVNO IN A
. USE ITEMS ORDER TAG INVNO IN B
. USE CUSTOMER ORDER TAG CUSTNO IN C
. USE INVENTRY ORDER TAG ITEMNO IN D
. SELECT INVOICE
. SET RELATION TO INVNO INTO ITEMS, CUSTNO INTO CUSTOMER
. SELECT ITEMS
. SET RELATION TO ITEMNO INTO INVENTRY
```

This creates the relations for the AJAX APPLIANCE order entry system. The INVOICE file is related to the CUSTOMER file by the customer number and to the ITEMS file by the invoice number. The ITEMS file is further related to the INVENTRY file by the item number.

In order to use the environment thus created, you would, in most languages, need to write an application program to make use of all the data items. The program would have to take care of advancing the record pointer on the ITEMS database, because more than one record exists on the ITEMS database for each invoice on the INVOICE database. The relationship only positions the record pointer at the first record in a series—in this example, the first of a group of ITEMS records that all have the same value in the INVNO field. Somehow, you need to capture the data on all of the ITEMS records that apply to a single invoice.

The SET SKIP TO command gives you this ability. This command tells dBASE to reposition the record pointer in the specified database until the key value in the related database changes. Only when this occurs does dBASE move the record pointer in the controlling database. SET SKIP TO, in effect, automatically repositions the record pointer in child databases without moving the record pointer in the controlling database. If you added the following command to the environment described earlier:

```
...
. SELECT INVOICE
. SET SKIP TO ITEMS
```

the ITEMS database would be repositioned until the relationship is no longer true—that is to say, until the value of INVNO changes on the current ITEMS record. Only after that happens is a new record accessed in the INVOICE database. If you set up the environment listed previously:

```
. USE INVOICE ORDER TAG INVNO IN A
. USE ITEMS ORDER TAG INVNO IN B
. USE CUSTOMER ORDER TAG CUSTNO IN C
. USE INVENTRY ORDER TAG ITEMNO IN D
. SELECT ITEMS
. SET RELATION TO ITEMNO INTO INVENTRY
. SELECT INVOICE
. SET RELATION TO INVNO INTO ITEMS, CUSTNO INTO CUSTOMER
. SET SKIP TO ITEMS
```

then you can use the REPORT FORM command to create all of the invoices at once, without using a program. SET SKIP TO affects the operation of all commands that use the FOR and/or WHILE options. Many dBASE commands use the FOR/WHILE options, including LIST/DISPLAY, REPORT FORM, and LOCATE.

Using SET SKIP, SET RELATION, the dBASE work areas, indexing, and the proper design techniques, the database environment that these commands have created can be used to create customer invoices by using a single dBASE command, instead of writing an application program to perform the same task.

Table lookup

An important part of any database management system is its ability to perform multiple database processes. Table lookup is just one of those types of processes. Using the FIND or LOCATE key words you can check a database to see if a value exists. For example, a customer number must exist on a customer database in order for the customer information to be retrieved. When you are selecting records you can use the FOR clause to retrieve all the records that match the FOR clause.

But, when you need to find the first record in a database that meets your criteria, how do you retrieve the records data and then go on to check other databases for a matching key? This is where the FIND and LOCATE commands are invaluable. You can perform database lookup with variables in report forms and LIST commands with the FOR clause, but you cannot process this data in any reasonable fashion.

LOCATE and CONTINUE When you are using dBASE IV as a database manager and are querying your data with commands such as LIST and DISPLAY, you are asking dBASE IV to search for records that meet certain criteria and then show the records on the screen. When you are using dBASE IV as a programming language, you will not use those commands because they do not give you very much flexibility when displaying the records on the screen.

When programming, you want to see if a record exists on the file. If it does exist, you want to know where it exists. Once you determine the location of a record, you can use standard programming techniques to retrieve the record and display it any way you want.

The LOCATE is one such command to help you to see if a record exists. The LOCATE command should only be used with non-indexed databases. Use this command like the LIST command, except all you can specify in the search criteria are the characters the desired entry should contain.

LOCATE normally searches the file beginning with the first record and continues either until it finds the record specified in the FOR clause or reaches the bottom of the file. If you use scope modifiers such as NEXT, REST, or the WHILE clause, it searches the database from the present record number. If your file is very large, it might take a long time to get there as it must read every record. If your record is on the bottom or not found, you might be in for a long wait.

LOCATE does not show you the record. If it finds the record, it responds by telling you the record number. If it doesn't find the record, it tells you End of locate scope. For example:

```
. LOCATE FOR NAME = 'SMITH'
Record =      25
```

and:

```
. LOCATE FOR NAME = 'JONES' AND STATE= 'MO'
End of locate scope
```

If the LOCATE command was successful and found the record, the function FOUND( ) is set to true. You could use the command:

```
. IF FOUND( )
```

to determine if the record was found. FOUND( ) can also be used in a loop or a CASE statement.

LOCATE also allows you to continue the search without returning to the top of the database. As you find a record, the record pointer moves to the record, and the record number is displayed. If you issue another LOCATE command, dBASE IV starts again from the top of the database.

The CONTINUE command allows you to keep searching as shown in Fig. 16-20. A record with the name of SMITH can be found in records 25, 104, and 684. You can then use the direct location to display those records, or, in programs, display the records before using the CONTINUE phrase. In programming, after the LOCATE or CONTINUE phrases, you would have to check to see if the record information is the information you were searching for. When dBASE IV reaches the "end of locate scope," the record pointer is pointing to the bottom of the file and the FOUND( ) function is set to .F..

```
. LOCATE FOR NAME = 'SMITH'
Record =      25

. CONTINUE
Record =      104

. CONTINUE
Record =      684

. CONTINUE
End of locate scope
```

16-20 Using LOCATE and CONTINUE.

FIND, SEEK, and SKIP   The FIND command is used like the LOCATE command but is used with indexed databases to find if the indexed key exists. The FIND command knows what the indexed key is. You do not have to specify the field name or names that created the key. The FIND command only tells if the record is not found. You must query the FOUND( ) function or the EOF( ) function. You can also query the internal record variable known to dBASE IV as RECNO( ) as shown in Fig. 16-21.

```
. USE CUSTOMER ORDER TAG LNAME
. FIND 'SMITH'
. ? FOUND()
  .T.
. ? EOF()
  .F.
. ? RECNO()
  25
```

16-21 Using FIND and the RECNO( ) function.

The first occurrence of SMITH is in record number 25. The ? RECNO( ) command allowed you to see if SMITH was in the database. The ? RECNO( )

command could have been followed by a DISPLAY command which would show you record number 25 where the current record pointer is.

You can see an example of a record not being in the database. The pointer is set to the bottom of the file and no record could be displayed as shown in Fig. 16-22.

```
. USE CUSTOMER ORDER TAG LNAME
. FIND 'SMITH'
. DISPLAY NAME,STATE
  SMITH   CT
. SKIP
.    RECNO()
            12
. DISPLAY NAME,STATE
  SMITH   VT
. SKIP
.    RECNO()
            56
. DISPLAY NAME,STATE
  SMITH   MA
. SKIP
.    RECNO()
           112
. DISPLAY NAME,STATE
  STEBBINS AZ
. SKIP
. ? RECNO()
           128
. DISPLAY NAME,STATE
  ZEBULAH MO
. SKIP
          No find
```

16-22 Not FINDING a record.

Using the LOCATE command, you are able to see subsequent occurrences of matching records with the CONTINUE phrase. In the FIND command, you must program this function. Because each keyed record is sequentially connected, you can use SKIP commands and check the data as shown in Fig. 16-22.

dBASE IV does not know if it has found other occurrences of SMITH. The SKIP command simply runs through the database sequentially by indexed key one record per SKIP.

When you reach the bottom of the database after you have "skipped" through all the records you get the message No find. Internal variables called EOF( ) and FOUND( ) are set on, to let you check for end of file or the not found condition in a program.

The FIND command lets you position the pointer and then search until there is no longer a match. However, you must use programming to determine when there is no longer a match or it reaches the end of file. Pseudocode for an indexed search appears in Fig. 16-23.

The FIND command lets you search on a literal value or a variable. If you use a variable you must use the macro substitution symbol & preceding the variable name. If SET EXACT ON is not set, the FIND finds index fields that contain the character string rather than is equal to the character string. Only

```
USE INDEXED DATABASE
FIND RECORD
IF FOUND()
   THEN
      DO WHILE FOUND()
         DISPLAY RECORD
         SKIP
      ENDDO
   ELSE
      RECORD NOT FOUND
ENDIF
```

16-23 Pseudocode for an indexed search.

the master index is used in the FIND command. Use the SET ORDER TO command to change the index before using the FIND.

The SEEK command works exactly as the FIND command, except that it works on expressions as well as literals and simple memory variables.

SET KEY

The command SET KEY TO allows for the specifying of a limiting range for accessing a database's index. It acts much like a SET FILTER command in that you can establish a range of expressions to be analyzed when accessing the database. The syntax is:

SET KEY TO *expr:match*/RANGE*expr:low,expr:hig* IN *alias*

What this command does is to limit the displaying of records to the RANGE specified within the command, taking immediate effect. It can be written in a number of ways: SET KEY TO *expr:match* will look only for an exact match. For example:

USE CUSTOMER
INDEX ON STATE TAG STATE
SET KEY TO 'CA','CT'
BROWSE

SET KEY TO RANGE *expr:low* or *expr:match* will look for values equal to or greater than the value given. For example:

USE EMPLOYEE
INDEX ON SALARY TAG SALARY
SET KEY TO RANGE 15000
BROWSE

SET KEY TO RANGE ,*expr:high* searches the index for all values equal to or less than the value sent. For example:

SET KEY TO RANGE ,50000

You can also set a key range to be between two numbers. For example:

SET KEY TO RANGE 15000,50000

The real advantage to this command is that it acts on the INDEX that is currently invoked, so that it acts much faster than a standard SET FILTER TO command, which acts upon each record of the database.

Printing commands

The commands discussed in this part help you control the printer.

SET DEVICE TO/SET PRINT

The SET PRINT ON command comes before the ? command if you want the output to go to the printer. The SET PRINT OFF command follows the output.

Another use of the ? command is to control the printer. Any printer code you might wish to send can be sent with the ? command:

```
. SET PRINT ON
. ? CHR(15)
.     'This would be compressed print'
. CHR(27) + CHR(69)
.     'This would be emphasized print'
. SET PRINT OFF
```

In dBASE IV, a new and better way to send printer control codes to the printer is the ?? command which sends control codes directly to the printer without the SET PRINT ON command preceding it. To send the compressed print command you would simply enter:

```
.?? CHR (15)        && This is for an Epson dot matrix printer
. ??? {ESC} (s16.66H && This is for a HP Laserjet II
```

The SET DEVICE TO PRINTER command comes before the @ SAY command if you want your output to go to the printer. The SET DEVICE TO SCREEN redirects all @ SAY commands to the screen after you are done printing. The initial default is to the screen, if no SET DEVICE TO command is used.

EJECT

The EJECT command advances the paper to the top of form on the printer and sets the line and column count to 1,1. It is a good idea to issue an EJECT before doing any printing. This will suppress an initial form feed that can be very annoying.

Logical constructs used in dBASE IV

The logical constructs explained in detail in Part One have various syntax (computer grammar) in dBASE IV. The basic constructs if-then-else, looping, case statements, and calling subroutines are shown here.

IF-THEN-ELSE-ENDIF

One of the most used logical constructs is the IF statement. The IF statement lets you make decisions during processing of your program.

The if-then-else logical construct allows a two way path of decision making. The IF clause is followed if the expression in the IF clause is true. If not, and there is an ELSE clause, then control passes to the ELSE clause.

There is no actual THEN clause in dBASE IV. It is implied that everything after the IF clause is part of the THEN clause until the ELSE clause is reached. Notice that all IF-THEN-ELSE statements end with an ENDIF.

You can have as many statements inside an IF statement as you want. You can also have IF statements inside of IF statements. These are known as *nested IFs*. The IF statement is used often in AJAX's code—AJAX makes a lot of decisions! Figure 16-24 shows three examples of the IF statement.

```
1)   STORE 'DEF' TO X
     IF X = 'ABC'
        'THEN CLAUSE'
     ENDIF


     NO OUTPUT

2)   STORE 'ABC' TO X
     IF X = 'ABC'
        'THEN CLAUSE'
     ELSE
        'ELSE CLAUSE'
     ENDIF
     THEN CLAUSE


3)   STORE 'DEF' TO X
     IF X = 'ABC'
        'THEN CLAUSE'
     ELSE
        'ELSE CLAUSE'
     ENDIF
     ELSE CLAUSE
```

16-24 The IF-THEN-ELSE construct.

The first example was only an IF-THEN clause. Because the condition X='ABC' is FALSE, there is no output and control passes out of the IF-THEN construct. The second example is TRUE and the THEN condition is executed. The final example is FALSE and control passes to the ELSE for execution.

Another way to do simple IF statements is the IIF function—this function can make it easier to use simple IF statements. It is described in the function library section.

DO WHILE-ENDDO

Looping is accomplished through a command known as DO WHILE. The DO WHILE loop is performed until the condition is no longer true. See Fig. 16-25.

In this example, a variable COUNTER is initialized to one. The loop is entered and the condition COUNTER $<= 5$ is checked to see if it is TRUE.

```
STORE 1 TO COUNTER
DO WHILE COUNTER <= 5
  @ COUNTER,COUNTER SAY COUNTER
  STORE COUNTER + 1 TO COUNTER
ENDDO
```

16-25 The DO WHILE loop.

Because it is TRUE, the loop continues. Each pass though the loop adds one to the variable COUNTER and outputs the value of COUNTER at screen location (counter,counter). The first pass puts it at (1,1), the next pass (2,2), the third pass (3,3) all the way to (5,5). Notice the diagonal pattern in the program output.

Any expression can be put in a DO WHILE loop. It can be a simple comparison or a complex conditional expression. You can even make the loop last forever (an *infinite loop*), if you never make the condition being tested false. Each DO WHILE ends with an ENDDO.

Next, you can see a complex loop. The SKIP command assumes we are moving through an indexed database:

```
DO WHILE CUSTNO='00001' .AND. DATE = '05/45/83'
@ 5,10 SAY AMOUNT
SKIP
ENDDO
```

Finally the following code shows an infinite loop caused by not incrementing the variable X:

```
STORE 1 TO X
DO WHILE X < 5
    @ 1,1 SAY 'HELLO'
ENDDO
```

SCAN

The SCAN command is a simple way to automatically select records from a data file and to apply processing commands to the selected records. It is used as an alternative to the DO WHILE command. It will cycle through an active data file and act on records that are within the *scope* that you have specified and that also meet the FOR and WHILE conditions.

If you use the default of the *scope* option, every record in the file, starting at the beginning, is scanned. NEXT or RECORD used as a scope begins scanning at the current record.

To specify which records within the *scope* are acted on, use FOR *condition*. WHILE *condition* puts more constraints on the records that can be acted on by allowing processing only as long as the WHILE conditional expression remains true.

To place control back at the beginning of the SCAN process, use LOOP. To end a scan process, use EXIT:

dBASE IV—WITH SCAN	dBASE III PLUS—BEFORE SCAN
USE ITEMS	USE ITEMS
SCAN FOR INVNO = '8808-010'	LOCATE FOR INVNO = '8808-010'
DO PRINTITEM	DO WHILE .NOT. EOF( )
ENDSCAN	DO PRINTITEM
	CONTINUE
	ENDDO

EXIT

The EXIT command is used to exit a DO WHILE construct regardless of what is between the EXIT and the ENDDO. For example, Fig. 16-26 shows an example of a loop with and without the EXIT command.

```
WITHOUT "EXIT"                    WITH "EXIT"

STORE 1 TO X                      STORE 1 TO X
DO WHILE X <= 5                      DO WHILE X <= 5
  STORE X+6 TO Y                      STORE X+6 TO Y
  @ X,X SAY 'HELLO'                   @ X,X SAY 'HELLO'
  @ X,Y SAY 'THERE'                   IF X = 3
ENDDO                                   EXIT
@ X,20 SAY X                          ENDIF
                                      @ X,Y SAY 'THERE'
                                    ENDDO
                                    @ X,20 SAY X


HELLO THERE                       HELLO THERE
  HELLO THERE                       HELLO THERE
    HELLO THERE                       HELLO          3
      HELLO THERE
        HELLO THERE     5
```

16-26   The EXIT command.

In the first example, the DO WHILE construct is performed five times as specified in the DO WHILE condition. The phrase HELLO and THERE keep repeating each time one character to the right. The second example contains an EXIT command. This tells the program that when X = 3 go immediately to the statement following the ENDDO, do not perform any of the other statements in the DO WHILE, do not collect two hundred dollars. As you can see, the statement following the ENDDO prints the value of X. In the second example, it is 3. The EXIT command caused a premature and immediate end to the DO WHILE loop.

The main use for the EXIT command is a quick way out when an error condition is signaled. If you are performing a series of IF statements and an error condition is signaled, using an EXIT statement is usually faster than a series of ELSE statements.

LOOP

The LOOP statement is very different from the EXIT statement in that LOOP returns control to the top of the DO WHILE while not processing any statements after the LOOP statement. The EXIT statement actually exits the loop and places control on the statement following the ENDDO.

The LOOP command usually comes after an error handling routine as it returns control to the DO WHILE. If the condition is not corrected before the program loops to the LOOP statement again, the error will occur again.

CASE-ENDCASE

The last logical construct is the CASE statement. This statement is used when an IF-THEN-ELSE is not sufficient to make a decision. IF-THEN-ELSE conditions only allow two paths, true and false. The CASE construct allows an infinite number of paths along with an OTHERWISE clause: Figure 16-27 shows pseudocode for a CASE statement.

16-27 An example of the CASE statement.

```
READ AN ANSWER
DO CASE
   CASE ANS = 1
      DO SOMETHING
   CASE ANS = 2
      DO SOMETHING
   CASE ANS > 2 .AND. ANS <= 10
      DO SOMETHING
   OTHERWISE
      DO SOMETHING
ENDCASE
```

This DO CASE statement allows four different paths of performance. If the answer was a 1, one path is performed, 2 performs another, an answer between 2 and 10 performs a third path, while anything else performs the OTHERWISE clause. These statements are especially used in selection menus. All DO CASE statements end with an ENDCASE statement. If there is no OTHERWISE clause, and none of the CASE statements are true, then no commands within the CASE structure are performed. The DO CASE construct is not a loop of any kind. It is performed only once unless inside a DO WHILE loop. A CASE construct can be built with many IF-THEN-ELSE statements, but then it is not as easy to use or understand.

Subroutines

Subroutines let you go off to another set of code and then return to exactly where you left off.

DO/RETURN The "Calling Subroutine" is implemented with the DO command:

MAIN.PRG	SUB1.PRG	SUB2.PRG
housekeeping	*some statements*	*some statements*
menu commands	*more statements*	*more statements*
DO SUB1	RETURN	RETURN
DO SUB2		

The command procedure (program) MAIN.PRG *calls* the subprocedures SUB1.PRG and SUB2.PRG. These can be programs by themselves, but probably they share common options and data with the main program. A subprocedure can call another subprocedure. The RETURN statement is dBASE IV's way of keeping track of where it is. The RETURN statement immediately returns control to the statement following the call. In the case of the RETURN statement in SUB1.PRG, it returns to the RUN SUB2 command. The RETURN in SUB2.PRG returns to the statement after RUN SUB2 in MAIN.PRG.

Most main menus are set to call subroutines to perform the processing for each menu choice. Programming with many subroutines makes your individual code modules much more manageable.

Return to master If you have a large set of subroutines where one subroutine calls another which calls another which calls another, you might find it slow as you finish with the last subroutine to get back to the original module because it must go through all the RETURNs in each subsidiary module. The command:

RETURN TO MASTER

automatically returns to the first module in the calling chain.

Procedures You can combine many modules into one file called a procedure file. Figure 16-28 shows an example of three simple procedures in a procedure file and a small program that would call them.

The example in Fig. 16-28 shows three separate procedures in a procedure file. On the disk would be the two files, MAIN.PRG and PROC1.PRC.

A procedure file can be named anything you want, as long as you use the same name in the SET PROCEDURE TO statement. The MAIN program sets up the procedure file PROC1.PRC. Only one procedure file can be active at one time.

The first subroutine is called, and if the entry was successful, the others are called. The first subroutine uses the PERSONNEL file and asks the user to enter his or her Social Security Number which is promptly checked against the personnel file. Once found the name is retrieved and the number of years in the company is calculated from the hire date.

A relation is set so the SSN is automatically found in the COMPANY file. Once the information is retrieved from the PERSONNEL file, control is

```
MAIN.PRG   && This is the main program file

    SET PROCEDURE TO PROC1.PRC
    DO GETPERS
    IF FOUND()
      DO GETCOMP
      DO BONUS
    ENDIF


PROC1.PRC   && This is the procedure file

    PROCEDURE GETPERS
      USE PERSONNEL
      ACCEPT "Enter Social Security Number ==> " TO SSN
      FIND &SSN
      IF FOUND()
        SELECT 2
        USE COMPANY
        SET RELATION TO SSN INTO COMPANY
        SELECT PERSONNEL
        STORE NAME TO PERSON
        STORE YEAR(DATE())-YEAR(HIREDATE) TO NUMYEARS
      ELSE
        'Invalid Social Security Number, Re-enter'
      ENDIF
      RETURN

    PROCEDURE GETCOMP
      USE COMPANY
      STORE SALARY TO SAL
      RETURN

    PROCEDURE BONUS
      BONUS = SAL * (1 + YRS/20)
        "Your Bonus is " + BONUS
      RETURN
```

16-28   An example of a procedure file.

returned to the MAIN program, and if the retrieval of the Social Security number is successful, the other subroutines in the procedure file are called.

Parameters   You can pass parameters or memory variables between programs with the PARAMETERS statement. If you want to use PARAMETERS it must be the first statement in a program. You can even pass parameters from outside of dBASE when you begin a program.

One use of the PARAMETERS statement is to pass the program the disk drive to use for data. Figure 16-29 shows a sample of this use of the PARAMETERS statement.

```
STORE 'A:' TO DR
DO ABC WITH DR
```

16-29   Using a PARAMETERS statement.

```
ABC.PRG
    PARAMETERS DR
    USE DR + NAMES
    LIST ALL
```

Before the program is run that contains the PARAMETERS statement, the parameters must be initialized. The memory variable DR is set to A:. The data is on the A drive. When the program is run, it will USE the NAMES file on the A drive due to the parameter statement.

RUN   The RUN command is used to execute any DOS command outside of dBASE. If you wanted to run Framework, and you had enough memory, you could enter the command:

    RUN C:\FW3\FW

This assumes that your Framework III program is on the directory FW3 and the name of the program is FW.

RUN( )

The RUN( ) function allows additional options to the RUN command. The syntax is:

    result = RUN(*expL1,expC,expL2*)

where *result* is the return code from the function as the completion code.

expC is the external command to run. *expL1*, if true, passes the previous command to the command processor, or, if false, loads the processor. *expL2*, if true, leaves space on disk for a swap file or, if false, uses available memory.

CANCEL

The CANCEL command stops processing of a command file and closes all open command files. Control is returned to the native dBASE dot prompt.

QUIT

The QUIT command closes all open files, including data, indexes, programs, and other files such as formats and terminates the dBASE IV session, returning control to the operating system.

There is an optional WITH *expN* option that will return the numeric value specified as a return exit code if dBASE IV has been invoked from a batch file or other outside program.

Procedural definitions and global procedure libraries

This section looks at the commands that allow for referencing other program files to run external routines, such as procedures and user-defined functions. dBASE IV allows for a program to run another program using the DO command.

If a DO command is in a program, dBASE IV looks in the program file currently in memory for a program of that name. If it is not found, it then looks in the current directory for a .PRG program of that name. After execution of the named program, control is returned to the calling program.

There are a number of different ways that you can specify where a certain program, procedure, or user-defined function is located. The following is a description of two commands that specify external program files.

SET PROCEDURE TO

This command specifies an external program file that contains a number of PROCEDUREs and/or FUNCTIONs. These mini-programs perform repetitious sets of commands that can be accessed by any of the programs within a system, providing the SET PROCEDURE TO command is prior to the program being run. The syntax is:

SET PROCEDURE TO *procset.prg*

When dBASE receives a command accessing a procedure or function, it first looks to see if it is present in the current .DBO file. If it is not, it loads the SET PROCEDURE file and looks for the procedure or function in that .DBO file. Once the command is processed, control is returned to the calling program.

To remove a reference to a particular procedure file you need to insert the command:

SET PROCEDURE TO

dBASE will remove the procedural reference.

SET LIBRARY TO

This command allows you to have a semi-permanent collection of procedures and functions to augment the ones stored in the SET PROCEDURE file or within the current .DBO file.

SET LIBRARY TO mylibr

This command will establish for dBASE that, if a procedure or function is accessed and is not present in the current .DBO file or in the SET PROCEDURE file, dBASE is to look in the SET LIBRARY file. To remove a library reference, you need to put in the command:

SET LIBRARY TO

SYSPROC

There is one other way to specify an existing external library of procedures and/or functions. That is in the CONFIG.DB file. There is a variable called the SYSPROC that, when set, will take precedence over all other library and procedure references. The syntax for the entry to CONFIG.DB is:

SYSPROC = *myprocs.prg*

The library specified in the SYSPROC= statement specifies a procedure library you create that could hold all external global routines. It's nothing but a program file that contains many procedures, but they would be available to all your programs.

To summarize, dBASE has a hierarchy of program accesses for external routines. It is as follows:

1. Look in the SYSPROC, if active
2. Look in currently active .DBO file
3. Look in a SET PROCEDURE TO file, if active
4. Look in other .DBO files in the call chain
5. Look in the SET LIBRARY TO file, if active
6. Search the disk for a .DBO file of that name
7. Search the disk for a .PRG file of that name to compile

Your application system must not only work to your expectations, it must work to everyone's expectations. The functions to be performed by the system are a part of the application design. The point of testing your application is to make sure that the functions are being performed correctly and accurately. dBASE provides a powerful debugging tool to aid in tracking down programming errors.

The dBASE IV debugging tools

Any error that dBASE finds within a program causes processing to be halted. dBASE then offers the choice of suspending processing, canceling the program, or ignoring the error and continuing with the next instruction.

SUSPENDed processing

A suspended program is one that is stopped between two instructions. The previous instruction has completed, and the current instruction is the one that caused the error. You can use dBASE to help find the problem by using the F1 (Help) feature, or you can use the LIST/DISPLAY commands to display the current status, memory, and settings. You can then use the RESUME command to allow processing to continue, if no program changes are required.

SUSPEND and RESUME are the heart of dBASE troubleshooting. These commands, and the "suspend" option of the error messages, are what allow you to debug dBASE programs interactively. You may SUSPEND a program at any point by just using the SUSPEND command; this leaves the current environment intact and presents the interactive mode prompt (i.e., the dot prompt). You may then query the contents of variables, DISPLAY STATUS, or any other command. Single-step mode may be initiated, or a command changed via the history feature. The RESUME command then picks up the program with the instruction following the SUSPEND. If single-stepping was started, you might then suspend the execution at any statement to display memory, and so forth.

You could add statements to your programs to help you with troubleshooting, but this is not recommended. Any debugging method that requires additional program code should be used as a last resort, and methods that use small amounts of change should be tried before using methods that require changing large amounts of code. Additional code requires debugging and syntax checking; if the time required for the additions is not worth it, another debugging method should be tried. dBASE IV allows you almost complete freedom from debugging, so that additional program code should not be necessary.

If additional code is added to a program for debugging purposes, comment lines should also be added to identify the temporary statements. The debugging statements can also be deactivated by placing an asterisk (*) in the first column of the statement, thus making it a comment. The asterisks may be removed to activate the debugging statements.

SET STEP ON is a dBASE SET command that causes only one instruction to be executed at a time. This is the same as SUSPENDing processing after each program statement. When you are stepping a program, you can examine the result of each statement before proceeding to the next. This sometimes means hours of hitting the spacebar to see the result of a specific calculation. STEP can be set on during a program, however, and stepping performed for only a part of the process.

Environment settings and commands

Also, several other dBASE IV SET commands can help you when troubleshooting a program. They can be set ON during the process, such as during a suspended program, or they can be set as default settings when you are testing a program.

SET ECHO ON   This is the command that makes dBASE "echo" each command to the screen as it is read. Using ECHO, the programmer can see the exact order in which statements are executed. This is also called *tracing* a program, and is very effective in finding logic and looping errors.

SET TALK ON   This dBASE parameter causes the results of various operations to be displayed on the screen. This can be helpful in finding the exact values of comparisons and calculations. TALK can also be used in determining where bottlenecks or slow-ups occur.

?   Another debugging technique can be used to discover the exact values contained in a variable at a specific time. The variable is printed on the console via the question mark (?) command, sometimes with an identifying message. The programmer can then use this information to discover the problem. This technique is called exhibiting a variable, and can be used directly from the dot prompt, instead of using LIST/DISPLAY MEMORY for a single variable.

LIST/DISPLAY MEMORY, LIST/DISPLAY STATUS, LIST/DISPLAY RECORD-RECNO( )   These commands can be used to monitor the status of the entire dBASE environment. DISPLAY MEMORY provides the complete picture of the contents of all current memory variables. The name, value, and the number and size of memory variable storage are displayed (Fig. 16-30). DISPLAY STATUS displays the status of all open database files and indexes, including any set relations and the current index key (Fig. 16-31). DISPLAY HISTORY displays the last 20 (default) commands that were executed. DISPLAY RECORD RECNO( ) displays the current database record. In dBASE, all of these commands also have the option to send their output directly to the printer by adding the words "TO PRINT" to the command.

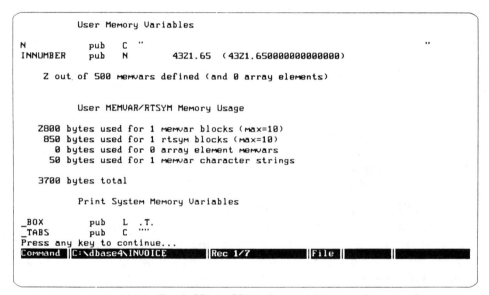

```
          User Memory Variables

N              pub    C  ''                                                    ''
INNUMBER       pub    N          4321.65  (4321.650000000000000)

    Z out of 500 memvars defined (and 0 array elements)


          User MEMVAR/RTSYM Memory Usage

   2800 bytes used for 1 memvar blocks (max=10)
    850 bytes used for 1 rtsym blocks (max=10)
      0 bytes used for 0 array element memvars
     50 bytes used for 1 memvar character strings

   3700 bytes total

          Print System Memory Variables

_BOX           pub    L  .T.
_TABS          pub    C  ''''
Press any key to continue...
Command  C:\dbase4\INVOICE        Rec 1/7              File
```

16-30   The DISPLAY STATUS output (first page).

SET HISTORY TO n   This tells dBASE to store *n* program statements in the command history. Normally, only 20 commands are stored in history; this default can be raised by issuing the SET HISTORY TO *n* command. The *n* may be between 0 and 16000. For most cases, 20 to 50 commands stored in history should be enough.

The dBASE debugging windows

Debug   DEBUG is a new dBASE IV command to create an environment for debugging programs. The window-type environment allows you to see the currently-executing statement, set breakpoints, display the values of selected memory variables, and to leave to the dot prompt and return to DEBUG quickly and easily, while the program remains suspended.

```
Currently Selected Database:
Select area:  1, Database in Use: C:\DBASE4\INVOICE.DBF   Alias: INVOICE
Production   MDX file:  C:\DBASE4\INVOICE.MDX
    Master Index TAG:     INVNO  Key: INVNO
           Index TAG:     INVDATE  Key: INVDATE
    Related into: ITEMS
    Relation: invno
    Related into: CUSTOMER
    Relation: custno

Select area:  2, Database in Use: C:\DBASE4\ITEMS.DBF   Alias: ITEMS
Production   MDX file:  C:\DBASE4\ITEMS.MDX
    Master Index TAG:     INVNO  Key: INVNO
    Related into: INVENTRY
    Relation: itemno

Select area:  3, Database in Use: C:\DBASE4\CUSTOMER.DBF   Alias: CUSTOMER
Production   MDX file:  C:\DBASE4\CUSTOMER.MDX
    Master Index TAG:     CUSTNO  Key: CUSTNO
           Index TAG:     COMPANY  Key: COMPANY
Press any key to continue...
Command  C:\dbase4\INVOICE          Rec 1/7          File
```

16-31 The DISPLAY MEMORY output (first page).

DEBUG has four windows—one that displays the program code, one that displays any breakpoints set, one that displays the values of variables or expressions, and the debug action window. The arrangement of these windows is shown in Fig. 16-32.

```
— C:\DBASE4\ENGNUM2.PRG —————————————————
  1 * Engnum2.prg
  2 PARAMETERS TRANSNUM, NUMSTRING
  3 SET ECHO OFF
  4 SET TALK OFF
  5   A1 = 'ONE '
  6   A2 = 'TWO '
  7   A3 = 'THREE '
  8   A4 = 'FOUR '
  9   A5 = 'FIVE '
 10   A6 = 'SIX '
 11   A7 = 'SEVEN '

— DISPLAY ——————————————        — BREAKPOINTS ——
                    :            1:
                    :            2:
                    :            3:
                    :            4:

— DEBUGGER ——————
Work Area: 1        Database file: INVOICE.DBF    Program file: engnum2.prg
Record:  1          Master Index: INVNO           Procedure:    ENGNUM2
ACTION:                                           Current line: 2

Stopped for step.
```

16-32 DEBUG windows.

You can leave the DEBUG windows to see how the screen would look to the user at any given point. You can also leave the window environment, returning to the dot prompt, so that you can enter your own commands while still in suspended mode. The action codes that are available in DEBUG are shown in Fig. 16-33.

Action code	Action
E	Edit program in Edit window
B	Set breakpoint in Breakpoint window
D	Display variables of expressions in Display window
S [n]S	Execute next instruction Execute next [n] instructions
N [n]N	Execute next instruction in current program (ignore sub-programs called by DOs) Execute next [n] instructions in current program (ignore sub-programs called by DOs)
R	Execute until breakpoint or end of program
X	Exit to dot prompt -- RESUME to resume DEBUG
Q	Quit DEBUG, cancelling program

16-33 The DEBUG actions.

You enter DEBUG by using the DEBUG in place of DO to start a program. The resulting command syntax looks like this:

. DEBUG <*prgname*> [WITH <*parameter list*>]

When you enter DEBUG, you are automatically suspended at the first program statement. This gives you a chance to set breakpoints or set up variable displays. You can then start the program with the "R" action code. The program runs until a breakpoint or a SUSPEND command is encountered. You can also execute just one statement at a time by using the "S" action code.

Another action is that you can return to the dot prompt while the program is still suspended by DEBUG. The action code "X" returns you to the dot prompt—the RESUME command will return you from the dot prompt to DEBUG. The action code "Q" leaves the debugger, canceling the program.

The F1 (Help) key displays a list of valid action codes while you are in DEBUG, as shown in Fig. 16-34. The F9 (Zoom) key shows you the screen as the user would see it. If there is a menu displayed, you would see the menu, for example. Pressing the F9 key again returns you to the DEBUG windows.

Breakpoint A breakpoint is the point where you want execution of a program to be suspended. You may want to suspend execution when a particular variable reaches a certain value, or when a specific record is accessed in a

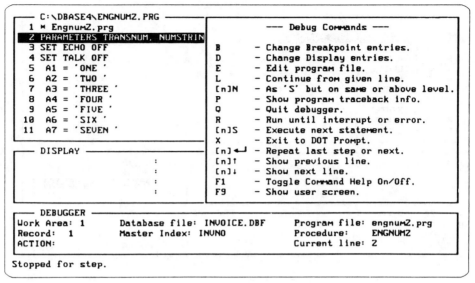

```
┌── C:\DBASE4\ENGNUM2.PRG ──────
│  1 × Engnum2.prg                        ┌──────── Debug Commands ────
│  2 PARAMETERS TRANSNUM, NUMSTRIN        │
│  3 SET ECHO OFF                    B    - Change Breakpoint entries.
│  4 SET TALK OFF                    D    - Change Display entries.
│  5  A1 = 'ONE '                    E    - Edit program file.
│  6  A2 = 'TWO '                    L    - Continue from given line.
│  7  A3 = 'THREE '                 [n]N  - As 'S' but on same or above level.
│  8  A4 = 'FOUR '                   P    - Show program traceback info.
│  9  A5 = 'FIVE '                   Q    - Quit debugger.
│ 10  A6 = 'SIX '                    R    - Run until interrupt or error.
│ 11  A7 = 'SEVEN '                 [n]S  - Execute next statement.
├── DISPLAY ──────────              X    - Exit to DOT Prompt.
│                            :      [n]◄┘ - Repeat last step or next.
│                            :      [n]↑  - Show previous line.
│                            :      [n]↓  - Show next line.
│                            :      F1    - Toggle Command Help On/Off.
│                                   F9    - Show user screen.
├── DEBUGGER ──────────────────────────────────────────────
│ Work Area: 1      Database file: INVOICE.DBF    Program file: engnum2.prg
│ Record:  1        Master Index: INVNO           Procedure:    ENGNUM2
│ ACTION:                                         Current line: 2
└──────────────────────────────────────────────────────────
Stopped for step.
```

16-34 The DEBUG Help screen.

database, or when the program has reached a certain statement. The dBASE IV DEBUG facility gives you the ability to set breakpoints to satisfy these requirements.

You can specify a program breakpoint by using any dBASE conditional expression as the breakpoint. When the expression becomes true, the execution of the program is suspended at that point. You can also, by using a dBASE built-in function, specify a particular statement number where execution is to be suspended.

To enter the breakpoint, use the "B" action code. The Breakpoint window will be activated, where you simply enter the breakpoint expression or expressions. When any of these expressions becomes true, program execution is suspended. Figure 16-35 shows breakpoint expressions entered in the Breakpoint window.

Note that the second expression in the Breakpoint window of Fig. 16-35 causes the program to be suspended at statement number 105. The LINENO( ) built-in function returns the current line number in the program, allowing you to easily set a positional breakpoint rather than a conditional breakpoint.

To leave the Breakpoint window, press either the Esc key or Ctrl–End. Either of these key combinations will return you to the DEBUG "Action:" prompt. You could then either issue the "R" action code to run the program until a breakpoint is encountered, or you could continue with any other action code.

Once the program is suspended, you can view the contents of various memory variables, or even return to the dot prompt (using the "X" action code) to perform LIST/DISPLAY commands.

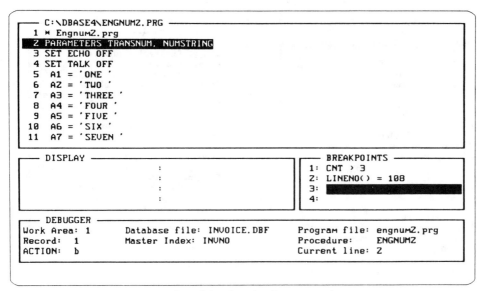

```
┌── C:\DBASE4\ENGNUM2.PRG ─────────────────────────────────────────┐
│  1 ⋈ Engnum2.prg                                                 │
│ ▐2 PARAMETERS TRANSNUM, NUMSTRING▌                               │
│  3 SET ECHO OFF                                                  │
│  4 SET TALK OFF                                                  │
│  5  A1 = 'ONE '                                                  │
│  6  A2 = 'TWO '                                                  │
│  7  A3 = 'THREE '                                                │
│  8  A4 = 'FOUR '                                                 │
│  9  A5 = 'FIVE '                                                 │
│ 10  A6 = 'SIX '                                                  │
│ 11  A7 = 'SEVEN '                                                │
├── DISPLAY ─────────────────────────┬── BREAKPOINTS ─────────────┤
│                         :          │ 1: CNT > 3                 │
│                         :          │ 2: LINENO( ) = 108        │
│                         :          │ 3: ▐▌                      │
│                         :          │ 4:                         │
├── DEBUGGER ─────────────────────────────────────────────────────┤
│ Work Area: 1      Database file: INVOICE.DBF  Program file: engnum2.prg │
│ Record:    1      Master Index: INVNO         Procedure:    ENGNUM2     │
│ ACTION:    b                                  Current line: 2          │
└──────────────────────────────────────────────────────────────────┘
```

16-35 Specifying breakpoint expressions.

Display You can display the values of memory variables or expressions in the Display window of DEBUG. You can open this window by using the "D" action code.

After entering the Display window, you can enter a dBASE expression on the left side of the colon (:) in the Display window. The result of that expression is displayed on the right side of the colon on the same line. You can enter several expressions in the display window, and you can use the arrow keys to scroll the window to see all of the expressions. Figure 16-36 shows the Display window with expressions in it.

At the beginning of the program, none of the memory variables entered in the Display window will be found, because they have not been created yet. As the program progresses, values are filled in as the expressions can be calculated. You can enter single-memory variables or field names in the Display window, or you can enter more complex calculations.

Edit The program window that displays your program statements can also be opened to allow editing of the program by using the "E" action code. The "E" action code opens the dBASE Editor in the window where the program statements are displayed. Figure 16-37 shows DEBUG with the Edit window opened.

All of the normal Editor commands are available in the Edit window of DEBUG. You can change program statements, modify expressions, and any other editing that you might need to perform on your source program code.

If you enter a new statement, the program would then have to be recompiled before DEBUG will recognize the new command. Remember that DEBUG is already running one version of your program, the .DBO version. You could not compile the program while you are still debugging it, because

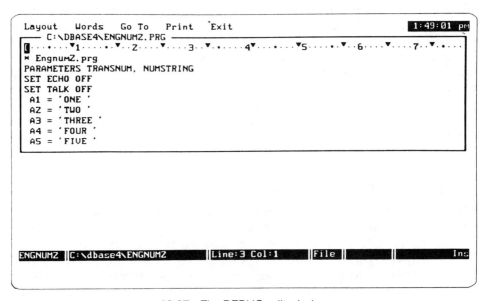

```
 ┌─── C:\DBASE4\ENGNUM2.PRG ──────────────────────────
 │  1  * Engnum2.prg
 │  2  PARAMETERS TRANSNUM, NUMSTRING
 │  3  SET ECHO OFF
 │  4  SET TALK OFF
 │  5  A1 = 'ONE '
 │  6  A2 = 'TWO '
 │  7  A3 = 'THREE '
 │  8  A4 = 'FOUR '
 │  9  A5 = 'FIVE '
 │ 10  A6 = 'SIX '
 │ 11  A7 = 'SEVEN '
 ├─── DISPLAY ─────────────────────┬─── BREAKPOINTS ──────
 │ TRANSNUM       :        4321.65  │ 1: CNT > 3
 │ A1             : Variable not found │ 2: LINENO() = 108
 │ ███████████████:                 │ 3:
 │                :                 │ 4:
 ├─── DEBUGGER ──────────────────────────────────────────
 │ Work Area: 1   Database file: INVOICE.DBF   Program file: engnum2.prg
 │ Record:    1   Master Index: INVNO          Procedure:    ENGNUM2
 │ ACTION:    d                                Current line: 3
 └───────────────────────────────────────────────────────
 Stopped for step.
```

16-36 The DEBUG display window.

```
 Layout   Words   Go To   Print   Exit                        1:49:01 pm
 ┌─── C:\DBASE4\ENGNUM2.PRG ──────────────────────────────────────
 █ · · · · ·▼1· · · · ·▼· ·2· · · ·▼· · ·3· ·▼· · · ·4▼· · · ·▼5· · · · ·▼· ·6· · · ·▼· · · ·7· ·▼· · · ·
 * Engnum2.prg
 PARAMETERS TRANSNUM, NUMSTRING
 SET ECHO OFF
 SET TALK OFF
 A1 = 'ONE '
 A2 = 'TWO '
 A3 = 'THREE '
 A4 = 'FOUR '
 A5 = 'FIVE '
 
 
 
 
 
 
 
 
 ENGNUM2  C:\dbase4\ENGNUM2         Line:3 Col:1      File              Ins
```

16-37 The DEBUG edit window.

that .DBO file is already in use by DEBUG. You would have to cancel the
program, then compile the new .PRG file into a .DBO program file, then
re-execute DEBUG.

If you do see that changes are needed to your program, the Edit window
of DEBUG gives you an easy way to change the code while the change is still
fresh in your mind.

17
Menus

dBASE IV introduced an entire new set of menu commands to the dBASE language. Previously, it required a lot of complicated code to create bar and pop-up menus.

In this section of the book, you will see how simple bar and pop-up menus take only a few statements to create. You also will see many tips and techniques for creating different types of menu interfaces. We will start with several tips for creating traditional full-screen menus, then go on to the new menu commands. You will see every conceivable type of menu as well as some custom variations that you might never have thought of.

Traversing the menu hierarchy

When you are creating dBASE programs, you probably create menus to act as a front end to your programs. Generally, you might have a menu hierarchy. The flowchart in Fig. 17-1 demonstrates a typical partial hierarchy.

The flowchart describes an order entry system for ABC Corporation. The main system is divided into several smaller systems: the customer system, sales orders, invoicing, inventory, and purchases. Each system is potentially divided into several functions. In this figure, only the customer system hierarchy is shown, including add, change, remove, view, print a customer directory, and print mailing labels.

This system could have three types of menus. The first type is a main menu screen that simply calls other menus of other systems. Another type is a working menu screen that calls other program modules, such as add, change, or remove. Finally, each function has a data entry or output screen to enter or view your data. With the new menu commands of dBASE IV, you also

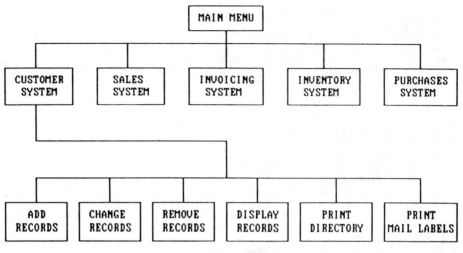

17-1 A system flowchart.

can perform all of the menu trees with one screen. You will see many variations of this in this chapter.

Steps to creating and using menus

As you saw in the Application Generator, you must go through several steps to create menus, then to assign actions to them. The same is true of creating menus from scratch. It is basically a two-step process:

- Define the menu
- Assign actions to each choice

Regardless of the type of menu that you are creating with the dBASE program statements or menu commands, you will have two distinct blocks of code. The first block creates the menu, while the second block decides what to do when the entry is chosen. In some menus, the blocks of code are intertwined, that is, a line of definition precedes a line of action statements. Usually, however, the blocks of code are separate.

Now, let's look at program code and results for creating each type of menu.

Using @ SAYs to create a menu

The most common and contemporary way to create menus is with @ SAYs commands. This command affords the greatest amount of control, because you can place the place menu text and input area anywhere on the screen you desire.

Figure 17-2 shows a very simple numeric pick menu. Figure 17-3 shows the code that produced it.

```
*****************************************************************
* Program......: @SAYMENU.PRG
* Author.......: Cary N. Prague
* Date.........: 03-24-92
* Description..: SAMPLE @ SAY CUSTOMER MENU
*****************************************************************

CLEAR
DO WHILE .T.
 sel = ' '
 @  1,  1  TO 24,78 DOUBLE
 @  3, 28  TO  5, 50
 @  4, 34  SAY "SAMPLE MENU"
 @  7, 29  SAY "Enter Selection ===>"
 @  7, 50  GET  sel
 @ 12, 29  SAY "1. Add Customer Record"
 @ 13, 29  SAY "2. Change Customer Record"
 @ 14, 29  SAY "3. Remove Customer Record"
 @ 15, 29  SAY "4. View Customer Record"
 @ 16, 29  SAY "5. Print Customer Directory"
 @ 17, 29  SAY "6. Print Customer Labels"
 @ 19, 29  SAY "X. Exit System"
 READ
 DO CASE
   CASE sel = '1'
    DO CUSADD
   CASE sel = '2'
    DO CUSCHG
   CASE sel = '3'
    DO CUSREM
   CASE sel = '4'
   ' DO CUSVEW
   CASE sel = '5'
    DO CUSDIR
   CASE sel = '6'
    DO CUSLBL
   CASE sel = 'X'
    RETURN
   OTHERWISE
    @ 9,29 SAY '*** INVALID SELECTION ***'
  ENDCASE
ENDDO
```

17-2 A menu using @ SAY'S.

As you can see, the menu is simply made up of the @ SAY commands that display the body of the menu and a single @ GET command to allow for the data entry. Because you are entering data into a memory variable that will be used to determine the choice you made, you must initialize the memory variable. That is why the:

    sel + ' '

statement is there. It stores a blank space (character) of length 1 to the memory variable that is created and named sel. You also could have used the statement:

    STORE SPACE(1) TO sel

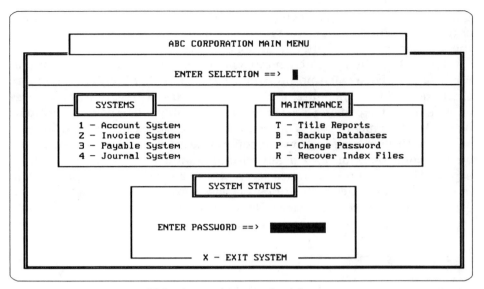

```
┌──────────────────────────────────────────────────────────┐
│        ┌──────────────────────────────────────────┐       │
│        │       ABC CORPORATION MAIN MENU           │       │
│  ┌─────────────────────────────────────────────────────┐  │
│  │         ENTER SELECTION ==>  █                       │  │
│  │  ┌─ SYSTEMS ──────────┐    ┌─ MAINTENANCE ────────┐  │  │
│  │  │  1 - Account System│    │ T - Title Reports    │  │  │
│  │  │  2 - Invoice System│    │ B - Backup Databases │  │  │
│  │  │  3 - Payable System│    │ P - Change Password  │  │  │
│  │  │  4 - Journal System│    │ R - Recover Index Files│ │  │
│  │  └────────────────────┘    └──────────────────────┘  │  │
│  │          ┌─ SYSTEM STATUS ───────────┐                │  │
│  │          │                           │                │  │
│  │          │  ENTER PASSWORD ==> █████  │                │  │
│  │          │                           │                │  │
│  │          └──── X - EXIT SYSTEM ──────┘                │  │
│  └─────────────────────────────────────────────────────┘  │
└──────────────────────────────────────────────────────────┘
```

17-3 A complex numeric pick menu.

or

```
STORE ' ' TO sel
```

All three of these statements do the same thing. The sel = ' ' form probably is the most universally understood and should be used. The STORE statement is really a remnant of dBASE II.

The READ statement is what tells dBASE to let you make an entry into the memory variable. That is all there is to creating the menu and allowing the choice to be made. Once the operator has done that, the second part of the menu program is run. This determines the action that each choice will perform.

A DO loop controls the entire module and allows the program to run over and over again until the user presses X to exit the system. As you can see from the bottom section of the code, a DO CASE construct controls all of the choices. Because the menu had seven choices, there are seven CASE statements—one for each choice. In this fictitious example, each choice calls another program with the DO command. At the end of the CASE statement is an OTHERWISE clause that is used in case the user pressed something other than a 1, 2, 3, 4, 5, 6, or X. It gives the user a message and lets the user re-enter the choice until he or she gets it right. The X choice exits the main loop and returns the user to the calling program. If the calling program is the main menu and the program was originally called from the dot prompt or Control Center, then the user will be returned there by a CANCEL statement instead of RETURN.

As you have seen, this menu can do one thing. That is to allow a single choice, then to perform a single action. That is what a menu does: it allows you to make a choice. Once you begin to enter your choice by answering a question or making a more complicated decision, the menu becomes a data entry screen. The techniques are no different than in a data entry screen, only the number and type of entry areas are different.

Figure 17-4 shows a much more complicated menu. The code is shown in Fig. 17-5. The code still is nothing but a series of @ SAYS, and there is more than one @ GET. There are also lines and boxes segregating the various choices. This type of menu is very busy and probably can be better handled by one of the other menu types. The menu shows a good use of lines and boxes to segregate the various functions. It could be argued that the password box, which is only used for one certain selection, should probably be a separate screen; however, it is sometimes acceptable to add some small entry area to menus such as date verifications or password checks. In the next few sections, you will see some alternatives to this problem. The password could be displayed in a window when needed and not be visible any other time.

```
STORE ' ' TO OPTION
CLEAR
DO WHILE .T.
   @  2,27 SAY 'ABC CORPORATION MAIN MENU'
   @  8,  7  TO 14, 37
   @  8, 42  TO 14, 72
   @  7, 45  TO  9, 59      DOUBLE
   @  7, 10  TO  9, 24      DOUBLE
   @ 16, 20  TO 23, 60
   @ 15, 31  TO 17, 49      DOUBLE
   @  4,  1  TO 24, 79      DOUBLE
   @  6,  2  TO  6, 78
   @  1,  9  TO  3, 69
   @  5, 28  SAY "ENTER SELECTION ==>"
   @  5, 49  GET OPTION
   @  8, 11  SAY "    SYSTEMS    "
   @  8, 46  SAY " MAINTENANCE "
   @ 10, 11  SAY "1 - Account System    "
   @ 11, 11  SAY "2 - Invoice System    "
   @ 12, 11  SAY "3 - Payable System    "
   @ 13, 11  SAY "4 - Journal System    "
   @ 10, 46  SAY "T - Title Reports"
   @ 11, 46  SAY "B - Backup Databases"
   @ 12, 46  SAY "P - Change Password"
   @ 13, 46  SAY "R - Recover Index Files"
   @ 16, 32  SAY "  SYSTEM STATUS   "
   @ 23, 31  SAY "  X - EXIT SYSTEM   "
   READ
   DO CASE
      CASE UPPER(OPTION) = 'P'
         STORE SPACE (10) TO PASW
         @ 18,22 CLEAR TO 22,59
         @ 20,25 SAY 'ENTER PASSWORD ==> ' GET PASW
         READ
      CASE UPPER(OPTION) = 'X'
         EXIT
   ENDCASE
   STORE ' ' TO OPTION
ENDDO
```

17-4 Complex numeric pick menu program code.

Techniques for dBASE IV menu commands

The *bar menu* is simply a horizontal menu that generally goes across the screen. The concept of being horizontal is from a design standpoint, because

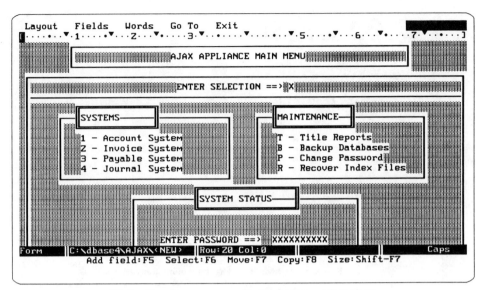

17-5 Creating a menu with the Forms work surface.

you can program the bar menu to go vertically on the screen or even diagonally or in a circle. If the individual choices (known as *pads*) are programmed in a non-linear manner, the cursor highlight will move in the programmed pattern. However, that is not what the bar menu is intended to be used for. Because the bar menu recognizes only the left and right arrows for pad to pad movement (just as the pop-up menu recognizes only the up and down arrows for bar to bar movement), you should create the bar menu in a horizontal fashion with each pad on the same line.

The bar menu example

Let's look at a normal bar menu. The screen is shown in Fig. 17-6. As you can see the choices are arranged straight across the screen in a single row. The highlight moves from one choice to another when the left or right arrow keys are pressed. Pressing Home or End takes you to the first or last selection.

You should always program the first selection first and the last selection (on the right) last. The cursor highlight moves in the order that you have programmed them.

As the cursor moves from choice to choice, an optional message can be displayed at the bottom of the screen for each option.

Now, its time to look at the code for this bar menu. The bar menu code is shown in Fig. 17-7.

Defining the bar menu: DEFINE MENU

The first task you must do is to define the overall bar menu name. This name will be the name that the menu is known by.

```
 Customer  Invoice  Inventory  Other  Exit




                    AAA    JJJJJ    AAA    X   X
                   A   A       J   A   A   X X
                   AAAAA       J   AAAAA    X
                   A   A   J   J   A   A   X X
                   A   A   JJJJJ   A   A   X   X

   AAA    PPPPP   PPPPP  L      IIIII    AAA    N   N   CCCCC  EEEEEE
  A   A   P    P  P    P L        I     A   A   NN  N   C      E
  AAAAA   PPPPP   PPPPP  L        I     AAAAA   N N N   C      EEEE
  A   A   P       P      L        I     A   A   N  N N  C      E
  A   A   P       P      LLLLL  IIIII   A   A   N   NN  CCCCC  EEEEEE


            Choose a selection for the Customer System
```

17-6   A BAR menu.

```
CLEAR
DEFINE MENU AJAXMAIN
DEFINE PAD PAD_1 OF AJAXMAIN PROMPT "Customer" AT 1,3
ON SELECTION PAD PAD_1 OF AJAXMAIN DO MAINPICK
DEFINE PAD PAD_2 OF AJAXMAIN PROMPT "Invoice" AT 1,13
ON SELECTION PAD PAD_2 OF AJAXMAIN DO MAINPICK
DEFINE PAD PAD_3 OF AJAXMAIN PROMPT "Inventory" AT 1,22
ON SELECTION PAD PAD_3 OF AJAXMAIN DO MAINPICK
DEFINE PAD PAD_4 OF AJAXMAIN PROMPT "Other" AT 1,33
ON SELECTION PAD PAD_4 OF AJAXMAIN DO MAINPICK
DEFINE PAD PAD_5 OF AJAXMAIN PROMPT "Exit" AT 1,40
ON SELECTION PAD PAD_5 OF AJAXMAIN DO MAINPICK
ACTIVATE MENU AJAXMAIN
```

17-7   Code for the BAR menu.

The DEFINE MENU command is used, along with other commands such as the DEFINE PAD command, to define a menu. This command is used as the first step in the process of creating a bar menu. It is not effective when used by itself. The function of DEFINE MENU is only to name a bar menu and associate an optional message with the menu name. You can define an optional MESSAGE that will appear centered and at the bottom of your screen. The message is limited to 79 characters. If you don't specify individual messages with each pad, then this message will be used.

Defining each choice: DEFINE PAD

The DEFINE PAD commands each define a single pad that is in the bar menu. If you want to define more than one pad in a menu, just repeat the command with the same menu name until all of your pads are defined. The only limit to the number of pads you can define is the amount of memory you have available.

To name the pad, follow the same rules as for fields or alias names (10 characters or less, first character must be a letter). If a name is used that already exists, the previous pad is overwritten. The OF *Menu_name* option needs to have been previously defined with the DEFINE MENU command.

Your PROMPT field is whatever text is displayed within the menu option. Menu prompts can be placed anywhere on the screen. To define the beginning point of the prompt text, use the optional screen coordinates. To have a vertical menu bar, use the same *X* coordinate for consecutive DEFINE PAD commands. However, you will find that the left and right arrow keys define bar menu movements and that the up and down arrow keys define a pop-up menu's movements. You should use a pop-up menu for vertical menu bars. This will be described later.

If no coordinates are specified, the first prompt will be placed in the upper left corner of the screen. Each prompt after that will be placed on this same line, with a space between each.

If you use the MESSAGE option, it will define a message and associate it with the PAD. You can make this message up to 79 characters long, with subsequent characters being truncated. This message will appear on the screen, centered and at the bottom, whenever the cursor is placed on the pad associated with it. This text will override any message that is defined with the DEFINE MENU command.

Once you have defined all of your pads you can define your actions.

Defining each action: ON SELECTION PAD

The ON SELECTION PAD command allows you to associate a command, procedure, or program with a bar menu pad. When that bar menu pad is selected, it will execute the specified command, procedure, or program. It executes whatever has been specified in the *command* clause. This command clause can contain any dBASE IV command or a DO *program name/procedure name* instruction.

Nothing happens until the Enter key is pressed. The action taken then will be the action specified in the ON SELECTION PAD statement. This form of the ON PAD statement is used for everything except the ability to automatically pop up (pull down) a menu when the highlight is placed on the PAD. You will see this command later in this chapter. It is the ON PAD statement that associates a pop-up menu with a menu pad, not the ON SELECTION PAD command presented here. Although you can pop up a menu using the ON SELECTION PAD command it first requires the user to press the Enter key.

Activating the menu: ACTIVATE MENU

Finally, once all of the menu options have been defined, the menu can be activated. The ACTIVATE MENU command activates an existing bar menu and displays it for use. This menu must be previously defined and is displayed over anything previously displayed on the screen. If the pad name is used along with the ACTIVATE MENU command, the highlight bar will appear on that pad. If a name is not used, then the first defined pad is used. The last menu that has been activated is the only active menu. Use the left and right arrow keys to move back and forth between the menu pads. Pads are accessed in the order that they were defined.

If you wanted to specifically activate the bar menu but choose the second option as the default pad to be highlighted you could code the command as:

```
ACTIVATE MENU AJAXMAIN PAD INVOICE
```

While the program is running, the active menu is deactivated. At the completion of the command, program, or procedure, the menu is once again active and you can use it to make another menu selection. If this command is used without a command or program, the named menu is deactivated.

Other bar menu commands

SHOW MENU   If you want to display a bar menu without activating it, use the SHOW MENU command with the desired menu name. It displays the menu named in the command on the screen, on top of any existing display. The displayed menu is inactive; you can't move the cursor in it or make a selection from it.

It is useful in program development to see what the menu you are designing will look like on the screen. It also can be used to show a totally dimmed set of menus when the previous choice is inappropriate for choices in the menu to be active.

DEACTIVATE MENU   The DEACTIVATE MENU command deactivates the active bar menu and erases it from the screen, but the menu remains intact in memory. It must be used with an ON SELECTION statement or in subsequent program code called from the ON SELECTION statement, because this is the only way it can be executed with an active menu. If there are no active menus, it has no effect such as from the dot prompt.

There is no required menu name for this command because it will deactivate only the active menu and erase it from the screen. Whatever was under the active menu then is displayed on the screen. DEACTIVATE MENU will return control to the level at which the menu was ACTIVATEd. If there is an ON PAD in effect, it also will deactivate any descendent pop-ups and menus.

It is used when the menu is no longer desired. If the menu is displayed inside a window, deactivating the window also deactivates the menu. Generally, you will deactivate a menu through a choice of Exit in the menu or when you are through performing the desired choice and a return to the menu is not the desired function.

Deactivating a menu does not remove the menu definition from memory. You can activate the menu again whenever you want and it will instantly appear. If you RELEASE or CLEAR the menu, you will have to define the menu again before activating it.

RELEASE MENU   The RELEASE MENUS command erases your bar menus from the screen and releases them from memory. It removes the menus in the menu name list from memory and deactivates any active menus. If no name list was used, it will clear all the menus from memory. It is recommended that you DEACTIVATE menus before you release them, so that any ON SELECTION and ON PAD commands that are associated with the menus are cleared. If you have defined your menus in procedures, you can release menus from memory at any time and then recover them by DOing the procedure that defines them.

Once you release a menu, you will have to define it again before you can activate it.

CLEAR MENUS   Use the CLEAR MENUS command to clear all bar menus from the screen and, at the same time, erase them from memory. This will free up the memory space used by menus for other operations. There is no difference between clearing menus and releasing them.

Bar menu functions

The MENU( ) function   MENU( ) returns the name of the active menu. It returns an alphanumeric string for the name of the most recent menu that was activated:

```
? MENU( )
EDIT
```

The MENU( ) function can be used in a program where all the menu options call a single program that then needs to know which option was chosen when the module was called.

One of the MENU( ) function's uses can be for help systems. If you use an ON KEY LABEL condition to call for help when the specified key is pressed, you can make the help system context sensitive by checking the value of MENU( ). However, you can't tell the value of the most recently selected PAD( ).

The PAD( ) function   The PAD( ) function returns the prompt PAD name of the most recently selected PAD of the active menu. Each menu option is located on a prompt PAD. When an option is entered, it becomes the most recently selected PAD:

```
? PAD( ) DATA_ENTRY
```

Like the MENU( ) function, this command displays the last chosen PAD, as shown in Fig. 17-8. It also is used to determine which was the chosen option.

This could be used to further support context-sensitive help or determine the last selected item for process checking. Unfortunately, it doesn't return the value of the pad you are on, just the value of the last PAD selected so that context-sensitive help might be somewhat limiting.

```
CLEAR
DEFINE MENU AJAXMAIN
DEFINE PAD PAD_1 OF AJAXMAIN PROMPT "Customer" AT 1,3
ON SELECTION PAD PAD_1 OF AJAXMAIN DO MAINPICK
DEFINE PAD PAD_2 OF AJAXMAIN PROMPT "Invoice" AT 1,13
ON SELECTION PAD PAD_2 OF AJAXMAIN DO MAINPICK
DEFINE PAD PAD_3 OF AJAXMAIN PROMPT "Inventory" AT 1,22
ON SELECTION PAD PAD_3 OF AJAXMAIN DO MAINPICK
DEFINE PAD PAD_4 OF AJAXMAIN PROMPT "Other" AT 1,33
ON SELECTION PAD PAD_4 OF AJAXMAIN DO MAINPICK
DEFINE PAD PAD_5 OF AJAXMAIN PROMPT "Exit" AT 1,40
ON SELECTION PAD PAD_5 OF AJAXMAIN DO MAINPICK
ACTIVATE MENU AJAXMAIN

PROCEDURE MAINPICK
  DO CASE
    CASE PAD() = PAD_1
      DO CUSTOMER
    CASE PAD() = PAD_2
      DO INVOICE
    CASE PAD() = PAD_3
      DO INVENTORY
    CASE PAD() = PAD_4
      DO OTHER
    CASE PAD() = PAD_5
    RETURN
  ENDCASE
RETURN
```

17-8 Using the PAD( ) Function.

The PROMPT( ) function PROMPT( ) returns the PROMPT of the most re-cently selected menu option. While the PAD( ) function returns the name of the PAD, the PROMPT( ) function displays the prompt of the menu pad that was last chosen:

```
? PROMPT( )
ENTER NEW RECORD
```

This could be used to feed back to the user help instructions or to let the user know what he or she has pressed and why that might not be correct. Because the PAD name is an internal name while the PROMPT( ) value is displayed on the screen, the PROMPT value can be more important than the PAD( ) value.

Techniques for dBASE IV pop-up menu commands

The pop-up menu creates a vertical menu that goes up and down the screen. Pop-up menus are used for a variety of reasons. They can become pull-down menus for bar menu choices or can be independent. They can have borders around them or can have no borders. They can be second-level menus. In this section, you will see several different types of pop-up menus.

The pop-up menu example

Let's look at a normal pop-up menu. The screen is shown in Fig. 17-9. As you can see, the choices are arranged up and down on the screen with a border around the menu. The highlight moves from one choice to another when the up or down arrow keys are pressed. Pressing Home or PgUp takes you to the first selection while pressing End or PgDn takes you to the last selection.

You should always program the first selection first and the last selection (on the right) last. The cursor highlight moves in the order that you have programmed them.

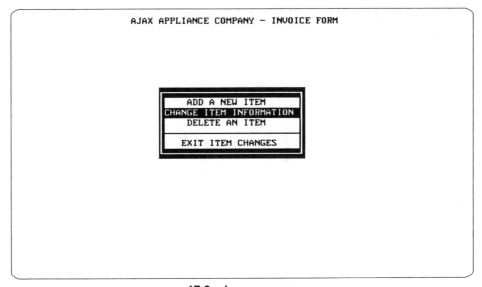

17-9   A pop-up menu.

As the cursor moves from choice to choice, an optional message can be displayed at the bottom of the screen for each option.

Now, it's time to look at the code for this pop-up menu. The pop-up menu code is shown in Fig. 17-10.

Defining the pop-up: DEFINE POPUP

The DEFINE POPUP command will define a pop-up window's name, location, prompts, and message line. The same naming rules as the alias and field names apply to pop-up menu names. The border around a pop-up menu is set

```
CLEAR
SET BORDER TO DOUBLE
DEFINE POPUP AJAXPOP FROM 6,28 TO 11,52
DEFINE BAR 1 OF AJAXPOP PROMPT "    ADD A NEW ITEM      "
DEFINE BAR 2 OF AJAXPOP PROMPT "CHANGE ITEM INFORMATION"
DEFINE BAR 3 OF AJAXPOP PROMPT "    DELETE AN ITEM      "
DEFINE BAR 4 OF AJAXPOP PROMPT "————————————————————————"  SKIP
DEFINE BAR 5 OF AJAXPOP PROMPT "   EXIT ITEM CHANGES    "
ON SELECTION POPUP AJAXPOP DO AJAXPICK

ACTIVATE POPUP AJAXPOP

PROCEDURE AJAXPICK
 DO CASE
   CASE BAR() = 1
     DO ADD
   CASE BAR() = 2
     DO CHANGE
   CASE BAR() = 3
     DO DELETE
   CASE BAR() = 5
     DEACTIVATE POPUP
 ENDCASE
RETURN
```

17-10 Code for the pop-up menu.

with the command:

SET BORDER TO NONE	No border around the menu choices
SET BORDER TO SINGLE	Draws a single line border
SET BORDER TO DOUBLE	Draws a double line border
SET BORDER TO PANEL	Draws a reverse video border

As you can see in Fig. 17-9, this pop-up has a double line border.

The most common form of the DEFINE pop-up is:

DEFINE pop-up AJAXMENU FROM 10,28 TO 16,52 ;
MESSAGE "Choose a Selection for the AJAX System"

This defines the name of the pop-up that it will then be known as. The size of the pop-up menu box is defined by the FROM and TO parameters. If you do not give the menu a large enough box to contain the bar options, then several things will happen. If the box is too narrow, then the bar options will be truncated. If the box is not tall enough, then the first few bar options will be displayed and the rest will scroll into sight when the down arrow is pressed.

Defining each choice: DEFINE BAR

Each DEFINE BAR command is used to define a single option in a pop-up menu. A *bar* is a single prompt or an option that appears in a defined pop-up menu or window.

If there is a missing BAR value, that row in the pop-up is left blank and the selection bar will skip over it. At least one bar must be defined in the pop-up window or the window will be empty and cannot be activated. If you want to place text, such as a message or separating line in the box, then you can follow the DEFINE BAR command with the SKIP parameter. This will skip the option and not allow it as a choice. In Fig. 17-9, you can see that the fourth bar is a horizontal line separating the first three choices from the other choices. In the code in Fig. 17-10, the SKIP parameter is used to tell dBASE to not allow it as a choice.

The SKIP parameter also can be used conditionally so that some options can be skipped for certain conditions. An example of this could be:

```
DEFINE BAR 2 OF AJAXMENU PROMPT "CHANGE ITEM INFORMATION" ;
    SKIP FOR EOF( )
```

If the database was at end of file that could check for no records, the change option could be skipped. This also could have applications for password and access level control.

Defining each action: ON SELECTION POPUP

Unlike the horizontal bar menus, you generally set up a separate procedure either within the program where the menu resides as a separate procedure or as a program by itself. The BAR( ) function then is used to determine which option was chosen. This is very different from the horizontal bar menus syntax. This is because you use the ON SELECTION command at the pop-up level not at the individual bar level, so you cannot assign actions here to the individual bars. In the bar menus, you assigned an action to each PAD.

The ON SELECTION POPUP command will specify the command or procedure that will execute when a pop-up menu selection is made. It associates any one of the prompts of the specified program menu with a dBASE IV command or procedure. If no command is specified with ON SELECTION POPUP, the active pop-up will be deactivated. If the name is ALL, then the command will apply to all of the pop-ups that are active. Later, when you see the code for some of the more complex examples, you will see how having many pop-ups defined at once can be advantageous. Then, using a nested (one within another) CASE statement, you can determine not only what BAR( ) was chosen but what POPUP( ) as well.

The AJAXMENU procedure is part of the program that contains the pop-up menu code. From this procedure the choices actually are made based on the value of the BAR( ) function.

Activating the pop-up menu: ACTIVATE POPUP

If you want to activate a previously defined pop-up for use, use the ACTIVATE POPUP command. Only one pop-up menu can be active at one time. Any active pop-up menu is deactivated when you issue a subsequent ACTIVATE POPUP command, press the Esc key, or issue the DEACTIVATE POPUP command.

You can have a pop-up open another pop-up, so, when a pop-up bar choice has many options, it can open another pop-up. When this occurs the first pop-up is suspended and still is displayed, but the cursor is active only in the first pop-up.

Other pop-up menu commands

SHOW POPUP   The SHOW POPUP command displays a pop-up menu without making it active. Because the pop-up menu is inactive, the cursor cannot be moved around in it (it stays at the dot prompt) and messages associated with the pop-up menu are not displayed. This is useful for developing programs.

DEACTIVATE POPUPS   Use the DEACTIVATE POPUP command to erase the active pop-up menu from the screen while leaving it intact in memory. If any of the text was covered by the pop-up menu, it will be displayed again. There will be no effect if this command is issued from the dot prompt. It can be used only as part of an ON SELECTION statement, because an active pop-up first must be deactivated.

CLEAR POPUPS   CLEAR POPUPS clears all the pop-up menus from the screen and also erases them from memory. You use this command to clear the screen of all the pop-up menus and to release the memory that was used up by pop-up menus. In addition, it also DEACTIVATEs the active pop-up and clears all ON SELECTION commands that are associated with the pop-up menus.

RELEASE POPUPS   The RELEASE POPUPS command erases the named pop-up menus from the screen and also from memory. The active pop-up menu is deactivated if you specify it from the pop-up name list. Any ON SELECTION pop-up commands that are associated with the pop-up menus that are in the names list are cleared before the pop-up menus are erased. If no pop-up name menu list has been used, the RELEASE POPUPS command will erase all pop-up menus from the screen and from memory.

Pop-up menu functions

The BAR( ) function   The BAR( ) function returns the BAR number of the last selected BAR from the current pop-up menu:

```
? BAR( )
3
```

As you have seen, this generally is used as part of a CASE statement to determine which bar was chosen.

The POPUP( ) function   The POPUP( ) function returns the name of the active pop-up menu. It returns a null string if no pop-up menu is active:

```
? pop-up( )
DATAENT
```

When more than one pop-up is active when one pop-up calls another, you might need to know which pop-up was last activated. This can tell you not only what menu bar was last chosen but also what pop-up it was chosen from.

The PROMPT( ) function   PROMPT( ) returns the PROMPT of the most recently selected menu pop-up:

```
? PROMPT( )
"ENTER NEW RECORD"
```

Other types of pop-ups: fields, file, structure

File lists   There are three other types of pop-up menus that can be created in dBASE IV. So far, you have seen how pop-up menus have hardcoded options within the menu box. There are three types of pop-up menus that have variable contents. These include the ability to display:

- The files on a disk or subdirectory of any type specified by using standard DOS wildcard characters
- The fields in a dBASE database structure
- The values of a specific field from the records in a database

When using the pop-up menu for the displaying of files, fields, and values, there is only the DEFINE POPUP command in the definition. There is no DEFINE BAR command for displaying these values in the pop-up.

Let's begin with the file list. File lists will list all of the files in the open catalog. The basic form of this command is:

```
DEFINE POPUP name FROM row1 col1 TO row2 col2 PROMPT FILES
```

You also can list specific files by using the LIKE option. Suppose you want to list only the database files in a pop-up called PICKNAME and wanted the pop-up to be whatever size it needs automatically, starting in position 10,25. You would enter:

```
DEFINE POPUP PICKNAME FROM 10,25 PROMPT FILES LIKE *.DBF
```

Examine the screen in Fig. 17-11. This is an example of the PROMPT FILES pop-up menu.

When you activate the pop-up, a box will appear with all of your database files that are in the active catalog. Your cursor will be placed in the box, and you can choose any of the database files. When you make a selection, the menu is deactivated and processing continues at the command after the

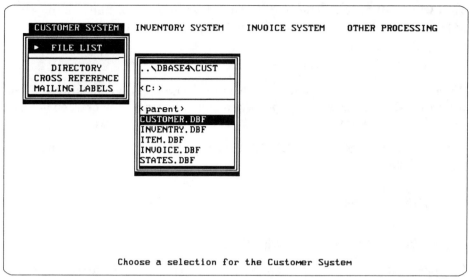

```
CUSTOMER SYSTEM    INVENTORY SYSTEM    INVOICE SYSTEM    OTHER PROCESSING

►  FILE LIST
                        ..\DBASE4\CUST
   DIRECTORY
   CROSS REFERENCE    <C:>
   MAILING LABELS
                      <parent>
                      CUSTOMER.DBF
                      INVENTRY.DBF
                      ITEM.DBF
                      INVOICE.DBF
                      STATES.DBF




           Choose a selection for the Customer System
```

17-11   A prompt files pop-up example.

activate statement. The PROMPT( ) function will contain the complete file-name of the file including drive, path, and extension in upper case.

Notice there is no TO clause in this example. This will automatically size the box as wide as the largest database filename and as tall as the number of filenames in the catalog. If the width of the largest filename doesn't fit in the box, then it will be truncated. If there are more files than the height of the pop-up, then the rest can be scrolled. The full filename will always fit into the PROMPT( ) function regardless of what is displayed in the pop-up menu.

Field lists   The next type of pop-up is the field list pop-up known as the STRUCTURE pop-up. This displays all of the fields in an open database or in the SET FIELDS to parameter. Examine the screen in Fig. 17-12. This is an example of the PROMPT STRUCTURE pop-up menu.

The single statement that defined the pop-up in Fig. 17-12 is:

DEFINE POPUP PICKFLD FROM 4,25 TO 15,35 PROMPT STRUCTURE

This displays all of the field names in the active database or view. A database or view must be open to use this parameter. Once again, the field name chosen will be the value of the PROMPT( ) function. This type of selection can be invaluable in building your own query system into dBASE applications when the QBE is either unavailable (in Runtime) or you simply want your own interface.

Value lists   The final type of pop-up menu is the values menu. This menu will list all of the values from a single field in the database. The simplest form of the DEFINE POPUP command is shown here. In this example, a pop-up called

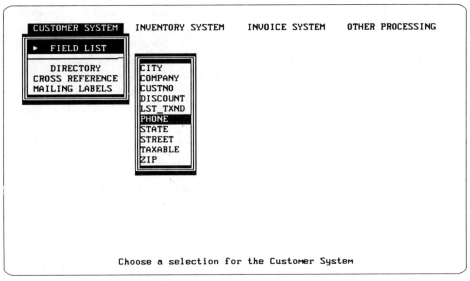

17-12 A prompt structure pop-up example.

PICKVAL is defined. When activated, it will contain all of the values from the name field of the open database or view.

DEFINE POPUP PICKVAL FROM 10,25 TO 20,35 PROMPT FIELD name

These types of menus can prove invaluable in allowing input beyond the multiple choice field or to allow the user to select fieldnames or fields they need to access in a program without worrying about hardcoding values. A multiple choice field can only be hardcoded where the PROMPT FIELD pop-up can show values from a user-defined database that can be maintained by the user and always be up to date.

dBASE IV pull-down menus

dBASE IV pop-up menus can be pull-downs or drop-downs. Depending on the commands you use, the menus will pop up automatically or will appear only when called up by the user.

Pull-downs vs. drop-downs

There are two ways to have a bar menu open a pop-up menu. If you use the ON SELECTION PAD command in the bar menu definition, then the user must make the selection for anything to happen. There is certainly nothing stopping you from making the ON SELECTION PAD action an ACTIVATE pop-up command. When the pop-up menu is positioned under the bar menu, this is referred to as a *drop-down menu*, because the menu appears to drop down when the user chooses the bar menu choice.

This is different from a true pull-down menu where the user merely moves the bar menu highlight from one pad to another and as each new pad is highlighted a pop-up menu appears. This is accomplished with the ON PAD command and doesn't require the user to press Enter for the pop-up menu to appear. Technically, this is called a *pull-down menu*.

Once the pop-up appears, there is no difference whether it was pulled down or dropped down. The next section of this chapter will deal with making a pop-up into a pull-down menu.

Making a pop-up menu into a pull-down menu

When you want a bar menu to automatically open a pop-up to make a pull-down menu, you must use a different version of the ON PAD command from the bar menu. Instead of the command ON SELECTION PAD, the command is simply ON PAD.

ON PAD names the pop-up menu and then activates this menu when the cursor is on the pad of the specified bar menu. It must be used with the ACTIVATE pop-up option or the prompt pad will be disabled.

By using the ACTIVATE POPUP option, you will be able to have both bar menus and pop-ups active on the screen at the same time. As you use the left and right arrow keys to move within the bar menus, you will activate various pop-up menus. You also can use the up and down arrow keys to move between the bars of the pop-up menus. This command cannot be used if you previously have used the ON SELECTION PAD command to associate a prompt or program with a pad.

An example of this is shown in Fig. 17-13. The first pop-up menu is

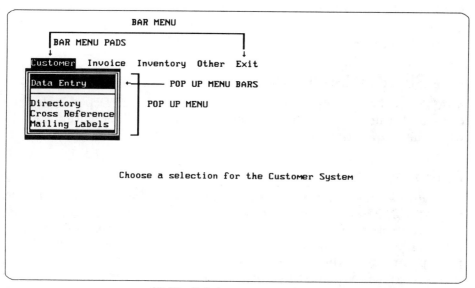

17-13 Pull-down menu screen.

pulled down. Each of the other bar menu options also has an associated pull-down menu. The program code for the bar menu and the first pull-down menu is shown in Fig. 17-14.

```
DEFINE MENU AJAXMAIN
DEFINE PAD PAD_1 OF AJAXMAIN PROMPT "Customer" AT 1,3
ON PAD PAD_1 OF AJAXMAIN ACTIVATE POPUP MAIN1
DEFINE PAD PAD_2 OF AJAXMAIN PROMPT "Invoice" AT 1,13
ON PAD PAD_2 OF AJAXMAIN ACTIVATE POPUP MAIN2
DEFINE PAD PAD_3 OF AJAXMAIN PROMPT "Inventory" AT 1,22
ON PAD PAD_3 OF AJAXMAIN ACTIVATE POPUP MAIN3
DEFINE PAD PAD_4 OF AJAXMAIN PROMPT "Other" AT 1,33
ON PAD PAD_4 OF AJAXMAIN ACTIVATE POPUP MAIN4
DEFINE PAD PAD_5 OF AJAXMAIN PROMPT "Exit" AT 1,40
ON PAD PAD_5 OF AJAXMAIN ACTIVATE POPUP MAIN5
*-- Popup
DEFINE POPUP MAIN1 FROM 2,2 ;
MESSAGE "Choose a selection for the Customer System"
DEFINE BAR 1 OF MAIN1 PROMPT "Data Entry"
DEFINE BAR 2 OF MAIN1 PROMPT "————————————————"   SKIP
DEFINE BAR 3 OF MAIN1 PROMPT "Directory"
DEFINE BAR 4 OF MAIN1 PROMPT "Cross Reference"
DEFINE BAR 5 OF MAIN1 PROMPT "Mailing Labels"
ON SELECTION POPUP MAIN1 DO MAIN1

ACTIVATE MENU AJAXMAIN

PROCEDURE MAIN1
 DO CASE
  CASE BAR() = 1
      DO CUSTMENU
  CASE BAR() = 3
      DO CUSTDIR
  CASE BAR() = 4
      DO CUSTCROS
  CASE BAR() = 5
      DO CUSTLBL
 ENDCASE
RETURN
```

17-14   Code for the pull-down menu.

As you can see, there would be quite a lot of code. First is the block of code to define the bar menu ABCMAIN. Each pad is defined along with the action which activates the different pop-ups.

There would be four pop-ups named MAIN1 through MAIN4. You can see only the first one in this figure. Each pop-up might have several bars defined. You might notice that the second bar of the menu is simply a line across the menu. The SKIP parameter keeps the cursor from moving onto the bar line that contains the line. Each pop-up menu calls a procedure. In this abbreviated example, you can see the first CASE statement for the CUSTOMER pop-up menu. The four bars, 1, 3, 4, and 5, have statements giving instructions.

In Fig. 17-14, only one pop-up menu is shown along with one routine to evaluate the action to be taken. For each pull-down menu you want to have, you must code both the pop-up menu definition and the case statement to handle the choice that is made. If you have a lot of bar menu pads and an equal number of pop-ups, you will end up with a lot of code. Each bar menu pad need not pull down a menu and each pop-up can have a different number of bar choices.

Creating a pop-up that calls another

Suppose that the customer menu program called another menu. In fact, it can. How might you program that. Figure 17-15 shows the screen that would be created. The changes to the previous program are minimal, as shown in Fig. 17-16.

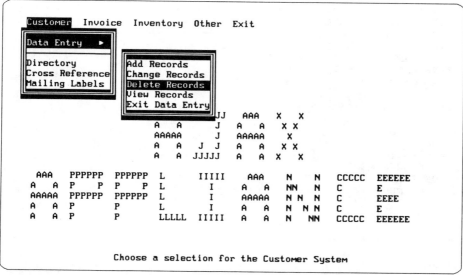

17-15 Screen for a pull-down menu that calls another pull-down menu.

The new pop-up is defined. It looks like any other pop-up menu. There is one small change to the original first pop-up. The option prompt for the first bar option has had a symbol added to it. The ASCII 16 symbol (▶) is an industry standard to tell the operator that this menu will call another pull-down menu. You also could use it to signify the calling of any menu that calls another menu.

The CASE statement is a little different. The CASE statement shows that, for the first choice, another pop-up menu will be opened. The ON SELECTION choice for that menu will call another program where the BAR( ) value that is active is evaluated.

You are not limited to two levels. You could continue to add a data entry level from the change or delete functions to determine which customer record

```
*-- Bar
DEFINE MENU AJAXMAIN
DEFINE PAD PAD_1 OF AJAXMAIN PROMPT "Customer" AT 1,3
ON PAD PAD_1 OF AJAXMAIN ACTIVATE POPUP MAIN1
DEFINE PAD PAD_2 OF AJAXMAIN PROMPT "Invoice" AT 1,13
ON PAD PAD_2 OF AJAXMAIN ACTIVATE POPUP MAIN2
DEFINE PAD PAD_3 OF AJAXMAIN PROMPT "Inventory" AT 1,22
ON PAD PAD_3 OF AJAXMAIN ACTIVATE POPUP MAIN3
DEFINE PAD PAD_4 OF AJAXMAIN PROMPT "Other" AT 1,33
ON PAD PAD_4 OF AJAXMAIN ACTIVATE POPUP MAIN4
DEFINE PAD PAD_5 OF AJAXMAIN PROMPT "Exit" AT 1,40
ON PAD PAD_5 OF AJAXMAIN ACTIVATE POPUP MAIN5

*-- Popup
DEFINE POPUP MAIN1 FROM 2,2 ;
MESSAGE "Choose a selection for the Customer System"
DEFINE BAR 1 OF MAIN1 PROMPT "Data Entry    ▶ "
DEFINE BAR 2 OF MAIN1 PROMPT "————————————"    SKIP
DEFINE BAR 3 OF MAIN1 PROMPT "Directory"
DEFINE BAR 4 OF MAIN1 PROMPT "Cross Reference"
DEFINE BAR 5 OF MAIN1 PROMPT "Mailing Labels"
ON SELECTION POPUP MAIN1 DO MAIN1

DEFINE POPUP CUSTD FROM 4,24 ;
MESSAGE "Choose a data entry operation for the Customer System"
DEFINE BAR 1 OF CUSTD PROMPT "Add Records     "
DEFINE BAR 2 OF CUSTD PROMPT "Change Records "
DEFINE BAR 3 OF CUSTD PROMPT "Delete Records "
DEFINE BAR 4 OF CUSTD PROMPT "View Records    "
DEFINE BAR 5 OF CUSTD PROMPT "Exit Data Entry"
ON SELECTION POPUP CUSTD DO CUSTDATA WITH BAR()

ACTIVATE MENU ABCMAIN

PROCEDURE MAIN1
 DO CASE
    CASE BAR() = 1
      ACTIVATE POPUP CUSTD
    CASE BAR() = 3
      DO CUSTDIR
    CASE BAR() = 4
      DO CUSTCROS
    CASE BAR() = 5
      DO CUSTLBL
 ENDCASE
RETURN
```

17-16 Code for a pull-down menu that calls another pull-down menu.

is to be changed. Remember that too many menu levels do get confusing, but it's nice to know that any interface can be programmed when needed.

Vertical bar menus: it's only a pop-up!

This menu can be implemented either as a bar menu or as a pop-up menu. If it is implemented as a bar menu, then there is one major problem. The up and down arrow keys do not move the cursor. A bar menu only recognizes the left and right arrow keys. This proves to be very confusing to the user, because, if the menu appears to be up and down, the user would want to press the up and down arrow keys. Because nothing would happen, this would prove confusing.

Creating a vertical bar menu in the middle of the screen, as shown in Fig. 17-17 actually is very simple. It is simply a pop-up menu without a border that has been double spaced and placed in the center of the screen.

The code for this menu is shown in Fig. 17-18. There is nothing special about the code. First, the border is set to NONE. Then, the pop-up is defined using a very large area. Each bar is placed on the odd numbered lines. There is no special reason for this. If the number of needed choices increased, the menu could be placed in single spacing to get more choices. Because there are no choices for the even numbered lines, those lines don't appear in the CASE statement.

```
                          ABC COMPANY
                     CUSTOMER DATA ENTRY




                    ADD CUSTOMER INFORMATION

                   CHANGE CUSTOMER INFORMATION

                      DELETE A CUSTOMER

                   VIEW CUSTOMER INFORMATION

                   EXIT CUSTOMER DATA ENTRY




          Choose a selection from the Customer Menu
```

17-17 Vertical bar menu screen.

Menus play one of the most important roles in a system because they control the navigation from one part of your system to another. In the next chapter, you will learn about windows and how they too are very valuable in shaping the user interface.

NEW MENU and POPUP COMMANDS

In version 2.0 of dBASE IV, there are a number of new menu and pop-up commands that allow you use the menu processing for more sophisticated uses other than just displaying a menu on the screen. The appendix C of this book describes the various commands and functions within the menu

```
CLEAR
SET BORDER TO NONE
DEFINE POPUP CUSMENU FROM 7,25 TO 17,55;
    MESSAGE "Choose a selection from the Customer Menu"
DEFINE BAR 1 OF CUSMENU PROMPT "   ADD CUSTOMER INFORMATION   "
DEFINE BAR 2 OF CUSMENU PROMPT "                             " SKIP
DEFINE BAR 3 OF CUSMENU PROMPT " CHANGE CUSTOMER INFORMATION "
DEFINE BAR 4 OF CUSMENU PROMPT "                             " SKIP
DEFINE BAR 5 OF CUSMENU PROMPT "      DELETE A CUSTOMER      "
DEFINE BAR 6 OF CUSMENU PROMPT "                             " SKIP
DEFINE BAR 7 OF CUSMENU PROMPT "  VIEW CUSTOMER INFORMATION  "
DEFINE BAR 8 OF CUSMENU PROMPT "                             " SKIP
DEFINE BAR 9 OF CUSMENU PROMPT "  EXIT CUSTOMER DATA ENTRY   "
ON SELECTION POPUP CUSMENU DO CUSTPICK

@ 1,28 TO 4,53
@ 2,30 SAY '       ABC COMPANY'
@ 3,30 SAY " CUSTOMER DATA ENTRY "

ACTIVATE POPUP CUSMENU
RETURN

PROCEDURE CUSTPICK
 DO CASE
   CASE BAR() = 1
     DO CUSTADD
   CASE BAR() = 3
     DO CUSTCHG
   CASE BAR() = 5
     DO CUSTDEL
   CASE BAR() = 7
     DO CUSTVEW
   CASE BAR() = 9
     DEACTIVATE POPUP
 ENDCASE
RETURN
```

17-18 Vertical bar menu screen code.

processing. The program shown in Fig. 17-18 shows a small program that uses a few of the new menu commands, and a non-standard use for the new options.

This small program will display a pop-up menu on the screen, then, based upon the bar that is displayed, will open the associated database file and display the structure of the file. When the highlight leaves a given bar, the database file is closed and the window is closed. This simple example shows how varied your processing can be when using the new menu and pop-up commands.

18
Windows

Windows give you the ability to handle errors, to have messages to the operator, and to have less code by not constantly redrawing previous screens. Windows also are used to display memo fields, so you can see the contents without having to go into the memo field entry area.

If you've never used a window in dBASE you are in for a new and fulfilling experience. The paragraph is our best definition of the power of a window.

Look at the floor where you are sitting or standing. Using your imagination (or a washable marker) draw a box on the floor precisely 24 inches across and 80 inches wide. That's your screen. In that box, you should visualize a data entry screen. Now, take a piece of paper. Cut it so it is rectangular and any size equal to or smaller than 24 inches across and 80 inches wide. Place an error message on that piece of paper. Place the paper on the floor inside your imaginary box. The paper will cover a portion of the "screen." Because the paper is opaque you cannot see the portion of the floor (screen) below it. Finally, lift the paper off the floor. The "screen" reappears. Because the paper was merely on top of the floor, it only covered it. When the paper was removed what was on the floor was again visible. The paper is a window.

Using windows in dBASE IV

Windows are rectangular areas that sit on top of whatever is on the screen at the time they are activated. Windows can be small areas that display a simple message or can fill the entire screen from positions 0,0 to 24,79. If data doesn't fit inside the window, it can be scrolled in any direction.

Anything that can be placed on a screen can go inside a window. In dBASE, this is limited to text, data, lines, boxes, and menus. However, what you can do inside a window is limited only by your imagination. Some of the tasks you can use a window for include:

- Help boxes, informational messages, error messages
- Data entry screens
- Menus
- Memo field edit and display
- Relational table lookup
- BROWSE tables for multi-record input or display
- Complete help or tutorial systems

In the AJAX appliance case study, you will see several different applications for windows. All error messages and warning messages are displayed in a window. In some of the modules, you will see how to practically implement a menu inside of a window to simulate push buttons.

Figure 18-1 shows an error window sitting on top of a data entry screen. The portion of the data entry screen under the window is covered by the window itself. When the window is removed the data entry screen can be seen again in its entirety.

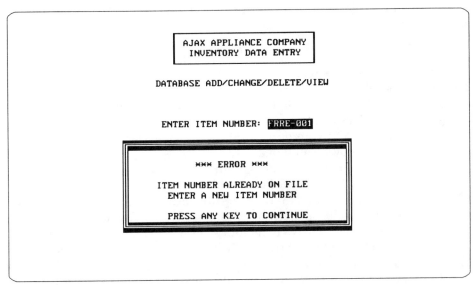

18-1 Screen dump of an error window.

Windows should be used whenever you want to place something on the screen temporarily. By placing windows on the screen, you can perform any task you want in them and not have to worry about what's on the screen under the window.

Windows give you the ability to handle errors, to display messages to the operator, and to have less code by not constantly redrawing previous screens.

Windows also are used to display memo fields, so you can see the contents without having to go into the memo field entry area.

Windows can be surrounded by a border or can be borderless and give you control of the extra two lines and columns normally used by the border.

Windows give your screen the ability to simulate multi-dimensions. Because you can have one window on top of another window, it appears that they float above the flat plane of your screen. When a window is placed on the screen, whatever is underneath cannot be seen. When you remove a window, you again can see whatever was obscured.

Before windows were part of dBASE IV, everything that was displayed by the system happened on the flat plane of your screen. If you wanted to display an error box on the screen, you had to place the box and text on the actual screen itself. You had to clear the area inside the box and then write your message in the box. Whatever you did became part of the screen. Once you were done displaying the box and its contents, you had to redraw the entire screen again or at least the portion where the box was.

Defining a window

Windows are defined in dBASE IV by using the command DEFINE WINDOW. You can define all of your windows at once or define them as you use them. A simple window definition might be:

```
DEFINE WINDOW win1 FROM 8,30 to 16,50
```

This command defines a window named WIN1 from row 8 column 30 to row 16 column 50. This would create a window 9 rows high and 21 columns across. Based on these coordinates, it also would be centered on the screen.

This in itself does not place the window on the screen. That is done with the ACTIVATE WINDOW command. The DEFINE WINDOW command merely establishes the window in memory.

You can define up to 20 windows in memory. When you define a window, it uses 44 bytes of memory regardless of its size, colors, or borders. However, when the window is activated, it uses significantly more memory. A check of one of my systems told me that a window that was 9 rows high and 40 columns across used 774 bytes of memory. A full-screen window from 0,0 to 24,79 used 4054 bytes when activated. If you run out of windows or memory, you will get an error message.

The name and placement of the window is not the only thing you specify when you define a window. You also enter the border and color information.

Window borders

To make your windows stand out, you have complete control of the area within and around the window. You can display the window with a border made up of several types of characters. These are the same type of visual effect you have when placing a box on a screen or report. Borders can be:

- Not displayed
- Single-line
- Double-line
- Inverse video lines (known as panels)
- Any user-defined ASCII character

To add the border definition to a window, you would add the appropriate border parameter to the definition.

The default border type is whatever the SET BORDER TO command defaults to. Normally, this is a single line. The other choices are:

- DOUBLE
- PANEL
- NONE

Placing no option after the window definition would default to the SET BORDER TO setting.

Optionally, you can specify the border definition string. This is a list of eight ASCII codes representing the eight different segments of any box. If you're not familiar with this, the normal single-line border definition string is 196, 196, 179, 179, 218, 191, 192, 217. These are the top and bottom horizontal characters, the left and right vertical characters, and the four corners in the order of top left, top right, bottom left, and bottom right. Figure 18-2 shows a representation of the border segments and the single-line ASCII equivalents. The inner digits represent the segment numbering scheme while the outer numbers are the ASCII codes for the different line segment types. The upper right corner, which is box segment number six, is an ASCII code of 191.

18-2 Single line border segments and their ASCII equivalents.

```
        218     196     191

                 5 1 6
                ┌───┐
        179    3 │   │ 4   179
                └───┘
                 7 2 8

        192     196     217
```

To define a window with a double-line border, you would enter:

DEFINE WINDOW win1 FROM 10,20 TO 14,60 DOUBLE

To define a window with a border of all dollar signs you would enter:

DEFINE WINDOW win1 FROM 10,20 TO 14,60 CHR(36),CHR(36),;
    CHR(36),CHR(36),CHR(36),CHR(36),CHR(36),CHR(36)

The CHR(36) parameter translates the decimal value 36 to its ASCII equivalent—a dollar sign.

It would be easier to use the SET BORDER TO command first to set the border to all dollar signs (ASCII 36) and then to use the default window definition:

```
SET BORDER TO 36,36,36,36,36,36,36,36 DEFINE WINDOW win1 ;
    FROM 10,20 TO 14,60 SET BORDER TO
```

In the SET BORDER TO command, the decimal to ASCII conversion is automatic and you do not have to use the CHR( ) function.

The final SET BORDER TO command resets the border to a single line so that the next menu or window defined does not have dollar signs for a border.

Finally, to define a window without a border, you would enter:

```
DEFINE WINDOW win1 FROM 10,20 TO 14,60 NONE
```

If you define a window without a border, you will have two extra rows and columns in which to place text or data. When a window has a border, you obviously can't write to the border itself.

Window colors

Window colors are defined with the COLOR option of the DEFINE WINDOW command. Without this option, the window will be the same color as your screen, because it uses the default colors.

You can define three types of colors:

- Standard
- Enhanced
- Frame (border)

Each type can have a foreground and background specified. Suppose, in our example, you want to have white on blue standard colors, white on red enhanced, green on white for a double-line border. (Yuch!) You would enter the window definition like this:

```
DEFINE WINDOW win1 FROM 10,20 TO 14,60 DOUBLE COLOR W/B,W/R,G/W
```

You do not have to specify all of the colors. You could use a comma in place of one that you didn't want to set. If you don't have a border, then the last color is ignored. When you display your text, data, and boxes within the window, they will be in the specified colors.

The coordinates of a dBASE IV window

There are 25 rows and 80 columns in a normal personal computer screen. You can run in 43-line EGA mode as well; however, for this book, we will discuss the more standard 18-line mode. The coordinates of the entire screen are from row 0, column 0 to row 24, column 79. This can be represented by 0,0 to 24,79. When you define the placement of a window on the screen, you define both the starting coordinate in terms of the row and column along with the ending row and column.

dBASE IV maintains a coordinate system inside a window separate from the coordinate system of the screen underneath. Once you activate a window and begin to write to the screen, you have to remember that the first usable position in the window is 0,0. If your window has a border, you will lose two rows and two columns. If you define a window from 12,19 to 20,59 that has a border you can only write in seven rows (13-19) and 39 columns (20-58).

Position 13,20 would be known as 0,0 while the last usable coordinate (19,58) would be known to the window as 6,38. So, in essence, your window is usable for window coordinates 0,0 to 6,38. This is shown in Fig. 18-3.

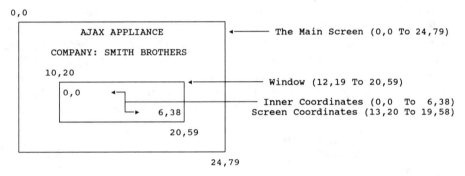

18-3 The dBASE window coordinate system.

If the window doesn't have a border, then you will reclaim the two rows and columns you otherwise would lose. In this example, you could write from window coordinates 0,0 to 8,40.

If you try to specify column coordinates outside the coordinate system of the window, an error message will be displayed. If you try to specify row coordinates outside the coordinate system of the window, the window will scroll up to display the text; however, you cannot scroll back to the original contents.

Tips for placing windows on the screen

Where you place a window on the screen is up to you. You can control its exact placement in terms of the FROM and TO coordinates. Because you also can separately control the color of the border (if you want one) and the inside of the window, you can control how visually appealing the window becomes.

Sometimes, centering a window on the screen is desired. You must look at where the window is going in relation to the screen itself. The center of a full screen is roughly 12,40. It's actually 12.5, 39.5; however, because you must work in whole character segments, you can choose to add or subtract one half to each of the coordinates. If you center a window in a full screen, then the center point still is the same. In our simple window definition, the midpoint of the coordinates 10,20 to 14,60 is about 12,40. If you place a window within a window, you would have to recalculate the center point. Often, you place a window on or near some specific place on the screen. An error window should be placed one or two lines below or above the error itself so as to not cover the data in error. A message window can be placed more towards the bottom of the screen to be visually appealing rather than to be visually obnoxious. Remember, windows should be used to convey messages or warn the operators of errors. Windows that constantly appear in the dead center of the screen seem to leap out and yell at the operator.

A single- or double-line border is used to define the bounds of the window. Inverse video should be used sparingly as it bleeds into the underlying screen and the window itself.

You can specify one color for the border and another for the inside of the window both for standard and enhanced text. You can specify both the foreground and background colors for text. Be careful to use colors that make the window stand out but do not contrast with the underlying screen. The border can be a different color than the inside, but it does not necessarily have to be. Choose colors that complement each other but do not conflict. If you don't use a border, then color can be essential to define the bounds of the window to the operator.

Finally, you can change the color of any part of the inside of the window as you write in it. Avoid the rainbow effect. A few colors is good. Trying to use them all is not.

Activating a window

Once you have defined a window, you can activate it. Activation means that the window appears on the screen. When you activate a window, it always is blank regardless of what you previously had in it.

The command to activate a window is simply:

```
ACTIVATE WINDOW win1
```

The ACTIVATE WINDOW command will activate and display the named window from memory and also will direct all screen output to that window. To use this command, you need to have defined the window previously.

The borders that appear around each window are in the format that you established when you defined the window. If no border string has been specified, then the SET BORDER setting will be used to determine window borders at activation time. Therefore, you always should specify a border setting when defining your windows.

One thing you will have to be careful about is that, once you activate a menu and begin to write to the screen, you have to remember that the first position in the window is 0,0. If your window takes up the entire screen and has a border, you will lose two rows and columns. Your window will be accessible (in screen coordinates) from 1,1 to 23,78 instead of the usual 0,0 to 24,79.

In the same way, if you create a window from 12,20 to 18,60 and you have a border, you will be able to write from screen coordinates 13,21 to 17,59 or window coordinates 0,0 to 5,39. If the window doesn't have a border, then you will reclaim the two rows and columns you otherwise would lose and you could then use window coordinates 0,0 to 7,41.

When you are through with the window, you can deactivate it. The DEACTIVATE WINDOW command deactivates the named window. The window is erased then from the screen. It still is defined in memory. To bring it back, simply use the ACTIVATE WINDOW command.

Remember, when you activate the window, it will be blank regardless if you had previously activated it and placed text, data, or boxes in it. You can save the window definition including its contents with the SAVE WINDOW command, which you will learn about later in this chapter.

Placing an error (or any) message inside a window

Now that you have seen how to define and activate a window, it is time to learn how to use one. One of the most common uses of a window is to simply convey a message. Messages can be simply informational (don't forget to do this or that) or can be a warning or even an error message telling you something is wrong and to allow you to take corrective action.

Remember, almost anything can be put inside a window. Let's begin with some simple text in an error window. One of the most common windows is the error window. This window generally is displayed in the center of a screen. Figure 18-4 shows a typical error window in a data entry screen. The program code for defining and using this error window is shown in Fig. 18-5.

The first statement defines the window. The window is named MSG1 and will be defined from row 12, column 19 to row 20, column 59. The window also is defined with a double-line border. Because the outside of the window is nine lines high (20−12+1), which is the standard formula (r2−r1+1), and the border takes two lines, you have seven lines in which to write to. These lines are numbered 0 to 6. The inside of the window is colored red so it will stand out more.

Once the window is defined, it can be activated. The ACTIVATE WINDOW msg1 command is all there is to it. The window then will appear on the screen on top of whatever was there before. The command ?? CHR( ) sounds a short beep to further get the user's attention. The next five lines of code display the error message. The @ 5,1 SAY ' ' command simply places the cursor at the beginning of the sixth window line (remember, the lines are numbered 0 to 6). The next command will start on the seventh and last line.

The WAIT command pauses execution until a key is pressed. Without this command, the window would flash on and off the screen. This pauses the display until the user acknowledges the error.

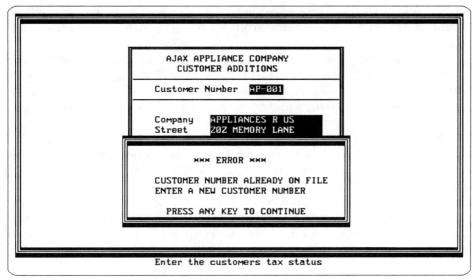

18-4 A typical error window.

```
DEFINE WINDOW msg1 FROM 12,19 TO 20,59 DOUBLE COLOR W+/R
?? CHR(7)
ACTIVATE WINDOW msg1
@ 1,05 SAY '         *** ERROR ***'
@ 3,05 SAY 'CUSTOMER NUMBER ALREADY ON FILE'
@ 4,05 SAY 'ENTER A NEW CUSTOMER NUMBER'
@ 5,1  SAY ' '
WAIT "        PRESS ANY KEY TO CONTINUE"
DEACTIVATE WINDOW msg1
```

18-5 Program for a typical error window.

Finally, once a key is pressed, the window is deactivated and removed from the screen and the screen's original contents underneath the window are redisplayed. Then, the user can go on and correct the input error.

Data entry in a window

An error message is simple text. In the last figure, the window that was displayed actually was the fourth active window at the same time. The first and second windows contained the main and customer menu, while the third window contained the data entry screen. The fourth window was the error window. Later in this chapter, we will discuss the problems of having more than one window active at the same time.

The next task you might want to do in a window is some simple (or complex) data entry. Windows can be used to get one specific value. Figure 18-6 shows the screen for an invoice data entry program where the line number of the record to change is being requested. The program code to display this window is no more difficult than the error window and is shown in Fig. 18-7.

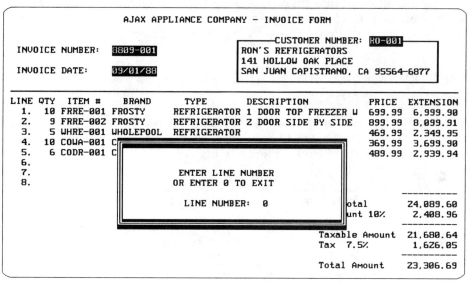

18-6 A typical data entry window.

```
LN = 0
?? CHR(7)
DEFINE WINDOW msg1 FROM 12,19 TO 20,59 DOUBLE
ACTIVATE WINDOW msg1
@ 1,05 SAY '     ENTER LINE NUMBER    '
@ 2,05 SAY '     OR ENTER 0 TO EXIT'
@ 4,05 SAY '        LINE NUMBER: ' GET LN PICTURE '9' RANGE 0,8
@ 5,1  SAY ' '
READ
DEACTIVATE WINDOW msg1
```

18-7 A typical data entry window program.

This example comes from an invoice data entry program. The operator has just chosen to change an invoice item. The window is being used to decide which item will be changed.

First, the data entry memory variable LN is set up. This memory variable will be used to compare to the displayed data so that the desired invoice item can be changed. Next, the window is defined and activated. You can assume that the same definition of the window MSG1 is used except that, because data entry will take place, the color of the window will be left alone.

Text is displayed within the window. On window line 5 (the sixth line), not only is an @ SAY used, but also a GET. The GET even has a PICTURE and a RANGE parameter. Any of the data validation commands can be used. As I have said throughout this chapter, anything that can be written to the screen can be written to a window.

A READ is used this time not only to pause the display of the window but also to get the data entry.

Again, although this small window is used for one data entry field, the larger window below is used for even more data entry. Any size window can support data entry. It's simply up to your imagination.

Placing a choice menu in a window: creating a dialog box

There really is nothing hard about placing a menu inside a window. The window commands are no different than without the menu commands. A typical window with a menu is shown in Fig. 18-8.

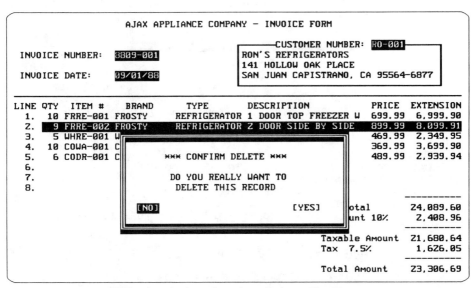

18-8 A typical confirmation window with a menu.

Nothing about the menu is automatic. It actually is a bar menu placed inside the window based on the window's coordinates, as shown in Fig. 18-9.

This type of window is called a dialog box because the user has a dialog with the system. Actually, all of the windows you have seen so far are dialog boxes; however, when a menu is added, it is more so. This window is used as a post-processor in systems to confirm that the operator really wants to delete the item listed on the screen. It serves as a final defense against the fatal deletion of data.

Like windows, a menu must be defined before it is used. Notice that each menu definition includes the brackets around the choices. Because the NO

```
?? CHR(7)
DEFINE WINDOW msg2 FROM 11,19 TO 20,59 DOUBLE
DEFINE MENU yesno
DEFINE PAD no OF yesno PROMPT "[NO]" AT 6,2
ON SELECTION PAD no OF yesno DEACTIVATE MENU
DEFINE PAD yes OF yesno PROMPT "[YES]" AT 6,30
ON SELECTION PAD yes OF yesno DO DELETE
ACTIVATE WINDOW msg2
@ 1,05 SAY '  *** CONFIRM DELETE ***      '
@ 3,05 SAY '    DO YOU REALLY WANT TO     '
@ 4,05 SAY '      DELETE THIS RECORD      '
ACTIVATE menu yesno
DEACTIVATE WINDOW msg2
```

18-9 Program code for a delete confirmation menu inside a
window.

choice is the default, it is listed first. Because this chapter is about windows
and not menus, it will suffice to say that these commands define this bar
menu with two choices. Once the menu is defined, the window is activated.

Inside the window are written the text lines that tell the operator what is
going on. Once the text is displayed, the menu is activated with coordinates
that place it inside the window.

Once the menu is activated, you cannot leave the menu until you make a
selection by pressing Enter. If [NO] is chosen, the menu is deactivated and the
window closed. If [YES] is chosen, a subroutine is called to delete the record
and the subroutine will deactivate the menu, allowing the program to
continue on where the window is deactivated.

Windows and memo fields

There are two ways to display memo fields in dBASE IV. The first way is as a
marker. This is the word *memo* in lowercase (if the record has no data in the
memo field) or the word MEMO in uppercase (if there is data in the memo field
for the current record). The memo marker was the only way to display the
memo field in previous versions of dBASE.

When the memo marker is selected and the operator presses one of the
keys to open the memo field for editing (Ctrl–Home or F9 in dBASE IV), the
memo editor opens the entire screen so that the memo data can be entered.

In dBASE IV, there is another way to view memo data without going into
the editor. Figure 18-10 shows a typical data entry screen with a memo
window. Although the window is inactive, you still can see the contents in the
open window.

As you can see, the memo field's data is visible in the window. The
window can be sized by the user. This allows the user to have any size window
for the memo data to be displayed. Once it is activated, the cursor moves into
the window for editing. If the user desires, the window still can be zoomed to
full screen size by another press of the zoom key, F9.

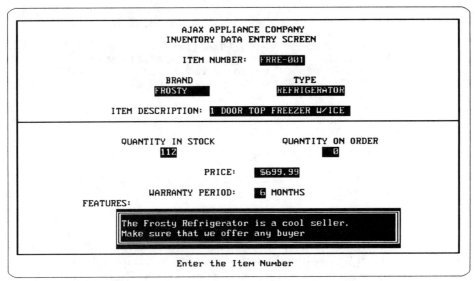

```
                AJAX APPLIANCE COMPANY
              INVENTORY DATA ENTRY SCREEN

            ITEM NUMBER:  FRRE-001

        BRAND                    TYPE
      FROSTY                REFRIGERATOR
    ITEM DESCRIPTION: 1 DOOR TOP FREEZER W/ICE

      QUANTITY IN STOCK       QUANTITY ON ORDER
            112                       0

            PRICE:     $699.99

        WARRANTY PERIOD:   6 MONTHS
   FEATURES:
        The Frosty Refrigerator is a cool seller.
        Make sure that we offer any buyer

              Enter the Item Number
```

18-10   A typical data entry window with a memo field.

Not only can the window be open all the time, but, if a marker is used, a window still can be used once the marker is opened. If you include a window command with an @ GET, then the window is used when the marker is opened. It might appear like this:

DEFINE WINDOW Wndow1 FROM 19,18 TO 22,68 DOUBLE
@ 19,18 GET *features* WINDOW Wndow1

The memo field still would appear as a marker but would open to the size specified in the DEFINE WINDOW command. However, the best way is to have the window always open. There are two ways to do this. The first way is simply to add the OPEN parameter to the GET command:

DEFINE WINDOW Wndow1 FROM 19,18 TO 22,68 DOUBLE
@ 19,18 GET *features* OPEN WINDOW Wndow1

This command will open the memo field specified in the @ GET command as a window that is always visible.

The second method is to use the command SET WINDOW OF MEMO TO command. This will globally set a window for all memo fields so that it only needs to be coded once:

DEFINE WINDOW Wndow1 FROM 19,18 TO 22,68 DOUBLE
SET WINDOW OF MEMO TO Wndow1
@ 19,18 GET *features*

The SET WINDOW OF MEMO TO command will allow you to use a window to edit memo fields while you still are using full-screen commands like APPEND, BROWSE, EDIT, CHANGE, and READ. The WINDOW clause that is specified with an @...GET command for editing memo fields will override this SET WINDOW command. The window name must be defined or an error message will appear. Although you still must press F9 (Zoom) or Ctrl–Home to edit the contents of the memo window, you will be able to see the data inside the window at all times.

Browse tables in a window

One final task that takes on special meanings in a window is a Browse screen. Figure 18-11 shows a Browse table in a window. Some of the main advantages can become evident in just a few words.

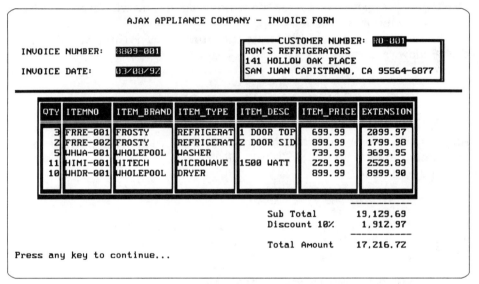

18-11 A BROWSE table inside a window.

By placing a Browse table within a window, you can perform multiple record data entry from the same file. The Browse table becomes a scrollable data entry screen. You even can perform relational lookups and displays with the technique. The BROWSE command features a WINDOW parameter that allows data entry to take place within the window.

The BROWSE command in its simple form might look like this:

BROWSE WINDOW win1

The window named in the BROWSE command must be already defined. It is activated automatically when used by the BROWSE command. The Browse table will be sized to fit within the window. Whatever doesn't fit will be able to be scrolled both horizontally and vertically.

This technique will be described in detail in the next chapter on screen design and programming.

Switching to full-screen mode

When you are in an active window, all output stays within the boundaries of the window. There might be times when your program will need to write to an area outside the window while still leaving the window on the screen.

dBASE IV provides a command to do just this. The command is:

ACTIVATE SCREEN

This command has no parameters. It leaves the window on the screen but lets you write anywhere on the physical screen. After you are done writing on the screen (or doing anything else you want), you can deactivate the window and it will disappear or else you can activate it again. Because it was never deactivated, it allows you to use the window again and whatever you placed inside the window still is there.

Remember, until you deactivate the window, everything you do inside the window remains intact.

Saving the window and its contents: save and restore window

Another set of commands that allow you to work with defined windows are the commands SAVE and RESTORE WINDOW.

The command:

SAVE WINDOW *winname* TO *filename*

will save the named window to a disk file named in the command. Not only is the window definition saved, but the contents are saved as well. When the window is restored by the command:

RESTORE WINDOW *winname* FROM *filename*

the window and all of its contents are restored to the screen. This way, you could save common window displays to disk files and recall them without issuing a series of @ SAY commands. This can be very handy in creating a window or error message library.

How messages and the status bar treat windows

Messages coming from menus or other automatic message generating code automatically are displayed on the last line of the screen (line 24 in normal mode). Even if you create a small window in the center of the screen, the message will be displayed on the last line of the physical window. Messages do not respect windows. If your window overlays that line, you still will see your message. However, if you have a border around the window, the message will obliterate the bottom of the border. All of line 24 is used to display the message.

Status bars also do not respect windows. The Status bar is always displayed on line 22. If you turn the status bar on, it also will obliterate all of line 22, including the border characters on that line.

The best advice we can suggest is to not use borders when you are using the status line and to keep anything off of line 22 through 24 in your programs.

Working with more than one active window

Much of the time, you have only one window active on the screen. However, there are many reasons why you would want more than one window active at the same time.

Figure 18-12 shows a conceptual view of several windows on the screen at once. While the main screen remains intact underneath, a small window sits on top of a larger window, both of which sit on top of the screen. By removing the windows separately or together, you can appear to restore the original contents of the screen.

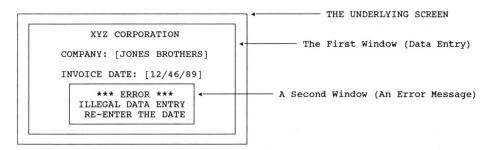

18-12 Conceptual view of multiple windows.

One of the main reasons for having more than one window on the screen at once is the way dBASE handles menus. When you activate a menu, you don't have complete control over what happens on the screen. The command to activate menus is self-contained. This means that, although you can branch to another routine, it automatically comes back to itself. Without windows, anything you display in the screen before you display the menu could not be easily redisplayed without additional coding.

Special tips for many layers of windows

When creating systems that will use many layers of windows, you might want to put everything in a window. This includes the very first screen. An example of a complex use of full-screen windows is when the main menu calls a secondary menu, the secondary menu calls a data entry screen, then the data entry screen detects an error and displays an error window. Each of these screens is placed within a window.

You might ask why place the very first screen, the main menu, in a window. Because the other screens are within windows themselves and all are sitting on top of the main menu, why waste the memory?

Occasionally, when those windows are removed, the original screen is blank. dBASE will clear the screen itself even though there is no CLEAR command ever issued and all other processing happens in one of the other windows. A workaround is simply to put each and every screen of a system in a window. This does not mean you have to define a window for every screen. You certainly can reuse windows. In my systems, I have one window for the main menu defined from 0,0 to 23,79 with a double border. The last line is left to display messages coming from the menu prompts. I have a calling window for second level menus that also is the same size. This window is used by all of the subsystems. There is a window defined from 0,0 to 24,79 with no border that is used for data entry. This window is used by 20 different modules. Finally, I have several message windows defined. A small one for simple messages, and a larger one to display toggle menus as previously shown.

An alternative to windows: save and restore screen

A better way to layer multiple screens is to save the screen in a SCREEN file. There are commands that allow you to save the entire screen and then, after you do anything you want to the screen, you can recall the original screen and its contents. This is called saving and restoring the screen.

The commands SAVE SCREEN and RESTORE SCREEN were added to dBASE IV 1.1, although they have existed since 1.0 but were undocumented. You save your screen to a file, perform some other functions on the original screen or on a completely different screen and, when you are done, simply restore the screen to its original state.

A common sequence of code might be:

```
SAVE SCREEN TO myscreen
DO DISPALL
RESTORE SCREEN FROM myscreen
```

Clearing windows from memory: release and clear windows

If you are through with a window, you can not only deactivate it but also remove it from memory. Removing a window from memory means that it is no longer defined. If you need to use it again, you would have to redefine the window. When you deactivate a window, you merely remove it from the screen. You do not remove it from memory.

The command:

```
RELEASE WINDOW winname
```

clears the named window from memory. This can be used to free up necessary space in memory or simply to clear memory of unneeded windows. The command:

    CLEAR WINDOWS

clears all windows from memory. This normally is used at the end of a program in the housekeeping section to clear the various objects from memory. Just as you can clear windows, you also can clear menus, pop-ups, and memory variables.

Moving windows around the screen: move window

The last window command to be mentioned is MOVE WINDOW. This command allows you to move a window either to a new starting coordinate or by a change factor listed in coordinate space. For example:

    MOVE WINDOW win1 TO 5,15

moves the window WIN1 so that the upper left corner would start in row 5 column 15. You also can move the window by a certain number of rows and columns:

    MOVE WINDOW win1 BY 3,−5

This would move the window WIN1 three rows down and five columns to the left from its presently defined position. If you try to move the window off the screen, you will get an error message.

Moving windows can give you the ability to use the same window for different locations without having to define new windows. Because moving a window also preserves the window's contents, it can be used to eliminate problems.

For example, suppose you have an error window that is used for different data entry screens and for different errors within different fields. You could have a problem if the window obscures the field that contains the error. By providing the user the ability to use the arrow keys to move the window left, right, up, or down, you could allow them to reposition the window. This would take some interesting code to read each keypress; however, with the INKEY( ) and READKEY( ) functions, it's not very hard. After the window is displayed in its final position and the window deactivated, it could be redefined with its original coordinates. An example of this code to read the user's keypress and reposition the window is illustrated in Fig. 18-13. Imagine that the window was positioned on a data entry screen and was part of an error procedure or UDF as part of a VALID clause of a GET.

As you have seen in this chapter, windows can do some wonderful things in allowing you to better manage the user interface. What you do with windows is limited only by your imagination. You will see many examples of window usage throughout the case studies.

```
DEFINE WINDOW msg1 FROM 12,20 TO 20,59 DOUBLE COLOR W+/R
ACTIVATE WINDOW msg1
?? CHR(7)
@ 1,05 SAY '          *** ERROR ***'
@ 3,05 SAY 'CUSTOMER NUMBER ALREADY ON FILE'
@ 4,05 SAY ' ENTER ANOTHER CUSTOMER NUMBER'
@ 5,05 SAY '   PRESS ANY KEY TO CONTINUE'
KEYP = 0
DO WHILE KEYP # 13
  KEYP = INKEY()
  DO CASE
   CASE KEYP = 5                    && up arrow
     MOVE WINDOW msg1 BY -1,0
   CASE KEYP = 24                   && down arrow
     MOVE WINDOW msg1 BY  1,0
   CASE KEYP = 4                    && right arrow
     MOVE WINDOW msg1 BY  0,1
   CASE KEYP = 19                   && left arrow
     MOVE WINDOW msg1 BY  0,-1
  ENDCASE
ENDDO
DEACTIVATE WINDOW msg1
RELEASE WINDOW msg1
```

18-13 Code to allow movement of windows.

19
Using the dBASE Compiler for DOS

A significant new development tool has been bundled with the new dBASE IV version 2.0—it is the dBASE Compiler for DOS. This new addition to the dBASE family of developer's tools will allow system developers to distribute their custom systems to end users that do not have a copy of dBASE IV.

It will compile and link dBASE program files (written in either dBASE III Plus or dBASE IV) into a single executable file that the end user can run. It combines all .PRG files with format files, report files, query files, and the like to form a single runtime program that a developer can distribute easily, not worrying if their end user has the latest copy of dBASE III or IV. It represents a significant enhancement to the development tools within dBASE IV.

Hardware requirements

To run the dBASE IV Compiler for DOS properly, your computer must contain the following minimum requirements:

- IBM or IBM-compatible 80286, 80386, or 80486 computer system
- A monitor compatible with CGA, EGA, or VGA
- A minimum of 2Mb of RAM
- At least 5.5Mb of hard disk space
- An additional 2Mb of hard disk space during installation only
- DOS 3.3, 4.01, 5.0, or 6.0

Installation of the Compiler

It is advisable to make a copy of all the Compiler diskettes prior to running the Installation program using the DOS DISKCOPY command. Use the copy as your installing disks, storing the original diskettes in a safe place. The following are the steps necessary to install the dBASE IV Compiler for DOS:

1. Insert Disk 1 into your floppy drive (either A or B).
2. Make the floppy drive the current drive by typing A: or B: and pressing the Enter key.
3. Type INSTALL and press the Enter key.
4. The Installation program will provide a series of instructions that you are to follow.

Note: The Installation program will, by default, place all the appropriate files concerned with the compiler in the C:\ BDCOMP directory. If you would like to store the Compiler files in a different directory, such as C:\ BASE\ COMPILER, you can specify the new directory during the installation. The compiler and linker will look for the corresponding system files in the current directory, as well as any directories within the DOS PATH statement. It is suggested that you update your PATH statement in your AUTOEXEC.BAT to include the Compiler directory name.

Code page selection

During the installation process, you will be asked by the Install program to select a code page value that the Compiler will use to select the proper character set to support during compilation and runtime. There are two choices: either 437 or 850.

It is important to select the code page value that your user systems are using. If you select an 850 value and you attempt to run the compiled program on a computer using the 437 code page value, the program might not run properly.

It should be noted that, even though you select a given code page value during the installation program of the compiler, the Installation program will not change the code page value within the version of DOS running on the development computer. You must load the DOS code page using DOS. Refer to your DOS manual for additional information concerning code page values.

Component overview

Once installed, the dBASE Compiler for DOS will contain the components described in the following sections.

BDC.EXE

This is the compiler that combines the specified source files into object files. These pseudo-code files are combined to form a set of pre-processed files, representing the initial source files with any compiler directives acted upon them. The pre-processor portion of the compiler allows for the execution of macro substitutions and conditional compilations. The significant options of the compiler are described in detail, later in this chapter.

BDL.EXE

This program is the linker that links the pseudocode object files created by the compiler with (optionally) the runtime library and resource files to create a single executable file (.EXE) of your application. There are two types of executable files that can be created by the linker:

- A standalone executable file that is a fully functional, self-contained .EXE file that users can run from DOS without any additional system files.
- A compact executable file that is a smaller .EXE file because it excludes the DBASE.RTL and DBASE.RES files. This option is especially useful when the user is operating a number of dBASE applications, because only one copy of the .RTL and .RES files is needed.

DSPLIT.EXE

This program is a utility that allows for the splitting of a single large file into several component files in order to easily store them on multiple floppy diskettes.

DJOIN.EXE

This utility program reassembles program segments created by dSPLIT into a single file.

MAKE.EXE

This program will allow for the creation of MAKE files for your application. It automatically will keep track of the latest object files and executable files from your latest source files. It will automate the build process for creating an executable application.

Compiling your system

There are several steps that you need to perform to create an executable file, including compiling and linking the files and assembling your application.

The compiler: BDC.EXE

The dBASE Compiler for DOS (BDC.EXE) compiles your dBASE source files into object files that the linker uses to create a single executable file. At the DOS prompt, use the BDC command to execute the compiler. The syntax for the command is shown here:

BDC [*compiler options*] [*linker options*] *file list* [*+file name*]

The following is a description of each option within the BDC command:

[*compiler options*]   These options are command-line switches that modify the compilation process. These options are described later in this chapter.

[*linker options*]   These options are command-line switches that modify the linking process. The BDC program calls the BDL program once the source files are compiled. If the -c option of the compiler is specified, then the BDL step will be skipped. A detailed list of the various linker options appears later in this chapter.

file list   This option of the BDC command specifies the files that you want to compile. This list can either be an explicit list or the name of the text file that contains all of the file components to be compiled. If you specify an explicit list of files, you must separate each file name with a single space.

If you use the text file name option, you must precede the file name with the @ character. The text file that contains the file names to be compiled must have each file name on a separate line with no delimiters. The BDC program will ignore any blank lines in your text file as well as any lines beginning with #, *, or ;.

[+*file name*]   This compiler option contains the name of the configuration file that stores options that control the compilation and/or link process. Later in this chapter, a detailed list of options for using a configuration file will be described.

Compiler options   The first option of the BDC command line is compiler options. These options specify the way that you want BDC to process your files. Options can be listed on the command line in any order, as long as you precede each option specified with a dash (-) or forward slash (/) and the correct upper- or lowercase letter. The following is a description of each compiler option:

Option	Description
-c	Compile source files but do not link
-D*macro name*	Define a preprocessor macro
-D*macro name=*	Define preprocessor macro to *macro expression*
-I*path*	Specify a search path for #include files
-n*path*	Specify path for generated object files
-P*path*	Specify path for preprocessed output without compiling
-p*path*	Specify path for preprocessed output with compile
-t	Display lines of code that generate warnings or errors
-w	Disable displaying warning messages
-X	Set LangTables on
-x	Set LangTables off

Compiler option narration   The -c option of the BDC command will allow you to compile your source files without proceeding with the link process. This is especially helpful in determining that there are no errors in your source files before continuing to the link program. You should use the -t option with the -c option so that any lines of code that generate an error or warning message will be displayed. In this way, you can use the BDC program to debug your source files.

The -D options allow for defining preprocessor macros. If you elect to use a configuration file, you can specify an unlimited number of macros to be included in the compilation process. It should be noted that any preprocessor macros that are defined in your source files will override macros defined within the command line.

As can be seen in the previous table, the -n, -P, and -p options within the BDC command line can be used to place the output of the BDC into whatever directories you desire. If no path is specified within the -n option, then all output files will be placed in the current directory. If any files exist with the same name as an output file, the BDC program will overwrite them. In addition, the -P option will generate a set of intermediate source files having a .DPP extension.

Under normal conditions, these preprocessed files will be deleted automatically once the compilation process is completed. The only way to preserve these intermediate files is to specify the -P or -p option. If no path is specified with either option, the BDC program will output these files to the current directory.

If your source files contain any characters that are within the extended ASCII character set, you must specify the -X option within the BDC command line. This setting will turn on the LangTable to allow the BDC program to properly process your source file. For United States versions of the BDC, LangTables defaults to OFF.

Compiler output files   During the compilation process, the dBASE IV Compiler for DOS creates a series of interim files, called *object files*. The compiler uses the extension of the source file to determine which object files to output. If no extension is specified or an extension is used that is not recognized by the dBASE Compiler, the .DBO extension will be generated. The following list details the output object files that are created by the compiler, based upon the input file extension:

File type	Source file	Object file
Form File	.FMT	.FMO
Report File	.FRG	.FRO
Label File	.LBG	.LBO
Program File	.PRG	.DBO
Query File	.QBE	.QBO
Update Query File	.UPD	.UPO

If an error occurs during the compilation step, the object file will not be generated. It will continue to process the other files within the system, until all source files have been processed. It should be noted that if there are any errors in any of the source files being processed, the compiler will not generate an executable file. You will receive an executable file only when all source files have been compiled successfully.

Note: The dBASE Compiler for DOS does not compile dBASE SQL source code files (.PRS). You must use dBASE to translate any .PRS files into .DBO files that can be later linked into the executable file. You can use the COMPILE instruction at the dot prompt with the RUNTIME option to create the proper .DBO files from the .PRS SQL files. The following statement is an example of the COMPILE instruction:

```
COMPILE filename.PRS RUNTIME
```

The resultant object file(s) then can be linked to the rest of the compiled source files using the BDL command later described in this chapter.

Unsupported commands   The dBASE IV Compiler for DOS creates files that are used at runtime; therefore, commands that are used interactively at the dot prompt are not supported within an .EXE file. The following is a list of the commands that are not supported by the compiler:

ASSIST	DISPLAY/LIST HISTORY
COMPILE	HELP
CREATE	MODIFY COMMAND
DEBUG	RESUME
DEXPORT	SUSPEND

plus SET (at full screen) and the following SET commands:

DEBUG	HISTORY
DEVELOPMENT	INSTRUCT
DOHISTORY	SQL
ECHO	STEP
FIXED	TRAP
HELP	

It should be noted that the RESUME and the SET SQL commands can be used only at the dot prompt and not within a program. If the Compiler encounters any of these instructions during the compilation step, it displays an error and does not create the output object file for the invalid source file.

Also, it is important to note that the Compiler does not support the macro (&) substitution of dBASE IV command verbs. It will support the substitution of memory variable macros, but the actual command verb must be present in its proper format. The following is an example of a valid, and an invalid command line:

```
Valid:   COPY TO &filename
Invalid:  m.br = "BROWSE"
          &m.br
```

The first example shows a macro substitution of a file name for the COPY TO command, which the compiler will properly compile, while the second example uses a memory variable to do a macro substitution of the command verb BROWSE, which is an invalid substitution.

Using the linker: BDL.EXE

Once the Compiler has done a clean pass of all source files within a system, it can be set to automatically call the dBASE Linker (BDL.EXE). The linker is used to combine all the object files of a compiled system into a single executable file (.EXE). If you are creating a standalone .EXE, the BDL.EXE combines the DBASE.RTL and DBASE.RES into the executable as well as the other object files. It is important to note that the linker does not combine data files such as .DBF, .DBT, .MDX, .NDX, or text files with the object files.

The BDL can link up to 2500 separate object files and the maximum size of the executable file can be up to 2,147,483,647 (2 gigabytes).

The syntax for calling the dBASE Linker for DOS is as follows:

BDL {*linker options*} *file list*

{*linker options*} are the command line switches that define the options required for the linking process. The detailed options are described later in this chapter.

file list can be an explicit list of the files you want to link or the name of a text file that contains the list of files to be linked. If an explicit list is entered, then each file name must be delimited by a space character.

In addition, if the text file option is used, you must, as with the compiler, precede the text file name with an @. Within the text file, each file name must be entered on a separate line, with no delimiters. The linker will ignore any blank lines within the text file, as well as any lines that are comment lines, where the first character of the line is #,*, or ;.

Linker options The linker options entered on the BDL command line determine how your object files are going to be processed. As with the compiler options, the following rules must be followed when entering the desired options. You can list the options in any order, but precede each option with either a dash or a forward slash and enter the option letter in the proper upper or lowercase letter format.

The following is a list of the different linker options that are available:

Option	Description
-B*program option*	Execute *program name* when the .EXE is started. If this option is skipped, the first .DBO file will be run when the .EXE is started.
-C*file name*	Link into the .EXE the specified file name as a CONFIG.DB. If no file is linked into the .EXE, then the .EXE, when run, will search in the user's current directory, then in the directories within the user's DOS PATH.

-E*file name*	The output name for the .EXE. If you do not specify a name for the output .EXE, the linker will use the name of the first .DBO file as the name.
-L	This option specifies that you want a large .EXE, a standalone .EXE.
-S	Specifies that you want a compact (small) .EXE output file. This is the default option.

Configuration file usage in linking   As with the dBASE Compiler, you can establish a configuration file that will contain all of the file names to be linked together to form your application. This option is especially useful when compiling and linking larger applications containing a large number of sources files of different types. It should be kept in mind that the DOS command line can contain only a maximum of 128 characters, so if you have a lengthy list of source files, it will be necessary for you to use the configuration file approach.

To set up a configuration file, you use your regular text editor and enter a list of the files that you need to link. You can group similar files within the configuration file for easy cross-reference, grouping all reports together, etc. If you want to have comment lines within the configuration files, precede the line with either an asterisk or a forward slash. These lines will be ignored by both the DOS Compiler and the DOS Linker. It is suggested that you give your configuration file a specific recognizable extension, such as .LST so that you can differentiate it from your other files.

As previously mentioned, you must precede the configuration file name with an @ within the BDL command line. The following example shows the usage of a configuration file for storing source file names:

BDL @PROGRAMS.LST

Another use for a configuration file is the storing of the actual linker options that correspond to the program list mentioned previously. As with the program list, you must put each linker option on a separate line of the text file, following the same syntax rules you use when you specify BDC options. It is suggested that you name the options configuration file the same name as the file list, but giving it a unique extension such as .CFG. The following instruction illustrates the use of both forms of configuration files.

BDL @PROGRAMS.LST +PROGRAMS.CFG

Note that the options configuration file is preceded by a plus (+) and that the program list is preceded by a @.

Language table considerations   dBASE IV uses language tables to determine how data is processed when characters with an ASCII value greater than 127 are present. Processes such as sorting data, converting characters from upper to lower case and back, as well as alphabetizing while indexing all must utilize language tables to determine correct processing activities.

As a dBASE IV user, you can change the setting of the language table by using LangTables=ON or LangTables=OFF in the CONFIG.DB file. By setting this option on, you allow dBASE IV to recognize and support extended ASCII characters. In the United States version of the dBASE IV Compiler and Linker, the LangTables option is off by default.

If the default remains when the Compiler encounters extended ASCII characters, a compilation error is generated. If this occurs, you can use the -X option at the BDC command line to turn the LangTables option on. Once you have created your executable file, it is important that you ensure that the same setting that you used to create the file is used at runtime. To do so, link into your executable file a CONFIG.DB file that specifies the LangTables setting.

Code page processing   During the installation of the Compiler and Linker for DOS, you will be asked to specify which code page you want the Compiler to use to process your program files, either 437 or 850. The code page determines the character set that the dBASE Compiler will support as it compiles your programs.

As you install the Compiler, the installation program maps the resource file for the code page you select, using either DBASE.437 or DBASE.850. This code page is mapped onto DBASE.RES, the resource file that the dBASE Compiler links into your executable file when you build a standalone .EXE. If you build a compact .EXE, you must include the DBASE.RES with the files you distribute.

Because the dBASE Resource File is different for each code page, executable files created on a system using code page 437 might not run on systems that use code page 850. To prevent incompatibility problems, be sure to run the dBASE Compiler using the code page that the end user is most likely to be using.

Assembling your application

In this section, we will cover the files that you must include with your application, the license restrictions involved in distributing these files, as well as different methods that you can use to segment large files and reassemble them for your end user.

Required files   As previously mentioned, you have the option to create either a standalone .EXE or a compact executable file. If you build a standalone file, you can distribute it without any additional dBASE system or runtime files. If, however, you want to build a compact .EXE, you must include DBASE.RTL and DBASE.RES with your compact .EXE. If your application requires other files such as data files, index files, and memo files, you should make sure to include them on your distribution disks because you cannot link these files into your .EXE.

License for distribution files   Borland has given consent to allow you to freely distribute any of the following files with your application programs. The selection of which files to distribute is dependent upon the needs of your application.

- DBASE.RTL—The dBASE runtime library.
- DBASE.RES—The dBASE resource file; this is the same as either DBASE.437 or DBASE.850, depending on the code page value you selected during installation.
- DBASE.437—The dBASE resource file supporting code page 437.
- DBASE.850—The dBASE resource file supporting code page 850.
- DJOIN.EXE—The program that reassembles file segments created by dSPLIT.

Breaking down large files   When preparing your applications for distribution, you might have a requirement to break down some of the larger files into more manageable sized files to fit easily on your distribution disks. A companion tool that is included with the dBASE Compiler is a program called DSPLIT.EXE. This development tool will divide a large file into smaller file segments and write them to floppy disks.

For example, the file DBASE.RTL does not fit on a single floppy disk and needs to be divided. With dSPLIT, you can specify the size of the file segments you want the main file broken down to, as well as the target directory. When dSPLIT segments a file, it assigns the resultant file segments with the name of the original file and adds a three digit extension. When dSPLIT segments the file DBASE.RTL, it will create a set of output files called DBASE.001, DBASE.002, DBASE.003, etc. The program DJOIN.EXE is the file that you will distribute with your application that will reconstruct the original DBASE.RTL. This program is described in the next section of this chapter.

To run dSPLIT, execute the following command at the DOS prompt using the following syntax:

DSPLIT [-S*first segment size* > [,*subsequent segment size*]]
[-O*target path name*] *file name*

file name is the name of the file that you want to divide.

The following table describes the DSPLIT command options:

Option	Description
-S*segment size* [,*subsequent segment size*]	The size of the file segments in kilobytes. Valid values range from 1 to the size of the file to be divided.
-O*target path name*	The location where the file segments are to be placed. You can specify a directory on your hard disk or floppy disk. The default is the current directory.

When specifying the size of the file segments, you have the option of assigning different sizes (in kilobytes) for each segment that dSPLIT is to create. This option is useful when you want the first file segment to be smaller than subsequent segments so that you can write it to a floppy disk containing other files.

If you specify only one value for the segment size, dSPLIT divides the file into equal segments of the specified value. If you do not specify the -S option at all, dSPLIT will divide the input file into 1200 kilobyte segments. Keep in mind that one kilobyte equals 1024 bytes.

If the output location where the file segments are to be placed is a floppy disk, dSPLIT will prompt you to insert new diskettes as each is filled.

Reassembling large files   dJOIN is a development tool that Borland allows you to freely distribute with your compiled application. If you elect to use dSPLIT to segment any of your large files, then you must include the DJOIN.EXE file with your distribution application.

To run dJOIN, execute the DJOIN command at the DOS prompt in the following syntax:

DJOIN [-O*target path name*] [-P [*message*]] *file name*

file name is the root name of the segmented files. For example, NEWAPP is the root name of file segment NEWAPP.001.

The following table describes the DJOIN command options:

Option	Description
-O*target path name*	The location where the reassembled file is to be placed. The default is the current directory.
-P [*message*]	Display a prompt message and pause for a key to be pressed before reading the next file segment from the floppy disk.

When you set up your installation procedure for your application, you can direct dJOIN to display a custom message with the -P option. For example, if you would like dJOIN to display Please Insert The Next Sequential Diskette, you can specify this using the -P option. If no message is specified, dJOIN will use as a default message the following:

Please insert disk ## into drive ?.
Press any key to continue.

Preprocessor directives

Preprocessor directives are statements that you insert into your dBASE programs to instruct the Compiler as to how to compile your code. Preprocessor directives must begin with a pound sign and are lower case by convention. As with regular commands, you can abbreviate preprocessor directives to the first four letters, such as #defi.

Overview

As with other preprocessors such as Borland's Turbo C and C++, the preprocessor included with the dBASE IV Compiler for DOS provides the ability to embed into your program code items such as source macro substitution, conditional compilation, and file inclusion. The following sections describe the various directives that you can insert into your program code in order to give you greater programming flexibility.

The Compiler for DOS considers any line of program code that begins with a # to be a preprocessor directive. The maximum length of a directive is limited to 1024 characters. Any spaces to the left of the directive # are ignored.

#define/#undef

The #define directive defines a macro for the compiler to process. Macros allow you to replace text in a program during compilation and are useful for specifying sets of instructions. To define a macro, you need to assign it a name, then specify the text that is to replace it. The preprocessor, as it processes your source file, will replace all occurrences of the name with the associated text.

As previously mentioned in the description of the Compiler options, you can define a macro within the command line of the Compiler (using the -D option), as opposed to putting it within your program file. Any macros defined within your source files that are being compiled will override any macros defined within the command line. Therefore, it is best that you decide where you want to consistently place your directives, keeping in mind the priority that the Compiler puts on the macros defined within your code.

The #undef directive is the method that you use to undefine a macro. The following examples show the use of both commands.

```
#define macro name [macro expression]
#undef macro name
```

#include

The #include directive will insert the entire contents of a file into your program at the location of the #include statement. A #include file might contain information such as constant information, global memory variables, and the like that are used by many programs within your application.

The syntax for the #include directive is:

```
#include "file name"/<file name>
```

If the file name is within quotes, the current directory is searched, followed by the set of directories specified within the -I option of the Compiler command line.

If the file name is enclosed within a set of angle brackets, then only the -I path is searched for the file to be included.

If, however, you specify a complete path for the include file, only that path will be searched.

The following are a few examples of different types of #include compiler directives:

```
#include "myheadr.prg"
#include "c: ÷ \ dbase\include\ myheadr.prg"
#include <myheadr.prg>
```

#if, #else, #elif, and #endif

This set of compiler directives allows you to embed conditional statements and processing into your code based upon a condition that can be tested for. These programming constructs allow for conditional compilation, giving you the ability to include or exclude certain parts of your code from your program object file. They are used much like the IF-ELSE-ENDIF constructs of dBASE IV. The following is the general syntax for using these compiler directives:

```
#if expression
.... commands
[#elif expression/#else
.... other commands]
#endif
```

As within dBASE IV, the *expression* portion of the directive can contain any combination of operators such as .AND., .OR., .NOT. etc. The only limitations in the directive statement are the substring comparison ($) and the exponentiation ($\wedge$).

#ifdef/#ifndef

This final set of compiler directives allows you to conditionally compile a command dependent upon whether or not a macro has been previously defined using the #define directive. Conversely, the #ifndef directive tests for a macro not being defined at that point within your program code. The syntax for using these directives is as follows:

```
#ifdef/#ifndef macro name
...commands
[#elif expression / #else
...commands
#endif
```

As can be seen in this syntax, the same #elif, #else, and #endif as is used within the #if directives are used with these directive commands.

Controlling your dBASE application with MAKE

The dBASE IV Compiler for DOS distribution package includes a utility program called MAKE. This utility is used to manage the source files that comprise your application. This same MAKE program is used in other Borland products to update executable files with the latest source code. It can also be used to set up complex macros and control structures for building dBASE applications.

Overview of MAKE

Whenever you compile a set of source files into an executable file, you will want to use the latest version of each source file. To insure that all source changes have been included in an executable file, it is necessary to control when each change is made. When defining an application to the MAKE utility, you will provide a description of how each of the source files are to be processed to create the finished product. MAKE compares the date and time of each source file to the eventual target file. It will only perform the steps necessary to bring the resultant file up to date.

In this way, if only one of thirty source files that comprise an application is changed, MAKE will reconstruct only the changed source file before linking to the final executable file. By processing your source files using the MAKE utility, you can not only insure that the latest files are used, but you also can save time by not recompiling all of the source files of the application being built.

How it works

When you run the MAKE utility, it will process your instructions that are stored within a makefile. A makefile is a standard ASCII text file that contains a series of statements that specify the dependency information needed to create an application. Makefiles contain statements called rules that specify the source and target files as well as the commands to create the target files. There are two types of rules, explicit and implicit.

Explicit rules specify the file names and the files they depend upon. Implicit rules specify only file extensions and imply to all files that have that extension. For example, the program CUST_IN.DBO would directly depend upon the file C CUST_IN.PRG. This would be an example of the explicit rule. On the other hand, an implicit rule might state that all .DBO files depend upon like-named .PRG files.

Macros also can be included within a makefile. Macros perform text replacement and can specify complex file name expansion. For example, you can create two different versions of a given application merely by specifying that the creation of the application is based upon the value of a controlling macro that contains the source directory for the input files.

Makefiles also can contain directives. Directives stored in a makefile perform various control functions, similar to the preprocessor directives described earlier in this chapter. By using these directives, you can set up conditional execution of portions of your makefile. In addition, some directives such as the .nosilent directive, which prints commands before executing them, can be embedded in your makefile.

MAKE options

To activate the MAKE utility, use the following syntax:

MAKE [*option* ...] [*target* ...]

option is a command-line option. The following list of rules below describes the command-line options. *target* is the name of a target file.

Observe these syntax rules:

- Separate each option from adjacent options with a space.
- Place options in any order and in any number, as long as there is room on the command line.
- Options that do not specify a string can have a − or + after them to turn the option off (−) or on (+).
- Follow the list of options with a space, then an optional list of targets.
- Separate each target from adjacent targets with a space. MAKE evaluates the target files in the order listed, rebuilding them as necessary.
- If the command line does not contain any target names, MAKE uses the first target file mentioned in an explicit rule.

Building files   In essence, creating a makefile is much like creating a program. You can use any text editor to create a makefile. Your makefile should contain a series of rules that specify the files and relationships that go into a given application.

As with the configuration files for the Compiler and Linker, MAKE considers all lines that are preceded with a # to be comment lines. If you require to extend a line onto the next line of text, you can use the backslash (\) to denote a continuation line. When you start the MAKE program, the first thing it looks for is the file BUILTINS.MAK. This file can contain any "built-in" rules and statements to evaluate each time you run MAKE.

It searches for the BUILTINS.MAK file first in the current directory, then in the directory where MAKE.EXE resides. If the MAKE program cannot find the BUILTINS.MAK file, then it begins to directly interpret Makefile (or MAKEFILE.MAK). If you have specified a file using the -f command line option, MAKE searches for makefiles only in the current directory.

The file BUILTINS.MAK has the same rules as the general make file. The BUILTINS.MAK file that is shipped with the dBASE IV Compiler for DOS contains a series of implicit rules for compiling dBASE IV files into object files. You can modify this file with any text editor to suit your specific needs. Generally, BUILTINS.MAK contains the standard implicit rules, macro definitions, and other statements used for building standard applications. When you install the compiler onto your hard disk, a sample .MAK file is placed in the compiler directory. You can use this sample file as an example of what you might include in your makefile to process your application.

Options   When you enter a MAKE command at the DOS prompt, you have options that you can specify that let you control the way MAKE processes your files. Options must be preceded with either a dash (-) or a forward slash (/), being sure you follow the case conventions described in the option descriptions listed here. You can enter the options that you desire either at the DOS prompt each time that you start the MAKE program or at the beginning of your makefile for your application.

Option	Description
-h **or** -?	Print a help message, indicating defaults in MAKE.EXE with a trailing plus sign.
-a	Check dependencies of include files and nested include files associated with object files (such as .DBO, .FMO); updates the object file if the include file has changed.
-B	Build all target files regardless of file dates.
-D*identifier*	Define *identifier* **as a single character, causing an expression !ifdef identifier written in the makefile to return true.**
[-D]*identifier*= *string*	Define *identifier* **as** *string*. **If** *string* **contains any spaces or tabs, enclose string in quotes. You don't have to enter the** -D.
-e	Ignore a macro if its name is the same as an external environment variable, which makes the external environment variable effective.
-f*filename*	Look first for a makefile called *filename* **or** *filename*.mak. **The space after the** -f **is optional.**
-i	Ignore the exit status of all programs run and continue the build process. Entering this option is like entering makefile commands with a leading minus symbol.
-I*directory*	Search for include files in *directory* **and in the current directory.**
-K	Save temporary files that MAKE created for debugging.
-m	Display the date and time stamp of each file as MAKE processes it.
-n	Print the commands but don't actually perform them; helpful when debugging a makefile.
-p	Display all macro definitions and implicit rules before executing the makefile.
-r	Ignore rules defined in BUILTINS.MAK, if any.
-s	Suppress printing of each command as MAKE executes it.
-U*identifier*	Cancel any previous definitions of *identifier*.
-W	Write instructions in MAKE.EXE to turn on the entered option or options by default, and don't build the program. To turn off a default option, enter it with a trailing minus symbol (−) and the -W option. The -h option shows what default options are set.

Exit codes   The MAKE process has the ability to be run from within a DOS batch control file. It can return standard DOS error codes that you can test for within your batch file using the DOS ERRORLEVEL statement. The following is a list of the exit codes that MAKE will set depending upon the result of the MAKE process.

Code	Description
0	No error encountered.
1	The build could not be completed properly. This error code is returned either when the -i option is entered or the .ignore directive is used.
2	An error occurred, such as an incorrect makefile syntax, a command execution error, or a user-break.
4	Insufficient memory is available to perform the build.

Rule processing

As previously mentioned, explicit rules deal with complete file names where implicit rules deal with only file extensions. Implicit rules allow you to apply a given rule to a series of like files (both target and dependent) that have the same base name, without specifying the specific base name. Therefore, an implicit rule can take the place of many explicit rules. You should attempt to use implicit rules wherever possible to limit the number of rules you must maintain.

The MAKE system will rely on implicit rules under the following situations:

- To get instructions for building a target file if it finds an explicit rule without a command line.
- To get instructions for building the dependent file if it can't find other build instructions (the name of the dependent specified as a target).
- When there is no makefile and you invoke MAKE with a target argument. In this case, MAKE looks for an implicit rule in BUILTINS-.MAK file.

Explicit rules   An explicit rule creates or updates a file called the target, using the specified dependent files and one or more commands. The format for this rule type is as follows:

```
target [target....] : [ : ] [ {paths} ] [ dependent .... ]
        [ modifier ] [ command ] [ {file-to-batch} ] [ operator ]
        [ modifier ] [ command ] [ {file-to-batch} ] [ operator ]
```

As shown here, the rules names one or more target files, followed by one or more colons. One colon denotes a single rule is written for the target file, while two indicate that two or more rules pertain to the particular target file.

Dependent files, if any, are listed at the right end of the dependency line, the first line of the rule that contains the target file name. A tab or whitespace preceding the line of text denotes a command line that can contains options such as an @, or in line file creation, or file redirection using standard DOS syntax. The MAKE program will distinguish the two types of input lines by the presence or absence of the tab or whitespace at the beginning of the line, so it is important to make sure you place these properly within your explicit rule entry.

The following is a brief description of the other components shown earlier in the explicit rule syntax lines:

Component	Description
target	The name of the file to be built.
: or ::	One colon means a single explicit rule, two means two or more rules.
path	A list of directories separated by ;, where a dependent file resides.
dependent	The file used to build a target file.
modifier	Refer to "Using modifier" section.
command	Any DOS command except the DOS PATH command.
operator	See "Using operators" section.
file-to-batch	A file name in braces—input for *command*
file	A file name or device optionally preceded by a path.

The following is a list of rules that must be observed when creating explicit rules:

- Include the file name of one or more target files, separated by spaces or tabs, in the dependency line.
- Include zero or more dependent file names in the dependency line.
- Don't indent the dependency line.
- Do indent the command line or lines; otherwise, MAKE can't distinguish the dependency line from the command line(s).
- Put the name of the first target at the beginning of the dependency line.
- If the dependency line and command line exceed the operating system's line length, extend it with the slash (\ ). Write the slash at a point on the line after a target or a dependent file name.
- Separate targets from the path and dependents with one or two colons. The colon or double colon can have whitespace before and after it.
- If the target file name is only one character, insert a space between it and the colon to distinguish it from a drive.
- Don't use a target file's name more than once in the target position of an explicit rule in a makefile.

If you want to have a makefile build multiple executable files, you can use a symbolic target name, listing the .EXE file names after the colon, as shown in the following example code. Note that the symbolic name MYFILES is the target file, even though the actual executable files being created are MYFILE1 and MYFILE2.

```
MYFILES: myfile1.EXE myfile2.EXE
myfile1.EXE: myfile1.DBO
    BDL myfile1.DBO
myfile2.EXE: myfile2.DBO
    BDL myfile2.DBO
```

Implicit rules An implicit rule allows you to write rules that are general in nature, grouping files with identical base names. An implicit rule begins with either a path or a period. The main components of an implicit rule are file extensions, delimited by a period.

Keep in mind that the first file extension of an implicit rule is the dependent's; the second is the target's extension.

The construct syntax of an implicit rule is as follows:

{{*depPath*}] . *depExtension* . [{*targetPath*}] *targetExtension* :
[*modifier*] [*command*] [*operator*]

The options within an implicit rule are described here:

Implicit rule component	Description
depPath	A directory location of the dependent files
.	Specifies that the next string is the source file name extension to be processed
depExt	The dependent file name extension
.	The beginning of a target file name extension, optionally prefaced by a path
tarPath	A directory location of the target executable file(s)
tarExt	The file name extension for the target(s)
:	End of the dependency line of the implicit rule
modifier	Refer to the "Modifiers" section later in this chapter
command	Any DOS command other than DOS PATH
operator	Refer to the "Operators" section later in this chapter

The following are two rules to follow when writing implicit rules:

- The base file name of the implicit rule's target and dependent must match.
- *depPath* and *tarPath* cannot specify multiple paths. Separate rules are needed to search multiple paths.

MAKE will update implicit dependent files by running the associated command line when either of two situations occur:

1. If the dependent file is out of date with respect to the target.
2. If the dependent file does not exist.

If, in a given makefile, a dependent file is a target file in a different dependency line of the makefile or if it is the target of an implicit rule, MAKE will update or create the file as a dependent first, before continuing.

Due to the flexibility of the MAKE processing, you can set up a general makefile that will process a given situation, using the command line to modify the particular process. For example, you can establish a general makefile that contains the following code:

```
.PRG.DBO:
    BDC -c $<
```

This makefile will wait for a parameter to be passed from the command line, specifying which .PRG file to process this time. A typical command line call of this makefile would look like this:

```
MAKE MYFILE.DBO
```

This command would pass the specific file name to the calling makefile, and the MAKE process would check to see if the .DBO called MYFILE.DBO exists. If it does not exist, MAKE would run the BDC command to create the new .DBO.

If, however, the MYFILE.DBO does exist, MAKE would check the time/date stamp of the .DBO and compare it to the MYPROG.PRG file's time/date stamp. If the .PRG is newer, MAKE then would run the makefile command to update the .DBO. Otherwise, MAKE would skip the command line process. The previous example illustrates the real value of the MAKE utility, being able to discern what processes need to be run at the time of the calling of the makefile.

Modifiers In the definitions of both the implicit and explicit rules, modifiers were referred to within the command line syntax. Basically, a modifier can be used in either rule type and are entered in front of the rule's command. As with other command lines, whitespace (or tab) is required prior to the text of the command line. The following list details the different modifiers that can be used within a makefile:

Option	Description
@	Do not display a command as it is executed.
-num	Stop processing commands in the makefile when the exit code that is returned from the command exceeds num.
-	Disregard nonzero exit codes—continue processing commands.
&	Expand the macro that means all dependent files ($**) or the macro ($?) meaning all dependent files stamped after the target.

It should be noted that normally, MAKE will abort if the exit code of a command is nonzero. If you want your makefile to completely process, regardless of the exit code returned from a command, be sure to use the dash, or dash with an error level to bypass this process.

Operators The following describes command-line operators, which are used in both implicit and explicit rules to redirect files or devices and create inline files. The operators are entered after the rule's command.

Operator	Description
<	Take the input for use by *command* from *file* rather than from standard input.
>	Send the output from *command* to *file*.
>>	Append the output from *command* to *file*.
<<	Create a temporary, inline file and use its contents as standard input to *command*.
&&	Create a temporary file and insert its name in the makefile.
delim	Use with << and && as a starting and ending delimiter for a temporary file. The closing *delim* is written on a line by itself. *delim* can be any unreserved character.

Batching MAKE's batching feature lets you accumulate the names of files to be processed by a command, combine them into a list, and invoke that command only once for the whole list.

MAKE will batch commands if you put braces around the file name in the command line. If the next command is identical except for what is in braces, MAKE combines the three commands by appending the file names that appear inside the braces.

The following example shows how the braces tell MAKE to issue one BDC command rather than invoking BDC three times to compile SOURCE1.PRG, SOURCE2.PRG, and SOURCE3.PRG:

```
Myapp.EXE: Source1.DBO Source2.DBO Source3.DBO
    BDC -EMyapp.EXE [Source1.PRG]
    BDC -EMyapp.EXE [Source2.PRG]
    BDC -EMyapp.EXE [Source3.PRG]
```

This rule invokes MAKE as follows:

```
BDC -EMyapp.EXE Source1.PRG Source2.PRG Source3.PRG
```

Macro processing

As previously described, a macro replaces one or more occurrences of a string in a makefile with a string you define. The use of macros allows for the creating of generalized "template-style" makefiles, that can be used in a number of different instances. In this way, there is no need to create a separate makefile for each application you are creating.

Overview of macros Macros can be very useful in makefile creation and processing. Oftentimes, you can define a set of macros in the front of your makefile to customize the makefile for a particular circumstance, using the bulk of the makefile as a standard set of entries. For example, you might have a macro that is called LIBRARY1 that is referred to throughout your makefile. In the beginning of the makefile, you could define it for this particular instance as follows:

```
LIBRARY1 = mylibr.DBO
```

The makefile would substitute the .DBO name throughout the makefile wherever the LIBRARY1 reference occurred.

MAKE will look for the macro definition within the makefile, but if it is not found, MAKE will look for an operating environment variable of that same name. If MAKE finds a definition of a macro name, then later in the makefile, it finds another definition, the new definition will take precedence.

Macros get defined within the makefile, each on a separate line or on the DOS command line when you invoke MAKE (using the -D command line option).

The general syntax for defining a macro within a makefile is as follows:

```
macro name = string
```

macro name consists of alphanumeric characters and is case sensitive and is limited to 512 characters for the DOS platform. *string* contains alphanumeric characters, punctuation, and whitespace when the macro is defined in a makefile. The string is limited to the line length, which is 4096 characters for the DOS platform.

Invoking macros Macros are processed within MAKE in much the same fashion as the macro substitution (&) command within dBASE IV. Whenever the processor encounters a macro, it substitutes the stored string for the macro occurrence. The difference in macro substitution within a makefile is that the precursor character is a dollar sign ($) as opposed to an ampersand (&). The syntax for invoking a macro is:

```
$(macro name)
```

MAKE processes macros depending upon what type of line they are on (rule, directive, or command) and whether they are nested or not. Nested macros will be expanded when the outer macro is invoked. Rule and directive line macros are immediately expanded while command line macros are expanded when the command is executed.

Macro substitution As previously stated, macro substitution occurs at various times throughout your makefile when a macro is encountered by MAKE. The expansion of the macro occurs after the characters are substituted, so it is not necessary to invoke a macro. The substitution and invocation occur in one step. The following is an example of substitution within a macro, using a single macro as a substitution for a series of file names, then using the macro name to link all of them:

```
INFILES - file1.PRG file2.PRG file3.PRG

myprog.EXE: $(INFILES)
    BDC -c $(INFILES)
    BDL -Emyprog.EXE $(INFILES:.PRG-.DBO)
```

Note that the substitution of the series of file names would allow for the compiling and linking of the files defined within the macro expression.

Defined test macro processing   The defined test macro $d is used with the !if conditional directive to perform some processing if a specific macro is defined. The $d is followed by a macro name, enclosed within parentheses. The following are both valid defined test macros:

```
!ifdef $(MyCode)
!if $d(MyCode)
```

File name macro processing   MAKE parses file names and paths within rules (both implicit and explicit) and expands certain parts of those names and paths. The following list details how MAKE expands the macros shown and how the expansion differs for implicit and explicit rules. Note that the word "file" means the file name and "ext" means the file name extension.

Macro	In implicit rules, macro expands to:	In explicit rules, macro expands to:
$*	path\dependent file	path\target file
$<	path\dependent file + ext	path\target file + ext
$:	path for dependents	path for target
$.	dependent file + ext	target file + ext
$&	dependent file	target file
$@	path\target file + ext	path\target file + ext
$**	path dependent file + ext	all dependents
$?	path\dependent file + ext	old dependents

When the file name macros do not provide exactly what you want, macro modifiers let you extract parts of the file names to suit your purposes.

The following example shows the syntax for modifying macros:

```
$ (macro [D] [F] [B] [R] )
```

The following is a list of macro modifiers and what part of a file name they expand:

Modifier	Part of file name expanded	Example
D	Drive and directory	$(<D)
F	Base and extension	$(<F)
B	Base only	$(<B)
R	Drive, directory and base	$(<R)

Predefined macros   MAKE automatically defines many useful macros. For example, the MAKEDIR macro returns the directory from which MAKE was invoked. The following is a list of predefined macros that you can use within your makefile:

Macro	Expands to:	Comment
__MSDOS__	1	If running under DOS
__MAKE__	0x0360	MAKE's hex version number
MAKE	make	MAKE's executable file name
MAKEFLAGS	options	If entered on command line
MAKEDIR	directory	Shows where MAKE was invoked

Directive processing

MAKE directives resemble directives in languages such as C and Pascal, and even within dBASE IV compiler options.

Overview   They provide various control functions, such as printing commands before executing them. As a general rule, MAKE directives begin either with an exclamation point or a period.

Conditional directives   MAKE provides conditional execution directives similar to those in dBASE, C, and other languages. These directives begin with an exclamation mark (!). The following list describes MAKE's conditional execution directives:

Directive	Description
!elif	Perform same action as a dBASE "elif."
!else	Perform same action as a dBASE "#else."
!endif	End a conditional statement.
!if	Begin a conditional statement.
!ifdef	Test for the existence of a macro.
!ifndef	A negated !ifdef.

In this list, the word *statement* refers to one or more lines containing macro definitions, an implicit or explicit rule, or one of three types of directives—!include, !error, or !undef. The word *condition* represents a conditional expression much like the dBASE conditional expressions.

Dot directives   You also can specify directives using the *dot directives*. These predefined directives cover specific commands within the makefile. The following list of dot directives details the corresponding commands for each:

Directive	Correspond Option	Description
.ignore	-I	Ignore any return value of a command until further notice
.noignore	-I	Turn off .ignore

.silent	-s	Execute commands with no printout
.nosilent	-s	Prints commands before executing them
.path.ext		Search for files in directories named in *.path* with an extension of *.ext*
.precious: *target*....		Saves target file(s) even if the build fails
.suffixes		Determine the implicit rule when a target's dependent is not clear

It should be kept in mind that the previous directives will override any corresponding command-line option. The .precious directive prevents MAKE from deleting target files if the build fails. For example, if you are adding a module to a library and the build fails, you do not want the MAKE program to delete the entire target library just because the addition of a single module failed.

Other directives   MAKE provides three other types of directives other than dot and conditional directives—they are use primarily for printing error messages, inserting files into a makefile, and undefining a given macro. The following list provides an overview of these other directives available within MAKE:

Directive	Description
!error	Stops the MAKE program and prints out the error message that caused the halt.
!include	As with other languages, MAKE will insert the file specified at the point of the directive
!undef	This directive merely clears the macro definition that was specified

The following examples illustrate simple uses for these directives:

```
!if $d(SPECMACRO)
     !error SPECMACRO is not present
!endif

!include: "MYHEADR"

!undef SPECMACRO
```

Part Four

Case Study
The custom system

At last, you have arrived in the last section where you will see the actual programs that make up the Ajax Appliance Company system. You will revisit your design from chapter 4 and see how to go from storyboard and pseudocode to actual dBASE IV program code.

The format for this section is a little different. You will examine the design that led to each module and then go over the pseudocode. You will examine the screen that is produced by the code and then in great detail section by section (or in some cases line by line) examine the code itself.

In Part Three, you saw how to use all the different programming commands and functions, but in this part you will see how to make the individual programming statements into working program code.

In chapter 4 you spent a great deal of time learning how to design a system from the ground up. In Fig. 4-1, you saw the 16-step design and programming method again. In chapter 4, we saw Steps 1 through 8. In chapter 7, we accomplished Step 9. All of the databases were designed and created in dBASE IV. In chapter 10, you saw how to relate the various databases and the program code that would eventually relate all of the databases as detailed in Step 10. A data entry form was created for the inventory system in chapter 12 conforming to Step 11 while the customer and invoice systems will use screens created with program code. Step 12 was to input test data. This was done in chapter 8, and the data was tested after chapter 12.

In Step 14, you were to create the report forms; you did this in chapter 13. In this part, you will use many of the report forms just as they are, and also you will create some reports directly from program code. Step 15 was to create menus using the application generator. You did that in chapter 15 but you will not use those menus. Rather, you will create all the menus and processes from scratch in this section--which brings us to Step 16. In this part, you will see how to create all of the modules designed and how to program the six major types of programs:

- Startup and Password Protection
- Main Menu
- Subsidiary Menu
- Data Entry
  - ~ Add
  - ~ Change
  - ~ Delete
  - ~ View
- Multiple File Data Entry
  - ~ One to One Relationships
  - ~ One to Many Relationships
- Reporting
  - ~ Report Preprocessors
  - ~ Simple Column
  - ~ Simple Form

~ Simple Mailmerge
~ Labels
~ Complex Form Reports
~ Complex Column Reports
~ Rollup Reports (Summaries)

If you need help remembering the fields in the different databases used in this book then look at appendix A. Appendix A contains a listing of all the databases used in this book. Appendix B contains a listing of all the programs demonstrated in this book.

20
Creating a
password-protected system

Before you start coding you should look at the overall flow of the modules again. Figure 20-1 shows a complete module flow chart of the system you are about to see created. This module chart known as a tree chart was done with Clear for dBASE, a software package from Clear Software in Brookline, Massachusetts.

The design for the system

As you can see in Fig. 20-1, the main module name is called AJAXPASS. This is the first module in the system and will be used to "call" the AJAXMAIN module after validating the password from the user. The AJAXMAIN module then calls five procedures called MAIN1, MAIN2, MAIN3, MAIN4, and MAIN5. Each of these are pull-down menu evaluators which call the specific actions for the CUSTOMER, INVOICE, INVENTORY, OTHER, and EXIT processing modules. We will refer back to this chart later as you build your system.

Storyboards, pseudocode, and flowcharts

The next step is to begin to code and test each module. In some modules, we show you the storyboard, pseudocode, and actual screen photograph before you actually see the code. In some modules, everything is presented in a different order. New ideas and programming techniques are always completely discussed, while ideas you have seen several times are presented in less detail.

In chapter 4, you saw a lot about storyboards and pseudocode. Let's begin by examining the storyboards and pseudocode for the password

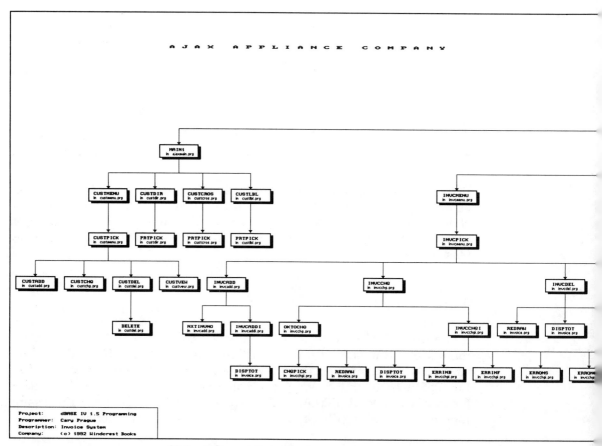

20-1 A Clear + Tree Chart.

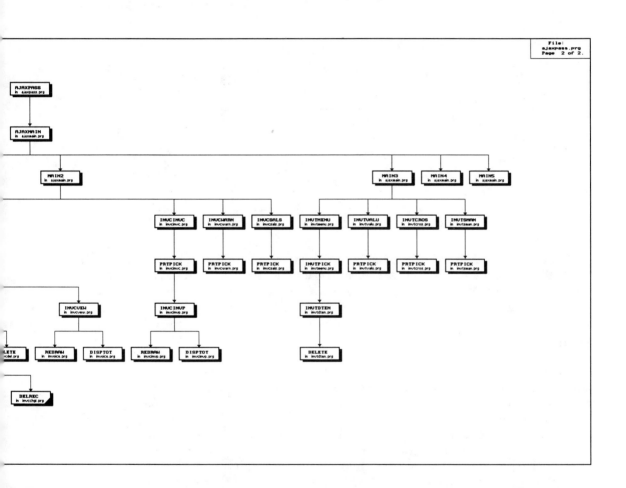

protection module. Figure 20-2 shows the storyboard for the password and date verification screen. This figure also shows the error window that was designed in case the password that is entered is invalid.

```
        AJAX APPLIANCE COMPANY
      PASSWORD AND DATE VERIFICATION


  ENTER PASSWORD:    ┌─────────────────┐
                     └─────────────────┘



ENTER/VERIFY DATE:   ┌─────────────┐
                     │  mm/dd/yy   │
                     └─────────────┘


        ┌─────────────────────────────────┐
        │        INVALID PASSWORD          │
        │     YOU HAVE 2 TRIES LEFT        │
        │                                  │
        │   PRESS ANY KEY TO CONTINUE      │
        └─────────────────────────────────┘
```

20-2 Storyboard for opening screen and error window.

The storyboard shows that a screen is displayed. A couple of lines at the top of the screen identify to the user the purpose of the screen. Then two lines will get the required input. The first line gets the password, while the next input line gets the date. The password data entry is not displayed. This is accomplished by changing the color to non-display. You will see this in the code as COLOR X/X,X/X.

The date is already displayed as the current system date. The DATE( ) function is used to do this. The user then either simply presses Enter to accept the current system date or changes it to the date he or she wants the system to think it is. This allows you to input your previous week's invoices the following Monday.

The error message is displayed inside a window that lays on top of the screen. The design called for the user to have three chances to input a correct password before the system returns them to the dot prompt.

All this is known not from the storyboard but because that is what was designed in chapter 4. As we go on, we assume that you have read chapter 4 and simply go over the most important parts. The pseudocode serves as a reminder as to the module flow.

As we will be seeing a lot of pseudocode, let's once again look at a flowchart. Figure 20-3 shows the flowchart for the opening screen.

First, the screen is displayed. Next, the data entry areas are displayed, and the input allowed into the fields. Finally the password is validated. If the password is valid, then the processing continues, and the main menu program is called. If the password is not valid, then a counter is updated, and

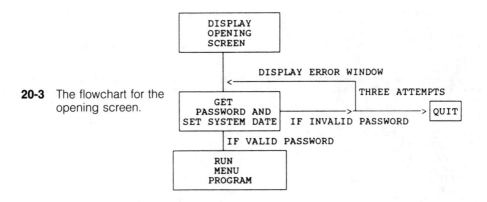

20-3 The flowchart for the opening screen.

the error window is displayed. The process is repeated until a valid password is input or until three invalid attempts are made.

Once the design is understood, it is time to start coding. As you look at the code that is displayed here for each function, remember that nobody just begins to code. We learned by looking at a lot of other code, just as you will in this book.

Starting to code comments

It is now time to begin to look at the code. The first module is the password system. The module in its entirety is shown in Fig. 20-4.

At the top of the code is the comment section. Each program should have a comment section. Notice that each comment line begins with an asterisk (*). The asterisk tells dBASE IV that the entire line is a comment and not to process it as part of the program. If you want a line to have program code followed by a comment on the same line, then you would write your program code and then begin the comment with a double ampersand (&& Comment goes after the code). The && tells dBASE that everything to the left of the && is part of the program and everything to the right is a comment.

The comment section shown in Fig. 20-4 is a dBASE standard. The comments section is separated from the rest of the code by an entire line of asterisks. Then comes information about the:

- Program
- Author
- Dates of creation and modification (if any)
- Module #
- dBASE version used
- Complete description of the module (as many lines as needed)

After the comments, it is time to begin the working code.

```
****************************************************************************
* Program......: AJAXPASS.PRG
* Author.......: Cary N. Prague
* Date.........: 9-04-88, Revision 12-26-88, Revision 8-8-90 Revision 3-12-92
* Module #.....: 00
* dBASE Ver....: IV 1.5
* Description..: AJAX APPLIANCE COMPANY SYSTEM PASSWORD AND DATE VERIFICATION
****************************************************************************
CLOSE ALL
CLEAR ALL
SET DELIMITER OFF
SET INTENSITY ON
SET ECHO OFF
SET TALK OFF
SET BELL OFF
SET CONFIRM OFF
SET EXACT ON
SET STATUS OFF
SET CLOCK OFF
SET SCOREBOARD OFF
SET DELETED ON
SET COLOR ON
SET COLOR TO W+/B,W+/R
SET COLOR OF MESSAGES TO W+/B
SET ESCAPE ON
CLEAR
PUBLIC DATE
STORE DATE() TO DATE
STORE 1 TO PTEST
STORE SPACE(10) TO PWORD
SET BORDER TO SINGLE
@ 0,0 TO 24,79
DEFINE WINDOW msg1 FROM 12,19 TO 20,59 DOUBLE color w+/r
DEFINE WINDOW msg2 FROM 11,19 TO 20,59 DOUBLE
DO WHILE PTEST <= 3 .AND. UPPER(PWORD) # 'TAB        '
   @  1,20 SAY '          AJAX APPLIANCE COMPANY              '
   @  3,20 SAY '            AUTHORIZATION CHECK              '
   @  6,28 SAY '*** ENTER PASSWORD *** '
   @  9,34 GET PWORD COLOR X/X,X/X
   @ 15,28 SAY '  *** ENTER DATE *** '
   @ 17,35 GET M->DATE PICTURE '99/99/99' ;
           RANGE {1/01/88},{12/31/99}
   READ
   IF UPPER(PWORD) # 'TAB        '
      ACTIVATE WINDOW msg1
      @ 2,10 SAY 'INVALID PASSWORD'
      @ 3,8  SAY 'YOU HAVE ' + STR((3-PTEST),1) + ' TRIES LEFT'
      @ 4,1  SAY " "
      WAIT "        PRESS ANY KEY TO CONTINUE"
      DEACTIVATE WINDOW msg1
      STORE SPACE(10) TO PWORD
   ENDIF
   PTEST = PTEST + 1
ENDDO
IF UPPER(PWORD) # 'TAB        '
   SET COLOR TO
   CANCEL
ENDIF
SET COLOR TO W+/B,W+/R
DO AJAXMAIN
```

20-4   The program code for AJAXPASS.PRG.

Setting the environment with SET statements

The first thing a program must do is operate in a known environment. You never know what was happening prior to running your program. You should begin by closing and clearing everything possible.

The two statements CLOSE ALL and CLEAR ALL do just that. CLOSE ALL closes all open databases, format files, indices, and procedure files and resets the work area to 1. The CLEAR ALL statement closes and clears items in memory as well. This includes database files, memory variables, array elements, pop-up and menu definitions, and window definitions. CLEAR ALL also closes the open catalog. CLEAR ALL does everything CLOSE ALL does and more. However, it is a good idea to use both commands.

Before coding begins, the environment must be set. The environment has global parameters that affect the rest of the program. The most important ones are:

SET DELIMITER OFF—If you are using the reverse video intensity you do not need delimiters. They show you the beginning and end of a field for data entry. The default is a ":" and would show a field like this:

Order Number : :

SET INTENSITY ON—Uses reverse video for data input areas.

SET ECHO OFF—Turns off commands from the command file. Without this off, the actual commands themselves show up on the screen. This is used only as a testing tool when all else fails.

SET TALK OFF—Turns off the displaying of database command results. When a database command is given such as DELETE, the message 1 Record Deleted appears on the screen. This eliminates this problem.

SET BELL OFF—This turns off the warning bell every time the end of a field is reached. In dBASE IV, one of the defaults is to sound the alarm each time the last character of a field is entered. It is used as a warning to tell you that you can't type anymore. The alarm is also most annoying if most of your entries will reach the end of the field.

SET CONFIRM OFF—When entering fields that fill the entire space allowed for the field, especially in one-character spaces of selection menus, this command automatically enters the input when the end of the field is reached. This saves the operator from hitting the Enter key every time the field is entered. This only works at the end of a field.

SET EXACT ON—This assures that only exact matches are found when searches are performed. Without it, there is no difference to the computer for "BILL SMITH" and "BILL SMITH JONES."

SET STATUS OFF—This eliminates the status line at the bottom of the screen. When you are using the entire screen you don't want the status line taking up three lines at the bottom.

SET SCOREBOARD OFF—With the STATUS bar off some information is still displayed at the top of the screen instead of in the STATUS bar. This includes the Ins, Num, and Caps key indicators. This will clear line 0 for use by your program. You might also have to SET CLOCK OFF if the clock remains in the upper right corner of the screen.

SET DELETED ON—This option makes deleted records invisible prior to packing them. If you use this option, you really don't need to check for deleted records when searching a file.

SET COLOR ON—If you have a color monitor, then it uses the color statements found in the program. If you don't you should turn this option off.

SET COLOR TO—This determines the overall colors for the system. In this program the statement is SET COLOR TO W+/B,W+/R. This means use bright white on a blue background for normal display and bright white on a red background for highlighted display such as GET fields and borders.

SET ESCAPE ON—This enables you to press Esc to break out of the program. It gives the user a way out should the system become hopelessly stuck.

The other major SET commands either are not used too often or are defaults that you would want in the programming mode. All of the set statements are briefly described in appendix D.

Finally, the CLEAR command clears the screen so the program starts with a blank screen.

Now that the environment has been set it is time to code the data entry.

Setting memory variables

Before data entry can begin for the password and the date, memory variables must be created to store the initial values for the data that will be entered. The statement:

PUBLIC DATE

tells dBASE to create a memory variable called DATE and let it be known to all subsequent modules in the system. Without the PUBLIC command, dBASE would only know about this memory variable in the AJAXPASS module and in modules directly called by it.

Next the value of DATE is initialized with the command:

STORE DATE( ) TO DATE

This stores the value of the function DATE( ) (the system date) to the memory variable DATE. Don't be confused by the similarities in the function name and the memory variable name. They don't have to be the same, but it makes it easier for the next programmer who comes along.

The variable PTEST is next initialized with the STORE 1 to PTEST statement. It could have also been written PTEST=1. This is used to test for password entry attempts. The password itself is entered into the memory variable PWORD and has been assigned a length of 10.

Getting ready for display with borders and windows

At this point, the program is displaying a blank screen. Memory variables have been set up, and everything is ready to go. A few more definitions are still necessary.

The BORDER is set to SINGLE. This means that anything that is defined that may use a border such as a pop-up menu or a window will have a single line border.

The command @ 0,0 TO 24,79 draws a box around the entire screen. Because this screen is not displayed inside a window, we must draw the box ourselves.

Next, two windows are defined. The first is needed by this module. The second is used by later modules. It is defined here because it makes it easier later to find all of the message window definitions. In reality, you probably would go back and enter the second window later after you realized you needed it. The only difference in the two windows is their size and names. The command:

```
DEFINE WINDOW msg1 FROM 12,19 TO 20,59 DOUBLE
```

defines a window from screen positions 12,19 to 20,59 and overrides the default border line which is a single line and draws a double line. The window is named msg1. You also could have changed the color of the inside of the window by adding a COLOR option if you desire. In this example, it is not necessary. Once the two windows are defined it is time to get to the heart of the logic.

A little logic

One loop is used to repeatedly ask for the password. This loop is repeated up to three times because of the counter PTEST. The memory variable PTEST has already been initialized to 1. Each time a new password is entered, it is incremented by 1. When the loop attempts to execute for a fourth time, the condition will be false, and processing will terminate.

The DO WHILE statement is actually testing two conditions:

```
DO WHILE PTEST <=3 .AND. UPPER(PWORD) # 'TAB
```

The first condition is the value of PTEST. As long as that is 3 or less, the second condition is checked. If the value of PTEST is greater than 3, then there is no need to even check the second condition. The .AND. joining the two conditions tells dBASE that both conditions must be met for the loop to continue. If either condition is false, the entire loop condition is false, and the program executes the statement following the ENDDO next.

The second condition tests whether the uppercase value of PWORD is not equal to 'TAB'. If the password has been entered that is invalid, then the loop continues. Once a valid password has been entered—whether it is the first, second, or third try—then the condition UPPER(PWORD) # 'TAB ' is no longer met and the loop ends.

The loop can only end for two reasons. First, the number of tries to enter a valid password exceeds three, or second, a correct password has been entered. The IF statement following the ENDDO checks for the correct password condition. If the condition is met then the program continues, and if not the program is canceled.

If the program continues, then the AJAXMAIN program is called. If the password was not 'TAB', then the program is canceled and the user is returned to the dot prompt.

Displaying the screen

Now we move inside the loop and display the screen and allow for data entry. Six statements display the screen and get the data input. Figure 20-5 displays the screen as it appears during data entry.

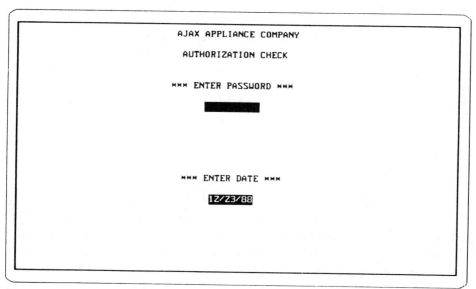

20-5 The password data entry screen.

The first two @ SAY statements display the title at the top of the screen. The third and fourth display a message to:

'*** ENTER PASSWORD ***'

and then to input the password. By using the GET statement with the COLOR X/X,X/X parameter, the input is invisible. You are entering the color blank on blank. Actually, any color that is displayed on top of the same color is invisible.

The last two @ SAY statements display the value of the DATE memory variable and allow input into it. Date range validation is accomplished with the RANGE parameter:

```
@ 17,35 GET M—>DATE ;
     PICTURE '99/99/99' RANGE {01/01/88}, {12/31/99}
```

This normal @ statement first positions the cursor at row 17 column 35 and allows data entry into the memory variable DATE. Because DATE is actually a reserved word, the M—> symbol tells dBASE to use the memory variable. The semicolon is used to continue the statement on the next line.

The PICTURE clause is unnecessary because the DATE memory variable is a date field type. If it were a character field type, it would be necessary to ensure that only valid dates were input and that the slashes were placed in the correct place.

The RANGE statement limits valid dates to between January 1, 1988, and December 31, 1999. The curly braces tell dBASE that you are specifying a date. When the turn of the century comes, you can SET CENTURY ON and use a four-digit year.

After the SAY and GET commands comes the READ statement. This opens up the screen for data input and allows the user to enter the password and date.

Handling errors

Once the data is entered, it can be evaluated. An IF statement evaluates the input. The date is verified at the field level, meaning that you cannot exit the field data entry area until you have entered a valid date. Once the date is entered the screen level edits are checked. There is only one check in this example—the password.

The IF statement is exactly the same as the second condition in the DO WHILE. If the password is not 'TAB', then this error logic is processed. Now the password has been hardcoded in this example. This means that it is part of the program. In reality the password is normally stored in a memory variable file or a database.

The error logic first activates the window 'msg1'. This was defined earlier in this module. Because the window definition included a border, activating the window displays a box on the screen from 12,19 to 20,59. Because it is a window, it 'sits on top of' the screen. When the window is deactivated, the screen returns to its previous state before the window was displayed. This window is shown in Fig. 20-6.

Once the window is activated, all display takes place inside the window, and the coordinates specified are in relation to the top corner of the window. The first statement displays the words INVALID PASSWORD in the second line of the window. Actually, row 2 is the third line because rows are numbered starting at 0, but that is the border row so row 2 is the second line inside the window.

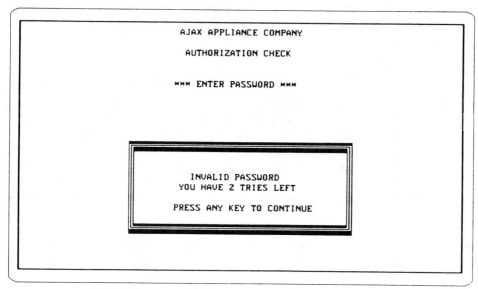

```
              AJAX APPLIANCE COMPANY

              AUTHORIZATION CHECK

         ***  ENTER PASSWORD  ***




              ┌─────────────────────────────┐
              │ ╔═════════════════════════╗ │
              │ ║                         ║ │
              │ ║     INVALID PASSWORD    ║ │
              │ ║   YOU HAVE 2 TRIES LEFT ║ │
              │ ║                         ║ │
              │ ║  PRESS ANY KEY TO CONTINUE ║ │
              │ ║                         ║ │
              │ ╚═════════════════════════╝ │
              └─────────────────────────────┘
```

20-6 The password data entry screen with error window.

The next line writes a message that tells the user how many tries are left. A formula is used to tell the user how many tries are left. The formula 3-PTEST calculates the number of tries left. As PTEST increases with each attempt the value of 3- PTEST decreases by 1 each time.

The actual statement is a little complex because it includes a concatenation, a conversion, and a calculation—the big 3:

- Concatenation—Combining two or more character strings
- Conversion—Transforming the data type from one to another
- Calculation—Using a formula to produce a new result

This statement reads:

@ 3,8 SAY 'YOU HAVE ' + STR((3-PTEST),1) + ' TRIES LEFT'

First, the cursor is positioned at row 3 column 8 inside the window. The string 'YOU HAVE ' is placed in memory and is the first part of three strings to be concatenated together. Notice the blank space after the E in HAVE. This is done to add a blank space after the word. Without it the concatenation would place the next string right against the word HAVE without any space.

The first string is now concatenated with the second string. The calculation of 3-PTEST returns a number—either 2, 1, or 0 depending on the value of PTEST. Because the value of this calculation is a number, it cannot be concatenated with a string. The number must first be converted to a string with the STR function. The string function requires you to determine the total length of the field and optionally any decimals. The ',1' indicates the length is one with no decimals. Normally, only one set of parentheses is needed. If you only wanted to convert the value of PTEST to a string, you would enter:

```
STR(PTEST,1)
```

Because the PTEST is a calculation, another set of parentheses delimits the calculation from the function.

The last concatenation joins the first two with the last part of the text. In this last concatenation, a blank space is added to the beginning of the text to avoid having it run into the back of the calculation.

The next two lines stop processing. First, the cursor is moved to row 4 column 1 of the window. Then the WAIT command is used to stop processing and center the message PRESS ANY KEY TO CONTINUE at the bottom of the window.

Now the user will see this window displayed. Until any key is pressed, nothing happens. Once a key is pressed, however, the processing continues.

The window is deactivated which removes the window and everything in it from the screen. What was under the window reappears instantly as the window "lifts off" the screen.

The offending password is erased by replacing the contents with 10 spaces. This is necessary, because you do not want to view the contents of the password data entry area. If the correct password was 5 characters and you had entered 6 incorrectly, you would never know that a bad character was in the field. This blanks out the entry area ready for you to try again.

After the ENDIF, the PTEST variable is incremented. This takes us to the ENDDO. If the password was entered correctly or if the value of PTEST is 4, then the loop ends. If not, it continues. Notice that the erasing of the PWORD value was done inside the IF statement, and only if the value was not matched. If you had erased the password regardless of its value, then it could not be used to check after the loop ended.

Calling the next menu

Once the loop ends, either the password is correct or it isn't. If it is not, then the statements inside the final IF is processed. This resets the colors and cancels the program. The user is returned to the dot prompt.

However, if the password was equal to 'TAB', then the last two statements are executed. First, the colors are reset. Finally, the AJAXMAIN module is called to display the main module.

Next, we will see the main module program and how it is created.

21
The Main menu

Now that the password screen is completed it is time to create the traffic cop—the Main menu. This is the module that controls all other modules.

Examining the design

Let's start by examining the design for this module. First, let's look at the design of the main module that you worked with in chapter 4. Figure 21-1 shows the storyboard for this module.

As you can see, both the bar menu and each of the pop-up menus have been defined. In the center of the screen is the name of the company in large letters—AJAX APPLIANCE. This is actually very easy to do as you will see. That part of the screen could also have been used to display a help box or to display an explanation of the system, a flowchart, navigational guides, or anything you want.

Each one of the five menus (the bar menu and four pop-ups) are defined separately. The large letters can be written anytime. Once you look at the design, you can code the individual menus. Before starting, you should review the pseudocode as it was designed.

Figure 21-2 again shows you the pseudocode that was created for the opening screen and the main menu. Once the password routine is valid, the menu is displayed and the many actions taken. The actions become a CASE statement because as each menu choice is made, an action must be taken.

Each choice in the first three pop-ups simply calls another module. The code tells us that you will work in the fourth module. There is no need to call a subsidiary module.

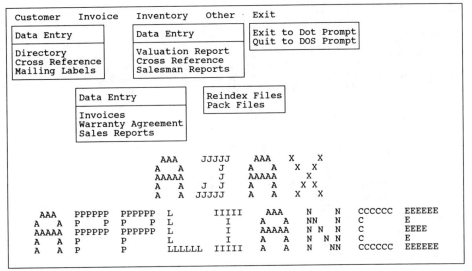

21-1 The main module storyboard screen.

Defining your windows

Because this is the main module, some things should happen which are particular to main menus. The environment has already been set in the password module. In this module, we don't have to worry about any of that.

Let's see the first page of the program. This first page defines the windows and all of the menus as shown in Fig. 21-3. (Windows were explained in chapter 18.)

First, the global BORDER setting is set to DOUBLE. This makes sure that all menus and windows will have a double-line border. The next command, SET message to " " AT 24, simply defines the bottom line of the screen (line 24) to display all messages from menus or data validation.

Next, the screen is cleared. This erases whatever is left on the screen from the password system. Next, a window must be defined in which to display the menus. Every screen must be placed in a window. This is an important concept. Unless you are planning to run the statements in previous modules when you return from subsequent modules that redraw the screen, you must put each screen in a window. If each window is the same size then they will fit on top of each other and hide what is underneath.

In this system, you will see some occurrences where four windows are on the screen at one time. The main menu is in one window. Each program it calls, such as the customer menu, is placed in a second window. When the customer menu calls the customer data entry screen, that is placed in a third window. When the delete confirmation window or an error window is displayed, a fourth window is active at the same time. There is no limit to how many windows you can have at once except as limited by memory. If you have no more than 10 windows defined or active at once, you should never have a problem.

```
OPENING SCREEN AND MAIN MENU

GET THE SYSTEM DATE FROM THE SYSTEM
RETRIEVE THE CURRENT SECRET PASSWORD FOR COMPARISON TO OPERATOR INPUT
LOOP FOR THREE TIMES OR UNTIL PASSWORD IS CORRECT AND DATE IS VALID
   DISPLAY A SCREEN TO GET THE PASSWORD AND VERIFY THE DATE
   IF PASSWORD IS NOT VALID DISPLAY WINDOW WITH PASSWORD ERROR MESSAGE
   AFTER THREE INVALID PASSWORD TRIES QUIT
END LOOP

IF PASSWORD IS VALID
    DISPLAY BAR MENU
      CASE CHOICE
        WHEN CUSTOMER SYSTEM
          DISPLAY PULL DOWN MENU
          CASE CHOICE
            WHEN DATA ENTRY DO CUSTOMER DATA ENTRY
            WHEN DIRECTORY DO CUSTOMER DIRECTORY
            WHEN CROSS REFERENCE DO PRINT CUSTOMER CROSS REFERENCE
            WHEN MAILING LABELS DO CUSTOMER MAILING LABELS
        WHEN INVOICE SYSTEM
          DISPLAY PULL DOWN MENU
          CASE CHOICE
            WHEN DATA ENTRY DO INVOICE DATA ENTRY
            WHEN PRINT INVOICES DO PRINT INVOICES
            WHEN WARRANTY AGREEMENTS DO PRINT WARRANTY AGREEMENTS
            WHEN SALES REPORTS DO SALES REPORTS
        WHEN INVENTORY SYSTEM
          DISPLAY PULL DOWN MENU
          CASE CHOICE
            WHEN DATA ENTRY DO INVENTORY DATA ENTRY
            WHEN VALUATION REPORT DO PRINT VALUATION REPORT
            WHEN CROSS REFERENCE DO INVENTORY CROSS REFERENCE
            WHEN SALESMAN REPORT DO PRINT SALESMAN REPORTS
        WHEN OTHER PROCESSING
          DISPLAY PULL DOWN MENU
          CASE CHOICE
            WHEN REINDEX FILES THEN REINDEX FILES
            WHEN PACK FILE THEN PACK FILES
        WHEN EXIT SYSTEM
          DISPLAY PULL DOWN MENU
          CASE CHOICE
            WHEN EXIT TO DOT PROMPT THEN CANCEL
            WHEN EXIT TO DOS PROMPT THEN QUIT
      ENDCASE
ENDLOOP
```

21-2   The main module pseudocode.

First, define all of the windows you will need in the system. You have already defined two windows, msg1 and msg2, for message display. In this module, only one window is needed; however, as you complete the coding you will see that a total of five windows are needed. Some are identical but most are different.

The first window defined is the "mainmenu" window. This is the window where the main menu is displayed. The command:

DEFINE WINDOW mainmenu FROM 0,0 TO 23,79 DOUBLE

defines this window. The window is smaller than the whole screen. In fact, it is one line shorter than the bottom of the screen. There is a reason for this.

```
********************************************************************
* Program......: AJAXMAIN.PRG
* Author.......: Cary N. Prague
* Date.........: 9-04-88, Revision 12-26-88, Revision 2-26-92
* Module #.....: 0
* dBASE Ver....: IV 1.5
* Description..: AJAX APPLIANCE COMPANY SYSTEM MAIN MENU
********************************************************************
SET BORDER TO DOUBLE
SET MESSAGE TO "" AT 24
CLEAR
DEFINE WINDOW mainmenu FROM 0,0 TO 23,79 DOUBLE
DEFINE WINDOW calling  FROM 0,0 TO 23,79 DOUBLE
DEFINE WINDOW data     FROM 0,0 TO 24,79 DOUBLE
DEFINE WINDOW data3    FROM 0,0 TO 23,79 DOUBLE
DEFINE WINDOW datan    FROM 0,0 TO 24,79 NONE
PUBLIC TAX_RATE
TAX_RATE = 7.5
*-- Bar
DEFINE MENU AJAXMAIN
DEFINE PAD PAD_1 OF AJAXMAIN PROMPT "Customer" AT 1,3
ON PAD PAD_1 OF AJAXMAIN ACTIVATE POPUP MAIN1
DEFINE PAD PAD_2 OF AJAXMAIN PROMPT "Invoice" AT 1,13
ON PAD PAD_2 OF AJAXMAIN ACTIVATE POPUP MAIN2
DEFINE PAD PAD_3 OF AJAXMAIN PROMPT "Inventory" AT 1,22
ON PAD PAD_3 OF AJAXMAIN ACTIVATE POPUP MAIN3
DEFINE PAD PAD_4 OF AJAXMAIN PROMPT "Other" AT 1,33
ON PAD PAD_4 OF AJAXMAIN ACTIVATE POPUP MAIN4
DEFINE PAD PAD_5 OF AJAXMAIN PROMPT "Exit" AT 1,40
ON PAD PAD_5 OF AJAXMAIN ACTIVATE POPUP MAIN5
*-- Popup
DEFINE POPUP MAIN1 FROM 2,2 ;
MESSAGE "Choose a selection for the Customer System"
DEFINE BAR 1 OF MAIN1 PROMPT "Data Entry"
DEFINE BAR 2 OF MAIN1 PROMPT "————————————————"    SKIP
DEFINE BAR 3 OF MAIN1 PROMPT "Directory"
DEFINE BAR 4 OF MAIN1 PROMPT "Cross Reference"
DEFINE BAR 5 OF MAIN1 PROMPT "Mailing Labels"
ON SELECTION POPUP MAIN1 DO MAIN1
*-- Popup
DEFINE POPUP MAIN2 FROM 2,12 ;
MESSAGE "Choose a selection for the Invoice System"
DEFINE BAR 1 OF MAIN2 PROMPT "Data Entry"
DEFINE BAR 2 OF MAIN2 PROMPT "————————————————————"    SKIP
DEFINE BAR 3 OF MAIN2 PROMPT "Invoices"
DEFINE BAR 4 OF MAIN2 PROMPT "Warranty Agreement"
DEFINE BAR 5 OF MAIN2 PROMPT "Sales Reports"
ON SELECTION POPUP MAIN2 DO MAIN2
*-- Popup
DEFINE POPUP MAIN3 FROM 2,21 ;
MESSAGE "Choose a selection for the Inventory System"
DEFINE BAR 1 OF MAIN3 PROMPT "Data Entry"
DEFINE BAR 2 OF MAIN3 PROMPT "————————————————————"    SKIP
DEFINE BAR 3 OF MAIN3 PROMPT "Valuation Report"
DEFINE BAR 4 OF MAIN3 PROMPT "Cross Reference"
DEFINE BAR 5 OF MAIN3 PROMPT "Salesman Report"
ON SELECTION POPUP MAIN3 DO MAIN3
*-- Popup
DEFINE POPUP MAIN4 FROM 2,32 ;
MESSAGE "Choose a selection for Other Processing"
DEFINE BAR 1 OF MAIN4 PROMPT "Reindex Files"
DEFINE BAR 2 OF MAIN4 PROMPT "Pack Files"
ON SELECTION POPUP MAIN4 DO MAIN4
*-- Popup
DEFINE POPUP MAIN5 FROM 2,39 ;
MESSAGE "Choose a selection for Exit Processing"
DEFINE BAR 1 OF MAIN5 PROMPT "Exit To Dot Prompt"
DEFINE BAR 2 OF MAIN5 PROMPT "Quit To DOS Prompt"
ON SELECTION POPUP MAIN5 DO MAIN5
```

21-3 The first page of code for the main menu module.

Messages from menus or data entry validation will always display on line 24 regardless of windows. Because the border would obscure line 24, you have two choices: either display the menu without a border or don't use line 24 by ending the window on line 23. The border is defined as a double-line border.

The next window defined is the window named "calling". This will be used to define submenus for the customer, invoice, and inventory modules. These will be another type of menu. It also is displayed from 0,0 to 23,79 with a double-line border.

Three data windows are necessary. The first is called "data" and is defined as the whole screen. This is used when all messages are handled through programmed windows and the standard messages or data validation are not. The second window is called "data3" and is only sized to line 23 for the same reasons as the menu windows. The final window "datan" takes up the whole screen but has no borders. This is used in the invoice program where every line on the screen is needed. The parameter BORDER NONE eliminates the border and frees up two extra lines for display.

A public memory variable called TAX_RATE is also defined and then initialized to 7.5. This is used to calculate the tax on taxable customers. In reality, you would probably keep another database of states and tax rates, but in order to simplify the example, we have a global tax rate.

Once the windows are defined the menus can be defined.

Creating the bar menu

A detailed explanation of menus is in chapter 17. If you need a refresher, read that chapter first.

The bar menu is created first. A comment in the program code shows where the bar menu definition begins. The first command DEFINE MENU defines the overall bar menu named AJAXMAIN. Once defined, the menu remains defined until it is released from memory. You can activate it or deactivate it as you desire. In this system, once it is activated, it is never deactivated until the program ends when the user chooses exit. The main bar menu never actually goes away. It is simply covered up by subsequent windows.

Once the menu itself is defined you can define the individual pads that make up the bar menu. As you have already learned, each of the choices are called pads and are defined separately. Let's look at the first pad definition:

```
DEFINE PAD PAD_1 OF AJAXMAIN PROMPT "CUSTOMER" AT 1,3
```

The first pad is defined and named PAD_1. The pad name can be anything you want, however, the OF clause must point back to a previously defined menu name. The PROMPT parameter is what is displayed on the screen. In this case, the prompt CUSTOMER is the first choice on the menu bar. The final parameter of the command is the placement of the beginning of the choice. This pad is displayed starting at row 1 column 3.

In order for a bar menu to be horizontal, all of the row definitions for the different pads must be the same. If they are not the same, the pads will not form a horizontal line. See chapter 17 for a more detailed explanation of these phenomena.

Once the pad is defined, you can determine what choosing it will do. The command ON PAD is used to select a pop-up menu and activate it. If you want to do an action other than to select a pop-up menu and make it a pull-down, you must use the ON SELECTION PAD command as described in chapter 17. Let's examine an ON PAD command:

```
ON PAD PAD_1 OF AJAXMAIN ACTIVATE POPUP MAIN1
```

This ON PAD command first defines the pad that it is creating an action for. This is the pad named PAD_1. The OF parameter tells which menu is being described. This way you can have menus with the same pad names. Once the pad is defined for the action, the action can be described. In this case the ACTIVATE POPUP action is taken. The pop-up that is activated is called MAIN1. In fact, at this time, the pop-up MAIN1 is not active or even defined. That comes later. As long as the pop-up is defined when the bar menu is activated, there are no problems.

That is all there is to defining a bar pad and an action for the pad. The order that these appear means very little. The order of the DEFINE PAD commands determines the order that the cursor moves. The ON_PAD commands can go anywhere. They do not need to follow the DEFINE PAD commands.

The other four pads are defined in this group of code. Each DEFINE PAD is followed by an ON PAD command. Each is named differently, is located at a different column position in row 1, and calls a different pop-up—all of which must still be defined.

Defining the pull-down menus

Once the bar menu is defined, you can define each of the five pop-up menus. The code for this is shown in Fig. 21-3. The code for each of the pop-ups is essentially the same. The POPUP is defined a little differently than the bar menu:

```
DEFINE POPUP MAIN1 FROM 2,2;
    MESSAGE 'Choose a selection from the Customer System'
```

The pop-up is defined by giving the coordinates of a box. In this code, only the starting coordinate is given. If you give an ending coordinate (to 8,20), this limits the menu. If the box is not wide enough for each menu bar, then the text is truncated. If the box is not tall enough to fit the entire text then it scrolls up and down within the box. If you only give the starting coordinate for the box, then the box is sized as large as necessary. Without a border parameter, the pop-up has the default border. In this example, in the

AJAXMAIN program the border is set to DOUBLE. Finally, a message is created for the entire menu. It can be overridden at the individual bar level if you want.

Once the pop-up itself is defined you can define the individual bars. Let's look at the first two bars:

```
DEFINE BAR 1 OF MAIN1 PROMPT " DATA ENTRY"
   DEFINE BAR 2 OF MAIN1 PROMPT "————————" SKIP
```

The first bar definition defines a bar that the user wants the cursor to move to. Each bar is defined with a number. The OF clause refers to a valid defined pop-up name. The PROMPT clause lists the choices that the user will see. The first bar inside the pop-up will be DATA ENTRY. The second bar will display a separating line across the pop-up. Because this is only a display bar, and the cursor really can't stop there (as the user can't choose it), it is skipped over by using the SKIP parameter.

The remaining three DEFINE BAR definitions define the other three options of the first pop-up. Once the pop-up is defined along with all of its bars, the action can be described. This is where bar menus and pop-up menus differ the most. While bar menus have a separate ON parameter to define each PAD action, pop-ups only have one ON parameter for the whole pop-up. A procedure is used as part of the module to determine the different choices. The command to select the procedure for the entire pop-up is:

```
ON SELECTION POPUP MAIN1 DO MAIN1
```

This calls a procedure called MAIN1. The procedure does not have to have the same name as the pop-up, but it makes it easier to attach the pop-up with its action procedure. As you are about to see, the procedure MAIN1 is part of this module. This is a good idea, although it could be a separate module.

The other four pop-ups are defined in the same way. Follow the example code in Fig. 21-3 or the storyboard in Fig. 21-1 to see these definitions.

Displaying other parts of the screen

The rest of the code activates the window and menu and displays the AJAX APPLIANCE logo on the screen. The rest of the code is shown in Fig. 21-4.

First, the logo part of the screen is displayed with a series of @ SAY commands. The large letters are simply created and then the @ SAY's are fitted around the text.

Once this is done, the AJAXMAIN menu is activated. This gives you the menus on the screen. The bar menu is the only menu activated. The bar menu actually activates each pop-up as you choose each bar menu pad.

Calling other modules

The last groups of code on the last two pages of the module are the subroutines MAIN1 through MAIN5. Let's look at the subroutine MAIN1.

```
@10,4 SAY "                        AAA    JJJJJ   AAA    X   X                    "
@11,4 SAY "                        A   A      J   A   A   X X                     "
@12,4 SAY "                        AAAAA      J   AAAAA    X                      "
@13,4 SAY "                        A   A   J  J   A   A   X X                     "
@14,4 SAY "                        A   A   JJJJJ  A   A   X   X                   "
@15,4 SAY "                                                                      "
@16,4 SAY " AAA    PPPPP   PPPPP   L    IIII    AAA    N    N   CCCCC  EEEEE"
@17,4 SAY "A   A   P   P   P   P   L     I    A   A   NN   N   C      E     "
@18,4 SAY "AAAAA   PPPPP   PPPPP   L     I    AAAAA   N N  N   C      EEE   "
@19,4 SAY "A   A   P       P       L     I    A   A   N  N N   C      E     "
@20,4 SAY "A   A   P       P       LLLLL IIII  A   A   N   NN   CCCCC  EEEEE"

ACTIVATE MENU AJAXMAIN


PROCEDURE MAIN1

  DO CASE
   CASE BAR() = 1
        SAVE SCREEN TO custscr
        CLEAR
        DO CUSTMENU
        RESTORE SCREEN FROM custscr
   CASE BAR() = 3
        SAVE SCREEN TO custscr
        CLEAR
        DO CUSTDIR
        RESTORE SCREEN FROM custscr
   CASE BAR() = 4
        SAVE SCREEN TO custscr
        CLEAR
        DO CUSTCROS
        RESTORE SCREEN FROM custscr
   CASE BAR() = 5
        SAVE SCREEN TO custscr
        CLEAR
        DO CUSTLBL
        RESTORE SCREEN FROM custscr
  ENDCASE

RETURN

PROCEDURE MAIN2

  DO CASE
   CASE BAR() = 1
        SAVE SCREEN TO invcscr
        CLEAR
        DO INVCMENU
        RESTORE SCREEN FROM invcscr
   CASE BAR() = 3
        SAVE SCREEN TO invcscr
        CLEAR
        DO INVCINVC
        RESTORE SCREEN FROM invcscr
   CASE BAR() = 4
        SAVE SCREEN TO invcscr
        CLEAR
        DO INVCWARN
        RESTORE SCREEN FROM invcscr
   CASE BAR() = 5
        SAVE SCREEN TO invcscr
        CLEAR
        DO INVCSALS
        RESTORE SCREEN FROM invcscr
  ENDCASE
```

21-4 The rest of the code for the main menu module.

```
RETURN

PROCEDURE MAIN3

 DO CASE
  CASE BAR() = 1
      SAVE SCREEN TO invtscr
      CLEAR
      DO INVTMENU
      RESTORE SCREEN FROM invtscr
  CASE BAR() = 3
      SAVE SCREEN TO invtscr
      CLEAR
      DO INVTVALU
      RESTORE SCREEN FROM invtscr
  CASE BAR() = 4
      SAVE SCREEN TO invtscr
      CLEAR
      DO INVTCROS
      RESTORE SCREEN FROM invtscr
  CASE BAR() = 5
      SAVE SCREEN TO invtscr
      CLEAR
      DO INVTSMAN
      RESTORE SCREEN FROM invtscr
 ENDCASE
RETURN

PROCEDURE MAIN4

 DO CASE
  CASE BAR() = 1
      USE CUSTOMER
      REINDEX
      USE INVENTRY
      REINDEX
      USE INVOICE
      REINDEX
      USE ITEMS
      REINDEX
  CASE BAR() = 2
      USE CUSTOMER
      PACK
      USE INVENTRY
      PACK
      USE INVOICE
      PACK
      USE ITEMS
      PACK

  ENDCASE

RETURN

PROCEDURE MAIN5

 DO CASE
  CASE BAR() = 1
      DEACTIVATE WINDOW mainmenu
      CLOSE ALL
      CANCEL
  CASE BAR() = 2
      DEACTIVATE WINDOW mainmenu
      CLOSE ALL
      QUIT
 ENDCASE

RETURN
```

Each subroutine begins with a PROCEDURE statement and the procedure name. PROCEDURE is a keyword known to dBASE IV and is automatically separated from the main part of the module. The subroutine itself is a single CASE statement. Each CASE statement lets the program make a decision. In the case of MAIN1, the CASE statement only has four choices. The BAR( ) function is used to determine which bar was chosen. There is no BAR( ) = 2 choice because the option is skipped by the menu program and can't be chosen.

The main menu screen is saved before the customer programs are called. The first choice BAR( ) = 1 is the Customer Data Entry choice. When this is chosen the CUSTMENU program is called to display the customer menu. Upon returning from that menu, the main menu screen is restored and the main menu is again displayed.

The other three choices display report processing screens. You will see each of these programs later in this part.

After the CASE statement and its choices is a RETURN statement. This returns the program to the calling module or, in this case, the main menu.

The procedures MAIN1, MAIN2, and MAIN3 are very similar. MAIN4 is very different; it has only two BAR( ) choices. The first choice is to reindex the databases. Rather than call another program, the first choice uses each database and executes the REINDEX command. The second choice packs the database.

The final routines in MAIN5 give the user the choice of exiting to the dot prompt or the DOS prompt.

Testing and debugging

Once the code is entered, it should be tested. The system is started by entering:

```
DO AJAXPASS
```

at the dot prompt or by choosing the AJAXPASS file from the applications panel in the Control Center. Remember, the password "hardcoded" in the example is TAB. This must be entered into the password entry area. Once this is done, the main menu should appear. The main menu and the first four pull-downs are shown in Fig. 21-5.

At this time, you have not coded any of the pull-down menu choices except the last choice. If you press Enter on any of the first four menus, you will get an error because the module is not found. You can display the menu and, using the cursor keys, pull down each menu and cycle through the options. You should see what is shown in Fig. 21-5.

Because we are designing from left to right, top to bottom, the next step is to define the CUSTMENU module that controls the data entry to the customer database.

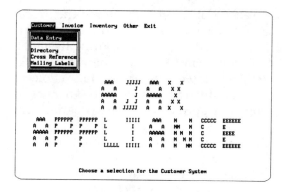
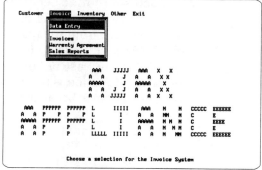
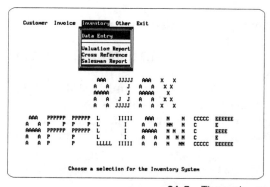
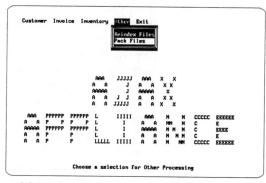

21-5 The main menu and the pull-downs.

22

Data-entry modules in the customer system

The Customer menu is another form of the pop-up. The "calling" window has already been activated on top of the "mainmenu" window. While the CUST-MENU is active, the main menu is dormant. It is still active, but now you are operating in a different window.

Remember, the commands that called the CUSTMENU menu simply activated the "calling" window and then called this module. The customer screen you will program is shown in Fig. 22-1. As you can see the screen has five choices with a space between each choice.

This menu is programmed by using a standard pop-up menu without a border. The code for this program is found in Fig. 22-2. Let's examine this code. First the screen is cleared. Because the window will be used by a lot of modules, you never know what may be left over in the window.

Once the CLEAR command is entered the menu can be defined. Since this menu won't have a border the command:

SET BORDER TO NONE

must first be entered. Then the pop-up is defined. As you can see, the pop-up is defined in the center of the screen. This is a true pop-up and not attached to a bar menu.

After the pop-up menu called CUSTMENU is defined, nine bars are defined. The odd numbered bars actually contain the menu choices. The even numbered bars are only blank lines and are skipped by using the skip

```
            AJAX APPLIANCE COMPANY
             CUSTOMER DATA ENTRY




         ┌─────────────────────────────┐
         │  ADD CUSTOMER INFORMATION   │
         └─────────────────────────────┘
          CHANGE CUSTOMER INFORMATION

             DELETE A CUSTOMER

           VIEW CUSTOMER INFORMATION

           EXIT CUSTOMER DATA ENTRY




      Choose a selection from the Customer Menu
```

22-1 The customer menu screen.

parameter in the even numbered lines. The five bars allow us to select the five normal functions of a database:

- Add
- Change
- Delete
- View
- Exit

Once the bars are defined, the ON SELECTION command calls the CUSTPICK procedure found at the bottom of Fig. 22-2.

Remember, defining the pop-up menu and the bars does not activate the menu. A few tasks still must be accomplished before the menu is activated.

Because this is a menu used to control data entry, it can also control the opening of the database. First, any open databases are closed to bring the system to a known state—no databases open. Then the CUSTOMER database is opened with the CUSTNO tag as the controlling index tag.

Next, the header information for the menu is displayed in a box. Once this is done, the pop-up CUSMENU is activated that displays the customer menu. The RETURN command returns to the main menu after the pop-up is deactivated. Because the window is not closed, the processing continues after the ACTIVATE POPUP command which executes the RETURN.

The CUSTPICK procedure contains a CASE statement that evaluates the value of BAR( ) for the odd-numbered bars. Each bar choice calls a different customer module for the four different data entry functions. The last item

```
*************************************************************************
* Program......: CUSTMENU.PRG
* Author.......: Cary N. Prague
* Date.........: 9-04-88, Final Revision 12-26-88 Revision 3-12-92
* Module #.....: 1.1
* dBASE Ver....: IV 1.5
* Description..: AJAX APPLIANCE COMPANY CUSTOMER MAIN MENU
*************************************************************************
CLEAR
*-- Popup
SET BORDER TO NONE
DEFINE POPUP CUSMENU FROM 7,25 TO 17,55 ;
MESSAGE "Choose a selection from the Customer Menu"
DEFINE BAR 1 OF CUSMENU PROMPT "   ADD CUSTOMER INFORMATION   "
DEFINE BAR 2 OF CUSMENU PROMPT "                              " SKIP
DEFINE BAR 3 OF CUSMENU PROMPT " CHANGE CUSTOMER INFORMATION "
DEFINE BAR 4 OF CUSMENU PROMPT "                              " SKIP
DEFINE BAR 5 OF CUSMENU PROMPT "      DELETE A CUSTOMER       "
DEFINE BAR 6 OF CUSMENU PROMPT "                              " SKIP
DEFINE BAR 7 OF CUSMENU PROMPT "  VIEW CUSTOMER INFORMATION   "
DEFINE BAR 8 OF CUSMENU PROMPT "                              " SKIP
DEFINE BAR 9 OF CUSMENU PROMPT "  EXIT CUSTOMER DATA ENTRY    "
ON SELECTION POPUP CUSMENU DO CUSTPICK

CLOSE DATABASES
USE CUSTOMER ORDER TAG CUSTNO
@ 1,28 TO 4,53
@ 2,30 SAY 'AJAX APPLIANCE COMPANY'
@ 3,30 SAY " CUSTOMER DATA ENTRY "

ACTIVATE POPUP CUSMENU
RETURN

PROCEDURE CUSTPICK
 DO CASE
   CASE BAR() = 1
    DO CUSTADD
   CASE BAR() = 3
    DO CUSTCHG
   CASE BAR() = 5
    DO CUSTDEL
   CASE BAR() = 7
    DO CUSTVEW
   CASE BAR() = 9
    SET BORDER TO SINGLE
    DEACTIVATE POPUP
 ENDCASE
 RETURN
```

22-2 The customer menu program.

which exits the customer data entry menu is done by deactivating the pop-up. Once the menu is programmed the various data entry screens can be programmed.

Checking the design

Now that the menu is done and the four data entry modules are defined, turn to the design of the data entry screen. Regardless of the function, the same screen is used to capture the data. While the add and change routines allow data entry, the delete and view routines only allow data display. Each module is somewhat different, as you will see when you look at the different pseudocode designs. The add routine doesn't enter data directly into the database. Data is entered into memory variables and after validation, a blank record is added to the database and the blank data values replaced with the data values from the memory variables. Changing data is done to the actual database, and therefore is a simpler process.

Regardless of the process, the data entry and display screen is the same. Let's examine the data entry screen as it was designed in our storyboard as shown in Fig. 22-3.

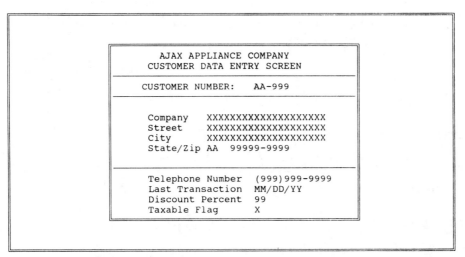

```
            AJAX APPLIANCE COMPANY
            CUSTOMER DATA ENTRY SCREEN

        CUSTOMER NUMBER:    AA-999


        Company    XXXXXXXXXXXXXXXXXXXX
        Street     XXXXXXXXXXXXXXXXXXXX
        City       XXXXXXXXXXXXXXXXXXXX
        State/Zip AA  99999-9999


        Telephone Number   (999)999-9999
        Last Transaction   MM/DD/YY
        Discount Percent   99
        Taxable Flag       X
```

22-3 The customer data entry screen storyboard.

As you can see there is nothing special about the screen. The data is arranged in a relatively vertical manner. Several header lines appear at the top of the screen. The key value—customer number—appears centered a few lines lower. The rest of the fields are placed under one another with spaces between the logical groupings. The address information appears together without any spacing.

The Add module

Once the screen is understood, it can be coded. In order to code, we must have a strategy.

Reviewing the pseudocode and error window

If you examine the new pseudocode in Fig. 22-4, you can see the strategy. First, the customer file is accessed. This is actually done in the customer menu. Next, memory variables are defined corresponding to each field in the database. Then the screen is displayed, and data entry allowed into the memory variables. Many of the variables have editing and validation statements associated with them. The key field is edited after the data is entered and any errors are handled by an error window.

```
ADD A CUSTOMER

ACCESS CUSTOMER FILE
CREATE MEMORY VARIABLES
DO WHILE CUSTOMER NUMBER NOT BLANK
   DISPLAY SCREEN
   ENTER DATA
      VERIFY CUSTOMER NUMBER
   IF BLANK
      RETURN TO MAIN MENU
   ENDIF
   IF NEW NUMBER
      THEN
         ADD CUSTOMER DATA
         CLEAR DATA FIELDS
      ELSE
         DISPLAY ERROR WINDOW - CUSTOMER NUMBER ALREADY ON FILE
   ENDIF
ENDDO
```

```
           *** ERROR ***

CUSTOMER NUMBER ALREADY ON FILE
   ENTER A NEW CUSTOMER NUMBER

     PRESS ANY KEY TO CONTINUE
```

22-4 The add customer record pseudocode and error window.

Once the data is input, several checks are made. First, the key field is checked. If it is blank, then the module loop is terminated, the data window closed, and control returned to the customer menu. If the key field is not blank, then it must be validated. If it is a new key value (one that is not already on file), then a blank record is added and the memory variables are used to replace the blank data. The memory variables are cleared and the next record can be entered. If the key value is found, then an error message is displayed and the data can be reentered. The error window has also been designed and is displayed in the pseudocode.

Now that the pseudocode has been examined it is time to begin the coding.

Creating the memory variables

The first page of the code for the CUSTADD program is shown in Fig. 22-5.

First, a window must be activated. Because you are going to be using dBASE error messages that display on line 24, you must use a window that only uses the first 23 lines. The data3 window was defined that way in the AJAXMAIN program.

```
************************************************************************
* Program......: CUSTADD.PRG
* Author.......: Cary N. Prague
* Date.........: 9-04-88, Revision 2-24-92
* Module #.....: 1.1.1
* dBASE Ver....: IV 1.5
* Description..: AJAX APPLIANCE COMPANY CUSTOMER ADD SCREEN
************************************************************************
ACTIVATE WINDOW data3
CLEAR
STORE SPACE(6)   TO CSN
STORE SPACE(20)  TO CMP
STORE SPACE(20)  TO STR
STORE SPACE(20)  TO CTY
STORE SPACE(2)   TO STT
STORE SPACE(10)  TO ZP
STORE SPACE(13)  TO PHN
STORE {  /  /  } TO LTD
STORE 0 TO DIS
STORE .F. TO TAX
DO WHILE .T.
   @ 2,19 TO 19,57 DOUBLE
   @ 3,26 SAY "AJAX APPLIANCE COMPANY"
   @ 4,26 SAY "  CUSTOMER ADDITIONS"
   @ 5,20 SAY "─────────────────────────────────"
   @ 6,23 SAY " Customer Number"
   @ 6,41 GET csn PICTURE "@! XX-999" ;
         MESSAGE "Enter a new customer number or <PgDn> to Return"
   @ 7,20 SAY "─────────────────────────────────"
   @ 9,24 SAY "Company"
   @ 9,34 GET cmp PICTURE "@!20" ;
         MESSAGE "Enter the company name"
   @ 10,24 SAY "Street"
   @ 10,34 GET str PICTURE "@! XXXXXXXXXXXXXXXXXXXX" ;
         MESSAGE "Enter the customers street address"
   @ 11,24 SAY "City"
   @ 11,34 GET cty PICTURE "@! XXXXXXXXXXXXXXXXXXXX" ;
         MESSAGE "Enter the customers city"
   @ 12,24 SAY "State/Zip"
   @ 12,34 GET stt PICTURE "@!M CA,CT,NM,NY,OK,PA" ;
         MESSAGE "Enter the customers state"
   @ 12,38 GET zp PICTURE "99999-####" ;
         MESSAGE "Enter the customers zip code"
   @ 14,20 SAY "─────────────────────────────────"
   @ 15,24 SAY "Telephone Number"
   @ 15,41 GET phn PICTURE "(###)999-9999" ;
         MESSAGE "Enter the customers phone number"
   @ 16,24 SAY "Last Transaction"
   @ 16,41 GET ltd ;
         RANGE {01/01/80},DATE()+60 ;
         WHEN .NOT. ISBLANK(ltd) ;
         MESSAGE "Enter the last transaction date"
   @ 17,24 SAY "Discount Percent"
   @ 17,41 GET dis PICTURE "99" ;
         VALID DIS >= 0 .AND. DIS <= 50 ;
         ERROR "The discount is not valid (0-50) Re-enter the discount" ;
         MESSAGE "Enter the customers discount"
   @ 18,24 SAY "Taxable Flag"
   @ 18,41 GET tax PICTURE "L" ;
         DEFAULT .T. ;
         MESSAGE "Enter the customers tax status"
   READ
```

22-5 The add customer record program—page 1.

Of course, the screen is then cleared. Next, each memory variable is defined. Character memory variables are defined by using the SPACE( ) function or by enclosing a number of spaces in quotes. Either of the following are functionally equivalent:

```
STORE SPACE(6) TO CSN
STORE '      ' TO CSN
CSN = SPACE(6)
CSN = '      '
```

In fact, it doesn't matter what the variable type is, you can either use the STORE form or the normal = sign equivalent.

Seven-character memory variables are defined in varying lengths. The lengths correspond to the lengths of the fields in the database. Each memory variable is named by creating the name as close to the real name as possible while shortening it substantially. CUSTNO becomes CSN, COMPANY becomes CMP, STREET becomes STR, etc. As long as you can recognize the name, you can work with it. You should create the memory variables in the same order that they are in the database. Because those three memory variables have the same data type and size, they could have been done in one statement:

```
STORE SPACE(20) TO COMP, STR, CTY
```

After the character memory variables are defined, a date memory variable is defined:

```
STORE {/ /} TO LTD
```

When you need a date memory variable just enclose a six-character string with two slashes within curly braces. This tells dBASE IV to define a date memory variable.

Numeric memory variables are defined by equating a number with a memory variable:

```
STORE 0 TO DIS
```

You can store any numeric value to a memory variable. You can also store or equate numeric formulas to create a memory variable. This places a 0 in a memory variable called DIS. If you wanted to create a numeric memory variable with two decimals, you could have entered STORE 0.00 TO DIS.

Finally, you can create a logical memory variable by using the logical .T. or .F.. The form:

```
STORE .F. TO TAX
```

creates a logical memory variable type named TAX and sets it to false.

Once the memory variables are created, you can begin to create the screen.

Displaying the screens: SAYs and GETs

Next, the DO WHILE statement sets up loop. Normally, the DO WHILE loop ends on a certain condition. In this example, you see a different form of the loop:

```
DO WHILE .T.
```

This creates an endless loop. The only way out of the loop is to use one of the special statements to leave a loop. These include:

- EXIT—Go to the next statement after the ENDDO.
- RETURN—Return to the calling module.
- CANCEL—Cancel the Program and return to the dot prompt.
- QUIT—Quit dBASE.

If you need a more detailed explanation back to chapter 16.

You will see how this example returns from the loop on the second page of the program code.

First, a box is drawn outside the outer box to display the data. Horizontal lines will be added to further highlight different data groups.

Now the various @ SAYs and @ GETs are programmed. First, the header lines are written to lines one and two. Then, the @ SAYs write the various text to the screen and the @ GETs get each memory variable for input. The customer number is first:

```
@ 6,45 GET csn PICTURE "@! AA-999" ;
    MESSAGE "Enter a new customer number"
```

The cursor is placed in row 6 column 45. The description has already been written by the @ SAY. Next, the GET places an entry area on the screen. Because "csn" was defined as SPACE(6), a 6-character box is created. The PICTURE clause determines what type of input can be put in the entry area. First, the @ sign as part of the picture clause signals the function. The ! function tells dBASE to convert the character portion of the input to uppercase. Next, comes the template. The AA tells dBASE to allow only character data. The dash says that a dash is automatically placed there and the cursor skips right over the "special symbol." Finally, the 999 tells dBASE to allow only numbers there. This is the format for the customer number data entry, and the system can edit for the form right away. It still checks the entry by looking for another customer number that is the same, but this starts the validation process.

Finally, the MESSAGE clause places a message at the bottom of the screen when the user places their cursor in the entry area. If you need to review the various picture templates and functions, see chapter 16. You can also review the data validation commands in chapter 12.

The CMP, STR, and CITY variables are the same. The XXX picture template means to allow any character. Actually, because this is the default, it isn't needed. The STT variable uses the multiple choice function:

```
@ 12,34 GET stt PICTURE "@M CA,CT,NM,NY,OK,PA"
```

The @M function lets you enter a list of acceptable fields. The first field becomes the default. When the cursor is placed on that field the CA appears. By pressing the Spacebar key, the values cycle through the list. After the PA value, the CA value reappears. You can also choose a value by typing it in. Entering O will immediately go to OK. To get to NY, you have to enter both characters, because dBASE can't tell whether you want NM or NY when you enter just N.

The ZIP variable and the PHONE variable also use picture templates to allow only certain characters in certain places. The dashes and parentheses are not defined as template characters, and are therefore skipped when input happens.

Evaluating the input

The last transaction date variable uses several other data validation parameters:

```
@ 16,41 GET ltd ;
RANGE {01/01/80},DATE( )+60 ;
WHEN .NOT. ISBLANK (ltd)
MESSAGE "Enter the last transaction date"
```

The RANGE option verifies that the date is between one value and another. In this case, the first range option is the minimum value of January 1, 1980. The second value is the maximum value which is the current system date plus sixty days.

The WHEN parameter lets you decide when to allow data entry and when to skip the field during certain conditions. In this example, you are telling dBASE to only allow data entry when the value of "ltd" is not blank. In this example, it is always blank because it is a new entry. However, it is used to illustrate the option.

Next, code the discount variable. The discount uses a few more options you haven't seen yet:

```
@ 19,40 GET dis PICTURE "99" ;
VALID dis >= 0 .AND. dis <= 50 ;
ERROR "The discount is not valid (0-50) Re-enter the discount" ;
MESSAGE "Enter the customers discount"
```

The VALID clause is used to validate the input. This example is simple, but any validation can be done no matter how complex. Even multiple conditions can be checked. If you can do it in an IF statement, you can validate it here. You can use any expression that returns a true or false condition.

Here, the value of dis must be between 0 and 50. The ERROR clause is activated if the expression in the VALID clause is false. The error message is displayed at the bottom of the screen. Any 79-character-or-less message can go in the ERROR clause.

The last GET on the screen is the customer's tax status. The DEFAULT clause is used to place a true condition (.T.) in the field. Once all the GETs are placed on the screen the READ statement is used to allow the data input to take place.

The screen shows an error message in Fig. 22-6.

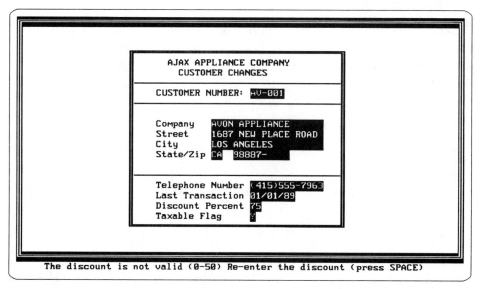

22-6 The add customer screen with error message.

Checking for a key value   Once the screen is displayed and valid data entered, still some more data needs to be validated. The second page of the CUSTADD program is shown in Fig. 22-7.

First, the key field is evaluated to see if anything was entered. Two checks are actually performed. If the field is either completely blank or has only the dashes, then it also is the same as nothing being entered. The dashes can get into the field if something was entered and then erased. The dashes would remain.

If nothing was entered, then the screen is cleared so the window will be blank when activated next. Then, deactivate the window to clear anything inside the window that was defined after the window was activated. Finally, the system returns to the customer menu (where it was called from) and the loop is automatically exited by this action.

Checking for duplicate data keys   Now that you have determined that something was entered, you must make sure it hasn't been entered before in the

```
IF CSN = '          ' .OR. CSN = '  -  '
     CLEAR
     DEACTIVATE WINDOW data3
     RETURN
ELSE
   SEEK TRIM(CSN)
   IF .NOT. FOUND()
        APPEND BLANK
        REPLACE CUSTNO WITH CSN,COMPANY WITH CMP,STREET WITH STR
        REPLACE CITY WITH CTY,STATE WITH STT,ZIP WITH ZP,PHONE WITH PHN
        REPLACE LST_TXND WITH LTD,DISCOUNT WITH DIS,TAXABLE WITH TAX
        @ 20,1
        WAIT '                    CUSTOMER ADDED-PRESS ANY KEY TO CONTINUE'
        CLEAR
        STORE SPACE(6) TO CSN
        STORE SPACE(20) TO CMP
        STORE SPACE(20) TO STR
        STORE SPACE(20) TO CTY
        STORE SPACE(2)  TO STT
        STORE SPACE(10) TO ZP
        STORE SPACE(13) TO PHN
        STORE {  /  /  } TO LTD
        STORE 0 TO DIS
        STORE .T. TO TAX
   ELSE
        ?? CHR(7)
        ACTIVATE WINDOW msg1
        @ 1,05 SAY '          *** ERROR ***'
        @ 3,05 SAY 'CUSTOMER NUMBER ALREADY ON FILE'
        @ 4,05 SAY 'ENTER A NEW CUSTOMER NUMBER'
        @ 5,1  SAY ' '
        WAIT "        PRESS ANY KEY TO CONTINUE"
        DEACTIVATE WINDOW msg1
   ENDIF
  ENDIF
ENDDO
```

22-7 The add customer record program—page 2.

ELSE clause of the IF statement. Remember, the "then" condition was nothing entered into the field.

The CUSTOMER database must be checked to see if the csn variable already exists, because the key value must be unique. This is how you can tell several locations of AVON APPLIANCE apart without looking at the address. The FIND (or SEEK) commands are used to search an indexed database for a specific value. The command:

SEEK TRIM(CSN)

is used to search the database. The database was opened in the customer menu program and the index tag CUSTNO was made the controlling index. For the SEEK command to find a value, the index must match the value being searched for. The TRIM(CSN) tells dBASE to search for the value of the variable CSN after removing any trailing blanks. The SEEK command always assumes that it is looking for a variable if there are no quotes around the characters.

With the SEEK command, any value can be located in an indexed database in less than 2 seconds regardless of the size of the database.

If the value is found, then the function FOUND( ) is .T.. You first check to see if it is not found. If the value is not found, the data entry was good and the record can be added to the database.

The IF statement controls the two possible conditions.

Appending a blank record

If the .NOT. FOUND( ) condition is met, you can begin the actual data entry into the database. A blank record is added to the bottom of the database. The command:

```
APPEND BLANK
```

adds a blank record to the database. Each of the fields in the database is in a null state. Character strings are blank, numeric fields have a zero in them, dates are blank, and logical fields are false.

Replacing the blank record in the database

Now you have a blank record in the database. To replace all of the blank fields with the values in the memory variables use the REPLACE command. You can continue REPLACE command across several lines, or you can have several different REPLACE commands as you have in this example.

Each field in the database has a replacement from a memory variable. After the replacements are accomplished, the fourth line is cleared with the @ 20,1 command with no parameters. Then a message is written to tell the user that the record was successfully added. Finally, the memory variables are all cleared in preparation for the next record.

Handling errors

The error is handled by the ELSE clause of the nested IF, the IF within an IF. You can have almost any number of nested IF's.

When you have an error you should make sure the user sees and hears it. The command:

```
? CHR(7)
```

sounds the alarm. This sounds a short beep tone from your computer's speaker.

Next, the window msg1 is activated, the error messages are written into the screen, and the cursor is placed at the beginning of the last line of the window. Then, the WAIT command is used to stop processing and display the last message. This causes the window to stay on the screen until the user presses any key.

Once any key is pressed, the program continues. The window is removed from the screen, restoring it to its original state, and then data entry continues. The user must enter a different value for the customer number or blank it out to cancel processing.

At the bottom of the screen are two ENDIF statements to close both IF statements and finally an ENDDO to close the DO WHILE command. This completes the customer add program. The screen with the error message is shown in Fig. 22-8.

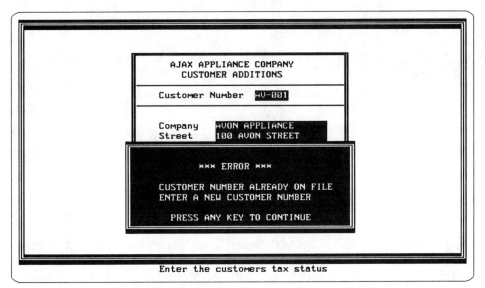

22-8 The add customer screen with error window.

The Change module

Essentially, the add, change, delete, and view modules are very similar. The change screen has the same basic statements, but in a slightly different order. Of course, in the change module we work with the data that is already in the database.

A different design

The main difference is that instead of filling out an entire screen of memory variables, you enter only one variable—the customer number. Before you can retrieve the data the user wants, you must determine which records they want to work with. Once you know the key field value (customer number), you can retrieve the record. Let's examine the pseudocode for this module as shown in Fig. 22-9.

Again, the customer file is accessed. The file was opened in the customer menu program and remains open while you are in that subsystem.

A memory variable is created with the same characteristics as the customer number. This is used to determine what customer number the user

```
CHANGE A CUSTOMER

ACCESS CUSTOMER FILE
SET CUSTOMER NUMBER TO NOT BLANK
DO WHILE CUSTOMER NUMBER NOT BLANK
   DISPLAY SCREEN
   ENTER CUSTOMER NUMBER
      VERIFY CUSTOMER NUMBER
   IF FOUND()
      THEN
         RETRIEVE CUSTOMER DATA
         CHANGE DESIRED FIELDS
         UPDATE RECORD
         CLEAR DATA FIELDS
      ELSE
         DISPLAY ERROR WINDOW-CUSTOMER NUMBER NOT ON FILE
   ENDIF
ENDDO
```

```
           *** ERROR ***

    CUSTOMER NUMBER NOT ON FILE
    ENTER ANOTHER CUSTOMER NUMBER

       PRESS ANY KEY TO CONTINUE
```

22-9   The change customer pseudocode.

wants to retrieve to edit. This is the only "fresh" data entry the module does. After a customer number is input, the database is searched to find the matching record. That record is then retrieved, and the edit screen is displayed so the values can be changed if desired. You are changing the data directly in the database exactly the same way as you use the edit screen.

If a "bad" customer number is requested, then an error message is displayed and another customer number can be requested.

A pre-processor

Let's examine the program code for this CUSTCHG module as shown in Fig. 22-10. Like the customer add program, a window is opened and the screen cleared.

A memory variable is created to get the customer number input. The endless loop is created and the program continues.

Now a *pre-processor* is created. A pre-processor is code that acts like a separate program but really isn't; it is a group of statements that must be executed before anything else can happen. In this example, the system must know what customer number you want to retrieve before it can display the screen.

The header lines are written to the screen and then only the customer number field is displayed along the memory variable entry area. The READ statement allows data input into that field. The pre-processor screen is shown in Fig. 22-11.

```
**********************************************************************
* Program......: CUSTCHG.PRG
* Author.......: Cary N. Prague
* Date.........: 9-04-88, Final Revision 12-26-88 Revision 3-12-92
* Module #.....: 1.1.2
* dBASE Ver....: IV 1.5
* Description..: AJAX APPLIANCE COMPANY CUSTOMER CHANGE SCREEN
**********************************************************************
ACTIVATE WINDOW data3
CLEAR
STORE SPACE(6) TO csn
DO WHILE .T.
  @ 2,19 TO 19,57 DOUBLE
  @ 5,20 SAY "─────────────────────────────────────"
  @ 3,26 SAY "AJAX APPLIANCE COMPANY"
  @ 4,26 SAY "  CUSTOMER CHANGES"
  @ 6,24 SAY "CUSTOMER NUMBER:"
  @ 6,41 GET csn PICTURE "@! AA-999" ;
    MESSAGE "Enter Customer Number or Press <Enter> to Return"
  READ
  IF csn = '       ' .OR. csn = '   -   '
      CLEAR
      DEACTIVATE WINDOW data3
      RETURN
    ELSE
      SEEK TRIM(CSN)
      IF FOUND()
        @ 6,41 GET custno PICTURE "@! XX-999" ;
          MESSAGE "Enter a new customer number or PgDn to Go Back"
        @ 7,20 SAY "─────────────────────────────────────"
        @ 9,24 SAY "Company"
        @ 9,34 GET company PICTURE "@!20" ;
          MESSAGE "Enter the company name"
        @ 10,24 SAY "Street"
        @ 10,34 GET street PICTURE "@! XXXXXXXXXXXXXXXXXXXX" ;
          MESSAGE "Enter the customers street address"
        @ 11,24 SAY "City"
        @ 11,34 GET city PICTURE "@! XXXXXXXXXXXXXXXXXXXX" ;
          MESSAGE "Enter the customers city"
        @ 12,24 SAY "State/Zip"
        @ 12,34 GET state PICTURE "@!M CA,CT,NM,NY,OK,PA" ;
          MESSAGE "Enter the customers state"
        @ 12,38 GET zip PICTURE "99999-####" ;
          MESSAGE "Enter the customers zip code"
        @ 14,20 SAY "─────────────────────────────────────"
        @ 15,24 SAY "Telephone Number"
        @ 15,41 GET phone PICTURE "(###)999-9999" ;
          MESSAGE "Enter the customers phone number"
        @ 16,24 SAY "Last Transaction"
        @ 16,41 GET lst_txnd ;
          RANGE {01/01/80},DATE()+60 ;
          WHEN .NOT. ISBLANK(lst_txnd) ;
          MESSAGE "Enter the last transaction date"
        @ 17,24 SAY "Discount Percent"
        @ 17,41 GET discount PICTURE "99" ;
          VALID discount >= 0 .AND. discount <= 50 ;
          ERROR "The discount is not valid (0-50) Re-enter the discount" ;
          MESSAGE "Enter the customers discount"
        @ 18,24 SAY "Taxable Flag"
        @ 18,41 GET taxable PICTURE "L" ;
          DEFAULT .T. ;
          MESSAGE "Enter the customers tax status"
```

22-10 The change customer program.

```
READ
@ 20,1
        WAIT '                    CUSTOMER CHANGED-PRESS ANY KEY TO CONTINUE'
        CLEAR
        STORE SPACE(6) TO CSN
      ELSE
        ?? CHR(7)
        ACTIVATE WINDOW msg1
        @ 1,05 SAY '       *** ERROR ***'
        @ 3,05 SAY ' CUSTOMER NUMBER NOT ON FILE'
        @ 4,05 SAY 'ENTER ANOTHER CUSTOMER NUMBER'
        @ 5,1  SAY ' '
        WAIT "       PRESS ANY KEY TO CONTINUE"
        DEACTIVATE WINDOW msg1
        STORE SPACE(6) TO CSN
      ENDIF
  ENDIF
  CLEAR
ENDDO
```

Next, the same check is made as in the add module to see if something was entered into the csn variable. If nothing was entered, then the screen is cleared, the window deactivated, and the user is returned to the customer menu. This also exits the user from the loop.

If something is entered (the ELSE clause), then processing continues. Again, the database must be searched for the customer number. This time the desired result is to find it. If it is FOUND( ), then the screen is displayed.

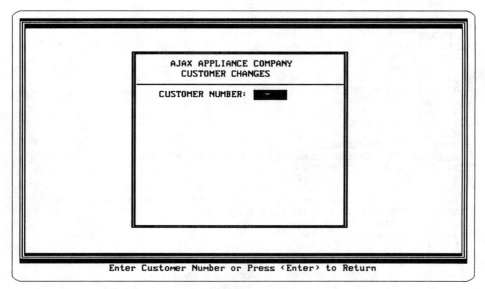

22-11 The change customer preprocessor screen.

Entering directly into the fields

As you can see, in the center portion of Fig. 22-10 is the code to display the screen and allow data entry directly into the fields. All of the fields should already have data in them as this is a change exercise. If you don't want to change the data, simply press Enter when the cursor comes to rest in that particular entry area. When you are through with the changes, you can press Ctrl–End or PgDn if you are not on the last field. This is true of any data entry screen.

Each field has a SAY and a GET in the database. Unlike the add module, the actual names from the database are used. When the record is found, the record pointer is positioned on the record in the database. You then have access to the actual data in the database. You also could have used the same validation commands from the add module.

Notice that the CUSTNO field can be changed. The key field, csn, is only used to select a record to retrieve. Once the record is retrieved, the key value can be changed. This might have implications if any invoices use this customer number.

The only difference between entering data directly into the fields or into memory variables is that you can always stop the REPLACE command when you are using memory variables. When you are entering directly into the database, whatever you enter is "final."

After the SAY and GET commands, READ is used to read the changes to the customer database. Because there is no validation here, a message is displayed indicating that the customer data has been changed.

The csn memory variable is cleared out to make way for the next entry of the customer number to be retrieved.

Handling errors

Just like the add module, the change module has an error window. However, the purpose for the window is very different. In the add module, the ELSE loop (error loop) is executed if the customer number is found. The check was IF .NOT. FOUND( ). Here, the ELSE loop (error loop) is executed if the customer number isn't found because the condition being tested for is IF FOUND( ).

The error window is exactly the same except for the middle two messages that are written to lines 3 and 4 of the window. Here the user is told that the customer number can't be found and to enter another number. The rest of the error window code is the same as the add module. Finally, both IF statements and the ENDDO close the program.

As you can see, the change module is derived from the add module. The delete and view modules are even more similar to the change module.

The Delete module

The delete module begins with the same philosophy as the change module and doesn't change much. The system must request the customer number to be processed. Once found, the screen can be displayed. This is one of the first two differences. The screen is displayed without any GETs. Therefore, no data entry is allowed. The idea of displaying the screen is to allow the user to view their data, not make changes to it.

A design for post-processing

Once the data is viewed, a *post-processor* occurs. A post-processor happens after everything else is done—in this case, after the screen is viewed. The post-processor in this case consists of a window with a menu inside asking the user to confirm that he or she wants to delete the record. If so, a subprocedure deletes the record and informs the user. This pseudocode is shown in Fig. 22-12.

```
DELETE A CUSTOMER

ACCESS CUSTOMER FILE
SET CUSTOMER NUMBER TO NOT BLANK
DO WHILE CUSTOMER NUMBER NOT BLANK
  DISPLAY SCREEN
  ENTER CUSTOMER NUMBER
    VERIFY CUSTOMER NUMBER
    IF FOUND()
      THEN
        RETRIEVE CUSTOMER DATA
        DISPLAY DELETE CONFIRMATION WINDOW
        IF CONFIRM
          DELETE RECORD
          MESSAGE = 'RECORD DELETED'
         ELSE
          MESSAGE = 'RECORD NOT DELETED'
        ENDIF
        CLEAR DATA FIELDS
      ELSE
        DISPLAY ERROR WINDOW-CUSTOMER NUMBER NOT ON FILE
    ENDIF
ENDDO
```

```
        *** CONFIRM DELETE ***

          DO YOU REALLY WANT TO
          DELETE THIS RECORD


    [NO]                        [YES]
```

```
          *** ERROR ***

      CUSTOMER NUMBER NOT ON FILE
      ENTER ANOTHER CUSTOMER NUMBER

        PRESS ANY KEY TO CONTINUE
```

22-12 The delete customer pseudocode and error windows.

The code for the delete window and menu is derived from the change program, with some subtle changes. This pseudocode shows that most of the processing occurs after the record is viewed. Several IF statements and menus control the final processing.

Retrieving and viewing the record

Displayed in Fig. 22-13 is the program code for the CUSTDEL program module. The system begins very similarly to the change routine. A window is opened and the customer number requested. If the customer number is blank, the program returns to the customer menu program. If the customer number is found, then the screen is displayed.

There are no GETs in the code. When you are about to delete a record, there is no reason to make changes to it. A READ statement acts like the WAIT command that pauses the program without displaying a message. Actually, a message to press any key is displayed near the top of the screen. Because you don't want to obscure the users' view of the screen when they are about to choose to delete the record, you must let them look at the whole screen. The message is written to line 20, where messages have been previously written to tell the user the record was successfully added or changed.

This takes care of the display part of the code. Once this happens, the task of deciding if the user really wants to delete the record begins.

The Delete post-processor

After the screen is viewed, the user presses a key. First, the message is cleared with the statement after the READ statement. Next, the bell is sounded to get the user's attention. Some SET statements determine the tone and frequency of the bell. This actually allows you to play music to really get their attention. See your dBASE manual for those ideas.

A menu must be defined before it can be used. This menu is called "yesno" and you are going to see a lot of it in later programs. It is defined each time it is used; however, once it is defined, it is always in memory until the program terminates. This could have been defined in the AJAXMAIN module, because it is actually a common routine. The menu is a simple bar menu:

```
DEFINE MENU yesno
DEFINE PAD no OF yesno PROMPT "[NO]" AT 6,2
ON SELECTION PAD no OF yesno DEACTIVATE MENU
DEFINE PAD yes OF yesno PROMPT "[YES]" AT 6,30
ON SELECTION PAD yes OF yesno DO DELETE
```

The two pads are [NO] and [YES]. By placing the menu choices in brackets, you make it easier for the user to see them. There is nothing special about the brackets. The [NO] selection comes first as the default. When you are deleting something, you want to make sure the user can't simply press Enter too fast

```
*********************************************************************
* Program......: CUSTDEL.PRG
* Author.......: Cary N. Prague
* Date.........: 9-05-88, Revision 12-26-88 REVISION 02-26-92
* Module #.....: 1.1.3
* dBASE Ver....: IV 1.5
* Description..: AJAX APPLIANCE COMPANY CUSTOMER DELETION SCREEN
*********************************************************************
ACTIVATE WINDOW data3
CLEAR
STORE SPACE(6) TO csn
DO WHILE .T.
  @ 2,19 TO 19,57 DOUBLE
  @ 3,26 SAY "AJAX APPLIANCE COMPANY"
  @ 4,26 SAY "  CUSTOMER DELETIONS"
  @ 5,20 SAY "─────────────────────────────────"
  @ 6,23 SAY " Customer Number"
  @ 6,41 GET csn PICTURE "@! XX-999" ;
    MESSAGE "Enter a Customer Number to Delete or Press <Enter> to Return"
  READ
  IF csn = '        ' .OR. csn = '   -   '
      CLEAR
      DEACTIVATE WINDOW data3
      RETURN
  ELSE
      SEEK TRIM(CSN)
      IF FOUND()
          @ 7,20 SAY "─────────────────────────────────"
          @ 9,24 SAY "Company"
          @ 9,34 SAY company PICTURE "@!20"
          @ 10,24 SAY "Street"
          @ 10,34 SAY street PICTURE "@! XXXXXXXXXXXXXXXXXXXX"
          @ 11,24 SAY "City"
          @ 11,34 SAY city PICTURE "@! XXXXXXXXXXXXXXXXXXXX"
          @ 12,24 SAY "State/Zip"
          @ 12,34 SAY state
          @ 12,38 SAY zip PICTURE "99999-####"
          @ 14,20 SAY "─────────────────────────────────"
          @ 15,24 SAY "Telephone Number"
          @ 15,41 SAY phone PICTURE "(###)999-9999"
          @ 16,24 SAY "Last Transaction"
          @ 16,41 SAY lst_txnd
          @ 17,24 SAY "Discount Percent"
          @ 17,41 SAY discount PICTURE "99"
          @ 18,24 SAY "Taxable Flag"
          @ 18,41 SAY taxable PICTURE "L"
          @ 20,23 SAY '*** PRESS ANY KEY TO CONTINUE *** '
          READ
          @ 20,1
          ?? CHR(7)
          DEFINE MENU yesno
          DEFINE PAD no OF yesno PROMPT "[NO]" AT 6,2
          ON SELECTION PAD no OF yesno DEACTIVATE MENU
          DEFINE PAD yes OF yesno PROMPT "[YES]" AT 6,30
          ON SELECTION PAD yes OF yesno DO DELETE
          ACTIVATE WINDOW msg2
          @ 1,05 SAY '  *** CONFIRM DELETE ***    '
          @ 3,05 SAY '   DO YOU REALLY WANT TO    '
          @ 4,05 SAY '    DELETE THIS RECORD      '
          ACTIVATE menu yesno
          DEACTIVATE WINDOW msg2
          @ 8,10 CLEAR TO 21,70
          STORE SPACE(6) TO CSN
```

22-13 The customer delete program.

```
      ELSE
      ?? CHR(7)
      ACTIVATE WINDOW msg1
      @ 1,05 SAY '        *** ERROR ***'
      @ 3,05 SAY ' CUSTOMER NUMBER NOT ON FILE'
      @ 4,05 SAY 'ENTER ANOTHER CUSTOMER NUMBER'
      @ 5,1  SAY ' '
      WAIT "         PRESS ANY KEY TO CONTINUE"
      DEACTIVATE WINDOW msg1
      STORE SPACE(6) TO CSN
    ENDIF
  ENDIF
  CLEAR
ENDDO

PROCEDURE DELETE
  DELETE
  CLEAR
  @ 1,5 SAY  ' *** CUSTOMER DELETED ***       '
  @ 3,1
  WAIT "         PRESS ANY KEY TO CONTINUE"
  DEACTIVATE MENU
  RETURN
```

and accidentally delete the record. This way, the user must consciously move the cursor to the right to [YES]. Figure 22-14 shows this window and menu on the screen.

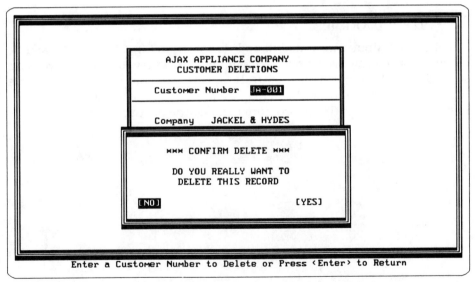

22-14 The delete confirmation window and menu.

The ON SELECTION PAD statement is used to define the actions. Unlike the main bar menu which uses ON PAD, you are not activating a pop-up here, you are choosing an action. If the choice is no, you deactivate the menu which closes the menu and continues processing beyond the ACTIVATE MENU command. If the user wants to delete the record, a subprocedure is run to do this and informs the user of that action.

Once the menu is defined the "msg2" window is activated. This window is slightly larger than the "msg" window, so there is room for the menu in the window. The text is written to the window telling the user to confirm the delete action. The menu is then activated. Notice there is no WAIT command as you have seen previously. The idea of a WAIT command is to pause processing. A menu on the screen does this as it waits for the user's response.

The two menu choices either close the menu and processing continues or the DELETE subprocedure is invoked. Let's look at Fig. 22-13 again. At the bottom of the program code is the DELETE procedure which deletes the record and changes the message inside the window. A WAIT pauses processing. The CLEAR command following the DELETE command also removes the menu from the window. Without the DEACTIVATE menu command, the menu would reappear after Enter is pressed.

After the menu is deactivated, control returns to the statement following the menu activation. This next statement deactivates the window, clears the display portion of the screen, and clears the CSN memory variable. The next record for deletion can then be entered.

The "customer not found" logic is unchanged from the customer change routine.

The View module

Finally, the customer view module code is shown in Fig. 22-15. This module is the simplest of all the code of the customer data entry routines. As you can see in Fig. 22-15, there are no new techniques here. The customer number is input, the record is retrieved and displayed, and processing continues. This is exactly like the CUSTDEL program without the post-processor.

```
*********************************************************************
* Program......: CUSTVEW.PRG
* Author.......: Cary N. Prague
* Date.........: 9-04-88, Final Revision 12-26-88 Revision 3-12-92
* Module #.....: 1.1.4
* dBASE Ver....: IV 1.5
* Description..: AJAX APPLIANCE COMPANY CUSTOMER VIEW SCREEN
*********************************************************************
ACTIVATE WINDOW data3
STORE SPACE(6) TO csn
DO WHILE .T.
   @ 2,19 TO 19,57 DOUBLE
   @ 3,26 SAY "AJAX APPLIANCE COMPANY"
   @ 4,26 SAY "    CUSTOMER VIEW"
   @ 5,20 SAY "─────────────────────────────────"
   @ 6,23 SAY " Customer Number"
   @ 6,41 GET csn PICTURE "@! XX-999" ;
      MESSAGE "Enter a Customer Number to View or Press <Enter> to Return"
   READ
   IF csn = '        ' .OR. csn = '    -    '
       CLEAR
       DEACTIVATE WINDOW data3
       RETURN
     ELSE
       SEEK TRIM(CSN)
       IF FOUND()
          @ 7,20 SAY "─────────────────────────────────"
          @ 9,24 SAY "Company"
          @ 9,34 SAY company PICTURE "@!20"
          @ 10,24 SAY "Street"
          @ 10,34 SAY street PICTURE "@! XXXXXXXXXXXXXXXXXXXX"
          @ 11,24 SAY "City"
          @ 11,34 SAY city PICTURE "@! XXXXXXXXXXXXXXXXXXXX"
          @ 12,24 SAY "State/Zip"
          @ 12,34 SAY state
          @ 12,38 SAY zip PICTURE "99999-####"
          @ 14,20 SAY "─────────────────────────────────"
          @ 15,24 SAY "Telephone Number"
          @ 15,41 SAY phone PICTURE "(###)999-9999"
          @ 16,24 SAY "Last Transaction"
          @ 16,41 SAY lst_txnd
          @ 17,24 SAY "Discount Percent"
          @ 17,41 SAY discount PICTURE "99"
          @ 18,24 SAY "Taxable Flag"
          @ 18,41 SAY taxable PICTURE "L"
          @ 20,23 SAY '*** PRESS ANY KEY TO CONTINUE *** '
          READ
          STORE SPACE(6) TO CSN
        ELSE
          ?? CHR(7)
          ACTIVATE WINDOW msg1
          @ 1,05 SAY '       *** ERROR ***'
          @ 3,05 SAY ' CUSTOMER NUMBER NOT ON FILE'
          @ 4,05 SAY 'ENTER ANOTHER CUSTOMER NUMBER'
          @ 5,1  SAY ' '
          WAIT "        PRESS ANY KEY TO CONTINUE"
          DEACTIVATE WINDOW msg1
          STORE SPACE(6) TO CSN
       ENDIF
   ENDIF
   CLEAR
ENDDO
```

22-15 The customer view program.

23

User-defined functions for data validation

In the previous chapters, you have seen how to program file maintenance programs for adding, deleting, changing, and viewing customer file data. You can set them up as separate program files, as we did with the customer file processing, or you can have them all in one program, as you will soon see with the inventory programs. dBASE IV has the flexibility to process your files as you feel most comfortable programming.

In this section, there are some file validation processing options that are more advanced than what has been presented thus far. They are various methods of using User-Defined Functions (UDFs) to provide the programmer with additional file processing tools to add to file maintenance programs and to potentially reduce the amount of code in the programs.

First, let us look at what UDFs are and how they work. Then, we will look at a few ways to use UDFs to enhance your file processing programs.

What is a UDF?

Although Borland has added a number of powerful functions to dBASE IV, you, as a programmer, will have occasion to require additional functions that are specific to the application you are developing. The purpose of a UDF is to help you to standardize many of the repetitious routines within your system while reducing the overall size of your code.

You should use a UDF as opposed to a procedure when the performance of the operation must return a specific value. There are some restrictions that Borland puts on UDFs. For example, they cannot contain any macro (&) commands, COPY commands, or DEFINE commands.

User-Defined Functions (UDFs) are stored as procedures and can be stored in a procedure file to allow all programs within a system to have access to them. The procedure file is identified in the main program with the SET PROCEDURE TO command. Menu UDFs are simply placed at the bottom of individual programs. They are differentiated from the main program with the keyword FUNCTION, which begins every UDF.

A UDF is called from a main program using the same syntax as the functions included with dBASE IV. The function acts on parameters passed from the main program, then returns a value to the calling program.

In the example in Fig. 23-1, the main program calls a function to determine the cube of a number called simply a. It is passed to the function CUBE. The cubed value is returned to the calling program and placed in the proper place in the @ SAY command. A function is used because the program code in the function can be used over and over again. This way, when the function needs to be changed, it has to be changed in only one place.

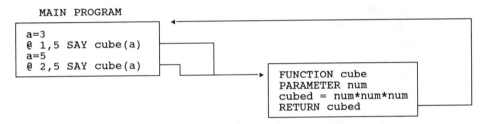

23-1 Calling a user defined function.

In the example, the first call passes a value of 3 to the function, which cubes it and returns the value of 27. The second call to the function passes a value of 5 and returns a value of 125.

Functions can be used for numeric, character, date, or logical parameter passing. A function need not have a parameter passed at all. Likewise, functions need to return only a logical .T. or .F. instead of a value.

In the examples in this chapter, you will see how a User-Defined Function can be used to center a string of text, create a pop-up menu of values to choose from, and create a browse table of multiple values to be used in validating a data entry error.

Centering text with a UDF

User-defined functions can be used to manipulate text strings. When displaying or printing character strings, it occasionally is necessary to center the text in a given area, such as the printing or displaying of a title.

UDFs can be passed more than one parameter. The UDF in Fig. 23-2 will accept any character string and center it in a larger character string, whose length is passed as the second parameter. It will append the proper number of spaces to the front of the text string so that it will be centered.

Main Program:

```
X="Customer Additions"
@ 1,0 SAY CENT(X,80)
```

Function Syntax:

```
FUNCTION cent                    && Function Name
PARAMETER ms,max                 && message and max length
   ms=ltrim(rtrim(ms))           && remove blanks on either side
   y = REPLACE(' ',(max-LEN(ms))/2) + ms   && Add spaces to center
RETURN y
```

23-2 A UDF to center a string.

The function CENT first removes any leading or trailing blanks from the passed string. It then inserts enough blanks in front of the text string to center it.

A string such as Customer Additions is 18 characters long. This string must be centered in an 80-character area. The center of an 80-character area is 40. Therefore, the center of the string must end within one character of the fortieth position.

The length of the trimmed string is determined to be 18. The formula (maxLEN(MS))/2 in this example equals $((80 - 18)/2) = 31$. So, 31 blanks are inserted in front of the string. The string is 18 characters long, so the center of the string falls squarely on the 40th position.

By using a formula to center text strings, you can alleviate the necessity of sitting and counting the proper number of spaces necessary for centering any text string.

Using a predefined function for data validation

In the customer file processing of the Ajax Appliance System, the program code in Fig. 23-3 was used in the customer additions program (CUSTADD-.PRG) to go to the Customer File and check to see if the customer number entered already was on file. It works fine and is a totally acceptable programming practice.

This approach processes the addition as long as the customer number (csn) was not found on the file. If it is found, then a window is opened and a message is sent to the operator saying that the number already is on file and must be corrected before going any further. This message is displayed after all fields have been entered onto the screen. However, this program code does not check for the duplicate key until after the entire screen is filled out.

A better way is to check for the duplicate key immediately after the customer number field is entered. If a function is used within the VALID statement of the GET instruction, the check is made before the cursor leaves the field. In the statement in the next paragraph, the customer number is checked as soon as it is entered as opposed to waiting until the whole record is entered before validating the number as in the customer add program.

```
@ 6,41 GET csn PICTURE "@! XX-999" ;
    MESSAGE "Enter a new customer number or <PgDn> to Return"

SEEK TRIM(CSN)              && Check for Duplicate Key on File

IF .NOT. FOUND()           && No Duplicate Found - Add New key
    APPEND BLANK
    REPLACE STATEMENTS .....
    MEMORY VARIABLE CLEAR
  ELSE                      && Duplicate Found - Display Error
    ?? CHR(7)
    ACTIVATE WINDOW msg1
    @ 1,05 SAY '       *** ERROR ***'
    @ 3,05 SAY 'CUSTOMER NUMBER ALREADY ON FILE'
    @ 4,05 SAY 'ENTER A NEW CUSTOMER NUMBER'
    @ 5,1  SAY ' '
    WAIT "       PRESS ANY KEY TO CONTINUE"
    DEACTIVATE WINDOW msg1
ENDIF
```

23-3 A program for duplicate key checking.

dBASE IV has a SEEK( ) function (which is very different from the SEEK command used in Fig. 23-3) that can be used within the VALID statement of a GET to verify that the code entered is not already in the database file. The syntax is simply:

```
@ 10,10 GET custno VALID .NOT. SEEK(custno, "customer") ;
    ERROR "Customer Number Already On File"
```

This statement will take the customer number entered and check that the key entered in custno is not in the associated file that is open for the alias customer. The .NOT. parameter returns the .F. state to the VALID if the SEEK is successful (the customer number is already found). If the number entered is already on file, the error message in the ERROR parameter will be displayed at the bottom of the screen.

When the operator presses the Spacebar to clear the message, the program automatically loops back to the customer number entry field so the operator can correct the number.

By using this validation method, the programmer can save a block of code in the program and give the operator immediate validation of the code entered. This is a good enhancement for validating that a key field does not already exist when adding new data keys.

In the change, view, and delete processing, the .NOT. would be removed to allow for validation that the customer number entered is on file so the rest of the data can be retrieved and edited, deleted, or viewed.

This however presents a more interesting problem. When validating a key field to make sure it is there (used in change, delete, or view) what should you do when the requested record is not found? Displaying an error message is not sufficient. You should show the user a list of valid keys to choose from. In the rest of this chapter, you will use UDFs to pop up a single field menu of customer numbers and a multi-field browse table of customer numbers and customer names.

Creating a pop-up list of values with a UDF

This problem can be solved not only by validating that the customer number entered is on file, but also by displaying a pop-up menu of customer numbers if the customer number is not on file. Figure 23-4 shows an enhanced version of the customer change program. If you have purchased the data disk, this program is on the disk and is called CUSTCHGP.

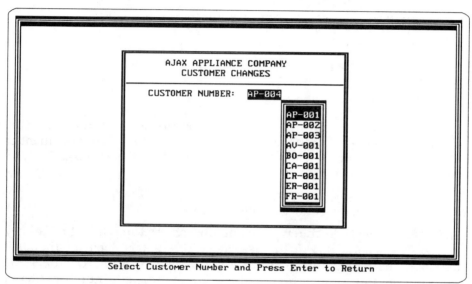

23-4 A screen showing a pop-up menu of choices.

To do this, you need a UDF. The CUSTCHG program is changed to replace the GET instruction for customer number. The new instruction is:

```
@ 6,41 GET csn PICTURE "@! XX-999" VALID GETCUS(csn) ;
    MESSAGE "Enter Customer Number or Press Enter to Return"
```

The UDF must check to see if the value is found before creating and displaying the pop-up menu. If the value is found there is no need to display the pop-up.

A UDF called GETCUS must be created to pop up the menu if the record is not found. Figure 23-5 shows this entire UDF.

The function begins with the FUNCTION keyword. One PARAMETER is passed called cnum in the UDF even though it is called csn in the main program. The names do not have to match, only the field types and values do.

Next, the CUSTOMER database file is checked to see if the value entered is found. If it is, the UDF ends and the value is validated by returning a .T.

```
FUNCTION getcus          && The function name
   PARAMETER cnum        && The parameter receiving the customer number
   SEEK TRIM(cnum)       && Finding the customer number
   IF FOUND()
      RETURN .t.         && The record was found
   ENDIF
   SET BORDER TO DOUBLE
   DEFINE POPUP cust FROM 7,47 TO 17,54
   cnt = 1
   GO TOP
   SCAN
      DEFINE BAR cnt OF cust PROMPT CUSTNO
      cnt = cnt + 1
   ENDSCAN
   ON SELECTION POPUP cust DEACTIVATE POPUP
   * Activate the popup menu
   SET MESSAGE TO 'Select Customer Number and Press Enter to Return'
   ACTIVATE POPUP cust
   IF BAR() = 0
      RETURN .f.
   ENDIF
   SEEK PROMPT()
   csn = custno
RETURN .T.
```

23-5 UDF to display a pop-up menu of choices.

from the UDF. The record then can be displayed. It is assumed that the CUSTOMER database file is open and that the index order is set to the CUSTNO field.

Once it is determined that the value is not found, the pop-up can be created and displayed. Notice that there is no ELSE as part of the program that checks for the existence of the key. This is because the RETURN ends the UDF. If the data is not found, the program continues without executing the first RETURN, so no ELSE statement is needed.

The pop-up is created dynamically by using a SCAN...ENDSCAN construct to read every value in the database and creating a separate bar of the pop-up for each record found. A SCAN...ENDSCAN is equivalent to all the following code:

```
GO TOP
DO WHILE .NOT. EOF ( )
   statements go here
   SKIP
ENDDO
```

When a SCAN is used, the database automatically is positioned at the top of the file and no SKIP is needed. Unless the SCAN command has a FOR or WHILE clause to limit the scope of the SCAN, it will begin with the first record in the database and continue until all of the records are processed. In dBASE IV 1.5, you should use a SCAN in place of a DO WHILE when reading the entire database. SCAN also issues an automatic skip between every record.

In this example, the program code in Fig. 23-6 creates a pop-up containing the customer numbers. First, a pop-up is DEFINEd from 7,47 to 17,54. The size of the pop-up is determined by the user to fit the width of the data and the bottom border of the screen. Once the pop-up menu itself is created, the bars must be created. This is done dynamically using the SCAN. The first BAR would be defined with the statement:

DEFINE BAR 1 OF cust PROMPT 'AP-001'

The statement is created by using the variable cnt to determine the bar number and the variable custno to determine the bar prompt. This continues for each of the records in the database by using the SCAN.

```
SET BORDER TO DOUBLE
DEFINE POPUP cust FROM 7,47 TO 17,54
cnt = 1
SCAN
 DEFINE BAR cnt OF cust PROMPT CUSTNO
 cnt = cnt + 1
ENDSCAN
```

23-6 Defining the pop-up.

Once the pop-up is defined, the action is determined when the selection is made. The action is to deactivate the pop-up and remove it from the screen with the DEACTIVATE pop-up command.

The pop-up then is activated with the ACTIVATE pop-up command. The value of BAR( ) is checked to make sure that a selection was made. If no selection is made, the value of BAR( ) is 0 and an .F. is returned to the program. A message that invalid input was entered is displayed, and the program will continue until a valid choice is made.

Finally, a SEEK command is used to position the record pointer on the chosen record in the database file. When the operator selects a pop-up menu bar, he or she is selecting only a copy of the data that was used to build the pop-up bars. This does not actually move the record pointer in the database file. The command SEEK PROMPT( ) is used because the PROMPT( ) function is used to retrieve the value of the prompt, which happens to be the customer number. If customer number 'AP-001' was selected, then SEEK 'AP-001' would position the CUSTOMER file record pointer to that specific record. The value of the database field custno then can be transferred to the memory variable csn so the rest of the data can be retrieved in the main program.

The pop-up method is very helpful for the operator, so he or she can see all the customer numbers that are on file. However, it might be even more helpful if not only the customer number is displayed, but the company name as well. To do this, you can modify the previous UDF, changing the pop-up menu to a pop-up browse table, showing both fields on the screen for reference.

Creating a browse table to see multiple values

Figure 23-7 shows an enhanced version of the customer change program. The program is found on the optional data disk as CUSTCHGB.

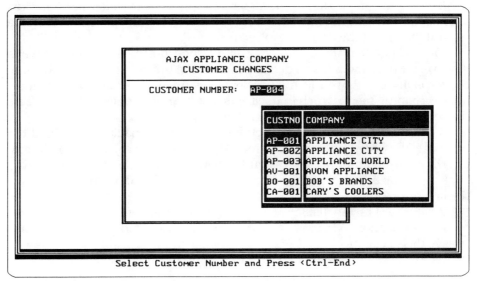

23-7 Using a browse table.

The program is very similar to the program to create the pop-up. The calling parameter is the same except that the name of the UDF is changed in case it is placed in a central library. The UDF is called with the statement:

@ 6,41 GET csn PICTURE "@! XX-999" VALID GETCUS2(csn) ;
   MESSAGE "Enter Customer Number or Press Enter to Return"

The call works the same as the pop-up call. The UDF GETCUS2 is called when the customer number is entered and the value of the memory variable csn is passed to the UDF. The entire UDF is shown in Fig. 23-8.

```
FUNCTION getcus2
  PARAMETER cnum
  SELECT customer
  SEEK TRIM(cnum)
  IF FOUND()
    RETURN .t.
  ENDIF
  DEFINE WINDOW custbrow FROM 9,44 TO 18,74 DOUBLE
  GO TOP
  SET MESSAGE TO 'Select Customer Number and Press <Ctrl-End>'
  BROWSE WINDOW custbrow FIELDS custno, company FREEZE custno
  IF .NOT. EOF()
    cnum=custno
  ENDIF
RETURN .T.
```

23-8 UDF to display a browse window of choices.

The UDF begins with the parameter passing. The database file is checked to see if the entered customer number is found. If it is, the program returns a .T. and the rest of the data is displayed.

Once it is determined that the value is not found, the Browse table is displayed. First, a window is defined to hold the browse table. A double-line border is displayed around the window. A window must be used because, unlike a pop-up menu which in itself acts like a window, a Browse table clears the screen and must be displayed in a window.

The GO TOP command moves the record pointer back to the top of the database file. Because the attempt to find a matching record was unsuccessful, the record pointer is currently at the bottom of the file. It must be moved back to the top or else, when the browse table is displayed, it would show only the last record.

A message is set to display at the bottom of the screen to tell the user how to make a selection. A browse table requires the Ctrl–End keys to be pressed to save the selection.

The browse table is defined with the command:

BROWSE WINDOW custbrow FIELDS custno, company FREEZE custno

The Browse table is displayed in the window CUSTBROW and displays the fields custno and company. The FREEZE parameter is used to keep the cursor in the custno field. This way the cursor cannot be moved into the company field name.

When the user presses Ctrl–End, the value of the customer number is returned to the main program. In the pop-up menu example, the record pointer had to be positioned on the chosen record in the database file. Unlike the pop-up menu, which uses only a copy of the data, the Browse table displays the actual records and the record is correctly positioned when the line in the Browse table is chosen.

The Browse table is very important when needing a cross reference of more than one field. When dealing with abstract key fields like a customer number, part number, or social security number, you need to show more than one field to understand the data. Customer name, part name, description, and price, or employee name and department are big helps in identifying the right record.

Asking questions with a UDF

A final UDF can be added to these programs to make sure that all the data was correctly entered before leaving the data entry screen. The UDFs described in this section remove a lot of operator interaction coding in a system by having the program pass the questions and answers to a generalized routine.

Throughout an application, various questions are asked of an operator, such as Is the Data OK?, Add More Records?, or Are You Sure? An easy way to eliminate repetitious coding such as this is to use a UDF to ask these questions. The code in Fig. 23-9 illustrates a way of asking a question of the operator, then, based upon the answer given, to perform an action.

```
IF ques("Is Everything Correct?")
   EXIT
ENDIF


FUNCTION ques
 PARAMETER msg
 DEFINE WINDOW message FROM 18,20 TO 20,58 DOUBLE
 ACTIV WIND message
 PRIV yn
 yn='Y'
 @ 0,2 SAY msg + "? (Y/N) " GET yn PICT "Y"
 READ
 DEACT WIND message
 RELEASE WINDOW message
 IF yn="Y"
    RETURN .T.
 ENDIF
RETURN .F.
```

23-9 UDF to ask a question.

Each time a question must be asked of the operator, the code containing the appropriate question must be written. Any text can be entered in the parameter to the function QUES.

The calling statement in Fig. 23-9 passes the question Is Everything Correct to the function QUES( ). The UDF will pass back an .F. if the operator answers with an N and .T. if the answer was Y.

By placing the previous UDF in your procedure file, you can eliminate repetitious coding in your system as well as add to your system a common look and feel to all error and question processing. When an operator sees a box appear at the bottom of the screen, he or she knows right away that a message is being sent or a question is being asked. This UDF also is found in the CUSTCHGB program.

As can be seen, there are no limits to the code that can be included within a UDF. You can keep it simple or make it as complex as you like, depending upon your needs. There are many possibilities to improve and enhance your dBASE IV programs using User-Defined Functions. The uses are limited only by your imagination. They are a powerful addition to a powerful language.

24
Alternate data-entry methods for the inventory

Now that you have seen the customer data entry system, turn your attention to another data entry system—the inventory system. The inventory system is another single file data entry system. Unlike the invoice system presented in chapter 26, the inventory system uses only one file. In chapter 22, you saw how each module of the customer system was separate. You also noticed that a lot of the code was exactly the same. We can take advantage of this and devise a data entry system that uses only one module. All of the common code is left common with the pre- and post-processors controlled by the one module.

The Inventory menu

Before we start that coding, let's see the inventory menu and see how it differs from the customer menu. Figure 24-1 shows the screen that the menu produces.

As you can see, this screen looks just like the customer menu. It has an add, change, delete, view, and an exit option. In fact, from the screen, you can't tell anything is different.

Examine the menu code in Fig. 24-2 to see how it differs. Again, the code starts by clearing the screen. The main menu screen already has been saved in the main menu module.

Like in the customer system, the border is set to none and a pop-up is created that fills most of the screen. The odd numbered items which are blank are skipped with the SKIP parameter.

The one ON SELECTION statement, which is normal for a pop-up, calls the INVTPICK when a selection is chosen.

```
                    AJAX APPLIANCE COMPANY
                    INVENTORY DATA ENTRY




                ┌────────────────────────────┐
                │        ADD NEW ITEM         │
                └────────────────────────────┘
                    CHANGE ITEM INFORMATION

                        DELETE AN ITEM

                    VIEW ITEM INFORMATION

                  EXIT INVENTORY DATA ENTRY




            Choose a selection from the Inventory Menu
```

24-1   The inventory data entry menu.

Finally, the title is written at the top of the screen, and the menu is activated.

What is different about this menu is the procedure. In the customer system, each item in the menu has a separate CASE statement. Here, there is one statement for all of the data entry choices, and one for the exit routine which deactivates the pop-up. The CASE statement uses .OR. to select the choices 1,3,5, or 7. When that choice is made, the data window is activated (the full-size window without a border) and the INVTDTEN (Inventory Data Entry) program is called.

Notice the DO statement:

```
DO INVTDTEN WITH BAR( )
```

This is a new parameter you haven't learned yet. The WITH parameter passes a value to the called program—in this case, the value of BAR( ). That means that a 1,3,5, or 7 is passed to the INVTDTEN program, depending on what the value of BAR( ) was. Remember, the value of BAR( ) is determined by which bar the highlight is on in the inventory pop-up menu when Enter is pressed.

That takes care of the menu. Now on to data entry.

Integrating format files and your code

In chapter 12, you saw the data entry forms. In fact, you created an inventory data entry form. In this part of the chapter, we are going to modify the code that was automatically generated by the Forms work surface, and then we will use the code for the inventory data entry. You will see how easy it can be to integrate format files and your code.

```
*************************************************************************
* Program......: INVTMENU.PRG
* Author.......: Cary N. Prague
* Date.........: 9-25-88, Final Revision 12-26-88 Revised 3-12-92
* Module #.....: 3.1
* dBASE Ver....: IV 1.5
* Description..: AJAX APPLIANCE COMPANY INVENTORY MAIN MENU
*************************************************************************
CLEAR
SET BORDER TO NONE
SET COLOR TO W+/B,W+/R
DEFINE POPUP INVMENU FROM 8,25 TO 18,51 ;
MESSAGE "Choose a selection from the Inventory Menu"
DEFINE BAR 1 OF INVMENU PROMPT "        ADD NEW ITEM          "
DEFINE BAR 2 OF INVMENU PROMPT "                              " SKIP
DEFINE BAR 3 OF INVMENU PROMPT " CHANGE ITEM INFORMATION "
DEFINE BAR 4 OF INVMENU PROMPT "                              " SKIP
DEFINE BAR 5 OF INVMENU PROMPT "       DELETE AN ITEM         "
DEFINE BAR 6 OF INVMENU PROMPT "                              " SKIP
DEFINE BAR 7 OF INVMENU PROMPT "   VIEW ITEM INFORMATION "
DEFINE BAR 8 OF INVMENU PROMPT "                              " SKIP
DEFINE BAR 9 OF INVMENU PROMPT "EXIT INVENTORY DATA ENTRY"
ON SELECTION POPUP INVMENU DO INVTPICK

@ 1,29 SAY "AJAX APPLIANCE COMPANY"
@ 2,29 SAY " INVENTORY DATA ENTRY"

ACTIVATE POPUP INVMENU

RETURN

PROCEDURE INVTPICK
  DO CASE
    CASE BAR() = 1  .OR. BAR() = 3 .OR. BAR() = 5 .OR. BAR() = 7
      SET BORDER TO SINGLE
      SAVE SCREEN TO invtp
      CLEAR
      DO INVTDTEN WITH BAR()
      RESTORE SCREEN FROM invtp
    CASE BAR() = 9
      DEACTIVATE POPUP
  ENDCASE
SET BORDER TO DOUBLE
RETURN
```

24-2 The inventory data entry menu program.

A lot of time has been spent designing this system. One thing that years of experience will teach you is that the simpler and smaller something is, the easier it should be to work with. After creating hundreds of programs with separate add, change, display, and delete modules, you may want to create one integrated module.

With dBASE IV, you will want to use a format file for data entry. The biggest complaint about using a format file for new additions to the database is that the system couldn't recognize if a record had already been entered. The reverse problem occurs when you try to use a format file for changing, deleting, or displaying data. When you enter the key field, you need the rest of the record to be displayed. Format files do not do that automatically like the code in the customer system does.

In Fig. 24-3, you can see the screen that was created in chapter 12. By using the database INVENTRY, setting the format file, and entering the command APPEND, you can quickly test the format file:

```
USE INVENTRY
SET FORMAT TO INVENTRY
APPEND
```

The screen in Fig. 24-3 comes into view. Let's now examine the modified format file code that you will use when you integrate the format file into your

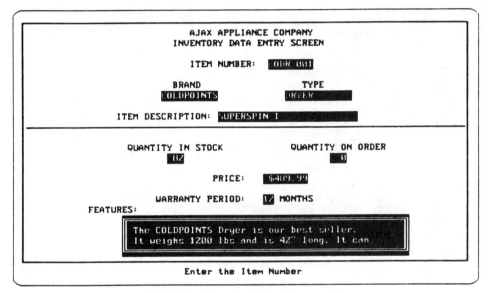

24-3 The inventory data entry screen.

program to add, change, display, and delete data. The modified format file is shown in Fig. 24-4.

Two sections of the format file were removed. When you create a format file from a screen form, several sections of code are generated. The first section, which is not shown in Fig. 24-4, is the 'Format file initialization code.' This code is actually housekeeping statements. A series of IF statements checks to see whether the status bar was on or off, and whether or not the system was processing in color when the screen was created. The code which has been removed, sets the environment to that state. However, when you integrate your format file into a program, you don't want the system resetting the environment.

The next section of the code (and the first section in Fig. 24-4) is a one line entry that creates a window that is used for the data entry of the memo field FEATURES.

```
************************************************************************
* Program......: INVENTRY.FMT
* Author.......: Cary N. Prague
* Date.........: 9-25-88, Final Revision 12-26-88 Revised 3-12-92
* Module #.....: ---
* dBASE Ver....: IV 1.5
* Description..: AJAX APPLIANCE COMPANY INVENTORY DATA ENTRY FORM
************************************************************************

*-- Window for memo field features.
DEFINE WINDOW Wndow1 FROM 19,18 TO 22,68 DOUBLE

*-- @ SAY GETS Processing. ----------------------------------------------------

*--   Format Page: 1

@ 0,0 TO 23,79
@ 1,30 SAY "AJAX APPLIANCE COMPANY"
@ 2,27 SAY "INVENTORY DATA ENTRY SCREEN"
@ 4,30 SAY "ITEM NUMBER:"
@ 4,44 SAY itemno PICTURE "@! AAAA-999" ;
   MESSAGE "Enter the Item Number"
@ 6,27 SAY "BRAND"
@ 6,50 SAY "TYPE"
@ 7,25 GET brand PICTURE "XXXXXXXXXX" ;
   MESSAGE "Enter a Brand Name"
@ 7,47 GET type PICTURE "@M REFRIGERATOR,DISHWASHER,WASHER,DRYER,RANGE,MICROWAVE
   MESSAGE "Press <spacebar> to Select a Type"
@ 9,17 SAY "ITEM DESCRIPTION:"
@ 9,35 GET desc PICTURE "XXXXXXXXXXXXXXXXXXXXXXXXXX" ;
   MESSAGE "Enter a Description for the Item"
@ 10,1 TO 10,78
@ 12,19 SAY "QUANTITY IN STOCK"
@ 12,48 SAY "QUANTITY ON ORDER"
@ 13,26 GET qty_stk PICTURE "999" ;
   RANGE -200,999 ;
   MESSAGE "Enter the Quantity in Stock"
@ 13,55 GET qty_ord PICTURE "999" ;
   RANGE 0,750 ;
   MESSAGE "Enter the Quantity On Order"
@ 15,34 SAY "PRICE:"
@ 15,43 GET price PICTURE "@$ 99999.99" ;
   RANGE 50,1999 ;
   VALID PRICE >= 50 .AND. PRICE <= 1999 ;
   ERROR "Price must be between $50 and $1999" ;
   MESSAGE "Enter the Price for the Item"
@ 17,24 SAY "WARRANTY PERIOD:"
@ 17,43 GET warranty PICTURE "99" ;
   RANGE 0,24 ;
   VALID WARRANTY >= 0 .AND. WARRANTY <= 24 ;
   ERROR "The length of the warranty is invalid " ;
   DEFAULT 12 ;
   MESSAGE "Enter the warranty period in months"
@ 17,46 SAY "MONTHS"
@ 18,12 SAY "FEATURES:"
@ 19,18 GET features OPEN WINDOW Wndow1
RELEASE WINDOWS Wndow1
```

24-4 The inventory file format file.

The middle section of code, which is unchanged in this figure, is called the '@ SAY GETs Processing.' This is simply the SAYs and GETs that make up the screen. It includes the text, fields, and picture templates and functions. It also includes the lines and boxes that are drawn on the screen. The last line in the code opens the memo window that was defined in the first section. When you place the cursor in the memo window and press Ctrl–Home, the window allows data entry. If you press it again, it expands to full screen size.

There is nothing in the format files @ SAYs or GETs that you haven't already seen in the customer file, so we will skip a detailed explanation.

Another section of code is generated that is not in the figure. After the SAY and GET section is a section that is called 'Format file exit code.' It performs the opposite of the initialization code; it resets the environment to its original state before the format file was run. By removing both the front and back parts of the code, we take control of the environment. It's not important for you at this time to know what is in those missing statements. We'll save that for a future learning experience.

Besides the change to the format file to remove the initialization and exit code, there is one more subtle change. The key field ITEMNO line has been changed to an @ SAY from an @ GET. When you code the routine that uses this format file, you will not allow the changing of the key field so you can maintain control. As you will see in the next section, a blank record is added to the file, then the key field is updated, and then the format file is used to add or change the other data items.

Combining ADD, CHANGE, DELETE, and DISPLAY

Now that you have used the Forms work surface to create your format file and have gone into the code to slightly modify it, you are ready to create a program to combine the functions of add, change, display, and delete and still give yourself complete control over testing for duplicate records or a record that should already exist. We begin by examining the pseudocode you created in chapter 4, as shown in Fig. 24-5.

The pseudocode shows two distinct sections. One is for adding new records while the other section would handle changes, displays, and deletes. Change and display are essentially the same function with the only difference being that in a display nothing is changed. The display and delete functions are also the same; either way there are no changes. However, a delete requires a back end process to confirm the delete.

Like the customer change, delete, or view routines, a pre-processor is used to get the value of the key field. In this case, the key field is ITEMNO. The pseudocode then splits into two sections. The "true" clause of the IF ADD statement handles the addition of a new item. A check is made to see if the key value already exists. If it does, an error window is displayed, and you can try again. If not, then a new record is added to the file, the key value replaced, and the format file opened in EDIT mode.

```
     DISPLAY MENU
       DO WHILE .NOT. EXIT
         CASE CHOICE
           WHEN ADD NEW ITEM DO INVENTORY DATA ENTRY WITH ADD
           WHEN CHANGE ITEM INFORMATION DO INVENTORY DATA ENTRY WITH CHANGE
           WHEN DELETE AN ITEM DO INVENTORY DATA ENTRY WITH DELETE
           WHEN VIEW ITEM INFORMATION DO INVENTORY DATA ENTRY WITH VIEW
           WHEN EXIT RETURN
       ENDDO


INVENTORY DATA ENTRY

DO WHILE NOT EXIT INVENTORY SYSTEM
  DISPLAY SCREEN TO ALLOW ENTRY OF ITEM NUMBER BEING USED
  ALLOW ENTRY INTO THE ITEMNO FIELD
  IF AN ENTRY IS MADE
    STORE INTO MEMORY VARIABLE
   ELSE
    EXIT OUT OF DO WHILES
  ENDIF
  ACCESS INVENTORY FILE
  IF ADD
    CHECK FOR ITEM NUMBER EXISTENCE
    IF FOUND()
       DISPLAY DATA ENTRY SCREEN WITH ERROR WINDOW
       LOOP BACK TO NEW DATA ENTRY
      ELSE
       ACCESS INVENTORY FILE
       APPEND BLANK RECORD
       REPLACE KEY FIELD WITH ITEM NUMBER
       USE FORMAT FILE ALLOWING GET'S IN NON-KEY FIELDS
       ALLOW DATA ENTRY DIRECTLY INTO FILE
    ENDIF
   ELSE    && CHANGE OR DELETE OR VIEW
    CHECK FOR ITEM NUMBER EXISTENCE
    IF .NOT. FOUND()
       DISPLAY DATA ENTRY SCREEN WITH ERROR WINDOW
       LOOP BACK TO NEW DATA ENTRY
      ELSE
       ACCESS INVENTORY FILE
       POSITION RECORD POINTER ON ITEM NUMBER RECORD
       USE FORMAT FILE ALLOWING GET'S IN NON-KEY FIELDS
       ALLOW DATA ENTRY DIRECTLY INTO FILE
        IF DELETE
           DISPLAY DELETE CONFIRMATION WINDOW
           GET CONFIRMATION
           IF Y
             DELETE RECORD
           ENDIF
        ENDIF
    ENDIF
  ENDIF
ENDDO
```

24-5 The combined function pseudocode.

The "false" clause means it is not an add. In any case, a check is made to make sure the item does exist. It must exist if you are to retrieve the data. The record is retrieved, and you can make changes to it. If you use the same format file for change as for delete and view, then you can actually change the data in delete or view mode. You must make the decision on how sophisticated you want the code. You can create another format file and change the GETs to SAYs if you want.

After the end of the change, view, or delete, there is one more check. If it is a delete, then a post-processor is run to check to make sure the record is to be deleted.

As you can see, all of the processes from the four modules in the customer system are combined into one module. When you review the code you will see that the code is almost exactly the same, too.

Let's now examine the INVTDTEN module that handles all of the data entry for the inventory system as shown in Fig. 24-6. The code begins by handling the passed parameter from the inventory menu. The command:

PARAMETERS CHOICE

takes the value of BAR( ) from the statement in the inventory menu DO INVTDTEN WITH BAR( ) and places the value into the variable CHOICE.

Next, the inventory file is opened with the ITEMNO tag active. You might notice that the TAG clause is missing from the second line of code in Fig. 24-6. The TAG parameter is actually optional. If you use only the ORDER clause, dBASE IV looks for a dBASE III PLUS index file named ITEMNO. If it doesn't find it, it then looks for an index tag named ITEMNO.

The screen is then cleared and the format is set to "nothing." This is important. An open format file is activated with a READ, EDIT, or APPEND command.

There is a misconception that when using a format file, only the commands APPEND (to enter as many new records as you want) or EDIT (to change all existing records) can be used. These commands let you work with many records, and therefore, do not maintain the strict control you must have in customized systems. One command lets you work only with the "current" record. The READ command is the third command that lets you use a format file.

You will be using a READ when you get the key field input. If the format file is active, then the entire screen will appear. Because you don't want that yet, you must make sure the format file is closed by using the command:

SET FORMAT TO

When used without a format file name, it closes any active format file.

The main loop is set up, and the key field data entry screen is displayed. The READ command allows entry into the item number field. This code is exactly the same as the customer change, delete, or view pre-processor code.

The first IF clause checks to see if something was entered in the key field. If it is blank, control is returned to the menu.

The SEEK TRIM(ITN) clause searches the inventory database file for the key field. Now, the results of the SEEK are either FOUND( ) equal to true or .NOT. FOUND( ) equal to false. The desired result is dependent upon the function being performed.

A CASE statement then decides whether the function is add, change, delete, or view. The add routine checks to make sure the key field is not found. Once this happens, the data entry can begin. The next four statements open the format file, add a blank record to the database, replace the key database value with the memory variable, and allow for data entry of all fields:

```
SET FORMAT TO INVENTRY
APPEND BLANK
REPLACE ITEMNO WITH ITN
READ
```

A message is then displayed indicating successful data entry. Going back to the other side of the IF .NOT. FOUND( ), if the item number is found, then an error message is displayed, and another item number must be entered.

```
**********************************************************************
* Program......: INVTDTEN.PRG
* Author.......: Cary N. Prague
* Date.........: 9-05-88, Final Revision 12-26-88 Revised 3-12-92
* Module #.....: 3.1.1
* dBASE Ver....: IV 1.5
* Description..: AJAX APPLIANCE COMPANY INVENTORY DATA ENTRY
**********************************************************************
PARAMETERS CHOICE
USE inventry ORDER itemno
CLEAR
SET FORMAT TO
STORE SPACE(8) TO ITN
DO WHILE .T.
   @ 1,28 TO 4,53
   @ 2,30 SAY 'AJAX APPLIANCE COMPANY'
   @ 3,30 SAY " INVENTORY DATA ENTRY "
   @ 6,25 SAY "DATABASE ADD/CHANGE/DELETE/VIEW"
   @ 10,26 SAY 'ENTER ITEM NUMBER: '
   @ 10,45 GET ITN PICTURE "@! AAAA-999"
   READ
   IF ITN = SPACE(8) .OR. ITN = '    -   '
      CLEAR
      RETURN
   ENDIF
   SEEK TRIM(ITN)
   DO CASE
      CASE CHOICE = 1              && ADD ITEM
         IF .NOT. FOUND()
            SET FORMAT TO INVENTRY
            APPEND BLANK
            REPLACE ITEMNO WITH ITN
            READ
            CLEAR
            @ 8,1
            @ 8,28 SAY '  *** ITEM ADDED *** '
         ELSE
            ?? CHR(7)
            ACTIVATE WINDOW msg1
            @ 2,05 SAY '       *** ERROR ***'
            @ 4,05 SAY 'ITEM NUMBER ALREADY ON FILE'
            @ 5,05 SAY '  ENTER A NEW ITEM NUMBER'
            @ 6,1  SAY ' '
            WAIT "       PRESS ANY KEY TO CONTINUE"
            DEACTIVATE WINDOW msg1
         ENDIF
```

24-6 THe inventory data entry combined function program.

```
       CASE CHOICE = 3 .OR. CHOICE = 5 .OR. CHOICE = 7
         IF FOUND()
           SET FORMAT TO INVENTRY
           READ
           CLEAR
           IF CHOICE =  3    && CHANGE ITEM
              @ 8,1
              @ 8,27 SAY '  *** ITEM CHANGED *** '
           ENDIF
           IF CHOICE =  5    && DELETE ITEM
              SET FORMAT TO
              ?? CHR(7)
              DEFINE MENU yesno
              DEFINE PAD no OF yesno PROMPT "[NO]" AT 6,2
              ON SELECTION PAD no OF yesno DEACTIVATE MENU
              DEFINE PAD yes OF yesno PROMPT "[YES]" AT 6,30
              ON SELECTION PAD yes OF yesno DO DELETE
              ACTIVATE WINDOW msg2
              @ 1,05 SAY '  *** CONFIRM DELETE ***    '
              @ 3,05 SAY '   DO YOU REALLY WANT TO     '
              @ 4,05 SAY '     DELETE THIS RECORD      '
              ACTIVATE menu yesno
              DEACTIVATE WINDOW msg2
              @ 8,10 CLEAR TO 21,70
              STORE SPACE(6) TO CSN
              ENDIF
         ELSE
           ?? CHR(7)
           ACTIVATE WINDOW msg1
           @ 2,05 SAY '        *** ERROR ***'
           @ 4,05 SAY '   ITEM NUMBER NOT ON FILE'
           @ 5,05 SAY ' ENTER ANOTHER ITEM NUMBER'
           @ 6,1  SAY ' '
           WAIT "       PRESS ANY KEY TO CONTINUE"
           DEACTIVATE WINDOW msg1
           STORE SPACE(8) TO ITN
         ENDIF
      ENDCASE
      STORE SPACE(8) TO ITN
      SET FORMAT TO
   ENDDO


   PROCEDURE DELETE
     DELETE
     @ 1,1 CLEAR TO 6,37
     @ 3,5 SAY  '  *** ITEM DELETED ***     '
     @ 5,1
     WAIT "      PRESS ANY KEY TO CONTINUE"
     DEACTIVATE MENU
   RETURN
```

The other CASE statement handles changes, deletes, and views. It makes sure that the key field is FOUND( ). Once it finds the field, the record pointer is automatically positioned on the retrieved record. The format file is activated and the READ instruction opens the file for data entry. In this example, the same format file is used for the change as well as delete and view. In a more complex system, there might be a different format file with no GETs.

After the READ, the screen is cleared and a message is displayed indicating that the record is changed. This message is displayed for either change or view, in this example.

Another IF statement checks to see if the function is DELETE. If so, the post-processor is run. This is the same post-processor you saw in the customer delete module. A window is placed on the screen with text and a confirmation menu. If the menu choice is yes, then the record is deleted.

Of course, the other side of the IF FOUND( ) statement for the change, delete, and view routine is that the record is not found. In that case, the processing is returned to the top of the loop to get another item number and try again.

At the bottom of the program just before the ENDDO is a SET FORMAT TO statement. Remember, before the single item number data entry can take place, the format file must be closed.

As you have seen, there are amazing similarities in this code and in the four modules of the customer system. And, why not? Programming is a science, not an art. You should not be constantly inventing new techniques unless they are getting easier to understand, easier to maintain, and—only after these two are true—faster and more efficient.

Throughout the rest of this book, you will see several more new techniques to handle many different situations. Consider these solid techniques developed over five years ago that are constantly improved to take advantage of each new version of dBASE.

Remembering testing techniques

Several testing techniques should be mentioned again. By now, you probably have discovered the command:

```
SET STEP ON
```

This command lets you see your program execute one step at a time. If you couple this with the commands:

```
SET TALK ON
SET ECHO ON
```

you can see the results of each and every line of a program. Unless you have major problems, you probably do not need to resort to this.

dBASE holds executed commands in a special buffer in memory. This buffer is called the command history. The main use of this feature is to allow the user to reenter commands at the dBASE prompt—a re-try editor. The command history can also be used as a part of the interactive debugging process.

Program commands can also be placed in the history buffer as a program executes. The SET DOHISTORY ON command enables this feature. Now, if an error occurs, you can choose to suspend the program's execution and review the commands in the history buffer. This alone might be enough to solve most problems.

When dBASE IV attempts to execute a statement that is in error, the operator sees three choices: Cancel, Suspend, and Ignore. Cancel returns you to the dBASE prompt with no other action. Ignore causes dBASE to attempt to continue program execution by ignoring the error, which will probably not work.

The Suspend option marks the beginning of interactive debugging. Choosing the Suspend option stops program execution and displays the dBASE prompt—but you now have the ability of continuing the program with the RESUME command. Another alternative is to issue the command SUSPEND in a dBASE program. If you SET DOHISTORY ON, the last 20 commands that have been executed are available with the command DISPLAY HISTORY. You can increase the number of stored commands by using SET HISTORY TO or the HISTORY = parameter in CONFIG.DB.

You can change commands stored in the history buffer and issue the RESUME command at that point. You can examine the values of memory variables and database fields; you might also DISPLAY STATUS or issue any other command necessary to troubleshooting. SET STEP ON allows you to "single-step" the program from that point on.

An advanced debugging technique (and one that we use) is to use the dBASE IV DEBUG command. See chapter 20 for a complete explanation of this tool.

You should now test all of your programs. Make sure that everything is working properly before continuing.

25

Reports with one database

dBASE IV features a complete report generator. Virtually any type of report can be created. This includes column reports, form reports, mail merge reports, and even labels. In chapter 13 you created the nine reports that are used in the AJAX Appliance system programs. If you need to refer back to any of those reports, take another look at chapter 13. In this chapter, we concentrate on getting the reports to come out not on the reports themselves.

Because the report form is so powerful, there is little need to program any report yourself. For this reason, we recommend that the report writer be used for 90% of your reports. You will see how to create a custom report in the last chapter of this book.

Report printing modules

You do, however, need to create a series of modules to control printing of the various reports. You designed many of these modules in chapter 4. In this chapter, we examine three of these modules in detail and mention the other three which are exactly the same.

A simple printing module

The simplest printing module is one that simply prints all of the records in the file. This is generally a simple column report. The customer cross-reference report is one such report. This is the second report in the customer system pull-down menu of the main module. Let's examine the

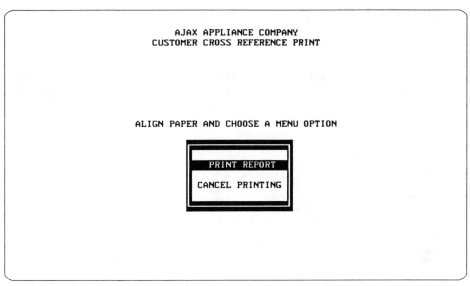

```
              AJAX APPLIANCE COMPANY
            CUSTOMER CROSS REFERENCE PRINT




        ALIGN PAPER AND CHOOSE A MENU OPTION

                  ┌─────────────────┐
                  │  PRINT REPORT   │
                  │ CANCEL PRINTING │
                  └─────────────────┘
```

25-1 Customer cross-reference print screen.

screen as it looks when you choose the Cross Reference choice from the customer system pull-down menu in the main program. Figure 25-1 shows this screen.

As you can see on the screen, a simple pop-up menu lets the user decide whether to print the report or cancel the printing. That's all. Let's examine the program code for this screen as shown in Fig. 25-2.

First, the screen is cleared, and any open databases are closed. Next, the CUSTOMER database is opened with the COMPANY index tag active. A cross-reference report should be in customer order.

Next, the pop-up is created. It has four bars of which only two are active. The second bar lets the user print the report, while the fourth bar returns back to the main customer system menu.

Some text is written to the screen telling the user which report was chosen and reminding the user to align their paper. Finally, the pop-up menu is activated and appears on the screen.

The PRTPICK procedure has two choices—either to print or not print the report. The command:

REPORT FORM CUSTCROS TO PRINT

actually handles the printing of the report. This is the same print command you could enter from the dot prompt. You might also notice the command:

SET CONSOLE OFF

This stops the output from being displayed on the screen at the same time it is printed on the printer. SET CONSOLE ON returns it to its normal state to handle screen interaction.

```
*********************************************************************
* Program......: CUSTCROS.PRG
* Author.......: Cary N. Prague
* Date.........: 9-25-88, Final Revision 12-26-88 Revised 3-12-92
* Module #.....: 1.3
* dBASE Ver....: IV 1.5
* Description..: AJAX APPLIANCE COMPANY CUSTOMER CROSS REFERENCE PRINT
*********************************************************************
CLEAR
CLOSE DATABASES
USE CUSTOMER ORDER COMPANY

*-- Popup
SET BORDER TO SINGLE
DEFINE POPUP PRTMENU FROM 12,31 TO 18,49
DEFINE BAR 1 OF PRTMENU PROMPT "                   " SKIP
DEFINE BAR 2 OF PRTMENU PROMPT "    PRINT REPORT "
DEFINE BAR 3 OF PRTMENU PROMPT "                   " SKIP
DEFINE BAR 4 OF PRTMENU PROMPT " CANCEL PRINTING "
ON SELECTION POPUP PRTMENU DO PRTPICK
SET CONSOLE OFF
@ 1,29 SAY "AJAX APPLIANCE COMPANY"
@ 2,25 SAY "CUSTOMER CROSS REFERENCE PRINT"
@ 10,22 SAY 'ALIGN PAPER AND CHOOSE A MENU OPTION'

ACTIVATE POPUP PRTMENU

RETURN


PROCEDURE PRTPICK
 DO CASE
   CASE BAR() = 2
     REPORT FORM CUSTCROS TO PRINT
     DEACTIVATE POPUP
   CASE BAR() = 4
     DEACTIVATE POPUP
 ENDCASE
 SET CONSOLE ON
 RETURN
```

25-2 Customer cross-reference print code.

That is all there is to this printing program. Two other reports use this same format and won't be shown here. They are the:

- Inventory Cross-Reference Report
  INVTCROS.PRG calls the ITEMCROS report form.
- Inventory Valuation Report
  INVTVALU.PRG calls the INVVALU report form.

Now that you have seen a simple printing process, let's move on to one that has a familiar pre-processor.

Choosing one record or all records

The Customer Directory program needs more than to print a simple column list of customers. It prints many pages of customers, one to a page with its information in a form type report. When you might want to print only a single customer rather than print an entire report, which might only be produced once a month, somehow you must have the ability to print only that one customer. Basically, you can use the same pre-processor you have used in the customer and the inventory systems.

Figure 25-3 shows this screen after the single customer number has been requested and the menu has been displayed. As you can see on the screen, a data entry line gets the customer number. After this is entered, then the simple pop-up menu appears letting the user decide whether to print the report or cancel the printing.

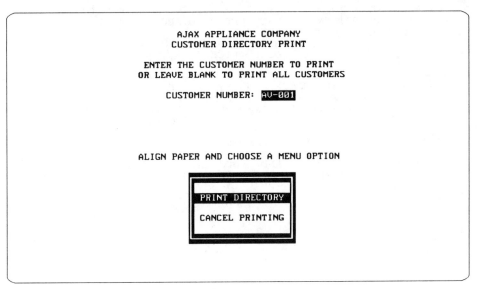

25-3 Customer directory print screen.

Let's examine the program code for this screen as shown in Fig. 25-4. The code is virtually the same in most places as the customer cross-reference report. The customer database is opened, but this time the CUSTNO field is the controlling index. A memory variable is created to allow for the customer number to be entered.

The same pop-up as in the cross-reference report is defined. In fact, you could actually define this pop-up once in the main menu and then activate it as you need it and deactivate it when you are through.

Because you have the ability to print one customer at a time, you also need the ability to print several customers one at a time. So, the print program is placed in a loop that continues until you cancel the printing. You can specify one customer, print it, and then specify another without returning to the main customer system menu.

The DO WHILE .T. loop that you have seen before is coded. Only when the RETURN is executed do you go back to the main customer menu.

```
**************************************************************************
* Program......: CUSTDIR.PRG
* Author.......: Cary N. Prague
* Date.........: 9-25-88, Final Revision 12-26-88 Revised 3-12-92
* Module #.....: 1.2
* dBASE Ver....: IV 1.5
* Description..: AJAX APPLIANCE COMPANY CUSTOMER DIRECTORY PRINT
**************************************************************************
CLEAR
CLOSE DATABASES
USE CUSTOMER ORDER CUSTNO
STORE SPACE(6)  TO CSN
STORE .T. TO MOREPRT
*-- Popup
SET BORDER TO SINGLE
DEFINE POPUP PRTMENU FROM 15,31 TO 21,49
DEFINE BAR 1 OF PRTMENU PROMPT "                " SKIP
DEFINE BAR 2 OF PRTMENU PROMPT " PRINT DIRECTORY "
DEFINE BAR 3 OF PRTMENU PROMPT "                " SKIP
DEFINE BAR 4 OF PRTMENU PROMPT " CANCEL PRINTING "
ON SELECTION POPUP PRTMENU DO PRTPICK
SET CONSOLE OFF
DO WHILE MOREPRT
  @ 1,29 SAY "AJAX APPLIANCE COMPANY"
  @ 2,28 SAY "CUSTOMER DIRECTORY PRINT"
  @ 4,22 SAY " ENTER THE CUSTOMER NUMBER TO PRINT"
  @ 5,22 SAY "OR LEAVE BLANK TO PRINT ALL CUSTOMERS"
  @ 7,27 SAY "CUSTOMER NUMBER:"
  @ 7,44 GET csn PICTURE "@! AA-999"
  READ
  @ 13,22 SAY 'ALIGN PAPER AND CHOOSE A MENU OPTION'
  ACTIVATE POPUP PRTMENU
ENDDO
RETURN

PROCEDURE PRTPICK
 DO CASE
   CASE BAR() = 2
     IF CSN = '      ' .OR. CSN = ' -   '
        REPORT FORM CUSTDIR TO PRINT
      ELSE
        SEEK TRIM(csn)
          IF FOUND()
             REPORT FORM CUSTDIR TO PRINT FOR CUSTNO = CSN
             STORE SPACE(6) TO CSN
           ELSE
             ?? CHR(7)
             ACTIVATE WINDOW msg1
             @ 2,05 SAY '       *** ERROR ***'
             @ 4,05 SAY ' CUSTOMER NUMBER NOT ON FILE'
             @ 5,05 SAY 'ENTER ANOTHER CUSTOMER NUMBER'
             @ 6,1  SAY ' '
             WAIT "       PRESS ANY KEY TO CONTINUE"
             DEACTIVATE WINDOW msg1
             STORE SPACE(6) TO CSN
             @ 13,1
          ENDIF
     ENDIF
     DEACTIVATE POPUP
   CASE BAR() = 4
     SET CONSOLE ON
     MOREPRT = .F.
     DEACTIVATE POPUP
 ENDCASE
RETURN
```

25-4 Customer directory print code.

Once inside the loop, a pre-processor is executed. It is the same pre-processor that you saw in the customer and inventory modules with a little more explanatory text around it. Once the customer number is input with the READ command, you can then display the align paper message and activate the pop-up. You can also reverse the order of the pop-up and the input of the customer number. You might notice that when you are done with printing, you have to press Enter on the blank customer number entry field before getting the menu to print or cancel. You might think the opposite way is better—display the menu first, and if printing is desired, then get the customer number.

Once the number or a blank is input the menu is displayed. If Print Directory is chosen, the CASE statement for that option is executed. If the customer number is left blank, then the report is simply printed. If one is entered, then first the customer number must be found. If it is found, the report is printed with the FOR option:

```
REPORT FORM CUSTDIR TO PRINT FOR CUSTNO = CSN
```

This limits the printing to one record. If it is not found, then a standard error window is displayed, and the user must try again.

The salesman report in the inventory system is also printed this way. That program is called INVTSMAN and calls the report form SALESMAN. A complete listing of all programs in their entirety is shown in appendix B.

Printing labels

The last type of report printing program is specifically for labels. Labels must be aligned before printing, especially on dot matrix printers that use continuous paper feeds. This requires a sample menu with three options. Figure 25-5 shows this screen.

It is basically the same screen as the other printing screen with the addition of the Alignment Test menu choice. The code for this menu is shown in Fig. 25-6.

As you can see, the menu has three choices instead of the two you have seen so far. The CASE statement shows two different ways to print the labels. If the Alignment Test option is chosen, the SAMPLE parameter is added:

```
LABEL FORM CUSTLBL TO PRINT SAMPLE5
```

When you use this command, the alignment labels are printed. dBASE then displays a window and automatically asks you if you want more alignment labels. When you finally answer no, the actual labels are printed.

If the Print Labels option is chosen, then the LABEL FORM command is used without the Sample option.

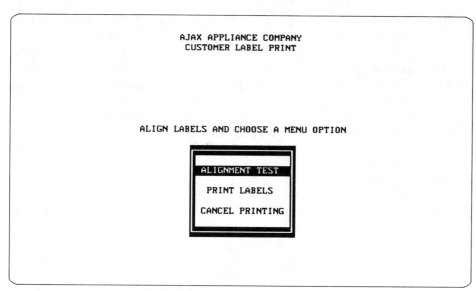

```
                    AJAX APPLIANCE COMPANY
                      CUSTOMER LABEL PRINT




              ALIGN LABELS AND CHOOSE A MENU OPTION


                    ┌─────────────────────┐
                    │ ALIGNMENT TEST      │
                    │                     │
                    │   PRINT LABELS      │
                    │                     │
                    │  CANCEL PRINTING    │
                    └─────────────────────┘
```

25-5   Customer label printing screen.

Specifying your printer

dBASE reports are hardware specific. That is, without special codes or intervention, it requires that you print the report on the same hardware you created it on. This is not realistic.

You can tell dBASE to set a specific print driver. It can be hardcoded anywhere in your program as:

    _pdriver = FX85_1.PR2

This assumes that your printer is an Epson dot matrix printer and that you have that driver set in your dBASE IV subdirectory. Other common printer drivers include:

- HPLAS100.PR2—Hewlett Packard Laserjet
- IBMQUIET.PR2—IBM Quietwriter
- GENERIC.PR2—A generic driver when you don't know

When you create reports with the dBASE IV Report Writer it uses whatever your default _pdriver is on the system that created the reports. However, when you run the system on another machine, that machine may not have the same print driver, and you might end up with a lot of garbage in the report. So, it is very important to specify the print driver in your report or to give the user a choice of print drivers. The GENERIC print driver is another possibility. This works with almost any printer but it ignores any special formatting

```
****************************************************************************
* Program......: CUSTLBL.PRG
* Author.......: Cary N. Prague
* Date.........: 9-25-88, Final Revision 12-26-88 Revised 3-12-92
* Module #.....: 1.4
* dBASE Ver....: IV 1.5
* Description..: AJAX APPLIANCE COMPANY CUSTOMER LABELS PRINT
****************************************************************************
CLEAR
CLOSE DATABASES
USE CUSTOMER ORDER COMPANY
STORE .T. TO MOREPRT

*-- Popup
SET BORDER TO SINGLE
DEFINE POPUP PRTMENU FROM 12,31 TO 20,49
DEFINE BAR 1 OF PRTMENU PROMPT "                  " SKIP
DEFINE BAR 2 OF PRTMENU PROMPT " ALIGNMENT TEST   "
DEFINE BAR 3 OF PRTMENU PROMPT "                  " SKIP
DEFINE BAR 4 OF PRTMENU PROMPT "   PRINT LABELS   "
DEFINE BAR 5 OF PRTMENU PROMPT "                  " SKIP
DEFINE BAR 6 OF PRTMENU PROMPT " CANCEL PRINTING  "
ON SELECTION POPUP PRTMENU DO PRTPICK
SET CONSOLE OFF
DO WHILE MOREPRT

   @ 1,29 SAY "AJAX APPLIANCE COMPANY"
   @ 2,29 SAY " CUSTOMER LABEL PRINT"
   @ 10,22 SAY 'ALIGN LABELS AND CHOOSE A MENU OPTION'

ACTIVATE POPUP PRTMENU

ENDDO

RETURN

PROCEDURE PRTPICK
 DO CASE
    CASE BAR() = 2
      LABEL FORM CUSTLBL TO PRINT SAMPLE
      DEACTIVATE POPUP
    CASE BAR() = 4
      LABEL FORM CUSTLBL TO PRINT
      DEACTIVATE POPUP
    CASE BAR() = 6
      SET CONSOLE ON
      MOREPRT = .F.
      DEACTIVATE POPUP
 ENDCASE
 RETURN
```

25-6 Customer label printing program.

like underlines, italics, and bold and might not produce the correct symbols
for underlining. However, the text should be perfect.

The _pdriver statement can be placed anywhere in the report process, but
it probably belongs in your main module as one of the very first statements.
_pdriver is not a command. It is actually a system memory variable that is
known to the system. Many of these variables are used for different things
such as keeping track of your environment. You can read about all of them in
Section 5 of your dBASE IV Language Reference Manual.

Printer control codes

You might have the need to pass control codes to your printer. These codes may include the ability to select compressed print or bold print or even to change laser printer fonts. In chapter 14, the print menus chapter, you learned how to send control codes through the menus. In this section of this chapter, you will see how to send control codes to the printer from the program itself.

The first way to send control codes is to use the ??? command. The triple question mark command's sole purpose is to send printer control codes. Suppose you want to send the commands to place an Epson or compatible dot matrix printer into compressed mode. You would enter:

```
??? CHR(15)
```

Suppose you wanted to send the equivalent laser printer command:

```
??? CHR(27) + '(s16.66H'
```

or

```
??? "{ESC} (s16.66H"
```

The CHR( ) function translates a decimal value to its ASCII equivalent. The CHR(27) is the Esc key. That is how most laser printer commands start. CHR(15) happens to be the code for compressed on a dot matrix while {ESC} (s16.66H is the code for compressed on a laser printer. Placing an ASCII code in a pair of curly braces is the same as using the CHR function. You should refer to your printer manual for a list of your supported codes.

The other way to send control codes to your printer is to use the system memory variables such as the variables _pscode (printer start code) and _pecode (printer end code). A good example of this is shown in the code for the inventory valuation program as shown in Fig. 25-7.

The fourth line of the program sends a printer control code to switch to compressed print:

```
_pscode = "{27} {40} {115} 16.66 {72}"
```

This is equivalent to:

```
_pscode = "{27}(s16.66H"
```

The second example shows some of the ASCII codes translated into the character equivalent of the ASCII codes. The Esc code cannot be translated.

After the program ends, the end code _pecode resets the printer as you can see at the bottom of Fig. 25-7:

```
_pecode = "{27} {69}"
```

These system memory variables are the easiest way to send codes but if you want, the ??? does the same thing for you.

```
**********************************************************************
* Program......: INVTVALU.PRG
* Author.......: Cary N. Prague
* Date.........: 10-03-88, Final Revision 12-26-88 Revised 3-12-92
* Module #.....: 3.2
* dBASE Ver....: IV 1.5
* Description..: AJAX APPLIANCE COMPANY INVENTORY VALUATION PRINT
**********************************************************************
CLEAR
CLOSE DATABASES
USE INVENTRY ORDER ITEMNO
SET CONSOLE OFF
_pscode = "{27}{40}{115}16.66{72}"
*-- Popup
SET BORDER TO SINGLE
DEFINE POPUP PRTMENU FROM 12,31 TO 18,49
DEFINE BAR 1 OF PRTMENU PROMPT "              " SKIP
DEFINE BAR 2 OF PRTMENU PROMPT "   PRINT REPORT "
DEFINE BAR 3 OF PRTMENU PROMPT "              " SKIP
DEFINE BAR 4 OF PRTMENU PROMPT " CANCEL PRINTING "
ON SELECTION POPUP PRTMENU DO PRTPICK

@ 1,29 SAY "AJAX APPLIANCE COMPANY"
@ 2,28 SAY "INVENTORY VALUATION PRINT"
@ 10,22 SAY 'ALIGN PAPER AND CHOOSE A MENU OPTION'

ACTIVATE POPUP PRTMENU


RETURN

PROCEDURE PRTPICK
 DO CASE
    CASE BAR() = 2
       REPORT FORM INVVALUE TO PRINT
       DEACTIVATE POPUP
    CASE BAR() = 4
       DEACTIVATE POPUP
 ENDCASE
 SET CONSOLE ON
 _pecode="{27}{69}"
 RETURN
```

25-7 An example of printer codes.

This completes a look at the various printing modules in the customer and inventory modules. In the final three chapters of this book, you will see the complex programming tasks of creating and modifying data in a multi-file environment. You will also see how to create front ends for complex reports and how to create a report from @ SAY and @ GET commands as you see how to create an invoice printing program.

26
Multi-file multi-record data entry for the invoice

The invoice system was designed using a two-file approach. The invoice file is actually made up of two databases, the main record file INVOICE and the item records file ITEMS. In the main file, there is only one record for each invoice number. In the items file, there are as many records for each invoice as there are items.

Design considerations

Typically in a relational database system, each record in the item file represents one item of the total invoice. This way there are no limits to the number of records that can appear in an invoice. Figure 26-1 shows the database structures for INVOICE and ITEMS.

As you can see the INVOICE file has data fields that appear once for an invoice. These include the invoice number, invoice date, customer number, and customer discount; even though the customer discount can be retrieved from the CUSTOMER file, it also can change. If the invoice was processed on January 10 and the customer had a 20% discount, you want to make sure that when you figure the total sale for profit that you do not retroactively give on March 31 the customer discount of 22%. The discount data can change, so you must take a "snapshot" of it when the invoice is created. If you have to rebill the customer in March because they haven't paid the invoice you want to make sure that the invoice looks exactly the same as it did in March. Unless you store this changeable data, you could mistakenly bill them at a lower rate.

Likewise, the customer address information can be retrieved at any time from the customer file. If this information changes however, you want to make the change. So, the customer address information remains only on the customer file.

```
Structure for database: C:\DBASE4\AJAX\INVOICE.DBF
Number of data records:       10
Date of last update    : 03/13/92
Field  Field Name  Type        Width    Dec    Index
    1  INVNO       Character      8               Y
    2  INVDATE     Date           8               Y
    3  CUSTNO      Character      6               N
    4  DISCOUNT    Numeric        2               N
** Total **                      25


Structure for database: C:\DBASE4\AJAX\ITEMS.DBF
Number of data records:       37
Date of last update    : 03/13/92
Field  Field Name  Type        Width    Dec    Index
    1  INVNO       Character      8               Y
    2  QTY         Numeric        3               N
    3  ITEMNO      Character      8               N
    4  PRICE       Numeric        7       2       N
** Total **                      27
```

26-1 The INVOICE and ITEMS database structure.

The ITEMS file contains all of those items which appear on each line of the invoice. The invoice number is used to relate the items back to the original invoice; it "ties" them together. The quantity and item number fields are all the invoice needs to know about the item. The program can retrieve any descriptive information or stock levels from the inventory file. The PRICE field falls into the same category as the DISCOUNT field. Prices constantly change. Even though the price field exists in the inventory file and data for the price is retrieved from the inventory file when the invoice is created, it isn't going to be accurate next week. Prices change frequently—up, down (usually up). You must make sure that the price they were charged when the invoice was created is the price in the file. By having the PRICE field in the ITEMS file, this happens.

In the next three chapters, you will see some fairly complicated code. Multiple file data entry and reports are not easy. However, by using our 16-step design and programming methodology, this can be accomplished even by the novice. In this chapter, you will see how to add a record to an invoice. You will see how it takes several forms and some interesting subroutines. A lot of the code in the different modules is common to all the modules and could be put in a "subroutine module." You will see how this works.

In the next chapter, you will see how to change, delete, and simply view an invoice. The change module demonstrates many new code techniques while the delete and view modules are variations on it just like the customer system.

Finally, in the last chapter you will see how to use the rollup sales report and the mail merge (word wrap) report you designed in chapter 13. You will also see how to code a custom report without the report writer as we code the invoice report.

Let's go on and create the invoice menu.

The Invoice menu

Now that you have seen the customer and inventory data entry systems, it is time to get a little more complicated—the invoice system. The invoice system is a multi-file, multi-record data entry system. In the customer system chapter, you saw how each module of the system was separate. In this system, the same is true.

Before we start coding, let's see the invoice menu and see how it differs from the customer or inventory menus. Figure 26-2 shows the screen that the menu produces.

```
                    AJAX APPLIANCE COMPANY
                     INVOICE DATA ENTRY




                    ┌───────────────────────┐
                    │    ADD NEW INVOICE     │
                    └───────────────────────┘
                     CHANGE INVOICE INFORMATION

                        DELETE AN INVOICE

                     VIEW INVOICE INFORMATION

                      EXIT INVOICE DATA ENTRY




                 Choose a selection from the Invoice Menu
```

26-2 The invoice data entry menu.

As you can see, it looks just like the other menus. It has an add, change, delete, view, and an exit option. In fact, from the screen you can't tell anything is different.

Let's examine the menu code to see how it differs. Figure 26-3 shows the invoice menu code.

Again the code starts by clearing the screen. Remember, that when this menu was called, the window "calling" was opened and the menu is being created inside the window named "calling."

Next, a procedure file is opened. A procedure file is a separate file that contains nothing but subroutines. These become external subroutines

```
********************************************************************
* Program......: INVCMENU.PRG
* Author.......: Cary N. Prague
* Date.........: 10-02-88, Final Revision 01-01-89 Revision 3-12-92
* Module #.....: 2.1
* dBASE Ver....: IV 1.5
* Description..: AJAX APPLIANCE COMPANY INVOICE MAIN MENU
********************************************************************
CLEAR
SET PROCEDURE TO INVOICE
USE INVOICE ORDER INVNO
USE CUSTOMER ORDER CUSTNO IN 2
USE INVENTRY ORDER ITEMNO IN 3
USE ITEMS ORDER INVNO IN 4
SET BORDER TO NONE
DEFINE POPUP INVCMENU FROM 8,23 TO 18,52 ;
MESSAGE "Choose a selection from the Invoice Menu"
DEFINE BAR 1 OF INVCMENU PROMPT "        ADD NEW INVOICE       "
DEFINE BAR 2 OF INVCMENU PROMPT "                              " SKIP
DEFINE BAR 3 OF INVCMENU PROMPT " CHANGE INVOICE INFORMATION   "
DEFINE BAR 4 OF INVCMENU PROMPT "                              " SKIP
DEFINE BAR 5 OF INVCMENU PROMPT "        DELETE AN INVOICE     "
DEFINE BAR 6 OF INVCMENU PROMPT "                              " SKIP
DEFINE BAR 7 OF INVCMENU PROMPT "    VIEW INVOICE INFORMATION  "
DEFINE BAR 8 OF INVCMENU PROMPT "                              " SKIP
DEFINE BAR 9 OF INVCMENU PROMPT "    EXIT INVOICE DATA ENTRY   "
ON SELECTION POPUP INVCMENU DO INVCPICK

@ 1,29 SAY "AJAX APPLIANCE COMPANY"
@ 2,29 SAY "  INVOICE DATA ENTRY"

ACTIVATE POPUP INVCMENU
CLOSE DATABASES

RETURN

PROCEDURE INVCPICK
 DO CASE
    CASE BAR() = 1
      DO INVCADD
    CASE BAR() = 3
      DO INVCCHG
    CASE BAR() = 5
      DO INVCDEL
    CASE BAR() = 7
      DO INVCVEW
    CASE BAR() = 9
      SET BORDER TO SINGLE
      DEACTIVATE POPUP
 ENDCASE
 RETURN
```

26-3 The invoice data entry menu program.

because they are called from different modules but are not part of the module itself. The procedure file takes routines common to many modules and puts them all in one place. Subroutines are called in dBASE with the DO command. When dBASE doesn't find the procedure in the open module, it searches any open procedure files for the program. The statement:

SET PROCEDURE TO *filename*

opens a procedure file. The procedure file should have a .PRG extension although it doesn't have to. You can specify the full drive, directory, and extension if you want. We will examine what is in this procedure file later in this chapter and the next.

Like in the customer system the border is set to none and a pop-up is created that fills most of the screen. The odd-numbered items which are blank are skipped with the SKIP parameter.

The one ON SELECTION statement which is normal for a pop-up calls the INVCPICK procedure when a selection is chosen.

The big difference is that all four databases are opened in the menu program. The form:

USE *database* ORDER *mdxfile* IN *workarea*

is used. Each database is opened in a separate work area with its key field index active. The files are then known by their default aliases (the database name) when they are used.

Finally, the title is written at the top of the screen, and the menu is activated.

The INVCPICK menu calls four different programs for each of the data entry options. We examine each of the programs in the next two chapters. That takes care of the menu. Now on to data entry.

A design for adding invoices: a two-screen process

Adding an invoice is actually a two-screen process. The first screen as designed is shown in Fig. 26-4. This screen looks like the top of the invoice and allows the input of all the data for the INVOICE file. The cursor only stops in three places: the invoice number, invoice date, and customer number fields. After the customer number is input and verified, the customer name and address are displayed.

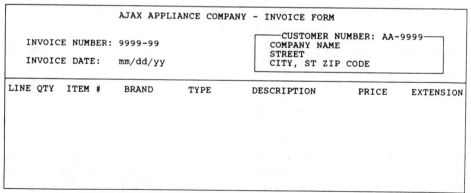

26-4 The top part of the INVOICE screen.

Notice that the discount field is not shown. That is because it is not input. Once the customer number is validated, all three of the data fields input (which are memory variables) are replaced to the INVOICE file where a new record is appended to the file. At the same time the memory variables are appended, the value of the discount field is retrieved from the customer file and also replaced in the INVOICE file.

The design philosophy

The basic philosophies behind creating the invoice and invoice items data entry routines are the same as the customer file. Memory variables are created, and after data is input into them and the data verified, a blank record is appended to the file and replaced by the values in the memory variables.

In this example, each data file is handled separately. However, you can "append blanks" to more than one database and then replace values in both databases from one screen of memory variables.

The top of the invoice screen is very simple because there are only a few fields, a box, and a line. The code is fairly short.

The main invoice screen

Getting started Let's look at the pseudocode that will help us program the code for the top part of the screen. As you build more complicated modules, you will find the pseudocode invaluable in creating your programs. The pseudocode is shown in Fig. 26-5.

The first item in the pseudocode is to "SELECT DATABASE FILES." Make sure that the file that you will work with the most is in the default work area. You can always reference the other work files later by name.

Designing an internal subroutine The second pseudocode instruction is to "DO CALCULATE NEXT INVOICE NUMBER." This is very important. Often the user will not know the next invoice number that is to be used. In the AJAX system, the design called for the invoices to have four digits followed by a dash and three more digits. The first group of digits tells us the date. The year is the first two digits while the month is the next two. The three numbers to the right of the dash are a sequence number. The first invoice of the month is 001, the next 002. At the end of the month, the numbers recycle. So, if there are three invoices in January 1989 and two in February 1989, they would be numbered:

8901-001, 8901-002, 8901-003, 8902-001, 8902-002

This is done as a subroutine. Because this code needs to be executed more than once and as you will see is fairly lengthy, it should not be repeated within the code. By placing it outside the main code as an "internal" subroutine, you only have to code it once. You save space in the program and if it has to be changed (like in the year 2000), it only has to be changed in one place—the subroutine.

```
INVOICE DATA ENTRY ADDITIONS (SCREEN 1)

SELECT DATABASE FILES
DO CALCULATE NEXT INVOICE NUMBER
CREATE BLANK MEMORY VARIABLES
DO WHILE MORE INVOICE NUMBERS
  DISPLAY EMPTY TOP OF THE INVOICE FORM
  ALLOW ENTRY INTO THE INVOICE, DATE, AND CUSTOMER NUMBER FIELDS
  IF INVOICE NUMBER IS BLANK
     EXIT BACK TO DATA ENTRY MENU
    ELSE
     VERIFY INVOICE NUMBER
     CHECK FOR INVOICE NUMBER EXISTENCE
     IF NOT FOUND()
        IF CUSTOMER NUMBER IS BLANK
           DISPLAY ERROR WINDOW
           LOOP BACK TO NEW DATA ENTRY
        ENDIF
        CHECK FOR CUSTOMER NUMBER EXISTENCE
        IF FOUND()
           GET CUSTOMER INFORMATION
           DISPLAY CUSTOMER INFORMATION
           APPEND BLANK RECORD
           REPLACE DATABASE FIELDS WITH MEMORY VARIABLE VALUES
           UPDATE LST_TXND IN CUSTOMER FILE
           DO ADD ITEMS ROUTINE
           DO CALCULATE NEXT INVOICE NUMBER
           EXIT BACK TO NEW DATA ENTRY
          ELSE
           DISPLAY CUSTOMER NUMBER NOT FOUND ERROR WINDOW
           LOOP BACK TO NEW DATA ENTRY
        ENDIF
       ELSE
        DISPLAY INVOICE NUMBER ON FILE ERROR WINDOW
        LOOP BACK TO NEW DATA ENTRY
     ENDIF
  ENDIF
ENDDO

CALCULATE NEXT INVOICE NUMBER

GET CURRENT DATE
STRIP THE MONTH AND YEAR AND BUILD THE LEFT SIDE
MAKE THE RIGHT SIDE '001' AND CONCATENATE WITH A DASH
IF THE RECORD IS FOUND IN THE FILE
  THEN
     DO WHILE THE RECORDS ARE FOUND IN THE FILE
        ADD ONE TO RIGHT SIDE
        REBUILD THE WHOLE FIELD
     END
     NEWRECORD IS FOUND WHEN THE LOOP IS EXITED
  ELSE
     NEWRECORD = LEFT SIDE CONCATENATED WITH "-001"
ENDIF
```

26-5 The invoice add pseudocode.

The subroutine is shown at the bottom of the pseudocode in Fig. 26-5. This is a perfect example of an algorithm—a logical computer solution. Unfortunately, this is not something that is easily taught. With new programmers, the problem is more often the algorithm to solve a particular problem than it is the coding itself. In large companies, people are employed strictly to write algorithms, usually as flowcharts or pseudocode. These people sometimes never program at all.

Let's look at the algorithm now and later we will look at the code.

First, the current date is retrieved from the system. Next the month and year are separated from the entire date and stored to build the left side of the invoice number. As you will see, you can take the year and the month, and the characters can then be concatenated together to make the left side of the invoice.

Once the left side is built (the current year and month) a dash is added followed by the characters "001". The logic here is to see if the 001 sequence record is found in the file. If it is not, then chances are it is a new month and that is the next record number. If it is found, then that month already has some invoices.

Using a loop, you can increment the right side sequence number and keep checking to see if the newly created number is found. Eventually, the number will not be found and that is the next invoice number. This routine even reuses invoice numbers that had been deleted and no longer exist.

Because of this ability, this routine would also have to be used to find the next invoice number after adding one. You couldn't be sure that if the first invoice number was 8901-034 that the next was 8901-035. If 8901-034 was an old invoice that had been deleted, then the next invoice could be a much later number. You will see later in the main pseudocode where this routine is used again.

The subroutine is called from the main program logic. Once the subroutine statements are executed and the next invoice number is known, the program returns to the main logic.

More pseudocode   After the invoice number is known, the three blank memory variables that are used for the top of the screen input are created. The invoice number that was calculated is stored into the invoice number memory variable. In fact, the memory variable that was used to build and store the invoice number is used to display the variable on the input screen.

Next, a loop is set up. As long as the user keeps entering new invoice numbers (or doesn't blank the one that is calculated out), the program continues letting them create new invoices. The blank (except for the invoice number) data entry form is displayed. The user can enter (or change) the invoice number, invoice date, and customer number. Once this is done, the data verification process begins for the top of the invoice.

If the invoice number has been erased, then the program ends, and the invoice module is redisplayed. If it is not blank, then it is reverified to make sure it doesn't exist already on the file. Even though the "Next Invoice Number" has been verified to make sure it doesn't exist, it can be changed and must be reverified.

Though not shown in the pseudocode, the invoice date is also filled in through the DEFAULT option as the system date. It, too, can be changed.

If the invoice number once again passes the "not found" verification and the invoice date passes a range check, then the customer number is verified. If the customer number is blank, then an error window is displayed telling the user to enter a customer number. If the customer number has been entered, then it must be verified to make sure it does exist.

If the customer number is not found, then another error window must be displayed telling the user to enter a different customer number.

Finally, if all the verification checks are passed, then the code in the center of the pseudocode is executed. First, the customer information (company name and address) is retrieved from the customer file. This is easy because the verification process positions the record pointer on the found record. The discount field is also retrieved but not displayed. Displaying the customer information is important because you can enter AV-001 when you meant to enter AV-002. Although both are found, it could still be wrong. When you see the name and address, you can visually verify the data is correct; if it's not, then change it.

Once the customer information is verified and displayed, a blank record is appended to the invoice file, and the blank database fields are replaced with the new values. The last transaction date in the customer file is also updated. A new invoice is a transaction, and the last transaction date in the customer file must be updated.

Next, the add items routine is called. We'll save that routine for the next part of this chapter. Once the bottom of the invoice is completed, the program returns to the main invoice program where the next invoice number is calculated (using the same subroutine as already designed) and the program continues. Until the invoice number is blanked out in the input area, the program continues to process new invoices.

The Items screen

The Add Items routine Once the main invoice information is added to the file, the individual items must be added to the items file. This requires the bottom portion of the invoice to be filled out. Figure 26-6 shows the complete invoice screen.

The top part of the invoice is separated from the bottom part of the invoice by a single line. The top part of the invoice is inactive; that is, the cursor cannot go there. You will work strictly in the bottom portion of the invoice.

In this design, you can see that space has been designed for eight items on one invoice. Now, in a more sophisticated system, you would probably allow for an unlimited number or at least as many as would fit on an invoice form. Because a screen has only 25 lines while a paper form has 66 lines, you can certainly fit a lot more on the printed page. This adds a dimension to the form called *scrolling*. When you can't see all the items at once, you scroll up and down in the items on the screen. Because we don't want to introduce that level of complexity in this book, let's just say that there will be a maximum of eight items in this example. When the eighth item is entered, the system will tell us to create a new invoice.

Figure 26-6 shows that below the displayed headings are the items. The

```
┌─────────────────────────────────────────────────────────────────────────┐
│              AJAX APPLIANCE COMPANY - INVOICE FORM                         │
│                                    ┌──CUSTOMER NUMBER: AA-9999──┐          │
│     INVOICE NUMBER: 9999-99        │COMPANY NAME                │          │
│                                    │STREET                      │          │
│     INVOICE DATE:    mm/dd/yy      │CITY, ST ZIP CODE           │          │
│                                    └────────────────────────────┘          │
│                                                                            │
│ LINE QTY  ITEM #    BRAND      TYPE      DESCRIPTION    PRICE    EXTENSION  │
│   9. 999 AAAA-999 X-BRAND-X X--TYPE--X X------DESC------X 9PRICE9 9QTY*PRI9 │
│   9. 999 AAAA-999 X-BRAND-X X--TYPE--X X------DESC------X 9PRICE9 9QTY*PRI9 │
│   9. 999 AAAA-999 X-BRAND-X X--TYPE--X X------DESC------X 9PRICE9 9QTY*PRI9 │
│   9. 999 AAAA-999 X-BRAND-X X--TYPE--X X------DESC------X 9PRICE9 9QTY*PRI9 │
│   9. 999 AAAA-999 X-BRAND-X X--TYPE--X X------DESC------X 9PRICE9 9QTY*PRI9 │
│   9. 999 AAAA-999 X-BRAND-X X--TYPE--X X------DESC------X 9PRICE9 9QTY*PRI9 │
│   9. 999 AAAA-999 X-BRAND-X X--TYPE--X X------DESC------X 9PRICE9 9QTY*PRI9 │
│   9. 999 AAAA-999 X-BRAND-X X--TYPE--X X------DESC------X 9PRICE9 9QTY*PRI9 │
│                                                          ----------        │
│                                          Sub Total      999,999.99         │
│                                          Discount 99%    99,999.99         │
│                                                          ----------        │
│                                          Taxable Amount 999,999.99         │
│                                          Tax 99.9%       99,999.99         │
│                                                          ----------        │
│                                          Total Amount   999,999.99         │
└─────────────────────────────────────────────────────────────────────────┘
```

26-6 The complete invoice screen.

line number on the invoice is displayed to make it easier for the user to interact with the screen. In the item change module, refer to your line items by number.

You actually only have to enter two fields in this example: quantity and item number. The rest of the information comes from the inventory file. Once the user inputs a quantity and item number, the system verifies that something has been entered and then verifies the item number. If the item number exists, several things happen. First, the quantity in stock is checked to make sure that there is enough in stock for the order. If not, an error window is displayed and the user can change the quantity, item number, or both. Once both fields are verified, the brand, type, description, and price are retrieved from the inventory file.

Only the price field is stored on the ITEMS file. The other data fields in the inventory file don't change and are not sensitive to time. The price, however, is. If you purchase the item today and next week the price goes up, you want the original price. Likewise if you purchase an item today at a certain price, and the price goes down, the store owners want to make sure you get the original price even if the invoice isn't produced for a few weeks. When the goods change hands (or the invoice is input) the price is set. So, along with the quantity and item numbers, the price field must be added to the items file.

After these fields are displayed for the line item, some calculations take place. First, the extension is calculated. This is simply QTY*PRICE. This is displayed at the end of the line.

Designing an external subroutine The display of the fields at the bottom of the screen are redone each time a new item is added. This is another good candidate for a subroutine. You will also learn that this routine is also used by the change, delete, and display modules. This then becomes known as a *common routine* because several modules use it. This can be placed in its own separate module known as a *procedure file*. This file contains subprocedures common to several modules in a system. This makes the main programs smaller and easier to maintain, and if the code changes for all of the modules, it only has to be changed in one place. When you see the program code, you will see that several subprocedures are placed in the procedure file you create, and the file is shared by all the data entry modules in the invoice system.

In the design for the first subroutine, each time a line item is entered, another more complicated calculation takes place. First, the extensions are summed to produce a subtotal. This can be accomplished by keeping a running total of the QTY*PRICE calculations, or, as each new item is added, a SUM function can be used. The subtotal is displayed.

Next, a discount is calculated. This requires a lot of work. If you notice on the form, both the discount percentage and the amount is displayed. The discount is retrieved from the customer file. This can happen either when the top part of the invoice is created or now because the record pointer in the customer file is still on the record being used. Remember, a separate record pointer is in each work area. As long as you don't do something to change it, it remains in the last place you left it. Once the percentage is retrieved, it can be displayed. Using the subtotal calculation, you can multiply subtotal times the discount amount (divided by 100) to display the discount. Because the discount is stored as a whole number (i.e., 20), it must be converted to its decimal equivalent (i.e., .20) before multiplying it times the subtotal field.

Once the discount is calculated, it can be subtracted from subtotal to display the taxable amount. Next, tax must be calculated. Tax is either some percentage, or it is 0 if the customer is exempt from tax. In the customer file is a field called TAXABLE. This is a logical field which holds the customer's tax status. If it is .F., then a 0 is entered both for the percentage and the tax amount. If it is .T., then the tax rate is used for the calculation. In reality, you should have another database with each state and their sales tax amount. In this example, we have stored 7.5 to tax rate in the AJAXMAIN module and will use that global memory variable. So, the tax rate (7.5) is retrieved (or actually just used because it is only a memory variable) and the tax is calculated after dividing the rate by 100 to get the decimal equivalent (.075). Tax can then be subtracted from taxable amount, and a total amount displayed. The underlines and all field positioning is controlled by the subroutine as well.

Any common routine can become an external subroutine. Many of your error windows are used over and over in different modules, such as the key fields blank or not found. In fact, you don't even need six different window programs to tell about three different fields being blank or not found. You could create one external routine and simply pass to it the parameters. Based on the parameters, the window could be displayed.

The same is true for the delete confirmation window used several times. This could also be a subroutine. For now, keep the windows in the code, but think about it as you see the programs created in the next few chapters.

Viewing the pseudocode Now that you understand the screen and what will take place, examine the pseudocode for the add items function. Figure 26-7 shows the pseudocode for adding items to the invoice.

```
INVOICE ITEMS ADD DATA ENTRY - SCREEN 2

DO WHILE MORE INVOICE ITEMS
   SET UP LINE COUNTERS
   ZERO OUT THE SUBTOTAL FIELD
   GET THE QUANTITY AND ITEM NUMBER FOR THE LINE ITEM
   SET ITEM COUNT BASED ON NUMBER OF ITEMS
   IF QUANTITY = 0
       EXIT ITEM DATA ENTRY
     ELSE
       VERIFY THE ITEM NUMBER
       IF ITEM NUMBER IS BLANK
          DISPLAY BLANK ITEM ERROR WINDOW
          LOOP BACK TO ITEM DATA ENTRY
       ENDIF
       IF ITEM NUMBER IS FOUND IN INVENTORY FILE
           RETRIEVE PRICE
           IF QUANITY DESIRED IS > QUANTITY IN STOCK
               DISPLAY INSUFFICIENT QUANTITY ERROR WINDOW
               LOOP BACK TO ITEM DATA ENTRY
           ENDIF
           REDUCE THE INVENTORY QUANTITY
           RETRIEVE THE DESCRIPTION INFORMATION
           DISPLAY THE COMPLETE LINE ITEM INCLUDING EXTENSION
           UPDATE THE SUBTOTAL
           DISPLAY TOTALS INCLUDING DISCOUNT AND TAX
           ADD THE RECORD TO THE ITEMS FILE
           UPDATE THE ITEM COUNTERS
           IF THAT IS THE EIGHTH ITEM
              DISPLAY INVOICE IS FULL ERROR WINDOW
              EXIT ITEM DATA ENTRY
           ENDIF
         ELSE
           DISPLAY ITEM NOT ON FILE ERROR WINDOW
       ENDIF
   ENDIF
ENDDO
```

26-7 The pseudocode for adding items to the invoice.

A loop is set up to continue as long as the user enters more quantities and item numbers. A blank quantity signals the end of data entry. A line counter must be set up to keep track of how many items have been entered and the subtotal field zeroed out to accumulate the sum of the extensions.

Next, data entry occurs. Statements must be coded to display the data entry portion of the screen for the current item number and then input for the two fields must be allowed. The current item count is used to position the cursor on the screen.

Quantity is checked to see if it is blank (0). If so, data entry is terminated, and the user is returned to the top of the now blank form to enter another invoice.

The item number must be verified if the quantity and item number were entered. Of course, the item number is verified to make sure it's not blank. Then it is checked against the inventory file. When found, the price is retrieved, and the quantity in stock is checked against the quantity desired.

If any of these tests fail, the user is given an error window, and the user can enter a new quantity or item number.

Once everything passes, it is simple sequence. The quantity is subtracted from the inventory quantity in stock. Then the description information is retrieved and displayed and the extension calculated. Next, the subtotal is updated. This is done by calling our external routine. The record is then added to the ITEMS file.

Item count is updated to check for the last item. Remember, only eight are allowed. If it is the eighth item, then a message is displayed and data entry terminates.

Message storyboards It is a good idea also to create and review the design of your messages before coding. This reduces the task to "busywork" and can be handled by someone else. Figure 26-8 shows the error windows that will be needed when adding items to the invoice.

```
        *** ERROR ***                        *** ERROR ***

  ITEM NUMBER CANNOT BE BLANK            INVOICE FORM IS FULL
     ENTER AN ITEM NUMBER               CREATE A NEW INVOICE

  PRESS ANY KEY TO CONTINUE          PRESS ANY KEY TO CONTINUE


        *** ERROR ***                        *** ERROR ***

 NOT ENOUGH QUANTITY IN STOCK          ITEM NUMBER NOT ON FILE
 REDUCE THE QUANTITY TO QTY_STK        ENTER ANOTHER ITEM NUMBER

  PRESS ANY KEY TO CONTINUE          PRESS ANY KEY TO CONTINUE
```

26-8 The error window storyboards for adding items to the invoice.

Four different windows are designed. The first is when a blank item number is entered, the next for an insufficient quantity. Notice how the message itself tells the user how many are in stock so they can decide whether to substitute another product or to use whatever is in stock and then substitute only a portion of the customer's needs. The other two messages tell the user about the full invoice and the item number not on the file.

It's now time to code!

The main screen program

The INVCADD program as shown in Fig. 26-9 follows the pseudocode that you have just reviewed. As you see, it is also very similar to the program code you wrote for the customer additions program. Let's begin by examining the beginning of the program as shown in Fig. 26-9.

First, the window "datan" is opened. This is the full screen window without the border. The screen is cleared, and the border default is set back to

```
*********************************************************************
* Program......: INVCADD.PRG
* Author.......: Cary N. Prague
* Date.........: 10-02-88, Final Revision 01-01-89 Revised 3-12-92
* Module #.....: 2.1.1
* dBASE Ver....: IV 1.5
* Description..: AJAX APPLIANCE COMPANY INVOICE ADDITIONS
*********************************************************************
ACTIVATE WINDOW datan
CLEAR
SET BORDER TO SINGLE
PUBLIC INVN
DO NXTINVNO

STORE SPACE(6) TO CSN
STORE M->DATE TO IDT
DO WHILE .T.
   @  0,20 SAY "AJAX APPLIANCE COMPANY - INVOICE FORM"
   @  3,1 SAY 'INVOICE NUMBER: ' GET INVN PICTURE "####-###"
   @  5,1 SAY 'INVOICE DATE:   ' GET IDT  RANGE CTOD('01/01/88'),CTOD('12/31/99')
   @  2,40 TO 6,76
   @  2,47 SAY 'CUSTOMER NUMBER:' GET CSN  PICTURE "@! AA-999"
   @  7,0 TO 7,79
   READ
   IF INVN = SPACE(8) .OR. INVN = '    -   '
      EXIT
   ELSE
      SELECT INVOICE
      SEEK TRIM(INVN)
      IF .NOT. FOUND()
         SELECT CUSTOMER
         IF CSN = SPACE(6) .OR. CSN = '  -   '
            ?? CHR(7)
            ACTIVATE WINDOW msg1
            @ 2,05 SAY '        *** ERROR ***'
            @ 4,05 SAY 'CUSTOMER NUMBER CANNOT BE BLANK'
            @ 5,05 SAY '   ENTER A CUSTOMER NUMBER'
            @ 6,1  SAY ' '
            WAIT "        PRESS ANY KEY TO CONTINUE"
            DEACTIVATE WINDOW msg1
            LOOP
         ENDIF
         SEEK TRIM(CSN)
         IF FOUND()
            SELECT CUSTOMER
            STORE DISCOUNT TO DIS
            REPLACE LST_TXND WITH DATE()
            @ 3,41 SAY COMPANY
            @ 4,41 SAY STREET
            @ 5,41 SAY TRIM(CITY) + ', ' + STATE + ' ' + ZIP
            @ 8, 0 SAY "LINE"
            @ 8, 5 SAY "QTY"
            @ 8,10 SAY "ITEM #"
            @ 8,20 SAY "BRAND"
            @ 8,31 SAY "TYPE"
            @ 8,42 SAY "DESCRIPTION"
            @ 8,64 SAY "PRICE"
            @ 8,71 SAY "EXTENSION"
            SELECT INVOICE
            APPEND BLANK
            REPLACE INVNO WITH INVN,CUSTNO WITH CSN,INVDATE WITH IDT, ;
                    DISCOUNT WITH DIS
            DO INVCADDI
            CLEAR
```

26-9 The add invoice (first screen) program.

```
                SELECT INVOICE
                DO NXTINVNO
                STORE SPACE(6) TO CSN
                STORE M->DATE TO IDT
            ELSE
                ?? CHR(7)
                ACTIVATE WINDOW msg1
                @ 2,05 SAY '        *** ERROR ***'
                @ 4,05 SAY '   CUSTOMER NUMBER NOT ON FILE'
                @ 5,05 SAY 'ENTER ANOTHER CUSTOMER NUMBER'
                @ 6,1  SAY ' '
                WAIT "        PRESS ANY KEY TO CONTINUE"
                DEACTIVATE WINDOW msg1
            ENDIF
        ELSE
            ?? CHR(7)
            ACTIVATE WINDOW msg1
            @ 2,05 SAY '        *** ERROR ***'
            @ 4,05 SAY 'INVOICE NUMBER ALREADY ON FILE'
            @ 5,05 SAY ' ENTER ANOTHER INVOICE NUMBER'
            @ 6,1  SAY ' '
            WAIT "        PRESS ANY KEY TO CONTINUE"
            DEACTIVATE WINDOW msg1
        ENDIF
   ENDIF
ENDDO
DEACTIVATE WINDOW datan
RETURN

 * CALCULATE NEXT AVAILABLE INVOICE NUMBER

PROCEDURE NXTINVNO

STORE DATE() TO CURDATE
LFTSIDE = SUBSTR(DTOS(M->DATE),3,2) + SUBSTR(DTOS(M->DATE),5,2)
RITSIDE = '001'
INVN = LFTSIDE + '-' + RITSIDE
SELECT INVOICE
GO TOP
SEEK TRIM(INVN)
IF FOUND()
    DO WHILE FOUND()
      NEWRIT = VAL(RITSIDE) + 1
      DO CASE
       CASE NEWRIT < 10
         RITSIDE = '00' + STR(NEWRIT,1)
       CASE NEWRIT >= 10 .AND. NEWRIT < 100
         RITSIDE = '0' + STR(NEWRIT,2)
      ENDCASE
      INVN = LFTSIDE + '-' + RITSIDE
      SEEK TRIM(INVN)
    ENDDO
ENDIF
RETURN
```

a single line. Without this, your lines and boxes won't appear. The invoice number memory variable used is declared public so it can be known to the invoice items program.

After this, the NXTINVNO (Next Invoice Number) internal subroutine is run. This is the routine that displays the next available invoice on the form. This code is shown at the bottom of the figure. Let's examine this first.

The system date is stored to a memory variable. Next, the left side of the invoice number is built. The SUBSTR( ) function is used to take part of the system data string. Notice that the DTOS( ) function is used. The DTOS( ) function returns the current system date as a character string in the form CCYYMMDD. This is normally used as a date index key because it always comes out in sorted order, but it can also be used to manipulate date data. The first SUBSTR( ) function:

```
SUBSTR(DTOS(M—>DATE),3,2)
```

takes apart the date from the third position for a length of two positions. The M—>DATE phrase tells dBASE to use the DATE memory variable created in the AJAXPASS program. The M—> parameter tells dBASE to use the memory variable DATE and not confuse it with a database field or the function DATE( ). Anytime you use a *reserved word* (a word with a specific meaning in dBASE) for a memory variable, you must tell dBASE you are specifically using the memory variable. M—> tells dBASE this. Although no database field is named DATE, if there were in the open work area, it would be used instead of the memory variable. Database fields have precedence over memory variables. M—> is created with the letter M, a hyphen, and a greater than symbol. The two SUBSTR( ) results are concatenated together to form the left side of the invoice number. The right side is initially set to 001. Finally, the left and right sides are concatenated together with a dash in the middle. You have created an invoice number. Now it must be checked against the file.

The invoice file is selected, and the record pointer is positioned to the top of the invoice. Next, use the FIND command to search the database for the record. If it is not found, then the subroutine ends and the "001" value is used for the next invoice number.

If it is found, a loop controls further searching. The loop runs as long as each successive invoice number is found. A new variable NEWRIT is created with the value of RITSIDE (the right side) plus one. The variable of RITSIDE must first be converted to a number from a character string before one can be added to it. Remember "+" means concatenation to character strings. The VAL( ) function converts the character string to a number. Now one can be added to it and stored in the new memory variable NEWRIT.

A CASE statement is needed to determine if RITSIDE is less than 10, between 10 and 99, or greater than 100. If NEWRIT is less than 10, then the new right side number is built as a character string with two zeros preceding the number. If NEWRIT is between 10 and 99, then only one zero must be concatenated to the front of the number. If the number is greater than 99, then the number is three characters already and no zeros are needed. The zeros are concatenated to the STR( ) function of the NEWRIT variable. The STR( ) function is known as the string function because it converts a numeric variable to a character string. It was converted from a character string in order to add one to it. Now it must be converted back to a character string so it can be concatenated with the left side of the invoice.

The SEEK command at the bottom of the loop checks the file for the new value built in the loop. The DO WHILE is once again checked to see if the value exists on the file. The loop ends when a value is found that is not on the file. This logic has fallacies because if that month already had 999 invoices, the subroutine would not work. We will assume that this number is never reached.

Now that we have examined the subroutine, let's return to the first part of the code. Once the next invoice number is calculated, it is time to display the top of the screen and get the input. The next command creates a memory variable to hold the customer number, and the memory variable DATE is assigned to another memory variable.

A main loop is set up as an endless loop and the screen, lines, and box are displayed. Picture functions and a date range are used in the input screen. A box is drawn from row 2 column 40 to row 6 column 76. A line is also drawn from row 7 column 0 to row 7 column 79. The READ statement lets you change any of the input. Even though the invoice number and invoice date are already displayed, you can still change them. Once the input is read, it can be evaluated. The screen that is displayed is shown in Fig. 26-10.

```
                    AJAX APPLIANCE COMPANY - INVOICE FORM

                                              ┌──────CUSTOMER NUMBER: ┌──────┐
  INVOICE NUMBER:   0901 001                  │                       │  -   │
                                              │
  INVOICE DATE:     01/01/89                  │
                                              │
```

26-10   The add invoice (first screen) display.

If the invoice number field was erased (by pressing Ctrl–Y), then the routine is exited to the statement following the ENDDO, the window deactivated, and the program returns to the invoice menu program.

If the invoice is filled in, then it is again checked to see if the invoice number is found on the file. This is done again because even though the program determines the next invoice number, the user is allowed to change it. So, it must be re-verified. If it was found, then an error window is displayed and the user can try again. If not, then the program continues.

The customer number is now checked to see if it is blank. The alarm is sounded and the message window is displayed if it was blank, and the LOOP command sends the program to the bottom of the loop to try again. If the customer number was entered, then it, too, must be verified. The customer number must exist on the file. If it isn't found, then another window is displayed, and you must reenter a valid customer number. Once it is found, then the main logic can finally be run.

The customer file is selected. The discount is stored to a memory variable so it can be added to the invoice file. The last transaction date field is updated with the system date. You could have used the memory variable date if you wanted. The company and address information is displayed along with the headers for the invoice items.

The INVOICE file is then re-selected. A blank record is appended. The blank database fields are then replaced by the invoice number, customer number, invoice date, and discount memory variables.

Then the items program is run to get the input of the individual items. When the program returns from the items data entry, the screen is cleared, and the next available invoice is calculated. The program clears the memory variables, and the program returns to the top of the loop to let you enter another invoice.

Now that the invoice add program is created, move on to the items program.

The Items screen program

The INVCADDI program is displayed in Fig. 26-11. This program is called from the INVCADD program once all of the input has been verified.

First, a counter is created for the LINCNT variable. This is the row number to display data to. Because you are going to have multiple data items and you don't know how many, you can't "hardcode" the row numbers; you must create and update a memory variable. In place of the row numbers in @ SAY and @ GETs, use the LINCNT variable. A counter called CNT keeps track of how many items you have entered. Remember, eight is the limit. Memory variables are created for the input of quantity (QNTY) and item number (ITMN). Finally, a subtotal field (SUBTOT) keeps track of the total of the extensions (QNTY*PRICE).

A standard loop is set up, and we begin. The item number is written on the screen with an @ SAY and the two input fields are opened with the @ GET. LINCNT has been substituted for the row number. Because LINCNT is initially set to 9, the display and input for the first item takes place in row 9. After each item has been entered, you will see that both LINECNT and CNT are incremented by one so the next line is line number 2 and data entry takes place in row 10. The READ command allows for the input.

Once the data is input, it can be verified. As always, the first field being blank (or 0) triggers the module to close by exiting from the loop and returning (in this case) to the main invoice module. This also happens after

```
****************************************************************
* Program......: INVCADDI.PRG
* Author.......: Cary N. Prague
* Date.........: 10-02-88, Final Revision 01-01-89 Revised 3-12-92
* Module #.....: 2.1.1.1
* dBASE Ver....: IV 1.5
* Description..: AJAX APPLIANCE COMPANY INVOICE ITEM ADDITIONS
****************************************************************
STORE 9 TO LINECNT
STORE 1 TO CNT
STORE 0 TO QNTY
STORE SPACE(8) TO ITMN
SUBTOT = 0
DO WHILE .T.
   @ LINECNT,1 SAY CNT PICTURE '99.'
   @ LINECNT,5 GET QNTY PICTURE '999'
   @ LINECNT,9 GET ITMN PICTURE '@! AAAA-999'
   READ
   IF QNTY = 0
      EXIT
   ELSE
      SELECT INVENTRY
      IF ITMN = SPACE(8) .OR. ITMN = '       -   '
         ?? CHR(7)
         ACTIVATE WINDOW msg1
         @ 2,05 SAY '       *** ERROR ***'
         @ 4,05 SAY ' ITEM NUMBER CANNOT BE BLANK'
         @ 5,05 SAY '   ENTER AN ITEM NUMBER'
         @ 6,1  SAY ' '
         WAIT "       PRESS ANY KEY TO CONTINUE"
         DEACTIVATE WINDOW msg1
         LOOP
      ENDIF
      SEEK TRIM(ITMN)
      IF FOUND()
         IF QNTY > QTY_STK
            ?? CHR(7)
            ACTIVATE WINDOW msg1
            @ 2,05 SAY '       *** ERROR ***'
            @ 4,05 SAY ' NOT ENOUGH QUANTITY IN STOCK'
            @ 5,05 SAY '  REDUCE THE QUANTITY TO ' + STR(QTY_STK,3)
            @ 6,1  SAY ' '
            WAIT "       PRESS ANY KEY TO CONTINUE"
            DEACTIVATE WINDOW msg1
            LOOP
         ENDIF
         STORE PRICE TO PRI
 *       REPLACE QTY_STK WITH QTY_STK-QNTY          && REDUCE THE INVENTORY
         @ LINECNT,5  SAY QNTY PICTURE '999'
         @ LINECNT,9  SAY ITMN
         @ LINECNT,18 SAY BRAND
         @ LINECNT,29 SAY TYPE
         @ LINECNT,42 SAY SUBSTR(DESC,1,20)
         @ LINECNT,62 SAY PRI PICTURE '99999.99'
         @ LINECNT,71 SAY QNTY*PRI PICTURE '99,999.99'
         SUBTOT = SUBTOT + (QNTY*PRI)
         DO DISPTOT
         SELECT ITEMS
         APPEND BLANK
         REPLACE INVNO WITH INVN, QTY WITH QNTY, ITEMNO WITH ITMN, ;
            PRICE WITH PRI
         STORE 0 TO QNTY
         STORE SPACE(8) TO ITMN
         STORE CNT + 1 TO CNT
```

26-11 The add invoice items (second screen) program.

26-11 Continued.

```
            STORE LINECNT + 1 TO LINECNT
            IF CNT = 9
               ?? CHR(7)
               ACTIVATE WINDOW msg1
               @ 2,05 SAY '        *** ERROR ***'
               @ 4,05 SAY '   INVOICE FORM IS FULL'
               @ 5,05 SAY '   CREATE A NEW INVOICE  '
               @ 6,1  SAY ' '
               WAIT "        PRESS ANY KEY TO CONTINUE"
               DEACTIVATE WINDOW msg1
               EXIT
            ENDIF
         ELSE
            ?? CHR(7)
            ACTIVATE WINDOW msg1
            @ 2,05 SAY '        *** ERROR ***'
            @ 4,05 SAY '   ITEM NUMBER NOT ON FILE'
            @ 5,05 SAY ' ENTER ANOTHER ITEM NUMBER'
            @ 6,1  SAY ' '
            WAIT "        PRESS ANY KEY TO CONTINUE"
            DEACTIVATE WINDOW msg1
         ENDIF
      ENDIF
   ENDIF
ENDDO
```

the eighth item has been added. The quantity can be made 0 for any item. If you have successfully added five items and that's all you want, then the value of quantity for the sixth item would be entered as 0, and the program would end.

If the quantity entered isn't zero, then the ELSE logic is run and the program continues. The inventory file is selected. First, the item number is checked to see if it's blank. If it is, an error window appears and the input for the item starts again. If the item was entered, it is checked to make sure it exists on the file. The SEEK does that, of course. If the item is FOUND( ), then all of the information about that item can be retrieved. However, another check must first be made.

The quantity desired must be compared to the quantity in stock. If the quantity requested is greater than the quantity in stock, then an error window is displayed. Look at the third line of the window:

@ 5,05 SAY 'REDUCE THE QUANTITY TO ' + STR(QTY_STK,3)

This concatenates the message with the quantity in stock. This is a way of giving the user more information. Remember that STR( ) converts the numeric value QTY_STK to a character string so it can be concatenated with the message. LINECNT is not used because the message is displayed in relation to the window, which is line 5 of that window.

If the quantity in stock is sufficient, then the program goes on. The value of price for the item is copied from the inventory file to a memory variable and used in the next few statements. The next statement replaces the present value of quantity in stock with the value after subtracting the quantity desired:

REPLACE QTY_STK WITH QTY_STK-QNTY

If QTY_STK is 50 and QNTY is 20, then the new value of QTY_STK is 30. Once the quantity is reduced, the rest of the record is displayed. The quantity and item number is redisplayed. This is because it was displayed by a GET in reverse video as it was input. Now a SAY is used to display it normally. Besides the quantity and item number, the BRAND and TYPE are displayed from the current record in the inventory file. The record pointer in the inventory file still points to the FOUND( ) inventory record. Because the inventory database is still the active work area, you can get the data directly from the database. After BRAND and TYPE are displayed, the first 20 characters of the description are displayed. The SUBSTR( ) function limits the display to 20 characters, because that is all that fits on the screen. The price is also displayed. Although the memory variable PRI is used, the inventory database field PRICE could have been used.

Finally, the extension is displayed. The calculation is:

@ LINECNT,71 SAY QNTY*PRI PICTURE '99,999.99'

The calculation is simply quantity times price. The picture template is used to add a comma between the thousands and the hundreds place.

Next, the subtotal is updated. The value of quantity times price plus the current value of subtotal is added together. This new value is then placed back into the subtotal field. As each line item is added the value of subtotal is updated with the item extension.

Next, the external subroutine DISPTOT is executed. This displays the bottom of the screen. We'll cover this routine after we finish the INVCADDI program. For now, let's look at Fig. 26-12.

Here we see the screen as it might look after adding a couple of items. The item extensions add up to the subtotal at the bottom, and the discount and

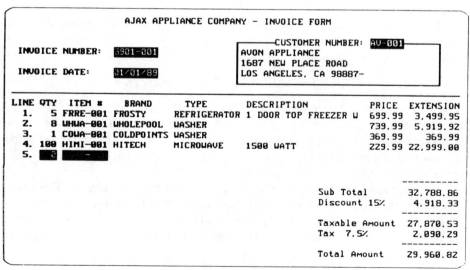

26-12 The add invoice items (second screen) display.

taxes are calculated. As each new quantity and item are input, the new totals are recalculated by the DISPTOT subroutine.

After the totals are displayed, add the item to the ITEMS database. The ITEMS file is selected once you are done with the inventory file. A blank record is appended. The four fields in the ITEMS file are replaced by the memory variables. Finally, the memory variables are zeroed out, and both the item counter (CNT) and the line counter (LINECNT) have one added to them.

If the CNT is nine an error message is displayed and the program terminates because there is no room for any more items. The appropriate message is displayed. Below this is the leftover Item not on file message routine from the ELSE clause above. Finally, the IFs and the DO are closed; that concludes the add item routine.

Coding the procedure file subroutine

Let's now look at the INVOICE.PRG procedure file (or at least part of it). The program with the DISPTOT procedure is shown in Fig. 26-13.

```
********************************************************************
* Program......: INVOICE.PRG
* Author.......: Cary N. Prague
* Date.........: 12-28-88, Final Revision 01-01-89 Revised 3-12-92
* Module #.....: 2.1.0
* dBASE Ver....: IV 1.5
* Description..: AJAX APPLIANCE COMPANY INVOICE PROCEDURE
********************************************************************
PROCEDURE DISPTOT
   @ 17,70 SAY '----------'
   @ 18,55 SAY 'Sub Total'
   @ 18,70 SAY SUBTOT PICTURE '999,999.99'
   @ 19,55 SAY 'Discount ' + STR(INVOICE->DISCOUNT,2) + '%'
DISC =  SUBTOT * (INVOICE->DISCOUNT/100)
   @ 19,70 SAY DISC PICTURE '999,999.99'
   @ 20,70 SAY '----------'
   @ 21,55 SAY 'Taxable Amount'
   @ 21,70 SAY SUBTOT-DISC PICTURE '999,999.99'
IF CUSTOMER->TAXABLE
   @ 22,55 SAY 'Tax ' + STR(TAX_RATE,4,1) + '%'
   TX = (SUBTOT-DISC) * (TAX_RATE/100)
   @ 22,70 SAY TX PICTURE '999,999.99'
  ELSE
   @ 22,55 SAY 'Tax - None'
   TX = 0
   @ 22,70 SAY TX PICTURE '999,999.99'
ENDIF
   @ 23,70 SAY '----------'
   @ 24,55 SAY 'Total Amount'
   @ 24,70 SAY SUBTOT-DISC+TX PICTURE '999,999.99'
   @ 17,1 SAY " "
RETURN
```

26-13 The invoice procedure file (DISPTOT routine only).

A procedure file has one use—to store many common subroutines in one place. Rather than have many program files, it can be easier to combine some common routines into a procedure file. As you already saw in this chapter, the file is opened with the command:

SET PROCEDURE TO *filename*

In this example, the procedure filename was INVOICE and was set in the INVCMENU (invoice menu) program. Now, in this figure, only the DISPTOT subroutine used to display the subtotal, discount, taxable amount, tax, and grand total is shown. The other routine in the procedure file is the REDRAW routine used to redraw all of the items in the invoice. This is used by the change, delete, and view routines and is shown in the next chapter.

Before you examine the DISPTOT code, note some other uses of external procedures. You have been creating groups of code that would be perfect for inclusion in a procedure file. Every time you write the code for an error window, you are writing code that is common to every module. So far in this book, you have seen many error windows for the same thing. This includes:

- Customer Number Not Found
- Customer Number Already on File
- Customer Number Cannot be Blank
- Item Number Not Found
- Item Number Already on File
- Item Number Cannot be Blank
- Invoice Number Not Found
- Invoice Number Already on File

Rather than coding these same windows over and over again, you could put them into a procedure file and DO them whenever you need them. For now, leave them in their respective modules, but if you want to make your programs shorter, feel free to move them.

Look at Fig. 26-13. The identification portion of the program is the same for a procedure file as a program file. A comment is always a comment when it begins with an asterisk.

The one thing that is different about this routine is that it begins with the PROCEDURE command. A procedure file is made up of nothing but procedures, just like when you create an internal subroutine, you have to identify each procedure file by its name. The command:

PROCEDURE DISPTOT

identifies the procedure file. The RETURN statement ends the procedure.

The DISPTOT procedure is composed almost completely of @ SAY commands. The first statement places an underline under the eighth item line. Instead of using the LINECNT variable, place the underline on a specific line. In fact, all of the totals go on specific lines.

After the underline goes the text for subtotal and the field itself. The PICTURE clauses align all of the decimals. The discount text is concatenated with the string of the discount percentage from the invoice file and the percent sign. Discount (DISC) is calculated as the subtotal times the discount in the invoice file divided by 100. Remember, whole number percentages have to be divided by 100 to transform them to their decimal equivalent before they can be used. After the discount is calculated, it can be displayed.

Another underline is displayed followed by the taxable amount label and calculation. Once the taxable amount is known, the tax can be figured. First, the taxable status is checked in the customer file. If it is true, then the tax is calculated; if not, then the tax is 0 and both the label and amount reflect that.

The tax is calculated by first subtracting the discount from the subtotal to once again get taxable amount. You could have created yet another memory variable to hold the taxable amount calculation, but if you can avoid creating hundreds of memory variables you are better off. The first part of the calculation is now multiplied by the tax rate divided by 100 to calculate the tax. The tax is then displayed.

Finally the total amount is calculated as SUBTOTAL-DISC+TX.

There is a lot to the invoice add procedure. There is even more to the invoice change procedure. When you need to do multi-file and multi-record input, it gets complicated. Move on to see how changing the invoice goes.

27

Changing the invoice with advanced data entry

Finally, look at the climax in data entry routines—multi-file, multi-record change routine. This is the most complex type of data entry routine you can write because it encompasses everything from the invoice add routine and adds the complexity of the customer add/change/delete logic in the change items logic. All this is accomplished in two modules.

The first of the two modules allows you to specify the invoice you want to change. After the information for the top of the invoice is retrieved, you can change the invoice date or the customer number. The same basic module is used as in the invoice add except that you have the invoice number pre-processor. Once the invoice is retrieved, a menu asks the user if they want to change the invoice items. This screen is shown in Fig. 27-1.

Once the user decides to change an invoice, the rest of the screen is displayed. All of the items are displayed on the screen. The REDRAW subroutine is used to do this. You will see this later. Essentially, it finds the first item in the file with the matching invoice number and then displays all the following records while the invoice numbers match. It doesn't matter if there are zero or eight items, a loop controls the display. After REDRAW does its display, the DISPTOT subroutine displays the totals at the bottom of the screen. That is the easy part. Once this happens, a menu is displayed, as you can see in Fig. 27-2.

The menu then controls the data entry. The user must choose whether they want to add, change, or delete an item, or exit the item data entry. Each choice runs a separate group of code in the program.

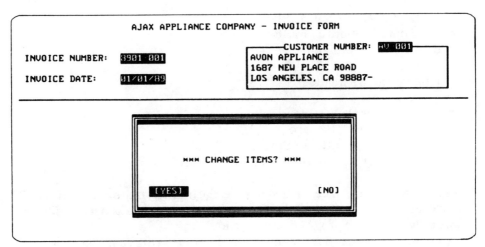

27-1 The invoice change module—screen 1.

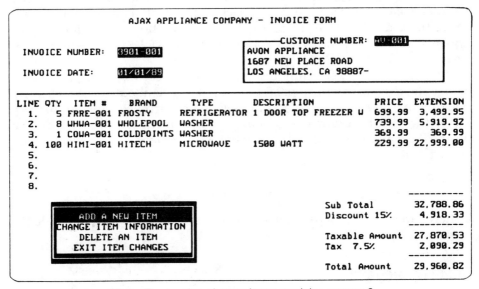

27-2 The invoice change items module—screen 2.

Some new design and coding techniques

Two techniques can make the coding simpler. Between the three groups of code (add, change, delete) there are eight error windows including some that are duplicate. These windows are divided into two groups: Add and Change. The Add windows include:

- Invoice Form Is Full—Create a New Invoice

- Item Number Cannot Be Blank
- Not Enough Quantity in Stock
- Item Number Not Found

The Change windows include:

- Item Number Cannot Be Blank
- Quantity Cannot Be Zero
- Not Enough Quantity in Stock
- Item Number Not Found

These error windows can be created as internal (or external) subroutines and simply called when needed. This can save some valuable space, and more importantly, make the programs more readable.

Another technique to make following the processing easier is to change the way the error-checking IF statements are coded. Instead of having many nested IF statements for all of these error-checking conditions, you will see that each condition is a separate IF check. A LOOP statement bypasses the rest of the code if an error is detected. This way, the code is almost pure sequence with a lot of calls, but the logic is easier to follow. You will see this when you look at the code.

By using these two techniques, you can reduce the main part of the change items code from five pages of code down to about three pages. By reducing the number of windows to only one occurrence, you can further reduce the code by another page. Each page is about 60 lines of code. By halving the main code section, you also halve the complexity. You will see this when it is displayed.

The inventory change programs

Rather than view a lot of pseudocode, let's get right to the program code for these modules.

The main program

Examine the main program code first. The code is shown in Fig. 27-3. The main part of the change program is very similar to the add invoice routine, so concentrate on the differences. By now you have seen that only about 20 commands are needed to accomplish most of what you need to in dBASE IV. You have seen most of the constructs:

- DO WHILE
- IF-THEN
- DO CASE
- SCAN

You have seen how to use the STORE command or just make one thing equal another, and you have seen @ SAY and @ GET commands. Besides this, there are the menu and window commands and subroutines. That's about it. About 90% of most of your programs use only these commands: it's how you put them together that counts.

The program starts by activating a window and then clearing it. The border is reset to single because the window has no border and lines are needed in the data entry screen. Next, some variables are made public so other modules can use them. A pre-processor is created to get the value of inventory number that needs to be changed.

The top of the form is built with @ SAYs. Unlike the add screen, the only GET is the invoice number field. Once the invoice number is input, the error checking can begin.

The invoice number data entry is checked to see if it is blank. If it is, then the routine is exited back to the main invoice menu. If not, the module continues. The INVOICE file is SELECTed, and the invoice number is found. If it is FOUND( ), then the invoice date and customer number is retrieved from the file. The customer number is used to position the record pointer in the CUSTOMER file. The customer information is retrieved and displayed in the customer box. After this group of code, the screen is reopened for input so you can change the invoice date or the customer number.

The invoice date is verified with the RANGE parameter. If the customer number is changed, it must be reverified. A loop is set up to verify the customer number. The customer number cannot be blank. This is verified first. If it is found, then the new customer information is displayed and the EXIT statement drops the program out of the loop to the statement following the ENDDO. If the customer number entered is not valid, then an error window is displayed. Another @ GET and a READ is placed at the bottom of the loop to get a new customer number until a valid customer number is entered.

Once everything passes validation, the program continues. First, the INVOICE file is selected. The CUSTNO field is replaced with the new value of the customer number.

The next step is to decide whether the user wants to change the items or not. A menu called "yesno" is defined as shown in Fig. 27-2. The menu has two choices, [YES] and [NO]. The yes choice sets the logical variable CHGITEM to .T., while the no choice doesn't. After the window and menu are deactivated, if the value of CHGITEM is .F., then the program returns to the beginning of the module to change a different invoice. If CHGITEM is .T., then the INVCCHGI program is called, which allows changes to the items. This module is covered next.

At the bottom of the code is an IF statement that checks the value of DELSW. This is a variable that is set to .T. if any of the items in the ITEMS file are deleted. This packs the file if necessary.

```
***********************************************************************
* Program......: INVCCHG.PRG
* Author.......: Cary N. Prague
* Date.........: 10-02-88, Final Revision 01-01-89 Revised 3-12-92
* Module #.....: 2.1.2
* dBASE Ver....: IV 1.5
* Description..: AJAX APPLIANCE COMPANY INVOICE CHANGES
***********************************************************************
ACTIVATE WINDOW datan
CLEAR
SET BORDER TO SINGLE
PUBLIC INVN,DELSW
STORE .F. TO DELSW
STORE SPACE(8) TO INVN
DO WHILE .T.
   @  0,20 SAY "AJAX APPLIANCE COMPANY - INVOICE FORM"
   @  3,1 SAY 'INVOICE NUMBER: ' GET INVN PICTURE "####-###"
   @  5,1 SAY 'INVOICE DATE:       '
   @  2,40 TO 6,76
   @  2,47 SAY 'CUSTOMER NUMBER:'
   @  7,0 TO 7,79
   READ
   IF INVN = SPACE(8) .OR. INVN = '    -   '
      EXIT
      ELSE
      SELECT INVOICE
      SEEK TRIM(INVN)
      IF FOUND()
         STORE INVDATE TO IDT
         STORE CUSTNO TO CSN
         SELECT CUSTOMER
         SEEK TRIM(CSN)
         STORE COMPANY TO CMP
         STORE STREET TO STR
         STORE TRIM(CITY) + ', ' + STATE + ' ' + ZIP TO CSZ
         @ 3,41 SAY CMP
         @ 4,41 SAY STR
         @ 5,41 SAY CSZ
         SELECT INVOICE
         @  5,1 SAY 'INVOICE DATE:     ' GET IDT  ;
             RANGE CTOD('01/01/88'),CTOD('12/31/99')
         @  2,47 SAY 'CUSTOMER NUMBER:' GET CSN  PICTURE "@! AA-###"
         READ
         ERRSW = .F.
         IF CSN # CUSTNO
           ERRSW = .T.
         ENDIF
         DO WHILE ERRSW
            IF CSN = '   -   '  .OR. CSN = SPACE(6)
               ?? CHR(7)
               ACTIVATE WINDOW msg1
               @ 2,05 SAY '        *** ERROR ***'
               @ 4,05 SAY 'CUSTOMER NUMBER CANNOT BE BLANK'
               @ 5,05 SAY '   ENTER A CUSTOMER NUMBER'
               @ 6,1  SAY ' '
               WAIT "        PRESS ANY KEY TO CONTINUE"
               DEACTIVATE WINDOW msg1
            ELSE
               SELECT CUSTOMER
               SEEK TRIM(CSN)
               IF FOUND()
                  @ 3,41 SAY COMPANY
                  @ 4,41 SAY STREET
                  @ 5,41 SAY TRIM(CITY) + ', ' + STATE + ' ' + ZIP
                  EXIT
```

27-3 The program code for changing invoices.

```
                        ELSE
                          ?? CHR(7)
                          ACTIVATE WINDOW msg1
                          @ 2,05 SAY '          *** ERROR ***'
                          @ 4,05 SAY '  CUSTOMER NUMBER NOT ON FILE'
                          @ 5,05 SAY 'ENTER ANOTHER CUSTOMER NUMBER'
                          @ 6,1  SAY ' '
                          WAIT "        PRESS ANY KEY TO CONTINUE"
                          DEACTIVATE WINDOW msg1
                        ENDIF
                   ENDIF
                   @  2,47 SAY 'CUSTOMER NUMBER:' GET CSN  PICTURE "@! AA-999"
                   READ
              ENDDO
              SELECT INVOICE
              REPLACE CUSTNO WITH CSN
              CHGITEM = .F.
              DEFINE MENU yesno
              DEFINE PAD yes OF yesno PROMPT "[YES]" AT 6,2
              ON SELECTION PAD yes OF yesno DO OKTOCHG
              DEFINE PAD no OF yesno PROMPT "[NO]" AT 6,31
              ON SELECTION PAD no OF yesno DEACTIVATE MENU
              ACTIVATE WINDOW msg2
              @ 3,05 SAY '    *** CHANGE ITEMS? ***        '
              @ 4,05 SAY '                                 '
              ACTIVATE menu yesno
              DEACTIVATE WINDOW msg2
              IF CHGITEM
                @ 8, 0 SAY "LINE"
                @ 8, 5 SAY "QTY"
                @ 8,10 SAY "ITEM #"
                @ 8,20 SAY "BRAND"
                @ 8,31 SAY "TYPE"
                @ 8,42 SAY "DESCRIPTION"
                @ 8,64 SAY "PRICE"
                @ 8,71 SAY "EXTENSION"
                DO INVCCHGI
              ENDIF
              CLEAR
              STORE SPACE(8) TO INVN
            ELSE
              ?? CHR(7)
              ACTIVATE WINDOW msg1
              @ 2,05 SAY '          *** ERROR ***'
              @ 4,05 SAY '   INVOICE NUMBER NOT FOUND'
              @ 5,05 SAY ' ENTER ANOTHER INVOICE NUMBER'
              @ 6,1  SAY ' '
              WAIT "        PRESS ANY KEY TO CONTINUE"
              DEACTIVATE WINDOW msg1
              STORE SPACE(8) TO INVN
            ENDIF
      ENDIF
  ENDIF
ENDDO
IF DELSW
  SELECT ITEMS
  PACK
ENDIF
DEACTIVATE WINDOW datan
RETURN

PROCEDURE OKTOCHG
  CHGITEM = .Y.
  DEACTIVATE MENU
RETURN
```

The Add/Change/Delete Items program

The Change Items program is the most complicated module of this system. Before looking at the code, reduce the code to its major sections. Figure 27-4 shows the major parts of the code.

```
DO WHILE MOREINVI
  SELECT ITEMS
  SEEK TRIM(INVN)
  IF REDRAW
    DO REDRAW
    DO DISPTOT
  ENDIF
  ACTIVATE POPUP CHGMENU
  IF SEL = 'ADD'                    && DETERMINE NEW LINE NUMBER TO ADD
  IF SEL = 'CHG' .OR. SEL = 'DEL'   && DETERMINE LINE NUMBER TO CHANGE OR DELETE
  SELECT ITEMS
  IF SEL = 'ADD'                    && ADD ITEM
  IF SEL = 'CHG'                    && CHANGE ITEM
  IF SEL = 'DEL'                    && DELETE ITEM
```

27-4 The major parts of the items change program.

There is one main loop. The items file is selected, and the REDRAW and DISPTOT procedures run. This displays the bottom part of the screen, including all of the calculations and totals. Once the screen is displayed, the menu can be activated, and the user can pick whether they want to add, change, delete, or exit. If exit is selected, the program terminates and control is returned to the main invoice change program. If ADD, CHG, or DEL is selected, then two things must happen. First, the cursor must be positioned on the right record. If ADD is chosen, then the cursor is moved to the first blank line. Of course, if there are already eight lines, the user receives an error window. If CHG or DEL is selected, the user is prompted for the line number to change or delete before the cursor is positioned. Once this block happens, then the ITEMS file is reselected and the process continues. While two different code groups position the cursor, three different groups actually do the work.

Add requires that a new record is appended to the file and the quantity and item number input to it. The price from the inventory file is also placed on the file using the exact same logic as the INVCADDI program. The change function changes the data directly in the database using the same logic as in the customer change program. The delete function is also the same as in the customer system. After the record is selected, it is highlighted and a menu appears within a window asking the user to confirm the delete.

Look at the program code for the INVCCHGI module. Notice that the commented major sections make it easier to follow the program logic. You will have to keep flipping back to see the program because it is a long one; if you try it, you will find it is an excellent design for multi-record input. In the back of the book is information about the disk with these programs if you wish to purchase it.

Figure 27-5 displays the main part of the program. The subroutines are not shown in this figure.

The program begins by setting the MOREINVI variable to .T.. You can't use an endless loop here, because there are too many complex conditions. The count (CNT) for the number of items and the selection that is chosen (SEL) are made public, because they are used in the external subroutines.

The pop-up menu that appears in the bottom left corner of the screen is defined. The user can choose one of the four choices. When the desired choice is selected, the CHGPICK internal subroutine is run. This simply sets the value of SEL to either ADD, CHG, or DEL and then deactivates the pop-up and removes it from the screen.

After the menu is defined, the ITEMS file is selected and the value of REDRAW is made true. After the record pointer is placed on the first occurrence of the invoice number in the ITEMS file, the REDRAW variable is checked. When it is true, all the records are displayed, and the descriptive values from the inventory file are also displayed. The price extension is also calculated and displayed. This subroutine is fully examined in the next section of this chapter. After displaying all of the items found, the totals are displayed using the same DISPTOT subroutine as in the invoice add program. Once the initial screen is displayed, the data entry can then commence. When each item is added, changed, or deleted, the menu reappears and control returns to the ACTIVATE POPUP command.

The first check is to see if the value of MOREINVI is .F.. This happens when the user chooses EXIT in the menu. This loops to the bottom of the main loop and out of the module.

The next IF statement checks to see if ADD was chosen. The line number must then be calculated. CNT stores the value of the number of items in the invoice. This is calculated when REDRAW runs. As long as the value of CNT is less than eight, the counter is updated. The variable LN is used to store the value of the line number where the cursor needs to be to add or change the record. If not, an error window is displayed, and the LOOP statement returns to the top of the DO loop where the menu is redisplayed. When there is an error, the memory variable REDRAW is left in the false state so there is no time wasted in redrawing the screen if nothing has changed.

Notice that each IF statement is a separate group. This avoids many complicated IF ELSE groups. When an error exists, it is easy to follow right in sequence in the code, and you don't have to skip down hundreds of lines to see the message or follow the logic. This is one of many ways to code complicated logic.

The next group of code determines the line to change or delete. A standard error loop is set up so you can't continue until you enter a "good" line number. A window is placed on the center of the screen. The window asks you to enter the line number. This is the first time you have seen a data entry within a small window. There is really no difference from the data entry you have been doing in the big windows. @ SAYs and an @ GET READ the line number. Notice that the memory variable LN is used to store the input. This

```
******************************************************************
* Program......: INVCCHGI.PRG (WITHOUT SUBROUTINES)
* Author.......: Cary N. Prague
* Date.........: 10-02-88, Final Revision 01-01-89 Revised 3-12-92
* Module #.....: 2.1.2.1
* dBASE Ver....: IV 1.5
* Description..: AJAX APPLIANCE COMPANY INVOICE ITEM CHANGES
******************************************************************
STORE .T. TO MOREINVI
PUBLIC CNT,SEL
*-- Popup
SET BORDER TO SINGLE
DEFINE POPUP CHGMENU FROM 18,6 TO 23,31
DEFINE BAR 1 OF CHGMENU PROMPT "    ADD A NEW ITEM       "
DEFINE BAR 2 OF CHGMENU PROMPT "CHANGE ITEM INFORMATION"
DEFINE BAR 3 OF CHGMENU PROMPT "     DELETE AN ITEM      "
DEFINE BAR 4 OF CHGMENU PROMPT "    EXIT ITEM CHANGES    "
ON SELECTION POPUP CHGMENU DO CHGPICK

SELECT ITEMS
REDRAW = .T.
DO WHILE MOREINVI
  SELECT ITEMS
  SEEK TRIM(INVN)
  IF REDRAW
    DO REDRAW
    DO DISPTOT
  ENDIF
  ACTIVATE POPUP CHGMENU
  IF MOREINVI = .F.
    LOOP
  ENDIF
  IF SEL = 'ADD'          && DETERMINE NEW LINE NUMBER TO ADD
    IF CNT < 8
      LN = CNT + 1
    ELSE
      ?? CHR(7)
      ACTIVATE WINDOW msg1
      @ 1,05 SAY '      *** ERROR ***'
      @ 3,05 SAY '   INVOICE FORM IS FULL'
      @ 4,05 SAY '   CREATE A NEW INVOICE  '
      @ 5,1  SAY ' '
      WAIT "      PRESS ANY KEY TO CONTINUE"
      DEACTIVATE WINDOW msg1
      LOOP
    ENDIF
  ENDIF
  IF SEL = 'CHG' .OR. SEL = 'DEL'   && DETERMINE LINE NUMBER TO CHANGE OR DELETE
    ERRSW = .T.
    DO WHILE ERRSW
      LN = 0
      ?? CHR(7)
      ACTIVATE WINDOW msg1
      @ 1,05 SAY '    ENTER LINE NUMBER    '
      @ 2,05 SAY '    OR ENTER 0 TO EXIT'
      @ 4,05 SAY '     LINE NUMBER: ' GET LN PICTURE '9' RANGE 0,8
      @ 5,1  SAY ' '
      READ
      DEACTIVATE WINDOW msg1
      IF LN = 0
        ERRSW = .F.
        LOOP
      ENDIF
```

27-5 The INVCCHGI program without the subroutines.

```
      IF LN > CNT
        ?? CHR(7)
        ACTIVATE WINDOW msg1
        @ 2,05 SAY '          *** ERROR ***'
        @ 4,05 SAY 'LINE NUMBER IS GREATER THAN'
        @ 5,05 SAY '    THE LAST LINE NUMBER '
        @ 6,1  SAY ' '
        WAIT "         PRESS ANY KEY TO CONTINUE"
        DEACTIVATE WINDOW msg1
        LOOP
      ENDIF
      ERRSW = .F.
    ENDDO
    IF LN = 0
      LOOP
    ENDIF
  ENDIF
  SELECT ITEMS
  IF SEL = 'ADD'                                              && ADD ITEM
    QNTY = 0
    ITMN = SPACE(8)
    DO WHILE .T.
      LINECNT = 8+CNT+1
      SELECT ITEMS
      @ LINECNT,5 GET QNTY PICTURE '999'
      @ LINECNT,9 GET ITMN PICTURE '@! AAAA-999'
      READ
      IF QNTY = 0
        EXIT
      ENDIF
      SELECT INVENTRY
      IF ITMN = SPACE(8) .OR. ITMN = '    -    '
        DO ERRINB
        LOOP
      ENDIF
      SEEK TRIM(ITMN)
      IF .NOT. FOUND()
        DO ERRINF
        LOOP
      ENDIF
      STORE PRICE TO PRI
      IF QNTY > QTY_STK
        DO ERRQNS
        LOOP
      ENDIF
*     REPLACE QTY_STK WITH QTY_STK-QNTY        && REDUCE THE INVENTORY
      SELECT ITEMS
      APPEND BLANK
      REPLACE INVNO WITH INVN, QTY WITH QNTY, ITEMNO WITH ITMN, ;
          PRICE WITH PRI
      STORE .T. TO REDRAW
      EXIT
    ENDDO
  ENDIF
  IF SEL = 'CHG'                               && CHANGE ITEM
    STORE 1 TO LOOPCNT
    SEEK TRIM(INVN)
    DO WHILE LOOPCNT < LN .AND. INVN = ITEMS->INVNO
      IF .NOT. DELETED()
        STORE LOOPCNT+1 TO LOOPCNT
      ENDIF
      SKIP
    ENDDO
    STORE 8+LOOPCNT TO LINECNT
```

```
DO WHILE .T.
  SELECT ITEMS
  @ LINECNT,5 GET QTY PICTURE '999'
  @ LINECNT,9 GET ITEMNO PICTURE '@! AAAA-999'
  READ
  STORE QTY TO QNTY
  STORE ITEMNO TO ITMN
  IF QNTY = 0
    DO ERRQN0
    LOOP
  ENDIF
  IF ITMN = SPACE(8) .OR. ITMN = '    -    '
    DO ERRINB
    LOOP
  ENDIF
  SELECT INVENTRY
  SEEK TRIM(ITMN)
  IF .NOT. FOUND()
    DO ERRINF
    LOOP
  ENDIF
  STORE PRICE TO PRI
  IF QNTY > QTY_STK
    DO ERRQNS
    LOOP
  ENDIF
  SELECT ITEMS
  REPLACE PRICE WITH PRI
  EXIT
ENDDO
STORE .F. TO ERRSW
REDRAW = .T.
ENDIF
IF SEL = 'DEL'                                  && DELETE ITEM
  SELECT ITEMS
  STORE 1 TO LOOPCNT
  SEEK TRIM(INVN)
  DO WHILE LOOPCNT <LN .AND. INVN = ITEMS->INVNO
    IF .NOT. DELETED()
      STORE LOOPCNT+1 TO LOOPCNT
    ENDIF
    SKIP
  ENDDO
  STORE 8+LOOPCNT TO LINECNT
  DO DELREC
  REDRAW = .T.
ENDIF
ENDDO
```

is the same variable that is used by the add routine that calculated it instead of letting the user enter it.

Once the line number is entered, it too must be validated. If LN is 0, then the process is exited and the menu reappears. If it is not 0, then it is compared to the value of CNT. If there are five item lines in the invoice, then the value of LN must be less than or equal to CNT. If the value of LN is greater than CNT, then an error window is displayed.

Notice that the IF LN=0 statement is in two places. The first time was inside the DO WHILE ERRSW loop. That first occurrence would take you out of the error loop. However, you are still in the main loop. Unless you exit that loop too, then the program continues into the next set of statements and tries to change or delete a line number that was never calculated. The second IF LN=0 and LOOP statement takes you out of both loops. The second statement is after the first ENDDO, because all the LOOP statement does is take you out of the current DO loop, not all the active loops.

Once a valid line number is calculated or entered, the next groups of code can be run. There are three groups of statements, one each for the add, change, and delete functions.

In the add function, the same logic is used as in the invoice add items program. In fact, it was copied almost exactly from the other module. Memory variables are created for quantity and item number. LINECNT is set to 8+CNT+1. The 8 is the line number where the column titles are placed. CNT is the number of items already in the invoice. Because the new item must be 1 greater than that, the equation becomes 8+CNT+1. It could have just as easily been CNT+9, but this way its easier for us to understand.

Once LINECNT is calculated, the quantity and item number fields can be input. After the READ statement, the four verification conditions are executed. First, QNTY must not be zero; if it is, then you exit from the data entry. Next, ITEMN cannot be blank. If it is, the procedure ERRINB is run and you loop to the bottom of the DO WHILE loop and are asked to input again. The DO WHILE loop that you are in is exclusively for the ADD function for getting the quantity and item number correct before going on. The only way out is to do this correctly or to enter a zero for the quantity and then data entry does not take place. If the "Item not blank" check passes, then the "Item not found" check must also pass. Finally, quantity input must be greater than quantity in stock or yet another error message is displayed. If everything passes, only then does data entry occur.

First, the inventory is reduced. Then a blank record is added to the ITEMS file and all of the fields are replaced with good data fields. REDRAW is set to true to redraw the screen and display new totals. The EXIT statement gets you out of the endless loop so you can continue.

The SEL = 'CHG' and SEL = 'DEL' are skipped if the function was add; the next statement to be run would be back at the top of the main loop.

Look at what is inside the SEL = 'CHG' code group. This gets executed when the user chooses CHANGE ITEM and then enters a valid line number to change. The variable LOOPCNT positions the cursor on a line that contains data. The line number can be easily calculated as the value of the line number input (LN) + 8. However, in order to figure out where to position the record pointer in the ITEMS file, you have to do a little more work. First, the SEEK statement positions the record pointer on the first item record in the ITEMS file for that record number. Now, all you have to do is SKIP to the correct record. This is still tricky. A loop is set up to SKIP through the records while LOOPCNT is less than the number of non-deleted lines and the invoice number is the same as the invoice you are processing. You must watch for DELETED( ) records which don't show up during the redraw procedure and are not counted; the records are counted with a simple SKIP command. If the record is deleted, then LOOPCNT is not updated. When LOOPCNT equals the value of LN (the input line number), then the cursor is correctly positioned. LINECNT is then equal to 8+LOOPCNT, and with the record pointer correctly positioned, changes can be made.

A data validation loop begins. The ITEMS file is reselected; at the current LINECNT position, you can change the current values of QTY and ITEMNO. After the READ, the new values are stored to memory variables. Quantity is checked to make sure it isn't zero.

If it is, an error window appears and you must reenter the quantity. The other same three checks from the add function are performed:

- Item cannot be blank
- Item must be found on the inventory file
- Quantity desired cannot exceed quantity in stock

If all this passes, then the price is updated and you are EXITed from the loop. REDRAW is again set to true, so the screen can be redrawn and the totals recalculated.

Finally, the delete function is very simple. Using the same positioning logic as the change routine, the record pointer is positioned on the desired record to delete. The subroutine DELREC is then executed. As you will see, this first highlights the record to be deleted and then confirms the delete. Now look at all the internal subroutines to see what each one does. The delete function uses DELREC which also uses DELETE, another internal subroutine.

The internal subroutines

Figure 27-6 shows the internal subroutines. There are four error subroutines. Each is nothing more than a window and some text. You have seen these same subroutines in many of the previous modules. Common routines like these probably belong in some common external procedure file.

The CHGPICK subroutine is what the menu calls when it needs to make a selection after the user has chosen the menu item.

Finally, we come to the delete procedures. DELREC is the procedure that the delete function called to actually perform the delete. First, the line is highlighted that is to be deleted. This is done by using the command:

@ LINECNT,5 FILL TO LINECNT,79 COLOR W+/R

This makes the whole line red where it was previously blue. Individual fields are not highlighted, because you are deleting the whole record. This visually tells the user that the whole record is being affected, not just some of the fields as when the add or change routines are run. The same window and menu in a window confirmation routine is then run. This screen is shown in Fig. 27-7.

```
************************************************************************
* Program......: INVCCHGI.PRG (SUBROUTINES)
* Author.......: Cary N. Prague
* Date.........: 10-02-88, Final Revision 01-01-89 Revised 3-12-92
* Module #.....: 2.1.2.1
* dBASE Ver....: IV 1.5
* Description..: AJAX APPLIANCE COMPANY INVOICE ITEM CHANGES
************************************************************************

PROCEDURE ERRINB    && ITEM CANNOT BE BLANK
 ?? CHR(7)
 ACTIVATE WINDOW msg1
 @ 2,05 SAY '      *** ERROR ***'
 @ 4,05 SAY ' ITEM NUMBER CANNOT BE BLANK'
 @ 5,05 SAY '  ENTER AN ITEM NUMBER'
 @ 6,1  SAY ' '
 WAIT "       PRESS ANY KEY TO CONTINUE"
 DEACTIVATE WINDOW msg1
RETURN

PROCEDURE ERRINF    && ITEM NOT FOUND
 ?? CHR(7)
 ACTIVATE WINDOW msg1
 @ 2,05 SAY '      *** ERROR ***'
 @ 4,05 SAY '   ITEM NUMBER NOT ON FILE'
 @ 5,05 SAY ' ENTER ANOTHER ITEM NUMBER'
 @ 6,1  SAY ' '
 WAIT "       PRESS ANY KEY TO CONTINUE"
 DEACTIVATE WINDOW msg1
RETURN


PROCEDURE ERRQN0    && QUANTITY CANNOT BE 0
 ?? CHR(7)
 ACTIVATE WINDOW msg1
 @ 2,05 SAY '      *** ERROR ***'
 @ 4,05 SAY '    QUANTITY CANNOT BE 0'
 @ 5,05 SAY '    CHANGE THE QUANTITY  '
 @ 6,1  SAY ' '
 WAIT "       PRESS ANY KEY TO CONTINUE"
 DEACTIVATE WINDOW msg1
RETURN

PROCEDURE ERRQNS    && QUANTITY NOT SUFFICIENT
 ?? CHR(7)
 ACTIVATE WINDOW msg1
 @ 2,05 SAY '      *** ERROR ***'
 @ 4,05 SAY ' NOT ENOUGH QUANTITY IN STOCK'
 @ 5,05 SAY '  REDUCE THE QUANTITY TO ' + STR(QTY_STK,3)
 @ 6,1  SAY ' '
 WAIT "       PRESS ANY KEY TO CONTINUE"
 DEACTIVATE WINDOW msg1
RETURN

PROCEDURE CHGPICK
 DO CASE
    CASE BAR() = 1
       SEL = 'ADD'
       DEACTIVATE POPUP
    CASE BAR() = 2
       SEL = 'CHG'
       DEACTIVATE POPUP
```

27-6 The INVCCHGI internal subroutines.

```
   CASE BAR() = 3
      SEL = 'DEL'
      DEACTIVATE POPUP
   CASE BAR() = 4
      MOREINVI = .F.
      DEACTIVATE POPUP
 ENDCASE
RETURN

PROCEDURE DELREC
   @ LINECNT,5 FILL TO LINECNT,79 COLOR W+/R
   ?? CHR(7)
   DEFINE MENU yesno
   DEFINE PAD no OF yesno PROMPT "[NO]" AT 6,2
   ON SELECTION PAD no OF yesno DEACTIVATE MENU
   DEFINE PAD yes OF yesno PROMPT "[YES]" AT 6,30
   ON SELECTION PAD yes OF yesno DO DELETE
   ACTIVATE WINDOW msg2
   @ 1,05 SAY '  *** CONFIRM DELETE ***     '
   @ 3,05 SAY '    DO YOU REALLY WANT TO     '
   @ 4,05 SAY '     DELETE THIS RECORD       '
   ACTIVATE menu yesno
   DEACTIVATE WINDOW msg2
   @ LINECNT,5 FILL TO LINECNT,79 COLOR W+/B
RETURN

PROCEDURE DELETE
   DELETE
   DELSW = .T.
   DEACTIVATE MENU
RETURN
```

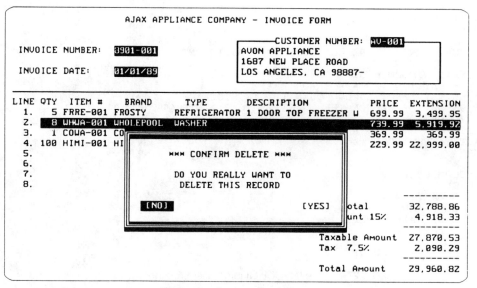

27-7 Confirming the delete.

If the user answers affirmatively, then the DELETE subroutine actually deletes the record. If a record is deleted, then DELSW is set to true so the INVCCHG main program can pack the items file.

That's it for the internal subroutines. Now look at the REDRAW subroutine in the external procedure file INVOICE.

The REDRAW external subroutine

The REDRAW subroutine is used to redraw the screen. The subroutine itself (taken out of the procedure file) is shown in Fig. 27-8. It is nothing more than a couple loops, relational display, and calculations.

```
PROCEDURE REDRAW
    PUBLIC SUBTOT
    STORE 0 TO CNT
    STORE 0 TO SUBTOT
    STORE 9 TO LINECNT
    STORE 1 TO LOOPCNT
    REDRAW = .F.
    @ LINECNT,1 CLEAR TO LINECNT+7,79
    DO WHILE INVN=ITEMS->INVNO .AND. .NOT. EOF()
       IF .NOT. DELETED()
          CNT = CNT + 1
          @ LINECNT,1 SAY CNT PICTURE '99.'
          @ LINECNT,5  SAY QTY PICTURE '999'
          @ LINECNT,9  SAY ITEMNO
          STORE QTY TO QNTY
          STORE ITEMNO TO ITN
          STORE PRICE TO PRI
          SELECT INVENTRY
          SEEK TRIM(ITN)
          @ LINECNT,18 SAY BRAND
          @ LINECNT,29 SAY TYPE
          @ LINECNT,42 SAY SUBSTR(DESC,1,20)
          SELECT ITEMS
          @ LINECNT,62 SAY PRI PICTURE '99999.99'
          @ LINECNT,71 SAY QNTY*PRI PICTURE '99,999.99'
          SUBTOT = SUBTOT + (QNTY*PRI)
          STORE LOOPCNT+1 TO LOOPCNT
          STORE LINECNT+1 TO LINECNT
       ENDIF
       SKIP
    ENDDO
    DO WHILE LINECNT < 17
       @ LINECNT,1 SAY LOOPCNT PICTURE '99.'
       STORE LOOPCNT+1 TO LOOPCNT
       STORE LINECNT+1 TO LINECNT
    ENDDO
RETURN
```

27-8 The REDRAW procedure.

The variable SUBTOT is made public because its value is needed by DISPTOT when it is called after the REDRAW procedure is finished from whatever program called REDRAW.

Next, several counters are set up. These include CNT (the number of items), SUBTOT (the total of quantity*price), LINECNT (the row number to display the records on the screen), and LOOPCNT (used to determine how many lines are left and to blank those out).

The value of the memory variable REDRAW is set back to .F. so that it won't be called again until one of the other modules sets it to .T.. As the invoice change, delete, or view program is looping, it only calls REDRAW when a change has been made to the data.

The screen is then cleared from row 9, column 1 to row 16, column 79. LINECNT is used in case only one line has to be changed—the value of LINECNT.

Now the loop begins. As long as there are records in the ITEM file with the same invoice number as the invoice being processed, this loop continues. It also stops when end-of-file is reached (EOF( ) = .T.). Only the non-deleted records are processed although, as you can see at the bottom of the ENDIF, the SKIP statement is outside the IF boundaries. All records must be skipped even if they are deleted. If the SKIP was inside the ENDIF, the system would stop when it came to a deleted record instead of bypassing it.

Each time a record is found, the value of CNT is increased by one. The item count, quantity, and item number are displayed. Then, the inventory file is selected and the matching item number found. The brand, type, and the first 20 characters of the description are displayed. Then the ITEMS file is reselected so the price can be displayed and the quantity*price calculation is displayed. Subtotal is updated by adding the current value of subtotal to the record's item extension. Both LINECNT and LOOPCNT are updated. The next record is then retrieved.

When the loop is exited, it means that there were no more records to process. One more loop is executed from the current value of LINECNT to 17. If it already is 17, nothing happens. What this does is clear the remainder of the screen and write in just the line numbers. If only three records were found, then the loop is run five times and writes the line numbers four through eight.

The invoice delete and view programs

The invoice delete and view programs are extremely similar to the change program. You can find these programs in appendix B.

28
Reports from multiple files

You have come a long way in this book. In this last chapter, you will produce three reports:

- Invoice
- Warranty Agreements
- Monthly Sales Report

Because of the "bugs" in the report writer discussed in chapter 13 and our desire to show you the difference between writing to the screen and writing to paper, you will see this report programmed without the report writer. The other reports are shown from the front ends that are needed to call the reports.

First, in this final chapter, let's produce a report from the invoice file, invoice item file, customer file, and inventory files. No, not all at once, but in order to produce this report, data is needed from all four files. The report looks like Fig. 28-1.

```
           AJAX APPLIANCE COMPANY - INVOICE FORM

INVOICE NUMBER: 8901-001          CUSTOMER NUMBER:AV-001
                                  AVON APPLIANCE
                                  1687 NEW PLACE ROAD
INVOICE DATE:    01/01/89         LOS ANGELES, CA 98887-


QTY  ITEM #    BRAND      TYPE         DESCRIPTION            PRICE  EXTENSION

  5 FRRE-001 FROSTY     REFRIGERATOR 1 DOOR TOP FREEZER W   699.99  3,499.95
  8 WHWA-001 WHOLEPOOL  WASHER                              739.99  5,919.92
  1 COWA-001 COLDPOINTS WASHER                              369.99    369.99
100 HIMI-001 HITECH     MICROWAVE    1500 WATT              229.99 22,999.00
```

28-1   The invoice output form.

- It looks a little different than the invoice report done with the report writer. Data comes from all four files to make up this report. The invoice file is the main driver for this report. The invoice file is accessed for a specific invoice number. This invoice contains the customer number from which the customer information is retrieved. The invoice number then points to the item file where the quantity, item numbers, and prices are found. The descriptions for the items are found in the inventory file. This program is a good example of the multiple-file environment.
- A report of this type is actually made up of four separate parts in two modules. The first part is the screen that simply allows the alignment of the paper and the confirmation to print. The second part prints the customer information on the top of the report. For this, use the main part of the second module. Part three prints the item records. A modified version of the REDRAW subroutine is used. The last part prints the total amount and discount using DISPTOT.

The invoice pre-processor

Look at the module that creates the front end. First, let's look at the screen that is produced as shown in Fig. 28-2.

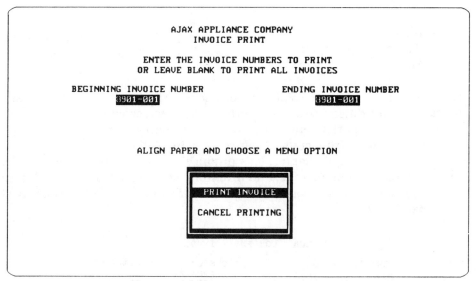

28-2 The invoice pre-processor screen.

As you can see, the input allows for two invoice numbers to be input. If no invoices are input, that means that all of the invoices are to be selected. Otherwise, the user must fill in the invoice numbers of both the first invoice to be printed and the last. If only one is desired, then the same number should be placed on both sides. The first invoice should be a lower number than the last, and both should exist on the file. In the code that you will see, only the first invoice number is checked for existence. If you wanted to make a more perfect system, you would need to check both numbers and also that the first number was lower than the second. Once the invoice numbers are entered, the menu appears. Like the other print menus that you have seen, this menu lets you either print the invoice or return to the main menu.

Let's first look at the code to produce this pre-processor screen. It is shown in Fig. 28-3.

As you can see, the code resembles other programs you have seen. By now you have realized that all of the programs in this book have a similar style. That is, once you have done a couple, they all look sort of alike. This is purposely done to make it easier for you to follow the various examples.

The program starts by opening the four databases necessary to the report. The relations are not set because SEEKs are used to position the record pointer in the different databases. When you are dealing with multiple occurrences of the same key, relations only can find the first occurrence. The SCAN construct which you learned about earlier can help, but it doesn't do everything.

Once the databases are opened and the memory variables defined, the pop-up menu can be defined. This pop-up is another good candidate for an external subroutine. It's used in almost all the report modules.

A loop is set up to handle the printing, the screen is displayed, and the input allowed. Notice that the headers are above the data entry areas instead of to their left as normally done.

The menu is then activated and the PRTPICK procedure run to print the invoice report. The PRTPICK procedure either prints the invoices or the printing is canceled and control returned to the main module AJAXPASS. If you need help remembering the module flow, see the diagram in Fig. 20-1.

If nothing was entered in the invoice entry areas, then the INVOICE file is selected and the record pointer placed at the top of the file. For each invoice in the file, the invoice printing program is called. Notice the statement SET CONSOLE OFF. This turns off the display to the screen by @ SAY commands. Because the printing program uses @ SAYs directed at the printer, there is no need to see them also on the screen. This also prevents the screen from being messed up. This is a good option to use whenever creating your own print programs.

If something was entered in the invoice file, then the first invoice number entered is found. If it is found, then the record pointer is set to that invoice. The print program is then called until the second invoice number entered is printed. If the first invoice number was not found, then an error window is displayed.

That's all there is to the invoice pre-processor. Now look at the invoice printing program.

The invoice report

The program and its subroutines are shown in Fig. 28-4. The program itself is very short. First, the command:

```
SET DEVICE TO PRINT
```

changes the target of @ SAY commands to the printer. The data from the current invoice is copied to memory variable fields. Then the top of the invoice is displayed. This code is the same as the change invoice screen except that there is no input. First, the customer file is selected

```
***********************************************************************
* Program.......: INVCINVC.PRG
* Author........: Cary N. Prague
* Date..........: 10-02-88, Final Revision 3-3-92 Revised 3-12-92
* Module #......: 2.2
* dBASE Ver.....: IV 1.5
* Description...: AJAX APPLIANCE COMPANY INVOICE PRINTING MENU PROGRAM
***********************************************************************
CLEAR
CLOSE DATABASES
USE INVOICE ORDER INVNO
USE CUSTOMER ORDER CUSTNO IN 2
USE INVENTRY ORDER ITEMNO IN 3
USE ITEMS ORDER INVNO IN 4
STORE .T. TO MOREPRT
STORE SPACE(8)  TO INVN1,INVN2

*-- Popup
SET BORDER TO SINGLE
DEFINE POPUP PRTMENU FROM 15,31 TO 21,49
DEFINE BAR 1 OF PRTMENU PROMPT "                " SKIP
DEFINE BAR 2 OF PRTMENU PROMPT "   PRINT INVOICE  "
DEFINE BAR 3 OF PRTMENU PROMPT "                " SKIP
DEFINE BAR 4 OF PRTMENU PROMPT " CANCEL PRINTING "
ON SELECTION POPUP PRTMENU DO PRTPICK

DO WHILE MOREPRT
   @ 1,22 SAY "       AJAX APPLIANCE COMPANY"
   @ 2,22 SAY "            INVOICE PRINT"
   @ 4,22 SAY " ENTER THE INVOICE NUMBERS TO PRINT"
   @ 5,22 SAY "OR LEAVE BLANK TO PRINT ALL INVOICES"
   @ 7,10 SAY "BEGINNING INVOICE NUMBER"
   @ 7,48 SAY "ENDING INVOICE NUMBER"
   @ 8,18 GET INVN1 PICTURE "@! ####-###"
   @ 8,54 GET INVN2 PICTURE "@! ####-###"
   READ
   @ 13,22 SAY 'ALIGN PAPER AND CHOOSE A MENU OPTION'

   ACTIVATE POPUP PRTMENU

ENDDO

RETURN

PROCEDURE PRTPICK
 DO CASE
   CASE BAR() = 2
      IF INVN1 = '        ' .OR. INVN1 = '      -   '
         SELECT INVOICE
         GO TOP
         DO WHILE .NOT. EOF()
          SET CONSOLE OFF
          DO INVCINVP
          SKIP
         ENDDO
         SET CONSOLE ON
```

28-3 The invoice printing menu program.

```
      ELSE
        SEEK TRIM(INVN1)
        IF FOUND()
            SCAN WHILE INVNO <= INVN2 .AND. .NOT. EOF()
             DO INVCINVP
            ENDSCAN
            STORE SPACE(8) TO INVN1
            STORE SPACE(8) TO INVN2
          ELSE
          ?? CHR(7)
          ACTIVATE WINDOW msg1
          @ 2,05 SAY '      *** ERROR ***'
          @ 4,05 SAY ' INVOICE NUMBER NOT ON FILE'
          @ 5,05 SAY 'ENTER ANOTHER INVOICE NUMBER'
          @ 6,1  SAY ' '
          WAIT "         PRESS ANY KEY TO CONTINUE"
          DEACTIVATE WINDOW msg1
          STORE SPACE(8) TO INVN1
          STORE SPACE(8) TO INVN2
        ENDIF
    ENDIF
    DEACTIVATE POPUP
  CASE BAR() = 4
    MOREPRT = .F.
    DEACTIVATE POPUP
ENDCASE
RETURN
```

and the customer data located so that the company name and address can be displayed. The ITEMS file is then selected and the first item found for that invoice number. The REDRAW and DISPTOT subroutines are then called.

The REDRAW program is virtually the same as the program used in the invoice change, delete, and view routines. There is no need to produce line numbers and those are not shown. It is reduced to a simple sequence of statements.

The DISPTOT program is unchanged except for the placement in a specific location and the addition of a double underline at the bottom of the report. DISPTOT could be changed to any position to meet the needs of any preprinted form.

After the DISPTOT program is run, control returns to the main invoice print program. The EJECT command ejects the paper by sending a form feed to the printer. The SET DEVICE TO SCREEN statement sends output back to the screen so the invoice pre- processor screen can display to the screen again. If there are still more invoices to print, the process is repeated.

The warranty agreement

Now that you have seen the code for the invoice pre-processor and the invoice printing program, you should understand one difference for the warranty program. The warranty program calls the warranty report you created in

```
**********************************************************************
* Program......: INVCINVP.PRG
* Author.......: Cary N. Prague
* Date.........: 10-03-88, Final Revision 01-01-89 Revised 3-12-92
* Module #.....: 2.2.1
* dBASE Ver....: IV 1.5
* Description..: AJAX APPLIANCE COMPANY INVOICE PRINT PROGRAM
**********************************************************************
   SET DEVICE TO PRINT
   STORE INVNO TO INVN
   STORE INVDATE TO IDT
   STORE CUSTNO TO CSN
   @  0,20 SAY "AJAX APPLIANCE COMPANY - INVOICE FORM"
   @  2,43 SAY 'CUSTOMER NUMBER:' + CUSTNO
   @  2,5 SAY 'INVOICE NUMBER: ' + INVNO
   SELECT CUSTOMER
   SEEK TRIM(CSN)
   @ 3,45 SAY COMPANY
   @ 4,45 SAY STREET
   @ 5,5 SAY 'INVOICE DATE:   ' + DTOC(IDT)
   @ 5,45 SAY TRIM(CITY) + ', ' + STATE + ' ' + ZIP
   @ 8, 5 SAY "QTY"
   @ 8,10 SAY "ITEM #"
   @ 8,20 SAY "BRAND"
   @ 8,31 SAY "TYPE"
   @ 8,42 SAY "DESCRIPTION"
   @ 8,64 SAY "PRICE"
   @ 8,71 SAY "EXTENSION"
   SELECT ITEMS
   SEEK TRIM(INVN)
   DO REDRAW
   DO DISPTOT
   EJECT
   SET DEVICE TO SCREEN
RETURN

PROCEDURE REDRAW
   PUBLIC SUBTOT
   STORE 0 TO CNT
   STORE 0 TO SUBTOT
   STORE 10 TO LINECNT
   DO WHILE INVN=ITEMS->INVNO .AND. .NOT. EOF()
    IF .NOT. DELETED()
       CNT = CNT + 1
       @ LINECNT,5  SAY QTY PICTURE '999'
       @ LINECNT,9  SAY ITEMNO
       STORE QTY TO QNTY
       STORE ITEMNO TO ITN
       STORE PRICE TO PRI
       SELECT INVENTRY
       SEEK TRIM(ITN)
       @ LINECNT,18 SAY BRAND
       @ LINECNT,29 SAY TYPE
       @ LINECNT,42 SAY SUBSTR(DESC,1,20)
       SELECT ITEMS
       @ LINECNT,62 SAY PRI PICTURE '99999.99'
       @ LINECNT,71 SAY QNTY*PRI PICTURE '99,999.99'
       SUBTOT = SUBTOT + (QNTY*PRI)
       STORE LINECNT+1 TO LINECNT
    ENDIF
    SKIP
   ENDDO
   SELECT INVOICE
RETURN
```

28-4 The invoice print program.

```
PROCEDURE DISPTOT
   @ 47,70 SAY '----------'
   @ 48,55 SAY 'Sub Total'
   @ 48,70 SAY SUBTOT PICTURE '999,999.99'
   @ 49,55 SAY 'Discount ' + STR(INVOICE->DISCOUNT,2) + '%'
   DISC =   SUBTOT * (INVOICE->DISCOUNT/100)
   @ 49,70 SAY DISC PICTURE '999,999.99'
   @ 50,70 SAY '----------'
   @ 51,55 SAY 'Taxable Amount'
   @ 51,70 SAY SUBTOT-DISC PICTURE '999,999.99'
   IF CUSTOMER->TAXABLE
      @ 52,55 SAY 'Tax ' + STR(TAX_RATE,4,1) + '%'
      TX = (SUBTOT-DISC) * (TAX_RATE/100)
      @ 52,70 SAY TX PICTURE '999,999.99'
    ELSE
      @ 52,55 SAY 'Tax - None'
      TX = 0
      @ 52,70 SAY TX PICTURE '999,999.99'
   ENDIF
   @ 53,70 SAY '----------'
   @ 54,55 SAY 'Total Amount'
   @ 54,70 SAY SUBTOT-DISC+TX PICTURE '999,999.99'
   @ 55,70 SAY '=========='
RETURN
```

chapter 13. However, this is the first report you see that has two possible choices for limiting the data. The pre-processor is just like the invoice program as you can choose one or more invoices to print. The one difference is the report statement:

```
REPORT FORM WARRANTY TO PRINT;
FOR INVNO >= INVN1 .AND. INVNO <= INVN2
```

This statement allows two conditions to be met. First, that the invoice number being processed is greater than or equal to the starting invoice number, and also that it is less than or equal to the ending number. This allows the invoice program to process a range of invoices. You can see this program in its entirety in appendix B.

The sales report

The sales report is very different than other reports and is shown in its entirety. In chapter 13, you designed and programmed the monthly sales report. This is a "rollup" report because you only wanted to see the totals and not the detail numbers. The report itself is handled by the report form. Let's look at the preprocessor for this report. Figure 28-5 displays the preprocessor screen.

The big difference here is that instead of using the invoice number as the selection, you are using year and month and comparing it to the year and month of the invoice date field. This involves "stripping" the year and month from the invoice date field and then comparing them to the value of the entered year and month.

Let's look at the program code for this module. The program code is shown in Fig. 28-6.

```
            AJAX APPLIANCE COMPANY
            MONTHLY SALES REPORT

        ENTER THE YEAR AND MONTH TO PRINT


        ENTER YEAR/MONTH:      89/01




        ALIGN PAPER AND CHOOSE A MENU OPTION


              ┌─────────────────────┐
              │  PRINT REPORT       │
              │  CANCEL PRINTING    │
              └─────────────────────┘
```

28-5 The sales report pre-processor screen.

The program begins with the usual clearing of the screen and creating the two memory variables that are used for input. Notice that both memory variables are created and initialized to two characters with the same statement. As long as you want to create variables with the same type and size, you can do it in one statement by separating the names with commas.

The standard pop-up is then created. The statements that are used to build the screen include some validity checking. The VALID clause is used to restrict the year entry to between 80 and 99, while the month is restricted to between 1 and 12. An error message at the bottom of the screen is displayed by the ERROR clause if the range isn't met. The VAL( ) function is used to convert the value of the input into a numeric field type so the VALID clause can do its checking.

When BAR( ) = 2, the user has chosen to print the report. If either YR or MN is blank, then an error window is displayed. If this check passes that, the print logic is executed. First, the view is set to SALES. This was created in the query chapter (chapter 11) of the book and reviewed in the reports chapter (chapter 13). It basically sorts the data by company and invoice number. The report is printed out by company and invoice number with just the totals shown for the total invoice, discount, and net profit displayed. In the report form, the detail is suppressed by closing the detail band.

The REPORT FORM command is a little complicated:

```
REPORT FORM SALESRPT TO PRINT ;
    FOR YEAR(INVDATE)-1900=VAL(YR) .AND.;
MONTH(INVDATE)=VAL(MN)
```

```
******************************************************************
* Program......: INVCSALS.PRG
* Author.......: Cary N. Prague
* Date.........: 10-02-88, Final Revision 01-01-89 Revised 3-12-92
* Module #.....: 2.4
* dBASE Ver....: IV 1.5
* Description..: AJAX APPLIANCE COMPANY MONTHLY SALES REPORT
******************************************************************
CLEAR
CLOSE DATABASES
STORE .T. TO MOREPRT
STORE SPACE(2) TO YR,MN
*-- Popup
SET BORDER TO SINGLE
DEFINE POPUP PRTMENU FROM 15,31 TO 21,49
DEFINE BAR 1 OF PRTMENU PROMPT "              " SKIP
DEFINE BAR 2 OF PRTMENU PROMPT "  PRINT REPORT  "
DEFINE BAR 3 OF PRTMENU PROMPT "              " SKIP
DEFINE BAR 4 OF PRTMENU PROMPT " CANCEL PRINTING "
ON SELECTION POPUP PRTMENU DO PRTPICK

DO WHILE MOREPRT
   @ 1,29 SAY "AJAX APPLIANCE COMPANY"
   @ 2,28 SAY " MONTHLY SALES REPORT"
   @ 4,22 SAY "ENTER THE YEAR AND MONTH TO PRINT"
   @ 7,23 SAY "ENTER YEAR/MONTH: "
   @ 7,45 GET YR PICTURE "##"  ;
      VALID VAL(YR) >= 80 .AND. VAL(YR) <=99  ;
      ERROR 'VALUE OF YR IS INVALID'
   @ 7,47 SAY '/'
   @ 7,48 GET MN PICTURE "##"  ;
      VALID VAL(MN) >= 1 .AND. VAL(MN) <=12  ;
      ERROR 'VALUE OF MN IS INVALID'
   READ
   @ 13,22 SAY 'ALIGN PAPER AND CHOOSE A MENU OPTION'

   ACTIVATE POPUP PRTMENU
ENDDO

RETURN

PROCEDURE PRTPICK
 DO CASE
   CASE BAR() = 2
     IF YR = '  ' .OR. MN = '  '
        ACTIVATE WINDOW msg1
        @ 2,05 SAY '        *** ERROR ***'
        @ 4,05 SAY '   YEAR AND MONTH NOT VALID'
        @ 5,05 SAY 'ENTER A VALID YEAR AND MONTH'
        @ 6,1  SAY '  '
        WAIT "        PRESS ANY KEY TO CONTINUE"
        DEACTIVATE WINDOW msg1
        STORE SPACE(2) TO YR,MN
      ELSE
        SET VIEW TO SALES
        REPORT FORM SALESRPT TO PRINT ;
           FOR YEAR(INVDATE) - 1900 = VAL(YR) .AND. MONTH(INVDATE) = VAL(MN)
        STORE SPACE(2) TO YR,MN
     ENDIF
     DEACTIVATE POPUP
   CASE BAR() = 4
     MOREPRT = .F.
     DEACTIVATE POPUP
 ENDCASE
 RETURN
```

28-6 The sales report pre-processor program.

The first line simply sends to print the form named SALESRPT. The FOR command is the key to the report. The idea is to print a single month's worth of data. This could easily be expanded to do a quarter, a year, or even any range of months by adding a second set of input values. The user has input the month and year to be selected. The value of year input must first be converted to numeric VAL(YR) and then compared against the year from INVDATE. The year is extracted from INVDATE with the YEAR function. Because the year is in the form YYYY you must subtract the century. That's why 1900 is subtracted from the YEAR(INVDATE). The same is done to the month using the MONTH( ) function. In that case, it can be compared directly to the value of month that was input.

If you need to remember what this report looked like, you can see it again in chapter 13. That completes our look at some reporting procedures for multiple files. You have now seen everything you will need to write complete systems using these programs as prototypes.

Summary

In this book, you have been given the tools to produce basic programs using dBASE IV. (That's basic as in simple, not the language BASIC; that's not used when you know dBASE IV.) Whether you are a novice or seasoned professional, hopefully this book has shown you tricks and techniques for contemporary program design for the nineties.

The programs and reports should serve as examples for all of your future work, but remember as you gain more experience to put some of your own ideas into the code. These programs have evolved over six years and four editions of this book into a set of very efficient programs that have remained as simplistic as possible.

You might wish to review each section as you begin to code in dBASE IV. A complete list of the databases used in this book can be found in appendix A. A complete list of the programs can be found in appendix B. Good luck in all your data processing endeavors—and remember, with dBASE IV, dPRO-GRAM is in dBAG!

A

The case studies database structure

```
Structure for database: C:\DBASE4\AJAX\CUSTOMER.DBF
Number of data records:     16
Date of last update   : 03/17/92
Field  Field Name  Type       Width    Dec    Index
    1   CUSTNO      Character      6             Y
    2   COMPANY     Character     20             Y
    3   STREET      Character     20             N
    4   CITY        Character     20             N
    5   STATE       Character      2             N
    6   ZIP         Character     10             Y
    7   PHONE       Character     13             N
    8   LST_TXND    Date           8             N
    9   DISCOUNT    Numeric        2             N
   10   TAXABLE     Logical        1             N
** Total **                      103

Structure for database: C:\DBASE4\AJAX\INVENTRY.DBF
Number of data records:     15
Date of last update   : 03/17/92
Field  Field Name  Type       Width    Dec    Index
    1   ITEMNO      Character      8             Y
    2   BRAND       Character     10             Y
    3   TYPE        Character     12             N
    4   DESC        Character     25             N
    5   PRICE       Numeric        7      2      N
    6   QTY_STK     Numeric        3             N
    7   QTY_ORD     Numeric        3             N
    8   WARRANTY    Numeric        2             N
    9   FEATURES    Memo          10             N
** Total **                       81

Structure for database: C:\DBASE4\AJAX\INVOICE.DBF
Number of data records:     10
Date of last update   : 03/17/92
Field  Field Name  Type       Width    Dec    Index
    1   INVNO       Character      8             Y
    2   INVDATE     Date           8             Y
    3   CUSTNO      Character      6             N
    4   DISCOUNT    Numeric        2             N
** Total **                       25

Structure for database: C:\DBASE4\AJAX\ITEMS.DBF
Number of data records:     37
Date of last update   : 03/17/92
Field  Field Name  Type       Width    Dec    Index
    1   INVNO       Character      8             Y
    2   QTY         Numeric        3             N
    3   ITEMNO      Character      8             N
    4   PRICE       Numeric        7      2      N
** Total **                       27
```

B
Program code for the case studies

```
********************************************************************************
* Program......: AJAXPASS.PRG
* Author.......: Cary N. Prague
* Date.........: 9-04-88, Revision 12-26-88, Revision 8-8-90 Revision 3-12-92
* Module #.....: 00
* dBASE Ver....: IV 1.5
* Description..: AJAX APPLIANCE COMPANY SYSTEM PASSWORD AND DATE VERIFICATION
********************************************************************************
CLOSE ALL
CLEAR ALL
SET DELIMITER OFF
SET INTENSITY ON
SET ECHO OFF
SET TALK OFF
SET BELL OFF
SET CONFIRM OFF
SET EXACT ON
SET STATUS OFF
SET CLOCK OFF
SET SCOREBOARD OFF
SET DELETED ON
*SET COLOR ON
*SET COLOR TO W+/B,W+/R
*SET COLOR OF MESSAGES TO W+/B
SET ESCAPE ON
CLEAR
PUBLIC DATE
STORE DATE() TO DATE
STORE 1 TO PTEST
STORE SPACE(10) TO PWORD
SET BORDER TO SINGLE
@ 0,0 TO 24,79
DEFINE WINDOW msg1 FROM 12,19 TO 20,59 DOUBLE color w+/r
DEFINE WINDOW msg2 FROM 11,19 TO 20,59 DOUBLE
```

```
DO WHILE PTEST <= 3 .AND. UPPER(PWORD) # 'TAB          '
   @  1,20 SAY '          AJAX APPLIANCE COMPANY              '
   @  3,20 SAY '          AUTHORIZATION CHECK                '
   @  6,28 SAY '*** ENTER PASSWORD *** '
   @  9,34 GET PWORD COLOR X/X,X/X
   @ 15,28 SAY '  *** ENTER DATE *** '
   @ 17,35 GET M->DATE PICTURE '99/99/99' ;
            RANGE {1/01/88},{12/31/99}
   READ
   IF UPPER(PWORD) # 'TAB          '
      ACTIVATE WINDOW msg1
      @ 2,10 SAY 'INVALID PASSWORD'
      @ 3,8  SAY 'YOU HAVE ' + STR((3-PTEST),1) + ' TRIES LEFT'
      @ 4,1  SAY " "
      WAIT "        PRESS ANY KEY TO CONTINUE"
      DEACTIVATE WINDOW msg1
      STORE SPACE(10) TO PWORD
   ENDIF
   PTEST = PTEST + 1
ENDDO
IF UPPER(PWORD) # 'TAB          '
   SET COLOR TO
   CANCEL
ENDIF
*SET COLOR TO W+/B,W+/R
DO AJAXMAIN
```

```
**************************************************************************
* Program......: AJAXMAIN.PRG
* Author.......: Cary N. Prague
* Date.........: 9-04-88, Revision 12-26-88, Revision 2-26-92
* Module #.....: 0
* dBASE Ver....: IV 1.5
* Description..: AJAX APPLIANCE COMPANY SYSTEM MAIN MENU
**************************************************************************
SET BORDER TO DOUBLE
SET MESSAGE TO "" AT 24
CLEAR
DEFINE WINDOW mainmenu FROM 0,0 TO 23,79 DOUBLE
DEFINE WINDOW calling  FROM 0,0 TO 23,79 DOUBLE
DEFINE WINDOW data     FROM 0,0 TO 24,79 DOUBLE
DEFINE WINDOW data3    FROM 0,0 TO 23,79 DOUBLE
DEFINE WINDOW datan    FROM 0,0 TO 24,79 NONE
PUBLIC TAX_RATE
TAX_RATE = 7.5
*-- Bar
DEFINE MENU AJAXMAIN
DEFINE PAD PAD_1 OF AJAXMAIN PROMPT "Customer" AT 1,3
ON PAD PAD_1 OF AJAXMAIN ACTIVATE POPUP MAIN1
DEFINE PAD PAD_2 OF AJAXMAIN PROMPT "Invoice" AT 1,13
ON PAD PAD_2 OF AJAXMAIN ACTIVATE POPUP MAIN2
DEFINE PAD PAD_3 OF AJAXMAIN PROMPT "Inventory" AT 1,22
ON PAD PAD_3 OF AJAXMAIN ACTIVATE POPUP MAIN3
DEFINE PAD PAD_4 OF AJAXMAIN PROMPT "Other" AT 1,33
ON PAD PAD_4 OF AJAXMAIN ACTIVATE POPUP MAIN4
DEFINE PAD PAD_5 OF AJAXMAIN PROMPT "Exit" AT 1,40
ON PAD PAD_5 OF AJAXMAIN ACTIVATE POPUP MAIN5
*-- Popup
DEFINE POPUP MAIN1 FROM 2,2 ;
MESSAGE "Choose a selection for the Customer System"
DEFINE BAR 1 OF MAIN1 PROMPT "Data Entry"
DEFINE BAR 2 OF MAIN1 PROMPT "————————————"    SKIP
DEFINE BAR 3 OF MAIN1 PROMPT "Directory"
DEFINE BAR 4 OF MAIN1 PROMPT "Cross Reference"
DEFINE BAR 5 OF MAIN1 PROMPT "Mailing Labels"
ON SELECTION POPUP MAIN1 DO MAIN1
*-- Popup
DEFINE POPUP MAIN2 FROM 2,12 ;
MESSAGE "Choose a selection for the Invoice System"
DEFINE BAR 1 OF MAIN2 PROMPT "Data Entry"
DEFINE BAR 2 OF MAIN2 PROMPT "————————————"    SKIP
DEFINE BAR 3 OF MAIN2 PROMPT "Invoices"
DEFINE BAR 4 OF MAIN2 PROMPT "Warrenty Agreement"
DEFINE BAR 5 OF MAIN2 PROMPT "Sales Reports"
ON SELECTION POPUP MAIN2 DO MAIN2
*-- Popup
DEFINE POPUP MAIN3 FROM 2,21 ;
MESSAGE "Choose a selection for the Inventory System"
DEFINE BAR 1 OF MAIN3 PROMPT "Data Entry"
DEFINE BAR 2 OF MAIN3 PROMPT "————————————"    SKIP
DEFINE BAR 3 OF MAIN3 PROMPT "Valuation Report"
DEFINE BAR 4 OF MAIN3 PROMPT "Cross Reference"
DEFINE BAR 5 OF MAIN3 PROMPT "Salesman Report"
ON SELECTION POPUP MAIN3 DO MAIN3
*-- Popup
DEFINE POPUP MAIN4 FROM 2,32 ;
MESSAGE "Choose a selection for Other Processing"
DEFINE BAR 1 OF MAIN4 PROMPT "Reindex Files"
DEFINE BAR 2 OF MAIN4 PROMPT "Pack Files"
ON SELECTION POPUP MAIN4 DO MAIN4
*-- Popup
DEFINE POPUP MAIN5 FROM 2,39 ;
```

```
MESSAGE "Choose a selection for Exit Processing"
DEFINE BAR 1 OF MAIN5 PROMPT "Exit To Dot Prompt"
DEFINE BAR 2 OF MAIN5 PROMPT "Quit To DOS Prompt"
ON SELECTION POPUP MAIN5 DO MAIN5


@10,4 SAY "                        AAA    JJJJJ   AAA    X   X                      "
@11,4 SAY "                        A   A      J  A   A    X X                      "
@12,4 SAY "                        AAAAA      J  AAAAA     X                       "
@13,4 SAY "                        A   A  J   J  A   A    X X                      "
@14,4 SAY "                        A   A  JJJJJ  A   A    X   X                    "
@15,4 SAY "                                                                       "
@16,4 SAY " AAA    PPPPP   PPPPP   L      IIIII   AAA    N   N   CCCCC   EEEEE"
@17,4 SAY "A   A   P    P  P    P  L        I    A   A   NN  N   C       E    "
@18,4 SAY "AAAAA   PPPPP   PPPPP   L        I    AAAAA   N N N   C       EEEE "
@19,4 SAY "A   A   P       P       L        I    A   A   N  NN   C       E    "
@20,4 SAY "A   A   P       P       LLLLL  IIIII   A   A   N   NN   CCCCC   EEEEE"


ACTIVATE MENU AJAXMAIN


PROCEDURE MAIN1

 DO CASE
   CASE BAR() = 1
       SAVE SCREEN TO custscr
       CLEAR
       DO CUSTMENU
       RESTORE SCREEN FROM custscr
   CASE BAR() = 3
       SAVE SCREEN TO custscr
       CLEAR
       DO CUSTDIR
       RESTORE SCREEN FROM custscr
   CASE BAR() = 4
       SAVE SCREEN TO custscr
       CLEAR
       DO CUSTCROS
       RESTORE SCREEN FROM custscr
   CASE BAR() = 5
       SAVE SCREEN TO custscr
       CLEAR
       DO CUSTLBL
       RESTORE SCREEN FROM custscr
 ENDCASE

RETURN

PROCEDURE MAIN2

 DO CASE
   CASE BAR() = 1
       SAVE SCREEN TO invcscr
       CLEAR
       DO INVCMENU
       RESTORE SCREEN FROM invcscr
   CASE BAR() = 3
       SAVE SCREEN TO invcscr
       CLEAR
       DO INVCINVC
       RESTORE SCREEN FROM invcscr
   CASE BAR() = 4
       SAVE SCREEN TO invcscr
       CLEAR
       DO INVCWARN
```

```
          RESTORE SCREEN FROM invcscr
   CASE BAR() = 5
       SAVE SCREEN TO invcscr
       CLEAR
       DO INVCSALS
       RESTORE SCREEN FROM invcscr
   ENDCASE

RETURN




PROCEDURE MAIN3

  DO CASE
   CASE BAR() = 1
       SAVE SCREEN TO invtscr
       CLEAR
       DO INVTMENU
       RESTORE SCREEN FROM invtscr
   CASE BAR() = 3
       SAVE SCREEN TO invtscr
       CLEAR
       DO INVTVALU
       RESTORE SCREEN FROM invtscr
   CASE BAR() = 4
       SAVE SCREEN TO invtscr
       CLEAR
       DO INVTCROS
       RESTORE SCREEN FROM invtscr
   CASE BAR() = 5
       SAVE SCREEN TO invtscr
       CLEAR
       DO INVTSMAN
       RESTORE SCREEN FROM invtscr
  ENDCASE
RETURN

PROCEDURE MAIN4

  DO CASE
   CASE BAR() = 1
       USE CUSTOMER
       REINDEX
       USE INVENTRY
       REINDEX
       USE INVOICE
       REINDEX
       USE ITEMS
       REINDEX
   CASE BAR() = 2
       USE CUSTOMER
       PACK
       USE INVENTRY
       PACK
       USE INVOICE
       PACK
       USE ITEMS
       PACK

  ENDCASE

RETURN
```

```
PROCEDURE MAIN5

DO CASE
  CASE BAR() = 1
       DEACTIVATE WINDOW mainmenu
       CLOSE ALL
       CANCEL
  CASE BAR() = 2
       DEACTIVATE WINDOW mainmenu
       CLOSE ALL
       QUIT
  ENDCASE

RETURN
```

```
*******************************************************************
* Program......: CUSTMENU.PRG
* Author.......: Cary N. Prague
* Date.........: 9-04-88, Final Revision 12-26-88 Revision 3-12-92
* Module #.....: 1.1
* dBASE Ver....: IV 1.5
* Description..: AJAX APPLIANCE COMPANY CUSTOMER MAIN MENU
*******************************************************************
CLEAR
*-- Popup
SET BORDER TO NONE
DEFINE POPUP CUSMENU FROM 7,25 TO 17,55 ;
MESSAGE "Choose a selection from the Customer Menu"
DEFINE BAR 1 OF CUSMENU PROMPT "   ADD CUSTOMER INFORMATION   "
DEFINE BAR 2 OF CUSMENU PROMPT "                              " SKIP
DEFINE BAR 3 OF CUSMENU PROMPT " CHANGE CUSTOMER INFORMATION  "
DEFINE BAR 4 OF CUSMENU PROMPT "                              " SKIP
DEFINE BAR 5 OF CUSMENU PROMPT "       DELETE A CUSTOMER      "
DEFINE BAR 6 OF CUSMENU PROMPT "                              " SKIP
DEFINE BAR 7 OF CUSMENU PROMPT "  VIEW CUSTOMER INFORMATION   "
DEFINE BAR 8 OF CUSMENU PROMPT "                              " SKIP
DEFINE BAR 9 OF CUSMENU PROMPT "   EXIT CUSTOMER DATA ENTRY   "
ON SELECTION POPUP CUSMENU DO CUSTPICK

CLOSE DATABASES
USE CUSTOMER ORDER TAG CUSTNO
@ 1,28 TO 4,53
@ 2,30 SAY 'AJAX APPLIANCE COMPANY'
@ 3,30 SAY " CUSTOMER DATA ENTRY "

ACTIVATE POPUP CUSMENU
RETURN

PROCEDURE CUSTPICK
 DO CASE
    CASE BAR() = 1
     DO CUSTADD
    CASE BAR() = 3
     DO CUSTCHG
   * DO CUSTCHGP
   * DO CUSTCHGB
    CASE BAR() = 5
     DO CUSTDEL
    CASE BAR() = 7
     DO CUSTVEW
    CASE BAR() = 9
     SET BORDER TO SINGLE
     DEACTIVATE POPUP
 ENDCASE
 RETURN
```

```
******************************************************************
* Program......: CUSTADD.PRG
* Author.......: Cary N. Prague
* Date.........: 9-04-88, Revision 2-24-92
* Module #.....: 1.1.1
* dBASE Ver....: IV 1.5
* Description..: AJAX APPLIANCE COMPANY CUSTOMER ADD SCREEN
******************************************************************
ACTIVATE WINDOW data3
CLEAR
STORE SPACE(6)   TO CSN
STORE SPACE(20)  TO CMP
STORE SPACE(20)  TO STR
STORE SPACE(20)  TO CTY
STORE SPACE(2)   TO STT
STORE SPACE(10)  TO ZP
STORE SPACE(13)  TO PHN
STORE {  /  /  } TO LTD
STORE 0 TO DIS
STORE .F. TO TAX
DO WHILE .T.
   @ 2,19 TO 19,57 DOUBLE
   @ 3,26 SAY "AJAX APPLIANCE COMPANY"
   @ 4,26 SAY "  CUSTOMER ADDITIONS"
   @ 5,20 SAY "————————————————————————"
   @ 6,23 SAY " Customer Number"
   @ 6,41 GET csn PICTURE "@! XX-999" ;
       MESSAGE "Enter a new customer number or <PgDn> to Return"
   @ 7,20 SAY "————————————————————————"
   @ 9,24 SAY "Company"
   @ 9,34 GET cmp PICTURE "@!20" ;
       MESSAGE "Enter the company name"
   @ 10,24 SAY "Street"
   @ 10,34 GET str PICTURE "@! XXXXXXXXXXXXXXXXXXX" ;
       MESSAGE "Enter the customers street address"
   @ 11,24 SAY "City"
   @ 11,34 GET cty PICTURE "@! XXXXXXXXXXXXXXXXXXX" ;
       MESSAGE "Enter the customers city"
   @ 12,24 SAY "State/Zip"
   @ 12,34 GET stt PICTURE "@!M CA,CT,NM,NY,OK,PA" ;
       MESSAGE "Enter the customers state"
   @ 12,38 GET zp PICTURE "99999-####" ;
       MESSAGE "Enter the customers zip code"
   @ 14,20 SAY "————————————————————————"
   @ 15,24 SAY "Telephone Number"
   @ 15,41 GET phn PICTURE "(###)999-9999" ;
       MESSAGE "Enter the customers phone number"
   @ 16,24 SAY "Last Transaction"
   @ 16,41 GET ltd ;
       RANGE {01/01/80},DATE()+60 ;
       WHEN .NOT. ISBLANK(ltd) ;
       MESSAGE "Enter the last transaction date"
   @ 17,24 SAY "Discount Percent"
   @ 17,41 GET dis PICTURE "99" ;
       VALID DIS >= 0 .AND. DIS <= 50 ;
       ERROR "The discount is not valid (0-50) Re-enter the discount" ;
       MESSAGE "Enter the customers discount"
   @ 18,24 SAY "Taxable Flag"
   @ 18,41 GET tax PICTURE "L" ;
       DEFAULT .T. ;
       MESSAGE "Enter the customers tax status"
   READ
```

```
IF CSN = '        '  .OR. CSN = '   -    '
     CLEAR
     DEACTIVATE WINDOW data3
     RETURN
ELSE
  SEEK TRIM(CSN)
  IF .NOT. FOUND()
        APPEND BLANK
        REPLACE CUSTNO WITH CSN,COMPANY WITH CMP,STREET WITH STR
        REPLACE CITY WITH CTY,STATE WITH STT,ZIP WITH ZP,PHONE WITH PHN
        REPLACE LST_TXND WITH LTD,DISCOUNT WITH DIS,TAXABLE WITH TAX
        @ 20,1
        WAIT '                     CUSTOMER ADDED-PRESS ANY KEY TO CONTINUE'
        CLEAR
        STORE SPACE(6) TO CSN
        STORE SPACE(20) TO CMP
        STORE SPACE(20) TO STR
        STORE SPACE(20) TO CTY
        STORE SPACE(2)  TO STT
        STORE SPACE(10) TO ZP
        STORE SPACE(13) TO PHN
        STORE {  /  /  } TO LTD
        STORE 0 TO DIS
        STORE .T. TO TAX
  ELSE
        ?? CHR(7)
        ACTIVATE WINDOW msg1
        @ 1,05 SAY '      *** ERROR ***'
        @ 3,05 SAY 'CUSTOMER NUMBER ALREADY ON FILE'
        @ 4,05 SAY 'ENTER A NEW CUSTOMER NUMBER'
        @ 5,1  SAY ' '
        WAIT "      PRESS ANY KEY TO CONTINUE"
        DEACTIVATE WINDOW msg1
  ENDIF
 ENDIF
ENDDO
```

```
****************************************************************************
* Program......: CUSTCHG.PRG
* Author.......: Cary N. Prague
* Date.........: 9-04-88, Final Revision 12-26-88 Revision 3-12-92
* Module #.....: 1.1.2
* dBASE Ver....: IV 1.5
* Description..: AJAX APPLIANCE COMPANY CUSTOMER CHANGE SCREEN
****************************************************************************
ACTIVATE WINDOW data3
CLEAR
STORE SPACE(6) TO csn
DO WHILE .T.
  @ 2,19 TO 19,57 DOUBLE
  @ 5,20 SAY "────────────────────────────────────────"
  @ 3,26 SAY "AJAX APPLIANCE COMPANY"
  @ 4,26 SAY "   CUSTOMER CHANGES"
  @ 6,24 SAY "CUSTOMER NUMBER:"
  @ 6,41 GET csn PICTURE "@! AA-999" ;
     MESSAGE "Enter Customer Number or Press <Enter> to Return"
  READ
  IF csn = '      ' .OR. csn = '   -   '
     CLEAR
     DEACTIVATE WINDOW data3
     RETURN
  ELSE
     SEEK TRIM(CSN)
     IF FOUND()
        @ 6,41 GET custno PICTURE "@! XX-999" ;
           MESSAGE "Enter a new customer number or PgDn to Go Back"
        @ 7,20 SAY "────────────────────────────────────────"
        @ 9,24 SAY "Company"
        @ 9,34 GET company PICTURE "@!20" ;
           MESSAGE "Enter the company name"
        @ 10,24 SAY "Street"
        @ 10,34 GET street PICTURE "@! XXXXXXXXXXXXXXXXXXXX" ;
           MESSAGE "Enter the customers street address"
        @ 11,24 SAY "City"
        @ 11,34 GET city PICTURE "@! XXXXXXXXXXXXXXXXXXX" ;
           MESSAGE "Enter the customers city"
        @ 12,24 SAY "State/Zip"
        @ 12,34 GET state PICTURE "@!M CA,CT,NM,NY,OK,PA" ;
           MESSAGE "Enter the customers state"
        @ 12,38 GET zip PICTURE "99999-####" ;
           MESSAGE "Enter the customers zip code"
        @ 14,20 SAY "────────────────────────────────────────"
        @ 15,24 SAY "Telephone Number"
        @ 15,41 GET phone PICTURE "(###)999-9999" ;
           MESSAGE "Enter the customers phone number"
        @ 16,24 SAY "Last Transaction"
        @ 16,41 GET lst_txnd ;
           RANGE {01/01/80},DATE()+60 ;
           WHEN .NOT. ISBLANK(lst_txnd) ;
           MESSAGE "Enter the last transaction date"
        @ 17,24 SAY "Discount Percent"
        @ 17,41 GET discount PICTURE "99" ;
           VALID discount >= 0 .AND. discount <= 50 ;
           ERROR "The discount is not valid (0-50) Re-enter the discount" ;
           MESSAGE "Enter the customers discount"
        @ 18,24 SAY "Taxable Flag"
        @ 18,41 GET taxable PICTURE "L" ;
           DEFAULT .T. ;
           MESSAGE "Enter the customers tax status"
```

```
      READ
      @ 20,1
      WAIT '                       CUSTOMER CHANGED-PRESS ANY KEY TO CONTINUE'
        CLEAR
        STORE SPACE(6) TO CSN
      ELSE
          ?? CHR(7)
          ACTIVATE WINDOW msg1
          @ 1,05 SAY '           *** ERROR ***'
          @ 3,05 SAY ' CUSTOMER NUMBER NOT ON FILE'
          @ 4,05 SAY 'ENTER ANOTHER CUSTOMER NUMBER'
          @ 5,1  SAY ' '
          WAIT "          PRESS ANY KEY TO CONTINUE"
          DEACTIVATE WINDOW msg1
          STORE SPACE(6) TO CSN
      ENDIF
  ENDIF
  CLEAR
ENDDO
```

```
*****************************************************************
* Program......: NEWCCHG.PRG
* Author.......: Cary N. Prague/P. Schickler
* Date.........: Final Revision 3-3-92
* Module #.....: 1.1.2
* dBASE Ver....: IV 1.5
* Description..: AJAX APPLIANCE COMPANY CUSTOMER CHANGE SCREEN
*****************************************************************
ACTIVATE WINDOW data3
CLEAR
STORE SPACE(6) TO csn
@ 2,18 TO 19,58 DOUBLE
@ 5,19 SAY "————————————————————————————————"
@ 3,26 SAY "AJAX APPLIANCE COMPANY"
@ 4,26 SAY "   CUSTOMER CHANGES"
@ 6,23 SAY "CUSTOMER NUMBER:"
@ 6,41 GET csn PICTURE "@! XX-999" VALID GETCUS(csn) ;
    MESSAGE "Enter Customer Number or Press Enter to Return"
READ
IF csn = '      ' .OR. csn = '  -   '
    CLEAR
    DEACTIVATE WINDOW data3
    RETURN
ENDIF
@ 6,41 SAY custno PICTURE "@! XX-999"
@ 7,19 SAY "————————————————————————————————"
@ 9,24 SAY "Company"
@ 9,34 GET company PICTURE "@!20" ;
    MESSAGE "Enter the company name"
@ 10,24 SAY "Street"
@ 10,34 GET street PICTURE "@! XXXXXXXXXXXXXXXXXXXX" ;
    MESSAGE "Enter the customers street address"
@ 11,24 SAY "City"
@ 11,34 GET city PICTURE "@! XXXXXXXXXXXXXXXXXXXX" ;
    MESSAGE "Enter the customers city"
@ 12,24 SAY "State/Zip"
@ 12,34 GET state PICTURE "@!M CA,CT,NM,NY,OK,PA" ;
    MESSAGE "Enter the customers state"
@ 12,38 GET zip PICTURE "99999-####" ;
    MESSAGE "Enter the customers zip code"
@ 14,19 SAY "————————————————————————————————"
@ 15,24 SAY "Telephone Number"
@ 15,41 GET phone PICTURE "(###)999-9999" ;
    MESSAGE "Enter the customers phone number"
@ 16,24 SAY "Last Transaction"
@ 16,41 GET lst_txnd ;
    RANGE {01/01/80},DATE()+60 ;
    WHEN .NOT. ISBLANK(lst_txnd) ;
    MESSAGE "Enter the last transaction date"
@ 17,24 SAY "Discount Percent"
@ 17,41 GET discount PICTURE "99" ;
    VALID DIS >= 0 .AND. DIS <= 50 ;
    ERROR "The discount is not valid (0-50) Re-enter the discount" ;
    MESSAGE "Enter the customers discount"
@ 18,24 SAY "Taxable Flag"
@ 18,41 GET taxable PICTURE "L" ;
    DEFAULT .T. ;
    MESSAGE "Enter the customers tax status"
READ
CLEAR
STORE SPACE(6) TO csn
DEACTIVATE WINDOW data3
RETURN
```

```
FUNCTION getcus        && The function name
   PARAMETER cnum      && The parameter receiving the customer number
   SEEK TRIM(cnum)     && Finding the customer number
   IF FOUND()
      RETURN .t.       && The record was found
   ENDIF
   SET BORDER TO DOUBLE
   DEFINE POPUP cust FROM 7,47 TO 17,54
   cnt = 1
   GO TOP
   SCAN
     DEFINE BAR cnt OF cust PROMPT CUSTNO
     cnt = cnt + 1
   ENDSCAN
   ON SELECTION POPUP cust DEACTIVATE POPUP
   * Activate the popup menu
   SET MESSAGE TO 'Select Customer Number and Press Enter to Return'
   ACTIVATE POPUP cust
   IF BAR() = 0
     RETURN .f.
   ENDIF
   SEEK PROMPT()
   csn = custno
RETURN .T.
```

```
***********************************************************************
* Program......: NEWCCHG2.PRG
* Author.......: Cary N. Prague/P. Schickler
* Date.........: Final Revision 3-3-92
* Module #.....: 1.1.2
* dBASE Ver....: IV 1.5
* Description..: AJAX APPLIANCE COMPANY CUSTOMER CHANGE SCREEN
***********************************************************************
ACTIVATE WINDOW data3
CLEAR
STORE SPACE(6) TO csn
@ 2,18 TO 19,58 DOUBLE
@ 5,19 SAY "————————————————————————————————————————"
@ 3,26 SAY "AJAX APPLIANCE COMPANY"
@ 4,26 SAY "    CUSTOMER CHANGES"
@ 6,23 SAY "CUSTOMER NUMBER:"
@ 6,41 GET csn PICTURE "@! XX-999" VALID GETCUS2(csn) ;
   MESSAGE "Enter Customer Number or Press Enter to Return"
READ
IF csn = '      ' .OR. csn = '  -   '
  CLEAR
  DEACTIVATE WINDOW data3
  RETURN
ENDIF
DO WHILE .t.
  @ 6,41 SAY custno PICTURE "@! XX-999"
  @ 7,19 SAY "————————————————————————————————————————"
  @ 9,24 SAY "Company"
  @ 9,34 GET company PICTURE "@!20" ;
     MESSAGE "Enter the company name"
  @ 10,24 SAY "Street"
  @ 10,34 GET street PICTURE "@! XXXXXXXXXXXXXXXXXXXX" ;
     MESSAGE "Enter the customers street address"
  @ 11,24 SAY "City"
  @ 11,34 GET city PICTURE "@! XXXXXXXXXXXXXXXXXXXX" ;
     MESSAGE "Enter the customers city"
  @ 12,24 SAY "State/Zip"
  @ 12,34 GET state PICTURE "@!M CA,CT,NM,NY,OK,PA" ;
     MESSAGE "Enter the customers state"
  @ 12,38 GET zip PICTURE "99999-####" ;
     MESSAGE "Enter the customers zip code"
  @ 14,19 SAY "————————————————————————————————————————"
  @ 15,24 SAY "Telephone Number"
  @ 15,41 GET phone PICTURE "(###)999-9999" ;
     MESSAGE "Enter the customers phone number"
  @ 16,24 SAY "Last Transaction"
  @ 16,41 GET lst_txnd ;
     RANGE {01/01/80},DATE()+60 ;
     WHEN .NOT. ISBLANK(lst_txnd) ;
     MESSAGE "Enter the last transaction date"
  @ 17,24 SAY "Discount Percent"
  @ 17,41 GET discount PICTURE "99" ;
     VALID DIS >= 0 .AND. DIS <= 50 ;
     ERROR "The discount is not valid (0-50) Re-enter the discount" ;
     MESSAGE "Enter the customers discount"
  @ 18,24 SAY "Taxable Flag"
  @ 18,41 GET taxable PICTURE "L" ;
     DEFAULT .T. ;
     MESSAGE "Enter the customers tax status"
  READ
  IF QUES("Is Everything Correct?")
     EXIT
  ENDIF
ENDDO
CLEAR
```

```
STORE SPACE(6) TO csn
DEACTIVATE WINDOW data3
RETURN


FUNCTION getcus2
  PARAMETER cnum
  SELECT customer
  SEEK TRIM(cnum)
  IF FOUND()
    RETURN .t.
  ENDIF
  DEFINE WINDOW custbrow FROM 9,44 TO 18,74 DOUBLE
  GO TOP
  SET MESSAGE TO 'Select Customer Number and Press <Ctrl-End>'
  BROWSE WINDOW custbrow FIELDS custno, company FREEZE custno
  IF .NOT. EOF()
    cnum=custno
  ENDIF
RETURN .T.

FUNCTION ques
  PARAMETER msg
  DEFINE WINDOW message FROM 18,20 TO 20,58 DOUBLE
  ACTIV WIND message
  PRIV yn
  yn='Y'
  @ 0,2 SAY msg + "? (Y/N) " GET yn PICT "Y"
  READ
  DEACT WIND message
  RELEASE WINDOW message
  IF yn="Y"
    RETURN .T.
  ENDIF
RETURN .F.
```

```
***********************************************************************
* Program......: CUSTDEL.PRG
* Author.......: Cary N. Prague
* Date.........: 9-05-88, Revision 12-26-88 REVISION 02-26-92
* Module #.....: 1.1.3
* dBASE Ver....: IV 1.5
* Description..: AJAX APPLIANCE COMPANY CUSTOMER DELETION SCREEN
***********************************************************************
ACTIVATE WINDOW data3
CLEAR
STORE SPACE(6) TO csn
DO WHILE .T.
  @ 2,19 TO 19,57 DOUBLE
  @ 3,26 SAY "AJAX APPLIANCE COMPANY"
  @ 4,26 SAY "  CUSTOMER DELETIONS"
  @ 5,20 SAY "————————————————————————"
  @ 6,23 SAY " Customer Number"
  @ 6,41 GET csn PICTURE "@! XX-999" ;
    MESSAGE "Enter a Customer Number to Delete or Press <Enter> to Return"
  READ
  IF csn = '        ' .OR. csn = '   -   '
      CLEAR
      DEACTIVATE WINDOW data3
      RETURN
  ELSE
      SEEK TRIM(CSN)
      IF FOUND()
         @ 7,20 SAY "————————————————————————"
         @ 9,24 SAY "Company"
         @ 9,34 SAY company PICTURE "@!20"
         @ 10,24 SAY "Street"
         @ 10,34 SAY street PICTURE "@! XXXXXXXXXXXXXXXXXXXX"
         @ 11,24 SAY "City"
         @ 11,34 SAY city PICTURE "@! XXXXXXXXXXXXXXXXXXXX"
         @ 12,24 SAY "State/Zip"
         @ 12,34 SAY state
         @ 12,38 SAY zip PICTURE "99999-####"
         @ 14,20 SAY "————————————————————————"
         @ 15,24 SAY "Telephone Number"
         @ 15,41 SAY phone PICTURE "(###)999-9999"
         @ 16,24 SAY "Last Transaction"
         @ 16,41 SAY lst_txnd
         @ 17,24 SAY "Discount Percent"
         @ 17,41 SAY discount PICTURE "99"
         @ 18,24 SAY "Taxable Flag"
         @ 18,41 SAY taxable PICTURE "L"
         @ 20,23 SAY '*** PRESS ANY KEY TO CONTINUE *** '
         READ
         @ 20,1
         ?? CHR(7)
         DEFINE MENU yesno
         DEFINE PAD no OF yesno PROMPT "[NO]" AT 6,2
         ON SELECTION PAD no OF yesno DEACTIVATE MENU
         DEFINE PAD yes OF yesno PROMPT "[YES]" AT 6,30
         ON SELECTION PAD yes OF yesno DO DELETE
         ACTIVATE WINDOW msg2
         @ 1,05 SAY '  *** CONFIRM DELETE ***   '
         @ 3,05 SAY '   DO YOU REALLY WANT TO    '
         @ 4,05 SAY '     DELETE THIS RECORD     '
         ACTIVATE menu yesno
         DEACTIVATE WINDOW msg2
         @ 8,10 CLEAR TO 21,70
         STORE SPACE(6) TO CSN
      ELSE
         ?? CHR(7)
```

```
         ACTIVATE WINDOW msg1
         @ 1,05 SAY '          *** ERROR ***'
         @ 3,05 SAY ' CUSTOMER NUMBER NOT ON FILE'
         @ 4,05 SAY 'ENTER ANOTHER CUSTOMER NUMBER'
         @ 5,1  SAY ' '
         WAIT "          PRESS ANY KEY TO CONTINUE"
         DEACTIVATE WINDOW msg1
         STORE SPACE(6) TO CSN
      ENDIF
   ENDIF
   CLEAR
ENDDO

PROCEDURE DELETE
   DELETE
   CLEAR
   @ 1,5 SAY  ' *** CUSTOMER DELETED ***      '
   @ 3,1
   WAIT "          PRESS ANY KEY TO CONTINUE"
   DEACTIVATE MENU
   RETURN
```

```
*****************************************************************
* Program......: CUSTVEW.PRG
* Author.......: Cary N. Prague
* Date.........: 9-04-88, Final Revision 12-26-88 Revision 3-12-92
* Module #.....: 1.1.4
* dBASE Ver....: IV 1.5
* Description..: AJAX APPLIANCE COMPANY CUSTOMER VIEW SCREEN
*****************************************************************
ACTIVATE WINDOW data3
STORE SPACE(6) TO csn
DO WHILE .T.
   @ 2,19 TO 19,57 DOUBLE
   @ 3,26 SAY "AJAX APPLIANCE COMPANY"
   @ 4,26 SAY "     CUSTOMER VIEW"
   @ 5,20 SAY "————————————————————————"
   @ 6,23 SAY " Customer Number"
   @ 6,41 GET csn PICTURE "@! XX-999" ;
      MESSAGE "Enter a Customer Number to View or Press <Enter> to Return"
   READ
   IF csn = '      ' .OR. csn = '   -   '
      CLEAR
      DEACTIVATE WINDOW data3
      RETURN
   ELSE
      SEEK TRIM(CSN)
      IF FOUND()
         @ 7,20 SAY "————————————————————————"
         @ 9,24 SAY "Company"
         @ 9,34 SAY company PICTURE "@!20"
         @ 10,24 SAY "Street"
         @ 10,34 SAY street PICTURE "@! XXXXXXXXXXXXXXXXXXXX"
         @ 11,24 SAY "City"
         @ 11,34 SAY city PICTURE "@! XXXXXXXXXXXXXXXXXXXX"
         @ 12,24 SAY "State/Zip"
         @ 12,34 SAY state
         @ 12,38 SAY zip PICTURE "99999-####"
         @ 14,20 SAY "————————————————————————"
         @ 15,24 SAY "Telephone Number"
         @ 15,41 SAY phone PICTURE "(###)999-9999"
         @ 16,24 SAY "Last Transaction"
         @ 16,41 SAY lst_txnd
         @ 17,24 SAY "Discount Percent"
         @ 17,41 SAY discount PICTURE "99"
         @ 18,24 SAY "Taxable Flag"
         @ 18,41 SAY taxable PICTURE "L"
         @ 20,23 SAY '*** PRESS ANY KEY TO CONTINUE *** '
         READ
         STORE SPACE(6) TO CSN
      ELSE
         ?? CHR(7)
         ACTIVATE WINDOW msg1
         @ 1,05 SAY '      *** ERROR ***'
         @ 3,05 SAY ' CUSTOMER NUMBER NOT ON FILE'
         @ 4,05 SAY 'ENTER ANOTHER CUSTOMER NUMBER'
         @ 5,1  SAY ' '
         WAIT "       PRESS ANY KEY TO CONTINUE"
         DEACTIVATE WINDOW msg1
         STORE SPACE(6) TO CSN
      ENDIF
   ENDIF
   CLEAR
ENDDO
```

```
**********************************************************************
* Program......: CUSTDIR.PRG
* Author.......: Cary N. Prague
* Date.........: 9-25-88, Final Revision 12-26-88 Revised 3-12-92
* Module #.....: 1.2
* dBASE Ver....: IV 1.5
* Description..: AJAX APPLIANCE COMPANY CUSTOMER DIRECTORY PRINT
**********************************************************************
CLEAR
CLOSE DATABASES
USE CUSTOMER ORDER CUSTNO
STORE SPACE(6)  TO CSN
STORE .T. TO MOREPRT
*-- Popup
SET BORDER TO SINGLE
DEFINE POPUP PRTMENU FROM 15,31 TO 21,49
DEFINE BAR 1 OF PRTMENU PROMPT "                   " SKIP
DEFINE BAR 2 OF PRTMENU PROMPT " PRINT DIRECTORY "
DEFINE BAR 3 OF PRTMENU PROMPT "                   " SKIP
DEFINE BAR 4 OF PRTMENU PROMPT " CANCEL PRINTING "
ON SELECTION POPUP PRTMENU DO PRTPICK
SET CONSOLE OFF
DO WHILE MOREPRT
   @ 1,29 SAY "AJAX APPLIANCE COMPANY"
   @ 2,28 SAY "CUSTOMER DIRECTORY PRINT"
   @ 4,22 SAY " ENTER THE CUSTOMER NUMBER TO PRINT"
   @ 5,22 SAY "OR LEAVE BLANK TO PRINT ALL CUSTOMERS"
   @ 7,27 SAY "CUSTOMER NUMBER:"
   @ 7,44 GET csn PICTURE "@! AA-999"
   READ
   @ 13,22 SAY 'ALIGN PAPER AND CHOOSE A MENU OPTION'
   ACTIVATE POPUP PRTMENU
ENDDO
RETURN

PROCEDURE PRTPICK
 DO CASE
   CASE BAR() = 2
     IF CSN = '      ' .OR. CSN = '   -   '
         REPORT FORM CUSTDIR TO PRINT
      ELSE
         SEEK TRIM(csn)
           IF FOUND()
              REPORT FORM CUSTDIR TO PRINT FOR CUSTNO = CSN
              STORE SPACE(6) TO CSN
            ELSE
              ?? CHR(7)
              ACTIVATE WINDOW msg1
              @ 2,05 SAY '       *** ERROR ***'
              @ 4,05 SAY ' CUSTOMER NUMBER NOT ON FILE'
              @ 5,05 SAY 'ENTER ANOTHER CUSTOMER NUMBER'
              @ 6,1  SAY ' '
              WAIT "       PRESS ANY KEY TO CONTINUE"
              DEACTIVATE WINDOW msg1
              STORE SPACE(6) TO CSN
              @ 13,1
           ENDIF
     ENDIF
     DEACTIVATE POPUP
   CASE BAR() = 4
     SET CONSOLE ON
     MOREPRT = .F.
     DEACTIVATE POPUP
 ENDCASE
RETURN
```

```
********************************************************************
* Program......: CUSTCROS.PRG
* Author.......: Cary N. Prague
* Date.........: 9-25-88, Final Revision 12-26-88 Revised 3-12-92
* Module #.....: 1.3
* dBASE Ver....: IV 1.5
* Description..: AJAX APPLIANCE COMPANY CUSTOMER CROSS REFERENCE PRINT
********************************************************************
CLEAR
CLOSE DATABASES
USE CUSTOMER ORDER COMPANY

*-- Popup
SET BORDER TO SINGLE
DEFINE POPUP PRTMENU FROM 12,31 TO 18,49
DEFINE BAR 1 OF PRTMENU PROMPT "                " SKIP
DEFINE BAR 2 OF PRTMENU PROMPT "    PRINT REPORT "
DEFINE BAR 3 OF PRTMENU PROMPT "                " SKIP
DEFINE BAR 4 OF PRTMENU PROMPT " CANCEL PRINTING "
ON SELECTION POPUP PRTMENU DO PRTPICK
SET CONSOLE OFF
@ 1,29 SAY "AJAX APPLIANCE COMPANY"
@ 2,25 SAY "CUSTOMER CROSS REFERENCE PRINT"
@ 10,22 SAY 'ALIGN PAPER AND CHOOSE A MENU OPTION'

ACTIVATE POPUP PRTMENU

RETURN


PROCEDURE PRTPICK
  DO CASE
    CASE BAR() = 2
      REPORT FORM CUSTCROS TO PRINT
      DEACTIVATE POPUP
    CASE BAR() = 4
      DEACTIVATE POPUP
  ENDCASE
  SET CONSOLE ON
  RETURN
```

```
********************************************************************
* Program......: CUSTLBL.PRG
* Author.......: Cary N. Prague
* Date.........: 9-25-88, Final Revision 12-26-88 Revised 3-12-92
* Module #.....: 1.4
* dBASE Ver....: IV 1.5
* Description..: AJAX APPLIANCE COMPANY CUSTOMER LABELS PRINT
********************************************************************
CLEAR
CLOSE DATABASES
USE CUSTOMER ORDER COMPANY
STORE .T. TO MOREPRT

*-- Popup
SET BORDER TO SINGLE
DEFINE POPUP PRTMENU FROM 12,31 TO 20,49
DEFINE BAR 1 OF PRTMENU PROMPT "                  " SKIP
DEFINE BAR 2 OF PRTMENU PROMPT " ALIGNMENT TEST   "
DEFINE BAR 3 OF PRTMENU PROMPT "                  " SKIP
DEFINE BAR 4 OF PRTMENU PROMPT "   PRINT LABELS   "
DEFINE BAR 5 OF PRTMENU PROMPT "                  " SKIP
DEFINE BAR 6 OF PRTMENU PROMPT " CANCEL PRINTING "
ON SELECTION POPUP PRTMENU DO PRTPICK
SET CONSOLE OFF
DO WHILE MOREPRT

   @ 1,29 SAY "AJAX APPLIANCE COMPANY"
   @ 2,29 SAY " CUSTOMER LABEL PRINT"
   @ 10,22 SAY 'ALIGN LABELS AND CHOOSE A MENU OPTION'

ACTIVATE POPUP PRTMENU

ENDDO

RETURN

PROCEDURE PRTPICK
  DO CASE
    CASE BAR() = 2
      LABEL FORM CUSTLBL TO PRINT SAMPLE
      DEACTIVATE POPUP
    CASE BAR() = 4
      LABEL FORM CUSTLBL TO PRINT
      DEACTIVATE POPUP
    CASE BAR() = 6
      SET CONSOLE ON
      MOREPRT = .F.
      DEACTIVATE POPUP
  ENDCASE
  RETURN
```

```
*************************************************************************
* Program......: INVTMENU.PRG
* Author.......: Cary N. Prague
* Date.........: 9-25-88, Final Revision 12-26-88 Revised 3-12-92
* Module #.....: 3.1
* dBASE Ver....: IV 1.5
* Description..: AJAX APPLIANCE COMPANY INVENTORY MAIN MENU
*************************************************************************
CLEAR
SET BORDER TO NONE
*SET COLOR TO W+/B,W+/R
DEFINE POPUP INVMENU FROM 8,25 TO 18,51 ;
MESSAGE "Choose a selection from the Inventory Menu"
DEFINE BAR 1 OF INVMENU PROMPT "        ADD NEW ITEM         "
DEFINE BAR 2 OF INVMENU PROMPT "                             " SKIP
DEFINE BAR 3 OF INVMENU PROMPT " CHANGE ITEM INFORMATION "
DEFINE BAR 4 OF INVMENU PROMPT "                             " SKIP
DEFINE BAR 5 OF INVMENU PROMPT "        DELETE AN ITEM       "
DEFINE BAR 6 OF INVMENU PROMPT "                             " SKIP
DEFINE BAR 7 OF INVMENU PROMPT "  VIEW ITEM INFORMATION  "
DEFINE BAR 8 OF INVMENU PROMPT "                             " SKIP
DEFINE BAR 9 OF INVMENU PROMPT "EXIT INVENTORY DATA ENTRY"
ON SELECTION POPUP INVMENU DO INVTPICK

@ 1,29 SAY "AJAX APPLIANCE COMPANY"
@ 2,29 SAY " INVENTORY DATA ENTRY"

ACTIVATE POPUP INVMENU

RETURN

PROCEDURE INVTPICK
  DO CASE
    CASE BAR() = 1  .OR. BAR() = 3 .OR. BAR() = 5 .OR. BAR() = 7
       SET BORDER TO SINGLE
       SAVE SCREEN TO invtp
       CLEAR
       DO INVTDTEN WITH BAR()
       RESTORE SCREEN FROM invtp
    CASE BAR() = 9
       DEACTIVATE POPUP
  ENDCASE
SET BORDER TO DOUBLE
RETURN
```

```
************************************************************************
* Program......: INVTDTEN.PRG
* Author.......: Cary N. Prague
* Date.........: 9-05-88, Final Revision 12-26-88 Revised 3-12-92
* Module #.....: 3.1.1
* dBASE Ver....: IV 1.5
* Description..: AJAX APPLIANCE COMPANY INVENTORY DATA ENTRY
************************************************************************
PARAMETERS CHOICE
USE inventry ORDER itemno
CLEAR
SET FORMAT TO
STORE SPACE(8) TO ITN
DO WHILE .T.
   @ 1,28 TO 4,53
   @ 2,30 SAY 'AJAX APPLIANCE COMPANY'
   @ 3,30 SAY " INVENTORY DATA ENTRY "
   @ 6,25 SAY "DATABASE ADD/CHANGE/DELETE/VIEW"
   @ 10,26 SAY 'ENTER ITEM NUMBER: '
   @ 10,45 GET ITN PICTURE "@! AAAA-999"
   READ
   IF ITN = SPACE(8) .OR. ITN = '    -   '
      CLEAR
      RETURN
   ENDIF
   SEEK TRIM(ITN)
   DO CASE
      CASE CHOICE = 1
         IF .NOT. FOUND()
            SET FORMAT TO INVENTRY
            APPEND BLANK
            REPLACE ITEMNO WITH ITN
            READ
            CLEAR
            @ 8,1
            @ 8,28 SAY '  *** ITEM ADDED *** '
          ELSE
            ?? CHR(7)
            ACTIVATE WINDOW msg1
            @ 2,05 SAY '       *** ERROR ***'
            @ 4,05 SAY 'ITEM NUMBER ALREADY ON FILE'
            @ 5,05 SAY '  ENTER A NEW ITEM NUMBER'
            @ 6,1  SAY ' '
            WAIT "          PRESS ANY KEY TO CONTINUE"
            DEACTIVATE WINDOW msg1
         ENDIF

      CASE CHOICE = 3 .OR. CHOICE = 5 .OR. CHOICE = 7
         IF FOUND()
            SET FORMAT TO INVENTRY
            READ
            CLEAR
            IF CHOICE =  3
               @ 8,1
               @ 8,27 SAY '  *** ITEM CHANGED *** '
            ENDIF
```

```
                IF CHOICE =  5
                    SET FORMAT TO
                    ?? CHR(7)
                    DEFINE MENU yesno
                    DEFINE PAD no OF yesno PROMPT "[NO]" AT 6,2
                    ON SELECTION PAD no OF yesno DEACTIVATE MENU
                    DEFINE PAD yes OF yesno PROMPT "[YES]" AT 6,30
                    ON SELECTION PAD yes OF yesno DO DELETE
                    ACTIVATE WINDOW msg2

                    @ 1,05 SAY '  *** CONFIRM DELETE ***      '
                    @ 3,05 SAY '   DO YOU REALLY WANT TO       '
                    @ 4,05 SAY '      DELETE THIS RECORD       '
                    ACTIVATE menu yesno
                    DEACTIVATE WINDOW msg2
                    @ 8,10 CLEAR TO 21,70
                    STORE SPACE(6) TO CSN
                    ENDIF
              ELSE
                ?? CHR(7)
                ACTIVATE WINDOW msg1
                @ 2,05 SAY '        *** ERROR ***'
                @ 4,05 SAY '   ITEM NUMBER NOT ON FILE'
                @ 5,05 SAY ' ENTER ANOTHER ITEM NUMBER'
                @ 6,1  SAY ' '
                WAIT "        PRESS ANY KEY TO CONTINUE"
                DEACTIVATE WINDOW msg1
                STORE SPACE(8) TO ITN
              ENDIF
          ENDCASE
        STORE SPACE(8) TO ITN
        SET FORMAT TO
  ENDDO


PROCEDURE DELETE
  DELETE
  @ 1,1 CLEAR TO 6,37
  @ 3,5 SAY '   *** ITEM DELETED ***     '
  @ 5,1
  WAIT "        PRESS ANY KEY TO CONTINUE"
  DEACTIVATE MENU
RETURN
```

```
***********************************************************************
* Program......: INVTCROS.PRG
* Author.......: Cary N. Prague
* Date.........: 10-02-88, Final Revision 12-26-88 Revised 3-12-92
* Module #.....: 3.3
* dBASE Ver....: IV 1.5
* Description..: AJAX APPLIANCE COMPANY INVENTORY CROSS REFERENCE PRINT
***********************************************************************
CLEAR
CLOSE DATABASES
USE INVENTRY ORDER BRAND

*-- Popup
SET BORDER TO SINGLE
DEFINE POPUP PRTMENU FROM 12,31 TO 18,49
DEFINE BAR 1 OF PRTMENU PROMPT "                  " SKIP
DEFINE BAR 2 OF PRTMENU PROMPT "    PRINT REPORT "
DEFINE BAR 3 OF PRTMENU PROMPT "                  " SKIP
DEFINE BAR 4 OF PRTMENU PROMPT " CANCEL PRINTING "
ON SELECTION POPUP PRTMENU DO PRTPICK

@ 1,29 SAY "AJAX APPLIANCE COMPANY"
@ 2,25 SAY "INVENTORY CROSS REFERENCE PRINT"
@ 10,22 SAY 'ALIGN PAPER AND CHOOSE A MENU OPTION'

ACTIVATE POPUP PRTMENU


RETURN

PROCEDURE PRTPICK
 DO CASE
   CASE BAR() = 2
     REPORT FORM ITEMCROS TO PRINT
     DEACTIVATE POPUP
   CASE BAR() = 4
     DEACTIVATE POPUP
 ENDCASE
 RETURN
```

```
**********************************************************************
* Program......: INVTVALU.PRG
* Author.......: Cary N. Prague
* Date.........: 10-03-88, Final Revision 12-26-88 Revised 3-12-92
* Module #.....: 3.2
* dBASE Ver....: IV 1.5
* Description..: AJAX APPLIANCE COMPANY INVENTORY VALUATION PRINT
**********************************************************************
CLEAR
CLOSE DATABASES
USE INVENTRY ORDER ITEMNO
SET CONSOLE OFF
_pscode = "{27}{40}{115}16.66{72}"
*-- Popup
SET BORDER TO SINGLE
DEFINE POPUP PRTMENU FROM 12,31 TO 18,49
DEFINE BAR 1 OF PRTMENU PROMPT "                    " SKIP
DEFINE BAR 2 OF PRTMENU PROMPT "    PRINT REPORT "
DEFINE BAR 3 OF PRTMENU PROMPT "                    " SKIP
DEFINE BAR 4 OF PRTMENU PROMPT " CANCEL PRINTING "
ON SELECTION POPUP PRTMENU DO PRTPICK

@ 1,29 SAY "AJAX APPLIANCE COMPANY"
@ 2,28 SAY "INVENTORY VALUATION PRINT"
@ 10,22 SAY 'ALIGN PAPER AND CHOOSE A MENU OPTION'

ACTIVATE POPUP PRTMENU


RETURN

PROCEDURE PRTPICK
  DO CASE
    CASE BAR() = 2
      REPORT FORM INVVALUE TO PRINT
      DEACTIVATE POPUP
    CASE BAR() = 4
      DEACTIVATE POPUP
  ENDCASE
  SET CONSOLE ON
  _pecode="{27}{69}"
RETURN
```

```
**************************************************************************
* Program......: INVTSMAN.PRG
* Author.......: Cary N. Prague
* Date.........: 10-02-88, Final Revision 12-26-88 Revised 3-12-92
* Module #.....: 3.4
* dBASE Ver....: IV 1.5
* Description..: AJAX APPLIANCE COMPANY INVENTORY SALESMAN REPORT
**************************************************************************
CLEAR
CLOSE DATABASES
USE INVENTRY ORDER ITEMNO
STORE .T. TO MOREPRT
STORE SPACE(8) TO ITN
SET CONSOLE OFF
*-- Popup
SET BORDER TO SINGLE
DEFINE POPUP PRTMENU FROM 15,31 TO 21,49
DEFINE BAR 1 OF PRTMENU PROMPT "                " SKIP
DEFINE BAR 2 OF PRTMENU PROMPT "  PRINT REPORT  "
DEFINE BAR 3 OF PRTMENU PROMPT "                " SKIP
DEFINE BAR 4 OF PRTMENU PROMPT " CANCEL PRINTING "
ON SELECTION POPUP PRTMENU DO PRTPICK

DO WHILE MOREPRT
  @ 1,29 SAY "AJAX APPLIANCE COMPANY"
  @ 2,28 SAY "SALESMAN INVENTORY PRINT"
  @ 4,22 SAY "   ENTER THE ITEM NUMBER TO PRINT"
  @ 5,22 SAY " OR LEAVE BLANK TO PRINT ALL ITEMS"
  @ 7,29 SAY "ITEM NUMBER:"
  @ 7,42 GET itn PICTURE "@! AAAA-###"
  READ
  @ 13,22 SAY 'ALIGN PAPER AND CHOOSE A MENU OPTION'
  ACTIVATE POPUP PRTMENU
ENDDO
RETURN

PROCEDURE PRTPICK
 DO CASE
   CASE BAR() = 2
     IF ITN = '        ' .OR. ITN = '     -   '
        REPORT FORM SALESMAN TO PRINT
     ELSE
        SEEK TRIM(ITN)
        IF FOUND()
           REPORT FORM SALESMAN TO PRINT FOR ITEMNO = ITN
           STORE SPACE(8) TO ITN
        ELSE
           ?? CHR(7)
           ACTIVATE WINDOW msg1
           @ 2,05 SAY '       *** ERROR ***'
           @ 4,05 SAY '   ITEM NUMBER NOT ON FILE'
           @ 5,05 SAY '  ENTER ANOTHER ITEM NUMBER'
           @ 6,1  SAY ' '
           WAIT "        PRESS ANY KEY TO CONTINUE"
           DEACTIVATE WINDOW msg1
           STORE SPACE(8) TO ITN
        ENDIF
     ENDIF
     DEACTIVATE POPUP
   CASE BAR() = 4
     MOREPRT = .F.
     SET CONSOLE ON
     DEACTIVATE POPUP
 ENDCASE
RETURN
```

```
*********************************************************************
* Program......: INVCMENU.PRG
* Author.......: Cary N. Prague
* Date.........: 10-02-88, Final Revision 01-01-89 Revision 3-12-92
* Module #.....: 2.1
* dBASE Ver....: IV 1.5
* Description..: AJAX APPLIANCE COMPANY INVOICE MAIN MENU
*********************************************************************
CLEAR
SET PROCEDURE TO INVOICE
USE INVOICE ORDER INVNO
USE CUSTOMER ORDER CUSTNO IN 2
USE INVENTRY ORDER ITEMNO IN 3
USE ITEMS ORDER INVNO IN 4
SET BORDER TO NONE
DEFINE POPUP INVCMENU FROM 8,23 TO 18,52 ;
MESSAGE "Choose a selection from the Invoice Menu"
DEFINE BAR 1 OF INVCMENU PROMPT "        ADD NEW INVOICE      "
DEFINE BAR 2 OF INVCMENU PROMPT "                             " SKIP
DEFINE BAR 3 OF INVCMENU PROMPT " CHANGE INVOICE INFORMATION "
DEFINE BAR 4 OF INVCMENU PROMPT "                             " SKIP
DEFINE BAR 5 OF INVCMENU PROMPT "        DELETE AN INVOICE    "
DEFINE BAR 6 OF INVCMENU PROMPT "                             " SKIP
DEFINE BAR 7 OF INVCMENU PROMPT "   VIEW INVOICE INFORMATION "
DEFINE BAR 8 OF INVCMENU PROMPT "                             " SKIP
DEFINE BAR 9 OF INVCMENU PROMPT "   EXIT INVOICE DATA ENTRY  "
ON SELECTION POPUP INVCMENU DO INVCPICK

@ 1,29 SAY "AJAX APPLIANCE COMPANY"
@ 2,29 SAY "  INVOICE DATA ENTRY"

ACTIVATE POPUP INVCMENU
CLOSE DATABASES

RETURN

PROCEDURE INVCPICK
 DO CASE
   CASE BAR() = 1
    DO INVCADD
   CASE BAR() = 3
    DO INVCCHG
   CASE BAR() = 5
    DO INVCDEL
   CASE BAR() = 7
    DO INVCVEW
   CASE BAR() = 9
    SET BORDER TO SINGLE
    DEACTIVATE POPUP
 ENDCASE
 RETURN
```

```
**********************************************************************
* Program......: INVOICE.PRG
* Author.......: Cary N. Prague
* Date.........: 12-28-88, Final Revision 01-01-89 Revised 3-12-92
* Module #.....: 2.1.0
* dBASE Ver....: IV 1.5
* Description..: AJAX APPLIANCE COMPANY INVOICE PROCEDURE
**********************************************************************
PROCEDURE REDRAW
    PUBLIC SUBTOT
    STORE 0 TO CNT
    STORE 0 TO SUBTOT
    STORE 9 TO LINECNT
    STORE 1 TO LOOPCNT
    REDRAW = .F.
    @ LINECNT,1 CLEAR TO LINECNT+7,79
    DO WHILE INVN=ITEMS->INVNO .AND. .NOT. EOF()
      IF .NOT. DELETED()
         CNT = CNT + 1
         @ LINECNT,1 SAY CNT PICTURE '99.'
         @ LINECNT,5  SAY QTY PICTURE '999'
         @ LINECNT,9  SAY ITEMNO
         STORE QTY TO QNTY
         STORE ITEMNO TO ITN
         STORE PRICE TO PRI
         SELECT INVENTRY
         SEEK TRIM(ITN)
         @ LINECNT,18 SAY BRAND
         @ LINECNT,29 SAY TYPE
         @ LINECNT,42 SAY SUBSTR(DESC,1,20)
         SELECT ITEMS
         @ LINECNT,62 SAY PRI PICTURE '99999.99'
         @ LINECNT,71 SAY QNTY*PRI PICTURE '99,999.99'
         SUBTOT = SUBTOT + (QNTY*PRI)
         STORE LOOPCNT+1 TO LOOPCNT
         STORE LINECNT+1 TO LINECNT
      ENDIF
      SKIP
    ENDDO
    DO WHILE LINECNT < 17
      @ LINECNT,1 SAY LOOPCNT PICTURE '99.'
      STORE LOOPCNT+1 TO LOOPCNT
      STORE LINECNT+1 TO LINECNT
    ENDDO
RETURN

PROCEDURE DISPTOT
    @ 17,70 SAY '----------'
    @ 18,55 SAY 'Sub Total'
    @ 18,70 SAY SUBTOT PICTURE '999,999.99'
    @ 19,55 SAY 'Discount ' + STR(INVOICE->DISCOUNT,2) + '%'
    DISC =  SUBTOT * (INVOICE->DISCOUNT/100)
    @ 19,70 SAY DISC PICTURE '999,999.99'
    @ 20,70 SAY '----------'
    @ 21,55 SAY 'Taxable Amount'
    @ 21,70 SAY SUBTOT-DISC PICTURE '999,999.99'
    IF CUSTOMER->TAXABLE
      @ 22,55 SAY 'Tax ' + STR(TAX_RATE,4,1) + '%'
      TX = (SUBTOT-DISC) * (TAX_RATE/100)
      @ 22,70 SAY TX PICTURE '999,999.99'
     ELSE
      @ 22,55 SAY 'Tax - None'
      TX = 0
      @ 22,70 SAY TX PICTURE '999,999.99'
    ENDIF
    @ 23,70 SAY '----------'
    @ 24,55 SAY 'Total Amount'
    @ 24,70 SAY SUBTOT-DISC+TX PICTURE '999,999.99'
    @ 17,1 SAY " "
RETURN
```

```
**********************************************************************
* Program......: INVCADD.PRG
* Author.......: Cary N. Prague
* Date.........: 10-02-88, Final Revision 01-01-89 Revised 3-12-92
* Module #.....: 2.1.1
* dBASE Ver....: IV 1.5
* Description..: AJAX APPLIANCE COMPANY INVOICE ADDITIONS
**********************************************************************
ACTIVATE WINDOW datan
CLEAR
SET BORDER TO SINGLE
PUBLIC INVN
DO NXTINVNO

STORE SPACE(6) TO CSN
STORE M->DATE TO IDT
DO WHILE .T.
   @  0,20 SAY "AJAX APPLIANCE COMPANY - INVOICE FORM"
   @  3,1 SAY 'INVOICE NUMBER: ' GET INVN PICTURE "####-###"
   @  5,1 SAY 'INVOICE DATE:    ' GET IDT  RANGE CTOD('01/01/88'),CTOD('12/31/99')
   @  2,40 TO 6,76
   @  2,47 SAY 'CUSTOMER NUMBER:' GET CSN  PICTURE "@! AA-999"
   @  7,0 TO 7,79
   READ
   IF INVN = SPACE(8) .OR. INVN = '    -   '
      EXIT
   ELSE
      SELECT INVOICE
      SEEK TRIM(INVN)
      IF .NOT. FOUND()
         SELECT CUSTOMER
         IF CSN = SPACE(6) .OR. CSN = '  -   '
            ?? CHR(7)
            ACTIVATE WINDOW msg1
            @ 2,05 SAY '        *** ERROR ***'
            @ 4,05 SAY 'CUSTOMER NUMBER CANNOT BE BLANK'
            @ 5,05 SAY '   ENTER A CUSTOMER NUMBER'
            @ 6,1  SAY ' '
            WAIT "          PRESS ANY KEY TO CONTINUE"
            DEACTIVATE WINDOW msg1
            LOOP
         ENDIF
         SEEK TRIM(CSN)
         IF FOUND()
            SELECT CUSTOMER
            STORE DISCOUNT TO DIS
            REPLACE LST_TXND WITH DATE()
            @ 3,41 SAY COMPANY
            @ 4,41 SAY STREET
            @ 5,41 SAY TRIM(CITY) + ', ' + STATE + ' ' + ZIP
            @ 8, 0 SAY "LINE"
            @ 8, 5 SAY "QTY"
            @ 8,10 SAY "ITEM #"
            @ 8,20 SAY "BRAND"
            @ 8,31 SAY "TYPE"
            @ 8,42 SAY "DESCRIPTION"
            @ 8,64 SAY "PRICE"
            @ 8,71 SAY "EXTENSION"
            SELECT INVOICE
            APPEND BLANK
            REPLACE INVNO WITH INVN,CUSTNO WITH CSN,INVDATE WITH IDT, ;
                 DISCOUNT WITH DIS
            DO INVCADDI
            CLEAR
            SELECT INVOICE
            DO NXTINVNO
            STORE SPACE(6) TO CSN
            STORE M->DATE TO IDT
```

```
            ELSE
                ?? CHR(7)
                ACTIVATE WINDOW msg1
                @ 2,05 SAY '        *** ERROR ***'
                @ 4,05 SAY '  CUSTOMER NUMBER NOT ON FILE'
                @ 5,05 SAY 'ENTER ANOTHER CUSTOMER NUMBER'
                @ 6,1  SAY ' '
                WAIT "        PRESS ANY KEY TO CONTINUE"
                DEACTIVATE WINDOW msg1
            ENDIF
        ELSE
            ?? CHR(7)
            ACTIVATE WINDOW msg1
            @ 2,05 SAY '        *** ERROR ***'
            @ 4,05 SAY 'INVOICE NUMBER ALREADY ON FILE'
            @ 5,05 SAY ' ENTER ANOTHER INVOICE NUMBER'
            @ 6,1  SAY ' '
            WAIT "        PRESS ANY KEY TO CONTINUE"
            DEACTIVATE WINDOW msg1
        ENDIF
    ENDIF
  ENDDO
DEACTIVATE WINDOW datan
RETURN

  * CALCULATE NEXT AVAILABLE INVOICE NUMBER

PROCEDURE NXTINVNO

STORE DATE() TO CURDATE
LFTSIDE = SUBSTR(DTOS(M->DATE),3,2) + SUBSTR(DTOS(M->DATE),5,2)
RITSIDE = '001'
INVN = LFTSIDE + '-' + RITSIDE
SELECT INVOICE
GO TOP
SEEK TRIM(INVN)
IF FOUND()
    DO WHILE FOUND()
        NEWRIT = VAL(RITSIDE) + 1
        DO CASE
          CASE NEWRIT < 10
            RITSIDE = '00' + STR(NEWRIT,1)
          CASE NEWRIT >= 10 .AND. NEWRIT < 100
            RITSIDE = '0' + STR(NEWRIT,2)
        ENDCASE
        INVN = LFTSIDE + '-' + RITSIDE
        SEEK TRIM(INVN)
    ENDDO
ENDIF
RETURN
```

```
**********************************************************************
* Program......: INVCADDI.PRG
* Author.......: Cary N. Prague
* Date.........: 10-02-88, Final Revision 01-01-89 Revised 3-12-92
* Module #.....: 2.1.1.1
* dBASE Ver....: IV 1.5
* Description..: AJAX APPLIANCE COMPANY INVOICE ITEM ADDITIONS
**********************************************************************
STORE 9 TO LINECNT
STORE 1 TO CNT
STORE 0 TO QNTY
STORE SPACE(8) TO ITMN
SUBTOT = 0
DO WHILE .T.
  @ LINECNT,1 SAY CNT PICTURE '99.'
  @ LINECNT,5 GET QNTY PICTURE '999'
  @ LINECNT,9 GET ITMN PICTURE '@! AAAA-999'
  READ
  IF QNTY = 0
     EXIT
   ELSE
     SELECT INVENTRY
     IF ITMN = SPACE(8) .OR. ITMN = '    -   '
        ?? CHR(7)
        ACTIVATE WINDOW msg1
        @ 2,05 SAY '        *** ERROR ***'
        @ 4,05 SAY ' ITEM NUMBER CANNOT BE BLANK'
        @ 5,05 SAY '   ENTER AN ITEM NUMBER'
        @ 6,1  SAY ' '
        WAIT "        PRESS ANY KEY TO CONTINUE"
        DEACTIVATE WINDOW msg1
        LOOP
     ENDIF
     SEEK TRIM(ITMN)
     IF FOUND()
        IF QNTY > QTY_STK
           ?? CHR(7)
           ACTIVATE WINDOW msg1
           @ 2,05 SAY '        *** ERROR ***'
           @ 4,05 SAY ' NOT ENOUGH QUANTITY IN STOCK'
           @ 5,05 SAY '  REDUCE THE QUANTITY TO ' + STR(QTY_STK,3)
           @ 6,1  SAY ' '
           WAIT "        PRESS ANY KEY TO CONTINUE"
           DEACTIVATE WINDOW msg1
           LOOP
        ENDIF
        STORE PRICE TO PRI
  *     REPLACE QTY_STK WITH QTY_STK-QNTY          && REDUCE THE INVENTORY
        @ LINECNT,5  SAY QNTY PICTURE '999'
        @ LINECNT,9  SAY ITMN
        @ LINECNT,18 SAY BRAND
        @ LINECNT,29 SAY TYPE
        @ LINECNT,42 SAY SUBSTR(DESC,1,20)
        @ LINECNT,62 SAY PRI PICTURE '99999.99'
        @ LINECNT,71 SAY QNTY*PRI PICTURE '99,999.99'
        SUBTOT = SUBTOT + (QNTY*PRI)
        DO DISPTOT
        SELECT ITEMS
        APPEND BLANK
        REPLACE INVNO WITH INVN, QTY WITH QNTY, ITEMNO WITH ITMN, ;
            PRICE WITH PRI
        STORE 0 TO QNTY
        STORE SPACE(8) TO ITMN
        STORE CNT + 1 TO CNT
        STORE LINECNT + 1 TO LINECNT
```

```
                    IF CNT = 9
                      ?? CHR(7)
                      ACTIVATE WINDOW msg1
                      @ 2,05 SAY '        *** ERROR ***'
                      @ 4,05 SAY '    INVOICE FORM IS FULL'
                      @ 5,05 SAY '    CREATE A NEW INVOICE  '
                      @ 6,1  SAY ' '
                      WAIT "        PRESS ANY KEY TO CONTINUE"
                      DEACTIVATE WINDOW msg1
                      EXIT
                    ENDIF
                ELSE
                    ?? CHR(7)
                    ACTIVATE WINDOW msg1
                    @ 2,05 SAY '        *** ERROR ***'
                    @ 4,05 SAY '   ITEM NUMBER NOT ON FILE'
                    @ 5,05 SAY ' ENTER ANOTHER ITEM NUMBER'
                    @ 6,1  SAY ' '
                    WAIT "        PRESS ANY KEY TO CONTINUE"
                    DEACTIVATE WINDOW msg1
                ENDIF
          ENDIF
ENDDO
```

```
******************************************************************
* Program......: INVCCHG.PRG
* Author.......: Cary N. Prague
* Date.........: 10-02-88, Final Revision 01-01-89 Revised 3-12-92
* Module #.....: 2.1.2
* dBASE Ver....: IV 1.5
* Description..: AJAX APPLIANCE COMPANY INVOICE CHANGES
******************************************************************
ACTIVATE WINDOW datan
CLEAR
SET BORDER TO SINGLE
PUBLIC INVN,DELSW
STORE .F. TO DELSW
STORE SPACE(8) TO INVN
DO WHILE .T.
   @  0,20 SAY "AJAX APPLIANCE COMPANY - INVOICE FORM"
   @  3,1 SAY 'INVOICE NUMBER: ' GET INVN PICTURE "####-###"
   @  5,1 SAY 'INVOICE DATE:   '
   @  2,40 TO 6,76
   @  2,47 SAY 'CUSTOMER NUMBER:'
   @  7,0 TO 7,79
   READ
   IF INVN = SPACE(8) .OR. INVN = '    -   '
      EXIT
      ELSE
      SELECT INVOICE
      SEEK TRIM(INVN)
      IF FOUND()
           STORE INVDATE TO IDT
           STORE CUSTNO TO CSN
           SELECT CUSTOMER
           SEEK TRIM(CSN)
           STORE COMPANY TO CMP
           STORE STREET TO STR
           STORE TRIM(CITY) + ', ' + STATE + ' ' + ZIP TO CSZ
           @ 3,41 SAY CMP
           @ 4,41 SAY STR
           @ 5,41 SAY CSZ
           SELECT INVOICE
           @  5,1 SAY 'INVOICE DATE:   ' GET IDT  ;
               RANGE CTOD('01/01/88'),CTOD('12/31/99')
           @  2,47 SAY 'CUSTOMER NUMBER:' GET CSN  PICTURE "@! AA-###"
           READ
           ERRSW = .F.
           IF CSN # CUSTNO
             ERRSW = .T.
           ENDIF
           DO WHILE ERRSW
             IF CSN = '  -   '  .OR.  CSN = SPACE(6)
                 ?? CHR(7)
                 ACTIVATE WINDOW msg1
                 @ 2,05 SAY '          *** ERROR ***'
                 @ 4,05 SAY 'CUSTOMER NUMBER CANNOT BE BLANK'
                 @ 5,05 SAY '    ENTER A CUSTOMER NUMBER'
                 @ 6,1  SAY ' '
                 WAIT "        PRESS ANY KEY TO CONTINUE"
                 DEACTIVATE WINDOW msg1
               ELSE
                 SELECT CUSTOMER
                 SEEK TRIM(CSN)
                 IF FOUND()
                    @ 3,41 SAY COMPANY
                    @ 4,41 SAY STREET
                    @ 5,41 SAY TRIM(CITY) + ', ' + STATE + ' ' + ZIP
                    EXIT
```

```
              ELSE
                 ?? CHR(7)
                 ACTIVATE WINDOW msg1
                 @ 2,05 SAY '          *** ERROR ***'
                 @ 4,05 SAY '    CUSTOMER NUMBER NOT ON FILE'
                 @ 5,05 SAY 'ENTER ANOTHER CUSTOMER NUMBER'
                 @ 6,1  SAY ' '
                 WAIT "          PRESS ANY KEY TO CONTINUE"
                 DEACTIVATE WINDOW msg1
              ENDIF
           ENDIF
           @  2,47 SAY 'CUSTOMER NUMBER:' GET CSN  PICTURE "@! AA-999"
           READ
        ENDDO
        SELECT INVOICE
        REPLACE CUSTNO WITH CSN
        CHGITEM = .F.
        DEFINE MENU yesno
        DEFINE PAD yes OF yesno PROMPT "[YES]" AT 6,2
        ON SELECTION PAD yes OF yesno DO OKTOCHG
        DEFINE PAD no OF yesno PROMPT "[NO]" AT 6,31
        ON SELECTION PAD no OF yesno DEACTIVATE MENU
        ACTIVATE WINDOW msg2
        @ 3,05 SAY '   *** CHANGE ITEMS? ***      '
        @ 4,05 SAY '                              '
        ACTIVATE menu yesno
        DEACTIVATE WINDOW msg2
        IF CHGITEM
           @ 8, 0 SAY "LINE"
           @ 8, 5 SAY "QTY"
           @ 8,10 SAY "ITEM #"
           @ 8,20 SAY "BRAND"
           @ 8,31 SAY "TYPE"
           @ 8,42 SAY "DESCRIPTION"
           @ 8,64 SAY "PRICE"
           @ 8,71 SAY "EXTENSION"
           DO INVCCHGI
        ENDIF
        CLEAR
        STORE SPACE(8) TO INVN
     ELSE
        ?? CHR(7)
        ACTIVATE WINDOW msg1
        @ 2,05 SAY '         *** ERROR ***'
        @ 4,05 SAY '    INVOICE NUMBER NOT FOUND'
        @ 5,05 SAY ' ENTER ANOTHER INVOICE NUMBER'
        @ 6,1  SAY ' '
        WAIT "          PRESS ANY KEY TO CONTINUE"
        DEACTIVATE WINDOW msg1
        STORE SPACE(8) TO INVN
     ENDIF
  ENDIF
ENDDO
IF DELSW
  SELECT ITEMS
  PACK
ENDIF
DEACTIVATE WINDOW datan
RETURN

PROCEDURE OKTOCHG
  CHGITEM = .Y.
  DEACTIVATE MENU
RETURN
```

```
***********************************************************************
* Program......: INVCCHGI.PRG
* Author.......: Cary N. Prague
* Date.........: 10-02-88, Final Revision 01-01-89 Revised 3-12-92
* Module #.....: 2.1.2.1
* dBASE Ver....: IV 1.5
* Description..: AJAX APPLIANCE COMPANY INVOICE ITEM CHANGES
***********************************************************************
STORE .T. TO MOREINVI
PUBLIC CNT,SEL
*-- Popup
SET BORDER TO SINGLE
DEFINE POPUP CHGMENU FROM 18,6 TO 23,31
DEFINE BAR 1 OF CHGMENU PROMPT "     ADD A NEW ITEM      "
DEFINE BAR 2 OF CHGMENU PROMPT "CHANGE ITEM INFORMATION"
DEFINE BAR 3 OF CHGMENU PROMPT "     DELETE AN ITEM      "
DEFINE BAR 4 OF CHGMENU PROMPT "   EXIT ITEM CHANGES   "
ON SELECTION POPUP CHGMENU DO CHGPICK

SELECT ITEMS
REDRAW = .T.
DO WHILE MOREINVI
  SELECT ITEMS
  SEEK TRIM(INVN)
  IF REDRAW
    DO REDRAW
    DO DISPTOT
  ENDIF
  ACTIVATE POPUP CHGMENU
  IF MOREINVI = .F.
    LOOP
  ENDIF
  IF SEL = 'ADD'          && DETERMINE NEW LINE NUMBER TO ADD
    IF CNT < 8
      LN = CNT + 1
    ELSE
      ?? CHR(7)
      ACTIVATE WINDOW msg1
      @ 1,05 SAY '        *** ERROR ***'
      @ 3,05 SAY '    INVOICE FORM IS FULL'
      @ 4,05 SAY '    CREATE A NEW INVOICE   '
      @ 5,1  SAY ' '
      WAIT "         PRESS ANY KEY TO CONTINUE"
      DEACTIVATE WINDOW msg1
      LOOP
    ENDIF
  ENDIF
  IF SEL = 'CHG' .OR. SEL = 'DEL'  && DETERMINE LINE NUMBER TO CHANGE OR DELETE
    ERRSW = .T.
    DO WHILE ERRSW
      LN = 0
      ?? CHR(7)
      ACTIVATE WINDOW msg1
      @ 1,05 SAY '     ENTER LINE NUMBER    '
      @ 2,05 SAY '     OR ENTER 0 TO EXIT'
      @ 4,05 SAY '      LINE NUMBER: ' GET LN PICTURE '9' RANGE 0,8
      @ 5,1  SAY ' '
      READ
      DEACTIVATE WINDOW msg1
      IF LN = 0
        ERRSW = .F.
        LOOP
      ENDIF
      IF LN > CNT
        ?? CHR(7)
```

```
          ACTIVATE WINDOW msg1
          @ 2,05 SAY '        *** ERROR ***'
          @ 4,05 SAY 'LINE NUMBER IS GREATER THAN'
          @ 5,05 SAY '    THE LAST LINE NUMBER '
          @ 6,1  SAY ' '
          WAIT "          PRESS ANY KEY TO CONTINUE"
          DEACTIVATE WINDOW msg1
          LOOP
       ENDIF
       ERRSW = .F.
     ENDDO
     IF LN = 0
       LOOP
     ENDIF
   ENDIF
ENDIF
SELECT ITEMS
IF SEL = 'ADD'                                            && ADD ITEM
   QNTY = 0
   ITMN = SPACE(8)
   DO WHILE .T.
     LINECNT = 8+CNT+1
     SELECT ITEMS
     @ LINECNT,5 GET QNTY PICTURE '999'
     @ LINECNT,9 GET ITMN PICTURE '@! AAAA-999'
     READ
     IF QNTY = 0
       EXIT
     ENDIF
     SELECT INVENTRY
     IF ITMN = SPACE(8) .OR. ITMN = '    -   '
       DO ERRINB
       LOOP
     ENDIF
     SEEK TRIM(ITMN)
     IF .NOT. FOUND()
       DO ERRINF
       LOOP
     ENDIF
     STORE PRICE TO PRI
     IF QNTY > QTY_STK
       DO ERRQNS
       LOOP
     ENDIF
 *   REPLACE QTY_STK WITH QTY_STK-QNTY          && REDUCE THE INVENTORY
     SELECT ITEMS
     APPEND BLANK
     REPLACE INVNO WITH INVN, QTY WITH QNTY, ITEMNO WITH ITMN, ;
         PRICE WITH PRI
     STORE .T. TO REDRAW
     EXIT
   ENDDO
ENDIF
IF SEL = 'CHG'                                            && CHANGE ITEM
   STORE 1 TO LOOPCNT
   SEEK TRIM(INVN)
   DO WHILE LOOPCNT < LN .AND. INVN = ITEMS->INVNO
     IF .NOT. DELETED()
       STORE LOOPCNT+1 TO LOOPCNT
     ENDIF
     SKIP
   ENDDO
   STORE 8+LOOPCNT TO LINECNT
   DO WHILE .T.
     SELECT ITEMS
     @ LINECNT,5 GET QTY PICTURE '999'
     @ LINECNT,9 GET ITEMNO PICTURE '@! AAAA-999'
```

```
                READ
                STORE QTY TO QNTY
                STORE ITEMNO TO ITMN
                IF QNTY = 0
                   DO ERRQN0
                   LOOP
                ENDIF
                IF ITMN = SPACE(8) .OR. ITMN = '      -   '
                   DO ERRINB
                   LOOP
                ENDIF
                SELECT INVENTRY
                SEEK TRIM(ITMN)
                IF .NOT. FOUND()
                   DO ERRINF
                   LOOP
                ENDIF
                STORE PRICE TO PRI
                IF QNTY > QTY_STK
                   DO ERRQNS
                   LOOP
                ENDIF
                SELECT ITEMS
                REPLACE PRICE WITH PRI
                EXIT
             ENDDO
             STORE .F. TO ERRSW
             REDRAW = .T.
          ENDIF
          IF SEL = 'DEL'                                        && DELETE ITEM
             SELECT ITEMS
             STORE 1 TO LOOPCNT
             SEEK TRIM(INVN)
             DO WHILE LOOPCNT <LN .AND. INVN = ITEMS->INVNO
                IF .NOT. DELETED()
                   STORE LOOPCNT+1 TO LOOPCNT
                ENDIF
                SKIP
             ENDDO
             STORE 8+LOOPCNT TO LINECNT
             DO DELREC
             REDRAW = .T.
          ENDIF
       ENDDO

PROCEDURE ERRINB    && ITEM CANNOT BE BLANK
?? CHR(7)
ACTIVATE WINDOW msg1
@ 2,05 SAY '        *** ERROR ***'
@ 4,05 SAY ' ITEM NUMBER CANNOT BE BLANK'
@ 5,05 SAY '   ENTER AN ITEM NUMBER'
@ 6,1  SAY ' '
WAIT "        PRESS ANY KEY TO CONTINUE"
DEACTIVATE WINDOW msg1
RETURN

PROCEDURE ERRINF    && ITEM NOT FOUND
?? CHR(7)
ACTIVATE WINDOW msg1
@ 2,05 SAY '        *** ERROR ***'
@ 4,05 SAY '  ITEM NUMBER NOT ON FILE'
@ 5,05 SAY ' ENTER ANOTHER ITEM NUMBER'
@ 6,1  SAY ' '
WAIT "        PRESS ANY KEY TO CONTINUE"
DEACTIVATE WINDOW msg1
RETURN
```

```
PROCEDURE ERRQN0    && QUANTITY CANNOT BE 0
 ?? CHR(7)
 ACTIVATE WINDOW msg1
 @ 2,05 SAY '       *** ERROR ***'
 @ 4,05 SAY '    QUANTITY CANNOT BE 0'
 @ 5,05 SAY '     CHANGE THE QUANTITY   '
 @ 6,1  SAY ' '
 WAIT "         PRESS ANY KEY TO CONTINUE"
 DEACTIVATE WINDOW msg1
RETURN

PROCEDURE ERRQNS    && QUANTITY NOT SUFFICIENT
 ?? CHR(7)
 ACTIVATE WINDOW msg1
 @ 2,05 SAY '        *** ERROR ***'
 @ 4,05 SAY ' NOT ENOUGH QUANTITY IN STOCK'
 @ 5,05 SAY '   REDUCE THE QUANTITY TO ' + STR(QTY_STK,3)
 @ 6,1  SAY ' '
 WAIT "         PRESS ANY KEY TO CONTINUE"
 DEACTIVATE WINDOW msg1
RETURN

PROCEDURE CHGPICK
 DO CASE
    CASE BAR() = 1
      SEL = 'ADD'
      DEACTIVATE POPUP
    CASE BAR() = 2
      SEL = 'CHG'
      DEACTIVATE POPUP
    CASE BAR() = 3
      SEL = 'DEL'
      DEACTIVATE POPUP
    CASE BAR() = 4
      MOREINVI = .F.
      DEACTIVATE POPUP
 ENDCASE
RETURN

PROCEDURE DELREC
    @ LINECNT,5 FILL TO LINECNT,79 COLOR W+/R
    ?? CHR(7)
    DEFINE MENU yesno
    DEFINE PAD no OF yesno PROMPT "[NO]" AT 6,2
    ON SELECTION PAD no OF yesno DEACTIVATE MENU
    DEFINE PAD yes OF yesno PROMPT "[YES]" AT 6,30
    ON SELECTION PAD yes OF yesno DO DELETE
    ACTIVATE WINDOW msg2
    @ 1,05 SAY '  *** CONFIRM DELETE ***       '
    @ 3,05 SAY '   DO YOU REALLY WANT TO       '
    @ 4,05 SAY '     DELETE THIS RECORD        '
    ACTIVATE menu yesno
    DEACTIVATE WINDOW msg2
    @ LINECNT,5 FILL TO LINECNT,79 COLOR W+/B
RETURN

PROCEDURE DELETE
  DELETE
  DELSW = .T.
  DEACTIVATE MENU
RETURN
```

```
**************************************************************************
* Program......: INVCDEL.PRG
* Author.......: Cary N. Prague
* Date.........: 10-02-88, Final Revision 01-01-89 Revised 3-12-92
* Module #.....: 2.1.3
* dBASE Ver....: IV 1.5
* Description..: AJAX APPLIANCE COMPANY INVOICE DELETES
**************************************************************************
ACTIVATE WINDOW datan
CLEAR
SET BORDER TO SINGLE
PUBLIC INVN,DELSW
STORE .F. TO DELSW
STORE SPACE(8) TO INVN
DO WHILE .T.
   @ 0,20 SAY "AJAX APPLIANCE COMPANY - INVOICE FORM"
   @ 3,1 SAY 'INVOICE NUMBER: ' GET INVN PICTURE "####-###"
   @ 5,1 SAY 'INVOICE DATE:   '
   @ 2,40 TO 6,76
   @ 2,47 SAY 'CUSTOMER NUMBER:'
   @ 7,0 TO 7,79
   READ
   IF INVN = SPACE(8) .OR. INVN = '    -   '
       EXIT
     ELSE
       SELECT INVOICE
       SEEK TRIM(INVN)
       IF FOUND()
           STORE INVDATE TO IDT
           STORE CUSTNO TO CSN
           @ 5,1 SAY 'INVOICE DATE:    ' + DTOC(IDT)
           @ 2,47 SAY 'CUSTOMER NUMBER:' + CSN
           SELECT CUSTOMER
           SEEK TRIM(CSN)
           STORE COMPANY TO CMP
           STORE STREET TO STR
           STORE TRIM(CITY) + ', ' + STATE + ' ' + ZIP TO CSZ
           @ 3,41 SAY CMP
           @ 4,41 SAY STR
           @ 5,41 SAY CSZ
           @ 8, 0 SAY "LINE"
           @ 8, 5 SAY "QTY"
           @ 8,10 SAY "ITEM #"
           @ 8,20 SAY "BRAND"
           @ 8,31 SAY "TYPE"
           @ 8,42 SAY "DESCRIPTION"
           @ 8,64 SAY "PRICE"
           @ 8,71 SAY "EXTENSION"
           SELECT ITEMS
           SEEK TRIM(INVN)
           DO REDRAW
           DO DISPTOT
           ?? CHR(7)
           DEFINE MENU yesno
           DEFINE PAD no OF yesno PROMPT "[NO]" AT 6,2
           ON SELECTION PAD no OF yesno DEACTIVATE MENU
           DEFINE PAD yes OF yesno PROMPT "[YES]" AT 6,30
           ON SELECTION PAD yes OF yesno DO DELETE
           ACTIVATE WINDOW msg2
           @ 1,05 SAY ' *** CONFIRM DELETE ***   '
           @ 3,05 SAY '  DO YOU REALLY WANT TO    '
           @ 4,05 SAY '    DELETE THIS RECORD     '
           ACTIVATE menu yesno
           DEACTIVATE WINDOW msg2
           CLEAR
```

```
                STORE SPACE(8) TO INVN
            ELSE
                ?? CHR(7)
                ACTIVATE WINDOW msg1
                @ 2,05 SAY '         *** ERROR ***'
                @ 4,05 SAY '    INVOICE NUMBER NOT FOUND'
                @ 5,05 SAY ' ENTER ANOTHER INVOICE NUMBER'
                @ 6,1  SAY ' '
                WAIT "         PRESS ANY KEY TO CONTINUE"
                DEACTIVATE WINDOW msg1
                STORE SPACE(8) TO INVN
            ENDIF
    ENDIF
ENDDO
IF DELSW
  SELECT INVOICE
  PACK
  SELECT ITEMS
  PACK
ENDIF
DEACTIVATE WINDOW datan
RETURN

PROCEDURE DELETE
  SELECT INVOICE
  SEEK TRIM(INVN)
  IF FOUND()
    DELETE
    SELECT ITEMS
    DELETE ALL FOR INVNO = INVN
    SELECT INVOICE
  ENDIF
  DEACTIVATE MENU
RETURN
```

```
*****************************************************************************
* Program......: INVCVEW.PRG
* Author.......: Cary N. Prague
* Date.........: 10-03-88, Final Revision 01-01-89 Revised 3-12-92
* Module #.....: 2.1.4
* dBASE Ver....: IV 1.5
* Description..: AJAX APPLIANCE COMPANY INVOICE VIEW
*****************************************************************************
ACTIVATE WINDOW datan
CLEAR
SET BORDER TO SINGLE
PUBLIC INVN,DELSW
STORE .F. TO DELSW
STORE SPACE(8) TO INVN
DO WHILE .T.
   @  0,20 SAY "AJAX APPLIANCE COMPANY - INVOICE FORM"
   @  3,1 SAY 'INVOICE NUMBER: ' GET INVN PICTURE "####-###"
   @  5,1 SAY 'INVOICE DATE:    '
   @  2,40 TO 6,76
   @  2,47 SAY 'CUSTOMER NUMBER:'
   @  7,0 TO 7,79
   READ
   IF INVN = SPACE(8) .OR. INVN = '    -   '
        MOREINV = .F.
        EXIT
     ELSE
        SELECT INVOICE
        SEEK TRIM(INVN)
        IF FOUND()
           STORE INVDATE TO IDT
           STORE CUSTNO TO CSN
           @  5,1 SAY 'INVOICE DATE:    ' + DTOC(IDT)
           @  2,47 SAY 'CUSTOMER NUMBER:' + CSN
           SELECT CUSTOMER
           SEEK TRIM(CSN)
           STORE COMPANY TO CMP
           STORE STREET TO STR
           STORE TRIM(CITY) + ', ' + STATE + ' ' + ZIP TO CSZ
           @  3,41 SAY CMP
           @  4,41 SAY STR
           @  5,41 SAY CSZ
           @  8, 0 SAY "LINE"
           @  8, 5 SAY "QTY"
           @  8,10 SAY "ITEM #"
           @  8,20 SAY "BRAND"
           @  8,31 SAY "TYPE"
           @  8,42 SAY "DESCRIPTION"
           @  8,64 SAY "PRICE"
           @  8,71 SAY "EXTENSION"
           SELECT ITEMS
           SEEK TRIM(INVN)
           DO REDRAW
           DO DISPTOT
           @ 19,6  SAY ' '
           WAIT "*** PRESS ANY KEY TO CONTINUE ***"
           CLEAR
           STORE SPACE(8) TO INVN
         ELSE
           ?? CHR(7)
           ACTIVATE WINDOW msg1
           @ 2,05 SAY '        *** ERROR ***'
           @ 4,05 SAY '    INVOICE NUMBER NOT FOUND'
           @ 5,05 SAY ' ENTER ANOTHER INVOICE NUMBER'
           @ 6,1 SAY ' '
           WAIT "       PRESS ANY KEY TO CONTINUE"
           DEACTIVATE WINDOW msg1
           STORE SPACE(8) TO INVN
        ENDIF
   ENDIF
ENDDO
DEACTIVATE WINDOW datan
RETURN
```

```
**********************************************************************
* Program......: INVCINVC.PRG
* Author.......: Cary N. Prague
* Date.........: 10-02-88, Final Revision 3-3-92 Revised 3-12-92
* Module #.....: 2.2
* dBASE Ver....: IV 1.5
* Description..: AJAX APPLIANCE COMPANY INVOICE PRINTING MENU PROGRAM
**********************************************************************
CLEAR
CLOSE DATABASES
USE INVOICE ORDER INVNO
USE CUSTOMER ORDER CUSTNO IN 2
USE INVENTRY ORDER ITEMNO IN 3
USE ITEMS ORDER INVNO IN 4
STORE .T. TO MOREPRT
STORE SPACE(8)   TO INVN1,INVN2

*-- Popup
SET BORDER TO SINGLE
DEFINE POPUP PRTMENU FROM 15,31 TO 21,49
DEFINE BAR 1 OF PRTMENU PROMPT "                " SKIP
DEFINE BAR 2 OF PRTMENU PROMPT "   PRINT INVOICE   "
DEFINE BAR 3 OF PRTMENU PROMPT "                " SKIP
DEFINE BAR 4 OF PRTMENU PROMPT " CANCEL PRINTING "
ON SELECTION POPUP PRTMENU DO PRTPICK

DO WHILE MOREPRT
   @ 1,22 SAY "        AJAX APPLIANCE COMPANY"
   @ 2,22 SAY "            INVOICE PRINT"
   @ 4,22 SAY " ENTER THE INVOICE NUMBERS TO PRINT"
   @ 5,22 SAY "OR LEAVE BLANK TO PRINT ALL INVOICES"
   @ 7,10 SAY "BEGINNING INVOICE NUMBER"
   @ 7,48 SAY "ENDING INVOICE NUMBER"
   @ 8,18 GET INVN1 PICTURE "@! ###-###"
   @ 8,54 GET INVN2 PICTURE "@! ###-###"
   READ
   @ 13,22 SAY 'ALIGN PAPER AND CHOOSE A MENU OPTION'

   ACTIVATE POPUP PRTMENU

ENDDO

RETURN

PROCEDURE PRTPICK
 DO CASE
   CASE BAR() = 2
     IF INVN1 = '          ' .OR. INVN1 = '     -   '
         SELECT INVOICE
         GO TOP
         DO WHILE .NOT. EOF()
          SET CONSOLE OFF
          DO INVCINVP
          SKIP
         ENDDO
         SET CONSOLE ON
     ELSE
        SEEK TRIM(INVN1)
        IF FOUND()
            SCAN WHILE INVNO <= INVN2 .AND. .NOT. EOF()
             DO INVCINVP
            ENDSCAN
            STORE SPACE(8) TO INVN1
            STORE SPACE(8) TO INVN2
           ELSE
```

```
                     ?? CHR(7)
                     ACTIVATE WINDOW msg1
                     @ 2,05 SAY '          *** ERROR ***'
                     @ 4,05 SAY ' INVOICE NUMBER NOT ON FILE'
                     @ 5,05 SAY 'ENTER ANOTHER INVOICE NUMBER'
                     @ 6,1  SAY ' '
                     WAIT "          PRESS ANY KEY TO CONTINUE"
                     DEACTIVATE WINDOW msg1
                     STORE SPACE(8) TO INVN1
                     STORE SPACE(8) TO INVN2
                  ENDIF
            ENDIF
            DEACTIVATE POPUP
         CASE BAR() = 4
            MOREPRT = .F.
            DEACTIVATE POPUP
   ENDCASE
   RETURN
```

```
**************************************************************************
* Program......: INVCINVP.PRG
* Author.......: Cary N. Prague
* Date.........: 10-03-88, Final Revision 01-01-89 Revised 3-12-92
* Module #.....: 2.2.1
* dBASE Ver....: IV 1.5
* Description..: AJAX APPLIANCE COMPANY INVOICE PRINT PROGRAM
**************************************************************************
   SET DEVICE TO PRINT
   STORE INVNO TO INVN
   STORE INVDATE TO IDT
   STORE CUSTNO TO CSN
   @  0,20 SAY "AJAX APPLIANCE COMPANY - INVOICE FORM"
   @  2,43 SAY 'CUSTOMER NUMBER:' + CUSTNO
   @  2,5 SAY 'INVOICE NUMBER: ' + INVNO
   SELECT CUSTOMER
   SEEK TRIM(CSN)
   @ 3,45 SAY COMPANY
   @ 4,45 SAY STREET
   @ 5,5 SAY 'INVOICE DATE:    ' + DTOC(IDT)
   @ 5,45 SAY TRIM(CITY) + ', ' + STATE + ' ' + ZIP
   @ 8, 5 SAY "QTY"
   @ 8,10 SAY "ITEM #"
   @ 8,20 SAY "BRAND"
   @ 8,31 SAY "TYPE"
   @ 8,42 SAY "DESCRIPTION"
   @ 8,64 SAY "PRICE"
   @ 8,71 SAY "EXTENSION"
   SELECT ITEMS
   SEEK TRIM(INVN)
   DO REDRAW
   DO DISPTOT
   EJECT
   SET DEVICE TO SCREEN
RETURN

PROCEDURE REDRAW
   PUBLIC SUBTOT
   STORE 0 TO CNT
   STORE 0 TO SUBTOT
   STORE 10 TO LINECNT
   DO WHILE INVN=ITEMS->INVNO .AND. .NOT. EOF()
     IF .NOT. DELETED()
        CNT = CNT + 1
        @ LINECNT,5  SAY QTY PICTURE '999'
        @ LINECNT,9  SAY ITEMNO
        STORE QTY TO QNTY
        STORE ITEMNO TO ITN
        STORE PRICE TO PRI
        SELECT INVENTRY
        SEEK TRIM(ITN)
        @ LINECNT,18 SAY BRAND
        @ LINECNT,29 SAY TYPE
        @ LINECNT,42 SAY SUBSTR(DESC,1,20)
        SELECT ITEMS
        @ LINECNT,62 SAY PRI PICTURE '99999.99'
        @ LINECNT,71 SAY QNTY*PRI PICTURE '99,999.99'
        SUBTOT = SUBTOT + (QNTY*PRI)
        STORE LINECNT+1 TO LINECNT
     ENDIF
     SKIP
   ENDDO
   SELECT INVOICE
RETURN
```

```
PROCEDURE DISPTOT
    @ 47,70 SAY '----------'
    @ 48,55 SAY 'Sub Total'
    @ 48,70 SAY SUBTOT PICTURE '999,999.99'
    @ 49,55 SAY 'Discount ' + STR(INVOICE->DISCOUNT,2) + '%'
    DISC =  SUBTOT * (INVOICE->DISCOUNT/100)
    @ 49,70 SAY DISC PICTURE '999,999.99'
    @ 50,70 SAY '----------'
    @ 51,55 SAY 'Taxable Amount'
    @ 51,70 SAY SUBTOT-DISC PICTURE '999,999.99'
    IF CUSTOMER->TAXABLE
       @ 52,55 SAY 'Tax ' + STR(TAX_RATE,4,1) + '%'
       TX = (SUBTOT-DISC) * (TAX_RATE/100)
       @ 52,70 SAY TX PICTURE '999,999.99'
     ELSE
       @ 52,55 SAY 'Tax - None'
       TX = 0
       @ 52,70 SAY TX PICTURE '999,999.99'
    ENDIF
    @ 53,70 SAY '----------'
    @ 54,55 SAY 'Total Amount'
    @ 54,70 SAY SUBTOT-DISC+TX PICTURE '999,999.99'
    @ 55,70 SAY '=========='
RETURN
```

```
*************************************************************************
* Program......: INVCWARN.PRG
* Author.......: Cary N. Prague
* Date.........: 10-02-88, Final Revision 01-01-89 Revised 3-12-92
* Module #.....: 2.3
* dBASE Ver....: IV 1.5
* Description..: AJAX APPLIANCE COMPANY INVOICE WARRANTY PRINTING PROGRAM
*************************************************************************
CLEAR
CLOSE DATABASES
SET CONSOLE OFF
USE INVOICE ORDER INVNO
USE ITEMS ORDER INVNO IN 2
STORE .T. TO MOREPRT
STORE SPACE(8)  TO INVN1,INVN2

*-- Popup
SET BORDER TO SINGLE
DEFINE POPUP PRTMENU FROM 15,31 TO 21,49
DEFINE BAR 1 OF PRTMENU PROMPT "                " SKIP
DEFINE BAR 2 OF PRTMENU PROMPT " PRINT WARRANTY " SKIP
DEFINE BAR 3 OF PRTMENU PROMPT "                " SKIP
DEFINE BAR 4 OF PRTMENU PROMPT " CANCEL PRINTING "
ON SELECTION POPUP PRTMENU DO PRTPICK

DO WHILE MOREPRT
  @ 1,22 SAY "      AJAX APPLIANCE COMPANY"
  @ 2,22 SAY "          WARRANTY PRINT"
  @ 4,22 SAY " ENTER THE INVOICE NUMBERS TO PRINT"
  @ 5,22 SAY "OR LEAVE BLANK TO PRINT ALL INVOICES"
  @ 7,10 SAY "BEGINNING INVOICE NUMBER"
  @ 7,48 SAY "ENDING INVOICE NUMBER"
  @ 8,18 GET INVN1 PICTURE "@! ####-###"
  @ 8,54 GET INVN2 PICTURE "@! ####-###"
  READ
  @ 13,22 SAY 'ALIGN PAPER AND CHOOSE A MENU OPTION'

  ACTIVATE POPUP PRTMENU

ENDDO

RETURN

PROCEDURE PRTPICK
 DO CASE
   CASE BAR() = 2
     IF INVN1 = '          ' .OR. INVN1 = '     -   '
        CLOSE DATABASES
        SET VIEW TO INVOICES
        REPORT FORM WARRANTY TO PRINT
     ELSE
       SEEK TRIM(INVN1)
         IF FOUND()
            CLOSE DATABASES
            SET VIEW TO INVOICES
            SET CONSOLE OFF
            REPORT FORM WARRANTY TO PRINT FOR INVNO >= INVN1 ;
               .AND. INVNO <= INVN2
            STORE SPACE(8) TO INVN1
            STORE SPACE(8) TO INVN2
          ELSE
            ?? CHR(7)
            ACTIVATE WINDOW msg1
            @ 2,05 SAY '         *** ERROR ***'
            @ 4,05 SAY ' INVOICE NUMBER NOT ON FILE'
```

```
                    @ 5,05 SAY 'ENTER ANOTHER INVOICE NUMBER'
                    @ 6,1  SAY ' '
                    WAIT "        PRESS ANY KEY TO CONTINUE"
                    DEACTIVATE WINDOW msg1
                    STORE SPACE(8) TO INVN1
                    STORE SPACE(8) TO INVN2
                ENDIF
            ENDIF
            DEACTIVATE POPUP
        CASE BAR() = 4
            MOREPRT = .F.
            SET CONSOLE ON
            DEACTIVATE POPUP
    ENDCASE
    RETURN
```

```
*****************************************************************
* Program......: INVCSALS.PRG
* Author.......: Cary N. Prague
* Date.........: 10-02-88, Final Revision 01-01-89 Revised 3-12-92
* Module #.....: 2.4
* dBASE Ver....: IV 1.5
* Description..: AJAX APPLIANCE COMPANY MONTHLY SALES REPORT
*****************************************************************
CLEAR
CLOSE DATABASES
STORE .T. TO MOREPRT
STORE SPACE(2) TO YR,MN
*-- Popup
SET BORDER TO SINGLE
DEFINE POPUP PRTMENU FROM 15,31 TO 21,49
DEFINE BAR 1 OF PRTMENU PROMPT "                " SKIP
DEFINE BAR 2 OF PRTMENU PROMPT "   PRINT REPORT   "
DEFINE BAR 3 OF PRTMENU PROMPT "                " SKIP
DEFINE BAR 4 OF PRTMENU PROMPT " CANCEL PRINTING "
ON SELECTION POPUP PRTMENU DO PRTPICK

DO WHILE MOREPRT
   @ 1,29 SAY "AJAX APPLIANCE COMPANY"
   @ 2,28 SAY " MONTHLY SALES REPORT"
   @ 4,22 SAY "ENTER THE YEAR AND MONTH TO PRINT"
   @ 7,23 SAY "ENTER YEAR/MONTH: "
   @ 7,45 GET YR PICTURE "##"  ;
      VALID VAL(YR) >= 80 .AND. VAL(YR) <=99  ;
      ERROR 'VALUE OF YR IS INVALID'
   @ 7,47 SAY '/'
   @ 7,48 GET MN PICTURE "##"  ;
      VALID VAL(MN) >= 1 .AND. VAL(MN) <=12  ;
      ERROR 'VALUE OF MN IS INVALID'
   READ
   @ 13,22 SAY 'ALIGN PAPER AND CHOOSE A MENU OPTION'

   ACTIVATE POPUP PRTMENU
ENDDO

RETURN

PROCEDURE PRTPICK
 DO CASE
   CASE BAR() = 2
     IF YR = '  ' .OR. MN = '  '
        ACTIVATE WINDOW msg1
        @ 2,05 SAY '        *** ERROR ***'
        @ 4,05 SAY '   YEAR AND MONTH NOT VALID'
        @ 5,05 SAY 'ENTER A VALID YEAR AND MONTH'
        @ 6,1  SAY ' '
        WAIT "        PRESS ANY KEY TO CONTINUE"
        DEACTIVATE WINDOW msg1
        STORE SPACE(2) TO YR,MN
     ELSE
        SET VIEW TO SALES
        REPORT FORM SALESRPT TO PRINT ;
           FOR YEAR(INVDATE) - 1900 = VAL(YR) .AND. MONTH(INVDATE) = VAL(MN)
        STORE SPACE(2) TO YR,MN
     ENDIF
     DEACTIVATE POPUP
   CASE BAR() = 4
     MOREPRT = .F.
     DEACTIVATE POPUP
 ENDCASE
 RETURN
```

C
dBASE IV commands

Copy commands

COPY TO *filename* [[TYPE]*file type*] / [[WITH] PRODUCTION]
  [FIELDS *field list*] [*scope*] [FOR *condition*] [WHILE *condition*]

Creates a new file (of optional type) by copying all or part of an active database.

COPY FILE *filename* TO *filename*

Creates a copy of a closed file of any type.

COPY INDEXES *.ndx file list* [TO *.mdx filename*]

Copies a list of index (.NDX) files into a single multiple index (.MDX) file as tags.

COPY MEMO *memo field* TO *filename* [ADDITIVE]

Copies the contents of the specified memo field of the current record to the file specified.

COPY STRUCTURE TO *file name* [FIELDS *field list*] [[WITH] PRODUCTION]

Copies all or part of the structure of the active database file to a new file without records.

COPY TO *filename* STRUCTURE EXTENDED

Creates a database comprised of records containing the structure of the current database.

COPY TAG *tag name* [OF .MDX filename] TO.*NDX filename*

Creates an index (.NDX) file from the specified tag of an open multiple index (.MDX) file.

COPY TO ARRAY *array name* [FIELDS *fields list*] [*scope*] [FOR *condition*]
  [WHILE *condition*]

Fills the specified existing array with the contents of the specified records from the active database.

Database and index creation/modification/ selection commands

APPEND [BLANK]/[NOORGANIZE]

Adds a new record(s) to the end of the active database and activates full screen editing. BLANK adds a blank record at the end of the database file without edit capability. NOORGANIZE brings up a menu bar without the organize menu.

APPEND FROM *filename*/?
  [[TYPE] *file type*][REINDEX][FOR *condition*]

Adds records from an existing database or file to the end of the active database. TYPE is used to specify non dBASE IV file types. REINDEX rebuilds noncontrolling indexes only after all new records are appended.

APPEND FROM ARRAY *array name*
  [REINDEX][FOR *condition*]

Adds records to the end of the active database from information in an array. REINDEX rebuilds noncontrolling indexes only after all new records are appended.

APPEND MEMO *memo field name* FROM *filename* [OVERWRITE]

Appends to or overwrites the named memo field contents of the current record with the contents of the specified filename.

BLANK [FIELDS *field list*/LIKE *skeleton*/EXCEPT *skeleton*]
  [REINDEX][*scope*] [FOR *condition*] [WHILE *condition*]

Fills fields and records with blanks according to their data type. REINDEX rebuilds noncontrolling indexes only after all specified records are BLANKed.

CREATE *filename* FROM *structure extended file*

Creates a new database from the specified structure extended file (database) which may have been created by COPY STRUCTURE EXTENDED.

DELETE [*scope*] [FOR *condition*] [WHILE *condition*]

Marks the specified record(s) in the active database for deletion.

DELETE TAG *tag name 1* [OF *.MDX filename*]
  [,*tag name 2* [OF *.MDX filename*]...]

Deletes the specified tag(s) from an active multiple index (.MDX) file.

INDEX ON *key expression* TO *.NDX filename* [UNIQUE]
or

INDEX ON *key expression* TAG *tag name* [OF *.MDX filename*]
   [FOR *condition*] [UNIQUE] [DESCENDING]

Creates a single (.NDX) or multiple index (.MDX) file from the active database ordering records alphabetically, chronologically, or numerically.

INSERT [BEFORE] [NOORGANIZE]/[BLANK]

Inserts a new record into the active database at the current record location and activates full screen editing. BLANK inserts without edit capability. BEFORE inserts before the current record. NOORGANIZE brings up a menu bar without the organize menu.

IMPORT FROM *filename* [TYPE] PFS/dBASEII/FW2/FW3/FW4/RPD/WKS/WK1

Creates dBASE IV files from foreign file formats.

JOIN WITH *alias* TO *filename* FOR *condition* [FIELDS *field list*]

Creates a new database by merging specified records and fields (excluding memo fields) from two open databases.

PACK

Removes records marked for deletion from the active database and reindexes associated open index files.

RECALL [*scope*] [FOR *condition*] [WHILE *condition*]

Recalls (records marked for deletion) the specified records in the active database.

REINDEX

Rebuilds all active index (.NDX) and multiple index (.MDX) files in the currently selected work area.

REPLACE *field 1* WITH *exp1* [ADDITIVE]
   [*,field 2* WITH *exp2* [ADDITIVE]...]
   [REINDEX][*scope*] [FOR *condition*] [WHILE *condition*]

Replaces the contents of the specified fields in the active database with the specified new contents. ADDITIVE issued with memo fields appends to the end of the existing memo field contents. REINDEX rebuilds noncontrolling indexes only after the specified records have been REPLACEd.

REPLACE FROM ARRAY *array name*
   [FIELDS *field list*][*scope*]
   [FOR *condition*] [WHILE *condition*] [REINDEX]

Replaces fields in the active database with data from an array. REINDEX rebuilds noncontrolling indexes only after the specified records have been REPLACEd.

SELECT *work area name or number/alias*

Selects the specified work area or the work area containing the specified open database.

SORT TO *filename* ON *field1* [/A] [/C] [/D]
    [,*field2* /A] [/C] [/D] ...] [ASCENDING]/[DESCENDING]
    [*scope*] [FOR *condition*] [WHILE *condition*]

Creates a new database by copying all or part of an active database in the order specified.

TOTAL ON *key field* TO *filename* [FIELDS *fields list*]
    [*scope*] [FOR *condition*] [WHILE *condition*]

Sums the specified numeric fields of the active database and creates a second database containing the results.

UPDATE ON *key field* FROM *alias* REPLACE *field name 1*
    WITH *expression 1* [,*field name 2* WITH *expression 2*...]
    [RANDOM] [REINDEX]

Replaces the contents of the specified field(s) in the current database with the contents of matching key field records in a second database. RANDOM requires only the current database to be indexed and sorted. REINDEX rebuilds noncontrolling indexes only after all records are UPDATEd.

USE [*database filename*/?] [IN *work area number*]
    [[INDEX *.NDX or .MDX file list*] [ORDER *.NDX filename*
    /[TAG] *.MDX tag* [OF *.MDX file name*]]
    [ALIAS *alias*] [EXCLUSIVE] [NOUPDATE] [NOLOG]
    [NOSAVE] [AGAIN]

Opens the specified database in the current or specified work area, automatically opens memo files (.DBT) where applicable and opens production and (optionally specified) indexes and sets the controlling order.

ZAP

Removes all records from the active database and reindexes all applicable open index files.

Design surface and menu-assisted commands

ASSIST

Activates the dBASE IV Control Center.

CREATE *filename*/MODIFY STRUCTURE

Provides access to the database design surface. CREATE builds a new database structure. MODIFY STRUCTURE modifies the structure of an existing database.

CREATE/MODIFY APPLICATION *filename*/?

Provides access to the dBASE IV Applications Generator for the creation/modification of application (.APP) files.

CREATE/MODIFY LABEL *filename*/?

Provides access to the label design surface for the creation/modification of label (.LBL) files.

CREATE/MODIFY QUERY *filename/?*

Provides access to the query design surface for the creation/modification of query (.QBE) and update query (.UPD) files.

CREATE/MODIFY REPORT *filename/?*

Provides access to the report design surface for the creation/modification of report form (.FRM) files.

CREATE/MODIFY SCREEN *filename/?*

Provides access to the screen forms design surface for the creation/modification of screen form (.SCR) files.

CREATE/MODIFY VIEW *filename/?* [FROM ENVIRONMENT]

Provides access to the query design surface for the creation/modification of view (.VUE) files. Issuing FROM ENVIRONMENT bypasses the design surface and utilizes the current environment.

DEBUG *filename/procedure name* [WITH *parameter list*]

Provides access to the dBASE IV debugger.

HELP [*dBASE IV keywords*]

Activates the dBASE IV help system.

MODIFY COMMAND/FILE *filename* [WINDOW *window name*]

Starts the dBASE IV text editor.

Display and printer commands

?/?? [*expression 1* [PICTURE *expC*] [FUNCTION *function list*] [AT *expN*] [STYLE *font number*]][,*expression 2* ...] [,]

Evaluates and displays the value of one or more expressions with optional formatting, styling, and positioning. Depending on system settings, output can go to the desktop, printer or file. ? sends a carriage return and line feed prior to the results of the expression. ?? sends only the expression results to the current line.

??? *expC*

Sends output directly to the printer.

DEFINE BOX FROM *column* TO *column* HEIGHT *expN*
    [AT LINE *print line*] [SINGLE/DOUBLE/*border definition string*]

Prints a box in the specified area of a report.

DIRECTORY/DIR [[ON *drive:*] [[LIKE] [*path*] *skeleton*]

Displays a listing of and information about databases or lists files matching the optional skeleton.

DISPLAY [FIELDS] [*expression list*] [OFF] [*scope*] [FOR *condition*]
  [WHILE *condition*] [TO PRINTER/FILE *filename*]

Displays/prints the current record or specified records, pausing after each screenful.

DISPLAY FILES [LIKE *skeleton*] [TO PRINTER/FILE *filename*]

Displays/prints directory information, pausing after each screenful.

DISPLAY HISTORY [LAST *expN*] [TO PRINTER/FILE *filename*]

Displays/prints a listing of commands stored in the history buffer, pausing after each screenful.

DISPLAY MEMORY [TO PRINTER/FILE *filename*]

Displays/prints information pertaining to and the contents of memory variables, pausing after each screenful.

DISPLAY STATUS [TO PRINTER/FILE *filename*]

Displays/prints information pertaining to the current dBASE IV session, pausing after each screenful.

DISPLAY STRUCTURE [IN *alias*] [TO PRINTER/FILE *filename*]

Displays/prints the structure of the current or specified database, pausing after each screenful.

DISPLAY USERS

Displays a listing of users in a multi-user dBASE IV environment, pausing after each screenful.

EJECT

Advances the printer to the top of the next page by issuing a form feed.

EJECT PAGE

Advances the streaming output to the ON PAGE handler or to the beginning of the next page.

LABEL FORM *label filename*/? [*scope*] [FOR *condition*]
  [WHILE *condition*] [SAMPLE] [TO PRINTER/FILE *filename*]

Displays/prints labels using the specified label format file.

LIST [FIELDS] [*expression list*] [OFF] [*scope*] [FOR *condition*]
  [WHILE *condition*] [TO PRINTER/FILE *filename*]

Displays/prints the current record or specified records without pausing.

LIST FILES [LIKE *skeleton*] [TO PRINTER/FILE *filename*]

Displays/prints directory information without pausing.

LIST HISTORY [LAST *expN*] [TO PRINTER/FILE *filename*]

Displays/prints a listing of commands stored in the history buffer without pausing.

LIST MEMORY [TO PRINTER/FILE *filename*]

Displays/prints information pertaining to and the contents of memory variables without pausing.

LIST STATUS [TO PRINTER/FILE *filename*]

Displays/prints information pertaining to the current dBASE IV session without pausing.

LIST STRUCTURE [IN *alias*] [TO PRINTER/FILE *filename*]

Displays/prints the structure of the current or specified database without pausing.

LIST USERS

Displays a listing of users in a multi-user dBASE IV environment without pausing.

REPORT FORM *report form filename*/? [PLAIN] [HEADING *expC*]
    [NOEJECT] [SUMMARY] [*scope*] [FOR *condition*]
    [WHILE *condition*] TO PRINT/FILE *filename*]

Displays/prints a report to the specified report format file.

TYPE *filename* [TO PRINTER/FILE *filename*] [NUMBER]

Displays/prints the contents of the specified ASCII text file with optional line numbering.

Event trapping (ON event) commands

ON BAR *expN* OF *popup name* [*command*]

Assigns a command to the specified bar of a pop-up that will be executed when the cursor is moved onto the bar. (New)

ON ERROR *command*

Executes the specified command or program if an error occurs.

ON ESCAPE *command*

Executes the specified command or program if the Esc key is pressed.

ON EXIT BAR *expN* OF *popup name* [*command*]

Assigns a command to the specified bar of a pop-up that will be executed when the cursor is moved off of the bar. (New)

ON EXIT MENU *menu name* [*command*]

Assigns a command to the pads of a menu (with no associated ON EXIT PAD) that will be executed when the cursor is moved off of the pad. (New)

ON EXIT PAD *pad name* OF *menu name* [*command*]

Assigns a command to the specified pad of a menu that will be executed when the cursor is moved off of the pad. (New)

ON EXIT POPUP *popup name* [*command*]

Assigns a command to the bars of a pop-up (with no associated ON EXIT BAR) that will be executed when the cursor is moved off of the bar. (New)

ON KEY [LABEL *key label name*] [*command*]

Executes the specified command or program if the specified *key label* is pressed. If no *key label* is specified, the specified command or program is executed when any key is pressed.

ON MENU *menu name* [*command*]

Assigns a command to the pads of a menu (with no associated ON PAD) that will be executed when the cursor is moved onto the pad. (New)

ON MOUSE *command*

Assigns a command that will be executed when the left mouse button is clicked and released. (New)

ON PAD *pad name* OF *menu name* [*command*] [ACTIVATE POPUP *popup name*]

Assigns a command (or pop-up) to the specified pad of a menu that will be executed (or activated) when the cursor is moved onto the pad. (Enhanced)

ON PAGE [AT LINE *expN command*]

Assigns a command that will be executed during the printing process when the specified print line is encountered.

ON POPUP *popup name* [*command*]

Assigns a command to the bars of a pop-up (with no associated ON BAR) that will be executed when the cursor is moved onto the bar. (New)

ON READERROR [*commands*]

Assigns a command for (or disables) error recovery that will be executed when invalid data is entered into a get field or full-screen editing operation.

ON SELECTION BAR *expN* OF *pop-up name* [*command*]

Assigns a command to the specified bar or a pop-up that will be executed when the bar is selected. (New)

ON SELECTION MENU *menu name* [*command*]

Assigns a command to the pads of a menu (with no associated ON SELEC-TION PAD) that will be executed when the pad is selected. (New)

ON SELECTION PAD *pad name* OF *menu name* [*command*]

Assigns a command to the specified pad of a menu that will be executed when the pad is selected. (Enhanced)

ON SELECTION POPUP *popup name*/ALL[BLANK][*commands*]

Assigns a command to the bars of a pop-up or all pop-ups (with no associated ON SELECTION BAR) that will be executed when the bar is selected. Optionally clears the pop-up prior to command execution. (Enhanced)

File commands

CLOSE ALL/ALTERNATE/DATABASES/FORMAT/INDEXES/ PRINTER/PROCEDURE
Closes files of the specified type. Specifying ALL closes all files of all types.

DELETE FILE *filespec*/?
Deletes the specified file; issuing ? in place of *filespec* activates a pop-up menu of file deletion choices.

DEXPORT SCREEN/REPORT/LABEL *filename* [TO *BNL filename*]
Creates a Binary Named List (BNL) file from a screen, report, or label file.

ERASE FILE *filespec*/?
Deletes the specified file; issuing ? in place of *filespec* activates a pop-up menu of file deletion choices.

EXPORT TO *filename*[TYPE] PFS/DBASEII/FW2/FW3/FW4/RPD/WKS/WK1 [FIELD *field list*] [*scope*] [FOR *condition*] [WHILE *condition*]
Creates a new file (of foreign format) by copying all or part of an active database.

RENAME *old filename* TO *new filename*
Changes the name of an existing (closed) file.

Full-screen editing commands

BROWSE [NOINIT] [NOFOLLOW] [NOAPPEND] [NOMENU]
    [NOORGANIZE] [NOEDIT] [NODELETE] [NOCLEAR]
    [COMPRESS] [FORMAT] [LOCK *expN*] [WIDTH *expN*]
    [FREEZE *field name*] [WINDOW *window name*]
    [FIELDS *field name 1* [/R] [*/column width*]
    /calculated field name 1 = expression 1
    [*,field name 2* [/R] [*/column width*]
    /calculated field name 2 = expression 2] ...]
A full-screen, menu-assisted command for editing and appending records in databases files and views.

CHANGE/EDIT [NOINIT] [NOFOLLOW] [NOAPPEND]
    [NOMENU] [NOORGANIZE] [NOEDIT] [NODELETE]
    [NOCLEAR] [*record number*] [FIELDS *field list*] [*scope*]
    [FOR *condition*] [WHILE *condition*]
Displays or changes the contents of a record in the active database or view.

EDIT [NOINIT] [NOFOLLOW] [NOAPPEND] [NOMENU]
    [NOORGANIZE] [NOEDIT] [NODELETE] [NOCLEAR]
    [*record number*] [FIELDS *field list*] [*scope*]
    [FOR *condition*] [WHILE *condition*]
Used to display and/or change the contents of a record in the active database or view.

READ [SAVE]

Activates all @...GETs issued since the last CLEAR, CLEAR ALL, CLEAR GETS, or READ command. Issuing READ SAVE does not clear GETs thus saving them for subsequent READs.

Memory variable, array, and keyboard input commands

ACCEPT [*prompt*] TO *memvar*

Prompts the user for keyboard input into a character memory variable.

AVERAGE [*expN list*] [*scope*] [FOR *condition*] [WHILE *condition*]
    [TO *memvar list*/TO ARRAY *array name*]

Computes the arithmetic mean of the specified numeric expressions.

CALCULATE [*scope*] *option list* [FOR *condition*] [WHILE *condition*]
    [TO *memvar list*/TO ARRAY *array name*]

Where *option list* can be any one of the following functions:

    AVG(*expN*)
    CNT( )
    MAX(*exp*)
    MIN(*exp*)
    NPV(*rate*),*flows*,*initials*)
    STD(*expN*)
    SUM(*expN*)
    VAR(*expN*)

Processes the specified records using financial and statistical functions.

COUNT [TO *memvar*] [*scope*] [FOR *condition*] [WHILE *condition*]

Counts the number of records in the active database matching the conditions specified.

DECLARE *array name1* [{*number of rows,*} *number of columns*]
    {*array name 2* [{*number or rows,*} *number of columns*]...}

Creates one or two dimensional arrays. (The square brackets are required syntax. The face brackets indicate optional items.)

INPUT [*prompt*] TO *memvar*

Prompts the user for keyboard input into a memory variable whose type can be determined by the input.

KEYBOARD *expC* [CLEAR]

Inserts simulated keystrokes into the (optionally CLEARed) type-ahead buffer.

PRIVATE ALL [LIKE/EXCEPT *skeleton*]

or

PRIVATE *memvar list*

Creates local memory variables in a lower-level program without disturbing the contents of a PUBLIC of higher level memory variable.

PUBLIC *memory variable list*/ARRAY *array name 1*
    [{*number of rows,*} *number of columns*]
    {,*array name 2* [{*number of rows,*} *number of columns*]...}

Defines the specified memory variables or arrays as global thus making them visible to all programs and subprograms. (When defining ARRAYS: The square brackets are required syntax. The face brackets indicate optional items.)

RELEASE *memvar list*/[ALL [LIKE/EXCEPT *skeleton*]]
    /[MODULE *module name list*]

Releases the specified memory variable(s) or LOADed module(s) from memory.

STORE *expression* TO *memvar list*/*array element list*

Creates and initializes the specified memory variable(s) or initializes existing array elements.

SUM [*expN list*] [TO *memvar list*/TO ARRAY *array name*]
    [*scope*] [FOR *condition*][WHILE *condition*]

Sums the specified numeric expressions to memory variables or arrays.

WAIT [*prompt*] [TO *memvar*]

Pauses program execution until a key is pressed and optionally stores the keyboard response in a character memory variable.

Multi-user and transaction tracking commands

CONVERT [TO *expN*]

Adds a field to a database's structure thus aiding in multi-user change/lock detection.

LOGOUT

Logs out the current user, closes files, and sets up a new log-in screen.

PROTECT

Provides access to the dBASE IV security system.

RESET [IN *alias*]

Removes the integrity tag from the current or specified database involved in an incomplete transaction.

ROLLBACK [*database filename*]

Restores the files within a transaction to the state that they were in before the transaction and terminates the transaction.

UNLOCK [ALL/IN *alias*]

Releases the record and file locks in effect within the current/specified/all databases.

Program execution commands and constructs

!/RUNDOS command

Executes a DOS command or program that can be executed by DOS from within dBASE IV.

BEGIN TRANSACTION [*path name*]
    dBASE IV commands
END TRANSACTION

Programming construct that defines a series of commands as a transaction ensuring that either all or none of the commands that affect database contents are processed.

CALL *module name* [WITH *expression list*]

Executes the specified LOADed binary file.

CANCEL

Stops program execution, closes all open programs (excluding procedure files), and returns to the dBASE IV dot prompt.

COMPILE *filename* [RUNTIME]

Compiles a file containing dBASE IV source code thus creating an executable object code (.DBO) file.

DO *program filename/procedure name* [WITH *parameter list*]

Executes (and optionally passes parameters to) a dBASE command file or procedure.

DO CASE
    CASE *condition*
        commands
    [CASE *condition*
        commands]
    [OTHERWISE
        commands]
ENDCASE

A programming construct that performs only one set (or none if OTHERWISE is excluded) of multiple sets of commands based on the specified conditions.

DO WHILE *condition*
    dBASE IV commands
    [LOOP]
    [EXIT]
ENDDO

A programming construct that repeats commands while the specified condition evaluates to true. EXIT when encountered exits the construct while LOOP branches to the beginning.

FUNCTION *UDF name*
[PARAMETERS]
dBASE IV commands
RETURN *expression*

A programming construct that defines a user-defined function within a procedure which can optionally accept parameters for the calling routine.

IF *condition*
    dBASE IV commands
[ELSE
    dBASE IV commands]
ENDIF

A programming construct that executes a set of commands when the specified condition evaluates to true. Use of the optional ELSE clause enables an alternate set of commands to be executed when the specified condition evaluates to false.

LOAD *binary filename*

Loads a binary program (.BIN) file into memory.

NOTE/* *text*

and

[*command* &&*text*

Allows notes and comments to be contained in a dBASE IV program (.PRG) file.

PARAMETERS *parameter list*

The first command within a function which assigns local variable names to data items passed to it from a calling program.

PLAY MACRO *macro name*

Executes a predefined macro.

PRINTJOB
dBASE IV commands
ENDPRINTJOB

A programming construct for defining and controlling a print job.

PROCEDURE *procedure name*
    dBASE IV commands
RETURN *expression*

A programming construct that defines a procedure (subroutine) within a program.

```
SCAN [scope] FOR condition] [WHILE condition]
    [dBASE IV commands]
    [LOOP]
    [EXIT]
ENDSCAN
```

A programming construct (containing an embedded skip) that repeats commands while the specified condition evaluates to true. EXIT, when encountered, exits the construct while LOOP branches to the beginning.

RESUME

Resumes SUSPENDed program execution.

RETRY

Retries the failed command that triggered the execution of the program called by ON ERROR DO program.

RETURN [expression/TO MASTER/TO procedure name]

Returns program control (with an optional expression) to the calling program (if any), the top level (master) program, or the specified calling program.

SUSPEND

A programming command (useful for debugging) that suspends program execution when encountered.

```
TEXT
    text characters
END TEXT
```

A programming construct that outputs blocks of text to the currently selected output device.

QUIT [WITHexpN]

Closes all open files, terminates the dBASE IV session, and returns control to the calling operating system and optionally returns an integer to the operating system.

Record location, retrieval, and movement commands

CONTINUE

Searches for the next record in the active database that meets the condition(s) specified by the last LOCATE command.

FIND literal key

Searches an indexed database for the first record with an index key matching the specified character string or number.

GO/GOTO BOTTOM/TOP [IN alias]

or

GO/GOTO [RECORD] *record number* [IN *alias*]

or

record number [IN *alias*]

Positions the record pointer to the top/bottom/specified record in the current or specified active database.

LOCATE [FOR *condition*] [*scope*] [WHILE *condition*]

Performs a sequential (non-indexed) search of the active database file for the first record that matches the specified condition.

SEEK *expression*

Searches an indexed database for the first record with an index key matching the specified expression.

SKIP [*expN*] [IN *alias*]

Moves the record pointer of the current or specified database *expN* records forward or backward.

SAVE and RESTORE commands

RESTORE FROM *filename* [ADDITIVE]

Restores memory variables from a memory (.MEM) file.

RESTORE MACROS FROM *macro file*

Restores macros from a macro (.KEY) file.

RESTORE SCREEN FROM *screen name*

Restores a previously saved screen image from memory.

RESTORE WINDOW *window name list*/ALL FROM *filename*

Restores window(s) definitions from a windows (.WIN) file.

SAVE TO *filename* [ALL LIKE/EXCEPT *skeleton*]

Saves the specified memory variables to a .MEM file.

SAVE MACROS TO *macro file*

Saves the currently defined macros to a .KEY file.

SAVE SCREEN TO *screen name*

Saves the current screen image to memory.

SAVE WINDOW *window name list*/ALL TO *filename*

Saves window(s) definitions to a .WIN file.

SET commands

SET

Activates a menu for changing SET command values.

SET ALTERNATE ON/OFF

Enables/Disables the recording of output to the text file specified by SET ALTERNATE TO.

SET ALTERNATE TO [*filename* [ADDITIVE]]

Creates/opens the specified text file for the recording of output. Output is appended to the specified file using the ADDITIVE clause.

SET AUTOSAVE ON/OFF

Enables/disables saving each record to the disk after each operation.

SET BELL ON/OFF

Enables/disables the audible beep sounded when invalid data is entered or a field is filled.

SET BELL TO [*frequency,duration*]

Sets the frequency (in hertz) and duration (in ticks) of the audible beep. Valid values for frequency are 19 through 10,000 with the default being 512. Valid values for duration are 1 through 19 with the default being 2.

SET BLOCKSIZE TO *expN*

Specifies the blocksize of memo fields and .MDX files in multiples of 512 bytes. Valid values are from 1 through 32 with the default being 1.

SET BORDER TO [SINGLE/DOUBLE/PANEL/NONE/ *border definition string*]

Specifies the default border of menus, windows, and pop-ups.

SET CARRY ON/OFF

Enables/disables the carrying forward of changes made to the last record during APPEND and INSERT.

SET CARRY TO [*field list* [ADDITIVE]]

Determines which fields are carried forward. ADDITIVE appends to the previous field list.

SET CATALOG ON/OFF

Enables/disables adding files to the current catalog.

SET CATALOG TO [*filename*/?]

Opens/creates the specified catalog.

SET CENTURY ON/OFF

Enables/disables the display/input of the century in a date field.

SET CLOCK ON/OFF

Displays/hides the system clock display.

SET CLOCK TO [*row,column*]

Specifies the position of the system clock display. The default position is 0,68.

SET COLOR ON/OFF

Sets monitor type to color/monochrome. The default is determined by the type in use at start-up.

SET COLOR TO [*standard*], [*enhanced*],{*perimeter*], [*background*]

Sets the general color attributes of the display.

SET COLOR OF NORMAL/MESSAGES/TITLES /HIGHLIGHT/BOX/INFORMATION/FIELDS TO [*attribute*]

Sets the color attributes of specific display elements.

SET CONFIRM ON/OFF

Enables/disables requiring a carriage return to exit a data entry element.

SET CONSOLE ON/OFF

Enables/disables output to the screen display from within a program.

SET CURRENCY LEFT/RIGHT

Specifies the position of the currency symbol relative to a numeric value.

SET CURRENCY TO [*expC*]

Specifies the currency symbol to be displayed.

SET CURSOR ON/OFF

Enables/disables display of the cursor.

SET DATE [TO] AMERICAN/ANSI/BRITISH/FRENCH/GERMAN /ITALIAN/JAPAN/USA/MDY/DMY/YMD

Specifies the format for date displays.

SET DBTRAP ON/OFF

Enables/disables protection against program errors when the execution of one command is interrupted to execute a second command.

SET DEBUG ON/OFF

Enables/disables the sending of ECHOed output to the current output device.

SET DECIMALS TO *expN*

Specifies the number of decimal places resulting from calculations. Valid values are from 1 through 18 with the default being 2.

SET DEFAULT TO [*drive*[:]]

Specifies the default (unless otherwise specified) drive.

SET DELETED ON/OFF

Specifies whether or not deleted records will be ignored in all but indexing operations.

SET DELIMITERS ON/OFF

Enables/disables the use of field delimiters.

SET DELIMITERS TO [expC/DEFAULT]

Specifies the character(s) to be used as field delimiters. The default character is a colon.

SET DESIGN ON/OFF

Enables/disables access to dBASE IV design surfaces.

SET DEVELOPMENT ON/OFF

Enables/disables automatic compilation of program source.

SET DEVICE TO SCREEN/PRINTER/FILE *filename*

Specifies where the results of @...SAY are to be sent.

SET DIRECTORY TO [[*drive:*] [*path*]]

Specifies the operating system working drive and directory.

SET DISPLAY TO COLOR/EGA25/EGA43/MONO/MONO43
    /VGA25/VGA43/VGA50

Specifies the video display mode of the monitor. (Enhanced)

SET ECHO ON/OFF

Enables/disables the echoing of commands as they are executed.

SET ENCRYPTION ON/OFF

Enables/disables file encryption in conjunction with PROTECT.

SET ESCAPE ON/OFF

Enables/disables the use of the escape key to interrupt program execution and ON ESCAPE processing.

SET EXACT ON/OFF

Enables/disables the requirement for an exact match in character string comparisons.

SET EXCLUSIVE ON/OFF

Enables/disables the requirement for exclusive access to files on a multi-user system.

SET FIELDS ON/OFF

Enables/disables the use of the SET FIELDS TO *field list*.

SET FIELDS TO [*field 1* [/R]/*calculated field id 1*]
    [,*field 2* [/R/calculated field id 2...*]
    /ALL [LIKE/EXCEPT *skeleton*]

Defines which fields can be accessed in one or more databases. Omitting all arguments removes the access restriction.

SET FILTER TO [FILE *filename*/?]/[*condition*]

Specifies which database records can be accessed based on the specified condition. Omitting all arguments removes the access restriction.

SET FORMAT TO [*format filename/?*]

Specifies a custom format file for data entry. Omitting the argument disables the use of the format file.

SET FULLPATH ON/OFF

Enables/disables return of the full path from the DBF( ), NDX( ) and MDX( ) functions.

SET FUNCTION *expN/expC/key label* TO [*expC*]

Programs the specified function key with a character expression. Omitting the TO clause expression clears the specified key.

SET HEADINGS ON/OFF

Enables/disables the display of column titles above the fields in AVERAGE, DISPLAY, LIST and SUM.

SET HELP ON/OFF

Enables/disables the help prompt if a syntax error is entered.

SET HISTORY ON/OFF

Enables/disables the storing of previously executed commands in the history buffer.

SET HISTORY TO *expN*

Specifies the number of previously executed commands to store in the history buffer. Valid values are from 0 through 16,000 with the default being 20.

SET HOURS TO [12/24]

Specifies 12- or 24-hour format for the clock display.

SET IBLOCK TO *expN*

Specifies the block size allocated to new multiple index (.MDX) files in multiples of 512 bytes. Valid values are from 1 through 63 with the default being 1 (although dBASE IV allocates a minimum of 1024 bytes). (New)

SET INDEX TO
SET INDEX TO *filename list* [ORDER *.ndx filename*
SET INDEX TO *filename list* [ORDER *.mdx tag* [OF *.mdx filename*]]

Opens the specified .NDX or .MDX file(s) and optionally specifies the controlling index. Omitting all arguments closes all .NDX and nonproduction .MDX files.

SET INSTRUCT ON/OFF

Enables/disables the display of prompt boxes when a file is selected from the dBASE IV Control Center and the display of generated code when screens, reports, or label forms are generated.

SET INTENSITY ON/OFF

Enables/disables the use of the enhanced screen attribute.

SET KEY TO [*exp:match*/RANGE *exp:low,exp:high*
    /*exp:low*[,]/,*exp:high*] [IN *alias*]

Specifies which database records can be accessed based on the controlling index key matching the specified condition(s). Omitting all arguments disables range checking.

SET LDCHECK ON/OFF

Enables/disables language driver ID checking. (New)

SET LIBRARY TO *filename*

Provides access to a library of procedures and/or functions that any program/application can execute. Omitting the argument closes the active library.

SET LOCK ON/OFF

Enables/disables automatic record/file locking in a multi-user environment.

SET MARGIN TO *expN*

Specifies the left margin for printed output. Default is 0.

SET MARK TO *expC*

Specifies the delimiter within date displays. Default is /. Omitting the argument restores the default.

SET MBLOCK TO *expN*

Specifies the block size allocated to new memo field (.DBF) files in multiples of 64 bytes. Valid values are from 1 through 511 with the default being 8. (New)

SET MEMOWIDTH TO *expN*

Specifies the width of memo field output in characters. Valid values are from 8 through 255 with the default being 50.

SET MESSAGE TO [*expC* [AT *expN* [,*expN*]]]

Specifies a message (and optionally its location) to be displayed during full-screen editing operations. Omitting all arguments resets the message to the null string.

SET MOUSE ON/OFF

Enables/disables the mouse cursor (if installed). (New)

SET NEAR ON/OFF

Enables/disables the positioning of the database record pointer to the record following the sought after key during a failed indexed record search.

SET ODOMETER TO *expN*

Specifies the update interval of the record counter for commands that display a record count. Valid values are from 1 through 200 with the default being 1.

SET ORDER TO
SET ORDER TO *expN*
SET ORDER TO *.ndx filename*
    /[TAG].*mdx tagname* [OF *.mdx filename*] [NOSAVE]

Specifies the controlling index number, name or tag. Omitting all arguments specifies no controlling index.

SET PATH TO [*path list*]

Specifies the directory path(s) used by dBASE IV to search for files not in the current directory. Omitting the argument clears the search path.

SET PAUSE ON/OFF

Enables/disables pausing between screenfuls of information by the SQL SELECT command.

SET POINT TO {*expC*]

Specifies the decimal place separator character. The default character is the period.

SET PRECISION TO [*expN*]

Specifies the precision used by dBASE IV in numeric math operations. Valid values are from 10 through 20 with the default being 16.

SET PRINTER ON/OFF

Enables/disables the direction of all non-@...SAY output to the print device.

SET PRINTER TO [*DOS device*]
SET PRINTER TO FILE *filename*
SET PRINTER TO \\ *computer name* \ *printer name* = *destination*
SET PRINTER TO \\ CAPTURE
SET PRINTER TO \\ SPOOLER

Specifies the local/shared printing device or file that will receive printer output.

SET PROCEDURE TO [*procedure filename*]

Provides access to a file of procedures and/or functions that any program/application can execute. Omitting the argument closes the active procedure file.

SET REFRESH TO *expN*

Specifies the time interval in seconds between checks (while BROWSEing or EDITing) to see if a record in a multi-user file has changed. Valid values are from 0 through 3,600 with the default being 0.

SET RELATION TO [*expression* INTO *alias* [,*expression* INTO *alias* ...]]

Specifies a link (relationship) between the active database and one or more open databases via a common key expression. Omitting all arguments clears the relationship.

SET REPROCESS TO *expN*

Specifies the number of times dBASE IV will retry a failed record/file lock in a multi-user environment. Valid values are from −1 to 32,000 with the default being 0.

SET SAFETY ON/OFF

Enables/disables the overwite/cancel prompt box before overwriting an existing file.

SET SCOREBOARD ON/OFF

Enables/disables the display of dBASE IV messages on line 0 when SET STATUS is OFF.

SET SEPARATOR TO [expC]

Specifies the numeric separator character. The default character is the comma.

SET SKIP TO [alias [,alias]...]

Provides access to all child records in the specified alias(es) when a one-to-many and/or many-to-many relationship has been established. Omitting all arguments restricts visibility to one child record per parent record.

SET SPACE ON/OFF

Enables/disables the printing/displaying of a space between comma delimited expressions passed to the ? and ?? commands.

SET SQL ON/OFF

Enables/disables SQL commands within dBASE IV.

SET STATUS ON/OFF

Enables/disables the display of the dBASE IV status bar.

SET STEP ON/OFF

Enables/disables the single step mode of program execution.

SET TALK ON/OFF

Enables/disables the display of command responses.

SET TITLE ON/OFF

Enables/disables prompting for the catalog title when adding new files.

SET TRAP ON/OFF

Enables/disables the calling of the dBASE IV debugger when an error occurs (or escape is pressed) during program execution. The ON ERROR routine takes precedence (when defined).

SET TYPEAHEAD TO expN

Specifies the size of the type-ahead buffer in characters. Valid values are from 0 through 32,000 with the default being 20.

SET UNIQUE ON/OFF

Specifies whether or not only records with unique key values will be contained in subsequently created indexes.

SET VIEW TO *query filename/?*

Specifies a query to be performed or sets the environment according to the contents of a previously created view (.VUE) file.

SET WINDOW OF MEMO TO [*window name*]

Specifies a previously defined window in which the editing of memo field contents will take place during full-screen editing operations.

SQL commands

ALTER TABLE *table name* ADD (*column name data type*
    [*,column name data type...*]);

Adds new columns to the specified table.

CLOSE *cursor name*;

Closes the specified cursor.

CREATE DATABASE [*path*]*database name*;

Creates the specified new database.

CREATE [UNIQUE] INDEX *index name* ON *table name*
    (*column name* [ASC/DESC] [*,column name* [ASC/DESC]...]);

Creates the specified index on the specified table.

CREATE SYNONYM *synonym name* FOR *table/view*;

Creates an alternate name (synonym) for a table or view.

CREATE TABLE *table name* (*column name data type*
    [*,column name data type...*]);

Creates the specified table and defines its structure.

CREATE VIEW *view name* [(*column name,column name..*)]
    AS *SELECT command* [WITH CHECK OPTION];

Creates a view based on data from one or more tables/views.

DBCHECK [*table name*];

Verifies that the information contained in the SQL catalog tables is current.

DBDEFINE [*filename*];

Creates SQL catalog table entries for databases.

DECLARE *cursor name* CURSOR FOR *SELECT command*
    [FOR UPDATE OF *column list/ORDER BY clause*];

Defines a cursor and specifies the result table on which it operates.

DELETE FROM *table name* [*alias name*] [*WHERE clause*];

Deletes the specified row(s) from a table.

DELETE FROM *table name* WHERE CURRENT OF *cursor name*;

Deletes the row pointed to by the cursor.

DROP DATABASE *database name*;
Deletes the specified SQL database.

DROP INDEX *index name*;
Deletes the specified SQL index.

DROP SYNONYM *synonym name*;
Deletes the specified table or view synonym.

DROP TABLE *table name*;
Deletes the specified SQL table.

DROP VIEW *view name*;
Deletes the specified SQL view.

FETCH *cursor name* INTO *memvar list*;
Advances the cursor pointer to the next row and copies values into memory variables.

GRANT ALL [PRIVILEGES]/*privilege list* ON [TABLE] *table list*
    TO PUBLIC/*user list* [WITH GRANT OPTION];
Grants access privileges to tables/views to other users.

INSERT INTO *table name* [(*column list*)]
    VALUES (*value list*)/*SELECT command*;
Adds rows to a table from a VALUE LIST or SELECT command.

LOAD DATA FROM [path]*filename* INTO TABLE *table name*
    [[TYPE] SDF/DIF/WKS/SYLK/FW2/RPD/dBASEII/
    /DELIMITED [WITH BLANK/WITH *delimiter*]];
Imports data into the specified SQL table from the specified foreign file format.

OPEN *cursor name*;
Opens a cursor and positions the pointer before the first row of the result table.

REVOKE ALL [PRIVILEGES]/*privileges list* ON [TABLE] *table list*
    FROM PUBLIC/*user list*;
Revokes access privileges to tables/views.

ROLLBACK [WORK];
Restores the tables within a transaction to the state they were in before the transaction and terminates the transaction.

RUNSTATS [*table name*];
Updates the database statistics in the SQL catalog tables.

SELECT *clause* [INTO *clause*]
    FROM *clause*
    [WHERE *clause*]
    [GROUP BY *clause*]
    [UNION *SELECT command...*];
    [ORDER BY *clause*
    / FOR UPDATE OF *clause*]
    [SAVE TO TEMP *clause*];

Retrieves data from one or more tables based on the specified selection criteria.

SHOW DATABASE;

Lists information pertaining to each SQL database.

START DATABASE *database name*;

Activates an existing SQL database.;

STOP DATABASE;

Deactivates the current SQL database.

UNLOAD DATA TO [path]*filename* FROM TABLE *table name*
    [[TYPE] SDF/DIF/WKS/SYLK/FW2/RPD/dBASEII
    [DELIMITED [WITH BLANK/WITH*delimiter*]]];

Exports data from the specified SQL table to the specified file of foreign file format.

UPDATE *table name* SET *column name* = *new value*
    [,*column name* = *new value...*] [WHERE *search condition*];

Changes data in the specified rows of a table/view.

UPDATE *table name* SET *column name* = *new value*
    [,*column name* = *new value...*]
    WHERE CURRENT OF *cursor name*;

Changes data in the row pointed to by the specified cursor.

User interface and menu definition commands

@ *row, col*
    [SAY *expression* [PICTURE *expC*]
        [FUNCTION*function list*]]
    [GET *variable*
        [[OPEN] WINDOW *window name*]
        [PICTURE *expC*] [FUNCTION *function list*]
        [RANGE [REQUIRED] [*low*] [,*high*]] [VALID
        [REQUIRED] *condition* [ERROR *expC*]]
        [WHEN *condition*] [DEFAULT *expression*]
        [MESSAGE *expC*]]
    [COLOR [*standard*][,*enhanced*]]

Used to create custom data input and output screens. SAY displays/GET accepts information in a specified format at a given set of screen coordinates.

@ *row1,col1* CLEAR [TO *row2,col2*]

Clears the portion of the screen or active window specified by the row and column coordinates supplied.

@ *row1,col1* FILL TO *row2,col2*
　　[COLOR *color attribute*]

Changes the color of the specified region of the desktop or active window.

@ *row1,col1* TO *row2,col2* SCROLL
　　[UP/DOWN/LEFT/RIGHT][BY *expN*][WRAP]

Shifts the contents of a specified region of the desktop up, down, left or right.

@ *row1,col1* TO *row2,col2* [DOUBLE/PANEL/*border definition string*]
　　[COLOR *color attribute*]

Draws a box on the desktop or active window with single lines or optionally double lines, panel (solid) or specified characters.

ACTIVATE MENU *menu name* [PAD *pad name*]

Activates an existing bar menu or highlights the specified pad.

ACTIVATE POPUP *popup name*

Activates a previously defined pop-up menu.

ACTIVATE SCREEN

Restores access to the entire desktop.

ACTIVATE WINDOW *window name list*/ALL

Activates and displays a user defined window, list of user defined windows or all user defined windows.

CLEAR [ALL/FIELDS/GETS/MEMORY/MENUS/POPUPS/SCREENS
　　/TYPEAHEAD/WINDOWS]

Clears the active window/desktop and repositions the cursor to the lower left-hand corner of the window/desktop. Can optionally release all pending GETS, close files, release memory variables, field lists, windows, pop-ups, and menus; and empty the type-ahead buffer.

DEACTIVATE MENU

Deactivates the active bar menu and erases it from the desktop without removing it from memory.

DEACTIVATE POPUP

Deactivates the active pop-up menu and removes it from the desktop without removing it from memory.

DEACTIVATE WINDOW *window name list*/ALL

Deactivates the specified windows and removes them from the desktop without removing them from memory.

DEFINE BAR *line number* OF *popup name* PROMPT *expC*
    [MESSAGE *expC*] [SKIP [FOR *condition*]]
Defines an option in a pop-up menu.

DEFINE MENU *menu name* [MESSAGE *expC*]
Defines a menu bar and is used in conjunction with DEFINE PAD to define a menu.

DEFINE PAD *pad name* OF *menu name* PROMPT *expC* [AT *row,col*]
    [MESSAGE *expC*]
Defines a single pad of the specified bar menu.

DEFINE POPUP *popup name* FROM *row1, col1*
    [TO *row2, col2*] [PROMPT FIELD *field name*
    /PROMPT FILES [LIKE *skeleton*]
    /PROMPT STRUCTURE] [MESSAGE *expC*]
Defines a pop-up menu/window's name, location, border, prompts, and message line.

DEFINE WINDOW *window name* FROM *row1,col1*
    TO *row2,col2* [DOUBLE/PANEL/NONE/*border definition string*]
    [COLOR [*standard*] [,enhanced] [,*frame*]]
Defines the specified window, its location, border and screen attributes.

MOVE WINDOW *window name* TO *row,column*
    /BY *delta row,delta column*
Moves the specified window to a new location.

RELEASE MENUS [*menu name list*]/POPUPS [*popup name list*]
    /SCREENS [*screen name list*]/WINDOW [*window name list*]
Removes the specified Menu(s), Pop-up(s), Screen(s) or Window(s) from the desktop and/or memory. All user-defined items of the specified type are released if *name list* is omitted.

SHOW MENU *menu name* [PAD *pad name*]
Displays the specified menu without activating it and optionally highlights the specified pad.

SHOW POPUP *popup name*
Displays the specified pop-up menu without activating it.

D
The dBASE IV function library

Many useful functions are in the dBASE IV function library. They are divided into eight main categories:

- Character—those dealing with character field and variables.
- Date—those dealing with date fields.
- Mathematical—those dealing with numeric fields and variables.
- Financial and Statistical—financial and statistical functions.
- Trigonometric—those dealing with SINE, COSINE, and TANGENTS.
- Database tests—tests of different database activities.
- Menu Functions—used in menu choice evaluation.
- Environment—checks of the outside environment.

In this part, you will see all of the functions demonstrated and some of the more important functions in more detail.

Most functions work in the same way. To use them requires knowing their name and the parameters that go inside them. For example, to convert a numeric to a character string, you would use the function STR. The correct form might be:

```
STORE STR(NUM,3) TO CHAR
```

Other functions are logical tests such as the EOF( ) function to test for end of file in a database. An example of this might be:

```
IF EOF( )
    "End of file has been reached"
```

As you see the various functions explained, try to think of how you might use these functions in the future.

Character functions

ASC/CHR   The ASC( ) function retrieves the ASCII code of the left-most character of a character string:

    STORE ASC('HELLO') TO LET
    ? LET
    72   && 72 is the ASCII code for H

    STORE ASC(753) TO NUM
    ? NUM
    55   && 55 is the ASCII code for 7

The CHR( ) function is an ASCII number to character conversion:

    STORE CHR(72) TO LET
    ? LET
    H   && H is the ASCII equivalent of 72

    STORE CHR(55) TO NUM
    ? NUM
    7   && 7 is the ASCII equivalent of 55

LEFT/RIGHT   The LEFT( ) and RIGHT( ) functions return a specified number of characters from the left or the right side of a character string:

    STORE 'Hello down there' TO CHRSTR

    ? LEFT(CHRSTR,9)
    Hello dow

    ? RIGHT(CHRSTR,9)
    own there

LOWER/UPPER   The LOWER( ) AND UPPER( ) functions convert character strings to upper- and lowercase regardless of the present case:

    STORE 'ABCdef' TO X

    ? LOWER(X)
    abcdef

    ? UPPER(X)
    ABCDEF

REPLICATE/SPACE   These functions create many characters from a single expression. The REPLICATE( ) command copies a character or group of characters over and over again:

    ? REPLICATE('-',80)

places 80 dashes across the screen or printer from the current pointer location.

The SPACE( ) function generates a character string with the specified number of blanks:

```
. STORE SPACE(15) TO BLANK
. DISPLAY MEMORY
BLANK      pub  C       "      "
   1 variable defined,    15 bytes used
253 variables available, 5985 bytes available
```

TRIM/LTRIM/RTRIM The TRIM( ) command removes ending blanks from character fields. This is especially useful when concatenating fields with ? commands. TRIM( ) works on character fields only:

```
STORE 'BILL      ' TO FIRST
STORE 'SMITH     ' TO LAST

      FIRST + LAST
BILL        SMITH

      FIRST—LAST
BILLSMITH

? TRIM(FIRST) + ' ' + LAST
BILL SMITH
```

The RTRIM( ) command is identical to the TRIM( ) command.

The LTRIM( ) command removes leading blanks from a character string created from a numeric expression:

```
? STR(235.65,8,2)
       235.65

? LTRIM(STR(235.65,8,2)
235.65
```

RAT/AT/SUBSTR/LEN/STUFF The AT( ) function is known as the substring search function. It returns the number that contains the starting position of a specified character string:

```
STORE "Hello down there" TO CHR
? AT("down",CHR)
7
```

The AT command has been enhanced in this version of dBASE. The format for the AT command is:

```
AT(expC1,expC2/memo field name[,expN])
```

AT returns the starting position (0 if not found) of the specified character string *expC1* within a second character expression *expC2* or memo field and returns the starting position of the nth occurrence when *expN* is specified. For example:

```
. ? AT("a", "dBaseIV Example")      && Find first occurrence of "a"
3                    = Position of first "a"
. ? AT("a", "dBaseIV Example", 2)     && Find second occurrence of "a"
11                   = Position of second "a"
```

The RAT command is new in this version of dBASE. The format for the RAT command is:

RAT(expC1,expC2/memo field name[,expN])

RAT performs a backwards search and returns the starting position (0 if not found) of the specified character string *expC1* within a second character expression *expC2* or memo field and returns the starting position of the nth occurrence when *expN* is specified.

The SUBSTR( ) command is called the substring command. It allows you to take only part of a character string. To use the substring function, you must specify the variable or literal, the starting character, and the length:

```
STORE 'BILL      ' TO FIRST
STORE 'SMITH     ' TO LAST

? FIRST + LAST
BILL     SMITH

     SUBSTR(FIRST,1,1) + '. ' + LAST
B. SMITH

? SUBSTR('ABCDEFG',3,4)
CDEF
```

The SUBSTR( ) and AT( ) functions can also be combined to manipulate character strings:

```
STORE "Smith, Bob" TO NAME

? SUBSTR(NAME,AT(",")+1) + " " + SUBSTR(NAME,1,AT(",")−1)
Bob Smith
```

This command string first finds the comma and knows that the first name is everything to the right of it. It then adds the first name to the last name, which is found by taking the NAME string from the first position to one position to the left of the location of the comma.

The LEN( ) function determines the length of a character string:

```
? LEN("Hello down there")
16

USE PAYROLL
? LEN(NAME)
20     && This is the field width

? LEN(TRIM(NAME))
12     && This is the actual length of the first name
```

The STUFF( ) function lets you change any part of a character string:

```
STORE "AJAX G. Dolphin" TO NAME
? STUFF(NAME,6,1,"F")
     NAME
AJAX F. Dolphin
```

The form of the STUFF( ) function is:

> STUFF(*char string,start position,number of chars,new chars*)

STR/VAL   The STR( ) command allows a numeric value to be used as a character string. Normally numbers are defined as numeric. You might want to use a number and place it in a database that has been defined as character. To do this you must use the "STR" command:

```
STORE 765 TO X
STORE STR(X,3) TO CHARX

STORE STR(633*265,4) TO CHARX
```

The opposite of the STR( ) function is the VAL( ) function. This translates legitimate numeric character strings into numbers of any length. The only characters that are considered legitimate are 0-9, one decimal point, and a minus sign in the beginning of the number:

```
STORE '765' TO X
STORE VAL(X) TO NUMX
```

LIKE   The LIKE( ) function is used for wildcard comparisons. The left side holds a pattern, including wildcard symbols, and the right side is compared to this pattern. Two wildcard characters are allowed in this string: the asterisk (any number of characters) and the question mark (single character). The LIKE( ) function lets you use wildcard symbols anywhere in the string and as often as is needed. This function returns a .T. or .F.:

```
ANYSTRING = 'THE PAYROLL DEPARTMENT'
? LIKE ("*PAY*", ANYSTRING)
.T.
```

This statement returns a logical true value if any string has the PAY sequence anywhere in it. The statement:

```
SCHEDULE = 'SATURDAY'
? LIKE ("*DAY", SCHEDULE)
.T.
```

will return a logical true value if the character variable of field schedule ends in the string DAY.

TRANSFORM   The TRANSFORM( ) function is used to add picture formatting to existing fields and memory variables:

```
STORE 1234567 TO NUM
? TRANSFORM(NUM,'$999,999,999.99')
$1,234,567.00
```

MEMLINES/MLINE   These functions bring up the number of lines (MEM-LINES) or extract a specific line of text (MLINE) from a memo field. MEM-LINES( ) uses the memo width setting established with the MEMOWIDTH( ) command to determine the number of lines in a memo field.

SET MEMOWIDTH changes the word wrap position, so the number of lines of text change with it:

```
SET MEMOWIDTH TO 10
? INVMEM
INVENTORY IS
CLASSIFIED AS TO
TYPE OF MATERIAL
AND STAGE OF
COMPLETION
? MEMLINES(INVMEM)
5
2SET MEMOWIDTH TO 25
? INVMEM
INVENTORY IS CLASSIFIED AS TO
TYPE OF MATERIAL AND STAGE
OF COMPLETION
? MEMLINES(INVMEM)
3
```

MLINE( ) is used to pull out a certain line of text in a memo field:

```
SET MEMOWIDTH TO 20
? INVMEM
INVENTORY IS CLASSIFIED
AS TO TYPE OF MATERIAL
AND STAGE OF COMPLETION
? MLINE(INVMEM,3)
AND STAGE OF COMPLETION
```

Date functions

CTOD/DTOC/DTOS   These three functions convert date fields to character strings and character strings to date fields:

```
STORE '01/25/86' TO CHR
STORE CTOD(CHR) TO HIREDATE

STORE DTOC(HIREDATE) TO CHR
```

Unlike the DTOC( ) function the DTOS( ) function keeps dates in their correct order. Use the DTOS( ) function to index on a date expression concatenated with a character expression. It converts the specified date to a character string of the form CCYYMMDD regardless of the SET CENTURY or SET DATE setting:

```
USE HIREDATE
INDEX ON DTOS(HIREDATE) + EMPID TO HIDATE
     100% INDEXED
LIST NEXT 7 HIREDATE, EMPID
```

RECORD #	HIREDATE	EMPID
6	01/07/89	R100
5	01/21/89	F202
4	01/28/89	S640
2	02/16/89	A200
3	02/16/89	B106
7	03/01/89	G903
1	03/08/89	D408

DATE The DATE( ) returns the current date:

? DATE( )
03/15/89

CDOW/CMONTH/DAY/DOW/MONTH/YEAR/DMY/MDY These functions convert dates to several forms:

? DATE( )
03/15/89

? CDOW(DATE( ))
Wednesday   && Returns day of the week

? CMONTH(DATE( ))
March   && Returns the present month

? DAY(DATE( ))
15   && Returns the number of the day

? DOW(DATE))
4   && Wednesday is the 4th day of the week

? MONTH(DATE( ))
3   && Returns the number of the month

? YEAR(DATE( ))
89   && Returns the number of the year

? DMY(03/15/89   && Converts the date to Day/Month/Year
15 MARCH 89   format from any valid expression

MDY(03/15/89)   && Converts the date format to
March 15▼89   Month/Day/Year

TIME The TIME function returns the current time:

? TIME( )
11:35:56

Mathematical

ABS/INT/MOD The ABS( ) function returns the absolute value of a numeric expression:

? ABS(−35)
35

The INT( ) function returns the integer of a numeric expression:

```
? INT(295.352)
295
```

The MOD( ) function returns the remainder of a division:

```
? MOD(36/7)
1           && 1 is the remainder of 5 and 1/7
```

EXP   The EXP( ) function returns the value of the exponential function:

```
EXP(1)
2.718
```

CEILING/FLOOR   CEILING( ) calculates and returns the smallest integer that is greater than or equal to a given value. (FLOOR( )) calculates and returns the largest integer that is less than or equal to a given value:

```
FIRST = 140
    140.00
SECOND = 25
    25.00

? CEILING (FIRST/SECOND)
    6.00

? FLOOR (FIRST/SECOND)
    5.00
```

FIXED/FLOAT   The FIXED( ) function converts long, real floating point numbers to binary coded decimal (fixed) numbers. This changes the format of the variable from float to numeric.

The FLOAT( ) function converts binary coded decimal type numbers to long, real, floating point numbers. This changes the format of the variable from numeric to float.

LOG/LOG10   The LOG( ) function returns the natural LOG of a number:

```
? LOG(2.718)
1
```

LOG10( ) returns the common log to the base 10 of a number.

MAX/MIN   The MAX( ) function returns the larger value of two numeric expressions while the MIN( ) function returns the smaller of two numbers:

```
? MAX(25,6*37)
222

? MIN(25,6*37)
25
```

PI   The PI( ) function brings up the irrational number 3.14159 (the approximate of the constant for the ratio between the circumference and the diameter of a circle):

```
? PI( )
3.14
```

The accuracy of the displayed number is determined by the SET DECIMALS and SET PRECISION parameters. To display more decimal places, increase the SET DECIMALS value:

```
SET DECIMALS TO 6
RADIUS = 3
AREA = PI( ) * (R**2)
28.274365
```

ROUND   The ROUND( ) function lets you choose the precision for any numeric expression. The form of the ROUND( ) function is:

```
? ROUND (expression,num places)
```

```
STORE 15364.4655 TO NUM
? ROUND(NUM,3)
15364.466
? ROUND(NUM,-2)
15400
```

SIGN   This function determines the sign of a numeric expression without calculating the value of the expression. It returns a 1 for a positive number, −1 for a negative number, and 0 for a zero:

```
X = 25
Y = 0
Z = -25
? SIGN (X), SIGN(Y), SIGN(Z)
      1      0      -1
```

SQRT   This function returns the square root of an expression:

```
? SQRT(36)
6
```

Financial and statistical functions

FV/PV   FV( ) calculates the future value of equal regular deposits into an ꞁvestment that yields a fixed interest for a certain number of time periods. ꞁ) calculates the present value of equal regular payments invested at a ꞌant interest rate for a given number of payment periods:

```
    ꞁent = number representing a constant regular payment
       = positive number that represents the interest rate
       = annual rate/365
       ꞌ annual rate/12
```

ꞁ

```
PAYMENT = 500
    500
RATE = .12
    0.12
PERIOD = 120
    120
? FV (PAYMENT,RATE/12,PERIOD)
    115019.34
? PV (PAYMENT,RATE/12,PERIOD)
    34850.26
```

PAYMENT   The PAYMENT( ) function returns the amount of payment to be made in each period to pay off the principal and interest in a number of payment periods:

```
Principal = balance of loan
Rate      = interest rate
Periods   = number of payment periods

PRINCIPAL = 100000
    100000
PERIODS = 360
    360
RATE = 12
    12
? PAYMENT (PRINCIPAL,RATE/12,PERIOD)
    1028.61
```

Trigonometric functions

COS/ACOS   COS( ) calculates and returns the cosine value for any size angle in radians:

```
? COS(.7854)
    0.7071
```

ACOS calculates and returns the angle size in radians for any given cosine value:

```
SET DECIMALS TO 4
X = 8.4852
    8.4852
Y = 12
    12.0000
MCOS = X/Y
    0.7071
ANGLE = ACOS(MCOS)
    0.7854
```

SIN/ASIN   SIN( ) returns the trigonometric sine of an angle. Values range from +1 to −1:

```
? SIN (3*PI( )/2)
    -1
```

The ASIN( ) function calculates and returns the angle size in radians for any given SIN( ) value:

```
? ASIN(.5000)
    .5236
```

TAN/ATAN/ATN2   TAN( ) returns the trigonometric tangent of an angle:

```
TAN(PI( ))
    0
```

The ATAN( ) function calculates and returns the angle size in radians for any tangent value:

```
? ATAN(1.000)
    0.7854
```

The ATN2( ) function calculates and returns the angle size in radians for all four quadrants. COSINE and SINE of a given point must be specified:

```
X = SIN(DTOR(30))
.50

Y = COS(DTOR(30))
.86

RTOD(ATN2(X,Y))
30.00
```

RAND   This function computes a random number with or without a numeric argument present. ( ) is an optional numeric expression used as the seed to generate a new random number:

```
? RAND(23)
    0.13
? RAND( )          && returns the next random number
    .57
```

DTOR/RTOD   DTOR( ) returns the angle size in radians, where( ) is the size of the angle measured in degrees:

```
? DTOR(180)
    3.14
```

The RTOD( ) function returns radians to degrees, where ( ) is a number representing an angle size in degrees:

```
X = 3 * PI( )/2
4.71
    RTOD(X)
270.
```

Database tests

BOF/EOF   Database tests are generally used with IF statements to determine if the test is true or false. You can determine processing based on the test. BOF( ) is true if the current record pointer is at the top of the database. EOF( ) is true if the record pointer has reached beyond the last record. EOF( ) may be false if the record pointer has just arrived at the last record.

COL/ROW/PCOL/PROW   These four variables determine the row and column of the current screen pointer ROW( ),COL( ) and the current values of the printer row and printer columns PROW( ), PCOL( ). You can use these to determine page breaks when printing or where to place messages on the screen.

DELETED   The DELETED( ) function is true if the current record that the pointer is pointing to in a database has been deleted.

DISKSPACE   The DISKSPACE( ) function returns the amount of free space on your default disk drive.

ERROR   The ERROR( ) function returns the error number of the error that dBASE has found. Based on the error number, you can take appropriate action. A list of error numbers and messages are found in your dBASE IV Manual.

FILE   The FILE( ) function tells you if the file entered exists on the disk:

```
FILE(CUSTOMER.DBF)
.T.
```

FLDLIST( )   FLDLIST is a new command that returns the specified field or expression from the SET FIELDS TO list. The format for FLDLIST is:

```
FLDLIST([expN])
```

Examples of the FLDLIST command are shown here:

```
. USE \ dbase \ data \ contact          && Open database
. SET FIELDS TO Name, Phone             && Set field list
.? FLDLIST( )                           && Query dBaseIV for entire
                                           field list

CONTACT—>NAME,CONTACT—>PHONE   = Entire field list
? FLDLIST(2)                            && Query dBaseIV for
                                           second field in the field
                                           list

CUSTOMER—>COMPANY              = Second field in the field list
```

FLDCOUNT( )   Returns the number of fields present in the database specified. If an alias or work area (1 to 40) is specified, the function returns the number of fields in that file, otherwise, the currently selected file is used:

```
USE customer
? FLDCOUNT( )
13
```

FOR( )   Returns the FOR condition used to create an .MDX file index tag. If no tag is specified, then the controlling tag is examined by the function. An optional alias or work area can be specified to be used instead of the currently selected work area:

```
USE customer
SET ORDER TO TAG oldbal
? FOR( )
custbal > 0
```

FOUND   The FOUND( ) function is set to true if the results of a FIND, SEEK, or LOCATE is true.

FSIZE( )   Returns the size of the specified file as reported by the operating system. If examining a file that has been modified during the dBASE IV session, it is suggested that the file be closed or flushed prior to examining it with FSIZE( ):

```
? FSIZE("CUSTOMER.DBF")
140450
```

HOME( )   Returns the path from which the current dBASE IV session was invoked. It includes the full path, the drive and the directory path to the dBASE IV system files invoked:

```
? home( )
C: \ DBASE \
```

IIF   The IIF function can take the place of a simple IF statement:

```
IIF(DELETED( ), 'Record has already been deleted',DELETE)
```

This command as shown here is equivalent to:

```
IF DELETED( )
     'Record has already been deleted'
ELSE
     DELETE
ENDIF
```

ISALPHA/ISCOLOR/ISLOWER/ISUPPER   ISALPHA( ) is true if the character string specified in the ISALPHA begins with a letter. ISCOLOR is true if the system is running in color mode. ISLOWER is true if the first character of the specified character string is a lowercase character, while ISUPPER is true if the first character is an uppercase character.

ISBLANK( )   Tests whether the specified expression is blank. Returns a logical TRUE if the valid expression specified evaluates to a blank value of any type. If the expression is not blank, a logical FALSE is returned:

```
? ISBLANK("▼")
.T.
? ISBLANK(" / / ")
```

INKEY/READKEY/LASTKEY The INKEY function returns the ASCII value of the last key pressed while the READKEY function returns the value of the last key pressed to exit from a full-screen command. The READKEY function also tells you if data has been changed. The LASTKEY function returns the decimal ASCII value of the last key that was pressed. The value it returns is the same as INKEY.

KEYMATCH( ) KEYMATCH is a new command that returns .T. if the specified expression is contained in the specified or controlling index of the specified or current work area. The format for KEYMATCH is:

KEYMATCH(exp[,index number[,alias>]])

An example of KEYMATCH is shown here:

. USE \ dbase\ samples \ customer	&& Open database
. INDEX ON cust_no TAG Cust OF Customer	&& Create index tag Cust
. INDEX ON LastName TAG Last OF Customer	&& Create index tag Last
. SET ORDER TO Cust	&& Set controlling index order
Master Index: CUST	= dBaseIV response with SET TALK ON
. ? TAGNO("Last")	&& Get tag number of LastName tag
2	= Tag number of LastName tag
. ? KEYMATCH("Long", 2)	&& Query whether "Long" is a key in tag # 2
.T.	= "Long" is a Key value in tag # 2

LOOKUP The LOOKUP( ) function searched for a record and returns a value from a field in a database file. The search is sequential unless it is used with an available look-in field index as its key expression:

```
USE ITEMS ORDER INVNO
SELECT 2
USE INVENTRY ORDER ITEMNO
SELECT 1
SET RELATION TO ITEMNO INTO INVENTRY
    ITEMNO, DESC=LOOKUP(INVENTRY—>DESC,ITEMNO,INVENTRY—>
    ITEMNO)
    CODR-001 SUPERSPIN I
```

LUPDATE LUPDATE returns the date of the last update to the currently selected database.

MESSAGE The MESSAGE( ) function returns the actual error message when an error occurs. You can store the message for later processing or for an error log.

RECCOUNT/RECNO/RECSIZE These three functions deal with the records in a database. RECCOUNT( ) returns the number of records in the database,

RECNO( ) returns the current record number, and RECSIZE( ) returns the size of the record in bytes.

TYPE   The TYPE( ) function returns the type of the expression, field, or memory variable. The various types are C, F, N, D, L, M, and U (for undefined).

ALIAS   ALIAS( ) returns the alias name of a specified work area. If no work area is specified, it returns the name of the current work area. This function allows the same database file to be opened in up to nine different work areas.

SEEK   SEEK( ) performs lookups in indexed database fields. This function moves a database file record pointer in an unselected work area. This is used to find out if a key field has a matching record in an unselected database file:

```
USE INVOICE ORDER INVNO
SELECT 2
USE ITEMS
DISPLAY ITEMNO/   QTY PRICE CUSTNO
      1      FRRE-001 15      699.99 AV-001
? INVOICE—>CUSTNO
     JA-001
     SEEK (CUSTNO, "INVOICE")
.T.
     INVOICE—>CUSTNO
     AV-001
```

SELECT   SELECT( ) returns the number of the highest unused work area. Numbers returned range from one to ten:

```
? SELECT( )
8

USE CUSTOMER IN SELECT( ) Opens a file in an unused work area
```

TAGCOUNT( )   Returns the number of active indexes (tags) in a specified work area or .MDX file. If no .MDX file is specified, it returns the total number of indexes in the specified work area. If no work area is specified, then it returns the number of indexes in the currently selected work area:

```
. myindex = mdx( )
C: \ PERSONL \ SALES \ PEOPLE.MDX

. ? TAGCOUNT(myindex)
5
```

TAGNO( )   Returns the index number for the specified index. If no .MDX name is specified, the current controlling .MDX is used. The optional alias parameter allows for examining .MDX files in other work areas:

```
USE customer
? TAGNO("CUSTNO")
1
```

VARREAD This function assists in creating context-sensitive help displays. It is used with the @ and full-screen editing commands. VARREAD( ) returns the name of a field or memory variable being edited and allows you to know what screen to display in a help system.

ORDER ORDER( ) returns the name of the controlling (primary) index for the active database file, or for the file specified with an alias name. It returns an .NDX file in uppercase, or if no .NDX is present, returns to .MDX tagname:

```
USE CUSTOMER ORDER CUSTNO
? ORDER( )
CUSTNO
```

SOUNDEX/DIFFERENCE SOUNDEX( ) returns a four-character phonetic match or sound-alike code to find a match when an exact spelling is not known. It drops all instances of aehiouwy in all positions except the first, and assigns numbers to the letters that remain. If there are two or more letters with the same code, it drops all but the first letter. SOUNDEX( ) provides a code in the form "letter-digit-digit-digit". Trailing zeros are added if there are less than three digits. All digits after the third place on the right are dropped. The first non-alpha character is a stopping point. SOUNDEX( ) skips over leading blanks. It returns "0000" if it finds the first non-blank character is non-alpha:

```
USE CUSTOMER
INDEX ON SOUNDEX (COMPANY) TO LIKENAME
100%        16
ACCEPT "ENTER A NAME TO LOOKUP:" TO NEWNAME
ENTER A NAME TO LOOKUP: AVN APPLNC

NEWNAME = SOUNDEX(NEWNAME)
SEEK NEWNAME
DISPLAY COMPANY

RECORD COMPANY
     1 AVON APPLIANCE
```

The DIFFERENCE( ) function finds the difference in two literal strings. It does this by first converting the literal strings to SOUNDEX codes and computing the difference between the two expressions. It returns a value from 0 to 4. Two closely matched codes return a difference of 4. Two codes that have nothing in common return a 0.

ISMARKED/ROLLBACK/COMPLETED ISMARKED( ) checks the current work area, or an alias if specified, to determine if a marker is present in the database file header. This marker indicates that the file is in a state of change and dBASE returns a logical true.

The ROLLBACK( ) function returns a logical true if the last ROLLBACK command was successful. It automatically restores data and index fields involved in an error to the condition before the transaction.

The COMPLETED( ) function is used to monitor transaction processing. The default is set to true, so if the transaction is in process, COMPLETED( ) is changed to false.

Mouse functions

ISMOUSE( )   ISMOUSE( ) is a new command that returns .T. if the system has a mouse driver installed. For example:

```
. ? ISMOUSE( )       && Query dBaseIV to see if a mouse driver is installed
.T.                   = Mouse driver is installed
```

MCOL( )   MCOL( ) returns the current column number of the mouse pointer (0 if no mouse driver is loaded). For example:

```
. ? MCOL( )         && Query dBaseIV for the current mouse column
34                   = Currently the mouse cursor is at Screen Column 34
```

MROW( )   MROW( ) returns the current row number of the mouse pointer (0 if no mouse driver is loaded). For example:

```
. ? MROW( )         && Query dBaseIV for the current mouse row
12                   = Currently the mouse cursor is at Screen Row 12
```

Menu functions

BAR   The BAR( ) function returns the BAR number of the last selected BAR from the current pop-up menu:

```
? BAR( )
3
```

MENU   MENU( ) returns the name of the active menu. It returns an alphanumeric string for the name of the most recent menu that was activated:

```
? MENU( )
EDIT
```

PAD   The PAD( ) function returns the prompt PAD name of the most recently selected PAD of the active menu. Each menu option is located on a prompt PAD. When an option is entered, it becomes the most recently selected PAD:

```
? PAD( )
DATA ENTRY
```

PROMPT   PROMPT( ) returns the PROMPT of the most recently selected menu option or pop-up. If PROMPT is used with the DEFINE POP-UP command, it returns different character strings for the FIELD, FILES, and STRUCTURE prompt options:

```
? PROMPT( )
"ENTER NEW RECORD"
```

POPUP The POPUP( ) function returns the name of the active pop-up menu. It returns a null string if no pop-up menu is active:

```
? POPUP( )
DATAENT
```

BARCOUNT( ) BARCOUNT is a new command that returns the number of bars in the specified or active pop-up menu (returns 0 if no active pop-up menu). It's format is:

```
BARCOUNT([expC])
```

An example of using the BARCOUNT command is shown here:

```
. DEFINE POPUP FilePop FROM 1,1 TO 10,20 PROMPT FILES LIKE
    c:\ dbase \ samples \*.dbf
. ? BARCOUNT("FilePop") && Query dBaseIV for the number of bars in popup
    "FilePop"
    37              = Popup "FilePop" has 37 bars defined
```

BARPROMPT( ) BARPROMPT is a new command that returns the text that appears in the specified bar of the specified or active pop-up menu. The format for BARPROMPT is:

```
BARPROMPT(expN[,expC])
```

An example of using the BARPROMPT command is shown here:

```
. DEFINE POPUP FilePop FROM 1,1 TO 10,20 PROMPT FILES LIKE
    c:\ data \*.dbf
. ? BARPROMPT(37,"FilePop")      && Query dBaseIV for the text in bar # 37 of
    popup "FilePop"
C:\ DATA \VENDORS.DBF     = Prompt text for bar # 37
```

PADPROMPT( ) PADPROMPT is a new command that returns the text of the specified pad in the current or specified menu. The format for PADPROMPT is:

```
PADPROMPT(pad name[,menu name])
```

An example of using the PADPROMPT command is shown here:

```
. DEFINE MENU Main                        && Define Main bar menu
. DEFINE PAD Pad1 OF Main PROMPT "File"    && Define first prompt pad
                                              of Main
. DEFINE PAD Pad2 OF Main PROMPT "Edit"    && Define second prompt
                                              pad of Main
. DEFINE PAD Pad3 OF Main PROMPT "Quit"    && Define third prompt pad
                                              of Main
. ? PADPROMPT("Pad2","Main")               && Get pad text of Pad2 of
                                              Main bar Menu
Edit                                       = Pad Text
```

Environment

CERROR   The CERROR( ) function returns the error number of the last compile-time error. This function would be used in a program that generates dBASE code and then executes it. Any errors could be identified and handled by the generating program. In the case of a compiler error, the ERROR( ) function returns "360" and the MESSAGE( ) function returns "Compilation error," which is not very useful for automatically handling the actual error. CERROR( ) returns the compiler error number, such as:

    93—Command not functional in dBASE IV
    348—Command not valid in RunTime environment

You can find a complete list of the compile-time error codes and their meanings in Appendix A of the dBASE IV Language Reference.

DBF/NDX/KEY/MDX/TAG   The DBF( ) function returns the name of the currently selected database. The NDX( ) function returns the currently selected index. The KEY( ) function returns the key expression for the specified index file. The MDX( ) function returns the filename for the open, active .MDX directory in the .MDX file list of the current work area. TAG( ) returns the TAG name for a specified index. It represents index files (.NDX) or .MDX tag.

FIELD   The FIELD( ) function returns the numeric position in the database of the field specified. This is necessary for array processing.

FKLABEL/FKMAX   These functions enable you to deal with the function keys on your terminal. FKLABEL( ) lets you set up your function keys by name instead of number. FKMAX( ) returns the number of function keys that your keyboard supports.

GETENV   The GETENV( ) function lets you check the environmental variables of the operating system. With this function you can check such things as the currently selected disk drive and path.

MEMORY( )   The MEMORY command has been enhanced in this version of dBASE. It returns the amount of available memory in kilobytes. The format for the MEMORY command is:

    MEMORY([expN])

Examples of using MEMORY are shown here:

    .? MEMORY( )   && or MEMORY(0)
        4286 = Approximate amount of available memory which is the sum of the
            values returned by MEMORY(3) and MEMORY(6).
    .? MEMORY(1)
        398 = Amount of available memory in the heap.
    .? MEMORY(2)
        471 = Amount of low DOS memory available for LOADing .BIN files.
    .? MEMORY(3)

> 1022 = *Amount of unallocated extended memory.*
> .? MEMORY(4)
> > 0 = *Amount of virtual and extended memory managed by the Virtual Memory Manager (VMM).*
>
> .? MEMORY(5)
> > 0 = *Amount of extended memory managed by the Virtual Memory Manager (VMM).*
>
> .? MEMORY(6)
> > 3264 = *Amount of memory used by the dBaseIV buffer manager.*
>
> .? MEMORY(7)
> > 0 = *Size of the swap file if the Virtual Memory Manager (VMM) created one.*

OS   The OS( ) function returns the name of the operating system. Possibilities include DOS and OS/2.

PCOUNT( )   Returns the number of parameters passed to a procedure or user-defined function. dBASE IV now does not return an error if the wrong number of parameters is sent to a procedure or UDF. PCOUNT( ) will return the number of parameters sent each time a function is accessed:

```
FUNCTION mysample
PARAMETER xname, xnumber
IF PCOUNT( ) <> 2
    ? "Wrong number of parameters sent"
    RETURN
ENDIF
```

VERSION   The VERSION function returns the version number of dBASE IV.

PRINTSTATUS   The PRINTSTATUS( ) function checks the status of the most recently selected print device, and returns a logical true if the device is ready to accept output. Printer selection is by SET PRINTER ON, SET DEVICE TO PRINTER, Ctrl–P or any command with a TO PRINTER clause.

PROGRAM   PROGRAM( ) returns the name of the program file or procedure that was being executed by the user when an error occurred. This function may be used from the Breakpoint or Display window of the Debugger, from within a program file, or from the dot prompt if the program is in suspension. No parameters are required.

LINENO   The LINENO( ) function returns the relative line number of the line that is about to be executed in a command or procedure file. It enables developers (from Debugger) to set breakpoint conditions to stop a program at a specific line. LINENO( ) can be used with ON ERROR routines to find the line number where a program error starts.

NETWORK   The NETWORK( ) function returns a logical true or false after determining if the system is running on a network, and to branch accordingly:

```
? NETWORK( )
.F.
```

SET( )   Returns the status of the SET command specified, such as FULL-PATH, HEADINGS, LIBRARY, MARK, PRINTER, RELATION, TALK, etc.:

```
? SET("TALK")
ON
```

TIME( )   The TIME command has been enhanced in this version of dBASE. It returns the system time (optionally to $\frac{1}{100}$ second precision) as a character string in HH:MM:SS.hh format. The format for TIME is:

```
TIME([any valid expression])
```

Examples of using the TIME command are shown here:

```
. ? TIME( )        && Query dBaseIV for the system time
10:45:01           = system time with 1 second precision
. ? TIME(1)        && Query dBaseIV for the system time
10:45:06.02        = system time with 1/100 second precision
```

Low-level file access

Low-level file I/O functions have been incorporated into dBASE IV version 1.5 to provide the advanced developer with greater flexibility when manipulating files. This can be particularly useful when the need arises to import or export data file formats not currently supported through dBASE IV. The following is an overview of the functions available for low level I/O processing.

FCLOSE(*file handle*)   Closes a low-level file. Returns a logical true (.T.) if successful or a logical false (.F.) if not successful.

FCREATE(*filename[,privilege]*)   Creates and opens a low-level file. It returns a file handle, or a null string for an error. Letters in quotes specify privilege level:

"r"	read only
"w"	write anywhere in the file
"a"	append to end of file only
"rw" or "wr"	read and write
"ar" or "ra"	read and append

FEOF(*file handle*)   Returns a logical true (.T.) if the file pointer is at the end-of-file. Returns a logical false (.F.) if the pointer is not at end-of-file.

FERROR( )   Returns the operating system error number of the last low-level file I/O operation. It returns zero if successful or never executed or if the I/O is intercepted by dBASE and does not reach the operating system.

FFLUSH(*file handle*)   Writes the contents of the buffer associated with the file handle to a disk file. FFLUSH( ) uses the filename assigned to that handle with FCREATE( ). Returns a logical true (.T.) if successful.

FGETS(*file handle[,bytes to read][,eol char(s)]*)   Returns a character string to dBASE IV. FGETS( ) reads to the specified number of bytes or until it encounters an end-of-line indicator, beginning at the file pointer.

FOPEN(*filename[,privilege]*)   Returns the operating system numeric file handle, or zero if an error occurs. Quoted letters specify privilege level:

"r"	read only
"w"	write anywhere in the file
"a"	append to end of file only
"rw" or "wr"	read and write
"ar" or "ra"	read and append

FPUTS(*file handle,string to write* [,*num chars to write*] [,*eolchar(s)*])   Beginning at the file pointer, FPUTS( ) writes the specified character string and appends an end-of-line indicator. It returns the number of bytes written or zero if an error occurs.

FREAD(*file handle,bytes to read*)   Beginning at the current file pointer, FREAD( ) reads the specified number of bytes or until it reaches the end-of-file. The file pointer is repositioned to the end of the read. FREAD( ) returns a string containing the number of characters read.

FSEEK(*file handle,bytes to move* [,*starting position*])   Moves the file pointer a specified number of bytes in an open low-level file. The starting position can be relative to the beginning of file, the end of file, or the current file pointer position.

FWRITE(*file handle,string to write* [,*bytes to write*])   Writes data from a character string to an open low-level file, beginning at the current file pointer. FWRITE( ) returns the number of characters written, or zero if an error occurs.

Index

help systems *cont.*
  boxes, 192
  creating, 515
  options, 192-193
hierarchy chart, 14, 36, 597

I

ID() function, 174
IF, 861
IF-THEN, 774
IF-THEN-ELSE, 25-29, 47, 52-53, 58-59
IF-THEN-ELSE-ENDIF, 580
implicit rules, 657-658
IMPORT FROM command, 851
IMPORT() function, 175
importing, data into memo fields, 271-272
INDEX command, 176
INDEX ON command, 372, 850-851
indexing, 168-169, 176, 221, 257, 260 (*see also* sorting)
  automatic, 232-233
  commands, 296-300
  concept, 276-277
  conditional, 293
  converting NDX files to MDX tags, 296
  creating new, 252
  descending order, 290-291
  displaying keys, 300-301
  multiple fields, 277-278, 291-293
  multiple-index files, 294-296
  one field only, 288-290
  production MDX files, 294-295
  related files, 372-373
  tags, 170, 295
  tree structure, 295
  types of files, 221
INKEY() function, 637
input, defining, 10-11
INPUT command, 556-557, 858
input/output (I/O), low-level, 172
INSERT command, 553-554, 851
INSERT INTO command, 872
INSTALL command, 179

dBASE IV, 179-181
dBASE IV 1.5 enhanced routine, 165-166
dBASE IV Compiler, 639-640
  printer configuration, 481-482
interactive processing, 22-23, 69-74
  conversational, 70
  real-time, 70
inventory, 87-90
  combining all data, 98-101
  cross referencing report, 89
  data design, 96-97
  data entry processes, 137-141
  data entry, 108-109
  menu, 120, 726-737
  reports, 79-80, 141
  salesperson report, 90
  screen design, 118
  test data, 113
invoice
  adding data, 143-146
  adding items, 146-148
  changing data, 149-150
  changing items, 150-153
  combining all data, 98-101
  data design, 97
  data entry, 110-111
  date, 142, 144
  deleting, 153-155
  multi-file data entry, 141-156
  preprocessor, 790-791
  reports, 79-80, 91-94, 464-470, 791-793
  sales report, 93-94, 475-478, 795-798
  screen design, 118-119
  screen process design, 141-142
  test data, 114
  viewing, 153-155
  warranty agreement report, 93, 470-475, 793-795
Invoice menu, 120, 748-771
  advanced data entry, 772-788
  coding procedure files, 769-771
  items screen, 756-760, 765-769

main screen, 753-756, 760-765
vs. Customer/Inventory menus, 750-752
ISBLANK() function, 172
ISMOUSE() function, 163
Item menu, 516-517

J

JOIN WITH command, 851

K

KEY() function, 300-301
KEYBOARD command, 173, 176-177, 261, 570, 858
KEYBOARD PgDn CLEAR command, 570
keyboards and keys
  application generator, 512
  dBASE function, 190
  duplicate data, 702-704
  EDIT key combinations, 250
  query design using, 329-330
  using with Control Center, 188-189
  value, 702
KEYMATCH() function, 163

L

LABEL FORM command, 463, 743, 854
labels
  adding fields, 460-463
  designing, 183, 187
  defining dimensions, 459-460
  differences between reports and, 458
  form, 458-459
  mailing, 49-50, 87, 414
  printing, 463-464, 488, 524-527, 743
  sample, 416
Layout menu, 384, 422-423, 450
libraries, 173-174
licensing agreement
  distribution files and, 647-648
  screen, 181
lines and boxes
  drawing, 560-561

browse tables in, 633
clearing from memory, 636-637
colors, 624
coordinates, 624-625
data entry, 628-630
dBASE IV, 620-622
debugging, 590-595
defining, 622
defining for Main menu, 683-686
dialog boxes, 630-631
errors, 696-697
error messages inside of, 627-628
full-screen mode, 634
layers of, 635-636
memo fields and, 631-633
messages and, 634
more than one active, 635
moving, 637-638
placing on the screen, 625-626
saving, 634
status bars and, 635
uses for, 122
word processors, 545-547
Words menu, 265, 384-385, 425, 543

Z

ZAP command, 246, 852

Other Bestsellers of Related Interest

SUPER VGA GRAPHICS: Programming Secrets—Steve Rimmer

Programming advice isn't generally considered witty, whimsical, or fun—except when it's from Steve Rimmer. In the latest of his computer graphics books, he not only provides the tools you need to make Super VGA graphics modes work for you, he makes them enjoyable, too. With very little math, indirect addressing or exponential notation, the examples Rimmer uses will let you access the Super VGA Graphics modes of most of the popular display cards, display pictures, print graphics, manage a mouse, use clickable buttons, draw graphic primitives, and more. 592 pages, 100 illustrations, 3.5″ disk. Book No. 053000-9, $36.95 paperback, Book No. 052999-X, $49.95 hardcover

VISUAL BASIC™ FOR DOS
—Namir C. Shammas

Program effectively with Visual Basic for DOS with this user-friendly, hands-on reference and accompanying 3.5″ disk by veteran computer author Namir C. Shammas. Designed so that you can develop professional looking DOS applications quickly and easily, this book contains 17 information-packed chapters on a wide range of Visual Basic topics. For easier access and comprehension, topics are logically organized into introductory, intermediate, and advanced sections. 360 pages, 218 illustrations, 3.5″ disk. Book No. 056860-X, $29.95 paperback only

PARADOX® PROGRAMMING—2nd Edition
—Patricia A. Hartman and Cary N. Prague

With more specific programming solutions than any other book, this guide details all of 4.0's new features—the Windows-like interface, drop-down menus, PAL extensions, memo fields, and enhanced query performance. You'll cover database and management techniques, from simple data entry and screen design to more complex functions like generating reports, sorting databases, and querying databases. Plus, you'll review PAL programming and script creation, screen design for data entry, multifile database systems, and more. 576 pages, 502 illustrations. Book No. 026978-5, $29.95 paperback only

CONVERTING MICROSOFT C TO MICROSOFT C/C++ 7.0—Len Dorfman

This book/disk package is designed to help real-world Microsoft C programmers make a smooth transition to Microsoft C/C++. It introduces you to the principles of object-oriented programming and shows you how to develop commercial-quality class libraries using Microsoft C/C++. Ready-to-run source code is included on the companion disk. The author also discusses many of C/C++ 7.0's most exciting new features, including High-Performance Object Technology (HOT), the inline assembler, and more. 288 pages, 100 illustrations, 3.5″ disk. Book No. 017829-1, $34.95 paperback only

MICROSOFT ACCESS PROGRAMMING—Namir C. Shammas

This hands-on introduction to Microsoft Access database programming is designed for anyone who's familiar with the BASIC language. It's a practical tutorial approach—complete with ready-to-use program code and professional tips, tricks, and warnings. You get information on the built-in online help that Microsoft Access offers, how to craft the visual interface of a form, how to fine-tune the control settings to alter their appearance of behavior, and more. 304 pages, 158 illustrations, 3.5″ disk. Book No. 056850-2, $32.95 paperback only

BUILD YOUR OWN LOW-COST POSTSCRIPT® PRINTER AND SAVE A BUNDLE—2nd Edition
—Horace W. LaBadie, Jr.

LaBadie shows you how to assemble your own inexpensive laser printer, upgrade, or replace a chip. You'll learn how to convert stock Canon CX and SX laser engines to full PostScript printing capability. Plus, you'll discover how to find, purchase, and assemble components. You'll understand engines, controllers, interfaces, power supplies, cabling lasers, toner cartridges, fuser mechanisms, memory upgrades, and more. 232 pages, 130 illustrations. Book No. 035887-7, $19.95 paperback only

LAN PERFORMANCE OPTIMIZATION—Martin A. W. Nemzow

Resolve your most stubborn network performance problems with this practical resource for LAN managers and consultants. This book-disk package will help you locate and eliminate bottlenecks in local area networks quickly. The diagnostic tools provided are equally effective with Banyan Vines, Novell Netware, UB Access One, Unix, Sun NFS, IBM LAN Server, Microsoft LAN Manager, Ethernet, Token Ring, and FDDI network operating systems. 230 pages, 90 illustrations, 5.25″ disk. Book No. 4310, $29.95 paperback only

GENERIC PROGRAMMING FOR BORLAND® C++—Namir C. Shammas

With this hands-on book/disk package, C++ programmers will learn how to code generic data structures that can be used over and over in a wide variety of applications. The author demonstrates the steps to follow when creating recyclable code and shows you how to enhance your generic code with techniques such as inheritance and polymorphism. Plus, you'll get a 3.5″ disk that includes all of the generic data structure class examples discussed in the book. 320 pages, 136 illustrations, 3.5″ disk. Book No. 056843-X, $34.95 paperback only

80386/80486 ASSEMBLY LANGUAGE PROGRAMMING
—Penn Brumm and Don Brum
"... A sheer masterpiece and a thorough reference ... worth every penny."
—Computing

Spending too much time writing assembly language code? Why reinvent the wheel when two of the industry's leading assembly language experts have compiled and documented the most complete set of fully tested, ready-to-use 80386/80486 programs and routines available? Penn and Don Brumm have put together this convenient, time-saving handbook that will give you the type of reusable, error-free code you need to develop reliable, high-powered applications for today's state-of-the-art PCs. 592 pages, 203 illustrations. Book No. 008616-8, $29.95 paperback, Book No. 008615-X, $39.95 hardcover

VIRTUAL REALITY: Through the new looking glass—Ken Pimental & Kevin Teixeira; Foreword by Gordon W. Moore, Chairman, Intel Corporation

Explore places that are not just uncharted, they're waiting to be created. This is the first truly accessible, easy-to-read introduction to this exciting new universe known as "cyberspace." No longer just a figment of hyperactive imaginations, the ability to experience first-hand the sights, sounds, and textures of worlds generated entirely by computer will soon be possible for almost all PC users. 336 pages, 148 illustrations. Book No. 063409-2, $22.95 paperback, Book No. 063410-6, $32.95 hardcover

UPGRADE YOUR COMPUTER PRINTER AND SAVE A BUNDLE
—Horace W. LaBadie, Jr.

Explore the affordable upgrade opportunities available for several popular printer makes and models, including Apple LaserWriters, the Hewlett-Packard Series, HP DeskJet, Canon Bubble Jets, Okidata, and others. You'll look at added font and graphics capabilities, spoolers and buffers, printer sharing and network boxes, interface converters, and caching drives, as well as software solutions such as PostScript and others. 288 pages, 245 illustrations. Book No. 035837-0, $19.95 paperback, Book No. 035836-2, $29.95 hardcover

BUILD YOUR OWN COMPUTER ACCESSORIES AND SAVE A BUNDLE
—Bonnie J. Hargrave and Ted Dunning

Here are step-by-step instructions for 27 useful network management and computer diagnostic devices. Practical guidance for building accessories make complex computer network operations easier and faster. Plus, you'll find a special section on the tools necessary for basic soldering and cabling operations, information on how to read circuit diagrams and schematics, a list of component suppliers, and estimated costs for each project. 376 pages, 222 illustrations. Book No. 026381-7, $19.95 paperback, Book No. 026380-9, $29.95 hardcover

Rx PC: The Anti-Virus Handbook
—Janet Endrijonas

This timely guide and its companion 3.5″ disk are an effective prescription for the prevention of computer viruses. Your lesson in preventive medicine starts with a brief introduction to what computer viruses are, where they come from, and how they can harm your computer. You'll discover how to install the proper virus protection software and how to perform regular system monitoring, maintenance, access control, and file backup—all of which can significantly reduce your risk of losing data to viral infection. 208 pages, 100 illustrations, 3.5″ disk. Book No. 019624-9, $29.95 paperback, Book No. 019623-0, $39.95 hardcover

DOS SUBROUTINES FOR C AND ASSEMBLER
—Leo J. Scanlon and Mark R. Parker

Fully tested and guaranteed to make programming faster and easier, this collection of subroutines will work on any IBM-compatible computer running DOS. It's a valuable source code toolbox that experienced C and assembly language programmers can draw on to save the hours or days it can take to create subroutines from scratch. Beginners also will appreciate this book because it's an easy-to-use source of pre-tested, error-free code that demonstrates the correct way to prepare programs. 360 pages, 125 illustrations, 3.5″ disk. Book No. 055022-0, $34.95 paperback, Book No. 055021-2, $44.95 hardcover

BUILD YOUR OWN 486/486SX AND SAVE A BUNDLE—2nd Edition—Aubrey Pilgrim

This hands-on guide makes it possible for you to build your own state-of-the-art, 100% IBM-compatible PC for about one-third of the retail costs or less with little more than a few parts, a screwdriver, and a pair of pliers. So don't shell out huge sums of money for a PC at your local retail outlet. This book will allow you to enjoy the speed and power of a 486—and still put food on the table. 256 pages, 58 illustrations. Book No. 050110-6, $19.95 paperback, Book No. 050109-2, $29.95 hardcover

WINDOWS® BITMAPPED GRAPHICS—Steve Rimmer

Stocked with ready-to-run source code in C, and illustrated with many fine examples of bit-mapped output, this complete programmer's reference gives you all the practical information you need to work effectively with Windows-compatible graphics formats, including Windows BMP, TIFF, PC Paintbrush, GEM/IMG, GIF, Targa, and MacPaint. You get a toolbox of portable source code designed to help you integrate these standards into your Windows applications plus a whole lot more. 400 pages, 82 illustrations. Book No. 4265, $26.95 paperback, $38.95 hardcover

Look for These and Other Windcrest/McGraw-Hill Books at Your Local Bookstore

To Order Call Toll Free 1-800-822-8158
(24-hour telephone service available.)

or write to Windcrest/McGraw-Hill, Blue Ridge Summit, PA 17294-0840.

Title	Product No.	Quantity	Price

☐ Check or money order made payable to Windcrest/McGraw-Hill

Charge my ☐ VISA ☐ MasterCard ☐ American Express

Acct. No. _____ Exp. _____

Signature: _____

Name: _____

Address: _____

City: _____

State: _____ Zip: _____

Subtotal	$ _____
Postage and Handling (\$3.00 in U.S., \$5.00 outside U.S.)	$ _____
Add applicable state and local sales tax	$ _____
TOTAL	$ _____

Windcrest/McGraw-Hill catalog free with purchase; otherwise send \$1.00 in check or money order and receive \$1.00 credit on your next purchase.

Orders outside U.S. must pay with international money in U.S. dollars drawn on a U.S. bank.

Windcrest/McGraw-Hill Guarantee: If for any reason you are not satisfied with the book(s) you order, simply return it (them) within 15 days and receive a full refund.

BC

dBASE IV 2.0 Programming

If you are intrigued with the possibilities of the programs included in *dBASE IV 2.0 Programming*, you should definitely consider having the ready-to-run disk containing the software applications. This software is guaranteed free of manufacturer's defects. (If you have any problems, return the disk within 30 days, and we'll send you a new one.) Not only will you save the time and effort of typing the data, but also the disk eliminates the possibility of errors in the data. Interested?

Available on either 5¼" or 3½" disk for only $19.95, plus $2.50 shipping and handling.

About the author

Cary N. Prague is an internationally best-selling author and lecturer. A previous version of this book won the Computer Press Association's award for Best Book of the Year. Cary recently left the corporate world after 15 years where he was Director of Software Productivity at Traveler's Insurance in Hartford, Connecticut.